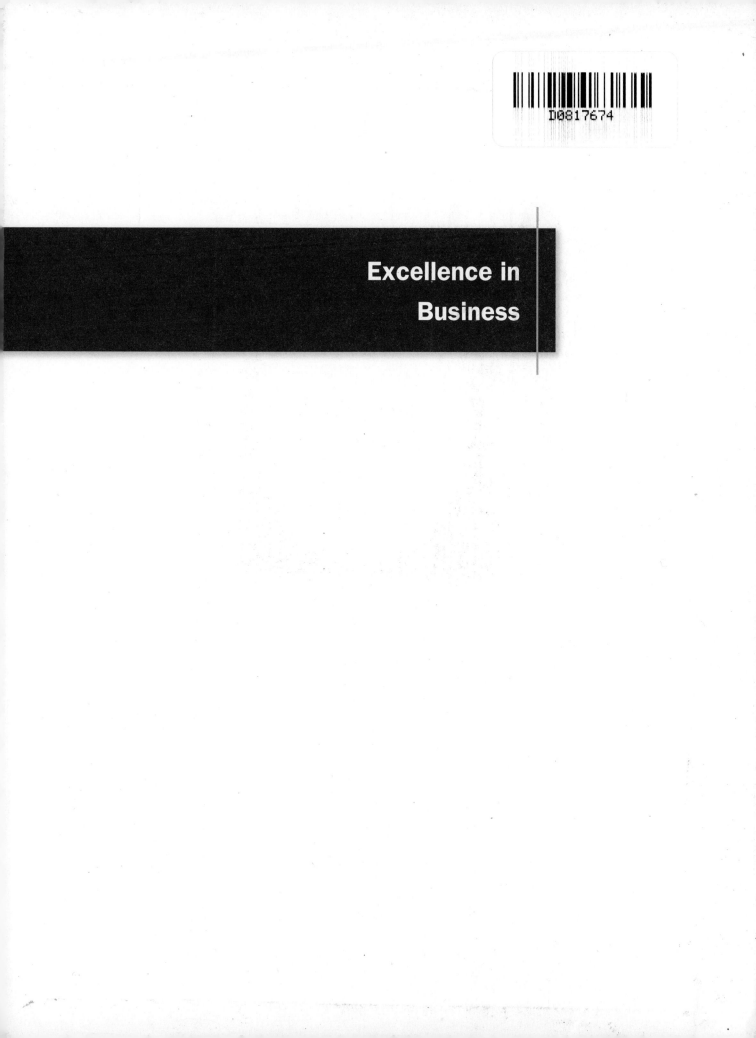

Excellence in
Business

Excellence in Business

Third Edition

Courtland L. Bovée

Professor of Business Administration

C. Allen Paul Distinguished Chair

Grossmont College

John V. Thill

Chief Executive Officer

Communication Specialists of America

Michael H. Mescon

Founder and Chairman, The Mescon Group

Atlanta, Georgia

Regents Professor of Management, Ramsey Chair of Private Enterprise

Andrew Young School of Policy Studies, Georgia State University

PEARSON
Prentice
Hall

Upper Saddle River, NJ 07458

Library of Congress Cataloging-in-Publication Data

Bovée, Courtland L.
  Excellence in business/Courtland L. Bovee, John Thill, Michael H. Mescon.—3rd ed.
    p. cm.
  Includes bibliographical references and index.
  ISBN 0-13-187047-5 (alk. paper)
  1. Business. 2. Management—United States. I. Thill, John V. II. Mescon, Michael H.
  III. Title.
  HF1008.M372 2007
  658—dc22   2005025765

AVP/Executive Editor: Jodi McPherson
VP/Editorial Director: Jeff Shelstad
Assistant Editor: Richard Gomes
Marketing Manager: Anne Howard
Associate Director, Production: Judy Leale
Managing Editor: Renata Butera
Production Editor: Marcela Boos
Permissions Supervisor: Charles Morris
Associate Director, Manufacturing: Vincent Scelta
Manufacturing Buyer: Diane Peirano
Art Director: Jayne Conte
Cover Design: Kevin Kall
Cover Photo: Alloy Photography
Manager, Multimedia Production/Design: Christy Mahon
Composition/Full Service Project Management: Lynn Steines, Carlisle Communications, Ltd.
Interior Printer/Binder: Courier – Kendallville
Cover Printer: Coral Graphics
Typeface: Times New Roman 10 pt.

Credits and acknowledgments borrowed from other sources and reproduced, with permission, in this textbook appear on page Ack-1.

Microsoft® and Windows® are registered trademarks of the Microsoft Corporation in the U.S.A. and other countries. Screen shots and icons reprinted with permission from the Microsoft Corporation. This book is not sponsored or endorsed by or affiliated with the Microsoft Corporation.

Pearson Education LTD.
Pearson Education Singapore, Pte. Ltd
Pearson Education, Canada, Ltd
Pearson Education–Japan

Pearson Education Australia PTY, Limited
Pearson Education North Asia Ltd
Pearson Educación de Mexico, S.A. de C.V.
Pearson Education Malaysia, Pte. Ltd

10 9 8 7 6 5 4 3 2 1
ISBN 0-13-187047-5

BRIEF CONTENTS

CONTENTS

Helping Students Make a Confident Leap from Consumers to Business Professionals

One of the primary challenges of any business course is helping students see business from the other side, from the perspective of the managers and entrepreneurs who make tough decisions in an increasingly complex environment. The Third Edition of *Excellence in Business* tackles that challenge head-on, from innovative new features to carefully selected examples that resonate with today's student-consumers.

Grasping the Big Picture

The real-world orientation starts right at the beginning, with a career-planning prologue that helps students understand what they need to offer in today's job market and where they can find opportunities that fit their needs and interests. Each chapter opens with an intriguing business story that connects to the chapter content by putting students in the driver's seat of major business decisions. Throughout each chapter, special care has been taken to present complex issues in simple ways and to put business concepts in a context that students can readily grasp.

Translating Consumer Experiences into Managerial Insights

When students' experiences as consumers are related to managerial challenges and decisions, they are often surprised to discover how much they already know about business. *Excellence in Business* emphasizes companies that students can relate to, starting on the very first page of Chapter 1 with Apple's phenomenally successful iPod and iTunes. Students will also learn how Toyota uses stealth marketing at trendy clubs and other hotspots to attract young buyers to its new Scion line and how *Rolling Stone* reinvented itself to recapture younger readers flocking to *Spin*, *Blender*, *Maxim*, and other upstart magazines.

Of course, any business text would be incomplete without a tough look at the controversies in business as well. Students will explore employee-management disputes at Electronic Arts and other video game companies, the health and environmental consequences of a socially conscious business such as Ben & Jerry's, and Procter & Gamble's army of unpaid teenage volunteers who promote products to their friends—often without their friends' knowledge.

Developing the Skills Needed in Today's Job Market

Excellence in Business minimizes theoretical discussions and highlights the practical business skills that students need to succeed. Every chapter offers a variety of activities that develop skills in research, problem solving, decision making, team building, and interpersonal communication. For those students who dream of starting their own companies, the new Minding Your Business boxes explain how to apply chapter concepts to small business challenges. And every student, whether destined for entrepreneurship or corporate management, benefits from the practical summaries found in the new chapter-ending checklist.

Expanding on Proven Pedagogy

Excellence in Business offers a feature set that is comprehensive yet fully integrated and easy to use. See how each chapter flows from start to finish as it helps students connect with the content, then identify and practice vital skills:

1
Orient

- **Learning objectives:** Give students a clear goal for the chapter and establish a framework for learning
- **Inside Business Today:** Vignette featuring a role model professional
- **Get Ready:** Encourages students to start thinking like the role model
- **Chapter Overview:** Links the vignette with chapter content to prepare students for reading

These chapter-opening features accomplish the vital task of raising students' curiosity about successful companies and products, including many they know and care about, such as Google, Jack in the Box, Nokia, Porsche, and Mountain Dew. That curiosity is then connected to the upcoming chapter concepts to motivate and prepare students for the material ahead.

Students have connected with a role model and grasp the context of major business challenges

2
Explore

- **Compelling examples:** Situations that are relevant and interesting to students, such as concert ticket pricing and tough ethical dilemmas
- **Critical Thinking Checkpoints:** Strategically placed, thought-provoking questions that verify learning
- **Keyed Learning Objectives:** Show students where each learning objective is addressed

Up-to-date chapter content is based on rigorous research and feedback from instructors and students, who have asked for practical business insights that feature a wide range of both familiar and unfamiliar companies. *Excellence in Business* also includes dozens of local and regional examples, so students might even recognize companies from their own hometowns.

Students have discovered the skills that their role model uses to succeed

3
Confirm

- **Apply These Ideas When You're the Boss:** Handy checklist of ways to use chapter concepts on the job
- **What's Next?:** Students revisit the chapter-opening vignette in light of what they've just learned and ponder the company's future
- **Summary of Learning Objectives:** Concise summaries help students verify what they've learned Students have three

opportunities to confirm the points they have just read in the chapter: (1) advice on applying chapter concepts when they become managers or entrepreneurs; (2) another look at the company featured in the chapter-opening vignette, explaining how it will use chapter concepts to face continuing challenges in the future; and (3) a helpful summary of each learning objective.

Students are ready to practice those skills for themselves

4
Apply

- Handling Difficult Situations on the Job
- Sharpening Your Communication Skills
- Building Your Team Skills
- Discovering Career Opportunities
- Developing Your Research Skills
- Exploring the Best of the Web
- Case for Critical Thinking
- Video Case

Students are now ready to practice the skills they have explored in the chapter. *Excellence in Business* offers a greater variety of student activities than any other leading business text, letting instructors vary assignments from chapter to chapter and shift emphasis between in-class, at-home, and online tasks.

Staying on the Leading Edge of Contemporary Business

The Third Edition is a cover-to-cover update based on the review of thousands of new source documents and hundreds of potential examples, issues, and trends. Students will explore the very same issues that today's professionals confront every day, from China's rise as an economic powerhouse to the social implications of offshoring to the pervasive role of technology. With its unmatched feature set and currency, *Excellence in Business* is the ideal resource for instructors who are guiding the next generation of business leaders.

Supporting Creative Instructors with a Host of Engaging Activities

We've always been impressed by the rich and varied approaches that instructors use to teach introduction to business, and we've fashioned this latest edition to support virtually any teaching style. *Excellence in Business* offers a greater variety of student activities than any other leading business text, so whether you emphasize in-class discussions, group interaction, individual tasks, or online assignments, you'll be sure to find a selection of activities that fit your methods.

Innovating to Help Students Connect with Today's Business World

Excellence in Business provides a wealth of features that facilitate both guided instruction and students' own reading. With far more resources than you'll ever need in a single course, you can mix and match from chapter-to-chapter, keeping the class fresh and interesting from the first day to the last.

	Feature	Major Benefits	Examples
New!	Inside Business Today	Chapter-opening vignette offers a slice-of-life look at a successful manager or entrepreneur; nearly half of the vignettes are new in this edition.	p. 25, 289, 485
New!	Get Ready	Integrates the opening vignette with the chapter content and puts students in the decision-making role.	p. 26, 290, 486
New!	Chapter Overview	Frames the upcoming material to facilitate reading and retention.	p. 62, 132, 458
New!	Box theme: *Minding Your Own Business*	Adapts chapter concepts to small business management and entrepreneurship.	p. 69, 238, 494
	Box theme: *Safety and Security in a Complex World*	Covering such hot topics as employee safety, identity theft, data security, terrorism, and privacy.	p. 154, 331, 375

(continued)

Feature	Major Benefits	Examples
Box theme: *Innovating for Business Success*	Highlights business innovations ranging from online training to individualized advertising.	p. 308, 431, 502
Box theme: *Thinking About Ethics*	Encourages students to ponder all sides of today's toughest ethical dilemmas.	p. 77, 296, 554
Box theme: *Competing in the Global Marketplace*	Helps students prepare for the complexities of international business.	p. 116, 183, 270
New! Minibox: *Technologies That Are Revolutionizing Business*	As part of the text's unmatched coverage of business technology, introduces students to such revolutionary developments as nanotechnology, wireless networking, virtual meetings, RFID, and assistive technologies for people with disabilities.	p. 202, 303, 364
New! Minibox: Learning from Business Blunders	Finds the lesson in such errors as Mitsubishi's effort to market to college-aged buyers with cut-rate financing—the company lost a half billion dollars when many of these young buyers defaulted on their loans.	p. 66, 310, 565
New! Critical Thinking Checkpoint	Help students gauge their learning progress and internalize chapter concepts.	p. 45, 244, 403
New! Business Buzz	Defines some of the latest buzzwords in business, from *e-mail hygiene* to *warm-chair attrition*.	p. 304, 402, 501
New! Checklist: Apply These When You're the Boss	Shows students how to apply text concepts to their own business ideas.	p. 52, 215, 508
New! What's Next?	Revisits the chapter-opening vignette and relates what students have just read to the challenges the company will face as it moves into the future.	p. 54, 315, 509
Handling Difficult Situations on the Job	Prepares students to resolve real-life scenarios, from workplace violence to mega-chain retail competitors to problems with business partners.	p. 158, 353, 452
New! Sharpening Your Communication Skills	Communication skills are one of the top concerns among today's hiring managers; this new exercise lets students practice listening, writing, and speaking in a variety of real-life scenarios.	p. 159, 452, 511
Building Your Team Skills	Teaches students important team skills, such as brainstorming, collaborative	p. 91, 125, 480

(continued)

		decision making, developing a consensus, debating, role playing, and resolving conflict.	
	Discovering Career Opportunities	Gives students the opportunity to explore career resources on campus, observe businesspeople on their jobs, interview businesspeople, and perform self-evaluations to assess their own career skills and interests.	p. 218, 422, 475
	Developing Your Research Skills	Familiarizes students with a wide variety of business reference material and offer practice in developing research skills.	p. 126, 354, 545
	Exploring the Best of the Web	Acquaints students with the wealth of information on the web that relates to the content of each chapter; includes online research and analysis activities.	p. 160, 254, 388
	A Case for Critical Thinking	Offers an in-depth look at a diverse range of issues, such as the endless turmoil in the airline industry, the disastrous AOL-Time Warner merger, and Wegmans' enlightened management in the ultra-tough retail grocery business.	p. 191, 254, 389
	Video Case	Takes students behind the scenes at a wide variety of small, medium, and large companies; each includes a synopsis, five discussion questions, and an online exploration exercise.	p. 95, 192, 391
New!	Career Profiles	Helps students evaluate the major career areas within business; includes skill and experience requirements, employment prospects, and sources of additional information.	p. 165, 224, 611
New!	E-Business in Action	Smart companies have learned the lessons of the dot-com bubble and are now using Internet technology and e-commerce techniques to boost productivity, hone marketing efforts, and improve virtually every aspect of business operations; this dedicated section expands student learning by explaining in depth the important challenges companies are facing in the world of e-business.	p. 163, 222, 516
New!	Appendix C: Personal Finance; Getting Set for Life	This major new appendix gives students practical advice for every stage in their financial lives, from college to planning for retirement. getting through Unlike personal finance sections in many other texts	p. A-25

(continued)

Feature	Major Benefits	Examples
	which are often little more than descriptive catalogs of financial topics, this appendix makes financial planning much more relevant by introducing students to the financial decisions they'll need to make as they transition from each life stage to the next. And in response to the debt crisis that affects so many college students today, this appendix highlights the serious problem of credit card debt and offers strategies for extricating oneself from a financial black hole.	

Additional Teaching and Learning Support

OneKey Online Courses

OneKey offers the best teaching and learning online resources in one place, with all the tools and resources that instructors need to plan and administer courses. OneKey also offers students anytime, anywhere access to online course material, including Learning Modules (section reviews, learning activities, and pretests and posttests), Student PowerPoints, and Research Navigator (four exclusive databases of reliable source content to help students understand the research process and complete assignments). Also included is The Big Picture, three special online features that provide annotated graphical overviews of complex business situations.

Conveniently organized by textbook chapter, these compiled resources save time and help students reinforce and apply what they have learned. *OneKey is available in three course-management platforms: Blackboard, CourseCompass, and WebCT.*

Instructor's Resource Center Available Online, in OneKey, or on CD-ROM

The Instructor's Resource Center, available on CD, at www.prenhall.com, or in your OneKey online course, provides presentation materials and other classroom resources. Instructors can collect the materials, edit them to create powerful class lectures, and upload them to an online course-management system.

Using the Instructor's Resource Center on CD-ROM, instructors can easily create custom presentations. Desired files can be exported for use in classroom presentations and online courses.

The Instructor's Resource Center offers a variety of faculty resources:

- **PowerPoints** Choose from a full set of PowerPoints or the concise, grab-and-go set with just the essentials.
- **TestGen Test-Generating Software** The test bank contains approximately 115 questions per chapter, including multiple-choice, true/false, fill-in, and essay questions.
- **Instructor's Manual** Designed to assist instructors in quickly finding and assembling the resources available for each chapter of the text, it includes Learning Objectives, Summary of Learning Objectives, Lecture Notes and Chapter Outline, Potential Difficulties and Suggested Solutions, Real-World Cases, Behind the Scenes, Answers to

End-of-Chapter Questions, Answers to Boxed Features, and Chapter Pop Quiz. (Print version also available.)
- **Test Item File** Printed version of the test bank (Microsoft Word file).

Companion Website

The text website at www.prenhall.com/bovee features chapter quizzes, suggested websites and student PowerPoints, which are available for review or can be conveniently printed three to a page for in-class note taking.

Acknowledgments

A key reason for the continued success of *Excellence in Business* is an extensive market research effort. The advice of hundreds of instructors around the country aided us in our attempt to create a textbook suited to the unique needs of the introductory business market. Our sincere thanks are extended to the individuals who responded to our surveys as well as to the individuals who provided us with their insights through detailed market reviews.

Survey Reviewers of Prior Editions

Lee Adami, Northern Wyoming College; **Robert Alliston,** Davenport College of Business; **Lorraine Anderson,** Marshall University; **Doug Ashby,** Lewis and Clark Community College; **Fay Avery,** Northern Virginia Community College; **Sandra Bailey,** Indiana Vocational Technical College; **James Baskfleld,** Northern Hennepin Community College; **Gregory Baxter,** Southeastern Oklahoma State University; **Charles Beavin,** Miami-Dade Community College; **Larry Beck,** Cohin County Community College; **Joseph Berger,** Monroe Community College; **James Boeger,** Rock Valley College; **Riccardo Boehm,** Hostos Community College; **Mary Jo Boehms,** Jackson State Community College; **Glennis Boyd,** Cisco Junior College; **Jeffrey Bruehl,** Bryan College; **Carl Buckel,** College of the Canyons; **Howard Budner,** Borough of Manhattan Community College; **John Bunnell,** Broome Community College; **Van Bushnell,** Southern Utah University; **William Carman,** Bucks County Community College; **Paul Caruso,** Richard Bland College; **Eloise Chester,** Suffolk County Community College; **Carmin Cimino,** Mitchell College; **Ellen Clemens,** Bloomsburg University of Pennsylvania; **James Cleveland,** Sage Junior College of Albany; **Debra Clingerman,** California University of Pennsylvania; **Herbert Coolidge,** Southern College of Seventh-Day Adventists; **Gary Cutler,** Dyersburg State Community College; **Giles Dail,** Edgecombe Community College; **Joe Damato,** Cuyamaca College; **James Day,** Shawnee State University; **Patrick Ellsberg,** Lower Columbia College; **Alfred Fabian,** Indiana Vocational College; **Jennifer Friestad,** Anoka-Ramsey Community College; **Joan Gailey,** Kent State University, East; **Joyce Goetz,** Austin Community College; **Barbara Goza,** Southern Florida Community College; **Phyllis Graff,** Kauai Community College; **Hugh Graham,** Loras College; **Vance Gray,** Bishop State Community College; **Gary Greene,** Manatee Community College; **Marciano Guerrero,** LaGuardia Community College; **Delia Haak,** John Brown University; **Maurice Hamington,** Mount St. Mary's College; **E.C. Hamm,** Tidewater Community College; **Carnella Hardin,** Glendale Community College; **Marie Hardink,** Anne Arundel Community College; **Diana Hayden,** Northeastern University; **Elizabeth Haynes,** Haywood Community College; **Sheila Devoe Heidman,** Cochise College; **Diana Henke,** University of Wisconsin at Sheboygan; **Norman Humble,** Kirkwood Community College; **Liz Jackson,** Keystone Junior College; **Michael Johnson,** Chippewa Valley Technical College; **Carol Jones,** Cuyahoga Community College; **Lonora Keas,** Del Mar College; **Sylvia Keyes,**

Northeastern University; **Sharon Kolstad,** Fort Peck Community College; **Ken LaFave,** Mt. San Jacinto Community College; **Richard Larsen,** University of Maine at Machias; **Philip Lee,** Campbellsville College; **Richard Lenoir,** George Washington University; **Martha Leva,** Pennsylvania State University; **Kathy Lorencz,** Oakland Community College; **James Loricchio,** Ulster County Community College; **Tricia McConville,** Northeastern University; **Cheryl Macon,** Butler County Community College; **Ann Maddox,** Angelo State University; **Marie Madison,** Harry S. Truman College; **Barry Marshall,** Northeastern University; **George Michaehides,** Franklin Pierce College; **Norman Muller,** Greenfield Community College; **Lucia Murphy,** Ursinus College; **Alita Myers,** Copiah-Lincoln Community College; **Eric Nielsen,** College of Charleston; **Patricia Parker,** Maryville University of St. Louis; **Clyde Patterson,** Shawnee State University; **Corey Pfaffe,** Marantha Baptist Bible College; **Noel Powell,** West Georgia College; **Allen Rager,** Southwestern Community College; **Roy Roddy,** Yakima Valley Community College; **Ehsan Salek,** Virginia Wesleyan College; **Bernard Saperstein,** Passaic County Community College; **Kurk Schindler,** Wilbur Wright College; **Mark Schultz,** Rocky Mountain College; **Arnold Scolnick,** Borough of Manhattan Community College; **David Shepard,** Virginia Western Community College; **Stephanie Smith,** Lander University; **Susan Smith,** Finger Lakes Community College; **George Stook,** Anne Arundel Community College; **David Stringer,** DeAnza College; **Ben Tanksley,** Sul Ross State University; **John Taylor,** University of Alaska, Fairbanks; **Chris Tomas,** Northeast Iowa Community College; **Palmina Uzzolino,** Montclair State University; **Martha Valentine,** Regis University; **Juanita Vertrees,** Sinclair Community College; **IngoVon Ruckteschel,** Long Island University; **Chuck Wall,** Bakersfield College; **Jay Weiner,** Adams State College; **Lewis Welshofer,** Miami University of Ohio; **Charles White,** Edison Community College; **Richard Williams,** Laramie County Community College; **Clay Willis,** Oklahoma Baptist University; **Ira Wilsker,** Lamar University; **Ron Young,** Kalamazoo Valley Community College; **Sandra Young,** Jones County Junior College; **Harold Zarr,** Des Moines Area Community College; **Nancy Zeliff,** Northwest Missouri State University; and **Gene Zeller,** Jordan College.

Market Reviewers of Prior Editions

Harvey Bronstein, Oakland Community College; **Debra Clingerman,** California University of Pennsylvania; **Bill Dempkey,** Bakersfield College; **John Heinsius,** Modesto Junior College; **Alan Hollander,** Suffolk Community College; **Bob Matthews,** Oakton Community College; **Jerry Myers,** Stark Technical College; **Dianne Osborne,** Broward Community College; **Mary Rousseau,** Delta College; **Martin St. John,** Westmoreland Community College; **Patricia Setlik,** William Rainey Harper College; **Richard Shapiro,** Cuyahoga Community College; and **Shafi Ullah,** Broward Community College; **Randy Barker,** Virginia Commonwealth University; **James D. Bell,** Southwest State University; **Joe Brum,** Fayetteville Technical Community College; **Steven Cassidy,** Howard University; **Jan Feldbauer,** Austin Community College; **Lorraine Hartley,** Franklin University; **Donald Johnson,** College for Financial Planning; **Jeffery Klivans,** University of Maine-Augusta; **Paul Londrigan,** Mott Community College; **Ted Valvoda,** Lakeland Community College; **William Warfeld,** Indiana State University; **Lewis Scholossinger,** Community College of Aurora; **Ronald Cereola,** James Madison University; **Mohammed Ahmed,** Webster University; **Dennis Foster,** Northern Arizona University; **Marshall Wick,** Gallaudet University; **Anthony Cafarelli,** Ursuline University; **Sandra Johnson,** Shasta College; **Robert Fouquette,** New Hampshire College; **Judy Domalewski,** Community College of Aurora, **Gerald Crawford,** University of North Alabama; **Gary Walk,** Lima Technical College; **Pamela Shindler,** Wittenburg University; **John Mozingo,** University of Wisconsin, Oshkosh, **C. Russell**

Edwards, Valencia Community College; and **David Sollars,** Auburn University, Montgomery.

Market Reviewers for *Excellence in Business*

Steven Huntley, Florida Community College; **Sara Huter,** Webster University; **Sally Wells,** Columbia College; **Roosevelt Martin,** Chicago State University; **George Crawford,** Clayton College and State University; **William Grimes,** Washtenaw Community College; **David DeCook,** Arapahoe Community College; **Ronald Akie,** Mount Ida College; **Barbara Van Syckle,** Jackson Community College; **Jeri Rubin,** University of Alaska; **Michael Scrivens,** Monroe Community College; **Marne David Schmitz,** Front Range Community College; **Janet Seggern,** Lehigh Carbon Community College; **Michael Shapiro,** Dowling College; **Cynthia Nicola,** Carlow College; **Robert Myers,** Palm Beach Atlantic College; **Don Richie,** Oregon Institute of Technology; **Richard Stewart,** Western Nevada Community College; **David Chandler,** Indiana University; **Lorena Edwards,** Belmont University; **Jaidev Singh,** University of Washington; **Rick Baldwin,** Prairie View A&M University **Pat Tadlock,** Horry-Georgetown Technical College; **P. K. Shukla,** Chapman University.

Personal Acknowledgments

A very special acknowledgment goes to George Dovel, whose superb editorial skills, distinguished background, and wealth of business experience assured this project of clarity and completeness. We are also grateful to Jackie Estrada for her remarkable talents and special skills.

The authors wish to acknowledge the contributions of Dr. David Rachman, including his work on the outline for the First Edition of *Business Today.* Dr. Rachman was a named author for editions One through Eight of *Business Today.*

The supplements package for *Excellence in Business* has benefited from the able contributions of numerous individuals. We would like to express our thanks to them for creating the finest set of instructional supplements in the field. The supplement authors include Barbara Gorski, University of St. Thomas; Martha Laham, Diablo Valley College; Myles Hassell, University of New Orleans; Tom Quirk, Webster University; and Channelle James, University of North Carolina, Greensboro.

We also wish to extend our warmest appreciation to the devoted professionals at Prentice Hall. They include Jerome Grant, president; Jeff Shelstad, vice president/editorial director; Jodi McPherson, executive editor; Richard Gomes, assistant editor; and Anne Howard, marketing manager, as well as all of Prentice Hall Business Publishing, and the outstanding Prentice Hall sales representatives. Finally, we thank Renata Butera, managing editor; Christy Mahon, manager of multimedia production/design; Judy Leale, associate director of production; and Marcela Boos, production editor, for their dedication, and we are grateful to Lynn Steines, project manager at Carlisle Communications; Marcia Craig, copy editor; Charles Morris, permissions coordinator; Melinda Alexander, photo researcher; and Kevin Kall, cover designer, for their superb work.

Courtland L. Bovée
John V. Thill
Michael H. Mescon

Excellence in
Business

may have helped you coordinate a winning presentation to your school's administration. As you analyze your achievements, you'll begin to recognize a pattern of skills. Which of them might be valuable to potential employers?

Next, look at your educational preparation, work experience, and extracurricular activities. What do your knowledge and experience qualify you to do? What have you learned from volunteer work or class projects that could benefit you on the job? Have you held any offices, won any awards or scholarships, mastered a second language?

Take stock of your personal characteristics. Are you aggressive, a born leader? Or would you prefer to let someone else lead? Are you outgoing, articulate, great with people? Or do you prefer working alone? Make a list of what you believe are your four or five most important qualities. Ask a relative or friend to rate your traits as well.

If you're having difficulty figuring out your interests, characteristics, or capabilities, consult your college placement office. Many campuses administer a variety of tests to help you identify interests, aptitudes, and personality traits. These tests won't reveal your "perfect" job, but they'll help you focus on the types of work best suited to your personality.

How Can You Make Yourself More Valuable?

While you're figuring out what you want from a job and what you can offer an employer, you can take positive steps toward building your career. You can do a lot before you graduate from college and even while you are seeking employment:

- ***Keep an employment portfolio.*** Collect anything that shows your ability to perform, whether it's in school, on the job, or in other venues. Your portfolio is a great resource for writing your résumé, and it gives employers tangible evidence of your professionalism. Many colleges now offer students the chance to create an *e-portfolio*, a multimedia presentation of your skills and experiences. It's an extensive résumé that links to an electronic collection of your student papers, solutions to tough problems, internship and work projects, and anything else that demonstrates your accomplishments and activities.[1] To distribute the portfolio to potential employers, you can burn a CD-ROM or store your portfolio on a website—whether it's a personal site, your college's site (if student pages are available), or a site such as www.collegegrad.com. (However, you *must* check with an employer before including any items that belong to the company or contain sensitive information.)
- ***Take interim assignments.*** As you search for a permanent job, consider temporary jobs, freelance work, or internships. These temporary assignments not only help you gain valuable experience and relevant contacts but also provide you with important references and with items for your portfolio.[2]
- ***Continue to polish and update your skills.*** Join networks of professional colleagues and friends who can help you keep up with your occupation and industry. Many professional societies have student chapters or offer students discounted memberships. Take courses and pursue other educational or life experiences that would be hard to get while working full-time.

Seeking Employment Opportunities and Information

Whether your major is business, biology, or political science, once you know what you want and what you have to offer, you can start finding an employer to match. If you haven't already committed yourself to any particular career field, review the career tables in the *Occupational Outlook Handbook,* a nationally recognized source of career information published by the U.S. Bureau of Labor Statistics. The handbook describes what workers do on the job, working conditions, the training and education needed, average earnings, and expected job prospects in a wide range of occupations. It is revised every two years and is available in print and online at www.bls.gov/oco.[3]

Here is a brief overview of the future outlook for a number of careers in business (also look for Career Profiles following Chapters 4, 6, 9, 11, 15, and 18):

- **Careers in management.** Today's business environment requires the skills of effective managers to reduce costs, streamline operations, develop marketing strategies, and supervise workers. As you'll read in Chapter 7, managers perform four basic functions: planning, organizing, leading, and controlling. Facing increased competition, many businesses are becoming more dependent on the expertise of outside management consultants—one of the fastest-growing occupations of all jobs. Outside management consultants perform many important tasks, but chief among them is evaluating operating conditions and making recommendations to improve effectiveness. To find out more about what you can do with a degree in management and the typical courses management majors take, log on to the Prentice Hall Student Success SuperSite at www.prenhall.com/success/MajorExp/mgmt.html.

- **Careers in human resources.** As Chapters 10 and 11 discuss, human resources managers plan and direct human resource activities that include recruiting, training and development, compensation and benefits, employee and labor relations, and health and safety. Additionally, human resources managers develop and implement human resources systems and practices to accommodate a firm's strategy and to motivate and manage diverse workforces. Large numbers of job openings are expected in the human resources field in the near future. Efforts to recruit quality employees and to provide more employee training programs should create new human resources positions. With a vast supply of qualified workers and new college graduates, however, the job market for human resources is likely to remain competitive. Learn more at www.prenhall.com/success/MajorExp/hrmgmt.html.

- **Careers in computers and information systems.** Job opportunities abound for trained information technology workers. As competition and advanced technologies force companies to upgrade and improve their computer systems, the number of computer-related positions continues to escalate. Within the computer field, only two categories of jobs are expected to decrease: computer operators and data-entry clerks. More user-friendly computer software has greatly reduced the need for operators and data-entry processors, but displaced workers who keep up with changing technology should have few problems moving into other areas of computer support. To find out more about careers in computer science and information systems, log on to the Prentice Hall Student Success SuperSite at www.prenhall.com/success/MajorExp/CSImajors.html, then explore the various specialties listed.

- **Careers in sales and marketing.** Increasing competition in products and services should create greater needs for effective sales and marketing personnel in the future. Employment opportunities for retail salespersons look good because of the need to replace the large number of workers who transfer to other occupations or leave the workforce each year. Opportunities for part-time work should be abundant. Employment for insurance and real estate agents, however, is expected to grow more slowly than average. Computer technology will allow established agents to increase their sales volume and eliminate the need for additional marketing personnel in these fields. For additional information on the types of courses marketing majors take and what you can do with a degree in marketing see Chapters 12 through 15 and log on to the Prentice Hall Student Success SuperSite at www.prenhall.com/success/MajorExp/mktg.html.

- **Careers in finance and accounting.** As Chapters 16 and 17 point out, accountants and financial managers are needed in almost every industry. Most positions in finance and accounting are expected to grow as fast as the average for all occupations in the near future, as continued growth in the economy and population is expected to create more demand for trained financial personnel. To find out more about careers in finance and accounting, log on to the Prentice Hall Student Success SuperSite at www.prenhall.com/success/MajorExp/acct.html, and select finance or accounting.

- **Careers in economics.** As Chapter 1 discusses, economists study how society distributes scarce resources such as land, labor, raw materials, and machinery to produce goods and services. They conduct research, collect and analyze data, monitor economic trends, and develop forecasts. Economists are needed in many industries and spend time applying economic theory to analyze issues that are important to their firms. For example, they might analyze the effects of global economic activity on the demand for the company's product, conduct a cost-benefit analysis of the projects the company is considering, or determine the effects of government regulations or taxes on the company. Employment of economists is expected to grow about as fast as the average for all occupations, with the best opportunities in private industry—especially research, testing, and consulting firms—as more companies contract out for economic research services. To find out more about what you can do with a degree in economics and the typical courses economics majors take, log on to the Prentice Hall Student Success SuperSite at **www.prenhall.com/success/MajorExp/econ.html.**

- *Careers in communications.* As businesses recognize the need for effective communications with their customers and the public, employment of communications personnel is expected to grow as fast or faster than the average for all occupations in the near future. Recent college graduates may face keen competition for entry positions in communications as the number of applicants is expected to exceed the number of job openings. Newly created jobs in the ever-expanding computer world—such as graphic designers for websites or technical writers for instruction manuals—are expected to improve the career outlook for new communications graduates.

Exhibit 1 lists the business occupations (including management positions) that are projected to grow the fastest between now and 2012. Keep in mind that most of the high-growth jobs require college degrees, and many of the hottest jobs in today's business world demand technological and computer skills. Even if you're interested in finance, human resources, or marketing positions, you'll need basic computer skills to snare the best jobs in your desired field of work.

Sources of Employment Information

One effective approach to the employment process is to gather as much information as you can, narrowing it as you go until you know precisely the companies you want to contact. Begin by finding out where the job opportunities are, which industries are strong, which parts of the country are booming, and which specific job categories offer the best prospects for the future.

From there you can investigate individual organizations, doing your best to learn as much about them as possible. Here are some good information sources:

- *Business and financial news.* If you don't already do so, subscribe to a major newspaper (print or online editions) and scan the business pages or a business news website frequently. Check your library for popular business magazines such as *Forbes, Fortune, BusinessWeek, Business 2.0, Fast Company*, and *Harvard Business Review*. Watch some of the television programs that focus on business, such as *Wall Street Week*. Of course, with all the business information available today, it's easy to get lost in the details. Try not to get too caught up in the daily particulars of business. Start by examining "big picture" topics, such as trends, issues, industrywide challenges, and careers, before delving into specific companies that look attractive.
- *Networking.* Networking is the process of making informal connections with a broad sphere of mutually beneficial business contacts. According to one recent survey, networking is the most common way that employees find jobs.[4] Networking takes place wherever and whenever people talk: at industry functions, social gatherings, sports events and recreational activities, online chat rooms (including sponsored online networking sites such as **http://network.monster.com**), alumni reunions, and so on. You may be able to network with executives in your field by joining or participating in student business organizations, especially those with ties to professional organizations such as the American Marketing Association or the American Management

Exhibit 1
The 25 Fastest-Growing Business Occupations
According to government estimates, these 25 business occupations are expected to grow the fastest in the near future. (The list does not include technical specialties such as engineering or computer programming.)

Occupation	2002 employment (thousands)	Projected increases by 2012	
		Number of new jobs (thousands)	% increase
Computer and information systems managers	284	103	36.1
Personal financial advisers	126	44	34.6
Sales managers	343	105	30.5
Management analysts	577	176	30.4
Medical and health services managers	244	71	29.3
Agents and business managers of artists, performers, and athletes	15	4	27.8
Human resources, training, and labor relations specialists	474	131	27.7
All other business operations specialists	1,056	290	27.5
Advertising and promotions managers	85	21	25.0
Public relations managers	69	16	23.4
Marketing managers	203	43	21.3
Meeting and convention planners	37	8	21.3
Administrative services managers	321	63	19.8
Transportation, storage, and distribution managers	111	22	19.7
Accountants and auditors	1,055	205	19.5
Human resources managers	202	39	19.4
Credit analysts	66	12	18.7
Financial analysts	172	32	18.7
Cost estimators	188	35	18.6
General and operations managers	2,049	376	18.4
Financial managers	599	109	18.3
Appraisers and assessors of real estate	88	16	17.6
Chief executives	553	93	16.7
Claims adjusters, appraisers, examiners, and investigators	241	34	14.0
Budget analysts	62	9	14.0

Association. Keep in mind that novice job seekers sometimes misunderstand networking and unknowingly commit breaches of etiquette. Networking isn't a matter of walking up to strangers at social events, handing over your résumé, and asking them to find you a job. Rather, it involves the sharing of information between people who might be able to offer mutual help at some point in the future. Think of it as an organic process, in which you cultivate the possibility of finding that perfect opportunity. Networking can take time, and it can operate in unpredictable ways. You may not get results for months, so it's important to start early and make it part of your lifelong program of career management.

Job fairs can be a great source of information about new career opportunities.

- *College placement offices.* Also known as career centers, college placement offices offer individual counseling, credential services, job fairs, on-campus interviews, and job listings. Staff members give advice on résumé writing and provide workshops in job-search techniques, interview techniques, and more.[5]

Employment Information on the Web

The web offers an amazing amount of company and employment information, both general and specific:

- *Discussion groups.* Using the web, you can locate and communicate with potential employers through numerous types of discussion groups dedicated to your field. Search for Usenet newsgroups in the fields you're interested in (visit www.google.com, click on Groups, then enter keywords such as "marketing" or "research"). Commercial systems such as AOL have numerous discussion groups as well.
- *Career counseling websites.* You can also find job counseling online. You might begin your self-assessment, for example, with the Keirsey Temperament Sorter, an online personality test at www.advisorteam.com. For excellent job-seeking pointers and counseling, visit college- and university-run online career centers. Major online job boards such as Monster.com also offer a variety of career planning resources.
- *Company websites.* Most companies, even small firms, offer at least basic information about themselves on their websites. Look for the "About Us" or "Company" part of the site to find a company profile, executive biographies, press releases, financial information, and information on employment opportunities. You'll often find information about an organization's mission, products, annual reports, and employee benefits. You can also e-mail organizations and ask for annual reports, descriptive brochures, or newsletters. Look for outside sources as well, including the business sections of local newspapers and trade publications that cover the company's industries and markets.
- *Job boards.* Online job boards have become an integral part of most companies' recruiting procedures, so be sure to check them out. In addition to the major sites such as Monster, Yahoo! HotJobs, and CareerBuilder, look for niche boards that address special-interest and specific career fields (see Exhibit 2). Your placement office probably has an up-to-date list as well.

Exhibit 2
Netting a Job on the Web
Begin your job search with these helpful online career resources.

Website*	URL	Highlights
Riley Guide	www.rileyguide.com	Vast collection of links to both general and specialized job sites for every career imaginable; don't miss this one—it'll save you hours or days of searching
America's CareerOneStop	www.careeronestop.org	Comprehensive, government-funded site that includes America's Career InfoNet and America's Job Bank; covers the workplace in general as well as specific careers; offers information on typical wages and employment trends and identifies education, knowledge, and skills requirements for most occupations
Monster	www.monster.com	World's largest job site with hundreds of thousands of openings, many from hard-to-find smaller companies; extensive collection of advice on the job-search process
MonsterTrak	www.monstertrak.com	Focuses on job searches for new college grads; your school's career center site probably links here
Yahoo! HotJobs	hotjobs.yahoo.com	Another leading job board, formed by recent merger of HotJobs and Yahoo! Careers
CareerBuilder	www.careerbuilder.com	Fast-growing site affiliated with more than 100 local newspapers around the country
USA Jobs	www.usajobs.opm.gov	The official job search site for the U.S. government, featuring everything from economists to astronauts to border patrol agents
IMDiversity	www.imdiversity.com	Good resource on diversity in the workplace, with job postings from companies that have made a special commitment to promoting diversity in their workforces
Dice.com	www.dice.com	One of the best sites for high-technology jobs
Net-Temps	www.nettemps.com	Popular site for contractors and freelancers looking for short-term assignments
InternshipPrograms.com	www.internships.wetfeet.com	Posts listings from companies looking for interns in a wide variety of professions

* Note: This list represents only a small fraction of the job-posting sites and other resources available online; be sure to check with your college's career center for the latest information.

Preparing Your Résumé

A **résumé** is a structured, written summary of a person's education, employment background, and job qualifications. Although many people have misconceptions about résumés (see Exhibit 3), the fact is that a résumé is a form of advertising. It is intended to stimulate an employer's interest in you—in meeting you and learning more about you. A successful résumé inspires a prospective employer to invite you to interview with the company. Thus,

résumé
Form of advertising that lists a person's education, employment background, and job qualifications in order to obtain an interview

Exhibit 3

Fallacies and Facts About Résumés

Many people incorrectly believe that a good résumé will get them the job they want; the real purpose of a résumé is to secure an invitation to a job interview.

Fallacy	Fact
✗ The purpose of a résumé is to list all your skills and abilities.	✓ The purpose of a résumé is to kindle employer interest and generate an interview.
✗ A good résumé will get you the job you want.	✓ All a résumé can do is get you in the door.
✗ Your résumé will be read carefully and thoroughly by an interested employer.	✓ Your résumé probably has less than 45 seconds to make an impression.
✗ The more good information you present about yourself in your résumé, the better.	✓ Too much information on a résumé may actually kill the reader's appetite to know more.
✗ If you want a really good résumé, have it prepared by a résumé service.	✓ Prepare your own résumé—unless the position is especially high-level or specialized. Even then, you should check carefully before using a service.

your purpose in writing your résumé is to create interest—*not* to tell readers everything about you. In fact, it may be best to only hint at some things and leave the reader wanting more. The potential employer will then have even more reason to contact you.[6]

Your résumé is one of the most important documents you'll ever write. You can help ensure success by remembering four things: First, treat your résumé with the respect it deserves. Until you're able to meet with employers in person, your résumé is all they have of you. Until that first personal contact occurs, you *are* your résumé, and a single mistake or oversight can cost you interview opportunities. Second, give yourself plenty of time. Don't put off preparing your résumé until the last second and then try to write it in one sitting. Let it "stew" between drafts and try out different ideas and phrases until you hit on the right combination. Also, give yourself plenty of time to proofread the résumé when you're finished—and ask several other people to proofread it as well. Third, learn from good models. You can find thousands of sample résumés online at college websites and job sites such as Monster.com. Fourth, don't get frustrated by the conflicting advice you'll read about résumés; they are more art than science. Consider the alternatives and choose the approach that makes the most sense in your specific situation.

By the way, if anyone asks to see your "CV," they're referring to your *curriculum vitae*, the term used instead of *résumé* in some professions and in many countries outside the United States. Résumés and CVs are essentially the same, although CVs can be more detailed. If you need to adapt a U.S.-style résumé to CV format, or vice versa, Monster.com has helpful guidelines on the subject.

Controlling the Format and Style

To give your printed résumé the best appearance possible, use a clean typeface on high-grade, letter-size bond paper in white or a very light earth tone. Avoid gimmicky preprinted papers (which can make you look unprofessional) or papers with speckled or other nonplain backgrounds (which can cause problems with scanning or photocopying). Your stationery and envelope should match. Leave ample margins all around, and make sure that any corrections are unnoticeable. Avoid hard-to read typefaces, and use a quality printer.

Try to keep your résumé to one page. If you have a great deal of experience and are applying for a higher-level position, you may need to prepare a somewhat longer résumé. The important thing is to have enough space to present a persuasive, but accurate, portrait of your skills and accomplishments.

Lay out your résumé so that the information is easy to grasp.[7] Break up the text with headings that call attention to various aspects of your background, such as work experience and education. Underline or boldface key points, or set them off in the left margin. Use indented lists to itemize your most important qualifications. Leave plenty of white space, even if you're forced to use two pages. Pay attention to mechanics and details. Make sure that headings and itemized lists are grammatically parallel and that grammar, spelling, and punctuation are correct.

Write in a simple and direct style to save your reader time. Use short, crisp phrases instead of whole sentences, and focus on what your reader needs to know. Avoid using the word *I*. Instead, you might say, "Led a team of volunteers that raised $45,000 for a community center" or "Managed a fast-food restaurant and four employees."

Think about your résumé from the employer's perspective. Ask yourself: What key qualifications will an employer be looking for? Which of these are my greatest strengths? What will set me apart from other candidates? What are my greatest accomplishments, and what was produced as a result? Then tailor your résumé to appeal to the employer's needs.

Keeping Your Résumé Honest

At some point in the writing process, you're sure to run into the question of honesty. A claim may be clearly wrong ("So what if I didn't get those last two credits—I got the same education as people who did graduate, so it's OK to say that I graduated too"). Or a rationalization may be more subtle ("Even though the task was to organize a department luncheon, I did a good job, so it should qualify as 'project management' "). Either way, the information is dishonest.

Somehow, the idea that "everybody lies on their résumés" has crept into popular consciousness, and dishonesty in the job search process has reached epidemic proportions. As many as half of the résumés now sent to employers contain false information. And it's not just the simple fudging of a fact here and there. Dishonest applicants are getting creative—and bold. Don't have the college degree you want? You can buy a degree from one of the websites that now offer fake diplomas. Better yet, pay a computer hacker to insert your name into a prestigious university's graduation records, in case somebody checks. Aren't really working in that impressive job at a well-known company? You can always list it on your résumé and sign up for a service that provides phony employment verification.[8]

Applicants with integrity know they don't need to stoop to lying to compete in the job market. If you are tempted to stretch the truth, bear in mind that professional recruiters have seen every trick in the book, and employers who are fed up with the dishonesty are getting more aggressive at uncovering the truth. Roughly 80 percent now contact references and conduct criminal background checks, and many do credit checks when the job involves financial responsibility.[9] And even if you get past these filters with fraudulent information, you'll probably be exposed on the job when you can't live up to your own résumé. Such fabrications have been known to catch up to people many years into their careers, with embarrassing consequences.

To maintain a high standard of honesty in your résumé, subject any questionable entries to two simple tests: First, if something is not true, don't include it—don't try to rationalize it, excuse it, or make it sound better than it is; simply leave it out. A second and more subtle test, helpful for those borderline issues, is asking whether you'd be comfortable sharing a particular piece of information face-to-face. If you wouldn't be comfortable saying it in person, don't say it in your résumé. These tests will help ensure a factual résumé that represents who you are and lead you toward jobs that are truly right for you.

Organizing Your Résumé Around Your Strengths

As you compose your résumé, try to emphasize the information that has a bearing on your career objective, and minimize or exclude any that is irrelevant or counterproductive. Call attention to your best features and downplay your weaknesses—but be sure you do so without distorting or misrepresenting the facts.[10] Do you have something in your history that might trigger an employer's red flag? Following are some common problems and some quick suggestions for overcoming them:[11]

- *Frequent job changes.* You can group similar contract positions and temporary jobs under one heading.
- *Gaps in work history.* Mention relevant experience and education gained during time gaps, such as volunteer or community work. If gaps are due to personal problems such as drug, alcohol abuse, or mental illness, offer honest but general explanations about your absences ("I had serious health concerns and had to take time off to fully recover").
- *Inexperience.* Do related volunteer work. List relevant course work and internships. Offer hiring incentives such as "willing to work nights and weekends."
- *Overqualification.* Tone down your résumé, focusing exclusively on pertinent experience and skills.
- *Long-term employment with one company.* Itemize each position held at the firm to show "interior mobility" and increased responsibilities. Don't include obsolete skills and job titles.
- *Job termination for cause.* Be honest with interviewers. Show you're a hard-working employee and address their concerns with proof such as recommendations and examples of completed projects.
- *Criminal record.* Consider sending out an introductory letter about your skills and experience, rather than a résumé and cover letter. Prepare answers to questions that interviewers will probably pose ("You may wonder whether I will be a trustworthy employee. I'd like to offer you a list of references from previous bosses and co-workers who will attest to my integrity. I learned some hard lessons during that difficult time in my life, and now I'm fully rehabilitated").

To focus attention on your strongest points, adopt the appropriate organizational approach—make your résumé chronological, functional, or a combination of the two. The "right" choice depends on your background and your goals.

chronological résumé
Most traditional type of résumé, listing employment history sequentially in reverse order so that the most recent experience is listed first

The Chronological Résumé In a **chronological résumé**, the work-experience section dominates and is placed in the most prominent slot, immediately after the name and address and optional objective. You develop this section by listing your jobs sequentially in reverse order, beginning with the most recent position and working backward toward earlier jobs. Under each listing, describe your responsibilities and accomplishments, giving the most space to the most recent positions. If you're just graduating from college with limited professional experience, you can vary this chronological approach by putting your educational qualifications before your experience, thereby focusing attention on your academic credentials.

The chronological approach is the most common way to organize a résumé, and many employers prefer it. This approach has three key advantages: (1) Employers are familiar with it and can easily find information, (2) it highlights growth and career progression, and (3) it highlights employment continuity and stability.[12] As vice president with Korn/Ferry International, Robert Nesbit speaks for many recruiters: "Unless you have a really compelling reason, don't use any but the standard chronological format. Your résumé should not read like a treasure map, full of minute clues to the whereabouts of your jobs and experience. I want to be able to grasp quickly where a candidate has worked, how long, and in what capacities."[13]

The chronological approach is especially appropriate if you have a strong employment history and are aiming for a job that builds on your current career path (see Exhibit 4).

functional résumé
Résumé organized around a list of skills and accomplishments, subordinating employers and academic experience in order to stress individual areas of competence; frowned on by many recruiters

The Functional Résumé A **functional résumé**, sometimes called a *skills résumé*, emphasizes your skills and capabilities, identifying employers and academic experience in subordinate sections. This pattern stresses individual areas of competence, so it's useful for people who are just entering the job market, want to redirect their careers, or have little continuous career-related experience. The functional approach also has three advantages: (1) Without having to read through job descriptions, employers can see what you can do for them, (2) you can emphasize earlier job experience, and (3) you can de-emphasize any lack of career progress or lengthy

Exhibit 4
Chronological Résumé

Roberto Cortez calls attention to his most recent achievements by setting them off in list form with bullets. The section titled "Intercultural and Technical Skills" emphasizes his international background, fluency in Spanish and German, and extensive computer skills—all of which are important qualifications for his target position.

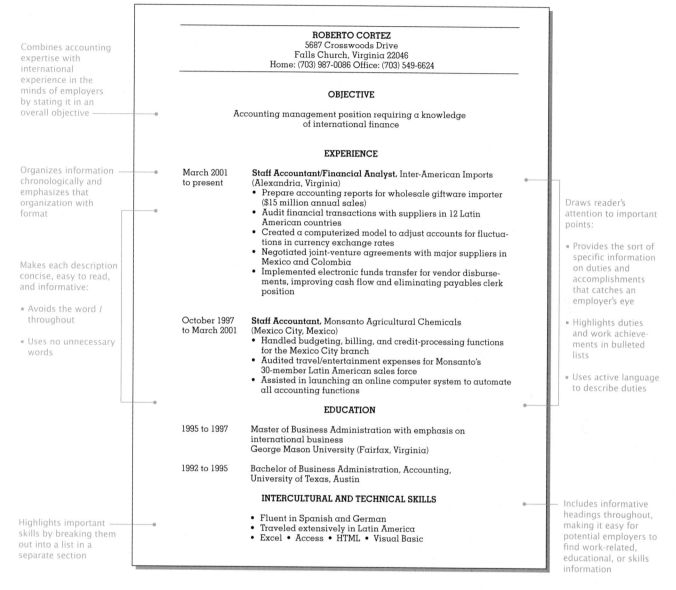

Combines accounting expertise with international experience in the minds of employers by stating it in an overall objective

Organizes information chronologically and emphasizes that organization with format

Makes each description concise, easy to read, and informative:

- Avoids the word *I* throughout

- Uses no unnecessary words

Highlights important skills by breaking them out into a list in a separate section

Draws reader's attention to important points:

- Provides the sort of specific information on duties and accomplishments that catches an employer's eye

- Highlights duties and work achievements in bulleted lists

- Uses active language to describe duties

Includes informative headings throughout, making it easy for potential employers to find work-related, educational, or skills information

ROBERTO CORTEZ
5687 Crosswoods Drive
Falls Church, Virginia 22046
Home: (703) 987-0086 Office: (703) 549-6624

OBJECTIVE

Accounting management position requiring a knowledge of international finance

EXPERIENCE

March 2001 to present — **Staff Accountant/Financial Analyst,** Inter-American Imports (Alexandria, Virginia)
- Prepare accounting reports for wholesale giftware importer ($15 million annual sales)
- Audit financial transactions with suppliers in 12 Latin American countries
- Created a computerized model to adjust accounts for fluctuations in currency exchange rates
- Negotiated joint-venture agreements with major suppliers in Mexico and Colombia
- Implemented electronic funds transfer for vendor disbursements, improving cash flow and eliminating payables clerk position

October 1997 to March 2001 — **Staff Accountant,** Monsanto Agricultural Chemicals (Mexico City, Mexico)
- Handled budgeting, billing, and credit-processing functions for the Mexico City branch
- Audited travel/entertainment expenses for Monsanto's 30-member Latin American sales force
- Assisted in launching an online computer system to automate all accounting functions

EDUCATION

1995 to 1997 — Master of Business Administration with emphasis on international business
George Mason University (Fairfax, Virginia)

1992 to 1995 — Bachelor of Business Administration, Accounting, University of Texas, Austin

INTERCULTURAL AND TECHNICAL SKILLS

- Fluent in Spanish and German
- Traveled extensively in Latin America
- Excel • Access • HTML • Visual Basic

unemployment. However, you should be aware that not all employers like the functional résumé, perhaps partly because it can obscure your work history and partly because it's less common. In any event, many seasoned employment professionals are suspicious of this résumé style, and some assume that candidates who use it are trying to hide something. In fact, Monster.com lists the functional résumé as one of employers' "Top 10 Pet Peeves."[14] If you don't have a strong, uninterrupted history of relevant work, the combination résumé might be a better choice.

The Combination Résumé A **combination résumé** includes the best features of the chronological and functional approaches. Nevertheless, it is not commonly used, and it has two major disadvantages: (1) It tends to be longer, and (2) it can be repetitive if you have to list your accomplishments and skills in both the functional section and the chronological job descriptions.[15]

combination résumé
A hybrid of a chronological and functional résumé that contains elements of both

As you look at a number of sample résumés, you'll probably notice variations on the three basic formats presented here. Study these other options in light of effective communication principles; if you find one that seems like the best fit for your unique situation, by all means use it.

Producing Your Résumé

With less than a minute to make a good impression, your résumé needs to look sharp and grab a recruiter's interest in the first few lines. A typical recruiter devotes 45 seconds to each résumé before tossing it into either the "maybe" or the "reject" pile. Few recruiters read every résumé from top to bottom; most give them a quick glance to look for keywords and accomplishments. If yours doesn't stand out—or stands out in a negative way—chances are a recruiter won't look at it long enough to judge your qualifications.[16]

Good design is a must, and it's not hard to achieve. Good designs feature simplicity, order, plenty of white space, and straightforward typefaces such as Times Roman or Arial (most of the fonts on your computer are not appropriate for a résumé). Make your subheadings easy to find and easy to read, placing them either above each section or in the left margin. Use lists to itemize your most important qualifications, and leave plenty of white space, even if doing so forces you to use two pages rather than one. Color is not necessary by any means, but if you add color, make it subtle and sophisticated, such as a thin horizontal line under your name and address. The most common way to get into trouble with résumé design is going overboard. If any part of the design "jumps out at you," get rid of it. You want people to be impressed with the information on your résumé, not the number of colors in your printer.

Until just a few years ago, producing résumés was a simple matter: You printed or photocopied as many as you needed and mailed them out. Not anymore. Depending on the companies you apply to, you might want to produce your résumé in as many as six forms:

- *Printed traditional résumé.* Format your traditional résumé simply but elegantly to make the best impression on your employer. Naturally, printed versions must be delivered by hand or by mail.
- *Printed scannable résumé.* Prepare a printed version of your résumé that is unformatted and thus electronically scannable so that employers can store your information in their database.
- *Electronic plain-text file.* Create an electronic plain-text file to use when uploading your résumé information into web forms or inserting it into e-mail messages.
- *Microsoft Word file.* Keep a Microsoft Word file of your traditional résumé so that you can upload it on certain websites.
- *HTML format.* By creating an HTML version, you can post your résumé on your own website, on a page provided by your college, or some of the many job board sites now available.
- *Electronic PDF file.* This is an optional step, but a portable document format (PDF) file of your traditional résumé provides a simple, safe format to attach to e-mail messages. Creating PDFs requires special software, but a PDF can be a helpful item to have on hand in case an employer asks you to e-mail your résumé.

Producing most of these formats is a straightforward task, but printing a scannable résumé and creating a plain-text file require careful attention to some important details.

Printing a Scannable Résumé To cope with the flood of unsolicited paper résumés in recent years, many companies now optically scan incoming résumés into a database. When hiring managers want to interview candidates for job openings, they search the database for the most attractive candidates, using keywords appropriate to a specific position. The system then displays a list of possible candidates, each with a percentage score indicating how closely the résumé reflects the employer's requirements.[17] Nearly all large companies now use these systems, as do many midsized companies and even some smaller firms.[18]

The emergence of such scanning systems has important implications for your résumé. First, computers are interested only in matching information to search parameters, not in artistic attempts at résumé design. A human being may never actually see the résumé as you submitted it, so don't worry about it looking depressingly dull; computers prefer it that way. Second, *optical character recognition (OCR) software* doesn't technically "read" anything; it merely looks for shapes that match stored profiles of characters. Although printing your name in some gothic font might look grand to you, it will look like nonsense to the OCR software. If the OCR software can't make sense of your fancy fonts or creative page layout, it will enter gibberish into the database (for instance, your name might go in as "W$..3r ?00!#" instead of "Walter Jones"). Third, even the most sophisticated databases cannot conduct a search with the nuance and intuition of an experienced human recruiter. Therefore, choosing the keywords for your résumé is a critical step. A human might know that "data-driven webpage design" means that you know XML, but the database probably won't make that connection.

The solution to these issues is twofold: (1) use a plain font and simplified design, and (2) compile your list of keywords carefully.

A scannable résumé contains the same information as your traditional résumé but is formatted to be OCR-friendly (see Exhibit 5):[19]

- Use a clean, common sans serif font such as Optima or Arial, and size it between 10 and 14 points.
- Make sure that characters do not touch one another (whether numbers, letters, or symbols— including the slash [/]).
- Don't use side-by-side columns (the OCR software reads one line all the way across the page).
- Don't use ampersands (&), percent signs (%), foreign-language characters (such as é and ö), or bullet symbols (use a dash—not a lowercase 'o'—in place of a bullet symbol).
- Put each phone number and e-mail address on its own line.
- Print on white, plain paper (speckles and other background coloration can confuse the OCR software).

Your scannable résumé will probably be longer than your traditional résumé because you can't compress text into columns and because you need plenty of white space between headings and sections. If your scannable résumé runs more than one page, make sure your name appears on every subsequent page (in case the pages become separated). Before sending a scannable résumé, check the company's website or call the human resources department to see whether it has any specific requirements other than those discussed here.

When adding a keyword summary to your résumé, keep your audience in mind. Employers generally search for nouns (since verbs tend to be generic rather than specific to a particular position or skill), so make your keywords nouns as well. Use abbreviations sparingly and only when they are well known and unambiguous, such as *MBA*. Include in your list between 20 and 30 words and phrases that define your skills, experience, education, professional affiliations, and so on. Place this list right after your name and address.

One good way to identify which keywords to include in your summary is to underline all the skills listed in ads for the types of jobs you're interested in. (Another advantage of staying current by reading periodicals, networking, and so on is that you'll develop a good ear for current terminology.) Be sure to include only those keywords that correspond with your skills and experience. Trying to get ahead of the competition by listing skills you don't have is unethical; moreover, your efforts will be quickly exposed when your keywords don't match your job experience or educational background.

Creating a Plain-Text File of Your Résumé An increasingly common way to get your information into an employer's database is by entering a *plain-text* version (sometimes referred to as an *ASCII text version*) of your résumé into an online form. This approach has the same goal as a scannable résumé, but it's faster, easier, and less prone to errors than the

Exhibit 5
Scannable Résumé
Because some of his target employers will be scanning his résumé into a database, and because he wants to submit his résumé via e-mail or post it on the Internet, Roberto Cortez created a scannable résumé by changing his formatting and adding a list of keywords. However, the information remains essentially the same.

Removes all boldfacing, rules, bullets, and two-column formatting

Roberto Cortez
5687 Crosswoods Drive
Falls Church, Virginia 22046
Home: (703) 987-0086
Office: (703) 549-6624
RCortez@silvernet.com

KEY WORDS

Includes carefully selected keywords that describe Cortez's skills and accomplishments

Financial executive, accounting management, international finance, financial analyst, accounting reports, financial audit, computerized accounting model, exchange rates, joint-venture agreements, budgets, billing, credit processing, online systems, MBA, fluent Spanish, fluent German, Excel, Access, Visual Basic, team player, willing to travel

Singles Cortez out from the crowd by including in the keyword section specific attributes such as "team player" and "willing to travel"

OBJECTIVE

Accounting management position requiring a knowledge of international finance

EXPERIENCE

Staff Accountant/Financial Analyst, Inter-American Imports (Alexandria, Virginia), March 2001 to present
— Prepare accounting reports for wholesale giftware importer, annual sales of $15 million
— Audit financial transactions with suppliers in 12 Latin American countries
— Created a computerized model to adjust for fluctuations in currency exchange rates
— Negotiated joint-venture agreements with suppliers in Mexico and Colombia
— Implemented electronic funds transfer for vendor disbursements, improving cash flow and eliminating payables clerk position

Uses dashes in place of bullet points

Staff Accountant, Monsanto Agricultural Chemicals (Mexico City, Mexico), October 1997 to March 2001
— Handled budgeting, billing, and credit-processing functions for the Mexico City branch
— Audited travel/entertainment expenses for Monsanto's 30-member Latin American sales force
— Assisted in launching an online computer system to automate accounting

Uses ample white space to make his plain-text résumé easier to scan

EDUCATION

Master of Business Administration with emphasis in international business, George Mason University (Fairfax, Virginia), 1995 to 1997

Bachelor of Business Administration, Accounting, University of Texas (Austin, Texas), 1992 to 1995

INTERCULTURAL AND TECHNICAL SKILLS

Fluent in Spanish and German
Traveled extensively in Latin America
Excel, Access, HTML, Visual Basic

scanning process. If you have the option of mailing a scannable résumé or submitting plain text online, go with plain text.

In addition, when employers or networking contacts ask you to e-mail your résumé, they'll often want to receive it in plain-text format in the body of your e-mail message. Thanks to the prevalence of computer viruses these days, many employers will refuse to open an e-mail attachment.

Plain text is just what it sounds like: no font selections, no bullet symbols, no colors, no lines or boxes, and so on. A plain-text version is easy to create with your word processor. Start with the file you used to create your traditional printed résumé, use the *save as* choice to save it as "plain text" or whichever similarly labeled option your software has, then verify the result.

The verification step is crucial because you can never be quite sure what happens to your layout. Open the text file to view the layout, but don't use your word processor; instead, open the file with a basic text editor (such as Notepad on Windows PCs). If necessary, reformat the page manually, moving text and inserting spaces as needed. For simplicity's sake, left justify all your headings, rather than trying to center them manually. You can put headings in all caps or underline them with a row of dashes to separate them from blocks of text.

Preparing Your Application Letter

Whenever you submit your résumé, accompany it with a cover, or application, letter to let readers know what you're sending, why you're sending it, and how they can benefit from reading it. Because your application letter is in your own style (rather than the choppy, shorthand style of your résumé), it gives you a chance to show your communication skills and some personality.

Always send your résumé and application letter together, because each has a unique job to perform. The purpose of your résumé is to get employers interested enough to contact you for an interview. The purpose of your application letter is to get employers interested enough to read your résumé.

Before drafting a letter, learn something about the organization you're applying to; then focus on your audience so that you can show you've done your homework. Imagine yourself in the recruiter's situation, and show how your background and talents will solve a particular problem or fill a specific need the company has. The more you can learn about the organization, the better you'll be able to capture the reader's attention and convey your interest in the company. During your research, find out the name, title, and department of the person you're writing to. Reaching and addressing the right person is the most effective way to gain attention. Avoid phrases such as "To Whom It May Concern" and "Dear Sir."

When putting yourself in your reader's shoes, remember that this person's in-box is probably overflowing with résumés and cover letters. So respect your reader's time. Steer clear of gimmicks, which almost never work, and include nothing in your cover letter that already appears in your résumé. Keep your letter straightforward, fact-based, short, upbeat, and professional (see Exhibit 6).

Following Up on Your Application

If your application letter and résumé fail to bring a response within a month or so, follow up with a second letter to keep your file active. This follow-up letter also gives you a chance to update your original application with any recent job-related information. Even if you've received a letter acknowledging your application and saying that it will be kept on file, don't hesitate to send a follow-up letter three months later to show that you are still interested. Such a letter can demonstrate that you're sincerely interested in working for the organization, that you're persistent in pursuing your goals, and that you're upgrading your skills to make yourself a better employee. And it might just get you an interview.

Interviewing with Potential Employers

Approach job interviews with a sound appreciation of their dual purpose: The organization's main objective is to find the best person available for the job; the applicant's main objective is to find the job best suited to his or her goals and capabilities.

In general, the easiest way to connect with a big company is through your campus placement office; the most efficient way to approach a smaller business is by contacting the firm directly. In either case, you move to the next stage and prepare to meet with a recruiter during an **employment interview**, a formal meeting during which an employer and an

employment interview Formal meeting during which an employer and an applicant ask questions and exchange information to see whether the applicant and the organization are a good match

Exhibit 6
Application Letter
In her unsolicited application letter, Glenda Johns manages to give a snapshot of her qualifications and skills without repeating what is said in her résumé.

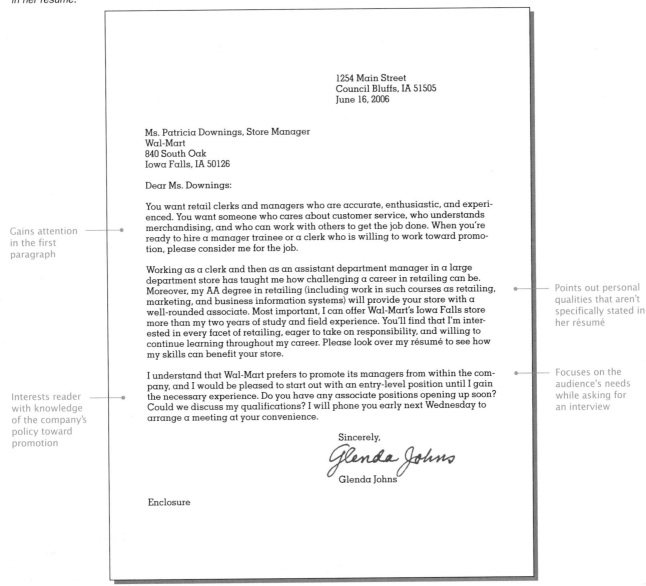

Gains attention in the first paragraph

Interests reader with knowledge of the company's policy toward promotion

Points out personal qualities that aren't specifically stated in her résumé

Focuses on the audience's needs while asking for an interview

1254 Main Street
Council Bluffs, IA 51505
June 16, 2006

Ms. Patricia Downings, Store Manager
Wal-Mart
840 South Oak
Iowa Falls, IA 50126

Dear Ms. Downings:

You want retail clerks and managers who are accurate, enthusiastic, and experienced. You want someone who cares about customer service, who understands merchandising, and who can work with others to get the job done. When you're ready to hire a manager trainee or a clerk who is willing to work toward promotion, please consider me for the job.

Working as a clerk and then as an assistant department manager in a large department store has taught me how challenging a career in retailing can be. Moreover, my AA degree in retailing (including work in such courses as retailing, marketing, and business information systems) will provide your store with a well-rounded associate. Most important, I can offer Wal-Mart's Iowa Falls store more than my two years of study and field experience. You'll find that I'm interested in every facet of retailing, eager to take on responsibility, and willing to continue learning throughout my career. Please look over my résumé to see how my skills can benefit your store.

I understand that Wal-Mart prefers to promote its managers from within the company, and I would be pleased to start out with an entry-level position until I gain the necessary experience. Do you have any associate positions opening up soon? Could we discuss my qualifications? I will phone you early next Wednesday to arrange a meeting at your convenience.

Sincerely,

Glenda Johns

Glenda Johns

Enclosure

preliminary screening interview
Meeting between an employer's representative and a candidate for the purpose of eliminating unqualified applicants from the hiring process

applicant ask questions and exchange information to see whether the applicant and the organization are a good match.

Most employers conduct two or three interviews before deciding whether to offer a person a job. The first interview, generally held on campus, is the **preliminary screening interview**, which helps employers eliminate unqualified applicants from the hiring process. Those candidates who best meet the organization's requirements are invited to visit company offices for further evaluation. Some organizations make a decision at that point, but many schedule a third interview to complete the evaluation process before extending a job offer.

Because the interview takes time, start seeking interviews well in advance of the date you want to start work. It takes an average of 10 interviews to get one job offer. If you hope to have several offers to choose from, you can expect to go through 20 or 30 interviews during your job search.[20] Some students start their job search a year or more before graduation. Early planning is even more crucial during downturns in the economy because many employers become more selective when times are tough.

What Employers Look For

Today's employers want candidates who are experienced, intelligent, good communicators, enthusiastic, creative, and motivated. In addition to these qualities, candidates must also fit in with the organization and meet the basic qualifications for the job.

To determine whether a candidate will be compatible with the other people in the organization, some interviewers may ask you questions about your interests, hobbies, awareness of world events, and so forth. Others may consider your personal style. You're likely to impress an employer by being open, enthusiastic, and interested. Still others may look for courtesy, sincerity, willingness to learn, and a style that is positive and self-confident. All of these qualities help a new employee adapt to a new workplace and new responsibilities.

When you're invited to interview for a position, the interviewer may already have some idea of whether you have the right qualifications, based on a review of your résumé. But during the interview, you'll be asked to describe your education and previous jobs in more depth so that the interviewer can determine how well your skills match the requirements. When describing your skills, be honest. If you don't know how to do something, say so. In many cases, the interviewer will be seeking someone with the flexibility to apply diverse skills in several areas.

What Applicants Need to Find Out

What things should you find out about the prospective job and employer? By doing a little advance research and asking the right questions during the interview (see Exhibit 7), you can probably find answers to these questions and more:

- Are these my kind of people?
- Can I do this work?
- Will I enjoy the work?
- Is this job what I want?
- Does the job pay what I'm worth?
- What kind of person would I be working for?
- What sort of future can I look forward to with this organization?

Questions About the Job	Questions About the Organization
What are the job's major responsibilities?	Who are your organization's major competitors, and what are their strengths and weaknesses?
What qualities do you want in the person who fills this position?	What makes your organization different from others in the industry?
Do you want to know more about my related training?	What are your organization's major markets?
What is the first problem that needs the attention of the person you hire?	Does the organization have any plans for new products? Acquisitions?
Would relocation be required now or in the future?	How would you define your organization's managerial philosophy?
Why is this job now vacant?	What additional training does your organization provide?
What can you tell me about the person I would report to?	Do employees have an opportunity to continue their education with help from the organization?
How do you measure success for someone in this position?	

Exhibit 7
Fifteen Questions to Ask the Interviewer
Learn as much as you can about potential employers by asking these questions.

How to Prepare for a Job Interview

It's perfectly normal to feel a little anxious before an interview. Don't worry too much, however; preparation will help you perform well. Learning about the organization and the job is important because it enables you to consider the employer's point of view. Here are some pointers to guide that preparation:

- *Think ahead about questions.* Most job interviews are essentially question-and-answer sessions: You answer the interviewer's questions about your background, and you ask questions of your own to determine whether the job and the organization are right for you. By planning for your interviews, you can handle these exchanges intelligently (see Exhibit 8). Of course, you don't want to memorize responses or sound overrehearsed.

Exhibit 8

Twenty-five Common Interview Questions

Prepare for an interview in advance by thinking about your answers to these questions.

Questions About College

1. What courses in college did you like most? Least? Why?
2. Do you think your extracurricular activities in college were worth the time spent on them? Why or why not?
3. When did you choose your college major? Did you ever change your major? If so, why?
4. Do you feel you did the best scholastic work you are capable of?
5. Which of your college years was the toughest? Why?

Questions About Employers and Jobs

6. What jobs have you held? Why did you leave?
7. What percentage of your college expenses did you earn? How?
8. Why did you choose your particular field of work?
9. What are the disadvantages of your chosen field?
10. Have you served in the military? What rank did you achieve? What jobs did you perform?
11. What do you think about how this industry operates today?
12. Why do you think you would like this particular type of job?

Questions About Personal Attitudes and Preference

13. Do you prefer to work in any specific geographic location? If so, why?
14. How much money do you hope to be earning in 5 years? In 10 years?
15. What do you think determines a person's progress in a good organization?
16. What personal characteristics do you feel are necessary for success in your chosen field?
17. Tell me a story.
18. Do you like to travel?
19. Do you think grades should be considered by employers? Why or why not?

Questions About Work Habits

20. Do you prefer working with others or by yourself?
21. What type of boss do you prefer?
22. Have you ever had any difficulty getting along with colleagues or supervisors? With instructors? With other students?
23. Would you prefer to work in a large or a small organization? Why?
24. How do you feel about overtime work?
25. What have you done that shows initiative and willingness to work?

- *Bolster your confidence.* By overcoming your tendencies to feel self-conscious or nervous during an interview, you can build your confidence and make a better impression. If some aspect of your background or appearance makes you uneasy, correct it or exercise positive traits to offset it, such as warmth, wit, intelligence, or charm. Instead of dwelling on your weaknesses, focus on your strengths so that you can emphasize them to an interviewer.

- *Polish your interview style.* Confidence helps you walk into an interview and give the interviewer an impression of poise, good manners, and good judgment. In the United States, you're more likely to be invited back for a second interview or offered a job if you maintain eye contact, smile frequently, sit in an attentive position, and use frequent hand gestures. These nonverbal signals convince the interviewer that you're alert, assertive, dependable, confident, responsible, and energetic.[21] Work on eliminating speech mannerisms such as "you know," "like," and "um" (simply pausing for a split second before you say something often helps). Speak in your natural tone, and try to vary the pitch, rate, and volume of your voice to express enthusiasm and energy.

- *Plan to look good.* The best policy is to dress conservatively. Wear the best-quality businesslike clothing you can, preferably in a dark, solid color. Avoid flamboyant styles, colors, and prints. Clean, unwrinkled clothes, well-shined shoes, neatly styled and combed hair, clean fingernails, and fresh breath help make a good first impression. Don't spoil the effect by smoking cigarettes before or during the interview. Finally, remember that one of the best ways to look good is to smile at appropriate moments.

- *Be ready when you arrive.* Be sure you know when and where the interview will be held. Take a small notebook, a pen, a list of your questions, a folder with two copies of your résumé, an outline of your research findings about the organization, and any correspondence about the position. You may also want to take a small calendar, a transcript of your college grades, a list of references, and, if appropriate, samples of your work. After you arrive, relax. You may have to wait, so bring something to read or to occupy your time (the less frivolous or controversial, the better).

How to Follow Up After the Interview

Touching base with the prospective employer after the interview, either by phone or in writing, shows that you really want the job and are determined to get it. It also brings your name to the interviewer's attention again and reminds him or her that you're waiting to know the decision.

The two most common forms of follow-up, the thank-you note and the inquiry, are generally handled by letter or e-mail. But a phone call can be just as effective, particularly if the employer favors a casual, personal style. Express your thanks within two days after the interview, even if you feel you have little chance for the job. In a brief message, acknowledge the interviewer's time and courtesy, convey your continued interest, and ask politely for a decision. If you're not advised of the interviewer's decision by the promised date or within two weeks, you might make an inquiry, particularly if you don't want to accept a job offer from a second firm before you have an answer from the first. Assume that a simple oversight is the reason for the delay, not outright rejection.

Building Your Career

In today's job market, employers seek people who are able and willing to adapt to diverse situations, who thrive in an ever-changing workplace, and who continue to learn throughout their careers. In addition, companies want team players with strong work records and leaders who are versatile. Many companies encourage managers to get varied job experience.[22] In some cases, your chances of being hired are better if you've studied abroad or learned another language. Many employers expect college graduates to have a sound understanding of international affairs, and they're looking for employees with intercultural sensitivity and an ability to adapt in other cultures.[23]

Compile an employment portfolio. If you aren't able to create an e-portfolio, get a three-ring notebook and a package of plastic sleeves that open at the top. Collect anything that shows your ability to perform, such as classroom or work evaluations, certificates, awards, and papers you've written. An employment portfolio serves as an excellent resource when writing your résumé and provides employers with tangible evidence of your professionalism.

As you search for a permanent job that fulfills your career goals, take interim job assignments, participate in an internship program, and consider temporary work or freelance jobs. Not only will these temporary assignments help you gain valuable experience and relevant contacts, but they will also provide you with important references and with items for your portfolio.[24] Employers will be more willing to find (or even to create) a position for someone they've learned to respect, and your temporary or freelance work gives them a chance to see what you can do.

If you're unable to find actual job experience, work on polishing and updating your skills. Network with professional colleagues and friends who can help you stay abreast of your occupation and industry. While you're waiting for responses to your résumé or your last interview, take a computer course or gain some other educational or life experience that would be difficult while working full-time. Become familiar with the services offered by your campus career center (or placement office). These centers offer individual placement counseling, credential services, job fairs, on-campus interviews, job listings, advice on computerized résumé-writing software, workshops in job-search techniques, résumé preparation, interview techniques, and more.[25]

Even after an employer hires you, continue improving your skills to distinguish yourself from your peers and to make yourself more valuable to current and potential employers:[26]

- Acquire as much technical knowledge as you can, build broad-based life experience, and develop your social skills.
- Learn to respond to change in positive, constructive ways; this will help you adapt if your "perfect" career path eludes your grasp.
- Keep up with developments in your industry and the economy at large; read widely and subscribe to free e-mail newsletters.
- Learn to see each job, even so-called entry-level jobs, as an opportunity to learn more and to expand your knowledge, experience, and social skills.
- Take on as much responsibility as you can outside your job description.
- Share what you know with others instead of hoarding knowledge in the hope of becoming indispensable; helping others excel is a skill, too.
- Understand the big picture; knowing your own job inside and out isn't enough any more.
- Understand that what counts isn't only who you know but also what you know and who knows you.

In Pursuit of Prosperity: The Fundamentals of Business and Economics

CHAPTER

1

LEARNING OBJECTIVES

After studying this chapter, you will be able to

1. Explain how the study of business will help you meet your career goals

2. Define what a business is and identify four key social and economic roles that businesses serve

3. Differentiate between goods-producing and service businesses and list five factors contributing to the increase in the number of service businesses

4. Identify the factors that affect demand and those that affect supply

5. Compare supply and demand curves and explain how they interact to affect price

6. Discuss the four major economic roles of the U.S. government

7. Explain how a free-market system monitors its economic performance

8. Identify five challenges you'll face as a business professional in today's global economy

www.prenhall.com/bovee

INSIDE BUSINESS TODAY

Making Dollars and Sense of Online Music at Apple iTunes

www.apple.com/itunes

Success in business is often a matter of connecting the dots: looking at your own strengths and weaknesses, exploring customer needs, and analyzing the various legal, technical, and social forces at work in the marketplace. You consider what you're capable of doing, what your competitors might do, what customers would like you to do—and what forces are reshaping the business landscape. Then you look for connections and opportunities. How can you capitalize on changing markets?

Apple Computer CEO Steve Jobs has spent his career connecting those dots, leading the development of innovations that have changed the way people work and play, including the way they listen to music. Although Apple didn't start out in the music business, by 2003 the company had become a significant force in music, at least indirectly. Many musicians and creative professionals favored Apple computers, and the company's sleek new iPod music players were a must-have item for trendsetting music consumers everywhere.

Meanwhile, though, the music industry was in a state of turmoil. Music fans, tired of buying entire CDs for just one or two favorite songs, were downloading millions of songs for free from the Internet—in spite of the fact that many people consider this practice unethical and the recording industry considers it illegal. Performers, songwriters, and music companies were all looking for better ways to address customer complaints while protecting their legal rights and financial assets. As is often the case, technology was one step ahead of business strategy and two steps ahead of legal developments. Amazon.com, eBay, and other companies had proven the potential for selling over the Internet, but was it possible to make money selling something as inexpensive as an individual song?

When Jobs surveyed the situation, he no doubt liked some of the things he saw more than others. On the plus side, Apple was a well-known and highly regarded presence in both the computer and music industries, so almost anything the company chose to do would have the support and respect of many consumers and potential business partners. Plus, 2 million people were already walking around with Apple iPods. Moreover, Apple's design team had a proven knack for making technology easier to use, a critical issue in the complicated arena of digital music.

On the minus side, Jobs knew there would be serious challenges in any effort to turn online music into a successful business venture. Seemingly every company from Wal-Mart and Microsoft to a reborn Napster and major cell phone companies wanted in on the digital music market. The technology would be complex, starting from the need to collect and store hundreds of thousands of songs and then make them easily available to thousands or even millions of online customers at once. The technology might've been the easiest part of the whole problem, however. The music business is a complex stew of strong personalities, strong traditions, tangled legal contracts, and lots of people who want a piece of the financial action, including performers, songwriters, music publishers, and record companies.

After 20 years of doing commercial battle with the likes of IBM and Microsoft, though, Steve Jobs has never been one to back down from a challenge. He added up those pluses and minuses, then decided to lead Apple into the fray. In 2003, the company launched iTunes.com, a web-based music store that offers more than a million legally downloadable songs, all for 99 cents each. iTunes enjoyed widespread media coverage when it was first launched and even more when it was expanded to support Windows-based personal computers (PCs). Industry experts have applauded its simplicity and breadth of musical offerings.

Music fans have responded by purchasing hundreds of millions of songs from iTunes, and Apple is now pushing hard to expand iTunes into markets around the world. The wild ride is sure to continue, as Jobs and company continue to navigate through a complex market full of demanding customers and hungry competitors.[1]

GET READY

No matter where you career takes you, you can learn by studying the decisions made by Steve Jobs and his iTunes team. Put yourself in their shoes as you read this chapter—how would you compete in the digital music business? How would you convince millions of file sharers to start paying for music? How would you build a multimillion-dollar business selling a 99-cent product? ▪

Chapter Overview

From a consumer's point of view, iTunes looks like a sleek product that offers access to music. Behind the scenes, though, is a complex operation that requires the efforts of accountants, lawyers, computer programmers, customer support specialists, managers, marketing experts, and other professionals. This chapter will help you understand the demanding environment in which Apple and all other businesses now function, from the basic laws of supply and demand to the influence of government agencies in the business arena. You'll learn how the U.S. economy got to where it is today and explore the challenges you'll face in today's global marketplace.

LEARNING OBJECTIVE 1

Explain how the study of business will help you meet your career goals

How This Course Will Help Your Career

No matter where your career plans take you, the dynamics of business will affect your work and life in innumerable ways. If you aspire to be a manager or an entrepreneur, knowing how to run a business is vital, of course. If you plan a career in a professional specialty such as law, engineering, or finance, knowing how businesses operate will help you interact with clients and colleagues more effectively and thereby contribute to your career success. Even if you plan to work in government, education, or some other noncommercial setting, business awareness can help you as well; many of these organizations look to business for new ideas and leadership techniques. And in your role as a consumer and taxpayer, knowing more about business will help you make better financial decisions.

In fact, your experiences as a consumer have already taught you a great deal about the business world. As you progress through this course, though, you'll begin to look at things from the eyes of an employee or a manager instead of a consumer. You'll develop a fundamental business vocabulary that will help you keep up with the latest news and make better-informed decisions. By participating in classroom discussions and completing the chapter exercises, you'll gain some valuable critical-thinking, problem-solving, team-building, and communication skills that you can use on the job and throughout your life.

This course will also introduce you to a variety of jobs in business fields such as accounting, economics, human resources, management, finance, marketing, and so on. You'll see how people who work in these fields contribute to the success of a company as a whole. You'll gain insight into the types of skills and knowledge these jobs require—and you'll discover that a career in business today is fascinating, challenging, and often quite rewarding.

In addition, a study of business management will help you appreciate the larger context in which businesses operate and the many legal and ethical questions managers must consider as they make business decisions. Both government regulators and society as a whole have numerous expectations regarding the ways businesses treat employees, shareholders, the environment, other businesses, and the communities in which they operate.

What Is a Business?

A **business** is an organized, profit-seeking activity that provides goods and services designed to satisfy customers' needs. Apple's iTunes, for example, satisfies an important aspect of consumers' entertainment needs. In addition to providing a society with necessities such as housing, clothing, food, transportation, communication, health care, and much more, businesses provide people with jobs and a means to prosper; they pay taxes that are used to build highways, fund education, and provide grants for scientific research; and they reinvest their profits in the economy, thereby creating a higher standard of living and quality of life for society as a whole.

The driving force behind most businesses is the prospect of earning a **profit**—money that remains after all expenses have been deducted from the sales revenue the business has brought in. Such a prospect is commonly referred to as a *profit motive*. Businesses may keep and use their profits as they wish, within legal limits. Still, not every organization exists to earn a profit. **Nonprofit organizations** (also known as *not-for-profit organizations*) such as museums, public schools and universities, symphonies, libraries, government agencies, and charities exist to provide society with a social, educational, or other service. The American Red Cross, for example, provides relief to victims of disasters and helps people prevent, prepare for, and respond to emergencies. Although nonprofit organizations do not have a profit motive, they must operate efficiently and effectively to achieve their goals. All nonprofit organizations, from a student club with only a few dozen members to a multibillion-dollar operation such as the Red Cross, can learn from business opportunities, challenges, and activities discussed throughout this course.

Goods-Producing Businesses Versus Service Businesses

Most businesses can be classified into two broad categories: goods-producing businesses and service businesses. **Goods-producing businesses** produce tangible goods by engaging in activities such as manufacturing, construction, mining, and agriculture. Boeing, the world's largest manufacturer of commercial jetliners, military aircraft, and satellites, is a goods-producing business. The company's Everett, Washington, factory is the largest building, by volume, in the world. Spanning 98 acres under one roof, the facility is big enough to handle construction of 20 wide-body jets at once.[2] Of course, most

LEARNING OBJECTIVE 2

Define what a business is and identify four key social and economic roles that businesses serve

business
A profit-seeking enterprise that provides goods and services that a society wants or needs

profit
Money left over after expenses and taxes have been deducted from revenue generated by selling goods and services

nonprofit organizations
Organizations whose primary objective is something other than returning a profit to their owners

goods-producing businesses
Businesses that produce tangible products

LEARNING OBJECTIVE 3

Differentiate between goods-producing and service businesses and list five factors contributing to the increase in the number of service businesses

manufacturing operations do not require a facility as big as Boeing's. Nonetheless, it's difficult to start a goods-producing business without substantial investments in buildings, machinery, and equipment. For this reason, most goods-producing businesses are **capital-intensive businesses**: they generally require large amounts of money or equipment to get started and to operate.

Service businesses, by contrast, produce intangible products (ones that cannot be held in your hand) and include those whose principal product is finance, insurance, transportation, construction, utilities, wholesale and retail trade, banking, entertainment, health care, repairs, or information. America Online, Nordstrom, Jiffy Lube, and eBay are examples of service businesses. Most service businesses are **labor-intensive businesses**. That is, they rely more on human resources than buildings, machinery, and equipment to prosper. A consulting firm is an example of a labor-intensive service business because its existence is heavily dependent on the knowledge and skills of its consultants. A group of consultants can go into business with little more than a few computers and some telephones—although the consultants must possess considerable knowledge and experience.

Goods and services are useful categories, but the line between the two is often blurry. For example, IBM is well known as a manufacturer of computers and other technological goods, but roughly half the company's sales now come from computer-related services such as systems design, consulting, and product support.[3] Similarly, Boeing provides flight training, fleet and logistics support, and a number of aviation services to supplement sales of its commercial aircraft. As more and more manufacturers such as Boeing and IBM focus on servicing and supporting their products, it becomes increasingly difficult to classify many companies as either goods-producing businesses or service businesses. In addition, economists don't always agree on what constitutes production of goods versus delivery of services. Does McDonald's "manufacture" hamburgers or simply provide the service of assembling and selling materials created elsewhere? Such questions might seem a bit silly, but they can have important implications for taxation and other economic decisions.[4]

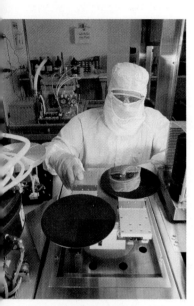

Computer-chip manufacturing is a capital-intensive business. A new state-of-the art factory costs about $2 billion to build and that's only the start. Add to that the costs of manufacturing equipment, supplies, equipment repairs, utilities, and skilled workers, and you can see why the barriers of entry into this industry are extraordinarily high.

Growth of the Service Sector

Over the past few decades, the U.S. economy has undergone a profound transformation from being dominated by manufacturing to being dominated by services. The service sector now accounts for 70 to 80 percent of the nation's economic output.[5] This trend will likely continue into the foreseeable future, with service businesses creating the vast majority of new jobs.[6] For instance, during a recent 12-month span when traditional high-tech and manufacturing regions such as Boston and the Silicon Valley in California lost jobs, the more service-oriented economy in Phoenix added 60,000 jobs in construction, health-care, and other industries.[7] Although the United States remains one of the world's manufacturing powerhouses, roughly two-thirds of the 100 largest U.S. companies are now service based.[8] The service sector is growing for a number of reasons:

- **Consumers have more disposable income.** The 76 million baby boomers in the United States (people born between 1946 and 1964) are in their peak earning years. These consumers find themselves with more disposable income and look for services to help them invest, travel, relax, and stay fit.
- **Services target changing demographic patterns and lifestyle trends.** As the population changes, businesses find opportunities in providing services that people can't or don't do for themselves, from in-home care for an increasingly aging population to self-storage units for people who've used their increasing incomes to buy more stuff than they can fit in their homes. Christopher Burdick and Jason Summerfield of Newton, Massachusetts, saw an opportunity in the anxiety that many consumers feel about buying a new car. The pair founded Autoheroes to do all the research, negotiating, and paperwork for a modest fee.[9]
- **Services are needed to support complex goods and new technologies.** Computers, home theater systems, recreational vehicles, security systems, and automated production

TECHNOLOGIES THAT ARE REVOLUTIONIZING BUSINESS | Instant Messaging

If you're a serious user of instant messaging (IM), do you remember what it was like those first few times you communicated? Chances are it changed the way you interacted with friends and family.

HOW IT'S CHANGING BUSINESS

IM may have started as a way for individual computer users to stay in touch, but it is quickly becoming a major communication tool for businesses worldwide. Businesses use IM to replace in-person meetings and phone calls, to supplement online meetings, and to interact with customers. Key benefits include rapid response to urgent messages and lower cost than both phone calls and e-mail.

Business-class IM systems offer a range of advanced capabilities in addition to basic chat, including *presence awareness* (the ability to quickly see who's at their desks and available to IM), remote display of documents, remote control of other computers, video, and even automated *bot* capabilities that mimic simple conversations with human beings.

WHERE YOU CAN LEARN MORE

To learn more about how IM works, check out www.computer.howstuffworks.com/instant-messaging.htm. For the latest on the business applications of IM, log on to www.instantmessagingplanet.com.

equipment are examples of products that often require specialized installation, repair, user training, or extensive support services.

- **Companies are increasingly seeking professional advice.** To compete in the global economy, many firms turn to consultants and professional advisers for help as they seek ways to cut costs, refine their business processes, expand overseas, and engage in **electronic commerce (e-commerce)**—buying and selling over the Internet (see Chapter 4).
- **Technology has lowered the barriers to entry for many service businesses.** Capital-intensive manufacturing businesses generally have high **barriers to entry**, which are the requirements a company must meet before it can start competing in a given market. Conditions vary widely by industry, but manufacturers sometimes need to invest many millions of dollars in facilities and equipment before they can produce a single product. Other barriers to entry can include government testing and approval, tightly controlled markets, strict licensing procedures, limited supplies of raw materials, and the need for

electronic commerce (e-commerce)
The general term for the buying and selling of goods and services on the Internet

barriers to entry
Factors that make it difficult to launch a business in a particular industry

The potential rewards available in a free-market economy encourage innovators to create new and exciting products such as the Apple iPod; a single innovative product can often revolutionize an entire industry.

highly skilled employees. Of course, many of these barriers apply to various service businesses as well, but in general, service businesses are easier to start than manufacturing businesses of comparable size—and the Internet has made it easier than ever to start service businesses in such areas as retailing, entertainment, and publishing.

Whether you're running a service or a goods-producing business, world economic situations affect all businesses that compete in the global economy. Consequently, running a successful business today requires a firm understanding of basic economic principles, of the various economic systems in the world, and of how businesses compete in the global economy.

What Is Economics?

Economics is the study of how a society uses its resources to produce and distribute goods and services. The study of economic behavior among consumers, businesses, and industries who collectively determine the quantity of goods and services demanded and supplied at different prices is commonly referred to as **microeconomics**. By contrast, the study of a country's larger economic issues, such as how firms compete, the effect of government policies, and how an economy maintains and allocates its scarce resources, is commonly referred to as **macroeconomics**.

Granted, economics doesn't strike everyone as the most fascinating subject on earth, but if you want to make it to the top of a corporation or launch your own successful business, you need a solid understanding of how and why money flows through the economy. A good place to start is understanding the different types of economic systems in use throughout the world.

All societies must deal with the same basic economic questions: How should limited economic resources be used to satisfy society's needs? What goods and services should be produced? Who should produce them? How should these goods and services be divided among the population? In some countries these decisions are made by individuals (or households) when they decide how to spend or invest their income and by businesses when they decide what kinds of goods and services to produce; in other countries these decisions are made by governments.

The resources that societies use to produce goods and services are called *factors of production*. To maximize a company's profit, businesses use five factors of production in the most efficient way possible:

- **Natural resources**—things that are useful in their natural state, such as land, forests, minerals, and water
- **Human resources**—anyone (from company presidents to grocery clerks) who works to produce goods and services
- **Capital**—resources (such as money, computers, machines, tools, and buildings) that a business needs to produce goods and services
- **Entrepreneurs**—innovative businesspeople who are willing to take the risks involved in creating and operating new businesses (see Exhibit 1.1)
- **Knowledge**—the collective intelligence of an organization

Traditionally, a business was considered to have an advantage if it was located in a country with a plentiful supply of natural resources, human resources, capital, and entrepreneurs. But in the global marketplace, intellectual assets are the key. Today companies can obtain capital from one part of the world, purchase supplies from another, and locate production facilities in still another. They can relocate their operations to wherever they find a steady supply of affordable workers. Thus, countries with the greatest supply of knowledge workers and ones with economic systems that give workers the freedom to pursue their own economic interests will have an advantage in the new economic landscape (see Exhibit 1.2).

Types of Economic Systems

The role that individuals and government play in allocating a society's resources depends on the society's **economic system**, the basic set of rules for allocating resources to satisfy its

---

economics
The study of how society uses scarce resources to produce and distribute goods and services

microeconomics
The study of how consumers, businesses, and industries collectively determine the quantity of goods and services demanded and supplied at different prices

macroeconomics
The study of "big picture" issues in an economy, including competitive behavior among firms, the effect of government policies, and overall resource allocation issues

natural resources
Land, forests, minerals, water, and other tangible assets usable in their natural state

human resources
All the people who work for an organization

capital
A collective term for both the funds used to finance a company's operations and its physical, human-made assets such as factories and computers

entrepreneurs
Businesspeople who create and run new businesses and accept the risks involved in the private enterprise system

knowledge
Expertise gained through experience or research

economic system
Means by which a society distributes its resources to satisfy its people's needs

The Company	Its Start
Amazon.com	In 1994 Jeff Bezos came across a report projecting annual web growth at 2,300 percent. He left his Wall Street job, headed to Seattle in an aging Chevy Blazer, and drafted his business plan en route. His e-business, Amazon.com, initially focused on selling books over the Internet but later expanded to include toys, consumer electronics, software, home improvement products, and more. Today Amazon.com generates over $5 billion in annual sales.
Clorox	In May 1913, five men pooled $100 each and started Clorox. The group had no experience in bleach-making chemistry but suspected that the brine found in salt ponds in San Francisco Bay could be converted into bleach.
Limited Brands	In 1963, 26-year-old Leslie Wexner left his family's retail business after having an argument with his father. He started with one small store in a strip mall in Columbus, Ohio, and today employs more than 100,000 people in a retailing group that includes The Limited, Victoria's Secret, Express, and Bath & Body Works.
Gateway	Using $10,000 borrowed from his grandmother, Ted Waitt started the company in his father's South Dakota barn in 1985. Today Gateway is a multibillion-dollar company and one of the largest PC manufacturers in the world.
Coca-Cola	Pharmacist John Pemberton invented a soft drink in his backyard in 1886. Asa Chandler bought the company for $2,300 in 1891. Current sales now exceed $20 billion every year.
Marriott	Willard Marriott and his fiancée-partner started a nine-seat A & W soda fountain with $3,000 in 1927. They demonstrated a knack for hospitality and clever marketing from the beginning.
Nike	In the early 1960s, Philip Knight and his college track coach sold imported Japanese sneakers from the back of a station wagon. Start-up costs totaled $1,000.
United Parcel Service	In 1907, two Seattle teenagers pooled their cash, came up with $100, and began a message and parcel delivery service for local merchants.
Wrigley's Gum	In 1891, young William Wrigley, Jr. started selling baking soda in Chicago. To entice new customers, he threw in two packages of chewing gum with every sale. Guess what the customers were more excited about?

Exhibit 1.1
Rags to Riches
Few start-up companies are resource rich. Still, they become successful because an entrepreneur substitutes ingenuity for capital resources.

citizens' needs. Economic systems are generally categorized as either *free-market systems* or *planned systems,* although these are really theoretical extremes; virtually every system in use today exhibits aspects of both approaches.

Free-Market Systems In a **free-market system**, individuals are free to decide what products to produce, how to produce them, whom to sell them to, and at what price to sell them. Thus, they have the chance to succeed—or to fail—by their own efforts. **Capitalism** and *private enterprise* are the terms most often used to describe the free-market system—one in which individuals own and operate the majority of businesses and where competition, supply, and demand determine which goods and services are produced. Capitalism owes its philosophical origins to 18th-century philosophers such as Adam Smith. According to Smith, in the ideal capitalist economy (pure capitalism), the *market* (an arrangement between buyer

free-market system
Economic system in which decisions about what to produce and in what quantities are decided by the market's buyers and sellers

capitalism
Economic system based on economic freedom, private ownership, and competition

Exhibit 1.2
What's New About
the New Economy?
*The new economy is
different from the old
economy in a number of
key ways. Besides being
faster and more volatile,
it's highly dependent on
the use of information
technology to gain a
competitive advantage.*

	Old Economy	**New Economy**
General characteristics	Competitive advantage based on physical assets	Competitive advantage based on intellectual assets
	Profits maximized by controlling costs	Profits maximized by adding value to products and services
Technology	Mechanical technology is main influence on economic growth	Information technology is main influence on economic growth
Workforce	Job-specific skills	Transferable skills and lifelong learning
Geography	Firms locate near resource to reduce costs	Firms locate near collaborators and competitors to boost innovation
Capital	Debt financing	Venture capital

and seller to trade goods and services) serves as a self-correcting mechanism—an "invisible hand" to ensure the production of the goods that society wants in the quantities that society wants, without regulation of any kind.[10]

Because the market is its own regulator, Smith was opposed to government intervention. He held that if anyone's prices or wages strayed from acceptable levels that were set for everyone, the force of competition would drive them back. In modern practice, however, the government sometimes intervenes in free-market systems to accomplish goals that leaders deem socially or economically desirable. This practice of limited intervention is characteristic of a *mixed economy* or *mixed capitalism,* which is the economic system of the United States and most other countries. For example, federal, state, and local governments intervene in the U.S. economy in a variety of ways, such as influencing particular allocations of resources through tax incentives, prohibiting or restricting the sale of certain goods and services, or setting *price controls.* Price controls can involve both maximum allowable prices (such as limiting rent increases or capping the price on gasoline or other products during emergencies and shortages) and minimum allowable prices (such as supplementing the prices of agricultural goods to ensure producers a minimum level of income or establishing minimum wage levels).[11]

Mixed economies, particularly those with a strong capitalist emphasis, offer opportunities for wealth creation but usually attach an element of risk to the potential reward. For instance, it's relatively easy to start a company in a mixed economic system such as the United States, but you could lose all of your start-up money if the company isn't successful. Entrepreneurs and investors willing to face these risks are a vital force in capitalist economies, and they can be rewarded handsomely when they are successful.

Planned Systems In a **planned system**, governments control all or part of the allocation of resources and limit the freedom of choice in order to accomplish government goals. Because social equality is a major goal of planned systems, private enterprise and the pursuit of private gain are generally regarded as unfair and exploitive.

The planned system that allows individuals the least degree of economic freedom is **communism**, which still exists in such countries as North Korea and Cuba. (Keep in mind that even though communism and socialism are discussed here as economic systems, they can be political and social systems as well.) The degree to which communism is actually practiced varies. In its purest form, almost all resources are under government control. Private ownership is restricted to personal and household items. Resource allocation is handled through rigid centralized planning by a handful of government officials who decide what goods to produce, how to produce them, and to whom they should be distributed.[12] Although pure communism still has its supporters, the future of communism is dismal. As economists Lester Thurow and Robert Heilbroner put it, "It's a great deal easier to design and assemble the skeleton of a mighty economy than to run it."[13]

planned system
Economic system in which
the government controls
most of the factors of
production and regulates
their allocation

communism
Economic system in which
the government owns and
operates all productive
resources and determines
all significant economic
choices

THINKING ABOUT ETHICS

SHOULD EMPLOYEES PAY TO KEEP THEIR JOBS?

When the economy is booming, job seekers tend to be in the driver's seat, and hiring managers will try signing bonuses, stock options, and other perks—doing whatever it takes to recruit and retain employees. However, when the economy heads south, negotiating power shifts back to employers, who sometimes have more workers than they can afford.

Facing a weakened economy, some companies immediately lay off employees. Others, who recognize that human capital is their most important asset, try to limit or avoid layoffs so they won't break the trust they've established with employees, lose experienced talent, then have to hastily rehire when the economy recovers. But maintaining huge payroll costs—which can account for two-thirds of most companies' expenses—is a challenge during an economic downturn. So some companies freeze wages or cut pay across the surviving workforce to distribute the pain more equitably.

Salary and benefit cuts "are the last thing you want to do in a down economy," warns one human resources expert. "It's never good to take away from the people you want to keep." In fact, many companies who imposed widespread pay cuts in past recessions say they would never do it again. The cuts generated millions in savings. But worker morale—and productivity —plummeted. These experts argue that it would be better for companies to lay off their least-productive workers so they can afford to keep more-productive employees. Not so, say others, who maintain that you can't have good morale unless all employees have confidence that a company will treat them fairly, which for some employees means avoiding layoffs at all costs, even if they have to swallow a pay cut.

The debate continues over which approach is the lesser of two evils: widespread layoffs or limited layoffs combined with across-the-board pay and benefits cuts for those who survive. From a company perspective, hiring and firing and then rehiring is an exercise they'd rather not repeat. But maintaining high payroll costs in poor economic times is also something they can't afford. From an employee's perspective, finding a new job in a recession is extremely difficult, so some are willing to pay to keep their jobs. But here's the twist: If employees feel they are being exploited by companies who are using an economic downturn to take back some of their hard-earned gains in the past decade or so, they will be the first to bolt when the economy strengthens.

Questions for Critical Thinking
1. How do the forces of supply and demand apply to employers and employees?
2. Why would a minimum wage law be considered a form of price control?

Socialism lies somewhere between capitalism and communism in the degree of economic freedom that it permits. Like communism, socialism involves a relatively high degree of government planning and some government ownership of land and capital resources (such as buildings and equipment). However, government involvement is limited to industries considered vital to the common welfare, such as transportation, utilities, medicine, steel, and communications. In these industries, the government owns or controls all the facilities and determines what will be produced and how the output will be distributed. Private ownership is permitted in industries that are not considered vital, and in these areas both businesses and individuals are allowed to benefit from their own efforts. Taxes are high in socialist states because the government must cover the costs of medical care, education, subsidized housing, and other social services.

socialism
Economic system characterized by public ownership and operation of key industries combined with private ownership and operation of less-vital industries

The Trend Toward Privatization

Although varying degrees of socialism and communism are practiced around the world today, several socialist and communist economies are moving toward free-market systems.

privatizing
The conversion of public
ownership to private
ownership

Anxious to unload unprofitable businesses for badly needed cash or to improve the efficiency of bureaucratic organizations, Great Britain, Mexico, Argentina, Israel, France, Sweden, China, and other countries are **privatizing** some of their government-owned enterprises by selling them to privately held firms. Great Britain, for example, has sold the national phone company, the national steel company, the national sugar company, Heathrow Airport, water suppliers, and the company that makes Rover automobiles. Although its communist government remains in firm control of the economy, China has taken dramatic steps to privatize major industries in order to compete more successfully in the global economy. And here in the United States, some free-market economists and political leaders believe that Social Security system and some other government programs would benefit from privatization.[14]

CRITICAL THINKING CHECKPOINT
1. Will a study of business help in your career, even if you don't pursue a career in the business field? Why or why not?
2. Could the U.S. economy reach a point when it becomes too dependent on the service sector for both jobs and economic output? Explain your answer.
3. Why does the United States use a mixed economy, rather than a pure free-market system?

L E A R N I N G
O B J E C T I V E 4

Identify the factors that
affect demand and those
that affect supply

Microeconomics: Understanding the Forces of Demand and Supply

At the heart of every business transaction is an exchange between a buyer and a seller. The buyer wants or needs a particular service or good and is willing to pay the seller in order to obtain it. The seller is willing to participate in the transaction because of the anticipated financial gains from selling the service or good. In a free-market system, the marketplace (composed of individuals, firms, and industries) and the forces of demand and supply determine the quantity of goods and services produced and the prices at which they are sold. **Demand** refers to the amount of a good or service that customers will buy at a given time at various prices. **Supply** refers to the quantities of a good or service that producers will provide on a particular date at various prices. Simply put, *demand* refers to the behavior of buyers, whereas *supply* refers to the behavior of sellers. Both work together to impose a kind of order on the free-market system.

On the surface, the theory of supply and demand seems little more than common sense. Customers should buy more when the price is low and buy less when the price is high. Producers would offer more when the price is high and offer less when the price is low. In other words, the quantity supplied and the quantity demanded continuously interact, and the balance between them at any given moment should be reflected by the current price on the open market. However, a quick look at any real-life market situation shows that balancing supply with demand by adjusting price isn't quite that simple, nor does it automatically guarantee profitability.

demand
*Buyers' willingness and
ability to purchase products*

supply
*Specific quantity of a
product that the seller is
able and willing to provide*

Understanding Demand

Consider the airline industry. When the economy is robust, consumers are willing to spend more on discretionary travel. When the economy falters, they cut back on such discretionary spending. Airlines can respond to changes in consumer demand by reducing ticket prices or by offering promotions. But factors other than price influence consumer demand, including

*   consumer income
*   consumer preferences (such as increased safety or reduced travel time for the airline industry)
*   the price of substitute products (such as rail or automobile travel or videoconferencing for the airline industry)

- the price of complementary goods (such as hotel accommodations or restaurant dining for the airline industry)
- advertising and promotional expenditures
- consumer expectations about future prices

Still, price generally is considered the most important variable. In most cases as the price of a good or service goes up, people buy less. In other words, as the price rises, the quantity demanded declines. Alternatively, at lower prices, consumers generally are willing to purchase more goods and services.

A **demand curve** is a graph showing the relationship between the amount of product that buyers will purchase at various prices. (Demand curves are not necessarily curved; they may be straight lines.) To draw the graph, we assume that all variables except price remain constant. Demand curves typically slope downward, which means that lower prices generally attract larger purchases. For instance, when airlines reduce their ticket prices, the demand for airline travel generally rises. Exhibit 1.3 shows a possible demand curve for the monthly number of economy tickets (seats) for an airline's Chicago to Denver route at different prices.

Note the difference between changes in the quantity demanded at various prices and changes in overall demand. A change in quantity demanded, such as the change that occurs at different airline ticket prices for a market, is simply movement along the demand curve. A change in overall demand resulting from changes in a number of variables besides price produces an entirely new demand curve. Exhibit 1.4 highlights the expected movement of the new demand curve in response to changing forces in the market place.

Looking back at the airline example, if consumer concerns for travel safety increase or the consumer income decreases, we would expect the original demand curve for airline tickets to drop at every price. As Exhibit 1.5 shows, such an overall drop in demand would result in a new demand curve for airline ticket sales for the same Chicago to Denver route. The

LEARNING OBJECTIVE 5

Compare supply and demand curves and explain how they interact to affect price

demand curve
Graph of the quantities of product that buyers will purchase at various prices

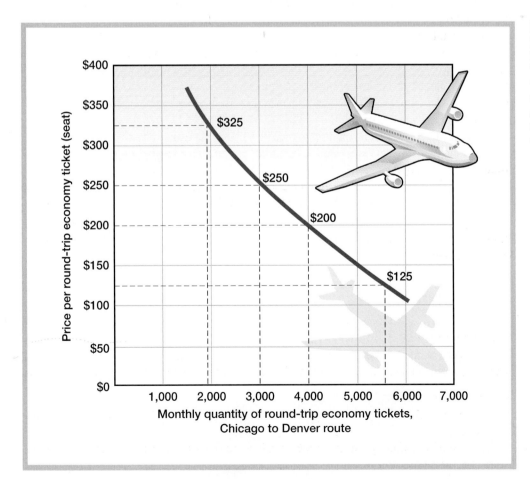

Exhibit 1.3
Demand Curve for Monthly Airline Tickets
This demand curve shows that the higher the ticket price, the smaller the quantity demanded, all else being equal.

Exhibit 1.4
The Influence of
Market Forces on the
Demand Curve
*The demand curve is
affected by changes
in these variables.*

| | Expected Shifts in Demand Curve | |
Variable	Shifts to the right when:	Shifts to the left when:
Consumers' incomes	increase	decrease
Consumer preferences	are more favorable toward product	are less favorable toward product
Prices of substitute products	increase	decrease
Prices of complementary goods	decrease	increase
Advertising or promotional expenditures	increase	decrease
Consumer expectations become more	optimistic	pessimistic
Number of buyers	increases	decreases

new demand curve shifts to the left of the original demand curve depicted in Exhibit 1.3. If conditions change and overall demand increases beyond the original demand depicted in Exhibit 1.3, the new demand curve would shift to the right of the original demand curve.

Understanding Supply

Demand alone is not enough to explain how a company operating in a free-market system sets its prices or production levels. In general, a firm's willingness to produce and sell a good or service increases as the price it can charge and its profit potential per item increase. In other words, as the price goes up, the quantity supplied generally goes up. The depiction

Exhibit 1.5
Shift in Demand
Curve for Monthly
Airline Tickets
*Heightened concerns
about travel safety and a
weakened economy are
two factors that have
decreased overall demand
for airline economy tickets
(seats) at all prices.*

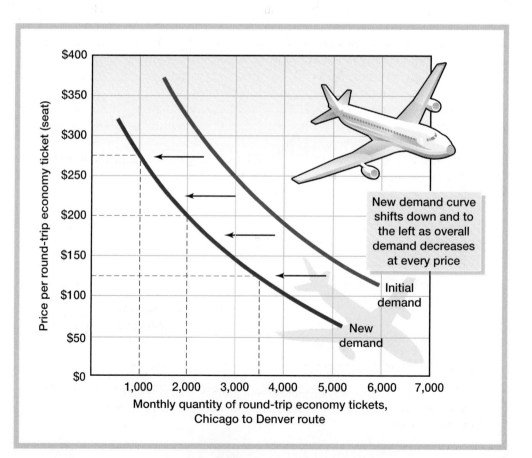

New demand curve shifts down and to the left as overall demand decreases at every price

Initial demand

New demand

Price per round-trip economy ticket (seat)

Monthly quantity of round-trip economy tickets,
Chicago to Denver route

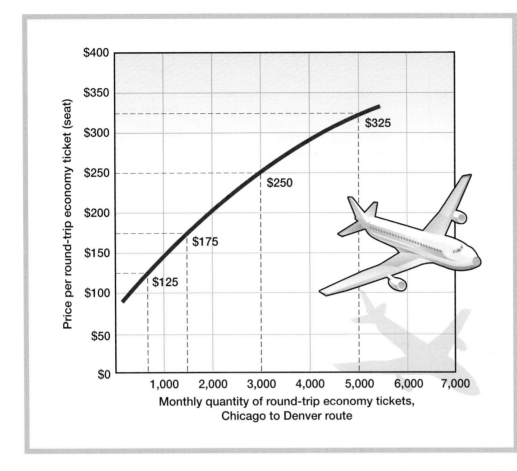

Exhibit 1.6
Supply Curve for
Monthly Airline
Tickets
*This supply curve shows
that the higher the price,
the larger the quantity of
economy tickets (seats)
airlines are willing to
supply, all else being
equal.*

of the relationship between prices and quantities that sellers will offer for sale, regardless of demand, is called a **supply curve**. Movement along the supply curve typically slopes upward. So as prices rise, the quantity sellers are willing to supply also rises. Similarly, as prices decline, the quantity sellers are willing to supply declines.

Exhibit 1.6 shows a possible supply curve for the monthly number of economy tickets (seats) supplied on an airline's Chicago to Denver route at different prices. The graph shows that increasing prices for economy tickets on that route should increase the number of tickets (seats) an airline is willing to provide for that route, because the airlines are motivated by the possibility of earning growing profits.

As with demand, several factors affect a seller's willingness and ability to provide goods and services at various prices. These variables include the cost of inputs (for example, pilot wages, fuel, and planes for the airlines), the number of competitors in the marketplace, and advancements in technology that allow companies to operate more efficiently. A change in any of these variables can shift the entire supply curve, either increasing or decreasing the amount available at every price, as Exhibit 1.7 suggests.

supply curve
*Graph of the quantities
that sellers will offer for
sale, regardless of
demand, at various prices*

Variable	Expected Shifts in Supply Curve	
	Shifts to the right when:	**Shifts to the left when:**
Costs of inputs	decrease	increase
Number of competitors	decreases	increases
New technology	decreases production costs	increases production costs
Suppliers expect that future sales prices	will decline	will increase

Exhibit 1.7
The Influence of
Market Forces on
the Supply Curve
*The supply curve is
affected by changes
in these variables.*

Exhibit 1.8
Shift in Supply Curve
for Monthly Airline
Tickets
*Airlines have responded
to heightened concerns
about travel safety and a
weakened economy by
reducing the supply of
airline tickets (seats) at all
prices. This new supply
curve shifts up and to
the left, signaling that
the quantity supplied
decreases at every price.*

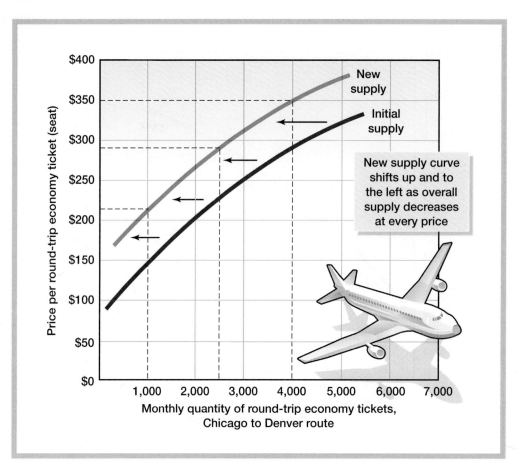

For example, if the cost of fuel rises, airlines may respond by cutting back the number of economy seats assigned to its routes, shifting the supply curve to the left (see Exhibit 1.8). But if new technologies allow the airline to save fuel or reduce the costs of training pilots, airlines may increase the number of economy seats assigned to its routes. Such increase in supply would shift the supply curve to the right.

Understanding How Demand and Supply Interact

In the real world, variables that affect demand and supply do not change independently. Instead, they change simultaneously and continually. Exhibit 1.9 shows the interaction of both supply and demand curves for monthly airline economy tickets (seats) on a single graph. The two curves intersect at the point marked E, or $250. This price is known as the **equilibrium price**. At that price the airline is willing to sell 3,000 round-trip economy tickets and consumers are willing to buy 3,000 economy tickets for its Chicago to Denver route. In other words, the quantity supplied and the quantity demanded are in balance.

equilibrium price
*Point at which quantity
supplied equals quantity
demanded*

As variables affecting supply and demand change, so will the equilibrium price. For example, increased concerns about passenger safety or longer lines at airport security checkpoints could encourage travelers to make alternative economic choices such as automobile travel or videoconferencing, thus reducing the demand for air travel at every price. Suppliers might respond to such a reduction in demand by either cutting the number of flights offered or lowering ticket prices in order to restore the equilibrium level. As this chapter's case study shows (see pages 58–59), several airlines are experimenting with a number of options to find a new equilibrium point because of an expected long-term decline in overall demand.

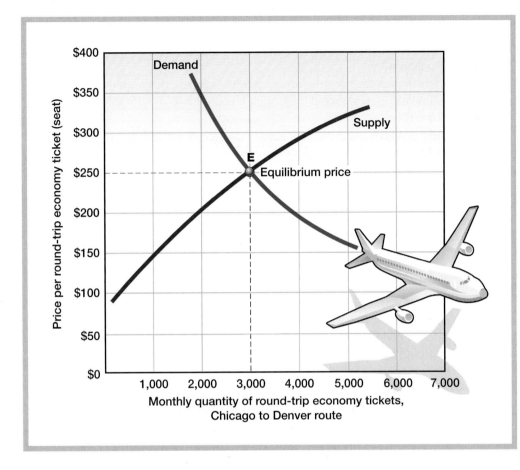

Exhibit 1.9
The Relationship
Between Supply and
Demand
*In a free-market system,
prices aren't set by the
government, nor do
producers alone have the
final say. Instead, prices
reflect the interaction of
supply and demand. The
equilibrium price (E) is
established when the
amount of a product that
producers are willing to sell
at a given price equals the
amount that consumers are
willing to buy at that price.*

In fact, questions of supply, demand, and equilibrium pricing are among the toughest issues you'll face as a manager. Imagine that you're a concert promoter planning for next year's summer season. You have to balance the potential demand for each performer across a range of prices in the hope of matching the supply you can deliver (the seating capacity of each venue and the number of shows)—and you have to make these predictions months in advance. Predict well, and you'll make a tidy profit. Predict poorly, and you could lose a pile of money. When ticket demand for many artists tailed off unexpectedly for the 2004 summer concert season, many promoters suffered losses because sales didn't cover the cost of renting the venues and paying the artists' minimum fees. People in the music business attribute the decline to a combination of sky-high ticket prices and oversupply (both too many concerts overall and too-frequent appearances by some performers who are touring more because their CD sales have dropped). Some big names played to a lot of empty seats over the summer, leading concert promoters to think more creatively about finding the equilibrium price. For instance, taking a cue from the airline industry, some are experimenting with last-minute discounts, selling seats for half price during the final 24 hours before a show.[15]

In some industries, managers must make multimillion- or even multibillion-dollar decisions about supply and demand years in advance. Boeing and Airbus start the design of a new aircraft years before anybody commits to buying it. In the electronics industry, manufacturers are placing a huge bet that demand for flat-panel televisions will surge if the price drops. To be able to meet that demand—and raise production volumes so they can lower the manufacturing cost enough to offer those lower prices—these companies have been forced to spend vast sums on new technologies and new factories long before they can prove the hypothesis about increased demand.[16]

CRITICAL THINKING CHECKPOINT

1. Can businesses create demand for a good or service that never existed before? Why or why not?
2. Why might a manufacturer of a luxury product keep a price high if a lower price would stimulate more demand (assuming it could be sold profitably at the lower price as well)?
3. When new products are launched, supply is often constrained as manufacturers work to build up production. During these times of tight supply, why would some consumers and businesses be willing to pay higher prices, when most probably know that prices will eventually drop as supply increases?

Macroeconomics: Understanding How an Economy Operates

The previous section discussed a variety of individual factors that affect the forces of supply and demand simultaneously. This section expands that discussion by showing how a number of larger economic forces also influence market behavior and ultimately affect supply and demand. These issues include how firms and industries compete in an economic system and the role government plays in fostering competition, regulating industries, protecting stakeholders, and contributing to economic stability.

Competition in a Free-Market System

In a free-market system, customers are free to buy whatever and wherever they please. Therefore, companies must compete with rivals for potential customers. Apple's iTunes service, for example, competes with other online music stores as well as CDs and even live music. **Competition** is the situation in which two or more suppliers of a product are rivals in the pursuit of the same customers.

The nature of competition varies widely by industry. In theory, the ideal type of competition is **pure competition**, which is characterized by three conditions: a marketplace of multiple buyers and sellers, a product or service with nearly identical features such as wheat or cotton, and low barriers of entry (that is, the ability to easily enter and exit the marketplace). When these three conditions exist, no single firm or group of firms in an industry becomes large enough to influence prices and thereby distort the workings of the free-market system. At the other extreme, in a **monopoly** there is only one supplier of a product in a given market, and thus the supplier is able to determine the price (within regulatory limits).

Most industries exist somewhere in between the extremes of pure competition and pure monopoly. For instance, commercial aircraft manufacturing is dominated by only a few suppliers (primarily Boeing and Airbus Industries), a situation known as an **oligopoly**. Like monopoly suppliers, oligopoly suppliers can sometimes exercise a degree of power over customers, based simply on the customer's lack of alternatives. For instance, toy maker Mattel encountered this situation when it threatened to stop buying advertising time on Nickelodeon because the cable TV channel wouldn't air a Mattel-produced Barbie movie in prime time. Nickelodeon's corporate parent Viacom responded by threatening not to sell Mattel advertising on *any* Viacom-owned media outlet, which includes MTV, VH-1, the CBS television network, billboards, and radio stations across the country. To avoid being cut off from so many advertising venues, Mattel relented.[17]

Most of the competition in advanced free-market economies is **monopolistic competition**, in which a large number of sellers (none of which dominates the market) offer products that can be distinguished from competing products in at least some small way. Toothpaste, cosmetics, soft drinks, Internet search engines, and restaurants are examples of products that can vary in the features each offers.

When markets become filled with competitors and products start to look alike, companies use price, speed, quality, service, or innovation to gain a **competitive advantage**—something that sets one company apart from its rivals and makes its products more appeal-

competition
Rivalry among businesses for the same customer

pure competition
Situation in which so many buyers and sellers exist that no single buyer or seller can individually influence market prices

monopoly
Market in which there are no direct competitors so that one company dominates

oligopoly
Market dominated by a few producers

monopolistic competition
Situation in which many sellers differentiate their products from those of competitors in at least some small way

competitive advantage
A company's ability to perform in one or more ways that competitors cannot match

ing to consumers. For example, Southwest Airlines competes on price, Jiffy Lube competes on speed, and Starbucks competes on quality. The risk/reward nature of capitalism promotes constant innovation in pursuit of competitive advantage, rewarding companies that do the best job of creating appealing goods and services.

Government's Role in a Free-Market System

Although the free-market system generally works well, it's far from perfect. If left unchecked, the economic forces that make capitalism succeed may also create severe problems for some groups or individuals. To correct these types of problems, the government serves four major economic roles: It enacts laws and creates regulations to foster competition; it regulates and deregulates certain industries; it protects stakeholders' rights; and it intervenes to contribute to economic stability.

Fostering Competition Because competition generally benefits the U.S. economy, the federal government and state and local governments create thousands of new laws and regulations every year to preserve competition and ensure that no single enterprise becomes too powerful. For instance, if a company has a monopoly, it can harm consumers by raising prices, cutting output, or stifling innovation. Furthermore, because most monopolies have total control over certain products and prices and the market share for those products, it's extremely difficult for competitors to enter markets where monopolies exist. For these reasons, over the last century or so, a number of laws and regulations have been established to help prevent individual companies or groups of companies from gaining control of markets in ways that restrain competition or harm consumers.

Antitrust Legislation. Antitrust laws limit what businesses can and cannot do to ensure that all competitors have an equal chance of producing a product, reaching the market, and making a profit. Some of the earliest government moves in this arena produced such landmark pieces of legislation as the Sherman Antitrust Act, the Clayton Antitrust Act, and the Federal Trade Commission Act, which generally sought to rein in the power of a few huge companies that had financial and management control of a significant number of other companies in the same industry. Usually referred to as *trusts* (hence the label *antitrust legislation*), these huge companies controlled enough of the supply and distribution in their respective industries to muscle smaller competitors out of the way.

More recently, government regulators have focused their attention on companies such as Microsoft, which has been accused by some competitors of using its dominance in the operating systems market (through Microsoft Windows) to unfairly influence competition and customer choice in the application software market (where it offers such products as Word and Excel). In 2000, a U.S. federal judge even ordered that Microsoft be split into two independent companies so that other application software companies could compete against it more effectively. This decision was overturned the following year, but the issues didn't fade away. In 2004, antitrust regulators in the European Union (EU) ordered the company to "unbundle" its Windows Media Player software from the Windows operating system. The EU asserted that making the media software part of the operating system put other media software companies (such as RealNetworks) at a competitive disadvantage.[18]

Mergers and Acquisitions. To preserve competition and customer choice, governments may occasionally prohibit two companies in the same industry from combining through a merger or acquisition. Over the years, regulators in the United States and other countries have halted some blockbuster deals, such as the proposed mergers between United Airlines and U.S. Airways and between book retailer Barnes & Noble and book wholesaler Ingram Book Group.[19] In other cases, regulators will allow the merger or acquisition, but only after the companies meet certain conditions. For instance, when America Online (AOL) wanted to merge with media giant Time Warner, the government stipulated that the companies make their powerful cable television and Internet networks available to competitors. Without such requirements, regulators were concerned that the combined AOL Time Warner (now known simply as Time Warner), by virtue of its enormous size, would have too much power and influence over access to the Internet.[20]

LEARNING OBJECTIVE 6

Discuss the four major economic roles of the U.S. government

Government regulators in both the United States and Europe have kept a close eye on industry giant Microsoft over the years, periodically responding to complaints that the company's dominance gives it unfair competitive advantages. CEO Steve Ballmer argues that the company should be free to innovate as long as it follows appropriate regulations.

Regulating and Deregulating Industries As part of their mandate to ensure fair competition, ethical business practices, safe working conditions, and general public safety, government bodies at the federal, state, and local levels impose a variety of regulations on many industries. For instance, in the wake of the terrorist attacks on September 11, 2001, the federal government established the Transportation Security Administration and took temporary control of U.S. airport security. In other cases, government agencies create regulations as a means to balance the often-conflicting interests of various segments of society.

In a *regulated industry,* close government control is substituted for free competition, and competition is either limited or eliminated. In extreme cases, regulators may even decide who can enter an industry, what customers they must serve, and how much they can charge. For years, the telecommunications, airline, banking, and electric utility industries fell under strict government control. However, the trend over the past few decades has been to open up competition in regulated industries by removing or relaxing existing regulations. Hopes are that such *deregulation* will allow new industry competitors to enter the market, create more choices for customers, and keep prices in check. But the debate is ongoing about whether deregulation achieves these goals. In some instances, deregulation has produced disastrous results. When the state of California deregulated some aspects of retail electricity in 2000, the result was a year's worth of skyrocketing prices and unreliable supply. The fiasco contributed heavily to a financial crisis that the state has yet to recover from.[21] If nothing else, the California experiment shows that deregulation needs to be approached with great care and a full understanding of the economic forces at work in any given industry.

Protecting Stakeholders In addition to fostering competition, another important role the government plays is to protect the stakeholders of a business. Businesses have many **stakeholders**—groups that are affected by (or that affect) a business's operations, including colleagues, employees, supervisors, investors, customers, suppliers, and society at large. In the course of serving one or more of these stakeholders, a business may sometimes neglect the interests of other stakeholders in the process. For example, managers who are too narrowly focused on generating wealth for shareholders might not spend the funds necessary to create a safe work environment for employees or to reduce waste. Similarly, a public company that withholds information about its true financial performance may hamper the ability of investors to make solid decisions and may even harm the wealth of stakeholders, as has happened in several high-profile instances in recent years, notably Enron and WorldCom (you'll read more about both companies in later chapters).

To protect consumers, employees, shareholders, and the environment from the potentially harmful actions of business, the government has established numerous regulatory agencies (see Exhibit 1.10). Many of these agencies have the power to pass and enforce

stakeholders
Individuals or groups to whom business has a responsibility

LEARNING FROM BUSINESS BLUNDERS

OOPS Filling out a loan application is always an unpleasant task; it's hard to avoid the feeling that you're being forced to divulge your most personal secrets and every mistake you ever made. Imagine how it must feel to see all those secrets on display on the World Wide Web. Dealerskins, a Nashville, Tennessee, company that hosts websites for car dealers, failed to take even the most basic steps to protect the private financial information of a thousand car-loan applicants. Anyone could view the applications simply by clicking on "View Source" in Internet Explorer.

WHAT YOU CAN LEARN In today's electronic economy, all businesses have an obligation to protect any confidential data they collect from customers. No system is absolutely foolproof, but readily available e-commerce systems provide secure, reliable ways to protect data.

Exhibit 1.10
Major Government
Agencies and What
They Do
*Government agencies
protect stakeholders by
developing and promoting
standards, regulating
and overseeing industries,
and enforcing laws and
regulations.*

Government Agency or Commission	Major Areas of Responsibility
Consumer Product Safety Commission (CPSC)	Regulates and protects public from unreasonable risks of injury from consumer products
Environmental Protection Agency (EPA)	Develops and enforces standards to protect the environment
Equal Employment Opportunity Commission (EEOC)	Protects and resolves discriminatory employment practices
Federal Aviation Administration (FAA)	Sets rules for the commercial airline industry
Federal Communications Commission (FCC)	Oversees communication by telephone, telegraph, radio, and television
Federal Energy Regulatory Commission (FERC)	Regulates rates and sales of electric power and natural gas
Federal Highway Administration (FHA)	Regulates vehicle safety requirements
Federal Trade Commission (FTC)	Enforces laws and guidelines regarding unfair business practices and acts to stop false and deceptive advertising and labeling
Food and Drug Administration (FDA)	Enforces laws and regulations to prevent distribution of harmful foods, drugs, medical devices, and cosmetics
Interstate Commerce Commission (ICC)	Regulates and oversees carriers engaged in transportation between states: railroads, bus lines, trucking companies, oil pipelines, and waterways
Occupational Safety and Health Administration (OSHA)	Promotes worker safety and health
Securities and Exchange Commission (SEC)	Protects investors and maintains the integrity of the securities markets
Transportation Security Administration (TSA)	Protects the national transportation infrastructure

rules and regulations within their specific area of authority. Such regulations are intended to encourage businesses to behave ethically and in a socially responsible way. Chapter 2 takes a closer look at society's concerns for ethical and socially responsible behavior, specific government agencies that regulate such behavior, and the efforts by businesses to become better corporate citizens.

Contributing to Economic Stability A nation's economy never stays exactly the same size. Instead, it expands and contracts in response to the combined effects of such factors as technological breakthroughs, changes in investment patterns, shifts in consumer attitudes, world events, and basic economic forces. *Economic expansion* occurs when the economy is growing and people are spending more money. Consumer purchases stimulate businesses to produce more goods and services, which in turn stimulates employment. *Economic contraction* occurs when such spending declines. Businesses cut back on production, employees are laid off, and the economy as a whole slows down.

If the period of downward swing is severe, the nation may enter into a **recession**, traditionally defined as two consecutive quarters of decline in real gross domestic product. When a downward swing or recession is over, the economy enters into a period of **recovery**: Companies buy more, factories produce more, employment is high, and workers spend their earnings.

recession
Period during which national income, employment, and production all fall

recovery
Period during which income, employment, production, and spending rise

These up-and-down swings are known as the **business cycle**. However, don't be misled by the term "cycle," which implies regular and predictable behavior. Every nation's economy is a complex and evolving creature, making it difficult to predict both the timing and the nature of the ups and downs in the business cycle. For instance, in 2004, the U.S. economy was recovering from a recession but didn't behave entirely as expected. Traditional economic thinking suggested that companies would start buying lots of new computers and other technology products to beef up their business systems in response to growing demand for their own products. However, the purchasing behavior of many corporate customers changed this time around. Having been burned by the infamous "irrational exuberance" of the dot-com era of the late 1990s (see page 49), many companies were much more careful about throwing money at technology as a way to solve business problems. Moreover, when they were forced to cut their budgets during the recession, many companies also learned to make better use of technology and discovered they didn't need to buy as much as previously thought. As a result, sales of technology equipment and software did not recover as quickly as anticipated.[22] Similarly, employment in some areas of the economy suffered the same fate, as companies learned they could get by with fewer employees. Employers were slow to add staff until well into the recovery phase, leading some to label it a "jobless recovery" for many months.[23]

While you're busy pondering your company's health throughout the business cycle, federal economists and bankers will be making their own predictions and "pulling the strings" of the national economy through monetary policy and fiscal policy.

Monetary Policy. Every economy has a certain amount of "spendable" money in it at any given time, a quantity known as the *money supply*. **Monetary policy** involves adjusting the nation's money supply by increasing or decreasing interest rates. In the United States, monetary policy is controlled primarily by the Federal Reserve Board (often called "the Fed"), a group of appointed government officials who oversee the country's central banking system.

With a variety of tools that you'll read about in Chapter 17, the Fed manages the money supply to make certain that enough money and credit are available to fuel a healthy economy, without providing so much money that purchasing heats up and leads to inflation. A good example of the Fed's influence on your life as a consumer and a business manager is its manipulation of the *discount rate,* the interest rate it charges commercial banks to borrow money. When you borrow money from a bank to buy a house or new manufacturing equipment, the interest rate you pay is heavily influenced by the discount rate, and your interest rate can have a profound effect on your purchasing behavior. For instance, if you can handle $2,000 a month for a house payment and interest rates are at 7 percent, you can afford a $300,000 house, roughly speaking. However, if rates climb to 10 percent, your price range suddenly drops to around $230,000. At 16 percent, you'll be shopping for a $150,000 house—only half the house you can buy with a 7 percent loan.

In addition to the initial impact that a change in the money supply can have, money injected into the economy also has a *multiplier effect* as it makes its way through the system. For example, if a company spends money to build a large office complex, thousands of construction workers will be gainfully employed and earn wages. If some of these workers decide to spend their extra income to buy new cars, car dealers will have more income. The car dealers, in turn, might invest their increased revenue in new equipment for the service department, and the sales staff (who earn commissions on the car sales) might buy new clothes, and so on. This *circular flow* of money through the economic system links all elements of the U.S. economy by exchanging goods and services for money, which is then used to buy more goods and services in a never-ending cycle.

Mortgage rates at 30-year lows sparked a wave of new-home construction at the beginning of the 21st century.

Fiscal Policy. **Fiscal policy** involves changes in the government's revenues and expenditures to stimulate a slow economy or dampen a growing economy that is in danger of overheating. On the revenue side, governments can adjust the revenue they bring in by changing tax rates and various fees collected from individuals and businesses (see Exhibit 1.11). When the federal government lowers the income tax rate, for instance, it

Type of Tax	Levied On
Income taxes	Income earned by individuals and businesses. Income taxes are the government's largest single source of revenue.
Real property taxes	Assessed value of the land and structures owned by businesses and individuals.
Sales taxes	Retail purchases made by customers. Sales taxes are collected by retail businesses at the time of the sale and then forwarded to the government.
Excise taxes	Selected items such as gasoline, tobacco, and liquor. Often referred to as "sin" taxes, excise taxes are implemented to help control potentially harmful practices.
Payroll taxes	Earnings of individuals to help fund Social Security, Medicare, and unemployment compensation. Corporations match employee contributions.

Exhibit 1.11
Types of Taxes
From road repair to regulation, running a government is an expensive affair. To fund government operations and projects, national governments, states, counties, and cities levy and collect a variety of revenue-raising taxes.

does so with the hope that consumers and businesses will spend and invest the additional money in their pockets.

On the expenditure side, local, state, and federal government bodies constitute a huge market for goods and services, with billions of dollars of collective buying power. Governments can stimulate the economy by increasing their purchases, sometimes even to the point of creating new programs or projects with the specific purpose of expanding employment opportunities and increasing demand for goods and services.

Fiscal policy decisions nearly always involve discussions of budget deficits, both annual deficits (when the government spends more than it takes in during any given year) and the accumulating national debt (the result of the many years in which the government spends more than it receives). In 2004, the federal budget rang up a record annual deficit of more than $500 billion, and the national debt is now over $7 trillion. These numbers are almost incomprehensible, but, like interest rates, they affect every business and every consumer in the country. The interest payment alone on the national debt costs U.S. taxpayers several hundred billion dollars a year, money that could be spent on health care, education, lower taxes, or dozens of other areas.[24]

CRITICAL THINKING CHECKPOINT
1. Apple's Steve Jobs was quoted as saying that iTune's real competition is piracy. What does he mean by this?
2. Why would the U.S. government grant an exclusive monopoly on mail delivery to the U.S. Postal Service when it works to prevent any single company from dominating most other industries?
3. Is it ever a wise move for a government body (federal, state, or local) to run a budget deficit? Explain your answer (think about the business cycle).

How a Free-Market System Monitors Its Economic Performance

Each day we are deluged with complex statistical data that depict the current status and past performance of the economy. Sorting, understanding, and interpreting these data are difficult tasks even for professional economists. **Economic indicators** include statistics such as interest rates, unemployment rates, housing data, and industrial productivity that are used to monitor and measure economic performance. Statistics that point to what may happen to the economy in the future are called *leading indicators;* statistics that signal a swing in the economy after the movement has begun are called *lagging indicators.*

LEARNING OBJECTIVE 7
Explain how a free-market system monitors its economic performance

economic indicators
Statistics that measure significant variables in the economy

Watching Economic Indicators

Economists monitor the performance of the economy by watching a variety of indicators. Unemployment statistics, for example, signal future changes in consumer spending. When unemployment rises, people have less money to spend, and the economy suffers. Housing starts, another leading indicator, show where several industries are headed. When housing starts drop, builders stop hiring and may even lay off workers. Meanwhile, orders fall for plumbing fixtures, carpets, and appliances, so manufacturers decrease production and workers' hours. These cutbacks ripple through the economy and lead to slower income and job growth and weaker consumer spending.[25] Another leading indicator is durable-goods orders, or orders for goods that typically last more than 3 years (which can mean everything from desk chairs to airplanes). A rise in durable-goods orders is a positive indicator that business spending is turning around. Informal indicators can also provide insights into economic health, such as the nature of buying and selling on Internet auction giant eBay. When buyers seem to be in a hopeful mood with cash to spend, luxury items are more popular. When times are tougher, people tend to shop for more run-of-the-mill, practical items.[26] In addition to all these indicators, economists closely monitor price changes and national output to get a sense of how well the economy is working.

Measuring Price Changes

Price changes, especially price increases, are another important economic indicator. In a period of rising prices, the purchasing power of a dollar erodes, which means that you can purchase fewer things with today's dollar than you could in a prior period. Over time, price increases tend to lead to wage increases, which in turn add pressures for higher prices, setting a vicious cycle in motion.

Inflation
Economic condition in which prices rise steadily throughout the economy

deflation
Economic condition in which prices fall steadily throughout the economy

Inflation and Deflation
Inflation is a steady rise in the prices of goods and services throughout the economy. When the inflation rate begins to decline, economists use the term *disinflation.* **Deflation**, on the other hand, is the sustained fall in the general price level for goods and services. It is the opposite of inflation; that is, purchasing power increases because a dollar held today will buy more tomorrow. In a deflationary period, investors postpone major purchases in anticipation of lower prices in the future. Keep in mind that although prices in the overall economy tend to increase year after year, not all industries and product categories necessarily follow this trend. The average price of a new computer might drop while the price of the electricity needed to power it increases.[27]

consumer price index (CPI)
Monthly statistic that measures changes in the prices of about 400 goods and services that consumers buy

Price Indexes
Price indexes offer a way to monitor the inflation or deflation in various sectors of the economy. The most well-known of these, the **consumer price index (CPI)**, measures the rate of inflation by comparing the change in prices of a representative basket of consumer goods and services, such as clothing, food, housing, and utilities, over time. A numerical weight is assigned to each item in the representative basket to adjust for each item's relative importance in the marketplace. The CPI has always been a hot topic because it is used by the government to index Social Security payments, and it is widely used by businesses in private contracts to calculate cost-of-living increases. But, like most economic indicators, the CPI is not perfect. The representative basket of goods and services may not reflect the prices and consumption patterns of the area in which you live or of your specific household. The U.S. Bureau of Labor Statistics periodically adjusts the mix of products used in the CPI, but the CPI should always be viewed as a general indicator of price trends, not as a specific measurement.[28]

producer price index (PPI)
A statistical measure of price trends at the producer and wholesaler levels

In contrast to the CPI, the **producer price index (PPI)** measures prices at the producer or wholesaler level. Three major categories of goods tracked in the PPI are finished goods sold to retailers, intermediate goods such as product components that require further processing, and crude goods or raw materials. In recent years, economists have noticed an important change in the relationship between the PPI and the CPI. Historically, cost increases at the producer level were generally passed along to the consumer level. For instance, if automakers had to pay more for steel, they would work that increase into the price of new cars. As global competition heats up, however, producers find they can't always pass along price increases and remain competitive. The alternatives include accepting lower profit levels or finding ways to improve productivity, such as by investing in more-efficient factories or clamping down on labor costs.[29]

Measuring a Nation's Output

The broadest measure of an economy's health is the **gross domestic product (GDP)**. The GDP measures a country's output—its production, distribution, and use of goods and services—by computing the sum of all goods and services produced for *final* use in a market during a specified period (usually a year). The goods may be produced by either domestic or foreign companies—as long as these companies are located within a nation's boundaries. Sales from a Honda assembly plant in California, for instance, would be included in the GDP. Although far from perfect, the GDP enables a nation to evaluate its economic policies and to compare its current performance with prior periods or with the performance of other nations.

GDP has largely replaced an earlier measure called the **gross national product (GNP)**, which excludes the value of production from foreign-owned businesses within a nation's boundaries and includes receipts from the overseas operations of domestic companies. GNP considers *who* is responsible for the production; GDP considers *where* the production occurs.

Is GNP, GDP, or any other strictly economic measure the best way to gauge how well a country is doing? The tiny Himalayan country of Bhutan now judges its success according to *gross national happiness*—GNH. The idea of measuring well-being, beyond mere financial facts, might sound frivolous, but it has caught the attention of social scientists and even a few economists around the world. To be sure, most of the factors that one would consider part of GNH, such as good health care, education, and ample leisure time, require the financial resources that only a healthy GDP can generate. However, the concept of GNH could at the very least encourage countries to consider *why* they're working so hard to generate all this wealth.[30]

Exhibit 1.12 summarizes the common indicators used to measure a nation's economic performance. By most of these measures, one could argue that the U.S. economy is in fair

gross domestic product (GDP)
Value of all the final goods and services produced by businesses located within a nation's borders; excludes receipts from overseas operations of domestic companies

gross national product (GNP)
Value of all the final goods and services produced by domestic businesses that includes receipts from overseas operations and excludes receipts from foreign-owned businesses within a nation's borders

Economic Measure	Description
Prime interest rate	Lowest interest rate that banks charge preferred borrowers on short-term loans
Unemployment rate	Percentage of a nation's workforce unemployed at any time
Housing starts	Number of building permits issued by private housing units
Durable-goods orders	New orders for goods that last more than three years
Labor productivity rate	Rate of increase or decrease in the average level of output per worker
Balance of trade	Total value of a country's exports minus the total value of its imports, over a specific period of time
Inflation rate	Percentage increase in prices of goods or services over a period of time
Producer price index	Monthly index that measures changes in wholesale prices
Consumer price index	Monthly index that measures changes in consumer prices of a fixed basket of goods and services
Gross domestic product	Dollar value of all final goods and services produced by businesses located within a nation's borders

Exhibit 1.12
Ten Common Indicators of a Nation's Economic Performance
Economists use a number of economic measures to evaluate a nation's economy. Here are 10 of the most significant measures.

shape, but as you'll read in Chapter 3, the *balance of trade* measurement has grown particularly worrisome to many observers. The country's ratio of imports to exports is higher than it's ever been, raising fears that the United States is becoming dangerously dependent on the economic decisions made by other countries.[31]

History of U.S. Economic Growth

To understand how the U.S. economy reached its current state—and the reasons it generates concern for some observers but not for others—it's necessary to take a quick look back at the country's unique economic history. Just how did we get here?

From Family Farms to Industrial Superpower

The first economic base in the United States was the small family farm. People grew enough food for their families and used any surplus to trade for necessary goods provided by independent craftspeople and merchants. Business operated on a small scale, and much of the population was self-employed. In the early nineteenth century, people began making greater use of rivers, harbors, and rich mineral deposits. Excellent natural resources helped businesspeople accumulate the capital they needed to increase production, fueling the transition of the United States from a farm-based economy to an industrial economy.

economies of scale
Savings gained from the increased efficiency of manufacturing, marketing, purchasing, or otherwise operating with large quantities

By the end of the nineteenth century, new technology had given birth to the factory and the industrial revolution. Millions of new workers came to the United States from abroad to work in factories where each person performed one simple task over and over. Separating the manufacturing process into distinct tasks and producing large quantities of similar products allowed businesses to achieve cost and operating efficiencies through **economies of scale**. The result was increasing prosperity—right up to the stock market crash in 1929 that triggered the Great Depression and generated unemployment rates reaching a record high of 25 percent.[32]

The economy was getting back on its feet by 1941, when the United States entered World War II. The war stimulated industrial capacity, then postwar reconstruction further revived the economy and renewed the trend toward large-scale enterprises. By 1950, the birth rate had accelerated, and the baby boom was on. By the end of the 1950s, nearly half of the world's manufacturing output bore the proud label "Made in the U.S.A."

The United States prospered throughout the 1960s, but rising inflation, an energy crisis, and the emergence of Japan as a manufacturing powerhouse in the 1970s combined to throw the U.S. economy back into a slump. During the 1980s, global competition continued to creep up on the United States. To regain a competitive edge, many U.S. companies restructured their operations. Some corporations merged with others to produce economies of scale; others splintered into smaller fragments to focus on a single industry or a narrower customer base. New companies such as Staples and Home Depot started popping up with founders who said, "We went to work for the safe, big company and it wasn't safe at all."[33] Meanwhile, new technologies continued to be embraced by entrepreneurial firms such as Microsoft, Cisco, and Oracle, who quickly rose to dominance in their markets.[34]

An Old Story About the New Economy

In the early 1990s, U.S. businesses got hit again. The U.S. economy went into a full-blown recession, and many companies that had loaded up on debt in the 1980s to expand their operations or to acquire other companies went bankrupt. During this period of upheaval, unemployment soared, as hundreds of thousands of jobs were eliminated. General Motors alone laid off 130,000 workers. Managers at IBM and AT&T breathed new life into these two U.S. manufacturing classics. Motorola struck back at Japan's growing dominance in the electronics field with its pagers and cell phones, Hewlett-Packard (HP) took over the market in low-cost computer printers, and Kodak challenged with digital and disposable cameras.[35] Investments in new technology and the promise of e-commerce ultimately pushed the U.S. economy into a remarkable period of prosperity.

During the energy crisis in the 1970s, gas shortages forced drivers to wait in long lines for fuel. Today, political instability in oil-producing regions has triggered new fears of energy shortages.

Faster growth, lower inflation, and technology-driven expansion ushered in a period in which businesses began viewing the Internet as a viable business resource. Meanwhile, a flood of money into new companies put pressure on older ones to raise productivity and innovate rapidly. For a good part of the 1990s the "new economy" became synonymous with rapid growth, improved living standards for millions, plentiful jobs, and glorious—or so it seemed—investment opportunities.

But by the turn of the century, the technology sector, which had led the economy upward led it right back down. The lure of instant wealth through *initial public offerings* (IPOs)—when a company begins selling stock to the public—created an unsustainable bubble in which vast sums of money were invested in start-up companies that often had unproven technologies, inexperienced managers, and untested business ideas. For a while, it seemed that all you needed to do was slap "dot-com" on the end of some quirky company name, and venture capitalists would hand you millions of dollars to start a company. In some cases, the fundamental business model was simply flawed, such as giving free PCs to people who would then agree to view online advertising. In others, entrepreneurs created wonderful websites on the "front end" but failed on the "back end," with the nitty-gritty details of warehousing, transportation, order fulfillment, and other nonexotic but crucial aspects of running a business. Overall, too many of these so-called new economy businesses believed that the Internet changed the nature of business so drastically that the rules of the *old economy* no longer applied.

While the overinflated stock prices of some dot-coms were fueling new rounds of investment in even more dot-coms, the telecommunications and information technology industries were expanding like mad to provide the new economy with all the networking and computers it would require. Unfortunately, it didn't take long for the era of "irrational exuberance," in Fed chairman Alan Greenspan's words, to come tumbling down. As always happens with bubbles, frenzied investors drive up prices (stock prices, in this case) until a few people start to notice that something is wrong—in this case, dot-com companies with no profits and telecommunication companies sinking into debt—and start selling. In the blink of an eye, irrational exuberance turned into irrational panic as investors unloaded their once-hot tech stocks, driving prices down even faster than they had driven them up. Dozens of dot-coms started going bankrupt every week. Massive layoffs throughout high tech were inevitable, and the effects rippled across the economy as not only jobs but investment fortunes disappeared overnight. By 2000, the country was once again in a full-on recession that continued into 2001. The terrorist attacks on September 11, 2001, delivered another staggering blow to the economy, as airlines and virtually every other part of the travel industry suffered sharp declines in demand.

Imagining the Future

The entrepreneurial spirit is hard to keep down, though, and businesses throughout the country got busy getting back on their feet. Investors regained a sense of sanity, and battle-scarred veterans of both the new and old economies learned valuable lessons from each other.

The economy began to improve, although sectors such as air travel continue to struggle (see this chapter's Case for Critical Thinking on pages 58–59). In fact, uncertainty might be the watchword of today's post-dot-com, post-9/11 universe. Assumptions that seemed rock solid just a few years ago, such as the steady expansion of U.S. firms around the world and the ability of new technology to redefine the very nature of business, look far less certain now. For instance, few people could have imagined that IBM, a symbol of U.S. dominance for decades and a pioneer in PCs, would end up selling its PC business to a Chinese manufacturer (Lenovo) because it was struggling to make money in an industry it helped create—and it needed a Chinese partner to help conquer the global computing market.[36]

Predicting the shape of the future is a risky venture, but five themes promise to shape the near future of business:

- ***The effects of terrorism.*** Terrorism continues to be a pervasive concern, affecting virtually every aspect of business from staffing to finance to transportation. You'll read more about terrorism's effects in Chapter 3.
- ***China's move onto the global stage.*** Given its sheer size and low labor costs, China has been a major presence in the world economy for some time now, but with furious industrial growth in recent years and the determination to compete head-to-head with the world's most advanced nations, it has joined the United States as the second anchor of the global economy. Not only is each of these two giant economies big enough to cause ripples throughout the world, they are also thoroughly interdependent, with China counting on the United States as a major export market, and the United States relying on these lower-cost imports to keep its own inflation in check.[37] China has yet to produce world-class companies on par with HP (United States), Samsung (South Korea), or Sony (Japan), which leads some experts to question the limits of the country's potential.[38] However, these other countries also had to learn, over time, how to develop great companies, and a few fast-rising firms such as Huawei (telecommunication equipment), Lenovo (computers), and Haier (home appliances) are taking their place on the world stage.[39] Moreover, China's ambitions in automobiles, wireless technology, computers, and other high-end markets are likely to stun any observers who might still be clinging to outdated notions of the country as nothing more than a supplier of cheap consumer goods.
- ***The mobility of work.*** One of the most profound changes brought by the Internet has been the ability to connect people virtually anywhere in the world. For some workers, this is a blessing, giving them the freedom to live where they want. For others, this advance has proven to be more of a curse because it puts them in competition with more of the global workforce. Technology and economic factors are also changing the very nature of work for many people as businesses replace permanent employment with temporary outsiders and connect them via the Internet.
- ***The dual deficits.*** The United States continues to post record deficits in both its federal budget and its trade balance with other nations. However, opinion is divided about just how dangerous this situation is—and if it is dangerous, how it should be fixed. On the one hand, the country has run deficits in both categories for years now. On the other, the United States has never racked up deficits this large, so we're entering uncharted waters.
- ***The normalization of e-business.*** During the first phase of the new economy, too many new businesses treated the Internet and other technologies as gateways to some magical new world in which the old rules of business no longer applied—and too many old-school businesses didn't fully appreciate how the Internet could both help and harm their ability to succeed. Moving into the future, smart managers are now merging tried-and-true business methods with the efficient technologies developed during the dot-com days—and realizing that for all its occasional razzle-dazzle, technology is just another tool in the business manager's toolkit.

INNOVATING FOR BUSINESS SUCCESS

THE ELECTRONIC ECONOMY: REDEFINING REALITY

Jumping on the Internet to check your test scores, reserve a plane ticket, or find an apartment might feel like business as usual to you these days, but the business and technology revolution that enabled these online conveniences has been anything but usual. And it's not over yet. No matter where your career takes you, inside the business arena or not, the electronic economy will affect you personally and professionally.

Throughout this course, you'll get insights into the interplay of technology and business. As you explore the ins and outs of business management, pay attention to the Internet's impact in areas such as these:

- *Competitive opportunities and threats.* The Internet creates new business opportunities for some companies and creates new competitive threats for others. Small companies can now reach customers halfway around the world—but the customers they used to have across the street can now shop just about anywhere as well.
- *The speed of business.* The good news is that technology can accelerate virtually every aspect of business. That's also the bad news. The faster things go, the faster everybody expects them to go. The pace can lead to rushed decision making and wear out both employees and managers.
- *Customer power.* Researching and shopping for many products used to be a laborious, time-consuming chore in many cases, leaving buyers wondering if they had really explored all their options and gathered enough information to make smart decisions. Not anymore. The Internet shifts power from sellers to buyers, who can usually gather mountains of information within minutes and jump from one seller to the next with the click of a mouse.
- *Security and privacy.* People who can't think of living without the Internet—a group that surely includes most college students—may find it hard to believe that a third of the U.S. population manages to get by without it quite nicely, thank you. Among their top reasons for staying away: fear of being barraged by online pornography and scammed by credit card thieves. Until these and other problems (including spam) are fixed, electronic business will never reach its full potential.

With the dot-com boom and collapse in the rearview mirror, technology is getting down to business, with an emphasis on sensible solutions to real-world problems. As you move into your career, you'll no doubt encounter all these issues—and perhaps make your mark somewhere in the ever-changing world of electronic business.

Questions for Critical Thinking
1. Select a business that you purchase from regularly; how could the Internet help or threaten this company?
2. How has the Internet helped (or perhaps hurt) your college experience?

CRITICAL THINKING CHECKPOINT
1. Deflation might sound like a great idea—but why can it be dangerous for an economy?
2. Why might the economic and social history of the United States have been different if the country had not been blessed with abundant natural resources?
3. What lessons did "old economy" and "new economy" businesses learn from each other?

LEARNING
OBJECTIVE 8

Identify five challenges
you'll face as a business
professional in today's
global economy

globalization
Tendency of the world's
economies to act as
a single interdependent
economy

The Challenges You'll Face in the Global Economy

No matter which direction the various elements of the economy move in the coming years, two things are certain. First, the U.S. economy is inextricably tied to the larger global economy. Globalization—the increasing tendency of the world to act as one market instead of a series of national ones—opens new markets for a company's goods and services and new sources of natural resources, labor, and skills. Second, your success will depend on how well you can handle some key challenges:

- *Producing quality goods and services that satisfy customers' changing needs.* Today's customer has access to considerable amounts of information about product choices and often has a wide range of goods and services from which to choose. For many businesses, competing in the global economy means competing on the basis of *speed* (getting products to market sooner), *quality* (doing a better job of meeting customer expectations), and *customer satisfaction* (making sure buyers are happy with every aspect of the purchase).
- *Thinking like an entrepreneur, even if you're an employee in a large company.* Entrepreneurial skills are more important than ever—embracing new ideas, finding and creating opportunities, taking decisive action even when faced with limited information, focusing with laser intensity on the core activities of the business, and directing all your energy toward satisfying customers and outperforming competitors.
- *Thinking globally and embracing a culturally diverse workforce.* As population patterns evolve and businesses continue to reach across national and cultural borders, businesses must also embrace the increasingly diverse workforce—both to support the needs of everyone in the workforce and to realize the benefits of having workers who represent a wider range of cultural backgrounds.
- *Behaving in an ethically and socially responsible manner.* As businesses become more complex through global expansion and technological change, they must deal with an increasing number of ethical and social issues. These include the marketing of unhealthful products, the use of questionable accounting practices to compute financial results,

CHECKLIST: Apply These Ideas When You're the Boss

✓ Whenever you have a bad experience as a consumer, figure out how you could do things better in your own business

✓ Don't underestimate the resources required to start a new business and survive the initial weeks and months; many businesses fail because they are *under-capitalized*

✓ Look for opportunities to offer new services when new technologies emerge or other developments occur in the marketplace

✓ Fight the temptation to relax if your business takes off; if you're successful, you're going to attract competition—and if you got over the barriers to entry, they probably can, too

✓ Understand what drives demand in your industry; if you don't know why people want your

goods or services, you won't know how to respond if customer needs change

✓ There's no such thing as permanent competitive advantage; if you don't keep improving, your competitors will catch you—and probably sooner rather than later

✓ No matter how exotic or exciting or different your business might be, it won't survive if it can't profitably deliver goods or services to customers who are willing to pay for them

✓ Pay attention to what's going on in the world so you don't get surprised by shifts in the global marketplace

✓ Conduct business in a way that makes you proud to look in the mirror every morning; your company will succeed faster and survive longer

and the pollution of the environment (as Chapter 2 discusses). In the future, businesses can expect continued pressure from environmental groups, consumers, employees, and government regulators to act ethically and responsibly.

- ***Keeping pace with technology and electronic commerce.*** Everywhere we look, technology is reshaping the world. The Internet and innovations in computerization, miniaturization, and telecommunication have made it possible for people anywhere in the world to exchange information and goods. Such technologies are collapsing boundaries and changing the way customers, suppliers, and companies interact. Technology is also changing the way people shop for books, cars, vacations, advice—even wash clothes. At the same time, technology can introduce unwanted complexities (no one ever had a typewriter crash in the middle of a term paper), security problems, and unwelcome elements such as *spam* (junk e-mail), *spim* (junk instant messages), and computer viruses.[40] In short, the Internet has touched every business and industry and is changing all facets of business life.

As these challenges suggest, doing business in the twenty-first century means working in a world of increasing uncertainty where change is the norm, not the exception. In the coming chapters, you'll explore specific challenges that businesses are facing in the global economy and learn how to apply the lessons of real-world companies to your own aspirations as an executive or entrepreneur.

Summary of Learning Objectives

1 **Explain how the study of business will help you meet your career goals.** Understanding business will help you in virtually any career, both inside and outside the business world. As a manager or an entrepreneur, naturally, understanding business concepts is vital to your success because you need to know how the various functions of a business operate. If you pursue a professional discipline such as accounting or marketing, you need to understand not only your own business function but also how that function contributes to the overall success of the organization. Outside the business world, many organizations find they can operate more efficiently and more effectively if they adapt techniques from business. Lastly, as a consumer and taxpayer, understanding business will help you make better financial decisions.

2 **Define what a business is, and identify four key social and economic roles that businesses serve.** A business is a profit-seeking activity that provides goods and services to satisfy consumers' needs. The driving force behind most businesses is the chance to earn a profit; however, nonprofit organizations exist to provide society with a social or educational service. Businesses serve four key functions: They provide society with necessities; they provide people with jobs and a means to prosper; they pay taxes that are used by the government to provide services for its citizens; and they reinvest their profits in the economy, thereby increasing a nation's wealth.

3 **Differentiate between goods-producing and service businesses, and list five factors that are contributing to the increase in the number of service businesses.** Goods-producing businesses produce tangible goods and tend to be capital-intensive; service businesses produce intangible goods and tend to be labor-intensive. The number of service businesses is increasing because (1) consumers have more disposable income to spend on taking care of themselves; (2) many services target consumers' needs brought about by changing demographic patterns and lifestyle trends; (3) consumers need assistance with using and integrating new technology into their business operations and lifestyles; (4) companies are turning to consultants and other professionals for advice to remain competitive; and (5) in general, barriers to entry are lower for service companies than they are for goods-producing businesses.

4 **Identify the factors that affect demand and those that affect supply.** In the simplest sense, supply and demand affect price in the following manner: When the price goes up, the quantity demanded goes down but the supplier's incentive to produce more goes up. When the price goes down, the quantity demanded increases, whereas the quantity supplied may (or may not) decline. When the interests of buyers and sellers are in balance, an equilibrium price is established. However, adjusting price or supply to meet or spur demand does not guarantee profitability; business may not be able to adjust costs and price far enough and quickly enough. The important thing to remember is that in a free-market system, the interaction of supply and demand determines what is produced and in what amounts.

5 **Compare supply and demand curves, and explain how they interact to affect price.** A demand curve is a graph showing the relationship between the amount of product that buyers will purchase at various prices. Because lower prices typically lead to larger purchases, demand curves usually slope downward as they move to the right. A change in overall demand shifts the demand curve further to the right if overall demand increases, or to the left if overall demand declines. A supply curve is a graph showing the relationship between various prices and quantities that sellers will offer for sale, regardless of demand. Because sellers are willing to supply more goods as prices rise, demand curves usually slope upward as they move to the right. Increases in overall supply shift the supply curve to the right; whereas decreases in overall supply shift the supply curve to the left. When the interests of buyers and sellers are in balance, an equilibrium price is established. This is the point at which the demand curve and supply curve intersect and represents the price at which buyers are willing to buy the same quantity as sellers are willing to sell.

6 **Discuss the four major economic roles of the U.S. government.** The U.S. government fosters competition by enacting laws and regulations, by enforcing antitrust legislation, and by approving mergers and acquisitions, with the power to block those that might restrain competition. It regulates certain industries where competition would be wasteful or excessive. It protects stakeholders from potentially harmful actions of businesses. And it contributes to economic stability by regulating the money supply and by spending for the public good.

7 **Explain how a free-market system monitors its economic performance.** Economists evaluate economic performance by monitoring a variety of economic indicators, such as housing starts, unemployment statistics, durable-goods orders, and inflation. They compute the consumer price index (CPI) to keep an eye on price changes—especially inflation. In addition, economists measure the productivity of a nation by computing the country's gross domestic product (GDP)—the sum of all goods and services produced by both domestic and foreign companies as long as those activities are located within a nation's boundaries.

8 **Identify five challenges you'll face as a business professional in today's global economy.** Throughout your career, you can be expected to (1) produce quality goods and services that satisfy customers' changing needs; (2) think like an entrepreneur, even if you're part of a large organization; (3) think globally and committing to a culturally diverse workforce; (4) behave in an ethically and socially responsible manner; and (5) keep pace with technology and electronic commerce.

Apple iTunes: What's Next?

Steve Jobs and his team at Apple iTunes have probably done about as good a job as anyone could in this wild new world of online music, but nobody knows yet if that is good enough. Recorded music is a multibillion-dollar industry, but success or failure in online music will literally come down to pennies. When Apple collects those 99 cents for each song it sells, it first hands over an estimated 70 cents to whichever company controls the rights to the song (typically a record company in the United States). This company then has to divide those 70 cents among music publishers, performers, and songwriters. From the 29 cents Apple keeps, it needs to cover its costs for advertising, staffing, computer systems, and other business expenses. A single nationwide advertising campaign can cost millions of dollars, so you can get an idea of how hard it is to stretch those 29 cents to cover costs and turn a profit.

In fact, some experts don't think online music will ever be profitable and that the only reason companies will continue to offer it is to help sell related goods and services. In Apple's case, iTune's best success might mean selling even more of those popular iPods. Either way, if online music does turn out to be a viable business long-term, you can expect to see Steve Jobs and iTunes leading the way.[41]

Critical Thinking Questions

1. If Steve Jobs decides to let iTunes operate at a loss in order to generate more sales of iPods, does iTunes still qualify as a profit-seeking business? Explain your answer.
2. Is the iTunes product line a goods-producing business or a service business? Why?
3. What barriers to entry did iTunes have to overcome in order to enter the online music business?

Learn More Online

Visit the iTunes website by going to Chapter 1 of this text's website at www.prenhall.com/bovee and clicking on the Apple iTunes hotlink. How does the website appeal to customers? What other goods and services are offered? In what ways does the website encourage visitors to make purchases?

Key Terms

barriers to entry (29)
business (27)
business cycle (44)
capital (30)
capital-intensive
   businesses (28)
capitalism (31)
communism (32)
competition (40)
competitive advantage (40)
consumer price index
   (CPI) (46)
deflation (46)
demand (34)
demand curve (35)
economic indicators (45)
economic system (30)
economics (30)
economies of scale (48)

electronic commerce
   (e-commerce) (29)
entrepreneurs (30)
equilibrium price (38)
fiscal policy (44)
free-market system (31)
globalization (52)
goods-producing
   businesses (27)
gross domestic product
   (GDP) (47)
gross national product
   (GNP) (47)
human resources (30)
inflation (46)
knowledge (30)
labor-intensive businesses (28)
macroeconomics (30)
microeconomics (30)

monetary policy (44)
monopolistic competition (40)
monopoly (40)
natural resources (30)
nonprofit organizations (27)
oligopoly (40)
planned system (32)
privatizing (34)
producer price index (PPI) (46)
profit (27)
pure competition (40)
recession (43)
recovery (43)
service businesses (28)
socialism (33)
stakeholders (42)
supply (34)
supply curve (37)

Test Your Knowledge

Questions for Review

1. Why do businesspeople study economics?
2. What are the five factors of production, and why are knowledge workers a key economic resource?
3. How is capitalism different from communism and socialism in the way it achieves economic goals?
4. Why is government spending an important factor in economic stability?
5. Why might a government agency seek to block a merger or acquisition?

Questions for Analysis

6. Why is it often easier to start a service business than a goods-producing business?
7. Why is competition an important element of the free-market system?
8. Besides price, what factors might influence consumers' demand for new automobiles? What factors, besides price, might influence manufacturers' supply of new automobiles?
9. How do countries know if their economic system is working?
10. **Ethical Considerations.** Because knowledge workers are in such high demand, you decide to enroll in an evening MBA program. Your company has agreed to reimburse you for 80 percent of your tuition. You haven't revealed, however, that once you earn your degree, you plan to apply for a management position at a different company. Is it ethical for you to accept your company's tuition reimbursement, given your intentions?

Questions for Application

11. Company sales are skyrocketing, and projections show that your computer consulting business will outgrow its current location by next year. What factors should you consider when selecting a new site for your business?
12. How would a decrease in Social Security benefits to the elderly affect the economy?
13. Graph a supply and demand chart for iTunes pricing structure. Make up any data you need, but show the equilibrium price for an individual song to be 99 cents.
14. Think about the many ways that technology has changed your life as a consumer. Record your thoughts on a sheet of paper. On that same sheet of paper, make a second list of how you envision technology will change your life in the near future. Compare your thoughts to those of your classmates.

Practice Your Knowledge

Handling Difficult Situations on the Job: Beating the Chains

You're a manager at the Blue Marble, an independent children's bookstore in Fort Thomas, Kentucky. Owner Tina Moore competes successfully with the big chains by supplying personalized service along with her products, thus earning customer loyalty. When your hand-picked staff sells a book, they draw on their extensive knowledge of children's literature to help customers choose.

But when it comes to the mega-best-selling *Harry Potter* series, Moore enters a global competition. Author J. K. Rowling's British and U.S. publishers coordinate a simultaneous release for every new book in the series (called a "strict on sale date"). Many stores stay open until midnight the night before so they can sell the hotly anticipated books the instant their agreements allow.

When the last *Harry Potter* came out, many of Moore's regular customers drove miles to reach the Barnes & Noble superstore, which threw a midnight pajama party, giving away "Harry Potter" spectacles, ladling out "butter beer" (ginger ale), and showcasing a live owl for the fans who showed up in droves. By the time you opened at 9 AM, your customers were already back at home, sipping hot chocolate and reading the gripping tome they'd purchased from your competitors.[42]

Your task: A new *Harry Potter* volume is on the way. Moore wants you to brainstorm ideas for drawing customers to the Blue Marble instead of losing them to the chains. What competitive advantages do you hold? How can you maximize and apply them to this situation? Since the product is identical, can you differentiate yourselves? How? Can you extend the excitement (and sales) beyond the release date? List your ideas, with points indicating benefits for each of them. Then finalize a plan for the next *Harry Potter* strict on sale date.

Sharpening Your Communication Skills

Select a local service business you are familiar with. How does that business try to gain a competitive advantage in the marketplace? Write a brief summary, as directed by your instructor, describing whether the company competes on speed, quality, price, innovation, service, or a combination of those attributes. Be prepared to present your analysis to your classmates.

Building Your Team Skills

Economic indicators help businesses and governments determine where the economy is headed. You may have noticed news headlines such as the following, each of which offers clues to the direction of the U.S. economy:

1. Housing Starts Lowest in Months
2. Fed Lowers Discount Rate and Interest Rates Tumble
3. Retail Sales Up 4 Percent Over Last Month
4. Business Debt Down from Last Year
5. Businesses Are Buying More Electronic Equipment
6. Industry Jobs Go Unfilled as Area Unemployment Rate Sinks to 3 Percent
7. Telephone Company Reports 30-Day Backlog in Installing Business Systems

Discuss each of those headlines with the other students on your team. Is each item good news or bad news for the economy? Why? What does each news item mean for large and small businesses? Report your team's findings to the class as a whole. Did all the teams come to the same conclusions about each headline? Why or why not? With your team, discuss how these different perspectives might influence the way you interpret economic news in the future.

Expand Your Knowledge

Discovering Career Opportunities

Thinking about a career in economics? Find out what economists do by reviewing the *Occupational Outlook Handbook* in your library or online at www.bls.gov/oco. This is an authoritative resource for information about all kinds of occupations. Search for "economists," then answer these questions:

1. Briefly describe what economists do and their typical working conditions.

2. What is the job outlook for economists? What is the average salary for starting economists?
3. What training and qualifications are required for a career as an economist? Are the qualifications different for jobs in the private sector as opposed to those in the government?

Developing Your Research Skills

Gaining a competitive advantage in today's marketplace is critical to a company's success. Look through recent copies of business journals and newspapers (online or in print) to find an article about a company whose practices have set that company apart from its competitors. Use your favorite online search engine or metacrawler (see Exhibit 4.3 on page 141 in Chapter 4 for a list if you don't already have a favorite) to find more information about that company online.

1. What products or services does the company manufacture or sell?
2. How does the company set its goods or services apart from those of its competitors? Does the company compete on price, quality, service, or innovation?
3. Does the company have a website, and if so, how does the company use it? What kinds of information does the company include on its website?

Exploring the Best of the Web

URLs for all Internet exercises are provided at the website for this book, www.prenhall.com/bovee. When you log on to this text's Companion Website, select Chapter 1. Then select "Featured Websites," click on the name of the featured website, and review the website to complete these exercises.

Explore these chapter-related websites, review their content, and answer the following questions for each website you visit:

1. What is the purpose of this website?
2. What kinds of information does this website contain? Please be specific.
3. How is the information provided at this website useful for businesspeople? Consumers?
4. How did you expand your knowledge of economics by reviewing the material at this website? What new things did you learn about this topic?

Find the Right Stuff

Learn about thousands of businesses around the world by visiting Corporate Information, a website with links to over 350,000 company profiles, data on 30 industries in 65 countries, and current economic information for over 100 countries. You'll also find research reports analyzing sales, dividends, earnings, and profit ratios on some thousands of companies, current foreign exchange rates, and the definitions of commonly used global company extensions such as GmbH, SA, de CV, and more. www.corporateinformation.com

Step Inside the Economic Statistics Briefing Room

Want to know where the economy is headed? Visit the Economic Statistics Briefing Room to get the latest economic indicators compiled by a number of U.S. agencies. Click on Federal Statistics by category to enter the room, and check out the stats and graphs for new housing starts; manufacturers' shipments, inventories, and orders; unemployment; average hourly earnings; and more. Are monthly housing starts, unemployment, and annual median household income increasing or decreasing? Make your own projections about which direction the economy is heading. www.whitehouse.gov/fsbr/esbr.html

Discover What's in the CPI

The CPI is an important tool that allows analysts to track the change in prices over time. But the CPI doesn't always match a given individual's inflation experience. Find out why by visiting the website maintained by the U.S. Bureau of Labor Statistics (look for Consumer Price Index). Be sure to check out how the CPI measures homeowners' costs, how the CPI is used, what goods and services it covers, and whose buying habits it reflects. http://stats.bls.gov

Learning Interactively

Companion Website

Visit the Companion Website at www.prenhall.com/bovee. For Chapter 1, take advantage of the interactive "Learning Modules" to test your chapter knowledge. Get instant feedback on whether you need additional studying. Complete the exercises as specified by your instructor.

A Case for Critical Thinking

Turmoil in the Airline Industry

Year in, year out, you'd be hard pressed to find an industry that generates more negative headlines than the airline business. From labor-management squabbles to massive financial losses to high-profile bankruptcies, the only time bad news gets chased off the front page is when worse news comes along. Since 1930, the industry has accumulated $5 billion in losses (individual companies make money now and then, but overall, the industry has been a money pit for over six decades).

Dramatic events such as the terrorist attacks on September 11, 2001, occasionally bring these troubles into sharp focus, but even during the best of times, running an airline profitably is a huge challenge, thanks in large part to two inescapable laws of nature: *product parity* and *high fixed costs*. Product parity exists when competitors in a given market are unable to distinguish their offerings in any meaningful way. And as a passenger, what could feel like more of the same than airline travel? From cramped seats to crowded baggage claims, it all tends to feel the same, no matter which airline you choose.

The danger of product parity is a virtual invitation to *price wars* (you'll read more about these in Chapter 13). If all airline service seems the same, passengers will naturally make selections based on price—and websites that rank flights from lowest price to highest make this sort of shopping a no-brainer. To attract enough customers, airlines have no choice but to constantly match the prices set by their competitors, even if that means setting prices so low that they lose money on every sale. And to the industry's eternal regret, somebody is always starting a price war. As former Continental CEO Gordon Bethune put it, "we are only as good as our dumbest competitor, and there have been numerous contestants for that honor."

Price wars are particularly vicious in an industry with high fixed costs—recurring expenses that must be paid even if the company isn't generating any revenue to cover them. For instance, airlines need to continue paying employees and making payments on their aircraft, even if those airplanes are flying around half full.

BUSINESS TRAVELERS CHANGE EXPENSIVE HABITS
Even as the industry struggles with parity and price wars, their customers are changing the way they buy and use air travel. Over the past few years, safety concerns and tighter corporate budgets have changed the behavior of the business travelers who typically generate about 70 percent of a major airline's revenue by buying expensive last-minute and flexible fares. Resourceful business travelers now use substitute products such as videoconferencing and online meetings or other transportation modes—even if it means putting up with inconveniences—to reduce travel expenses.

AIR TRAVEL GETS "WAL-MARTED"
But wait; its gets even worse. Just as Wal-Mart did in retailing, the discounters of the air such as Southwest and JetBlue are squeezing the major airlines from every angle. Since coming on the scene in the wake of industry deregulation in the late 1970s, low-cost carriers have been able to sell tickets for less because they have many cost advantages over full-service rivals. To begin with, as newer companies themselves, they often have younger fleets, which require less maintenance, and younger labor forces that aren't tied to complicated, inefficient labor contracts. Moreover, low-fare carriers typically fly one airplane model, thus minimizing maintenance, operating, and training costs. By contrast, big carriers typically fly six or seven types of aircraft.

In addition, discounters aren't saddled with the high cost of *hub-and-spoke* systems, which major carriers use to funnel flights through a small number of high-volume airports. This practice helps them to serve small markets and offer passengers more destinations and more frequent flights, but it's a more complex and more expensive way to run an airline. By using a *point-to-point* approach, discounters minimize unproductive downtime for both aircraft and employers.

FLYING INTO AN UNCERTAIN FUTURE
Even as upstarts saw some degree of success, between 2001 and 2004, U.S. airlines collectively lost some $30 billion dollars and laid off well over 100,000 employees. In one year alone, from 2003 to 2004, the price of airline fuel jumped 70 percent. The majors continue to struggle under expensive union contracts, animosity between labor and management, crushing debt, and pension plans they claim they can't afford to support.

Some are making drastic moves in the struggle to survive. Delta convinced its pilots to accept a $1 billion reduction in compensation and benefits, and both Delta and U.S. Airways are trying to back out of pension commitments made to now-retired employees. Other moves are more positive, including United's recent launch of a premium service between New York and Los Angeles and more aggressive expansion by several majors into overseas markets.

Of course, this *is* the airline industry, so nothing is simple. Today, even the discounters who dished out trouble for the majors are having trouble of their own. For instance, Southwest Airlines, the first significant discounter and still the largest, is no longer a young rebel but a middle-aged corporation whose employees want to be paid as well as anyone else.

Where will it all end? Even an industry accustomed to losing money can't keep dishing it out at the rate these companies have been the past few years. Experts warn that some of the major carriers could disappear if they can't get their costs under control soon. When it filed for bankruptcy protection (for the second time) in 2004, U.S. Airways admitted that "it did not anticipate the magnitude of the structural shift" in the business brought about by discounters—although one could certainly ask why it took the company 25 years to figure out that deregulation and the discounters had changed the business forever.

Critical Thinking Questions

1. What supply and demand factors have changed the equilibrium point for airline ticket sales?
2. How has information technology affected the airline industry?
3. How are complementary products affected by problems in the airline industry?
4. Several of the major airlines say that with their very survival at stake, they can no longer afford to pay the pensions of retired employees. If the government allows them to back out of these agreements, the burden will fall on a federal pension guarantee agency that is funded by industry—but not funded well enough to cover so many pensions. Should taxpayers be asked to help pay the pensions of retired employees whose former employers are unwilling or unable to pay them? Why or why not?

Video Case

Helping Businesses Do Business: U.S. Department of Commerce

Learning Objectives

The purpose of this video is to help you:

1. Understand world economic systems and their effect on competition.
2. Identify the factors of production.
3. Discuss how supply and demand affect a product's price.

Synopsis

The U.S. Department of Commerce seeks to support U.S. economic stability and help U.S.-based companies do business in other countries. In contrast to the planned economy of the People's Republic of China, the United States is a market economy where firms are free to set their own missions and buy from and sell to any other business or individual. In the United States, companies must comply with government regulations that set standards such as minimum safety requirements. When doing business in other countries, they must consider tariffs and other restrictions that govern imports to those markets. In addition, supply and demand affect a company's ability to set prices and generate profits.

Discussion Questions

1. *For analysis:* If a U.S. company must pay more for factors of production such as human resources, what is the likely effect on its competitiveness in world markets?
2. *For analysis:* Is the equilibrium price for a company's product likely to be the same in every country? Explain your answer.
3. *For application:* To which factors of production might a small U.S. company have the easiest access? How would this affect the company's competitive position?
4. *For application:* Is a company likely to see more competitors enter a market when supply exceeds demand or when demand exceeds supply?
5. *For debate:* Should the U.S. Department of Commerce, funded by citizens' tax payments, be providing advice and guidance to U.S. companies that want to profit by doing business in other countries? Support your chosen position.

Online Exploration

Visit the U.S. Department of Commerce website at www.commerce.gov and follow some of the links from the homepage to see some of this government agency's resources for businesses. Also follow the link to read about the DOC's history. What assistance can a U.S. business expect from this agency? How have the agency's offerings evolved over the years as the needs and demands of business have changed?

Business Done Right: Ethics and Social Responsibility

CHAPTER 2

LEARNING OBJECTIVES

After studying this chapter, you will be able to

1. Define corporate social responsibility and ethics

2. Highlight three factors that influence ethical behavior

3. Identify three steps that businesses are taking to encourage ethical behavior and explain the advantages and disadvantages of whistle-blowing

4. List four questions you might ask yourself when trying to make an ethical decision

5. Explain the difference between an ethical dilemma and an ethical lapse

6. Compare the three major perspectives on corporate social responsibility

7. Discuss how businesses can become more socially responsible

8. Outline activities the government and businesses are undertaking to protect the environment

www.prenhall.com/bovee

Even Patagonia's stores are recycled in many cases. The Portland, Oregon, store is housed in a building that dates from 1895; when it was remodeled in 1998, 97 percent of the building materials were reclaimed or recycled.

INSIDE BUSINESS TODAY

Patagonia Trades Rampant Growth for Environmentally Friendly Operations

www.patagonia.com

Like many entrepreneurs, Yvon Chouinard transformed a personal passion—mountaineering, in his case—into a profitable business. Unlike many business leaders, he also transformed his company into a living embodiment of his personal values.

As the founder and owner of Patagonia, a leading producer of outdoor gear and clothing, Chouinard worked hard to build a successful company that catered to extreme sports enthusiasts like himself (and to less-adventuresome people who like the image of outdoor adventure, he readily admits). Along the way, he incorporated his personal passion for limiting the environmental damage done by contemporary business into Patagonia's operating principles.

Chouinard put those principles to work by instituting such policies as a self-imposed "earth tax" (amounting to the greater of 1 percent of sales or 10 percent of pretax profits) with the proceeds being donated to a variety of environmental causes. As sales continued to grow throughout the 1980s—as much as 30 percent every year—the company expanded its offerings to include 375 products.

However, several events during the 1990s challenged Chouinard to reexamine both his philosophy of business and the way Patagonia was run. Sales slowed during a recession, and the company's bank called in a loan, forcing it to come up with the cash in a hurry. The double blow compelled Patagonia to scale back its operations and lay off one-fifth of its workforce. Consultants advised Chouinard to sell the company and create a charitable foundation for environmental causes, but he wanted to do more than simply give money away. He also refused advice to generate cash by taking the company public, selling stock to investors. He knew those investors would start calling the shots and probably force the company to put profitable growth above all else. Chouinard wanted to "use the company as a tool for social change," and he wanted to do so on his own terms. Somehow or another, Patagonia had to stay in business and remain a private company.

The other life-changing event occurred when the company analyzed the environmental impact of the materials used in its products. Chouinard had assumed that polyester and other petroleum-based fabrics would be the biggest culprits, so he was stunned to learn that cotton was the worst of the bunch. The problem: the massive amounts of chemical pesticides used in commercial cotton farming. In fact, 25 percent of all pesticides in use today are used on cotton fields.

Chouinard addressed the multiple challenges by aligning Patagonia even more closely with his personal ideals. To avoid the financial volatility often brought on by rapid growth and constant debt, the company would no longer grow for the sake of growth, but rather would grow only at a rate that was safely sustainable. He simplified the product line and reduced the staff by 20 percent to bring costs in line. And he was determined that Patagonia would lead the apparel industry into a new era of chemical-free organic cotton—even to the extent of lending money to farmers when their banks refused to help finance them through the transition to pesticide-free farming.

The effort to find environment-friendly fabric also included the formulation of Synchilla fleece, made from recycled plastic soda bottles, which is featured in a variety of Patagonia products and accounts for the recycling of millions of plastic bottles every year. Not only does Patagonia use these fabrics itself, it also helps educate competitors such as Gap and Nike on incorporating them into their own product lines.

Organic cotton and recycled fleece have proven to be huge hits with consumers, but at Patagonia conscientious management isn't limited to the environment. For instance, employees who are new parents get two months of fully paid time off, and the company was one of the first in the United States to provide onsite day care to help minimize the stress on both parents and children. As a result, the company benefits from extremely low employee turnover—replacing employees who get frustrated or stressed-out and leave is more expensive than day-care facilities and family-friendly policies—and has been recognized by *Fortune*, *Working Mother*, and the Society for Human Resource Management as a great place to work.[1]

GET READY

Yvon Chouinard acknowledges that every company has an impact on the environment and that the best any company can do is to work diligently to minimize that impact. Patagonia pursues that goal in every facet of operations, from solar energy in its offices to earth-friendly fabrics. He also knows that the pursuit of ideals often involves sacrifice and change. However, Chouinard and his colleagues have proven that profitability and ideology can coexist. Patagonia offers much to think about, not only in the context of business and the environment, but also the larger issue of the relationship between business and society in general. Could you successfully apply Patagonia's approach to other causes, such as education or religion? What stumbling blocks might you encounter if you tried? When you're managing a department or running a company yourself, how will you approach the challenges of ethics and social responsibility? ■

Chapter Overview

Every company has the potential to affect the world around it in both negative and positive ways. Patagonia works hard to minimize its negative impact on the natural environment while influencing positive changes that align with the founder's values. Thousands of other companies demonstrate their commitment to responsible behavior in countless other ways, from treating customers with respect to communicating honestly with investors to supporting their local communities. This chapter explains what it means to conduct business in an ethically and socially responsible manner and discusses the importance of doing so. You'll explore the factors that influence ethical behavior and learn ways to make ethical decisions as a manager or business owner. The chapter also provides an overview of the efforts being made to ensure that businesses treat society, the natural environment, their customers, their investors, their employees—and each other—fairly. Unfortunately, the actions of a small number of companies around the world have tainted the entire business profession in the eyes of some observers in recent years. According to a recent *BusinessWeek*/Harris poll, some 79 percent of Americans believe corporate executives put their own personal interests ahead of workers' and shareholders'.[2] However, as a future business leader yourself, you can be a catalyst for positive change.

Ethics and Social Responsibility in Contemporary Business

Yvon Chouinard is one of many thousands of managers today who wrestle with the sometimes-competing demands of running a profitable business and running a socially responsible company. He would probably be the first to tell you that a company can't take action or make decisions; only the individuals within a company can do that. From the CEO to the newest college hire, every individual in an organization makes choices and decisions that have moral implications and can affect thousands of people.

In discussions of *social responsibility* and *ethics,* you'll often hear the two terms used interchangeably, but they are not the same. **Corporate social responsibility** is the idea that business has certain obligations to society beyond the pursuit of profits. **Ethics**, by contrast, is defined as the principles and standards of moral behavior that are accepted by society as right versus wrong. To make the right choice, or at least the best choice from among competing alternatives, individuals must think through the consequences of their actions. *Business ethics* is the application of moral standards to business situations.

Thanks to a number of high-profile scandals involving finances and product safety, corporate social responsibility and managerial ethics have been pushed to center stage in recent years. Several of these scandals have painfully demonstrated that corporate responsibility and ethics are not just intriguing philosophical questions but real-life issues, where mistakes by just a handful of people can erase billions of dollars of shareholder value (including the life savings of many employees), destroy tens of thousands of jobs, and affect families and communities for years. Throughout your business studies and into your career, you'll continue to hear references to the following cases (note that civil and criminal lawsuits are still active in several, so the final outcomes have yet to be determined):

- **Enron.** Once the nation's seventh-largest company and a poster child for new economy companies, Houston-based energy conglomerate Enron all but collapsed in 2001 thanks to a complex stew of hidden partnerships (designed to overstate profits and hide losses from investors), management mistakes, and insider trading. Thousands of employees lost their jobs, and many lost their life savings when Enron stock became almost worthless. More than 20 executives have been investigated by the Justice Department; at least a dozen have been indicted, and several pled guilty before they could be indicted. Charges were also brought against several of Enron's banks for their role in hiding financial information from investors.[3] See this chapter's Case for Critical Thinking on pages 93–94 for an in-depth look at the Enron scandal.
- **Arthurs Andersen.** Once one of the world's oldest and most distinguished public accounting firms, Arthur Andersen served as both Enron's independent financial auditor and management adviser (Chapter 16 discusses this *conflict of interest* in more detail). The company was indicted for shredding Enron accounting documents and later convicted of obstruction of justice for hiding information about Enron finances, making it the first major accounting firm ever convicted of a felony. Although the conviction was later overturned by the U.S. Supreme Court, at this point it is unlikely that Arthur Anderson can rebuild.[4]

LEARNING OBJECTIVE 1

Define corporate social responsibility and ethics

corporate social responsibility
The concern of businesses for the welfare of society as a whole

ethics
The rules or standards governing the conduct of a person or group

Business Buzz
enronomics
Suspect business practices that rely on impossibly optimistic forecasts, dubious accounting, or unsustainable spending

- *Marsh & McLennan.* Shock waves rolled through the insurance business when Marsh & McLennan's insurance brokerage unit, which helps corporations find insurance for various business needs, was accused of cheating customers by making favorable deals for itself at their expense. New York Attorney General Eliot Spitzer agreed not to press criminal charges on the condition that Marsh change its business practices and that CEO Jeffrey Greenberg resign, but the company was forced to pay $850 million to compensate defrauded customers and had to lay off 3,000 employees when sales plunged.[5]
- *WorldCom.* Telecommunications giant WorldCom (which now goes by the name MCI) filed for bankruptcy and cut more than 22,000 jobs after revealing accounting frauds totaling $11 billion. In 2005, founder and former CEO Bernard Ebbers was convicted on nine criminal charges stemming from the fraud.[6] You'll read more about the WorldCom case in Chapter 16.
- *Citigroup.* Citigroup's troubles didn't enter the public consciousness quite as much as these other examples, but the world's largest financial services company made ethical missteps from New York to Tokyo. In addition to controversial banking work for both Enron and WorldCom, Citigroup was forced by Japanese regulators to shut down its private banking unit (a specialized bank for individuals with high net worth). The tab so far: roughly $10 billion dollars in fines, fees, and lawsuits.[7]

Although these cases involve only a few companies, the fallout from their actions continues to affect managers in thousands of companies. As you'll see in Chapter 16, for instance, publicly traded companies (those that sell stock to investors) must now comply with new federal regulations, the Sarbanes-Oxley Act of 2002, that require much more stringent financial reporting. This new level of information may be a good thing for investors, but it comes at a cost. Estimates vary, but U.S. businesses will probably spend several billion dollars and countless hours of employee and executive time to ensure compliance with the new regulations—time and money that could've been invested in creating better products, improving customer service, and other productive activities.[8] And consumers ultimately pay the price when these added costs are passed along. Even though those new costs are a small fraction of the amount investors lost in these scandals, the unethical behavior of a small group of executives raised costs for everyone else.

The news is not all bad, of course, not by a long shot. As you read about illegal or unethical behavior on the part of a few managers, bear in mind that the vast majority of

Following Japanese tradition, executives from Citigroup bowed during a press conference in which the company expressed remorse for unethical business dealings in Japan.

businesses are run by ethical managers and staffed by ethical employees who make positive contributions to their communities. When Cummins Engine, a multinational engine manufacturer based in Columbus, Indiana, discovered that poor children without a school were sneaking into its Brazilian factory to steal metal to sell, the company funded the construction of a school that now serves 800 kids—and their parents in the evenings.[9] When John Wheeler, CEO of Rockford Construction, found out how poorly inner-city students in Grand Rapids, Michigan, were being treated, he mobilized his entire company to help. The 60 or 70 projects the company has initiated range from building a playground to buying two dilapidated schools and spending $18 million to resurrect them to simply handing one principal an envelope with $5,000 in it, to be used whenever a low-income student's family can't afford to pay a gas or electricity bill.[10] Moreover, even when businesses are simply engaged in the normal course of business—and do so ethically—they contribute to society in such ways as making useful products, providing gainful employment, and paying taxes. Businesses catch a lot of flak these days, some of it rightly deserved, but overall, the contributions of business to the health, happiness, and well-being of society are practically beyond measure.

Like all managers, these people face issues that aren't always clear-cut either, so identifying the "right" choice is not always easy. You can start to appreciate the dilemmas these managers face by first understanding what constitutes ethical behavior.

What Is Ethical Behavior?

As Patagonia's Yvon Chouinard knows, wanting to be an ethical corporate citizen isn't enough; people in business must actively practice ethical behavior. In business, besides obeying all laws and regulations, practicing good ethics means competing fairly and honestly, communicating truthfully, and not causing harm to others.

Competing Fairly and Honestly Businesses are expected to compete fairly and honestly and not knowingly deceive, intimidate, or misrepresent themselves to customers, competitors, clients, or employees. While most companies compete within the boundaries of the law, some do knowingly break laws or take questionable steps in their zeal to maximize profits and gain a competitive advantage. For example, to get ahead of the competition, some companies have engaged in spying on other companies, stealing patents, hiring employees from competitors to gain trade secrets, and eavesdropping electronically. Although businesses need to gather as much strategic information as they can, ethical companies steer clear of such practices.

Communicating Truthfully Today's companies communicate with a wide variety of audiences, from their own employees to customers to government officials. Most people would agree that honesty is its own reward, but it's also good business. Be honest with employees, and they'll serve the company well. Be honest with customers, and they'll keep buying your products and services. Year after year, Bryan Burk of Matrix Healthcare in Cincinnati, Ohio, continues to engage Majid Samarghandi and his team at Tritonservices whenever Matrix needs mechanical design or construction at one of its facilities. Burk explains why he continues to do business with Samarghandi: "One of the main reasons I keep going back is his honesty. If the man tells you something, you can take it to the bank. A handshake and his word mean something."[11]

Communicating truthfully is a simple enough concept: tell the truth, the whole truth, and nothing but the truth. However, matters sometimes aren't so clear. For instance, if you plan to introduce an improved version of a product next year, do you have an obligation to tell customers who are buying the existing product this year? Suppose you do tell them, and so many decide to delay their purchases that you end up with a cash flow problem that forces you to lay off several employees. Would that be fair for customers but unfair for your employees?

The timing and content of business messages aren't the only aspect of honesty. Has a friend or classmate ever encouraged you to try a product, and perhaps even given you discount coupons or free samples—for no apparent reason? The reason might be that he or she is one of the several hundred thousand young people across the United States who now promote products to their friends in exchange for free goods and services, inside information about upcoming products, and other benefits. Some 280,000 unpaid teenagers spread marketing messages for Tremor, a promotional company that is part of Proctor & Gamble, the consumer goods giant. Similarly, BzzAgent has engaged 20,000 adult agents, also unpaid, to push goods and services ranging from brew pubs to magazines.[12] Even if the information is completely truthful, is the communication honest if you aren't aware that the friendly conversation you think you're having is actually a carefully planned marketing campaign? The rapid growth of blogs (see Chapter 4) is presenting a similar issue online. If a company pays a blogger to write about its products, does the blogger have an ethical obligation to share that fact with his or her audience?[13]

Whenever you face a dilemma about what to say and when to say it, think about the decisions your audience is facing. What information do they need in order to make an intelligent decision? You may encounter situations when, for a valid reason such as protecting confidential financial information, you can't give people all the information they'd like to have. However, by focusing on your audience's needs, you'll find it much easier to clarify what constitutes truthful communication.

Not Causing Harm to Others All businesses have the capacity to cause harm to employees, customers, other companies, their communities, and investors. Problems can start when managers make decisions that put their own interests above those of other stakeholders, underestimate the risks of failure, or neglect to consider potential affects on other people and organizations. Of course, harm can also result even when managers have acted ethically—but they're still responsible for these negative outcomes.

As business and technology grow ever more complex, the potential for harm increases. For instance, although genetic engineering has contributed to food production with strains that are resistant to sometimes-devastating diseases, uncertainty remains about the long-term effects of these new plants on both human health and the environment. As a result, many consumers choose to purchase conventional or organic foods in the belief that they are safer (and some countries have banned bioengineered food entirely). Recently, however, biologists have raised concerns over "gene flow," a condition in which genetically engineered crops have begun to cross-pollinate with conventional and organic crops. Rice farmers in California and papaya growers in Hawaii who sell nonengineered crops are among those concerned that

LEARNING FROM BUSINESS BLUNDERS

OOPS When KFC launched a new ad campaign that presented fried chicken as an acceptable part of a "healthy, balanced diet" (or at least healthier than other fast-food alternatives), consumer advocates were quick to point out that the bucket of chicken being advertised contained more than 3,000 calories. *Advertising Age* magazine attacked the campaign, calling it "laughable." KFC quickly pulled the ads.

WHAT YOU CAN LEARN Whether people can occasionally enjoy fried chicken as part of a generally healthy diet is probably an issue for dieticians to resolve, but one thing is clear: Showing a 3,000-calorie, deep-fat fried product while talking about healthy diets is only asking for criticism. Many businesses now operate under constant scrutiny, so any suspect product claims are likely to come under close, critical examination from any number of regulators and advocacy groups.

their businesses will suffer. If their plants become interbred with genetically engineered plants, they won't be able to sell their crops to those consumers—or to entire countries such as Japan, which currently prohibits the sale of genetically modified foods.[14]

In nearly every company, the manner in which employees and executives handle information is key to avoiding harm to others. Because these people often have access to information that outsiders don't have, they have a responsibility not to take advantage of the situation. Specifically, buying or selling a company's stock based on information that outside investors lack is known as **insider trading**, which is not only unethical but also illegal.

Insider trading is a good example of the ethical trouble that businesspeople can get into when they face a **conflict of interest**, a situation in which a choice that promises personal gain compromises a more fundamental responsibility. If you're in charge of buying a new computer system for your company and you select the vendor who gave you Super Bowl tickets instead of the vendor who offered a better deal, you would be guilty of a conflict of interest.

The most common conflicts of interest are *insider deals* or *related-party deals,* such as when Company A purchases from or sells to Company B, which is owned or controlled by an executive from Company A. If the same person is involved in both ends of the transaction, whose interest is he or she looking out for? Another example is a company lending money to top executives or investing in companies owned by insiders. Even when these deals are legal (and most are, although loans to executives are now illegal), in the aftermath of Enron and other scandals that involved insider deals of various types, some find it surprising that so many corporations still make deals that invite accusations of conflict of interest.[15]

insider trading
The use of unpublicized information that an individual gains from the course of his or her job to benefit from fluctuations in the stock market

conflict of interest
Situation in which a business decision may be influenced by the potential for personal gain

---

CRITICAL THINKING CHECKPOINT

1. What role does ethics play in the practice of corporate social responsibility?
2. Do companies contribute to society just by being in business? Explain your answer.
3. How would you distinguish ethical behavior from unethical behavior?

Factors Influencing Ethical Behavior

Although a number of factors influence the ethical behavior of businesspeople, three in particular appear to have the most impact: cultural differences, knowledge, and organizational behavior.

LEARNING OBJECTIVE 2

Highlight three factors that influence ethical behavior

Cultural Differences Globalization exposes businesspeople to a variety of cultures and business practices. What does it mean for a business to do the right thing in Thailand? In Nigeria? In Norway? What may be considered unethical in the United States may be an accepted practice in another culture. Managers may need to consider a wide range of issues, including acceptable working conditions, minimum wage levels, product safety issues, and environmental protection. Chapter 3 explores these issues in more detail.

Knowledge As a general rule, the more you know and the better you understand a situation, the better your chances are of making an ethical decision. In the often frantic churn of daily business, though, it's easy to shut your eyes and ears to potential problems. However, as a business leader, you have the responsibility to not only pay attention but to actively seek out information regarding potential ethical issues. Ignorance is never an acceptable defense in the eyes of the law, and it shouldn't be in questions of ethics, either.

With information in hand, your next responsibility is to act in a timely and effective manner. Purdue Pharma, maker of the OxyContin prescription painkiller (known as "hillbilly heroin" in some rural areas), was criticized for its slow initial response when word spread that OxyContin was being distributed illegally through local pharmacies and over the

Internet. Purdue has since donated nearly $2 million to local law enforcement agencies to combat the problem, particularly in hard-hit areas such as Eastern Kentucky.[16]

Organizational Behavior The foundation of an ethical business climate is ethical awareness and clear standards of behavior. Organizations that strongly enforce company codes of conduct and provide ethics training help employees recognize and reason through ethical problems. Similarly, companies with strong ethical practices set a good example for employees to follow. On the other hand, companies that commit unethical acts in the course of doing business open the door for employees to follow suit.

To avoid such ethical breaches, many companies proactively develop programs designed to improve their ethical conduct, often under the guidance of a chief ethics officer or other top executive. These programs typically combine training, communication, and a variety of other resources to guide employees. More than 80 percent of large companies have also adopted a written **code of ethics**, which defines the values and principles that should be used to guide decisions (see Exhibit 2.1 for an example). By itself, however, a code of ethics can't accomplish much. "You can have grand motives, but if your employees don't see them, they aren't going to mean anything," says one ethics manager.[17] To be effective, a code must be supported by employee communications efforts, a formal training program, employee commitment to follow it, and a system through which employees can get help with ethically difficult situations.[18]

In addition to setting a good example, top executives must also be sensitive to ethical pressures they may be placing on their employees. For instance, a number of U.S. employers, including Wal-Mart, Pep Boys, Family Dollar, Taco Bell, and Toys "R" Us, have recently been accused of "time shaving," a practice in which supervisors alter employees' work records in order to cut costs (typically to avoid paying overtime when employees log more than 40 hours a week). All of these companies have formal policies prohibiting time shaving, but some supervisors say they are under such intense pressure to control costs that they fear they'll lose their own jobs if they don't shave time off their

---

LEARNING OBJECTIVE 3

Identify three steps that businesses are taking to encourage ethical behavior and explain the advantages and disadvantages of whistle-blowing

code of ethics
Written statement setting forth the principles that guide an organization's decisions

---

Exhibit 2.1
eHealth Code of Ethics
The Internet Healthcare Coalition, which represents companies and organizations that provide online health care information, encourages its members to abide by these ethical principles.

Candor	Disclose information that if known by consumers would likely affect consumers' understanding or use of the site or purchase or use of a product or service.
Honesty	Be truthful and not deceptive.
Quality	Provide health information that is accurate, easy to understand, and up to date.
	Provide the information users need to make their own judgments about the health information, products, or services provided by the site.
Informed consent	Respect users' right to determine whether or how their personal data may be collected, used, or shared.
Privacy	Respect the obligation to protect users' privacy.
Professionalism	Respect fundamental ethical obligations to patients and clients.
	Inform and educate patients and clients about the limitations of online health care.
Responsible partnering	Ensure that organizations and sites with which they affiliate are trustworthy.
Accountability	Provide meaningful opportunity for users to give feedback to the site.
	Monitor their compliance with the *eHealth Code of Ethics*.

MINDING YOUR OWN BUSINESS

LEAD YOUR TEAM WITH ETHICAL BEHAVIOR

A written code of ethics, an ethics hot line, employee training, and other tactics are important parts of any effort to ensure strong ethics in your company, but nothing is more crucial than the behavior of the company's owners and managers—and if you're the top executive, you're the most important part of the equation. Your actions say more about the company's virtues than any program or poster.

The gap between talk and action has led to a credibility crisis in U.S. companies. In one survey, more than 80 percent of top managers said they consider ethics in their decision making, but 43 of employees expressed the belief that managers routinely overlook ethics. When leaders make decisions that show profits winning out over ethics, employees not only lose faith in their leaders but begin to assume that all the glorious talk about ethics is just that—talk. And in an era when many corporate executives can earn staggering sums of money in pay and bonuses that are based on company profits and stock prices, skeptical employees might just assume that the unethical behavior is done is pursuit of personal gain.

Moreover, questionable behavior at the top creates an environment ripe for ethical abuse throughout the organization. If employees see that bending or breaking the rules is not only accepted but the best way to succeed, some will be tempted to start emulating their leaders. Then as other employees see those people getting away with it and getting ahead, they'll jump on the bandwagon. The unethical bandwagon doesn't need too many people on it to bring down an entire corporation, either, as Enron, WorldCom, and others have shown.

As a leader, you have a moral—and in many cases, legal—responsibility for the actions of your organization.

- **Lead by example.** Again, nothing is more important than demonstrating your commitment to ethics than behaving ethically yourself.
- **Don't tolerate unethical behavior.** At the same time, you have to show that poor decisions won't be accepted. Let one go without correction, and you'll probably see another one before long.

- **Inspire concretely.** Tell employees how they will personally benefit from participating in ethics initiatives. People respond better to personal benefits than to company benefits.
- **Acknowledge reality.** Admit errors. Discuss what went right, what went wrong, and how the company can learn from the mistakes. Solicit employee opinion and act on those opinions. If you only pretend to be interested, you'll make matters worse.
- **Communicate, communicate, communicate.** Ethics needs to be a continuous conversation, not a special topic brought up only in training sessions or when a crisis hits. Harold Tinkler, the chief ethics and compliance officer at the accounting firm Deloitte & Touche, says that "Companies need to turn up the volume," when it comes to talking about ethics.
- **Be honest.** Tell employees what you know as well as what you don't know. Talk openly about ethical concerns and be willing to accept negative feedback.
- **Hire good people.** Alan Greenspan, recent chairman of the Federal Reserve Board, put it nicely: "rules are no substitute for character." If you hire good people (not people who are good at their jobs, but people who are good, period) and create an ethical environment for them, you'll get ethical behavior. If you hire people who lack good moral character, you're inviting ethical lapses, no matter how many rules you write.

Questions for Critical Thinking

1. How does building trust, even when you've done so by admitting mistakes, encourage your employees to be more ethical?
2. How can you balance the business need to inspire employees to compete aggressively with the moral need to avoid competing unethically?

employees' time cards. Compensation experts say the practice is far more common than most people believe.[19]

Codes of ethics are so important that according to the Federal Sentencing Guidelines (1991), a company found to be violating federal law might not be prosecuted if it has the proper ethics policies and procedures in place.[20] Another way companies support ethical behavior is by establishing a system for reporting unethical or illegal actions at work, such as an ethics hot line. Companies that value ethics will try to correct reported problems. United Technologies, a large aerospace and defense manufacturer based in Hartford, Connecticut, has long had an ethics hot line as part of a comprehensive ethics communication program. During the last two decades, employees have made nearly 60,000 queries, and 41 percent of these queries led to some sort of change. Of the remaining queries, 23 percent didn't need or ask for a change, and the remaining 36 percent were deemed to require no action by management.[21]

If a serious problem persists, or in cases where management may be involved in the act, an employee may choose to blow the whistle. **Whistle-blowing** is an employee's disclosure to the media or government authorities of illegal, unethical, or harmful practices by the company. Both the Enron and WorldCom fraud cases came to light through the efforts of whistle-blowers: Sherron Watkins at Enron and Cynthia Cooper at WorldCom (both of whom strongly dislike the term whistle-blower, by the way; they don't see themselves as tattle-tales but as good employees doing their jobs).[22]

Whistle-blowing can bring high costs: Public accusation of wrongdoing hurts the business's reputation, requires attention from managers who must investigate the accusations, and damages employee morale. Moreover, whistle-blowers risk being fired or demoted, and they often suffer career setbacks, financial strain, and emotional stress. The fear of such negative repercussions may allow unethical or illegal practices to go unreported. Still, all things considered, many employees do the right thing, as Exhibit 2.2 suggests.

How Do You Make Ethical Decisions?

Determining what's ethically right in any given situation can be difficult, as you've no doubt experienced from time to time in your personal life. For instance, is it right to help a friend get a passing grade, even though you know he or she doesn't understand what's going on in the class? One helpful approach is to measure your choices against standards. These standards are usually grounded in universal teachings such as "Do not lie" and "Do not steal" that are aimed at assuring **justice**—the resolution of ethical issues in a way that is consistent with those generally accepted standards or right and wrong. Another place to look for ethical guidance is the law. If saying, writing, or doing something is clearly illegal, you have no decision to make; you obey the law.

whistle-blowing
The disclosure of information by a company insider that exposes illegal or unethical behavior on the part of the organization

justice
The resolution of ethical questions and other dilemmas in a manner that is consistent with generally accepted standards of right and wrong

Exhibit 2.2
Doing the Right Thing
According to a recent survey of 1,002 randomly selected adults, when it comes to ethics in the workplace, most employees try to do the right thing.

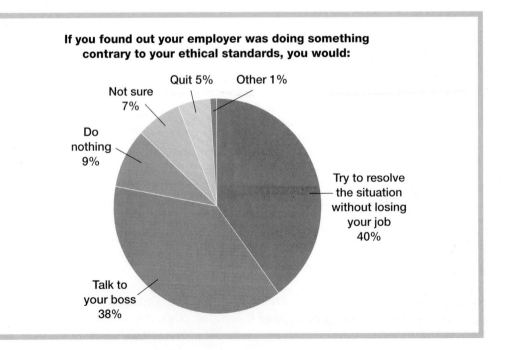

If you found out your employer was doing something contrary to your ethical standards, you would:

Quit 5%   Other 1%
Not sure 7%
Do nothing 9%
Talk to your boss 38%
Try to resolve the situation without losing your job 40%

Even though legal considerations will resolve some ethical questions, you'll often have to rely on your own judgment and principles. For example, what are your motives in a given situation? If your intent is honest, the decision is ethical; however, if your intent is to mislead or manipulate, your decision is unethical. Don't automatically assume you're viewing a situation fairly and objectively, either. Psychological research suggests that many people are influenced by unconscious biases that may even run counter to their stated beliefs.[23] Moreover, don't assume that other people think the way you do. The time-honored "Golden Rule" of treating others the way you want to be treated can get you into trouble when others don't want to be treated the same way you do. You might also consider asking yourself a series of questions:

1. Is the decision legal? (Does it break any laws?)
2. Is it balanced? (Is it fair to all concerned?)
3. Can you live with it? (Does it make you feel good about yourself?)
4. Is it feasible? (Will it actually work in the real world?)

When you need to determine the ethics of any situation, these questions will get you started. The decision-making tools in the right-hand column of Exhibit 2.3 can also help. One of the most practical and widely accepted methods is **utilitarianism**, an approach that seeks the greatest good for the greatest number of people involved. These approaches are not mutually exclusive alternatives. On the contrary, most businesspeople combine them to reach decisions that will satisfy as many stakeholders as possible without violating anyone's rights or treating anyone unjustly.

LEARNING OBJECTIVE 4

List four questions you might ask yourself when trying to make an ethical decision

utilitarianism
A decision-making approach that seeks to create the greatest good for the greatest number of people affected by the decisions

Is the Decision Ethical?	Does It Respect Stakeholders?	Does It Follow a Philosophical Approach?
IS IT LEGAL?	WILL OUTSIDERS APPROVE?	IS IT A UTILITARIAN DECISION?
Does it violate civil law?	Does it benefit customers, suppliers, investors, public officials, media representatives, and community members?	Does it produce the greatest good for the greatest number of people?
Does it violate company policy?		
IS IT BALANCED?		DOES IT UPHOLD INDIVIDUAL, LEGAL, AND HUMAN RIGHTS?
Is it fair to all concerned, in both the short and the long term?	WILL SUPERVISORS APPROVE?	Does it protect people's own interests?
	Did you provide management with information that is honest and accurate?	
CAN YOU LIVE WITH IT?		Does it respect the privacy of others and their right to express their opinion?
Does it make you feel good about yourself?	WILL EMPLOYEES APPROVE?	
	Will it affect employees in a positive way?	Does it allow people to act in a way that conforms to their religious or moral beliefs?
Would you feel good reading about it in a newspaper?		
IS IT FEASIBLE?	Does it handle personal information about employees discreetly?	DOES IT UPHOLD THE PRINCIPLES OF JUSTICE?
Does it work in the real world?		
Will it improve your competitive position?	Did you give proper credit for work performed by others?	Does it treat people fairly and impartially?
Is it affordable?		Does it apply rules consistently?
Can it be accomplished in the time available?		Does it ensure that people who harm others are held responsible and make restitution?

Exhibit 2.3
Guidelines for Making Ethical Decisions
Companies with the most success in establishing an ethical structure are those that balance their approach to making decisions.

L E A R N I N G
O B J E C T I V E 5

Explain the difference
between an ethical
dilemma and an ethical
lapse

ethical dilemma
*Situation in which both
sides of an issue can
be supported with valid
arguments*

ethical lapse
*Situation in which an
individual makes a decision
that is morally wrong,
illegal, or unethical*

When making ethical decisions, keep in mind that most ethical situations can be classified into two general types: ethical dilemmas and ethical lapses. An **ethical dilemma** is a
situation in which one must choose between two conflicting but arguably valid sides. All
ethical dilemmas have a common theme: the conflict between the rights of two or more
important groups of people. The second type of situation is an **ethical lapse**, in which an
individual makes a decision that is clearly wrong, such as divulging trade secrets to a competitor. Be careful not to confuse ethical dilemmas with ethical lapses. A company faces an
ethical dilemma when it must decide whether to continue operating a production facility that
is suspected, but not proven, to be unsafe. A company makes an ethical lapse when it continues to operate the facility even after the site has been proven unsafe. Other examples of
ethical lapses would include inflating prices for certain customers, hiring employees from
competitors to gain trade secrets, selling technological secrets to unfriendly foreign governments, switching someone's long-distance service without his or her consent (a practice
known as *slamming*), slipping unauthorized charges into phone bills (a practice known as
cramming), and using insider information to profit on the sale of company securities—
something Enron executives were accused of doing.

CRITICAL THINKING CHECKPOINT

1. Are cultural differences a legitimate reason for behavior by one group that
   another group finds unethical? Explain your answer.
2. Is ignorance a valid excuse for unethical behavior? Why or why not?
3. What questions can you ask to judge the ethics of your business decisions?
4. How does an ethical lapse differ from an ethical dilemma?

L E A R N I N G
O B J E C T I V E 6

Compare the three major
perspectives on corporate
social responsibility

Perspectives on Corporate Social Responsibility

Conflicts over ethics and social responsibility are often fueled by differing perspectives on the
issues at hand. People with equally good intentions can arrive at different conclusions based
on different assumptions about business's role in society. These perspectives can be grouped
into three general categories: (1) the only responsibility of business is to make money,
(2) business has a larger responsibility to society—and ethical behavior leads to financial
success, and (3) businesses must balance social responsibility and financial objectives.

The Traditional Perspective: The Business of Business Is Making Money The
classic perspective on this issue states that the sole responsibility of business is to make
money for the investors who put their money at risk to fund companies. This stance seems
blunt, but it can be more subtle than you might think at first glance. In the 19th and early 20th
centuries, the prevailing view among U.S. industrialists was that business had only one
responsibility: to make a profit. "The public be damned," said railroad tycoon William
Vanderbilt, "I'm working for the shareholders."[24] *Caveat emptor*—"Let the buyer beware"—
was the rule of the day. If you bought a product, you paid the price and took the consequences.

In 1970, influential economist Milton Friedman updated this view by saying "There is
only one social responsibility of business: to use its resources and engage in activities
designed to increase its profits so long as it stays within the rules of the game, which is to
say, engages in open and free competition without deception or fraud." Friedman argued
that only real people, not corporations, could have responsibilities and that dividends and
profit maximization would allow the shareholders to contribute to the charities and causes
of their choice.[25] As he saw it, the only social responsibility of business was to provide jobs
and pay taxes.

The subtlety that is sometimes overlooked by critics of business is that companies cannot
fund the many good things businesses today are expected to provide—decent wages, health
care, child care, community assistance, philanthropy, and so on—if they don't make enough
money to do so. The benefits of a healthy economy are numerous, from lower crime rates to

better education, but socially healthy economies cannot exist without financially healthy companies because business is the primary generator of wealth in the economy.

The Contemporary Perspective: Ethics Pays Most people in the United States, as much as 95 percent of the population according to one survey, now reject the notion that a corporation's only role is to make money.[26] In the last couple of decades, a new view of corporate social responsibility has replaced the classic view in the minds of many people both inside and outside business. This perspective states that not only do businesses have a broader responsibility to society, doing good for society helps companies do well for themselves. In other words, ethics pays.

Many investors and managers now support a broader view of social responsibility. They argue that a company has an obligation to society beyond the pursuit of profits and that becoming more socially responsible can actually improve a company's profits. This line of thinking is best captured by a *New York Times* headline: "Do Good? Do Business? No, Do Both!" "You can't put one in front of the other. You can't be successful if you can't do both," says Seth Goldman, cofounder of Honest Tea, a company that manufactures barely sweetened ice tea and totally biodegradable tea bags. In other words, companies must be profitable businesses to advance their social mission, and their socially responsible activities should enhance the business.

Companies that support this line of thinking link the pursuit of socially responsible goals with their overall strategic planning. Such socially responsible companies are just as dedicated to building a viable, profitable business as they are to hewing to a mission—and they think strategically to make both happen. Increasingly, companies and employees are caring about their communities and want to be a part of the greater cause (see Exhibit 2.4). They want to be good corporate citizens and satisfy shareholders' needs for a return on their investment. Still, finding the right balance can be challenging.

Exactly how much can businesses contribute to social concerns? This is a difficult decision for most companies because they have limited resources. They must allocate their resources to a number of goals, such as upgrading facilities and equipment, developing new products, marketing existing products, and rewarding employee efforts, in addition to contributing to social causes. This juggling act is a challenge that every business faces. For example, if a company consistently ignores its stakeholders, its business will suffer and eventually fold. If the company disregards society's needs (such as environmental concerns),

Percentage of executives who "strongly agree" or "agree" that companies should	
Be environmentally responsible	100%
Be ethical in operations	100
Earn profits	96
Employ local residents	94
Pay taxes	94
Encourage and support employee volunteering	89
Contribute money and leadership to charities	85
Be involved in economic development	75
Be involved in public education	73
Involve community representatives in business decisions that impact community	62
Target a proportion of purchasing toward local vendors	61
Help improve quality of life for low-income populations	54

Exhibit 2.4
Civic Responsibilities
Executives generally support the notion that companies should serve their communities and be socially responsible citizens in a number of ways.

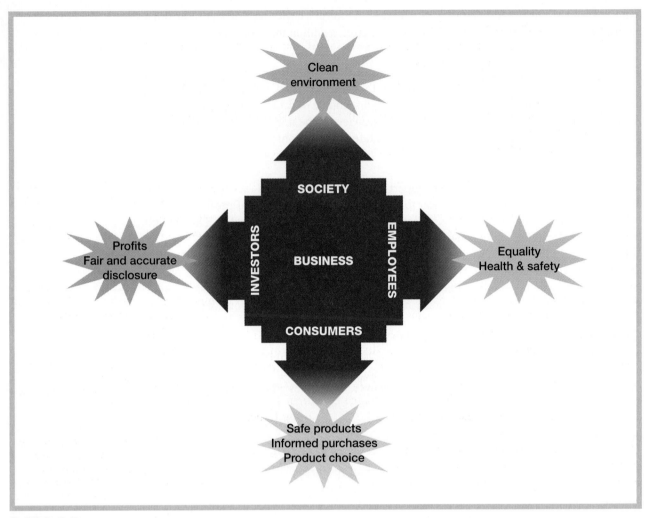

Exhibit 2.5
Balancing Business and Stakeholders' Rights
Balancing the individual needs and interests of a company's stakeholders is one of management's most difficult tasks.

voters will clamor for laws to limit the offensive business activities, consumers who feel their needs and values are being ignored will spend their money on a competitor's products, investors who are unhappy with the company's performance will invest elsewhere, and employees whose needs are not met will become unproductive or will quit and find other jobs. As Exhibit 2.5 shows, stakeholders' needs sometimes conflict. In such cases, which stakeholders should be served first—society, consumers, investors, or employees?

An Emerging Perspective: Dynamically Balancing Ethics and Profits Some business theorists now promote a third view, that ethics needs to be one of the cornerstones of business but that in the real world, profits and ethics are often at odds. Managers need to evaluate every situation within the context of the organization's "moral personality." In some cases, the ethical approach will pay off financially as well, but in others it won't.[27] The decision by 3M to discontinue Scotchgard Fabric Protector is a noteworthy example of this perspective. The government did not order 3M to stop manufacturing products (such as Scotchgard) containing perfluorooctane sulfonate (PFOs), and there was no evidence as yet that PFOs harmed humans. But when traces of the chemical showed up in humans, 3M decided to pull the plug on the product and not wait until scientific evidence might someday link PFOs to a disease. This decision cost 3M $500 million in annual sales because the company did not have a substitute product to fill Scotchgard's void.[28] Even though the decision had painful financial implications, it fit the moral personality that 3M's leaders want to maintain for the organization.

CRITICAL THINKING CHECKPOINT

1. Do you agree with Milton Friedman's assessment of the social responsibilities of a corporation? Why or why not?
2. Is the notion that "ethics pays" a cynical way to view social responsibility? Explain your answer.
3. What role does the CEO or owner of a business have in establishing the company's moral personality?

Business's Efforts to Increase Social Responsibility

Particularly in times of highly publicized corporate scandals, it's important to remember that thousands of socially responsible businesses remain committed to having a positive impact on their local communities, the nation, and the world as a whole. *IndustryWeek*'s 100 Best Managed Companies all actively engage in socially responsible activities. Some work to curb child abuse or domestic violence. Others provide generous benefits packages for employees. Still others have strong recycling programs to help keep the environment clean. Microsoft's Bill Gates is admired by many and criticized by some for his aggressive competitive approach to business, but through the Bill and Melinda Gates Foundation, he has become one of the world's most generous executives. The foundation supports health and education efforts in poorer countries with billions of dollars' worth of grants. In fact, one expert in international health issues predicts that Gates will ultimately be known more for what he's doing to improve world health than for what he does in the computer industry.[29]

Few businesses have the resources that Bill Gates can bring to bear in his charitable activities, but every business can make choices that benefit its stakeholders beyond the bottom line. Many companies now approach this challenge by starting with a **social audit**, a systematic evaluation and reporting of the company's social performance. The report typically includes objective information about how the company's activities affect its various stakeholders.

With the social audit as a guide, owners and managers can then decide how and where they would like to make a difference. In some cases, the effort will be purely charitable, such as donating money to a favorite cause. In others, the effort will be linked in some way to the company's own business efforts, bringing benefits to both the business and one or more groups in society. A common approach is **cause-related marketing**, in which a portion of product sales helps support worthy causes.

Similarly, managers can make business decisions that affect other businesses or communities in a positive way. For instance, in response to pressure from environmental activists, Home Depot persuaded its lumber suppliers in Chile to adopt tree farming methods that protected native forests. By using its power as a huge customer (the company buys 10 percent of the wood exported from Chile, for example), Home Depot was able to influence other companies for a positive outcome.[30]

Some companies choose to be socially responsible corporate citizens by engaging in **philanthropy**: donating money, time, goods, or services to religious, charitable, humanitarian, or educational institutions. Corporations such as Microsoft, General Electric, Dell, and Wal-Mart donate millions of dollars in cash, products, and employee time to charity each year. A number of companies also offer their expertise to charitable causes. Pharmaceutical giant Pfizer sends its Global Health Fellows, a 30-member team of business and medical professionals, around the world to help developing countries deal with pressing public health issues.[31]

To be sure, corporate philanthropy often promises some benefit for the giver as well, from boosting morale to attracting new employees to building a presence in international regions that hold promise as future markets.[32] An endless ethics debate could be waged about whether such "reverse benefits" reduce the goodness of the gift-giving, but unless the gifts are deceitful or harmful, it's hard to argue that corporate gifts don't help those who receive them.

LEARNING OBJECTIVE 7

Discuss how businesses can become more socially responsible

social audit
Assessment of a company's performance in the area of social responsibility

cause-related marketing
Marketing campaigns that donate a portion of their proceeds to a charitable organization or other public cause

philanthropy
Altruistic actions such as donating money, time, goods, or services to charitable, humanitarian, or educational institutions

Bill Gates made his name as the co-founder and guiding force behind Microsoft, but in recent years he and his wife Melinda (not pictured) have become increasingly well known for their generous contributions to worldwide health care and education.

Responsibility Toward Society and the Environment

L E A R N I N G
O B J E C T I V E

Outline activities the
government and businesses
are undertaking to protect
the environment

The three-way relationship among business, the natural environment, and the human beings who rely on that environment is a great example of the complex ethical decisions that managers often face. People want products that make their lives safer, simpler, or more enjoyable. However, the creation, delivery, and use of those products virtually always generates pollution—which can make peoples' lives less safe, more complicated, and less enjoyable. Moreover, the process of business consumes natural resources, either directly or indirectly. Yvon Chouinard has taken effective and even inspiring steps toward reducing the impact that Patagonia has on the environment while making products that satisfy consumer demands. But could he make the same progress if he were building the cars that people drive to the store to buy Patagonia products or refining the gasoline they put in those cars? Those products are surely more essential to modern life than climbing gear—and a lot more difficult to manufacture.

Few issues in the public dialog have become as heated and politicized as pollution has in the past few decades. Environmentalists and their political allies sometimes portray business leaders as heartless profiteers who would strip the Earth bare for a few bucks. Corporate leaders and their political allies, on the other hand, sometimes cast environmentalists as tree-hugging fringe lunatics who want to send civilization back to the stone ages. As is too often the case, real problems and real solutions get lost in all the noise.

No matter what role you end up playing inside or outside of the business world, try to keep two important points in mind. First, we all consume natural resources and generate pollution to some degree, so we are all part of the problem—and U.S. consumers haven't shown much willingness to make sacrifices in the interest of the environment. In a 2002 survey, only 15 percent said they make financial or behavioral sacrifices in the interest of protecting the environment (such as buying more-expensive but environmentally friendly versions of products). Another 31 percent support environmental causes, but usually not if it means paying more. The remaining groups—roughly half the population—might be best described as "don't know and don't care" when it comes to the environment.[33] Second, causes that environmentalists take on are often as much about human health and safety as they are about forests and rivers and wildlife, so they matter to everyone, not just people concerned with wild spaces.

The Pervasiveness of Pollution   For decades, environmental and public health experts have warned about the dangers of **pollution**, the contamination of the natural environment by the discharge of harmful substances. Our air, water, and land can easily be tainted by industrial discharges, aircraft and motor vehicle emissions, and chemicals that spill out into the environment as industrial waste products. Moreover, the pollution in any one element can easily taint the others. For instance, when emissions from coal-burning factories and electric utility plants react with air, they can cause acid rain, which damages lakes and forests. No business is immune from pollution issues, either. Internet-based companies such as Yahoo! and Google strike some people as "clean" because there seems to be no visible pollution, but the Internet and all the computers attached to it have a voracious appetite for electricity, and the generation of electricity nearly always affects the environment—two-thirds of the electricity used in the United States is generated by burning coal, oil, or natural gas.[34]

pollution
Damage to or destruction of the natural environment caused by the discharge of harmful substances

The Government Effort to Reduce Pollution   Widespread concern for the environment has been growing since the 1960s with the popularization of **ecology**, or the study of the relationship between organisms and the natural environment. In 1963, federal, state, and local governments began enacting laws and regulations to reduce pollution (see Exhibit 2.6). In 1970, the federal government established the Environmental Protection Agency (EPA) to regulate air and water pollution by manufacturers and utilities, supervise the control of automobile pollution, license pesticides, control toxic substances, and safeguard the purity of drinking water. A landmark piece of legislation, the

ecology
Study of the relationships among living things in the water, air, and soil; their environments; and the nutrients that support them

THINKING ABOUT ETHICS

BEN & JERRY'S: A DOUBLE SCOOP OF IRONY?

Few companies have a better reputation for environmental and social responsibility than Ben & Jerry's Homemade, the folksy, irreverent ice cream company. Since its inception in 1978, the company has donated 7.5 percent of pretax profits to various causes, including saving the family farm, promoting world peace, saving the world's rain forests, and keeping French nuclear testing out of the South Pacific. Even as the company grew, it managed to stay focused on Ben Cohen and Jerry Greenfield's mission and their intent to be a different kind of company. Cohen and Greenfield brought in professional management to balance the desire to do good with the need to maintain financial viability. To the surprise of many, the vision even survived a corporate buyout in 1999, when the company was purchased by Unilever, a $45 billion global colossus. Today, Ben & Jerry's continues to put its money where its mouth is, promoting a variety of admirable causes.

Here's the catch. Well, three of them, actually. First, even with the company's high standards of environmental responsibility—and you'd have to look far and wide to find a company with higher standards—it can be hard to make a case that the production of ice cream is an environmentally friendly endeavor. For instance, ice cream requires refrigeration at every step of the manufacturing and distribution process, refrigeration requires prodigious amounts of electricity, and nearly all the electricity in this country is generated by coal-fired, natural gas, nuclear, or hydroelectric power plants. And while the company has done a great job of removing chlorine and other nasty elements from the production of its ice cream cartons, those cartons are delivered to your local grocery store by fume-spewing diesel trucks. Second, obesity has become one of the nation's top health problems, and most of Ben & Jerry's products are high-fat, high-calorie concoctions. Third, all of this discussion concerns products that no one really needs. After all, this is ice cream, not medical supplies or drinking water.

Ben & Jerry's may well be the most environmentally and socially responsible ice cream company in history, but that still leaves the question: Should *anybody* be in the ice cream business?

Questions for Critical Thinking

1. Could Ben & Jerry's environmental stance be considered hypocritical, given the electricity demands of the ice cream industry? Why or why not?
2. How might Ben & Jerry's respond to the three issues discussed above while still remaining true to its philosophical roots?

Clean Air Act, was also passed that year. Many individual states and cities have also passed their own tough clean-air laws.

Cleaning up major industrial pollution sources is a complex technical and financial task with costs that can run into the billions of dollars, however, and the clean-air effort has been bogged down in lawsuits and political wrangling for years. For instance, in 2003, EPA officials modified a key maintenance standard for coal-burning power plants, one of the most significant sources of air pollution in the country; the EPA's own inspector general later said this change has hampered efforts to enforce clean air laws.[35] The situation is not likely to be resolved for years.[36]

In addition, the country's love affair with the automobile has slowed progress toward cleaner air. Three of the most popular types of vehicles—pickups, minivans, and sport utility vehicles (SUVs)—are considered light trucks by government regulators and therefore aren't required to meet the more stringent pollution standards set for passenger cars. The situation is not helped by the runaway success of large SUVs, which consume far more fuel than the average car, or moves such as the one Subaru recently made to get its popular Outback sedan reclassified as a small truck in order to skirt passenger car fuel-efficiency requirements.[37] The EPA blames the popularity of SUVs and a dramatic increase in the miles being driven for the lack of progress in reducing smog in the past 10 or 15 years.[38]

Legislation	Provision
National Environmental Policy Act (1999)	Establishes a structure for coordinating all federal environmental programs
Clean Air Act and amendments (1963, 1965, 1970, 1977, 1990)	Assists states and localities in formulating control programs; sets federal standards for auto-exhaust emissions; sets maximum permissible pollution levels; authorizes nationwide air-pollution standards and limitations to pollutant discharge; requires scrubbers in new coal-fired power plants; directs EPA to prevent deterioration of air quality in clean areas; sets schedule and standards for cutting smog, acid rain, hazardous factory fumes, and ozone-depleting chemicals
Solid Waste Disposal Act and amendments (1965, 1984)	Authorizes research and assistance to state and local control programs; regulates treatment, storage, transportation, and disposal of hazardous waste
Resource Recovery Act (1970)	Subsidizes pilot recycling plants; authorizes nationwide control programs
Federal Water Pollution Control Act and amendments (1972)	Authorizes grants to states for water-pollution control; gives federal government limited authority to correct pollution problems; authorizes EPA to set and enforce water-quality standards
Safe Drinking Water Act (1974, 1996)	Sets standards for drinking-water quality; requires municipal water systems to report on contaminant levels; establishes funding to upgrade water systems
Noise Control Act (1972)	Requires EPA to set standards for major sources of noise and to advise Federal Aviation Administration on standards for airplane noise
Toxic Substances Control Act (1976)	Requires chemicals testing; authorizes EPA to restrict the use of harmful substances
Oil Pollution Act (1990)	Sets up liability trust fund; extends operations for preventing and containing oil pollution

Exhibit 2.6
Major Federal Environmental Legislation
Since the early 1960s, major federal legislation aimed at the environment has focused on providing cleaner air and water and reducing toxic waste.

global warming
A gradual rise in average temperatures around the planet; caused by increases in carbon dioxide emissions

Regardless of its source, air pollution is now a global problem, as evidenced by the threat of **global warming**, a gradual rise in average temperatures around the planet caused by increases in carbon dioxide (one of the major components of engine exhaust). According to the American Geophysical Union, www.agu.org, a nonprofit, nonpartisan organization whose membership includes more than 40,000 scientists in 130 countries, "It is virtually certain that increasing atmospheric concentrations of carbon dioxide and other greenhouse gases will cause global surface climate to be warmer."[39] In response to such concerns, 124 countries have signed the Kyoto Protocol, which mandates reductions in carbon dioxide. The United States has not signed the agreement; many business and political leaders believe the costs of complying with the treaty outweigh the potential benefits.[40]

In contrast to air pollution, a good deal of progress has been made in reducing water pollution, thanks in large part to the Clean Water Act passed in 1972. As with the Clean Air Act, though, the conflict between environmental and commercial forces rages on when it comes to such issues as the dumping of mining wastes into rivers and streams and the annual discharge of millions of gallons of animal waste from large "factory" farms.[41] Drinking water quality has improved somewhat in the past couple of decades but still varies considerably across the country.[42] On the negative side, reports of mercury pollution in rivers and lakes, which is primarily the result of air pollution from coal-burning power plants and waste incinerators, are on the rise. Since this mercury gets into the human food chain through fish consumption and is toxic to children, most states now issue warnings to

A modern economy needs metals, minerals, and fules, but the effort to extract these materials—such as this open-pit mine—can create unsafe conditions for nearby populations.

children and pregnant woman to limit the number of fish eaten from some or all of their rivers and lakes.[43]

The complex war on toxic waste on land has marked a number of successes over the years, although as with air and water pollution, overall results are mixed. The EPA's Superfund program, designed to clean up the worst toxic waste dumps in the country, is now cleaning up only 40 or 50 sites a year, with more than a thousand left to go.[44] Some of these sites date from decades ago, when environmental awareness and corporate accountability were far below today's presumed standards. Some of the companies that created the worst messes no longer exist, and cleanup at many sites has been mired in lawsuits.

The Business Effort to Reduce Pollution "Someday people like me will go to jail."

That's not a hardened criminal talking, but the CEO of Interface, the world's largest producer of carpet tiles, based in Atlanta, Georgia. In the early 1990s, Ray Anderson says he suddenly realized that his company was a "plunderer," taking natural resources that didn't belong to it and leaving behind a mess that future generations would be forced to clean up. He changed course in dramatic fashion, pledging to transform Interface by 2020 into a company that would stop using natural resources (including oil) and stop generating harmful wastes and emissions. Calling this goal ambitious is an understatement, but by 2004, he was already well on the way, having reduced the company's consumption of water by 78 percent, its use of petroleum by 28 percent, and its generation of waste by 80 percent.[45]

Ray Anderson represents one end of a spectrum of responses to the problem of pollution and resource consumption. Overall, business efforts to reduce pollution range from corporations that must be forced into taking action to those that take the initiative on their own. DuPont, once labeled the country's biggest polluter, has shifted its corporate strategy to focus on *sustainable growth*, developing businesses that can operate forever without depleting natural resources. Among its current efforts: creating clothing fabrics with corn instead of petroleum as a key ingredient.[46] Many other companies are addressing environmental concerns by taking a variety of positive actions:[47]

- Considering environmental issues a part of everyday business and operating decisions
- Accepting environmental staff members as full-fledged partners in improving the company's competitiveness

- Measuring environmental performance
- Tying compensation to environmental performance
- Determining the long-term environmental costs *before* such costs occur
- Considering environmental impact in the product-development process
- Challenging suppliers to improve environmental performance
- Conducting environmental training and awareness programs

In addition to these actions, companies are reducing the amount of solid waste they send to landfills by companywide recycling programs, a key effort in grappling with the millions of pounds of solid waste that consumers and businesses generate every year. The proliferation of electronic waste—discarded computers, cell phones, music players, and other technology products—is a particular concern these days, given the millions of electronic products thrown out every year and the number of toxic materials they contain. Every time you upgrade your phone, for example, do you know what happens to the old one? In the United States, it is estimated that only 13 percent of computers are recycled each year, while 27 percent end up in landfills, even though this disposal is illegal in many locations. The European Union now requires producers in its 25 member states to establish systems to take back electronic products for recycling, and companies such as HP and Dell in the United States have set their own programs as well. The processing of "e-waste" is becoming an industry on its own, in fact. One critical issue that remains to be solved, however, is the amount of electronic waste that is currently exported to countries with more lenient regulations, rather than being recycled here at home.[48]

green marketing
Marketing strategies that highlight a company's efforts to minimize damage to the natural environment

Businesses that recognize the link between environmental performance and sustained financial well-being are discovering that spending now to prevent pollution can end up saving more money down the road (by reducing cleanup costs, litigation expenses, and production costs). From building eco-industrial parks to improving production efficiency, these activities are a part of the **green marketing** movement, in which companies distinguish themselves by using fewer packaging materials, recycling more waste, developing new products that are easier on the environment—and communicating these efforts to consumers. In addition to ethical and financial concerns, green marketing efforts can also help companies build goodwill with customers, communities, and other stakeholders.

Most of the electronic waste generated in the United States is shipped to countries with weaker environmental regulations. Electronics recycling centers like this one near the Lianjiang River in China are releasing toxic pollutants, environmental groups say.

CRITICAL THINKING CHECKPOINT

1. How would you resolve an argument between someone who says that Internet retailing is better for the environment and someone who says traditional stores are better? (Hint: Think all the way through the distribution process.)
2. Every company damages the natural environment to some degree, no matter how careful it might be. Wouldn't the responsible course of action be simply to go out of business? Explain your answer.
3. Is *green marketing* simply a cynical ploy to boost sales among environmentally conscious consumers? Explain your answer.

Responsibility Toward Consumers

The 1960s activism that awakened business to its environmental responsibilities also gave rise to **consumerism**, a movement that put pressure on businesses to consider consumer needs and interests. Consumerism prompted many businesses to create consumer affairs departments to handle customer complaints. It also prompted state and local agencies to set up bureaus to offer consumer information and assistance. At the federal level, President John F. Kennedy announced a "bill of rights" for consumers, laying the foundation for a wave of consumer-oriented legislation (see Exhibit 2.7). These rights include the right to safe products, the right to be informed, the right to choose, and the right to be heard.

consumerism
Movement that pressures businesses to consider consumer needs and interests

Legislation	Provision
Food, Drug, and Cosmetic Act (1938)	Puts cosmetics, foods, drugs, and therapeutic products under Food and Drug Administration's jurisdiction; outlaws misleading labeling
Cigarette Labeling Act (1965)	Mandates warnings on cigarette packages and in ads
Fair Packaging and Labeling Act (1966, 1972)	Requires honest, informative package labeling; labels must show origin of product, quantity of contents, uses or applications
Truth-in-Lending Act (Consumer Protection Credit Act) (1968)	Requires creditors to disclose finance charge and annual percentage rate; limits cardholder liability for unauthorized use
Fair Credit Reporting Act (1970)	Requires credit-reporting agencies to set process for assuring accuracy; requires creditors to explain credit denials
Consumer Product Safety Act (1972)	Creates Consumer Product Safety Commission
Magnuson-Moss Warranty Act (1975)	Requires complete written warranties in ordinary language; requires warranties to be available before purchase
Alcohol Labeling Legislation (1988)	Requires warning labels on alcohol products, saying that alcohol impairs abilities and that women shouldn't drink when pregnant
Nutrition Education and Labeling Act (1990)	Requires specific, uniform product labels detailing nutritional information on every food regulated by the FDA
American Automobile Labeling Act (1992)	Requires carmakers to identify where cars are assembled and where their individual components are manufactured
Deceptive Mail Prevention and Enforcement Act (1999)	Establishes standards for sweepstakes mailings, skill contests, and facsimile checks to prevent fraud and exploitation
Controlling the Assault of Non-Solicited Pornography and Marketing Act (2003)	Known as CAN-SPAM, attempts to protect online consumers from unwanted and fraudulent e-mail

Exhibit 2.7
Major Federal Consumer Legislation
Major federal legislation aimed at consumer protection has focused on food and drugs, false advertising, product safety, and credit protection.

The Right to Safe Products The United States and many other countries go to considerable lengths to ensure the safety of the products sold within their borders. The U.S. government imposes many safety standards that are enforced by the Consumer Product Safety Commission (CPSC), as well as by other federal and state agencies. Theoretically, companies that don't comply with these rules are forced to take corrective action. Moreover, the threat of product-liability suits and declining sales motivates companies to meet safety standards. After all, a poor safety record can quickly damage a hard-won reputation. However, unsafe goods and services remain a constant concern, given the ever-changing array of products available and the sheer magnitude of the monitoring effort.

Unsafe toys and automobiles grab a lot of the headlines, but the range of product safety issues in today's complex economy is extremely broad, as these examples suggest:

- Millions of people benefited from Merck's pain reliever Vioxx after it was introduced in 1999, but the company pulled it from the market in 2004 after an independent test showed that it increased the risk of heart attacks and strokes. Merck clearly did the right thing in removing the drug from the market, although critics contend it should've acted three years earlier, when other data suggested at least the possibility of the heightened risk. The company maintains it acted promptly as soon as it had conclusive evidence. Merck is expected to face billions of dollars' worth of Vioxx-related lawsuits in coming years.[49]
- In 2003, the Westin Bonaventure hotel in Los Angeles lost a $2.8 lawsuit brought by a woman who blamed poor security after she was assaulted in the hotel. This case and others are prompting hotels nationwide to find ways to improve safety for women traveling alone.[50]
- Millions of U.S. consumers and businesses are now victims of the fastest-growing crime in the country: **identity theft**, in which criminals steal personal information and use it to take out loans and commit other fraud, and some critics say that banks and others who collect this information aren't doing enough to stop it. For instance, ChoicePoint, a company in Alpharetta, Georgia, that has personal files on nearly every U.S. consumer (information that it sells to landlords, lenders, and other businesses), was recently scammed by a group of identity thieves who set up dozens of front companies to pose as legitimate ChoicePoint customers.[51]

identity theft
Crimes in which thieves steal personal information and use it to take out loans and commit other types of fraud

As you can see from even this short list, the concept of product safety involves a lot more than just toys and other tangible items, and it is constantly evolving as technology advances and society changes.

The Right to Be Informed Consumers have a right to know what they're buying, how to use it, and whether it presents any risks to them. They also have a right to know the sales price of goods or services and the details of any purchase contracts. In 2004, several insurance companies were accused of misleading military personnel at Fort Benning in Georgia, Camp Pendleton in California, and other bases around the country. Many of these young men and women thought they were signing up for savings programs when in fact they were buying extremely expensive and frequently unnecessary life insurance policies. The policies were often sold during mandatory financial training session for the soldiers, who were given no time to read the documents they signed. After the situation was brought to national attention by the *New York Times* and other news media, one of the companies involved, American Amicable Life Insurance, of Waco, Texas, began issuing full refunds, and officials began investigating other companies involved.[52]

For many consumers, labels are one of the most important information sources about products. The Food and Drug Administration, the Federal Trade Commission, and the Agriculture Department are the federal agencies responsible for regulating product labels to make sure no false claims are made. These agencies are concerned not only with safety but also with accurate information. If a product is sufficiently dangerous, a warning label is required by law, as in the case of cigarettes. However, warning labels can be a mixed blessing for consumers. To some extent, the presence of a warning protects the manufacturer

TECHNOLOGIES THAT ARE REVOLUTIONIZING BUSINESS Location and Tracking Technologies

Science fiction movies sometimes feature amazing technologies that can track people anywhere in the universe. They might still be amazing, but they're no longer science fiction; a variety of tracking devices can now keep tabs on both people and products.

HOW THEY'RE CHANGING BUSINESS

Location and tracking technologies cover a wide range of capabilities, some already in use and some just now hitting the market. Here are some of the more common uses and a few examples:

- ***Personal security and medical care.*** Parents and caregivers can use tracking technologies to check on elderly relatives, pets, or children. The Food & Drug Administration recently approved an implantable device that uses radio frequency identification (RFID) technology to store medical information that emergency personnel could retrieve with a quick scan, even if the patient is unconscious. The Great America amusement park in Santa Clara, California, offers RFID bracelets for $5 so parents and children can reconnect if they get separated in the crowds.
- ***Inventory management.*** Retail giant Wal-Mart is moving to require its suppliers to attach RFID tags

to incoming merchandise in order to enhance inventory management; with Wal-Mart's vast reach, this innovation will ripple through many sectors of the economy.

- ***Location-based services and marketing campaigns.*** Customers who are on the move can benefit from instant information that reflects their immediate shopping needs—and marketers would love to offer the right information at the right time, including notifications of nearby sales.

These new capabilities present considerable technological, social, and ethical issues, however, so expect to hear plenty of discussion about them in the coming years, both for and against RFID. For instance, Consumers Against Supermarket Privacy Invasion and Numbering (CASPIAN) is active in the fight against what it terms "spychips." Worries range from abusive marketing tactics to invasions of privacy based on tags embedded in library books.

WHERE YOU CAN LEARN MORE

This is a broad and dynamic field, with new information available nearly every day. Here are a few of the many sources online: MIT's Auto-ID Lab, autoidlabs.mit.edu, *RFID Journal*, www.rfidjournal.com, the Federal Communications Commission, www.fcc.gov/911/enhanced, and CASPIAN, www.nocards.org and www.spychips.com.

from product-liability suits, but the label may not deter people from using the product or from using it incorrectly. The billions of dollars a year still spent on cigarettes in the United States illustrate this point.

The Right to Choose Which Products to Buy Especially in the United States, the number of products available to consumers is truly amazing. But how far should the right to choose extend? Are we entitled to choose products that are potentially harmful, such as cigarettes, liquor, or guns? Consumer groups and businesses are concerned about these questions, but no clear answers have emerged. Moreover, some consumer groups say that government does not do enough. For example, when a product has been proven to be dangerous, does the fact that it is legal justify its sale? Should the government take measures to make the product illegal, or should consumers be allowed to decide for themselves what they buy?

Consider cigarettes, for example. Scientists determined long ago that the tar and nicotine in tobacco are both harmful and addictive. In 1965, the Federal Cigarette Labeling and Advertising Act was passed, requiring all cigarette packs to carry the now-famous Surgeon General's warnings. Over the years, tobacco companies have spent billions of dollars to defend themselves in lawsuits brought by smokers suffering from cancer and respiratory diseases. As recently as 1996, the Liggett Group (a major U.S. tobacco company) admitted publicly that cigarettes cause cancer, are addictive, and have been promoted to encourage

Media blitzes by antismoking organizations have appeared in magazines, on billboards, and in television commercials. The hope is that ads such as this one will elevate consumer awareness about the health problems cigarette smoking causes.

smoking among minors. And in 1997 the tobacco industry agreed to pay $368.5 billion over 25 years and an additional $15 billion per year after that to settle lawsuits brought by smoking victims and 40 state governments. Lawsuits and legislative activity surrounding tobacco products continue to this day—and are likely to continue for years into the future. Meanwhile, consumers can still purchase cigarettes in the marketplace. As RJR Nabisco chairman Steve Goldstone put it, "behind all the allegations . . . is the simple truth that we sell a legal product."[53]

The Right to Be Heard Many companies have established toll-free numbers for consumer information and feedback and print these numbers on product packages. In addition, more and more companies are establishing websites to provide product information and a vehicle for customer feedback. Companies use such feedback to improve their products and services and to make informed decisions about offering new ones. Technology has been a boon to consumers in this respect, with the opportunity to share information and voice their complaints via websites and online newsgroups.

Responsibility Toward Investors

Given the scandals of recent years, a growing number of investors are concerned about the ethics and social responsibility of the companies in which they invest. Allegations range from executives dumping stock ahead of bad news to companies using dirty accounting tricks to misrepresenting investments.

The job of looking out for a company's investors falls to its board of directors. Lately, more investors are turning up the heat on the individuals who sit on those boards (as you'll explore in Chapter 5). Concerned investors are targeting board members who fail to attend meetings, who sit on the boards of too many companies, who are underinvested (own very little stock in the companies they direct), and who sit on boards of companies with which their own firms do business. Aggrieved investors are also filing lawsuits not just against the management of companies that admit to "accounting irregularities" but against their boards of directors and their audit committees.

The audit committee signs off on all financial statements and is supposed to protect shareholders, acting as a check on management's corporate reporting methods and asking tough questions about accounting practices. Looking out for investors is no easy task, but investors are finding that holding individual directors more accountable improves overall performance.[54] Of course, any action that cheats the investors out of their rightful profits or exposes them to risks that were hidden from them is unethical.

CRITICAL THINKING CHECKPOINT

1. Why isn't market pressure considered enough to ensure safe products?
2. How far should a company go in informing buyers about any dangers associated with its products? Why?
3. Financial accounting in any large, public corporation is almost unfathomably complex; how much responsibility does a corporation have to explain all the financial details that might affect investors in the company's stock? Consider the implications when you explain your answer.

Responsibility Toward Employees

Patagonia's Yvon Chouinard has always emphasized employee relationships that are ethical and supportive. For some companies, the past 30 years have brought dramatic changes in the attitudes and composition of the workforce. These changes have forced businesses to modify their recruiting, training, and promotion practices, as well as their overall corporate values and behaviors. (Consult Chapter 11 for an in-depth discussion of the staffing and demographic challenges employers are facing in today's workplace.)

The Push for Equality in Employment The United States has always stood for economic freedom and the individual's right to pursue opportunity. Unfortunately, in the past, many people were targets of economic **discrimination**, were relegated to low-paying, menial jobs, and were prevented from taking advantage of many opportunities solely on the basis of their race, gender, disability, or religion.

discrimination
In a social and economic sense, denial of opportunities to individuals on the basis of some characteristic that has no bearing on their ability to perform in a job

The Civil Rights Act of 1964 established the Equal Employment Opportunity Commission (EEOC), the regulatory agency that battles job discrimination. The EEOC is responsible for monitoring the hiring practices of companies and for investigating complaints of job-related discrimination. It has the power to file legal charges against companies that discriminate and to force them to compensate individuals or groups who have been victimized by unfair practices. The Civil Rights Act of 1991 extended the original act by allowing workers to sue companies for discrimination and by granting women powerful legal tools against job bias.

Affirmative Action. In the 1960s, **affirmative action** programs were developed to encourage organizations to recruit and promote members of groups whose economic progress had been hindered through either legal barriers or established practices. Affirmative action programs address a variety of situations, from college admissions to executive promotions to conducting business with government agencies (businesses that want to sell goods or services to the federal government are generally required to have an affirmative action program in place, for instance). Note that while affirmative action programs address a variety of population segments, from military veterans with disabilities to specific ethnic groups, in popular usage, "affirmative action" usually refers to programs based on race.

affirmative action
Activities undertaken by businesses to recruit and promote women and minorities, based on an analysis of the workforce and the available labor pool

Affirmative action remains one of the most controversial and politicized issues in business today, with opponents claiming it creates a double standard and can encourage reverse discrimination against white males, and proponents saying that it remains a crucial part of the effort to ensure equal opportunities for all. One of the key points of contention is whether affirmative action programs are still needed, given the various anti-discrimination laws now in place. Opponents assert that everyone has an equal shot at success now, so the programs are unnecessary and if anything, should be based on income, not race; proponents argue that laws can't remove every institutionalized barrier and that discrimination going back decades has left many families and communities at a long-term disadvantage.[55]

Part I: Conducting Business in the Global Economy

CHECKLIST: Apply These Ideas When You're the Boss

✓ Periodically review the mission of your team or company with respect to your role in the community and society as a whole; are your actions and progress consistent with your views on corporate social responsibility?

✓ Whenever you hear about a manager in another company making a poor ethical choice, ask yourself if you might be unwittingly committing a similar error.

✓ Examine your business practices to make sure that aggressive competition doesn't turn into unethical competition.

✓ Ask an impartial observer to judge whether your various communication efforts (such as your company website) communicate truthfully with your target audiences.

✓ When you find yourself in a potential conflict of interest, stop and ask where your most important responsibilities lie.

✓ Assess the impact of your products and services in the marketplace; are they being abused or used incorrectly in ways that can cause harm?

✓ Make sure you understand the laws and regulations that apply to your business so that you don't unknowingly break the law.

✓ Establish a clear code of ethics and make sure everyone on your team understands and follows it.

✓ Analyze the methods you use to make decisions with important ethical ramifications; do you consider the needs of all your stakeholders?

✓ Examine your company's operations from start to finish, looking for ways to reduce resource consumption and waste output; it's good for business and good for the environment.

✓ Ask yourself if you are following the *spirit* of the law (what it was really meant to say) as well as the *letter* of the law (what it actually says); don't succumb to the temptation to split hairs in order to get away with something that the law was intended to prevent.

✓ Lead by example; if you conduct yourself with honor, your employees probably will, too.

Summary of Learning Objectives

1 **Define corporate social responsibility and ethics.** Corporate social responsibility is the idea that companies have an obligation to society, beyond simply making profits. Ethics encompasses the principles and standards of moral behavior that a society accepts as right versus wrong.

2 **Highlight three factors that influence ethical behavior.** Of the many factors that influence ethical behavior, the three most common are cultural differences, knowledge of the facts and consequences involving a decision or action, and the organization's ethical practices and commitment to ethical behavior.

3 **Identify three steps that businesses are taking to encourage ethical behavior, and explain the advantages and disadvantages of whistle-blowing.** Businesses are adopting codes of ethics, appointing ethics officers, and establishing ethics hot lines. In spite of these efforts, if illegal, unethical, or harmful practices persist, an employee may need to blow the whistle or disclose such problems to outsiders. Doing so may force the company to stop the problematic practices. But bringing these issues into the public eye has consequences. It can hurt the company's reputation, take managers' time, damage employee morale, and impact the informant's job with the company.

4 **List four questions you might ask yourself when trying to make an ethical decision.** When making ethical decisions ask yourself: (1) Is the decision legal? (2) Is it balanced and as fair as possible to all concerned? (3) Can you live with the consequences of the decision? (4) Is it a feasible answer to a real-world problem?

5 **Explain the difference between an ethical dilemma and an ethical lapse.** An ethical dilemma is an issue with two conflicting but arguably valid sides, whereas an ethical lapse occurs when an individual makes a decision that is illegal, immoral, or unethical.

6 **Compare the three major perspectives on corporate social responsibility.** Over the years, three major perspectives on corporate social responsibility have gained a foothold in the business world: (1) the only responsibility of business is to make money, (2) business has a larger

responsibility to society, and ethical behavior leads to financial success, and (3) businesses must balance social responsibility and financial objectives, even if that means taking a less-profitable course of action at times.

7 **Discuss how businesses can become more socially responsible.** Companies can conduct social audits to assess whether their performance is socially responsible; they can engage in cause-related marketing by using a portion of product sales to help support worthy causes; and they can become philanthropic by donating their money, time, goods, or services to charitable, humanitarian, or educational institutions. Companies can also protect and improve the environment by taking a variety of actions to reduce pollution. They can become good citizens by considering consumers' needs and respecting their four basic rights: the right to safe products; the right to be informed— which includes the right to know a product's contents, use, price, and dangers; the right to choose which products to buy; and the right to be heard, such as the right to voice a complaint or concern. They can look out for a company's investors and protect the value of their interests. And they can foster good employee relationships by treating employees fairly and equally and by providing a safe working environment.

8 **Outline activities the government and businesses are undertaking to protect the environment.** In 1970, the government set up the Environmental Protection Agency to regulate the disposal of hazardous wastes and to clean up polluted areas. Many individual states have also passed their own clean-air laws. Companies are taking these steps to improve the environment: (1) considering them a part of everyday business and operating decisions, (2) making environmental staff members full-fledged partners in improving competitiveness, (3) measuring environmental performance, (4) tying compensation to environmental performance, (5) determining environmental costs *before* they occur, (6) considering the environmental impact of the product-development process, (7) helping suppliers improve their environmental performance, and (8) conducting training and awareness programs.

Patagonia: What's Next?

Patagonia's Yvon Chouinard has effected change not only in his own company but throughout the apparel industry. Competitors are waking up to the environmental benefits and consumer interest in more sustainable production techniques, and recyclers and cotton farmers are benefiting from the demand for new fabrics.

With the zeal common to both entrepreneurs and activists, though, Chouinard is not content to sit still. Patagonia and its suppliers are now working on such innovations as clothing articles that are completely recyclable—right down to the zipper. The company envisions a complete cycle in which consumers could return worn out clothes, which could then be quickly and efficiently recycled into fabric for new garments.

Whatever the innovation, as long as Yvon Chouinard is in command, you can be sure that Patagonia will keep seeking ways to serve its customers while minimizing the footprints the company leaves behind.[63]

Critical Thinking Questions

1. Could any of Patagonia's various stakeholders be negatively affected by the company's slow-growth, low-impact approach to conducting business? Explain your answer.
2. How does Patagonia's environmentalism relate to the consumer's right to safety?
3. Couldn't Patagonia completely eliminate its impact on the environment by simply going out of business? Explain why you agree or disagree with this notion.

Learn More Online

Patagonia's environmentalism is communicated through the company's catalog, product labels, and website. Go to Chapter 2 of this text's website at www.prenhall.com/bovee, and click on Patagonia to read about the company. Click on Enviro Action to read current and older reports on environmental issues. What types of environmental concerns are being addressed and supported? Do you agree with the causes Patagonia supports? Explain your answer.

Key Terms

affirmative action (85)
cause-related marketing (75)
code of ethics (68)
conflict of interest (67)
consumerism (81)
corporate social
   responsibility (63)
discrimination (85)
ecology (76)

ethical dilemma (72)
ethical lapse (72)
ethics (63)
green marketing (80)
global warming (78)
identity theft (82)
insider trading (67)
justice (70)

philanthropy (75)
pollution (76)
social audit (75)
utilitarianism (71)
whistle-blowing (70)

Test Your Knowledge

Questions for Review

1. Who shapes a company's ethics?
2. What is a conflict of interest situation?
3. What can companies do to support ethical behavior?
4. How are businesses responding to the environmental issues facing society?
5. What can a company do to assure customers that its products are safe?

Questions for Analysis

6. Why can't legal considerations resolve every ethical question?
7. How do individuals employ philosophical principles in making ethical business decisions?
8. Why does a company need more than a code of ethics to be ethical?
9. Why is it important for a company to balance its social responsibility efforts with its need to generate profits?
10. **Ethical Considerations.** How do business scandals such as the Enron and WorldCom cases impact all businesses?

Questions for Application

11. You sell musical gifts on the web and in quarterly catalogs. Your 2-person partnership has quickly grown into a 27-person company, and you spend all your time on quality matters. You're losing control of important environmental choices about materials suppliers, product packaging, and even the paper used in your catalogs. What steps can you take to be sure your employees continue making choices that protect the environment?
12. Several friends have asked you to give them copies of software that your company has provided for the laptop computer you were issued when you started work. How would you respond?
13. **Integrated.** Chapter 1 identified knowledge workers as a key economic resource of the twenty-first century. If an employee leaves a company to work for a competitor, what types of knowledge would be ethical for the employee to share with the new employer and what types of knowledge would be unethical to share?
14. **Integrated.** Numerous local governments around the United States have been applying the concept of *eminent domain* to enable "big box" retailers such as Costco and Wal-Mart to move into areas already occupied by smaller businesses. Under the concept of eminent domain, landowners are legally required to sell, but this power has traditionally been used only to acquire land for public infrastructure such as new highways. Cities that use eminent domain for big retailers say their use of the power is justified because they're bringing in businesses that will generate more tax revenue, provide more jobs, and stimulate local economies. Costco executives also defend the practice, saying that such decisions benefit the greater number of people, and if they don't get the land, one of their competitors (other big-box retailers) will.[64] Do you believe that cities' use of eminent domain is ethical in this case? Is it ethical for big retailers to ask cities to invoke eminent domain on their behalf?

Practice Your Knowledge

Handling Difficult Situations on the Job: Children at Risk

This morning Perrigo Company discovered that a batch of its cherry-flavored children's painkiller contains more than the label-indicated amount of acetaminophen. Marketing department reports indicate that 6,500 four-ounce bottles of the "children's nonaspirin elixir" (a Tylenol lookalike) are already in the hands of consumers; 1,288 bottles remain on store shelves. The problem is that the acetaminophen contained in the painkilling liquid is up to 29 percent more than labels state, enough to cause an overdose in young children, which can cause liver failure and even death. So far, thankfully, no injuries have been reported. Only lot number 1AD0228 contains the excess dosage.

Your job responsibility in the Customer Support and Service Department is to the retailers who sell Perrigo's 900 over-the-counter pharmaceuticals and nutritional products as "store brands." These are the "better buys" found beside brand-name products such as Tylenol, Motrin, Aleve, Centrum, or Ex-Lax, featuring such store names as Kroger or Hy-Vee. They're priced a bit lower and they offer "comparable quality and effectiveness." Retailers yield higher profits from them, while consumers save money by buying them.[65]

Your task: Perrigo has publicly announced its recall of the product. Consumers can return bottles from the faulty batch to stores, and stores can return them to Perrigo for full refunds. Your job is to notify stores in writing, as legally mandated. What information should you include in your letter? What information should you omit, if any? How can you use your letter to preserve Perrigo's fine reputation?

Sharpening Your Communication Skills

All organizations, not just corporations, can benefit from having a code of ethics to guide decision making. But whom should a code of ethics protect, and what should it cover? In this exercise, you and your team are going to draft a code of ethics for your school.

Start by thinking about who will be protected by this code of ethics. What stakeholders should the school consider when making decisions? What negative effects might decisions have on these stakeholders? Then think about the kinds of situations you want your school's code of ethics to cover. One example might be employment decisions; another might be disclosure of confidential student information.

Next, using Exhibit 2.1 as a model, draft your school's code of ethics. Write a general introduction explaining the purpose of the code and who is being protected. Next, write a positive statement to guide ethical decisions in each situation you identified earlier in this exercise. Your statement about promotion decisions, for example, might read: "School officials will encourage equal access to job promotions for all qualified candidates, with every applicant receiving fair consideration."

Compare your code of ethics with the codes drafted by your classmates. Did all the codes seek to protect the same stakeholders? What differences and similarities do you see in the statements guiding ethical decisions?

Building Your Team Skills

Choosing to blow the whistle on your employees or co-workers can create all kinds of legal, ethical, and career complications. Here are five common workplace scenarios that might cause you to search your soul about whether or not to go public with potentially damaging charges. Read them carefully and discuss them with your teammates. Then decide what your team would do in each situation.[66]

1. You believe your company is overcharging or otherwise defrauding a customer or client.
2. With all of the headlines generated by sexual harassment cases lately, you'd think employees wouldn't dare break the law, but it's happening right under your company's nose.
3. You discover that your company, or one of its divisions, products, or processes, presents a physical danger to workers or to the public.
4. An employee is padding overtime statements, taking home some of the company's inventory, or stealing equipment.
5. You smell alcohol on a co-worker's breath and notice that individual's work hasn't been up to standard lately.

Expand Your Knowledge

Discovering Career Opportunities

Businesses, government agencies, and not-for-profit organizations offer numerous career opportunities related to ethics and social responsibility. How can you learn more about these careers?

1. Search the Occupational Handbook at http://stats.bls.gov/oco (a printed version might also be available in your library) to identify jobs related to ethics and social responsibility. One example is occupational health and safety manager, a job concerned with a company's responsibility toward its employees. What are the duties and qualifications of the jobs you have identified? Are the salaries and future outlooks attractive for all of these jobs?
2. Select one job for further consideration. What other sources of employment information might provide more details about this job? Which of these sources are available in your school or public library? What additional sources can you consult for more information about the daily activities of this job and for ideas about locating potential employers?
3. What skills, educational background, and work experience do you think employers are seeking in applicants for the specific job you are researching? What keywords do you think employers would search for when scanning electronic résumés submitted for this position?

Developing Your Research Skills

Articles on corporate ethics and social responsibility regularly appear in business journals and newspapers. Look in recent issues (print or online editions) to find one or more articles discussing one of the following ethics or social responsibility challenges faced by a business:

- Environmental issues, such as pollution, acid rain, and hazardous-waste disposal
- Employee or consumer safety measures
- Consumer information or education
- Employment discrimination or diversity initiatives
- Investment ethics
- Industrial spying and theft of trade secrets
- Fraud, bribery, and overcharging
- Company codes of ethics

1. What was the nature of the ethical challenge or social responsibility issue presented in the article? Does the article report any wrongdoing by a company or agency official? Was the action illegal, unethical, or questionable? What course of action would you recommend the company or agency take to correct or improve matters now?
2. What stakeholder group(s) is affected? What lasting effects will be felt by (a) the company and (b) this stakeholder group(s)?
3. Writing a letter to the editor is one way consumers can speak their mind. Review some of the letters to the editor in newspapers or journals. Why are letters to the editor an important feature for that publication?

Exploring the Best of the Web

URLs for all internet exercises are provided at the website for this book, www.prenhall.com/bovee. When you log on to this text's Companion Website, select Chapter 2. Then select "Featured Websites," click on the name of the featured website, and review the website to complete these exercises.

Explore these chapter-related websites, review their content, and answer the following questions for each website you visit:

1. What is the purpose of this website?
2. What kinds of information does this website contain? Please be specific.
3. How is the information provided at this website useful for businesspeople? Consumers?
4. How did you expand your knowledge of ethics and social responsibility in business by reviewing the material at this website? What new things did you learn about this topic?

Build a Better Business

One way to distinguish your business as an ethical organization is to join the Better Business Bureau (BBB). Members of this private, not-for-profit business group agree to maintain specific standards for operating ethically and addressing customer complaints. The BBB website is packed with information about the organization, member businesses, and programs that benefit businesses and consumers alike. You can find reports on companies, register complaints, get help with consumer problems, and access publications on all kinds of consumer issues, such as avoiding business scams and investigating charitable organizations. www.bbb.org

Surf Safely

Although the majority of telemarketing and online businesses are legitimate, unethical businesses bilk consumers out of billions of dollars every year. Fortunately, the National Fraud Information Center (NFIC) can help consumers fight back. The center was established by the National Consumers League (NCL) to safeguard consumers against telemarketing and Internet fraud. Resources on the center's website include reports about current online and telephone scams, tips for online safety, advice on how to file a fraud report, statistics about telemarketing fraud, and special advice for seniors, who are targeted by con artists. Even if you consider yourself a savvy consumer, the site contains a lot of valuable information to help you avoid being ripped off. www.fraud.org

Protect the Environment

For 30 years, the United States Environmental Protection Agency (EPA) has been working for a cleaner, healthier environment for the American people. Visit the agency's website to get the latest information on today's environmental issues. Become familiar with the major environmental laws and proposed regulations and learn how to report violations. Expand your knowledge about air pollution, ecosystems, environmental management, and hazardous waste. Visit the EPA newsroom to get regional news. Read the current articles and follow the links to hot lines, publications, and more. This site is a must for all businesses. www.epa.gov

Learning Interactively

Companion Website

Visit the Companion Website at www.prenhall.com/bovee. For Chapter 2, take advantage of the interactive "Learning Modules" to test your chapter knowledge. Get instant feedback on whether you need additional studying. Complete the exercises as specified by your instructor.

A Case for Critical Thinking

Enron: A Case Study in Unethical Behavior

Perhaps no company in history can match the spectacular rise—and cataclysmic fall—of Houston-based Enron. The company started out in 1985 as a distributor of natural gas, then evolved into a leading *market maker,* trading everything from electricity to broadband access. Few people really understood how this new business model worked or what Enron actually did, but it did everything in a big way. In the three-year period from 1998 to 2000, reported revenues tripled to $100 billion and landed Enron in the number-seven slot on the *Fortune* 500 list of the largest companies in the country.

Along the way, Enron became widely admired in the business world and was cited by *Fortune* as one of the "100 best companies to work for in America." Enron's past chairman Kenneth Lay boasted to the press that "our corporate culture and our world-class employees make Enron a great place to work." He added, "We are proud to receive recognition as a top workplace; it's a reflection of our commitment to our employees and their key role in our company's success." The company's stock price shot up along with its reputation, making fortunes for top executives and secure retirements for many Enron employees—or so they thought.

When the truth about Enron started to come out, the company's empire unraveled and exposed one of the biggest business scandals in U.S. history. Unlike most other scandals, though, Enron fundamentally changed the way many people look at the business world and directly contributed to sweeping changes in the way public companies are run in the United States.

WHO'S ACCOUNTABLE?

Enron's collapse began in March 2001, when another *Fortune* article posed a seemingly simple question: Was that Enron stock, which was making so many people so rich, overpriced? (Internet message posters had been sounding warnings for a couple of years before that, but no one had paid attention.) Since stock prices are based, at least in theory, on the amount of cash that a company generates, the question about stock price quickly led to another: How exactly does this company make money? Wall Street analysts had been complaining that Enron's financial reporting was inscrutably complex, and no one on the outside seemed quite sure how the company made money. As long as the stock kept climbing, though, not too many people complained. However, to *Fortune* writer Bethany McLean, who broke the story, it didn't appear that the company was making *any* money, in spite of its public financial reports.

The full details of Enron's ethical and legal missteps are still being uncovered through multiple investigations and criminal trials. However, the short version of the story is that a handful of Enron executives engaged in a series of financial frauds—aided by those financial reports that few people could understand—to cover up the fact that the company was actually losing money and wasn't quite the brilliant, revolutionary company everyone thought it was. The frauds included hidden partnerships that took over Enron debt to make its financials look better, encouragement from executives to keep buying the stock even as they were bailing out of it themselves, and assurances to employees (many of whom had much of their life savings tied up in Enron stock) that everything was going to be fine. CEO Kenneth Lay told Wall Street analysts that "the continued excellent prospects in Enron's market position make us very confident in our strong earnings outlook," after he was advised by Enron vice president Sherron Watkins that questionable accounting practices could sink the company. "I am incredibly nervous that we will implode in a wave of accounting scandals," she wrote. Upon receiving the letter, Lay asked Watkins not to blow the whistle while he tried to deal with the situation. But Lay did nothing, and Watkins, believing that he would investigate as promised, did not inform outside authorities.

When investor confidence evaporated following the *Fortune* article, though, the end came quickly. Terrified investors dumped the stock, and a $100 billion company quickly became just about worthless.

ONE COZY BUNCH

As you might expect, perpetrating fraud on such a galactic scale requires some outside help, and Enron seems to have had plenty. The accusations and arrests soon extended to such highly respected companies as Arthur Andersen (a public accounting firm) and Citigroup and Merrill Lynch (both banking and investment firms). For instance, long before Enron's collapse, Andersen accountants knew of the company's growing losses, but they continued to bend to the wishes of Enron executives who didn't want to recognize the losses or make them public.

Once the losses were disclosed, Andersen managers began a massive shredding campaign of Enron documents—which they claimed was standard company procedure. On June 15, 2002, a federal jury convicted Arthur Andersen on a single felony count of obstruction of justice for interfering with a federal investigation of its failed client, Enron. Although the accounting firm was originally indicted for shredding Enron-related documents, the firm was convicted because an Andersen lawyer ordered critical deletions to an internal memo for the purpose of impeding an official proceeding. The conviction will forever stain the legacy of this once-revered American institution. In August 2002 the 89-year-old, 85,000-employee firm was ordered to stop auditing public companies—the core of its worldwide business. What's left of Andersen now faces a raft of Enron-related lawsuits.

Near the end of 2004, the first wave of convictions hit, when four executives from Merrill Lynch and one from Enron were convicted of fraud. As other trials continue, you can expect to be hearing about Enron for years.

THE RIPPLE EFFECT

Enron serves as an example of how negligent conduct by a company's managers and advisors and the failure to communicate truthfully to stakeholders can severely harm employees, investors, customers, and other innocent stakeholders. Enron's 21,000 employees lost their jobs, and many saw their retirement savings wiped out. And tens of thousands of shareholders—including some of the nation's biggest institutional investors—lost billions of dollars when Enron's stock value plummeted from $80 to pennies a share.

Critical Thinking Questions

1. What unethical acts did Enron's managers and auditors commit?
2. How did such acts affect the company's stakeholders?
3. What factors may have influenced Enron's unethical behavior?
4. What role did whistle-blowing play in the collapse of Enron?

Video Case

Doing the Right Thing: American Red Cross

Learning Objectives

The purpose of this video is to help you:

1. Identify some of the social responsibility and ethics challenges faced by a nonprofit organization.
2. Discuss the purpose of an organizational code of ethics.
3. Understand the potential conflicts that can emerge between an organization and its stakeholders.

Synopsis

The American Red Cross is affiliated with the worldwide International Red Cross and Red Crescent Movement, which is dedicated to helping victims of war, natural disasters, and other catastrophes. The Red Cross was been instrumental in helping millions of people, from victims of World War I up through the Asian tsunami disaster in 2004 and beyond. The organization's nearly 1,000 chapters across the United States are governed by volunteer boards of directors who oversee local activities and enforce ethical standards in line with the Red Cross's code of ethics and community norms. Over the years, the Red Cross has been guided in its use of donations by honoring donor intent. This helped the organization deal with a major ethical challenge after the terrorist attacks of September 11, 2001. The Red Cross received more than $1 billion in donations and initially diverted some money to ancillary operations such as creating a strategic blood reserve. After donors objected, however, the organization reversed its decision and—honoring donor intent—used the contributions to directly benefit people who were affected by the tragedy.

Discussion Questions

1. *For analysis:* What are the social responsibility implications of the American Red Cross's decision to avoid accepting donations of goods for many local relief efforts?
2. *For analysis:* What kinds of ethical conflicts might arise because the American Red Cross relies so heavily on volunteers?
3. *For application:* What can the American Red Cross do to ensure that local chapters are properly applying the nonprofit's code of ethics?
4. *For application:* How might a nonprofit such as the American Red Cross gain a better understanding of its stakeholders' needs and preferences?
5. *For debate:* Should the American Red Cross have reversed its initial decision to divert some of the money donated for September 11th relief efforts to pressing but ancillary operations? Support your chosen position.

Online Exploration

Visit the American Red Cross site at www.redcross.org and scan the headlines to read about the organization's response to recent disasters. Also look at the educational information available through links to news stories, feature articles, and other material. Next, carefully examine the variety of links addressing the needs and involvement of different stakeholder groups. What kinds of stakeholders does the American Red Cross expect to visit its website? Why are these stakeholders important to the organization? Do you think the organization should post its code of ethics prominently on this site? Explain your answer.

Wild World: Competing in the Global Economy

CHAPTER 3

LEARNING OBJECTIVES

After studying this chapter, you will be able to

1. Discuss why nations trade

2. Explain why nations restrict international trade and list four forms of trade restrictions

3. Highlight three protectionist tactics nations use to give their domestic industries a competitive edge

4. Explain how trading blocs affect trade

5. Highlight the opportunities and challenges you'll encounter when conducting business in other countries

6. List five ways you can improve communication in an international business relationship

7. Identify five forms of international business activity

8. Discuss terrorism's impact on globalization

www.prenhall.com/bovee

INSIDE BUSINESS TODAY

Trek Bikes: Trekking Around the Globe

www.trekbikes.com

Every global market leader suffers production delays from to time, but Trek Bikes is probably the only one forced to delay a factory opening so that the farmer who owned the land could harvest his corn. But that's life in rural Waterloo, Wisconsin, home to one of the world's most innovative bicycle manufacturers. You can now find people riding one of Trek's market-leading bikes from the mountains of New Zealand to the streets of Paris during the final stage of the prestigious Tour de France—every time Lance Armstrong crossed the finish line in his record-setting string of seven victories from 1999 through 2005, he was riding a Trek.

During the company's first few years, Trek sold its bicycles exclusively in the United States. But all that changed in 1985 when Joyce Keehn, now Trek's worldwide sales director, received several inquiries about exporting Treks to Canada. A novice in international trade, Keehn consulted the state's export agency and sought advice from local exporters at state-sponsored trade seminars. After considering Trek's close proximity to Canada, Keehn decided that selling directly to Canadian bicycle shops was the company's best option for international expansion.

As more exporting opportunities opened up, Keehn experimented with other foreign distribution methods. For instance, to minimize cultural and language barriers, she relied on the expertise and knowledge of local distributors instead of approaching retailers directly. In other countries, she advised Trek to create wholly owned subsidiaries for handling sales, inventory, warranties, customer service, and direct distribution to retail outlets. Such subsidiary offices allowed Trek to maintain higher profits and more control over how its products were marketed.

Still, Keehn hit some bumps in the road as she ventured into the global marketplace. For example, customs delays created frequent insurance and financial problems; some shipments even disappeared during customs clearances in Mexico. On one occasion, Trek halted distribution of its catalog after discovering that a featured cartoon character was offensive to Germans. And customizing bikes for the European markets increased Trek's production costs.

Online retailing presented even more challenges for Keehn. Trek's international dealers must charge higher prices than those charged by U.S. sellers to cover costs such as shipping and tariffs. Moreover, international prices must take into consideration fluctuating foreign exchange rates. To minimize confusion and protect its international sellers, Trek does not sell bicycles or reveal prices on its website. Instead, the company refers customers to authorized dealers in their area.

Today, whether you're in Cincinnati or Cyprus, you won't have to travel far to find a Trek. Keehn has established a network of distributors on six continents and seven wholly owned subsidiaries in Europe and Japan. From its humble beginnings in Waterloo, Trek is now the world's largest maker of racing bikes, mountain bikes, and other types of specialty bikes. The company sells more than a half million bikes in more than 70 countries every year. In 10 years, annual revenues have grown from $18 million to over $400 million, of which 40 percent now comes from international business.[1]

GET READY

Trek's story began the way thousands of companies get started in the United States, with a small group of people who are passionate about an idea. What sets Trek apart from most is the dominant position the company now has in the global marketplace. Even if your business ideas won't carry you to the finish line in the Tour de France, you can learn from Trek's experience. As you explore the concepts of international trade in this chapter, imagine how you might follow in the path of successful international executives such as Trek's Joyce Keehn. How would you cope with the complexities of diverse markets? How would you fare against competitors from India, South Korea, Italy, China—and every other country with global ambitions?

Chapter Overview

Thanks to the Internet and booming economies in China, India, and other markets, the idea of international business has gone from exotic to commonplace in recent years. This chapter helps you explore the fundamentals of international trade, including the risks and rewards of conducting business across national borders, the organizations that influence international trade, and the all-important factor of currency exchange rates. Following that introduction, you'll learn how successful companies navigate international markets, including such key issues as cultural and legal differences, the forms of business available to them, and the way that companies need to adjust their strategies in various markets. The chapter concludes with the sobering but impossible-to-ignore effects of terrorism on international business.

Fundamentals of International Trade

Wherever you're reading this, stop and look around for a minute. You might see cars that were made in Japan running on petroleum from Russia or Saudi Arabia, cell phones made in South Korea, food from Canada or Mexico or Chile, a laptop computer made in China, clothing from Italy, industrial equipment made in Germany—and dozens of other products from every corner of the globe. Conversely, if you or a family member work for a midsize or large company, chances are it gets a significant slice of its revenue from sales to other countries. In short, we live and work in a global marketplace.

Just as employees compete with one another for jobs and companies compete for customers, countries and regions compete with one another for both. The ability of firms such as

Trek to buy and sell across national borders depends on the complex economic relationships the United States maintains with other countries. Naturally, the U.S. government promotes and protects the interests of U.S. companies, U.S. workers, and U.S. consumers. Other countries are trying to do the same thing. As you might expect, the many players in world trade sometimes have conflicting goals, making international trade a never-ending tug of war.

Why Nations Trade

International trade is rarely simple, but it's a fact of life for all countries for two reasons. First, no single country, even a country as vast as the United States, has the resources and capabilities to produce everything its citizens want or need at prices they're willing to pay. In some cases, it's a matter of simply not having the resources or capabilities. For instance, the United States doesn't produce enough oil to meet its needs, so we buy oil from Russia, Saudi Arabia, Venezuela, and other countries that produce more than they can use. Conversely, most countries lack the ability to make commercial aircraft, so many of them buy planes from Boeing, a U.S. company. In other cases, buyers prefer products made in other countries even though similar products are available from domestic companies. Teenagers in Europe like the style of Red Wing work boots (made in Red Wing, Minnesota), while young people in the United States can't seem to get enough of Japanese anime cartoons and films. A variety of luxury cars are available in China, including models from local leader Shanghai Automotive, but many drivers from China's rising middle class buy good old American Buicks when they want a luxury car.[2]

The second major reason countries trade is that many companies have ambitions that are too large for their own backyards. Well-known U.S. companies such as Microsoft and Boeing would be a fraction of their current sizes if they were limited to the U.S. marketplace. Swedish mobile phone maker Ericsson, which already does business in 140 countries, wants to reach 1 *billion* new customers by 2009 and is pinning its hopes on countries with large populations but relatively low phone usage, including India, Russia, and Pakistan.[3]

Of course, overseas companies view the U.S. market as a giant, tasty target as well. For instance, German's DHL is making a major push to compete here with FedEx and UPS, and Mexico's Televisa has its sights set on the U.S. television, publishing, and Internet markets.[4] In fact, competition could strike your company from just about anywhere. Romania is a leader in antivirus software, Israel is a leader in software that protects computer networks, and there's a good chance the disk drive in your computer came from Singapore.[5] Hungary wants a larger piece of the U.S. film production business, which might seem far-fetched until you realize that Hungarian immigrants played a central role in the development of the Hollywood movie machine in its early days.[6] Ever heard of India's Bajaj? It's the world's largest maker of two-wheeled motor vehicles, and its economical scooters are starting to take U.S. sales away from Italy's Vespa and Japan's Honda.[7]

All this international activity involves more than just sales growth, of course. By expanding their markets, companies can benefit from **economies of scale** when they purchase, manufacture, and distribute in higher quantities.[8] If you build 1,000 cars a year, you can't afford to invest in automated factories, large advertising campaigns, and a vast network of dealers. However, if you build 100,000 cars a year, you can do all these things, which allows you to produce and sell each car for less money. In addition to helping companies, international trade also helps consumers by giving them more options and lower prices, and it helps governments by generating more revenue.

The motivation to trade is clear, but how does a country know which products it should make and which it should trade for with other countries? If a country can produce something more efficiently than every other country, or it has a natural resource that no other country has, it would have an **absolute advantage** in the world marketplace. In practice, however, virtually no country has an absolute advantage in any industry. Instead, **comparative advantage theory** suggests that each country should specialize in those areas where it can produce more efficiently than other countries, and it should trade for goods and services that it can't produce as economically.

LEARNING OBJECTIVE 1

Discuss why nations trade

economies of scale
Savings from buying parts and materials, manufacturing, or marketing in large quantities

absolute advantage
A nation's ability to produce a particular product with fewer resources per unit of output than any other nation

comparative advantage theory
Theory that states that a country should produce and sell to other countries those items it produces most efficiently

For example, the United States and Brazil can each produce both steel and coffee, but the United States is more efficient at producing steel than coffee, while Brazil is more efficient at producing coffee than steel. According to the comparative advantage theory, the two countries will be better off if each specializes in the industry in which it is more efficient and if the two trade with each other, with the United States selling steel to Brazil and Brazil selling coffee to the United States.[9] The basic argument behind the comparative advantage theory is that such specialization and exchange will increase a country's total output and allow both trading partners to enjoy a higher standard of living.

Comparative advantage is both relative and dynamic. In other words, no matter how good you are, you only have an advantage if you are better than someone else, and no advantage is preordained to last forever. The U.S. auto industry was once the unquestioned world leader, but over the course of just a couple of decades, Japan was able to reduce that advantage with quality products at lower prices. Now South Korea is repeating the Japanese strategy with its own brands, most notably Hyundai. Similarly, the United States has long been a hotbed of technology, but India is becoming a strong competitor in fields that require advanced engineering and computer skills. Not only are Indian colleges and universities turning out talented people in higher numbers, but observers here in the United States worry that lower investments in basic research and restrictive immigration policies in the wake of the September 11, 2001, terror attacks will damage U.S. competitiveness even further.[10] The United States remains one of the world's most competitive countries, to be sure, but dozens of other countries now compete for the same employees and customers (see Exhibit 3.1).

The comparative advantage theory has been a cornerstone of economic thinking for nearly 200 years, but a few economists are starting to question whether it still holds true in a world that has been transformed by technology. For example, over the past few decades, globalization has had a traumatic impact on much of the U.S. manufacturing sector. Many lower-skilled jobs in labor-intensive industries disappeared when U.S. manufacturers either moved their operations to lower-wage countries or stopped trying to compete in those industries altogether. Conventional economic thinking acknowledged that this was temporarily painful for those U.S. workers and companies but positive for the economy overall, since those people could then focus on higher-skilled, higher-paying work in computer programming, aerospace engineering, medical technology, and other areas where the United States holds a comparative advantage. However, when *those* jobs started to move to lower-wage countries as well, some economists started to wonder if all this rampant globalization is really going to be good for the United States after all. The question is still unanswered, but it affects thousands of companies and millions of workers, so you can expect it to be a hot topic in the coming years.[11]

How International Trade Is Measured

Chapter 1 discussed how economists monitor certain key economic indicators to evaluate how well a country's economic system is performing, and several of these indicators measure international trade. As Exhibit 3.2 illustrates, the United States imports more goods

Exhibit 3.1
The World's Most Competitive Countries
According to the World Economic Forum, Finland is currently the world's most competitive country, based on its ability to sustain its economic growth.

Rank	Country	Rank	Country
1.	Finland	6.	Norway
2.	USA	7.	Singapore
3.	Sweden	8.	Switzerland
4.	Taiwan	9.	Japan
5.	Denmark	10.	Iceland

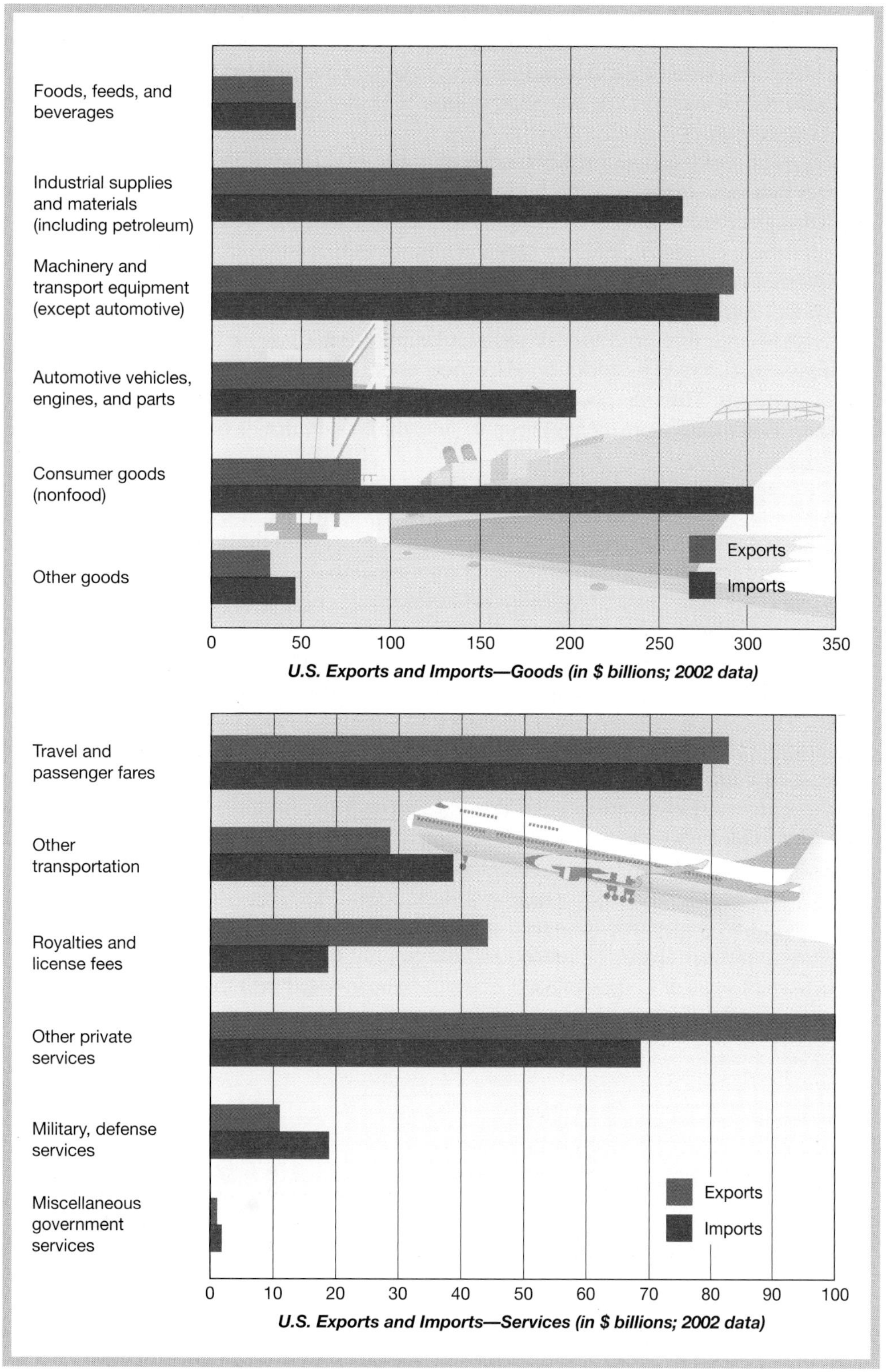

Exhibit 3.2
U.S. Exports and
Imports
*The United States actively
participates in global trade
by exporting and importing
goods and services.*

U.S. Exports and Imports—Goods (in $ billions; 2002 data)

Foods, feeds, and beverages
Industrial supplies and materials (including petroleum)
Machinery and transport equipment (except automotive)
Automotive vehicles, engines, and parts
Consumer goods (nonfood)
Other goods

Exports
Imports

0   50   100   150   200   250   300   350

U.S. Exports and Imports—Services (in $ billions; 2002 data)

Travel and passenger fares
Other transportation
Royalties and license fees
Other private services
Military, defense services
Miscellaneous government services

Exports
Imports

0   10   20   30   40   50   60   70   80   90   100

than it exports, but it exports more services than it imports. Two key measurements of a nation's level of international trade are the *balance of trade* and the *balance of payments*.

The total value of a country's exports *minus* the total value of its imports, over some period of time, determines its **balance of trade**. In years when the value of goods and services exported by the United States exceeds the value of goods and services it imports, the U.S. balance of trade is said to be positive: People in other countries buy more goods and services from the United States than the United States buys from them, creating a **trade surplus**.

balance of trade
*Total value of the products
a nation exports minus the
total value of the products
it imports, over some
period of time*

trade surplus
*Favorable trade balance
created when a country
exports more than it
imports*

trade deficit
Unfavorable trade balance created when a country imports more than it exports

balance of payments
Sum of all payments one nation receives from other nations minus the sum of all payments it makes to other nations, over some specified period of time

Explain why nations restrict international trade and list four forms of trade restrictions

free trade
International trade unencumbered by restrictive measures

Conversely, when the people of the United States buy more from foreign countries than the foreign countries buy from the United States, the U.S. balance of trade is said to be negative. That is, imports exceed exports, creating a **trade deficit**. As Exhibit 3.3 shows, in 2003 the U.S. trade deficit soared to nearly $500 billion.[12] That record-setting pace continued into 2004 as well.

The **balance of payments** is the broadest indicator of international trade. It is the total flow of money into the country *minus* the total flow of money out of the country over some period of time. The balance of payments includes the balance of trade plus the net dollars received and spent on foreign investment, military expenditures, tourism, foreign aid, and other international transactions. For example, when a U.S. company buys all or part of a company based in another country, that investment is counted in the balance of payments but not in the balance of trade. Similarly, when a foreign company such as Daimler-Benz buys a U.S. company such as Chrysler or purchases U.S. stocks, bonds, or real estate, those transactions are part of the balance of payments. The U.S. government, like all governments, desires a favorable balance of payments. That means more money is coming into the country than is flowing out.

Free Trade and Fair Trade

The benefits of the comparative advantage model are based on the assumption that nations don't take artificial steps to minimize their own weaknesses or to blunt the advantages of other countries. For instance, if the United States wanted to negate Brazil's cost efficiencies in coffee, it could place a fee on every pound of imported coffee to artificially bring its price up to the price of U.S.-grown coffee (you'll read more about these trade restrictions on page 103). Trade that takes place without these artificial interferences is known as **free trade**.

Free trade is not a universally welcomed concept, in spite of the positive connotation of the word "free." For instance, free trade can be a jarring experience for companies and workers who suddenly find themselves at a competitive disadvantage in the world market. Seaman Paper in Gardiner, Massachusetts, which makes crepe paper streamers and other decorative items, found that even with extensive automation to offset much lower labor costs in China, it still couldn't compete with Chinese suppliers—whose prices for finished products are below Seaman's cost of raw materials.[13] The free-trade argument that China should make crepe paper because it has a comparative advantage and Seaman should make something else at which it has a comparative advantage is probably of little comfort to the employees who count on paychecks from Seaman or to the company's owners, who invested their money in automation.

Exhibit 3.3
Trade Deficit on the Rise
U.S. officials say the exploding trade deficit is evidence that the United States maintains the world's most open markets.

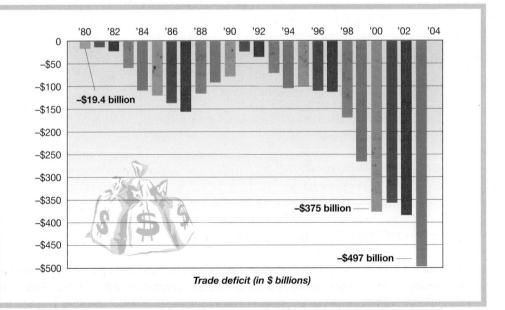

Trade deficit (in $ billions)

In addition, some critics argue that free trade makes it too easy for companies to exploit workers around the world by pitting them against one another in a "race to the bottom," in which production moves to whichever country has the lowest wages and fewest restrictions regarding worker safety and environmental protection.[14] This complaint has been at the heart of recent protests over free trade and globalization in general. A similar criticism involves the negotiating advantages that large international companies can have when buying from small farmers and other producers in multiple countries. The result, it is argued, is that prices get pushed so low that those producers struggle to earn enough money to survive because somebody, somewhere is always willing to work for less or sell for less. One response to this situation is the concept of **fair trade**, in which buyers voluntarily agree to pay more than the prevailing market price in order to help producers earn a *living wage*, enough money to satisfy their essential needs.[15]

Trade Restrictions

Unlike fair trade, which is a voluntary reaction to perceived inequalities in international free trade, governments can also mandate restrictions on various aspects of international trade. These restrictions are collectively known as **protectionism** since they often seek to protect a specific industry or groups of workers. Governments can also take protectionist steps to shield industries that are key to their national defense, to protect the health and safety of their citizens, and to give new or weak industries an opportunity to grow and strengthen before facing the full brunt of international competition.[16]

Are trade restrictions a good idea or a bad idea? Study after study has shown that in the long run, they hurt a country because they remove competition, stifle innovation, and allow domestic producers to charge more for their goods. However, short-term pressures on politicians, from both business owners and labor groups, can override long-term thinking on occasion. The most commonly used trade restrictions are *tariffs, quotas, embargoes*, and *sanctions*.

- **Tariffs. Tariffs** are taxes, surcharges, or duties levied against imported goods. Sometimes tariffs are levied to generate revenue for the government, but more often they are imposed to restrict trade or to punish other countries for disobeying international trade laws.

- **Quotas. Quotas** limit the amount of a particular good that countries can import during a given year. The United States puts ceilings on imports of sugar, peanuts, and dairy products, for instance. During the 1970s, the federal government moved to protect the textiles and garment industries by setting import quotas on foreign products. While these limits can protect industries, they raise prices for consumers—an estimated $14 billion a year for textiles and garments alone. Under international agreement, these quotas were phased out over a 10-year period and were removed completely on January 1, 2005. The impact on the U.S. textile and garment industries was immediate, with companies such as National Spinning in North Carolina laying off half its workforce. Similar cutbacks occurred throughout Latin America as well, where garment factories play a major role in national economies.[17]

- **Embargoes.** In its most extreme form, a quota becomes an **embargo**, a complete ban on the import or export of certain products. For example, Canada forbids the importation of oleomargarine in order to protect its dairy industry, and the United States bans the importation of toys with lead paint because of health concerns. The U.S. government has had a full trade embargo with Cuba for more than 40 years, but recently allowed CancerVax in Carlsbad, California, to import three experimental drugs developed by Cuban researchers.[18]

- **Sanctions.** Sanctions are politically motivated embargoes that revoke a country's normal trade relations status; they are often used as forceful alternatives short of war. Sanctions can include arms embargoes, foreign-assistance reductions and cutoffs, trade limitations,

Automobiles are just one of the many products that have been subject to trade restrictions by various governments over the years.

LEARNING OBJECTIVE 3

Highlight three protectionist tactics nations use to give their domestic industries a competitive edge

tariff increases, import-quota decreases, visa denials, air-link cancellations, and more. Most governments (including the United States) use sanctions sparingly, because studies show that sanctions are ineffective at getting countries to change.[19]

In addition to restricting foreign trade, governments sometimes give their domestic producers a competitive edge by using these protectionist tactics:

- **Restrictive import standards.** Countries can assist their domestic producers by establishing restrictive import standards, such as requiring special licenses for doing certain kinds of business and then making it difficult for foreign companies to obtain such a license. For example, Saudi Arabia restricts import licenses for a variety of products, including chemicals, pasteurized milk, and information technology products.[20] Other countries restrict imports by requiring goods to pass special tests.

- **Subsidies.** Rather than restrict imports, some countries subsidize domestic producers so that their prices can compete favorably in the global marketplace. Subsidies continue to be one of the most hotly contested aspects of international business, and farm subsidies often top the list of the most disputed items. The world's richest countries currently subsidize their farmers to the tune of $300 billion every year (including the $19 billion the United States currently gives its farmers every year), making it virtually impossible for poorer countries to compete in world markets. Negotiations have been under way for several years to reduce these payments, and in 2004, the United States agreed to start reducing its cotton subsidies in response to complaints by Benin, Burkina Faso, Chad, and Mali (all cotton-growing countries in Africa).[21] Another high-profile subsidy issue is the ongoing tussle between the United States (on behalf of Boeing) and the European Union (on behalf of Airbus, Boeing's primary competitor). Both sides accuse each other of unfairly subsidizing the multibillion-dollar cost of developing new aircraft. The situation is particularly complex in the aircraft business, since the two companies share the same customer base and many of the same suppliers, so any financial penalties levied against one or both companies could ripple through the entire industry.[22]

dumping

Charging less than the actual cost or less than the home-country price for goods sold in other countries

- **Dumping.** The practice of selling large quantities of a product at a price lower than the cost of production or below what the company would charge in its home market is called **dumping**. This tactic is most often used to try to win foreign customers or to reduce product surpluses. If a domestic producer can demonstrate that the low-cost imports are

TECHNOLOGIES THAT ARE REVOLUTIONIZING BUSINESS Telepresence

Telepresence systems start with the basic idea of video-conferencing but go far beyond with imagery so real that colleagues thousands of miles apart appear to be in the same room together. Business executives dissatisfied with the delays and image quality of conventional video-conferencing are turning to telepresence systems to stay connected with colleagues and customers—while avoiding the disruptions, costs, or perceived risks of international travel.

HOW IT'S CHANGING BUSINESS

Telepresence enhances communication for teams spread around the country or around the world. For example, Duke University's Fuqua School of Business installed a telepresence system to link its campuses in Durham, North Carolina, and Frankfurt, Germany. When meeting participants sit down at a table in one city, virtual participants from the other city appear to be sitting on the other side of the table. The effect is so real that some people think it's downright eerie. Not only can participants make eye contact across the Atlantic, but "you can stick your head in the room in Durham and hear the traffic of downtown Frankfurt," says associate dean Nevin Fouts.

Developers are even working on robotic telepresence, in which you'll be able to control a robot surrogate hundreds or thousands of miles away. Before long, you'll be able to run your global empire from the conference room down the hall.

WHERE YOU CAN LEARN MORE

Teliris is one of the early innovators in telepresence technology; check out the company's website at www.teliris.com.

damaging its business, most governments will seek redress on their behalf through international trade organizations. Dumping is often a tricky situation to resolve, however; buyers of the product being dumped benefit from the lower prices, and proving what a fair price is in the country of origin can be difficult.[23]

CRITICAL THINKING CHECKPOINT
1. How does international trade affect the lives of U.S. citizens?
2. Why do governments occasionally resort to protectionist tactics in their dealings with other countries?
3. What affect does dumping have on the U.S. economy?

Agreements and Organizations Overseeing International Trade

Solving business disputes within a country is fairly simple, since all parties are subject to the rules of the same government. However, disputes between countries are another matter entirely, often involving complicated negotiations that can take years to resolve. In an effort to ensure equitable trading practices and iron out the inevitable disagreements over what is fair and what isn't, governments around the world have established a number of important agreements and organizations that address trading issues, including GATT, WTO, APEC, IMF, and the World Bank.

The General Agreement on Tariffs and Trade (GATT) The General Agreement on Tariffs and Trade (GATT) is a worldwide pact that was first established in the aftermath of World War II. The pact's guiding principle is nondiscrimination: Any trade advantage a GATT member gives to one country must be given to all GATT members, and no GATT nation can be singled out for punishment. In 1995, GATT established the World Trade Organization (WTO), which has replaced GATT as the world forum for trade negotiations.

The World Trade Organization (WTO) The World Trade Organization (WTO), www.wto.org, is a permanent forum for negotiating, implementing, and monitoring international trade procedures and for mediating trade disputes among its member countries (of which there are currently 148). The organization's primary goal is to improve the welfare of people worldwide by helping international trade function more efficiently. Critics of globalization and free trade often direct their ire at the WTO, but the organization says these criticisms are unjustified and based on misunderstandings of what the WTO does.[24]

The Asia Pacific Economic Cooperation Council (APEC) The Asia Pacific Economic Cooperation Council (APEC), www.apec.org, is an organization of 18 countries that is making efforts to liberalize trade in the Pacific Rim (the land areas that surround the Pacific Ocean). Among the member nations are the United States, Japan, China, Mexico, Australia, South Korea, and Canada. In 1994, the members agreed to eliminate all tariffs and trade barriers among industrialized countries of the Pacific Rim by 2010 and among developing countries by 2020.[25]

The International Monetary Fund (IMF) The International Monetary Fund (IMF), www.imf.org, was founded in 1945 and is now affiliated with the United Nations. Its primary function is to provide short-term loans to countries that are unable to meet their budgetary expenses. As such, the IMF is often looked upon as a lender of last resort. For example, the IMF provided a combined total of over $150 billion in loans to South Korea, Indonesia, Brazil, Thailand, and other countries to help rescue them from a global financial crisis at the end of the 20th century.[26]

The World Bank Officially known as the International Bank for Reconstruction and Development, the World Bank (www.worldbank.org) is a United Nations agency owned by its 184 member nations. It was founded to finance reconstruction after World War II, and is now involved in hundreds of projects around the world aimed at alleviating poverty and improving health in developing countries. The World Bank is affiliated with several other agencies that also play a role in international trade, such as the International Finance Corporation, which provides financing assistance to companies in developing countries.[27]

LEARNING OBJECTIVE 4

Explain how trading blocs affect trade

trading blocs
Organizations of nations that remove barriers to trade among their members and that establish uniform barriers to trade with nonmember nations

Trading Blocs

Trading blocs are regional organizations that promote trade between member nations. Although specific rules vary from group to group, their primary objective is to ensure the economic growth and benefit of members. As such, trading blocs generally promote trade inside the region while creating uniform barriers against goods and services entering the region from nonmember countries. Trading blocs are becoming a significant force in the global marketplace.[28]

Trading blocs can be advantageous or disadvantageous in promoting world trade, depending on one's perspective. Some economists are apprehensive about the growing importance of regional trading blocs. They fear that the world is splitting into three camps, revolving around the Americas, Europe, and Asia, with each camp working to protect its own trade at the expense of the others. Others claim that trading blocs should improve world trade, particularly for smaller or younger nations that are trying to build strong economies. The lack of trade barriers within a bloc could help member industries compete with producers in more-developed nations, and, in some cases, member countries could reach a wider market than before.[29]

The four most powerful trading blocs today are the Association of Southeast Asian Nations (ASEAN), South America's Mercosur, the North American Free Trade Agreement (NAFTA), and the European Union (EU), with the latter two being the largest and most powerful (see Exhibit 3.4). Because many trading nations see Latin America as an area for large-scale economic growth in the future, they are eager to establish ties with Mercosur,

European Union (EU)	North American Free Trade Agreement (NAFTA)	Association of Southeast Asian Nations (ASEAN)	Mercosur
Austria	Canada	Brunei	Argentina
Belgium	Mexico	Cambodia	Brazil
Cyprus	United States	Indonesia	Paraguay
Czech Republic		Laos	Uruguay
Denmark		Malaysia	
Estonia		Myanmar	
Finland		Philippines	
France		Singapore	
Germany		Thailand	
Great Britain		Vietnam	
Greece			
Hungary			
Ireland			
Italy			
Latvia			
Lithuania			
Luxembourg			
Malta			
Netherlands			
Poland			
Portugal			
Slovakia			
Slovenia			
Spain			
Sweden			

Exhibit 3.4
Members of Major Trading Blocs
As the economies of the world become increasingly linked, many countries have formed powerful regional trading blocs that trade freely with one another and limit foreign competition.

which links Argentina, Brazil, Paraguay, and Uruguay and encompasses a population of 210 million people who produce more than $1 trillion in goods and services.[30]

NAFTA In 1994, the United States, Canada, and Mexico formed a powerful trading bloc, the North American Free Trade Agreement (NAFTA). The agreement paved the way for the free flow of goods, services, and capital within the bloc by eliminating tariffs and quotas on trade among the three nations.[31]

Now, after more than a decade in action, has NAFTA lived up to its promises, particularly regarding trade between the United States and Mexico? That depends on where you look and whom you ask. Mexico has tripled its exports, and U.S. and other foreign companies have invested billions of dollars in the country. Some companies are thriving, thanks to those export opportunities, while others, particularly in agriculture, have been hurt severely by low-cost imports from the United States. Many of the manufacturing jobs Mexico hoped to attract wound up in China instead. And outside the business sphere, hoped-for improvements in education and health care haven't materialized to the extent NAFTA backers expected, either, although they place the blame on government inaction, not on the free-trade agreement. In the United States, critics of NAFTA claim that much of the promised benefits of lower consumer prices and steady export markets for small farmers didn't materialize, and that benefits of NAFTA have gone mostly to huge agribusiness corporations.[32]

Another NAFTA-like agreement, the Central American Free Trade Agreement (CAFTA), which proposes to link the United States and five countries in Central America, is currently in development. Ultimately, NAFTA's supporters would like to see the agreement expanded to include all of Central and South America—making this Free Trade Association of the Americas (FTAA) the largest free-trade zone on the planet. However, Mexico's experience has soured many workers throughout the United States and Latin America on the prospects of free trade.[33]

The European Union One of the largest trading blocs is the European Union (EU), www.europa.eu.int, which now combines 25 countries and nearly a half billion people. Talks are under way to admit several more countries in 2007.[34] EU nations have eliminated hundreds of local regulations, variations in product standards, and protectionist measures that once limited trade among member countries. As a result, trade now flows among member countries in much the same way as it does among states in the United States. The EU's reach extends far beyond the borders of Europe, in fact; to simplify design and manufacturing for world markets, many companies now create their products to meet EU specifications. If you've seen the "CE" marking on any products you may own, that stands for *Conformitié Europiéene* and indicates that the product has met EU standards for safety, health, and environmental responsibility.

The EU has taken a significant step beyond all other trading blocs in the area of money. In 1999, 12 of the 15 countries that were EU members at that time formed an economic and monetary union and turned over control of their individual monetary policies to the newly created European Central Bank. With a combined population of about 376 million people, these 12 countries account for about 20 percent of the world's gross domestic product (GDP), making them the world's second-largest economy.[35] These countries also adopted a unified currency called the **euro**. By switching to a common currency, the 12 countries vastly simplify commerce for both consumers and businesses by removing the hassle and expense of changing money, maintaining catalogs with multiple currencies, calculating prices for online orders, and so on. Some of the newer member states, such as Poland and Hungary, are likely to adopt the euro in the coming years, once their economies meet EU financial standards.[36]

euro
A unified currency used by most nations in the European Union

The euro eases price comparisons for products sold in the member countries of the European Union.

CRITICAL THINKING CHECKPOINT

1. What might happen in the relationships between countries if the World Trade Organization didn't exist to help mediate commercial disputes?
2. Why are some people concerned about the emergence of three strong trading blocs in Asia, Europe, and the Americas?
3. Why are some observers critical of NAFTA and wary of any expansion of trading blocs across North, Central, and South America?

Foreign Exchange Rates and Currency Valuations

The euro was designed to solve one of the most complex issues that bedevil international commerce: exchange rates and currency valuations. When companies buy and sell goods and services in the global marketplace, they complete the transaction by exchanging currencies. For instance, if a Japanese company borrows money from a U.S. bank to build a manufacturing plant in Japan, it must repay the loan in U.S. dollars. Or if a South Korean car manufacturer imports engine parts from Japan, it must pay for them in yen (Japan's currency). The process is called *foreign exchange*, the conversion of one currency into an equivalent amount of another currency. The number of units of one currency that must be exchanged for a unit of the second currency is known as the **exchange rate** between the currencies.

exchange rate
Rate at which the money of one country is traded for the money of another

Most international currencies operate under a *floating exchange rate system*; thus, a currency's value or price fluctuates in response to the forces of global supply and demand. The supply and demand of a country's currency are determined in part by what is happening in the country's own economy. Moreover, because supply and demand for a currency are always changing, the rate at which it is exchanged for other currencies may change a little each day. Japanese currency might be trading at 107.6 yen to the U.S. dollar on one day and 106.8 on the next.

A currency is called *strong* relative to another when its exchange rate is higher than what is considered normal and called *weak* when its rate is lower than normal (("normal" itself is a relative term here). A *strong dollar* means that relative to most currencies around the world, the U.S. dollar buys more units of those other currencies than it has in the recent past. For instance, if a dollar bought 100 yen in January and 105 yen in March, it would be strengthening or rising relative to the yen. A *weak dollar* means the opposite. Note that "strong" isn't necessarily good, and "weak" isn't necessarily bad when it comes to currencies, as Exhibit 3.5 illustrates.

Exchange rates can dramatically affect a company's financial results. In 2004, a strong yen relative to the U.S. dollar reduced Honda's annual profits by $889 million (the U.S. market accounts for 80 percent of the company's profits).[37] For instance, if Honda makes $1,000 profit on a car sold here when the yen is trading at 108 to the dollar, it brings 108,000 yen home to Japan. However, if the yen is trading at 103 to the dollar, Honda's profit drops to 103,000 yen in its home currency—even though it still made $1,000 in the United States when it sold the car. Of course, a weak dollar generally helps U.S. exporters, such as Markel Corporation, a small manufacturing company in Plymouth Meeting, Pennsylvania. When the dollar was weak against the euro in 2004, Markel earned enough extra profit to hand out holiday bonuses, raises, and retirement account increases.[38]

Even though most governments let the value of their currency respond to the forces of supply and demand, sometimes a government will intervene and adjust the exchange rate of its country's currency. **Devaluation**, a move by one government to drop the value of its currency relative to the value of other currencies, can at times boost a country's economy because it makes the country's products and services more affordable in foreign markets while it increases the price of imports, as Exhibit 3.5 indicated.

devaluation
A move by one government to drop the value of its currency relative to the value of other currencies

Some countries fix, or peg, the value of their currencies to the value of more stable currencies, such as the dollar or the yen, instead of letting it float freely. The Chinese yuan, for instance, while no longer strictly pegged, is allowed to float only within a very tight range

Exhibit 3.5
Strong and Weak
Currencies: Who
Gains, Who Loses?
*A strong dollar and a weak
dollar aren't necessarily
good or bad; each
condition helps some
people and hurts others.*

		Strong Dollar	**Weak Dollar**
How it helps		U.S. buyers pay less for imported goods and services	U.S. products more price-competitive in foreign markets
		Lower-cost imports help keep inflation in check	U.S. firms under less price pressure from imports in U.S. market
		Travel to others countries is cheaper	Overseas tourists encouraged to visit the U.S.
		Foreign investments are cheaper	Investments in U.S. stocks and bonds more attractive to international investors
How it hurts		U.S. exports more expensive to buyers in other countries	Prices of imported products are higher for U.S. consumers and businesses
		U.S. companies must compete with lower-priced imports in the U.S. market	Higher import prices raises cost of living; contributes to inflation
		Overseas tourists discouraged from visiting the U.S.	International travel more expensive for U.S. residents
		International investors less likely to invest in the U.S. capital markets (stocks, bonds, etc.)	Expansion and investment in other countries more difficult for U.S. firms and investors

versus the U.S. dollar. If a currency is pegged, its value fluctuates proportionately with the value of the foreign currency to which it is linked. So if the U.S. dollar declines, so will the yuan and other currencies that are pegged to it. This system works well as long as the proportionate relationship between the two currencies remains valid. But if one partner suffers economic hardship, demand for its currency will decline significantly and the exchange rate at which the two are pegged will become unrealistic. Such was the case with Thailand's currency (the baht), Indonesia's currency (the rupiah), and Argentina's currency (the peso). When these countries unpegged their currencies from the U.S. dollar to let them gradually seek their true value, the currencies went into a free fall. Conversely, the Chinese economy has grown so strong in recent years that many are calling on the Chinese government to completely unpeg its currency from the dollar so that goods imported into China would be less expense to local buyers and goods exported from China would be more expensive in overseas markets (a situation that would help the United States in both directions, for example).[39]

CRITICAL THINKING CHECKPOINT
1. How can a fixed exchange rate distort financial interaction between two countries?
2. Is a strong dollar good for U.S. exporters? Why or why not?
3. Is a strong dollar good for U.S. consumers? Why or why not?

LEARNING
OBJECTIVE 5

Highlight the opportunities
and challenges you'll
encounter when conducting
business in other countries

The Global Business Environment

Doing business internationally clearly isn't easy, but it's become essential for thousands of U.S. companies. Even small firms such as Trek have discovered that they can tap the sales potential of overseas markets with the help of overnight delivery services, e-mail, and the Internet. Selling goods and services in foreign markets can generate increased sales, produce operational efficiencies, expose companies to new technologies, and provide greater consumer choices. But venturing abroad also exposes companies to many new challenges. Every country has unique ways of doing business, which must be learned: laws, customs, consumer preferences, ethical standards, labor skills, and political and economic stability. All these factors can affect a firm's international prospects. Furthermore, volatile currencies, international trade relationships, and the threat of terrorism can make global expansion a risky proposition. Still, in most cases the opportunities of the global marketplace greatly outweigh the risks. When UPS began its rapid global expansion program in the 1980s, it had to attain air rights into each country, unravel a patchwork of customs laws, learn how to deal with varying work ethics and employment policies, and so on. But the company's efforts paid off. Today UPS delivers over 13 million documents and packages daily in more than 200 countries.[40]

Of course, not every business is a candidate for international sales. Some industries, such as consumer electronics and apparel, are highly globalized. These products are easy to make just about anywhere, and they don't cost much to ship. Others, including products that are expensive to ship relative to their sales value (such as steel) are less globalized. Services are among the least-globalized product categories, given the obvious costs and difficulties of delivering most services at long distances.[41]

Cultural Differences in the Global Business Environment

Cultural differences present a number of challenges in the global marketplace. Successful companies recognize and respect differences in language, social values, ideas of status, decision-making habits, attitudes toward time, use of space, body language, manners, and ethical standards. Above all else, avoid falling into the twin traps of **stereotyping**, assigning a wide range of generalized (and often superficial or even false) attributes to an individual on the basis of membership in a particular culture or social group without considering the individual's unique characteristics, and **ethnocentrism**, the tendency to judge all other groups according to your own group's standards, behaviors, and customs.

The best way to prepare yourself for doing business with people from another culture is to study that culture in advance. Learn everything you can about the culture's history, religion, politics, and customs—especially its business customs. Who makes decisions? How are negotiations usually conducted? Is gift giving expected? What is the proper attire for a business meeting? In addition to the suggestion that you learn about the culture, seasoned international businesspeople offer the following tips for improving intercultural communication:

- *Be alert to the other person's customs.* Expect the other person to have values, beliefs, expectations, and mannerisms different from yours. For instance, don't be surprised when businesspeople in Pakistan excuse themselves in the middle of a meeting to conduct prayers. Moslems pray five times a day.
- *Deal with the individual.* Don't stereotype the other person or react with preconceived ideas. Regard the person as an individual first, not as a representative of another culture.
- *Clarify your intent and meaning.* The other person's body language may not mean what you think, and the person may read unintentional meanings into your message. Clarify your true intent by repetition and examples. Ask questions and listen carefully. The Japanese are generally appreciative when foreigners ask what is proper behavior, because it shows respect for the Japanese way of doing things.[42]
- *Adapt your style to the other person's.* If the other person appears to be direct and straightforward, follow suit. If not, adjust your behavior to match. In many African countries, people are suspicious of others who seem to be in a hurry. Therefore, you should allow plenty of time to get to know the people you are dealing with.
- *Show respect.* Learn how respect is communicated in various cultures—through gestures, eye contact, and so on. For example, in Spain let a handshake last five to seven strokes; pulling away too soon may be interpreted as a rejection. In France, however, the preferred handshake is a single stroke.

stereotyping
Assigning a wide range of generalized attributes, which are often superficial or even false, to an individual based on his or membership in a particular culture or social group

ethnocentrism
Judging all other groups according to your own group's standards, behaviors, and customs.

L E A R N I N G
O B J E C T I V E 6

List five ways you can improve communication in an international business relationship

COMPETING IN THE GLOBAL MARKETPLACE

HOW TO AVOID BUSINESS MISTAKES ABROAD

Doing business in another country can be extremely tricky. Here are some issues to consider when you conduct business abroad.

THE IMPORTANCE OF PACKAGING

Numerous problems result from the failure to adapt packaging for other cultures. Sometimes only the color of the package needs to be altered to enhance a product's sales. For instance, white symbolizes death in Japan and much of Asia; green represents danger or disease in Malaysia. Using the wrong color in these countries might produce negative reactions.

THE LANGUAGE BARRIER

Some product names travel poorly. For instance, the gasoline company Esso found out that its name means "stalled car" in Japan. However, some company names have traveled well. Kodak may be the most famous example. A research team deliberately developed this name after searching for a word that was pronounceable everywhere but had no specific meaning anywhere.

PROBLEMS WITH PROMOTIONS

In its U.S. promotion, one company had effectively used this sentence: "You can use no finer napkin at your dinner table." The U.S. company decided to use the same commercials in England because, after all, the British do speak English. To the British, however, the word *napkin* or *nappy* actually means "diaper." The ad could hardly be expected to boost sales of dinner napkins in England.

LOCAL CUSTOMS

Social norms vary greatly from country to country, and it is difficult for any outsider to be knowledgeable about all of them, so local input is vital. For example, one firm promoted eyeglasses in Thailand with commercials featuring animals wearing glasses. However, in Thailand animals are considered a low form of life; humans would never wear anything worn by an animal.

TRANSLATION PROBLEMS

The best translations of an advertising message convey the concept of the original but do not precisely duplicate the original. PepsiCo learned this lesson when it reportedly discovered that its slogan "Come alive with Pepsi" was translated into German as "Come alive out of the grave with Pepsi." In Asia, the slogan was once translated as "Bring your ancestors back from the dead."

THE NEED FOR RESEARCH

Proper market research may reduce or eliminate most international business blunders. Market researchers can uncover needs for product adaptations, potential name problems, promotional requirements, and useful market strategies. Good research may even uncover potential translation problems.

As you can see, doing business in other cultures can be risky if you're unprepared. However, awareness of differences, consultations with local people, and concern for host-country feelings can reduce problems and save money.

Questions for Critical Thinking

1. If you were thinking of selling a breakfast cereal in Japan, what issues might you want to consider?
2. What steps can companies take to avoid business blunders abroad?

These are just a few tips for doing business in the global marketplace. Successful international businesses learn as much as they can about political issues, cultural factors, and the economic environment before investing time and money in new markets. Exhibit 3.6 can guide you in your efforts to learn more about a country's culture before doing business abroad.

Legal Differences in the Global Business Environment

Differences in national legal systems may not be as immediately obvious as cultural differences, but they can have a profound effect on international business efforts. For instance, the legal systems in the United States and the United Kingdom are based on *common law*, in which tradition, custom, and judicial interpretation play important roles. In contrast, the

Exhibit 3.6

Checklist for Doing Business Abroad

Use this checklist as a starting point when investigating a foreign culture.

UNDERSTAND SOCIAL CUSTOMS

✓ How do people react to strangers? Are they friendly? Hostile? Reserved?

✓ How do people greet each other? Should you bow? Nod? Shake hands?

✓ How are names used for introductions?

✓ What are the attitudes toward touching people?

✓ How do you express appreciation for an invitation to lunch or dinner or to someone's home? Should you bring a gift? Send flowers? Write a thank-you note?

✓ How, when, or where are people expected to sit in social or business situations?

✓ Are any phrases, facial expressions, or hand gestures considered rude?

✓ How close do people stand when talking?

✓ How do you attract the attention of a waiter? Do you tip the waiter?

✓ When is it rude to refuse an invitation? How do you refuse politely?

✓ What are the acceptable patterns of eye contact?

✓ What gestures indicate agreement? Disagreement? Respect?

✓ What topics may or may not be discussed in a social setting? In a business setting?

✓ How is time perceived?

✓ What are the generally accepted working hours?

✓ How do people view scheduled appointments?

LEARN ABOUT CLOTHING AND FOOD PREFERENCES

✓ What occasions require special clothing? What colors are associated with mourning? Love? Joy?

✓ Are some types of clothing considered taboo for one sex or the other?

✓ What are the attitudes toward human body odors? Are deodorants or perfumes used?

✓ How many times a day do people eat?

✓ How are hands or utensils used when eating?

✓ What types of places, food, and drink are appropriate for business entertainment?

✓ Where is the seat of honor at a table?

ASSESS POLITICAL PATTERNS

✓ How stable is the political situation? Does it affect businesses in and out of the country?

✓ How is political power manifested? Military power? Economic strength?

✓ What are the traditional government institutions?

LEARN ABOUT ECONOMIC AND BUSINESS INSTITUTIONS

✓ Is the society homogeneous?

✓ What minority groups are represented?

✓ What languages are spoken?

✓ Do immigration patterns influence workforce composition?

✓ What are the primary resources and principal products?

✓ What vocational/technological training is offered?

✓ What are the attitudes toward education?

✓ Are businesses generally large? Family controlled? Government controlled?

✓ Is it appropriate to do business by telephone? By fax? By e-mail?

✓ Do managers make business decisions unilaterally, or do they involve employees?

✓ How are status and seniority shown in an organization? In a business meeting?

✓ Must people socialize before conducting business?

(Continued)

Exhibit 3.6
Continued

APPRAISE THE NATURE OF ETHICS, VALUES, AND LAWS

✓ Is money or a gift expected in exchange for arranging business transactions?

✓ What ethical or legal issues might affect business transactions?

✓ Do people value competitiveness or cooperation?

✓ What are the attitudes toward work? Toward money?

✓ Is politeness more important than factual honesty?

✓ What qualities are admired in a business associate?

---

system in countries such as France and Germany is based on *civil law*, in which legal parameters are specified in detailed legal codes. One everyday consequence of this difference is that business contracts tend to be shorter and simpler in civil law systems, since the existing legal code outlines more aspects of the transaction or relationship. A third type of legal system, *theocratic law*, or laws based on religious principles, predominates in such countries as Iran and Pakistan. Companies doing business in such countries need to be aware of legal differences, some of which can be markedly different from U.S. law. For instance, Islamic law prohibits banks from charging interest on loans, so many international banks have established Islamic banking divisions.[43]

Beyond the differences in legal philosophies, the business of contracts, copyrights, and other legal matters can vary considerably from one country to another. For example, the International Monetary Fund and the World Bank have found that legal processes in countries such as Turkey and Russia are currently unpredictable enough to discourage many foreign companies from doing business there.[44]

Perhaps no issue in international business law generates as much confusion and consternation as bribery. In some countries, payments to government officials are so common that they are considered by some businesspeople to be standard operating practice. These payments are used to facilitate a variety of actions, from winning contracts for public works projects (such as roads or power plants) to securing routine government services (such as customs inspections) to getting preferential treatment (such as the approval to raise prices).[45] These payment systems discourage much-needed investment in developing countries, weaken trust in government, and raise prices for consumers by inflating business costs. Some businesspeople have argued that critics of such payoffs are trying to impose U.S. values on other cultures, but Transparency International, a watchdog group that works to reduce business-government corruption around the world, discredits that argument by saying that all countries have laws against corruption, so it can hardly be considered a cultural issue.[46] (To learn more about Transparency International's work, visit www.transparency.org.)

All U.S. companies are bound by the Foreign Corrupt Practices Act (FCPA), which outlaws payments with the intent of getting government officials to break the laws of their own countries. Lucent Technologies, a large manufacturer of telecommunications equipment, recently fired four executives from its Chinese subsidiary after an internal analysis of potential FCPA allegations in 27 countries. The company is also under investigation for possible bribery in a $5 billion telecom contract in Saudi Arabia.[47] However, the FCPA does allow payments that expedite actions that are legal, such as clearing merchandise through customs, a distinction that could be considered unethical because it still permits private profits to be gained from public trust.[48] Other types of payments can also be considered forms of influence but aren't covered by the FCPA, such as foreign aid payments from one government to another, made with the intent of securing favorable decisions for business.

Critics of the FCPA complain that payoffs are a routine part of business in some parts of the world, so forbidding U.S. companies to follow suit cripples their ability to compete. Others counter that U.S. exports haven't been affected by this law and that companies can conduct business abroad without violating antibribery rules. Regardless of whether they agree or disagree with the law, some companies have had to forgo opportunities as a result of it. For example, a consortium led by IBM lost a contract to build air traffic control systems for the Mexican government because it was unable to make such payments.[49]

Forms of International Business Activity

Beyond cultural and legal concerns, companies that plan to go international also need to think carefully about the right organizational approach to support these activities. The five common forms of international business are *importing and exporting, licensing, franchising, strategic alliances and joint ventures,* and *foreign direct investment,* and each has a varying degree of ownership, financial commitment, and risk.

Importing and Exporting
Importing, the buying of goods or services from a supplier in another country, and **exporting,** the selling of products outside the country in which they are produced, have existed for centuries. In the last few decades, however, the increased level of these activities has caused the economies of the world to become tightly linked.

Exporting, one of the least risky forms of international business activity, permits a firm to enter a foreign market gradually, assess local conditions, then fine-tune its product offerings to meet the needs of foreign consumers. In most cases, the firm's financial exposure is limited to the costs of researching the market, advertising, and either establishing a direct sales and distribution system or hiring intermediaries. Such intermediaries include *export management companies,* which are domestic firms that specialize in performing international marketing services on a commission basis, and *export trading companies,* which are general trading firms that will buy your products for resale overseas as well as perform a variety of importing, exporting, and manufacturing functions. Still another alternative is to use foreign distributors.

Working through a foreign distributor with connections in the target country is often helpful to both large and small companies because such intermediaries can provide you with the connections, expertise, and market knowledge you will need to conduct business in a foreign country.[50] In addition, many countries now have foreign trade offices to help importers and exporters interested in doing business within their borders. Other helpful resources include professional agents, local businesspeople, and the International Trade Administration of the U.S. Department of Commerce (www.export.gov). This trade organization offers a variety of services, including political and credit-risk analysis, advice on entering foreign markets, and financing tips.

International Licensing
Licensing is another popular approach to international business. License agreements entitle one company to use some or all of another firm's intellectual property (patents, trademarks, brand names, copyrights, or trade secrets) in return for a royalty payment. Underwear manufacturer Jockey licenses the rights to use the Jockey name to certain foreign manufacturers of women's active wear, sleepwear, and slippers. Jockey licenses its products in more than 120 countries but is careful that all such arrangements add value to the Jockey name.[51]

Many firms choose licensing as an approach to international markets because it involves little out-of-pocket cost. A firm has already incurred the costs of developing the intellectual property to be licensed. Pharmaceutical firms, for instance, routinely use licensing to enter foreign markets. Once a pharmaceutical firm has developed and patented a new drug, it is often more efficient to grant existing local firms the right to manufacture and distribute the patented drug in return for royalty payments. Israel's Teva Pharmaceutical Industries, for example, has a license to manufacture and market Merck's pharmaceutical products in Israel. This arrangement saves Merck the expense of establishing its own Israeli salesforce.[52] Of course, licensing agreements are not restricted to international business. A company can also license its products or technology to other companies in its domestic market.

International Franchising
Some companies choose to expand into foreign markets by *franchising* their operation. International franchising is among the fastest-growing forms of

LEARNING OBJECTIVE 7

Identify five forms of international business activity

importing
Purchasing goods or services from another country and bringing them into one's own country

exporting
Selling and shipping goods or services to another country

licensing
Agreement to produce and market another company's product in exchange for a royalty or fee

COMPETING IN THE GLOBAL MARKETPLACE

CHINA'S COUNTERFEIT ECONOMY

The vast economy in the People's Republic of China has come alive in recent years, with the communist government embracing many principles of free-market economics. The quality of Chinese products has already risen dramatically, and many of the world's best-known companies now rely on Chinese manufacturers to build some of their products for them.

Unfortunately, the Chinese manufacturing phenomenon is not limited to legitimate products. China also produces more counterfeit products than any other nation—everything from autos to aircraft parts to medicines. China isn't the only nation that produces counterfeit goods (the Philippines, Russia, Vietnam, and Pakistan are among the many others involved), but as the source of nearly two-thirds of the counterfeit goods in the world, China is the focus of special attention. For instance, nearly half of the world's 14 billion batteries made every year are produced in China. But most of them are fake versions of Panasonic, Gillette, and other big brands. Cycles with names that include Yamaha zip along the roads from Beijing to Tibet, but Yamaha didn't make a lot of them. Procter & Gamble (P&G) claims counterfeiters sell $150 million of fake P&G products annually. More than 90 percent of all music CDs sold in China are pirated copies, joining $168 million worth of pirated movies on DVD, according to industry experts. Microsoft has invested several billion dollars in China but has yet to generate a nickel of profit, since more than 90 percent of the application software sold in the country is counterfeit.

Most counterfeiters work at small to midsized factories, but many stay at home, doing things like filling Head & Shoulders bottles with concoctions from large vats in their living rooms or translating subtitles for pirated movies. Overall, the amount of China's manufacturing base that is dependent on illegal knockoffs is estimated to be 10 percent to 30 percent—and growing.

Raids do occur daily, but even the government's efforts aren't cracking down on the number of counterfeiters. Local officials are hesitant to stop the pirates because they create millions of jobs. "Entire villages live off counterfeiting. If you suddenly throw these people out of work, you'll have riots," says one spokesperson for a leading private anticounterfeiting agency. Shutting down counterfeiters in the city of Yiwu—China's largest wholesale distribution center, where it is estimated that 80 percent of the consumer goods sold are counterfeits—would cripple the city's economy because many hotels, restaurants, and other businesses cater to the trade.

The sale of fake or pirated products is not limited to the Chinese market, either; these items are exported around the globe—to Europe, Russia, the Middle East. Unilever says that fake Dove soap is making its way from China into Europe. Bose, a maker of high-end audio systems, is finding Chinese fakes in overseas markets. These exports are made possible by the growing sophistication of Chinese manufacturing. Ten years ago, China's knockoffs were below Western standards. Now, many fake Duracell batteries look so genuine that Gillette has to send them to a forensics lab to analyze them.

So what are pirated brand owners to do? For the most part, companies hope to encourage greater government enforcement, but it's a tough task. Although U.S. sunglasses maker Oakley has gotten Chinese authorities to close counterfeiters' factories, new ones pop up in their place. Officials have confiscated and destroyed millions of DVDs and CDs, but the counterfeiters continue to churn them out in ever greater numbers. U.S. business groups say the problem is getting worse, not better, and 90 percent of companies in a recent survey said they see "virtually no enforcement" by Chinese authorities.

Some multinationals are shutting down or shrinking product lines in China because these products are overrun by counterfeits. But China's market is so vast and promising, few companies are willing to pull out entirely. Given the magnitude of the problem and the number of people who are dependent on this shadow economy, the situation won't be solved anytime soon, if ever.

Questions for Critical Thinking

1. Honda recently set up a joint venture to make and sell motorcycles with a Chinese company that used to produce Honda knockoffs. Why would Honda do this?
2. How might product counterfeiting in China affect consumers in the United States?

international business activity today. Under this arrangement, a franchisor enters into an agreement whereby the franchisee obtains the rights to duplicate a specific product or service—perhaps a restaurant, photocopy shop, or video rental store—and the franchisor obtains a royalty fee in exchange. Holiday Inn Worldwide has used this approach to reach customers in over 65 countries. So have KFC, McDonald's, and scores of others. Smaller companies have also found that franchising is a good way for them to enter the global marketplace.[53] By franchising its operations, a firm can minimize the costs and risks of global expansion and bypass certain trade restrictions. (The advantages and disadvantages of franchising in general will be discussed in detail in Chapter 5.)

International Strategic Alliances and Joint Ventures A **strategic alliance** is a long-term partnership between two or more companies to jointly develop, produce, or sell products in the global marketplace. To reach their individual but complementary goals, the companies typically share ideas, expertise, resources, technologies, investment costs, risks, management, and profits. In some cases, a strategic alliance might be the only way to gain access to a market, which was the reason Viacom (which owns CBS, MTV, and other media) decided to form an alliance with Beijing Television in order to expand its presence in China.[54]

strategic alliance
Long-term relationship in which two or more companies share ideas, resources, and technologies in order to establish competitive advantages

Strategic alliances are a popular way to expand globally. The benefits of this form of international expansion include ease of market entry, shared risk, shared knowledge and expertise, and synergy. Companies that form a strategic alliance with a foreign partner can often compete more effectively than if they entered the foreign market alone. When the French retail giant Carrefour attempted to enter the Japanese market without a local partner, it had trouble getting land for new stores; land in Japan is often held in complex partnerships that outsiders find difficult to penetrate. The company pulled out of Japan within five years.[55]

A **joint venture** is a special type of strategic alliance in which two or more firms join together to create a new business entity that is legally separate and distinct from its parents. In some countries, foreign companies are prohibited from owning facilities outright or from investing in local business. Thus, establishing a joint venture with a local partner may be the only way to do business in that country. In other cases, foreigners may be required to move some of their production facilities to the country to earn the right to sell their products there.

joint venture
Cooperative partnership in which organizations share investment costs, risks, management, and profits in the development, production, or selling of products

Foreign Direct Investment Exporting, licensing, franchising, and strategic alliances allow a firm to enter the global marketplace without investing in foreign factories or facilities. However, many firms prefer to enter international markets through partial or whole ownership and control of assets in foreign countries, an approach known as **foreign direct investment (FDI)**. Some facilities are set up through FDI to exploit the availability of raw materials; others take advantage of low wage rates; still others minimize transportation costs by choosing locations that give them direct access to markets in other countries. In almost all cases, at least part of the workforce is drawn from the local population. Companies that establish a physical presence in multiple countries through FDI are called **multinational corporations (MNCs)**.

foreign direct investment (FDI)
Investment of money by foreign companies in domestic business enterprises

FDI typically gives companies greater control, but it carries much greater economic and political risk and is more complex than any other form of entry in the global marketplace. Consequently, most FDI takes place between the industrialized nations (a group that includes such large, stable economies as the United States, Canada, Japan, and most countries in Europe), which tend to offer greater protection for foreign investors. The top three countries in which U.S. companies own facilities through FDI are the United Kingdom, Canada, and the Netherlands, and the top three countries whose companies invest in U.S. facilities through FDI are the United Kingdom, Japan, and the Netherlands.[56]

multinational corporations (MNCs)
Companies with operations in more than one country

Companies that engage in FDI can either establish facilities in the countries where they want to operate or purchase existing foreign firms, as Wal-Mart did when it acquired large retail stores in Germany and Great Britain and later converted them into Wal-Mart Supercenters.[57] In contrast, Intel spent nearly $1 billion to build two semiconductor facilities in China to capitalize on that country's voracious appetite for electronic products.[58]

Yahoo! Japan is just one of the many U.S. companies that expand internationally through foreign direct investment.

Strategic Approaches to International Markets

Choosing the right form of business to pursue is the first of many decisions that companies need to make when moving into other countries. Virtually everything you learn about in this course, from human resources to marketing to financial management, needs to be reconsidered carefully when going international. Some of the most important decisions involve products, customer support, pricing, promotion, and staffing:

- **Products.** You face two primary dilemmas regarding products. First, which products should you try to sell in each market? For instance, before China and Russia began to liberalize their economies, it made little sense for luxury goods suppliers to offer many products there. Now, with personal incomes on the rise in both countries, luxury brands from Gucci to Ferrari are racing in with new stores and expanded product offerings.[59] Second, should you *standardize* your products, selling the same product everywhere in the world, or *customize* your products to accommodate the lifestyles and habits of local target markets? Customization seems like an obvious choice, but it can increase costs and operational complexity, so the decision to customize is not automatic. The degree of customization can also vary. A company may change only the product's name or packaging, or it can modify the product's components, size, and functions. Of course, understanding a country's regulations, culture, and local competition plays into the decisions. Britain's Vodaphone, the world's largest cell phone operator, entered the Japanese market with the same relatively mundane lineup of phones it offered elsewhere and promoted the phones worldwide compatibility. However, Japanese consumers accustomed to constant innovation and flashy new features shunned the Vodaphone lineup.[60] Similarly, McDonald's, KFC, and Frito-Lay learned to customize their product offerings, sometimes dramatically, to appeal to Chinese consumers. For instance, Frito-Lay now offers "warmer" tasting potato chips in the winter and "cooler" flavors in the summer, which Chinese consumers expect.[61]
- **Customer support.** Cars, computers, and other products that require some degree of customer support add another layer of complexity to international business. Many customers are reluctant to buy foreign products that don't offer some form of local support, whether it's a local dealer, a manufacturer's branch office, or a third-party organization that offers support under contract to the manufacturer.
- **Promotion.** Advertising, public relations, and other promotional efforts also present the dilemma of standardization versus customization. As you'll see in Chapter 12, consistency is

Even with the worldwide power of the Disney brand, the company learned that it needed to adapt its products and services to the local tastes of the European market.

one of the keys to successful promotion, making sure the audience receives the same message from all sources, time after time. However, after years of trying to build global brands, many U.S. companies are putting new emphasis on crafting customized messages for each country. As Martin Sorrell, head of the UK advertising conglomerate WPP, puts it, "One size doesn't fit all. Consumers are more interesting for their differences rather than their similarities."[62] Pepsi-Cola didn't catch on in India until the company started featuring Indian movie star Shahrukh Khan and cricket player Sachin Tendulka in its TV commercials.[63]

- **Pricing.** Even a standardized strategy adds costs, from transportation to communication, and customized strategies add even more costs. Before moving into other countries, businesses need to make sure they can cover all these costs and still be able to offer competitive prices.
- **Staffing.** Depending on the form of business a company decides to pursue in international markets, staffing questions can be major considerations. Many companies find that a combination of U.S. and local personnel works best, mixing company experience with local knowledge and connections. In Latin American markets, U.S. companies such as Home Depot, Payless, and Marriott have been successful transferring Spanish-speaking employees, many of whom are immigrants from Latin America, back to the region to establish and manage facilities.[64]

Given the number and complexity of the decisions to be made, you can see why successful companies plan international expansion with great care.

CRITICAL THINKING CHECKPOINT

1. Why do some U.S. companies criticize the Foreign Corrupt Practices Act?
2. Why might a U.S. company hesitate to pursue foreign direct investment in a country with hostile political values or an unstable government?
3. Why wouldn't every U.S. company customize its products for every overseas market in which it wants to do business?

Terrorism's Impact on the Global Business Environment

LEARNING OBJECTIVE 8

Discuss terrorism's impact on globalization

The continuing threat of terrorist acts is a concern for business managers in nearly every industry. The attacks on September 11, 2001, specifically included a well-known symbol of global commerce, the World Trade Center in New York City, and were partly intended to wreak havoc on the economies of Western countries. However, the impact of terrorism

CHECKLIST: Apply These Ideas When You're the Boss

✓ Recognize that fewer and fewer businesses are immune from the dynamics of global trade these days; even small companies can find opportunities and threats all over the world

✓ Look for economies of scale—buying raw materials in greater quantity, manufacturing at higher volumes, or marketing and selling in quantity

✓ Pay attention to political developments that could affect your business; the battles over protectionism are never ending in some industries

✓ Carefully study the cultures in the markets in which you plan to do business; U.S. companies

have made some embarrassing, expensive mistakes by rushing into new markets without understanding local languages and cultures

✓ Pay particular attention to communication; it's a complex challenge in international business

✓ Take the time to explore all the forms of business you might be able to use; this decision can make or break you

✓ Consider every aspect of your operations, from product design through customer support, before you enter a new market

Summary of Learning Objectives

1 **Discuss why nations trade.** Nations trade to obtain raw materials and goods that are unavailable to them or too costly to produce and to find markets for their own output. International trade benefits nations by increasing a country's total output, offering lower prices and greater variety to its consumers, subjecting domestic oligopolies and monopolies to competition, and allowing companies to expand their markets and achieve production and distribution efficiencies.

2 **Explain why nations restrict international trade, and list four forms of trade restrictions.** Nations restrict international trade to boost local economies, to shield domestic industries from head-to-head competition with overseas rivals, to save specific jobs, to give weak or new industries a chance to grow strong, and to protect a nation's security. The four most commonly used forms of trade restrictions are tariffs (taxes, surcharges, or duties levied against imported goods), quotas (limitations on the amount of a particular good that can be imported), embargoes (the banning of imports and exports of certain goods), and sanctions (politically motivated embargoes).

3 **Highlight three protectionist tactics that nations use to give their domestic industries a competitive edge.** From time to time, countries give their domestic producers a competitive edge by imposing restrictive import standards, such as requiring special licenses or unusually high product standards, by subsidizing certain domestic producers so they can compete more favorably in the global marketplace, and by dumping or selling large quantities of a product at a lower price than it costs to produce the good or at a lower price than the good is sold for in its home market.

4 **Explain how trading blocs affect trade.** Trading blocs are regional groupings of countries within which trade barriers have been removed. These alliances ease trade among bloc members and strengthen barriers for nonmembers. Critics of trading blocs fear that as members become more protective of their regions, those not in the bloc could suffer. Proponents see them as a way to help smaller or younger nations compete with producers in more-developed nations. The four most powerful trading blocs today are the Association of Southeast Asian Nations (ASEAN), the Mercosur, the North American Free Trade Agreement (NAFTA), and the European Union (EU).

5 **Highlight the opportunities and challenges you'll encounter when conducting business in other countries.** Conducting business in other countries can provide such opportunities as increased sales, operational efficiencies, exposure to new technologies, and consumer choices. At the same time, it poses challenges such as the need to learn unique laws, customs, and ethical standards. Furthermore, it exposes companies to the risks of political and economic instabilities, volatile currencies, international trade relationships, and the threat of global terrorism.

6 **List five ways you can improve communication in an international business relationship.** To improve international communication, learn as much as you can about the culture and customs of the people you are working with; keep an open mind and avoid stereotyping; anticipate

misunderstandings and guard against them by clarifying your intent; adapt your style to match the style of others; and learn how to show respect in other cultures.

7 **Identify five forms of international business activity.** Importing and exporting, licensing, franchising, strategic alliances and joint ventures, and foreign direct investment are five of the most common forms of international business activity. Each provides a company with varying degrees of control and entails different levels of risk and financial commitment.

8 **Discuss terrorism's impact on globalization.** Terrorism could prompt companies to withdraw from the global marketplace and focus more on doing business within their national borders. But the likelihood of moving in that direction is remote. Most multinational organizations have too much at stake to move backward; they see globalization as the key to their future. Global terrorism, however, does pose new challenges to world trade. Tighter security, border crossing delays, cargo restrictions, higher transportation costs, and difficulties in hiring foreign talent are having an impact on the free flow of goods in the global marketplace. These obstacles are forcing some companies to rethink their inventory and manufacturing strategies.

Trek Bikes: What's Next?

Joyce Keehn and her colleagues at Trek wrestle with virtually every issue you read about in this chapter, from the basic economics of international business to the intricacies of consumer demand in dozens of different countries.

Even with a strong record of success, things never get simple when it comes to international business. For instance, in 2004 the company moved its European manufacturing facility from Ireland to Germany in an effort to consolidate facilities, 6 years after the Irish Development Agency had given it a start-up grant in exchange for a commitment to staying in Ireland for at least 10 years. The Irish government is seeking full repayment of the grant.

Trek's distribution strategy continues to evolve as it develops market share in various markets as well. After using a local distributor in France for 7 years to market its bikes to French retailers, for example, Trek hired a manager to handle this function internally. As the global market grows ever more complex, expect to see Trek apply the same innovative thinking to its business efforts that it applies to its highly regarded bikes.[72]

Critical Thinking Questions

1. Why would Trek opt for a manufacturing facility in Europe, when a key element of its brand image is "Made in the USA"?
2. In countries such as the Netherlands, bicycles are a more widely accepted part of daily transportation than in countries such as the United States (the Netherlands is crisscrossed with well-maintained bike paths, for instance). Should Trek market its products differently in such a country? Why or why not?
3. What factors should a company such as Trek consider before it would agree to license its product designs and brand name to a manufacturer in another country?

Learn More Online

Find out how Trek is faring in the global cycle market. Go to Chapter 3 of this text's website at www.prenhall.com/bovee, and click on the Trek hotlink to read the latest news releases about Trek's products, its continuing technical innovations, its involvement with world-class athletes such as Lance Armstrong. Compare the company's U.S. and UK websites to see how it adapts its marketing approach for other markets.

Key Terms

absolute advantage (99)	comparative advantage	dumping (104)
balance of payments (102)	theory (99)	economies of scale (99)
balance of trade (101)	devaluation (109)	embargo (103)

ethnocentrism (111)	free trade (102)	quotas (103)
euro (108)	importing (115)	stereotyping (111)
exchange rate (109)	joint venture (117)	strategic alliance (117)
exporting (115)	licensing (115)	tariffs (103)
foreign direct investment	multinational corporations	trade deficit (102)
(FDI) (117)	(MNCs) (117)	trade surplus (101)
fair trade (103)	protectionism (103)	trading blocs (106)

Test Your Knowledge

Questions for Review

1. How can a company use a licensing agreement to enter world markets?
2. What two fundamental product strategies do companies choose between when selling their products in the global marketplace?
3. What is the balance of trade, and how is it related to the balance of payments?
4. What is dumping, and how does the United States respond to this practice?
5. What is a floating exchange rate?

Questions for Analysis

6. Why would a company choose to work through intermediaries when selling products in a foreign country?
7. How do companies benefit from forming international joint ventures and strategic alliances?
8. What types of situations might cause the U.S. government to implement protectionist measures?
9. How do tariffs and quotas protect a country's own industries?
10. **Ethical Considerations.** Should the U.S. government more closely regulate the practice of giving trips and other incentives to foreign managers to win their business? Is this bribery?

Questions for Application

11. Suppose you own a small company that manufactures baseball equipment. You are aware that Russia is a large market, and you are considering exporting your products there. What steps should you take? Who might be able to give you assistance?
12. Your Brazilian restaurant caters to North American businesspeople and tourists, so much of the food you buy is imported from the United States. Lately, the value of the *real* (Brazil's currency) has been falling relative to the dollar. This change makes your food imports much more costly, and it negatively affects your profitability. You have three options: (a) Raise menu prices across the board. (b) Accept only U.S. dollars from customers. (c) Try to purchase more of your food items locally. Which would you choose? Why?
13. **Integrated.** Review the theory of supply and demand discussed in Chapter 1. Using this theory, explain how a country's currency is valued and why governments sometimes adjust the values of their currency.
14. **Integrated.** You just received notice that a large shipment of manufacturing supplies you have been waiting for has been held up in customs for two weeks. A local business associate tells you that you are expected to give customs agents some "incentive money" to see that everything clears easily. How will you handle this situation? Evaluate the ethical merits of your decision by answering the questions outlined in Exhibit 2.3.

Practice Your Knowledge

Handling Difficult Situations on the Job: English Only—Defending a Tough Policy

When Frances Torres read the memo announcing that employees should speak only English on the job, she was outraged. Torres, a lens inspector for Signet Amoralite, a lens-manufacturing firm in southern California, is fluent in both English and Spanish but feels that the English-only rules constitute discrimination. Now Torres and a group of her co-workers have brought their complaints to you, a manager in human resources.

More than half of Signet Amoralite's 900 employees are Asian, Filipino, or Hispanic. The company policy states that "speaking in another language that associates cannot fully understand can lead to misunderstandings, is impolite, and can even be unsafe." While the policy carries no punishment, it is considered by some critics to violate federal discrimination laws.

Your task: You know that you must defend the company's English-only policy to Torres and the others; you've been told by upper management that it will not be eliminated or altered. To help clarify your thinking and see things from the employees' perspective, imagine that you have been hired by a company in another country that uses a language different from your own. How would you feel if you were required to learn and use that language exclusively, even if some of your co-workers were able to speak and understand your native tongue? To defend Signet Amoralite's policy, what can you do or say or write that will help Torres and her co-workers accept it? Also, what do you think will be the

Skills

is. When doing business in the global marketplace, fic, literal meaning. Avoid using slang or idioms their individual components when translated liter- yptian executive that a certain product "doesn't cut l fail.

xamples of slang (in your own language) that would uring a business conversation with someone from ther words you might use to convey the same mes- same as the original slang or idiom. Compare your

raction of going global, but these savings are possible es from country to country. MTV has become one of ut to do so it creates localized versions that meet local zes love songs and promotes family values with a programming five times a day with calls to prayer in order to meet the expectations of the country's largely Muslim population. Italy's high-style MTV includes food shows. MTV in gadget-crazy Japan emphasizes the latest technological marvels.[74]

Many of these country- or region-specific channels do leverage selected content from the U.S. MTV operation, so MTV does get some advantages of scale. However, your boss has just given your team an interesting assignment in reverse: find international MTV programming that you think might succeed in the U.S. market.

With your team, visit the following websites and assess the programs shown on MTV in that country or region, then review the bios of the VJs (called "presenters" in Great Britain). These four sites are in English, but if someone on your team speaks another language, check out MTV International at **www.mtv.com/mtvinternational** and select the appropriate link to a country or regional website that's in a language other than English.

- India: **www.mtvindia.com**
- Great Britain: **www.mtv.co.uk**
- Australia: **www.mtv.com.au**
- Northern Europe: **www.mtve.com**

Answer the following questions as you review these sites:

1. Can you find any programs that are available in a particular country or region that aren't available on MTV in the United States?
2. From this collection of non-U.S. programs, which one would be most likely to succeed in the U.S. market? Why?
3. Which VJ from all the sites you've visited would be most likely to succeed in the U.S. market? Why?

Present your analysis to the class and explain why you think the program and the VJ you've identified will succeed in the United States.

Expand Your Knowledge

Discovering Career Opportunities

If global business interests you, consider working for a U.S. government agency that supports or regulates international trade. For example, here are the duties performed by an international trade specialist at the International Trade Administration of the U.S. Department of Commerce: "The incumbent will assist senior specialists in coordination and support of government trade programs and events; perform research and analysis of trade data and information on specific topics or issues within a larger project or assignment; and disseminate trade information and materials on government products/services to U.S. businesses and associations. Incumbent will attend meetings and engage in other activities for developmental purposes. As a condition of employment, applicants must be available for reassignment and relocation within the United States."[75]

1. On the basis of this description, what education and skills (personal and professional) would you need to succeed as an international trade specialist? Why? How does this job description fit your qualifications and interests?
2. Given their duties, where would you expect international trade specialists to be situated or transferred? Would you be willing to move to another city or state for this type of position?
3. What sources would you contact to locate trade-related jobs with government agencies such as the International Trade Administration?

Developing Your Research Skills

Companies involved in international trade have to watch the foreign exchange rates of the countries in which they do business. Use your research skills to locate and analyze information about the value of the Japanese yen relative to the U.S. dollar. As you complete this exercise, make a note of the sources and search strategies you used.

1. How many Japanese yen does one U.S. dollar buy right now? Find yesterday's foreign exchange rate for the yen in the *Wall Street Journal* or on the Internet. (Note: One Internet source for foreign exchange rates is www.xrates.com.)
2. Investigate the foreign exchange rate for the yen against the dollar over the past month. Is the dollar growing stronger (buying more yen) or growing weaker (buying fewer yen)?
3. If you were a U.S. exporter selling to Japan, how would a stronger dollar be likely to affect demand for your products? How would a weaker dollar be likely to affect demand?

Exploring the Best of the Web

URLs for all Internet exercises are provided at the website for this book, www.prenhall.com/bovee. When you log on to this text's Companion Website, select Chapter 3. Then select "Featured Websites," click on the name of the featured website, and review the website to complete these exercises.

Explore these chapter-related websites, review their content, and answer the following questions for each website you visit:

1. What is the purpose of this website?
2. What kinds of information does this website contain? Please be specific.
3. How is the information provided at this website useful for businesspeople? Consumers?
4. How did you expand your knowledge of conducting business in the global environment by reviewing the material at this website? What new things did you learn about this topic?

Navigating Global Business Differences
In today's global marketplace, knowing as much as possible about your international customers' business practices and customs could give you a strategic advantage. To help you successfully conduct business around the globe, navigate the resources at the U.S. Government Export Portal. Start at www.export.gov, then click on "Market Research," then "Country Information—Quick Reference (TIC)." Click anywhere on the world map to learn more about each country. www.export.gov

Going Global
Have you ever thought about getting into the world of exporting? Where would you go for information and help? Many small and large companies have gotten valuable export assistance from online material such as the *Basic Guide to Exporting*, offered by the U.S. Department of Commerce. Visit www.export.gov, click on "The Export Basics," then click on "Basic Guide to Exporting" for a wealth

of information about export procedures; foreign markets, industries, companies, and products; export financing; unfair trade practices; trade statistics; and more. www.export.gov

Banking on the World Bank

The World Bank plays an important role in today's fast-changing, closely meshed global economy. Do you know what this organization of five closely associated institutions does? Do you know who runs the bank, where the bank gets its money, and where the money goes? Learn how this organization's programs and financial assistance help poorer nations as well as affluent ones. Log on to the World Bank website and find out why global development is everyone's challenge. www.worldbank.org

Learning Interactively

Companion Website

Visit the Companion Website at www.prenhall.com/bovee. For Chapter 3, take advantage of the interactive "Learning Modules" to test your chapter knowledge. Get instant feedback on whether you need additional studying. Complete the exercises as specified by your instructor.

A Case for Critical Thinking

Doing Everybody's Wash—Whirlpool's Global Lesson

The small city of Benton Harbor, Michigan, might seem an unlikely center of a global industry, but that's where you'll find the world headquarters of Whirlpool, the $12 billion home appliance giant. In the mid-1980s, CEO David Whitwam launched Whirlpool on a multiyear expansion plan that took the company from its Michigan roots to every corner of the world.

THE RIGHT WAY TO GO GLOBAL

Determined to convert Whirlpool from a U.S. company to a major global player, Whitwam started by purchasing Philips's European appliance business in 1989. The CEO's first challenge was to integrate and coordinate the many European operations with the U.S. operation. Some companies accomplish this task by imposing the parent's systems on acquired companies, but Whitwam started down a more ambitious path. He created cross-cultural teams with members from the European and North American operations, and together they designed a program to ensure quality and productivity throughout Whirlpool's worldwide operation. In the eyes of other corporate leaders, Whirlpool was doing everything right. The company was even featured in a *Harvard Business Review* article titled "The Right Way to Go Global."

SPINNING OUT OF CONTROL

Whitwam soon discovered, however, that developing global strategies was easier than executing them. Whirlpool had not counted on the difficulty in marketing appliances—a process that is consistent in local markets all across the United States—to the fragmented cultures of Europe, Asia, and Latin America. For instance, clothes washers sold in colder, northern European countries such as Denmark must spin-dry clothes much better than washers in southern Italy, where consumers often line-dry clothes in warmer weather. And consumers in India and southern China prefer small refrigerators because they must fit in tight kitchens.

Despite these challenges, Whitwam was convinced that he could remake Whirlpool into a truly global company. But Whirlpool's timing couldn't have been worse. Just as the company was planting its feet in international markets, economic turmoil hit Asia and Europe. Wildly fluctuating foreign exchange rates wreaked havoc in Asia, where Whirlpool had participated in several joint ventures. Fortunately, less than 5 percent of Whirlpool's sales came from Asia at the time, so the company was not seriously hurt. Still, ongoing global economic woes contributed to Whirlpool's multimillion dollar losses overseas.

REARRANGING THE GLOBAL LOAD

The global economic crisis forced Whitwam to fine-tune his expansion plans. Whirlpool dropped one joint venture in China (costing the company $350 million) and rearranged others as intense competition and weak economic conditions drove appliance prices down and sapped profits. "The thing we misjudged was how rapidly Chinese manufacturers could improve their quality," notes Whitwam.

In Brazil, where Whirlpool had long been profitable, a currency crisis coupled with inflation worries slowed appliance sales to a trickle. Still, Whitwam remained committed to the market. Anticipating future growth opportunities in this emerging market, Whirlpool invested hundreds of millions of dollars to modernize operations, cut costs, and solidify its position as the country's market leader in refrigerators, room air conditioners, and washers.

David Whitwam's global strategy, however, was not widely copied by rivals. As Whirlpool continued to expand in Europe, Latin America, and Asia, the company's major competitor, Maytag, was selling its European and Australian businesses to refocus on the lucrative North American market. Nevertheless, Whitwam was willing to ride out the storm, even as international economic troubles dragged on.

To succeed on a global scale in markets as different as the United States, Brazil, India, and Germany, Whitwam knew that Whirlpool would need to take advantage of its worldwide capabilities without falling into the trap of enforcing a one-size-fits-all approach. Accordingly, functions such as procuring raw materials, developing new technologies, and designing generic product "platforms" are conducted with a more global reach, then these platforms are customized for the unique demands of various local markets. Appliances that may look quite different from the outside can share as many as 70 percent of the same parts inside. The result is global efficiency with local effectiveness.

NO REST FOR THE SUCCESSFUL

By carefully adapting strategies to the complex variations of global business, Whitwam transformed Whirlpool from an inward-looking U.S. company into the world's leading manufacturer of major home appliances. In 2004, he turned the reins over to Jeff Fettig, a seasoned executive who had been instrumental in Whirlpool's successes in Europe and Asia. Building on the global foundation—Whirlpool now designs and manufactures at nearly 50 locations around the world and claims customers in more than 170 countries—Fettig leads the company into a future that will be every bit as challenging as the past.

High up on his list of enduring challenges is the growing international power of China's industrial sector. From computers to cars to just about every product Whirlpool makes, Chinese manufacturers are no longer content to compete at the low end of the market or assemble goods for other companies. They want to be global brands themselves, and Fettig and company will no doubt continue to run into them in appliance stores the world over.

While he's busy competing with other manufacturers, Fettig also needs to keep Whirlpool's costs under control—a difficult task in today's volatile markets. Whirlpool can control some of this by improving internal efficiencies wherever possible, but it can't control international markets for such vital material as steel and petroleum. For instance, when UK steel giant Mittal Steel hiked its prices, Whirlpool was forced to raise its prices by as much as 10 precent to cover the increase. As Fettig explained, "I don't think any company can overcome that magnitude of raw-material price increases with productivity." Historically high oil prices also affect transportation costs and the cost of plastic, nearly all of which is currently derived from petroleum. Whirlpool has an enviable international foundation, but Fettig will need all the smart thinking that took Whirlpool from Benton Harbor to the world stage.[76]

Critical Thinking Questions

1. What did Whirlpool find to be the advantages and disadvantages of doing business around the world?
2. How did global expansion affect Whirlpool's products?
3. Should Whirlpool be concerned about a currency devaluation in a country where it sells few appliances?
4. Find out how Whirlpool is faring with its global strategy. Go to Chapter 3 of this book's website at **www.prenhall.com/bovee**, and click on the Whirlpool hotlink to read more about Whirlpool's financial performance, international operations, and plans for expansion. How are Whirlpool's sales doing outside the United States? Where is the company strongest? Where is it struggling? What changes, if any, is the company making to its global strategy?

Video Case

Entering the Global Marketplace: Lands' End and Yahoo!

Learning Objectives

The purpose of this video is to help you:

1. Understand the different reasons that businesses undertake international expansion.
2. Identify the financial and marketing issues of selling goods and services internationally.
3. Recognize the influence of culture on business decisions in an international firm.

Synopsis

Yahoo! is an Internet company headquartered in Santa Clara, California, with offices around the world. The company's service offerings have expanded from a search engine and web directory to a wide array of content and e-commerce offerings. Yahoo! now counts more than 200 million users worldwide. Lands' End began in 1963 by selling sailing equipment by catalog. Today the firm (which is now owned by retailing giant Sears, which is in turn owned by Kmart) is one of the largest apparel brands in the United States, with a variety of catalogs and a high-volume e-commerce site. This video segment shows how these two very different companies approached the same goal: expansion into international business. You will see how each copes with cultural, financial, monetary, and marketing differences as well as differences in language and method of payment. See whether you can identify those areas in which each firm chose to adapt to the needs and expectations of the international marketplace, and where it maintained its original product or policy.

Discussion Questions

1. *For analysis:* Compare the different reasons why Lands' End and Yahoo! decided to expand internationally.
2. *For analysis:* How did Lands' End succeed in establishing itself in the United Kingdom and Japan?
3. *For application:* In addition to hiring local employees in countries such as France and China, how could Yahoo! help educate U.S. employees about the nuances of doing business in these countries?
4. *For application:* How should Lands' End alter its online marketing efforts in countries that have different expectations of personal modesty?
5. *For debate:* Both Yahoo! and Lands' End expect their employees to behave in an ethical manner in all business dealings. However, experienced managers recognize that definitions of ethical behavior can vary from country to country? Should both companies demand a consistent ethical code in all cases across all regions of the world? Why or why not?

Online Exploration

Visit Yahoo!'s website (www.yahoo.com) and explore some of the features and functions that appeal to you. Then select one of the international sites listed at the bottom of the Yahoo! homepage and compare it to the U.S. site. Identify the changes that have been made to suit the particular country's language and customs, and observe what elements of the site have *not* been changed. What do you think is the motivation behind the design and content choices Yahoo! made in the overseas site? Do you think it is successful in its market?

Business at the Speed of Light: Information Technology and E-Commerce

CHAPTER 4

LEARNING OBJECTIVES

After studying this chapter, you will be able to

1. Differentiate data, information, and insight

2. Explain how information quality is measured

3. Identify four key areas where businesses use information

4. Discuss five important ways the Internet is changing business

5. Explain the differences between search engines, web directories, and research databases

6. Differentiate between operational systems and professional and managerial systems

7. Identify seven current challenges that managers face with respect to information technology

www.prenhall.com/bovee

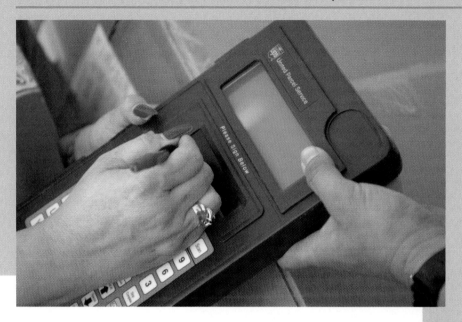

INSIDE BUSINESS TODAY

Technology Delivers New Business Opportunities for UPS

From the outside, United Parcel Service (UPS) may look like a delivery company that moves packages from point A to point B. But on the inside, UPS is really an information technology company. That may seem like an odd way to describe a company with nearly 100,000 vehicles and enough airplanes to qualify as the world's 11th-largest airline, but information technology is one of UPS's most important strategic assets. UPS uses technology to improve its own business and to help other companies with everything from supply chain management to product repair.

Technology has always played a key role at UPS, even back in 1907, when leading-edge technology meant a telegraph machine and a sturdy bicycle. Nineteen-year-old founder Jim Casey and his crew started out delivering handwritten messages and telegrams around Seattle. As another new technology—the telephone—caught on and took business away from the telegraph, Casey shifted the company from messages to packages, offering home delivery services for local retail stores. Sure enough, the automobile caught on next and people started taking their purchases home themselves, so Casey shifted again, this time to the general package-delivery model that is still the core of the company's business.

For a long time, however, UPS saw investments in new technology as little more than a monitoring system to make sure the birthday sweater from Grandma arrived on time. When it finally caught on to the real power of information, UPS began using technology to explore the millions of transactions it made every day to look for ways to make its routes more efficient, optimize truck sizes, and improve delivery time. Company drivers ditched their clipboards and paper in favor of wireless handheld computers, known as the Delivery Information Acquisition Device (DIAD). These mobile devices capture electronic signatures and delivery details and feed this information into the company's data centers in New Jersey and Georgia, which house 14 mainframe computers and 140 terabytes of company and customer data (roughly seven times the amount of information stored in the Library of Congress's book collection). Initially, this system allowed UPS managers to pinpoint the whereabouts of a package and to deliver that information to customers over the telephone. But this was just the first step in a bigger plan.

In 1995, UPS began offering package tracking on its website. "We were so efficient at getting packages through on time and on schedule, we could never really understand why people wanted tracking or other information about packages," says UPS vice chairman Mike Eskey. But once UPS started turning that information over to customers, it learned that access to data was more than a convenience; it was a phenomenon. On an average day, customers track 10 million packages via the UPS website, and corporate customers can even integrate some of UPS's own web software into their own websites to simplify importing, exporting, and e-commerce.

After assessing how important information had become to its own operations, UPS realized it could gain a competitive edge by giving other corporations access to similar kinds of information about their own companies. The company formed a subsidiary, UPS Logistics, to sell distribution and information management and warehousing expertise to other companies. Today Ford Motor Company engages UPS Logistics to manage the transportation and distribution of 4.5 million vehicles a year—from 21 manufacturing sites, through five railroad yards, to 55 destination railroads, to 6,000 dealers in North America. Ford now saves $125 million a year through faster deliveries while increasing dealer and customer satisfaction. Samsung and Nike are among the other well-known companies that have turned to UPS for warehousing and distribution expertise. And UPS offers to help when products go in reverse, too, managing returns and even product repairs for the likes of Toshiba and Lexmark.

As UPS celebrates its one hundredth birthday with 370,000 employees and nearly $40 billion in revenue, technology continues to drive the company in new directions. Those humble brown trucks rumbling through your neighborhood don't look much fancier than Jim Casey's original bicycle, but they're now guided by one of the most sophisticated information systems on the planet.[1]

GET READY

UPS is a clear example of how a company that may seem far removed from the world of electronic business can use the Internet to improve operations and build competitive advantages. If you were in charge of information technology at UPS, how would you handle the avalanche of data the company generates every single day? How would you convert all that raw data into useful strategic information? How would you address the numerous ethical and legal issues that new technologies create? ▪

Chapter Overview

LEARNING OBJECTIVE 1

Differentiate data, information, and insight

data
Facts, numbers, statistics, and other individual bits and pieces that by themselves don't necessarily constitute useful information

information
Useful knowledge, often extracted from data

insight
A deep level of understanding about a particular subject or situation

Information represents one of the most intriguing challenges you'll face as a manager. Many companies now find themselves drowning in an ocean of data—but struggling to find the handful of crucial bits that can mean the difference between success and failure. This chapter explains how companies use information and how the Internet continues to change contemporary business. The chapter then takes you into the various types of information systems and the hardware, software, and networking components in those systems. The chapter concludes with a look at some of the most important technology-related issues you'll need to address as a manager or an entrepreneur.

From Data to Information to Insight

The first step in turning information into a competitive advantage is understanding the difference between **data** (recorded facts and statistics), **information** (useful knowledge, often extracted from data), and **insight** (a deep level of understanding about a particular situation). The transformation from data to insight requires a combination of technology, information-management strategies, creative thinking, and business experience—and

Exhibit 4.1
From Data to Information to Insight

Businesses generate massive amounts of data, but a key challenge is transforming all those individual data points into useful information, then applying creative thinking (sometimes with the additional help of computers) to extract deeper insights from the information.

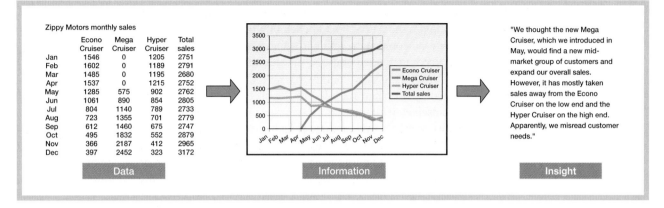

Zippy Motors monthly sales

	Econo Cruiser	Mega Cruiser	Hyper Cruiser	Total sales
Jan	1546	0	1205	2751
Feb	1602	0	1189	2791
Mar	1485	0	1195	2680
Apr	1537	0	1215	2752
May	1285	575	902	2762
Jun	1061	890	854	2805
Jul	804	1140	789	2733
Aug	723	1355	701	2779
Sep	612	1460	675	2747
Oct	495	1832	552	2879
Nov	366	2187	412	2965
Dec	397	2452	323	3172

Data

Information

"We thought the new Mega Cruiser, which we introduced in May, would find a new mid-market group of customers and expand our overall sales. However, it has mostly taken sales away from the Econo Cruiser on the low end and the Hyper Cruiser on the high end. Apparently, we misread customer needs."

Insight

companies that excel at this transformation have a huge advantage over their competitors. In fact, entire industries can be created when a single person looks at the same data and information everyone else is looking at but sees things in a new way, yielding insights that no one has ever had before (see Exhibit 4.1).

Businesses collect data from a wide array of sources, from checkout scanners and website clicks to telephone calls, research projects, and electronic sensors. As you can imagine from the diagram in Exhibit 4.2, a single customer order can generate hundreds of data points, from a credit card number to production statistics to accounting totals that end up on

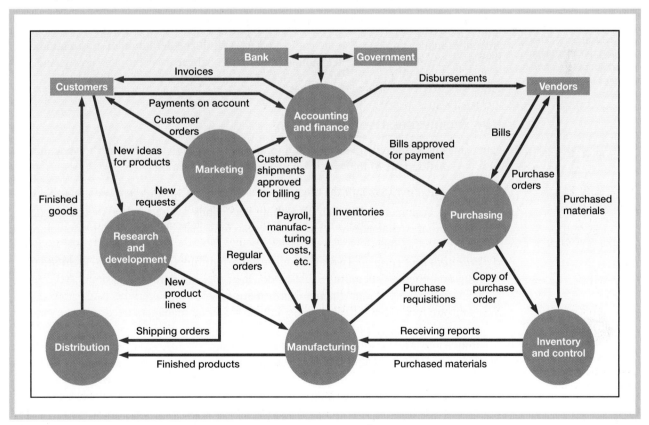

Exhibit 4.2
Information Flow Inside a Typical Manufacturing Company

From daily operations to long-term decision making, the flow of data and information around the organization is vital to every company's success.

a tax form. Even a small business can quickly amass thousand or millions of individual data points; large companies such as UPS generate billions and even trillions of data points. Visa now processes a billion credit card transactions every single day.[2]

To keep all these data points under control and to extract useful information from them, companies rely on **databases**, computerized files that collect, sort, and cross-reference data. In addition to the daily chores of sending out bills, ordering new parts, and everything else that keeps the company running, databases can also be used for **data mining**, a powerful computerized analysis technique that identifies previously unknown relations among individual data points.[3]

Unfortunately, just like they found themselves with too much data, many companies now find themselves with too many databases—perhaps one in marketing, one in manufacturing, one in accounting, others in regional sales offices, and so on. Taikang Life, an insurance company based in China, created several hundred separate databases in the span of just four years.[4] To coordinate multiple databases, companies have two basic choices. The first is to create a *virtual database*, a smart program that knows how to dig information out of all those separate databases.[5] The second is to create a *data warehouse*, which merges all the current and historical data from around the organization. These warehouses can grow to such massive scale that they require specialized computers, such as the behemoth from Netezza that contains 650 disk drives and costs $10 million.[6] Managers can also create smaller *data marts* from these warehouses, extracting subsets of information for specific purposes, such as marketing and sales.[7]

Most large organizations employ a top-level manager, often called a **chief information officer (CIO)**, whose job is to understand the company's information needs and to create systems and procedures to deliver that information to the right people at the right time. In smaller companies, the role of the CIO might be filled by a data services manager, information systems manager, or someone with a similar title. These managers are expected to deliver quality information, which can be defined as *relevant* (the information delivered to each person relates directly to his or her needs), *accurate* (it's both current and free from errors), *timely* (delivered in time to make a difference), and *cost effective* (costs a reasonable amount of money compared to the value it offers). While the definition of information quality may be easy to grasp, the technology required to deliver it is complex, costly, and constantly evolving, making the CIO's job one of the most challenging in business today.

How Businesses Use Information

Companies invest heavily in information for the simple reason that they can't live without it. Here's a small sample of the ways managers rely on information:

- **Research and development.** In a sense, the cycle of information usage starts with understanding customer needs, then developing new goods and services to meet those needs. Information is vital at every step, from researching markets to analyzing competitors to testing new products.
- **Planning and control.** Two of the most important functions of management are planning and control—deciding what to do, then making sure it gets done. Accounting managers need accurate financial information, sales managers need to know if their teams are meeting their sales goals, human resource managers need to make sure the company has enough of the right kind of employees, and so on. Some industries have unique needs that require specialized information systems. For example, both UPS and archrival FedEx employ their own weather forecasters to get the most accurate and most timely weather information possible. FedEx says its 14 forecasters give it a significant competitive advantage, particularly in such challenging areas as offering overnight service to Asia.[8]
- **Marketing and sales.** Thanks to technology, marketing and sales have evolved from "gut feel" activities to scientific, information-driven functions. The convenience store chain 7-Eleven recently pulled itself up from bankruptcy to solid financial health,

---

databases
Computerized files that collect, sort, and cross-reference data

data mining
A method of extracting previously unknown relationships among individual data points in a database

LEARNING OBJECTIVE 2

Explain how information quality is measured

chief information officer (CIO)
A high-level executive responsible for understanding the company's information needs and creating systems and procedures to deliver that information to the right people at the right time

LEARNING OBJECTIVE 3

Identify four key areas where businesses use information

Vital business information comes in many forms; here forecasters at FedEx's Memphis control center monitor the weather around the globe to ensure the safe and timely arrival of hundreds of flights every day.

thanks in large part to one of the most sophisticated information systems in the industry. For instance, store managers can instantly tap into information on hot sales trends around the country and change the merchandise offerings in their stores overnight.[9]

- *Communication and collaboration.* Throughout the organization, employees, managers, and teams of every size and shape rely on information to communicate and collaborate. In fact, as you'll see in the following section, information technology is changing the very definition of what an organization means, thanks to the Internet's ability to connect people from every corner of the globe. For instance, InnoCentive, www.innocentive.com, links scientists and companies around the world. Companies (called "seekers") post problems they need to solve and the financial rewards they're offering, and scientists (called "solvers") can post solutions. Seekers then select the best solution and compensate the solver accordingly.[10]

How the Internet Is Changing Business

No single technology in recent decades has reshaped the business world as much as the Internet has—and continues to do. The Internet has helped many companies reach wider markets but has also exposed them to more competitors. It has created new business capabilities, such as online meetings and automated shopping, but has also raised the constant threat of viruses, hacking, and other malicious technology. It has even helped shift the balance of commercial power from sellers to buyers by giving buyers more information and more choices than they ever had before.

If you grew up with the Internet, these may not seem like changes at all, since for you that's the way it's always been done, from shopping online to e-mailing your homework to your instructor. In fact, the Internet might be such a central element in your school and personal lives that a network outage can cause a mild panic. In contrast, if you worked in the business world before the mid-1990s, you probably have a clear sense how different things are today from the way they were just a few years ago.

As you move into (or back into) the business world, you'll find the Internet being put to use all over the place, in virtually every part of many companies. As a business professional, manager, or entrepreneur, you can expect to use the Internet in a variety of beneficial ways: to accelerate commerce, erase borders, control costs, enhance communication and collaboration, and simplify research.

LEARNING OBJECTIVE 4

Discuss five important ways the Internet is changing business

Accelerating Commerce　Amazon.com and eBay are well-known symbols of the retailing transformation brought about by the Internet. Thousands of companies, from solo entrepreneurs working in their sweatpants to multinational corporations, are now engaged in this electronic commerce, or **e-commerce**. E-commerce offers tremendous advantages for both buyers and sellers. Buyers can shop from the comfort of their homes or offices, quickly gather comparative information about products, and learn from other customers through online product reviews. Benefits to sellers include the ability to reach thousands or millions of potential customers without the enormous expenses involved in building physical retailing outlets and the opportunity to customize messages for narrow groups of customers or even individual shoppers.

Companies such as Amazon and eBay were formed specifically to take advantage of the Internet, and their very youth gave them a key advantage in one important sense: They didn't need to undo established processes, tear out existing technology, or change old habits. On the other hand, pre-Internet companies such as Sears, Wal-Mart, and Gap often had more experience in the nuts and bolts of business—customer service, warehousing, transportation, and so on—giving them that advantage over the upstarts. In just the past few years, both camps have learned from each other, and online retailing from both old companies and new has finally begun to mature into a stable, profitable business with endless variety to offer both consumers and business customers.[11]

E-commerce comes in four basic flavors:

- **Business-to-consumer e-commerce**. Referred to as *B2C*, *electronic retailing*, or *e-tailing*, this form of e-commerce involves interactions and transactions between companies and consumers.
- **Business-to-business e-commerce**. Known as *B2B*, this form of e-commerce involves a company and its suppliers, distributors, manufacturers, retailers, and other corporate customers, but not individual consumers. Virtually every kind of business product imaginable is sold online today, from semiconductors to advertising services.
- **Consumer-to-consumer e-commerce**. Often called *C2C*, this category of e-commerce involves consumers who sell products directly to each other using the Internet as the intermediary. Online auctions are the most dominant form of C2C.
- **Mobile commerce (m-commerce)**. This emerging category of e-commerce uses wireless Internet access and wireless handheld devices, such as cell phones and **personal digital assistants (PDAs)**, to transact business. Purchasing ring tones for your cell phone is a good example of mobile commerce, but the possibilities range from restaurant recommendations to electronic coupons for stores you happen to be walking past. Currently, m-commerce is more widely available in Europe and Asia than in the United States, where the companies that control wireless services and those that offer mobile content have been slow to coordinate their efforts.[12]

Product sales aren't the only big business online. Online advertising is now a multibillion-dollar business as well. In fact, online advertising is expected to surpass magazine advertising by 2008, thanks to the web's ability to precisely target customers and the enormous popularity of search-engine advertising (those "sponsored links" that appear when you do a search on Google and similar sites).[13] Along the way, this growth in web-based promotion is reshaping the advertising industry as well, with new Internet specialists such as Aquantive and ValueClick sharing the stage with classic "Madison Avenue" ad agencies.[14]

Controlling Costs　Generating revenue through e-commerce is only one side of the Internet's financial story. Companies are also finding creative ways to reduce costs through online technologies. Sometimes the savings are dramatic, as when companies can forgo entire facilities or accomplish far more with fewer people. In other cases, the savings might not sound like much but can add up quickly. For instance, online training can save thousands of dollars every time employees need updated information or skills. Documentation is another area that can yield considerable savings. Boeing saves millions of dollars a year by

e-commerce
Short for electronic commerce, which refers to marketing and selling products over the Internet

business-to-consumer e-commerce
E-commerce between a company and consumers; often referred to as B2C

business-to-business e-commerce
E-commerce between companies; often referred to as B2B

consumer-to-consumer e-commerce
E-commerce between consumers; often referred to as C2C

mobile commerce (m-commerce)
E-commerce that uses wireless Internet access and wireless handheld devices

personal digital assistants (PDAs)
Handheld computers; some smartphones now have PDA capabilities as well

giving its airline customers online access to technical manuals, parts lists, and other maintenance documents, rather than printing, shipping, and constantly updating paper documents.[15] Speaking of airlines, major carriers are currently trying to coax travel agents to move from electronic reservation systems that predate the Internet to web-based systems that can reduce the processing cost of booking a flight from $10 to $1. It's only a $9 savings—until you multiply it by millions of passenger flights every year.[16]

Erasing Borders One of the Internet's most profound changes has been its ability to erase borders—borders between departments, between companies, and even between countries. Thanks to e-mail, instant messaging, and a variety of *virtual meeting* technologies that let groups conduct meetings online, people across town or across the country can work together more efficiently. Not only does this ability offer more flexibility in employment, since employees have more freedom to live where they want to live and companies can hire people who may not want to move, but it helps companies address the costs, security concerns, and productivity losses that are a part of air travel these days. Instead of hopping on a plane and spending a couple of days and a few thousand dollars for a meeting, you can now hop on the Internet and have that meeting for a fraction of the cost and time commitment. For instance, more than 9,000 companies now conduct long-distance meetings using WebEx (www.webex.com), the leading provider of online meeting services. Agilent Technologies, a large manufacturer of scientific and engineering equipment, has more than 4,000 online meetings a month.[17] Online meetings are also a common part of **telecommuting**, working at home while staying in touch with the office via information technology.

telecommuting
Working at home while staying connected to the office via electronic networking

Enhancing Communication and Collaboration Virtual meetings are a great example of how the Internet helps businesspeople connect in ways never before possible. You may already be familiar with some of the many other Internet tools that businesses use to communicate and collaborate:

- **E-mail and instant messaging.** If you live by e-mail and **instant messaging (IM)**, which provides real-time text conversations between computers, you already know how effective these two tools can be. At computer giant IBM, up to 5 million instant messages fly around the company every day.[18] IM is also used extensively in e-commerce and online customer support as a cost-effective way to communicate with multiple customers at once.[19]

- **Mail server lists and newsgroups.** *Mail server lists* (commonly but improperly called by the trademarked name *listserv*), are discussion groups to which you subscribe by sending a message to the list's e-mail address. In contrast, *newsgroups* consist of posted messages on a particular subject and the responses to them. Both mail server lists and newsgroups are frequently used by people in professional specialties who need to stay up to date with industry developments or get advice from peers.

- **Intranets and extranets.** Companies use a variety of specialized websites to help groups of employees and business partners stay in touch. **Intranets**, websites accessible by employees only, carry a wide range of information, from production-line updates to health insurance sign-up forms. **Extranets** are a similar concept but allow trusted outside business partners to log on as well as employees. Both intranets and extranets are sometimes called *portals*, particularly when they amass information from a variety of sources. General Motors built a centralized portal for its 275,000 employees after "a couple of hundred different, independent" intranets and regular websites popped up throughout the huge company (communication had become so fragmented that employees sometimes simply waited to hear major company announcements on the evening news).[20] The latest twist on intranets and extranets is *darknets*, small, invitation-only networks that are typically more secure than other networks. Although they are popular with people sharing pirated music files, darknets have legitimate business uses as well, primarily to exchange highly confidential information.[21]

instant messaging (IM)
Real-time text conversations between computers; IM is similar in concept to text messaging on cell phones, but it's a more powerful and more flexible technology

intranets
Websites that are accessible by employees only

extranets
Websites that are similar to intranets but also allow access by trusted outside business partners

INNOVATING FOR BUSINESS SUCCESS

LIVEPERSON PUTS A PULSE ON THE WEB

You're shopping online, but you'd like some more information. Does that sweater come in red? Will those tires fit your motocross bike? Before you click and buy, sometimes you need the help of a real, live person. That's why Robert LoCascio developed LivePerson.com, a New York software company that puts the human touch in online shopping.

LoCascio knows that many retail websites are ineffective. They confuse and frustrate shoppers and force them to sift through page after page of detail to find the information they need. As a result, many consumers give up and abandon their electronic shopping carts. But Lo Cascio's LivePerson helps companies doing business on the Internet maximize their online shopping experience. Websites with LivePerson services invite online shoppers to chat with a real, live person. Shoppers simply click on the LivePerson icon, and a pop-up window appears on the screen. Type in your name, and you're instantly greeted by a customer service rep who asks, "What can I do for you?" Because pre-scripted responses to common questions are prepared in advance, customer service reps can chat with four or five customers at the same time.

The reps can also help customers with their unique product questions and selections. For instance, LivePerson reps can suggest alternatives to customers by clicking on different webpages to show similar products. They can also supply customers with valuable information about their past purchases and previous visits to the website. As LoCascio explains, the reps "embrace the customer and help them through the process of shopping."

All in all, LoCascio's LivePerson helps e-commerce companies compete by providing a high level of customer service. "If you walk into a store, and there's no person there to help you, the experience is pretty bad," says LoCascio. "The same thing is true online."

Questions for Critical Thinking

1. How can a service such as LivePerson help Internet retailers gain a competitive advantage?
2. A business is a profit-seeking activity that provides goods and services that satisfy customer needs. What needs does LivePerson try to satisfy?

---

blogs
Web-based logs or journals

- **Virtual workspaces.** *Shared workspaces* are "virtual offices" that give everyone on a team access to the same set of resources and information: databases, calendars, project plans, IM and e-mail exchanges, shared reference materials, and team-created documents. These workspaces enable geographically dispersed team members to access shared files anytime, anywhere. For instance, Alaska Indoor Sports Distribution turned to Groove Workspace when staffers in the company's Anchorage and Ketchikan offices were getting buried in faxes—and losing orders in the process.[22]

- **Blogs.** **Blogs** are web-based logs or journals first used by web enthusiasts but now embraced as a communication tool by many companies. Managers use blogs to communicate with employees and employees use them to share ideas. Even some top executives, such as Sun Microsystems president Jonathan Schwartz, write blogs to share information and viewpoints. Seattle's Findory, itself a maker of blogging software, uses a blog to connect with potential employees. Increasingly, companies also use blogs to communicate with customers; the personal feel of a blog can be a welcome alternative to the "corporate" feel of typical business communication. And naturally, anything that attracts an audience attracts advertisers, which are starting to place ads on popular blogs. *Video blogs (vlogs or vblogs)* and *mobile blogs (moblogs)* are the latest developments in this exciting new medium.[23]

- **Wikis.** In the same way that blogs allow an individual to communicate online, a *wiki* allows teams to write collaboratively online ("wiki" is Hawaiian for "quick"). In fact, a wiki effort has created an entire encyclopedia online, the Wikipedia (www.wikipedia.com). Wiki technology can also be used to create simple web-based programs and customize commercial software.[24]

- ***Internet telephone service.*** **Internet telephone service** (also known as *Internet telephony* or by the technical term *VoIP*) converts voice to digital data for transmission across the Internet. Although still in its infancy, Internet phone service is catching on with customers attracted to its flexible features and lower costs (and with services such as Skype, PC-to-PC phone calls are even free). The disadvantages include the requirement of a broadband Internet connection, occasional problems with sound quality, and a vulnerability to power outages (which aren't a problem with regular phone service).[25]

Internet telephone service
Telephone service that converts voice to digital data for transmission across the Internet; also known as Internet telephony or VoIP

CRITICAL THINKING CHECKPOINT

1. Would individual quality control measurements on a production line be considered data or information? Why?
2. Saving on printing costs is a key benefit of the Internet, which implies a loss of business for printing companies; how might printers themselves also take advantage of the Internet?
3. How might shared online workspaces help reduce confusion and communication problems?

Simplifying Research In much the same way that you now use the Internet to research assignments, you'll use the Internet for business research as well—studying competitors, learning about new products, uncovering business opportunities, and doing much more. Of course, you'll need to exercise the same degree of caution; experienced business researchers know that the Internet can be a tremendous source of both data and information—and it can waste hours and hours of precious time and deliver inaccurate or biased information, exaggerated claims, and unsubstantiated rumors. Always keep in mind that much of the information available online hasn't been verified by the editorial boards and fact checkers commonly used in traditional publishing.

Online information can be found in unexpected places. For instance, Amazon.com's "Search inside the book" capability lets you look within the content of published books (the words highlighted in this example were the keywords in the search). This feature can help you quickly identify books that will make good sources for your business research.

If possible, try to learn something about an unfamiliar topic from a trusted source (such as an industry journal or an experienced colleague) before you start searching online. You'll be better able to detect skewed or erroneous information, and you can be more selective about which websites and documents to use. One good place to start on the web is the Internet Public Library at www.ipl.org. Modeled after a real library, this site provides you with a carefully selected collection of links to high-quality business resources that offer such information as company profiles, trade data, business news, corporate tax and legal advice, small-business information, prepared forms and documents, biographies of executives, financial reports, job postings, online publications, and so on.

LEARNING OBJECTIVE 5

Explain the differences between search engines, web directories, and research databases

search engines
Web-based research tools that identify individual webpages containing specific words or phrases

web directories
Categorized lists of suggested websites on specific topics

metacrawlers
Online tools that format search requests for the specific requirements of multiple search engines

Understanding Search Engines, Web Directories, and Research Databases. Search engines, web directories, and databases all provide access to online source material (or in some cases to information on a CD-ROM), but each operates in a unique way and therefore has distinct advantages and disadvantages for business researchers. You may find yourself using all three resources to get the best perspective on business questions.

Search engines identify individual webpages that contain a specific word or phrase you've asked for. Search engines have the advantage of scanning millions or billions of individual pages, and the best engines use powerful ranking algorithms to present the pages that are probably the most relevant to your search request. However, search engines have three disadvantages that could affect the quality of your research. First, the process they use to find and present lists of webpages is computerized, with no human editors involved to evaluate the quality of the content you find on these pages. Second, search engines can't reach the content held in limited-access collections, such as the back issues of many newspapers, magazines, and professional journals. Third, various search engines use different techniques to find, classify, and present pages, so you might be able to find certain pages through one engine but not through another.

The good news is that you can get around all three shortcomings when conducting research—although you have to pay for access in some cases. **Web directories** address the first major shortcoming of search engines by using human editors to categorize and evaluate websites. Directories such as those offered by Yahoo! About, and the Open Directory at http://dmoz.org present lists of websites chosen by a team of editors. For instance, the Open Directory lists more than 200,000 business-related websites by category, from individual companies to industry associations, all of which have been evaluated and selected by a team of volunteer editors.[26] Several directories (such as www.invisible-web.net and www.completeplanet.com) specialize in the *invisible web*, those sites that contain information not reachable by search engines.

Research databases address the second shortcoming of search engines by offering access to the newspapers, magazines, and journals that you're likely to need for many research projects. You can access such sources as *BusinessWeek* and the *Wall Street Journal* either through the individual publishers' own sites or through a commercial database that offers access to multiple sources. Individual publisher sites sometimes require a subscription to that publication for anything beyond the current issue or charge a per-article fee, and commercial databases require subscriptions to access all content. Some commercial databases, such as HighBeam, www.highbeam.com (formerly elibrary), are priced to attract individual users, whereas others, such as LexisNexis and ProQuest, are intended for use by libraries and corporations. In addition to databases that primarily feature content from newspapers and periodicals, specialized databases such as Hoover's (www.hoovers.com) and OneSource's CorpTech (www.corptech.com) offer detailed information on thousands of individual companies. You can also obtain company news releases from the free databases maintained by PRNewswire (www.prnewswire.com) and Business Wire (www.businesswire.com). News releases are good places to look for announcements of new products, management changes, earnings, dividends, mergers, acquisitions, and other company information.

Metacrawlers, or *metasearch engines,* address the third shortcoming of search engines by formatting your search request for the specific requirements of multiple search engines and then telling you how many hits each engine was able to find for you. The more popular metacrawlers include Dogpile.com and Mamma.com. Exhibit 4.3 lists some of the more popular search engines, directories, metacrawlers, and other tools available today.

Exhibit 4.3
Best of Internet Searching
Search engines, metacrawlers, directories, and other online research tools provide multiple ways to find vital business information.

Major Search Engines

AllTheWeb	www.alltheweb.com
Alta Vista	www.altavista.com
Ask Jeeves	www.askjeeves.com
Google	www.google.com
Lycos	www.lycos.com
MSN	http://search.msn.com
Teoma	www.teoma.com

Metacrawlers and Hybrid Sites

Answers.com	www.answers.com
Dogpile	www.dogpile.com
Infonetware RealTerm Search	www.infonetware.com
IXQuick	www.ixquick.com
Kartoo	www.kartoo.com
LookSmart	www.looksmart.com
Mamma	www.mamma.com
MetaCrawler	www.metacrawler.com
Fazzle	www.fazzle.com
ProFusion	www.profusion.com
Query Server	www.queryserver.com
Search.com	www.search.com
Surfwax	www.surfwax.com
Vivismo	www.vivisimo.com
Web Brain	www.webbrain.com
WebCrawler	www.webcrawler.com
Yahoo!	www.yahoo.com
Zapmeta	www.zapmeta.com
Zworks	www.zworks.com

Web Directories

About	www.about.com
Beaucoup	www.beaucoup.com
Internet Public Library	www.ipl.org
Open Directory	http://dmoz.org

News Search Engines

AllTheWeb News	www.alltheweb.com/?cat=news
AltaVista News	http://news.altavista.com
Daypop	www.daypop.com
Google News	http://news.google.com
NewsTrove.com	www.newstrove.com
World News Network	www.wn.com
Yahoo News	http://news.yahoo.com

Magazine and Periodical Search Engines

FindArticles.com	www.findarticles.com
MagPortal	www.magportal.com

As often happens in technology and business, the lines between these three types of tools are beginning to blur. For instance, Dogpile.com provides both metacrawler and directory functions, and LookSmart.com provides features of all three: a search engine, a directory, and a database of articles (although the database is limited to publications that provide free access to articles).[27]

Using Search Tools Effectively. Search engines, metacrawlers, and databases offer a variety of ways to find information. That's the good news. The bad news is that no two of them work in exactly the same way, so you might have to modify your search techniques as you move from one tool to the next. The most basic form of searching is a *keyword search*, in which the engine or database attempts to find items that include all of the words you enter. A *Boolean search* expands on this capability by using search *operators* that let you define a query with greater precision. Common operators include AND (the search must include both words before and after the AND), OR (it can include either or both words), or NOT (the search ignores items with whatever word comes after NOT). For example:

- *corporate AND profits* finds webpages or database entries that contain both *corporate* and *profits*.
- *corporate OR profits* finds items that contain either *corporate* or *profit* but not necessarily both.
- *corporate NOT profit* finds items that contain *corporate* but excludes all those that contain the word *profit*.

Boolean searches can also include operators that let you find a particular word in close proximity to other words or use *wildcards* to find similar spellings (such as *profit, profits*, and *profitability*).

To overcome the perceived complexity of Boolean searches, some search engines and databases offer *natural language searches*, which let you ask questions in normal, everyday English ("Which videogame companies are the most profitable?"). For instance, HighBeam lets you select either Boolean or natural language searches.

Recently, search engines such as Google, Yahoo! and AllTheWeb have implemented *forms-based searches* that help you create powerful queries without the need to learn any special techniques.[28] As the name implies, you simply fill out an online form that typically lets you specify such parameters as date ranges, word to include or exclude, language, Internet domain name, and even file and media types. To access these forms, look for "advanced search" or a similar option.

To make the best use of any search engine or database, keep the following points in mind:

- ***Read the instructions.*** Unfortunately, there is no universal set of instructions that apply to every search tool, and search engines in particular are in a constant race to add new capabilities. You can usually find a "Help" page that explains how to use a particular tool most effectively. Also, look for special features that can help with your research, such as A9.com's diary function, which lets you record notes about each website you visit.[29]
- ***Pay attention to the details.*** Details can make all the difference in a search. For instance, some engines and databases interpret the question mark as a wildcard to let you search for variations of a given word, but Google does not (Google searches for word variations automatically). Again, you need to know how to operate each search engine or database, and don't assume they all work in the same way.
- ***Review the search and display options carefully.*** Some sites and databases let you make a variety of choices to include or exclude specific types of files and pages from specific sites. Also, pay attention to whether you are searching in the title, subject, or document field of the database. Each will return different results. When the results are displayed, verify the presentation order. On Highbeam, for instance, you can choose to sort the results by either date or relevancy.

- *Try variations of your terms.* If you can't find what you're looking for, try abbreviations (*CEO, CPA*), synonyms (*man, male*), related terms (*child, adolescent, youth*), different spellings (*dialog, dialogue*), singular and plural forms (*woman, women*), nouns and adjectives (*manager, management, managerial*), and open and compound forms (*online, on line, on-line*).
- *Adjust the scope of your search if needed.* If a search yields little or no information, broaden your search by specifying fewer terms. If you're inundated with too many hits, use more terms to narrow your search.

Using RSS. For years, Internet users have been dreaming of intelligent software agents that automatically prowl the online world and bring back high-quality information. You can't hire a research robot yet, but you can use *really simple syndication (RSS)* to automatically collect new material from multiple websites (including blogs) without the time-consuming chore of repeatedly visiting every site looking for fresh content. By using a *news aggregator*, you can have new content delivered to your computer as frequently as every hour. Businesspeople who need to monitor competitors or industry developments can save hours of time with RSS, and companies that want to reach potential customers and other audiences can easily publish their messages by making it RSS-compatible. You can learn more at such sites as NewsGator (www.newsgator.com), NewzCrawler (www.newzcrawler.com), Bloglines (www.bloglines.com), FeedDemon (www.feeddemon.com), or Pluck (www.pluck.com). Be careful about signing up for too many RSS feeds, though; many first-timers find themselves inundated by more new material than they can ever hope to read.[30]

CRITICAL THINKING CHECKPOINT
1. What are the risks of limiting your online research to search engines?
2. What steps could you take if an initial online search doesn't produce any relevant results?
3. How could RSS help a company that sells home furnishings online?

Enabling the Electronic Business From commerce to communication, various Internet capabilities help an organization move toward becoming an **electronic business (e-business)**, in which all major business functions take full advantage of the capabilities and efficiencies of information technology. Note that *e-commerce* and *e-business* are sometimes used interchangeably, but e-commerce refers specifically to buying and selling online, whereas e-business is a much broader term that encompasses every facet of the business operation.

e-business
Taking advantage of information technology, particularly the Internet, across all major business functions

Business Systems

All these Internet capabilities work best when they are used in the context of *business systems*—that is, as integrated solutions to business problems, rather than as discrete pieces of technology. Over the years, the collective label for these technologies and processes has changed; what used to be called *data processing* is now called **information systems (IS)** or, more recently, **information technology (IT)**. This section offers a brief overview of the various types of business systems in use today and the components that make those systems work.

information systems (IS)
A collective label for all technologies and processes used to manage business information; many organizations now refer to this as information technology (IT)

Types of Business Systems

The types of information systems used by a company generally fall into two major categories: (1) operational systems and (2) professional and managerial systems. (Of course, the specific systems you'll encounter in your career are likely to have their own

information technology (IT)
A generally accepted substituted term for information systems

management information system (MIS)
A system that provides managers with information and support for making routine decisions; sometimes used to describe information systems in general

A **management information system (MIS)** provides managers with information and support for making routine decisions. (Note that *MIS* is sometimes used synonymously with both *IS* and *IT* to describe the entire information technology effort.) An MIS takes data from a database and summarizes or restates the data into useful information such as monthly sales summaries, daily inventory levels, product manufacturing schedules, employee earnings, and so on.

Whereas a management information system typically provides structured, routine information for managerial decisions, a *decision support system (DSS)* assists managers in solving highly unstructured and nonroutine problems through the use of decision models and specialized databases. Compared with an MIS, a DSS is more interactive (allowing the user to interact with the system instead of simply receiving information), and it usually relies on both internal and external information. Similar in concept to a DSS is an *executive support system (ESS)*, which helps top executives make strategic decisions. Most of these systems can be equipped with an *executive dashboard*, which is a simplified, graphical display of the key variables that measure business performance, such as revenue and profitability, in much the same way that an automobile dashboard tells you how the various systems in your car are functioning.

One of the more intriguing applications for computers in decision making and problem solving is the development of **artificial intelligence**—the ability of computers to solve problems through reasoning and learning and to simulate human sensory perceptions. For instance, an *expert system* mimics the thought processes of a human expert to help less-knowledgeable individuals make decisions.

artificial intelligence
The ability of computers to solve problems through reasoning and learning and to simulate human sensory perceptions

Business System Technology

At the heart of all these business systems lie the hardware, software, and networking technologies that make it all happen. Although you don't need to be a technical expert to use most of these systems, understanding the basic terminology and ideas can make you more productive and self-sufficient.

hardware
The tangible equipment used in information systems

Hardware **Hardware** is the tangible equipment used in a computer system, such as disk drives, keyboards, modems, printers, scanners, PDAs, and so on. Hardware falls into three categories: input, processing, and output. Input devices range from conventional keyboards to new *speech recognition* devices that convert human speech to digital data. You may have encountered speech recognition in automated phone systems that ask you to speak your requests. Speech recognition is also one of a growing number of *assistive technologies* (see Chapter 11) designed to help people with physical disabilities use computer systems. Processing devices are at the heart of most every electronic product these days, from the cell phone in your pocket to the computer on your desk. The primary processing device is an integrated circuit "chip" called the *central processing unit (CPU)*, although some people use *CPU* to refer to the main body of a desktop computer as well. Output devices include printers, displays, and speakers. Systems equipped with speech recognition often have *speech synthesis* on the output, converting digital data back to human-sounding speech.

Computers themselves come in a variety of shapes and sizes but generally fall into the categories of *clients* (desktops, laptops, PDAs, and other end-user devices) and *servers* (the more powerful computers that run many business systems). When you retrieve information from the World Wide Web, for instance, your PC, the client, is accessing data stored on a server. Corporate data centers often employ *mainframe computers* as well, a general term for any large computer system. For example, in addition to its 14 mainframes, UPS has 6,100 servers and 125,000 clients.[33]

A *thin client,* which is essentially just a keyboard, display, and mouse, lacks the ability to run software on its own. Word processing, spreadsheets, and other software run on the server, and the client interacts with them via a network connection. A growing number of companies, wary of employees downloading viruses and installing unauthorized software on their traditional PCs, are moving to thin clients to reduce infection risks and support costs.[34]

The traditional desktop PC has given way to laptops, PDAs, and even smartphones for businesspeople on the go.

Exhibit 4.5
Common Business Application Software

You're probably familiar with the most of the basic types of application software used in business today; here are types you're most likely to encounter on the job. Note that the major applications, including word processing, spreadsheets, and presentation graphics, are often packaged together in suites, *such as Microsoft Office.*

Word processing: You probably use Microsoft Word or one of its competitors already. The ability to use the basic functions of word processing software is almost universally expected in business jobs today. Chances are you'll also be expected to use templates and style sheets in order to make your documents conform to company standards.

Desktop publishing: Desktop publishing software goes a step beyond typical word processors by allowing designers to lay out printer-ready pages that incorporate artwork, photos, and a large variety of typographic elements. Together with scanners and other specialized input devices, publishing programs let businesspeople create sophisticated documents on their computers in a fraction of the time it once took. In many companies, desktop publishing is handled by specialists who are trained to use the software (which requires more skill and knowledge than word processing).

Web publishing systems: Sometimes known as content management systems, these systems help companies manage the many documents and graphics that make up a typical corporate website. As a site contributor, you typically submit content to the system, which then formats it and posts it to the website more or less automatically (saving you the time and trouble of learning the details of webpage formatting).

Spreadsheets: A spreadsheet is a program designed to let you organize and manipulate data in a row-column matrix. The intersection of each row-and-column pair is called a *cell*, and every cell can contain a number, a mathematical formula, or text used as a label. Among the spreadsheet's biggest strengths is the ability to quickly update masses of calculations when conditions change—it will automatically update a record if one of the records to which it is linked is changed. Businesspeople use spreadsheets to solve a wide variety of problems, ranging from statistical analysis to simulation models used in decision support systems.

Databases: Database management software lets you create, store, maintain, rearrange, and retrieve contents of databases. Almost anywhere you find a sizable amount of data in electronic format, you'll find a database management program at work. Such programs help users produce useful information by allowing them to look at data from various perspectives.

Presentation and graphics software: Presentation software such as Microsoft PowerPoint is used extensively in business today, so you'll do well to become familiar with its capabilities. You may also need to use graphics software to create diagrams for presentations and documents (many of the charts and graphs you'll use can be created more easily in a spreadsheet).

Personal information managers (PIMs): Sometimes known as contact managers, these specialized database programs help you track communication with your business contacts, organize e-mail, maintain a work calendar and appointment schedules, store contact information, and much more.

Software Hardware is of little value without **software**, the programmed instructions that direct the activity of the hardware. Software comes in two main varieties:

- *Application software.* This is the outermost layer of software in a system, the software that you see as a user on your computer, PDA, cell phone, or other device. Literally thousands of software applications are now available for business use, from those for writing memos and surfing the web to programs for managing inventory and testing new employees (see Exhibit 4.5). When you hear IT specialists speak of "applications," they can be talking about either the application software itself or the business task that the software applies to.
- *System software.* This class of software operates between the hardware and the application software, so it's not usually seen by regular business users. The most common type of system software is the operating system, the layer of software that directly manages the hardware in a system. The best-known operating systems are Microsoft Windows, the Apple Macintosh operating system, Unix, and Linux (usually pronounced "linn icks"), a variation on Unix. For desktops and laptops, Microsoft Windows is the king of corporate operating systems, although Linux is gaining ground. However, a legal battle being waged by the company that owns the rights to Unix could stall the rise of Linux.[35]

software
The programmed instructions that direct the activity of the hardware; the intangible part of information systems

Networking Nearly all of the information technology benefits described in this chapter require multiple computers to be connected in some fashion. A **network** is a collection of specialized hardware and software that links computers. Networks come in a variety of configurations, some with a single, central server, others with multiple servers that coordinate their activities, and *peer-to-peer networks*, in which multiple client computers share information directly or collaborate on large computing tasks. Networks can also be wired, wireless, or a combination of both. Networks are generally classified by range of geographic coverage:

network
A collection of specialized hardware and software that links computers together to share data and information

- A **local area network (LAN)** connects computers within a limited local range, such as within a single department or single building. You may hear the term *Ethernet* applied to LANs; that's the type of networking technology used in nearly all office LANs.
- A *wide area network (WAN)* covers larger areas, up to entire countries. Telecommunication networks are a good example of WANs. Some WANs are shared by multiple customers; others, called *private lines*, are owned by or leased to a single organization. Companies can also create a *virtual private network (VPN)* that "tunnels" through the public Internet but prevents outsiders from gaining access to it.
- A *municipal area network (MAN)* typically covers a city or a town and surrounding areas.
- The **Internet** is actually a network of networks spanning the entire globe. The forerunner to the Internet was originally funded by the U.S. government, but its operation and maintenance were eventually turned over to a group of large **Internet service providers (ISPs)**, including Sprint and MCI. These large services maintain the *backbone*, the primary lines that link regional and local ISPs to the Internet. Exhibit 4.6 lists some common Internet terms you might encounter on the job; you can explore other definitions at TechTarget, http://whatis.techtarget.com, and the TechWeb TechEncyclopedia at www.techweb.com/encyclopedia.

local area network (LAN)
A network that connects computers within a limited local range, such as within a single department or single building

Internet
A network of networks that spans the entire globe

Internet service providers (ISPs)
Companies that provide access to the Internet through dial-up, DSL, cable, or wireless networking

In addition to the security issues addressed later in the chapter, current developments in the area of networking are dominated by three issues: bandwidth, wireless, and convergence.

broadband
A term applied to higher speed network connections

Bandwidth. If you've ever twiddled your thumbs waiting for your e-mail to download or a webpage to appear, you know all about the issue of *bandwidth*, which is simply a measure of the speed of a network connection. **Broadband** is a rather vague term used to describe higher-speed network connections. The U.S. Federal Communications Commission (FCC) defines broadband as anything faster than 200 kilobits (200,000 bits) per second, or roughly the low end of a digital subscriber line (DSL) connection. However, South Korea, which currently leads the world in broadband coverage, doesn't consider anything below 1 megabit (1 million bits) per second to be broadband. A typical broadband connection in South Korea is 20 megabits per second, and 75 percent of homes have this level of broadband, compared to fewer than 25 percent in the United States.[36]

Bandwidth is a concern both for the connections that individual users and companies have with the Internet and for the overall speed of the Internet itself. For many businesses, a slow Internet connection is more than an inconvenience—it can be a major strategic issue that affects where companies locate, which products they can develop, and more. A number of smaller cities and towns across the country, such as Danville, Virginia, and Provo, Utah, are building their own high-speed MANs as a way to attract business and help their communities with better access to long-distance educational resources.[37]

Although it's hard to imagine now, the Internet was never designed to connect the billion or more users and devices that it is rapidly approaching, to handle huge multimedia files such as movies, or to support the vast commercialization of global e-commerce. Between this overload and the twin scourges of spam and viruses, the Internet no longer meets the needs of many advanced scientific and engineering endeavors. In response, more than 200 universities and several dozen technology companies have joined the *Internet2* initiative, which is building an ultra-high-speed global network that will meet the demands of research institutions.[38]

Exhibit 4.6
Important Internet Terms

You'll encounter these terms and acronyms as you browse around the World Wide Web, send and receive e-mail, and perform other tasks on the Internet.

Bookmark	A browser feature that places selected URLs in a file for quick access, allowing you to automatically return to the website by clicking on the site's name (called "Favorites" in Microsoft's Internet Explorer)
Browser	Software, such as Internet Explorer or Firefox, that enables a computer to search for, display, and download information that appears on the World Wide Web
Domain name	The portion of an Internet address that identifies the host and indicates the type of organization it is. The abbreviation following the *period* is the top-level domain (TLD). The original seven TLDs identified businesses (com), educational institutions (edu), government agencies (gov), international sources (int), the military (mil), network resources (net), and nonprofit organizations (org). To keep up with demand, additional TLDs (such as pro, biz, info, coop, museum, and name) have been introduced. For Internet sites outside the United States, two-level TLDs identify the country, such as jp (Japan), ca (Canada), and fr (France).
Download	Transmitting a file from one computer system to another; on the Internet, bringing data from the Internet into your computer
File Transfer Protocol (FTP)	A method for transferring files; FTP software lets you copy or move files from a remote computer, known as an FTP site
Homepage	The top-level page on a website
Hyperlink	An onscreen linkage between two webpages or other elements; allow you to jump from one page to another, launch programs, or download files; links can be configured as either text (usually presented as one or more underlines words in a special color) or graphics (such as specific areas in a diagram that link to other elements)
Hypertext Markup Language (HTML)	The software language used to create, present, and link pages on the World Wide Web
Hypertext Transfer Protocol (HTTP)	A method for transferring files over the World Wide Web; HTTP is used whenever you load a webpage, for instance
Uniform Resource Locator (URL)	Web address that gives the exact location of an Internet resource
Upload	To send a file from your computer to a server or host system
Webpage	An individual page on a website; can consist of a single text document or a group of related multimedia files
Website	A collection of related webpages on the World Wide Web
World Wide Web (WWW or web)	A hypertext-based system for finding and accessing Internet resources such as text, graphics, audio, and other multimedia resources

Wireless Networking. By combining mobility with the power of networked information, wireless promises to change business and daily life as much as just about anything in the history of technology. You might encounter dozens of different wireless technologies, but here are the most significant from a business perspective:[39]

- ***Wi-Fi.*** You may already be using **Wi-Fi** (short for *wireless fidelity*), which is a wireless alternative for LANs, around your campus or in the thousands of coffee shops, airports, and other locations that provide wireless *hotspots*. If you encounter the technical designation 802.11, that's referring to Wi-Fi as well. Several variations on this form of wireless networking exist and others are in development. In addition to providing

Wi-Fi
A wireless alternative for LANs; short for wireless fidelity

untethered access for computers and PDAs, Wi-Fi is increasingly being used for Internet phone service.[40]

- **WiMAX.** Designed for higher bandwidth and wider range than Wi-Fi, *WiMAX* provides wireless broadband connections to the Internet. WiMAX promises to help solve the "last mile" problem in Internet access, the expensive step of connecting individuals' homes and businesses to the Internet.[41]

- **GPS.** The *Global Positioning System (GPS)* uses a ring of satellites around the earth to precisely identify locations virtually anywhere on the planet. Many businesses have already adopted GPS solutions in such areas as monitoring trucking fleets. The location and tracking services you read about in Chapter 2 often employ GPS.

- **Bluetooth.** Bluetooth is a short-range wireless technology for connecting digital devices, such as sending documents from a PDA to a printer or exchanging phone books between cell phones.

- **SMS.** Short Messaging Service (SMS) is the technical name of the text messaging capability now available on many cell phones. SMS provides the same basic function as instant messaging on computers, although with shorter messages and limited features.

- **3G.** *3G* stands for a collection of "third-generation" mobile phone systems that promise data transmission rates high enough to enable music downloads and other features. (Roughly speaking, the original cell phones were the first generation, and the digital cell phones now in widespread use are the second generation.)

- **RFID.** **Radio frequency identification (RFID)** tags (see Chapter 2) combine a memory chip with a tiny antenna; these tags can be scanned by wireless reading devices.

Businesses around the world are putting all these wireless capabilities to work, both in offering new services and in managing their operations more efficiently, but business and society have only just begun to realize the possibilities—both helpful and potentially harmful—that wireless can offer.

Digital Convergence. Internet companies offering phone service, cable TV companies offering Internet service, satellite TV companies offering phone service, phone companies offering TV service, electrical utilities offering Internet service, software companies getting into the movie business—if this all sounds chaotic, welcome to *digital convergence*, the tendency for digitally oriented goods and services that were once separate to combine into new forms. Entertainment, communication, and computing used to be three fairly distinct industries, but everybody is invading everybody else's markets nowadays. Some of these changes will certainly benefit consumers and businesses, but they are driven more by competitive concerns as suppliers try to protect their own markets and find new opportunities in other markets. As a business manager, keep your eyes open for ways to take advantage of these new technologies, particularly as bandwidth increases and networks show up everywhere.[42]

Given all these possibilities, where will the Internet take us in the years to come? It's an interesting question that is impossible to answer with any certainty because to a large degree, no one controls the Internet—and everybody controls the Internet. Technology aficionados have been chatting online for years, but it took only a few new pieces of blogging software to make it easy for everybody to join the conversation, and within months, the very nature of journalism changed. Or take the case of Skype's Internet telephone service. An entrepreneur from Denmark and another from Sweden hired some hot programming talent from Estonia, and suddenly millions of people all over the world began making free phone calls over the Internet.

Three bits of advice for your own business ventures: (1) View promises of amazing new technologies with healthy skepticism—but don't get trapped into thinking something can't happen just because it hasn't happened yet. (2) Don't base an entire business plan on the way technology is today because it won't be that way tomorrow. (3) Change can hurt when you don't see it coming or you resist it because you don't like it, but it can make you a fortune if you view it as an opportunity and a new way to create and satisfy customers.

> **CRITICAL THINKING CHECKPOINT**
> 1. How does a customer relationship management system differ from a transaction processing system?
> 2. How could effective knowledge management help an organization?
> 3. Why is network bandwidth a concern for many businesses?

Technology Issues for Today's Managers

As you already know from your experiences as a student and a consumer, technology can deliver some amazing benefits, and every year seems to bring new technical miracles. As a business manager or entrepreneur, you can capitalize on all these benefits as well, but you'll also be responsible for a variety of legal, ethical, and administrative issues, starting with the challenge of ensuring privacy and security.

Ensuring Security and Privacy

Linking computers via networking technology creates enormous benefits for businesses and consumers, but there's a dark side to connecting everyone everywhere. Managers need constant vigilance these days to make sure their computer systems remain secure and that data on them remain private. It's a staggering challenge, with tens of thousands of known computer viruses circling the globe and everybody from small-time crooks to international crime syndicates using the Internet to steal.[43] Three major categories of concern are malware, security breaches, and privacy.

Malware, short for *malicious software*, is the term often applied to the diverse and growing collection of computer programs that are designed to disrupt websites, destroy information, or enable criminal activity. **Viruses** are invasive programs that reproduce by infecting legitimate programs; *worms* are a type of virus that can reproduce by themselves. Between 1999 and 2004, six of the worst computer viruses and worms caused an estimated $20 billion of financial damage.[44] Another variety, *Trojan horses,* allow outsiders to hijack infected computers and use them for purposes such as retransmitting spam e-mail. Many viruses and worms are able to wreak havoc because computer owners haven't bothered to install available security patches in their software or haven't installed *firewalls*, hardware or software devices that block access to intruders. However, a troubling new twist appeared in 2004, when the Witty worm destroyed a specific target group of 12,000 computers by attacking the very security products used to defend these systems. Witty worked on a smaller scale than some of the more widely known viruses and worms, but it was 100 percent successful and remarkably fast because it was launched simultaneously from a network of 100 "pre-infected" computers. Experts worry that Witty could be a sign of more lethal malware to come.[45] And as the networking options multiply, so do the areas of risk; new areas of concern include viruses sent through Internet phone service, viruses on cell phones (including viruses downloaded from ring tone websites and viruses transmitted from phone to phone over Bluetooth wireless), and nasty things lurking on public wireless networks.[46]

Information technology products are also vulnerable to a wide range of security breaches and sabotage attacks, in which individual systems are invaded for potentially malicious or criminal purposes. For instance, a new variety of malware known as **spyware** sneaks onto computers with the intent of capturing passwords, credit card numbers, and other valuable information. Chances are you've already met spyware's less-malicious cousin, *adware*, which creates pop-up ads on your computer screen. Another new worry is theft by Wi-Fi, in which a thief installs an "evil twin" wireless access point to impersonate legitimate wireless service in public areas, then tries to capture credit card information from anyone who connects.[47] These worries are in addition to good old-fashioned *hacking*, in which someone electronically breaks into a computer network (many computer professional call this illegal activity *cracking*, not hacking, but *hacking*

LEARNING OBJECTIVE 7

Identify seven current challenges that managers face with respect to information technology

malware
Short for malicious software; an umbrella term for illicit software with destructive, invasive, or criminal intent

viruses
Invasive computer programs that reproduce by infecting legitimate programs

spyware
Malware that sneaks onto computers with the intent of capturing passwords, credit card numbers, and other valuable information

Spyware detection programs such as Spy Sweeper have become essential tools in the battle against malicious software. In this scan, Spy Sweeper found 11 suspicious programs residing on this computer.

is the more commonly used term). Hacking remains a huge problem. Acxiom, a Little Rock, Arkansas, company that compiles personal data on U.S. consumers, has been infiltrated at least twice by hackers who copied personal information on millions of people.[48] These problems aren't limited to outsiders, either; by some estimates, 70 percent of system intrusions are orchestrated by company insiders.[49] Sometimes it doesn't even require actual hacking. In the new sport of "Google hacking," curious web users have used search engines to find everything from financial records to top-secret government information on poorly guarded websites.[50]

Data security is also a part of a larger ethical question that all companies face regarding consumer and employee privacy. Businesses have the responsibility to ensure that private information in its control stays private, but they also need to address some tough questions regarding the information they should collect in the first place. Technologies such as web *cookies*, small data files that record aspects of your web sessions, are a good example of this dilemma. Cookies can make life easier for you as a consumer by customizing your web experiences, but cookies and other web technologies raise difficult questions. For instance, is it ethical to track your habits in order to display online ads that mirror the products you seem to be interested in, without personally identifying who you are? What about linking those web habits with other sources of consumer information such as credit reports to tailor the advertising even more precisely? Right now, the generally accepted ethical boundary is somewhere between these two capabilities.[51]

Inside the organization, an even wider range of techniques are being used to monitor employee behavior. For instance, a significant number of companies—30 percent, according to one recent survey—now automatically monitor employee e-mail. Employers are legitimately worried about such employee activities as divulging business secrets (intentionally or not) or sharing sexually explicit materials that could open the company to lawsuits. In a typical monitoring scenario, software flags messages that contain certain words or types of attached files, then alerts the employees of the potential problem so they can modify their behavior.[52] Wireless has created another opportunity to monitor employees—and another ethical dilemma. Products such as Aligo's Worktrack system let employers track the location of mobile workers through GPS-equipped cell phones.[53]

LEARNING FROM BUSINESS BLUNDERS

OOPS Mailing a catalog is always a nerve-wracking experience; you spend thousands of dollars, sometimes millions, then can't do much but wait by the phone or website to see if anybody responds. With good planning and a bit of luck, the orders start rolling in within a few days. The experience has been compared to farming, where you work for months planting crops then have to hope nothing bad happens before harvest. Eziba, a North Adams, Massachusetts, marketer of handcrafted goods from around the world, recently sent out a catalog and then did the customary nail-biting, then kept waiting . . . and waiting . . . and waiting—and nothing happened. The problem? A service provider the company relies on for mailing had accidentally sent the catalogs to the names in Eziba's database *least* likely to purchase, rather than *most* likely. The resulting financial hit was so bad that it forced Eziba to halt operations (although company owners hope to sell to outside investors and restart business soon).

WHAT YOU CAN LEARN This heartbreaking error demonstrates how it doesn't take much of a mistake to bring a company down—particularly when information systems multiply the error by thousands of customers. When the company's survival is at stake, check, double-check, then check once again.

Whether it's human issues such as background checks on new hires and ongoing security training or technical issues such as firewalls, encryption, or disaster recovery plans, all managers need to devote time and energy to potentially harmful side effects of information technology. Sadly, as long as criminals can profit from digital theft and malware writers can amuse themselves by destroying the hard work of others, the problems are likely to only get worse.

Protecting Property Rights

Digital technology has also increased concerns over the protection of both digital products (including software and entertainment products available in digital format) and **intellectual property**, a term that covers a wide range of creative outputs with commercial value, such as design ideas, manufacturing processes, brands, and chemical formulas. One of the most controversial issues in this area is *digital rights management (DRM)*, the protection of owners' rights in products that are in digital format. DRM limits the ways consumers can use music files, movies, and other digital purchases, and critics worry that major corporations are using DRM to stifle creativity and control popular culture. Intellectual property protection remains a contentious and complex issue, as copyright owners, privacy advocates, and consumers groups battle over how digital products can or can't be used. You can expect to see more lawsuits and legislation regarding these issues for years to come.

*intellectual property
A wide range of creative outputs with commercial value, such as design ideas, manufacturing processes, brands, and chemical formulas*

Guarding Against Information Overload

From simple RSS newreaders to enterprise-wide sales reporting systems, it's not uncommon for businesspeople to be stunned by how quickly their computerized systems start piling up data and information. Once you open the floodgates, it's difficult to stem the tide, so think carefully before you start collecting any data. Work backward from your most important decisions and separate the information you really need to have from the information that is merely interesting or potentially useful. Then analyze the needs of each decision maker to identify what information each person needs and the best way to present it. Fortunately, new tools such as *data visualization*, presenting data in visual formats, help simplify this challenge by showing trends and relationships that are difficult to see in plain numerical data. These tools go beyond simple charts and graphs to show three-dimensional and even animated models of complex data.[54]

SAFETY AND SECURITY IN A COMPLEX WORLD

SAY, IS THAT STOLEN DATA YOU'RE LISTENING TO ON YOUR IPOD?

The iPod's massive storage and easy connectivity to your computer via FireWire or Universal Serial Bus (USB) make it a great device for listening to music on the go. And according to some security experts, these features also make it a great device for stealing confidential data from desktop and laptop PCs. The concern also includes small, portable USB data-storage units, variously known as *flash drives, thumb drives,* or *key drives.*

Cell phones with built-in cameras have created another new security concern: that people will photograph valuable secrets, from manufacturing processes to prototypes of new products. For instance, in industries such as cars and consumer electronics, where companies work hard to keep new product designs away from the prying eyes of competitors, General Motors, DaimlerChrysler, and Samsung now ban camera phones in research and engineering facilities (ironically enough in Samsung's case, since it's one of the world's leading manufacturers of camera phones). Camera phones also present privacy issues, leading a number of businesses and other organizations to ban them in restrooms and locker rooms.

How real are these threats? When it comes to stealing secrets, iPods, flash drives, and camera phones can't really do anything new, since thieves have been able to steal data via floppy disks and CD-ROM burners for years

now, and industrial spies could smuggle in tiny film cameras. However, the concern in both cases is how fast and easy these devices are to use in nefarious schemes. With a camera phone, for instance, someone could snap a photo of your top-secret design and transmit it to a competitor's engineering lab halfway around the world in a matter of seconds—and no one looks suspicious walking around with a cell phone these days. Similarly, it's not at all uncommon for employees to walk around listening to their iPods, and thumb drives are so tiny that they're much easier to conceal than disks or CD-ROMs.

Debate continues about just how real or widespread this threat is, but don't be surprised to see a sign in the next office building you walk into—including your own—asking you to leave your iPod or camera phone in the car.

Questions for Critical Thinking

1. Would careful screening during the hiring process be a better approach to the potential problem of employees who steal confidential information? Explain your answer.
2. Do employers have the right to ban the use of personal entertainment devices that might be used in inappropriate ways in the workplace, even if no one in the company has done so? Why or why not?

Monitoring Productivity

Avoiding information overload is a key part of the larger challenge of ensuring the overall productivity of your organization in its use of information technology. Two issues highlight the complexity of this challenge: spam and misuse of technology.

If you use e-mail regularly, you already know what an annoyance **spam**, unsolicited bulk e-mail, can be. (And if you ever wished you were billionaire Bill Gates, take heart in the fact that he receives four million e-mails a day, and most of that is spam.) You may also have received *spim* (junk IM) and even junk mail on your cell phone.[55]

Spam is more than an annoyance for business, however; it's a massive headache that wastes billions of dollars every year. Information technology departments spend time and money trying to filter it out, employees waste time deleting it, and a business can even lose its e-mail service entirely if a spammer takes over an unprotected PC, leading an ISP to *blacklist* the company's e-mail addresses. Filters can help, but keeping them up to date requires constant work, and they create the risk of *false positives*, when a spam filter deletes legitimate messages. Major ISPs are trying to fight back with authentication schemes, but some experts are skeptical that a solution is even possible at this point. (How are spammers

spam
Unsolicited bulk e-mail

Business Buzz

zombie PC
A home PC that has been unwittingly taken over by spammers using Trojan horse viruses for the purpose of resending junk e-mail; millions of zombie PCs now contribute to the daily flood of spam

able to get away with all this, you might ask? The people who invented e-mail several decades ago were all friends and colleagues who respected one another, so they didn't see a need to design in security features.)[56]

How employees use information technology is another important productivity issue. The Internet and e-mail are key parts of what has been called the "information technology paradox," in which tools designed to save time can waste as much time as they save. A commonly cited problem is employees who simply don't realize how much time they're wasting or how much this wasted time costs their employers. So many employers are concerned about productivity losses from personal use of the Internet and e-mail at work that thousands now place restrictions on how employees can use them. For instance, a common tactic is installing software that limits Internet access to business-related sites during working hours. And it's not merely a productivity issue, either; employee misuse of information technology can expose a company to a lawsuits over such matters as sexual harassment and expose systems to malicious software.[57]

Managing Total Cost of Ownership

The true costs of information technology are a concern for every company. The *total cost of ownership (TCO)* of IT systems, which includes the purchase costs of hardware, software, and networking plus expenses for installation, customization, training, upgrades, and maintenance, can be three to five times higher than the purchase price.[58] As expensive as IT can be, however, that's not the end of it. Too many companies are prone to buying technology they don't need, a result of poor planning or the fear of being left behind. The results are eye-opening: The financial services firm Morgan Stanley estimates that between 2000 and 2002, corporations tossed out some $130 billion worth of information technology.[59] Sometimes companies spend millions of dollars building systems that are junked before they're even finished. These cautionary tales highlight the difficulty of managing vital business resources in the midst of competing budget demands, dynamic markets, and ever-changing technology.

Developing Employee Skills

With the pervasiveness of information technology, virtually everyone from the mailroom to the executive suite is expected to have some level of skills with information technology. Not only will you need to keep your own skills up to date so that you can manage yourself and others efficiently, you'll need to make sure your employees have the skills they need. And don't overlook the fundamentals, either—with the importance that e-mail and IM have taken on in recent years, the ability to write well is more vital than ever.[60]

Maintaining the Human Touch

Even in the best circumstances, technology can't match the rich experience of person-to-person contact. For instance, e-mail, IM, and voicemail can't always convey the necessary emotional and nonverbal aspects of communication, which can cause unnecessary confusion and aggravation.[61]

Moreover, all human beings need to connect with other people, and as technological options increase, people seem to need the human touch even more. When Alan Hassenfeld, the CEO of game maker Hasbro, implored his employees to interact more in person and rely less on technological communication, they gave him a standing ovation.[62] Several companies have improvised on the "casual Friday" idea by instituting "e-mail-free Fridays." If people want to communicate with colleagues, they have to pick up the phone or walk down the hall. "This is really about trying to get people to collaborate," says Andrew McCarthy of Veritas Software in Mountain View, California, one of the companies that has begun banning e-mail in some departments on Fridays.[63]

CRITICAL THINKING CHECKPOINT
1. Is it ethical for a company to monitor employee e-mail? Why or why not?
2. How does spam reduce productivity?
3. Reducing the "human touch" is a common worry with technology-based communication; how can technology increase the human touch?

CHECKLIST: Apply These Ideas When You're the Boss

✓ Understand the differences between data and information and between information and insights, as they apply to your business needs

✓ Look beyond sales transactions for ways to incorporate the Internet into your entire operation

✓ Apply a healthy dose of skepticism whenever you or your employees conduct research online; biased, inaccurate, outdated information is an unfortunate part of the online experience

✓ Look for opportunities in technological change; for instance, what could you do differently if you could switch to wireless networking?

✓ Don't get too "hard-wired" to current technology; it will change sooner or later

✓ Pay attention to the ethical and legal ramifications of privacy and security issues

✓ With any new information technology, don't be blinded by the coolness factor; understand the business pros and cons before you adopt it

✓ With communication and collaboration technology, remember that people are still on either end—don't lose the human touch

Summary of Learning Objectives

1 **Differentiate data, information, and insight.** People often use *data* and *information* interchangeably, but it's helpful to distinguish the two. Think of data as recorded facts, statistics, numbers—bits and pieces that by themselves don't really mean all that much. In contrast, information is useful knowledge extracted from data. Insight goes beyond mere information, representing a deeper understanding of a given subject.

2 **Explain how information quality is measured.** Information quality can be measured in a number of ways, but a good general rule of thumb is that information should be *relevant* (the information delivered to each person relates directly to his or her needs), *accurate* (it's both current and free from errors), *timely* (delivered in time to make a difference), and *cost effective* (costs a reasonable amount of money compared to the value it offers).

3 **Identify four key areas where businesses use information.** Businesses use information in every decision and every facet of operations, but the four highlighted in the chapter are research and development (from understanding customer needs to developing new products), planning and control (assembling plans then monitoring how well the business executes them), marketing and sales (connecting with customers), and communication and collaboration (sharing information and working together throughout the organization).

4 **Discuss five important ways the Internet is changing business.** The Internet is changing business in the following ways: (1) accelerating commerce through e-commerce (B2B, B2C, C2C, and m-commerce); (2) erasing borders by allowing people to work across organizational and geographical boundaries; (3) controlling costs by reducing costs for travel, printing, physical facilities, and other traditional expenses; (4) enhancing communication and collaboration through a variety of tools, from e-mail to intranets to blogs, and (5) simplifying research through search engines, web directories, and research databases.

5 **Explain the differences between search engines, web directories, and research databases.** Search engines look for keywords, phrases, or other search terms (depending on the engine) in publicly accessible webpages; they can't access all the pages on the World Wide Web, and they

don't take advantage of human reviewers or editors to screen out or prioritize pages (although the best use sophisticated programs to rank pages in terms of potential relevance or quality). In contrast, web directors are reviewed lists of websites. A human editor has reviewed and selected various sites, and he or she often provides some commentary on each site's strengths and weaknesses. Research databases provide access to information that often isn't available through search engines or web directories, such as the archives of many publications.

6 **Differentiate between operational systems and professional and managerial systems.** Operational systems collect and process the data and information that represent the daily business of the enterprise, from sales receipts to production data to accounting records. The most common types are transaction processing systems, process and production control systems, office automation systems, and customer relationship management systems. In contrast, professional and managerial systems assist with analysis and decision making in both the professional and managerial ranks of the organization. Among the many varieties of these systems are knowledge management systems, management information systems, decision support systems, and executive support systems.

7 **Identify seven current challenges that managers face with respect to information technology.** Managers in virtually all industries need to address these seven technology-related challenges: ensuring privacy and security, protecting property rights, guarding against information overload, monitoring productivity, managing total cost of ownership, helping employees develop the necessary technical skills, and maintaining the human touch in interactions with both employees and customers.

UPS: What's Next?

UPS continues to innovate as both a transportation company and an information technology company. Along with long-time archrival FedEx, UPS faces a new challenge in the U.S. market from DHL. DHL, which was started in the United States, has long been a leader in overseas markets, but ironically enough, never placed much emphasis on the U.S. market until its recent purchase by Deutsche Post, the privatized German postal service. One of DHL's objectives is to pursue small and midsized customers by promoting a more personal level of service, which could prove a strong selling point as UPS continues to build its automated, e-commerce capabilities. For its part, UPS continues to expand its business services in a number of directions, offering everything from wireless package tracking to e-commerce software to business financing. In every effort, you can expect to see information technology play a central role.[64]

Critical Thinking Questions

1. Visit UPS's website at **www.ups.com** and explore the ways UPS offers to help small businesses. If you were starting a company that would sell sports memorabilia or original artwork (choose either one), how might you use UPS's small-business services?
2. An executive from DHL claims that both UPS and FedEx are losing the personal touch as they become increasingly automated and efficient. As a UPS executive, what steps could you take to ensure that customers can still make "human contact" with your company?
3. Can you identify any potential risks in UPS's efforts to diversify into e-business software, consulting, and other areas outside of its core transportation business?

Key Terms

artificial intelligence
(146)
blogs (138)
broadband (148)
business-to-business
e-commerce (136)
business-to-consumer
e-commerce (136)
chief information officer
(CIO) (134)

consumer-to-consumer
e-commerce (136)
data (132)
data mining (134)
databases (134)
e-business (143)
e-commerce (136)
extranets (137)
hardware (146)
information (132)

information systems (IS)
(143)
information technology (IT)
(143)
insight (132)
instant messaging (IM) (137)
intellectual property (153)
Internet (148)
internet service providers
(ISPs) (148)

Internet telephone service (139)   mobile commerce   software (147)
intranets (137)   (m-commerce) (136)   spam (154)
local area network (LAN)   network (148)   spyware (151)
    (148)   personal digital assistants   telecommuting (137)
malware (151)   (PDAs) (136)   viruses (151)
management information   radio frequency identification   web directories (140)
    system (MIS) (146)   (RFID) (150)   Wi-Fi (149)
metacrawlers (140)   search engines (140)

Test Your Knowledge

Questions for Review

1. What are the purposes of data warehousing and data mining?
2. Why do companies need information and information management systems?
3. How are companies using the Internet to generate revenues?
4. What kinds of information are companies placing on intranets?
5. How does business-to-business e-commerce differ from business-to-consumer e-commerce?

Questions for Analysis

6. Would employee records be considered data or information? Explain your answer.
7. What concerns might you have when citing information from a website?
8. Is information more important than data? Explain your answer.
9. Why is new technology sometimes considered both a benefit and a curse?
10. **Ethical Considerations.** You finally saved enough money to buy a CD-RW drive so you can burn your own CDs and save lots of money. You log onto the Internet but before you can download your favorite tunes you must first agree to all those WARNING messages. Of course, you're in too much of a hurry to actually read them, so you simply check "agree" and begin downloading songs. What do you think is the purpose of these warning messages? Is it ethical for you to agree to them without understanding what you are agreeing to? What happens if you disagree?

Questions for Application

11. Select a well-known e-commerce website, review its content, and answer these questions:
    a. What kinds of product and company information does the website provide?
    b. What information does the website ask customers to provide about themselves?
    c. What are some of the features the website includes to facilitate the ordering of products? (For example, can you check the status of your order? Does the site advise you if the product is out of stock?)
    d. How does the website provide customers with assistance if they have a question or need help?
12. How has the Internet changed the way that you personally interact with businesses?
13. **Integrated.** The business you started just last year is already getting e-mail inquiries from potential customers in other countries. These opportunities are intriguing, but you don't have the time or money right now to expand your e-commerce website to include local-language versions. On the other hand, you don't want to lose customers to your competitors. What should you do?
14. **Integrated.** How might an increased interest in m-commerce (from a consumer perspective) stimulate the economy?

Practice Your Knowledge

Handling Difficult Situations on the Job: Controlling Techno-Tantrums

This is the third time in a month your company, Metro Power, has had to escort an employee from the building after a violent episode. Frankly, everyone is a little frightened by this development, and as a department manager, you have the unhappy task of trying to quell the storm. All of these episodes began with some failure of company technology to perform as expected.

One man punched out his computer screen after the system failed. Another threw his keyboard across the room when he couldn't get access to the company's intranet. A woman started kicking her stalled printer and screaming obscenities before terrified co-workers stopped her. You're afraid these incidents may be just the beginning.

Your business depends on technology at all levels. Common as they are, technology failures are sometimes seen as disastrous and unacceptable by tired, stressed, and overworked employees. Tempers flare and physical violence too often follows. You're just grateful that, so far, none of that anger or frustration has been taken out on co-workers.[65]

Your task: You need to decide how to reduce the rising tide of temper tantrums over technology failure. How can you help your workers deal with this fairly routine frustration? Equipment failures are inevitable; what can you suggest to help frazzled employees respond more calmly? What steps might they take before (prevention), during (response), and after (repair) techno glitches? You need to be prepared if another employee explodes in a violent outburst against company equipment. How will you handle that worker? Can you think of ways to defuse such a situation?

Sharpening Your Communication Skills

As a training specialist in your company's human resources department, you listen carefully to feedback from supervisors around the company to identify new training needs. Over the past few years, the tide of complaints about the writing skills of new employees has grown from a whisper to a roar. Senior managers in particular are tired of getting memos from junior staffers that read like text messages "sent by teenagers at the mall," as one executive put it. You'd like to design a training course for new employees that addresses communication skills, but you don't have time this year. A memo of your own will have to do. Write a short (2–3 paragraph) memo explaining why the casual style that many younger employees are accustomed to from personal e-mail, IM, and text messaging is not appropriate in a corporate setting.

Building Your Team Skills

A virus shut down the computer system of your major competitor last month, and you heard from a friend that they are still experiencing serious problems. So you decide to learn from their experience. As manager of the IT department you have assembled your team of top thinkers to brainstorm a list of precautions and steps your department should take to protect the company's data against computer viruses. Generate this list of recommendations and then group the recommendations into logical categories. Compare your team's recommendations with those generated by the other teams in your class.

Expand Your Knowledge

Discovering Career Opportunities

You love technology but cringe at the thought of sitting in front of the computer all day, writing miles of code for new programs or designing complicated networks. But before you prejudge what you may or may not have to do at work if you pursue a career in information management, why not consult an expert. Log onto Prentice Hall's Student Success SuperSite at www.prenhall.com/success/MajorExp and select the Information Technology major. What courses do you need to take for this major? What can you do with a degree in Information Technology? How might you use these courses to prepare you for a general business career?

Developing Your Research Skills

Scan recent business journals and newspapers (print or online edition) for an article showing how computers or other new technology helped a company gain a competitive advantage or improve its profitability.

1. What new technology did the company acquire and how did managers use it to gain a competitive advantage or improve profitability?
2. Did the article mention any problems the company had implementing its new technology? What were they? Do you think the problems could have been avoided? How?
3. Did the technology require employees to learn new skills? If so, what were they?

Exploring the Best of the Web

URLs for all Internet exercises are provided at the website for this book, www.prenhall.com/bovee. When you log on to this text's Companion Website, select Chapter 4. Then select "Featured Websites," click on the name of the featured website, and review the website to complete these exercises.

Explore these chapter-related websites, review their content, and answer the following questions for each website you visit:

1. What is the purpose of this website?
2. What kinds of information does this website contain? Please be specific.
3. How is the information provided at this website useful for businesspeople? Consumers?
4. How did you expand your knowledge of information management, the Internet, and e-commerce by reviewing the material at this website? What new things did you learn about these topics?

Stay Informed with CIO

Chief information officers make smart business decisions by staying current in the field of information technology. Resources such as CIO Online, a leading resource for information managers, provides expert advice and links to many industry-related resources. Log onto the journal and research critical information topics, listen to industry experts, receive career advice, get the latest Internet survey information, visit the reading room, join a discussion forum, and more. Don't worry if you missed an issue or two—access to the archives is as easy as a click of the mouse. www.cio.com

Ride the Technology Wave

Computer technology advances at a dizzying pace. Today's industry standards in hardware and software can become dinosaurs almost overnight. This situation can be especially problematic for businesses that spend thousands, or even millions, of dollars on computer systems intended to improve productivity. Fortunately, a number of excellent resources are available on the Internet to help both businesspeople and home computer users stay on top of the advancing waves of technology. *PC Magazine Online* is one such resource. This website offers news on future technologies, reviews of current hot products, and hints for effective information and technology management, as well as hundreds of free software downloads. Take some time to explore this resource. In business today, any extra information you can get about technology trends may become a competitive advantage. www.pcmag.com

Learn the Rules of the Road

The road to creating a successful online store can be a difficult and confusing one if you are unaware of the concepts and principles behind e-commerce. Learn how e-commerce works and how to get started in the exciting world of e-commerce by visiting the eCommerce Guidebook. Discover how to get an Internet merchant bank account. Search for available domain names. Get the latest Internet and e-commerce statistics. And stay on top of the latest e-commerce news by clicking on one of the featured e-magazines, by visiting an industry association, or by following the online resource links provided at this website. www.online-commerce.com

Learning Interactively

Companion Website

Visit the Companion Website at www.prenhall.com/bovee. For Chapter 4, take advantage of the interactive "Learning Modules" to test your chapter knowledge. Get instant feedback on whether you need additional studying. Complete the exercises as specified by your instructor.

A Case for Critical Thinking

Nokia Dials Up Wireless Innovations

Hold up one of Nokia's innovative mobile phones, and it's hard to picture the Finnish company's humble beginnings as a maker of everything from toilet paper to tires. Founded in 1865 as a forest products company, Nokia saw more than 125 years of profitable operations skid to a halt in the early 1990s when a global recession and the Soviet Union's collapse stalled demand for the company's rubber, paper, and chemical products. Nokia was making mobile phones by that time, but it couldn't match competitors' mass-production techniques. When Jorma Ollila took over as CEO in 1992, Nokia was floundering.

STRONG CONNECTIONS

In a bold move to survive, Ollila ditched the conglomerate's other interests to focus on wireless tele-com. His hands-off management style inspired innovation and creativity, and employees worked in teams to turn the company around. Nokia beefed up its research and development efforts and designed the 2100 series with stylish, contemporary features. The company had predicted sales of 400,000 units when it launched the 2100 series in late 1993. Actual sales were 20 million.

Operating profits soared to $1 billion in 1995, but Ollila was determined to stay ahead of the competition. Nokia began introducing models that appealed to specific market segments, from user-friendly phones that required only one hand to operate to models with switchable covers and selectable ring tones. A series of market winners pushed Nokia past Motorola as the world's top mobile maker by the end of the 1990s, with roughly a third of the global market.

NOKIA'S SECRET CODE

From the beginning of Nokia's dramatic turnaround, the company realized that teamwork, focus, and innovation were key to success. At annual meetings known as the Nokia Way, employees now help determine Nokia's priorities. Nokia executives then translate these priorities into a strategic plan and make sure they stay on track by monitoring annual revenue growth. If growth of a product line falls below 25 percent, employees shift their focus to other products with more potential.

Another element of Nokia's success is the company's ability to innovate with an eye on the future. More than a third of its employees work in research and development, fostering new technologies, creating new products, and even envisioning new business models. Smart strategy and fast, creative implementation continued to pay off, cementing Nokia's position as the world's number one phone supplier.

A MISSTEP THAT COSTS MILLIONS

Ollila knows that sustaining phenomenal growth requires constant attention and reinvention. As he once put it, "This isn't a business where you do one big strategic thing right and you're set for the next five years." Those words came painfully true in 2004, when Nokia suddenly slipped from its lofty perch, and the company's stock price tumbled as a result. In less than a year, its worldwide market share plunged from nearly 40 percent to around 30 percent, primarily a consequence of being slow to market with "clamshell" style phones made popular by Motorola and sold with increasing success by South Korean competitors Samsung and LG.

How could a company that had done so much so right make such a mistake? Anssi Vanjoki, the executive in charge of multimedia, was blunt: "We read the signs in the marketplace a bit wrong." Nokia may be been blinded by success, too. First, having risen to the top with an emphasis on quality and technical capability, the company might've been slow to recognize the phone market's transition from functional electronic product to fashion accessory. Second, a key part of Nokia's success has been its ability to mass-produce phones in its own factories, rather than relying on contract manufacturers. However, to manage these factories efficiently, the company has often taken a wait-and-see approach to adopting new features and technologies—to make sure the wide-scale demand is there to support mass production. In a slow-moving market, this can be a great strategy, but as cell phones became toys and fashion accessories, consumer demand became as fickle as it is in those two industries—and a production system designed for high volumes but limited variety can became a liability.

REINVENTING NOKIA—ONCE AGAIN

Having once survived the collapse of its biggest market and having completely recast the company as a high-tech powerhouse, Ollila is hardly someone who shrinks from a challenge. Nokia moved quickly, simplifying the structure of the company from nine down to five market-focused divisions and retooling manufacturing to produce a wider variety of phones in less time, including customized versions for major cell phone service providers.

Maintaining profitability is going to be one of the biggest ongoing challenges. Nokia used to hold a strong lead in unique phone technologies, but as often happens in electronics, many of these once-unique features and functions are now available off the shelf in inexpensive integrated circuits. Several companies even sell "phone kits" that are ready to assemble, making it much easier for Nokia's competitors to build phones. Such advances help lower prices for consumers but blunt Nokia's advantages and put tremendous pressure on profit margins.

If anyone has demonstrated the ability to make it happen, though, it's the experienced management team at Nokia. In 2006, Ollila retired and turned the reins over to 20-year Nokia veteran Olli-Pekka Kallasvuo. It's now up to Kallasvuo to help Nokia carry on the proud Finnish tradition of *sisu*, which roughly translates as a combination of courage and perseverance. Up against several world-class companies fighting for market share, Nokia will need all the sisu it can muster.

Critical Thinking Questions

1. Why did Nokia shift its focus to wireless communications?
2. Why is mass production capability a potential liability in some consumer markets?
3. How could Nokia use information technology to avoid missing another shift in consumer preferences?
4. Visit Nokia's website and answer these questions: Has Nokia managed to continue growth and maintain profits? How does Nokia encourage consumers to try new features and functions such as digital photography? How does Nokia explore new technologies and business possibilities that aren't in its immediate corporate focus? How does the Nokia Research Center help the rest of the company?

VIDEO CASE

Space Age Information Systems: Boeing Satellite Systems

Learning Objectives

The purpose of this video is to help you:

1. Recognize why a business must manage information.
2. Consider the role of information systems within an organization.
3. Recognize how information systems and communication technology contribute to a company's efficiency and performance.

Synopsis

The world's leading manufacturer of commercial communications satellites, Boeing Satellite Systems is a wholly owned subsidiary of Boeing and serves customers in 14 countries. Each of the company's more than 8,000 employees is equipped with a personal computer or laptop, which can also serve as a television to receive broadcasts about company activities. The company's information system collects data from all departments, analyzes the information, and then disseminates the results to help management make decisions that will boost performance, productivity, and competitiveness. The chief information officer also oversees security precautions and disaster recovery plans to safeguard the company's valuable data.

Discussion Questions

1. *For analysis:* What role do information systems play in the Boeing Satellite Systems division?
2. *For analysis:* What are some of the ways in which information technology can improve productivity and performance at Boeing Satellite Systems?
3. *For application:* What potential problems might Boeing Satellite Systems have encountered when introducing computer kiosks into factory operations?
4. *For application:* In addition to showing Boeing-made satellites being launched, what else should the company broadcast to employees' computers? Why?
5. *For debate:* Should Boeing Satellite Systems use software to prevent potential abuses by monitoring how its employees use their personal computers and laptops? Support your chosen position.

Online Exploration

Visit the Boeing Satellite Systems website at www.boeing.com/satellite and follow links or search the site to learn more about its state-of-the-art integration and test facility. Also browse the site to see what the company says about its use of information systems and communication technology. Why would the company discuss technology in detail on a public website? What specific benefits of information systems does Boeing Satellite Systems highlight? Why are these benefits important to customers who buy satellites?

E-Business in Action

THE BIGGEST AUDIENCE IN THE WHOLE WIDE WORLD WIDE WEB

As signs of progress go, it's not one that will make anybody happy, but it's a sign of progress nonetheless: The Peoples' Republic of China is now the world's number two receiver of junk e-mail, second only to the United States. The dubious distinction goes hand in hand with China's rapid rise as an online market. More than 80 million Chinese residents were online in 2004, and that number is expected to soon reach 150 or 200 million. At that point, China will have more Internet users than the United States (and, presumably, more spam).

The game company Kingsoft is a good example of how rapidly Chinese consumers embrace new online offerings. After attempting to sell software to consumers for years, the company gave up and shifted to putting games on the Internet, starting with an action game called Sword Online. Within six months, Kingsoft had signed up 1.7 million customers and has plans to keep growing into a technology leader. Forecasters expect the online game market in China to surpass $800 million by 2007.

Internet + Mobile Phones = Profits

The marriage of the Internet and wireless technology promises to be another hot business across China. The country already has twice as many mobile phone subscribers as the United States, and online portals now deliver a variety of information and entertainment services to phone users—news, games, dating services, even voice greeting cards featuring NBA star Yao Ming. The wireless multimedia market alone jumped from $200 million in 2001 to $3 billion in 2004. Kingsoft is among the companies developing phone games that combine movies, voice, and data.

Multimedia phone services proved to be an enormous blessing for China's leading web portals, which include Sina, Sohu, and NetEase. (A web portal is a multifaceted website such as www.yahoo.com, which provides a variety of information and entertainment offerings, along with site directories, search engines, and other services.) Because advertising opportunities in China were so minuscule to begin with, Sina and the other Chinese portals avoided a misstep that hobbled many U.S. e-commerce companies during the early days of the Internet boom—trying to support themselves by selling online advertising. That business model never really took off in the United States and, in fact, proved to be the financial undoing of many promising young companies that invested millions of dollars in the untested hope that ad dollars would show up sooner or later. In contrast, the Chinese portals are already profitable, thanks to wireless content services.

Rapid Evolution

This sizzling growth is a far cry from just a few years ago, when the Chinese government generally viewed e-commerce as a threat to its tight control over the economy and consumer behavior. Now, the country's leadership is intent on making China a global technology leader, showing strengths in both networking and wireless technologies. The country is rapidly evolving from a low-cost manufacturer to a high-quality manufacturer and is on its way to being a technical innovator as well. As Robert Mao, CEO of greater China operations for networking giant Nortel, put it, China is now "part of the leading edge."

This isn't to say that growth is easy, by any means. Peggy Lu, head of DangDang.com, which roughly models itself after Amazon.com, faced the challenge of selling products online without a financial feature that marketers in many countries take for granted—credit cards (most Chinese citizens don't have them yet). To get around this hurdle, Lu's company accepts money orders and lets customers pay in cash when products are delivered.

Internet entrepreneurs such as Lu are becoming role models for a new generation who see that they can get ahead on their own initiative, without relying on official connections. In an economy under tight state control, "people used to think you could only get rich with stocks or smuggling," says one Chinese CEO. "Now, with the Internet, they know they can get rich using their intelligence."

Freedom to Profit, Not Freedom of the Press

Does all this free-market fervor mean that China's communist government is relaxing its control over the country's citizens? Hardly. Site operators are forbidden to publish information about Falun Gong, an outlawed religious group, or to raise the call for political reform, for instance. The instant message service QQ is reported to filter out more than 1,000 politically sensitive names and terms. Moreover, the government has been known to demand free advertising space on portal sites.

Blogs, the newest online rage in the United States, also came under close scrutiny in China. In 2004, for instance, the government shut down two blogs for carrying content it deemed objectionable—rumored to be discussions relating to the 1989 crackdown on a student protest in Beijing's Tiananmen Square. A year earlier, officials blocked access to Blogspot, a popular site in the United States that helps people build their own blogs.

In addition, Internet cafés, popular with students and travelers all over the world, can prompt government crackdowns. Officials recently banned the establishment of any new Internet cafés close to primary or middle schools or within residential buildings, out of fear that illegal online content might corrupt young minds.

Building a Bubble?

In spite of the technical and political challenges, the World Wide Web is in China to stay. The Internet economy may have taken a while to catch a spark in China, but it's been on fire ever since. In fact, market watchers liken the frantic growth to the dot-com boom in the United States in the late 1990s. Stock prices for China's leading Internet companies are growing as fast as their markets, leading some to worry that the bubble will soon burst, as the dot-coms did in the United States a few years ago. However, executives such as NetEase's Ted Sun insist things are different in China. Not only are the companies already making money, but they tend not to be saddled by much debt and they run their operations in a much more frugal manner than their U.S. counterparts did.

Speaking of U.S. Internet firms, where do such giants as Yahoo! and AOL show up in the list of China's most popular online sites? Not much more than a blip on the radar screen, actually. Yahoo! China ranks a distant fourth in popularity, behind Sina, Sohu, and NetEase. As one investor put it, "Everybody thought AOL was going to take over the world. They didn't." Experts and users both say that foreign-owned sites don't yet seem to have a good feel for the Chinese market. With the

world's largest Internet population in their sights, though, you can bet that the world's leading Internet companies aren't about to ignore China's vast online market.

Questions for Critical Thinking

1. What advantages do U.S. e-commerce companies have over their Chinese counterparts? What disadvantages?
2. Why is a country's infrastructure an important factor in e-commerce development and success?
3. How might government control of information affect the growth of e-commerce in China?

Career Profiles

Here are brief glimpses at two career paths that relate to the chapters in Part I. You'll find other career profiles following Chapters 6, 9, 11, 15, and 18.

Business Economist

Economists work in a variety of capacities, often specializing in such areas as market dynamics, labor trends and issues, international markets, and finance.

Nature of the Work   Business economist is generally a research and advisory position in which you identify forces and trends in the business environment, analyze the threats and opportunities suggested by these trends, and recommend a course of action in response to those threats and opportunities. Other common projects include analyzing the economic impact of government regulations, forecasting labor demand and supply, and studying the effects of interest rates and other monetary factors.

The profession is well suited to people with analytical minds, strong curiosity about how the world operates, and the ability to pay close attention to details while simultaneously keeping the "big picture" in sight. The work involves lots of research, statistical analysis, report writing, and presentations. Because you spend so much time studying the external environment, business economics can give you a comprehensive view of industries and markets often not available in other professions.

Qualifications   With a bachelor's degree, you can qualify for some entry-level positions (such as a research assistant), but a master's degree is usually required for most positions in business economics—and a Ph.D. is expected for many top-level jobs. In addition to understanding principles of economics and business, you'll be expected to have strong math and computer skills in virtually any area of business economics. Because so much of the work involves sharing research results and recommendations with people who aren't specialists in the field, written and oral communication skills are essential.

Where the Jobs Are   Roughly half of all economists work in private industry, typically for large corporations or consulting firms that offer either economic analysis services or strategic advice. The remainder work in teaching positions or for government agencies and various other not-for-profit organizations, such as labor unions and industry associations.

Where to Learn More   National Association for Business Economics, www.nabe.com; Canadian Association for Business Economics, www.cabe.ca.

Information Technology Manager

Information technology (IT) managers oversee the systems that capture, organize, process, protect, and redistribute an organization's vital data and information. Positions within this field range from departmental network manager and data center manager on up to chief technology officer (CTO) and chief information officer (CIO).

Nature of the Work   If you enjoy solving complex problems, leading talented teams, staying on top of the latest technologies, and working at the very heart of the modern corporation, an IT management job might be perfect for you.

IT management often has both an ongoing operational component (keeping systems running smoothly) and a project-oriented component (creating new systems or modifying existing systems). The nature of the work varies with the specific responsibilities of the team or department but usually involves a mix of technology, business, and human resource elements, so the ability to grasp, analyze, and solve multidimensional problems is crucial. The pace can be hectic, particularly with *mission-critical* technologies such as e-commerce and production systems.

Qualifications   IT management is demanding field, so it should come as no surprise that the qualifications are rigorous. The combination of a technical undergraduate degree and an MBA is a common expectation (many students planning to enter the field opt for one of the specialized IT-focused MBA programs now available). All positions in IT management require some level of technical acumen, although the work generally becomes less hands-on and more business-oriented as you rise through the organization. Jobs in IT require constant learning, keeping up with not only new technologies but also important issues such as data security, privacy, and intellectual property laws. Many IT managers first gain experience as *systems analysts*, a position that involves studying the information needs of a given set of users, then designing cost-effective solutions to deliver that information in a timely manner.

Communication skills are vital at every level, from practicing active listening in order to understand user needs to helping top executives understand how IT fits in the overall strategic picture to writing proposals.

Where the Jobs Are   IT management jobs exist just about everywhere that IT systems exist, in virtually every industry and in all but the smallest companies. Roughly 300,000 IT management jobs exist in the United States alone, and that number is expected to keep growing in the foreseeable future. Management opportunities can be found in both the organizations that manage their own IT systems and *outsourcers* that provide IT services to organizations without their own IT resources.

Where to Learn More   Association of Information Technology Professionals, www.aitp.org (AITP has hundreds of local chapters around the country; chances are your college or university has a student chapter); *InformationWeek*, www.informationweek.com; *CIO*, www.cio.com; *InfoWorld*, www.infoworld.com; *ComputerWorld*, www.computerworld.com.

Building the Foundation: Forms of Business Ownership

CHAPTER 5

LEARNING OBJECTIVES

After studying this chapter, you will be able to

1. List five advantages and four disadvantages of sole proprietorships

2. List five advantages and two disadvantages of partnerships

3. Explain the differences between common and preferred stock from a shareholder's perspective

4. Highlight the advantages and disadvantages of public stock ownership

5. Cite four advantages and three disadvantages of corporations

6. Delineate the three groups that govern a corporation and describe the role of each

7. Identify the synergies that companies hope to achieve by combining their operations

www.prenhall.com/bovee

INSIDE BUSINESS TODAY

Growing Pains at Kinko's

www.kinkos.com

All big companies were small at one point, but Paul Orfalea's photocopy shop near the University of California, Santa Barbara, was literally so small he had to wheel the single copier onto the sidewalk to make room for customers. From those humble beginnings in the early 1970s, Orfalea built Kinko's (the name was inspired by his own curly hair) into a far-flung empire. By 1995, Kinko's had 815 stores operating in five countries.

Unlike the typical growing company, however, Kinko's wasn't managed as a single entity but instead consisted of 130 separate partnerships, each operating groups of stores. Even though Orfalea retained a majority interest in each partnership, the partners were free to operate their stores as they saw fit. As a result, the facilities and service level varied dramatically from one Kinko's to the next. Some owners reinvested their earnings in high-tech equipment while others cashed in their profits. Traveling customers would find color copiers and high-speed Internet access at spruced-up outlets in one city and dilapidated storefronts with little more than black-and-white copy machines in another.

Orfalea realized that to succeed in an increasingly high-tech marketplace, he needed to replace this patchwork management structure with a real corporate organization so that Kinko's customers could rely on consistency throughout the chain. Moreover, with more and more people working at home, in cars, in airports, or in other remote locations, the stores would have to invest in expensive equipment such as digital printers, high-speed copiers, fast Internet connections, and even videoconferencing equipment to service the growing needs of a new generation of knowledge workers.

In need of both managerial expertise and financial backing, Orfalea selected private investors Clayton, Dublier & Rice (CD&R) in 1997 to help turn things around. Orfalea sold one-third of his partnership interests to CD&R for $220 million. Meanwhile, CD&R organized a massive "roll-up," in which individual partnerships swapped their interests for shares of stock in the new private Kinko's corporation. This structure allowed CD&R to centralize operations and bring in professional managers (Orfalea stepped aside to became chairman of the board). The original partners needed some time to adjust to the new corporate structure—after all, they were accustomed to being their own bosses. But eventually they came around, realizing that a private equity stake in Kinko's could be worth a sizable fortune if the company went public some day.

Store managers lobbied aggressively for new equipment and expanded their services to include on-site computer rentals, document binding and finishing, custom printing, passport photos, mailing services (including overnight delivery drop-off), videoconference facilities, and a computer network that lets customers transmit information from one Kinko's site to another—a huge bonus for traveling businesspeople.

Restructuring the partnerships helped turn Kinko's into the world's leading provider of document solutions and business services, and the chain soon grew past 1,000 stores. The public stock offering many partners hoped for never happened, however, and Orfalea and other shareholders accused CD&R of preventing them from cashing out their shares. Rather than taking the company public, CD&R began buying up partners' shares of stock, first reaching 40 percent ownership, then paying an additional $175 million to acquire 73 percent ownership in 2003. CD&R's investment paid off—in a major way—when Federal Express purchased the entire Kinko's operation in early 2004 for $2.4 billion. Although some analysts were surprised at the price tag, FedEx saw the acquisition as an opportunity to expand its retail presence and compete more effectively with arch-rival UPS, which had recently expanded *its* retail presence with the acquisition of Mail Boxes Etc.[1]

GET READY

Imagine that, like Paul Orfalea, you've nurtured one of your own business ideas until it grew into a large company, but you've reached a point where you need outside help. Would you be able to surrender control in exchange for managerial expertise and financing? How would you convince thousands of employees at hundreds of Kinko's branches worldwide that changing to a corporate structure would provide the operating efficiencies and funds the shops would need to survive and thrive? What steps would you take to make sure that the transition from seat-of-the-pants entrepreneurship to organized corporate life would add these benefits without destroying the independent spirit that helped the company grow in the first place? ■

Chapter Overview

Kinko's long journey represents about every possible form of business ownership, from a single individual with an entrepreneurial idea to a business unit tucked inside a major multinational corporation. In this chapter you'll explore one of the most fundamental and important questions in business: What legal form should the company take? You'll start by considering the three major types of ownership—sole proprietorships, partnerships, and corporations—then look at current trends in mergers and acquisitions. The chapter concludes with an overview of joint ventures and strategic partnerships.

Choosing a Form of Business Ownership

As Paul Orfalea knows, one of the most fundamental decisions you must make when starting a business is selecting a form of business ownership. This decision can be complex and have far-reaching consequences for owners, employees, and customers. Picking the right ownership structure involves knowing your long-term goals and how you plan to achieve them. Your choice also depends on your desire for ownership and your tolerance for risk.

Exhibit 5.1

Characteristics of the Forms of Business Ownership

The "best" form of ownership depends on the objectives of the people involved in the business.

Structure	Ownership Rules and Control	Tax Considerations	Liability Exposure	Ease of Establishment and Termination
Sole proprietorship	One owner has complete control.	Profits and losses flow directly to the owners and are taxed at individual rates.	Owner has unlimited personal liability for business debts.	Easy to set up but leaves owner's personal finances at risk. Owner must generally sell the business to get his or her investment out.
General partnership	Two or more owners; each partner is entitled to equal control unless agreement specifies otherwise.	Profits and losses flow directly to the partners and are taxed at individual rates. Partners share income and losses equally unless the partnership agreement specifies otherwise.	Personal assets of any operating partner are at risk from business creditors.	Easy to set up. Partnership agreement recommended but not required. Partners must generally sell their share in the business to recoup their investment.
Limited partnership	Two or more owners; the general partner controls the business; limited partners don't participate in the management.	Same as for general partnership.	Limited partners are liable only for the amount of their investment.	Same as for general partnership.
Corporation	Unlimited number of shareholders; no limits on stock classes or voting arrangements. Ownership and management of the business are separate. Shareholders in public corporations are not involved in daily management decisions; in private or closely held corporations, owners are more likely to participate in managing the business.	Profits and losses are taxed at corporate rates. Profits are taxed again at individual rates when they are distributed to the investors as dividends.	Investor's liability is limited to the amount of his or her investment.	Expense and complexity of incorporation vary from state to state; can be costly from a tax perspective. In a public corporation, shareholders may trade their shares on the open market; in a private corporation shareholders must find a buyer for their shares to recoup their investment.

Furthermore, as your business grows, chances are you may change the original form you selected, as Orfalea did.

The three most common forms of business ownership are sole proprietorship, partnership, and corporation. Each form has its own characteristic internal structure, legal status, size, and fields to which it is best suited. Each has key advantages and disadvantages for the owners (see Exhibit 5.1).

Sole Proprietorships

A **sole proprietorship** is a business owned by one person (although it may have many employees), and it is the easiest and least expensive form of business to start. Many farms, retail establishments, and small service businesses are sole proprietorships, as are many home-based businesses (such as caterers, consultants, and computer programmers). Many of the local businesses you frequent around your college campus are likely to be sole proprietorships.

Advantages of Sole Proprietorships A sole proprietorship has many advantages, starting with ease of establishment. About the only legal requirement is obtaining the necessary business licenses. Another advantage is the satisfaction of working for yourself. As a sole proprietor, you can make your own decisions, such as which hours to work (beware the old joke that working for yourself means you get to choose which 80 hours you work every week), whom to hire, what prices to charge, whether to expand, and whether to shut down. You also get to keep all the after-tax profits, and, depending on your filing status and taxable income, you may be obligated to pay less as a sole proprietor, compared to what you would pay as a corporation (although you are also obligated to pay self-employment tax as a sole proprietor).

As a sole proprietor, you also have the advantage of privacy; you do not have to reveal your performance or plans to anyone. Although you may need to provide financial information to a banker if you need a loan, and you must provide certain financial information when you file tax returns, you do not have to prepare any reports for outsiders as you would if the company were a public corporation.

Disadvantages of Sole Proprietorships One major drawback of a sole proprietorship is the proprietor's **unlimited liability**. From a legal standpoint, the owner and the business are one and the same. Any legal damages or debts incurred by the business are the owner's responsibility. As a sole proprietor, you might have to sell personal assets, such as your home, to satisfy a business debt. And if someone sues you over a business matter, from dissatisfaction with a product to slipping on ice in your parking lot, you might lose everything you own if you do not have the proper business insurance.

In some cases, the sole proprietor's independence can also be a drawback because it means that the business depends on the talents and managerial skills of one person. If problems crop up, the sole proprietor may not recognize them or may be too proud to seek help, especially given the high cost of hiring experienced managers and professional consultants. Other disadvantages include the difficulty of a single-person operation obtaining large sums of capital and the limited life of a sole proprietorship. Although some sole proprietors pass their businesses on to their heirs as part of their estate, the owner's death may mean the demise of the business. And even if the business does transfer to an heir, the founder's unique skills may have been crucial to the successful operation of the business.

Partnerships

If starting a business on your own seems a little intimidating, you might decide to share the risks and rewards of going into business with a partner. In that case, you would form a **partnership**—a legal association of two or more people as co-owners of a business for profit. You and your partners would share the profits and losses of the business and perhaps the management responsibilities. Your partnership might remain a small, two-person operation or it might have multiple partners, as Kinko's did before it was purchased by FedEx.

Partnerships are of two basic types. In a **general partnership**, all partners are considered equal by law, and all are liable for the business's debts. For instance, when the accounting firm Laventhol and Horwath plunged into bankruptcy, the partners had to dig into their own pockets to satisfy creditors.[2] To guard against personal liability exposure, some organizations choose to form a **limited partnership**. Under this type of partnership, one or more persons act as *general partners* who run the business, while the remaining partners are passive investors (that is, they are not involved in managing the business). These partners are called *limited partners* because their liability (the amount of money they can lose) is limited to the amount of their capital

TECHNOLOGIES THAT ARE REVOLUTIONIZING BUSINESS Groupware

Groupware is an umbrella term for systems that let people communicate, share files, present materials, and work on documents simultaneously.

HOW IT'S CHANGING BUSINESS

Groupware is changing the way employees interact with one another—and even the way businesses work together. In fact, groupware is changing the way many companies are structured. *Shared workspaces* are "virtual offices" that give everyone on a team access to the same set of resources and information: databases, calendars, project plans, archived instant messages and e-mails, reference materials, and team documents. These workspaces (which are typically accessible through a web browser) let you and your team organize your work files into a collection of electronic folders, making it easy for geographically dispersed team members to access shared files anytime, anywhere. Employees no longer need to be in the same office or even in the same time zone. They don't even need to be employees. Groupware makes it easy for companies to pull together partners and temporary contractors on a project-by-project basis.

Groupware is often integrated with web-based meeting systems that combine instant messaging, shared workspaces, videoconferencing, and other tools such as *virtual whiteboards* that let teams collaborate in real time.

WHERE YOU CAN LEARN MORE

Log on to **www.zdnet.com**, click on "Tech Update," then "Software Infrastructure," then "Groupware."

contribution. Many states now recognize *limited liability partnerships* (LLPs) in which all partners in the business are limited partners and have only limited liability for the debts and obligations of the partnership. The limited liability partnership was invented to protect members of partnerships from being wiped out by claims against their firms. Most states restrict LLPs to certain types of professionals such as attorneys, physicians, dentists, and accountants.[3] Of the three forms of business ownership, partnerships are the least common (see Exhibit 5.2).

Advantages of Partnerships Proprietorships and partnerships have some of the same advantages. Like proprietorships, partnerships are easy to form. Partnerships also provide the same potential tax advantages as proprietorships.

LEARNING OBJECTIVE 2

List five advantages and two disadvantages of partnerships

Exhibit 5.2
Popular Forms of Business Ownership
The most popular form of business ownership is sole proprietorship, followed by corporations, then partnerships.

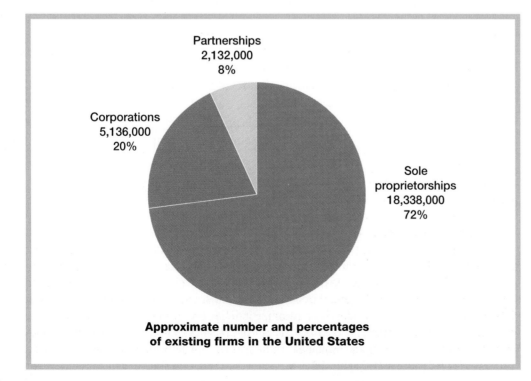

Partnerships
2,132,000
8%

Corporations
5,136,000
20%

Sole proprietorships
18,338,000
72%

Approximate number and percentages of existing firms in the United States

However, in a couple of respects, partnerships are superior to sole proprietorships, largely because there's strength in numbers. When you have several people putting up their money, you can start a more ambitious enterprise. In addition, the diversity of skills that good partners bring to an organization leads to innovation in products, services, and processes, which improves your chances of success.[4] The partnership form of ownership also broadens the pool of capital available to the business. Not only do the partners' personal assets support a larger borrowing capacity but the ability to obtain financing increases because general partners are legally responsible for paying off the debts of the group. Finally, by forming a partnership you increase the chances that the organization will endure, because new partners can be drawn into the business to replace those who die or retire. For example, even though the original partners in the several accounting firms that eventually became industry giant KPMG (the roots of which stretch back to 1870) died many years ago, the company continues.

Disadvantages of Partnerships Except in limited liability partnerships, at least one member of every partnership must be a general partner. All general partners have unlimited liability. Thus, if one of the firm's partners makes a serious mistake and is sued by a disgruntled client, all general partners are financially accountable. General partners are also responsible for any debts incurred by the partnership.

Another disadvantage of partnerships is the potential for interpersonal problems. Difficulties can arise when each partner wants to be responsible for managing the organization. Electing a managing partner to lead the organization may diminish the conflicts, but disagreements are still possible. Moreover, the partnership may have to face the question of what to do with unproductive partners. And if a partner wants to leave the firm, conflicts can arise over claims on the firm's profits and on capital the partner invested. Provisions for handling the departure and addition of partners are usually covered in the partnership agreement.

Keeping It Together: The Partnership Agreement A *partnership agreement* is a written document that states all the terms of operating the partnership by spelling out the partners' rights and responsibilities. Although the law does not require a written partnership agreement, it is wise to work with a lawyer to develop one. One of the most important features of such an agreement is to address sources of conflict that could result in battles between partners. The agreement spells out such details as the division of profits, decision-making authority, expected contributions, and dispute resolution. Moreover, a key element of this document is the buy/sell agreement, which defines the steps a partner must take to sell his or her partnership interest or what will happen if one of the partners dies.

Avis has never paid cash dividends to shareholders. The company believes that shareholders are best served by reinvesting profits back into the company to foster long-term growth.

CRITICAL THINKING CHECKPOINT

1. Can a sole proprietorship outlive its original owner?
2. Is a partnership more or less risky than a sole proprietorship? Explain your answer.
3. Why is it important for a partnership agreement to spell out managerial responsibilities and financial arrangements?

Corporations

corporation
Legally chartered enterprise having most of the legal rights of a person, including the right to conduct business, to own and sell property, to borrow money, and to sue or be sued

A **corporation** is a legal entity, distinct from any individual persons, with the power to own property and conduct business. Regardless of how many owners a corporation has (some have thousands of owners), the law generally treats the corporation the same way it treats an individual person. The modern corporation evolved in the nineteenth century when large sums of capital were needed to build railroads, steel mills, and manufacturing plants. Such endeavors required so much money that no single individual or group of partners could hope to raise it all. The solution was to sell *shares* in the business to numerous investors, who would get a cut of the profits in exchange for their money. These investors got a chance to vote on certain issues that might affect the value of their investment, but they were not involved in managing day-to-day operations. The investors were protected from the risks associated with such large undertakings by having their liability limited to the amount of their investment.

It was a good solution, and the corporation quickly became a vital force in the nation's economy. As rules and regulations developed to define what corporations could and could not do, corporations acquired the legal attributes of people. Like you, a corporation can receive, own, and transfer property; make contracts; sue; and be sued. Unlike the case with sole proprietorships and partnerships, a corporation's legal status and obligations exist independently of its owners.

Ownership The corporation is owned by its **shareholders**, who are issued shares of stock in return for their investments. These shares are represented by a **stock certificate**, and they may be bequeathed or sold to someone else. As a result, the company's ownership may change drastically over time while the company and its management remain intact (as long as the company is economically sound). The corporation's unlimited life span, combined with its ability to raise capital, gives it the potential for significant growth.

Common Stock. Most stock issued by corporations is **common stock**. Owners of common stock have voting rights and get one vote for each share of stock they own. Depending on the corporation, they can elect the company's board of directors in addition to voting on major policies that will affect ownership—such as mergers and acquisitions. Besides conferring voting privileges, common stock frequently pays **dividends**, payments to shareholders from the company's profits. Dividends can be paid in cash or stock (called *stock dividends*). They are declared by the board of directors but their payment is not mandatory. For example, some companies, especially young or rapidly growing ones, pay no dividends. Instead, they reinvest their profits in new product research and development, equipment, buildings, and other assets so they can grow and earn future profits.

In addition to dividends, common shareholders can earn a return on their investment. If shareholders sell their stock in good times for more than they paid for it, they stand to pocket a handsome gain. But because the value or price of a company's common stock is subject to many economic variables besides the company's own performance, common-stock investments are risky and shareholders run the risk of losing some or even all of their investment.

Preferred Stock. In contrast to common stock, **preferred stock** does not usually carry voting rights. It does, however, give preferred shareholders the right of first claim on the corporation's assets (in the form of dividends) after all the company's debts have been paid. This right is especially important if the company ever goes out of business. Moreover, preferred shareholders get their dividends before common shareholders do. The amount of preferred dividend is usually set (or fixed) at the time the preferred stock is issued and can provide investors with a source of steady income. Like common stock, however, dividends on preferred stock may be omitted in times of financial hardship. Still, most preferred stock is *cumulative preferred stock,* which means that any unpaid dividends must be paid before dividends are paid to common shareholders.

Public Versus Private Ownership. The ownership of corporations can be arranged in several ways, which occasionally leads to some confusion about terminology. The stock of a **private corporation**, such as Kinko's was before its purchase by FedEx, is held by only a few individuals or companies and is not publicly traded. By withholding their stock from public sale, the owners retain complete control over their operations and ownership. Such famous companies as Hallmark and Hyatt Hotels have opted to remain private corporations (also referred to as *closed corporations* or *closely held companies*). These companies finance their operating costs and growth from either company earnings or other sources, such as bank loans. Doctors, lawyers, and some other professionals often join forces in a special type of private corporation called a *professional corporation*. As with other private corporations, shares in these professional corporations are not available to the public.

Business Buzz
painting the tape
Unscrupulous attempt to generate interest in a stock, such as by splitting a large purchase into multiple small purchases to create the illusion that many investors are interested in the stock

shareholders
Owners of a corporation

stock certificate
Document that proves stock ownership

common stock
Shares whose owners have voting rights and have the last claim on distributed profits and assets

dividends
Distributions of corporate assets to shareholders in the form of cash or other assets

LEARNING OBJECTIVE 3

Explain the differences between common and preferred stock from a shareholder's perspective

preferred stock
Shares that give their owners first claim on a company's dividends and assets after paying all debts

private corporation
Company owned by private individuals or companies

Volkswagen executives address shareholders at the company's annual meeting.

In contrast, the stock of a **public corporation** is held by and available for sale to the general public (including not only individual investors but also mutual funds, nonprofit organizations, and other companies); thus, the company is said to be *publicly held* or *publicly traded*. Whenever you hear discussions about "corporations," people are nearly always talking about public corporations. These are the stocks you see listed in the newspaper stock tables and on various websites that offer investing information (you'll learn about these in Chapter 18).

As you'll read in Chapter 6, the primary reason for "going public" is to help finance the enterprise. In addition to providing a ready supply of capital, public ownership has other advantages and disadvantages. Among the advantages are increased liquidity, enhanced visibility, and the establishment of an independent market value for the company. Moreover, having a publicly traded stock gives companies flexibility to use such stock to acquire other firms. This was one of the primary reasons UPS recently decided to sell 10 percent of its stock to the public after nearly a century of remaining a privately held organization.[5]

Nevertheless, selling stock to the public also has distinct disadvantages: (1) The cost of going public is high (up to hundreds of thousands of dollars or more), (2) the filing requirements with the Securities and Exchange Commission (SEC) are burdensome, (3) ownership control is reduced, (4) management must be ready to handle the administrative and legal demands of heightened public exposure, and (5) the company is subjected to the stock market's incessant demand for quarterly results. Some companies find it just isn't worth the trouble anymore, particularly with Sarbanes-Oxley and other regulatory changes. Kohler, a highly regarded maker of kitchen and bath fixtures based in Kohler, Wisconsin, has been in family hands for more than a hundred years—and plans to stay that way so it can develop strategies over decades without quarterly stock market pressures. The New York grocery chain Gristede's has been a publicly traded company, but CEO John A. Castimatidis is tired of struggling for recognition from investment analysts and complying with new regulations. "We'll just take the company private," he said in 2004.[6]

Advantages of Corporations No other form of business ownership can match the success of the corporation in bringing together money, resources, and talent; in accumulating assets; and in creating wealth. As it grows, a corporation gains from a diverse labor pool, greater financing options, and expanded research-and-development capabilities. The corporation has certain inherent qualities that make it the best vehicle for reaching those objectives, including limited liability. Although a corporate entity can assume tremendous liabilities, it is the corporation that is liable and not the various shareholders.

In addition to limited liability, corporations that sell stock to the general public have the advantage of **liquidity**, which means that investors can easily convert their stock into cash by selling it on the open market. This option makes buying stock in a corporation attractive to many investors. In contrast, liquidating the assets of a sole proprietorship or a partnership can be difficult. Moreover, shareholders of public corporations can easily transfer their ownership by selling their shares to someone else. Thus, corporations tend to be in a better position than proprietorships and partnerships to make long-term plans, with their unlimited life span and funding available through the sale of stock. As they grow, corporations can benefit from the diverse talents and experience of a large pool of employees and managers. Moreover, large corporations are often able to finance projects internally.

liquidity
The level of ease with which an asset can be converted to cash

Creating the opportunity to seek outside funding was one of the key reasons why Marty Ambuehl and Neil Clark decided on a corporate structure for their business, ATM Express, based in Billings, Montana. Along the way, the pair learned that the more-detailed process of incorporation also forced them to think hard about important issues surrounding their company's future.[7]

Keep in mind that a company need not be large to incorporate. Most corporations, like most businesses, are relatively small, and most small corporations are privately held. The big ones, however, are *really* big (see Exhibit 5.3). A half-dozen of the largest corporations in the United States now generate more than $100 billion in annual revenue.[8] The workforce at Wal-Mart, the biggest U.S. corporation, is larger than the population of a dozen U.S. states.[9]

Rank	Company	2003 Revenue ($millions)
1	Wal-Mart Stores	258,681.0
2	Exxon Mobil	213,199.0
3	General Motors	195,645.2
4	Ford Motor	164,496.0
5	General Electric	134,187.0
6	ChevronTexaco	112,937.0
7	ConocoPhillips	99,468.0
8	Citigroup	94,713.0
9	IBM	89,131.0
10	American International Group	81,300.0
11	Hewlett-Packard	73,061.0
12	Verizon Communications	67,752.0
13	Home Depot	64,816.0
14	Berkshire Hathaway	63,859.0
15	Altria Group	60,704.0
16	McKesson	57,129.2
17	Cardinal Health	56,829.5
18	State Farm Insurance	56,064.6
19	Kroger	53,790.8
20	Fannie Mae	53,766.9
21	Boeing	50,485.0
22	AmerisourceBergen	49,657.3
23	Target	48,163.0
24	Bank of America	48,065.0
25	Pfizer	45,950.0

Exhibit 5.3
U.S. Corporate Titans
Here are the 25 largest public corporations in the United States, as ranked by Fortune *magazine.*

Disadvantages of Corporations Corporations are not without some disadvantages. The paperwork and costs associated with incorporation can be burdensome, particularly if you plan to sell stock to the public. The complexity varies from state to state, but regardless of where you live, it is wise to consult an attorney and an accountant before incorporating. In addition, corporations are taxed twice. They must pay federal and state corporate income tax on the company's profits, and individual shareholders must pay income taxes on their share of the company's profits received as dividends.

Another drawback pertains to publicly owned corporations. As mentioned earlier, such corporations are required by the government to publish information about their finances and operations. Disclosing financial information increases the company's vulnerability to competitors and to those who might want to take over control of the company against the wishes of the existing management. Entrepreneurs who've spent years building companies can even be kicked out of the company if enough other shareholders think it's time for a leadership change. Disclosure also increases the pressure on corporate managers to achieve short-term growth and earnings targets in order to satisfy shareholders and to attract potential investors. Some cite such earnings pressure as the driving force behind the questionable accounting practices you read about in Chapter 1 and will explore in more detail in Chapter 17.

Special Types of Corporations Certain types of corporations enjoy special privileges provided they adhere to strict guidelines and rules. One special type of corporation is known as the **S corporation** (or subchapter S corporation). An S corporation distinction is made only for federal income tax purposes; otherwise, in terms of legal characteristics, it is no different from any other corporation. Basically, the owners receive the tax advantages of a partnership while they raise money through the sale of stock. In addition, income and tax deductions from the business flow directly to the owners, who are taxed at individual income tax rates, just as they are in a partnership. Corporations seeking "S" status must meet certain criteria: (1) They must have no more than 75 investors, none of whom may be nonresident aliens; (2) they must be a domestic (U.S.) corporation; and (3) they can issue only one class of common stock, which means that all stock must share the same dividend and liquidation rights (but may have different voting rights).[10]

Limited liability companies (LLCs) are flexible business entities that combine the tax advantages of a partnership with the personal liability protection of a corporation. Furthermore, LLCs are not restricted in the number of shareholders they can have, and members' participation in management is not restricted as it is in limited partnerships. Members of an LLC normally adopt an operating agreement (similar to a partnership agreement) to govern the entity's operation and management. These agreements generally are flexible and permit owners to structure the allocation of income and losses any way they desire, as long as certain tax rules are followed. In addition, the agreements can be designed to meet the special needs of owners, such as special voting rights, management controls, and buyout options. The only limit to what can be done is the owners' imagination.[11] The advantages of LLCs over other forms have made them quite popular in recent years. In New Hampshire, for instance, new LLCs are forming at four times the rate of regular corporations.[12] Although LLCs are favored by many small companies, they are by no means limited to small firms. Some fair-sized and well-known firms have gone the LLC route, including BMW of North America, Segway (makers of the high-tech Segway Human Transporter), Freightliner (trucks, fire engines, and other vehicles), and CMP Media (a leading publisher of professional journals and websites).

Some corporations are not independent entities; that is, they are owned by a single entity. **Subsidiary corporations**, for instance, are partially or wholly owned by another corporation known as a **parent company**, which supervises the operations of the subsidiary. A *holding company* is a special type of parent company that owns other companies for investment reasons and usually exercises little operating control over those subsidiaries.

S corporation
Corporation with no more than 75 shareholders that may be taxed as a partnership; also known as a subchapter S corporation

limited liability companies (LLCs)
Organizations that combine the benefits of S corporations and limited partnerships without the drawbacks of either

subsidiary corporations
Corporations whose stock is owned entirely or almost entirely by another corporation

parent company
Company that owns most, if not all, of another company's stock and that takes an active part in managing that other company

To further complicate matters, corporations can also be classified according to where they do business. An *alien corporation* operates in the United States but is incorporated in another country. A *foreign corporation*, sometimes called an *out-of-state corporation*, is incorporated in one state (frequently the state of Delaware, where incorporation laws are more lenient) but does business in several other states where it is registered. And a *domestic corporation* does business only in the state where it is chartered (incorporated).

Corporate Governance Although a corporation's common shareholders own the business, they are rarely involved in managing it, particularly if the corporation is publicly traded. Instead, the common shareholders elect a board of directors to represent them, and the directors, in turn, select the corporation's top officers, who actually run the company (see Exhibit 5.4). The term **corporate governance** can be used in a broad sense to describe all the policies, procedures, relationships, and systems in place to oversee the successful and legal operation of the enterprise; media coverage tends to define governance in a more narrow sense: as the responsibilities and performance of the board of directors specifically.

The center of power in a corporation usually lies with the **chief executive officer (CEO)**. Together with the chief financial officer (CFO) and other "c-level" executives, such as the chief technology officer (CTO), chief information officer (CIO), and the chief operating officer (COO)—titles vary from one corporation to the next—the CEO is responsible for establishing company policies, managing corporate direction, and making the big decisions that will affect the company's growth and competitive position, as Chapter 7 discusses in detail. The CEO may also be the chairman of the board, the president of the corporation, or sometimes all three.

Shareholders. Shareholders of a corporation can be individuals, other companies, nonprofit organizations, pension funds, and mutual funds. All shareholders who own voting shares are invited to an annual meeting where top executives present the previous year's results and plans for the coming year and shareholders vote on various resolutions that may be before the board. Those who cannot attend the annual meeting in person vote by **proxy**, signing and returning a slip of paper that authorizes management to vote on their behalf. Because shareholders elect the directors, in theory they are the ultimate governing body of the corporation. In practice, however, most individual shareholders in large corporations—where the shareholders may number in the millions—usually accept the recommendations of management.

The more shareholders a company has, the less tangible the influence each shareholder has on the corporation. However, some shareholders have more influence than others. In recent years, *institutional investors* (such as pension funds, insurance companies, mutual funds, and college endowment funds), which now own half the stock in U.S. corporations, have begun to exert considerable influence over management. For instance, as the largest public pension fund in the country, California Public Employees Retirement System (CalPERS) is one of those institutions with enough influence to get the attention of major corporations. One of its recent moves was withholding its votes for three board members of the Safeway grocery chain, citing several years of poor financial results.[13]

LEARNING OBJECTIVE 6

Delineate the three groups that govern a corporation and describe the role of each

corporate governance
In a broad sense, describes the policies, procedures, relationships, and systems in place to oversee the successful and legal operation of the enterprise; in a narrow sense, describes the responsibilities and performance of the board of directors

chief executive officer (CEO)
Person appointed by a corporation's board of directors to carry out the board's policies and supervise the activities of the corporation

proxy
Document authorizing another person to vote on behalf of a shareholder in a corporation

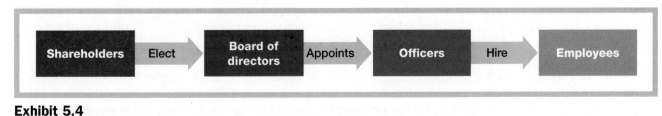

Exhibit 5.4
Corporate Governance
In theory the shareholders of a corporation own the business, but in practice they elect others to run it.

board of directors
Group of people, elected by the shareholders, who have the ultimate authority in guiding the affairs of a corporation

Board of Directors. The **board of directors** in a corporation represents the shareholders and is responsible for declaring dividends, guiding corporate affairs, reviewing long-term strategic plans, selecting corporate officers, and overseeing financial performance. Depending on the size of the company, the board might have anywhere from 3 to 35 directors, although 15 to 25 is the typical range for traditional corporations and perhaps 5 to 10 for smaller, newer corporations. Directors are usually paid a combination of an annual fee and stock options, the right to buy company shares at a specified price.

The board typically has the power to vote on major management decisions, such as building a new factory, hiring a new CEO, or buying a subsidiary. However, the board's actual involvement in running the business varies from one company to another, from passive boards that contribute little to the management of the organization to extremely involved boards that participate in strategic decision making.[14] At Intel, for instance, the board's role has shifted in the past few years from primarily one of passive oversight to one of active involvement. The job is demanding: Directors are expected to understand the company's complex technologies and to be able to analyze the management of Intel facilities worldwide. Directors spend an average of 300 hours a year on Intel business, a significant amount of time for people who have companies of their own to run.[15]

In sharp contrast, the board at failed telecom giant WorldCom (now MCI) once approved a $6 billion acquisition of another company during a 35-minute conference call—with no documents to review. And without even knowing it had done so, the board gave two top executives the authority to borrow unlimited amounts of money from the company. Investigators assert that if the board had questioned WorldCom's growing debt load, it could've stopped or at least slowed the company's descent into bankruptcy.[16]

Much of the attention focused on corporate reform in recent years has zeroed in on boards, but the challenge is not a simple one. In response to both outside pressure and management's recognition of how important an effective board is, corporations are wrestling with a variety of board-related issues:

- **Composition.** Simply identifying the type of people who should be on the board can be a major challenge. Ideally, you want a balanced group of seasoned executives, each of whom can "bring something to the table" that helps the corporation, such as extensive contacts in the industry, manufacturing experience, insight into global issues, and so on. The ratio of insiders (executives) to outsiders (independent directors) is another hot topic. Sarbanes-Oxley requires that the majority of directors be independent so they can

Every Home Depot director must make formal visits to at least 20 stores each year to gain hands-on knowledge of the company's operation.

provide an objective counterbalance to the CEO and other executives, but in order to be effective, these outsiders must also have enough knowledge about the inner workings of the organization to make informed decisions. Diversity is also important, to ensure that adequate attention is paid to issues that affect stakeholders who have been historically underrepresented on corporate boards.[17]

- **Education.** Overseeing the modern corporation is an almost unimaginably complex task. Board members are expected to understand everything from government regulations to financial management to executive compensation strategies—in addition to the inner workings of the corporation itself. A key area of concern is the number of directors who aren't well versed enough in finance to understand their companies' financial statements; this problem has led a number of companies to start educational programs for directors.[18]
- **Liability.** One of the more controversial reform issues has been the potential for directors to be held legally and financially liable for misdeeds of the companies they oversee. In a few extreme cases, directors have even been forced to pay fines out of their own pockets, although this is quite rare.[19]
- **Recruiting challenges.** By now, you've probably gathered that being an effective director in today's business environment is a tough job—so tough that good candidates may start to think twice about accepting directorships. Good board members are more vital than ever, though, so corporate and government leaders have no choice but to solve these challenges.

CRITICAL THINKING CHECKPOINT

1. Why do many corporations choose to remain private when selling shares to the public can raise millions of dollars?
2. Why are corporations considered more liquid than partnerships or sole proprietorships?
3. Why are boards of directors sometimes blamed when corporations lose money or commit ethical or legal violations?

Understanding Business Combinations

Companies have been combining in various configurations since the early days of business. Joining two companies is a complex process because it involves virtually every aspect of both organizations. For instance, executives have to agree on how the combination will be financed and how the power will be transferred and shared. Marketing departments need to figure out how to blend advertising campaigns and sales forces. Incompatible information systems often need to be rebuilt or replaced in order to operate together seamlessly. Companies often must deal with layoffs, transfers, and changes in job titles and work assignments. And through it all, the enterprise needs to keep its eye on customer service, accounting, and every other function.

Mergers and Acquisitions

Businesses can combine permanently through either *mergers* or *acquisitions*. The two terms are often discussed together, usually with the shorthand phrase "M & A," or used interchangeably (although they are technically different). In fact, sometimes an acquisition will be announced to the public and to employees as a merger to help the acquired company save face.[20] The business intentions and outcomes of a merger or an acquisition are usually the same, although the legal and tax ramifications can be quite different, depending on the details of the transaction.

In a **merger**, two companies join to form a single entity. Traditionally, mergers took place between companies of roughly equal size and stature, but mergers between companies of vastly difference sizes is common today. Companies can merge either by pooling their

merger
Combination of two companies in which one company purchases the other and assumes control of its property and liabilities

consolidation
Combination of two or
more companies in
which the old companies
cease to exist and a new
enterprise is created

acquisition
Form of business
combination in which one
company buys another
company's voting stock

hostile takeovers
Situations in which an
outside party buys enough
stock in a corporation to
take control against the
wishes of the board of
directors and corporate
officers

leveraged buyout (LBO)
Situation in which
individuals or groups of
investors purchase
companies primarily with
debt secured by the
company's assets

resources or by one company purchasing the assets of the other.[21] Although not strictly a merger, a **consolidation**, in which two companies create a new, third entity that then purchases the two original companies, is often lumped together with the other two merger approaches.[22] (Note that businesspeople and the media often use "consolidation" in two general senses: to describe any combination of two companies, merger or acquisition, and to describe situations in which a wave of mergers and acquisitions sweeps across an entire industry, reducing the number of competitors.)

In an **acquisition**, one company simply buys a controlling interest in the voting stock of another company. Unlike the real or presumed marriage of equals in a merger, the buyer is definitely the dominant player in an acquisition. In most acquisitions, the selling parties agree to be purchased; management is in favor of the deal and encourages shareholders to vote in favor of it as well. Since buyers frequently offer shareholders more than their shares are currently worth, sellers often have a motivation to sell. However, in a minority of situations, a buyer attempts to acquire a company against the wishes of management. In these **hostile takeovers**, the buyer tries to convince enough shareholders to go against management and vote to sell.

Buyers can offer sellers cash, stock in the acquiring company, or a combination of the two. Another option involves debt. A **leveraged buyout (LBO)** occurs when one or more individuals purchase a company's publicly traded stock by using borrowed funds. The debt is expected to be repaid with funds generated by the company's operations and, often, by the sale of some of its assets. For an LBO to be successful, the acquired company must have a reasonably priced stock, and the acquirer must have easy access to borrowed funds. Unfortunately, in many cases, the buyer must make huge interest and principle payments on the debt, which then depletes the amount of cash that the company has for operations and growth.

Whether it's technically a merger or an acquisition, the combination can take one of several forms (usually all referred to as "mergers" for simplicity's sake):

- A *vertical merger* occurs when a company purchases a complementary company at a different level in the "value chain," such as when a company purchases one of its suppliers or one of its customers. For instance, a car manufacturer acquiring a windshield manufacturer would be a vertical merger since the two companies complement each other in the creation of automobiles.

- A *horizontal merger* involves two similar companies at the same level, such as a combination of two car manufacturers, two windshield manufacturers, two banks, or two retail chains—such as when Kmart acquired Sears in the hopes of competing more effectively against Wal-Mart.[23] Because these mergers are often between two competitors, regulators review them closely to make sure the combined firm won't have monopoly power.

- In a *conglomerate merger*, the two firms offer dissimilar products or services, often in widely different industries.[24] Conglomeration was a popular strategy in the 1950s and 1960s, based on the hope that by diversifying into a variety of industries at once, the company could survive market downturns in one or a few of them. The stock prices of conglomerates often didn't live up to the hope, and the strategy's popularity declined in the 1970s.[25] Conglomerates didn't disappear, of course; the current list includes a number of large and successful companies, such as United Technologies and General Electric. In addition, a new twist on the conglomerate model has appeared in recent years, in which a company that is good in a particular area of business acquires underperforming companies that can benefit from that skill set. For instance, Danaher, an industrial company based in Washington, D.C., has acquired multiple companies that take advantage of Danaher's ability to improve operating efficiency.[26]

- A *market extension merger* combines firms that offer similar products and services in different geographic markets. Bank of America, which already had a strong presence in the West and Southeast, gained an instant presence in the Northeast when it acquired FleetBoston in 2004.[27]

- Companies pursue a *product extension merger* when they need to round out a product line. This approach is common in the computer industry, where larger customers expect suppliers to provide a wide range of goods and services. If a company doesn't have the time or resources to develop all the products, it will try to buy another entity that has already developed the missing pieces.

Advantages of Mergers and Acquisitions Companies pursue mergers and acquisitions for a wide variety of reasons: They might hope to reduce costs by eliminating redundant resources; increase their buying power as a result of their larger size; increase revenue by cross-selling products to each other's customers; increase market share by combining product lines to provide more comprehensive offerings; eliminate manufacturing overcapacity; or gain access to new expertise, systems, and teams of employees who already know how to work together. Often these advantages are grouped under umbrella terms such as *economies of scale, efficiencies,* or *synergies,* which generally mean that the benefits of working together will be greater than if each company continued to operate independently. For instance, as the costs of creating new video games keep escalating, companies such as Electronic Arts view acquisitions of other game companies as a way to keep development costs in check.[28]

The recent combination of two large computer companies, HP and Compaq, illustrates the challenge of combining two large organizations successfully. The numbers were staggering: 145,000 employees, factories and offices in 160 countries, and 163 product lines—many of which overlapped. In addition, mergers and acquisitions in the technology industry are particularly difficult because these firms depend so heavily on the brainpower of individual scientists, engineers, and other specialists. However, HP CEO Carly Fiorina was convinced that the merger was vital to HP's efforts to compete with IBM and that the combined organization could reduce costs by as much as $3 billion. The highly controversial merger succeeded in reducing costs, but HP's board grew impatient with the company's continuing lackluster performance in other aspects and ousted Fiorina in 2005.[29]

Disadvantages of Mergers and Acquisitions HP's experience highlights the risks inherent in all mergers and acquisitions. In fact, mergers often fail to meet their stated goals (see "Hey, Wanna Lose a Few Billion? We Have a Sure Deal for You"). Every situation is unique, of course, but there are recurring themes. For instance, companies often borrow immense amounts of money to acquire a firm, and the loan payments on this corporate debt gobble up cash needed to run the business. Moreover, managers must help combine the operations of the two entities, pulling them away from their normal day-to-day responsibilities. Another obstacle that companies face when combining forces is that they tend to underestimate the difficulties of merging two cultures.

As you'll read in Chapter 7, a company's *culture* is a general term that describes the way people in a given organization approach the day-to-day business of running a company. Culture includes not only management style and practices but even the way people dress and how they communicate. *Culture clash* occurs when two joining companies have different beliefs about what is really important, how to make decisions, how to supervise people, how to communicate, and so on (see "DaimlerChrysler: Merger of Equals or Global Fender Bender?"). Experts note that in too many deals the acquiring company imposes its values and management systems on the acquired company without any regard to what worked well there.

Given the less-than-stellar record of mergers and acquisitions, one might be tempted to ask why so many deals continue to happen, year in and year out. In some cases, the managers involved believe that the potential advantages outweigh the risks. In others cases, executives believe they need to combine companies in order to stay competitive in a changing marketplace; this was the primary motivation behind the HP-Compaq merger, for instance.

Current Trends in Mergers and Acquisitions Every year, a few megadeals catch everyone's attention, but in reality, several thousand mergers and acquisitions occur every year in the United States, and thousands more take place in other countries. As Exhibit 5.5

CEO Dick Heckmann led K2 Sports on an acquisition binge to expand beyond winter skis into a sporting goods company for all seasons.

LEARNING OBJECTIVE

Identify the synergies that companies hope to achieve by combining their operations

THINKING ABOUT ETHICS

HEY, WANNA LOSE A FEW BILLION? WE HAVE A SURE DEAL FOR YOU

If you were about to make a multibillion-dollar deal with the financial well-being of thousands of people on the line, but statistics suggested you had an 80 percent chance of failure, would you go for it? Sure you would, if you work in the slightly wacky world of corporate mergers and acquisitions.

Studies consistently show that the vast majority of mergers and acquisitions fail to meet their primary goal of increasing shareholder value—and half actually decrease value. During the deal-crazy period from 1995 to 2000, for instance, businesses around the world bought and sold each other to the tune of more than $12 trillion. Guess how much all that deal making increased shareholder value? It *decreased* net value by at least $1 trillion—that's more financial destruction than even the dot-com crash managed to generate. In many cases, the only people who win in these deals are the shareholders in acquired companies, when eager buyers shell out more for shares than they're really worth. It's no surprise that lots of investors are starting to wonder whose interests these boards have at stake.

Ethical concerns aside, how can so many otherwise talented people keep making so many mistakes? Although no one answer applies to every situation, experts cite these common mistakes:

- Companies often rush into deals in search of synergies but then fail to develop them. Once the merger is done, management doesn't follow through to make sure that the computer programmers, sales representatives, engineers, and others responsible for carrying out the details are able to cut costs and boost revenues according to plan. For instance, integrating diverse software packages, whether it's the systems that run the businesses or actual commercial products themselves, in the case of software company mergers, can take months or years.
- Mergers can drive customers away if they feel neglected while the two companies are busy with all the internal chores of stitching themselves together. In a recent *BusinessWeek* survey, half of

all customers involved in mergers were less satisfied with service after the merger than before.
- Companies pay excessively high premiums for the companies they acquire. According to one expert, any time an acquiring company pays a premium of 25 percent or more over the trading price of the acquired company's stock, the acquiring company is exposing itself and its shareholders to substantial risk.
- Companies are unable to reconcile differences in corporate cultures. A successful merger requires more than respecting each partner's differences. Procedures must be established to settle disputes and to integrate workforces and product lines strategically.

Without question, some mergers and acquisitions are beneficial to companies and shareholders in both the short term and the long term. Even the controversial HP-Compaq achieved significant cost efficiencies. However, managers need to approach mergers and acquisitions with caution by answering these questions: Will the regulatory environment change? How will competitors respond? Do the expected gains justify the up-front costs and disruption to business operations? Will the cultures, systems, processes, and product lines of the two companies blend well? Executives will continue to believe they can beat the odds and craft successful deals, but without seeking honest answers to these questions first, they're likely to only find themselves adding to the depressing statistics about mergers and acquisitions.

Critical Thinking Questions
1. If you were on the board of directors at a company and the CEO announced plans to merge with a competitor, what types of questions would you want answered before you gave your approval? How would you view your ethical responsibilities in this situation?
2. If a CEO has the opportunity to merge with or acquire another company and is reasonably certain that the transaction will benefit shareholders, is the CEO obligated to pursue the deal? Why or why not?

shows, merger activity tapered off through the 1970s, during the waning years of the conglomeration age. The 1980s saw a brief surge in activity but nothing like the boom of the late 1990s, which was fueled by the rapid price increases in dot-com and other technology stocks. Tens of thousands of mergers and acquisitions took place during this period,

COMPETING IN THE GLOBAL ECONOMY

DAIMLERCHRYSLER: MERGER OF EQUALS OR GLOBAL FENDER BENDER?

On paper, it seemed like a perfect fit. The German automaker Daimler-Benz and the U.S. automaker Chrysler were both doing well, but each had strengths that would complement the other's weaknesses. Daimler's engineering was legendary, and it was strong in technology. Chrysler excelled at new-product design and development. Complementary products and geographical mix would allow them to challenge rivals around the world. Moreover, anticipated synergies would save the combined operation $3 billion annually. Optimism was running high when the $36 billion merger was announced in May 1998, creating the world's third-largest automaker.

Charged with excitement and curious about each other's cars and culture, the two companies began the integration process. But fundamental differences in managerial, operational, and decision-making styles made the transition difficult. For example, a German decision would work its way through the bureaucracy for final approval at the top. Then it was set in stone. By contrast, the Americans valued consensus building and shared decision making. Moreover, they allowed midlevel employees to proceed on their own initiative, sometimes without waiting for executive-level approval.

Turf battles also bogged down the combination process. Managers from both sides spent more time defending their way of doing things than promoting the integration of systems. Issues that should have been resolved by managers were bumped up to the company's board of directors. Differences in salary levels and management perks fueled an undercurrent of tension. The Americans earned two, three, and in some cases four times as much as their German counterparts. But the expenses of U.S.

workers were tightly controlled compared with those of the German system. Daimler-Benz employees thought nothing of flying to Paris or New York for a half-day meeting, then capping the visit with a fancy dinner and a night in an expensive hotel. The Americans blanched at such extravagances.

Within months, the stock price fell to half its post-merger peak. Friction led to the departure of talented Chrysler midlevel managers and of several top Chrysler executives—including Chrysler's president Thomas Stallkamp, who had played an instrumental role in orchestrating the merger. Soon the management board was scaled down from 17 members to 13 (8 Germans and 5 Americans), and the reality became clear: Daimler executives were indeed running the show. A joke making the rounds in Chrysler offices said it all:

Q: How do you pronounce "DaimlerChrysler"?
A: "Daimler." The "Chrysler" is silent.

The merger of equals turned out to be anything but. For all intents and purposes, Daimler-Benz had acquired Chrysler, and an American icon had lost its independence. And shareholders lost once again: By the end of 2004, the company's market value had plunged by $60 billion.

Critical Thinking Questions

1. What prevented DaimlerChrysler from achieving the promised synergies?
2. Which of these stakeholders benefited the most from the merger: the original Chrysler shareholders or the new DaimlerChrysler shareholders? Explain your answer.

including a number of huge deals in such major industries as news and entertainment media (AOL and Time Warner), automobiles (Chrysler and Daimler-Benz), oil (Exxon and Mobil), and banking (Travelers and Citicorp).[30] However, when the stocks that financed so much of this activity cooled or collapsed, the number of mergers and acquisitions fell off rapidly as well. Then as the stock market began to show signs of recovery in 2003 and 2004, deal activity began to pick up again.

The number of deals can vary widely from year to year, based on both general economic conditions (such as the health of the stock market) and the dynamics of specific industries. For instance, when a new industry or business model emerges, the market often fills up quickly with more suppliers than the number of customers can support. The stronger players then frequently acquire smaller, weaker players, reducing the number of suppliers left in the market (this is the *industry consolidation* referred to earlier).

Exhibit 5.5

Mergers and
Acquisitions Involving
U.S. Companies
*Rising stock prices during
the dot-com boom of the
late 1990s fueled a surge
in merger-and-acquisition
activity among U.S.
companies, which fell off
quickly when those stock
prices collapsed.*

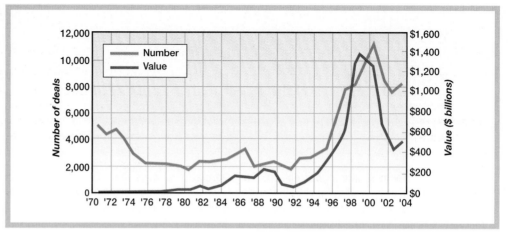

Merger-and-Acquisition Defenses Every corporation that sells stock to the general public is potentially vulnerable to takeover by any individual or company that buys enough shares to gain a controlling interest, although as mentioned earlier, most takeovers are friendly acquisitions welcomed by the acquired company. A hostile takeover can be launched in one of two ways: by tender offer or by proxy fight. In a *tender offer*, the buyer, or *raider*, as this party is sometimes called, offers to buy a certain number of shares of stock in the corporation at a specific price. The price offered is generally more, sometimes considerably more, than the current stock price so that share-holders are motivated to sell. The raider hopes to get enough shares to take control of the corporation and to replace the existing board of directors and management. In a *proxy fight*, the raider launches a public relations battle for shareholder votes, hoping to enlist enough votes to oust the board and management. Proxy fights usually favor insiders, however; corporate boards and executives have devised a number of schemes to defend themselves against unwanted takeovers:

- *The poison pill.* This plan, triggered by a takeover attempt, makes the company less valuable in some way to the potential raider; the idea is to discourage the takeover from actually happening. A good example is a special sale of newly issued stock to current stockholders at prices below the market value of the company's existing stock. Such action increases the number of shares the raider has to buy, making the takeover more expensive. Many shareholders believe that poison pills are bad for a company, because they can entrench weak management and discourage takeover attempts that would improve company value. Southwest Airlines and Yahoo! are among the companies whose shareholders have been trying to convince management to drop poison pills in recent years.[31]
- *The shark repellent.* This tactic is more direct; it is simply a requirement that stockhold-ers representing a large majority of shares approve of any takeover attempt. Of course, such a plan is viable only if the management team has the support of the majority of shareholders.
- *The white knight.* A white night is a third company that steps in to acquire a company that is in danger of being swallowed up in a hostile takeover. The takeover target is still purchased, but at least it happens on more positive terms.

Companies that don't want to be acquired can be quite aggressive when they need to be. To fight off a takeover attempt by a private investor, the British retail chain Marks & Spencer convinced shareholders not to sell out by demonstrating that it was serious about improving performance: The company quickly fired its CEO and other senior executives, abandoned costly plans to launch a chain of home furniture stores, and sold a credit card company it owned and gave the proceeds to shareholders as dividends.[32]

LEARNING FROM BUSINESS BLUNDERS

OOPS Would you pay $2 billion to get *out* of a business relationship? What if the alternative was being forced to buy a company that was more than $10 billion in debt, burning through a couple of billion more in cash every year, and worth virtually nothing? That was the unpleasant choice facing General Motors in early 2005, when its hand was forced by Fiat SpA, an Italian industrial conglomerate that was the primary owner of Fiat Auto, the company in question. Five years earlier, GM and Fiat SpA had entered into a complex partnership that gave GM partial owner-ship of Fiat Auto—but gave Fiat SpA the option of requiring GM to buy the rest of the company at some point in the future. After they signed the agreement, Fiat Auto's mar-ket position and finances deteriorated so badly that Fiat SpA eventually decided to exercise the option to unload it.

GM initially argued that circumstances had changed so much that it was no longer bound by the agreement, but Fiat threatened to launch what surely would've been a long and costly legal battle. GM opted to shell out $2 billion in order to get released from the partnership agreement instead.

WHAT YOU CAN LEARN Wall Street analysts believed that Fiat SpA's "put option," as it's called, was a bad idea for GM from the start, and they turned out to be painfully right. Even if you never get involved in multibillion-dollar deals to buy car companies, always consider the worst-case scenario before signing any agreement. As GM exec-utives would tell you, sometimes the worst possible thing really does come true.

Strategic Alliances and Joint Ventures

Chapter 3 discussed strategic alliances and joint ventures from the perspective of inter-national expansion, defining a *strategic alliance* as a long-term partnership between companies to jointly develop, produce, or sell products and a *joint venture* as a separate legal entity established by the strategic partners. Strategic alliances can accomplish many of the same goals as a merger, consolidation, or acquisition without requiring a painstaking process of integration.[33] They can help a company gain credibility in a new field, expand its market presence, gain access to technology, diversify offerings, and share best practices without forcing the partners to become permanently entangled. For instance, in the information technology business, computer giant IBM recently struck an alliance with Cisco, a leader in networking technology, in order to supply Internet tele-phony and video solutions.[34] In other cases, companies team up to share the benefits of powerful brand names. The luxury jeweler Bulgari joined forces with Marriott's Ritz-Carlton chain to create a new super-deluxe hotel brand, Bulgari Hotels & Resorts, com-bining Bulgari's strong brand name with Ritz-Carlton's expertise in running hotels. Bulgari gained a new venue for promoting its products, and Ritz-Carlton bolstered its image as a luxury brand.[35]

Strategic alliances may be simpler than full-scale mergers and acquisitions, but they need to be entered into with equal care: roughly half of all alliances fail to meet their objectives.[36] Details matter, too. When the first Bulgari hotel opened in Milan, Italy, some Ritz-Carlton executives were dismayed to find that the Ritz-Carlton name was nowhere to be found.[37]

CRITICAL THINKING CHECKPOINT
1. What are the risks of a leveraged buyout?
2. Why does customer service frequently suffer after a merger or acquisition?
3. Why would FedEx choose to acquire Kinko's rather than entering into a strategic alliance?

CHECKLIST Apply These Ideas When You're the Boss

✓ No matter what size or stage your business is in, consider the ownership possibilities with extreme care; this could be the single most important decision in the life of your company.

✓ Don't overlook the financial risks inherent in sole proprietorship; unlimited liability could put your entire future at risk.

✓ Don't rush through the partnership agreement if you're considering this form of business ownership—clearly spell out management responsibilities and financial details.

✓ Even if you're a small company, consider the many benefits of incorporating but remaining privately held.

✓ If you incorporate, choose your board of directors with great care; a compliant board might make life easier in the short term, but a lack of vigorous oversight can be disastrous in the long term.

✓ View merger and acquisition possibilities from a worst-case perspective: Will the deal still make sense if an optimistic projection doesn't come true?

✓ Explore strategic partnerships and joint ventures with the same care you'd take when buying another company; the downsides can be just as traumatic.

Summary of Learning Objectives

1 List five advantages and four disadvantages of sole proprietorships. Sole proprietorships have five advantages: (1) They are easy to establish, (2) they provide the owner with control and independence, (3) the owner reaps all the profits, (4) profits are taxed at individual rates, and (5) the company's plans and financial performance remain private. The four main disadvantages of a sole proprietorship are (1) the company's financial resources are usually limited, (2) management talent may be thin, (3) the owner is liable for the debts and damages incurred by the business, and (4) the business may cease when the owner dies.

2 List five advantages and two disadvantages of partnerships. In addition to being easy to establish and having profits taxed at individual rates, partnerships offer a greater ability to obtain financing, longevity, and a broader base of skills. The two main disadvantages of partnerships are unlimited liability for general partners and the potential for personality and authority conflicts.

3 Explain the differences between common and preferred stock from a shareholder's perspective. Common shareholders can vote and can share in the company's profits through discretionary dividends and adjustments in the market value of their stock. In other words, they can profit from their investment if the value of the stock rises above the price they paid for it, or they can lose money if the value of the stock falls below the price they paid for it. In contrast, preferred shareholders cannot vote, but they can get a fixed return (dividend) on their investment and a priority claim on assets after creditors.

4 Highlight the advantages and disadvantages of public stock ownership. Public stock ownership offers a company increased liquidity, enhanced visibility, financial flexibility, and an independently established market value for the stock. The disadvantages of public stock ownership are high costs, burdensome filing requirements, loss of ownership control, heightened public exposure, and loss of direct control over the market value of the company's stock.

5 Cite four advantages and three disadvantages of corporations. Because corporations are a separate legal entity, they have the power to raise large sums of capital, they offer the shareholders protection from liability, they provide liquidity for investors, and they have an unlimited life span. In exchange for these advantages, businesses pay large fees to incorporate, and they are taxed twice on company profits—corporations pay tax on profits and individuals pay tax on dividends (distributed corporate profits). Finally, if publicly owned, corporations must adhere to strict government reporting requirements.

6 **Delineate the three groups that govern a corporation, and describe the role of each.** Shareholders are the basis of the corporate structure. They elect the board of directors, who in turn elect the officers of the corporation. The corporate officers carry out the policies and decisions of the board. In practice, the shareholders and board members have often followed the lead of the chief executive officer. However, some board members are more active than others. This is especially true of young dot-com corporations that appoint directors for their management expertise and industry connections.

7 **Identify six main synergies companies hope to achieve by combining their operations.** By combining their operations, companies hope to eliminate redundant costs, increase their buying power, increase their revenue, improve their market share, eliminate manufacturing overcapacity, and gain access to new expertise and personnel.

FedEx Kinko's: What's Next?

The story of Kinko's and its acquisition by FedEx in 2004 is a common one in business today: An entrepreneur with a dream builds a company that grows so large that it grows beyond the founder's ability to manage it efficiently. At the same time, an established, larger corporation looks around for opportunities to strengthen its own market presence and expand its product offerings. These acquisitions are never simple, however, even when well planned and well executed. FedEx spent an enormous amount of money to buy Kinko's from leveraged-buyout specialists CD&R, then had to spend even more to rebrand the chain as part of the FedEx corporate family. While photocopying and overnight delivery might seem to be two unrelated businesses, FedEx (like archrival UPS) had already expanded beyond its original business into supply chain management, helping companies organize the sourcing and delivery of parts and raw material, so managing the flow of documents and information isn't as big a stretch as it might seem at first. Plus, the delivery business requires a widespread retail presence, giving customers convenient places to drop off and pick up packages, so the far-flung Kinko's chain was a natural fit there. With both globalization and "virtualization" continuing to reshape the business world, the FedEx Kinko's combo should be a strong fit.

Critical Thinking Questions

1. Why did Kinko's change its structure from individual partnerships to a single corporate entity?
2. Why is it important for all FedEx Kinko's stores to have the same equipment and offer the same services?
3. What are the potential advantages and disadvantages of being purchased by FedEx?

Learn More Online

Go to Chapter 5 of this text's website at www.prenhall.com/bovee, and click on the FedEx Kinko's hotlink to learn about the company's many services. Why does FedEx Kinko's provide extensive information on how to prepare documents, brochures, posters, presentations, and more? Notice how the website urges customers to "Make It, Print It, Pack It, Ship It." How does this take advantage of the synergies created by the acquisition?

Key Terms

acquisition (180)
board of directors (178)
chief executive officer
  (CEO) (177)
common stock (173)
consolidation (180)
corporate governance (177)
corporation (172)
dividends (173)
general partnership (170)

hostile takeover (180)
leveraged buyout (LBO) (180)
limited liability companies
  (LLCs) (176)
limited partnership (170)
liquidity (175)
merger (179)
parent company (176)
partnership (170)
preferred stock (173)

private corporation (173)
proxy (177)
public corporation (174)
S corporation (176)
shareholders (173)
sole proprietorship (170)
stock certificate (173)
subsidiary corporations (176)
unlimited liability (170)

Test Your Knowledge

Questions for Review

1. What are the three basic forms of business ownership?
2. What is the difference between a general and a limited partnership?
3. What is a closely held corporation, and why do some companies choose this form of ownership?
4. What is the role of a company's board of directors?
5. What is culture clash?

Questions for Analysis

6. Why is it advisable for partners to enter into a formal partnership agreement?
7. To what extent do shareholders control the activities of a corporation?
8. How might a company benefit from having a diverse board of directors that includes representatives of several industries, countries, and cultures?
9. Why do so many mergers fail?
10. **Ethical Considerations.** Your father sits on the board of directors of a large, well-admired public company. Yesterday, while looking for an envelope in his home office, you stumbled on a confidential memorandum. Unable to resist the temptation to read the memo, you discovered that your father's company is talking with another publicly traded company about the possibility of a merger, with Dad's company being the survivor. Dollar signs flashed in your mind. Should the merger occur, the value of the other company's stock is likely to soar. You're tempted to log on to your E*Trade account in the morning and place an order for 1,000 shares of that company's stock. Better still, maybe you'll give a hot tip to your best friend in exchange for the four Dave Matthews Band tickets your friend has been flashing in your face all week. Would either of those actions be unethical? Explain your answer.

Questions for Application

11. Suppose you and some friends want to start a business to take tourists on wilderness backpacking expeditions. None of you has much extra money, so your plan is to start small. However, if you are successful, you would like to expand into other types of outdoor tours and perhaps even open up branches in other locations. What form of ownership should your new enterprise take, and why?
12. Selling antiques on the Internet has become more successful than you imagined. Overnight your website has grown into a full-fledged business—now generating some $200,000 in annual revenue. It's time to think about the future. Several competing online antique dealers have approached you with a proposal to merge their website with yours to create the premier online antique store. The money sounds good, but you have some concerns about joining forces. What might they be? What other growth options should you consider before joining forces with another business?
13. **Integrated.** Chapter 3 discussed international strategic alliances and joint ventures. Why might a U.S. company want to enter into those types of arrangements instead of merging with a foreign concern?
14. **Integrated.** You've developed considerable expertise in setting up new manufacturing plants, and now you'd like to strike out on your own as a consultant who advises other companies. However, you recognize that manufacturing activity tends to expand and contract at various times during the business cycle (see Chapter 1). Do you think a single-consultant sole proprietorship or a small corporation with a half dozen or more consultants would be better able to ride out tough times at the bottom of a business cycle?

Practice Your Knowledge

Handling Difficult Situations on the Job: Determining Accountability in a Crisis

Like other board members, you agreed to management's recommendation that the Westlake Therapy and Rehabilitation Center invest in an Endless Pool. This new invention by a Philadelphia manufacturer produces an adjustable current flow, so that physical therapy patients can swim "endlessly" against it. Westlake could offer patients year-round water therapy, in an indoor pool small enough to fit a standard living room.

Management chose the optional six-foot depth, which required (1) a special platform and (2) installation in a room with a high ceiling. Westlake's old gymnasium would become the new Water Therapy Pavilion. Total cost: $20,080, plus $8,000 budgeted for installation. According to the manufacturer, the Endless Pool could be assembled by "two reasonably handy people with no prior installation experience following detailed procedural videos." Playing it safe, management hired professionals—Abe's Pool Installation—to build the platform and install the pool. Owner Abe Hanson was given the instructional videos, the manufacturer's hotline number, and told that Endless Pool would provide free, pre-installation engineering consultations.

Weeks later, Westlake's chief administrator flipped the switch at the dedication ceremony and the new pool's hydraulic motor started moving 5,000 gallons of water a minute through a grill at the front of the pool. But instead of entering the turning vane arrays, the wave surged out the back, onto the platform and gathered board members, staff, patients, and reporters. Final damage: a collapsed platform, a ruined floor, an incorrectly installed pool, and numerous dry-cleaning bills. Fortunately, no injuries. Estimated cost with floor repair: $10,000. Local newscasters aired the footage on the evening news; they're coming back tomorrow for an interview. Abe is not returning management's calls.[38]

Your task: You must help to decide how to handle this much-publicized fiasco. What actions should the board take, and what should it leave to management's discretion? Consider the impact on company image, profitability, liability, and daily operations. Whom will you hold accountable? How?

Sharpening Your Communication Skills

You have just been informed that your employer is going to merge with a firm in Germany. Because you know very little about German culture and business practices, you think it might be a good idea to do some preliminary research—just in case you have to make a quick trip overseas. Using the Internet or library sources, find information on the German culture and customs and prepare a short report discussing such cultural differences as German social values, decision-making customs, concepts of time, use of body language, social behavior and manners, and legal and ethical behavior.

Building Your Team Skills

Directors often have to ask tough questions and make difficult decisions, as you will see in this exercise. Imagine that the president of your college or university has just announced plans to retire. Your team, playing the role of the school's board of directors, must decide how to choose a new president to fill this vacancy next semester.

First, generate a list of the qualities and qualifications you think the school should seek in a new president. What background and experience would prepare someone for this key position? What personal characteristics should the new president have? What questions would you ask to find out how each candidate measures up against the list of credentials you have prepared?

Now list all the stakeholders that your team, as directors, must consider before deciding on a replacement for the retiring president. Of these stakeholders, whose opinions do you think are most important? Whose are least important? Who will be directly and indirectly affected by the choice of a new president? Of these stakeholders, which should be represented as participants in the decision-making process?

Select a spokesperson to deliver a brief presentation to the class summarizing your team's ideas and the reasoning behind your suggestions. After all the teams have completed their presentations, discuss the differences and similarities among credentials proposed by all the teams for evaluating candidates for the presidency. Then compare the teams' conclusions about stakeholders. Do all teams agree on the stakeholders who should participate in the decision-making process? Lead a classroom discussion on a board's responsibility to its stakeholders.

Expand Your Knowledge

Discovering Career Opportunities

Are you best suited to working as a sole proprietor, as a partner in a business, or in a different role within a corporation? For this exercise, select three businesses with which you are familiar: one run by a single person, such as a dentist's practice or a local landscaping firm; one run by two or three partners, such as a small accounting firm; and one that operates as a corporation, such as Target.

1. Write down what you think you would like about being the sole proprietor, one of the partners, and the corporate manager or an employee in the businesses you have selected. For example, would you like having full responsibility for the sole proprietorship? Would you like being able to consult with other partners in the partnership before making decisions? Would you like having limited responsibility when you work for other people in the corporation?
2. Now write down what you might dislike about each form of business. For example, would you dislike the risk of bearing all legal responsibility in a sole proprietorship? Would you dislike having to talk with your partners before spending the partnership's money? Would you dislike having to write reports for top managers and shareholders of the corporation?
3. Weigh the pluses and minuses you have identified in this exercise. In comparison, which form of business most appeals to you?

Developing Your Research Skills

Review recent issues of business newspapers or periodicals (print or online editions) to find an article or series of articles illustrating one of the following business developments: merger, acquisition, consolidation, hostile takeover, or leveraged buyout.

1. Explain in your own words what steps or events led to this development.
2. What results do you expect this development to have on (a) the company itself, (b) consumers, (c) the industry the company is part of? Write down and date your answers.
3. Follow your story in the business news over the next month (or longer, as your instructor requests). What problems, opportunities, or other results are reported? Were these developments anticipated at the time of the initial story, or did they seem to catch industry analysts by surprise? How well did your answers to question 2 predict the results?

Exploring the Best of the Web

URLs for all Internet exercises are provided at the website for this book, www.prenhall.com/bovee. When you log on to this text's Companion Website, select Chapter 5. Then select "Featured Website," click on the name of the featured website, and review the website to complete these exercises.

Explore these chapter-related websites, review their content, and answer the following questions for each website you visit:

1. What is the purpose of this website?
2. What kinds of information does this website contain? Please be specific.
3. How is the information provided at this website useful for businesspeople? Consumers?
4. How did you expand your knowledge of forms of business ownerships and business combinations by reviewing the material at this website? What new things did you learn about this topic?

Choose a Form of Ownership
Which legal form of ownership is best suited for a new business? Answering this question can be a challenge—especially if you're not familiar with the attributes of sole proprietorships, partnerships, and corporations. That's where Nolo Self-Help Centers can help. Because there's no right or wrong choice for everyone, your job is to understand how each legal structure works and then pick the one that best meets your needs. Start your research by browsing the small-business law center at Nolo. Be sure to check out the FAQs and Legal Encyclopedia. www.nolo.com

Follow the Fortunes of the Fortune 500
Quick! Name the largest corporation in the United States, as measured by annual revenues. Give up? Just check *Fortune* magazine's yearly ranking of the 500 largest U.S. companies. For years, General Motors has topped the list with its $170 billion-plus in annual revenues, but now Wal-Mart has taken over with over $200 billion in annual revenues. The Fortune 500 not only ranks corporations by size but also offers brief company descriptions along with industry statistics and additional measures of corporate performance. You can search the list by ranking, by industry, by company name, or by CEO. And to help you identify the largest international corporations, there's a special Global 500 list as well. www.fortune.com

Build a Great Board
Want a great board of directors? This Inc.com guide contains the best resources for entrepreneurs who are ready to recruit outside directors for their boards. Find out how to recruit board members and how

to persuade top-notch people to come on board. Once you've selected your members, learn how to maximize your board's impact and resolve conflicts among board members. Check out one expert's five practical tips for good nuts-and-bolts boardsmanship. www.inc.com/guides/growth/20672.html

Learning Interactively

Companion Website
Visit the Companion Website at www.prenhall.com/bovee. For Chapter 5, take advantage of the interactive "Learning Modules" to test your chapter knowledge. Get instant feedback on whether you need additional studying. Complete the exercises as specified by your instructor.

A Case for Critical Thinking

AOL Time Warner: Deal of the Century Turns into Disaster of a Lifetime

Industry experts laughed in his face. The Silicon Valley elite sneered at his audacity. Back in 1995, Steve Case's predictions about the future of his fledgling company, America Online (AOL), seemed outrageous to everyone—except Steve Case. Nonetheless, Case doggedly pursued his dream, turning AOL into one of the darlings of Wall Street during the height of the dot-com boom. "We could be bigger than AT&T," Case predicted. "The future is online." It was a vision that Case refused to abandon, in spite of the odds against him.

Near the end of the 20th century, AOL was a profitable Internet giant, serving over 22 million customers around the globe and delivering more mail than the U.S. Postal Service. Its high-flying stock price gave it the financial clout to grow its customer base by acquiring such companies as Netscape Communications, rival CompuServe, and ICQ with its instant messaging software. But CEO Case knew AOL needed access to compelling content and the high-speed cable TV lines that could zap information and entertainment into homes at lightning speed.

DEAL OF THE CENTURY
Determined to transform itself into a global communications company, AOL orchestrated the deal of the century. When AOL approached publishing and cable TV giant Time Warner about the merger possibility, Time Warner was reeling from its own costly, repeated, and failed efforts to move into the digital era. Hitching a ride into the future with AOL seemed like an attractive option. For AOL, capturing Time Warner, a respected, old-school company with five times its revenues, seemed to herald the dawning of the digital century. Melding AOL's Internet empire with the diverse and revenue-rich Time Warner colossus (which included Time Warner Cable, HBO, CNN, TBS, Warner Bros. Pictures, Warner Music Group, and such magazines as *Time, People,* and *Sports Illustrated*) would produce the first fully integrated media and communications company.

VISIONS OF A BLOCKBUSTER—BUT PLENTY OF DOUBTERS
In January 2000, the two announced their intention to merge. The new AOL Time Warner promised grand synergies and slam-dunk revenues from its unrivaled combination of print and television content with cable and online distribution. Together, the companies could pipe a dazzling array of movies, music, magazines, and more to their combined 100 million customers. And the merged companies could reap economies of scale by promoting and selling each other's products and by eliminating duplicate operating costs.

Not everyone was excited about the prospects of the merger. Critics feared that merging AOL, a "new economy" Internet company based in Virginia, with Time Warner, an "old economy" media company headquartered in New York City, could create communication and cultural problems. At worst, they feared, the merger would shackle AOL's flexibility, speed, and entrepreneurial drive and sink its rapidly rising stock price. And Time Warner's shareholders, who were getting paid in AOL stock, worried that the share price was highly inflated.

Regulators and members of Congress were concerned that an AOL Time Warner would be too big and too powerful—that it might be able to single-handedly dominate and control the coming era of broadband access to the Internet. They wanted to ensure that the cable TV system, just like the federal highways, would be open to everyone.

IT ALL COMES UNGLUED
The wrangling with regulators, shareholders, and other stakeholders lasted a full year, but the government finally approved the largest merger in U.S. history on January 11, 2001. The celebration didn't last long. The purchase was made with hyperinflated dot-com stock that was ripe for a collapse (along

with the rest of the dot-com economy), and the success of the deal was predicated on the unproven assumption that advertisers would flock en masse to online media outlets, which didn't happen. Case later admitted that the company had been "too aggressive" in its promises.

The online bonanza that never happened was bad enough, but the dot-com shakeout also helped push the entire economy into a slump, which then triggered the worst advertising recession in a decade—meaning that the company's magazine and television businesses suffered right along with its online business. The following year, the company reported the biggest annual corporate loss in history: $98.7 billion. Along the way, tens of thousands of employees lost their jobs, and the stock that was ripe for a collapse collapsed in a breathtaking way, vaporizing $200 billion of shareholder wealth, rendering employee stock options nearly worthless and confirming doubters' fears that Time Warner made a huge mistake by merging with AOL. Throughout it all, AOL and Time Warner executives continued to clash, compounding the new giant's troubles. In other words, just about everything that could go wrong with the deal did go wrong.

BUT WAIT; THERE'S MORE

As often happens when a company's stock collapses, investors and government regulators wanted a closer look at AOL Time Warner's finances. Sure enough, investigators found accounting irregularities in the AOL business. The company reached a settlement with the Justice Department at the end of 2004, and negotiations continued with the Securities and Exchange Commission. The final tab should run around $500 million in fines.

Most of the senior executives associated with the merger have since left the company, including Steve Case, who resigned in 2003 after stating that he did not want his presence to continue to be a distraction. In a move that could be a symbol of old-economy titans taking the stage back from new-economy upstarts, the company dropped "AOL" from its name, and AOL is now simply another one of Time Warner's business units. With most of its troubles in the rearview mirror, Time Warner entered 2005 with recovering finances and a healthy skepticism for promises of miracles in the new digital economy.

Critical Thinking Questions

1. Why did the media refer to the merger as the deal of the century?
2. Why was Time Warner eager to merge with AOL?
3. What challenges did AOL Time Warner face as a merged company?
4. Visit the Time Warner website. Review the site to get the latest news about the fate of the merger. How is the company doing financially? How much turnover has occurred among high-level executives? If any parts of the business have been sold off, what has the acquiring company said about future prospects?

Video Case

Doing Business Privately: Amy's Ice Cream

Learning Objectives

The purpose of this video is to help you:

1. Distinguish among the types of corporations.
2. Consider the advantages and disadvantages of incorporation.
3. Understand the role that shareholders play in a privately held corporation.

Synopsis

Amy's Ice Creams, based in Austin, Texas, is a privately held corporation formed in 1984 by Amy Miller and owned by Miller and a small group of family members and friends. At the outset, one of the most important decisions Miller faced was choosing an appropriate legal ownership structure for the new business. Fueled by the founder's dedication to creating happy ice cream memories for customers, Amy's has continued to evolve and grow. The company now operates 11 stores and rings up close to $3.5 million in annual sales. Applying for a job is an adventure in creativity, and Miller welcomes employees' suggestions for new flavors and new promotions to keep sales growing.

Discussion Questions

1. *For analysis:* How does Amy's Ice Creams differ from a publicly held corporation?
2. *For analysis:* What are some of the particular advantages of corporate ownership for a firm such as Amy's Ice Creams?

3. *For application:* How well do you think Amy's is working to ensure its continued survival and success? Looking ahead to future growth, what marketing, financial, or other suggestions would you make?

4. *For application:* What are some of the issues that Amy Miller may have to confront because her 22 investors are family members and friends?

5. *For debate:* Should Amy's Ice Creams become a publicly held corporation? Support your chosen position.

Online Exploration

Find out what is required to incorporate a business in your state. You might begin by searching the CCH Business Owner's Toolkit site at www.toolkit.cch.com. If you were going to start a small business, would you choose to incorporate or choose a different form of legal organization? List the pros and cons that incorporation presents for the type of business you would consider.

skills and improved the operation along the way. For example, she redesigned her website to make it easier to find through Internet search engines and discontinued international sales when she realized the company couldn't satisfy overseas customers to the standard she wanted. Dropping international sales also meant she and her family could scale back their hours a bit, approaching something like a normal life at times.

Without the huge marketing budgets that many dot-coms have (or had) GeniusBabies.com emphasizes positive word of mouth, cooperative online marketing with similar companies, and a personal touch that keeps customers happy. Donahue-Arpas knows that simple moves such as personal notes and thank-you messages with orders can pay back big time in customer satisfaction and positive referrals. She says that consumers are so used to impersonal treatment from large corporations that they're pleasantly shocked when her small company communicates in such an intimate way.

Success naturally leads to growth, but Donahue-Arpas has kept it a mom-friendly, family affair. The staff now includes two full-time moms, two-part moms, and the newest addition to the GeniusBabies.com family: her husband George. Her mother and grandmother even pitch in, along with a small army of temporary help during the holiday season.

Managing with limited resources, learning on the fly, digging deep for inspiration—these are all classic elements of the entrepreneurial experience. And so is hard work. Donahue-Arpas routinely works nights and weekends to keep customers satisfied and to manage the many facets of a growing business. Like most entrepreneurs, she has to put more into her work than the average job, but she wouldn't have it any other way. From staying at home to being her own boss to doing work she truly believes in, Michelle Donahue-Arpas has made her personal dream of entrepreneurship come true.[1]

GET READY

Since you're studying business, chances are you've already had an idea or two for a new business. Is your objective to create a company that fits your lifestyle, as Michelle Donahue-Arpas has done, or do you have dreams of creating a major enterprise? Are you ready to wear a half dozen hats at once and do whatever it takes to get your company off the ground? Should you start something from scratch or buy an existing business? Maybe a franchise is the right choice for you instead. If you plan to join the millions of small business owners around the United States, be prepared to answer all these questions and a whole lot more. ▪

Chapter Overview

GeniusBabies.com is a great example of two major trends in small business today: the growing number of women starting their own businesses and the nearly endless opportunities presented by e-commerce technologies. You'll read about these trends and more in this chapter, starting with an overview of the world of small business, what small businesses are like, and why they continue to pop up all over the place. Following that, you'll take a closer look at the process of starting a business, from judging whether you have what it takes to be an entrepreneur to deciding which of the three basic paths to business ownership is right for you. The chapter concludes with a look at a critical issue that most entrepreneurs and small business owners need to address: finding the money to make your dream a reality.

Understanding the World of Small Business

Many small businesses start out like GeniusBabies.com: with an entrepreneur, an idea, and a drive to succeed. Since the founding of the United States, small businesses have been a vital part of the national economy. Small businesses play a role in virtually every sector of the economy, from e-commerce companies such as GeniusBabies.com to the independent contractors who drive routes for FedEx Ground, the freight arm of FedEx.[2] Many well-known entertainers, from singer Ani DiFranco to comedian/actor Bernie Mac, became small-business owners as a way to take control of their careers.[3] The opportunities for small business ownership are as diverse as the U.S. economy.

Defining just what constitutes a small business is surprisingly tricky because *small* is a relative term. For example, a manufacturing firm with 500 employees might be considered small if it competes against much larger companies, but a retail establishment with 500 employees might be classified as big when compared with its competitors. The distinction is more than a statistical curiosity; billions of dollars are at stake in such areas as employment regulations, from which the smallest companies are often exempt, and government contracts reserved for small businesses.[4]

The U.S. Small Business Administration (SBA) currently defines a **small business** as a firm that (a) is independently owned and operated, (b) is not dominant in its field, (c) is relatively small in terms of annual sales, and (d) has fewer than 500 employees (although the agency's exact standards vary from industry to industry, adjusting for the competitive makeup of each industry). By this definition, the United States is home to approximately 23 million small businesses. The SBA reports that 80 percent of all U.S. companies have annual sales of less than $1 million and that about 60 percent of the nation's employers have fewer than five workers.[5]

small business
Company that is independently owned and operated, is not dominant in its field, and meets certain criteria for the number of employees and annual sales revenue

Economic Roles of Small Businesses

Small businesses are the cornerstone of the U.S. economy. They bring new ideas, processes, and vigor to the marketplace. They generate about half of private sector output,[6] and they fill niche markets that often are not served by large businesses. Here are just some of the important roles small businesses play in the economy:

LEARNING OBJECTIVE 1

Highlight the major contributions small businesses make to the U.S. economy

- ***They provide jobs.*** Small businesses employ about half of the private-sector workforce in this country and create somewhere between two-thirds and three-quarters of new jobs. However, it's important to recognize that most of this job growth comes from that subset of small businesses whose goal is to grow into midsize or large businesses; the overwhelming majority of small businesses have no employees at all.[7]
- ***They introduce new products.*** The freedom to innovate that is characteristic of many small firms continues to yield countless advances in both technologies and marketable goods and services. In some cases, the innovation is a new way of looking at marketing opportunity, as when the founders of Zipcar, based in Cambridge, Massachusetts, recognized a need for hourly car rentals, which wasn't being met by the standard practices of established rental car companies.[8] In other cases, innovators develop new technologies then either build a growth company around it (such as Google's search engine technology) or sell the entire business to a larger company that wants to fold the technology into its product line (Microsoft has purchased several dozen companies in the past few years with this plan in mind).[9]
- ***They supply the needs of larger organizations.*** Many small businesses act as distributors, servicing agents, and suppliers to large corporations. In addition, government agencies often reserve a certain percentage of their purchasing contracts for small businesses.
- ***They inject a considerable amount of money into the economy.*** If U.S. small businesses were a separate country, they would constitute the third-largest economy in the world.[10]
- ***They take risks that larger companies sometimes avoid.*** Entrepreneurs play a significant role in the economy as risk takers, the people willing to try new and unproven ideas. A larger company might be afraid to start a chain of cereal shops, but Cereality (www.cereality.com), based in Boulder, Colorado, is betting the consumers will take to the idea of stopping in for a bowl of cereal the same way they visit other places for coffee or frozen yogurt.[11]
- ***They provide specialized goods and services.*** Small businesses frequently spring up to fill niches that aren't being served by existing companies. For instance, Seattle entrepreneur Michael Eastman founded the online music service Chondo (www.chondo.net) to give customers access to the incredible array of African-influenced music from artists all over the world. From Brazilian reggae to Tanzanian hip-hop to the *soukous* pop music of Congo, Chondo offers music that is difficult or impossible to find elsewhere.[12]

Japanese clothing designer and entrepreneur Risa Koyanagi has built a multimillion-dollar business on the strength of her unique fashions.

**L E A R N I N G
O B J E C T I V E** 2

Identify the key
characteristics (other than
size) that differentiate
small businesses from
larger ones

Business Buzz
social entrepreneur
*Someone who applies
entrepreneurial
business skills and
experience to a social
or charitable cause*

Characteristics of Small Businesses

The majority of small businesses are modest operations with little growth potential, although some have attractive income potential for the solo businessperson. The self-employed consultant, the corner florist, the family-owned neighborhood pizza parlor, and many e-commerce ventures (including GeniusBabies.com) are sometimes called *lifestyle businesses* because they are built around the personal and financial needs of an individual or a family. In contrast, other firms are small simply because they are young, but they have ambitious plans to grow. Many well-known companies—such as FedEx, Microsoft, and Papa John's (see this chapter's Case for Critical Thinking on pages 223–224)—start out as small entrepreneurial firms but quickly outgrow their small-business status. These *high-growth ventures* are usually run by a team rather than by one individual, and they expand rapidly by obtaining a sizable supply of investment capital and by introducing new products or services to a large market. In the past few years, a new subcategory of high-growth venture has emerged, too—the *quick-flip start-up*. Such companies are built to be sold within a couple of years or even less. For instance, Lucinda Duncalfe Holt and David Brussin started TurnTide, which develops anti-spam software, with an initial investment of $775,000. Six months later, they sold the company to Symantec—for $28 million.[13]

Regardless of their primary objectives, small companies tend to differ from large enterprises in a variety of important ways. First, most small firms have a narrower focus, offering fewer goods and services to fewer market segments. This can be both a blessing and a curse—a narrow focus can help you out-compete companies that serve multiple market needs, but it can also limit you in ways such as getting attention from distributors and retailers. Second, unless they are launched with generous financial backing, which is rare, small businesses get by with limited resources, which can mean anything from getting comfortable with used furniture and equipment to juggling a half-dozen different jobs at once (see Exhibit 6.1). Professionals who've spent their careers working for large companies can be shocked to discover how many tasks they need to accomplish as entrepreneurs.

The third major difference between small and large companies is also one of the most common—and exciting—reasons people go into business for themselves: having the

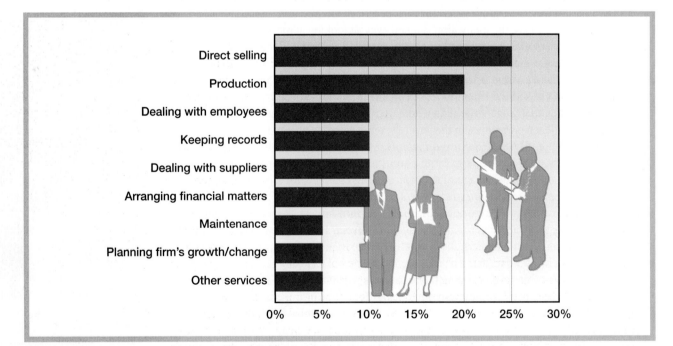

Exhibit 6.1
How Entrepreneurs Spend Their Time
The men and women who start their own companies are jacks-of-all-trades, but they devote the lion's share of their time to selling and producing the product.

freedom to innovate and move quickly. As they grow in size, companies also tend to grow in both complexity and bureaucracy. Decision making becomes slower and more difficult as more departments get involved and various groups compete internally for resources and recognition. In contrast, entrepreneurial firms usually find it easier to operate "on the fly," making decisions quickly and reacting to changes in the marketplace.

The entrepreneur's innovative spirit is so compelling, in fact, that many large companies and individuals within companies now try to duplicate it through *intrapreneurship*, a term coined by business consultant Gifford Pinchot to designate intracorporate entrepreneurship.[14] In some cases, companies designate specific groups to work on new ideas. Schneider Electric, a global supplier of electrical parts and supplies, is one of many large firms to establish internal *incubators* (see page 211) to give employees the opportunity to work on innovative business projects.[15] In other cases, an individual with an innovative idea develops and promotes the idea internally until the organization embraces it. For instance, several years ago Wendy Bohling convinced the management team at Avaya that Internet telephone service was going to be a major opportunity in the near future. It was a risky idea at the time, but Bohling persevered, and now Internet telephone products are a major part of Avaya's business.[16]

Factors Contributing to the Increase in the Number of Small Businesses

LEARNING OBJECTIVE 3
Discuss three factors contributing to the increase in the number of small businesses

Three factors are contributing to the increase in the number of small businesses today: e-commerce and other technological advances, the growing diversity in entrepreneurship, and corporate downsizing and outsourcing.

E-Commerce and Other Technologies E-commerce and other technologies have spawned thousands of new business ventures in recent years—both firms that create the technology and firms that use it. GeniusBabies.com is a perfect example of a small business enabled by the Internet. Consider the difference it has made in Michelle Donahue-Arpas's life: Without the Internet, she would have to either sacrifice family time and run her business out of a traditional retail store or find a considerable source of money to finance the catalog operations of a traditional mail-order company.

Growing Diversity in Entrepreneurship Small-business growth is also being fueled by women, minorities, immigrants, and young people who want alternatives to traditional employment. For instance, women now own some 10 million U.S. businesses—in fact, one of every 11 women in the country owns a business of some kind. Moreover, businesses owned by women are increasing both revenue and employment faster than the national average.[17]

As Exhibit 6.2 shows, women are starting small businesses for a number of reasons. Some choose to run their own companies so they can enjoy a more flexible work arrangement; others start their own business because of barriers to corporate advancement, known as the *glass ceiling*. This trend isn't limited to the United States, either, as women around the world seek a greater degree of financial independence and security through entrepreneurship, sometimes against considerable odds. When Kiran Mazumdar-Shaw started the biotechnology company Biocon in Bangalore, India, she struggled to find employees, office space, and raw materials—all because she was a woman. After nearly three decades of hard work, her company now employees hundreds of research scientists, and she's the richest woman in India.[18]

Between 1987 and 1997, the number of firms owned by minorities grew 168 percent—more than triple the 47 percent rate of U.S. businesses overall.[19] Minorities now own 15 percent of all U.S. businesses, double the number of a decade ago.[20] Part of this growth is attributed to firms that do a better job of marketing to specific segments of the population. For example, Hispanic-owned businesses have been doing better than the economy as a whole in recent years, thanks in large part to their success at marketing to the growing Hispanic American population.[21]

Kiran Mazumdar-Shaw worked for years to overcome biases against women as entrepreneurs and is now the richest woman in India.

MINDING YOUR OWN BUSINESS

DAVID COMPETES WITH GOLIATH ONLINE

You may not have the plush offices or fancy retail space of a large company in the physical world, but you can look just as impressive in the online world. Follow these tips to create a powerful online presence:

- *Present a professional image.* Be sure to provide a corporate profile that tells people something about your company in order to remove their fear of the unknown. Include news releases or articles about your business so that customers can see how well known or successful you are in your industry. Make sure your material is accurate, interesting, and focused on your audience's needs, not your own.
- *Make your website easy to use.* Web surfers have a short attention span, and large companies spend a significant amount of time and money making their sites easy to use. Give users a clear and obvious pathway through your site, and be sure to have several people test the navigation before you go live. Review other sites to see which terms are in common use. For instance, most sites now put company background information on a page entitled "About Us" so many web surfers expect to see such a page.
- *Make it sticky.* "Sticky" websites keep people coming back again and again; they're sites that people bookmark, visit frequently, and tell their friends about. To make your site sticky, make it relevant, interactive, and above all, fresh. People wouldn't read a newspaper that printed the same news every morning, and they won't revisit websites that don't provide new material constantly.

- *Anticipate your customers' needs.* Plan ahead. By including answers to frequently asked questions, you'll address many common concerns. So be sure to include an active customer feedback mechanism such as e-mail, open feedback forms, or structured survey forms, but don't require people to register before they can see your site or access useful information; most will simply click away to one of your competitors.
- *Don't forget the basics.* Always give visitors a person to call and a place to send for information. Be sure to list your postal and e-mail addresses and phone and fax numbers. And remember, because the Internet is international, list the nation(s) where your company or its dealers are located.
- *Promote your website.* Be sure to list with numerous search engines and online industry directories. Stay on top of the latest developments in online promotion, such as sponsored listings on search engines. Seek out related but noncompetitive companies that might attract the same customers you want to attract, then offer to link to each others' sites. Make sure your URL is included in all your advertising, signs, business cards, letterhead, and anywhere else potential customers might see it.

Questions for Critical Thinking
1. Why do web surfers have a short attention span?
2. If you're a tiny company competing against much larger firms, should you play up or play down your size? Explain your answer.

The tradition of immigrants starting small companies stretches back to the first days of the United States and continues strong today. With help from programs such as StartSmart, run by Coastal Enterprises in Wicasset, Maine, immigrants and political refugees get coaching and assistance on achieving financial independence through business ownership.[22]

Finally, young people are one of the strongest forces in entrepreneurship today. In fact, so-called Generation X, those people born between 1965 and 1980, now start some 70 percent of all new businesses.[23] Following in the tradition of Michael Dell, who started Dell Computer from his dorm room, many young entrepreneurs start businesses before they finish college. Heather Waibel started DirtDiggers Background Checks as an informal service to help her roommates learn more about prospective dates, then began growing it into a formal business that helps companies and nonprofit organizations perform background checks on new hires.[24]

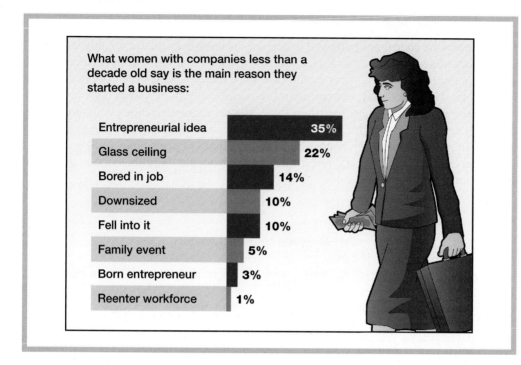

Exhibit 6.2
Women Starting
Businesses
*More than half of all
women business owners
started their own
businesses because they
had an entrepreneurial
idea or wished to further
advance their careers.*

Downsizing and Outsourcing Contrary to popular wisdom, business start-ups often soar when the economy sours. During hard times, many companies downsize or lay off talented employees, who then have little to lose by pursuing self-employment. In fact, several well-known companies were started during recessions. Tech titans William Hewlett and David Packard joined forces in Silicon Valley in 1938 during the Great Depression. Bill Gates started Microsoft during the 1975 recession. And the founders of Sun Microsystems, Compaq Computer, Adobe Systems, Silicon Graphics, and Lotus Development started their companies in 1982—in the midst of a recession and high unemployment.[25]

To make up for layoffs of permanent staff, some companies use **outsourcing**, the subcontracting of special projects and secondary business functions to experts outside the organization. Others turn to outsourcing as a way to permanently eliminate entire company departments. Regardless of the reason, the increased use of outsourcing provides opportunities for smaller businesses to service the needs of larger enterprises.

outsourcing
*Subcontracting work to
outside companies*

CRITICAL THINKING CHECKPOINT
1. Why might a small business be more willing to take a risk that a larger company would avoid?
2. Why would a successful corporation need to resort to intrapreneurship efforts in order to create innovative new products?
3. What effect is a more diverse group of entrepreneurs and small business owners likely to have on the overall U.S. economy?

Starting a Small Business

Are you ready to join the hundreds of thousands of people who start businesses in the United States every year? A good place to start is by exploring the most common characteristics of others who've taken the entrepreneurial plunge.

**L E A R N I N G
O B J E C T I V E 4**

Cite the key
characteristics common
to most entrepreneurs

Characteristics of Entrepreneurs

Entrepreneurs are sometimes portrayed in popular media as charismatic, slightly larger than life characters, people such as Sir Richard Branson, head of the Virgin entertainment, travel, and communications empire—people who have some secret success gene that protects them from failure. Or more darkly, entrepreneurs are occasionally portrayed as a greedy, predatory lot who're out to take more than their share. Neither characterization accurately reflects the multifaceted world of entrepreneurship, of course, and the entrepreneurial myth is just that, a myth.[26] In any event, it's impossible to lump millions of people into a single category; successful entrepreneurs are as diverse as the rest of the population, although they do tend to share a number of characteristics:[27]

- They are highly disciplined.
- They have a high degree of confidence.
- They have plenty of physical energy and emotional stamina.
- They like to control their destiny.
- They relate well to others and have a talent for organizing team efforts in pursuit of a common goal.
- They are eager to learn whatever skills are necessary to reach their goals.
- They learn from their mistakes.
- They stay abreast of market changes.
- They are willing to exploit new opportunities.
- They are driven by a passion to succeed—but they often don't measure success in strictly financial terms.
- They think positively and are able to overcome failure and adversity; they are tenacious in pursuit of their goals.
- Contrary to popular stereotype, they are not compulsive gamblers who thrive on high-risk situations; rather, they embrace moderate risk when it is coupled with the potential for significant rewards.

The story of Craig Tanner illustrates the range of personal characteristics that a successful entrepreneur must have. After working as a stock broker and sales manager, Tanner recognized his real opportunity when he watched Tiger Woods win yet another amateur golf

---

TECHNOLOGIES THAT ARE REVOLUTIONIZING BUSINESS Social Network Applications

Social networking sounds like the time you spend wandering around a party trying to meet people, but it's actually a new category of technology that is changing the way many professionals communicate. Social network applications, which can be either stand-alone software products or websites, help identify potential business connections by indexing e-mail and instant messaging address books, calendars, and message archives. For instance, you might find that the sales lead you've been struggling to contact at a large customer is a golf buddy of one of your suppliers or a relative of your child's soccer coach.

HOW THEY'RE CHANGING BUSINESS
One of the biggest challenges small-business owners face is finding the right people and making those connections,

whether you're looking for a new employee, an investor, a potential customer, or anyone else who might be important to the future of your business. With social network applications, businesspeople can reach more people than they could ever hope to reach via traditional, in-person networking.

WHERE YOU CAN LEARN MORE
Visit the websites of LinkedIn (**www.linkedin.com**), Ryze (**www.ryze.com**), and Spoke (**www.spoke.com**) to learn more about their products. To find other products and information about social network applications, enter "business networking" or "social networking" in your favorite search engine.

Exhibit 6.3

Why Entrepreneurs Go into Business

Entrepreneurs seldom cite "making more money" as a primary reason for going into business.

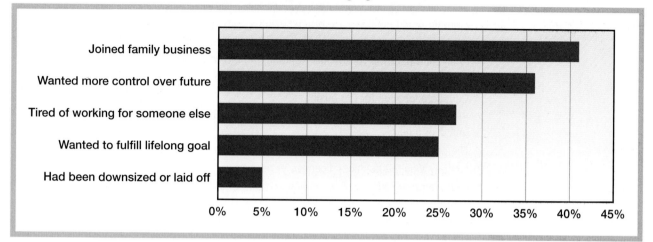

title early in his career. Woods hadn't yet become the global superstar he is today, but Tanner saw the future: "I knew that people of color and kids would get into golf." He founded Urban Golf Gear (www.urbangolfgear.com) in Oakland, California, with the goal of producing golf attire that combined the technical performance of athletic wear with the contemporary style of urban culture. Initial financing, all $1,500 of it, came from selling a car he had refurbished; he eventually took on more than $50,000 in credit card debt to grow the business. The products are attractive, and the market seemed to be there, but Tanner immediately ran into two obstacles. First, his products fell somewhere between the traditional golf apparel market and the urban apparel market, so working his way into retail outlets proved almost impossible. Second, no one would invest in a new company chasing an as-yet unproven opportunity. As tenacious as all successful entrepreneurs, Tanner created his own distribution channels, selling products to associates who would then resell them to consumers, displaying his wares at golf tournaments and events held by a variety of African American organizations, and working with promoters to get UGG gear featured in a variety of TV shows and movies. Gradually, satisfied customers began to spread the word, and sales took off.[28]

Entrepreneurs and small business owners go into business for a variety of reasons (see Exhibit 6.3). Most have diverse backgrounds in terms of education and business experience. Some come from companies unlike the ones they start; others use their prior knowledge and skills—such as editing, telemarketing, public relations, or selling—to start their own businesses. Still others have less experience but an innovative idea or a better way of doing something. They find an overlooked corner of the market, exploit a demographic trend unnoticed by others, or meet an unsatisfied consumer need through better service or a higher-quality product.

Importance of Preparing a Business Plan

Getting started in a new business requires a lot of work (see Exhibit 6.4), not the least of which is planning. Although many successful entrepreneurs claim to have done little formal planning, they all have at least *some* intuitive idea of what they're trying to accomplish and how they hope to do it. In other words, even if they haven't produced a formal printed document, chances are they've thought through the big questions, which is just as important. Jeff Bezos, founder of Amazon.com, planned the world's first online bookstore in the backseat of his car as his wife drove them from New York to Seattle. As Bezos and other entrepreneurs know, planning is essential for success. As FedEx founder Fred Smith put it, "Being entrepreneurial doesn't mean [you] jump off a ledge and figure out how to make a parachute on the way down."[29]

Exhibit 6.4
Business Start-Up
Checklist
You have many tasks to
perform before you start
your business. Here are
just a few.

✓ Choose a business name, verify the right to use it, and register it.

✓ Reserve a corporate name if you will be incorporating.

✓ Register a domain name for your website.

✓ Register or reserve state or federal trademarks.

✓ Apply for a patent if you will be marketing an invention.

✓ Write a business plan.

✓ Choose a location for the business.

✓ Identify and understand all the costs you're likely to encounter, both at start-up and over time.

✓ File partnership or corporate papers.

✓ Get any required business licenses or permits.

✓ Check local zoning laws.

✓ Identify any health, safety, or other special regulations that will apply to your business.

✓ Have business phone lines installed.

✓ Check into business insurance needs.

✓ Apply for a sales tax number.

✓ Apply for a federal employer identification number if you will have employees.

✓ Open business bank account(s).

✓ Have business cards and stationery printed.

✓ Purchase equipment and supplies.

✓ Order inventory, if needed.

✓ Order signs for the business, if needed.

✓ Produce your promotional materials (a website, brochures, etc., as needed).

✓ Send out publicity releases.

✓ Call everyone you know and tell them you are in business.

Planning forces you to think ahead. Before you rush in to supply a product, you need to be sure that a market exists. You must also try to foresee some of the problems that might arise and figure out how you will cope with them. For instance, what will you do if one of your suppliers suddenly goes out of business? Can you locate another supplier quickly? What if the neighborhood starts to change—even for the better? An influx of wealthier neighbors may lead to such a steep increase in rent that your business must move. Also, tough competition may move into the neighborhood along with the fatter pocketbooks. Do you have an alternative location staked out? What if styles suddenly change? Can you switch products quickly if consumer demand changes?

One of the first steps you should take toward starting a new business is to develop a **business plan**, a written document that summarizes an entrepreneur's proposed business venture, communicates the company's goals, highlights how management intends to achieve those goals, and shows how customers will benefit from the company's products or services. Writing the business plan can be a daunting task, but you can get help from a wide variety of websites, books, classes, and software products that guide you through the process.[30] Keep an eye out for business plan competitions, too; they're a popular way for entrepreneurs to get feedback from professionals—and win some start-up capital to boot. For instance, the team at Vertebration won $89,000 for their plan (for a product that would simplify spinal surgery) in Ohio State University's annual MBA business plan competition.[31]

Preparing a business plan serves two important functions: First, it guides the company operations and outlines a strategy for turning an idea into reality; second, it helps persuade lenders and investors to finance your business. In fact, if you don't have a

business plan
A written document that
provides an orderly
statement of a company's
goals and a plan for
achieving those goals

LEARNING FROM BUSINESS BLUNDERS

OOPS Carol Skonberg's company, Swasko Jewels, made sterling silver charms that dinner guests could wrap around the stems of their wineglasses to prevent confusion over which glass belongs to whom. Not a life-and-death problem, to be sure, but one of the things people would readily pay a few dollars to avoid, she figured. Her hunch proved correct, and she soon convinced 90 retailers in her home state of Texas to carry the products. Sales looked promising—then quickly plummeted as competitors with similar products but more aggressive marketing appeared out of nowhere. Skonberg and her business partner disbanded the company soon after.

WHAT YOU CAN LEARN According to small-business experts, Skonberg made several common rookie mistakes.

The first was believing she had a unique product. It's not unusual for more than one company to come up with the same solution to a given problem. The second mistake was failing to investigate legal protection earlier. Although she couldn't patent her designs (jewelry usually can't be patented), she could've come up with a catchy brand name and eye-catching logo, then trademarked those. The third—and probably biggest—mistake was not being prepared to go expand rapidly. Two competitors did go nationwide quickly, signing up sales reps around the country and getting into catalogs with wide distribution. The story has a happy ending, though. Skonberg learned from her experience and tried again, this time with a jewelry company called Hiplce that makes chains that drape off beltlines. So far, so good.

business plan, many investors won't even grant you an interview. Keep in mind that sometimes the greatest service a business plan can provide an entrepreneur is the realization that "the concept just won't work." Discovering this reality on paper can save you considerable time and money.

As important as planning is, it's equally important to monitor the market and be ready to adjust once you start moving. You don't want to be so locked into your plan that you fail to see changes in the market or new opportunities along the way.

Small-Business Ownership Options

Once you've done your research and planning, if you decide to take the risk, you can get into business for yourself in three ways: Start from scratch, buy an existing business, or obtain a franchise. Roughly two-thirds of business founders begin **start-up companies**; that is, they start from scratch rather than buying an existing operation or inheriting a family business. Starting a business from scratch has many advantages and disadvantages (see Exhibit 6.5); in many cases it can be the most difficult option.

Another way to go into business for yourself is to buy an existing business. This approach tends to reduce the risks—provided, of course, that you check out the company carefully. When you buy a healthy business, you generally purchase an established customer base, functioning business systems, a proven product or service, and a known location. You don't have to go through the challenging period of building a reputation, establishing a clientele, finding suppliers, and hiring and training employees. In addition, financing an existing business is often much easier than financing a new one; lenders are reassured by the company's history and existing assets and customer base. With these major details already settled, you can concentrate on making improvements.

Still, buying an existing business is not without disadvantages. For one thing, the business may be overpriced. For another, inventories and equipment may be obsolete. Furthermore, the location may no longer be satisfactory, the previous owner may have created ill will, your personality may clash with those of existing managers and employees, and outstanding bills owed by customers may be difficult to collect. Keep in mind that no matter how fast you learn

LEARNING OBJECTIVE 5

List three ways of going into business for yourself

start-up companies
New business ventures

*Prospective Subway
franchisees must
attend company training
classes and pass a
final exam before they
can own a Subway
sandwich shop.*

equipment—and most important of all, evaluating the franchisor. In addition to the questions in Exhibit 6.6, consult *Consumer Guide to Buying a Franchise*, a free publication from the FTC (www.ftc.gov).

Nevertheless, some people find out too late that franchising isn't the best choice for them. They make a mistake common among prospective franchisees—buying without really understanding the day-to-day business. Often, prospects simply don't get beyond the allure of the successful name or concept or the mistaken notion that a franchise brings instant success. Experts caution that you need to have cash set aside for both personal and business expenses so that you can survive until your new franchise begins to turn a profit.[34]

Advantages of Franchising Why is franchising so popular? For one thing, when you invest in a franchise, you know you are getting a viable business, one that has "worked" many times before. If the franchise is well established, you get the added benefit of instant name recognition, national advertising programs, standardized quality of goods and services, and a proven formula for success. Buying a franchise also gives you access to

Exhibit 6.6

Ten Questions to Ask Before Signing a Franchise Agreement
A franchise agreement is a legally binding contract that defines the relationship between the franchisee and the franchisor. Because the agreement is drawn up by the franchisor, the terms and conditions generally favor the franchisor. Before signing the franchise agreement, be sure to consult an attorney.

1. What does the initial franchise fee cover? Does it include a starting inventory of supplies and products?
2. How are the periodic royalties calculated and when are they paid?
3. Are all trademarks and names legally protected?
4. Who provides and pays for advertising and promotional items?
5. Who selects the location of the business?
6. Is the franchise assigned an exclusive territory?
7. If the territory is not exclusive, does the franchisee have the right of first refusal on additional franchises established in nearby locations?
8. Is the franchisee required to purchase equipment and supplies from the franchisor or other suppliers?
9. Under what conditions can the franchisor and/or the franchisee terminate the franchise agreement?
10. Can the franchise be assigned to heirs?

a support network and in many cases a ready-made blueprint for building a business. For an initial investment (from a few thousand dollars to upward of a million, depending on the franchise), you get services such as site-location studies, market research, training, and technical assistance, as well as assistance with building or leasing your structure, decorating the building, purchasing supplies, and operating the business during your initial ownership phase. Some franchisors also assist franchisees in financing the initial investment.

Disadvantages of Franchising Although franchising offers many advantages, it is not the ideal vehicle for everyone. First, owning a franchise is no guarantee of wealth. Even though it may be a relatively easy way to get into business, not all franchises are hugely profitable. Some franchisees barely survive, in fact. One of the biggest disadvantages of franchising is the monthly payment, or royalty, that must be turned over to the franchisor. Royalties are not necessarily bad as long as the franchisee gets ongoing assistance in return. Royalty fees vary from nothing at all to 20 percent of sales. Papa John's, for example, charges franchisees a monthly royalty fee of 4 percent of net sales.[35]

Another drawback of franchises is that many allow individual operators little independence. Franchisors can prescribe virtually every aspect of the business, down to the details of employee uniforms and the color of the walls. Furthermore, when a chain loses its cutting edge in the marketplace, being stuck with a franchise can be painful. By contrast, if independent retailers run into trouble with their product lines, they can change suppliers or perhaps switch rapidly to a whole new line of business. Franchisees can't. They're usually bound by contracts to sell only authorized products, often at a price set by the franchisor. Philip Castaldo, a 7-Eleven franchisee in Commack, New York, has found his sense of independence diminishing as 7-Eleven fine-tunes product choices throughout the store chain. He used to be able to choose many of his products and negotiate with local distributors, but all those decisions are under central control now. "I am not in charge of my destiny anymore," he says.[36]

Although franchisors can make important decisions without consulting franchisees, the days of franchisors' exercising unlimited control are ending. In many cases the relationship between franchisor and franchisee is becoming more of a joint venture. Some franchisors are rewriting contracts to become less dictatorial, says the CEO of U.S. Franchise Systems. Newer contracts offer stock options, automatic contract renewals, and empowerment through franchise advisory boards. Great Harvest Bread, for instance, promotes innovation among its franchisees. Owners are free to run their bakeries as they see fit, on just one condition: They must share what they learn along the way with other franchise owners. Great Harvest facilitates this collaboration through annual workshops and an extranet for franchisees.[37]

Why New Businesses Fail

Even if you carefully evaluate a prospective franchise or write a winning business plan, you have no guarantee of success. In fact, you may have heard some depressing statistics about the number of new businesses that fail. Some reports say your chances of succeeding are only one in three; others claim that the odds are even worse, stating that 85 or 90 percent of all new business ventures fail within 10 years. Actual statistics, however, show otherwise. Among all companies that close their doors, only about one in seven actually fails—that is, goes out of business leaving behind unpaid debts. And even in the ultra-competitive restaurant business, the failure rate is much less than the often-quoted 90 percent; one carefully conducted study says it's more along the lines of 60 percent.[38] Moreover, the true failure rate is much lower if you remove those operations that business analysts say aren't "genuine businesses." For instance, a freelance writer who writes one article for a magazine and then stops writing would be counted as a failed business under the traditional measurement (which is based on tax returns).[39]

Businesses can fail for any number of reasons, as Exhibit 6.7 suggests. Lack of management skills, experience, and proper financing are among the top 10 reasons for failure. Jumping on a hot trend without considering the long-term picture is another way to risk

Starting a business is a risky venture with no guarantee of success, but you can improve the odds dramatically with careful planning.

everything. Brad Salzman and Stephen Bikoff figured the low-carb diet craze was a sure bet for a specialty retail store chain, so they quickly signed leases on retail space in Santa Monica and Beverly Hills, California, figuring that figure-conscious Los Angeles was the perfect place to start. Unfortunately, things went downhill just as quickly. In addition to several planning missteps, such as selecting locations that weren't near consumers' other grocery and errand stops, the small stores simply couldn't compete with large grocery chains that buy in vast quantities and offer lower prices. Any food product that gains popularity is likely to be picked up by Wal-Mart, Safeway, and other national chains. Salzman and Bikoff are trying to recoup their $400,000 initial investment (most of it supplied by relatives) with a line of gourmet frozen foods they plan to pitch to the same grocery chains that trounced their retailing dreams.[40]

Although it sounds counterintuitive, growing *too* quickly is also a significant source of business failures, for several reasons. First, the entrepreneurial skills needed to get a business off the ground are not the same skills required to transform a hot start-up into a stable business

- Managerial incompetence
- Lack of relevant experience
- Inadequate financing
- Poor cash management
- Lack of strategic planning
- Ineffective marketing
- Uncontrolled growth
- Poor location
- Poor inventory control
- Inability to make the transition from corporate employee to entrepreneur

Exhibit 6.7
Why New Businesses Fail
Businesses can fail for a wide variety of reasons; here are 10 of the most common.

organization. Inventive minds who are stimulated by the joy of discovery and the puzzle-solving aspects of assembling a company can grow bored with the day-to-day work of managing a maturing business. In some cases, entrepreneurs have been able to reinvent themselves along the way and become successful executives. In others, they recognize their limitations and hire seasoned executives to take over, as eBay founder Pierre Omidyar did when he replaced himself with Meg Whitman—who has since led the company to dominance in online auctions.[41]

Second, growth puts tremendous pressure on every aspect of a company, and businesses can literally grow themselves into bankruptcy if they're not careful. Andi L. Brown, founder of Halo, Purely for Pets, a maker of high-quality pet foods and products in Palm Harbor, Florida, recently faced that exact dilemma. An opportunity to get shelf space at retail giant Petco is exciting, but she figures she'll need to double her staff and borrow up to the $2 million to meet Petco's volume needs. What if Petco drops her after she's built up her organization? Time will tell if she can manage the transition.[42]

Third, as small companies begin to grow, they often find themselves butting heads with much larger competitors—without having the resources of these larger companies. Consultant Doug Tatum describes this dilemma as "being too big to be small and too small to be big."[43] For instance, customers start to miss the personal attention and flexible response they enjoyed when the company was small, but the company isn't yet able to compensate with the comprehensive customer support systems that larger competitors can afford.

If you go into business for yourself, you'll probably make mistakes. But they don't have to be fatal; plenty of entrepreneurs make mistakes, learn from them, and go on to succeed. Also, the number of resources now available to entrepreneurs means you can learn from other people's experiences (including their mistakes).

Sources of Small-Business Assistance

Many local business professionals are willing to serve as mentors and can help you avoid the most common pitfalls. A number of smaller companies assemble advisory boards to help them review plans and decisions. Some executives meet regularly in small groups to analyze each other's progress month by month. Many colleges and universities also offer entrepreneurs programs. In addition, consider the assistance available from three other sources: the Service Corps of Retired Executives (SCORE), incubators, and the Internet. These resources can help you evaluate your business idea, develop a business plan, locate start-up funding sources, and promote your business more effectively.

LEARNING OBJECTIVE 6

Identify four sources of small-business assistance

SCORE Some of the best advice available to small businesses costs little or nothing. It's delivered by thousands of volunteers at SCORE (a resource partner of the Small Business Administration). These experienced business professionals offer advice and one-to-one counseling sessions on topics such as developing a business plan, securing financing, and managing business growth. Every year, SCORE counselors help some 400,000 U.S. businesses, such as *Virginia Horse Journal*, a magazine published by the husband-and-wife team of Dean and Darlene Jacobsen in Charlottesville, Virginia. Two SCORE counselors, both seasoned publishing industry professionals, helped the Jacobsens turn their struggling magazine into a thriving business.[44] You can contact a local SCORE counselor or learn more about available programs at www.score.org.

Incubators Incubators are centers that provide "newborn" businesses with just about everything a company needs to get started, from office space to information technology to management coaching, usually at sharply reduced costs. Most are nonprofit organizations (often partnerships between local governments, universities, and established businesses), although a number of for-profit incubators now exist as well. Incubators have spread rapidly in the past two decades; there are about 1,000 in North America and another 4,000 around the world. The objectives of specific incubators vary, such as facilitating the transfer of new technologies from universities to the commercial sector or developing local economies. For example, the Louisiana Technology Park in Baton Rouge, Louisiana, helps Internet,

incubators
Facilities that house small businesses during their early growth phase

With help from SCORE, Wayne Erbsen turned his passion for preserving and performing traditional music into a business that reaches customers all over the world from his home in Asheville, North Carolina. Native Ground Books & Music (www.nativeground. com) offers books and recordings of songs and folklore from the Civil War, the Old West, Appalachia, railroading, gospel, and many other elements of America's heritage.

e-commerce, and biotechnology start-ups that show promise of making substantial contributions to the state economy. Like most incubators, the Louisiana Technology Park wants to help companies that are close to launching their products, so it sets time limits of 12 to 24 months for companies in the program. Nationwide, the success rate of incubators is extremely high—nearly 90 percent of companies that "graduated" from incubators are still in business.[45] To learn more about incubators or to find one in your home state or country, visit the National Business Incubation Association website at www.nbia.org.

The Internet The Internet is another source of small-business assistance. Both informal chat rooms and membership organizations such as Young Entrepreneur (www.young entrepreneur.com) and the Young Entrepreneurs Organization (www.yeo.org) can help you learn from people who've already been down the path you're on. In addition, use all the online research techniques described in Chapter 4 to learn as much as you can about the markets and industries you want to enter. It's a fast and inexpensive way to avoid expensive mistakes—and discover lucrative opportunities.

CRITICAL THINKING CHECKPOINT

1. Some entrepreneurs view creating a company from nothing to be less risky than working in a corporate job. Why might that be?
2. Some businesspeople reject the idea of formal business plans because they say that plans can lock a company onto a fixed track while the world around them might be changing radically. How would you answer this criticism?
3. If you wanted to run a pizza restaurant, would you prefer to buy an existing operation or would you rather start from scratch? Would you prefer to own a franchise or an independent restaurant? Why?

LEARNING OBJECTIVE 7

Discuss the principal sources of small-business private financing

Financing a New Business

Even the simplest home-based businesses require some start-up capital, the costs for a retail shop or small manufacturing facility can run to several hundred thousand dollars, and a more complex business might require millions of dollars of invested cash before it can begin to generate sales revenue. Of all the mistakes that first-time business owners make, underestimating the amount of money it takes to get rolling is one of the most common. This mistake can happen in several areas: overestimating sales, overestimating how quickly money will come in from those sales (corporate customers often take 30 to 60 days or longer to pay, for instance), and underestimating expenses. Entrepreneurs are optimists by nature, but experts strongly recommend against using best-case scenarios when estimating your financing needs. Lower your sales expectations, raise your expense estimates, and run your numbers past an experienced professional (such as a SCORE advisor) to make sure you've identified all the potential costs. And even when things work as planned, you might have to survive for several months before you can start putting money in the bank. Follow the example of Ross McDowell, who borrowed enough money to keep his new running-shoe store in Oshkosh, Wisconsin, going for three months without a single sale. Fortunately, he began to generate revenue sooner, so he banked the leftover startup cash for emergency expenses down the road.[46]

Figuring out *how much* you'll need requires good insights into the particular industry you plan to enter. Figuring out *where* to get the money is a creative challenge no matter which industry you're in. As you can imagine, financing a business enterprise is a complex undertaking, and chances are you'll need to piece together funds from multiple sources, possibly using a combination of *equity* (in which you give investors a share of the business in exchange for their money) and *debt* (in which you borrow money that must be repaid). You'll read more about equity and debt financing in Chapter 17. Again, use the resources available today for advice; they can point you in the right direction for seeking both *private financing* and *public financing*.

Seeking Private Financing

Private financing covers every source of funding except selling stock to the public via a stock market. Virtually every company starts with private financing, even companies that eventually go public. The range of private finance options is diverse, from personal savings to investment funds set up by large corporations looking for entrepreneurial innovations. Many firms get *seed money*, their very first infusion of capital, through family loans. If you go this route, be sure to make the process as formal as a bank loan would be, complete with a specified repayment plan. Otherwise, problems with the loan can cause problems in the family.[47]

Four common categories of private financing, each of which requires its own special approach in order to be successful, are banks and microlenders, venture capitalists, angel investors, and that old standby of the entrepreneur—credit cards.

Banks and Microlenders Bank loans are one of the most important sources of financing for small business—but there's an important catch: In most cases, banks won't lend money to a start-up that hasn't established a successful track record.[48] As your company grows, a bank will nearly always be a good long-term partner, helping you finance expansions and other major expenses. However, as a start-up, about your only chance of getting a bank loan is by putting up marketable collateral, such as buildings or equipment, to back the loan.[49] You'll learn more about working with banks in Chapter 17.

In response to the needs of entrepreneurs who don't qualify for standard bank loans or who don't need the amount of a regular loan, a number of organizations now serve as *microlenders*, offering loans or grants ranging from several hundred dollars up to several thousand or more to help very small operations get started. For instance, the worldwide Trickle Up program, **www.trickleup.org**, helps low-income people with grants to start businesses. When Renee Turning Heart, a member of the Cheyenne River Sioux Lakota Nation in South Dakota, was injured and lost her job, Trickle Up provided a small grant to help her start a business selling quilts. Two years later, Turning Heart's business was doing well enough that she qualified for a bank loan to expand.[50] Similarly, the Association for Enterprise Opportunity, **www.microenterpriseworks.org**, provides links to microlenders throughout the United States and Mexico. While the companies that use microlenders may never grow up to be corporate giants, microlending is proving to be an effective way to help people move out of poverty and off public assistance.[51]

Venture Capitalists Venture capitalists (VCs) are investment specialists who raise pools of capital from large private and institutional sources (such as pension funds) to fund ventures that have high growth potential and a need for large amounts of capital. Given the amounts of money involved and the expectations of sizable returns, VCs typically invest in high-potential areas such as information technology, biotechnology, and digital media. For instance, Mforma Group of Kirkland, Washington, has received more than $60 million in VC backing to develop videogames for mobile phones.[52] Unlike banks or most other financing sources, VCs do more than simply provide money. They also provide management expertise in return for a sizable ownership interest in the business. Once the business becomes profitable, VCs reap the reward by selling their interest to long-term investors, usually after the company goes public.

Because they risk considerable amounts of money, usually $10 million or more, VCs are quite selective when it comes to investing and quite demanding of the management teams in the companies in which they do invest—and even more so after the dot-com, telecom, and biotech boom-and-bust years of the late 1990s. Unlike in those crazy days, VCs today are no longer willing to hand millions of dollars over to unproven firms led by recent college grads (sorry!); they now insist on experienced management running the company. Moreover, they want to invest in companies that are already profitable or that can show a strong possibility of becoming profitable if they receive funding. For instance, VCs investing in biotechnology are no longer content to fund years of unfocused research; they want their money going into specific products that show near-term potential. As an example, Nucleonics, based in Malvern, Pennsylvania, was unable to attract VCs until it narrowed its focus down to a single drug that promises to treat hepatitis B.[53]

Angel Investors Start-up companies that can't attract VC investment often look for *angel investors*, private individuals who put their own money into start-ups with the goal of eventually selling their interest for a large profit. These wealthy individuals are willing to invest smaller amounts than VCs usually invest and to stay involved with the company for a longer period of time. Many of these investors join *angel networks* or *angel groups* that invest together in chosen companies. Angel investing tends to have a more local focus than venture capitalism, so you can search for angels through local business contacts and organizations. You can also find many angel networks online or through *Inc.* magazine's *Directory of Angel-Investor Networks* at www.inc.com.[54]

Credit Cards Just like U.S. consumers, U.S. small business owners are crazy about credit cards; roughly half of all small businesses are now financed with them. It's an easy way to get money for your business, particularly with credit card companies pitching you new cards all the time. It's also an incredibly easy way to get into trouble if things don't work out. Unfortunately, there is no simple answer about using credit cards; some entrepreneurs have used them to launch successful, multimillion-dollar businesses, while others have destroyed their credit ratings and racked up debts that will take years to pay off. For example, twin brothers Jason and Matthew Olim used credit cards to launch CDnow in their parents' basement in Ambler, Pennsylvania, and eventually sold the company for an estimated $117 million after it hit the big time. On the other hand, Sam and Renée Beckley used credit cards to build Gremlin Studios, a small recording studio in Aurora, Illinois, but their story doesn't have quite such a happy ending. High debt coupled with medical expenses put them in a financial hole that will take them several years to climb out of. Fortunately, the studio has proven to be a solid, if not spectacular, enterprise, and the Beckleys are on the road to recovery.[55]

Small Business Administration Assistance If your business doesn't fit the profile of high-powered venture-capital start-ups, or you can't find an angel, you might be able to qualify for a bank loan backed by the Small Business Administration. SBA financing has helped launch some of the best-known companies in the United States, including FedEx, Intel, and Apple Computer. To get an SBA-backed loan, you apply to a regular bank, which actually provides the money; the SBA guarantees to repay between 50 to 85 percent of the loan (depending on the program) if you fail to do so. The upper limit on SBA-backed loans is currently $2 million.[56]

In addition to operating its primary loan guarantee program, known as the 7(a) program, the SBA also manages a microloan program, known as 7(m), in conjunction with nonprofit, community-based lenders.[57] Another option for raising money is one of the investment firms created by the SBA. These Small Business Investment Companies (SBICs) offer loans, venture capital, and management assistance, although they tend to make smaller investments and are willing to consider businesses that VCs or angel investors may not want to finance.[58]

Going Public

In contrast to private financing, in which you request funds from a specific individual or institution, companies with solid growth potential may also seek funding from the public at large. Whenever a corporation offers its shares of ownership to the public for the first time, the company is said to be *going public*. The initial shares offered for sale are the company's **initial public offering (IPO)**. Going public is an effective method of raising needed capital, but it can be an expensive and time-consuming process with no guarantee you'll get the amount of money you need. Public companies must meet a variety of regulatory requirements, as you'll explore in more detail in Chapter 17.

initial public offering (IPO)
Corporation's first offering of stock to the public

CRITICAL THINKING CHECKPOINT

1. Why do most entrepreneurs need to arrange financing from multiple sources throughout the life of their businesses?
2. Why do banks view start-up companies differently from the way venture capitalists view them?
3. Why are credit cards a risky way to finance an unproven start-up venture?

CHECKLIST: Apply These Ideas When You're the Boss

✓ Before you consider implementing any business idea, make sure you have a clear understanding of what the business really entails, day in and day out.

✓ Don't let tough economic conditions scare you away from entrepreneurship; good ideas and good managers can usually survive and succeed no matter what is happening in the world around them.

✓ Business plans require work—sometimes a lot of work—but if you cut corners in the planning stage, you could end up paying the price after you launch the business.

✓ Don't forgot to analyze yourself before you start a business; if you have any shortcomings

as an entrepreneur, find a way to fix them—or find partners who are strong in areas where you are weak.

✓ Explore every financing option you can find before deciding how to fund your new business; don't jump on the first solution you find.

✓ Learn from others' mistakes—with all the resources and information so readily available today, there's no good reason to repeat mistakes that other businesspeople have already made.

✓ Don't let a lack of experience or resources squash your dreams; if you truly want to run your own business, you can probably find a way to get the experience and resources you need.

Summary of Learning Objectives

1 **Highlight the major contributions small businesses make to the U.S. economy.** Small businesses bring new ideas, processes, and vigor to the marketplace. They generate about half of private sector output, employ over half of the private nonfarm U.S. workforce, and create a significant number of new jobs. Small businesses introduce new goods and services, provide specialized products, and supply the needs of large corporations. Additionally, they spend almost as much as big businesses in the economy each year.

2 **Identify the key characteristics (other than size) that differentiate small businesses from larger ones.** In general, small businesses tend to sell fewer products and services to a more targeted group of customers. They have closer contact with their customers and many tend to be more open-minded and innovative because they have less to lose than established companies. Small-business owners generally make decisions faster and give employees more opportunities for individual expression and authority. Because they have limited resources, however, small-business owners often must work harder and perform a variety of job functions.

3 **Discuss three factors contributing to the increase in the number of small businesses.** One factor is the advancement of technology in general and the Internet in particular, which makes it easier to start a small business, compete with larger firms, or work from home. A second factor is the increase in the number of women and minorities who are interested in becoming entrepreneurs. Third, corporate downsizing and outsourcing have made self-employment or small-business ownership a more attractive and viable option.

4 **Cite the key characteristics common to most entrepreneurs.** Successful entrepreneurs are highly disciplined, intuitive, innovative, ambitious individuals who are eager to learn and like to set trends. They enjoy the thrill of being in business and are willing to take calculated risks to reap the rewards. Few start businesses for the sole purpose of making money.

5 **List three ways of going into business for yourself.** You can start a new company from scratch, you can buy a going concern, or you can invest in a franchise. Each option has its advantages and disadvantages when it comes to cost, control, certainty, support, and independence.

6 **Identify four sources of small-business assistance.** One source for small-business assistance is SCORE—an organization staffed by retired executives and active small-business owners who provide counseling and mentoring for free. Incubators are another source. They provide facilities, business resources, and all types of start-up support. The Internet is an excellent resource for product and market research, business leads, advice, and contacts. And many small-business owners try to take advantage of mentors and advisory boards.

7 **Discuss the principal sources of small-business private financing.** Bank loans are a principal source of private financing, although they are difficult for many small businesses to obtain; new mini-lenders offer opportunities for companies that need small amounts. Microlenders fill the need for smaller loans and grants in many cases. Family and friends are another source. Other alternatives include big businesses, venture capitalists, angel investors, and credit cards. Finally, the Small Business Administration, though not an actual source, can assist entrepreneurs by partially guaranteeing small bank loans.

GeniusBabies: What's Next?

As a private business, GeniusBabies.com doesn't report financial results to the public, but all signs suggest that Michelle Donahue-Arpas's at-home e-commerce enterprise is running just fine. She also operates a second, related e-commerce site called BabyGiftsCo.com, which focuses on gifts that families and friends of parents with young children would be interested in buying. As long as she continues to provide the quality products and superb customer service that she's become known for—and giant e-commerce sites such as Amazon.com aren't able to lure customers away—Donahue-Arpas's entrepreneurial dream should continue for as long as she wants to run her company.

Critical Thinking Questions

1. Explore the GeniusBabies.com and BabyGiftsCo.com sites then analyze why Donahue-Arpas would want to operate these two sites separately. (Note that www.babygifts.com is an unrelated site; Donahue-Arpas's second site is www.babygiftsco.com.)

2. Both the GeniusBabies.com and BabyGifts.com sites proudly display the Yahoo! Shopping 5 Star award for customer service (both sites are hosted by Yahoo!'s Small Business e-commerce services). Visit Yahoo! Small Business at http://smallbusiness.yahoo.com;

why would Donahue-Arpas choose Yahoo! to host her online businesses, rather than creating her own e-commerce sites?

3. One of the risks that every small e-commerce retailer faces is that popular products are likely to be picked up by giants such as Amazon.com, which can probably offer lower prices. How can Donahue-Arpas ensure that her customers will keep buying from her if the products she carries start appearing on Amazon.com?

Key Terms

business plan (204)	incubators (211)	small business (197)
franchise (207)	initial public offering	start-up companies (205)
franchisee (207)	(IPO) (215)	venture capitalists (VCs) (214)
franchisor (207)	outsourcing (201)	

Test Your Knowledge

Questions for Review

1. What are two essential functions of a business plan?
2. What are the advantages of buying a business rather than starting one from scratch?
3. What are the advantages and disadvantages of owning a franchise?
4. What are the key reasons for most small-business failures?
5. What is a business incubator?

Questions for Analysis

6. Why is writing a business plan an important step in starting a new business?
7. Why is it important to establish a time limit for a new business to generate a profit?
8. What things should you consider when evaluating a franchise agreement?
9. What factors should you consider before selecting financing alternatives for a new business?
10. **Ethical Considerations.** You're thinking about starting your own hot dog and burger stand. You've got the perfect site in mind, you've analyzed the neighborhood, and you understand the costs and resources required. It looks as if all systems are go. Uncle Pete is even going to back you on this one. You really understand the fast-food market. In fact, you've become a regular at a competitor's operation (down the road) for over a month. The owner thinks you're his best customer. He even wants to name a sandwich creation after you. But you're not there because you love Frannie's fancy fries. No, you're actually spying. You're learning everything you can about the competition so you can outsmart them. Is this behavior ethical? Explain your answer.

Questions for Application

11. Briefly describe an incident in your life in which you failed to achieve a goal you set for yourself. What did you learn from this experience? How could you apply this lesson to a future experience as an entrepreneur?
12. Lack of industry experience is one of the most common reasons for failure of new businesses. If you wanted to start a new business that provides catering and other services for corporate events (office parties, executive retreats, public open houses, and so on), how might you gain the experience needed to succeed in such a venture?
13. **Integrated.** Entrepreneurs are one of the five factors of production as discussed in Chapter 1. Review that material plus Exhibit 1.1 (Rags to Riches), and explain why entrepreneurs are an important factor for economic success.
14. **Integrated.** Pick a local small business or franchise that you visit frequently and discuss whether that business competes on price, speed, innovation, convenience, quality, or any combination of those factors. Be sure to provide some examples.

Practice Your Knowledge

Handling Difficult Situations on the Job: Getting the Inside Scoop on a Franchise

You know that franchises can be a smart first move for aspiring business owners. But you've also read that they demand long hours, steep investments, and rigid rule following. Still, you're seriously investigating buying into an existing franchise system. You've narrowed down the choices and this week, you're investigating the Subway franchise, hoping for a location near your hometown of Bartlesville, Oklahoma. *Entrepreneur* magazine has just ranked Subway as the best franchise opportunity, and it seems like a good investment—but you need to be certain.

When you called Subway's headquarters and asked for references, you were told about Tharita Jones, who operates a Subway store in Tulsa, about 30 miles from Bartlesville. "She's been with us for about five years now," said the woman as she gave you Jones's name and number. Jones generously agreed to meet with you for a brief time next week, despite her daily avalanche of work (watching over employees, doing paperwork, ordering supplies, talking to customers, checking restrooms, fixing problems . . .). You want to make the meeting as efficient as possible, for your sake and hers.[59]

Your task: Considering all you've learned in this chapter about franchise advantages and disadvantages, and small businesses in general, what questions will be most pertinent for your meeting with Jones? Jot them down as you think of them so you'll be prepared. Remember, you won't want to waste Jones's time with questions you can get answered from other sources, so focus on eliciting her unique insights as a franchisee.

Sharpening Your Communication Skills

Effective communication begins with identifying your primary audience and adapting your message to your audience's needs. This is true even for business plans. One of the primary reasons for writing a business plan is to obtain financing. With that in mind, what do you think are the most important things investors will want to know? How can you convince them that the information you are providing is accurate? What should you assume investors know about your specific business or industry?

Building Your Team Skills

The 10 questions shown in Exhibit 6.6 cover major legal issues you should explore before plunking down money for a franchise. In addition, however, there are many more questions you should ask in the process of deciding whether to buy a particular franchise.

With your team, think about how to investigate the possibility of buying a Papa John's franchise. First, brainstorm with your team to draw up a list of sources (such as printed sources, Internet sources, and any other suitable sources) where you can locate basic background information about the franchisor. Also list at least two sources you might consult for detailed information about buying and operating a particular franchise. Next, generate a list of at least 10 questions any interested buyer should ask about this potential business opportunity.

Choose a spokesperson to present your team's ideas to the class. After all the teams have reported, hold a class discussion to analyze the lists of questions generated by all the teams. Which questions were on most teams' lists? Why do you think those questions are so important? Can your class think of any additional questions that were not on any team's lists but seem important?

Expand Your Knowledge

Discovering Career Opportunities

Would you like to own and operate your own business? Whether you plan to start a new business from scratch or buy an existing business or a franchise, you will need certain qualities to be successful. Start your journey to entrepreneurship by reviewing this chapter's information on entrepreneurs. Now you are ready to delve deeper into the career opportunities of owning and running a small business.

1. Which of the entrepreneurial characteristics mentioned in the chapter describe you? Which of those characteristics can you develop more fully in advance of running your own business?
2. Using library sources, find a self-test on entrepreneurial qualities or use the entrepreneurial test at the website www.onlinewbc.gov/docs/starting/test.html. Analyze the test's questions. Which of

the characteristics discussed in this chapter are mentioned or suggested by the questions included in the test?

3. Answer all the questions in the self-test you have selected. Which questions seem the most critical for entrepreneurial success? How did you score on this self-test and on the questions you think are most critical? Before you go into business for yourself, which characteristics will you need to work on?

Developing Your Research Skills

Scan issues of print or online editions of business journals or newspapers for articles describing problems or successes faced by small businesses in the United States. Clip or copy three or more articles that interest you and then answer the following questions.

1. What problem or opportunity does each article present? Is it an issue faced by many businesses, or is it specific to one industry or region?
2. What could a potential small-business owner learn about the risks and rewards of business ownership from reading these articles?
3. How might these articles affect someone who is thinking about starting a small business?

Exploring the Best of the Web

URLs for all Internet exercises are provided at the website for this book, www.prenhall.com/bovee. When you log on to this text's Companion Website, select Chapter 6. Then select "Featured Websites," click on the name of the featured website, and review the website to complete these exercises.

Explore these chapter-related websites, review their content, and answer the following questions for each website you visit:

1. What is the purpose of this website?
2. What kinds of information does this website contain? Please be specific.
3. How is the information provided at this website useful for businesspeople? Consumers?
4. How did you expand your knowledge of information management, the Internet, and e-commerce by reviewing the material at this website? What new things did you learn about these topics?

Guide Your Way to Small-Business Success
Inc.com has an outstanding selection of articles and advice on buying, owning, and running a small business that you won't want to miss. If you're considering a franchise, the tools and tips at this site will help you find your ideal business. Concerned about financing? Check out the articles on raising start-up capital, finding an angel, or attracting venture capital. You can also find information on how to create or spruce up a website, set up your first office, develop entrepreneurial savvy, and overcome burnout. Running a small business is no easy feat, so get a head start by reading the Inc.com guides online. www.inc.com/guides

Start a Small Business
Thinking about starting your own business? The U.S. Small Business Administration (SBA) website puts you in touch with a wealth of resources to assist you in your start-up. Perhaps you would like some professional business counseling, financial assistance, or advice on developing a business plan. Starting a new business or buying an existing one can be an overwhelming process. But you can increase your chances of success by taking your first steps with the SBA's Startup Kit. So log on to find out if entrepreneurship is for you. Then do your research and discover some of the secrets of success. www.sba.gov

Learn the ABCs of IPOs
Taking a company public is not for the faint of heart. But like a Broadway opening, a successful debut can launch a relatively unknown company into stardom—or allow it to quietly disappear from the public eye. Even today's largest corporations were at some point small start-ups looking for public financing. Which company is the next AOL, Xerox, or Microsoft? How do IPOs work? How does a young company play the IPO game? You can find the answer to these questions and more by checking out the Beginners Guide to IPOs at Hoover's IPO Central. www.hoovers.com (click on IPO Central)

Learning Interactively

Companion Website
Visit the Companion Website at www.prenhall.com/bovee. For Chapter 6, take advantage of the interactive "Learning Modules" to test your chapter knowledge. Get instant feedback on whether you need additional studying. Complete the exercises as specified by your instructor.

A Case for Critical Thinking

Why Is Papa John's Rolling in Dough?

As a high school student working at a local pizza pub, John Schnatter liked everything about the pizza business. "I liked making the dough; I liked kneading the dough; I liked putting the sauce on; I liked putting the toppings on; I liked running the oven," recalls Schnatter. "From the get-go, I fell in love with the business." Working his way through college by making pizzas, Schnatter was obsessed with perfect pizza topping placement and bubble-free melted cheese. But he knew that something was missing from national pizza chains: a superior-quality pizza delivered to the customer's door. And his dream was to one day open a pizza restaurant that would fill that void.

HUMBLE BEGINNINGS

Schnatter got his chance shortly after graduating from Ball State University with a business degree. His father's tavern was $64,000 in debt and failing. So Schnatter sold his car, purchased some used restaurant equipment, knocked out a broom closet in the back of his father's tavern, and began selling pizzas to the tavern's customers. Soon the pizza became the tavern's main attraction and helped turn his father's business around.

With a recipe for success, Schnatter opened the first Papa John's restaurant in 1985 in Louisville, Kentucky. Then he set about growing his business. After all, he was no novice. He knew the grass-roots of the pizza business, had an intuitive grasp on what customers wanted, and knew how to make pizzas taste a little bit better than the competition's.

EXPANDING THE PIE CHART

John Schnatter used franchising to grow the business. Today about 75 percent of Papa John's are franchised; the rest are company-owned. But Papa John's doesn't just move into an area and open up 200 stores. It expands one store at a time. Before a single pizza hits the ovens, franchisees spend six months to a year assessing an area's potential. Once a store is up and running, the company puts enormous effort into forecasting product demand. Franchisees project demand one to two weeks in advance. They factor in anything from forthcoming promotions to community events to the next big high school football game. If a major sports event is on TV, store owners are ready for the surge in deliveries.

Papa John's made its European debut in 1999 by acquiring Perfect Pizza Holdings, a 205-unit delivery and carryout pizza chain in the United Kingdom. The acquisition gave Papa John's instant access to proven sites that would have been difficult to obtain. Besides the real estate, Perfect Pizza had a good management team that Schnatter could fold into his organization.

THE PERFECT CRUST

If one strength rises above the others in Schnatter's path to success, it's his ability to recruit and retain the right people. "There's nothing special about John Schnatter except the people around me," Schnatter says. "They make me look better" and they make Papa John's what it is—committed to its heritage of making a superior-quality, traditional pizza.

Quality control is another important part of Schnatter's secret recipe for success. To ensure a high-quality product, owners are trained to remake any pies that rate less then 8 on the company's 10-point scale. If the cheese shows a single air bubble or the crust is not golden brown, out the offender goes. To make sure everything is in order, Schnatter visits four to five stores a week. His attention to detail has helped the company earn awards. Papa John's was twice voted number one in customer satisfaction among all fast-food restaurants in the American Consumer Satisfaction Index.

PIPING-HOT PERFORMANCE

Now the third-largest pizza chain, Papa John's has 3,000 stores in 49 states and 20 international markets. Annual sales have mushroomed to about $1.7 billion. But like many companies today, Papa John's faces challenges. Although Americans consume pizza at the rate of 350 slices a second, restaurant pizza sales are as flat as a thin-crust pie. Papa John's opens new restaurants and closes unprofitable outlets all the time to keep profitability in line. But it's becoming increasingly difficult to expand the company's share of the pie in a highly competitive and stagnant industry. Which means that to succeed, Papa John's must grab market share from giants such as Pizza Hut, Little Caesar's, and delivery king Domino's. To help in that effort, in 2005 Schnatter hired Nigel Travis from Blockbuster Video to serve as Papa John's new president and CEO. Schnatter is staying on as chairman of the board, but you can bet his attention to the details of quality pizza and competitive entrepreneurship won't diminish one bit.

Critical Thinking Questions

1. What steps did John Schnatter take to turn Papa John's into a successful pizza chain?
2. If you were drafting Papa John's initial business plan, what would you need to know about competition?
3. Why does Papa John's rely on franchising to grow its concept?
4. Go to Chapter 6 of this text's website at www.prenhall.com/bovee. Click on the Papa John's link to read about Papa John's franchise system. What kind of assistance does Papa John's provide new franchisees? What are Papa John's minimum requirements for new franchisees? How much does it cost to open a Papa John's restaurant?

Video Case

Managing Growth at Student Advantage

Learning Objectives

The purpose of this video is to help you:

1. See how a company is successfully making the transition away from being a small business.
2. Understand some of the pitfalls of growing beyond a small, entrepreneurial organization.
3. Recognize how important partnerships with established companies can be for many small businesses.

Synopsis

Many students are familiar with the Student Advantage discount card, saving them up to 50 percent on everyday purchases on and off campus, including air and ground transportation. Keeping pace with the growing consumer base among high school and college students, Student Advantage, Inc. has successfully implemented an aggressive growth strategy. Working with hundreds of colleges, universities and campus organizations, and more than 15,000 merchant locations, the company reaches customers offline through the Student Advantage Membership and online through its website. Eleven acquisitions in its first 10 years of existence have taught this company and its young CEO, Ray Sozzi, that communication is the key to growing beyond a small business without losing the original entrepreneurial vision.

Discussion Questions

1. *For analysis:* Even though Student Advantage may have started as a small company, it was clearly created with an eye on growth, rather than as a lifestyle business designed to support one family. In a company that must partner with dozens of other companies and provide services to more than a million customers, what are the risks of growing quickly?
2. *For analysis:* Based on what you learned in the video, what steps did Student Advantage take to avoid the potential problems of a high-growth strategy based on frequent acquisitions?
3. *For analysis:* How does the "buddy system" help Student Advantage integrate employees from acquired companies?
4. *For application:* Student Advantage's corporate lawyer made a strong case for a go-slow approach to growing internationally. Given the millions of students in other countries who might want to use the company's services—and who might find other alternatives before Student Advantage becomes available in their respective countries—why would it be wise to grow slowly and carefully, rather than jumping into new markets quickly, before competitors can spring up?
5. *For debate:* One of the Student Advantage executives describes the challenge of growing into the job without the benefit of previous managerial or executive experience. What are the pros and cons of bringing in experienced outside managers to help a small company, versus giving existing employees the opportunity to grow into managerial jobs?

Online Exploration

Visit Student Advantage's website at www.studentadvantage.com. Based on the types of services you see, what sort of companies does Student Advantage seek out as partners? How does the company promote its services to students? How does the website try to appeal to student lifestyle concerns, such as summer vacation or spring break?

E-Business in Action

THE RISE, FALL, AND RISE OF DOT-COMS

On April 8, 1999, Craig Winn, founder of Value America, became a dot-com billionaire. Investors flocked to his idea of a "Wal-Mart" on the Internet, where shoppers could order jars of caviar along with their gas barbecues or desktop computers. The company served as a go-between: It transmitted customer orders immediately to manufacturers, which would ship the merchandise directly to buyers. Value America's IPO was a success. The stock closed the first day at $55 a share, valuing the three-year-old profitless company at $2.4 billion.

Running on Empty

Twelve months later, Value America filed for Chapter 11 bankruptcy protection, and the price of the company's stock had fallen to 72 cents. The cyberstore was supposed to harness every efficiency promised by the Internet: no inventory, no shipping costs, no warehouse, no physical store. But like many Internet entrepreneurs, Winn tried to do too much too soon. Company computers crashed, customers waited to get their orders filled, returned merchandise piled up in the halls of the company's offices, and discounting and advertising drained the company's cash, wiping out any chance of profitability.

Instant Paper Billions

Value America's rise and fall is symbolic of an era of unbridled optimism. For much of the 1990s, U.S. businesses and their investors displayed an appetite for risk that would have been considered reckless just a few years earlier. A raging bull market, free-flowing capital, and technological advances created so many opportunities at the turn of the millennium that it was sometimes difficult to separate a calculated risk from a wild grab at the brass ring.

Just about any dot-com company that wanted to hawk wares over the Net found plenty of eager investors hoping to reap huge profits from the dot-com craze. The web was like a vast, underdeveloped prairie; web entrepreneurs even used the word "landgrab" to describe their mad attempts at capturing market share—at any cost. The new-economy boom led many to believe that the rules of business had changed. Venture capitalists, flush with wealth from skyrocketing stock prices, threw too many millions at inexperienced entrepreneurs with untested ideas and unproven technology. Enthusiastic investors raced to claim a stake in the new frontier at Internet speed. Most went in with their eyes wide shut, driving stock prices even higher—which gave VCs that much more money to throw at new businesses.

The Lights Go Out

Like a thrill ride at an amusement park, however, the whole affair soon screeched to a halt. Entrepreneurs learned the hard way that successfully launching a public company was much different from successfully running one. Cyberspace got crowded. New dot-coms went unnoticed. Desperate to get consumers' attention and business, e-tailers spent lavishly on advertising. Some pumped out discount offers and free-shipping promises—hemorrhaging cash and piling up losses. This turn of events prompted investors to take a second look and change their minds—overnight. Profits, it seemed, mattered after all. Many investors watched in shock as dot-com stock prices fell through the floor.

Some, of course, had predicted the dot-com fallout. History, they said, would repeat itself. After all, from 1855 to 1861, the number of start-up telegraph companies in the United States shrank by 87 percent—from 50 to 6. The Internet, they predicted, would not escape a shakeout of its own. Why did the dot-coms run out of steam? Experts now cite these reasons:

- *Poor management.* Many dot-coms were founded by people with little or no experience running a business. Some entrepreneurs were in such a rush to go public they forgot one small detail: They needed a sound business plan. They were more attracted by the potential to get rich than by the need to create a company "built to last." Craig Winn's business background, for instance, consisted mainly of leading another public company into bankruptcy. His technology experience? None. Only during a period of a seeming suspension of the "rules of business" could someone with Winn's background amass the funds to launch such a risky venture.

- *Unrealistic goals.* Many dot-com start-ups were dedicated to achieving the impossible—launching companies in weeks and attracting millions of customers in months. But the evolution of consumers was far slower than most people predicted. People were not ready to buy mortgages and new cars in volume over the Internet. In fact, most Internet firms found that hoped-for volume simply wasn't there. Take online grocers, for example. Buying groceries online requires consumers to make a big change in the way they shop for basic household goods. Moreover, to build up a base of customers from scratch, the newcomers had to spend heavily on advertising and other types of marketing. Webvan, for instance, spent 25 to 35 percent of its revenue on advertising, compared with an average of about 1 percent spent by traditional grocers. Another unrealistic goal, and one that doomed a number of dot-coms, was the assumption that a herd of advertisers would migrate from television and other traditional venues as soon as enough websites attracted enough "eyeballs."

- *Going public too soon.* Venture capitalists, eager to back the next AOL or Amazon, tossed huge sums of money at companies that had barely a prayer of prospering. In many cases, the VCs took the dot-coms public way too soon. Instead of waiting the customary four to five years, dot-coms were taken public in two years or less—long before the company or its management could prove consistent performance to the public. Nonetheless, investors overlooked business fundamentals and continued to scoop up these stocks, driving prices into the stratosphere.

- *Fighting the laws of supply and demand.* Demand-driven start-ups are born to fulfill existing needs of consumers or businesses. By contrast, supply-driven start-ups are born in the mind of the entrepreneur with little more than a gut feeling that someone will eventually need or want the company's product or service. Thus, supply-driven start-ups leave the company with the enormous task of establishing a new market rather than participating in an existing one. Moreover, with relatively low barriers to entry in many cases, other dot-coms could easily copy a good idea.

- *Extravagant spending.* Companies spent recklessly to lure customers with special promotions and silly marketing campaigns—no matter the cost. For instance, drkoop.com, an online health site, burned through three-quarters of the $84 million it raised in an IPO in less than one year. Losses, of course, were excused as necessary in the pursuit of new customers. Some dot-coms even began to act like conventional retailers—building costly warehouses and adding staff—to compete. Webvan officials argued in the company's early stages that the centers, which could handle up to 8,000 orders a day (many times more than a traditional warehouse) would give it a big cost advantage over its bricks-and-mortar competitors. But it never gained the sales volume to take full advantage of the efficiencies, and so its profit margins trailed those of large traditional grocers. After chewing through $830 million in start-up and IPO funds, Webvan filed for bankruptcy protection.

- *Locked out of cash.* Most dot-coms were started with venture capital. When they burned through that money, they had to find new funding or go public. For many, neither happened. As the dot-com failure rate grew, investors forced companies to cut costs vigorously, look for merger candidates, postpone or scrap their plans to go public, find a buyer at any price, or simply close up shop.

As quickly as they'd jumped on the bandwagon, investors, the press, and the general public turned on the whole idea of dot-coms. VCs and individual investors licked their wounds and looked for safer places to invest whatever money they had left. Workers who had been lured away from big-company jobs with the dream of IPO riches tried to return. Most people seemed to write it off as some big, crazy experiment that went wildly wrong.

Internet entrepreneurs learned a lot during the dot-com boom, everything from fundamentals of supply and demand (when there's no demand, there's not much point in having supply) to the truth about those traditional business models they once scoffed at as outmoded (there's a reason those models have been in use for years . . . they work!). Online companies learned how hard it was to compete in businesses that often had razor-thin profit margins, such as retailing, and how hard it was to change consumer habits.

A Funny Thing Happened on the Way to the Trash Heap

A year or two after the bleakest point of the dot-com story, an amazing thing began to happen: Some of the dot-coms started to succeed. Amazon.com became a multibillion-dollar retailer that started to turn a profit on its massive investment in e-commerce. eBay reinvented the world of flea markets and auctions on its way to becoming the most popular shopping site in the world and continues to show strong profits. Yahoo! attracts more than 200 million visitors a month to its global network of web portals. Google has become a household name, synonymous with searching online. And old-school retailers such as Wal-Mart and manufacturers such as Dell learned from dot-com mania and now harness the Internet successfully themselves. So while the dot-com party certainly got out of control in the late 1990s, it seems there were some ideas worth celebrating after all.

Critical Thinking Questions

1. Why did so many dot-com businesses fail at the beginning of the twenty-first century?
2. How did the attitude of dot-com investors change? Why did it change?
3. If you had the opportunity to invest in a dot-com business today, what questions would you ask before investing your money?

Career Profiles

Here are brief glimpses at two career paths that relate to the chapters in Part II. You'll find other career profiles following Chapters 4, 9, 11, 15, and 18.

Marketing Researchers and Research Managers

Marketing researchers and the managers who oversee research teams are responsible for gathering market intelligence and transforming it into "actionable" information and advice that companies can use to guide strategy.

Nature of the Work   Do you often wonder why other people behave the way they do? If so, a career in marketing research could be a fascinating option for you. Marketing researchers help executives answer questions about the future: what competitors will do next, what will be the next hot consumer trend, how customer expectations will change, and so on. The work involves a cycle of identifying information needs; designing surveys, experiments, and other information collection methods appropriate to the task at hand; analyzing the results; and presenting summaries, conclusions, and recommendations to managers (either within your own firm or for clients).

Qualifications   A master's degree is expected in most research jobs, particularly for specialists and managers. Solid skills in math, statistics, and survey design are essential, and familiarity with behavioral psychology, sociology, and basic economic and marketing concepts is important as well. Communication skills are vital at every stage of research, including understanding what clients or managers need to learn, carefully listening to and observing research subjects, and communicating results simply and clearly.

Where the Jobs Are   Marketing research takes place in virtually every industry, and you have three basic options for the type of company to work for: (1) a company that conducts its own research—these jobs tend to be found more in midsize and large companies; (2) an advertising agency or other services firm that conducts a lot of research in the course of its work for clients; or (3) a firm that specializes in marketing research. Many ad agencies and research firms also further specialize by product type (such as high technology or automobiles) or target markets (such as young adults, Hispanic Americans, and so on). And some firms and individual researchers also specialize in the type of research they do, such as focus groups, behavioral studies, or advanced statistical analysis.

Where to Learn More   Marketing Research Association, www.mra-net.org; American Marketing Association, www.marketingpower.com (search for collegiate chapters); World Association of Research Professionals (ESOMAR), www.esomar.org.

Administrative Services Managers

This is a broad category that covers all the managerial jobs—outside of marketing, finance, manufacturing, and other core functions—that keep business organizations humming day after day.

Nature of the Work   The nature of these management jobs varies widely depending on the size of the company and the type of facilities and systems it uses, from overseeing administrative support staff to managing facilities to helping in the planning of telecommuting strategies and systems for virtual organizations. Managerial positions range from department supervisor up to the vice president of administrative services in some larger corporations. Although these positions generally aren't involved in setting and implementing core business strategy, they provide the infrastructure and services that allow the company to function. Depending on the position, you can get involved in a wide range of activities, including security, real estate, facilities management, architectural planning, contract negotiation and administration, employee health and safety issues, and workflow and space planning.

Qualifications   With such a diverse range of job descriptions that fall under the administrative services umbrella, it's hard to define a single set of qualifications. However, all successful managers in this area of business possess both good leadership skills and experience with the various processes they are expected to manage. Given the importance of hands-on experience, many administrative managers rise through the ranks after working in staff positions, although large organizations sometimes hire managers with advanced degrees and professional certifications. Some industries expect education or certification in industry-specific disciplines (such as billing specialists in health care).

Where the Jobs Are   Service industries such as finance, insurance, and health care are among the primary employers of administrative managers whose responsibilities emphasize staff leadership. Companies that depend on large, complex facilities, such as manufacturers and hospitals, also rely on administrative managers whose emphasis is on physical facilities, real estate planning, and so on. As corporations outsource many noncore functions, administrative management opportunities can now be found in consulting or outsourcing firms.

Where to Learn More   International Facility Management Association, www.ifma.org.

From Planning to Inspiration: The Functions of Management

C H A P T E R

7

LEARNING OBJECTIVES

After studying this chapter, you will be able to

1. Define the four basic management functions

2. Outline the strategic planning process

3. Explain the purpose of a mission statement

4. Discuss the benefits of SWOT analysis

5. Explain the importance of setting long-term goals and objectives

6. Cite five common leadership styles and explain why no one style is best

7. Identify and explain important types of managerial skills

8. Summarize the six steps involved in the decision-making process

www.prenhall.com/bovee

Founder Michael Dell (left) and CEO Kevin Rollins have invested Dell with a renewed sense of purpose and clear corporate values.

INSIDE BUSINESS TODAY

Adding Soul to the Winning Ways of Dell

www.dell.com

It's a true story that sounds like a Texas-sized tall tale. In 1984, 19-year-old Michael Dell started selling personal computers from his dorm room at the University of Texas at Austin. He began with a simple but radical idea: purchase computer components from suppliers, assemble the components, cut out the intermediaries, and sell PCs directly to customers. A mere eight years later, Dell Computer Corporation joined the ranks of the Fortune 500—*Fortune* magazine's annual roster of the largest companies in the United States. By 2001, the company led all PC manufacturers in global market share and posted annual revenues of over $32 billion.

One secret to Michael Dell's success has been to always push the company to be self-critical in its quest for ever-greater efficiency in everything it does. He also has an uncanny ability to visualize and then capitalize on changes in the business world before they occur.

However, no one's foresight is perfect, and the company struggled to sustain its amazing growth during an economic downturn that stretched from 2000 into 2003. Every computer company got hit hard, and Dell was no exception.

When growth slows, managers face tough decisions: How could the company boost revenues? Where could it cut expenses? How could it hang on to talented people? True to Michael Dell's aggressive spirit, the company pursued solutions in all three areas. One of the most difficult choices was to cut expenses by laying off nearly 6,000 people. The most daring move was to boost revenues by launching several new product lines. Dell had already offered more than just PCs, but these other items were products made by Cisco, Palm, Hewlett-Packard (HP), and others that Dell simply resold. So in 2002 Dell began applying its own name to printers and other items previously manufactured by others. The move grew revenues, but it also caused former partners to sever their ties with Dell. The most farsighted initiative was the search for a larger purpose that would help Dell inspire and retain its remaining employees.

This search for a larger purpose was a sign of a maturing senior management team. In the aftermath of a large layoff, a typical company would respond by encouraging its people to work harder, do more, and still produce good results. In other words, do the same old things but faster. However, Dell applied its find-a-better-way mentality and started searching for answers to a bigger question: Beyond pure financial performance, what does it mean to be a great company? The program, called "The Soul of Dell," examined the company's culture and looked for ways to make Dell into more than just the world's most efficient and competitive computer maker.

Leading the way was president and chief operating officer Kevin Rollins, a former management consultant who had advised Michael Dell during the company's vigorous growth days. Rollins searched for models of success, starting with other companies that were recognized as being great places to work. All had a strong culture, a well-defined leadership model, and an overarching purpose that went beyond financial rewards. He also studied the ideas and habits of Thomas Jefferson, Theodore Roosevelt, and other great leaders.

The results of this search are captured in five core elements that expanded the company's vision: (1) create loyal customers by providing a superior experience at great value and by outperforming the competition; (2) base continued success on teamwork and the opportunity for each team member to learn and grow; (3) be direct in all ways—business model, ethics, communication, relationships, and more; (4) participate responsibly in the global marketplace; and (5) maintain a passion for winning.

Examining and clarifying something as amorphous as the soul of a huge organization is no simple challenge, but Dell's efforts have proven to be successful. The company weathered the downturn and moved into the middle of the decade stronger than ever, the clear market leader in the U.S. PC market and aggressively challenging top seller HP in the rest of the world.[1]

GET READY

It's only appropriate that a company founded in a college dorm room has become one of the most studied corporations in the world. With the twin ideas of assembling computers from ready-made components and selling directly to customers, Dell almost singlehandedly redefined the personal computer industry. However, one can argue that Michael Dell's transformation as a manager is every bit as remarkable as his company's success. From a bold teenage entrepreneur who announced to his father that he was going to take on IBM, he has developed into a first-class business leader at the head of one of the world's most admired companies. And Kevin Rollins, now the CEO, has smoothly taken the reins to continue Dell's amazing run. If you were leading an organization such as Dell, what skills would you need to be successful? How would you guide the organization through the nonstop twists and turns of the hypercompetitive PC industry?

Chapter Overview

Innovative decision making is just one of many managerial skills that Michael Dell and Kevin Rollins continue to demonstrate year after year. In this chapter, you'll explore the four basic functions of management—planning, organizing, leading, and controlling. Along the way, you'll see how managers get their companies pointed in the right direction by starting with a vision and a mission statement, the anchors of the strategic planning process. Following a brief look at crisis planning, the chapter dives into organization, leading, and controlling, then concludes with a discussion of the skills you'll need in order to be an effective manager.

The Four Basic Functions of Management

LEARNING OBJECTIVE 1

Define the four basic management functions

Managers play a vital role in every organization, and the job is far from simple. According to one recent survey, more than a third of the people who take on new managerial positions fail within the first 18 months.[2] A key step in avoiding this unpleasant fate is gaining a thorough

Exhibit 7.1
The Four Basic Functions of Management

To varying degrees at different times, all managers engage in the four primary functions of planning, organizing, leading, and controlling. Although these functions tend to occur in a somewhat progressive order, they often occur simultaneously, and often the process is ongoing.

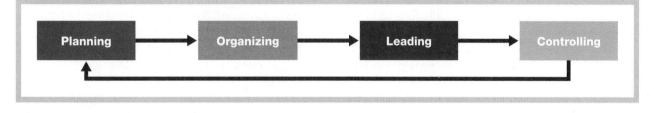

understanding of what being a manager really entails, starting with the four basic functions of **management**: planning, organizing, leading, and controlling resources (land, labor, capital, and information) to efficiently reach a company's goals (see Exhibit 7.1).[3]

In the course of performing the four management functions, managers play a number of *roles* that fall into three main categories:

- *Interpersonal roles.* Management is largely a question of getting work accomplished through the efforts of other people, so managers must play a number of interpersonal roles, including providing leadership to employees, building relationships, and acting as a liaison between groups and individuals both inside and outside the company (such as suppliers, competitors, government agencies, consumers, special-interest groups, and interrelated work groups).
- *Informational roles.* Managers spend a fair amount of time gathering information from sources both inside and outside the organization. They also distribute information to employees, other managers, and other stakeholders.
- *Decisional roles.* From deciding how to respond to a customer complaint to deciding whether to acquire another company or develop a new product line, managers up and down the organizational ladder face an endless stream of decisions. Many of these decisions are fairly routine, such as deciding which of several job candidates to hire or setting the prices of new products. Other decisions, however, might occur only once or twice in a manager's career, such as responding to a product-tampering crisis or the threat of a hostile takeover.

Being able to move among these roles while performing the four basic management functions is just one of the many skills that managers must possess. But these functions are not discrete; they overlap and influence one another. The following sections provide a closer look.

The Planning Function

Managers engage in **planning** when they develop strategies for success, establish goals and objectives for the organization, and translate their strategies and goals into action plans. Planning can be considered the primary management function because it drives all the other functions. To develop long-term strategies and goals, managers must be well informed on a number of key issues and topics that could influence their decisions. A closer look at the strategic planning process will give you a clearer idea of the types of information managers need to help them plan for the company's future.

Understanding the Strategic Planning Process **Strategic plans** outline the firm's long-range (often two to five years) organizational goals and set a course of action the firm will pursue to reach its goals. One of the most important questions at this stage is the company's **business model**—a clear, simple outline of how the business intends to generate revenue. For instance, Dell's business model emphasizes *process* innovations such as e-commerce and customized manufacturing, rather than innovative *product* research, as some of its competitors emphasize. Business models often change over time, too. Marvel Enterprises, which owns the rights to Spider-Man, the X-Men, and more than 5,000 other characters, started as a comic book

management
Process of coordinating resources to meet organizational goals

planning
Establishing objectives and goals for an organization and determining the best ways to accomplish them

LEARNING OBJECTIVE 2

Outline the strategic planning process

strategic plans
Plans that establish the actions and the resource allocation required to accomplish strategic goals; they are usually defined for periods of two to five years and are developed by top managers

business model
The fundamental design of the company, explaining how the enterprise plans to generate revenue

When Wendelin Wiedeking took over as CEO of Porsche, the company was racing toward record losses of $150 million. Few people believed that Wiedeking could get Porsche back on track. But Wiedeking had a clear vision for the company—one that adopted lean and efficient Japanese production systems at Porsche. Thanks to Wiedeking's vision and leadership, Porsche is back in the fast lane.

publisher in 1939, but today comic books contribute just 15 percent of the company's revenue. Marvel's business model now emphasizes licensing deals with toymakers, movie producers, videogame creators, and other companies that purchase the right to use Marvel characters.[4]

Beyond the fundamental business model, a good strategic plan answers such important questions as: Where are we going? How do we get there? What is the business environment going to be like?[5] Not only are these questions often difficult to resolve, but many top executives struggle to find enough time to ponder and discuss them. In one recent survey of large companies, top executives spent an average of only three hours a month discussing vital strategic questions, so simply finding the time and mental energy to do it is one of the key challenges of strategic planning.[6]

The *strategic planning process* consists of seven interrelated steps: developing a clear vision, creating a mission statement, performing a SWOT analysis, developing forecasts, analyzing the competition, establishing goals and objectives, and developing action plans (see Exhibit 7.2).

The circular arrangement of Exhibit 7.2 is no coincidence, by the way. Strategic planning should be a never-ending process, as you establish strategies, measure outcomes, monitor changes in the business environment, and make adjustments as needed. The history of business is full of companies that no longer exist because they were unwilling or unable to redirect their strategies as the world changed around them.

vision
A viable view of the future that is rooted in but improves on the present

Develop a Clear Vision. Most organizations are formed in order to realize a **vision**, a realistic and achievable view of the future that grows out of and improves on the present.[7] For instance, Seattle-based Hydrogen Power sees "the world on the threshold of a new economy—one based on hydrogen fuel, eventually replacing fossil fuel."[8] Such visions can be startling to people whose views of the world are locked in the present, but many industries that everyone takes for granted today, from air travel to computers, were also viewed with skepticism and even derision in their formative days. In fact, business visionaries who've been able to see beyond the way things are to the way things could be can rightly take much of the credit for the standard of living that developed countries such as the United States now enjoy. (Of course, visionaries do miss the mark from time to time; we don't yet have the flying cars and personal robots that some bold thinkers predicted a few decades ago.)

LEARNING OBJECTIVE 3

Explain the purpose of a mission statement

Translate the Vision into a Meaningful Mission Statement. A vision statement gives the company a clear target, but to translate that vision into reality, managers must define specific organizational goals, objectives, and philosophies. A good starting point is to

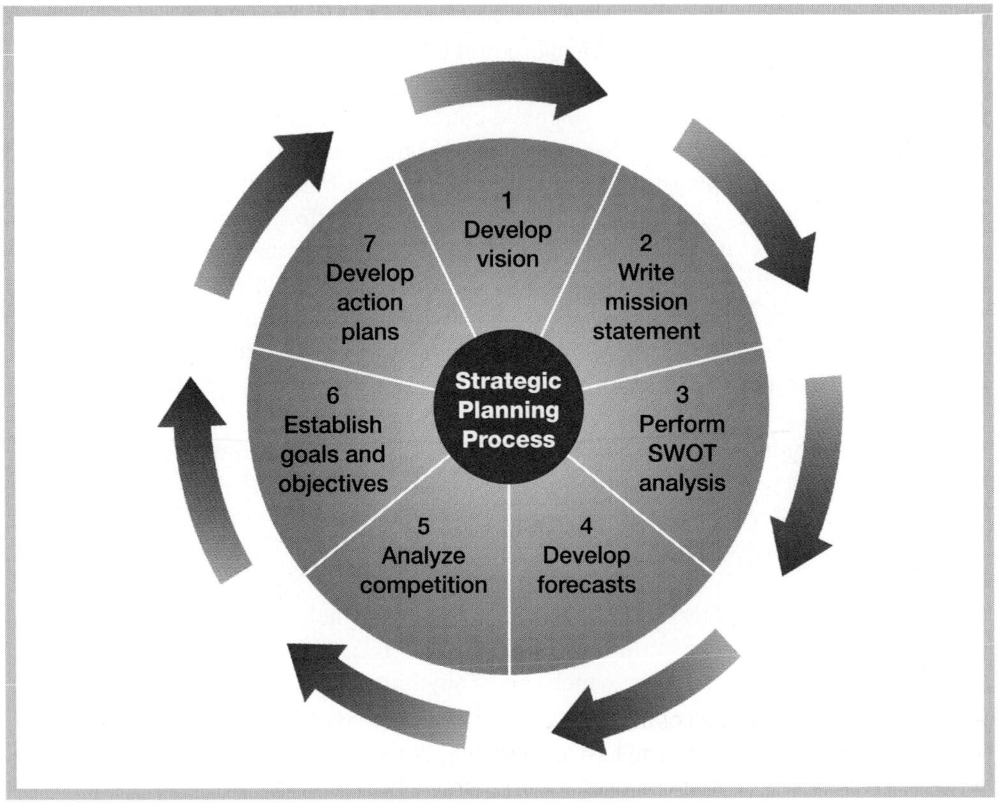

Exhibit 7.2
Seven Steps in the Strategic Planning Process
For most firms, strategic planning in today's nonstop business environment is an ongoing process involving these seven steps.

write a **mission statement**, a brief articulation of why your organization exists, what it seeks to accomplish, and the principles that the company will adhere to as it tries to reach its goals (see Exhibit 7.3). In other words, a mission statement communicates what the company is, what it does, and where it's headed. Typical components of a mission statement include the company's product or service; primary market; fundamental concern for survival, growth, and profitability; managerial philosophy; and commitment to quality and social responsibility. (Note that some organizations use the terms *vision* and *mission statement* rather loosely and even interchangeably at times.)

mission statement
A statement of the organization's purpose, basic goals, and philosophies

---

Kodak's corporate values:

- We show respect for the dignity of the individual.
- We uphold uncompromising integrity.
- We give and receive unquestionable trust.
- We prove and maintain constant credibility.
- We support continual improvement and personal renewal.
- We recognize and celebrate achievement.

Kodak's mission:

With the above mentioned values in mind, we plan to grow more rapidly than our competitors by providing customers with the solutions they need to capture, store, process, output and communicate images—anywhere, anytime. We will derive our competitive advantage by delivering differentiated, cost-effective solutions—including consumables, hardware, software, systems and services—quickly and with flawless quality. All this is thanks to our diverse team of energetic, results-oriented employees with the world-class talent and skills necessary to sustain Kodak as the world leader in imaging.

Exhibit 7.3
Mission Statement
Kodak defines its mission statement in the context of clearly stated corporate values.

A well-written mission statement is a powerful call to action. Consider this from Translink, a consortium of public transportation companies in Belfast, Northern Ireland: "To provide a transformed network of coordinated bus and rail services which attracts a growing number of passengers, enjoys public confidence and is recognized for its quality and innovation."[9] Virtually every word in this statement is packed with importance and challenge, from transforming the existing transportation infrastructure to building public confidence through safety and dependability. The collective effort of an entire organization springs forth from this single sentence. Translink employees can use the mission statement to align their own work with the organization's mission, and executives can use it to make sure the decisions they make stay true to the stated mission. For instance, a proposal to open a theme park might have the compelling argument of increasing passenger traffic for Translink, but such a business venture would be outside the company's stated mission.

LEARNING OBJECTIVE 4

Discuss the benefits of SWOT analysis

Assess the Company's Strengths, Weaknesses, Opportunities, and Threats. Before establishing long-term goals, you need to have a clear assessment of your firm's strengths and weaknesses compared with the opportunities and threats it faces. Such analysis is commonly referred to as *SWOT*, which stands for strengths, weaknesses, opportunities, and threats.

Identifying a firm's internal strengths and weaknesses helps management understand its current abilities so it can set proper goals. *Strengths* are positive internal factors that contribute to a company's success, which can be anything from a team of expert employees to financial resources to unique technologies. *Weaknesses* are negative internal factors that inhibit the company's success, such as obsolete facilities or inadequate financial resources. Sometimes, inventive companies can turn a perceived weakness into a strength. When Malibu, California, toymaker Jakks Pacific purchased another toymaker, the mish-mash of products it acquired included a low-tech videogame unit that looked hopelessly out of date in a world of PlayStations and Xboxes. However, the company figured the device might have some goofy retro appeal, not to mention a bargain price, and programmed it with yesteryear arcade games such as Ms. Pac-Man. The result: Jakks now sells more than $60 million a year of its TV Games line.[10]

Excelling in many areas at once is unrealistic for most firms, so managers frequently choose to focus on developing a small number of strengths, known as *core competencies*. A core competence is a bundle of skills, technologies, and other resources that enable a company to provide a particular benefit to customers. It sets the company apart from its competitors and is difficult for competitors to duplicate. For instance, one of Dell's core competencies is the rapid assembly of highly customized computers.

Once you've taken inventory of your company's internal strengths and weaknesses, your next step is to identify the external opportunities and threats that might affect your ability to attain desired goals. *Opportunities* are positive external situations that represent the possibility of generating new revenue. Shrewd managers and entrepreneurs recognize opportunities before others do and then promptly act on their ideas (see Exhibit 7.4). Some opportunities are found in existing markets, going against established competitors by offering more attractive products. In other instances, an innovator creates something so radically different that it redefines a market, as Cirque du Soleil did with its inventive reinterpretation of the circus. Cirque du Soleil is now a multimillion-dollar enterprise in an industry that had been in serious, long-term decline.[11] In still other cases, entrepreneurs or managers envision markets that don't even exist yet, such as Hydrogen Power's development of a hydrogen-based fuel source. Creating new markets is usually an expensive, complicated, and risky move, but if you're successful, you instantly become the industry leader.

Threats are negative forces that could inhibit the firm's ability to achieve its objectives. Most threats are external, but a few, such as workplace violence, can appear internally as well. External threats include new competitors, new government regulations, economic recession, disruptions in supply, technological advances that render products obsolete, theft of intellectual property, product liability lawsuits, and even the weather. Some threats appear out of nowhere: Parsons Manufacturing, a metal fabricator in Roanoke, Illinois, was humming along just fine

Coca-Cola

During WWII, Robert Woodruff, president of Coca-Cola, committed to selling bottles of Coke to members of the armed services for a nickel a bottle. Customer loyalty never came cheaper.

Diners Club

In 1950, when Frank McNamara found himself in a restaurant with no money, he came up with the idea of the Diners Club Card. The first credit card changed the nature of buying and selling throughout the world.

Holiday Inn

When the Wilson family of Memphis went on a motoring vacation, they discovered it was not much fun staying in motels that were either too expensive or too slovenly. So Kemmons Wilson built his own. The first Holiday Inn opened in Memphis in 1952.

Honda

When Honda arrived in America in 1959 to launch its big motorbikes, customers weren't keen on their problematic performance. However, they did admire the little Supercub bikes Honda's managers used. So Honda bravely changed direction and transformed the motorbike business overnight.

Weight Watchers

After Jean Nidetch was put on a diet by the Obesity Clinic at New York Department of Health, she invited six dieting friends to meet in her apartment every week. In 1961, she started Weight Watchers and helped create the diet industry.

CNN

Ted Turner launched the Cable News Network in 1980. Few thought a 24-hour news network would work, but CNN has become a fixture in global news media.

Sony

Sony chief Akito Morita noticed that young people liked listening to music wherever they went. So in 1980 he and the company developed what became the Walkman, the forerunner of all portable music players.

Tylenol

When Johnson & Johnson pulled Tylenol from store shelves in 1982 after capsules were found to be poisoned, the company put customer safety before corporate profit. And it provided a lesson in media openness.

Dell

In 1984, Michael Dell decided to sell PCs direct and built to order. Now everybody in the industry is trying to imitate Dell Computer's strategy.

Amazon.com

With relentless focus on the mundane, behind-the-scenes details, such as warehousing, packaging, and shipping, Jeff Bezos proved that large-scale e-commerce can work.

Exhibit 7.4
Some of the Greatest Management Decisions Ever Made
Great business decisions can change the world. Here are some of the greatest management decisions made in the last 100 years.

until the summer of 2004, when a freak storm with softball-sized hailstones flattened the entire facility.[12] Other threats build up over time: Microsoft now faces what *Forbes* magazine calls the biggest threat in its history—the Linux operating system (see Chapter 4). This struggle is being played out all over the world as Microsoft works to keep its Windows operating system in the lead while competitors such as IBM push Linux as hard as possible.[13]

The Windows-Linux battle is a good example of how companies sometimes inadvertently create threatening situations for themselves, in a scenario identified by Harvard professor Clayton Christensen as the "innovator's dilemma." A successful firm can get locked into meeting the expanding needs of its current customers with increasingly expensive and sophisticated products, leaving the low end of the market unprotected. New competitors step into this void with less-expensive products, such as Linux, gradually gaining experience and market share. The original firm often dismisses these new entrants as cheap, unsophisticated, or just "too different"—until customers start to find the new products appealing and jump to the competition. Before long, the new offerings can upset the competitive balance in an entire industry, which is why they're called *disruptive* products or technologies.[14]

Develop Forecasts. Planning requires managers to predict the future, but forecasting is notoriously difficult and prone to errors. Not only do you need to predict *what* will (or will not) occur, but *when* it will occur and *how* it will affect your business. At the same time, forecasting is crucial to every company's success because it influences virtually every important decision. As Bernardo Huberman, a manager at HP who is involved in the company's efforts to improve forecasting, puts it, "A company that can predict the future is a company that is going to win."[15]

Managerial forecasts fall under two broad categories: *quantitative forecasts,* which are typically based on historical data or tests and often involve complex statistical computations, and *qualitative forecasts,* which are based more on intuitive judgments. Analyzing cycles of economic growth and recession over several decades to predict when the economy will take a downward turn is an example of quantitative forecasting. Predicting the response of competitors to a new product is an example of qualitative forecasting.

Regardless of the type of forecast or the variables being predicted, reliable inputs are key. Forecasters collect pertinent data and information in a wide variety of ways, such as reviewing internal data, conducting surveys and other research, purchasing industry forecasts from research companies, and reviewing projections from the many periodicals, industry organizations, and government agencies that publish forecasts on business and economic issues. In the past few years, several companies have been experimenting with an intriguing addition to the forecasting toolkit: a *prediction market*. With this method, a group of people who have insights into the question at hand are given a small sum of money and asked to bet on the likelihood of various outcomes. The theory here is that such markets can be an efficient way to distill the wisdom of a group, rather than relying on a single manager or planner. In early tests, prediction markets at HP have improved the accuracy of sales forecasts, and pharmaceutical company Eli Lilly was able to correctly predict the most successful new drugs from a group of six candidates then under development.[16]

Analyze the Competition. Every effort to implement strategy takes place in a competitive context, even if it's competing against totally unrelated companies for a share of the customer's budget. With insight into its own capabilities and those of its competitors, a company can then work to gain a competitive edge through at least one of three basic strategies:

- *Differentiation.* A company using differentiation develops a level of service, a product image, unique product features (including quality), or new technologies that distinguish its product from competitors' products. Even though it nearly always matches Wal-Mart on prices of most products, for instance, arch-rival Target works hard to differentiate itself through a more stylish brand image and better insights into what consumers consider hip at any given moment.[17]
- *Cost leadership.* The premier example of cost leadership is Wal-Mart, which revolutionized retailing with business processes that constantly seek to improve efficiency and cost-effectiveness.
- *Focus.* When using a focus strategy, companies concentrate on a specific segment of the market, seeking to develop a better understanding of those customers and to tailor products specifically to their needs. For instance, Nike competes in a variety of sporting goods segments, but Calloway and Tommy Armour focus solely on the golf segment of the sports market.

Many firms gain a competitive advantage by excelling in two of these areas at once, such as Toyota's efforts to excel at both quality (a differentiation strategy) and lower cost. However, pursuing more than one strategic focus at a time can be risky if it leads to mediocre efforts across the board.[18]

You won't find cheap frying pans at Williams-Sonoma. This retailer competes by focusing on a narrow marketing: top-of-the-line cookware for gourmet cooks.

Establish Company Goals and Objectives. As mentioned earlier, establishing goals and objectives is the key task in the planning process. Although these terms are often used interchangeably, a **goal** is a broad, long-range accomplishment that the organization wants to attain in typically five or more years, whereas an **objective** is a specific, short-range target designed to help reach that goal. For Dell, a *goal* might be to capture 10 percent of the U.S. market for flat-screen TVs over the next five years, and an *objective* might be to sell 500,000 laptop computers in the U.S. in the next 12 months. To be effective, organizational goals and objectives should be specific, measurable, relevant, challenging, attainable, and time limited. For example, "substantially increase our sales" is a poorly worded statement because it doesn't define what *substantial* means or when it should be measured.

Setting appropriate goals has many benefits: It increases employee motivation, establishes standards for measuring individual and group performance, guides employee activity, and clarifies management's expectations. By establishing organizational goals, managers set the stage for the actions needed to achieve those goals. If actions aren't planned, the chances of reaching company goals are slim.

Develop Action Plans. Once you've established long-term strategic goals and objectives, your next step is to develop a plan of execution. **Tactical plans** lay out the actions and the allocation of resources necessary to achieve specific, short-term objectives that support the company's broader strategic plan. Tactical plans typically focus on departmental goals and cover a period of one to three years. Their limited scope permits them to be changed more easily than strategic plans. **Operational plans** designate the actions and resources required to achieve the objectives of tactical plans. Operational plans usually define actions for less than one year and focus on accomplishing specific objectives, such as securing additional financing or opening a new retail channel.

Keep in mind that many highly admired entrepreneurs and executives have stumbled not because they didn't have strategies for success, but because they didn't execute their strategies or deliver on their commitments. Coming up with a brilliant strategy is only a small part of the equation of succession; executing is what counts. Everyone knows Dell's direct-business model, for example, but no one has been able to duplicate it on the same scale or with the same success as Dell.

Planning for a Crisis No matter how well a company plans for its future, any number of problems can arise to threaten its existence. An ugly fight for control of a company, a product failure, a breakdown in routine operations, or an environmental accident could develop into a serious and crippling crisis. In 2005, consumers across the nation were outraged to

LEARNING OBJECTIVE 5

Explain the importance of setting long-term goals and objectives

goal
Broad, long-range target or aim

objective
Specific, short-range target or aim

tactical plans
Plans that define the actions and the resource allocation necessary to achieve tactical objectives and to support strategic plans; they are usually defined for a period of one to three years and are developed by middle managers

operational plans
Plans that lay out the actions and the resource allocation needed to achieve operational objectives and to support tactical plans; they are usually defined for less than one year and are developed by middle managers

learn that Alpharetta, Georgia-based ChoicePoint had inadvertently sold access to its highly confidential consumer information files to a group of identity thieves, who then used the data to defraud hundreds of people. Privacy advocates and government officials immediately began calling for investigations and tighter regulation of the data-collection industry, and CEO Derek Smith started working "around the clock" to rebuild the trust of company investors, customers, legislators, and the public.[19]

Managers can help a company survive these setbacks through **crisis management**, a plan for handling such unusual and serious problems. The goal of crisis management is to keep the company functioning smoothly both during and after a crisis. Successful crisis management requires both comprehensive contingency plans to help managers make important decisions and communication plans to reach affected parties quickly. During a crisis, employees, their families, the surrounding community, and others will demand information. Moreover, rumors can spread unpredictably and uncontrollably, particularly online. You can expect the news media to descend instantly as well, asking questions of anyone they can find.

Companies that respond quickly with the information people need tend to fare much better in these circumstances than those that go into hiding or release bits and pieces of uncoordinated or inconsistent information. The crisis management plan should outline communication tasks and responsibilities, which can include everything from media contacts to news release templates. The plan should clearly specify the people who are authorized to speak for the company, contact information for all key executives, and the media outlets and technologies that will be used to disseminate information. Many companies now go one step further by regularly testing crisis communications in realistic practice drills lasting a full day or more.[20]

CRITICAL THINKING CHECKPOINT
1. Would Boeing and Old Navy develop strategic plans over the same time horizon? Why or why not?
2. How does the vision statement guide the planning process?
3. Why is it considered risky to pursue two or more avenues of competitive differentiation simultaneously?

The Organizing Function

organizing

Process of arranging resources to carry out the organization's plans

Organizing, the process of arranging resources to carry out the organization's plans, is the second major function of managers. During the organizing stage, managers think through all the activities that employees carry out (from programming the organization's computers to mailing its letters), as well as all the facilities and equipment employees need in order to complete those activities. They also give people the ability to work toward organizational goals by determining who will have the authority to make decisions, to perform or supervise activities, and to distribute resources.

The organizing function is particularly challenging because most organizations undergo constant change. Long-time employees leave, and new employees arrive. Technologies that were once on the leading edge of innovation grow out of date. The public's tastes and interests change, and the organization has to reevaluate its plans and activities. Shifting political and economic trends can lead to cutbacks or perhaps expansion. Long-time competitors take unexpected actions, and new competitors enter the market. Every week the organization faces new situations, so management's organizing tasks are never finished.

management pyramid

Organizational structure comprising top, middle, and lower management

top managers

Those at the highest level of the organization's management hierarchy; they are responsible for setting strategic goals, and they have the most power and responsibility

Chapter 8 discusses the organizing function in detail; for now, it's sufficient to recognize the three levels of a typical corporate hierarchy—top, middle, bottom—commonly known as the **management pyramid** (see Exhibit 7.5). In general, **top managers** are the upper-level managers who have the most power and who take overall responsibility for the organization. An example is the chief executive officer (CEO). Top managers establish the structure for the organization as a whole, and they select the people who fill the

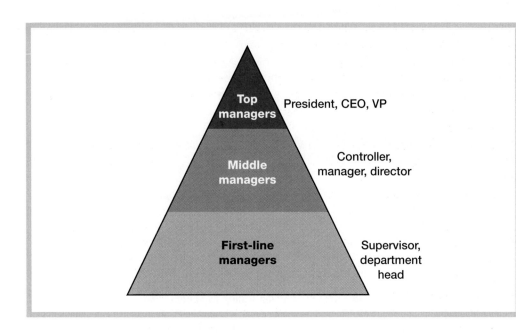

Exhibit 7.5
The Management
Pyramid
*Separate job titles are
used to designate the
three basic levels in the
management pyramid.*

upper-level positions. Top managers also make long-range plans, establish major policies, and represent the company to the outside world at official functions and fundraisers. The term *executive* applies to top managers.

Middle managers have similar responsibilities but on a smaller scale, such as for an individual department or facility. The term *middle management* is somewhat vague, but in general, managers at this level report upward to top executives, while first-line managers report to them. In other words, they usually manage other managers, not workers. A smaller company might have a single layer of middle management (or none at all, in many cases), whereas a large corporation could have a half dozen or more layers of middle managers. As you'll see in Chapter 8, though, many companies are *flattening* their organizational structures, largely by removing layers of middle management.

In addition to being vague, *middle management* is sometimes used as a disparaging term, suggesting layers of bureaucracy that slow things down without adding value. However, many innovative companies today take full advantage of the skills of this middle layer—as project managers, team leaders, and the driving forces behind intrapreneurial ventures within larger organizations. In addition, middle managers in some corporations now have considerable responsibility, overseeing entire product divisions and business initiatives.

At the bottom of the management pyramid are **first-line managers** (or *supervisory managers*). They oversee the work of operating employees, and they put into action the plans developed at higher levels. Positions at this level include supervisor, department head, and office manager.[21] As you'll see in Chapter 8, reducing the number of first-line managers is another step companies are taking to flatten their organizational pyramids. For instance, a company might remove a department supervisor and have the employees manage themselves as a team or may have the employees report up to someone who was previously considered a middle manager.

middle managers
*Those in the middle
of the management
hierarchy; they develop
plans to implement the
goals of top managers
and coordinate the work
of first-line managers*

first-line managers
*Those at the lowest
level of the management
hierarchy; they supervise
the operating employees
and implement the plans
set at the higher
management levels*

The Leading Function

Leading—the process of influencing and motivating people to work willingly and effectively toward company goals—is the third basic function of management. Managers with good leadership skills have greater success in influencing the attitudes and actions of others, through both the demonstration of specific tasks and the manager's own behavior and spirit. Furthermore, effective leaders are good at *motivating,* or giving employees a reason to do the job and to put forth their best performance (see Chapter 10).

All managers have to be effective leaders to be successful, but management and leadership are not the same thing. The easiest way to distinguish the two is to view management as the rational, intellectual, and practical side of guiding an organization and to view leadership as the

leading
*Process of guiding and
motivating people to work
toward organizational goals*

MINDING YOUR OWN BUSINESS

DO YOU HAVE WHAT IT TAKES TO BE A LEADER?

The fact that thousands upon thousands of books and articles have been written on the subject of leadership and hundreds more appear every year suggests a couple of things: (1) it's an important and popular topic, and (2) nobody has quite figured it out yet. Recent research suggests that effective leaders are as diverse as the organizations and people they lead; there is no single set of traits that define the ideal leader. Moreover, the media image of the all-seeing, all-knowing CEO who has movie star charisma (and movie star pals) and superhuman powers of persuasion is just that—a media image. All that really matters is whether you can help an organization achieve the right goals in the right way.

While there is no standard set of traits that define great leaders, successful leaders do tend to share a number of skills. Assess your leadership readiness by pondering these questions:

- **Can you listen?** Can you truly listen to what people mean to say, not just what they actually say or what you want to hear?
- **Can you communicate?** If you find yourself frequently being misunderstood, for whatever reason, consider this a warning that you need to improve your communication skills.
- **Can you lead by example?** Are you a living, breathing example of what you want the organization to be?
- **Are you dedicated to the organization's success above your own?** Leaders who put personal power or wealth ahead of the organization's success may shine brightly, but they usually shine briefly.
- **Do you know what makes other people tick?** Knowing what motivates the diverse people around you is crucial to leading them all in the same direction.

- **Do you manage yourself well?** If you can't get your own work done, whether it's meeting deadlines or develop the skills that you lack, your shortcomings will be amplified throughout the organization. For instance, if you're constantly late when making major decisions, you'll slow down every employee affected by those decisions.
- **Are you willing to accept responsibility?** Business leaders sometimes need to make tough decisions that affect the lives of hundreds or thousands of people; will you be ready when it's time to make the tough call or to accept blame for company mistakes?
- **Can you face reality?** Whether they're blinded by their own egos or just simple optimism, leaders who refuse to see the world the way it really exists usually set their companies up for failure.
- **Can you solve problems but stay focused on opportunities?** Leaders who get mired in problems miss opportunities; those who look only at opportunities can get bitten by problems that they should've solved.
- **Are you willing to trust your employees?** If you can't delegate responsibility, you'll swamp yourself with too much work and hinder the growth of your employees.

Questions for Critical Thinking
1. Would it be wise to start a company right out of college, without having gained any experience as an employee in another company? Why or why not?
2. Does leadership experience in school activities (such as student government and athletics) help prepare you for business leadership? Why or why not?

inspirational, visionary, and emotional side. Oversimplifying somewhat, management is the head and leadership is the heart. Both management and leadership involve the use of power, but management involves *position power* (so called since it stems from the individual's position in the organization), whereas leadership involves *personal power* (which stems from a person's own unique attributes, such as expertise or charisma).[22] For instance, Jim Press of Toyota Motor Sales USA has position power by virtue of his title as executive vice president and chief operating officer. He also has considerable personal power with the company's technical staff, thanks to his intimate knowledge of Toyota's world-class engineering and manufacturing systems.[23]

As the box "Do You Have What It Takes to Be a Leader" indicates, leadership can be a difficult concept to pin down. Researchers have been studying effective leaders for years, trying to figure out (a) what makes them effective, (b) how to identify potential leaders who possess the same traits as successful leaders, and (c) how to train or develop leadership skills in both current and future leaders. Successful leaders tend to share many of the same traits, but no magic set of personal qualities automatically destines someone for leadership. Nevertheless, in general, good leaders possess a good balance of several different types of intelligence. IQ, the widely known but often misunderstood *intelligence quotient*, measures a fairly narrow set of human capabilities, such as problem-solving logic. Although IQ is often touted as the standard of intelligence, it is an incomplete measure of human intelligence and a poor predictor of success in leadership.[24] People with high IQs can fail miserably as leaders, in fact, while people with more modest IQs can succeed brilliantly.

Research in the last decade or so, much of it pioneered by Daniel Goleman, has highlighted the importance of *emotional intelligence*, or *emotional quotient (EQ)*, in both leadership and life in general. The characteristics of a high EQ include:[25]

- *Self-awareness.* Self-aware managers have the ability to recognize their own feelings and the effect those feelings have on their own job performance and on the people around them.
- *Self-regulation.* Self-regulated managers have the ability to control or reduce disruptive impulses and moods. Self-awareness and self-regulation are vital to keeping executive egos in check. Michael Dell, for instance, is exemplary in this respect, leading *BusinessWeek* to refer to his style as "nearly egoless management."[26]
- *Motivation.* Motivated managers are driven to achieve beyond expectations, both their own and everyone else's.
- *Empathy.* Empathetic managers thoughtfully consider employees' feelings, along with other factors, in the process of making intelligent decisions.
- *Social skill.* Socially skilled managers tend to have a wide circle of acquaintances, and they have a knack for finding common ground with people of all kinds.

In addition to IQ and EQ, successful managers also possess good *social intelligence*. This *social quotient (SQ)* goes beyond the social skills that are part of EQ by looking outward to understand the dynamics of social situations and the emotions of other people, in addition to your own.[27] Finally, researcher James Clawson has identified a fourth key leadership intelligence, which he calls *change quotient (CQ)* and defines it as the ability to recognize the need for change and to manage that change in an efficient, effective way.[28] For more on this important topic, see "Managing Change" on page 241.

Looking at these four types of intelligence, you can easily see how people who might be logically brilliant (high IQ) could fail as leaders if, for instance, they can't manage their own emotions in the face of frustration (low emotional quotient), can't understand what makes other people "tick" and therefore can't motivate them (low social quotient), or fear change so much that they disrupt the organization's efforts to grow and adapt (low change quotient).

Developing an Effective Leadership Style These leadership traits can manifest themselves in a variety of *leadership styles*. Every manager has a definite style, although an individual's style might vary over time and from situation to situation. Management theorists have identified quite a variety of styles; the major categories are *autocratic, democratic, laissez-faire, contingent,* and *situational.*

Autocratic leaders control the decision-making process in their organizations, often reserving the right to make all major decisions by themselves and restricting the decision-making freedom of subordinates. Autocratic leadership has a bad reputation, and when it's overused or used inappropriately, it can certainly produce bad results or stunt an organization's growth. However, companies can find themselves in situations where autocratic leadership is needed to stave off collapse. When Carol Bartz took over as CEO of Autodesk (maker of the widely used AutoCAD design software), she inherited a firm that was growing out of control, with immature business practices and insufficient management talent.

LEARNING OBJECTIVE 6

Cite five common leadership styles and explain why no one style is best

autocratic leaders
Leaders who do not involve others in decision making

Meg Whitman, CEO of
eBay, is a great example
of a democratic leader.
She attributes much
of eBay's success
to involvement of
employees and
managers in decision
making. "I'm really proud
of what we've created at
eBay, but I haven't done
it alone," says Whitman.

Moreover, many of the programmers were more loyal to the departed company founder than they were to Bartz. In short, she faced a dire situation that demanded quick action—and she faced it head on, letting everyone know who was in control: "I'm not here to appease anyone. I'm here to build a company," she told employees. Thanks to her strong leadership, Autodesk now dominates its industry and has grown into one of today's most successful high-tech companies.[29]

In contrast, **democratic leaders** delegate authority and involve employees in decision making. Meg Whitman, another CEO hired to bring discipline to a rapidly growing young firm—eBay, in this case—is a great example of a democratic leader. Even though she is considered one of the most influential executives in business today, she is well-known for delegating decision-making authority and claims that she doesn't consider herself to be powerful.[30] By spreading power around, Whitman is also practicing **participative management**.

The third leadership style, laissez-faire, is sometimes referred to as free-rein leadership. The French term *laissez-faire* can be translated as "leave it alone," or more roughly as "hands off." **Laissez-faire leaders** take the role of consultants, encouraging employees' ideas and offering insights or opinions when asked, and they emphasize **employee empowerment**—giving employees the power to make decisions that apply to their specific aspects of work. The laissez-faire style may fail if workers pursue goals that do not match the organization's. However, with the right employees in the right environment, this style can be quite effective. Wegmans, the Rochester, New York-based grocery chain that you can read about in this chapter's Case for Critical Thinking, emphasizes this style of leadership with great success. As one Wegmans executive joked, "We're a $3 billion company run by 16-year-old cashiers."[31]

More and more businesses are adopting democratic and laissez-faire leadership as they reduce the number of management layers in their corporate hierarchies and increase the use of teamwork and technology. However, experienced managers know that no one leadership style works every time. In fact, new research shows that leaders with the best results adapt their approach to match the requirements of the particular situation.[32] Adapting leadership style to current business circumstances is called *contingency leadership.* One of the more important contingency styles is *situational leadership*, in which leaders adapt their style based on the readiness of employees to accept the changes or responsibilities the manager wants them to accept.[33] You can think of leadership styles as existing along a continuum of possible leadership behaviors, as suggested by Exhibit 7.6.

Aside from these styles, leaders also differ in the degree to which they try (or need) to reshape their organizations. *Transactional leaders* tend to focus on meeting established goals, making sure employees understand their roles in the organization, making sure the correct resources are in place, and so on. In contrast, some leaders can "take it up a notch," inspiring their employees to perform above and beyond the everyday, expected responsibilities of their jobs. These *transformational leaders* can reshape the destinies of their organizations by inspiring employees to see the world in new ways, to find creative solutions to business challenges, to rise above self-interest, and to create new levels of success for the company as a whole.[34] Well-known transformational leaders include Jeff Bezos of Amazon.com and Bill Gates of Microsoft, both of whom have inspired thousands of employees to feats that have reshaped the world economy.

Coaching and Mentoring Leadership also carries an important responsibility for education and encouragement, resulting in the roles of coaching and mentoring. **Coaching** involves taking the time to meet with employees, discussing any problems that may hinder their ability to work effectively, and offering suggestions and encouragement to help them find their own solutions to work-related challenges. (Be aware that the term *executive coaching* usually refers to hiring an outside management expert to help senior managers.)

Exhibit 7.6
Continuum of Leadership Behavior

Leadership style occurs along a continuum, ranging from boss-centered to employee-centered. Situations that require managers to exercise greater authority fall toward the boss-centered end of the continuum. Other situations call for a manager to give workers leeway to function more independently.

Boss-centered leadership						Employee-centered leadership
Use of authority by the manager						**Area of freedom for workers**
Manager makes decision, announces it.	Manager "sells" decision.	Manager presents ideas, invites questions.	Manager presents tentative decision subject to change.	Manager presents problems, gets suggestions, makes decisions.	Manager defines limits, asks group to make decision.	Manager permits workers to function within defined limits.

Mentoring is similar to coaching but is based on long-term relationships between senior and junior members of an organization. The mentor is usually an experienced manager or employee who can help guide other managers and employees through the corporate maze. Mentors have a deep knowledge of the business and can explain office politics, serve as a role model for appropriate business behavior, and provide valuable advice about how to succeed within the organization. Mentoring programs are used in a variety of ways, such as helping newly promoted managers make the transition to leadership roles and helping women and minorities prepare for advancement. Cigna, a large insurance company headquartered in Philadelphia, emphasizes bringing more women and minorities into its managerial and executive ranks, and mentoring is a vital part of that effort. In fact, mentoring has become so popular in some companies that executives have been forced to resort to group mentoring, since they don't have enough senior staff to work with all the employees who want to participate.[35]

mentoring
Formal program of career guidance in which an experienced manager or employee with a wide network of industry colleagues explains office politics, serves as a role model for appropriate business behavior, and helps other employees negotiate the corporate structure

Managing Change The stimulus for change can come from any direction, both inside and outside the organization. Internally, a shift in strategy might require changes to the structure of the organization and to the jobs of many people within the company. In others cases, managers might identify a need to improve performance or fix organizational weaknesses. For instance, when Rick Wagoner took over as CEO of General Motors, he inherited problems that had been growing for decades, including lagging productivity, a severely underfunded pension program, a bureaucratic corporate hierarchy, and products that many considered bland. To attack these problems, Wagoner had to institute an array of changes, including bringing in executives from other companies to implementing rigorous financial controls.[36]

Outside the organization, changes can come from many directions, in many flavors. Some develop over time and are relatively easy to prepare for, such as shifts in demographics. For instance, if your company markets exclusively to teenagers and you observe that birth rates have been declining, you know it won't be too many years before your market will start to shrink. Other times, you know that change is heading your way but you can't reliably predict the effects it will have on your organization. This is often the case with new competitors, new technologies, new regulations, and shifts in political influence. Still other changes come without warning, such as natural disasters and terrorist attacks.

Change presents a major leadership challenge for one simple reason: Most people don't like it. They may fear the unknown, they may be unwilling to give up current habits or benefits, they may believe that the change is bad for the organization, or they may not trust the motives of the people advocating change.[37] As a result, many—perhaps most—change initiatives fail, according to one study.[38] To improve the chances of success when the organization needs to change, managers can follow these steps:[39]

1. **Identify what needs to change.** Changes can involve the structure of the organization, technologies and systems, or people's attitudes, beliefs, skills, or behaviors.[40]
2. **Identify the forces acting for and against the change.** By understanding these forces, managers can work to amplify the forces that will facilitate the change and remove or diminish the negative forces. Helping people understand the need for change is often called *unfreezing* existing behaviors.
3. **Choose the approach, or combination of approaches, best suited to the situation.** Managers can institute change through a variety of techniques, including communication, education, participation in the decision making, negotiation with groups opposed to the change, visible support from top managers or other opinion leaders, or coercive use of authority (usually recommended only for crisis situations).
4. **Reinforce changed behavior and monitor continued progress.** Once the change has been made, managers need to reinforce new behaviors and make sure old behaviors don't creep back in. This effort is commonly called *refreezing* new behaviors.

In many industries and markets, change now appears to be a constant aspect of business, making change management a vital skill for leaders at all levels of the organization.

Building a Positive Organizational Culture Strong leadership is a key element in establishing a productive *organizational culture*— the set of underlying values, norms, and practices shared by members of an organization. When you visit an organization, observe how the employees work, dress, communicate, address each other, and conduct business. Each organization has a special way of doing things. In corporations, this force is often referred to as **corporate culture**.

> **corporate culture**
> A set of shared values and norms that support the management system and that guide management and employee behavior

Just as your social culture influences the way you think, what you believe, and how you behave, so too do company cultures influence the way people treat and react to each other and to customers and suppliers. Cultures shapes the way employees feel about the company and the work they do; the way they interpret and perceive the actions taken by others; the expectations they have regarding changes in their work or in the business; and their ability to lead, be productive, and choose the best course of action. For example, TechTarget, an interactive media company based in Needham, Massachusetts, has established a culture that emphasizes employee responsibility and accountability. Rather than defining working hours, vacation time, and other standard policies, TechTarget lets employees decide when they come to work and how much vacation to take, as long as they meet their agreed-upon performance objectives.[41]

Positive cultures create an environment that encourages employees to make ethical decisions for the good of the company and its customers. At companies with legendary corporate cultures, such as Nordstrom and Southwest Airlines, employees routinely go the extra mile to make sure customers are treated well. In contrast, negative, dysfunctional cultures can lead employees to make decisions that are bad for customers, bad for the company—and even unethical or illegal.

Corporate cultures are established and maintained through the countless actions and decisions of leaders, year after year. When Southwest Airlines employees saw former CEO Herbert Kelleher emphasizing fun, teamwork, and sacrificing for the common good, they followed suit. However, as the company has grown and the airline industry has come under considerable cost pressures, even Southwest's culture is starting to show signs of wear and tear. The company is now taking steps to reinvigorate the culture through better communication, but some longtime employees are wondering if the magic of the early days is gone.[42]

The Controlling Function

> **controlling**
> Process of measuring progress against goals and objectives and correcting deviations if results are not as expected

Controlling involves monitoring a firm's progress toward meeting its goals and objectives, resetting the course if goals or objectives change, and correcting deviations if goals or

MINDING YOUR OWN BUSINESS

CREATING THE IDEAL CULTURE IN YOUR COMPANY

You can't create a culture directly, but you can establish the behaviors and values that in turn do create a culture. Use this list of questions to explore the many ways you can foster a positive culture—and avoid the growth of a negative culture.

COMPANY VALUES

- Have you articulated a compelling vision for the company?
- Have you defined a mission statement, based on the vision that employees understand and can implement?
- Do employees know how their work relates to this vision?
- Is there a common set of values that bind the organization together?
- Do you and other executives or owners demonstrate these values day in and day out?

PEOPLE

- How are people treated?
- Do you foster an atmosphere of civility and respect?
- Do you value and encourage teamwork, with all ideas welcomed?
- Do you acknowledge, encourage, and act upon (when appropriate) ideas from employees?
- Do you give employees credit for their ideas?
- Have you shown a positive commitment to a balance between work and life?

COMMUNITY

- Have you clarified how the company views its relationship with the communities it affects?
- Do your actions support that commitment to community?

COMMUNICATION

- Do you practice and encourage open communication?
- Do you share operating information throughout the company so that people know how the company is doing?
- Do you regularly survey employees on workplace issues and ask for their input on solutions?
- Is there an open-door policy for access to management?

EMPLOYEE PERFORMANCE

- Do you handle personnel issues with fairness and respect?
- Do employees receive feedback regularly?
- Are employee evaluations based on agreed-upon objectives that have been clearly communicated?

Questions for Critical Thinking

1. How might a job candidate find the answers to these questions?
2. Why is it important to learn about the company's culture before accepting a job?

---

objectives are not being attained. Rather than focus primarily on financial results, many companies now use a *balanced scorecard*, which monitors the performance from four perspectives: finances, operations, customer relationships, and the growth and development of employees and intellectual property.[43]

One of the most important performance variables that fall under managerial control is **quality**—a measure of how closely goods or services conform to predetermined standards and customer expectations. Many firms control for quality through a four-step cycle that involves all levels of management and all employees (see Exhibit 7.7). In the first step, top managers set **standards**, or criteria for measuring the performance of the organization as a whole. At the same time, middle- and first-line managers set departmental quality standards so they can meet or exceed company standards. Establishing control standards is closely tied to the planning function and depends on information supplied by employees, customers, and

quality
A measure of how closely a product conforms to predetermined standards and customer expectations

standards
Criteria against which performance is measured

Exhibit 7.7

The Control Cycle

The control cycle has four basic steps: (1) On the basis of strategic goals, top managers set the standards by which the organization's overall performance will be measured. (2) Managers at all levels measure performance. (3) Actual performance is compared with the standards. (4) Appropriate corrective action is taken (if performance meets standards, nothing other than encouragement is needed; if performance falls below standards, corrective action may include improving performance, establishing new standards, changing plans, reorganizing, or redirecting efforts).

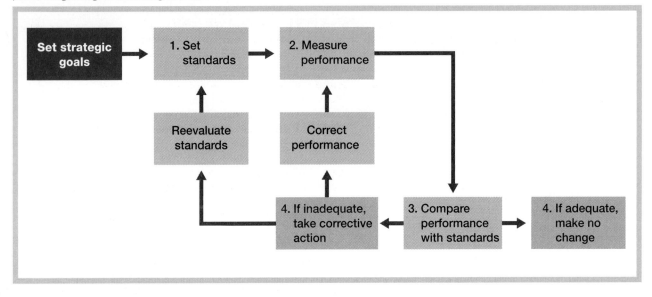

other external sources. Examples of specific standards might be "Produce 15,000 circuit boards monthly with less than 1 percent failures."

In the second step of the control cycle, managers assess performance, using both quantitative (specific, numerical) and qualitative (subjective) performance measures. In the third step, managers compare performance with the established standards and search for the cause of any discrepancies. If the performance falls short of standards, the fourth step is to take corrective action. If performance meets or exceeds standards, no corrective action is taken. If results are below expectations, controls help managers take any necessary action, which can range from a minor adjustment in a food recipe to a complete strategic shift. For instance, as Toys "R" Us continues to lose sales to Wal-Mart and Target in its declining toy business but take sales away from department stores in its growing Babies "R" Us chain, the company is considering whether to downplay or even exit the toy business.[44]

In other cases, executives discover that the monitoring and control system itself needs fixing, as Citigroup learned after assembling a banking empire that now employs 275,000 people in 100 countries. As you read in Chapter 2, regulators in Japan shut down Citigroup's private banking arm there after repeated violations. CEO Charles Prince later admitted that he was too busy trying to manage revenue and profit across the sprawling company and wasn't paying enough attention to regulatory compliance. In response, compliance managers throughout the company now answer directly to headquarters, rather than to individual division or country managers.[45]

You'll read more about control methods, including the important concept of *total quality management*, in Chapter 9.

CRITICAL THINKING CHECKPOINT

1. Are management and leadership the same thing? If not, why not?
2. Can a single individual be an autocratic, democratic, *and* laissez-faire leader? Why or why not?
3. Why is it critical to "unfreeze" existing behaviors or other variables before attempting to change them?

LEARNING FROM BUSINESS BLUNDERS

OOPS When the worst blackout in North American history shut off electrical power to 50 million people in the eastern United States and Canada and drained up to $10 billion from the U.S. and Canadian economies in the summer of 2003, both countries discovered just what a complicated managerial challenge the power industry faces. Electrical suppliers and customers are connected via a complex grid of transmission lines that ensure continued power even as supply and demand ebb and flow in various parts of the grid. Every power station has automatic controls that prevent the grid from drawing too much power, which can happen when demand rises across the grid or when other stations reduce the power they make available to the grid. The system can usually respond to localized power shortages by managing availability, but power station operators need to know what's going on to make these decisions.

Believe it or not, this economic disaster was triggered by a few trees. Three high-voltage lines in Ohio, owned by power company FirstEnergy, shorted out when they came into contact with trees that should have been trimmed but weren't. Then FirstEnergy's monitoring facility didn't detect the problem because its computer system wasn't operating properly and employees weren't trained adequately. Because the company didn't respond to its own problems or alert other power generators, a surge of unmet demand for electricity began to roll through the grid—which set off automatic protection systems at other stations across the grid and continued to compound the problem until it rolled all the way to the East Coast.

WHAT YOU CAN LEARN The 2003 blackout yielded several key business lessons: (1) Monitoring and control, based on reliable data, are essential to the operation of every business; (2) unless they are detected and dealt with quickly, relatively small mistakes can mushroom into huge problems—moreover, complex systems need vigorous, constant scrutiny; (3) employee training and system maintenance are crucial—managers can't just assume that people or systems will work properly; (4) when various independent business entities are connected (either literally connected, as in the power industry, or financially connected, as in banking, for instance), problems can spread quickly. The bottom line: Know yourself—and your business partners.

Management Skills

Managers rely on a number of skills to perform their functions and maintain a high level of quality in their organizations. These skills can be classified into three basic categories: *interpersonal skills*; *technical, administrative,* and *conceptual skills*; and *decision making skills.* As managers rise through the organization's hierarchy, they may need to strengthen their abilities in one or more of these skills. Such managers may also need to de-emphasize skills that helped them in lower-level jobs and develop different skills.[46] After Kenneth Freeman, CEO of Teterboro, New Jersey-based Quest Diagnostics, handpicked Surya Mohapatra as his successor, both men knew that Mohapatra's considerable scientific and technical skills would not be enough in his eventual role as CEO of the medical testing company. Over the course of five years, the two worked to help Mohapatra communicate better, delegate more effectively, and trade his "deep thinking" habits in favor of faster decision making.[47]

Interpersonal Skills

The various skills required to communicate with other people, work effectively with them, motivate them, and lead them are **interpersonal skills**. Because managers mainly get things done through people at all levels of the organization, they need interpersonal skills in countless situations. Encouraging employees to work together, interacting with employees and other managers, negotiating with partners and suppliers, developing employee trust and loyalty, and fostering innovation—all these activities require interpersonal skills.

LEARNING OBJECTIVE 7

Identify and explain important types of managerial skills

Business Buzz
snoopervision
An intrusive control style in which managers pry into every last detail of their employees' daily work

interpersonal skills
Skills required to understand other people and to interact effectively with them

Communication, or exchanging information, is the most important and pervasive interpersonal skill that managers use. Effective communication not only increases the manager's and the organization's productivity but also shapes the impressions made on colleagues, employees, supervisors, investors, and customers. In your role as a manager, communication allows you to perceive the needs of these stakeholders (your first step toward satisfying them), and it helps you respond to those needs.[48] Moreover, as the workforce becomes more and more diverse—and as more and more companies recognize the value of embracing diversity in their workforces—managers need to adjust their interactions with others, communicating in a way that considers the different needs, backgrounds, experiences, and expectations of their workforces.

Technical, Administrative, and Conceptual Skills

technical skills
Ability and knowledge to perform the mechanics of a particular job

A person who knows how to operate equipment, prepare a financial statement, or program a computer has **technical skills**, the knowledge and ability to perform the mechanics of a particular job. Technical skills are most important at lower organizational levels because managers at these levels work directly with employees who are using the tools and techniques of a particular specialty. At any level, however, today's managers must have some technology background, not only to make good decisions about investments in their own facilities and systems but also to understand changes in the external environment.

administrative skills
Technical skills in information gathering, data analysis, planning, organizing, and other aspects of managerial work

Managers at all levels use **administrative skills**, which are the skills necessary to manage an organization. Administrative skills include the abilities to define schedules, create and monitor budgets, and manage projects from start to finish. Managers often develop such skills through education and then improve them by working in one or more functional areas of an organization, such as accounting or marketing.[49]

conceptual skills
Ability to understand the relationship of parts to the whole

Managers need **conceptual skills** to see the organization as a whole, in the context of its environment, and to understand how the various parts interrelate. Conceptual skills are especially important to the top managers who define goals and craft strategies. Managers use their conceptual skills to acquire and analyze information, identify problems and opportunities, understand the competitive environment, develop strategies, and make decisions.

decision-making skills
The ability to make decisions by following the process of identifying a decision situation, analyzing the problem, weighing the alternatives, choosing an alternative and implementing it, and evaluating the results

Decision-Making Skills

Decision-making skills involve the ability to define problems and select the best course of action. Most managers make decisions by following a process such as the one highlighted in Exhibit 7.8. Using a formal process helps ensure that the best decision is made—a critical success factor for most companies. The product-development decisions made by Boeing illustrate the complexity of the decision-making process. Developing a

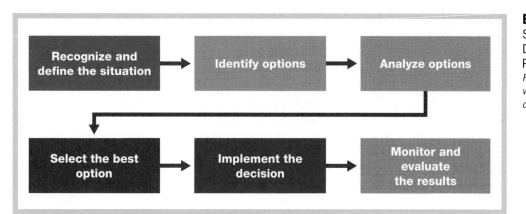

Exhibit 7.8
Steps in the Decision-Making Process
Following these six steps will help you make better decisions.

new airplane takes years and billions of dollars, and a single poor decision can cause serious, long-term damage to the company. However, Boeing doesn't have the luxury of immediately judging the quality of these decisions and taking corrective action. "You make decisions and then you don't find out whether they make sense until 10 years later," notes one Boeing executive.[50] Needless to say, the decision of what kinds of planes to build is crucial for this company.

Recognizing and Defining the Problem or Opportunity The first step in the decision-making process is to recognize that an opportunity or a problem exists. Most companies look for problems or opportunities by gathering customer feedback, conducting studies, or monitoring such warning signals as declining sales or profits, excess inventory buildup, or high customer turnover. Such was the case with Boeing.

For years, Boeing built the vast majority of the world's jetliners. But in the 1990s Boeing began to steadily lose ground to rival Airbus, as the popularity of the European jet maker's single-aisle airplanes took off. By 1994, Airbus had increased its total market share for new jets from 30 percent to nearly 50 percent, while Boeing's market share dropped from 85 percent to 50 percent. Then in 1999 rival Airbus sold twice as many planes as Boeing. It was a huge wake-up call for Boeing. One year later, Airbus announced its plans to go after Boeing's lucrative 747 market by building the A380, a state-of-the-art, 555-passenger, double-decker flying behemoth. The A380, eventually introduced in 2005, uses the latest technology such as lightweight materials, making it cheaper to operate per seat-mile than Boeing's 747-400 (which seats 416 passengers). However, the superjumbo flies no faster than today's jets and cost more than $12 billion to develop.[51]

Identifying and Developing Options Once a problem or opportunity has been defined, the next step is to develop a list of alternative courses of action. Boeing knew that to regain its decisive market lead, it would have to develop a new airplane. Management identified several options: It could build a similar superjumbo plane to compete with the A380; it could build a larger version of its 747-400 to accommodate more passengers; it could build the Sonic Cruiser, a technologically advanced version of a midsize plane that travels at a speed just below the sound barrier and could cut travel time by 20 percent; or it could build a cheaper, fuel-efficient jet that is more economical to operate.[52]

Analyzing Options Once the ideas have been generated, most companies develop criteria such as cost, feasibility, availability of existing resources, market acceptance, potential for revenue generation, and compatibility with the company's mission and vision, to evaluate the options. Some companies rank their criteria by importance, assigning a numerical value to criteria so that important criteria receive more weight in the decision-making process. This weighting is especially important in cases in which certain criteria, such as cost, labor, or implementation time, are scarce. As you can imagine, this step involves a great deal of discussion and debate among managers.

LEARNING OBJECTIVE 8

Summarize the six steps involved in the decision-making process

After analyzing the relevant information, challenges, opportunities, and competitive environment, and applying specific criteria, Boeing concluded that the superjumbo was too risky and too expensive. Boeing saw demand for new jets in the 400-plus passenger category increasing slightly but felt it could service this demand with its current 747 model. Moreover, Boeing thought the challenges posed by the superjumbo were too risky. One such challenge is the need for airports to spend hundreds of millions of dollars to upgrade terminals and taxiways to service the A380 and its two levels of jetways.

Selecting the Best Option After all options have been analyzed and debated, management selects the best one. Some companies turn to customers and employees for feedback before finalizing their decision. This process can be cumbersome but rewarding. For instance, Boeing initially concluded that the company's best option was to build a new version of the 747 that could match or beat the A380's economics and cost only $4 billion to develop versus the $12 billion or more to develop a superjumbo. But after presenting this option to potential customers, Boeing discovered that the market acceptance for a modified 747 did not exist. So the company investigated an alternative option—developing a Sonic Cruiser. But that option was thrown off course after the September 11 terrorist attacks and the resulting drop in passenger traffic. With travelers becoming more price-sensitive and with airlines in deep financial trouble, potential buyers were reluctant to endorse a plane that could cost more to operate.[53]

After reviewing all the available information and making informed assumptions about the airline business years into the future, Boeing opted to focus its commercial aircraft development efforts on the new mid-sized 787 Dreamliner, scheduled for first service in 2008. The company's description of the new plane's benefits resonates with everything they've learned about the economy in general and air travel in particular—it will be more fuel efficient while offering flight speeds similar to today's wide body jumbo jets and the opportunity for airlines to increase their air cargo revenues.[54] In other words, it represents a carefully reasoned response to all the information the company gathered from the outside, along with an assessment of its own strengths and weaknesses. Airbus and Boeing reached different decisions about the future of the air travel industry, and only time will tell which company made the best choice.

TECHNOLOGIES THAT ARE REVOLUTIONIZING BUSINESS Business Intelligence Systems

One of the maddening ironies of contemporary business is that many decision makers are awash in data but starved for true information and insights. *Business intelligence* (BI) systems aim to harness all that data and turn it into the information and insights that managers need.

The good news is that a number of companies now offer solutions to this problem. The bad news is there's a dizzying array of terminology in use today. The wide range of technologies that fall under the BI umbrella include the executive information systems and decision support systems that you encountered in Chapter 4, and you'll also encounter such terms as *performance metrics* (systems that measure and report on progress toward organizational goals) and *online analytical processing (OLAP)* and *business analytics* (data analysis tools that help managers discover trends and relationships in operating data).

HOW THEY'RE CHANGING BUSINESS

Business intelligence systems are helping managers and professionals in many industries grapple with both strategic and tactical problems. For instance, Boeing tracks the staggeringly complex process of custom-building each of its aircraft, and DaimlerChrylser analyzes millions of owner contact records to learn more about customer needs and expectations.

WHERE YOU CAN LEARN MORE

Because business intelligence is a broad term that describes a variety of approaches, technologies, and specific products, you can expect to find a wide range of information. Start with Business Intelligence.com, www.businessintelligence.com, then try several of the leading vendors, including Cognos, www.cognos.com; Business Objects, www.businessobjects.com; and Hyperion, www.hyperion.com.

Implementing the Decision and Monitoring the Results Once a final option has been selected, it's time to implement the decision. This step generally requires the development of action plans that may be similar in scope to those developed for a strategic plan. Next, managers monitor the results of decisions over time to see whether the chosen alternative works, whether any new problems or opportunities arise because of the decision, and whether the decision should be modified to meet changing circumstances. Boeing and Dell, for example, must always keep a close eye on the changing nature of their respective industries.

In the next chapter, you'll see how a company's managerial structure influences the way decisions are made. Today's flatter organizations, for example, allow infor-mation to flow more freely among all levels of the organization, and they push decision making down to lower organizational levels. Moreover, as more and more organizations empower their employees, they delegate the task of decision making to teams.

CRITICAL THINKING CHECKPOINT

1. Why might a manager need to de-emphasize skills that he or she honed in previous positions?
2. Why is trust a vital aspect of a manager's interpersonal skills?
3. What are the risks of defining problems or opportunities poorly prior to making decisions?

CHECKLIST: Apply These Ideas When You're the Boss

✓ Recognize that strategic planning is a never-ending process; always keep eyes open for market conditions that could dictate a change in your strategic plans.

✓ Make sure your vision statement is meaningful and specific to your organization; bland, generic statements do little to guide effective planning.

✓ Be wary of all forecasts—and the further out into the future a forecast reaches, the more wary you need to be.

✓ You can't anticipate every specific crisis you might encounter, but you can establish plans for responding to various types of crises.

✓ Remember that leadership always involves the exercise of power—use it wisely.

✓ Plan changes carefully; most people and most organizations resist change, even when it's in their best interests.

✓ Realize that you can't change a company culture directly; instead, try to change behaviors, organizational structures, beliefs, goals, and the other elements that create culture.

✓ Never assume that you have all the skills needed to manage and lead effectively; the good news is that virtually all the skills you need can be developed.

Summary of Learning Objectives

1. **Define the four basic management functions.** The four management functions are: (1) planning—establishing objectives and goals for the organization and translating them into action plans; (2) organizing—arranging resources to carry out the organization's plans; (3) leading—influencing and motivating people to work effectively and willingly toward company goals; and (4) controlling—monitoring progress toward organizational goals, resetting the course if goals or objectives change in response to shifting conditions, and correcting deviations if goals or objectives are not being attained.

2 **Outline the strategic planning process.** The strategic planning process begins with a clear vision for the company's future. This vision is then translated into a mission statement so it can be shared with all members of the organization. Next, managers assess the company's strengths, weaknesses, opportunities, and threats; they develop forecasts about future trends that affect their industry and products; and they analyze the competition—paying close attention to their strengths and weaknesses so that they can use this information to gain a competitive edge. Managers use this information to establish company goals and objectives. Finally, they translate these goals and objectives into action plans.

3 **Explain the purpose of a mission statement.** A mission statement defines why the organization exists, what it does, what it hopes to achieve, and the principles it will abide by to meet its goals. It is used to bring clarity of focus to members of the organization and to provide guidelines for the adoption of future projects.

4 **Discuss the benefits of SWOT analysis.** An organization identifies its strengths, weaknesses, opportunities, and threats prior to establishing long-term goals. Identifying internal strengths and weaknesses gives the firm insight into its current abilities. The organization must then decide whether new abilities must be learned to meet current or more ambitious goals. Internal strengths become a firm's core competence if they are a bundle of skills and technologies that set the company apart from competitors. Identifying a firm's external opportunities and threats helps prepare it for challenges that might interfere with its ability to reach its goals.

5 **Explain the importance of setting long-term goals and objectives.** Goals and objectives establish long- and short-range targets that help managers fulfill the company's mission. Setting appropriate goals increases employee motivation, establishes standards by which individual and group performance can be measured, guides employee activity, and clarifies management's expectations.

6 **Cite five common leadership styles, and explain why no one style is best.** Five common leadership styles are autocratic, democratic, laissez-faire, contingent, and situational. Each may work best in a given situation: autocratic when quick decisions are needed, democratic when employee participation in decision making is desirable, and laissez-faire when fostering creativity is a priority. Good leaders are flexible enough to respond with the best approach for the situation.

7 **Identify and explain important types of managerial skills.** Managers use interpersonal skills to communicate with other people, work effectively with them, and lead them; technical skills to perform the mechanics of a particular job; administrative skills to manage an organization efficiently; conceptual skills to see the organization as a whole, to see it in the context of its environment, and to understand how the various parts interrelate; and decision-making skills to ensure that the best decisions are made.

8 **Summarize the six steps involved in the decision-making process.** The first step in the decision-making process is recognizing that a problem or opportunity exists. Second, managers identify and develop options using a variety of brainstorming techniques. Third, managers analyze those options using the criteria they've established for that particular decision. The fourth step is then selecting the best option, the fifth step is implementing the decision, and the sixth step is monitoring the results and making changes as needed.

Dell: What's Next?

In a telling move, the name Dell Computer was changed several years ago to simply Dell, paving the way for a future beyond personal computers. The company's move into the printer business was only a first step. Other key growth areas are engineering workstations, networking equipment, servers, storage (specialized computers that contain data warehouses and other large databases), and consumer items such as music players and flat-screen TVs. Michael Dell and Kevin Rollins don't jump into just any market, however. For instance, Microsoft has been pressuring Dell to develop a tablet computer, but Dell and Rollins don't see a significant growth opportunity in that area yet. No matter where the company does decide to grow, the decisions will be consistent with Dell's business model and reflective of the company's success-generating soul.[55]

Critical Thinking Questions

1. Dell now evaluates the performance of its managers not only on whether they reach their objectives, but *how* they reach those objectives. For instance, a manager who meets his or her sales targets but damages team morale in the process would receive a mixed performance rating. How does this reflect the soul of Dell?
2. What message did Michael Dell likely send to his employees when he replaced himself as CEO?
3. Dell invests far less in the development of new technology than typical high-tech companies. Is this risky for an electronics company? Why or why not?

Learn More Online

Go to Chapter 7 of this text's website at www.prenhall.com/bovee, and click on the hotlink to Dell's website. Review the website to answer these questions: How is the "Soul of Dell" presented to the public? What is the "Dell Effect" and how does it relate to the company's business model? Why do you think the company explains its business model to the public?

Key Terms

administrative skills (246)
autocratic leaders (239)
business model (229)
coaching (240)
conceptual skills (246)
controlling (242)
corporate culture (242)
crisis management (236)
decision-making skills (246)
democratic leaders (240)
employee empowerment (240)

first-line managers (237)
goal (235)
interpersonal skills (245)
laissez-faire leaders (240)
leading (237)
management (229)
management pyramid (236)
mentoring (241)
middle managers (237)
mission statement (231)
objective (235)

operational plans (235)
organizing (236)
participative management (240)
planning (229)
quality (243)
standards (243)
strategic plans (229)
tactical plans (235)
technical skills (246)
top managers (236)
vision (230)

Test Your Knowledge

Questions for Review

1. What is management? Why is it so important?
2. What is forecasting, and how is it related to the planning function?
3. What is the goal of crisis management?
4. What are some common characteristics of effective leaders?
5. Why are interpersonal skills important to managers at all levels?

Questions for Analysis

6. Is the following statement an example of a strategic goal or an objective? "To become the number-one retailer of computers and computer accessories in terms of revenue, growth, and customer satisfaction." Explain your answer.
7. How do the three levels of management differ?
8. How do autocratic, democratic, and laissez-faire leadership differ?

9. Why are coaching and mentoring effective leadership techniques?

10. **Ethical Considerations.** When an organization learns about a threat that could place the safety of its workers or its customers at risk, is management obligated to immediately inform these parties of the threat? Explain your answer.

Questions for Application

11. What are your long-term goals? Develop a set of long-term career goals for yourself and several short-term objectives that will help you reach those goals. Make sure your goals are specific, measurable, and time limited.

12. Do you have the skills it takes to be an effective manager? Find out by taking the Keirsey Temperament Sorter II personality test at www.keirsey.com.

13. **Integrated.** Using Dell's mission statement in Exhibit 7.3 as a model and the material you learned in Chapter 2, develop a mission statement that balances the pursuit of profit with responsibility to employees and community. Choose either a manufacturer of musical instruments or a retailer of children's clothing as the company.

14. **Integrated.** What is the principal difference between a business plan (as discussed in Chapter 6) and a strategic plan?

Practice Your Knowledge

Handling Difficult Situations on the Job: Managing Fraud Risks

"Isn't there anything consumers can do to protect themselves?" you ask in disbelief. You're a midlevel manager at Capital One, where vice president Shauna Perkins has just concluded a presentation on *skimming*, the latest twist in credit card fraud.

"What we don't want customers to do is become afraid to use their credit cards," Perkins replies. "They can monitor accounts through our online or toll-free services, reporting discrepancies immediately. They're not liable for charges they didn't make, but they'll have to prove the fraud. And if they wait for mailed statements, the crooks may have 30–60 days to ring up charges!"

The crooks she's referring to are using small devices, about the size of a pager, to skim vital information from a credit card's magnetic strip, including cardholder name, account number, expiration date, and the invisible verification codes introduced in the early 1990s to foil counterfeit cards. (Readers can be purchased for as little as $100 over the Internet and are intended for legitimate use by banks, restaurants, retailers, and hotels.) With the verification codes, an electronically indistinguishable duplicate card can be created.

The actual skimming is accomplished either manually by a dishonest waiter or store clerk who has been paid to conceal the device or automatically by readers secretly installed in private ATMs often found in gas stations and convenience stores. Either way, the stolen credit card data are then downloaded into a computer and transmitted via the Internet, often to Europe, Asia, or Latin America. Phony cards are embedded with the stolen codes and within hours, the thieves can make purchases anywhere in the world.[56]

Your task: Since you manage the consumer fraud division, Perkins has assigned you the decision-making task: Should you warn customers about this new scam? New technologies may soon solve the problem: Visa is trying a tape with a stronger magnetic pull, and MasterCard is experimenting with embedding the last three digits of the account number in the plastic, not the magnetic stripe. Fingerprinting may also be used. If you do warn customers, what will you say? What might be the drawbacks for Capital One if you speak up? What will be the benefits?

Sharpening Your Communication Skills

As the manager of Richter's Restaurant Supply, you see a huge potential for selling company products on the Internet to customers around the world. Your company already has a website but it's geared to U.S. sales only. Before you propose your ideas to senior management, however, you're going to do your homework. Studies show that companies selling in the global marketplace benefit by modifying their websites to accommodate cultural differences. For instance, a mailbox with a raised flag has no meaning in many foreign countries.

Your task is to review the websites of several leading global companies and take notes on how they adapt their websites for global audiences. Once you've gathered your notes, write a short memo to management highlighting (via bullet points) some of the ways these leaders make their websites effective for a global audience.

Building Your Team Skills

A good mission statement should define the organization's purpose and ultimate goals and outline the principles that are to guide managers and employees in working toward those goals. Using library sources such as annual reports or Internet sources such as organizational websites, locate mission statements from one nonprofit organization, such as a school or a charity, and one company with which you are familiar.

Bring these statements to class and, with your team, select four mission statements to evaluate. How many of the mission statements contain all five of the typical components (product or service; primary market; concern for survival, growth, and profitability; managerial philosophy; commitment to quality and social responsibility)? Which components are most often absent from the mission statements you are evaluating? Which components are most often included? Of the mission statements your team is analyzing, which is the most inspiring? Why?

Now assume that you and your teammates are the top management team at each organization or company. How would you improve these mission statements? Rewrite the four mission statements so that they cover the five typical components, show all organization members how their roles are related to the vision, and inspire commitment among employees and managers.

Summarize your team's work in a written or oral report to the class. Compare the mission statement that your team found the most inspiring with the statements that other teams found the most inspiring. What do these mission statements have in common? How do they differ? Of all the inspiring mission statements reported to the class, which do you think is the best? Why? Does this mission statement inspire you to consider working for or doing business with this organization?

Expand Your Knowledge

Discovering Career Opportunities

If you become a manager, how much of your day will be spent performing each of the four basic functions of management? This is your opportunity to find out. Arrange to shadow a manager (such as a department head, a store manager, or a shift supervisor) for a few hours. As you observe, categorize the manager's activities in terms of the four management functions and note how much time each activity takes. If observation is not possible, interview a manager in order to complete this exercise.

1. How much of the manager's time is spent on each of the four management functions? Is this the allocation you expected?
2. Ask whether this is a typical workday for this manager. If it isn't, what does the manager usually do differently? During a typical day, does this manager tend to spend most of the time on one particular function?
3. Of the four management functions, which does the manager believe is most important for good organizational performance? Do you agree?

Developing Your Research Skills

Find two articles in business journals or newspapers (print or online editions) that profile two senior managers who lead a business or a nonprofit organization.

1. What experience, skills, and business background do the two leaders have? Do you see any striking similarities or differences in their backgrounds?
2. What kinds of business challenges have these two leaders faced? What actions did they take to deal with those challenges? Did they establish any long-term goals or objectives for their company? Did the articles mention a new change initiative?
3. Describe the leadership strengths of each person as they are presented in the articles you selected. Is either leader known as a team builder? Long-term strategist? Shrewd negotiator? What are each leader's greatest areas of strength?

Exploring the Best of the Web

URLs for all Internet exercises are provided at the website for this book, www.prenhall.com/bovee. When you log on to this text's Companion Website, select Chapter 7. Then select "Featured Websites," click on the name of the featured website, and review the website to complete these exercises.

Explore these chapter-related websites, review their content, and answer the following questions for each website you visit:

1. What is the purpose of this website?
2. What kinds of information does this website contain? Please be specific.
3. How is the information provided at this website useful for businesspeople? Consumers?
4. How did you expand your knowledge of management by reviewing the material at this website? What new things did you learn about this topic?

Become a Better Manager

ManagementFirst.com can help you become a better manager. Focused on management theory and practice, this website is a management portal that explores in-depth management issues including leadership, time management, training, strategy, knowledge management, personal development, customer relationship management, and more. Each channel provides lengthy articles, advice, and a collection of carefully annotated links. Log on today and join ManagementFirst.com to become information rich and well organized. Learn why knowledge management is important. Discover what emotional intelligence is all about. And find out why companies form strategic alliances. www.managementfirst.com

Linking to Organizational Change

Looking for more information on every aspect of organizational change management? You'll find a comprehensive collection of links on the website of the Management Assistance Program for Nonprofits. This is the place to access articles, discussion groups, and other resources related to organizational change in businesses and in not-for-profit organizations. Start with the overview, which sets the stage for browsing the many links devoted to exploring management and employee perspectives on the challenges and goals of managing change. www.managementhelp.org/org_chng/org_chng.htm

Learn From the Best—and the Worst

Every year, *BusinessWeek* magazine profiles the managers who've done the best and worst jobs of leading their respective companies. See who the magazine's editors and reporters select each year, and find out what they've done. www.businessweek.com/magazine (then click on "Special Reports" and look for "The Best and the Worst Managers of the Year").

Learning Interactively

Companion Website

Visit the Companion Website at www.prenhall.com/bovee. For Chapter 7, take advantage of the interactive "Learning Modules" to test your chapter knowledge. Get instant feedback on whether you need additional studying. Complete the exercises as specified by your instructor.

A Case for Critical Thinking

Wegmans Satisfies Customers by Putting Employees First

Thousands of companies repeat "the customer is king" and similar slogans, proclaiming in various ways that customers are their number one priority. Not Wegmans, a regional grocery store based in Rochester, New York. Wegmans makes a clear statement of its priorities: employees first, customers second.

What do customers think about this, you ask? They love it. Customers routinely drive miles out of their way, past other grocery stores, to shop at Wegmans. The company receives several thousand letters of praise every year from current customers—and several thousand more letters from consumers in cities where it doesn't have stores, begging the chain to open a Wegmans nearby.

A CLEAR WINNER IN A CHALLENGING INDUSTRY

Such enthusiasm has helped the company post a solid record of success since its founding back in 1915. As a private company, Wegmans isn't required to report its financial results to the public, but the numbers that are available are impressive. Its operating margin (a measure of profitability) is twice as high as national chains such as Safeway and Kroger. Sales per square foot, a key measure of selling efficiency, are estimated to be 50 percent higher than the industry average. The *Wall Street Journal* once called Wegmans the "best chain in the country, maybe in the world."

Such results would be impressive in any industry, but they're almost unfathomable in the grocery retailing business, one of the toughest industries on earth. Most grocery retailers struggle with constant price wars that guarantee paper-thin profit margins (making one or two cents on every dollar of revenue is typical), frequent labor troubles, high employee turnover, and a customer base that views most grocery stores as virtually indistinguishable. And as if those problems weren't enough, groceries across the country face the steamrolling cost efficiencies of Wal-Mart and other discount mass merchandisers, which have already captured about a third of the grocery business in the United States.

A STRATEGIC PLAN FOR LONG-TERM SUCCESS

A conventional response to all these challenges would be to just keep squeezing everything— customer service, wages, employee benefits, training, and anything else to keep prices low and still eke out a profit. However, joining the discounters in a never-ending race to cut, cut, cut is not the Wegmans way. Instead, the company defines its mission as being "the very best at serving the needs of our customers." In pursuit of that mission, the company makes employees its number one priority and counts on employees to then meet the needs of customers. To compete successfully against both traditional grocers and Wal-Mart, Wegmans strategy emphasizes a huge selection of products and employees who know food and love serving customers. The cheese department is a good example. Unlike the typical selection of two or three dozen varieties at most, Wegmans shoppers find four or five *hundred* varieties—and a knowledgeable staff that can help them select and serve the perfect cheese. In fact, chances are the department manager has been sent on a research tour of cheese-producing areas in Europe so that he or she has firsthand knowledge of the tastes and traditions of each region.

Such training is expensive, to be sure. Add in higher-than-average wages and employee benefits, and Wegmans labor costs are higher than those of its competitors. Moreover, Wegmans managers exhibit a degree of personal concern for employees not often found in the hectic retail industry. As an example, when one manager whose job required frequent out-of-town travel learned that her mother had been diagnosed with cancer, Wegmans executives modified her responsibilities so that she could stay in town to care for her mother—before she even asked.

This investment in employees pays off in important ways. For starters, customers buy more when they understand how to use various products and are successful and satisfied with them. These positive experiences with Wegmans employees also help shoppers build emotional bonds with the store, further increasing customer loyalty. And employees who enjoy their work and feel they are treated with respect are more productive and less likely to leave in search of other jobs. Employee turnover (the percentage of the workforce that leaves and must be replaced every year) is a major expense for more retailers, but turnover at Wegmans is a fraction of the industry average.

DEMOCRATIC—BUT DISCIPLINED—DECISION MAKING

The mission to be the best at serving consumers extends to the company's decision-making style as well. For day-to-day decisions, laissez-faire management is widespread; executives want front-line employees to make whatever choices are needed to keep customers happy. For more strategic decisions, executives use the freedom of being a private company to move carefully and deliberately. Most retailers try to grow as quickly as possible, largely to meet the expectations of investors, but the strain on employees, managers, and various business systems can damage customer service and cause other problems. In contrast, Wegmans takes a much slower approach to growth, typically opening only one or two new stores a year as it continues to expand beyond New York State. Stores don't open until employees are fully trained and all systems are in top-notch order.

However, being careful doesn't mean Wegmans is afraid of new ideas—far from it. The company has innovated from the beginning and continues to adopt new technologies and policies that benefit employees, customers, and the company. For instance, Wegmans was one of the first U.S. retailers to join the new Global Data Synchronization Network, an industrywide effort to reduce costs and improve accuracy by coordinating electronic product data from manufacturers to distributors to retailers.

THE ACHIEVEMENT OF A LIFETIME

Over the years, Wegmans has won an impressive array of awards, as everything from the best apple merchandiser to the most family-friendly store in the country. However, none of them made the Wegman family as proud as being named by *Fortune* magazine in 2005 as the best company to work for in the United States. Board chairman and current family patriarch Robert Wegman called the award "the culmination of my life."

Critical Thinking Questions

1. Wegmans has always been managed by members of the Wegman family. Do you think the company could continue its winning ways if the next generation doesn't want to take over, forcing the company to hire someone from outside the family as CEO? Explain your answer.
2. Wegmans has proven that putting employees first can be a successful strategy, but does it create any risks? Explain your answer.
3. Would the Wegmans approach work for an car dealer? A bookstore? A manufacturer of industrial goods? Explain your answers.
4. How does low employee turnover contribute to Wegmans distinct and positive corporate culture?

Video Case

Creative Management: Creative Age Publications

Learning Objectives

The purpose of this video is to help you:

1. Understand how and why managers set organizational goals.
2. Identify the basic skills that managers need to be effective.
3. Discuss how corporate culture can affect an organization.

Synopsis

Creative Age Publications uses creativity in managing its beauty-industry publications. With offices or franchised operations in Europe, Japan, Russia, and other countries, the company has expanded rapidly—thanks to sound management practices. One of the company's goals is to avoid overtaxing its management team by growing slowly in the near future. The CEO is working toward delegating most or all of the decisions to her management team rather than making these decisions herself. As Creative Age's managers moved up through the ranks, they honed their technical skills as well as their skills in working with others. "Having heart" is a major part of the company's culture—an important element that, in the CEO's opinion, many companies lack.

Discussion Questions

1. *For analysis:* How does global growth affect Creative Age's emphasis on the management skill of interacting well with other people?
2. *For analysis:* How does moving Creative Age's managers up through the ranks help them develop their conceptual skills?
3. *For application:* How would you suggest that the CEO spread Creative Age's culture throughout its global offices?
4. *For application:* How might the CEO manage Creative Age's growth through the process of controlling?
5. *For debate:* Do you agree with the CEO's policy of allowing managers and employees to work on any company magazine they choose? Support your position.

Online Exploration

Visit Creative Age's website www.creativeage.com and follow the link to *NailPro* magazine. Scan the magazine's homepage and then click on the "About Us" link to read more about the magazine and its parent company. Why would Creative Age call attention to each magazine's goals and market rather than focusing on the parent company? How might Creative Age use a corporate website to communicate with other people and organizations that affect its ability to achieve its goals?

We're All in This Together: Organization and Teamwork

CHAPTER 8

LEARNING OBJECTIVES

After studying this chapter, you will be able to

1. Discuss the function of a company's organization structure
2. Explain the concepts of accountability, authority, and delegation
3. Define five major types of organization structure
4. Describe the five most common forms of teams
5. Highlight the advantages and disadvantages of working in teams
6. List the characteristics of effective teams
7. Review the five stages of team development
8. Highlight six causes of team conflict

www.prenhall.com/bovee

INSIDE BUSINESS TODAY

Reinventing the Retail Experience at The Container Store

www.containerstore.com

Let's face it: frontline jobs in retail sometimes don't have the greatest reputation. From an employee's perspective, these sales positions often combine low pay with high stress, leading to rapid burnout and frequent turnover. From a customer's perspective, frontline retail employees in some stores seem to fall into two categories: poorly trained and poorly motivated rookies or aggressive sellers who seem more intent on getting their commissions than helping customers.

What if you wanted to put a new face on retailing? What if you wanted shopping to be a pleasant, welcome experience for both employees and customers? Too much to ask for, perhaps?

This is the challenge Garrett Boone and Kip Tindell set for themselves when they opened their first Container Store in Dallas, Texas, with the ambition to be the "best retail store in the United States." The chain, which now numbers more than 30 locations across the country, carries a staggering array of products—more than 10,000 at last count—that help customers organize their lives. Store employees are expected to help customers solve every storage problem imaginable, from sweaters to DVDs to rubber stamps to tax records, using a variety of boxes, baskets, hangers, hooks, closet organizers, and more.

As millions of frustrated consumers know all too well, though, delivering great customer service in retail environments isn't easy. The Container Store does it with strong company values, respect for employees, and a structure that promotes teamwork over individual competition.

When selecting new employees, for instance, the company engages in a comprehensive interviewing and selection process to find the perfect person for each position, driven by the belief that one great person equals three good ones. Most employees are college educated, almost half come from employee referrals, and most have been customers of the store. They are also self-motivated, team-oriented, and passionate about customer service.

Once those new hires are on board, they are immersed in an environment far different from that in most retail operations. Full-time employees receive well over 200 hours of training in their first year and 160 hours per year after that. In comparison, most retailers give new workers less than 10 hours of training per year. The Container Store also pays wages as much as 50 to 100 percent above those of other retailers, building long-term employee loyalty that further ingrains the company culture and the sense of team. Moreover, salespeople are also not paid commissions, which is unusual in retailing, so they have no urge to pressure customers—or compete with other employees. To top it off, part-time employees, which are sometimes treated as second-class citizens in other companies, are granted the same respect as full-timers, so they feel part of the team as well.

That emphasis on teamwork is reinforced twice a day, before opening and after closing, through a meeting called "the huddle." Similar to a huddle in football, it helps to give everyone a common purpose: set goals, share information, boost morale, and bond as a team. Morning sessions feature spirited discussions of sales goals and product applications and may include a chorus of "Happy Birthday" for celebrating team members. Evening huddles include more team building and friendly competitions, such as guessing the daily sales figures. Tindell believes that full, open communication with employees takes courage but says, "The only way that people feel really, really a part of something is if they know everything." Team-building efforts are further encouraged by participation in community outreach activities, such as school supply drives for local schools, and through purely recreational activities dreamed up by the employees on the Fun Committee.

By aligning its corporate values with its management practices and its organization structure, The Container Store paves the way for its employees to deliver great customer service. People outside the company are starting to notice, too. The Container Store has become a consistent winner in such nationwide forums as the annual Performance Through People Award, presented by Northwestern University, and *Fortune* magazine's annual list of The 100 Best Companies to Work For.[1]

GET READY

If you were in Boone and Tindell's shoes, what steps would you take to break out of the retail rut and create a company that is satisfying for both customers and employees? How would you attract the best and the brightest employees and pull off a minor miracle in retailing—hanging on to them year after year? (The company's first salesperson, Barbara Anderson, still works there, 25 years later; she's now the community service director.) How would you organize the staffs in your stores? How much information would you share with them, and how would you communicate it? No matter what kind of company you envision joining after college, the principles of organization and teamwork that you can learn from The Container Store can benefit you as an employee, a manager, and an entrepreneur. ■

Chapter Overview

Garrett Boone and Kip Tindell's emphasis on teamwork is just one of the many decisions that managers need to make regarding the organization of their companies. Although organization may seem like an unexciting subject at first, the way companies organize themselves can have a tremendous impact on decision making, communication, productivity, and other vital measures of competitive performance. In this chapter, you'll explore the most important issues to consider in designing an organization structure, along with the most common structures in use today, including the latest: matrix, network, and hybrid designs. The second half of the chapter addresses the vital subject of teamwork, including common types of teams, the pluses and minuses of working in teams, the development of effective teams, and conflict resolution. The chapter concludes with some good advice on conducting effective meetings—a crucial skill for every manager.

Designing an Effective Organization Structure

As Garrett Boone and Kip Tindell can tell you, a company's **organization structure** has a dramatic influence on the way employees and managers make decisions, communicate, and accomplish important tasks. This structure helps the company achieve its goals by providing a framework for managers to divide responsibilities, effectively distribute the authority to make decisions, coordinate and control the organization's work, and hold employees accountable for their work. In contrast, a poorly designed structure can create enormous waste, confusion, and frustration for employees, suppliers, and customers. When Michael Jordan took over as CEO at Electronic Data Systems (EDS), he was appalled by the inefficiencies brought on in part by the organization structure. "It was [like] 2,000 separate companies with a financial overlay," as he put it. As one example of the problems this created, as many as 22 separate EDS divisions were calling on some of the same customers.[2]

When managers design the organization's structure, they use an **organization chart** to provide a visual representation of how employees and tasks are grouped and how the lines of communication and authority flow. Exhibit 8.1 shows the organization chart for a grocery store chain. An organization chart depicts the official design for accomplishing tasks that

LEARNING OBJECTIVE 1

Discuss the function of a company's organization structure

organization structure
Framework enabling managers to divide responsibilities, ensure employee accountability, and distribute decision-making authority

organization chart
Diagram showing how employees and tasks are grouped and where the lines of communication and authority flow

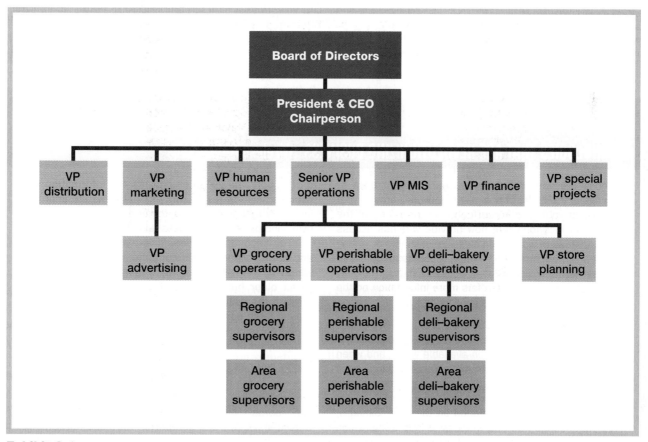

Exhibit 8.1
Organization Chart for Food Lion Grocery Store Chain

Many organization charts look like this one for Food Lion. The traditional model of an organization is a pyramid in which numerous boxes form the base and lead up to fewer and fewer boxes on higher levels, ultimately arriving at one box at the top. A glance at Food Lion's organization chart reveals who has authority over whom, who is responsible for whose work, and who is accountable to whom.

departmentalization can also increase costs by duplicating the use of resources such as facilities and personnel. Furthermore, poor coordination between divisions may cause them to focus too narrowly on divisional goals and neglect the organization's overall goals. Finally, divisions may compete with one another for resources and customers, causing rivalries that hurt the organization as a whole.[19]

matrix structure
Structure in which employees are assigned to both a functional group and a project team (thus using functional and divisional patterns simultaneously)

Matrix Structures A **matrix structure** is an organizational design in which employees from functional departments form teams to combine their specialized skills (see Exhibit 8.5). This structure allows the company to pool and share resources across divisions and functional groups. The matrix may be a permanent feature of the organization's design, or it may be established to complete a specific project. In Dell's case, for instance, sales regions and product groups are linked in a permanent matrix structure; within that framework, *business councils* also focus on specific types of customers, such as small-business owners.[20]

The matrix structure can help big companies function like smaller ones by allowing teams to devote their attention to specific projects or customers without permanently reorganizing the company's structure. A matrix can also make it easier to deploy limited resources where they're needed the most and to bring a mix of skills to bear on important tasks. On the downside, people in a matrix structure have to get used to reporting to two bosses, more communication and coordination is usually required, and struggles over resources can foster unhealthy competition between the two sides of the matrix.[21]

network structure
Structure in which individual companies are connected electronically to perform selected tasks for a small headquarters organization

Network Structures A **network structure** stretches beyond the boundaries of the company to connect a variety of partners and suppliers that perform selected tasks for a headquarters organization. Also called a *virtual organization*, the network organization can *outsource* engineering, marketing, research, accounting, production, distribution, or other functions. The design of a network structure stems from decisions about core competencies, with executives deciding which functions to focus on internally and which to outsource.

The network structure presents an intriguing blend of benefits and risks. A virtual structure can lower costs and increase flexibility, allowing you to react more quickly to market demands. It can also boost competitiveness by taking advantage of specific skills and technologies available in other companies. On the other hand, relying too heavily on outsiders can render you vulnerable to events beyond your control, such as key suppliers going out of business, offering the same goods and services to your competitors, or going into direct competition with you. Moreover, outsourcing too many fundamental tasks such as product design can leave a company without any real competitive distinctions to speak of.[22]

Exhibit 8.5
Matrix Structure
In a matrix structure, each employee is assigned to both a functional group (with a defined set of basic functions, such as production management) and a project team (which consists of members of various functional groups working together on a project, such as bringing out a new consumer product).

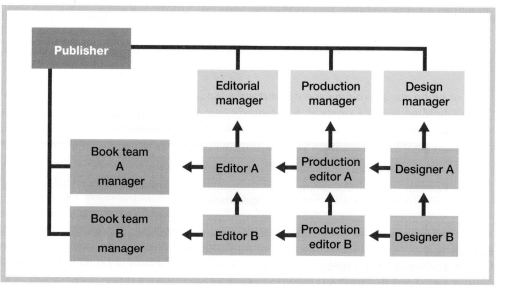

Hybrid Structures Some companies find it most effective to adopt a **hybrid structure**, combining various elements from the four standard types of structure. For example, Inergy Automotive Systems, a Paris-based manufacturer of fuel and energy subsystems for automobiles and other vehicles, has both functional groups (such as research and development) and six geographic customer groups that give the firm a local presence in Japan, North America, and other major automotive assembly regions.[23]

hybrid structure
Structure that combines elements of functional, divisional, matrix, and network organizations

---

CRITICAL THINKING CHECKPOINT

1. Should The Container Store use the same organization structure in each of its stores around the country? Why or why not?
2. Why does a matrix structure create potential problems in the chain of command?
3. What are some of the factors that might convince a company to modify an organization structure that has worked well in the past?

Working in Teams

While the vertical chain of command is a tried-and-true method of organizing for business, it is limited by the fact that decision-making authority is often located high up the management hierarchy while real-world feedback from customers is usually located at or near the bottom of the hierarchy. Companies that organize vertically may become slow to react to change, and high-level managers may overlook many great ideas for improvement that originate in the lower levels of the organization. In addition, many business tasks and challenges demand the expertise of people who work in many parts of the company, isolated by the formal chain of command. To combat these issues, organizations such as The Container Store work to involve employees from all levels and functions of the organization in the decision-making process, using a variety of *team formats* in day-to-day operations.

Even though the team approach has many advantages, shifting to a team structure often requires a fundamental shift in the organization's culture. Teams must also have clear goals that are tied to the company's strategic goals, and their outcomes need to be measured and compared with benchmarks. Moreover, employees must be motivated to work together in teams. Such motivation requires extensive training and a compensation system that is based, at least in part, on team performance. This last objective is sometimes accomplished by using stock options, profit sharing, performance bonuses, and other employee incentives, as Chapter 10 discusses.

Companies that emphasize teamwork often design office spaces to encourage casual interaction between team members.

team
A unit of two or more people who share a mission and collective responsibility as they work together to achieve a goal

What Is a Team?

A **team** is a unit of two or more people who work together to achieve a shared goal. Teams differ from work groups in that work groups interact primarily to share information and to make decisions to help one another perform within each member's area of responsibility. In other words, the performance of a work group is merely the summation of all group members' individual contributions.[24] In contrast, the members of a team have a shared mission and are collectively responsible for their work. By coordinating their individual efforts, the members of successful teams accomplish more together than they could individually, a result known as *synergy*.[25]

Although the team's goals may be set by either the team itself or someone in the formal chain of command, it is the job of the team leader to make sure the team stays on track to achieve those goals. Team leaders are often appointed by senior managers, but sometimes they emerge naturally as the team develops. Some teams complete their work and disband in a matter of weeks or months, while those working on complex projects can stay together for years. In one of the more extreme examples of team longevity, pairs of advertising copywriters and art directors (the two creative halves of a typical ad development team) in England are usually hired—and fired—as a team and often work together for many years.[26]

COMPETING IN THE GLOBAL MARKETPLACE

E-SOFTSYS STAYS CONNECTED AROUND THE GLOBE

It's tough enough to schedule meetings and coordinate team efforts when your partners work across the hall. Imagine what it's like when they work on the other side of the planet. The potential for misunderstandings, missed assignments, and mistrust could easily derail any project. And these are just some of the obstacles facing Kat Shenoy, president and CEO of E-SoftSys. His company employs offshore teams of engineers in China, India, Russia, and elsewhere to develop software for other companies.

When potential customers think about using E-SoftSys for offshore software development, most need reassurance that the firm can successfully manage and monitor its far-flung team. As one customer asks: "How will it operate from so far away? Will we be able to communicate effectively?" To address their concerns and ensure effective teamwork, Shenoy offers customers a mix of human interaction and electronic collaboration (tools such as e-mail, instant messaging, and NetMeeting online software).

Keeping the project on track requires plenty of communication with the customer and within the team. Team members in the United States and other countries rely on frequent, informal communication to avoid misunderstanding one another, missing assignments, and forcing the project off schedule. The project manager uses regular, formal communication with the customer—typically through weekly status reports—to build trust and provide reassurance that the international team is making progress toward timely completion of the software.

However, technology can't address all the communication challenges. E-SoftSys teams often pull together people from diverse cultural backgrounds with different language abilities, and the company has found that face-to-face communication is critical when these teams are forming. For instance, during the early stages of most projects, a U.S.-based project manager travels to the E-SoftSys office in Bangalore, India, to collaborate with the Indian staff in designing the software and planning the work. By working side by side, even temporarily, these intercontinental colleagues establish a rapport that bridges time and space when the U.S. personnel return home.

Questions for Critical Thinking

1. How might a lack of trust between U.S. and international team members threaten E-SoftSys's ability to meet customer needs?
2. Why couldn't the company introduce teams via instant messaging, rather than through expensive, time-consuming in-person meetings?

LEARNING OBJECTIVE 4

Describe the five most common forms of teams

Types of Teams

The type, structure, and composition of individual teams within an organization depends on the organization's strategic goals and the objective for forming the team. The five most common forms of teams are *problem-solving teams, self-managed teams, functional teams, cross-functional teams*, and *virtual teams*. Such classifications are not exclusive. For example, a problem-solving team may also be self-managed and cross-functional. Similarly, some teams are established on an informal basis. That is, they are designed to encourage employee participation but do not become part of the formal organization structure.

problem-solving team
Informal team that meets to find ways of improving quality, efficiency, and the work environment

Problem-Solving Teams A **problem-solving team** is a group assembled to find ways of improving quality, efficiency, or other performance issues. For instance, to address concerns of U.S. car buyers, the German automaker Audi pulled together U.S. and German personnel to collaborate on a range of quality and reliability issues.[27] Such teams are examples of *quality circles;* these problem-solving teams were common in U.S. businesses in the 1980s and 1990s, but their popularity declined when companies realized that many teams weren't delivering the desired improvements in quality. The general ineffectiveness of quality circles highlights a critical issue with problem-solving teams: Teams that are given the responsibility to identify solutions but aren't given the authority to implement the necessary changes aren't likely to solve anything in the long run.

Self-Managed Teams Self-managed teams take problem-solving teams to the next level. As the name implies, **self-managed teams** manage their own activities and require minimum supervision. Typically, they control the pace of work and determination of work assignments. Fully self-managed teams select their own members. As you might imagine, some managers are reluctant to embrace self-managed teams because it requires them to give up significant control.

self-managed teams
Teams in which members are responsible for an entire process or operation

Functional Teams **Functional teams**, or *command teams*, are organized along the lines of the organization's vertical structure and thus may be referred to as *vertical teams*. They are composed of managers and employees within a single functional department, and the structure of a vertical team typically follows the formal chain of command. In some cases, the team may include several levels of the organizational hierarchy within the same functional department.[28]

functional teams
Teams whose members come from a single functional department and that are based on the organization's vertical structure

Cross-Functional Teams In contrast to functional teams, **cross-functional teams**, or *horizontal teams*, draw together employees from various functional areas and expertise. To develop its 777 airplane, Boeing assembled 238 "design-build" teams that integrated design engineers, production workers, and suppliers. The development of the 787 Dreamliner is now following a similar plan.[29] Cross-functional teams have many potential benefits: (1) They facilitate the exchange of information between employees, (2) they generate ideas for how to best coordinate the organizational units that are represented, (3) they encourage new solutions for organizational problems, and (4) they aid the development of new organizational policies and procedures.[30]

cross-functional teams
Teams that draw together employees from different functional areas

Cross-functional teams can take on a number of formats:

- *Task forces.* A **task force** is a type of cross-functional team formed to work on a specific activity with a completion point. Several departments are usually involved so that all parties who have a stake in the outcome of the task are able to provide input. Task forces are also commonly used when business and government leaders coordinate efforts that involve a particular industry or community. For example, the Blue Ribbon Task Force on Nanotechnology is working to promote California's Silicon Valley region as the worldwide center of research and development in nanotechnology (see Chapter 9).[31]

task force
Team of people from several departments who are temporarily brought together to address a specific issue

- *Special-purpose teams.* Like task forces, **special-purpose teams** are created as temporary entities to achieve specific goals. However, special-purpose teams are different because they exist outside the formal organization hierarchy. Such teams remain a part of the organization but have their own reporting structures, and members view themselves as separate from the normal functions of the organization. For instance, to help the scientists and engineers at Ford who were developing the Escape Hybrid SUV meet an extremely tight schedule for a product launch in the summer of 2004, managers exempted the team from the normal corporate procedures for budget approvals and project update reports.[32]

special-purpose teams
Temporary teams that exist outside the formal organization hierarchy and are created to achieve a specific goal

- *Committees.* In contrast to a task force, a **committee** usually has a long life span and may become a permanent part of the organization structure. Committees typically deal with regularly recurring tasks. For example, a grievance committee may be formed as a permanent resource for handling employee complaints and concerns. Because many committees require official representation in order to achieve their goals, committee members are sometimes selected on the basis of their titles or positions rather than their personal expertise.

committee
Team that may become a permanent part of the organization and is designed to deal with regularly recurring tasks

Virtual Teams **Virtual teams** are groups of physically dispersed members who work together to achieve a common goal. Virtual team members communicate using a variety of means, from instant messaging to electronic meeting software. Occasionally, they may meet face-to-face, particularly when they start working together, to help establish and maintain rapport. In many cases, virtual teams are as effective as teams that function under a single

virtual teams
Teams that use communication technology to bring geographically distant employees together to achieve goals

By pulling together the diverse viewpoints and expertise of their various members, effective teams can accomplish far more than a collection of individuals working solo.

cause individual team members to withhold contrary or unpopular opinions. The result can be decisions that are worse—not better—than the team members might've made individually.

- *Diminished individual motivation.* Balancing the need for team harmony with individual motivation is a constant issue with teams. This can be a particularly strong concern in areas such as sales or software development, where the contributions of top performers can far exceed the group average. Without the promise of individual recognition and reward, these high-performance individuals may feel less incentive to keep working at such high levels.
- *Structural disruption.* Teams can become so influential within an organization that they compete with the formal chain of command, in effect superimposing a matrix on the existing structure. For example, a team charged with solving quality problems in the company's current products might be tempted to start brainstorming new and better product designs, which could lead to conflict with the research and engineering staffs who already have the responsibility for product design.
- *Excessive workloads.* The time and energy required to work on teams isn't free, and when team responsibilities are layered on top of individuals' regular job responsibilities, the result can be overload.

**L E A R N I N G
O B J E C T I V E**

List the characteristics of effective teams

Characteristics of Effective Teams

To be successful, teams need to be designed as carefully as any other part of the organization structure. Establishing the size of the team is one of the most important decisions; the optimal size for teams is generally thought to be between 5 and 12 members. Teams smaller than 5 may be lacking in skill diversity and may, therefore, be less effective at solving problems. Teams of more than 12 may be too large for group members to bond properly or communicate efficiently and may discourage some members from sharing their ideas. Larger groups are also prone to disagreements and factionalism because so many opinions must be considered, thus making the team leader's job more difficult. Moreover, people in larger teams can start to feel that their individual contribution is less valuable, so they fall to the temptation of skipping meetings and reducing their overall contribution.

The types of individuals on the team is also vital. People who assume the *task-specialist role* focus on helping the team reach its goals. In contrast, members who take on the *socio-emotional role* focus on supporting the team's emotional needs and strengthening the team's

Exhibit 8.6
Team Member Roles
Team members assume one of these four roles. Members who assume a dual role often make effective team leaders.

	Member social behavior	
High	**Task specialist role** • Focuses on task accomplishment over human needs • Important role, but if adopted by everyone, team's social needs won't be met	**Dual role** • Focuses on task and people • May be a team leader • Important role, but not essential if members adopt task specialist and socioemotional roles
Member task behavior	**Nonparticipator role** • Contributes little to either task or people needs of team • Not an important role—if adopted by too many members, team will disband	**Socioemotional role** • Focuses on people needs of team over task • Important role, but if adopted by everyone, team's tasks won't be accomplished
Low	Low	High

social unity. Some team members are able to assume dual roles, contributing to the task and still meeting members' emotional needs. These members often make effective team leaders. At the other end of the spectrum are members who are *nonparticipators*, contributing little to reaching the team's goals or to meeting members' emotional needs. These **free riders** are team members who don't contribute their fair share to the group's activities, often because they aren't being held individually accountable for their work. Obviously, a team staffed with too many free riders isn't going to accomplish anything. Exhibit 8.6 outlines the behavior patterns associated with each of these roles.

Beyond the right number of the right sort of people, effective teams share a number of other characteristics:[37]

- *Clear sense of purpose.* Team members clearly understand the task at hand, what is expected of them, and their respective roles on the team.
- *Open and honest communication.* The team culture encourages discussion and debate. Team members speak openly and honestly, without the threat of anger, resentment, or retribution. They listen to and value feedback from others. As a result, all team members participate. Conversely, members who either don't share valuable information because they don't understand that it's valuable—or worse, withhold information as a way to maintain personal power—can undermine the team's efforts.[38]
- *Creative thinking.* Effective teams encourage original thinking, considering options beyond the usual.
- *Accountability.* Team members commit to being accountable to each other.
- *Focus.* Team members get to the core issues of the problem and stay focused on key issues.
- *Decision by consensus.* All decisions are arrived at by consensus. But this point comes with a warning: Teams that worry too much about consensus can take forever to make decisions. In many cases, team members need to commit to the group's decision even though they may not all support it 100 percent.

For a brief review of characteristics of effective teams, see Exhibit 8.7.

Five Stages of Team Development

Developing an effective team is an ongoing process. Like the members who form them, teams grow and change as time goes by; teams typically go through five definitive stages of development, nicknamed *forming, storming, norming, performing,* and *adjourning.*[39]

free riders
Team members who do not contribute sufficiently to the group's activities because members are not being held individually accountable for their work

LEARNING OBJECTIVE

Review the five stages of team development

Exhibit 8.7
Characteristics of
Effective Teams
*Effective teams practice
these good habits.*

Build a sense of fairness in decision making

✓ Encourage debate and disagreement without fear of reprisal

✓ Allow members to communicate openly and honestly

✓ Consider all proposals

✓ Build consensus by allowing team members to examine, compare, and reconcile differences

✓ Avoid quick votes

✓ Keep everyone informed

✓ Present all the facts

Select team members wisely

✓ Involve stakeholders

✓ Limit team size to the minimum number of people needed to accomplish the task at hand

✓ Select members with a diversity of views

✓ Select creative thinkers

Make working in teams a top management priority

✓ Recognize and reward individual and group performance

✓ Provide ample training opportunities for employees to develop interpersonal, decision-making, and problem-solving skills

✓ Allow enough time for the team to develop and learn how to work together

Manage conflict constructively

✓ Share leadership

✓ Encourage equal participation

✓ Discuss disagreements

✓ Focus on the issues, not the people

✓ Keep things under control

Stay on track

✓ Make sure everyone understands the team's purpose

✓ Communicate what is expected of team members

✓ Stay focused on the core assignment

✓ Develop and adhere to a schedule

✓ Develop rules and obey norms

- *Forming.* The forming stage is a period of orientation and ice-breaking. Members get to know each other, determine what types of behaviors are appropriate within the group, identify what is expected of them, and become acquainted with each other's task orientation.
- *Storming.* In the storming stage, members show more of their personalities and become more assertive in establishing their roles. Conflict and disagreement often arise during the storming stage as members jockey for position or form coalitions to promote their own perceptions of the group's mission.
- *Norming.* During the norming stage, these conflicts are resolved, and team harmony develops. Members come to understand and accept one another, reach a consensus on who the leader is, and reach agreement on what each member's roles are.
- *Performing.* In the performing stage, members are really committed to the team's goals. Problems are solved, and disagreements are handled with maturity in the interest of task accomplishment.
- *Adjourning.* Finally, if the team has a specific task to perform, it goes through the adjourning stage after the task has been completed. In this stage, issues are wrapped up and the team is dissolved.

As the team moves through these various stages of development, two important developments occur. First, the team develops a certain level of **cohesiveness**, a measure of how committed the members are to the team's goals. The team's cohesiveness is reflected in meeting attendance, team interaction, work quality, and goal achievement. Cohesiveness is influenced by many factors, although the two primary factors are competition and evaluation. If a team is in competition with other teams, cohesiveness increases as the team strives to win. In addition, if a team's efforts and accomplishments are recognized by the organization, members tend to be more committed to the team's goals. Strong team cohesiveness generally results in high morale. Moreover, when cohesiveness is coupled with strong management support for team objectives, teams tend to be more productive.

cohesiveness
A measure of how committed the team members are to their team's goals

The second development is the emergence of **norms**, informal but often powerful standards of conduct that members share and use to guide their behavior. Norms define acceptable behavior by setting limits, identifying values, and clarifying expectations. By encouraging consistent behavior, norms boost efficiency and help ensure the group's survival. Individuals who deviate from these norms can find themselves ridiculed, isolated, or even removed from the group entirely (this fear is the leading cause of groupthink, by the way). Norms can be established in various ways: from early behaviors that set precedents for future actions, from significant events in the team's history, from behaviors that come to the team through outside influences, and from a leader's or member's explicit statements that have an impact on other members.[40]

norms
Informal standards of conduct that guide team behavior

Team Conflict

Of all the skills needed to make a team successful, none is more important than the ability to handle *conflict*—which can range from simple creative differences to all-out battles—resulting from differences in ideas, opinions, goals, or methods of work. Conflict can be *constructive* if it generates creative solutions to problems or encourages team members to understanding opposing viewpoints, but it can be *destructive* if it creates a poisonous emotional atmosphere or distracts the team's performance.[41]

Causes of Team Conflict Team conflicts can arise for a number of reasons. First, individuals may feel they are in competition for scarce or declining resources, such as money, information, and supplies. Second, team members may disagree about who is responsible for a specific task; this type of disagreement is usually the result of poorly defined responsibilities and job boundaries. Third, poor communication can lead to misunderstandings and misperceptions about other team members or other teams. In addition, intentionally withholding information can undermine trust among members. Fourth, basic differences in values, attitudes, and personalities may lead to clashes. Fifth, power struggles may result when one party questions the authority of another or when people or teams with limited authority attempt to increase their power or exert more influence. Sixth, conflicts can arise because individuals or teams are pursuing different goals.[42]

Highlight six causes of team conflict

Keep in mind that while "conflict" sounds negative, in many cases it is simply the result of different perspectives. And until quirky human beings are replaced by groups of matching robots, teams will *always* have some level of conflict. When Ford was developing the Escape Hybrid SUV, management staffed the cross-functional team with both research scientists and product engineers. The scientists were accustomed to taking as much time as needed to invent new solutions or solve problems, but the engineers were more accustomed to schedule-driven work. When launch team leader Mary Ann Wright made it clear that the August 2004 date for starting production was non-negotiable, the diverse team members focused on the common goal and completed the design in time.[43]

Solutions to Team Conflict As with any human relationship, the way a team approaches conflict depends to a large degree on how well the team was functioning in the first place. A strong, healthy team is more likely to view a conflict as simply another challenge to overcome—and can emerge from the conflict even stronger than before. In contrast, a generally dysfunctional team can disintegrate even further when faced with a new source of conflict.

Teams handle conflict in variety of ways. Depending on the strength of the team leadership and the urgency of the situation, a team may simply force a resolution to the conflict, bringing it out in the open and resolving it as quickly as possible. At the other extreme, the team leadership may choose to ignore the conflict and wait for it to subside naturally—which may only serve to quiet the arguments temporarily without actually solving the problem. Other alternatives including negotiating compromises or reminding the team to refocus on its shared goals.[44] In the worst cases, a team may need to be disbanded or reformed with different members.

Attempts at conflict resolution come into play after a conflict has developed, but team members and team leaders can take several steps to prevent conflicts. First, by establishing clear goals that require the efforts of every member, the team reduces the chance that members will battle over their objectives or roles. Second, by developing well-defined tasks for each member, the team leader ensures that all parties are aware of their responsibilities and the limits of their authority. And finally, by facilitating open communication, the team leader can ensure that all members understand their own tasks and objectives as well as those of their teammates. Communication builds respect and tolerance, and it provides a forum for bringing misunderstandings into the open before they turn into full-blown conflicts.

Productive Team Meetings

Meetings are the primary communication venue for business teams, whether they take place in formal conference rooms or on the Internet in virtual meetings. Well-run meetings can help you solve problems, develop ideas, and identify opportunities. Much of your workplace communication will take place in small-group meetings; therefore, your ability to contribute to the company and to be recognized for those contributions will depend on your meeting participation skills.

Unfortunately, many meetings are unproductive because they are either poorly planned or poorly conducted. Ineffective meetings can waste hundreds or thousands of dollars an hour in lost work time and travel expenses, so it's no wonder that managers today focus on making their team meetings more productive. Companies can make better use of valuable meeting time by following these steps:

- *Clarify the purpose of the meeting.* Although many meetings combine purposes, most focus on one of two types: *Informational meetings* involve sharing information and perhaps coordinating action. *Decision-making meetings* involve persuasion, analysis, and problem solving. They often include a brainstorming session, followed by a debate on the alternatives. Moreover, decision-making meetings require that each participant be aware of the nature of the problem and the criteria for its solution. Whatever your purpose, make sure it is clear and clearly communicated to all participants.
- *Select participants carefully.* With a clear purpose in mind, it's easier to identify the right participants. If the session is purely informational and one person will do most of the talking, you can invite a large group. For problem-solving and decision-making meetings, invite only those people who are in a direct position to help the meeting reach its objective. The more participants, the more comments and confusion you're likely to get, and the longer the meeting will take. However, make sure you invite all the key decision makers, or your meeting will fail to satisfy its purpose.
- *Establish a clear agenda.* The success of any meeting depends on the preparation of the participants. Distribute a carefully written agenda to participants, giving them enough time to prepare as needed. A productive agenda answers three key questions: (1) What do we need to do in this meeting to accomplish our goals? (2) What issues will be of greatest importance to all participants? (3) What information must be available in order to discuss these issues? In addition to improving productivity, this level of agenda detail shows respect for participants and the other demands on their time.[45]

Effective teams know how to keep meetings on track while ensuring full participation from everyone involved.

- *Keep the meeting on track.* A good meeting draws out the best ideas and information the group has to offer. Good leaders occasionally guide, mediate, probe, stimulate, and summarize, but mostly they encourage participants to share. Experience will help you recognize when to be dominant and press the group forward and when to step back and let people talk. If the meeting lags, you'll need to ask questions to encourage participation. Conversely, there will be times when you have no choice but to cut off discussion in order to stay on schedule.
- *Follow agreed-upon rules.* Business meetings run the gamut from informal to extremely formal, complete with detailed rules for speaking, proposing new items to discuss, voting on proposals, and so on. The larger the meeting, the more formal you'll need to be to maintain order. Whatever system of rules you employ, make sure everyone is clear about the expectations.
- *Encourage participation.* As the meeting gets under way, you'll discover that some participants are too quiet and others are too talkative. The quiet participants might be shy, they might be expressing disagreement or resistance, or they might be answering e-mail or instant messages on their laptop computers or PDAs. Draw them out by asking for their input on issues that particularly pertain to them. For the overly talkative, simply say that time is limited and others need to be heard from.
- *Close effectively.* At the conclusion of the meeting, verify that the objectives have been met; if not, arrange for follow-up work as needed. Either summarize the general conclusion of the discussion or list the actions to be taken. Make sure all participants agree on the outcome and give people a chance to clear up any misunderstandings.

CRITICAL THINKING CHECKPOINT
1. Should new hires with no business experience be assigned to virtual teams? Why or why not?
2. What are the risks of not giving new teams the time and opportunity to "storm" and "norm" before tackling the work they've been assigned?
3. Should meetings always follow a strict agenda? Why or why not?

CHECKLIST: Apply These Ideas When You're the Boss

✓ Make sure that the structure of your organization serves its mission, not the other way around.

✓ Strive for a healthy balance between the efficiencies of work specialization and benefits of cross-training.

✓ Beware of assigning employees responsibility without giving them the authority needed to meet those responsibilities.

✓ Make sure that efforts to decentralize don't create chaos and confusion by eliminating important links in the chain of command.

✓ Carefully weigh the costs of changing the organizational structure; the loss of productivity as people figure out new responsibilities and develop new relationships can be considerable.

✓ Make sure that all teams have a clear purpose—and that they don't outlive that purpose.

✓ Don't let an emphasis on teamwork obscure the contribution of individual performers.

✓ Remember that conflict is a natural part of every team scenario; the difference between teams that succeed and those that fail is how they handle conflict.

✓ Understand the true cost of meetings, and make sure they are both necessary and productive.

Summary of Learning Objectives

1 **Discuss the function of a company's organization structure.** An organization structure provides a framework through which a company can coordinate and control the work, divide responsibilities, distribute authority, and hold employees accountable. An organization chart provides a visual representation of this framework.

2 **Explain the concepts of accountability, authority, and delegation.** Accountability is the obligation to report work results to supervisors or team members and to justify any outcomes that fall below expectations. Authority is the power to make decisions, issue orders, carry out actions, and allocate resources to achieve the organization's goals. Delegation is the assignment of work and the transfer of authority and responsibility to complete that work.

3 **Define five major types of organization structure.** Companies can organize in four primary ways: by function, which groups employees according to their skills, resource use, and expertise; by division, which establishes self-contained departments formed according to similarities in product, process, customer, or geography; by matrix, which assigns employees from functional departments to interdisciplinary project teams and requires them to report to both a department head and a team leader; and by network, which connects separate companies that perform selected tasks for a headquarters organization. In addition, many companies now combine elements of two or more of these designs into hybrid structures.

4 **Describe the five most common forms of teams.** The five most common forms of teams are (1) problem-solving teams, which seek ways to improve a situation and then submit their recommendations; (2) self-managed teams, which manage their own activities and seldom require supervision; (3) functional teams, which are composed of employees within a single functional department; (4) cross-functional teams, which draw together employees from various departments and expertise in a number of formats such as task forces, special-purpose teams, and committees; and (5) virtual teams, which bring together employees from distant locations.

5 **Highlight the advantages and disadvantages of working in teams.** Teamwork has the potential to produce higher-quality decisions, increase commitment to solutions and changes, lower stress and destructive internal competition, and improve flexibility and responsiveness. The potential disadvantages of working in teams include inefficiency, groupthink, diminished individual motivation, structural disruption, and excessive workloads.

6 **List the characteristics of effective teams.** Effective teams have a clear sense of purpose, communicate openly and honestly, build a sense of fairness in decision making, think creatively, stay focused on key issues, manage conflict constructively, and select team members wisely by involving stakeholders, creative thinkers, and members with a diversity of views. Moreover, effective teams have an optimal size of between 5 and 12 members.

7 **Review the five stages of team development.** Teams typically go through five stages of development. In the forming stage, team members become acquainted with each other and with the group's purpose. In the storming stage, conflict often arises as coalitions and power struggles develop. In the norming stage, conflicts are resolved and harmony develops. In the performing stage, members focus on achieving the team's goals. In the adjourning stage, the team dissolves upon completion of its task.

8 **Highlight six causes of team conflict.** Conflict can arise from competition for scarce resources; confusion over task responsibility; poor communication and misinformation; differences in values, attitudes, and personalities; power struggles; and goal incongruity.

The Container Store: What's Next?

With a corporate culture built around teamwork, The Container Store has built a reputation for delivering extraordinary customer service. Kip Tindell and Garrett Boone's intention of hiring only "great people" continues to pay off as the company expands around the United States. Expansion is methodical, to say the least. After more than a quarter century, the company had fewer than three dozen stores. As with Wegmans (Chapter 7), careful expansion is key to keeping the culture intact and ensuring a positive customer experience in every store. Meanwhile, e-commerce lets The Container Store reach customers nationwide; www.containerstore.com gives shoppers the opportunity to plan projects and order storage systems and supplies online. With the home remodeling boom and redecorating boom showing no signs of abating anytime soon, Tindell and Boone's team should continue to delight customers well into the future.[46]

Critical Thinking Questions

1. Based on what you've learned about the way The Container Store employees interact with customers, do you think that the company emphasizes centralized or decentralized decision making? Explain your answer.
2. How might the company's emphasis on teamwork affect accountability and authority?
3. What effect might a change to commission-based compensation have on the team structure at The Container Store?

Learn More Online

Effective teamwork and communication have helped The Container Store earn consistent acclaim as one of the best companies to work for in the United States. Go to Chapter 8 of this text's website at www.prenhall.com/bovee and click on the "Best Places to Work" hotlink. Read through the profiles of recent winners. How have the winners improved quality or customer satisfaction through better teamwork? What role does communication play in their success? How does the structure of the organization help the company succeed?

Key Terms

accountability (263)	formal organization (262)	organization structure (261)
authority (263)	free riders (275)	problem-solving team (270)
centralization (265)	functional structure (266)	process divisions (267)
chain of command (263)	functional teams (271)	product divisions (267)
cohesiveness (277)	geographic divisions (267)	responsibility (263)
committee (271)	hybrid structure (269)	self-managed teams (271)
cross-functional teams (271)	informal organization (262)	span of management (263)
customer divisions (267)	line organization (263)	special-purpose teams (271)
decentralization (265)	line-and-staff organization (263)	tall organizations (264)
delegation (263)	matrix structure (268)	task force (271)
departmentalization (266)	network structure (268)	team (269)
divisional structure (267)	norms (277)	virtual teams (271)
flat organizations (264)	organization chart (261)	work specialization (262)

Test Your Knowledge

Questions for Review

1. Why is organization structure important?
2. What are the characteristics of tall organizations and flat organizations?
3. What are the advantages and disadvantages of work specialization?
4. What are the advantages and disadvantages of functional departmentalization?
5. What are the advantages and disadvantages of working in teams?

Questions for Analysis

6. Why would you expect a manager of a group of nuclear physicists to have a wide span of management?
7. How can a virtual organization reduce costs?
8. What can managers do to help teams work more effectively?
9. How can companies benefit from using virtual teams?
10. **Ethical Considerations.** You were honored that you were selected to serve on the salary committee of the employee negotiations task force. As a member of that committee, you reviewed confidential company documents listing the salaries of all department managers. You discovered that managers at your level are earning $5,000 more than you, even though you've been at the company the same amount of time. You feel that a raise is justified on the basis of this confidential information. How will you handle this situation?

Questions for Application

11. You are the leader of a cross-functional work team whose goal is to find ways of lowering production costs. Your team of eight employees has become mired in the storming stage. They disagree on how to approach the task, and they are starting to splinter into factions. What can you do to help the team move forward?
12. Your warehouse operation is currently functioning at capacity. To accommodate anticipated new business, your company must either build a major addition to your current warehouse operation or build a new warehouse that would be located at a distant site. As director of warehouse operations, you would like several people to participate in this decision. Should you form a task force, a committee, or a special-purpose team? Explain your choice.
13. **Integrated.** One of your competitors has approached you with an intriguing proposition. The company would like to merge with your company. The economies of scale are terrific. So are the growth possibilities. There's just one issue to be resolved. Your competitor is organized under a flat structure and uses lots of cross-functional teams. Your company is organized under a traditional tall structure that is departmentalized by function. Using your knowledge about culture clash, what are the likely issues you will encounter if these two organizations are merged?
14. **Integrated.** Chapter 7 discussed several styles of leadership, including autocratic, democratic, and laissez-faire. Using your knowledge about the differences in these leadership styles, which style would you expect to find under the following organization structures: (a) tall organization—departmentalization by function; (b) tall organization—departmentalization by matrix; (c) flat organization; (d) self-directed teams?

Practice Your Knowledge

Handling Difficult Situations on the Job: Dehiring Campus Recruits

As the human resources manager at Intel, you've grown accustomed to the cyclical nature of the semi-conductor industry, with business growing and shrinking in response to demand for chips and other components throughout the economy. You've forecasted the start of a slowdown coming soon, so you've stopped hiring to fill vacancies; you've deferred payment of management raises for six months; and you've split the rank-and-file raises into "half now, half in six months." You're trying to hit the numbers management has targeted for immediate cuts in staff and salary expenses. But you know that others' sacrifices will be small consolation to the talented college graduates Intel recruited last winter. They're about to feel the pinch of a soft economy.

You've seen the days in which the quest for college talent was so hot that you fought with competitors to hire the best recruits—and then figured out later what jobs to put them in. Times have changed. Today you've learned a new buzz phrase: "reverse hiring."

Should Intel do as others are now doing and "dehire" the grads you recruited last winter? Or should you let them come on board as planned, get placed in lesser jobs than expected, and risk finding themselves "reorganized" out of work? Being last hired, they could easily wind up in the growing pool of laid-off Intel employees awaiting new positions.

Some of your competitors are offering "reverse hiring bonuses," say two months' worth of the promised salary, if recruits will dismiss all legal claims and agree not to come to work. Some also let recruits keep their signing bonuses. Like Intel, these companies are trying to meet job-reduction goals, but they want their reputations on campus to remain strong. As soon as the economy picks up, you'll all be battling over the same individuals getting de-hired today.[47]

Your task: Determine the best course of action. Should Intel dehire recruits? How might dehiring recruits impact the firm's organizational structure? What alternatives can you offer? If you choose reverse hiring, what will you say to recruits and how will you reach them (letters, phone calls, e-mail)? What offers will you make, if any? How can you prevent hard feelings against Intel?

Sharpening Your Communication Skills

Write a brief memo to your instructor describing a recent conflict you had with a peer at work or at school. Be sure to highlight the cause of the conflict and steps you took to resolve it. Which of the three conflict-resolution styles discussed in this chapter did you use? Did you find a solution that both of you could accept?

Building Your Team Skills

What's the most effective organization structure for your college or university? With your team, obtain a copy of your school's organization chart. If this chart is not readily available, gather information by talking with people in administration, then draw your own chart of the organization structure.

Analyze the chart in terms of span of management. Is your school a flat or a tall organization? Is this organization structure appropriate for your school? Does decision making tend to be centralized or decentralized in your school? Do you agree with this approach to decision making?

Finally, investigate the use of formal and informal teams in your school. Are there any problem-solving teams, task forces, or committees at work in your school? Are any teams self-directed or virtual? How much authority do these teams have to make decisions? What is the purpose of teamwork in your school? What kinds of goals do these teams have?

Share your team's findings during a brief classroom presentation, then compare the findings of all teams. Is there agreement on the appropriate organization structure for your school?

Expand Your Knowledge

Discovering Career Opportunities

Whether you're a top manager, first-line manager (supervisor), or middle manager, your efforts will impact the success of your organization. To get a closer look at what the responsibilities of a manager are, log on to the Prentice Hall Student Success SuperSite at www.prenhall.com/success. Click on Majors Exploration, and select "management" in the drop-down box. Then scroll down and read about careers in management.

1. What can you do with a degree in management?
2. What is the future outlook for careers in management?
3. Follow the link to the American Management Association website, and click on Research. Then scroll down and click on Administrative Professionals Current Concerns Survey. According to the survey, what has affected administrative professionals most recently? On which five tasks do managers spend most of their time?

Developing Your Research Skills

Although teamwork can benefit many organizations, introducing and managing team structures can be a real challenge. Search past issues of business journals or newspapers (print or online editions) to locate articles about how an organization has overcome problems with teams.

1. Why did the organization originally introduce teams? What types of teams are being used?
2. What problems did each organization encounter in trying to implement teams? How did the organization deal with these problems?
3. Have the teams been successful from management's perspective? From the employees' perspective? What effect has teamwork had on the company, its customers, and its products?

Exploring the Best of the Web

URLs for all Internet exercises are provided at the website for this book, www.prenhall.com/bovee. When you log on to this text's Companion Website, select Chapter 8. Then select "Featured Websites," click on the name of the featured website, and review the website to complete these exercises.

Explore these chapter-related websites, review their content, and answer the following questions for each website you visit:

1. What is the purpose of this website?
2. What kinds of information does this website contain? Please be specific.
3. How is the information provided at this website useful for businesspeople? Consumers?
4. How did you expand your knowledge of organizing and working in teams by reviewing the material at this website? What new things did you learn about these topics?

Build Teams Online

Let Teamworks, the Virtual Team Assistant, help you build a more effective team, resolve team conflict, manage projects, solve team problems, be a team leader, encourage team feedback, and teach with teams. Each of the site's nine information modules contains background information, self-assessment vehicles, skill development exercises, and links to helpful resources. Log on now and increase your effectiveness as a team member by learning more about why teams work, the stages of team development, tips for communicating with team members during a project, and some creative problem-solving techniques. www.vta.spcomm.uiuc.edu

Be Direct

If you want to learn more about building effective teams, you can read many excellent books on the subject. But you might be surprised by just how much information on team building you can find on the Internet. One good starting point is the Self-Directed and Self-Managed Work Teams page. This site's designers are passionate about teamwork, and they want to make it easier for people to work effectively in teams. Read the Frequently Asked Questions (FAQs) about self-managed teams. Then explore some of the links to discover more about teams and teamwork. www.mapnp.org/library/grp_skll/slf_drct/slf_drct.htm

Resolve Conflict Like a Pro

The field of conflict resolution has been growing very quickly and includes practices such as negotiation, mediation, arbitration, international peace building, and more. Learn more about each of these topics along with basic information about conflict resolution by visiting CRInfo. Be sure to check out the web resources, where you'll find links to communication and facilitation skills, consensus building, and more. Find out why BATNA is important. Discover what a mediator does. Learn how to conduct effective meetings. And don't leave without testing your knowledge of common negotiation terms. www.crinfo.org

Learning Interactively

Companion Website

Visit the Companion Website at www.prenhall.com/bovee. For Chapter 8, take advantage of the interactive "Learning Modules" to test your chapter knowledge. Get instant feedback on whether you need additional studying. Complete the exercises as specified by your instructor.

A Case for Critical Thinking

Harley-Davidson Drives from Dysfunctional to Cross-Functional

Richard Teerlink knows what it's like being at the bottom looking up. When he joined Harley-Davidson in 1981 as chief financial officer, the motorcycle manufacturer was as low as it could go. The company had acquired a poor reputation for quality and reliability. It was behind the curve on product design and development. And its big-iron cruisers and long-distance touring bikes were heavy, chrome-laden, and expensive. Moreover, they leaked oil and they vibrated excessively. Some customers even joked that they should buy two Harleys—one to ride and one for parts. Tired of tolerating frequent breakdowns, motorcycle buyers turned to smooth-riding and smooth-running imports.

HARLEY GOES FULL THROTTLE

Facing some of the toughest competition in the world from such companies as Honda, Suzuki, and Yamaha, Harley-Davidson had to improve quality, introduce new products, and cut costs. So Teerlink and the management team set out to rebuild the company's production processes from the ground up.

Harley had survived several arduous years of crisis and had overcome its obstacles under the direction of a very strong hierarchical, centralized leadership group. By 1986, Harley's future looked bright. New products were coming to market, quality had improved, and products were snapped up as quickly as they could be cranked out. In fact, product demand rebounded so strongly that dealers reported long waiting lists of riders eager to climb on a Harley. Some fiercely loyal fans even tattooed the company's logo on their chests.

Harley-Davidson's inspiring comeback was a cheering symbol of American industrial renaissance. So when Teerlink climbed into the CEO saddle in 1989, he thought the hard work of saving the company was behind him. But competition from Japanese companies soon heated up.

MORE POTHOLES AHEAD

Japanese competitors fumbled in their first few attempts at unseating Harley, but learned quickly. By 1995, they were producing virtual Harley clones, with one exception—these new bikes had many technical improvements. Once again, Harley faced a daunting challenge. In spite of its many improvements, Harley's quality standards were not on a par with those of its foreign competitors. Moreover, Harley's cost structure was among the highest in the industry. Teerlink had his work cut out for him—again.

HARLEY REVS UP ITS ENGINES

Teerlink knew that the best way to improve quality and reliability and lower production costs was to create an environment in which everyone took responsibility for the company's present and future. Of course, such an approach would not come naturally to Harley. The previous crisis had been managed with an unmistakable top-down approach, as is so often the case with turnarounds.

But times had changed, and Teerlink flattened the corporate hierarchy and established teams of cross-functional leaders to work collaboratively and provide senior leadership with direction. This is the structure under which Harley currently operates. At the heart of the organizational structure are three cross-functional teams called Circles—the Create Demand Circle, the Produce Product Circle, and the Provide Support Circle. Each Circle includes design engineers, purchasing professionals, manufacturing personnel, marketing personnel, and others. The cross-functional teams are responsible for every motorcycle produced by Harley—from product conception to final design. Within each team, the leadership role moves from person to person, depending on the issue being addressed.

Recognizing that suppliers' input is crucial to Harley's new-product development, all cross-functional teams include key suppliers who work elbow-to-elbow with Harley personnel. "Suppliers are the experts. They have expertise in not only what they're developing today but also what's going on in their industry," says one Harley purchasing director. "The more input we have up front, the better our products will be."

MAKING A U-TURN

Cross-functional teamwork indeed paid off for Harley. Output and productivity soon soared, as did sales around the world. In 1997, the company added a new production facility in Kansas City, Missouri, and another in Manuas, Brazil, the following year. Teerlink retired as CEO in 1999, but under the leadership of his replacement, Jeffrey Bleustein, Harley stayed on course. As vice president of engineering during Teerklink's reign, Bleustein had been instrumental in improving product quality and repairing Harley's public image. By the time he retired as CEO in 2005, annual revenues had passed the $5 billion mark and the growth in unit sales was on track to meet a goal of 400,000 bikes by 2007.

With big bikes more popular than ever, the company is riding a wave of success. However, competitors aren't about to let Harley have all the glory; even without Harley's unique brand mystique, they continue to challenge with well-engineered products. Harley also faces the challenge of an aging customer base—the average buyer in 2004 was 47 years old. For the past several years, the company has been targeting younger buyers with the sleeker, sportier V-Rod—its first smaller bike in two decades. Women are a key target as well; female buyers made up just 2 percent of the customer base in 1985 but are 10 percent today. With one of the strongest brand names in the world, a range of popular products, and membership in the Harley Owners Group (HOG) pushing up toward one million, it's now up to new CEO James Ziemer and the rest of the Harley team to continue one of the great turnaround stories in the history of American business.

Critical Thinking Questions

1. During Teerlink's tenure as Harley's CFO was the organizational structure flat or tall? Centralized or decentralized? Explain your answers
2. As CEO, how did Teerlink change the organizational structure?
3. Why does Harley-Davidson include outside suppliers on its cross-functional teams?
4. Go to Chapter 8 of this text's website at **www.prenhall.com/bovee** and click on the hot link to get to the Harley-Davidson website. Navigate the site to answer the following questions: How many motorcycles did Harley produce in the most recent quarter? What is the output trend? What is the trend in Harley's worldwide sales?

Video Case

Juicing Up the Organization: Nantucket Nectars

Learning Objectives

The purpose of this video is to help you:

1. Recognize how growth affects an organization's structure.
2. Discuss why businesses organize by departmentalization.
3. Understand how flat organizations operate.

Synopsis

Tom Scott and Tom First founded Nantucket Nectars in 1989 with an idea for a peach drink. In the early days, the two ran the entire operation from their boat. These days, Nantucket Nectars has more than 130 employees split between headquarters in Cambridge, Massachusetts, and several field offices. As a result, management has developed a more formalized organization structure to keep the business running smoothly. The company relies on cross-functional teams to handle special projects such as the implementation of new accounting software. These strategies have helped Nantucket Nectars successfully manage its rapid growth.

Discussion Questions

1. *For analysis:* What type of organization is in place at Nantucket Nectars?
2. *For analysis:* How would you describe the top-level span of management at Nantucket Nectars?
3. *For application:* Nantucket Nectars may need to change its organization structure as it expands into new products and new markets. Under what circumstances would some form of divisional departmentalization be appropriate for the firm?
4. *For application:* Assume that Nantucket Nectars is purchasing a well-established beverage company with a tall structure stressing top-down control. What are some of the problems that management might face in integrating the acquired firm into the existing organization structure of Nantucket Nectars?
5. *For debate:* Assume that someone who is newly promoted into a management position at Nantucket Nectars cannot adjust to delegating work to lower-level employees. Should this new manager be demoted? Support your chosen position.

Online Exploration

Visit the Nantucket Nectars site at www.juiceguys.com and follow the links to read about the company and its products. Then use your favorite search engine to find recent news about the company (which is formally known as Nantucket Allserve). Has it been acquired by a larger company or has it acquired one or more smaller firms? What are the implications for the chain of command, decision making, and organization structure of Nantucket Nectars?

Creating Value: Producing Quality Goods and Services

LEARNING OBJECTIVES

After studying this chapter, you will be able to

1. Explain what production and operations managers do

2. Outline the unique challenges of delivering quality services

3. Identify key tasks involved in designing a production process

4. Define the supply chain and distinguish it from the value chain

5. Discuss the role of computers and automation technology in production

6. Explain the strategic importance of managing inventory

7. Distinguish among JIT, MRP, and MRP II inventory management systems

8. Highlight the differences between quality control and quality assurance

www.prenhall.com/bovee

INSIDE BUSINESS TODAY
Fulfilling Customized Dreams at Carvin Guitars

www.carvin.com

When beginning guitarists have mastered the nuances of "Mary Had a Little Lamb" and set their sights on making serious music, they often encounter a serious equipment problem. Low-cost, beginner guitars lack the materials and workmanship needed to produce top-quality sounds. They are difficult to keep in tune, and they cannot produce true notes all the way up and down the neck. Plus, they just aren't very cool. Nobody is going to step on stage and face 10,000 adoring fans with a guitar purchased at the local discount store.

And so the shopping begins, as these aspiring guitarists look to upgrade. As with just about every product category these days, the array of choices is dizzying. For a few hundred dollars, budding musicians can buy imports that offer improved quality. Moving up toward a thousand dollars, they can enter the world of such classic American brands as Fender, Gibson, and Martin—a world that extends up to $8,000 or $10,000 for limited-edition models. Musicians with that much to spend and several months to wait can also hire skilled instrument builders known as *luthiers* to create custom guitars that reflect their individual personalities and playing styles.

Musicians who look hard enough will find another alternative, the semi-custom guitars made by Carvin, of San Diego, California. Carvin has built a successful business filling the gap between mass-produced and fully custom guitars by perfecting the art and science of *mass customization*, the ability to adapt standardized products to the tastes of individual customers. In two to six weeks, and for roughly $700 to $1,500, Carvin can customize one of several dozen models of guitars and basses. All are available in a wide variety of woods, paints, stains, finishes and electronics—so many choices that the discussion boards on Carvin's website buzz with debates about which combinations are "best" for specific styles of music.

Carvin's factory combines old-world craftsmanship with new-world technologies. Because the custom guitars are built on a standard set of body shapes and styles, Carvin can use computer-controlled cutting and milling machines that cut and shape the bodies and necks quickly and precisely. A diamond-surface finishing machine mills fingerboards (the playing surface of the neck) to tolerances of a thousand of an inch. Experienced craftspeople with sensitive eyes and ears take over from there, performing such tasks as matching veneer pieces on guitar tops (veneers are thin sheets of wood, usually exotic or expensive species), adjusting the action (the feel of the strings against the frets), and listening to the tone quality of finished instruments.

As with any customized offering, the buyer's involvement in the production process is a vital step in ensuring customer satisfaction. Carvin has several retail stores, but all are located in Southern California, so most buyers interact with the company online. The company's website presents each guitar on a page that lists standard features, provides an interactive list of customization options, and computes the total price for the desired configuration. A pop-up window called the "virtual custom shop" lets online shoppers preview the many woods, paints, and stains. Buyers can quickly see what their dream instruments would look like in every shade from natural maple to translucent blue.

With this blend of automation and human touch, Carvin produces instruments that win rave reviews from appreciative customers. "Nothing can touch it in terms of sound quality and workmanship" and "I haven't seen anything close to this price that can outperform it" are typical of the comments that Carvin customers post online. Upon hearing a salesperson in another music store speak disparagingly of the brand, one indignant Carvin owner retrieved his guitar from his car and put on an impromptu concert for the store's sales staff to demonstrate just how good the Carvin product sounded. With a proven manufacturing approach and customer loyalty like that, Carvin will be fulfilling the musical dreams of guitarists for years to come.[1]

GET READY

Carvin's guitar business is a great example of a dilemma facing millions of businesses today: how to satisfy customers who want unique products at mass-market prices. If you were running Carvin, what strategies would you put in place to manufacture semi-custom guitars that have unbeatable quality but don't carry the high price tags of fully custom products? How would you integrate the precision of computer-controlled machinery with the human feel of experienced technicians and musicians? Most of all, how would you use manufacturing as a key strategic strength to stay profitable in a hotly competitive business? ▪

Chapter Overview

Although an artistic endeavor such as creating musical instruments might not strike you as "manufacturing," Carvin Guitars demonstrates the competitive advantages companies can gain today by exploring a variety of strategic and technology options in the world of production. This chapter gives you an overview of the many elements that make up a production strategy, starting with the important concept of the value chain, then moving on to the unique challenges of service delivery, the varieties of mass production and customization, and the hot topic of outsourcing. Following that is a look at the steps involved in designing the production process, from establishing your supply chain to scheduling work. The final two sections explore the major technologies used in product design and production and outline the important aspects of managing the production process.

Understanding Production and Operations Management

As the managers of Carvin know, the extremely competitive nature of the global business environment requires companies to produce high-quality goods and services in the most efficient way possible. Fast production, low costs, few defects, excellent customer service, broad market reach, innovative products and processes, less waste, and high flexibility are all objectives that improve quality by adding value to the good or service being produced. Companies pursue these objectives to maintain a competitive advantage.[2] Moreover, managers understand that the level of quality that a company aspires to in the production of goods and services affects its long-term ability to address the needs of its customers, its employees, and its shareholders.

Like most aspects of business, production tends to get more complex and technologically advanced with each passing year. To get a sense of what production means today and how it might affect your career, it's important to first clarify what production really is, explain how it fits in the value chain, identify the unique challenges of service production, distinguish between mass production and customization, and explore the impact that outsourcing is having on businesses and employers all over the world.

What Is Production?

To many people, the term *production* suggests images of factories, machines, and assembly lines staffed with employees making automobiles, computers, furniture, motorcycles, or other tangible goods. That's because in the past people used the terms *production* and *manufacturing* interchangeably. With the growth in the number of service-based businesses and their increasing importance to the economy, however, the term **production** is now used to describe the transformation of resources into goods and services that people need or want. The broader term **production and operations management (POM)**, or simply *operations management,* refers to all the activities involved in producing a firm's goods and services.

Like other types of management, POM involves the basic functions of planning, organizing, leading, and controlling. It also requires careful consideration of a company's goals, the strategies for attaining those goals, and the standards against which results will be measured. In both manufacturing and service organizations, the production and operations manager is the person responsible for performing these functions. One of the principal responsibilities of the production and operations manager is to design and oversee an efficient conversion process—one that lowers costs by optimizing output from each resource used in the process. These resources include money, materials, inventories, people, buildings, and time.

The Value Chain and the Conversion Process

Every business, from neighborhood coffeehouses to motorcycle manufacturers, tries to create value by transforming inputs (such as labor, information, and raw materials) into outputs (goods and services that customers want to purchase). This transformation, often called the *conversion process,* is at the core of the company's **value chain**, the linked sequence of processes that add value to those inputs until the final output—the product offered to the customer—is realized.[3] For instance, the process of combining flour and other ingredients to produce bread adds value to those raw materials. A critical measure of success for every management team is **productivity**, or the efficiency with which they can convert inputs to outputs throughout the value chain. (Put another way, productivity is equal to outputs divided by inputs.) Productivity is vital not only because it drives the return that investors get but also because it determines how price-competitive the company can be in its chosen markets. In the automotive industry, for example, Nissan sets the productivity pace by manufacturing its Altima model with only 15.33 hours of labor per car.[4] Because Nissan spends less to build a vehicle than its competitors, it has more flexibility in setting its prices while still generating healthy profits. Of course, productivity alone isn't enough to ensure success; cranking out shoddy products or vast quantities of the wrong product isn't going to get you anywhere.

LEARNING OBJECTIVE 1

Explain what production and operations managers do

production
Transformation of resources into goods or services that customers need or want

production and operations management (POM)
Coordination of an organization's resources for the manufacture of goods or the delivery of services

value chain
All of the functions required to transform inputs into outputs (goods and services), along with the business functions that support the transformation process

productivity
A measure of the efficiency with which a company transforms inputs into outputs

Exhibit 9.1
The Conversion Process
Production of goods or services is essentially a process of conversion. Inputs *(the basic ingredients) are* transformed *(by the application of labor, equipment, and capital) into* outputs *(the desired product or service).*

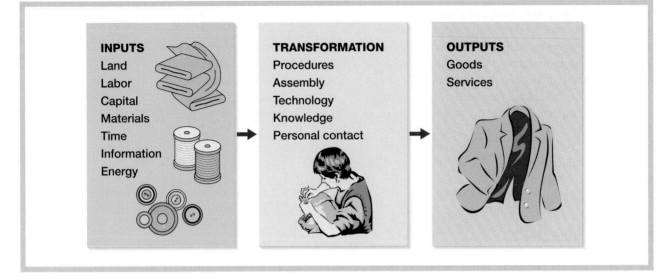

This transformation concept applies to both tangible goods and intangible services. An airline, for example, uses such processes as booking flights, flying airplanes, maintaining equipment, and training crews to transform tangible and intangible inputs such as the plane, pilot's skill, fuel, time, and passengers into the delivery of customers to their destinations. For a clothing manufacturer to produce a jacket, inputs such as cloth, thread, and buttons are transformed by the seamstress into the finished product (see Exhibit 9.1).

Conversion is of two basic types. An **analytic system** breaks raw materials into one or more distinct products, which may or may not resemble the original material in form and function. To create *dimensional lumber*, for example, a sawmill cuts whole logs down to various sizes of lumber. A **synthetic system** combines two or more materials to form a single product. Various types of *engineered lumber* are created by combining wood chips or sawdust and glue to form sheets, joists, and other building components.

analytic system
Production process that breaks incoming materials into various component products and divisional patterns simultaneously

synthetic system
Production process that combines two or more materials or components to create finished products; the reverse of an analytic system

L E A R N I N G
O B J E C T I V E 2

Outline the unique challenges of delivering quality services

The Unique Challenges of Service Delivery

The conversion processes for services and goods are similar in terms of *what* is done—transforming inputs into outputs—but the two differ in *how* the processes are performed (see Exhibit 9.2). That's because the production of goods results in a tangible output—something you can see or touch, such as a jacket, motorcycle, desk, or bicycle—while the production of a service results in an intangible act. Most of the concepts associated with goods manufacturing apply to services as well, although service providers do face some unique issues:[5]

- Customers are usually involved in—and can affect the quality of—the service delivery. Personal trainers can instruct clients in the proper way to work out, but if the clients don't follow directions, the result will be unsatisfactory.
- Unlike goods, which can usually be built ahead of time and stored in inventory until customers buy them, most services are consumed at the same time they are produced. For instance, if a 200-seat airline flight takes off half empty, those 100 sales opportunities are lost forever; they can't be stored in inventory for later sale. This attribute can have a dramatic impact on the way service businesses are managed, from staffing (making sure enough people are on hand to help with peak demands) to pricing (using discounts to encourage people to buy services when they are available). Note that some technology-based services don't have to deal with this constraint. Online data backup services, for example, are available whenever customers want to use them.

Exhibit 9.2

Input-Transformation-Output Relationships for Typical Systems

Both goods and services undergo a conversion process, but the components of the process vary to accommodate the differences between tangible and intangible outputs.

System	Representative Inputs	Transformation Components	Transformation Function	Typical Desired Output
Hospital	Patients, medical supplies	Physicians, nurses, equipment	Health care	Healthy individuals
Restaurant	Hungry customers, food	Chef, waitress, environment	Well-prepared and well-served food	Satisfied customers
Automobile factory	Sheet steel, engine parts	Tools, equipment, workers	Fabrication and assembly of cars	High-quality cars
College or university	High school graduates, books	Teachers, classrooms	Impart knowledge and skills	Educated individuals
Department store	Shoppers, stock of goods	Displays, salesclerks	Attract shoppers, promote products, fill orders	Sales to satisfied customers

- Services are usually people-intensive, whether they require manual skills (carpentry, landscaping) or intellectual or creative energy skills (advertising, freelance writing). Much of the investment in e-commerce in recent years has been aimed at offering services that don't require as much human activity to compete, such as Amazon.com in online retailing. On the other hand, technology can also be used to restore the human touch in services that have become increasingly impersonal in recent years. For instance, few doctors make house calls anymore and often have only a few minutes to devote to patients who come to their offices. However, by adopting e-mail to communicate with patients, some doctors are finding that they are more productive and communicate better with their patients—and patients like e-mail because it gives them more time to explain their conditions and express their concerns.[6]

- Customers often dictate when and where services are performed. The equipment and food ingredients used in a restaurant can be produced just about anywhere, but the restaurant itself needs to be located close to customers and be open when customers want to eat.

- Service quality can be more subjective than goods quality. If you create a pair of scissors, for instance, both you and the customer can measure and agree on the hardness of the steel, the sharpness of the blades, the smoothness of the action, and so on. If you create a haircut using those scissors, however, you and the customer might disagree on the attractiveness of the style or the quality of the salon experience.

With the majority of workers in the United States now involved in the service sector, managers in thousands of companies need to pay close attention to these factors when designing service-delivery systems.

Mass Production, Mass Customization, and Customized Production

Both goods and services can be created through mass production, mass customization, or fully customized production, depending on the nature of the product and the desires of target customers. In **mass production**, identical goods or services are created, usually in large quantities, such as when Apple churns out 10,000 identical iPod music players. Although not normally associated with services, mass production is what American Airlines is doing when it offers hundreds of opportunities for passengers to fly from, say, Dallas to Chicago every day—every customer on these flights gets the same service at the same time.

At the other extreme is **customized production**, sometimes called *batch-of-one production* in manufacturing, in which the producer creates a unique good or service for each customer. If you order a piece of furniture from a local craftsperson, for instance, you can specify

mass production
Production of uniform products in large quantities

customized production
Production of individual goods and services for individual customers

everything from the size and shape to the types of wood and fabric used. Or you can hire a charter pilot to fly you wherever you want, whenever you want. Both products are customized to your unique requirements.

Mass production has the advantage of economies of scale, but it can't deliver many of the unique goods and services that today's customers demand. On the other hand, fully customized production can offer uniqueness but usually at a much higher price. An attractive compromise in many cases is **mass customization**, in which part of the product is mass produced, then the remaining features are customized for each buyer. Carvin guitars are an ideal example; customers get the same basic guitar bodies but their own individual combinations of woods, finishes, and electronic components.

Technology continues to increase the options for mass customization. For instance, Meridian Golf mass customizes golf clubs in 1,100 different combinations for shoppers who visit its two locations in Golden Valley and Oakdale, Minnesota. Customers are fitted by swinging a club on a special in-store platform where computers measure 14 aspects of their golf swing. Thanks to such mass customization, Meridian Golf boasts a 99.5 percent customer satisfaction rate.[7] Other catchy examples of mass customization include the ability to imprint M&M candies or the soles of Nike shoes with your personal slogan.[8]

Outsourcing

Chapter 6 introduced the concept of corporate outsourcing as a source of opportunity for small businesses. Nearly every aspect of a business has the potential to be outsourced, from product design and manufacturing to human resources to marketing and sales. For instance, some companies choose to focus on design and hand some or all of the manufacturing duties off to companies that specialize in that phase of the value chain. A good example of this process is DaimlerChrysler's Smart line of cars. Just about everything in Smartville, the production center in France where the Smart cars are assembled, is relegated to suppliers—from inventorying nuts and bolts on the assembly line to delivering cars to dealers in Europe and out to Japan. Over half the people working in Smartville aren't even on the manufacturer's payroll. The biggest suppliers are right on-site, building most of the car in the form of large modules—body, doors, rear section with engine, and so on. Conveyors link major suppliers' plants directly to the assembly building where the cars are bolted together. Suppliers carry much of the cost of work-in-progress inventory, since they don't get paid until each car comes off the line and is accepted for sale by inspectors—about every 90 seconds, which is quick time for the auto industry. Meanwhile, DaimlerChrysler hopes to incorporate what it has learned about suppliers, modules, pay-on-build, and new technologies into its global operation. "We are getting more and more into learning from others," says one Smart car plant manager. "We take good things in other places and install them at our plant."[9]

Outsourcing all or part of the manufacturing function has several potential advantages. For one thing, it allows companies to redirect the capital and resources spent on manufacturing to new product research and development, marketing, and customer service. For another, many contract manufacturers are industry specialists with state-of-the art facilities and production efficiencies that would be costly to duplicate on an individual scale. After AMD designed its Personal Internet Communicator, a low-cost device aimed at giving consumers in developing countries computing and Internet capabilities, it turned manufacturing for the device over to Solectron, a global contract manufacturer that builds everything from surgical robots to videogame systems.[10]

With all its potential financial and technical advantages, however, outsourcing is not without problems. Some companies that outsourced important functions have pulled them back in house after being disappointed by the quality or cost. Everdream, a Fremont, California, software company, outsourced customer support to a company in Costa Rica but brought it back in house after encountering a variety of problems, from telephone static to low productivity.[11] Companies take on a different sort of potential trouble when they outsource work to prisons; at least 2,000 inmates of U.S. prisons now perform call center tasks for corporations and government agencies. Concerns include the privacy of personal information—in at least one instance, prisoners shared personal information about the people they'd called—to unfair wage competition (prisoners are paid far less than the going rate for such work).[12] For an international look at the implications of outsourcing, see "Offshoring: Profits, Yes, But at What Cost?"

In automotive manufacturing circles, the way the Smart car is built has attracted as much attention as the vehicle. Outsourcing the manufacturing function integrates the Smart car supply chain to the maximum.

CRITICAL THINKING CHECKPOINT

1. Using Exhibit 9.2 as a model, identify the inputs, transformation components and functions, and desired outputs of an online health information resource such as WebMD (www.webmd.com) or the Mayo Clinic (www.mayoclinic.com).

2. If customers are involved in a service, do they share responsibility for the quality of the outcome? Why or why not?

3. Is your college education an example of mass production or mass customization? Explain your answer.

Designing the Production Process

Designing an effective production process is one of the key responsibilities of production and operations managers. It involves six important tasks: establishing the supply chain, forecasting demand, planning for capacity, choosing a facility location, designing a facility layout, and scheduling work.

LEARNING OBJECTIVE 3

Identify key tasks involved in designing a production process

Establishing the Supply Chain

The value chain and the conversion process that it incorporates rely on supplies at every step of the way. Next time you visit a coffeehouse, whether it's a local independent or a chain such as Starbucks, take a second to look around at all the goods and services required to operate such a business. Even for a relatively simple business such as a coffeehouse, the list is long: the many different types of coffee beans, flavor additives, chocolate shavings, sugar, sweetener, cream, half-and-half, cow's milk, soy milk, cinnamon, water, electricity, workers' aprons, maintenance for espresso machines, coffee cups, lids, placemats, napkins, stirrers, and so on. And that doesn't include all the goods and services that aren't directly involved in making coffee, such as accounting software to pay taxes and print paychecks, heating, security

THINKING ABOUT ETHICS

OFFSHORING: PROFITS, YES, BUT AT WHAT COST?

Few business issues in recent years have generated the emotional intensity that outsourcing has stirred up. Outsourcing has been going on for about as long as businesses have existed, but it has become a hot topic as the outsourcing movement expands from mostly lower-paying assembly positions to higher-paying technical and professional positions.

When companies outsource any function in the value chain, they often eliminate the jobs associated with that function as well. And, increasingly, those jobs aren't going across the street to another local company but rather around the world, a variation on outsourcing known as *offshoring*. (Offshoring can shift jobs to either another company or an overseas division of the same company.) HP, IBM, Dell, Microsoft, and Accenture are among the many U.S. technology firms that have already moved thousands of technical jobs to India, which has a large pool of educated workers willing to work for far less than U.S. workers are typically paid. Offshoring is a possibility whenever firms can find less-expensive labor in another country, whether it's Japanese manufacturers moving work to China or U.S. firms moving work to Thailand.

Proponents say that offshoring is crucial to the survival of many U.S. companies and that it saves other U.S. jobs. Plus, offshoring helps raise the standard of living in other countries and thereby expands opportunities for U.S. companies to export their products. And some observers say that like it or not, offshoring is going to continue for generations, so everyone might as well start adapting to the idea.

Opponents say that companies are selling out the U.S. middle class in pursuit of profits and starting a trend that can only harm the country. When jobs in engineering, medicine, finance, scientific research, architecture, journalism, and law can move overseas, they ask, what jobs are going to be left in the United States? Their anger isn't helped when terminated U.S. employees are forced to train their own overseas replacements, an apparently common practice. Offshoring that involves crucial health and safety issues is a big concern, too—for instance, half of all the "heavy" maintenance performed on U.S. commercial aircraft is now offshored to places such as Hong Kong and El Salvador as U.S. airlines struggle mightily to control costs.

Uncertainty is only fueling the controversy, because nobody can be entirely certain just how far the offshoring trend will go or what impact it will have on employees, communities, or companies themselves. Estimates vary widely about the number of jobs that have moved or could move to other countries. A U.S. government analysis of job losses in 2004 suggested that offshoring accounts for only a small fraction of jobs lost in the United States. Moreover, aside from cases in which a particular job was moved to another country, it's often difficult to identify the specific reasons that one country gained jobs or another lost jobs. The emergence of new technology, phasing out of old technology, shifts in consumer tastes, changes in business strategies, and other factors can all create and destroy jobs. And in a new twist, a few U.S. start-ups aren't even bothering hiring in the United States to begin with; rather, they build their organizations by hiring or subcontracting overseas.

Moreover, traditional economic theory suggests that outsourcing lower-level jobs to countries with lower wages is good for U.S. companies because it frees up money and employees to work on more valuable activities. To some degree, this did in fact happen when many U.S. manufacturing jobs moved overseas in previous decades. However, when those more valuable activities themselves started to move overseas, quite a few people began to question the theory.

Some economists continue to assert that short-term pains will lead to long-term gains—that the jobs lost this time around will once again be replaced by other jobs. Here again, though, there's more uncertainty: no one has yet identified what those new jobs are going to be. Paul Craig Roberts, a former assistant treasury secretary, says the traditional economists are wrong because they're using 200-year-old assumptions about comparative advantage (see Chapter 3) that don't apply to a highly mobile, information-based economy. With companies trying to reduce costs wherever possible but workers trying to protect as many jobs as possible, offshoring promises to be a hot topic for years to come—not only for businesses and employees but for governments and society as a whole.

Questions for Critical Thinking

1. Some economists have suggested "wage insurance" to help workers whose income declines after their high-paying jobs go overseas. Do you agree? Why or why not? If you do agree, who should pay for the insurance, taxpayers or the companies that offshore jobs?
2. Will global labor markets eventually balance out, with workers in comparable positions all over the world making roughly the same wages? Explain your answer.

systems, advertising, phone service, window washers, paint, restroom supplies, and furniture repair. Now just imagine what it must be like to keep track of the millions of aircraft parts that Boeing receives from over 1,000 suppliers worldwide.[13]

A company's ability to deliver quality products and services is often tied to the dynamics of its suppliers. One faulty part, one late shipment, can send rippling effects through the production system and can even bring operations to a grinding halt. To avoid such problems, every company has to carefully manage its **supply chain**, the collection of suppliers and systems that provide all the various materials required to make a finished product. (*Supply chain* and *value chain* are sometimes used interchangeably, but it's helpful to distinguish the supply chain as the part of the overall value chain that acquires and manages the goods and services needed to produce whatever it is the company produces and then deliver it to the final customer. Everyone in the company is part of the value chain, but not everyone is involved in the supply chain.[14]) The supply chain begins with the provider of raw materials and ends with the company that produces the finished product that is delivered to the final customer. The members of the supply chain vary according to the nature of the operation and type of product but typically include suppliers, manufacturers, distributors, and retailers.

Before a company can produce a single product, it must first create a supply chain. Managers need to identify which materials and other supplies they need, who can supply them, where they should be stored, and a host of other variables. When TiVo, the maker of the popular personal video recorders that capture television programming, started up several years ago, executives figured they needed to get products on the market as quickly as possible. They established a supply chain almost overnight by outsourcing manufacturing, distribution, retailer recruiting, public relations, advertising, and customer support.[15]

The best supply chains function as true partnerships, with buyers and sellers coordinating their efforts in a win-win approach. For instance, both Toyota and Honda have developed close, cooperative relationships with U.S. parts suppliers as these Japanese firms have expanded their manufacturing presence in North America (60 percent of all Toyotas and 80 percent of all Hondas sold in North America are built in North America). In the Japanese tradition of *keiretsu*, the two companies have spent years "growing" a close-knit supply network that meets their needs—and helps their suppliers run their businesses more successfully as well. The process is neither easy nor simple, but the result is positive relationships in which suppliers go the extra mile for Honda and Toyota because they're confident the carmakers will treat them fairly in return. Among the benefits: Toyota and Honda have been able to design new cars in half the time it takes Ford, GM, and Chrysler—all of which have a reputation for more adversarial relationships with their suppliers.[16]

Supply-chain decision making might not sound as glamorous as high-level corporate strategy or innovative e-commerce, but it is every bit as crucial to a company's success. For instance, the public face of Amazon.com is a website that has all the hallmarks of a leading-edge Internet company; behind the scenes, though, are some of the world's most sophisticated warehouses and supply-chain technologies. In fact, more than a few dot-com pioneers in the 1990s learned to their dismay just how important supply chains are when their razzle-dazzle web company ideas faltered because of nuts-and-bolts supply-chain problems.

Forecasting Demand

A smooth-running supply chain can provide the inputs a company needs, but managers need to figure out how much to buy. And to make that decision, they need to forecast demand for the goods they'll be manufacturing or the services they'll be delivering. Using customer feedback, sales orders, market research, past sales figures, industry analyses, and educated guesses about the future behavior of the economy and competitors, operations managers prepare **production forecasts**, estimates of future demand for the company's products. These estimates are then used to plan, budget, and schedule the use of resources. Of course, many factors in the business environment cannot be predicted or controlled with certainty. For this reason, managers must regularly review and adjust their forecasts to account for these uncertainties. Forecasts that are too high can waste money if the company

LEARNING OBJECTIVE 4

Define the supply chain and distinguish it from the value chain

supply chain
The collection of suppliers and systems that provide all of the materials and supplies required to create finished products and deliver them to final customers; can refer to both the supply chain of an individual company and the supply chain of an entire industry

production forecasts
Estimates of how much of a company's goods and services must be produced in order to meet future demand

invests in production capacity that it doesn't need. Forecasts that are too low—meaning the company winds up selling more than it expected—are a better problem to have, but a problem nonetheless. Racing to produce higher-than-expected volumes can raise costs if overtime wages need to be paid, can frustrate customers if products are delayed, and can put added stress on machinery, information systems, and employees.

Planning for Capacity

Once product demand has been estimated, management must determine the company's capacity to produce the goods or services. The term *capacity* refers to the volume of manufacturing or service capability that an organization can handle. For example, a doctor's office with only one examining room limits the number of patients the doctor can see each day. And a cruise ship with 750 staterooms limits the number of passengers that the ship can accommodate in any given week. Similarly, a beverage bottling plant with only one conveyor belt and one local warehouse limits the company's ability to manufacture beverage products.

capacity planning
The long-term strategic decisions that determine the level of resources available to an organization to meet customer demand

Capacity planning is the collection of long-term strategic decisions that establish the overall level of resources needed to meet customer demand. When managers at Boeing plan for the production of an airliner, they have to consider not only the staffing of thousands of people but also massive factory spaces, material flows from hundreds of suppliers around the world, internal deliveries, cash flow, tools and equipment, and dozens of other factors. Because of the potential impact on finances, customers, and employees—and the difficulty of making large-scale changes or reversing major decisions quickly—capacity choices are among the most important decisions that top-level managers make.[17]

Choosing a Facility Location

Choosing the location of production facilities is one of the most important decisions managers face when designing the production process for goods and services. Just like buying a house is usually the biggest purchase decision consumers ever make, so to is the decision to buy land, build factories, lease office space, and so on. The goal is to choose a location that minimizes costs while increasing operational efficiencies and product quality, and managers must consider such factors as land, construction, labor, local taxes, energy, local living standards, and transportation for both raw materials and finished products.

Creative thinking and careful management can overcome seemingly insurmountable odds when it comes to location. Vegpro Kenya, one of Kenya's largest produce growers, has seven farms within a two-hour drive of the country's main airport in Nairobi and a packing facility right at the airport itself. Every morning, trucks load up vegetables that have just been picked on the farms and shuttle them to the airport, where Vegpro workers prepare them for immediate transport on overnight flights to London, Paris, and other cities. In just a day or two, fresh vegetables from the middle of Africa show up in European supermarkets thousands of miles away—compared to the week it typically takes for produce grown here in the United States to reach U.S. supermarkets.[18]

Location considerations may be different for some service organizations. Although they may also take regional costs into consideration, the main objective for many service firms is to locate where profit potential is greatest. Unlike manufacturing operations, in which low production costs are an important consideration, services tend to focus on more customer-driven factors.[19] Because they often require one-on-one contact with customers, service organizations such as gas stations, restaurants, department stores, and charities must locate where their target market is large and sustainable. Therefore, market research often plays a central role in site selection. However, for service companies that reach customers primarily by telephone, mail, or the Internet, proximity to customers is less of a consideration.

Support from local communities and governments often plays a key role in location decisions as well. To provide jobs and expand their income and sales tax bases, many governments offer companies generous packages of financial relief, from reduced property taxes to free land. Puerto Rico has convinced a number of medical and pharmaceutical companies to build

Whenever transportation costs are a major expense in the production of a product or service, access to railroads and other means of transport becomes an important consideration.

plants there through a combination of tax incentives and a stable, educated workforce.[20] When the South Korean automaker Kia recently explored locations for building its first factory in Europe (partly to avoid the European Union's high import duties on cars), Slovakia made the most attractive offer, outbidding Poland, the Czech Republic, and Hungary.[21]

Designing a Facility Layout

Once a site has been selected, managers must turn their attention to *facility layout,* the arrangement of production work centers and other elements (such as materials, equipment, and support departments) needed to process goods and services. Layout planning includes such decisions as how many steps are needed in the process, the amount and type of equipment and workers needed for each step, how each step should be configured, and where the steps should be located relative to one another.[22]

The overall goal of facility layout design is arranging production resources in a way that makes the best use of space, machinery, materials, and staff. Well-designed facilities help companies operate more productively by reducing wasted time and wasted materials, but that is far from the only benefit. Smart layouts support close communication and collaboration among employees and help ensure their safety, both of which are important for employee satisfaction and motivation. In the delivery of services, facility layout can be a major influence on customer satisfaction in some important aspects as the amount of time that customers are forced to wait to be served.[23] Facilities can be laid out in an endless variety of ways, but four typical facility layouts are the *process layout, product layout, cellular layout,* and *fixed-position layout* (see Exhibit 9.3).[24]

A **process layout**, also called a *functional layout,* concentrates everything needed to complete one phase of the production process in one place. Specific functions, such as drilling or welding, are performed in one location for different products or customers (see Exhibit 9.3A). The process layout is often used in machine shops as well as in service industries. For example, a medical clinic might dedicate one room to X rays, another room to routine examinations, and still another to outpatient surgery.

An alternative to the process layout is the **product layout**, also called the *assembly-line layout,* in which the main production process occurs along a line, and products in progress move from one workstation to the next. Materials and subassemblies of component parts may feed into the main line at several points, but the flow of production is continuous. Automotive and personal-computer manufacturers are just two of many industries that typically use this layout (see Exhibit 9.3B).

process layout
Method of arranging a facility so that production tasks are carried out in separate departments containing specialized equipment and personnel

product layout
Method of arranging a facility so that production proceeds along a line of workstations

Exhibit 9.3
Types of Facility Layouts

Facility layout is often determined by the type of product. **(A) Process layout:** *Typically used for producing made-to-order products; arranged according to the specialized employees and materials involved in various phases of the production process.* **(B) Product layout:** *Used to produce large quantities of just a few products; the developing product moves in a continuous sequence from one workstation to the next.* **(C) Cellular layout:** *Works well for mass customization; parts with similar shapes or processing requirements are processed together in work centers to aid teamwork and flexibility.* **(D) Fixed-position layout:** *Requires employees and materials to be brought to the product; used when the product is too large to move easily.*

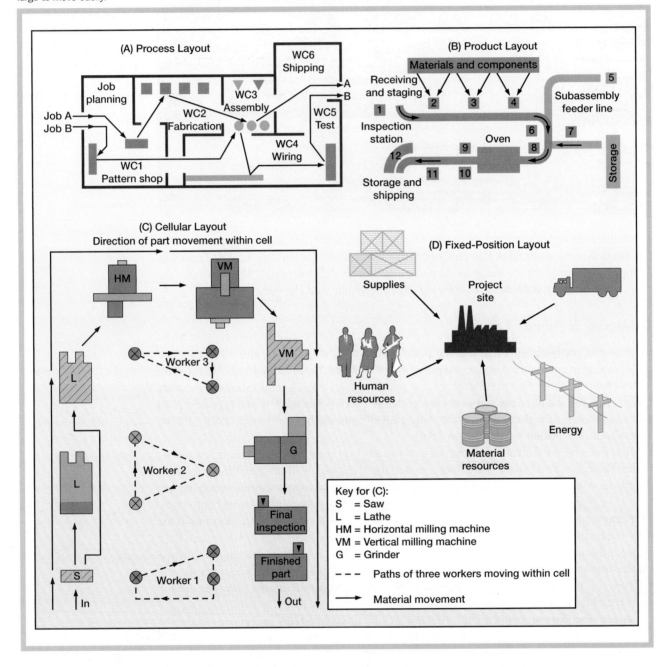

Some production of services is also organized by product. For example, when you go to your local department of motor vehicles to get a driver's license, you usually go through a series of steps administered by several people: registering, taking a written or computerized test, having an eye exam, paying a cashier, and getting your picture taken. You emerge from this system a licensed driver (unless, of course, you fail one of the tests).

A **cellular layout** groups dissimilar machines into work centers (or cells) to process parts that have similar shapes and processing requirements (see Exhibit 9.3C). Arranging work flow by cells can improve the efficiency of a process layout while maintaining its flexibility. At the same time, grouping smaller numbers of workers in cells facilitates teamwork and joint problem solving. Employees are also able to work on a product from start to finish, and they can move between machines within their cells, thus increasing the flexibility of the team. Cellular layouts are commonly used in computer chip manufacture and metal fabricating.[25]

cellular layout
Method of arranging a facility so that parts with similar shapes or processing requirements are processed together in work centers

Finally, the **fixed-position layout** is a facility layout in which labor, materials, and equipment are brought to the location where the good is being produced or the customer is being served. Buildings, roads, bridges, airplanes, and ships are examples of the types of large products that are typically constructed using a fixed-position layout (see Exhibit 9.3D). Many service companies also use fixed-position layouts; for example, a plumber goes to a job site bringing the tools, material, and expertise needed to repair a broken pipe.

fixed-position layout
Method of arranging a facility so that the product is stationary and equipment and personnel come to it

Routing is the task of specifying the sequence of operations and the path through the facility that the work will take. The way production is routed depends on the type of product and the layout of the plant. A table-manufacturing company, for instance, uses a process layout because it has three departments, each handling a different phase of the table's manufacture and each equipped with specialized tools, machines, and employees. Department 1 cuts wood into tabletops and legs. These pieces are then sent to department 2, where holes are drilled and rough finishing is done. Finally, the individual pieces are routed to department 3, where the tables are assembled and painted.

Scheduling Work

In any production process, managers must use *scheduling*—determining how long each operation takes and setting a starting and ending time for each. A master schedule, often called a *master production schedule (MPS),* is a schedule of planned completion of items. In services such as a doctor's office, the appointment book serves as the master schedule.

When a job has relatively few activities and relationships, many production managers keep the process on schedule with a **Gantt chart**. Developed by Henry L. Gantt in the early 1900s, the Gantt chart is a bar chart showing the amount of time required to accomplish each part of a process. It allows managers to see at a glance whether the process is in line with the schedule they had planned (see Exhibit 9.4).

Gantt chart
Bar chart used to control schedules by showing how long each part of a production process should take and when it should take place

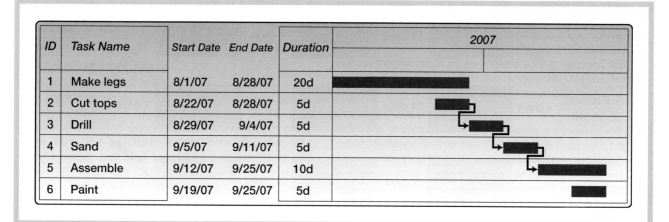

ID	Task Name	Start Date	End Date	Duration	2007
1	Make legs	8/1/07	8/28/07	20d	
2	Cut tops	8/22/07	8/28/07	5d	
3	Drill	8/29/07	9/4/07	5d	
4	Sand	9/5/07	9/11/07	5d	
5	Assemble	9/12/07	9/25/07	10d	
6	Paint	9/19/07	9/25/07	5d	

Exhibit 9.4
A Gantt Chart
A chart like this one enables a production manager to immediately see the dates on which production steps must be started and completed if goods are to be delivered on schedule. Some steps may overlap to save time. For instance, after three weeks of cutting table legs, cutting tabletops begins. This overlap ensures that the necessary legs and tops are completed at the same time and can move on together to the next stage in the manufacturing process.

computers can access each other's databases to get whatever information they need.) Because EDI and XML can solve the same problems, supply-chain managers in many companies are now faced with the dilemma of which technology to use. XML promises to be less expensive and easier to implement, but EDI is firmly entrenched in thousands of companies around the world. As a result, XML will likely be used in most new systems, but some companies will continue to invest in EDI, and both schemes will coexist in the supply chain for years to come.[37]

Managing and Controlling the Production Process

During the production design phase, operations managers establish the supply chain, forecast demand, plan for capacity, choose facility locations, design facility layouts and configurations, and develop production schedules and sequences. With the process in place, now it's time to "flip the switch" and start producing goods and services. Two major responsibilities at this point are coordinating the supply chain and assuring product quality.

Coordinating the Supply Chain

By now you have a sense of how many pieces must fit together—in the right place, at the right time—for successful production. Unfortunately, you can't just pile up huge quantities of everything you might eventually need because **inventory**, the goods and materials kept in stock for production or sale, costs money to purchase and store. On the other hand, not having an adequate supply of inventory can delay production and result in unhappy customers. That's why more and more companies are changing the way they purchase and handle the materials they use to produce goods and services.

Purchasing, or *procurement*, is the acquisition of the raw materials, parts, components, supplies, and finished products required to produce goods and services. The goal of purchasing is to make sure that the company has all of the materials it needs, when it needs them, at the lowest possible cost. To accomplish this goal, a company must always have enough supplies on hand to cover a product's *lead time*—the period that elapses between placing the supply order and receiving materials. This balancing act is the job of **inventory control**, which tries to determine the right quantities of supplies and products to have on hand, then tracks where those items are.

LEARNING OBJECTIVE 6

Explain the strategic importance of managing inventory

inventory
Goods kept in stock for the production process or for sales to final customers

purchasing
Acquiring the raw materials, parts, components, supplies, and finished products needed to produce goods and services

inventory control
System for determining the right quantity of various items to have on hand and keeping track of their location, use, and condition

---

Today's supply chains often span the globe, pulling in parts and materials from multiple countries.

Simply controlling what's in inventory is not enough for many companies, however, and over the years, operations specialists have developed several approaches to coordinating the supply chain, including *just-in-time systems, material requirements planning, manufacturing resource planning,* and *supply-chain management.*

Just-in-Time Systems **Just-in-time (JIT)** systems are designed to have only the right amounts of materials arrive at precisely the times they are needed. Because supplies arrive just as they are needed, and no sooner, inventories are theoretically eliminated and waste is reduced. Reducing stocks of parts to practically nothing also encourages factories to keep production flowing smoothly, from beginning to end, without any holdups. And a constant production flow requires good teamwork. On the other hand, JIT exposes a company to greater risks, as a disruption in the flow of raw materials from suppliers can slow or stop the production process. A JIT system also places a heavy burden on suppliers because they must be able to meet the production schedules of their customers.

Thus, to be effective, JIT systems must be designed to include multifunctional teamwork, flexible manufacturing, small-batch production, strict production control, quick setups, consistent production levels, preventive maintenance, and reliable supplier networks. Furthermore, poor quality simply cannot be tolerated in a stockless manufacturing environment because one defective part can bring production to a halt. In other words, JIT cannot be implemented without a commitment to total quality control.[38] When all of these factors work in sync, the manufacturer achieves *lean production,* improving productivity and quality while reducing defects.[39]

However, efforts to achieve lean production can collide with efforts to offer mass customization. Predicting material needs is easy when you know exactly what you're going to be building next week or next month, but it's more challenging when customers can visit your website and order personalized versions of your products at all hours of the day and night. Toyota, one of the pioneers of the JIT concept, is now adapting its vaunted lean production system to make it easier for buyers to order customized cars and trucks. Because the various options on the 10 models Toyota builds in North America add up to some 60,000 possible combinations, the company spent several years developing sophisticated software that analyzes each custom order, estimates how quickly the right components can be pulled together, and determines the effect the production of each custom order will have on the rest of the manufacturing flow. Toyota's goal is to strike a balance, maintaining the efficiency of its operations while offering customized models with only a reasonable waiting period.[40]

Material Requirements Planning **Material requirements planning (MRP)** is another inventory-control technique that helps a manufacturer get the correct materials where they are needed, when they are needed, and without unnecessary stockpiling. Managers use computer programs to calculate when certain materials will be required, when they should be ordered, and when they should be delivered so that storage costs will be minimal. These systems are so effective at reducing inventory levels that they are used almost universally in both large and small manufacturing firms.

A more automated form of material requirements planning is the *perpetual inventory system,* in which computers monitor inventory levels and automatically generate purchase orders when supplies fall below a certain level. The price scanners found at the checkout counters of many stores are part of perpetual inventory systems. Every time a product is purchased, the scanner deletes that particular item from the computer system's inventory data. When inventory of the product reaches a predetermined level, the system generates an order for more. Often, the store's system is linked to the supplier's own computer system, which enables the order to be placed with virtually no human involvement.

Manufacturing Resource Planning The MRP systems on the market today are made up of various modules, including inventory control, purchasing, customer order entry, production planning, shop-floor control, and accounting. With the addition of more and more modules that focus on capacity planning, marketing, and finance, an MRP system evolves into a **manufacturing resource planning (MRP II)** system.

L E A R N I N G
O B J E C T I V E 7

Distinguish among JIT, MRP, and MRP II inventory management systems

just-in-time (JIT)
Continuous system that pulls materials through the production process, making sure that all materials arrive just when they are needed with minimal inventory and waste

material requirements planning (MRP)
Method of getting the correct materials where they are needed, on time, and without carrying unnecessary inventory

manufacturing resource planning (MRP II)
Computer-based system that integrates data from all departments to manage inventory and production planning and control

INNOVATING FOR BUSINESS SUCCESS

YOUR INVENTORY WANTS TO TALK TO YOU

Next time you find yourself digging under the sofa to find the remote control for your TV or excavating your desk to find batteries for your calculator, imagine what it's like trying to keep track of a thousand remote controls or a million batteries. That's the challenge faced by manufacturers, distributors, and retailers throughout the supply chain: keeping track of inventory as it travels around inside companies, transfers between companies, waits in warehouses and stockrooms, and sits on retail shelves as it tries to catch a shopper's eye—and tries to protect itself from the occasional shopper or employee in search of a five-finger discount.

The electronic solution to this Herculean challenge is *radio frequency identification (RFID)*, a technology that combines a small antenna and a microchip in a *tag* that is attached to either individual products or cases and containers of products and a *reader* that scans for any tags within a given area. Think of RFID as the next generation of barcodes that you see scanned when you pass through a checkout line, with two important differences: (1) RFID readers don't need to physically "see" each item in the same way that barcode scanners do, and (2) RFID tags carry much more information than simple barcodes can, including where and when the product was manufactured, how long it has sat on store shelves, whether it's beyond its expiration date, when it needs to be reordered, and even whether it's been misplaced or stolen.

This seemingly simple capability of knowing which products are where, without manually inspecting every single item, has profound implications for inventory management, information systems, and personal privacy. In an RFID-enabled supply chain, truckloads of products can announce their arrival to workers on the loading dock.

Readers can then automatically record every time these items are moved, and missing items can be located quickly by tracking their electronic fingerprints. Empty store shelves signal when it's time to haul out a few more cases from the stockroom, and when inventories run low vendors receive an automated announcement that it's time to ship more product.

RFID is just beginning to have an impact in a number of industries. Widespread implementation will require companies that use it to weave this new data stream into existing transaction processing systems (RFID can inundate an information system with billions of new data points) and address privacy concerns (such as assuring customers that they won't be tracked and monitored once they leave the store). Suppliers of RFID technology also need to reduce the price of the tags themselves in order to make it a cost-effective alternative to simply barcodes. All these efforts are gaining steam, though, thanks in large part to the push from Wal-Mart. The country's largest retailer has a strong record of making intelligent investments in technologies that reduce costs and increase sales. After testing RFID technology in a handful of stores, Wal-Mart began rolling it out on a wider scale in 2005 and continues to work with suppliers to help them implement RFID with their products. RFID may never help you find the remote, but it'll soon be helping thousands of companies keep track of their essential goods.

Questions for Critical Thinking

1. How can RFID tags help companies manage their inventory?
2. What effect will RFID likely have on the managers and employees of retail companies?

---

enterprise resource planning (ERP)
A comprehensive database system that expands beyond the production function to include other groups such as sales and accounting

Because it draws together all departments, an MRP II system produces a company-wide game plan that allows everyone to work with the same numbers (see Exhibit 9.6). Employees can now draw on data, such as inventory levels, back orders, and unpaid bills, once reserved for only top executives. Moreover, the system can track each step of production, allowing managers throughout the company to consult other managers' inventories, schedules, and plans. In addition, MRP II systems are capable of running simulations (models of possible operations systems) that enable managers to plan and test alternative strategies.[41] Many companies have extended the MRP II concept to include functions outside of manufacturing, such as accounting and sales, an approach known as **enterprise resource planning (ERP)**.

Exhibit 9.6
MRP II

An MRP II computer system gives managers and workers in every department easy access to data from all other departments, which in turn makes it easier to generate—and adhere to—the organization's overall plans, forecasts, and schedules.

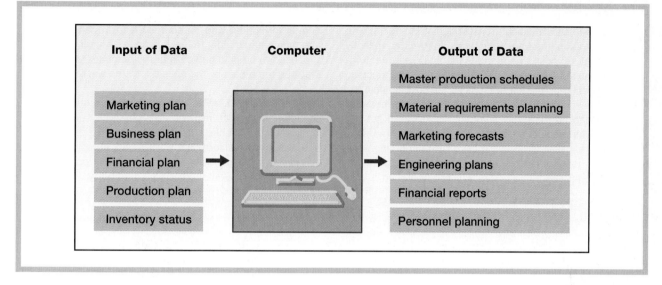

Supply-Chain Management Whereas MRP II and ERP seek to incorporate more functions with the business, **supply-chain management (SCM)**, focuses on the movement and coordination of goods, services, information, and capabilities all the way through the supply chain, from raw materials to finished products delivered to the final consumer.[42] SCM combines business procedures and policies with a comprehensive software solution that integrates the various elements of the supply chain into a cohesive system, even if the supply chain involves a wide variety of outside suppliers and distribution partners. (ERP and SCM are similar in many respects, and the terminology in the industry can be rather confusing; for instance, vendors of ERP software are adding modules that handle SCM tasks.[43])

Although SCM sounds like basic inventory control on the surface, it has the potential to have a much more profound strategic impact on companies in three important ways:[44]

- *Managing risks.* SCM can help companies manage the complex risks involved in a supply chain, risks that include everything from cost and availability to health and safety issues.
- *Managing relationships.* It can also coordinate the numerous relationships in the supply chain and help managers focus their attention on the most important company-to-company relationships. For instance, General Motors buys massive quantities of both steel and aluminum, but the nature of the two markets puts a higher priority on GM's relationship with its aluminum supplier, Alcan. GM uses SCM to forge a close relationship with Alcan, including stabilizing prices in ways that help both companies.
- *Managing trade-offs.* Finally, SCM helps managers address the many trade-offs in the supply chain. These trade-offs can be a source of conflict within the company, and SCM helps balance the competing interests of the various functional areas. This holistic view helps managers balance both capacity and capability along the entire chain. For instance, to deliver a complex, multiple-computer system to a customer, Sun Microsystems used to consolidate all the components at a staging facility, then repackage the entire system and have it shipped to the customer. After analyzing the time and cost involved, the company realized it made more sense to have Federal Express take care of the consolidation, in addition to the shipping.[45]

Successful applications of SCM can yield increased sales, cost savings, inventory reductions, improved quality, accelerated delivery time, and improved customer service.[46] In fact, the potential of SCM is so great that businesses now spend roughly $20 billion a year on SCM software and related technology. Unfortunately, nearly half the companies in one recent survey

supply-chain management (SCM)
An approach to coordinating and optimizing the flow of goods, services, information, and capabilities throughout the entire supply chain, including outside business partners

LEARNING FROM BUSINESS BLUNDERS

OOPS A freelance medical transcriptionist (someone who types doctors' notes from audiotapes) in Pakistan recently threatened to post confidential medical records from patients at the University of California at San Francisco Medical Center on the Internet unless the hospital paid her for her transcription work. The hospital had never heard of her and had no idea how someone in Pakistan got her hands on its medical records in the first place. The solution to this mystery? It was a case of outsourcing gone mad: The hospital first outsourced the project to a company called Transcription Stat, which outsourced it to a

woman in Florida, who outsourced it to a man in Texas, who then outsourced it to the woman in Pakistan (who was supposed to be paid one-sixth of the amount Transcription Stat was to be paid by the hospital, by the way).

WHAT YOU CAN LEARN Whenever work is outsourced, particularly when it involves something as sensitive as medical records, make sure you know where it's going and who's going to perform the work. Many outsourcers put clauses in their contracts that specifically prohibit the work from being re-outsourced to a third party.

said they were disappointed in their SCM efforts. Some experts pin the blame on the approach people take to SCM, not on the concept itself. To ensure success, managers need to view SCM at a strategic level, look at trade-offs across the entire supply chain, and make sure that the various groups in the chain have the training and tools required to cooperate effectively.[47]

Assuring Product Quality

LEARNING OBJECTIVE 8

Highlight the differences between quality control and quality assurance

Besides maintaining optimal inventory levels, companies today must produce high-quality goods and services as efficiently as possible. In almost every industry you can name, this global challenge has caused companies to re-examine their definition of quality and re-engineer their production processes. In some industries, quality is literally a matter of life and death. Nearly 100,000 deaths in the United States every year are attributed to medical errors; in Canada, a quarter of all patients who seek medical care wind up getting another illness as a result of medical mistakes.[48]

As companies try to compete with lower prices, more sophisticated products, or sometimes both at once, the strain on quality can be considerable. In a recent survey, *Consumer Reports* found that the least reliable sedan sold in the United States is the sumptuous, $100,000 S-Class Mercedes (Daimler-Benz, the manufacturer, vigorously disputes the survey results). High up on the list were two other Mercedes models and a pair of BMWs. How could cars from companies that are the very epitome of quality have so many problems? Some observers say it is because the cars have become too complex, with too many automated systems and too much software—too many things to go wrong, in other words.[49]

quality control
Routine checking and testing of a finished product for quality against an established standard

quality assurance
System of policies, practices, and procedures implemented throughout the company to create and produce quality goods and services

The traditional means of maintaining quality is called **quality control**—measuring quality against established standards after the good or service has been produced and weeding out any defects. A more comprehensive approach is **quality assurance**, a system of companywide policies, practices, and procedures to ensure that every product meets preset quality standards. Quality assurance includes quality control as well as doing the job right the first time by designing tools and machinery properly, demanding quality parts from suppliers, encouraging customer feedback, training employees, empowering them, and encouraging them to take pride in their work. In 1999, Hyundai chairman Chung Mong Koo set out to improve the automaker's rather dismal quality record, with the goal of equaling Toyota within five years. Some of the many steps he took included creating a "quality team" of 865 employees who have the authority to stop production if they find problems, training nearly every employee in the company on quality methods, and conducting frequent meetings in which Hyundai models are compared in close detail with competitors' cars. Sure enough, by 2004, Hyundai was in a second-place tie with Toyota in the widely respected J.D. Powers survey of initial quality.[50]

Statistical Quality Control and Continuous Improvement Quality assurance also includes the now widely used concept of **statistical quality control (SQC)**, in which all aspects of the production process are monitored so that managers can see whether the process is operating as it should. The primary tool of SQC is **statistical process control (SPC)**, which involves taking samples from the process periodically and plotting observations of the samples on a *control chart*. A large enough sample provides a reasonable estimate of the entire process. By observing the random fluctuations graphed on the chart, you can identify whether such changes are normal or whether they indicate that some corrective action is required in the process.[51]

In addition to using SQC, companies can empower each employee to continuously improve the quality of goods production or service delivery. The Japanese word for continuous improvement is *kaizen*. Japanese manufacturers learned long before many U.S. manufacturers that continuous improvement is not something that can be delegated to one or a few people. Instead, it requires the full participation of every employee. This approach means encouraging all workers to spot quality problems, halt production when necessary, generate ideas for improvement, and adjust work routines as needed.[52]

Total Quality Management and Six Sigma The most comprehensive approach to quality is known as **total quality management (TQM)**, which is both a management philosophy and a strategic management process that focuses on delivering the optimal level of quality to customers by building quality into every organizational activity (see Exhibit 9.7). Implementing TQM requires six elements:[53]

- Management commitment to supporting TQM at every level in the organization
- Clear focus on customers and their needs
- Employee involvement throughout the organization
- Commitment to continuous improvement
- Willingness to treat suppliers as partners
- Meaningful performance measurements

TQM was one of the hot management topics in the 1980s and 1990s, and some businesses that tried to establish TQM failed, for reasons ranging from an inability to change the corporate culture to ineffective measurement techniques.[54] TQM doesn't receive the attention that it once did in the business media, either, and some observers now dismiss it as another management fad that came and went. However, the principles of TQM infuse much of today's managerial practice, even if managers don't always use the TQM label.[55]

An alternative approach to focusing an organization on quality processes and products is **Six Sigma**, which began as a statistical approach to eliminating defects but has evolved into a "fully integrated management system" that "aligns business strategy with improvement efforts," in the words of Motorola, where the concept was first formalized. (*Six sigma* is a statistical term that indicates 3.4 defects per million opportunities—near perfection, in other words.) Six Sigma is a highly disciplined, systematic approach to reducing the deviation from desired goals in virtually any business process, whether it's eliminating defects in the creation of a product or improving a company's cash flow.[56] Six Sigma efforts typically follow a five-step approach, known as DMAIC for short:[57]

1. **D**efine the problem that needs to solved
2. **M**easure current performance to see how far it deviates from desired performance
3. **A**nalyze the root causes of this deviation from the ideal
4. **I**mprove the process by brainstorming, selecting, and implementing changes
5. **C**ontrol the process long-term to make sure performance continues to meet expectations

statistical quality control (SQC)
Monitoring all aspects of the production process to see whether the process is operating as it should

statistical process control (SPC)
Use of random sampling and control charts to monitor the production process

total quality management (TQM)
A management philosophy and strategic management process that focuses on delivering the optimal level of quality to customers by building quality into every organizational activity

Six Sigma
A quality management program that strives to eliminate deviations between the actual and desired performance of a business system

Exhibit 9.7
Total Quality
Management
These 14 points, based on the work of W. Edwards Deming, can help managers improve their goods and services through total quality management (TQM).

1. **Create constancy of purpose for the improvement of goods and services.**

   The organization should constantly strive to improve quality, productivity, and consumer satisfaction to improve performance today and tomorrow.

2. **Adopt a new philosophy to reject mistakes and negativism.**

   Customers, managers, and employees all need to change their attitudes toward unacceptable work quality and sullen service.

3. **Cease dependence on mass inspection.**

   Instead of inspecting products after production to weed out bad quality, improve the process to build in good quality.

4. **End the practice of awarding business on price alone.**

   Create long-term relationships with suppliers who can deliver the best quality.

5. **Improve constantly and forever the system of production and service.**

   Improvement is not a one-time effort; managers must lead the way to continuous improvement of quality, productivity, and customer satisfaction.

6. **Institute training.**

   Train all organization members to do their jobs consistently well.

7. **Institute leadership.**

   Managers must provide the leadership to help employees do a better job.

8. **Drive out fear.**

   Create an atmosphere in which employees are not afraid to ask questions or to point out problems.

9. **Break down barriers between units.**

   Ensure that people in organizational departments or units do not have conflicting goals and are able to work as a team to achieve overall goals.

10. **Eliminate slogans, exhortations, and targets for the workforce.**

    These alone cannot help anyone do a better job, and they imply that employees could do better if they tried harder; instead, management should provide methods for improvement.

11. **Eliminate numerical quotas.**

    Quotas count only finished units, not quality or methods, and they generally lead to defective goods, wasted resources, and demoralized employees.

12. **Remove barriers to pride in work.**

    Most people want to do a good job but are prevented from doing so by misguided management, poor communication, faulty equipment, defective materials, and other barriers that managers must remove to improve quality.

13. **Institute a vigorous program of education and retraining.**

    Both managers and employees have to be educated in the new quality methods.

14. **Take action to accomplish the transformation.**

    With top-management commitment, have the courage to make the changes throughout the organization that will improve quality.

Six Sigma shares the same focus on the customer and emphasis on employee involvement as TQM, but provides a simpler and widely accepted set of methods for business teams to follow. Thousands of companies now use Six Sigma in various guises, and a small industry of consultants and trainers has grown up around it.

Global Quality Standards In addition to meeting the quality expectations of their customers, many companies now face the need to meet international quality standards as well. For instance, many companies in Europe require that suppliers comply with standards set by the International Organization for Standardization (ISO), a nongovernment entity based in Geneva, Switzerland. ISO oversees a vast array of product standards, but the two of most general concern to businesses are the *ISO 9000* family, which concerns quality and customer satisfaction, and *ISO 14000*, which concerns environmental issues. More than 600,000 organizations in over 150 countries have now implemented ISO standards, making it a universally recognized indicator of compliance. The ISO 9000 and ISO 14000 families both focus on management systems, the processes and policies that companies use to create their goods and services, rather than on the goods and services themselves. Achieving ISO certification sends a reassuring signal to other companies that your internal processes meet these widely accepted international standards.[58]

ISO standards help companies become *world-class manufacturers,* a term used to describe the level of quality and operational effectiveness that puts a company among the top performers in the world. Some companies view ISO standards as a starting point to achieving national quality awards such as Japan's Deming Prize, a highly regarded industrial quality award, or the U.S. Malcolm Baldrige National Quality Award, which honors the quality achievements of companies. Of course, even if an organization doesn't want to actually apply for an award, it can improve quality by measuring its performance against an award's standards and working to overcome any problems uncovered by this process.

CRITICAL THINKING CHECKPOINT
1. Would a just-in-time approach to inventory be a wise choice for a hospital? Why or why not?
2. Why is quality assurance considered a more effective long-term approach than quality control?
3. Why is employee involvement a critical part of total quality management?

CHECKLIST: Apply These Ideas When You're the Boss

✓ Periodically examine every aspect of your production operations, looking for opportunities to reduce costs, create new sales, and build competitive advantage.

✓ Be sure to include your entire value chain when you try to improve operations; everything from hiring policies to accounting practices can help—or hurt—your ability to produce quality goods and services.

✓ If you're in a services business, keep an eye on emerging technologies that might help you create new or improved services at lower costs.

✓ Mass customization will continue to influence a wide variety of consumer and commercial markets; look for ways to build competitive advantages by efficiently creating unique products and services.

✓ Always consider outsourcing when developing production strategies; it might not be the right choice in every case, but the advantages are often compelling.

✓ At the same time, don't be blind to the potential disadvantages of outsourcing and offshoring; cost is not the only factor to consider.

✓ Follow the example of industry leaders in treating the supply chain as a major strategic element in any production operation.

✓ Recognize the importance—and difficulty—of both demand forecasting and capacity planning.

✓ Don't think you're too small to learn from industry giants such as Wal-Mart, Toyota, and Dell; you can always learn something from their investments in and experiments with new techniques and technologies.

Summary of Learning Objectives

1 **Explain what production and operations managers do.** Production and operations managers design and oversee an efficient conversion process—the sequence of events that convert resources into goods and services. To do this, they must coordinate a firm's resources and optimize output from each resource. Additionally, production and operations managers perform the four basic functions of planning, organizing, leading, and controlling, but the focus of these activities is the production of a company's goods and services.

2 **Outline the unique challenges of delivering quality services.** The perishable and intangible nature of services presents a number of challenges: (1) customers are often involved in and can affect the quality of service delivery; (2) most services cannot be created in advance and stored in inventory awaiting sale, so creation and consumption usually happen simultaneously; (3) services are usually people-intensive; (4) customers often dictate when and where services should be performed; and (5) service quality can be more subjective than goods quality.

3 **Identify key tasks involved in designing a production process.** Managers must first prepare production forecasts, or estimates of future demand for the company's products. Next they must consider capacity, which is a business's volume of manufacturing or service delivery. The next step is to find a facility location that minimizes regional costs (land, construction, labor, local taxes, leasing, energy), transportation costs, and raw materials costs. Once a location has been selected, managers need to consider facility layout—the arrangement of production work centers and other facilities (such as material, equipment, and support departments) needed for the processing of goods and services. Finally, managers must develop a master production schedule.

4 **Define the supply chain and distinguish it from the value chain.** The supply chain consists of all companies involved in making a finished product. The members of the chain vary according to the nature of the operation and the type of product but typically include suppliers, manufacturers, distributors, and retail outlets. In contrast, the value chain represents all the business functions that support the process of transforming inputs into finished outputs (the goods and services that customers buy). For instance, the accounting function is part of the value chain because it provides necessary support to the transformation process, but accounting isn't part of the supply chain.

5 **Discuss the role of computers and automation technology in production.** Computers and automation technology improve the production process in several ways: (1) Robots perform repetitive or mundane tasks quickly and with great precision; (2) CAD and CAE systems allow engineers to design and test virtual models of products; (3) CAM systems easily translate CAD data into production instructions; (4) CIM systems link the people, machines, databases, and decisions involved in each step of producing a good; and (5) flexible manufacturing systems (FMSs) reduce setup costs and time by linking programmable, multifunctional machine tools through a computer network and an automated materials-handling system.

6 **Explain the strategic importance of managing inventory.** The goods and materials kept in stock for production or sale make up inventory, which must be managed to minimize costs and ensure that the right supplies are in the right place at the right time. Having too much inventory is costly and increases the risk that products will become obsolete. Having too little inventory can result in production delays and unfilled orders.

7 **Distinguish among JIT, MRP, and MRP II inventory management systems.** Just-in-time (JIT) systems reduce waste and improve quality by producing only enough to fill orders when they are due, thus eliminating finished-goods inventory. Furthermore, under the JIT system, parts or materials are ordered only when they are needed, thus eliminating supplies inventories. Material requirements planning (MRP) and perpetual inventory systems are used to determine when materials are needed, when they should be ordered, and when they should be delivered. A more advanced system is manufacturing resource planning (MRP II), which brings together data from all parts of a company (including financial, design, and engineering departments) to better manage inventory and production planning and control.

8 **Highlight the differences between quality control and quality assurance.** Quality control focuses on measuring finished products against a preset standard and weeding out any defects. On the other hand, quality assurance is a system of companywide policies, practices, and procedures that build quality into a product and ensure that each product meets quality standards.

Carvin Guitars: What's Next?

Carvin continues to emphasize its customized guitar business and its proud heritage as an American manufacturer, but even it has joined the outsourcing and offshoring parade. In order to offer customers a slightly less expensive line of standard guitars (customization isn't available on these models), Carvin turned to a subcontractor in South Korea, a country that is rapidly building a reputation for producing top-quality musical instruments. This line of guitars is built to Carvin's demanding specifications, then the almost-finished products are sent to Carvin's customizers at headquarters in San Diego for final tune-up. Judging from overwhelmingly positive customer feedback, the dual strategy of mass production in South Korea and mass customization in the United States seems to be paying off.[59]

Critical Thinking Questions

1. If Carvin wanted to benchmark its manufacturing against other guitar makers but was unable to visit other factories, what steps could it take to measure its quality relative to the competitors?

2. If Carvin experienced an increase in orders from its website over a period of two weeks, should it expand its production capacity to make sure it can handle increased demand in the future? Why or why not?

3. Wooden musical instruments have been carved by hand for hundreds of years. Why wouldn't Carvin want to continue this tradition?

Learn More Online

Visit the Carvin website by clicking on the hotlink at Chapter 9 of this text's website at **www.prenhall.com/bovee**. How does the company promote its customized products? How does it use e-commerce technology to simplify the shopping experience? Take the virtual factory tour to see both computer-controlled machinery and guitar builders in action. Visit the discussion boards; what are Carvin customers talking about these days?

Key Terms

analytic system (292)
capacity planning (298)
cellular layout (301)
computer-aided design (CAD) (304)
computer-aided engineering (CAE) (304)
computer-aided manufacturing (CAM) (304)
computer-integrated manufacturing (CIM) (304)
critical path (302)
customized production (293)
electronic data interchange (EDI) (305)
enterprise resource planning (ERP) (308)
fixed-position layout (301)
Gantt chart (301)

inventory (306)
inventory control (306)
just-in-time (JIT) systems (307)
manufacturing resource planning (MRP II) (307)
mass customization (294)
mass production (293)
material requirements planning (MRP) (307)
process layout (299)
product layout (299)
product lifecycle management (PLM) (304)
production (291)
production and operations management (POM) (291)
production forecasts (297)
productivity (291)

program evaluation and review technique (PERT) (302)
purchasing (306)
quality assurance (310)
quality control (310)
Six Sigma (311)
statistical process control (SPC) (311)
statistical quality control (SQC) (311)
supply chain (297)
supply-chain management (SCM) (309)
synthetic system (292)
total quality management (TQM) (311)
value chain (291)

Test Your Knowledge

Questions for Review

1. What is the conversion process?
2. What is mass customization?
3. What factors need to be considered when selecting a site for a production facility?
4. Why is an effective system of inventory control important to every manufacturer?
5. Why might a company want to outsource its manufacturing function?

Questions for Analysis

6. Why is capacity planning an important part of designing operations?
7. How do JIT systems go beyond simply controlling inventory?
8. Why have companies moved beyond quality control to quality assurance?
9. How can supply chain management (SCM) help a company establish a competitive advantage?
10. **Ethical Considerations.** How does society's concern for the environment affect a company's decisions about facility location and layout?

Questions for Application

11. Assume you are the production manager for a small machine shop that manufactures precision parts for industrial equipment. How can you use CAD, CAE, CAM, CIM, FMS, and EDI or XML to manufacture better parts more easily?
12. If your final product requires several unique subunits that are all produced with different machinery and in differing lengths of time, what facility layout will you choose and why?
13. **Integrated.** Review the discussion of franchises in Chapter 6. From an operational perspective, why is purchasing a franchise such as Wendy's or Jiffy Lube an attractive alternative for starting a business?
14. **Integrated.** Review the discussion of corporate cultures in Chapter 7. What things could you learn about a company's culture by observing the layout and design of its production facility? Discuss both goods and services operations.

Practice Your Knowledge

Handling Difficult Situations on the Job: Giving Suppliers a Report Card

Just when you thought there was nothing left to measure and evaluate, your boss at Microsoft, Roxanna Frost, suggested something new. Frost, who is the program manager for Microsoft's Executive Management and Development Group, thinks that, like employees who get performance reviews, suppliers also need improved clarity in terms of goals and expectations, accomplishments, and improvements. "There's a gap between what we want our suppliers to do and the feedback they're getting," says Frost.

Thinking about this observation, you realize that 60 percent of the employee services your group monitors (travel assistance, retirement plans, the library at Microsoft's Redmond, Washington, campus) are outsourced to independent suppliers. This is nothing unusual at Microsoft, where many departments outsource both goods and services. What is new is Frost's idea of providing suppliers with performance feedback.

Frost suggested at a recent meeting that it would be a good idea to periodically evaluate all the outside suppliers that serve the company. When she asks for a volunteer to coordinate this new project, you raise your hand. This is just the kind of challenge you relish.[60]

Your task: To get the project underway, you'll first need to resolve several issues. For instance, what criteria should Microsoft departments use for evaluating suppliers? List four to six of these criteria (such as on-time delivery). How often should suppliers be evaluated? Why? What response should Microsoft expect from suppliers after their evaluation? What will you do to encourage positive responses?

Sharpening Your Communication Skills

As the newly hired manager of Campus Athletics—a shop featuring athletic wear bearing logos of colleges and universities—you are responsible for selecting the store's suppliers. Merchandise with team logos and brands can be very trendy. When a college team is hot, you've got to have merchandise. You know that selecting the right supplier is a task that requires careful consideration, so you have decided to host a series of selection interviews. Think about all the qualities you would want in a supplier, and develop a list of interview questions that will help you assess whether that supplier possesses those qualities.

Building Your Team Skills

Facility layout is one of the most critical decisions production managers must make. In this exercise, you and your team are playing the role of production managers for the following companies, some producing a specific good and some producing a specific service:

- PepsiCo—soft drinks
- H&R Block—tax consultation
- Bob Mackie—custom-made clothing
- Burger King—fast food
- Boeing—commercial jets
- Massachusetts General Hospital—medical services
- Hewlett-Packard—personal computers
- Toyota—sport-utility vehicles

For each company on the list, discuss and recommend a specific facility layout, referring to Exhibit 9.3 for an overview of the four layouts. Why does your team believe the recommended layout is best suited to the product or service each company produces? How would the recommended layouts affect the movement of resources and inventory for the manufacturers on the list? How would the layouts affect customer interaction for the service providers on the list?

Expand Your Knowledge

Discovering Career Opportunities

Whether you prefer to work with products or services, many possible careers await you in production and operations. From input to transformation to output, companies are looking for resourceful, results-oriented employees able to meet the demands of ever-changing schedules and specifications. Start your research by scanning the help-wanted classified and display ads in your local newspaper and in the *Wall Street Journal*; also check help-wanted ads in business magazines such as *Industry Week*. Go online and search the production and manufacturing jobs listed in America's Job Bank, www.ajb.org, or Monster, www.monster.com.

1. As you read through these want ads, note all the production-related job titles you find. How many of these jobs include quality or technology (or both) among the duties and responsibilities?
2. Select two job openings that interest you. Reread the ads for those jobs to find out what kind of work experience and educational background are required. What further preparation will you need to qualify for these jobs?
3. Assume you have the qualifications for the two jobs you have selected. What keywords should you include on your electronic résumé to show the employers that you are a good job candidate?

Developing Your Research Skills

Seeking increased efficiency and productivity, a growing number of producers of goods and services are applying technology to improve the production process. Find an article in business journals or newspapers (print or online edition) that discusses how one company used CAD, CAE, robots, XML, or other technological innovations to refit or reorganize its production operations.

1. What problems led the company to rethink its production process? What kind of technology did it choose to address these problems? What goals did the company set for applying technology in this way?
2. Before adding the new technology, what did the company do to analyze its existing production process? What changes, if any, were made as a result of this analysis?

3. How did technology-enhanced production help the company achieve its goals for financial performance? For customer service? For growth or expansion?

Exploring the Best of the Web

URLs for all Internet exercises are provided at the website for this book, www.prenhall.com/bovee. When you log on to this text's Companion Website, select Chapter 9. Then select "Featured Websites," click on the name of the featured website, and review the website to complete these exercises.

Explore these chapter-related websites, review their content, and answer the following questions for each website you visit:

1. What is the purpose of this website?
2. What kinds of information does this website contain? Please be specific.
3. How is the information provided at this website useful for businesspeople? Consumers?
4. How did you expand your knowledge of economics by reviewing the material at this website? What new things did you learn about this topic?

Step Inside ISO Online

The International Organization for Standardization (ISO) is a worldwide federation of national standards bodies from some 130 countries, one from each country. Established in 1947, ISO is a nongovernmental organization with the following mission: to promote the development of standardization and related activities in the world with a view to facilitating the international exchange of goods and services and to developing cooperation in the spheres of intellectual, scientific, technological, and economic activity. Step inside ISO Online and take a closer look at how ISO standards are developed, why international standardization is needed, and what fields are covered by ISO standards. www.iso.ch

Make Quality Count

In today's competitive business environment, companies have to be concerned about the quality of their goods and services. For information and advice, many turn to the American Society for Quality (ASQ). There you can find out about ISO 9000 and the Malcolm Baldrige Award. Find out who Malcolm Baldrige was and why the award was established. Discover how winning companies are selected, which companies have won the award, and how the award differs from ISO 9000. Follow the links to other quality-related websites. At the ASQ, quality is only a click away. www.asq.org

Follow This Path to Continuous Improvement

The business of manufacturing is more complex than ever before. Today's operations managers must address the conflicting needs of customers, suppliers, employees, and shareholders. Discover why many operations managers turn to *IndustryWeek* magazine to stay on top of trends, technologies, and strategies to help drive continuous improvement throughout their organization. Log on to this magazine's website and read about the world's best-managed companies. Find out which manufacturing plants have won awards. Check out the surveys and special industry reports. Take a peek at the factories of the future. Don't leave without browsing the current articles or reviewing the glossary of manufacturing terms. www.industryweek.com

Learning Interactively

Companion Website

Visit the Companion Website at www.prenhall.com/bovee. For Chapter 9, take advantage of the interactive "Learning Modules" to test your chapter knowledge. Get instant feedback on whether you need additional studying. Complete the exercises as specified by your instructor.

A Case for Critical Thinking

Porsche—Back in the Fast Lane

The German automaker Porsche enjoyed a long ride of success with its sleek, high-performance sports cars, cruising straight into the hearts of both consumers and racing fans with the introduction of its first model back in 1948. Producing such classics as the 356, the 550 Spyder, and the legendary 911, Porsche garnered a winning reputation for engineering excellence and for its victories in the racing world. Owning a Porsche became the ultimate fantasy for many car lovers around the world, and the company's annual sales grew to more than 50,000 cars by the mid-1980s.

Then the recession of the early 1990s hit, and consumers postponed buying cars—especially expensive sports cars. Demand dropped sharply for Porsche's 911 model, and sales plummeted by nearly 75 percent. By the time Wendelin Wiedeking took over in 1993, Porsche was racing toward record losses of $150 million. Few people believed Wiedeking could get Porsche back on track. After all, the German engineer was the fourth person in five years to manage the company. But Wiedeking was determined to save Porsche from bankruptcy. "It was a question of 'to be or not to be'—as simple as that," Wiedeking recalls.

STEERING AWAY FROM DISASTER

To start the process of implementing changes, Wiedeking obtained benchmarks on every aspect of production by measuring the amount of time, money, and effort that was being spent on making a Porsche. Then he compared Porsche's production methods to those of Japanese automakers. After touring the production facilities of Honda, Toyota, and Nissan, Wiedeking and his managers were convinced they could apply the Japanese's lean, efficient production system at Porsche and turn the company around by slashing production costs and increasing productivity. Back at home, Wiedeking launched an improvement program to eliminate waste and to establish standards for quality and efficiency. Moreover, he paved the way for change by simplifying the management structure and assigning new responsibilities to every employee.

MEETING CHALLENGES HEAD-ON

Despite Wiedeking's efforts, Porsche's losses continued to mount. Drastic measures were needed to save the company, and Wiedeking had to act fast. He needed to overhaul the entire production system, and he needed the full cooperation of every worker to implement the changes. So he consulted a team of former Toyota managers who were experts in the concept of *kaizen*, a system developed by Toyota that emphasized continuous improvement in the quality of production.

The consultants quickly pointed out ways to save time and effort in Porsche's production assembly process. Under the existing system, for example, workers searched through shelves crammed with 30 days of inventory to find the components for assembling an engine. To save time and distance, the consultants replaced the shelves with robotic carts that carried the necessary parts for one engine straight to workers on the assembly line.

A NEW SENSE OF DIRECTION

Wiedeking worked swiftly to implement the new production methods throughout the entire assembly process. He slashed the company's spiraling costs and introduced leaner, more flexible production processes. Then to keep things even leaner, Porsche began outsourcing most of the manufacturing of its models, keeping a core set of manufacturing activities—and all of the all-important research and development—in house. The results were immediate and dramatic, slashing production time and costs while giving Porsche more flexibility to respond to shifts in market demands.

As the company began to recover, Wiedeking instructed Porsche's engineers to apply the concepts of lean production to the development process. Instead of building expensive prototypes, for instance, the engineers used computer simulation to revamp the 911 model and to design a new two-seat roadster, the Boxster. They also incorporated the 911's basic engine and parts into the new Boxster and created a common assembly line to produce the two cars, eliminating waste and saving time and money. After implementing the production changes, the company slashed production time for each 911 from 120 to 30 hours, built more engines with half the space, decreased the number of manufacturing defects, and cut its stockpiles of inventory from seven days to one. The company even established a new division, Porsche Consulting, to advise other businesses on improving productivity through lean manufacturing and efficient supply chain management. By 2003, the tenth year of Wiedeking's tenure as CEO, Porsche had boosted sales from less than 15,000 cars a year to more than 70,000 and become one of the world's most profitable car companies.

DRIVING THE FUTURE

Thanks to Wiedeking's dramatic turnaround, Porsche continues to grow and looks healthier than ever. Wiedeking's tenth anniversary as CEO was also highlighted by the introduction of the Cayenne SUV, Porsche's first foray into the family market. Many Porsche purists and insiders agonized at the idea of one of the world's great sports car companies introducing an SUV, but the Cayenne has proved to be wildly popular. Moreover, the Cayenne generates enough cash flow to fund continuing development of new sports cars. Plus, any doubts about the company's commitment to sports cars were probably erased in 2004, when the exotic Carrera GT supercar hit the streets, boasting a top speed of 205 MPH and a price tag of $440,000. Meanwhile, back on Earth, in 2005 Porsche introduced the Cayman mid-level sports car and continued churning out new variations on the venerable 911, the Cayenne, and the Boxster.

Wiedeking isn't content to rest on these successes, however, and he continues to push for productivity improvements every year. In fact, he still meets regularly with his Japanese counterparts in what he terms a friendly competition to see who can become the most productive. With an unbeatable combination of world-class research and development, high-productivity manufacturing, and the financial independence that comes with a decade of careful cash management, Wiedeking and his team at Porsche are looking at a wide-open road ahead.

Critical Thinking Questions

1. Why did Porsche run into problems during the early 1990s?
2. What steps did Wiedeking take to overhaul Porsche's production methods?
3. Why does Porsche outsource manufacturing functions to suppliers?
4. Go to Chapter 9 of this text's website at www.prenhall.com/bovee and click on the hot link to get the Porsche website. Review the website so you can answer these questions: What has Porsche learned from its past mistakes? Is Porsche prepared to meet the competitive and business challenges of the future? Does Porsche consider its relatively small company size an advantage or disadvantage? Why?

Video Case

Managing Production Around the World: Body Glove

Learning Objectives

The purpose of this video is to help you:

1. Recognize the production challenges faced by a growing company.
2. Understand the importance of quality in the production process.
3. Discuss how and why a company may shift production operations to other countries and other companies.

Synopsis

Riding the wave of public interest in water sports, Body Glove began manufacturing wet suits in the 1950s. The founders, dedicated surfers and divers, came up with the idea of making the wet suits from neoprene, offering more comfortable insulation than the rubber wet suits of the time. The high costs of neoprene and labor were major considerations in Body Glove's eventual decision to have its wet suits made in Thailand. The company's constant drive for higher quality was also a factor. Now company management can focus on building Body Glove's image as a California-lifestyle brand without worrying about inventory and other production issues. In licensing its brand for a wide range of goods and services—from cell phone cases to flotation devices, footwear, resorts, and more—Body Glove has created a network of partners around the world.

Discussion Questions

1. *For analysis:* Even though Body Glove makes its wet suits in Thailand, why must its managers continually research how U.S. customers use its products?
2. *For analysis:* Which aspects of product quality would wet suit buyers be most concerned about?
3. *For application:* When deciding whether to license its name for a new product, what production issues might Body Glove's managers research in advance?
4. *For application:* How might Body Glove's Thailand facility use forecasts of seasonal demand to plan production?
5. *For debate:* Should the products that Body Glove does not manufacture be labeled to alert buyers that they are produced under license? Support your chosen position.

Online Exploration

Visit the Body Glove website www.bodyglove.com and follow the links to read the Body Glove story and see the variety of products sold under the Body Glove brand. Also look at the electronics products, including the cell phone cases. Then browse the contacts listing to find out which U.S. and international companies have licensed the Body Glove brand for various products. How do these licensed products fit with the Body Glove brand image? What challenges might Body Glove face in coordinating its work with so many different companies and licensed products?

E-Business in Action

WHATEVER HAPPENED TO B2B EXCHANGES?

Of all the innovative ideas that bubbled up in the heady days of the dot-com boom, online business-to-business (B2B) exchanges seemed like one of the few that actually made economic sense. The idea behind these exchanges was to bring buyers and sellers together in huge online trading hubs where purchasing, selling, and other supply-chain transactions for the entire industry could take place under one virtual roof—it would all be fast, efficient, and good for just about anybody.

It sounded so good, in fact, that some 37,000 B2B exchanges opened for business by the end of 2000, serving just about every industry imaginable. Some were run by independent third parties; others were set up by industry players who joined forces to form new ventures. The two most common types of B2B exchanges are *buyer exchanges* and *supplier exchanges*. Buyer exchanges are marketplaces formed by large groups of buyers (even competitors) who purchase similar items. By joining forces and aggregating demand for a product, they can achieve economies of scale that are not possible individually. Supplier exchanges are formed by suppliers who band together to create marketplaces to sell their goods online. These groups of suppliers typically sell complementary products, offering buyers one-stop shopping for most of their needs.

Another Dot-Com Dream Up in Smoke

B2B exchanges promised to save members billions of dollars annually and to transform the way companies bought and sold. Unfortunately, nearly all of them went out of business—95 percent of them by one estimate—and only a few of the survivors have serious backing from major global corporations. Among the casualties: small exchanges such as Foodusa.com, which tried to link slaughterhouses, distributors, and brokers of beef and poultry; big exchanges such as PetroCosm, an online buying site formed by Chevron and Texaco for the petroleum industry; and Zoho.com for the hotel industry. These start-ups learned that the path to B2B prosperity was full of unanticipated roadblocks:

- *Member rivalry.* For large, public B2B exchanges to work effectively, competitors must be willing to expose business processes—processes that often give them a competitive advantage. Some companies were concerned that participation in public exchanges would put sales information and other critical data in the hands of customers and competitors. For instance, using a public exchange to purchase goods could tip a company's hand to competitors who were monitoring buying patterns.
- *Supplier resistance.* It was easy to see how buyers would benefit by joining forces, but suppliers worried that online marketplaces, auctionlike pricing, and easy access to cheaper goods would drive down the prices of their goods. Many refused to join.
- *Customer resistance.* Many companies were unwilling to dump the network of suppliers they'd built up over the years. Larger companies such as Dell, Intel, and Wal-Mart, for example, already get the best prices possible from suppliers and have no plans to join public marketplaces. Moreover, many manufacturers have long-term buying contracts and didn't see how the exchanges would get them lower prices or offer additional benefits.
- *Incompatible systems.* One of the biggest challenges facing B2B exchanges was the need to seamlessly blend the operating systems used by exchange members. This included dozens of software packages, accounting systems, data management systems, and manufacturing schedules. Different customs, languages, and laws from country to country further complicated the endeavors. For the truly giant endeavors, such as Covisint.com, set up by the major U.S. automakers, this proved an insurmountable hurdle. As one participant put it, "Relationship behavior is more important than people thought."

To Be or Not To Be?

Despite these roadblocks, a few public B2B exchanges are making progress, such as exchanges for health-care supplies (Broadlane.com), steel and metals (e-Steel.com), chemicals (ChemConnect.com), and shipping (LevelSeas.com).

The real news, however, might be in a new generation of B2B exchanges based on the concept of "one-to-many." Instead of having many buyers and many sellers in the exchange, this new format connects a single buyer with multiple sellers. For instance, IBM Canada has a private B2B exchange with a number of travel-related suppliers, including American Express, Air Canada, Hertz, and Delta Hotels. Because the suppliers don't compete with one another, and there's only one buyer to coordinate technology with, the system works quite well.

Are the mighty public B2B exchanges a thing of the past, though? Some observers believe the economic benefits are still there, if only people would cooperate. Until that glorious day arrives, private exchanges such as IBM Canada's and smaller public exchanges in niche markets will keep the dream alive.

Questions for Critical Thinking

1. Why would a buyer want to participate in a B2B exchange?
2. Would sellers ever have any incentive to participate? Explain your answer.
3. Why does a private B2B exchange such as IBM Canada's work?

Lighting the Fire: Employee Motivation, Workforce Trends, and Labor Relations

CHAPTER

10

LEARNING OBJECTIVES

After studying this chapter, you will be able to

1. Compare Maslow's hierarchy of needs and Herzberg's two-factor theory, then explain their application to employee motivation

2. Explain why expectancy theory is considered by some to be the best description of employee behavior

3. Discuss four staffing challenges employers are facing in today's workplace

4. Explain the challenges and advantages of a diverse workforce

5. Discuss four alternative work arrangements that a company can use to address workplace challenges

6. Cite three options unions can exercise when negotiations with management break down

7. Cite three options management can exercise when negotiations with a union break down

www.prenhall.com/bovee

INSIDE BUSINESS TODAY
Learning the Art of Motivation at Atlas Container

www.atlascontainer.com

Picture your dream job.

Now erase that picture. *Your* job is all about cardboard. You come to work every day facing the prospect of converting giant rolls of corrugated paper into cardboard boxes. Hundreds, thousands, millions of boxes—one box after another, day after day after day. It's difficult, noisy, sweaty work in a no-growth industry populated mostly by small companies that usually can't offer the opportunities and benefits that major corporations can use to motivate their employees. How could you possibly get excited about a job like this?

Now imagine that you're a manager in such a firm, and it's your responsibility to motivate those people who come to work every day to make cardboard boxes. Such was the challenge facing brothers Peter and Paul Centenari when they purchased Atlas Container, based in Severn, Maryland. When they bought the company, these well-connected Harvard Business School graduates were investment bankers, not industrialists, and their goal was to buy a small company, apply their financial smarts to grow it into a slightly larger company, then resell it at a tidy profit.

A funny thing happened on the way to the auction block, however. For starters, the brothers stumbled badly, mismanaging a profitable business into a financial mess. "Basically, we drove it into the ground," says Paul, who serves as the company's CEO. Then somehow during the painful process of learning how to run the business and return it to fiscal health, they got excited about the box business and decided to keep the company rather than sell it. But these brothers weren't going to run just any old company; they wanted to redefine what it meant to be an employee and what it meant to be a manager. They wanted people to be excited about making cardboard boxes.

As the Centenaris rebuilt their company, they built a new management philosophy as well, based on respect for employees. Their philosophy rests on four pillars: employee stock ownership,

325

open-book management, continuous learning, and deep employee involvement that gives employees a strong voice in the decisions that affect their work and their future. These pillars are not unique in the business world, of course, but the way Atlas implements them is highly unusual. The Centenaris believe their employees can make better decisions and involve themselves more deeply in the company if they know everything there is to know about the company's financial health. This open-book management is supported with financial training for everyone in the company, so employees know what the numbers mean and how they all contribute to those results. Paul explains that "If you can somehow create a line of sight from what they do every day and how it affects the financial statement, you're going to create a passionate workforce that wants to make a difference and a profit."

The final pillar, employee involvement, is what truly sets Atlas apart. Rather than making decisions in a closed room, the Centenaris let employees vote on everything from health insurance plans to new production machinery—a level of employee involvement that is almost unheard of. The employees even outvoted the owners regarding the selection of some major new equipment. As in the best democracies, voting works best when the people are truly informed, and Atlas's commitment to training and open-book management ensures that the employees know what they're talking about when they cast their votes.

The results speak for themselves. On-time delivery is in the 90 to 95 percent range, well above the industry average of 75 percent. Costs stay under control because employees are careful with the company's money—after all, it's their money, too. And sales continue to grow at a rapid clip.

Financial success helps the company offer generous benefits to its employees, even to funding tutoring services for employees' children. Helping employees not only gives the brothers personal satisfaction, but as Paul explains, "The more we give, the more we get." It's enough to get employees excited to come to work, even in the tough business of making cardboard boxes.[1]

GET READY

Peter and Paul Centenari are living proof that intelligent, employee-centered leadership can motivate employees to high performance in even the most challenging circumstances. If you found yourself in their shoes, what steps would you take to create an environment in which people could flourish and find meaning in their work? How would you respond to the demographic shifts that continue to change the face of the global workforce? How would you deal with pressure from unions, which are increasingly trying to recruit workers in small, industrial firms such as Atlas? ▪

Chapter Overview

Companies with vast resources in growing industries can fail without it, while scrappy companies in tough circumstances can succeed with it. *It* is motivation, an almost magical force that divides achievers from people who just show up for work. This chapter introduces you to both classic and current thinking in the field of workforce motivation and shows how smart companies such as Atlas Containers bring these theories to life. If you have your sights set on management or entrepreneurship, understanding motivation is one of the most important discoveries you'll make in this entire course. After exploring the theories, you'll encounter the complex realities of today's workforce—and some of the key reasons that motivation is a never-ending effort, from staffing challenges to shifting demographics to the pros and cons of setting people free from the confines of 9-to-5 office life through alternative work arrangements. The chapter wraps up with a look at the role unions play in business today and the sometimes-contentious relationship between organized labor and business owners.

Motivating Employees

Peter and Paul Centenari would be the first to tell you that Atlas Container's success stems directly from its employees' strong sense of **engagement**, which is both a rational and an emotional commitment to their work. This commitment leads to higher-quality work and increased productivity while sharply reducing the likelihood that employees will leave the company in search of more satisfying opportunities.[2] Employees who are thoroughly engaged in their work generally exhibit high **morale**, a positive attitude toward both their jobs and their employers.

engagement
An employee's rational and emotional commitment to his or her work

morale
Attitude an individual has toward his or her job and employer

You already understand these concepts from your experiences as a student. For instance, you've surely experienced a few assignments that you just couldn't get excited about, for whatever reason. Without a strong intellectual or emotional connection to the work, chances are you expended the minimum amount of effort required. Conversely, let's hope you've had more than a few assignments in which the opposite was true: You poured your heart and soul into these projects because you made a commitment to excel, and at some level, you even enjoyed what you were doing. In other words, you were *engaged* with the work and *motivated* to do your best.

Making sure that employees are engaged and motivated is one of the most important challenges you'll face as a manager. It's also one of the most complex; human beings are complicated creatures to begin with, and today's demanding business environment makes the challenge that much greater. You can start to appreciate the challenge by first exploring what motivation is, then by considering some of the many theories proposed over the years to explain motivation in the workplace.

What Is Motivation?

Motivation is the combination of forces that moves individuals to take certain actions and avoid others in pursuit of individual objectives. The notion of movement is vital here; motivational strategies have little value if they don't translate into action that helps the business enterprise. A diverse range of theories has attempted to explain motivation, but every theory or motivational approach must consider three basic steps:

motivation
The combination of forces that moves individuals to take certain actions and behaviors and avoid other actions or behaviors

1. *Need.* The employee senses a need of some sort, from the basic need to earn enough money for food to a need for recognition or self-respect. We are all born with certain needs but can acquire other needs as we grow up, such as a need for achievement, a need for power, or a need to affiliate with compatible friends and colleagues.[3]
2. *Action.* To fulfill the need, the employee takes actions or adopts behaviors that he or she believes will result in the need being satisfied. The *quality* of the action is a matter of choosing which action to take, deciding how much effort to put into the action, and deciding how long to sustain that effort.[4]
3. *Outcome.* The employee observes the outcome of the action (sometimes called the *reward*) and determines whether the effort was worthwhile. Actions that result in positive outcomes are likely to be repeated; those that result in negative outcomes are less likely to be repeated.

Even from this extremely simple model you can start to grasp the challenges involved. For instance, what if two or more needs conflict, leading to incompatible actions? It's hard to balance the need to have fun with the need to generate enough money to pay the rent. Or what if an employee's need for recognition motivates him or her to work hard in the hopes of getting a promotion, but thanks to a tough economy, the company isn't growing and can't offer the promotion? Or what if top management doesn't notice the hard work—or worse yet, credits it to someone else? Think about these three steps the next time you encounter an employee in action. Maybe that unhelpful sales clerk actually started the job full of desire to help people but soon learned that management rewarded productivity more than customer satisfaction.

Before moving into specific theories, it's important to consider the role of money as a motivator, since it's a central issue for most employees. Money obviously plays a critical role in

Satisfied, motivated employees tend to be more productive and more effective, leading to higher rates of customer satisfaction and repeat business.

most everyone's work life, but it is not the ultimate motivator for many people, because money often can't compensate for the lack of other satisfying factors. In other words, it's important but not enough to truly motivate people toward peak performance. Today, employees also expect to be treated fairly and want the opportunity to pursue satisfying, meaningful work while balancing the demands of their professional and personal lives.

Theories of Motivation

Motivation has been a topic of interest to managers and researchers for more than a hundred years. A number of theories have evolved over the years, some that describe *what* motivates people and others that describe *how* they go about fulfilling their needs. No single theory offers a complete and proven picture of motivation, but each can offer some perspective. As you read about these theories, bear in mind that motivational theory is a broad field in which researchers continue to piece together this complex puzzle. As a manager, don't settle on a single theory to the exclusion of all others, and pay attention to new developments and ideas.

One of the earliest motivational researchers, Frederick W. Taylor, a machinist and engineer from Philadelphia, studied employee efficiency and motivation in the late nineteenth and early twentieth centuries. He is credited with developing **scientific management**, an approach that sought to improve employee efficiency through the scientific study of work. In addition to analyzing work and business processes in order to develop better methods, Taylor also popularized compensation schemes that emphasized financial incentives for good performance. His work truly revolutionized business and had a direct influence on the rise of the United States as a global industrial power in the first half of the twentieth century.[5]

Although money proved to be a significant motivator, scientific management didn't consider other motivational elements, such as opportunities for personal satisfaction. For instance, scientific management can't explain why someone still wants to work even though that person's spouse already makes a good living or why a successful executive will take a hefty pay cut to serve in government. Therefore, other researchers have looked beyond money to discover what else motivates people. The most widely recognized theories include Maslow's hierarchy of needs, Herzberg's two-factor theory, Theory X and Theory Y, Theory Z, equity theory, and expectancy theory.

Maslow's Hierarchy of Needs In 1943 psychologist Abraham Maslow proposed the theory that behavior is determined by a variety of needs. He organized these needs into five categories and then arranged the categories in a hierarchy. As Exhibit 10.1 shows, the most basic needs are at the bottom of this hierarchy and the more advanced needs are toward the top. In Maslow's hierarchy, all of the requirements for basic survival—food, clothing, shelter, and the like—fall into the category of *physiological needs.* These basic needs must be satisfied before the person can consider higher-level needs such as *safety needs, social needs* (the need to give and receive love and to feel a sense of belonging), and *esteem needs* (the need for a sense of self-worth and integrity).[6]

At the top of Maslow's hierarchy is *self-actualization*—the need to become everything one can become. (You may recall the advertising tagline used by the U.S. Army for many years, "Be all that you can be," which was a direct appeal to the self-actualization impulse.) This need is also the most difficult to fulfill—and even to identify in many cases. Employees who reach this point work not only to make money or to impress others but also because they feel their work is worthwhile and satisfying. Self-actualization needs partially explain why some people make radical career changes or strike out on their own as entrepreneurs. Conversely, when faced with tough or unstable economic conditions, employees may temporarily downplay higher-order needs and focus on the physiological and safety needs—making a steady paycheck more important than personal fulfillment.

Although Maslow's hierarchy is a convenient way to classify human needs, it would be a mistake to view it as a rigid sequence. A person need not completely satisfy each level of

scientific management
Management approach designed to improve employees' efficiency by scientifically studying their work

LEARNING OBJECTIVE 1

Compare Maslow's hierarchy of needs and Herzberg's two-factor theory, then explain their application to employee motivation

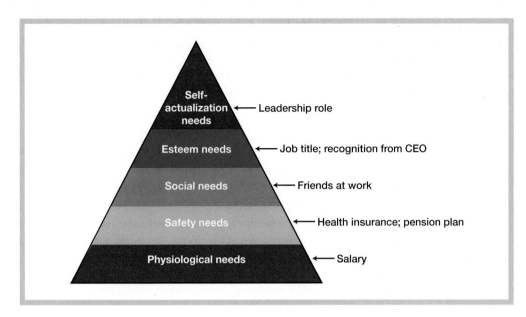

Exhibit 10.1
Maslow's Hierarchy
of Needs
*According to Maslow,
needs on the lower levels
of the hierarchy must
be satisfied before
higher-level needs can be
addressed.*

needs before being motivated by a higher need. Indeed, at any one time, most people are motivated by a combination of needs.

Herzberg's Two-Factor Theory In the 1960s, Frederick Herzberg and his associates asked accountants and engineers to describe specific aspects of their jobs that made them feel satisfied or dissatisfied. They found that two entirely different sets of factors were associated with dissatisfying and satisfying work experiences: *hygiene factors* and *motivators* (see Exhibit 10.2). What Herzberg called **hygiene factors** are associated with

hygiene factors
*Aspects of the work
environment that are
associated with
dissatisfaction*

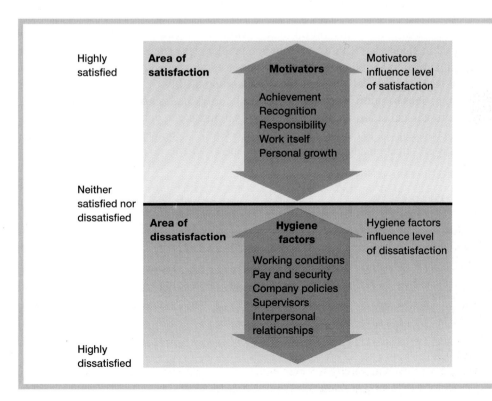

Exhibit 10.2
Two-Factor Theory
*Hygiene factors such as
working conditions and
company policies can
influence employee
dissatisfaction. On the
other hand, motivators
such as opportunities for
achievement and
recognition can influence
employee satisfaction.*

dissatisfying experiences. The potential sources of dissatisfaction include working conditions, company policies, pay, and job security. Management can decrease worker dissatisfaction by improving hygiene factors, but such improvements seldom increase satisfaction. On the other hand, managers can help employees feel more motivated and, ultimately, more satisfied by paying attention to **motivators** such as achievement, recognition, responsibility, and other personally rewarding factors.[7] (Comparing Herzberg to Maslow, you can see that Herzberg's motivators closely resemble Maslow's higher-level needs, while the hygiene factors resemble the lower-level needs.) Simple recognition can be an extraordinarily powerful motivator, even leading people to leave otherwise satisfactory jobs in search of better recognition for their efforts.[8] To make sure its top performers don't leave, KeySpan, an energy company based in Brooklyn, New York, acknowledges employee efforts through a variety of programs, such as the CEO Award, given to employees who are selected by their peers for outstanding contributions toward company goals.[9]

According to Herzberg's model, managers need to focus on removing dissatisfying elements (such as unpleasant working conditions or low pay) and adding satisfying elements (such as interesting work and professional recognition). The specific areas to address vary from one situation to the next. A skilled, well-paid, middle-aged employee may be motivated to perform better if motivators are supplied. However, a young, unskilled worker who earns low wages or an employee who is insecure will probably still need the support of strong hygiene factors to reduce dissatisfaction before the motivators can be effective.

McGregor's Theory X and Theory Y In the 1960s psychologist Douglas McGregor identified two radically different sets of assumptions that underlie most management thinking, which he classified as *Theory X* and *Theory Y* (see Exhibit 10.3). According to McGregor, **Theory X**-oriented managers believe that employees dislike work and can be motivated only by the fear of losing their jobs or by *extrinsic rewards*—those given by other people, such as money, promotions, and tenure. This management style emphasizes physiological and safety needs and tends to ignore the higher-level needs in Maslow's hierarchy. In contrast, **Theory Y**-oriented managers believe that employees like work and can be motivated by working for goals that promote creativity or for causes they believe in. Consequently, Theory Y-oriented managers seek to motivate employees through *intrinsic rewards*—which employees essentially give themselves.[10] For example, creating products known for high quality is a powerful intrinsic reward. At Cobalt Boats, a motorboat manufacturer based in Neodesha, Kansas, veteran boatbuilders take such pride in their work that they've been known to hound each other (and newer employees in particular) to make sure nothing is done to tarnish Cobalt's reputation for sterling quality.[11]

The assumptions behind Theory X emphasize authority; the assumptions behind Theory Y emphasize growth and self-direction. However, it's a mistake to conclude that Theory X is necessarily a bad approach and that Theory Y is necessarily a good approach. Effective managers assess every situation and use their judgment and experience to apply the right methods.

---

motivators
In Herzberg's two-factor model, factors that may increase motivation

Theory X
Managerial assumption that employees are irresponsible, are unambitious, and dislike work and that managers must use force, control, or threats to motivate them

Theory Y
Managerial assumption that employees like work, are naturally committed to certain goals, are capable of creativity, and seek out responsibility under the right conditions

---

Exhibit 10.3
Theory X and Theory Y
McGregor proposed two distinct views of human nature: The assumptions of Theory X are basically negative, whereas those of Theory Y are basically positive.

Theory X	Theory Y
1. Employees inherently dislike work and will avoid it whenever possible.	1. Employees like work and consider it as natural as play and rest.
2. Because employees dislike work, they must be threatened with punishment to achieve goals.	2. People naturally work toward goals they are committed to.
3. Employees will avoid responsibilities whenever possible.	3. The average person can learn to accept and even seek responsibility.
4. Employees value security above all other job factors.	4. The average person's intellectual potential is only partially realized.

SAFETY AND SECURITY IN A COMPLEX WORLD

WHICH THEORY WILL SOLVE THE PROBLEM OF EMPLOYEE THEFT?

In a world where many managers go out of their way to keep employees happy, the rather bleak assumptions regarding the motives and behavior of the average employee expressed in Theory X almost sound like something from the Dark Ages. After all, today's Theory Y managers are supposed to treat employees with respect, give them plenty of freedom, and trust them to make the right decisions and look out for the best interests of customers and the company.

But there's one small problem: Some employees abuse that trust and steal from their employers. Actually, it's not a small problem at all. Employee theft and embezzlement is a *huge* problem, costing U.S. companies hundreds of billions of dollars a year—that's *billions* with a *b*. (Legally speaking, embezzlement differs slightly from regular theft. The FBI defines it as "misappropriation or misuse of money or property entrusted to one's care, custody, or control," as opposed to simply taking something that doesn't belong to you. A payroll manager who puts fictitious employees on the books, then pockets their paychecks commits embezzlement, for instance.)

Employee thievery ranges from the simple to the complex, from taking office supplies to stealing retail products (in the retail business, theft by employees is often a bigger problem than shoplifting) to creating fictitious companies that then bill the employer for equally fictitious goods or services. The financial damage is considerable, although exact amounts are difficult to pin down—partly because some companies are embarrassed to report such losses. In rough terms, simple theft of supplies and inventory costs companies somewhere between $15 and $90 billion every year. Throw in intellectual property theft, and the number jumps to $240 billion a year or so. Embezzlement more than doubles that, to some $600 billion a year.

Who pays for all this? You do—you and every other employee, investor, and customer. Not only do companies suffer the direct financial damage, but they also incur billions of dollars in additional costs for everything from extra insurance to security guards to legal expenses to an array of technological controls. The result is higher costs for customers, less money to spend on employee wages and benefits, and additional restrictions on all employees—including the honest ones. Moreover, some experts estimate that 30 to 50 percent of all business failures are a result of employee theft and embezzlement.

Against those odds, even the most enlightened modern managers may need to exercise some good old-fashioned Theory X skepticism about their workforces.

Questions for Critical Thinking
1. How should managers explain to their workforces the necessity to implement security controls?
2. Could Herzberg's hygiene factors help explain employee theft and embezzlement? Why or why not?

Ouchi's Theory Z In the 1980s, when U.S. businesses began to feel a strong competitive threat from Japanese companies, William Ouchi proposed another approach to motivation that was based on his comparative study of Japanese and U.S. management practices. His **Theory Z** merged the best of both systems, as expressed in seven principles: long-term employment, consensus-based decision making, individual responsibility, slow evaluation and promotion, informal control with formal measurements, a moderate degree of career specialization, and a holistic concern for the individual.[12]

Theory Z
Leadership approach that emphasizes involving employees at all levels and treating them like family

Although the phrase "Theory Z" isn't used as much today, many of the principles embodied in the theory have been widely embraced. Atlas Container is a classic example of a company that has succeeded by applying these principles. Mark Cuban, owner of the Dallas Mavericks basketball team, demonstrates Theory Z principles as well—sometimes in slightly outlandish fashion. For instance, Cuban has been repeatedly fined by the National Basketball Association (a half-million dollars in one instance) for criticizing the efforts of referees. His isn't just the usual courtside griping, however; in Cuban's eyes, the failures to call penalties on opposing players was endangering the health and safety of his players.[13] By showing that he'll do whatever it takes to protect and support his employees, including everyone from players to coaches to office workers, Cuban embraces the holistic concern for employees that Ouchi promoted.

equity theory
A theory that suggests employees base their level of satisfaction on the ratio of their inputs to the job and the outputs or rewards they receive from it

Equity Theory **Equity theory** contributes to the understanding of motivation by suggesting that employee satisfaction depends on the perceived ratio of inputs to outputs. If you work side by side with someone, doing the same job and giving the same amount of effort, only to learn that your colleague earns more money, would you be satisfied in your work and motivated to continue working hard? You perceive a state of *inequity,* so you probably won't be happy. In response, you might ask for a raise, decide not to work as hard, try to change perceptions of your efforts or their outcomes, or simply quit and find a new job—any one of these steps might bring your perceived input/output ratio back into balance.[14] In the aftermath of large-scale layoffs in many sectors of the economy in the past few years, many of the employees left behind feel a sense of inequity in being asked to shoulder the work of those who left, without getting paid more for the extra effort.[15] Equity also plays a central role in complaints about gender pay fairness (see page 340) and many unionizing efforts, whenever employees feel they aren't getting a fair share of corporate profits or are being asked to shoulder more than their fair share of hardships (see "Learning from Business Blunders").

LEARNING OBJECTIVE 2

Explain why expectancy theory is considered by some to be the best description of employee behavior

expectancy theory
Suggests that the effort employees put into their work depends on expectations about their own ability to perform, expectations about the rewards that the organization will give in response to that performance, and the attractiveness of those rewards relative to their individual goals

Expectancy Theory **Expectancy theory**, considered by many experts to offer the best available explanation of employee motivation, links an employee's efforts with the outcome he or she expects from that effort. Like equity theory, expectancy theory focuses less on the specific forces that motivate employees and more on the process they follow to seek satisfaction in their jobs. Expectancy theory expands on earlier theories in several important ways, including linking effort to performance and linking rewards to individual goals (see Exhibit 10.4). The effort employees will put forth depends on (1) their expectations about their own ability to perform, (2) their expectations about the rewards that the organization will give in response to that performance, and (3) the attractiveness of those rewards relative to their individual goals.[16]

Imagine that you're a carpenter assigned to a home remodeling project. If you don't think you have the skills necessary to do an absolutely perfect job on the kitchen cabinets (maybe you specialize in framing, not finish work), or you do have the skills but you don't think your boss will reward you for putting in the extra effort, your motivation may suffer. Or perhaps you do have the skills and the boss will recognize your efforts with a cash bonus, but you'd rather receive an extra day off to spend with your family. Expectancy theory

LEARNING FROM BUSINESS BLUNDERS

OOPS In a move that is not unusual when a company is struggling, American Airlines CEO Donald Carty asked the company's unions for $1.8 billion in wage and benefit concessions, explaining that the company was on the edge of bankruptcy. His plea was successful—until the unions learned that at the same time Carty was asking them to accept pay cuts, he had arranged generous bonuses for top executives and a $40 million plan that would protect their pensions in case the company did in fact slide into bankruptcy. Union leader John Ward expressed what many union members probably felt: "It's the equivalent of an obscene gesture from management."

The unions agreed to the pay cuts on the condition that Carty resign, which he did.

WHAT YOU CAN LEARN The American Airlines pay situation was a classic example of equity theory in action. When most employees know the company is in trouble, they're willing to accept some short-term pain in exchange for keeping their jobs, but they expect everyone in the company to suffer equally. (In contrast to Carty's actions, executives in several other companies in recent financial trouble have reduced or even eliminated their own salaries, and a few have even given back bonuses previously earned.)

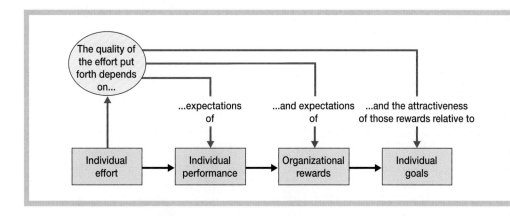

Exhibit 10.4
Expectancy Theory
Expectancy theory suggests that employees base their efforts on expectations of their own performance, expectations of rewards for that performance, and the value of those rewards.

points out several areas in which motivation can suffer and so gives managers more insight into how to successfully motivate employees.

Motivational Strategies

Once managers have some idea of what motivates—or de-motivates—employees, they can devise policies and procedures that attempt to keep workforce morale at a productive level. Even in professions that have a reputation for poorly motivated workers, creative and committed managers can foster environments that motivate employees and contribute to business success. For example, the pay-television industry (both cable and satellite) is infamous for poor service when customers phone in with problems or questions. In a recent survey by the American Customer Satisfaction Index, three large cable companies, AT&T, Charter Communications, and Comcast, scored customer satisfaction ratings that were "among the lowest ever recorded, across all companies and all industries." And yet, Directv, which competes in the same industry—and even uses the same outsourcing firm for customer service calls that some of its competitors use—earns significantly higher customer satisfaction scores with a motivational strategy that emphasizes such key points as soliciting employees' input, providing workers with the tools they need to perform well, and giving them the authority to make decisions on their own.[17] Being good to employees (even if they're employees of an outsourcer) is good for Directv's business, too: Higher customer satisfaction scores translate to greater customer loyalty.

The range of motivational decisions managers face is almost endless, from redesigning jobs to make them more interesting to offering recognition programs for high achievers. Whether it's a basic award program for salespeople or an entirely new way to structure the workforce, though, every motivational strategy needs to consider two critical aspects: setting goals and reinforcing behavior.

Setting Goals As mentioned earlier, successful motivation involves action. To be successful, that action needs to be directed toward a meaningful goal. Accordingly, **goal-setting theory** suggests the idea that goals can motivate employees. For example, retail chain Eddie Bauer rewards its store employees with a 35-cent-per-hour bonus if a store meets its sales goals, and a 65-cent bonus if sales exceed the goal by 5 percent. These amounts may not seem all that significant and probably wouldn't be much of a motivator for higher-paid workers, but for people who work at low-paying jobs, such bonuses can be a powerful motivator.[18]

The process of setting goals is often embodied in the technique known as **management by objectives (MBO)**, a companywide process that empowers employees and involves them in goal setting and decision making. This process consists of four steps: setting goals, planning actions, implementing plans, and reviewing performance (see Exhibit 10.5). Because employees at all levels are involved in all four steps, they learn more about company objectives and feel that they are an important part of the companywide team. Furthermore, they understand how their individual job function contributes to the organization's long-term success. Jointly setting clear and challenging—but achievable—goals can encourage employees to reach higher levels of performance.

goal-setting theory
Motivational theory suggesting that setting goals can be an effective way to motivate employees

management by objectives (MBO)
A motivational approach in which managers and employees work together to structure personal goals and objectives for every individual, department, and project to mesh with the organization's goals

Exhibit 10.5
Management by Objectives
The MBO process has four steps. This cycle is refined and repeated as managers and employees at all levels work toward establishing goals and objectives, thereby accomplishing the organization's strategic goals.

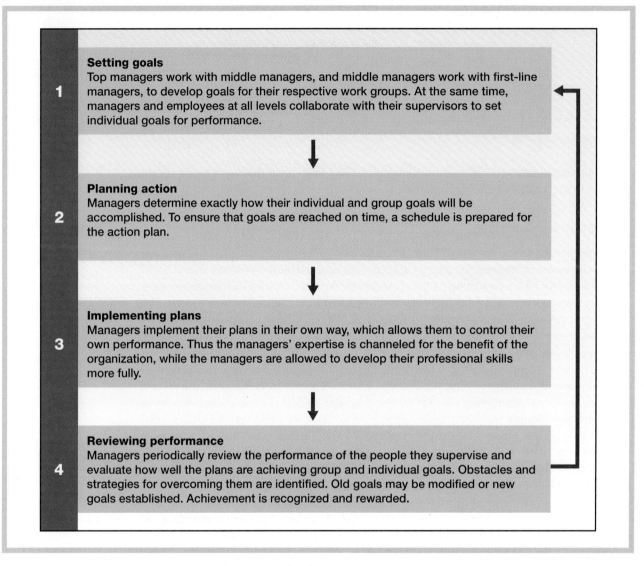

Setting goals
1 Top managers work with middle managers, and middle managers work with first-line managers, to develop goals for their respective work groups. At the same time, managers and employees at all levels collaborate with their supervisors to set individual goals for performance.

Planning action
2 Managers determine exactly how their individual and group goals will be accomplished. To ensure that goals are reached on time, a schedule is prepared for the action plan.

Implementing plans
3 Managers implement their plans in their own way, which allows them to control their own performance. Thus the managers' expertise is channeled for the benefit of the organization, while the managers are allowed to develop their professional skills more fully.

Reviewing performance
4 Managers periodically review the performance of the people they supervise and evaluate how well the plans are achieving group and individual goals. Obstacles and strategies for overcoming them are identified. Old goals may be modified or new goals established. Achievement is recognized and rewarded.

reinforcement theory
A motivational approach based on the idea that managers can motivate employees by influencing their behaviors with positive and negative reinforcement

behavior modification
Systematic use of rewards and punishments to change human behavior

Reinforcing Behavior Employees in the workplace, like human beings in all aspects of life, tend to repeat behaviors that create positive outcomes. **Reinforcement theory** suggests that managers can motivate employees by controlling or changing their actions through **behavior modification**. Managers systematically encourage those actions that are desirable by providing pleasant consequences and discourage those that are not by providing unpleasant consequences.

Positive reinforcement offers pleasant consequences for completing or repeating a desired action. Experts recommend the use of positive reinforcement because it emphasizes the desired behavior rather than the unwanted behavior. By contrast, *negative reinforcement* allows people to avoid unpleasant consequences by behaving in the desired way.[19] For example, fear of losing a job (unpleasant consequences) may move an employee to finish a project on time (desired behavior). Such negative motivation, however, is less effective than encouraging an individual's own sense of direction, creativity, and pride in doing a good job.

Managers and the organizations they represent in today's global economy take a variety of approaches to motivation, some more enlightened than others. However, all these managers face the challenge of motivating a workforce that is diverse, dynamic, and at times demanding, as you'll see in the following section.

CRITICAL THINKING CHECKPOINT

1. What is likely to happen if an employee initiates a certain action or adopts a certain behavior without first believing that there is a need for that action or behavior?
2. According to equity theory, could an employee making $50,000 a year feel fairly compensated if the company's CEO makes $2 million a year?
3. How does self-esteem play into the notion of expectancy theory?

Keeping Pace with Today's Workforce

LEARNING OBJECTIVE 3

Discuss four staffing challenges employers are facing in today's workplace

Even as the external business environment undergoes constant change, managers must wrestle with a variety of internal workforce issues, including a number of staffing challenges, demographic shifts in the workforce, and alternatives to the traditional 9-to-5 office arrangement.

Staffing Challenges

Managers in every organization that hires employees face an ongoing array of staffing challenges. The most significant of these include aligning the workforce with ever-evolving organizational needs, fostering employee loyalty in an uncertain job market, adjusting workloads and monitoring for employee burnout, and helping employees balance their work and personal lives.

Aligning the Workforce with Organizational Needs Matching the right employees to the right jobs at the right time is a constant challenge for most companies. Outside the company, changing market needs, the emergence and exit of various competitors, advances in technology, and new government regulations can all affect the ideal size and composition of the workforce. Inside the company, shifts in strategy, changes to information and production sytems, and growing or declining product sales can force managers to realign their workforces. And while external and internal forces shape workforce needs, individual employees also pursue their own professional and personal goals, whether it's leaving for better jobs, temporarily stepping out of the workforce for personal reasons, or retiring permanently. Losing the valuable skills and knowledge of experienced employees is often referred to as **brain drain**.

brain drain
Term used to describe the loss of experienced employees from an organization

Rightsizing is a term generally used to describe periodic realignments or shakeups, implying that the organization is making changes in the workforce to match its business needs more precisely. Although rightsizing usually involves *downsizing*—reducing the workforce, sometimes by thousands of employees in a single move—companies sometimes add workers even while they eliminate other jobs. Such was the case at Hewlett-Packard when the company shed marketing jobs but added new positions in consulting and sales. "In many cases, companies are trying to upgrade their talent," says one human resources expert.[20] In other cases, companies are simply trying to reduce costs, as Circuit City recently did when it dismissed 3,900 of its highest-paid (and most-experienced) salespeople in a single day. Losing a competitive battle with Best Buy and other electronics retailers, the company believed the move was "the best thing long-term."[21]

Fostering Employee Loyalty For decades, many employees and employers had an implicit agreement that employment was for life: New hires would join a firm right out of high school or college, progress through the ranks, and retire after 40 years or so. Employees were loyal to their companies because their companies were usually loyal in return. While this is a somewhat oversimplified and romanticized view of the "good old days," the situation is clearly different today. Even stalwarts such as Hewlett-Packard, which had a no-layoff policy for many years and avoided roller-coaster business opportunities (such as large military contracts) that would force it to hire then fire large groups of employees, eventually had to acknowledge the brutal new landscape of global competiton.

With the notion of lifetime employment long gone, employees have been forced to devote more time and energy to looking out for their own careers, knowing that they could be forced to seek other work at any time. As you can imagine, this new scenario presents a considerable challenge for managers: They usually can't guarantee long-term employment, but they want employees to commit themselves to the company even in the face of this uncertainty. Moreover, many employees no longer *want* to work for the same company for life, even if given the opportunity.[22] Managers can respond to this challenge in a variety of ways:

- ***Manage their companies effectively and ethically.*** While this might sound obvious, one of the simple truths of business is that managerial blunders can devastate workforces.
- ***Give employees a stake in the success of the firm.*** Make it clear that employees not only share the responsibility for the success of the company—thereby increasing the probability of continued career opportunities—but will also share in the rewards, through profit sharing, stock options, and other programs.
- ***Take better care of their employees.*** Employees who believe they are being treated well will tend to stay with their current employers—and to engage enthusiastically with their work while they're there.
- ***Work with employees to align their career goals with the company's goals.*** By having regular and honest discussions with employees regarding their career goals, managers can work with employees to create plans that benefit both parties—even if it will be for only a few years.[23]

Monitoring Workloads and Avoiding Employee Burnout If you grew up playing videogames, working for a videogame developer might seem like about the best job on Earth. However, before you hone your programming skills and polish up that résumé, you might want to speak with a few industry insiders—including the several game developers who've filed lawsuits against their employers for making them work long hours without overtime pay. The suits hinge on whether these employees should be exempt from overtime laws, which you'll read about in Chapter 11, but they've brought to light working conditions inside such firms as Electronic Arts (EA) and Vivendi Universal Games. For example, some employees at EA claim that the company established regular working schedules of more than 82 to 84 hours per week.[24]

The pressure to get more done with fewer employees is raising concerns about employee burnout.

Eighty-hour weeks are the exception, of course, but many employees seem to be feeling the strain of extra work these days. The problem is common after downsizing, when employees who still have jobs are sometimes expected to pick up the "ghost work" of the people who've been let go. Other employees cite the inability to ever truly get away from work, now that they're connected via cellphones, laptop computers, and PDAs with wireless e-mail access. These multiple stresses create the risk of *employee burnout,* a state of physical and emotional exhaustion that can result from constant exposure to stress over a long period of time.[25]

The prospect of overwork and widespread burnout raises two vital questions. First, how bad is the problem? Although many people now work more hours per year, according to the University of Chicago's National Opinion Research Center, overall workplace stress has actually declined in recent years.[26] Second, when employees are expected to work long hours, does all that extra time really help companies over the long run—particularly in professional and managerial jobs, where analysis, creativity, and decision-making skills are so important? The *quality* of this work is often more important than the *quantity.* Unfortunately, "seat time" is often much easier to measure than work quality, creating situations in which the number of hours worked becomes a de facto measure of employee loyalty and commitment. Critics of long work hours also point to European companies such as Airbus that compete successfully in world markets, even though Europeans typically work far fewer hours than their North American and Asian counterparts.[27]

work-life balance
Efforts to help people balance the competing demands of their professional and personal lives

Managing Work-Life Balance The concerns over workloads is one of the factors behind the growing interest in **work-life balance**, the idea that employees, managers, and entrepreneurs need to balance the competing demands of their professional and personal lives. Even younger employees who might be more willing to devote most of their waking hours to work early in their careers usually want to pull back as their personal responsibilities (such as caring for children or elderly relatives) or outside interests grow over time.[28] Unfortunately, their career demands usually increase at the same time as they move into positions of greater and greater responsibility, leading some observers to wonder whether permanent balance is even possible. A more realistic approach might be to acknowledge that things will be out of balance from time to time and so design careers around that fact, rather than adding to the stress even more by trying to "have it all" all the time.[29]

Regardless of how realistic balance may or may not be, many companies are trying to make it easier for employees to juggle multiple responsibilities with on-site daycare facilities, flexible work schedules, and other options designed to improve **quality of work life (QWL)**. "There is a philosophy here of supporting an employee's entire lifestyle because it will make for a better employee and facility productivity, which it does," explains Cynthia Edwards of Genencor, a biotech company based in Palo Alto, California. Toward this end, Genencor has taken such steps as providing on-site dry cleaning and offering loaner bikes and cars so that employees who use public transportation to get to and from work can run errands during work breaks. While this assistance may sound expensive, it helps Genencor maintain lower turnover and higher productivity than its competitors.[30] In addition to benefits such as these, companies can also improve QWL through **job enrichment**, which reduces specialization and makes work more meaningful by expanding each job's responsibilities, and **job redesign**, which restructures work to provide a better fit between employees' skills and their jobs.

quality of work life (QWL)
Overall environment that results from job and work conditions

job enrichment
Reducing work specialization and making work more meaningful by adding to the responsibilities of each job

job redesign
Designing a better fit between employees' skills and their work to increase job satisfaction

MINDING YOUR OWN BUSINESS

ARE WE HAVING FUN YET?

When you're putting your business together, don't forget to plan to have fun, too.

"Because we spend more of our waking hours working than doing anything else, fun should be a very fundamental part of work," notes one expert on human behavior. In fact, workplace fun is increasingly important because today's jobs are more insecure and more competitive than they once were. Furthermore, camaraderie is diminishing as employees spend more and more time relating to machines than to each other, eat lunch at their desks, or work from home.

Having fun at work isn't just a matter of fun and games, either. Employees who enjoy their work and their workplaces tend to be more productive and more committed. For one thing, a little wisecracking and laughs can go a long way toward relieving stress. Moreover, fun can raise a company's bottom line by improving health, reducing absenteeism, boosting morale, building teamwork, releasing creativity, improving productivity, and increasing enthusiasm. So while the pursuit of fun may seem frivolous to the serious-minded, more and more companies are beginning to see the value of a good hearty laugh or a little giggle now and then.

At Sprint, company-sponsored fun days encourage employees to wear clothes backward and to go on a photo safari with disposable cameras, taking candid photos of other employees. At Lands' End—voted as one of the best places to work—employees can participate in the company's "Cruise Room," where workers can enjoy calypso music and fruit punch on their breaks. Other companies have organized employee costume parties, hosted goofy birthday celebrations, and sponsored fun-filled weekends at hotels. These companies and others recognize that if work is fun, people will want to come to work. As George Zimmer, CEO of the Men's Wearhouse and a major advocate of trying to make work more enjoyable, puts it, "If the employees are happy and make the stores fun, then that will make it fun for the customers. If they're happy, business will follow, and shareholders will be happy. It all starts with the employees and making it fun for them. Why does work have to be dull?"

Questions for Critical Thinking

1. Under which level of Maslow's hierarchy of needs would you place having fun at work?
2. Does fun have any role in serious workplaces such as hospitals or power plants? Explain your answer.

L E A R N I N G
O B J E C T I V E 4

Explain the challenges
and advantages of a
diverse workforce

Demographic Challenges

The workforce is always in a state of demographic change, whether from a shift in global immigration patterns or from the changing balance of age groups within a country's population. The companies that are most successful at managing and motivating their employees take great care to understand the diversity of their workforces and establish programs and policies that both embrace that diversity and take full advantage of diversity's benefits.

Workforce Diversity Issues Today's workforce is diverse in race, gender, age, culture, family structures, religion, sexual orientation, mental and physical ability, and educational backgrounds. Smart business leaders recognize the competitive advantages of diverse workforces: They bring a broader range of viewpoints and ideas, they help companies understand and identify with diverse markets, and they enable companies to tap into the broadest possible pool of talent. Diversity is simply a fact of life for all companies—even if it's nothing more than a mix of men and women of various ages working together.

Differences in everything from religion to ethnic heritage to geography and military experience enrich the workplace, but all can create managerial challenges. A diverse workforce brings with it a wide range of skills, traditions, backgrounds, experiences, outlooks, and attitudes toward work—all of which can affect employee behavior on the job. Supervisors face the challenge of communicating with these diverse employees, motivating them, and fostering cooperation and harmony among them. Teams face the challenge of working together closely, and companies are challenged to coexist peacefully with business partners and with the community as a whole. Some of the most important diversity issues today include the immigration and globalization of the workforce, the aging of the U.S. workforce, gender and race issues, and religion in the workplace.

Immigration and Globalization. For many companies, both large and small, managing the workforce is now an international challenge, whether it involves offshoring work to other countries, hiring employees to establish operations in other countries, or hiring workers who have immigrated to the United States from other countries. The United States has been a nation of immigrants from the beginning, and that trend continues today. The western and northern Europeans who made up the bulk of immigrants during the nation's early years now share space with people from across Asia, Africa, Eastern Europe, and other parts of the world. By 2010, recent immigrants will account for half of all new U.S. workers.[31] Nor is this pattern of immigration unique to the United States: Workers from Africa, Asia, and the Middle East are moving to Europe in search of new opportunities, while workers from India, the Philippines, and Southeast Asia contribute to the employment base of the Middle East.[32] This international, intercultural nature of the workforce yields a number of important benefits, including cost advantages, specialized talents, and local market knowledge, but it often gives managers a more complex employee base to supervise and motivate.

Age. Against this backdrop of global immigration and outsourcing, the workforce within the United States is aging. The baby boom generation, which currently dominates the middle and upper tiers of the workforce, is nearing retirement age and triggering a host of age-related issues. Perhaps the most important of these is the age at which boomers will actually retire. Reversing a long-term trend toward earlier and earlier retirement, employment rates among older workers have recently increased, along with the number of people who plan to continue working well into their 60s, 70s, and even 80s.[33] Economists cite a number of reasons: rising health-care costs, reductions in company pension plans, and the desire to stay active longer. Many employers are happy to hire older workers, too, citing their greater flexibility in work hours and pay, lower rates of absenteeism, lower turnover rate, and ability to train younger workers.[34] The Home Depot, one of the most active employers of the

COMPETING IN A GLOBAL MARKETPLACE

TOO MANY WORKERS? NOT FOR LONG

One of the biggest challenges all managers face is trying to juggle short-term reality with long-term predictions. It's hard to keep one eye on the things you need to do today and another on the changes that could affect your business in the future—particularly when tomorrow promises to be radically different from today.

With the economy still reeling from a recession, the nation tangled up in an ongoing argument about global off-shoring, and millions of employees worried about their jobs, talk of a labor shortage seems almost far-fetched. As they struggle to reduce their workforces, many managers find it hard to believe that they're going to be facing the exact opposite problem in just a few years, that they'll be struggling to find enough qualified workers. Similarly, workers who have been downsized surely find it hard to believe that they'll be hot commodities a few years from now.

The reason is simple demographics: The huge baby boom generation (those born between 1946 and 1964) ballooned the workforce during the 1980s and 1990s, but by 2010, many of those workers will be retired, and the generations coming behind them aren't nearly large enough to fill the empty slots the boomers will leave behind. Declining college enrollment in high-tech fields and a rise in the number of young mothers who choose not to work outside the home further complicate the situation. Moreover, if college tuitions continue to rise and financial aid continues to shrink, the ranks of college graduates may not grow as rapidly as in the past.

But while a labor shortage presents tremendous hurdles for employers, it brings opportunity for employees.

A slower-growing workforce could indeed shift the balance of power to workers, forcing employers to hike wages, add day-care centers, increase flexible work hours, provide more training, and develop innovative ways to attract and retrain existing employees. Moreover, older workers could suddenly take on value as a skilled pool of labor. Bottom line: Employers that refit the work environment to appeal to both young and old, experienced and inexperienced, native and immigrant, will end up in the best position. And forward-thinking employers realize that they need to address the problem now, before they're left shorthanded. For instance, Cigna Systems is retraining workers for such jobs as database administrators, which are likely to face severe talent shortages, teaming younger workers with older colleagues before that experience walks out the door into retirement. Stratus Technologies continues to offer its new hires attractive wages and benefits, even though it could pay them less in a tough job market. The company figures that employers who squeeze employees during tough times aren't creating enough loyalty to hang on to those workers when job opportunities start to grow again.

Questions for Critical Thinking

1. In the United States and other developed nations, the average age of the workforce is higher than in many developing nations in Asia, Africa, and the Middle East. How is this likely to affect U.S. competitiveness in global markets in the coming years?
2. What can employers do to prepare for a future skilled-labor shortage?

formerly retired, is particularly keen on the customer service skills of many older workers. As one store manager explains, "They bring respect and knowledge, and they tend to be very friendly."[35]

Although older workers are making some employment gains, the workplace is not always a welcoming environment. Even though the 1967 Age Discrimination in Employment Act (ADEA) makes workers over 40 a protected class, charges of age discrimination filed with the Equal Employment Opportunity Commission (EEOC) are on the rise.[36] For instance, a group of older employees laid off by the consumer electronics chain Best Buy sued the company for age discrimination, claiming that nearly two-thirds of the 126 employees affected by that particular round of layoffs were past age 40.[37] Finding the evidence to prove that age really was the deciding factor in such terminations is often difficult, but in 2005, the U.S. Supreme Court ruled that employers can be held liable for age discrimination even if the

Judy McGrath, the chairman and CEO of MTV Networks, is not only a dominant influence in contemporary popular culture but one of the most powerful women in global business.

sexism
Discrimination on the basis of gender

glass ceiling
Invisible barrier attributable to subtle discrimination that keeps women out of the top positions in business

discrimination wasn't intentional. This change is expected to further increase the number of age-bias lawsuits and make them easier to win.[38]

Age-related issues aren't solely a concern for older workers, however. Some younger workers claim they suffer discrimination in various ways as well, such as being criticized for a lack of loyalty to their employers and an unwillingness to "pay their dues" as older workers did. More than a few younger workers respond to this criticism by saying that companies no longer look out for their workers, so the workers need to look out for themselves.[39] As with all diversity issues, the solution to age-related conflicts can be found in respecting one another and working toward common goals. As Virginia Byrd, a veteran career counselor from Encinitas, California, put it, "It's a real blessing to have different generations in our workplaces. There is so much we can share, if we make the effort."[40]

Gender. From warehouses to the plush offices on Wall Street, compensation and career opportunities for women continue to be contentious issues, more than 40 years after the Civil Rights Act of 1964 made it illegal for employers to practice **sexism**, or discrimination on the basis of gender. A number of recent gender-discrimination lawsuits at such companies as Boeing, Wal-Mart, Morgan Stanley, and Costco suggest that these issues aren't going to disappear any time soon, either.[41]

For instance, without admitting any wrongdoing, stockbroker Merrill Lynch has already paid out more than $100 million in gender bias cases, with more cases pending.[42] And in the largest private civil rights case in U.S. history, women from Wal-Mart stores across the country filed suit in 2004 alleging a consistent pattern of gender discrimination at the company. According to the suit, female managers make less than male managers at every level, and, on average, men are promoted faster than women, despite the fact that the women have higher average performance rankings. Wal-Mart denies the allegations but has modified its compensation policies to make sure women are paid more fairly.[43]

The statistical picture of men and women in the workforce is complex, but three general themes are clear. First, both year to year and over the course of their careers, women earn less on average than men, although the gap has closed from less than 60% to about 80% in recent decades. Second, even in occupations that have traditionally been served primarily by women, such as teaching and nursing, women still earn less than men on average. Third, the higher up you go in most corporations, the fewer women you'll find in positions of authority. Women hold roughly 10 percent of the board seats in the 1,000 largest corporations, and a quarter of these firms have no female directors at all.[44]

A lack of opportunities to advance into the top ranks is often referred to as the **glass ceiling**, implying that women can see the top but can't get there. On the positive side, women now hold top positions or are in line for the top job at a number of the leading corporations, including eBay, Avon, MTV, Lucent Technologies, and Xerox. And although Wal-Mart is the subject of gender bias complaints, two female vice presidents from the company, Linda Dillman (information technology) and Claire Watts (merchandising), are considered among the most influential executives in the United States.[45]

Companies that do treat women equally are discovering that it's not only the right thing to do but also better for business. Studies suggest a strong correlation between gender diversity in managerial ranks and financial success. From 1996 to 2000, for instance, companies in the Fortune 500 that had the highest percentage of women as senior executives significantly outperformed those that had the lowest percentage.[46] However, it's important to note this is a correlation, not necessarily a causation; managing gender diversity successfully may be just one of many things that successful companies do well.[47]

With laws against employment discrimination, a society that is much more supportive of women in professional roles than it was just a few decades ago, and strong evidence that companies in which women are given opportunities to lead outperform companies that don't, why do these gaps still exist? In addition to instances of simple discrimination, analysts suggest a variety of reasons, including lower levels of education and job training, different occupational choices, the need to juggle the heavy demands of both career and parenthood, and the career hit that parents often take when they step out of the workforce for extended periods, since more women than men choose to be stay-at-home parents.

Beyond pay and promotional opportunities, many working women also have to deal with **sexual harassment**, defined as either an obvious request for sexual favors with an implicit reward or punishment related to work, or the more subtle creation of a sexist environment in which employees are made to feel uncomfortable by lewd jokes, remarks, or gestures. Even though male employees may also be targets of sexual harassment and both male and female employees may experience same-sex harassment, sexual harassment of female employees by male colleagues continues to make up the majority of reported cases. Recent surveys suggest that anywhere from 21 to 45 percent of women and 7 to 19 percent of men reported being sexually harassed at work. In response, most corporations now publish strict policies prohibiting harassment, both to protect their employees and to protect themselves from lawsuits.[48]

Race. In many respects, the element of race in the diversity picture presents the same concerns as gender: equal pay for equal work, access to promotional opportunities, and ways to break through the glass ceiling. However, while the ratio of men and women in the workforce remains fairly stable year to year, the ethnic composition of the United States has been on a long-term trend of greater and greater diversity. Even the term "minority," as it applies to nonwhite residents, makes less and less sense every year: In two states (California and New Mexico) and several dozen large cities, Caucasian Americans no longer constitute a clear majority.[49]

Unfortunately, as with average wages between women and men, disparity still exists between minority households and white households. For instance, African American males earn roughly 75 percent of what white males earn, and that ratio has barely budged in the last decade.[50] One bright spot: African Americans now hold more than 300 board seats in the largest U.S. corporations, leading to hope that people in these positions can use their influence to level the playing field for minority employees.[51]

Religion. The effort to accommodate employees' life interests on a broader scale has led a number of companies to address the issue of religion in the workplace. As one of the most personal aspects of life, of course, religion does bring potential for controversy in a work setting. On the one hand, some employees feel they should be able to express their beliefs in the workplace and not be forced to "check their faith at the door" when they come to work. On the other hand, companies want to avoid situations in which openly expressed religious differences might cause friction between employees or distract employees from their responsibilities. To help address such concerns, firms such as Ford, Intel, Texas Instruments, and American Airlines allow employees to form faith-based employee-support groups as part of their diversity strategies. In contrast, Proctor & Gamble is among those companies that don't allow organized religious activities at its facilities.[52] As more companies work to establish inclusive workplaces, and as more employees seek to integrate religious convictions into their daily work, you can expect to see this issue being discussed at a wide range of companies in the coming years.

Diversity Initiatives   To respond to these many challenges—and to capitalize on the business opportunities offered by both diverse marketplaces and diverse workforces—companies across the country are finding that embracing diversity in the richest sense is simply good business. As the U.S. population becomes more diverse, a diverse workforce can be a significant competitive advantage by bringing more ideas and broader perspectives to bear on business challenges. In response, thousands of U.S. companies have established **diversity initiatives**, which can include such steps as contracting with more suppliers owned by women and minorities, adding more women and minorities to boards of directors, and targeting a more diverse customer base. Many companies also offer employees diversity training to promote understanding of the unique cultures, customs, and talents of all employees.

For example, IBM established executive-led task forces to represent women, Asian Americans, African Americans, Hispanic Americans, Native Americans, people with disabilities, and individuals who are gay, lesbian, bisexual, and transgender. Recommendations from these task forces helped transform IBM's recruiting, training, leadership, and development

Managers have the responsibility to educate their employees on the definition and consequences of sexual harassment.

sexual harassment
Unwelcome sexual advance, request for sexual favors, or other verbal or physical conduct of a sexual nature within the workplace

diversity initiatives
Efforts to attract and support diverse workforces, expand supplier bases, and reach out to diverse markets

The number of U.S. workers over 65 has been growing in recent years, creating both opportunities and challenges for managers.

Discuss four alternative work arrangements that a company can use to address workplace challenges

flextime
Scheduling system in which employees are allowed certain options regarding time of arrival and departure

practices. Today, diversity is embraced at the employee level through 133 networking groups that unite people with a variety of talents and interests. As part of a broader effort to include as many employees as possible in its available talent pool, the company views its diversity efforts as a way to produce the best products in a competitive marketplace. For instance, women and minorities are a significant presence in the small-business marketplace, and having women and minorities on product development and marketing teams helps IBM understand the needs of these customers.[53]

However, opinions differ on whether support groups for specific groups of employees help or hurt efforts to embrace diversity. For instance, UPS doesn't have such employee-support groups, nor does it have a diversity officer, an increasingly common executive position. As the company's senior vice president of human resources, Lea Soupata, explains, "We don't want to accentuate differences among us. We're all part of the same team."[54]

Although encouraging sensitivity to employee differences is an important step, a company stands to benefit most when it incorporates its employees' diverse perspectives into the organization's work. This assimilation enables the company to uncover new opportunities by rethinking primary tasks and redefining markets, products, strategies, missions, business practices, and even cultures. Reneé Wingo of Virgin Mobile USA, a cell phone operator based in Warren, New Jersey, summarized this nicely when she advised, "You're not going to create any magic as a manager unless you bring together people with diverse perspectives who aren't miniversions of you."[55]

Alternative Work Arrangements

To meet today's staffing and demographic challenges, many companies are adopting alternative work arrangements to better accommodate the needs of employees—and to reduce costs in many cases. Four of the most popular arrangements are flextime, telecommuting, job sharing, and flexible career paths.

Flextime Flextime is a scheduling system that allows employees to choose their own hours, within certain limits. For instance, a company may require everyone to be at work between 10:00 A.M. and 2:00 P.M., but employees may arrive or depart whenever they want as long as they work a total of 8 hours every day. Another popular flextime schedule is to work four 10-hour days each week, taking one prearranged day off. The benefits include the opportunity for workers to align their schedules with other family members and to avoid the worst slowdowns during morning and afternoon commutes. More than half of U.S. companies offer employees some flexibility in choosing their work hours, although the number of companies offering flextime tends to rise and fall as the job market strengthens or weakens.[56] In addition, the feasibility of flextime differs from industry to industry and from position to position within individual companies. For instance, jobs that involve customer contact can require fixed working hours.

Telecommuting Telecommuting, or *telework*—working from home or another location using computers and telecommunications equipment to stay in touch with colleagues, suppliers, and customers—provides another dimension of flexibility. Telecommuting helps employees balance their professional and personal commitments by spending less time in transit between home and work, and it helps companies reduce facility costs while reaching a wider pool of potential employees. Sun Microsystems, one of the most extensive adopters of telecommuting among large corporations, saved $255 million on real estate during a recent four-year period. All employees, including top managers, are eligible to participate in the company's iWork program. Nearly half of Sun's 35,000 worldwide employees work from home or from one of several drop-in telework centers at least part of the time.[57]

Telecommuting does have potential limitations. One of the most commonly expressed concerns is work-life balance, with employees struggling to shut down their work lives so they can participate in their home lives. Some managers struggle with a perceived loss of control over employees they can't see. Others are concerned that people working at home

TECHNOLOGIES THAT ARE REVOLUTIONIZING BUSINESS Telecommuting Technologies

In simplest form, telecommuting doesn't require much more than a computer, a telephone, and access to the Internet and e-mail. However, most corporate employees need a more comprehensive connection to their offices, with such features as secure access to confidential files, groupware (see Chapter 4), and web-based virtual meetings that let people communicate and share information over the Internet. Some of the other technologies you'll encounter in telecommuting include broadband Internet connections (cable, DSL, or satellite), some form of file access (including shared workspaces), security (including user authentication and access control), Internet-based telephones, and wireless networking.

HOW THEY'RE CHANGING BUSINESS

When they're used successfully, telecommuting technologies can reduce facility costs, put employees closer to customers, reduce traffic and air pollution in congested cities, give companies access to a wide range of independent talent, and let employees work in higher-salary jobs while living in lower-cost areas of the country. In the future, these technologies have the potential to change business so radically they could even influence the design of entire cities. With less need to pull millions of workers into central business districts, business executives, urban planners, and political leaders have the opportunity to explore such new ideas as *telecities*—virtual cities populated by people and organizations who are connected technologically, rather than physically.

WHERE YOU CAN LEARN MORE

Start with the International Telework Association and Council, **www.telecommute.org**. Companies that supply hardware, software, and services for telecommuting—or that use extensive telecommuting themselves—often have information as well; see Sun Microsystems (**www. sun.com/aboutsun/iwork**), AT&T (**www.att.com/telework**), and AgilQuest (**www.agilquest.com**) for examples.

will slack off (although some studies show that telecommuters actually work *more* hours, not fewer) or that telecommuting could cause resentment among office-bound colleagues or weaken company loyalty.[58] Some companies find that the lack of face-to-face communication hinders decision making, in spite of the best technology available. Accel, a venture-capital firm based in London, has cut down on its use of telecommuting because "we were becoming dysfunctional," in the words of one partner.[59]

Defining the precise number of telecommuters in the United States is difficult, since some surveys include people who work from home as infrequently as once a month. However, telecommuting has clearly become a major element in the work life of U.S. employees. More than 20 million U.S. employees now work from home at least part of the time; about a quarter of these work at home every day or nearly every day.[60] Some two-thirds of Fortune 1000 companies now offer telecommuting arrangements to at least some of their employees.[61] Telecommuting is on the rise around the world, too; Europe is now home to 20 million teleworkers as well.[62]

Job Sharing **Job sharing**, which lets two employees share a single full-time job and split the salary and benefits, can be attractive an alternative for people who want part-time hours in situations normally reserved for full-time employees. Job sharing can be more challenging to implement than other flexible work arrangements, given the complexities of two individuals interacting with colleagues and customers instead of one. The benefits can be impressive, however, particularly for companies facing a brain drain as new parents leave the workforce. After the British drugstore chain Boots implemented job sharing, the percentage of women who returned to the company after maternity leave jumped from 7 to 77 percent.[63] Banking executives Cynthia Cunningham and Shelley Murray shared a position at Fleet Bank (now Bank of America) for six years and plan to apply for their next position as a team as well. One of their key selling points is offering a broader mix of skills than any one person is likely to offer.[64]

job sharing
Splitting a single full-time job between two employees

Flexible Career Paths Perhaps the most challenging of all alternative work arrangements are situations in which employees want to leave the workforce for an extended period of time to return to school, work for a charity, raise children, or pursue other interests—with the intention of returning to work at some point in the future. (The phrases "mommy track" and "daddy track" are often applied when an employee leaves a permanent, full-time position in order to raise children.) In the past, stepping out of the workforce for several years or more usually meant a significant blow to one's career. Skills can date quickly in fast-moving fields, networks of industry contacts can grow stale, and employees who "opted out" for a while sometimes got the stigma of being less than fully committed to their companies and careers.

However, the pressure to accommodate such moves is now coming from multiple angles: Companies that have invested in developing star employees want them back, many women who leave to raise children want to regain their career momentum when they return to work, and today's generation of new fathers frequently want to spend more time with their young children, even if that means putting their careers on hold for a while.[65] More than 40 percent of women and nearly a quarter of all men now opt out at some point in their careers, creating a potentially huge talent shortage for companies that are unable to reintegrate these employees.[66] To recapture as many of these employees as possible, IBM allows employees to take a *leave of absence* for up to three years, then return to either full-time or part-time work.[67]

CRITICAL THINKING CHECKPOINT

1. Is quality of work life a motivator or a hygiene factor? Why?
2. How can efforts to embrace and support diversity give companies a competitive edge?
3. Do you think that promoting women and minorities into positions of power makes companies more successful, or is it simply one of many signs of a successful company? Explain your answer.

Working with Labor Unions

labor unions
Organizations of employees formed to protect and advance their members' interests

Although they work toward common goals in most cases, managers and employees do face an inherent conflict over resources: Managers, as representatives of company ownership, want to minimize the costs of operating the business, whereas employees want to maximize salaries and ensure good benefits and safe, pleasant working conditions. If employees believe they are not being treated fairly or don't have a voice in how the company is run, they may have the option of joining **labor unions**, organizations that seek to protect employee interests by negotiating with employers for better wages and benefits, improved working conditions, and increased job security. Historically, labor unions have played an important role in U.S. employee-management relations and are largely responsible for the establishment of worker's compensation, child-labor laws, overtime rules, minimum-wage laws, severance pay, and more. (See Exhibit 10.6 for a summary of the most significant laws relating to labor unions.)

The history of labor-management relationships is long, complex, and often hostile. Unions can trace their history back nearly a thousand years, to early guilds in Europe that gave craftspeople bargaining power over merchants. In the United States, the Industrial Revolution in the second half of the 1800s and the Great Depression of the 1930s were formative events in the history of unionization. Responding to worker complaints about unsafe working conditions, long hours, child labor, and other concerns, unions gained a strong foothold in the United States. At the peak of unionization in the 1950s, about a third of the U.S. workforce belonged to unions.[68]

How Unions Are Structured

locals
Relatively small union groups, usually part of a national union or a labor federation, that represent members who work in a single facility or in a certain geographic area

Many unions are organized at local, national, and international levels. **Locals**, or local unions, represent employees in a specific geographic area or facility; an example is

Exhibit 10.6
Key Legislation Relating to Unions

Most major labor legislation was enacted in the 1930s and 1940s. Subsequent legislation amends and clarifies earlier laws.

Legislation	Provision
Norris-La Guardia Act of 1932	Limits companies' ability to obtain injunctions against union strikes, picketing, membership drives, and other activities.
National Labor Relations Act of 1935 (Wagner Act)	Gives employees the right to form, join, or assist labor organizations; the right to bargain collectively with employers through elected union representatives; and the right to engage in strikes, pickets, and boycotts. Prohibits certain unfair labor practices by the employer and union. Established the National Labor Relations Board to supervise union elections and to investigate charges of unfair labor practices by management.
Labor-Management Relations Act of 1947 (Taft-Hartley Act)	Amends Wagner Act to reaffirm employees' rights to organize and bargain collectively over working conditions. Establishes specific unfair labor practices both for management and for unions, and prohibits strikes in the public sector.
Landrum-Griffin Act of 1959	Amends Taft-Hartley Act and Wagner Act to control union corruption and to add the secondary boycott as an unfair labor practice. A secondary boycott occurs when a union appeals to firms or other unions to stop doing business with an employer who sells or handles goods of a company whose employees are on strike. The act requires all unions to file annual financial reports with the U.S. Department of Labor, making union officials more personally responsible for the union's elections, the right to sue unions, and the right to attend and participate in union meetings.
Plant-Closing Notification Act of 1988	Requires employers to give employees and local elected officials 60 days advance notice of plant shutdowns or massive layoffs.

United Auto Workers Local 1853 in Spring Hill, Tennessee, which represents GM's Saturn employees and those of several other companies in the area.[69] The members in a local are often referred to as the *rank and file*. Each department or facility also elects a **shop steward**, who works in the facility as a regular employee and serves as a go-between with supervisors when a problem arises. In large locals and in locals that represent employees at several locations, an elected full-time **business agent** visits the various work sites to negotiate with management and enforce the union's agreements with those companies.

A **national union** is a nationwide organization composed of many local unions that represent employees in specific locations; examples are the United Auto Workers (UAW) of America and the United Steelworkers of America. *International unions* have members in more than one country, such as the Union of Needletrades, Industrial, and Textile Employees (UNITE). A national union is responsible for such activities as organizing in new areas or industries, negotiating industrywide contracts, assisting locals with negotiations, administering benefits, lobbying Congress, and lending assistance in the event of a strike. Local unions send representatives to the national delegate convention, submit negotiated contracts to the national union for approval, and provide financial support in the form of dues. They have the power to negotiate with individual companies or plants and to undertake their own membership activities. The AFL-CIO is a **labor federation** consisting of a variety of national unions and of local unions that are not associated with any other national union.

How Unions Organize

Unions are required by law to follow a specific process for gaining the right to represent a given group of workers, known as a *bargaining unit* (see Exhibit 10.7). Employees who

shop steward
Union member and employee who is elected to represent other union members and who attempts to resolve employee grievances with management

business agent
Full-time union staffer who negotiates with management and enforces the union's agreements with companies

national union
Nationwide organization made up of local unions that represent employees in locations around the country

labor federation
Umbrella organization of national unions and unaffiliated local unions that undertakes large-scale activities on behalf of their members and that resolves conflicts between unions

Exhibit 10.7

The Union-Organizing Process

This diagram summarizes the steps a labor union takes when organizing a group of employees and becoming certified to represent them in negotiations with management. The certification election is necessary only if management is unwilling to recognize the union.

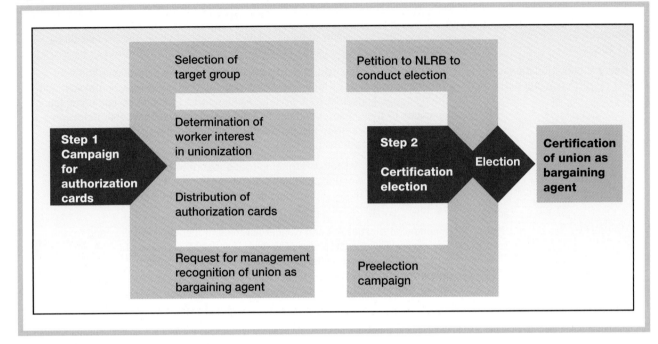

authorization cards
Sign-up cards designating a union as the signer's preferred bargaining agent

certification
Process by which a union is officially recognized by the National Labor Relations Board as the bargaining agent for a group of employees

decertification
Process employees use to take away a union's official right to represent them

express interest are sent information about the union, along with **authorization cards**—sign-up cards used to designate the union as their bargaining agent. If 30 percent or more of the employees in the group sign the union's authorization cards, the union may ask management to recognize it. Usually, however, unions do not seek to become the group's bargaining agent unless a majority of the employees sign.

Often the company's management is unwilling to recognize the union at this stage. The union can then ask the National Labor Relations Board (NLRB), an independent federal agency created in 1935, to administer and enforce the National Labor Relations Act, to supervise a **certification** election, the process by which a union becomes the official bargaining agent for a company's employees. If a majority of the affected employees choose to make the union their bargaining agent, the union becomes certified. If not, that union and all other unions have to wait a year before trying again.

Once a company becomes aware that a union is seeking a certification election, management may mount an active campaign to point out the disadvantages of unionization, from the company's perspective. A company is not allowed, however, to make specific threats or promises about how it will respond to the outcome of the election, and it is not allowed to change general wages or working conditions until the election has been concluded.

Even when a union wins a certification election, there's no guarantee that it will represent a particular group of employees forever. Sometimes employees become dissatisfied with their union and no longer wish to be represented by it. When this happens, the union members can take a **decertification** vote to take away the union's right to represent them. If the majority votes for decertification, the union is removed as the bargaining agent. After Atlas Container acquired another container plant, which had been unionized for 40 years, employees in that plant eventually decided that the Centenari brothers' approach to management met their needs better than the union could and voted in favor of decertification.[70]

The Collective Bargaining Process

As long as a union has been recognized as the exclusive bargaining agent for a group of employees, its main job is to negotiate employment contracts with management. In a process known as **collective bargaining**, union and management negotiators work together to forge the human resources policies that will apply to all employees covered by the contract. Most labor contracts are a compromise between the desires of union members and those of management. The union pushes for the best possible deal for its members, and management tries to negotiate agreements that are best for the company (and the shareholders, if a corporation is publicly held). Exhibit 10.8 illustrates the collective bargaining process.

collective bargaining
Process used by unions and management to negotiate work contracts

Meeting and Reaching an Agreement When the negotiating teams made up of representatives of the union and management sit down together, they state their opening positions and each side discusses its position point by point. In a cooperative atmosphere, the real issues behind the demands gradually come to light. For example, management may begin by demanding the right to determine the sizes of work crews when all it really wants is smaller work crews; the union, however, wants to protect the jobs of its members and keep crew sizes as large as possible but may agree to certain reductions in exchange for, say, higher pay. After many stages of bargaining, each party presents its package of terms, and any gaps between labor and management demands are then dealt with.

mediation
Process for resolving a labor-contract dispute in which a neutral third party meets with both sides and attempts to steer them toward a solution

If negotiations reach an impasse, outside help may be needed. The most common alternative is **mediation**—bringing in an impartial third party to study the situation and make recommendations for resolution of the differences. Mediators are generally well-respected community leaders whom both sides will listen to. However, mediators can only offer suggestions, and their solutions are not binding. When a legally binding settlement is needed, the negotiators may submit to **arbitration**—a process in which an impartial referee listens to both sides and then makes a judgment by accepting one side's view. In *compulsory arbitration,* the parties are required by a government agency to submit to arbitration; in *voluntary arbitration,* the parties agree on their own to use arbitration to settle their differences.

arbitration
Process for resolving a labor-contract dispute in which an impartial third party studies the issues and makes a binding decision

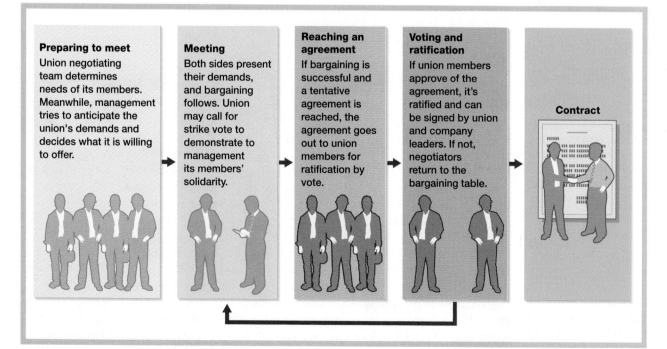

Preparing to meet
Union negotiating team determines needs of its members. Meanwhile, management tries to anticipate the union's demands and decides what it is willing to offer.

Meeting
Both sides present their demands, and bargaining follows. Union may call for strike vote to demonstrate to management its members' solidarity.

Reaching an agreement
If bargaining is successful and a tentative agreement is reached, the agreement goes out to union members for ratification by vote.

Voting and ratification
If union members approve of the agreement, it's ratified and can be signed by union and company leaders. If not, negotiators return to the bargaining table.

Contract

Exhibit 10.8
The Collective Bargaining Process
Contract negotiations go through the four basic steps shown here.

LEARNING OBJECTIVE 6

Cite three options unions can exercise when negotiations with management break down

Exercising Options When Negotiations Break Down The vast majority of management-union negotiations are settled without the need for either side to take further action. However, negotiations occasionally reach an impasse, and neither side is willing to compromise. Both labor and management are able to draw on many powerful options when negotiations or mediation procedures break down.

Labor's Options. Strikes and picket lines are perhaps labor's best-known tactics, but other options are also used.

strike
Temporary work stoppage by employees who want management to accept their union's demands

picketing
Strike activity in which union members march before company entrances to communicate their grievances and to discourage people from doing business with the company

boycott
Union activity in which members and sympathizers refuse to buy or handle the product of a target company

- *Strike.* The most powerful weapon that organized labor can use is the **strike**, a temporary work stoppage aimed at forcing management to accept union demands. The basic idea behind the strike is that, in the long run, it costs management more in lost earnings to resist union demands than to give in. An essential part of any strike is **picketing**, in which union members positioned at entrances to company premises march back and forth with signs and leaflets, trying to persuade nonstriking employees to join them and to persuade customers and others to stop doing business with the company.
- *Boycott.* A less direct union weapon is the **boycott**, in which union members and sympathizers refuse to buy or handle the product of a target company. Millions of union members form an enormous bloc of purchasing power, which may be able to pressure management into making concessions. In fact, the AFL-CIO maintains a website that lists companies it would like consumers to boycott (**www.unionlabel.org/boycott.asp**).
- *Publicity.* Increasingly, labor is pressing its case by launching publicity campaigns, often called *corporate campaigns,* against the target company and companies affiliated with it. These campaigns might include sending investors alerts that question the firm's solvency, staging rallies during peak business hours, sending letters to charitable groups questioning executives' motives, handing out leaflets that allege safety and health-code violations, and stimulating negative stories in the press.

Labor's other options include *slowdowns,* in which employees continue to do their jobs but at a slow enough pace to disrupt operations, and *sickouts,* in which employees feign illness and stay home.

Management's Options. From its side, management can use a number of legal methods to pressure unions when negotiations stall:

When contract talks broke down between grocery workers and major grocery chains in Southern California in late 2003, the result was a strike that lasted four and a half months.

- *Strikebreakers.* When union members walk off their jobs, management can legally replace them with **strikebreakers**, nonunion workers hired to do the jobs of striking workers. (Union members brand them as "scabs.")
- *Lockouts.* The U.S. Supreme Court has upheld the use of **lockouts**, in which management prevents union employees from entering the workplace, in order to pressure the union to accept a contract proposal. A lockout is management's counterpart to a strike. It is a preemptive measure designed to force a union to accede to management's demands. Lockouts are legal only if the union and management have come to an impasse in negotiations and the employer is defending a legitimate bargaining position. During a lockout, the company may hire temporary replacements as long as it has no antiunion motivation and negotiations have been amicable.[71] In extreme instances, the company will cease operations, as the National Hockey League did when it canceled the 2005 season after owners and players failed to reach agreement on new contract terms.[72]
- *Injunctions.* An **injunction** is a court order prohibiting union workers from taking certain actions. Management used this weapon without restriction in the early days of unionism, when companies typically sought injunctions to order striking employees back to work on the grounds that the strikers were interfering with business. Today, injunctions are legal only in certain cases. For example, the president of the United States has the right, under the Taft-Hartley Act, to obtain a temporary injunction to halt a strike deemed harmful to the national interest, such as a wide-scale transportation strike.

The Labor Movement Today

In certain industries, including transportation, retailing, and manufacturing, unions remain a significant force in employee-management relations in the United States. But their membership continues to decline, from more than a third of the workforce in the 1950s to less than 15 percent today.[73] True to the often combative nature of the relationship, each side blames organized labor's decline on the other. Some business leaders say unions don't have anything relevant to offer workers in today's environment of more enlightened and supportive management, while union leaders say managers use every tactic they can think of, both legal and illegal, to thwart unionization efforts. According to one source, in a quarter of all certification campaigns in 1988 and 1989, union supporters were illegally fired by their employers. Unions also point to surveys suggesting that nearly half of U.S. workers would vote for a union if given the opportunity.[74]

Meanwhile, the labor movement is also in a state of internal turmoil, highlighted by a major split within the AFL-CIO in 2005. After criticizing the national federation for being too slow to adapt to the changing world of business, four unions—including the Service Employees International Union, which is both the largest union in the United States and one of the few unions to experience strong membership growth in recent years—took steps to end their affiliation with the AFL-CIO.[75]

What does the future hold for unions? Predictions are risky, but two key issues highlight the continuing complexity of union-management relations:

- *Health-care costs.* By just about any measure, health-care costs in the United States are spiraling out of control, climbing much faster than the general inflation rate. These costs have become a major point of contention in labor negotiations, with employers saying that employees need to pay a larger share of health-care costs and employees saying they can't afford to. Much of this attention focuses on Wal-Mart, the nation's largest private employer and a company famous—or infamous, depending on whose side you're on—for cutting costs to the bone. Wal-Mart typically pays its workers less than other chains, which tends to drive down wages across the industry, and many employees say they can't afford the health insurance the company offers. Wal-Mart workers are not unionized— although the United Food and Commercial Workers union is campaigning hard for certification—but the company is such a dominant force in retail that many competitors feel they have no choice but to cut their own operating costs in order to survive.[76]

• *International competition.* In industries that face vigorous international competition, such as autos, steel, and aircraft, some union and business leaders are trying to work more cooperatively than they have in years past. In the steel industry, for instance, union leaders have made significant concessions and even helped arrange the consolidation of three battered steel companies in the hopes of competing more effectively with overseas suppliers.[77]

Both health-care costs and international competition are staggeringly complex challenges with no clear solutions, but attempts to solve them may well influence the progress of unions in the coming years.

CRITICAL THINKING CHECKPOINT

1. If a company's workforce has been unionized for years as a result of poor policies toward employees in the past, how might the current management regain the workers' trust?
2. Why might a union choose a boycott over a strike?
3. What are the risks of initiating a lockout?

CHECKLIST: Apply These Ideas When You're the Boss

✓ Recognize the importance of employee morale, in both good times and bad; motivated employees can accomplish far more than people who simply show up for work.

✓ Whenever you face a motivational challenge, revisit the basic needs-action-outcome model of motivation; it can help you identify, understand, and respond to a variety of motivational issues.

✓ Don't settle on a single theory of motivation or a single motivational strategy; each can offer some important insights, but none is a complete picture of complex human behavior.

✓ Remember that perceptions of unequal treatment or rewards can breed tremendous resentment in a workforce.

✓ Pay close attention to the expectancy theory model when designing motivational strategies and programs; for instance, if people don't value the rewards you offer, they'll have little motivation to improve their performance.

✓ Understand the negative effects of uncertainty and fear regarding job stability; people worried about their jobs might work extra hard—or they might adopt negative, self-protective behaviors or simply start looking for another job.

✓ Pay attention to the diverse expectations—and potential contributions—of today's multifaceted workforce.

✓ No matter what your opinions about unionization are, keep in mind that a negative long-term relationship between a union and an employer isn't going to help anybody.

Summary of Learning Objectives

1 **Compare Maslow's hierarchy of needs and Herzberg's two-factor theory, then explain their application to employee motivation.** Maslow's hierarchy organizes individual needs into five categories and proposes that the individual must satisfy the most basic needs before being able to address higher-level needs. Based on the assumption that employees want to "climb to the top" of Maslow's pyramid, managers should provide opportunities to satisfy those higher-level needs. Herzberg's two-factor theory covers the same general set of employee needs but divides them into two distinct groups. His theory suggests that hygiene factors—such as working conditions, company policies, and job security—can influence employee dissatisfaction, but an improvement in these factors will not motivate employees. Only motivational factors such as recognition and responsibility can improve employee performance.

2 **Explain why expectancy theory is considered by some to be the best description of employee behavior.** Expectancy, which suggests that the effort employees put into their work depends on expectations about their own ability to perform, expectations about the rewards that the organization will give in response to that performance, and the attractiveness of those rewards relative to their individual goals, is considered a good model because it considers the linkages between effort and outcome. For instance, if employees think a linkage is "broken," such as having doubts that their efforts will yield acceptable performance or worries that they will perform well but no one will notice, they're likely to put less effort into their work.

3 **Discuss four staffing challenges employers are facing in today's workplace.** The four challenges identified in the chapter are (1) aligning the workforce with the organization's needs; (2) fostering employee loyalty in a time when most companies can no longer guarantee lifetime employment; (3) monitoring employee workloads and making sure employee are in danger of burnout; and (4) helping employee find a balance, at least temporarily, between the demands of their personal and professional lives.

4 **Explain the challenges and advantages of a diverse workforce.** Smart business leaders recognize diverse workforces bring a broader range of viewpoints and ideas, they help companies understand and identify with diverse markets, and they enable companies to tap into the broadest possible pool of talent. Supervisors face the challenge of communicating with these diverse employees, motivating them, and fostering cooperation and harmony among them. Teams face the challenge of working together closely, and companies are challenged to coexist peacefully with business partners and with the community as a whole.

5 **Discuss four alternative work arrangements that a company can use to address workplace challenges.** To meet today's staffing and demographic challenges, companies are offering their employees flextime (the ability to vary their work hours), telecommuting (the ability to work from home or another location), job sharing (the ability to share a single full-time job with a co-worker), and flexible career paths (the opportunity to leave the workforce for an extended period then return).

6 **Explain the two steps unions take to become the bargaining agent for a group of employees.** First, unions distribute authorization cards to employees, which designate the union as the bargaining agent, and if at least 30 percent (but usually a majority) of the target group sign the cards, the union asks management to recognize it. Second, if management is unwilling to do so, the union asks the National Labor Relations Board to sponsor a certification election. If a majority of the employees vote in favor of being represented by the union, the union becomes the official bargaining agent for the employees.

7 **Cite three options unions can exercise when negotiations with management break down.** Unions can conduct strikes, organize boycotts, and use publicity to pressure management into complying with union proposals. A strike is a temporary work stoppage, which the union hopes will cost management enough in lost earnings so that management will be forced to accept union demands. A boycott is a union tactic designed to pressure management into making concessions by convincing sympathizers to refuse to buy or handle the product of the target company. A negative publicity campaign against the target company is a pressure tactic designed to smear the reputation of the company in hopes of gaining management's attention.

8 **Cite three options management can exercise when negotiations with a union break down.** To pressure a union into accepting its proposals, management may continue running the business with strikebreakers (nonunion workers hired to do the jobs of striking workers), institute a lockout of union members by preventing union employees from entering the workplace, or seek an injunction against a strike or other union activity.

Atlas Container: What's Next

"A rising tide lifts all boats." Business professionals like to share that old nugget to explain how a growing industry makes it easy for just about any company to increase its sales.

Well, the tide's not rising in the cardboard container business, and when a company such as Atlas Container continues to increase its revenues, you can be fairly certain that it's doing more than a few things better than the competition. Through both acquisitions of other box companies and *organic growth*—increases of sales through existing operations—Atlas manages to increase its sales 20 to 25 percent a year. Plus, with workforce morale higher than it is in many competitive firms, employee turnover is much lower—about 15 percent a year, compared to 50 percent for the industry. That keeps continuity and customer satisfaction high and costs low as well.

Competitors can use the same raw materials that Atlas uses, buy the same machinery, implement the same production methods, and even copy its marketing and sales approach. But you can't fake soul. And the soul of Atlas Container, built on fundamental respect for employees, is its most sustainable competitive advantage.[78]

Critical Thinking Questions

1. Why does involving employees in decision making help raise their morale?
2. What are the challenges involved in giving employees the opportunity to vote on major business decisions?
3. What problems might Atlas run into as it continues to acquire other companies and instill its management style in those new facilities?

Learn More Online

Visit the Atlas Container website by clicking on the hotlink at Chapter 10 of this text's website at **www.prenhall.com/bovee**. Explore the company, product, and employment information on the site. How does Atlas Container describe itself? How does the company try to distinguish itself from its competitors? What kind of people is the company looking to hire?

Key Terms

arbitration (347)
authorization cards (346)
behavior modification (334)
boycott (348)
brain drain (335)
business agent (345)
certification (346)
collective bargaining (347)
decertification (346)
diversity initiatives (341)
engagement (327)
equity theory (332)
expectancy theory (332)
flextime (342)
glass ceiling (340)

goal-setting theory (333)
hygiene factors (329)
injunction (349)
job enrichment (337)
job redesign (337)
job sharing (343)
labor federation (345)
labor unions (344)
locals (344)
lockouts (349)
management by objectives (MBO) (333)
mediation (347)
morale (327)
motivation (327)

motivators (330)
national union (345)
picketing (348)
quality of work life (QWL) (337)
reinforcement theory (334)
scientific management (328)
sexism (340)
sexual harassment (341)
shop steward (345)
strike (348)
strikebreakers (349)
work-life balance (336)
Theory X (330)
Theory Y (330)
Theory Z (331)

Test Your Knowledge

Questions for Review

1. What is motivation?
2. In what way are Maslow's hierarchy and Herzberg's two-factor theory similar?
3. What is expectancy theory?
4. What is the glass ceiling?
5. What is quality of work life, and how does it influence employee motivation?

Questions for Analysis

6. Why do managers often find it difficult to motivate employees who remain after downsizing?
7. How can diversity initiatives benefit a company?
8. What are some of the advantages and disadvantages of alternative work arrangements?

9. Why do employees choose to join labor unions? Why do they not join labor unions?

10. **Ethical Considerations.** You've got a golf game scheduled for Sunday afternoon, and you've worked all weekend to write a proposal to be presented Monday morning. The proposal is more or less finished, but a few more hours of work would make it polished and persuasive. Do you cancel the game?

Questions for Application

11. Some of your talented and hardworking employees come to you one day and say they do not feel challenged. They expected to be able to diversify their skills more and take on greater responsibility than they now have. How do you respond?

12. Assume you are the plant manager for a company that manufactures tires for cars and light trucks. To compete more economically in the global market, the company is seriously considering closing the plant within the next year and moving manufacturing operations to Southeast Asia. Upon hearing about the possible plant closing, the union votes to launch a strike in one week if its demands for job security aren't met. Because of a recent surge in orders, the company is not in a position to close the plant yet. What are your options as you continue to negotiate with union representatives? Which option would you choose and why?

13. **Integrated.** How do economic concepts such as profit motive and competitive advantage (see Chapter 1) affect today's workforce?

14. **Integrated.** Why is it sometimes difficult for small businesses to allow employees to telecommute, share jobs, and work flexible hours?

Practice Your Knowledge

Handling Difficult Situations on the Job: Removing the Obstacles from the On Ramp

Like many companies these days, the accounting firm Ernst & Young is fighting a brain drain as experienced executives and professionals leave in mid-career to pursue charitable interests, spend more time with family, or pursue a variety of other dreams or obligations. The problem is particularly acute among women, since on average they step off the career track to pursue outside interests more often than men do. As general manager of the largest division in the company, you've been tapped to draft a set of guidelines to make it easier for employees who've taken some time off to move back into the company.

However, as soon as word gets out about what you're planning, several of your top performers, people who've never left the company for personal time off—or "taken the off ramp," in current buzzword-speak—march into your office to complain. They fear that encouraging the "off-rampers" to return isn't fair to the employees who've remained loyal to the firm, as they put it. One goes as far to say that anyone who leaves the company doesn't deserve to be asked back. Two others claim that the additional experience and skills they've gained as they continued to work should guarantee them higher pay and more responsibilities than employees who took time off for themselves.[79]

Your task: This is a managerial dilemma if there ever was one. On the one hand, you need to attract as many of these people back as you can, precisely because you need their high levels of skill and experience. On the other hand, if you reward them for that skill and experience, some of your other employees may accuse you of giving the returnees special treatment. How should you handle this thorny situation? What points would you make to the workforce in order to educate them on the company's need for these talented people and to assure them everyone will be treated fairly? How can you resolve this without making either group feel that they've been treated unfairly?

Sharpening Your Communication Skills

As the director of public relations for a major airline, one of your less-pleasant responsibilities is preparing news releases should the pilots decide to strike. This is a challenging task because many people will be affected by the strike. Being a good communicator, you know that one of the first things you must do before preparing a message is to analyze the audience. Think about an airline strike and answer these questions briefly to practice this important communication technique:

1. What groups of people do you think would be interested in the information about the airline strike?
2. What do you think each of these groups would want to know about most?
3. How might they react to the information you will provide? Summarize your answers to these three questions in a short memo to your instructor.

Building Your Team Skills

Debate the pros and cons of telecommuting for an accounting, computer programming, or graphics design firm. Break into groups of four students, with two students taking the employees' pro side and the other two taking management's con side. As you prepare for this debate, consider the following factors: employee motivation, staffing challenges, quality of work life, costs, control, and feasibility.

During your team's debate, let one side present its arguments while the other side takes notes on the major points. After both sides have completed their presentations, discuss all the supporting points and try to reach a consensus as to whether or not your firm will support telecommuting. Draft a one-page statement outlining your team's conclusion and reasoning, and then share it during a class discussion.

Compare your team's conclusion and reasoning with those of other teams. Do most teams believe telecommuting is a good or bad idea? What issues do most teams agree on? What issues do they disagree on?

Expand Your Knowledge

Discovering Career Opportunities

Is an alternative work arrangement such as flextime, job sharing, or telecommuting in your career future? This exercise will help you think about whether these work arrangements fit into your career plans.

1. Look at the list of possible business careers in the Prologue (see page 2). Of the careers that interest you, which seem best suited to flextime? To job sharing? To telecommuting?
2. Select one of the careers that seems suited to telecommuting. What job functions do you think could be performed at home or from another remote location?
3. Thinking about the same career, do you think it would be possible to split the job's responsibilities with a co-worker under a job-sharing arrangement? What issues, if any, might you need to resolve first?

Developing Your Research Skills

Select one or two articles from recent issues of business journals or newspapers (print or online editions) that relate to employee motivation or morale.

1. What is the problem or trend discussed in the article(s), and how is it influencing employee attitudes or motivation?
2. Is this problem unique to this company, or does it have broader implications? Who is affected by it now, and who do you think might be affected by it in the future?
3. What challenges and opportunities does this situation present to the company or industry? The employees? Management?

Exploring the Best of the Web

URLs for all Internet exercises are provided at the website for this book, **www.prenhall.com/bovee**. When you log on to this text's Companion Website, select Chapter 10. Then select "Featured Websites," click on the name of the featured website, and review the website to complete these exercises.

Explore these chapter-related websites, review their content, and answer the following questions for each website you visit:

1. What is the purpose of this website?
2. What kinds of information does this website contain? Please be specific.
3. How is this information provided at this website useful for businesspeople? Consumers?
4. How did you expand your knowledge of managing employees by reviewing the materials at this website? What new things did you learn about this topic?

Working Hard on the Web

Frustrated workers and managers now have a place to go to voice their opinions, commiserate with others, and get advice on how to motivate employees. The place is Hard@Work, a website created "to reduce the oversupply of fear and alienation in the workplace by meeting the pent-up demand for constructive communication about what's happening on the job." Visitors can hang around the "Water Cooler" to chat with others about work issues and careers; play "Stump the Mentor," which offers suggestions for handling sticky work situations; or dig into the "Rock Pile," which features realistic case studies. Hard@Work offers something for workers and job seekers alike. www.hardatwork.com

Learn the Language of Equal Opportunity

The Equal Employment Opportunity Commission (EEOC) offers an extensive array of information online for both employees and employers. Explore the categories of employment discrimination and learn how the government defines each type. Learn more about the employment laws that employers are expected to follow, or see the steps employees can take when they feel they have been discriminated against. www.eeoc.gov

Spreading the Union Message

Of all the websites devoted to union causes, the AFL-CIO's site offers perhaps the most extensive collection of statistics, information, and commentaries on union issues and programs. The site is designed to educate members and prospective members about union activities and campaigns. Topics include union membership campaigns, safety and family issues, and much more. The AFL-CIO also maintains online directories with the e-mail addresses of members of Congress plus sample letters to encourage communication with legislators. Browse this site to get the latest on union initiatives as well as information about trends in the labor movement today. www.aflcio.org

Learning Interactively

Companion Website

Visit the Companion Website at www.prenhall.com/bovee. For Chapter 10, take advantage of the interactive "Learning Modules" to test your chapter knowledge. Get instant feedback on whether you need additional studying. Complete the exercises as specified by your instructor.

A Case for Critical Thinking

Brewing Up People Policies at Starbucks

Hiring, training, and compensating a diverse workforce of 40,000 employees worldwide would be a difficult task for any company. But it was an especially daunting challenge in an industry whose annual employee turnover rate approached 300 percent. It was even more of a challenge for a company that was striving to open a new store every day.

This was the high-pressure situation facing Starbucks Coffee Company in the 1990s, when CEO Howard Schultz set a torrid pace for global expansion. The rich aroma of fresh-brewed espresso was already wafting through hundreds of neighborhoods all over North America, and new stores were planned for the United Kingdom, Japan, even China. But Schultz and his management team knew that good locations and top-quality coffee were just part of the company's formula for success.

To keep up with its ambitious schedule of new store openings, Starbucks had to find, recruit, and train 700 new employees every month, no easy feat "when there is a shortage of labor and few people want to work behind a retail counter," as Schultz noted. Moreover, Starbucks employees had to deliver consistently superior customer service in every store and every market. In other words Starbucks employees (known internally as partners) had to do more than simply pour coffee—they had to believe passionately in the product and pay attention to all the details that can make or break the retail experience for the chain's 10 million weekly customers. In short, Starbucks managers had to ensure that their stores provided the best service along with the best coffee.

PERKING UP BENEFITS

Schultz, of course, knew that attracting and motivating employees would take more than good pay and company declarations to "provide a great work environment and treat each other with respect and dignity." So, guided by the company mission statement, the CEO and his managers designed a variety of human resources programs to motivate Starbucks partners.

First they raised employees' base pay. Next, management bucked the trend in the industry by offering full medical, dental, life, and disability insurance benefits to every partner who worked at least 20 hours per week. These partners were also eligible for paid vacation days and retirement savings plans, benefits not commonly available to part-time restaurant workers. To help partners better balance their work and family obligations—another priority for Starbucks—the human resources department designed a comprehensive work-life program. This program featured flexible work schedules, access to employee assistance specialists, and referrals for child-care and elder-care support.

A TASTE OF THE GOOD LIFE

The most innovative benefit brewed up by management, however, was its Bean Stock, a program offering stock options not just to upper-echelon managers but to all partners who worked 20 or more hours per week. "We established Bean Stock in 1991 as a way of investing in our partners and creating ownership across the company," explained Bradley Honeycutt, vice president of human resources. "It's been a key to retaining good people and building loyalty." For those who wanted to enlarge their financial stake in Starbucks, management devised a program that permitted partners to buy company stock at a discount. Owning a piece of the company motivated employees to take customer service to an even higher level of excellence.

THE PERFECT BLEND

Of course, Starbucks recognizes that good pay and benefits, while attractive, are not enough to meet the company's future growth plans. So to stay on schedule and on top, Starbucks continually invests in its workforce, including training in not only the finer points of coffee brewing but also the company's culture and values. To encourage more and better feedback and communication, management holds a series of open forums in which company performance, results, and plans are openly discussed. Finally, Starbucks honors employees whose achievements exemplify the company's values.

BUBBLING INTO THE FUTURE

Focusing on its employees has helped Starbucks grow from 17 coffee shops in Seattle to a multibillion-dollar operation with thousands of outlets around the world—while maintaining a strong record of profitability. The record is stunning, all things considered, but success always brings new challenges, particularly for a company that has set its sights on having 30,000 coffee shops worldwide (Starbucks hasn't publicly announced a target date for achieving this goal). In a sign of the times, Starbucks recently dismissed an employee who wrote critical comments about his boss on a personal blog site. Some employees occasionally grumble about being overworked, but in general, such complaints seem to be less widespread than in the typical food service or retail operation.

Starbucks still innovates in its search for better ways to support its workforce. One great example is the series of award-winning computer games to introduce younger employees to the importance and nuances of retirement planning, including the company's FutureRoast retirement savings program. The first principle of the Starbucks mission statement—"Provide a great work environment and treat each other with respect and dignity"—still guides the company in its approach to hiring and caring for its partners. That mission statement is no dusty document sitting on a shelf at company headquarters, either. Employees are encouraged to bring up anything they see that could violate the mission. Some two hundred employees raise concerns every month, and every concern is looked into. Under the leadership of new CEO Jim Donald, Starbucks continues to pay close attention to the employees who are responsible for the worldwide phenomenon of the Starbucks coffee shop experience.

Critical Thinking Questions

1. Why do Starbucks human resources managers need to be advised of company plans for new store openings?
2. What are the advantages and disadvantages of employing so many part-timers?
3. How does Starbucks use generous employee benefits to motivate its employees?
4. Go to Chapter 10 of this text's website at www.prenhall.com/bovee and click on the hot link to get to the Starbucks website. Then visit the site's job section to see how Starbucks presents its HR policies to potential employees. Browse the pages that discuss working at Starbucks. Read about company culture, diversity, benefits, and learning and career development. Why would Starbucks post information about company culture in this section of the website? Why would job candidates be interested in learning about the culture as well as the employee benefits and training at Starbucks?

Video Case

Feeling Like Part of the Family: Kingston Technology

Learning Objectives

The purpose of this video is to help you:

1. Understand the importance of motivating employees.
2. Consider how financial and nonfinancial rewards can motivate employees.
3. Explain how high morale can affect organizational performance.

Synopsis

Kingston Technology, based in California, is the world's largest independent manufacturer of computer memory products. Founded by John Tu and David Sun, Kingston employs more than 2,000 people—yet makes each employee feel like part of the family. The company returns 10 percent of its company profits to employees every year through a profit-sharing program. Just as important, it fosters mutual trust and respect between employees and management. Senior managers stay in touch with employees at all levels and conduct surveys to obtain employee feedback. For their part, employees report high job satisfaction and develop both personal and professional connections with their colleagues—boosting morale and motivation.

Discussion Questions

1. *For analysis:* After the sale to Softbank, employees learned from news reports that Kingston's $100 million profit-sharing distribution was one of the largest in U.S. history. What was the likely effect of this publicity on employee morale?
2. *For analysis:* Are Kingston's managers applying Theory X or Theory Y to their employees? How do you know?
3. *For application:* What kinds of questions should Kingston ask through employee surveys to gauge satisfaction and morale?
4. *For application:* What else might Kingston's management do to motivate employees by offering opportunities to satisfy higher-level needs such as self-actualization?
5. *For debate:* Do you agree with Kingston's policy of giving new employees profit-sharing bonuses even when they join the company just one week before profits are distributed? Support your position.

Online Exploration

Visit Kingston Technology's website at www.kingston.com and follow the link to browse company information and read about its awards. From the company information page, follow the link to learn about the organization's values. How do these values support the founders' intention to create a family feeling within the company? How do they support employees' achievement of higher-level needs? Why would Kingston post this listing of milestones on its website, starting with the company's founding and continuing with honors bestowed by Fortune and others?

Taking Care of Employees: Managing Human Resources

C H A P T E R

11

LEARNING OBJECTIVES

After studying this chapter, you will be able to

1. List six main functions of human resources departments

2. Cite eight methods recruiters use to find job candidates

3. Identify the six stages in the hiring process

4. Discuss how companies incorporate objectivity into employee performance appraisals

5. List six popular types of financial incentive programs for employees

6. Highlight five popular employee benefits

7. Describe four ways an employee's status may change and discuss why many employers like to fill job vacancies from within

www.prenhall.com/bovee

INSIDE BUSINESS TODAY

Blending a Successful Workforce: Jamba Juice Whips Up Creative Recruiting Strategies

www.jambajuice.com

Finding and keeping employees is no easy feat—especially for a high-growth company in the fast-food industry. But as a leading retailer of smoothies, freshly squeezed juices, healthy soups, and breads, San Francisco–based Jamba Juice meets the challenge of building a successful workforce with an appealing blend of savvy recruiting strategies and creative incentive tools.

Since founder Kirk Perron opened his first smoothie store in 1990, Jamba Juice has grown to hundreds of outlets nationwide, with dozens more added every year. The majority of Jamba's 4,000 employees are part-time workers, primarily high school and college students who whip up healthy concoctions between classes and during school breaks. To attract part-time "team members," Perron promoted the key ingredients of the company's success: nutrition, fitness, and fun. And he was quick to point out that the company's name reflected the enjoyable working environment—jamba is a West African word meaning "to celebrate."

As Jamba Juice expands its operations under the guidance of new CEO Paul Clayton, the human resources (HR) staff works closely with the company's real estate committee to forecast demand for the number of workers needed in specific locations. HR begins the search at least four months before an official store opening, allowing time for finding, interviewing, and training new employees.

Searches are conducted using a variety of resources, and they are customized for each market. For instance, to attract young candidates who fit the profile of a typical Jamba employee, HR managers make extensive use of community events and the Internet, including such recruiting websites as www.restaurantrecruit.com, a site popular with managers in the food industry. In turn, these sites provide a direct link to Jamba Juice's website so that job seekers can find out more about the company or send an e-mail requesting additional information.

Of course, Internet ads can generate responses from applicants who live as far away as Australia and France. So the HR staff must sift through the piles of applications and identify the strongest candidates to interview. Initial interviews are conducted by telephone. During 30-minute phone screenings, interviewers look for personable candidates with a strong work ethic—the type of candidate who wants to stick with the company.

But recruiting new staff is only one of the challenges Jamba Juice faces. Clayton must also retain current store managers. To do that, he starts by giving each new assistant general manager 500 stock options and each new general manager 2,500 stock options. (Stock options are opportunities to buy company stock at attractive prices, but employees must stay with the company for several years before they are able to take full advantage of this benefit.) Then he offers incentives to reward store performance, giving managers a percentage of their store's sales every eight weeks. Furthermore, managers accrue retention bonuses for building the store's business. After accumulating three years of retention bonuses, managers receive a cash payment for their efforts. And managers who sign up for three more years of employment are rewarded with a three-week paid sabbatical.

The combination of efforts to recruit and retain employees while immersing them in a positive corporate culture is paying dividends. Not only has Jamba Juice been able to successfully staff its nationwide expansion, but also it's gaining recognition from the restaurant industry, including the Winning Workforce Award from the National Restaurant Association.[1]

GET READY

Paul Clayton and his executive team at Jamba Juice devote much of their time and energy to one of the most pressing problems in business today: finding, recruiting, training, and retaining productive employees. In an industry that's notorious for high turnover, they've crafted a corporate culture that attracts good workers and good managers—and encourages them to stay longer than industry averages. If you were a top executive at Jamba Juice, where would you go to find employees and how would you convince them to join your company? What steps would you take to retain your best employees, particularly as the job market heats up in the coming years and the best workers and managers will have multiple career options to choose from? And how would you institute all these benefits and programs without letting costs get out of control?

Chapter Overview

Companies such as Jamba Juice demonstrate repeatedly that attracting and keeping the right employees is often the difference between failure and success. This chapter offers an overview of the human resources function, from planning a company's staffing needs to recruiting and training new employees to appraising employee performance. You'll also get a look at current practices in compensation and benefits, two topics that will surely interest you in the short term as an employee and in the long term as a manager or entrepreneur. The chapter concludes with a discussion of how companies manage changes in employment status, from the pleasant task of promoting employees to the unpleasant task of terminating them.

LEARNING OBJECTIVE 1

List six main functions of human resources departments

human resources management (HRM) Specialized function of planning how to obtain employees, oversee their training, evaluate them, and compensate them

Understanding What Human Resources Managers Do

No matter what the industry, hiring the right people to help a company reach its goals and then overseeing their training and development, motivation, evaluation, and compensation are critical to a company's success. These activities are known as **human resources management (HRM)**, which encompasses all the tasks involved in acquiring, maintaining, and developing an organization's human resources, as well as maintaining a safe working environment that meets current legal requirements and ethical expectations.[2] Because of the accelerating rate at which today's workforce, economy, corporate cultures, and legal environment are being transformed,

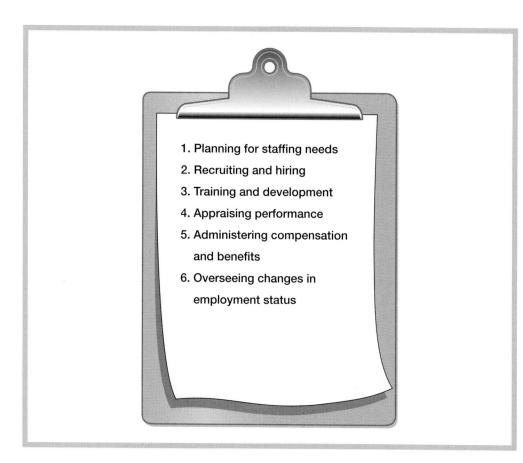

Exhibit 11.1
The Functions of the
Human Resources
Department
*Human resources
departments are
responsible for these six
important functions.*

1. Planning for staffing needs
2. Recruiting and hiring
3. Training and development
4. Appraising performance
5. Administering compensation
   and benefits
6. Overseeing changes in
   employment status

the role of human resources is increasingly viewed as a strategic one. More than half of employers now say that it plays a full or substantial role in the company's strategic planning efforts.[3]

Human resources (HR) managers must figure out how to attract qualified employees from the available pool of entry-level candidates, how to train employees in the skills the company needs to succeed, how to keep experienced employees who may have few opportunities for advancement, and how to adjust the workforce equitably when rightsizing is necessary. They must also retrain employees to cope with increasing automation and computerization, manage increasingly complex (and often expensive) employee benefits programs, shape workplace policies to address changing workforce demographics and employee needs (as discussed in Chapter 10), and cope with the challenge of meeting government regulations in hiring practices and equal opportunity employment.

In short, human resources managers and staff members help keep the organization running smoothly at every level by planning for a company's staffing needs, recruiting and hiring employees, training and developing employees and managers, appraising employee performance, and retaining valuable employees. (Note that in most organizations, HR shares these responsibilities with other functional departments. For instance, to train new accountants, HR will typically coordinate with the accounting department to provide the *content expertise* for training classes while specialists in HR provide the *training expertise*.) The HR staff also administers compensation and employee benefits and oversees changes in employment status (promotion, reassignment, termination or resignation, and retirement). This chapter explores each of these human resources responsibilities, beginning with planning (see Exhibit 11.1).

Planning for a Company's Staffing Needs

One of the six functions of the human resources department is to plan for a company's staffing needs. Proper planning is critical because a miscalculation could leave a company without enough employees to keep up with demand, resulting in customer dissatisfaction

Exhibit 11.2

Steps in Human Resources Planning
Careful attention to each phase of this sequence helps ensure that a company will have the right human resources when it needs them.

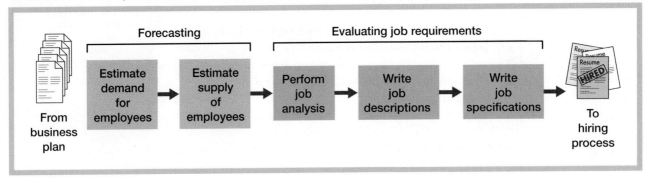

and lost business. Yet if a company expands its staff too rapidly, profits may be eaten up by payroll, or the firm may have to lay off people who were just recruited and trained at considerable expense. The planning function consists of two steps: (1) forecasting supply and demand and (2) evaluating job requirements (see Exhibit 11.2).

Forecasting Supply and Demand

Planning begins with forecasting *demand,* the numbers and types of employees who will be needed at various times. HR managers consider a number of variables when estimating demand, including (1) predicted sales of the company's goods and services; (2) the expected *turnover rate,* the percentage of the workforce that leaves every year; (3) the current workforce's skill level, relative to the company's future needs; (4) impending strategic decisions that might affect the number and type of workers needed; (5) changes in technology or other business factors that could affect the number and type of workers needed; and (6) the company's current and projected financial status.[4] Juggling all these variables in a dynamic business environment can get so complex that many HR managers, particularly in larger companies, rely on computer models to help predict workforce demands.

In addition to overall workforce levels, every company has a number of employees and managers who are considered so critical to the company's ongoing operations that HR managers work with top executives to identify potential replacements in the event of the loss of any of these people, a process known as **succession planning**. Such plans can cover owners, senior executives, researchers, top sales staff, and other vital members of the organization.[5] A **replacement chart** identifies these key employees and lists potential replacements, along with any current vacancies in key positions and other planning details (such as the number of years before the CEO is expected to retire, for instance).

With some idea of future workforce demands, the HR staff then tries to estimate the *supply* of available employees. In many cases, that supply is within the company already— perhaps just needing training to fill future requirements. For instance, Jamba Juice may well find that the assistant manager at an existing store can be promoted to manage the new store and that one of the current employees can be moved up to assistant manager.

To ensure a steady supply of experienced employees for new opportunities and to maintain existing operations, successful companies focus heavily on **employee retention**, the degree to which they are able to keep desired employees. A good way to understand the retention challenge is to review Herzberg's two-factor theory from Chapter 10. Both hygiene factors (dissatisfiers) and motivators contribute to retention efforts. For example, both higher pay (removing a dissatisfier) and the opportunity to lead a new project (adding a motivator) are steps that could increase employee retention. The factors vary by employee, too; some favor predictability in the work environment, while others place a much higher emphasis on opportunities for growth, even if that means higher stress.[6] The steps employers take also fluctuate with the economy. In contrast to the on-site massage therapists, free espresso, game rooms,

succession planning
Workforce planning efforts that identify possible replacements for specific employees, usually senior executives

replacement chart
A planning tool that identifies the most vital employees in the organization and information about their potential replacement

employee retention
Efforts to keep current employees

and other, sometimes frivolous offerings from the 1990s, many employers now emphasize more meaningful work-life benefits that help employees balance their work and home lives, including flexible work schedules, telecommuting, and career planning assistance.[7]

Temporary Employees More and more businesses try to save money and increase flexibility by augmenting their core workforces with temporary employees. Today's temporary ranks now include computer systems analysts, human resources managers, accountants, doctors, and even CEOs.[8] Depending on the position and the industry, such workers can be called *temps, independent contractors, freelancers,* or *consultants.* The term **contingent employee** is often used to describe any such person employed on a temporary basis. Some companies hire contingent staff themselves, whereas others "lease" workers from temporary staffing agencies.

In addition to smoothing out workload demands (such as hiring more retail staff around the holidays), more companies now incorporate temporary workers into their strategic HR plans. For instance, the use of temps can be an excellent recruiting technique because it allows companies to try out employees before hiring them permanently.[9]

However, contingent workforces are by no means a simple solution to staffing requirements. The challenges include motivating workers who don't feel they have a stake in the organization's long-term success, investing in training for workers who may not be around in the near future, and dealing with a variety of legal risks. The most significant of these risks is the frequent uncertainty about what constitutes employment; the guidelines for determining whether a worker is an employee or an independent contractor are complicated and not always clear, yet they have significant tax repercussions for both the worker and the company.[10] In a landmark case involving temporary workers at Microsoft, a court awarded a group of temps and freelancers $97 million after finding they had been denied a variety of employee benefits because Microsoft improperly classified them as independent contractors.[11] Moreover, regulatory agencies and courts can apply the concept of "dual employment" when a temporary worker breaks the law; both the temp agency and the employer can be held liable in such cases.[12]

A special category of foreign temporary workers has generated its own controversy in recent years as well. Usually known as "H-1B" workers for the type of *work visa* they've been granted by the U.S. government, a limited number of these workers (currently 65,000) are allowed to work in the United States for three years and one three-year extension (a similar program, H-2B, lets lower-skilled workers in the country for up to 10 months). The purpose of the H-1B program is to give U.S. companies, primarily in high technology, access to people with specific talents that may be in short supply in the United States at any particular time.[13] Many U.S. companies claim that they need H-1B workers to remain competitive, but some U.S. employees complain that the program is allowing in more foreign workers than it was designed for and that some companies may be manipulating the program to replace high-paid native employees with less-expensive foreign workers.[14] Nonetheless, companies continue to make full use of the H-1B option: The entire 65,000-visa allotment for 2005 was filled in a single day.[15]

Outsourcing Just as companies can opt to outsource parts of the production function, they can also use outsourcing as a way to meet staffing needs throughout the organization without hiring permanent employees. Some companies outsource an entire function, such as sales or product design, whereas others outsource selected jobs or projects. In fact, various elements of the human resources department itself, including retirement plans, health benefits, training, and payroll are now among the most commonly outsourced functions.[16] Many companies even outsource work to former employees who've set themselves up as independent contractors or started companies that perform the same functions they used to perform for employers.[17]

Evaluating Job Requirements

The second step of the planning function is to evaluate job requirements. If you were the owner of a small business, you might have a good grasp of the requirements of all the jobs in your company. However, in large organizations where hundreds or thousands of employees

contingent employee
As a general term applies to any nonpermanent employee, including temporary workers and independent contractors; also applied specifically to workers hired on a probationary basis

Retailers and other companies with fluctuating seasonal demand often rely on temporary employees during peak periods

TECHNOLOGIES THAT ARE REVOLUTIONIZING BUSINESS Assistive Technologies

The term *assistive technologies* covers a broad range of devices and systems that help people with disabilities perform activities that might otherwise be difficult or impossible. These include technologies that help people communicate orally and visually, interact with computers and other equipment, and enjoy greater mobility, along with myriad other specific functions.

HOW THEY'RE CHANGING BUSINESS

Assistive technologies create a vital link for thousands of employees with disabilities, giving them the opportunity to pursue a greater range of career paths and giving employers access to a broader base of talent. With the United States heading for a potentially serious shortage of workers in a few years, the economy will benefit from everyone who can make a contribution, and assistive technologies will be an important part of the solution.

WHERE YOU CAN LEARN MORE

AssistiveTech.net, www.assistivetech.net, is a great place to search for the many categories of assistive technologies now available; it also provides links to a variety of other sites. The Business Leadership Network, www.usbln.com, "recognizes and promotes best practices in hiring, retraining, and marketing to people with disabilities." For a look at the government's efforts to promote these technologies, visit the National Institute on Disability and Rehabilitation Research, www.ed.gov/about/offices/list/osers/nidrr. If you'd like to explore a career in assistive technologies, visit the Rehabilitation Engineering and Assistive Technology Society of North America, www.resna.org. Technology companies such as IBM and Microsoft also devote significant resources to developing assistive technologies and making information technology more accessible.

---

job analysis
Process by which jobs are studied to determine the tasks and dynamics involved in performing them

job description
Statement of the tasks involved in a given job and the conditions under which the holder of the job will work

job specification
Statement describing the kind of person who would be best for a given job—including the skills, education, and previous experience that the job requires

are performing a wide variety of jobs, management needs a more formal and objective method of evaluating job requirements. Through the process of **job analysis**, employers try to identify both the nature and demands of each position within the firm and the optimal employee profile to fill each position.[18]

To obtain the information needed for a job analysis, the human resources staff asks employees or supervisors several questions: What is the purpose of the job? What tasks are involved in the job? What qualifications and skills are needed to do it effectively? In what kind of setting does the job take place? Is there much public contact involved? Does the job entail much time pressure? Sometimes they obtain job information by observing employees directly. Other times they ask employees to keep daily diaries describing exactly what they do during the workday.

Once job analysis has been completed, the human resources staff develops a **job description**, a formal statement summarizing the tasks involved in the job and the conditions under which the employee will work. In most cases, the staff will also develop a **job specification**, which identifies the type of personnel a job requires, including the skills, education, experience, and personal attributes that candidates need to possess[19] (see Exhibit 11.3).

CRITICAL THINKING CHECKPOINT

1. Why should companies treat human resources as one of the most vital strategic functions in the organization?
2. How could HR work with functional managers in other parts of the company to forecast staffing demands?
3. Some companies prohibit former employees from providing outsourced services for an extended period after they leave the company (such as six months or a year). Is this a good idea? Why or why not?

Job Title

Director of E-Marketing

Location

Denver, CO

Reports to

Vice President of Marketing

Job Detail

Soccer Scope is a leading retailer of soccer equipment, apparel, and accessories based in Denver, Colorado, with retail locations in 23 states. We seek to expand our online presence under the guidance of a director of e-marketing, a new managerial position to be based in our Denver headquarters.

The candidate who fills this position will be responsible for all nonstore aspects of our retailing efforts, including Soccer Scope's primary U.S. website and our country and region websites around the world, search-related advertising strategies, search engine optimization strategies, e-mail marketing campaigns, clicks-and-bricks integration strategy, affiliate marketing campaigns, customer retention efforts, and all aspects of online marketing research. The director of e-marketing will also work closely with the director of information technology to ensure the successful deployment of e-marketing platforms and with the director of retail operations to ensure a smooth clicks-and-bricks integration of offline and online retailing operations.

In addition to developing e-marketing strategies and directing e-marketing operations, the director is also responsible for leading a team of marketing and technical specialists who will implement and manage various programs.

Responsibilities

- Develop e-marketing strategies and plans consistent with Soccer Scope's overall business strategy and brand imperatives
- Establish and achieve aggressive customer acquisition and retention goals
- Coordinate efforts with technology and retailing counterparts to ensure successfully integrated online and offline marketing operations
- Assemble, lead, and develop an effective team of e-marketing professionals

Skills and Experience

- BA or BS in business, advertising, marketing, or related discipline required; MBA preferred
- Minimum 8 years of marketing experience, with at least 3 years in e-commerce
- Current and thorough understanding of e-marketing strategies
- Demonstrated proficiency in developing and executing marketing strategies
- Excellent communication skills in all media

Exhibit 11.3
Job Description and Specification
As you can see from this excerpt, a well-written job description and specification tells potential applicants what to expect from the job and what employers will expect from them.

Recruiting, Hiring, and Training New Employees

LEARNING OBJECTIVE 2

Cite eight methods recruiters use to find job candidates

recruiting
Process of attracting appropriate applicants for an organization's jobs

Having forecast a company's supply and demand for employees and evaluated job requirements, the human resources manager's next step is to match the job specification with an actual person or selection of people. This task is accomplished through **recruiting**, the process of attracting suitable candidates for an organization's jobs. The recruiting function is often judged by a combination of criteria known as *quality of hire,* which measures how closely incoming employees meet the company's needs.[20]

Recruiters are use a variety of methods and resources, including internal searches, newspaper and Internet advertising, public and private employment agencies, union hiring halls, college campuses and career offices, trade shows, corporate "headhunters" (outside agencies that specialize in finding and placing employees), and referrals from employees or colleagues in the industry (see Exhibit 11.4). Both large and small companies now make extensive use of Internet-based technologies to find candidates. For instance, Impinj, a Seattle semiconductor manufacturer (www.impinj.com/blog), uses a recruiting blog to attract candidates.[21] Others constantly prowl the Internet looking for strong candidates. Using powerful artificial intelligence software, Cambridge, Massachusetts-based Zoom Information (www.zoominfo.com) has built a massive database of information on corporate executives and managers; corporate recruiters pay an annual fee to search the listings.[22] You can learn more about online recruiting in the "E-Business in Action" feature at the end of this chapter.

LEARNING OBJECTIVE 3

Identify the six stages in the hiring process

The Hiring Process

The first stage in the hiring process is to select a small number of qualified candidates from all of the applications received. Finalists may be chosen on the basis of a standard application form that all candidates fill out or on the basis of a résumé—a summary of education, experience, and personal data compiled by each applicant (see "Preparing Your Résumé" in the Prologue for further details). Sometimes both sources of information are used. Many organizations now use *applicant tracking systems* to help them quickly sort through résumés and identify the most attractive candidates for each job; the systems contain résumés submitted electronically and paper résumés that have been scanned in.[23]

The second stage in the hiring process is to interview each candidate to clarify qualifications and to fill in any missing information (see "Interviewing with Potential Employers" in the Prologue for further details). Another goal of the interview is to get an idea of the applicant's personality and ability to work with others. For instance, interviewers can judge

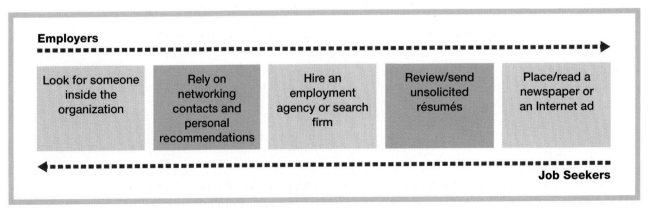

Exhibit 11.4
How Employers and Job Seekers Approach the Recruiting Process
Studies show that employers prefer to fill job openings with people from within their organization or from an employee's recommendation. Placing want ads is often viewed as a last resort. In contrast, typical job seekers begin their job-search process from the opposite direction (starting with reading newspaper or Internet ads).

how well the applicant relates to them as individuals, using this behavior as a sign for how well the person will get along with colleagues in general.[24] A growing number of companies, from the Woman & Infants Hospital of Rhode Island to delivery giant UPS, realize that the right attitude can be as vital as job experience or technical qualifications.[25] Depending on the type of job at stake, candidates may also be asked to take a test or a series of tests.

In the third stage, the best candidates may be asked to meet with someone in the human resources department who will conduct a more probing interview. For higher-level positions, candidates may go through a series of interviews with managers, potential co-workers, and the employees who will make up the successful candidate's staff.

After all the interviews have been completed, the process moves to the final stages. In the fourth stage, the department supervisor usually evaluates the candidates, sometimes in consultation with a higher-level manager, the human resources department, and staff. During the fifth stage, the employer checks the references of the top few candidates. The employer may also research the candidates' background, as the following section describes. In the sixth stage, the supervisor selects the most suitable person for the job.

Background Checks Bringing in a new employee is often one of the riskiest moves you'll have to make as a manager. After all, you're adding someone who is probably a complete stranger to a group of people who already know and presumably trust one another. To remove some of the mystery and reduce the chances of hiring people with the potential to damage the firm in some way, businesses now conduct a variety of background checks on job applicants, including verifying all educational credentials and previous jobs, accounting for any large time gaps between jobs, and checking references. Background checks are particularly important for jobs in which employees are in a position to harm others or handle large amounts of cash, for instance.

Roughly 70 to 80 percent of U.S. employers now conduct criminal background checks, and a third conduct credit checks. These checks can prevent serious hiring errors—according to one firm that does criminal background checks for employers, 9 percent of its searches uncover felony records that applicants failed to disclose—although some applicants and privacy advocates have expressed concerns about both invasion of privacy and the chance of errors in both criminal and credit histories.[26]

Hiring and the Law Federal and state laws and regulations govern many aspects of the hiring process (see Exhibit 11.5 for a list of some of the most important employment-related laws). In particular, employers must be careful to avoid discrimination in the wording of their application forms, in interviewing, and in testing. Employers must also respect the privacy of applicants. Consider the dilemma this situation presents for employers.

On the one hand, asking questions about unrelated factors such as citizenship, marital status, age, and religion violates the Equal Employment Opportunity Commission's regulations because such questions may lead to discrimination. In addition, employers are not allowed to ask questions about whether a person has children, whether a person owns or rents a home, what caused a physical disability, whether a person belongs to a union, whether a person has ever been arrested, or when a person attended school. The exception is when such information is related to a bona fide occupational qualification for the specific job.

On the other hand, employers must obtain sufficient information about employees to avoid becoming the target of a negligent-hiring lawsuit. Moreover, the Immigration Reform and Control Act (passed in 1986) forbids almost all U.S. companies from hiring illegal aliens. The act also prohibits discrimination in hiring on the basis of national origin or citizenship status. This creates a difficult situation for employers who must try to determine their applicants' citizenship, so they can verify that the newly hired are legally eligible to work, without asking questions that violate the law.

SAFETY AND SECURITY IN A COMPLEX WORLD

WHEN EMPLOYEES TURN ON EACH OTHER

Few events in a company's history can be as traumatic as extreme workplace violence, when employees exact revenge or take out frustrations by attacking or killing their colleagues. Every year, dozens of employees are killed by their fellow workers, and hundreds more are seriously injured.

Although murders of employees by employees represent a small fraction of workplace violence, they can have a dramatic effect on company morale. "No organization is ever completely the same after a tragedy like this," emphasizes Mary Tyler, a psychologist with the federal government's Office of Personnel Management. Survivors and witnesses of attacks frequently quit, and productivity within the firm can suffer for months afterward. Even when murder isn't involved, assaults and intimidation create a dangerous, poisonous work environment for everyone involved. Moreover, these incidences of violence can subject employers to tremendous legal damages for failing to provide employees with safe workplaces.

What causes workers to explode with such rage? The key to understanding this problem is to recognize that workplace murder is unlike the often-random violence that afflicts society in general. As security consultant Doug Kane explains, "Workplace violence is one of the few types of violent behavior that follows a clear pattern. It is never spontaneous and almost always avoidable." According to the FBI, no specific personality profile can identify potentially violent attackers, but a consistent pattern of circumstances does appear in many cases, including a recent firing, a demotion, or an argument with co-workers or supervisors. In addition, employees who speak openly about suicide should be considered risks

as well, since many workplace murderers take their own lives after killing one or more co-workers.

Experts recommend five steps to protect workers. First and foremost, take the problem seriously. Too many workers die because managers don't think violence can happen at their facilities. Second, perform thorough background checks on all potential hires, looking specifically for a history of substance abuse, conflicts with co-workers, or convictions for violent crimes (80 percent of U.S. employers now conduct criminal background checks). Third, implement protection policies, such as prohibiting any kind of weapons on company grounds and deciding in advance how to handle conflicts before they escalate into violence. (At present, most U.S. companies do not have comprehensive, formal programs to prevent workplace violence.) Fourth, train everyone—and particularly front-line supervisors, since they often bear the brunt of attacks—to watch for the telltale warning signs. Fifth, respond instantly to those warning signs. In many cases, attackers made threats or exhibited other evidence of impending disaster, but most of the companies involved failed to respond.

Questions for Critical Thinking

1. Debate continues regarding the use of zero-tolerance policies for aggressive behavior. Some experts say employees who exhibit violent tendencies should be fired immediately, but others say that doing so would discourage co-workers from reporting seemingly minor incidents. What is your opinion?
2. Should a company be held liable for financial damages if an employee kills one or more colleagues? Why or why not?

Testing One much-debated aspect of the hiring process is testing—using not only the tests that prospective employers give job applicants but any devices that can evaluate employees when making job decisions. Tests are used to gauge abilities, intelligence, interests, and sometimes even physical condition and personality. Employers that receive high volumes of applications also use tests as screening devices to sort through the deluge of applications. For instance, Boeing recently received 1.2 million applications in a year during which it had only 20,000 job openings and relied on testing to narrow down the list of candidates.[27]

Many companies rely on preemployment testing to determine whether applicants are suited to the job and whether they'll be worth the expense of hiring and training. Companies use three

Exhibit 11.5
Major Employment Legislation
Here are a few of the most significant sets of laws that affect employer-employee relations in the United States.

Category	Legislation	Highlights
Labor and unionization	National Labor Relations Act, also known as the Wagner Act	Establishes the right of employees to form, join, and assist unions and the right to strike; prohibits employers from interfering in union activities
	Labor-Management Relations Act, also known as the Taft-Hartley Act	Expands union rights; gives employers free speech rights to oppose unions; gives the president the right to impose injunctions against strikes
	Labor-Management Reporting and Disclosure Act, also known as the Landrum-Griffin Act	Gives union members the right to nominate and vote for union leadership candidates
	State right-to-work laws	Gives individual employees the right to choose not to join a union
	Fair Labor Standards Act	Establishes minimum wage and overtime pay for nonexempt workers; sets strict guidelines for child labor
	Immigration Reform and Control Act	Prohibits employers from hiring illegal immigrants
Workplace safety	State workers' compensation acts	Require employers (in most states) to carry either private or government-sponsored insurance that provides income to injured workers
	Occupational Health and Safety Act	Empowers the Occupational Safety and Health Administration (OSHA) to set and enforce standards for workplace safety
Employee benefits	Employee Retirement Income Security Act	Governs the establishment and operation of private pension programs
	Consolidated Omnibus Budget Reconciliation Act (usually known by the acronym COBRA)	Requires employers to let employees or their beneficiaries buy continued health insurance coverage after employment ends
	Federal Unemployment Tax Act and similar state laws	Requires employers to fund programs that provide income for qualified unemployed persons
	Social Security Act	Provides a level of retirement, disability, and medical coverage for employees and their dependents; jointly funded by employers and employees

main procedures: job-skills testing, psychological testing, and drug testing. Job-skills tests are the most common type, designed to assess competency or specific abilities needed to perform a job. For instance, TopCoder (www.topcoder.com), based in Glastonbury, Connecticut, conducts regular programming contests to help employers identify skilled software engineers.[28] Psychological tests usually take the form of questionnaires. These tests can be used to assess overall intellectual ability, attitudes toward work, interests, managerial potential, or personality characteristics— including dependability, commitment, and motivation. For example, thousands of employers have used the Wonderlic Personnel Test (www.wonderlic.com) to measure cognitive ability.[29] Employers who favor psychological tests say they help weed out people

LEARNING FROM BUSINESS BLUNDERS

OOPS In late October 2003, federal agents raided 61 Wal-Mart locations in 21 states, rounding up 250 to 300 illegal aliens who worked for companies that Wal-Mart contracted to clean its stores at night. The public and regulators would probably overlook one or two instances of this nature, but Wal-Mart has made quite a few headlines in recent years, with several cases of illegal aliens working for cleaning contractors and multiple accusations of violating child labor laws and overtime laws, discriminating against women, and locking employees in stores at night (the company claims this policy was intended to protect employees in high-crime areas, but some employees have complained they couldn't get out of the building when they were sick or injured, when hurricanes hit in Florida, or when their wives went into labor). In all of these cases, Wal-Mart has defended itself by saying that any wrong actions taken on the part of employees or outside firms are against company policy.

WHAT YOU CAN LEARN Managing a company as large as Wal-Mart is a complex task, to be sure, and mistakes are bound to happen. Big companies are also big targets, so based on numbers alone, Wal-Mart is going to attract more complaints and more lawsuits than smaller employers. Moreover, Wal-Mart wasn't accused of hiring illegal aliens itself (whether or not Wal-Mart knew its contractors hired illegal aliens is a point of dispute). However, in the court of public opinion, such distinctions are often lost on many people. In addition, the public and government officials aren't always going to accept the defense that company policy forbids all these wrong actions and that the problems were caused by a few rogue managers acting on their own. When mistakes are repeated or occur in multiple places throughout the company, people get suspicious. As Jeffrey Garten, dean of the Yale School of Management, recently wrote in reference to Wal-Mart's troubles, "For me, there is too much smoke for there not to be a fire." Every business organization needs to clearly communicate explicit policies that forbid illegal activity and managers also need to review the culture of the organization to see if it is intentionally or unintentionally promoting bad behavior. For instance, if a supervisor picks up the message to "cut costs or you'll lose your job," even if it's never expressed in those exact words, he or she might be sorely tempted to cut ethical or legal corners.

who won't be able to perform on the job, and some 40 percent of large employers now use them. However, critics say that such tests often fail to meet accepted standards for reliability.[30]

Drug and alcohol testing is one of the most controversial issues in business today. Some employers believe such testing is absolutely necessary to maintain workplace safety, whereas others view it as an invasion of employee privacy and a sign of disrespect. Even within a single industry, you can find widely divergent opinions on the subject. Computer maker Dell tests every employee, whereas rival HP doesn't test anyone. Some companies test only applicants but not current employees.[31] Not only does evidence show that drug use costs employers (through lost productivity, increased health care, and on-the-job mistakes), but companies are also liable for negligent hiring practices if an employee harms an innocent party on the job. Although drug testing has declined somewhat in recent years and the direct financial payback of testing programs is difficult to measure, many companies are likely to continue their testing programs.[32]

Training and Development

Even the best applicants rarely begin a job knowing everything they need to know or possessing all the skills they need in order to succeed in a specific position, company, or industry. Moreover, with the pace of change in everything from government regulations to consumer tastes to technology, knowledge and skills need to be constantly updated. Consequently, the most successful companies place a heavy emphasis on employee training and development efforts, for everyone from entry-level workers to the CEO. Overall, U.S. companies now spend some $50 billion a year on training.[33]

Training sometimes begins before new hires even start working. For example, General Mills is one of a growing number of companies that send liberal arts graduates to a "business finishing school" after graduation to learn business fundamentals before they report to work.[34]

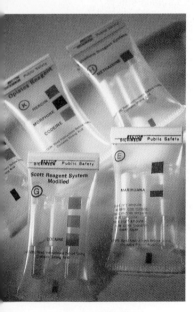

Drug testing is a controversial but common pre-employment screening tactic.

A growing number of companies now use a variety of web-based and computer-based tools to train employees.

In most cases, though, the training process starts as soon as new employees join the workforce, with **orientation programs** designed to ease the new hire's transition into the company and to impart vital knowledge about the organization and its rules, procedures, and expectations. Effective orientation programs help employees become more productive in less time, help eliminate confusion and mistakes, and can significantly increase employee retention rates.[35]

orientation programs
Formal programs for acclimating new employees to an organization

Training and other forms of employee development continue throughout the employee's career in most cases. Many HR departments maintain a **skills inventory**, which identifies both the current skill levels of all the employees and the skills the company needs in order to succeed. Depending on the industry, some of the most common subjects for ongoing training include problem solving, new products, sales, customer service, safety, sexual harassment, supervision, quality, strategic planning, communication, time management, and team building.[36]

skills inventory
A list of the skills a company needs from its workforce, along with the specific skills that individual employees currently possess

In addition, companies use a variety of methods to deliver training. Self-paced, computer-based training (see "Click and Learn: E-Training Today's Employees") is gaining momentum, but the majority of training courses in most companies still involve an instructor, either in person in a classroom or long distance via videoconferencing or webcasting.[37]

CRITICAL THINKING CHECKPOINT

1. If you were hired to start the HR department in a young and fast-growing company, would you focus your attention on recruiting or retention first? Why?

2. Why do many companies consider advertising to be one of the least preferred methods of finding new employees?

3. Why will many companies continue to conduct employee drug tests, even if such testing has unclear financial impact?

Appraising Employee Performance

How do employees (and their managers) know whether they are doing a good job? How can they improve their performance? What new skills should they learn? Most human resources managers attempt to answer these questions by developing **performance appraisals** to objectively evaluate employees according to set criteria.

performance appraisal
Evaluation of an employee's work according to specific criteria

INNOVATING FOR BUSINESS SUCCESS

CLICK AND LEARN: E-TRAINING TODAY'S EMPLOYEES

Employers from automakers and software firms to hospitals and pharmaceutical companies are turning to computers to train today's employees. Electronic training, or e-learning, uses computers and live or recorded webcasts, web-based self-paced tutorials, and other forms of electronic media such as CD-ROMs to instruct employees on new products, customer service, sales techniques, and more.

Dell Computer expects 90 percent of its learning solutions to be totally or partially technology enabled. General Motors University uses interactive satellite broadcasts to teach salespeople the best way to highlight features on new cars. Pharmaceutical companies such as Merck use live interactive Internet classes to instruct sales reps on the latest product information rather than fly them to a conference center. Semiconductor maker Texas Instruments uses simulators to help employers understand how disruptive it is when TI misses shipment commitments to its customers. And IBM has moved online virtually all the content of the first three phases of management training for its first-line managers—eliminating the need to send them to off-site locations over the course of a training period that stretched out over six months.

As these companies have learned, e-training has many benefits:

- **Reduced costs.** Much of the cost savings comes from reduced travel expenses and time savings. "If we save our 70,000 employees just 20 minutes a year, that alone is $1 million in savings," says one Intel training manager. Home Depot has used e-training to cut a full day from the time required to train new cashiers—a huge savings when multiplied by the 60,000 cashiers it hires every year.
- **Increased productivity.** "Our salesforce can't come in for three-day conferences anymore," says one Black & Decker vice president. "But they still need to understand the company's new products and features." So the company has instituted

online training courses—which means the company's 700-person salesforce can spend a combined 12,000 more days a year with customers.
- **Individualized pace.** E-learning allows you to learn at your own pace—skipping over material you already know and spending more time learning material that meets your specific needs.
- **Increased consistency.** Companies can create one set of instructional materials that is used consistently by everyone in the organization. Thus, all employees are learning the same thing—regardless of their location.

Like many other Internet-related efforts in recent years, e-learning saw a rapid rise followed by a period of rethinking, when corporate trainers moved past the "gee whiz" factor and took a more objective look at what training technology really could—and couldn't—offer. They began to appreciate the value of e-learning but also realized it wasn't the solution to every training challenge and that impressive technology was no substitute for good instructional planning. As a result, many companies now emphasize *blended learning,* which is a combination of delivery methods. Wendy O'Brien of 3Com, a computer networking firm based in Massachusetts, says her team examines the content and audience of each training effort, along with parameters such as budgets and deadlines, before they choose a delivery method. By combining the best available methods in each individual case, 3Com maintains the focus on the learner, rather than on the technology, while still using e-learning to its fullest potential.

Questions for Critical Thinking
1. Why is e-learning an increasingly popular training approach for companies?
2. How might an economic slowdown or global terrorism affect e-learning?

LEARNING OBJECTIVE 4

Discuss how companies incorporate objectivity into employee performance appraisals

The ultimate goal of performance appraisals is not to judge employees but rather to improve their performance. Thus, experts recommend that performance reviews be an ongoing discipline, particularly in today's project-driven, results-oriented workplace. Employees need fast feedback so they can correct their deficiencies in a timely manner.

Most companies require regular written evaluations of each employee's work. The evaluation criteria are in writing so that both employee and supervisor understand what is expected and are therefore able to determine whether the work is being done adequately (see Exhibit 11.6). Written evaluations also provide a record of the employee's performance, which may protect the company in cases of disputed terminations. An increasing number of companies now conduct evaluations online, using password-protected websites to record and analyze information.[38]

Most jobs are evaluated in several areas, including tasks specific to the position, contribution to the company's overall success, and interaction with colleagues and customers. A production-line technician might be evaluated on such factors as work quality, productivity, innovation and problem solving, teamwork, job knowledge, and reliability. In contrast, the production manager might be evaluated on the basis of communication skills, people management, leadership, teamwork, recruiting and employee development, delegation, financial management, planning, and organizational skills.[39]

Many performance appraisals require the employee to be rated by several people (including more than one supervisor and perhaps several co-workers). This practice further promotes fairness by correcting for possible biases. The ultimate in multidimensional reviews is the *360-degree review,* in which a person is given feedback from subordinates, peers, and superiors. To ensure anonymity and to compile the multiple streams of information, 360-degree reviews are often conducted via computer. At Dell, even Michael Dell himself is subjected to 360-degree reviews. When subordinates complained that his style seemed too detached, Dell committed himself to engaging with people at a more emotional level.[40] As you can imagine, however, this review format presents some serious risks, including employees who have an ax to grind, and managers who don't welcome criticism from their employees. Experts recommend that 360-degree reviews not be used to set salaries and that reviewers be thoroughly trained in the technique.[41]

With so many companies emphasizing teamwork, evaluating individual performance fairly is becoming a bigger challenge for many employers. Assessments by the team leader are important, but they can't always sort out how much each member contributed to the overall output. A good way to address this problem is to have each team member evaluate his or her own contribution and that of every other team member. A manager who oversees the team can then compare all the assessments (which are done anonymously) to look for patterns—who contributes the bulk of the new ideas, who's just along for the ride, and so on.[42]

In addition to formal, periodic performance evaluations, many companies evaluate some workers' performance continuously, using **electronic performance monitoring (EPM)**, sometimes called *computer activity monitoring.* For instance, customer service and telephone sales representatives are often evaluated by the number of calls they complete per hour and other variables. Newer software products extend this monitoring capability, from measuring data input accuracy to scanning for suspicious words in employee e-mails. As you can imagine, EPM efforts can generate controversy in the workplace, elevating employee stress levels and raising concerns about invasion of privacy.[43]

electronic performance monitoring (EPM)
Real-time, computer-based evaluation of employee performance

Administering Compensation and Employee Benefits

In many companies, payroll is the single biggest expense in the entire company, and the cost of benefits, particularly health care, continues to climb. Consequently, **compensation**, the combination of direct payments such as wages or salary and indirect payments through employee benefits, is one of the HR manager's most significant responsibilities.

compensation
Money, benefits, and services paid to employees for their work

Salaries and Wages

Most employees receive the bulk of their compensation in the form of **salary**, if they receive a fixed amount per year, or **wages**, if they are paid by the unit of time (hourly, daily, or weekly) or by the unit of output (often called "getting paid by the piece" or "piecework"). The Fair Labor Standards Act, introduced in 1938 and amended many times since then, sets specific guidelines for administering salaries and wages, including setting a minimum wage and paying overtime for time worked beyond 40 hours a week. However, most professional and

salary
Fixed cash compensation for work, usually by yearly amount; independent of the number of hours worked

wages
Cash payment based on the number of hours the employee has worked or the number of units the employee has produced

Exhibit 11.6
Sample Performance Appraisal Form
Many companies use forms like this (either printed or online) to ensure that performance appraisals are as objective as possible.

Name _____ Title _____ Service Date _____ Date _____

Location _____ Division _____ Department _____

Length of Time in Present Position   Period of Review   Appraised by _____

_____   From: ____ To: ____   Title of Appraisor _____

Area of Performance	Comment	Rating
Job Knowledge and Skill Understands responsibilities and uses background for job. Adapts to new methods/techniques. Plans and organizes work. Recognizes errors and problems.		5 4 3 2 1
Volume of Work Amount of work output. Adherence to standards and schedules. Effective use of time.		5 4 3 2 1
Quality of Work Degree of accuracy–lack of errors. Thoroughness of work. Ability to exercise good judgment.		5 4 3 2 1
Initiative and Creativity Self-motivation in seeking responsibility and work that needs to be done. Ability to apply original ideas and concepts.		5 4 3 2 1
Communication Ability to exchange thoughts or information in a clear, concise manner. Dealing with different organizational levels of clientele.		5 4 3 2 1
Dependability Ability to follow instructions and directions correctly. Performs under pressure. Reliable work habits.		5 4 3 2 1
Leadership Ability/Potential Ability to guide others to the successful accomplishment of a given task. Potential for developing subordinate employees.		5 4 3 2 1

5. Outstanding   Employee who consistently exceeds established standards and expectations of the job.

4. Above Average   Employee who consistently meets established standards and expectations of the job. Often exceeds and rarely falls short of desired results.

3. Satisfactory   Generally qualified employee who meets job standards and expectations. Sometimes exceeds and may occasionally fall short of desired expectations. Performs duties in a normally expected manner.

2. Improvement Needed   Not quite meeting standards and expectations. An employee at this level of performance is not quite meeting all the standard job requirements.

1. Unsatisfactory   Employee who fails to meet the minimum standards and expectations of the job.

I have had the opportunity to read this performance appraisal.   How long has this employee been under your supervision?

Signature   Date   Signature of Supervisor   Date

SAFETY AND SECURITY IN A COMPLEX WORLD

SOMEBODY'S WATCHING (AND LISTENING AND READING AND MONITORING AND RECORDING)

If you've grown accustomed to saying anything about anybody in e-mail and instant messaging, get ready for some major culture shock when you enter (or re-enter) the corporate world. For a number of reasons, the majority of mid- to large-size companies now monitor employee e-mail and IM—using both increasingly sophisticated monitoring software and, in some cases, human beings who actually intercept and read outgoing messages. Roughly a quarter of these companies have fired employees for violating e-mail usage policies.

To get an idea of the monitoring capabilities now available, consider just some of the features in TrueActive Monitor, a monitoring product used by nearly 100,000 employers: keystroke logging (records everything a person types), chat room and IM recording, website tracking (records which websites a person visits), text scanning (monitors messages for particular words or phrases), file management activity (which can tell if someone deletes or copies files), and webcam control (which can activate a webcam for video evidence of who was using a computer at specific times).

Now, if the idea of someone scanning your messages raises your hackles, you're not alone. However, companies have a variety of valid concerns regarding how their employees use information technology:

- Protecting corporate information, including client records, strategic plans, and product design details.
- Making sure employees don't inadvertently break the law when communicating with customers.

- Protecting company networks from viruses, spyware, and other malware.
- Preventing the transmission of pornographic material, which can open a company to lawsuits over sexual harassment.
- Making sure employees don't use the Internet for personal reasons when they are on company time.

Privacy advocates raise valid concerns about employers going too far to check up on employees. However, the risks of not monitoring are so great—a few poor choices by a single employee can cost millions—that the use of monitoring tools is only going to increase in the coming years.

As an employee, you can avoid trouble by remembering one simple thought: all of the information technology you use at work is company property, provided by your employer for your use in engaging in company business. For anything else, it's best to use your own Internet service and your own personal e-mail and IM accounts.

Questions for Critical Thinking

1. What affect is workplace monitoring likely to have on employee morale? Do you think most workers blame management or their own misbehaving colleagues for the use of these monitoring technologies.
2. At present, only two states (Delaware and Connecticut) require employers to notify employees that their e-mail messages are being monitored. Should all states enact this requirement? Why or why not?

managerial employees are considered exempt from these regulations. Although the potential for long hours with no extra pay is a disadvantage of being exempt (some professionals and executives often work as many as 50 hours a week or more), these employees often enjoy other advantages, such as higher pay and more flexibility in setting their own schedules. The distinction between *exempt employees* and *nonexempt employees* is based on job responsibilities and pay level. In general, salaried employees are exempt, although there are many exceptions.[44] As you read in the cases involving video game companies in Chapter 10, a growing number of workers are claiming they've been misclassified as exempt employees and have therefore missed out on significant amounts of overtime pay. In other recent cases, employees at Farmers Insurance (claims adjusters), Pacific Bell (engineers), and Radio Shack (store managers) successfully challenged their exempt status.[45] In 2004, the federal government tried to clarify the classification issue but appears to have generated more confusion and controversy. As thousands of employees face reclassification—which will lower their pay in some instances and raise it in others—the situation is likely to take several years and numerous lawsuits to iron out.[46]

Compensation has become a hot topic in recent years, at both ends of the pay scale. At the low end, for instance, many businesses, employees, and unions are wrestling with the downward pressure on wages and benefits exerted by Wal-Mart's enormous presence in the economy. With a million and a half employees (1 out of every 20 new jobs in this country is at Wal-Mart), the company's cost-conscious strategy indirectly affects thousands of people who've never worked there. For instance, as Safeway, Albertsons, and other grocery stores try to compete with Wal-Mart, they feel they have no choice but to pay their employees less and offer fewer benefits. Consumers benefit from Wal-Mart's lower prices, and their patronage benefits Wal-Mart's stockholders, but some critics charge that Wal-Mart employees who can't afford the company's health insurance and those who are on food stamps are increasing the burden on taxpayers. Lower wages also mean Wal-Mart employees themselves are able to spend less on consumer goods and services, and consumer spending is a major factor in the strength of the U.S. economy. As one researcher puts it, "You can't have every company adopt a Wal-Mart strategy. It isn't sustainable."[47] You can read Wal-Mart's responses to such criticisms at **www.walmartfacts.com**.

Not all of Wal-Mart's competitors are following the "race to the bottom," as some people call it. For example, Wegmans and Costco are two retail chains that are succeeding with a markedly different approach to compensation. Wegmans, which offers most employees free health care coverage and higher wages than Wal-Mart, follows the belief that "If we take care of our employees, they will take care of our customers," in the words of vice president Karen Shadders. Costco, which competes with Wal-Mart's Sam's Club chain of superstores, also offers higher wages and better benefits—and yet still generates better financial results than Sam's Club. Costco attributes much of its success to satisfied, motivated employees who are more productive and more eager to help customers (to be fair, Costco also sells many higher-priced products and caters to a more affluent clientele, both of which enable it to pay workers more and which contribute to its attractive financial results).[48]

At the upper end of the pay scale, executive compensation, and the pay of CEOs in particular, has generated its own brand of controversy. CEOs typically receive complex compensation packages that include a base salary plus a wide range of benefits and bonuses, including *golden handshakes* when they join a company and *golden parachutes* when they leave. Part of the controversy stems from the widening compensation gap between CEOs and their employees; with the average compensation of CEOs at large companies now in the $15 million range, it's not uncommon for CEOs to earn several hundred times more than their lowest-paid employees.[49] Even the pay for CEOs of European firms, which has historically been far below that of their U.S. counterparts, has risen enough in recent years to prompt calls for government regulation in several countries.[50]

A second aspect of the controversy can be the disparity between results and compensation. Even though CEOs are supposed to be evaluated by such factors as stock price appreciation, some continue to earn large salaries even as their companies' stocks decline. Comparing compensation packages is difficult because they are so complex, and some include potential income that executives haven't actually received yet, but critics still find the numbers staggering. The boards of directors who grant these packages generally defend them as necessary to retain key executives, but critics respond that many other CEOs earn far less and don't leave in search of greener pastures.[51]

LEARNING OBJECTIVE 5

List six popular types of financial incentive programs for employees

incentives
Cash payments to employees who produce at a desired level or whose unit (often the company as a whole) produces at a desired level

Incentive Programs

To encourage employees to be more productive, innovative, and committed to their work, many companies provide managers and employees with **incentives**, cash payments linked to specific individual, group, and companywide goals; overall productivity; and company success. In other words, achievements, not just activities, are made the basis for payment.

The success of these programs often depends on how closely incentives are linked to actions within the employee's control:

- **Bonuses.** For both salaried and wage-earning employees, one type of incentive compensation is the **bonus**, a payment in addition to the regular wage or salary. Performance-based bonuses have become an increasingly popular approach to compensation as more companies shift away from automatic annual pay increases.[52]

- **Commissions.** In contrast to bonuses, **commissions** are a form of compensation that pays employees a percentage of sales made. Used mainly for sales staff, they may be either the sole compensation or an incentive payment in addition to a regular salary.

- **Profit sharing.** Employees may be rewarded for staying with a company and encouraged to work harder through **profit sharing**, a system in which employees receive a portion of the company's profits. Depending on the company, profits may be distributed quarterly, semiannually, or annually. Expeditors International, a freight forwarding firm with offices in 182 countries around the world, allots 20 percent of each office's net income to profit sharing; local managers decide how to distribute the funds.[53]

- **Gain sharing.** Similar to profit sharing, **gain sharing** ties rewards to profits (or cost savings) achieved by meeting specific goals such as quality and productivity improvement.

- **Pay for performance.** A variation of gain sharing, **pay for performance** requires employees to accept a lower base pay but rewards them with bonuses, commissions, or stock options if they reach production targets or other goals. Pay for performance must be re-earned each year and doesn't permanently increase base salary. Individuals can be evaluated on a number of variables, including whether they show partnership, demonstrate teamwork, or improve their skills. Proponents of the incentive say that rigorous, long-term pay-for-performance systems offer effective methods of helping companies continually improve the workforce while getting and keeping the best employees. Opponents argue that such pay plans tend to pit employees against one another, erode trust and teamwork, and create white-collar sweatshops.[54]

- **Knowledge-based pay.** Another approach to compensation being explored by companies is **knowledge-based pay**, also known as *competency-based pay* or *skill-based pay*, which is tied to employees' knowledge and abilities rather than to their job per se. Typically, the pay level at which a person is hired matches that person's current level of skills; as the employee acquires new skills, the pay level goes up. More than half of all large U.S. companies now use some variation on this incentive.[55]

bonus
Cash payment, in addition to regular wage or salary, that serves as a reward for achievement

commissions
Employee compensation based on a percentage of sales made

profit sharing
The distribution of a portion of the company's profits to employees

gain sharing
Plan for rewarding employees not on the basis of overall profits but in relation to achievement of goals such as cost savings from higher productivity

pay for performance
Incentive program that rewards employees for meeting specific, individual goals

knowledge-based pay
Pay tied to an employee's acquisition of knowledge or skills; also called competency-based pay or skill-based pay

Sales professionals usually earn at least part of their income through commissions; the more they sell, the more they earn.

These incentive programs are so popular in today's workplace that many employees consider their financial value as part of their overall salary package. However, many companies are still unsure about the value of such programs. For instance, only 17 percent in a recent survey said that their pay-for-performance initiatives were showing a clear impact on company performance.[56] Poorly administered programs can easily cost more than help, but companies that design and implement programs well do see beneficial results.[57]

Employee Benefits and Services

employee benefits
Compensation other than wages, salaries, and incentive programs

cafeteria plans
Benefit plans that let employees choose from a flexible menu of health care, retirement, and other benefits.

LEARNING OBJECTIVE 6

Highlight five popular employee benefits

Companies also regularly provide **employee benefits**—elements of compensation other than wages, salaries, and incentives. These benefits may be offered as either a preset package—that is, the employee gets whatever insurance, paid holidays, pension plan, and other benefits the company sets up—or as flexible plans, sometimes known as **cafeteria plans**. Cafeteria plans (so called because of the similarity to choosing items from a menu) recognize that people have different priorities and needs at different stages of their lives. An employee with a young family might feel a more immediate need for extra health insurance over retirement benefits, whereas a single employee might choose to "buy" an extra week of vacation time by giving up some other benefit.

The benefits most commonly provided by employers are insurance, retirement benefits, employee stock-ownership plans, stock options, and family benefits. As you read about these in the following sections, try to consider them from the perspectives of both an employee and an employer. You'll begin to understand why the field of benefits has become such a complex area in business today, and why benefits often figure strongly in union contract negotiations, strategic planning decisions, and even national public policy debates.

Insurance Employers can offer a range of insurance plans to their employees, including life, health, dental, vision, disability, and long-term-care insurance. Although employers are under no general legal obligation to provide insurance coverage (except in union contracts, for instance), many companies view these benefits as a competitive necessity, to attract and retain good employees. For example, following the lead of other fast-food retailers as Jamba Juice and Starbucks, Jack in the Box recently began offering health insurance to all its hourly employees, both part-time and full-time, at company-owned restaurants. Although the program adds costs, the company figures the reduction in employee turnover—which in turn reduces hiring and training costs while improving workforce stability—will make the expense worthwhile.[58]

Perhaps no other issue illustrates the challenging economics of business today than health insurance. With insurance premiums and other costs rising quickly, employers are taking a variety of steps to control costs, including forcing employees to pick up more of the cost (a practice often known as *cost shifting*), reducing or eliminating coverage for retired employees, auditing employees' health claims more carefully, inquiring into employees' health and habits more closely, dropping spouses from insurance plans, or even firing employees who are so sick or disabled that they are no longer able to work. At the same time, however, workers' earnings aren't increasing fast enough to cover a rising share of these expenses, either. The situation is particularly acute for small businesses, which don't have the purchasing power of large corporations.[59] For a look at why health care costs so much, see "The Big Picture: The Unhealthy Economics of Health Care" online at **www.prenhall.com/bovee**.

The tension is likely to continue, prompting calls for more government intervention, spurring unionizing efforts, pitting healthy employees against their less-healthy colleagues, and extending the reach of companies into their employees' personal lives. For instance, Weyco, a small employer in Okemos, Michigan, recently took the highly unusual step of forbidding its employees to smoke—even on their own time—and enforces the policy through random breathalyzer testing. The fact that Weyco is in the business of administering health benefit programs for other companies gives it front-line insights into the rising costs of health care, including the statistic that smokers incur several thousand dollars a year on average in extra productivity and health care costs.[60] Exhibit 11.7 shows a sample of many creative ways employers, insurers, and public officials are trying to offer adequate coverage at manageable costs.

Exhibit 11.7
Creative Approaches to Skyrocketing Health Care Costs
For a variety of reasons—cost control, competitiveness, and concern for their employees—U.S. companies are tackling high health care costs in a variety of ways.

High-deductible insurance	One of the simplest changes is switching to high-deductible insurance, in which the employee must pay more of his or her medical expenses directly before insurance kicks in. This not only lowers insurance premiums, but advocates say it forces employees to use health care services more carefully.
Health Savings Accounts (HSAs)	Higher deductibles are a feature of the new Health Savings Accounts (HSAs) introduced in 2003. HSAs let employees sock away parts of their salaries tax-free and use the money to pay for medical care or spend it on other things if they stay healthy.
In-house clinics	A few companies have saved by opening their own private clinics on site, giving them more control over costs and removing the insurance layer from the health care model. However, this option is attractive only to companies with large, geographically concentrated workforces.
Health insurance buying groups	Smaller employers can band together to increase their purchasing power. After joining the employers' group Presidion, the Tampa, Florida, restaurant chain Ragin' Ribs cut its health care costs by 25 percent. Similar organizations also exist to help independent contractors save on insurance.
Employer-driven quality improvements	An even more comprehensive cooperative effort is the Leapfrog Group, a nonprofit coalition representing a variety of employers and health care plans; Leapfrog offers incentives to hospitals and health care providers to reduce preventable medical errors, improve the quality of care, and in doing so also cut costs dramatically.
Insurance for the uninsured	A coalition of large employers recently formed the Affordable Health Care Solution, a giant purchasing cooperative that lowers the cost of insurance for independent contractors, part-timers, and others who can't afford insurance.
Sliding-scale plans	With a sliding-scale program, employers charge for health insurance based on salary, making insurance more affordable for lower-wage workers.
Wellness programs	Many employers have discovered that a great way to cut health care costs is to keep employees healthier in the first place; wellness programs can include everything from dietary advice to exercise facilities to smoking-cessation classes.

Over the next few years, you'll hear a lot of discussion regarding major structural changes in the U.S. health care system. Consensus is growing that the country needs some way to provide basic health coverage for the 40-plus million people who currently can't afford it, but agreement about how to accomplish that goal is a long way off.[61] An overall lack of money is not the problem; the United States spends enough money to provide adequate care for everyone, but there is considerable waste, inefficiency, and imbalance in the system. Moreover, every attempt at restructuring health care quickly runs into philosophical debates about the social and economic responsibilities of the federal government and the vested interests of the many companies that have a stake in the multibillion-dollar medical industry.

Retirement Benefits Social Security was created by the federal government following the Great Depression of the 1930s to provide basic support to those who could not accumulate the retirement money they would need later in life. Today, nearly everyone who works regularly is eligible for Social Security payments during retirement. This income is paid for by the Social Security tax, part of which is withheld by the employer from employees' wages and part of which is paid by the employer. As Chapter 1 noted, however, some changes must be made to the Social Security system in the coming years to allow it to continue meeting its obligations to future retirees.

In addition to Social Security, many employees benefit from **retirement plans** set up by their employers. These plans are regulated by the Employees' Retirement Income Security Act of 1974 (ERISA), which established a federal agency to insure the assets of pension plans, along with newer laws that address specific types of retirement plans.[62]

Company-sponsored retirement plans can be categorized as either *defined benefit plans,* in which the company specifies how much it will pay employees upon retirement, or *defined contribution plans,* in which companies specify how much they will put into the retirement fund for their employees, without guaranteeing any specific payouts during retirement. Although both types are technically **pension plans**, when most people speak of pension plans, they are referring to traditional defined benefit plans.[63] In the past two decades, the number of companies offering defined benefit plans has dropped from 170,000 to less than 30,000.[64] Moreover, many of these plans are now in serious financial trouble. To meet their current and future obligations to employees, pension fund managers invest some of the company's cash and assume those investments will grow enough to cover future retirement needs. However, dramatic stock market losses in recent years have left many plans underfunded, some by billions of dollars, forcing those companies to redirect cash from other purposes. For instance, Delphi Automotive, a large auto parts manufacturer, has had to divert $600 million a year from expansion and hiring in order to cover gaps in its pension plan.[65]

Changing existing pension programs is a complex and risky move. When IBM attempted to transfer 140,000 employees from a defined-benefit plan to a plan that paid them less, the dispute led to a $300 million court settlement and Congressional hearings. Moreover, companies that renege on promises made to employees can create long-lasting mistrust of management that hampers morale and productivity.[66] Another major problem is brewing with the Pension Benefit Guaranty Corporation (PBGC), a federal agency that essentially acts as an employer-funded insurance program to cover pension costs whenever a company is unable or unwilling to pay its retirees. After a number of large pension defaults in recent years, the PBCG is paying out more than it takes in, and healthy companies such as IBM and GE are paying far more than unhealthy or bankrupt companies (mostly steel companies and airlines at this point).[67]

Some 8 million U.S. employees are now enrolled in another type of defined benefit plan known as an **employee stock-ownership plan (ESOP)**, in which a company places a certain amount of its stock in trust for some or all of its employees, with each employee entitled to a certain share. These plans allow employees to later purchase the shares at a fixed price. If the company does well, the ESOP may provide a substantial employee benefit. In addition to potential retirement benefits, an ESOP also provides a means for employees to have a representative on the board of directors, a situation now found in more than 300 U.S. corporations.[68]

Employers can choose from several different types of defined contribution plans, the most common of which is known as a *401(k) plan.* In a 401(k) plan, employees contribute a percentage of their pretax income, and employers often match that amount or some portion of it. In addition to the money their employers invest, employees enjoy tax reductions based on their annual contributions to the fund.[69] Unfortunately, stock market declines, reductions in company contributions, and accounting scandals have reduced the attractiveness of 401(k) plans in the eyes of some employees, particularly in the all-too-common situation where employees invested most of their 401(k) fund in their own employer's stock. Enron employees alone lost an estimated $1 billion of retirement savings when that stock collapsed.[70] Overall, employees have a fairly poor record of managing their own retirement funds—a situation that concerns some experts during the national debate about shifting more responsibility from Social Security to individual account holders.[71]

Stock Options A related method for tying employee compensation to company performance is the stock option plan. **Stock options** grant employees the right to purchase a set number of shares of the employer's stock at a specific price, called the *grant* or *exercise price,* during a certain time period. Options typically "vest" over five years, at a rate of 20 percent

retirement plans
Company-sponsored programs for providing retirees with income

pension plans
Generally refers to traditional, defined benefit retirement plans

employee stock-ownership plan (ESOP)
Program enabling employees to become partial owners of a company

Charles Prestwood is one of the many former Enron employees whose retirement savings were virtually wiped out when the company's stock collapsed. The value of his Enron stock plunged from $1.3 million to just $8,000.

stock options
Contract allowing the holder to purchase or sell a certain number of shares of a particular stock at a given price by a certain date

annually. This means that at the end of one year employees can purchase up to 20 percent of the shares in the original grant, at the end of two years 40 percent, and so on. If the stock's market price exceeds the exercise price, the option holder can exercise the option and sell the stock at a profit. If the stock's price falls below the exercise price, the options become worthless, at least temporarily (such options are often referred to as being "under water").

Stock options can benefit both employers and employees. From the employer's perspective, stock options cost little, provide long-term incentives for good people to stay with the company, and encourage employees to work harder because they have a vested interest in the company doing well. From the employee's perspective, stock options can generate a handsome profit if the stock's market price exceeds the grant price. But stock options lose their appeal when the stock does not perform as expected.

Options were quite popular in the technology boom in the 1980s and 1990s, when start-ups would frequently lure new employees with low salaries but thousands of stock option shares. In the cases where those stocks enjoyed healthy growth, some employees became quite wealthy. Practically an entire generation of Microsoft employees earned enormous sums of money this way. However, employees in many other companies, particularly in dot-coms in the late 1990s, saw their dreams of stock-option riches turn to dust as stock prices collapsed. Stock options have also come under attack from regulators and financial reformers in recent years, who claim they can tempt executives into decisions that boost stocks prices in the short term but harm the company in the long term. In a sign of what could be a major shift in compensation strategies, Microsoft announced in 2003 that it would stop awarding employees with stock options.[72]

Family Benefits The Family Medical and Leave Act (FMLA), signed into law in 1993, requires employers with 50 or more workers to provide up to 12 weeks of unpaid leave per year for childbirth, adoption, or the care of oneself, a child, a spouse, or a parent with serious illness.[73] Many employees can't afford to take extended periods of time off without pay, but at least the law creates the opportunity for those who can. However, employer complaints about excessive use of the FMLA under questionable circumstances have led some to nickname it the "Far More Leave than anyone intended Act" and push for a clearer definition of what constitutes a serious medical problem.[74]

Day care is another important family benefit, especially for single parents and two-career couples. In fact, half of all working families now rely on day care.[75] Nearly half of all companies now offer some sort of childcare assistance, including flexible savings accounts (which let employees put aside some of their pay for childcare and other services), referral programs, discounted rates at nearby childcare centers, and on-site day-care centers.[76] Although the number of companies with on-site day-care centers remains fairly low, recent research led by Bowdoin College economist Rachel Connelly shows that such facilities don't have to be the financial burden many perceive them to be—and can even generate profits. Moreover, day-care facilities also send a message to the entire workforce, including employees without children, that the company cares about its workers and their struggles to balance personal and professional responsibilities.[77]

Another family benefit of growing importance is elder care, assisting employees with the responsibility of caring for aging parents. Many employers now offer some form of elder-care assistance, ranging from referral services that help find care providers to dependent-care allowances. Some companies will even agree to move elderly relatives when they transfer an employee to another location.[78]

Other Employee Benefits Although sometimes overlooked, paid holidays, sick pay, premium pay for working overtime or unusual hours, and paid vacations are important benefits. To provide incentives for employee loyalty, most companies grant employees longer paid vacations after they've been with the organization for a prescribed number of years. And rather than separating time off by vacation, sick days, and other reasons, some companies present employees with a block of "general-purpose" time that they are free to use for whatever reason they wish. For example, Agilent Technologies takes this approach with a program called Flexible Time Off.[79]

CEO Jim Goodnight of SAS Institute (a software development firm) takes a snack break with children at the company's on-site day-care center.

employee assistance program (EAP)
Company-sponsored counseling or referral plan for employees with personal problems

Among the many other benefits that companies sometimes offer are sabbaticals (time off to spend at the employee's discretion, usually after a certain length of service to the employer), tuition loans and reimbursements, financial counseling and legal services, even assistance with buying homes in areas with high housing costs.[80] One of the most cost-effective benefits employers can establish is an **employee assistance program (EAP)**, which offer private and confidential counseling to employees who need help with issues related to drugs, alcohol, domestic violence, finances, stress, family issues, and other personal problems. Studies by the National Council on Alcoholism and Drug Dependence (NCADD) show that the average annual cost for EAP services runs from $12 to $20 per employee. However, these services save between $5 and $16 for each dollar spent as a result of improved safety and productivity, as well as reduced employee turnover.[81] Domestic violence alone leads to some $700 million a year in lost productivity and another $4 billion in health care costs, prompting companies such as the clothing firm Liz Claiborne and the electronics firm Harman International to include domestic violence counseling as part of their EAPs.[82]

In addition to these benefits, companies can offer a wide array of other goods, services, and discounts, generally known as *perks* (short for *perquisite*). These can range from the use of company cars to health club memberships to free parking.

CRITICAL THINKING CHECKPOINT

1. Why is it considered poor management to give employees feedback only once a year?
2. Do employers have any business trying to influence the lifestyles of their employees in an effort to contain health care costs? Why or why not?
3. Why do managers in different companies disagree about the use of stock options as an employee incentive?

LEARNING OBJECTIVE 7

Describe four ways an employee's status may change and discuss why many employers like to fill job vacancies from within

attrition
Loss of employees for reasons other than termination

Overseeing Changes in Employment Status

Of course, providing competitive compensation and good employee benefits is no guarantee that employees will stay with the company. Every company experiences some level of **attrition**, when employees leave for reasons other than termination, including retirement, new job opportunities, long-term disability, or death. Virtually all companies also find themselves with the need to terminate employment of selected workers from time to time. Whatever the reason, when a vacancy occurs, companies must go to the trouble and expense of finding a replacement, whether from inside or outside the company.

Promoting and Reassigning Employees

As Exhibit 11.5 shows, many companies prefer to look within the organization to fill job vacancies. In part, this "promote from within" policy allows a company to benefit from the training and experience of its own workforce. This policy also rewards employees who have worked hard and demonstrated the ability to handle more challenging tasks. In addition, morale is usually better when a company promotes from within because employees see that they can advance. For example, Enterprise Rent-A-Car, one of the nation's largest employers of new college graduates, has used its strong tradition of promoting from within as a major selling point to potential employees.[83]

Terminating Employees

A company invests time, effort, and money in each new employee it recruits and trains. This investment is lost when an employee is removed by **termination**—permanently laying off the employee because of cutbacks or firing the employee for poor performance or other reasons. Many companies facing a downturn in business have avoided large-scale layoffs by cutting other costs, but sometimes a company has no alternative but to reduce the size of its workforce.

Layoffs are the termination of employees for economic or business reasons unrelated to employee performance. Companies are free to make layoffs in any manner they choose, just as long as certain demographic groups are not disproportionately affected. But as Michael Dell puts it, making cuts "is one of the hardest, most gut-wrenching decisions you can make as a leader." Layoffs are "an admission that we screwed up" by over-hiring.[84]

To help ease the pain of layoffs, many companies provide laid-off employees with job-hunting assistance. *Outplacement* aids such as résumé-writing courses, career counseling, office space, and secretarial help are offered to laid-off executives and blue-collar employees alike. Large-scale outplacement efforts are often outsourced to specialist firms such as Challenger, Gray & Christmas (**www.challengergray.com**), which boasts a record of helping laid off employees find jobs in much less time than they can usually do on their own.[85]

Terminating employment by firing an employee is a complex subject with many legal ramifications, and the line between a layoff and a firing can be blurry. For instance, many employees would be surprised to learn that every state except Montana supports the concept of *at-will employment*, meaning that companies are free to fire nearly anyone they choose. Exceptions to this vary from state to state, but in general, employers cannot discriminate in firing (such as by firing someone because he or she is of a certain race or a certain age), nor can they fire employees for whistle-blowing, filing a worker's compensation claim, or testifying against the employer in harassment or discrimination lawsuits.[86] If the employee believes any of these principles have been violated, he or she can opt to file a *wrongful discharge* lawsuit against the employer. In addition, employers must abide by the terms of an employment contract, if one has been entered into with the employee (these are much more common for executives than they are for lower-level employees). In spite of the leeway provided by at-will employment, many employers offer written assurances that they will terminate employees only *for cause,* which usually includes such actions as committing crimes or violating company policy.

One of the newest and most controversial trends in employee termination is known informally as the *rank and yank,* in which a company ranks the performance of all its employees, then fires the bottom 5 or 10 percent in an effort to improve overall corporate performance. Former General Electric CEO Jack Welch, who pioneered the tactic years ago (and prefers to call it *differentiation*) says that it's a honest and humane way to let lower performers know that they might have better opportunities elsewhere. According to one estimate, 20 percent of all large employers now use the *rank and yank* method from time to time.[87]

Business Buzz
warm-chair attrition
A situation in which employees have mentally checked out from their current jobs but are waiting for the economy to improve before finding better jobs

termination
Process of getting rid of an employee through layoff or firing

layoffs
Termination of employees for economic or business reasons

Retiring Employees

As Chapter 10 discussed, the U.S. workforce is aging rapidly. For the business community, an aging population presents two challenges. The first is to give job opportunities to people who are willing and able to work but who happen to be past the traditional retirement age. Many older citizens are concerned about their ability to live comfortably on fixed retirement incomes. Others simply prefer to work. For several decades, many companies and industries had **mandatory retirement policies** that made it necessary for people to quit working as soon as they turned a certain age. As you read in Chapter 10, however, in 1967, the Age Discrimination in Employment Act outlawed discrimination against anyone between the ages of 40 and 65. Subsequent amendments raised the upper age to 70, outlawed mandatory retirement (some professions, such as airline pilots are still governed by such rules, however), and forbade employers to stop benefit contributions or accruals because of age.[88]

The second challenge posed by an aging workforce is to find ways to encourage older employees to retire early if the company needs to balance its workforce. One method a company may use is to offer older employees financial incentives to resign, such as enhanced retirement benefits or onetime cash payments. Inducing employees to depart by offering them financial incentives is known as a **worker buyout**. This method can be a lot more expensive than firing or laying off employees, but it has several advantages: The morale of the remaining employees is preserved because they feel less threatened about their own security, younger employees see increased chances for promotion, and the risk of age-discrimination lawsuits is minimized.

mandatory retirement policies
Required dismissal of an employee who reaches a certain age

worker buyout
Distribution of financial incentives to employees who voluntarily depart; usually undertaken in order to reduce the payroll

---

CRITICAL THINKING CHECKPOINT
1. Managers brought in to rejuvenate a failing division or company have been known to fire the entire staff and require everyone to reapply for his or her job. What are the benefits and risks of such a dramatic move?
2. What affect would a "promote from within" policy have on employee motivation?
3. Why can layoffs be considered an instance of management failure?

CHECKLIST: Apply These Ideas When You're the Boss

✓ Remember that recruiting new employees is nearly always more expensive and more risky than retaining proven employees.

✓ Add new employees to your organization with great care; never hire in response to short-term blips in workloads, but always with an eye on longer-term needs.

✓ Use job analysis to identify the true needs of every position before you start to recruit for it.

✓ Don't overlook your own customers when you're looking for new talent; these people already know about your business and they can bring valuable perspectives (however, note that in business-to-business markets, it is sometimes frowned upon to "poach" employees from one's own customers)

✓ Unless you already know a candidate thoroughly, always perform background checks to make sure you're not bringing potential trouble on board.

✓ View training as an investment, not a cost—but make sure training is based on identified business needs.

✓ Maintain a current skills inventory of everyone in the company; it'll help you forecast staffing needs, align the workforce with changing business requirements, and guide employees in their own career development.

✓ Virtually every aspect of human resources management is covered by laws and regulations; staying up to date on the laws is one of your responsibilities as a business owner or manager.

✓ Many industries conduct salary surveys to help employees figure out competitive wage levels; these reports can be expensive, but they can also save money and help attract the right hires.

✓ Implement incentive programs with great care and make sure you'll be able to afford them through the ups and downs of the business cycle.

Summary of Learning Objectives

1 **List six main functions of human resources departments.** Human resources departments plan for a company's staffing needs, recruit and hire new employees, train and develop employees, appraise employee performance, administer compensation and employee benefits, and oversee changes in employment status.

2 **Cite eight methods recruiters use to find job candidates.** Recruiters find job candidates by (1) promoting internal candidates, (2) advertising in newspapers and on the Internet, (3) using public and private employment agencies, (4) contacting union hiring halls, (5) recruiting at college campuses and career placement offices, (6) attending trade shows, (7) hiring corporate "headhunters," and (8) soliciting referrals from employees or colleagues in the industry.

3 **Identify the six stages in the hiring process.** The stages in the hiring process are (1) narrowing down the number of qualified candidates, (2) performing initial screening interviews, (3) administering a series of follow-up interviews, (4) evaluating candidates, (5) conducting reference checks, and (6) selecting the right candidate.

4 **Discuss how companies incorporate objectivity into employee performance appraisals.** Employee performance appraisals are an effective way to inform employees if they are doing a good job and how they can improve their performance. To ensure objectivity and fairness, most firms use a standard, companywide format, provide a written record of appraisals for future reference, and solicit several perspectives by engaging superiors, peers, and colleagues at different levels in the organization in the review process.

5 **List six popular types of financial incentive programs for employees.** The most popular employee incentive programs are bonuses, commissions, profit sharing, gain sharing, pay for performance, and knowledge-based pay.

6 **Highlight five popular employee benefits.** The two most popular employee benefits are insurance (health, life, disability, and long-term care) and retirement benefits, such as pension plans that help employees save for later years. Employee stock-ownership plans and stock options, two additional benefits, allow employees to receive or purchase shares of the company's stock and thus obtain a stake in the company. Family benefits programs, also popular, include maternity and paternity leave, child-care assistance, and elder-care assistance.

7 **Describe four ways an employee's status may change, and discuss why many employers like to fill job vacancies from within.** An employee's status may change through promotion or through reassignment to a different position, through termination (removal from the company's payroll), through voluntary resignation, or through retirement. Employers like to fill vacancies created from such changes by promoting from within for these reasons: The employee has been trained by the company and knows the ropes, it boosts employee morale, and it sends a message to other employees that good performance will be rewarded.

Jamba Juice: What's Next

As a classic service business, Jamba Juice relies heavily on the talent, commitment, and stability of its workforce. No amount of clever strategy or high-tech gadgetry can keep the business going strong if the right people aren't in place on the front lines. So far, Jamba Juice has shown considerable talents for attracting good employees and keeping them content with a variety of benefits and a positive, people-centered work environment.

Those talents will be put to the test in a major way in the next few years, as the restaurant industry's demand for workers grows—restaurants already employ nearly 10 percent of the U.S. workforce—and retiring waves of baby boomers create talent shortages throughout the economy. Other companies will be dialing up the competition for workers, but they'll have a long way to go to outrun Jamba Juice in the race for human resources.[89]

Critical Thinking Questions

1. So far, Jamba Juice has refused to sell franchises to individual entrepreneurs because it doesn't want to run the risk of damaging its Jamba Juice brand through poorly managed operations bearing its name. However, franchising could be one way to keep expanding without the constant headache of finding new employees. If expansion has to slow because the company can't hire enough new people, should it change its stance on franchising in order to keep growing? Why or why not?

2. Which questions would you ask potential employees in order to assess their attitude toward customer service?

3. How might Jamba Juice's community involvement help the company deal with labor shortages?

Learn More Online

Visit the Jamba Juice website by clicking on the hotlink at Chapter 11 of this text's website at www.prenhall.com/bovee. Explore the company, product, and employment information on the site. What language does Jamba Juice use to describe itself and how does this help the company appeal to potential employees? What benefits does the company offer? If you were interested in a managerial job at Jamba, does the site provide enough information to help you decide whether to apply?

Key Terms

attrition (382)
bonus (377)
cafeteria plans (378)
commissions (377)
compensation (373)
contingent employee (363)
electronic performance
    monitoring (EPM) (373)
employee assistance
    programs (EAPs) (382)
employee benefits (378)
employee retention (362)
employee stock ownership
    plan (ESOP) (380)

gain sharing (377)
human resources
    management (HRM) (360)
incentives (376)
job analysis (364)
job description (364)
job specification (364)
knowledge-based pay (377)
layoffs (383)
mandatory retirement (384)
orientation programs (371)
pay for performance (377)
pension plans (380)
performance appraisals (371)

profit sharing (377)
recruiting (366)
replacement chart (362)
retirement plans (380)
salary (373)
skills inventory (371)
stock options (380)
succession planning (362)
termination (383)
wages (373)
worker buyout (384)

Test Your Knowledge

Questions for Review

1. What do human resources managers do?
2. What are some strategic staffing alternatives that organizations use to avoid overstaffing and understaffing?
3. What is the purpose of conducting a job analysis? What are some of the techniques used for gathering information?
4. Why do some companies use preemployment drug testing while others don't?
5. What functions do orientation programs serve?

Questions for Analysis

6. How do incentive programs encourage employees to be more productive, innovative, and committed to their work?
7. Why do some employers offer comprehensive benefits even though the costs of doing so have risen significantly in recent years?

8. What are the advantages and disadvantages of 401(k) retirement plans?

9. The 1986 Immigration Reform and Control Act forbids companies to hire illegal aliens but at the same time prohibits discrimination in hiring on the basis of national origin or citizenship status. How can companies satisfy both requirements of this law?

10. **Ethical Considerations.** Corporate headhunters have been known to raid other companies of their top talent to fill vacant or new positions for their clients. Is it ethical to contact the CEO of one company and lure him or her to join the management team of another company?

Questions for Application

11. If you were on the human resources staff at a large health care organization that was looking for a new manager of information systems, what recruiting method(s) would you use and why?

12. Assume you are the manager of human resources at a manufacturing company that employs about 500 people. A recent cyclical downturn in your industry has led to financial losses, and top management is talking about laying off workers. Several supervisors have come to you with creative ways of keeping employees on the payroll, such as exchanging workers with other local companies. Why might you want to consider this option? What other options exist besides layoffs?

13. **Integrated.** Of the five levels in Maslow's hierarchy of needs, which is satisfied by offering salary? By offering health care benefits? By offering training opportunities? By developing flexible job descriptions?

14. **Integrated.** What are some of the human resources issues managers are likely to encounter when two companies (in the same industry) merge?

Practice Your Knowledge

Handling Difficult Situations on the Job: Juggling Diversity and Performance

As billing adjustments department manager at SBC Pacific Bell, you've been trained to handle a culturally diverse workforce. One of your best recent hires is 22-year-old Jorge Gutierrez. In record time, he was entering and testing complex price changes, mastering the challenges of your monumental computerized billing software. He was a real find—except for one problem: His close family ties often distract him from work duties.

His parents immigrated from Central America when Jorge and his sisters were young children, and you understand and respect the importance that family plays in the lives of many Hispanic Americans. However, every morning Gutierrez's mother calls to be sure he got to work safely. Then his father calls. And three times this month, his younger sister has called him away from work with three separate emergencies. Friends and extended family members seem to call at all hours of the day.

Gutierrez says he's asked friends and family not to call his office number. Now they dial his cell phone instead. He's reluctant to shut off his cell phone during work hours, in case someone in his family needs him.

Your task: How should you approach Gutierrez on this issue? Should you wait for a formal performance appraisal or do it sooner? Why? Should you terminate him (after all, his family responsibilities do distract him from work at times)? Would alternative work arrangements be a good idea for Gutierrez? Why or why not?

Sharpening Your Communication Skills

A visit to CCH's SOHO Guide at www.toolkit.cch.com can help you reduce your legal liability whether you are laying off or firing a single employee or are contemplating a companywide reduction in your workforce. Log on to the website and scroll down to the CCH Small Business Guide, then click on Table of Contents. Scroll down to People Who Work for You, and click on Firing and Termination to find out the safest way to fire someone from a legal standpoint before it's too late. Learn why it's important to document disciplinary actions. Then use the information at this website to write a short memo to your instructor summarizing how to set up a termination meeting and what you should say and do at the meeting when you fire an employee.

Building Your Team Skills

Team up with a classmate to practice your responses to interview questions. Use the list of common interview questions provided in the Prologue, and take turns posing and responding to those questions. Which questions did you find most difficult to answer? What insights did you gain about your strengths and weaknesses by answering those questions? Why is it a good idea to rehearse your answers before going to an interview?

Expand Your Knowledge

Discovering Career Opportunities

If you pursue a career in human resources, you'll be deeply involved in helping organizations find, select, train, evaluate, and retain employees. You have to like people and be a good communicator to succeed in HR. Is this field for you? Using your local Sunday newspaper, the *Wall Street Journal,* and online sources such as Monster (www.monster.com), find ads seeking applicants for positions in the field of human resources.

1. What educational qualifications, technical knowledge, or specialized skills are applicants for these jobs expected to have? How do these requirements fit with your background and educational plans?
2. Next, look at the duties mentioned in the ad for each job. What do you think you would be doing on an average day in these jobs? Does the work in each job sound interesting and challenging?
3. Now think about how you might fit into one of these positions. Do you prefer to work alone, or do you enjoy teamwork? How much paperwork are you willing to do? Do you communicate better in person, on paper, or by phone? Considering your answers to these questions, which of the HR jobs seems to be the closest match for your personal style?

Developing Your Research Skills

Locate one or more articles in business journals or newspapers (print or online editions) that illustrate how a company or industry is adapting to changes in its workforce. (Examples include retraining, literacy or basic-skills training, flexible benefits, and benefits aimed at working parents or people who care for aging relatives.)

1. What changes in the workforce or employee needs caused the company to adapt? What did the company do to respond to these changes? Was the company's response voluntary or legally mandated?
2. Is the company alone in facing these changes, or is the entire industry trying to adapt? What are other companies in the industry doing to adapt to the changes?
3. What other changes in the workforce or in employee needs do you think this company is likely to face in the next few years? Why?

Exploring the Best of the Web

URLs for all Internet exercises are provided at the website for this book, www.prenhall.com/bovee. When you log on to this text's Companion Website, select Chapter 11. Then select "Featured Websites," click on the name of the featured website, and review the website to complete these exercises.

Explore these chapter-related websites, review their content, and answer the following questions for each website you visit:

1. What is the purpose of this website?
2. What kinds of information does this website contain? Please be specific.
3. How is the information provided at this website useful for businesspeople? Consumers?
4. How did you expand your knowledge of economics by reviewing the material at this website? What new things did you learn about this topic?

Explore the Latest Workforce Management Ideas
Visit *Workforce Management* online to see what management leaders are thinking about month by month (requires registration to read most articles, but it's free). The Community Center hosts a number of forums in which you can read questions, answers, and commentary from working HR managers. The Research Center lists a wide range of topics to explore in the HRM field. www.workforce.com

Digging Deeper at the Bureau of Labor Statistics

By now you're probably aware that the U.S. government has an agency for almost every purpose. Many of these agencies gather facts and statistics on trends in the United States, and the Bureau of Labor Statistics is no exception. When you need to research detailed information about national or regional employment conditions—such as wages, unemployment, productivity, and benefits—point your web browser to this site: www.bls.gov

Maximizing Your Earning Potential

You know you should be making more money. So now what? Log on to Salary.com to find out what you are worth. Then maximize your earning potential by exploring the basics of negotiation. Sharpen your skills so you can get the job, salary, and benefits you want. Contemplating a move? Use the cost-of-living wizard to find out if it makes economic sense. You may even want to prepare for your next performance review by taking one of the site's self-tests. Finally, don't leave without learning how to manage your take-home pay or getting some facts about tuition assistance. Many companies will reimburse you for your career course work. But you may not get it if you don't ask. www.salary.com

Learning Interactively

Companion Website

Visit the Companion Website at www.prenhall.com/bovee. For Chapter 11, take advantage of the interactive "Learning Modules" to test your chapter knowledge. Get instant feedback on whether you need additional studying. Complete the exercises as specified by your instructor.

A Case for Critical Thinking

General Motors: Will Taking Care of Employees Sink This Industrial Titan?

WHAT'S KEEPING RICK WAGONER AWAKE THESE NIGHTS?

Care to guess which strategic business issue sits at the top of General Motors CEO Rick Wagoner's worry list? The roller coaster price of steel? The image of Toyota getting closer in the rearview mirror? New product designs? Safety?

None of the above. The cost of GM's employee benefits is his top-of-mind issue—and health care in particular. On average, health care costs add $1,500 to the price of every GM car, putting it at a serious disadvantage in the battle with super-efficient competitors such as Toyota. In 2005, GM spent nearly $6 billion on health care for 1.1 million current and retired employees and their families, and those costs are going nowhere but up. The drain on GM's finance is so severe that it risks getting a junk bond credit rating (meaning that it would be considered a high credit risk) if things get much worse. A few observers have even mentioned the potential for bankruptcy, although the company still has billions of dollars in the bank.

A PROBLEM NEARLY A CENTURY IN THE MAKING

How did the mighty General Motors find itself in such dire financial straights? As with seemingly everything related to health care, the answer is complex, but three issues figure prominently in GM's case:

- *GM's age.* At nearly 100 years old, the company has been adding to its retiree pool for longer than most companies have been in existence. To give you an idea of just how long GM has been around, more than 200 GM retirees are past the age of 100, meaning they've been drawing retirement benefits for 40 or 50 years. The pool of retirees is so large that for every active employee GM needs to generate enough revenue to support 2.5 retirees.
- *Labor contracts.* GM's benefit costs are defined in large part by its labor contracts with the United Auto Workers (UAW), which over the years has done a mighty good job of negotiating benefits for its members. According to *Fortune* magazine, GM's UAW-member employees and retirees have better health care plans than most CEOs. In late 2005, the company was able to negotiate with the UAW for $1 billion in annual cost reductions for health care, but Wagoner admits this isn't enough to stem the firm's financial losses. Health care and retirement costs will continue to be major points of contention in the company's relationship with unions.

- **The U.S. health care crisis.** GM's problems are set against a growing health care crisis in the United States, as costs continue to climb much faster than inflation in general, even as the quality of care lags in many respects. For instance, as a percentage of GDP, the United States pays far more for health care than any other nation, and half of that is wasted, according to researchers at Boston University. And adding injury to insult, U.S. health care buyers get far less in return—the United States ranks 12th out of 13 industrialized nations on an array of health quality indicators such as longevity and infant mortality.

In other words, GM has a huge problem on its hands, a problem that could threaten the company's survival if these costs can't be brought under control in the coming years.

COMPANIES COMPETING AGAINST GOVERNMENTS

In an important sense, GM and the other two U.S. carmakers, Ford and Chrysler, aren't just competing against Toyota, Honda, and Nissan, they're competing against the entire country of Japan. That's because the Japanese government, not private industry, funds most of the health care costs of workers there. The Japanese automakers also employ thousands of workers at their facilities in the United States, but these operations are much newer and therefore have few retired employees to support. Consequently, while GM is pumping billions of dollars into employee and retiree benefits, Toyota and other rivals are pumping their money into new car designs, new production technologies, and other competitive advantages.

In addition, GM and everyone else who pays for medical insurance indirectly subsidizes care for the more than 40 million Americans who have no health insurance. In Japan and many other countries, those costs are spread across the entire population, not just the segment that can afford health insurance.

A LOOK INTO THE FUTURE OF U.S. BUSINESS?

GM's troubles sound a lot like the woes of the steel and airline industries, but the crisis is hardly limited to these old-line industries. From small firms to high-tech icons such as IBM, thousands of U.S. companies are struggling to meet commitments they've made to both active employees and retirees. As Sean McAlinden of the Center for Automotive Research puts it, "There are many, many more companies out there in trouble because of health care costs."

Unfortunately, the inefficient U.S. health care system is so fragmented that forcing meaningful change is a mammoth challenge. Moreover, discussions about fixing health care too often degenerate into philosophical shouting matches between advocates of universal health care, who claim that a national, government-managed system is the best solution, and advocates of free-market economics, who claim that such universal health care smacks of socialism and isn't as great as the other side claims it to be anyway.

In the meantime, companies at risk of collapse are already taking dramatic steps, such as sharply reducing health care benefits or even dropping them entirely. Such changes are hard enough on current employees, but they can be devastating to retirees who've counted on this coverage and can't afford alternatives.

Rick Wagoner has become a visible and vocal proponent for fixing the problem, however, and if enough voices like his join forces, corporate America may just have the market influence needed to solve this crisis before it engulfs too many more U.S. companies.

Critical Thinking Questions

1. To a larger degree than any other industrialized country, the United States depends on employers to provide such critical services as health insurance and retirement funds. Should the government step in and take over more of these services? Why or why not?
2. Do you think it is appropriate for Rick Wagoner to use his position as the CEO of one of the largest companies in the country to press for changes in the health care system? Why or why not?
3. If GM or any other company has to make the difficult choice between reneging on a promised benefit to retirees or active employees, which groups should it favor? Why?
4. Go to Chapter 11 of this text's website at www.prenhall.com/bovee and click on the hot link to get to the GM website, then find the section on employee benefits. What message does GM send to potential employees regarding health care and retirement benefits? Also visit the United Auto Workers website at www.uaw.org for the union's perspective on these issues. Find the section on Auto Contract Summaries, then click on the General Motors & Delphi link. What does the union say about its health care and pension benefits in its latest contract?

Video Case

Channeling Human Resources at Showtime

Learning Objectives

The purpose of this video is to help you

1. Identify the many ways in which human resources managers can actively develop employees
2. Appreciate the role of mentoring in employee development
3. Understand how a performance appraisal system can be designed and administered

Synopsis

Showtime Networks Inc. (SNI), which is a wholly owned subsidiary of media conglomerate Viacom, operates the premium television networks Showtime, The Movie Channel (TMC), Flix, and Showtime Event Television. It also operates the premium network Sundance Channel, a joint venture with Robert Redford and Universal Studios. One of the biggest challenges at SNI, as anywhere, is attracting, retaining, and motivating a committed workforce. Demographic changes, work and family issues, and increasing diversities of age, race, and lifestyle call forth the dedication and creativity of its human resources staff. This video introduces various Showtime executives who discuss the company's human resources policies and challenges. The firm is a leader in creating a broad training and career development program that serves many different kinds of employee needs. It also uses a performance appraisal system that employees have helped design and has a formal program for encouraging mentoring.

Discussion Questions

1. *For analysis:* Among the organizational changes recently made at Showtime are the combining of the legal and the human resources departments and the appointment of one particular human resources manager to each SNI division. Comment on the advantages or disadvantages of these changes.

2. *For analysis:* Is Showtime doing a good job of offering its employees chances to develop and improve their skills? Can you suggest additional programs it could undertake to achieve this goal?

3. *For analysis:* Do you think the performance appraisal system at Showtime is an effective one? Why or why not?

4. *For application:* Could you apply Showtime's approach to a company with only three or four employees? Why or why not?

5. *For debate:* Do companies have a responsibility, beyond their own business needs, to mentor and develop employees? Why or why not?

Online Exploration

Visit the online job board of Showtime's parent company Viacom at https://jobhuntweb. viacom.com/Viacom/main/jobhome_viacom.asp (online applications for all Viacom companies are handled through this central site). Consider the information available on this site and the manner in which it is presented. Does Viacom sound like the sort of company you'd like to work for? Why or why not? What advice would you give the company to improve recruiting of college graduates, if any?

E-Business in Action

JOB RECRUITING MOVES TO THE NET

In just the past few years, e-cruiting (recruiting over the Internet) has become an integral part of the recruiting strategy for companies of all sizes. Companies have discovered that the Internet is a fast, convenient, and inexpensive way to find prospective job candidates. And job candidates are finding that the Internet is a convenient way to gather company information, search for job vacancies, and post résumés on both high-volume career websites such as Monster, Yahoo! HotJobs, and CareerBuilder (also known as job boards) and on more focused websites such as Dice (for high-tech jobs) and InternshipPrograms.com (for intern opportunities).

The Traditional Path Versus E-Cruiting

Before the advent of the Internet, recruiting followed a traditional path: When a company had exhausted internal possibilities, it would "announce" a job opening to the marketplace (through a classified ad, an executive recruiter, employee referral incentives, a job fair, or other medium), and recruiters made endless rounds of cold telephone calls to identify potential job candidates. Then, after a lengthy process of sorting through faxed and mailed résumés, someone from human resources called the most promising candidates and interviewed them. The process is slow and expensive.

Thanks to the Internet, however, the recruiting process is changing. Companies are using the Internet to search for résumés of promising candidates, take online applications, accept electronic résumés, conduct interviews, and administer tests. Recruiters at Amazon.com, for example, post ads on job boards and actively search the web for résumés. "To be a recruiter at Amazon.com, you have to like the thrill of the hunt," says Amazon's manager of technical recruiting. Amazon's recruiters sort through hundreds of candidates they consider for every position by using a tool to presort and categorize résumés.

Benefits and Drawbacks of E-Cruiting

In comparison to traditional recruiting methods, the benefits of Internet recruiting are many:

- **Speed.** The Internet allows job seekers to search for jobs quickly and to communicate via e-mail with potential employers. Companies can also save time in the hiring process by using the Internet to become a 24-hour, seven-days-a-week recruiter and give applicants quick responses to their queries. Determined nocturnal headhunters can snap up hot résumés posted on the Internet before dawn and contact candidates immediately by e-mail.

Some companies report receiving responses and résumés only minutes after posting a job opening.

- **Reach.** The Internet allows employers to contact a broader selection of applicants more quickly, target specific types of applicants more easily, and reach highly skilled applicants more efficiently. Some company websites bring in thousands of résumés in one week, a volume that would be far too cumbersome to manage through traditional means.
- **Cost savings.** Electronic ads typically cost much less than traditional print ads, career fairs, and open houses. Moreover, processing electronic application forms is more efficient than processing paper forms. Intelligent automated search agents can filter or prescreen potential applicants and find résumés that match job descriptions and specific employer criteria.

Of course, e-cruiting is not without drawbacks. The biggest complaint voiced by companies is that the Internet is flooding them with résumés from unqualified applicants. "People will send their résumé because it's very simple to cut and paste. But, they're no way qualified for the position," notes one HR director. And online recruiting will probably never replace employers' favorite methods of finding new hires: their own workforces or referrals from current employees.

The Future of E-Cruiting

In spite of these drawbacks, the future of e-cruiting looks promising. In addition to the big three (Monster, Yahoo! HotJobs, and CareerBuilder), thousands of other job boards now try to match employers and employees in specific areas. Some of these specialty boards include HireDiversity.com, Vets4Hire, and Attorneyjobs. For instance, Maureen Kelleher, a recruiting director for Ernst & Young, uses a group of 20 specialty boards to find more-experienced professionals. Job searchers also have a great new tool at their disposal, *employment search engines* such as www.simplyhired.com and www.indeed.com that connect them directly to job openings on thousands of employers' websites and other listings.

Questions for Critical Thinking

1. How are job seekers and employers using the Internet in the recruiting process?
2. What are the benefits and drawbacks of Internet recruiting?
3. What steps would you take to make your résumé stand out among the thousands that are transmitted electronically? (*Hint:* Think of content.)

Career Profiles

Here are brief glimpses at two career paths that relate to the chapters in Part IV. You'll find other career profiles following Chapters 4, 6, 9, 15, and 18.

Human Resources Managers

Human resources (HR) management covers a wide range of managerial possibilities, including *employment and placement managers*, *equal employment opportunity (EEO) officers*, *compensation and benefit managers*, *labor relations managers*, and *training and development managers*. In many organizations, these managers report to a *director of human resources* (a position traditionally called the *personnel manager*).

Nature of the Work   HR managers oversee the people and processes that organizations use to recruit, develop, and support their workforces. Each of the managerial positions listed above is responsible for a specific area of HR, but each usually requires extensive interaction with employees and the careful application of both company guidelines and government regulations.

Qualifications   The educational backgrounds of HR professionals and managers range from general business degrees to specialized degrees (in human resources or labor relations, for instance). Because these positions combine business fundamentals with sociology, psychology, human learning, and other areas, multidisciplinary study is extremely helpful. In addition, some of the specializations require advanced study.

Aside from academic qualifications, HR professionals must possess good people skills and have a genuine interest in helping people succeed on the job. The HR department participates in both the high points (such as getting hired or promoted) and low points (such as poor performance evaluations or employee grievances) of every employee's career, so sensitivity is a key attribute. Privacy and discretion are vital, too, since HR departments have access to extensive personal information on employees.

Where the Jobs Are   HR jobs can be found in virtually every company with more than a few employees. In smaller firms, a single individual might be responsible for all of the HR tasks, whereas larger firms usually have specialists who cover each of the functions within HR. Individual HR activities are outsourced in many companies (and the entire HR function in some firms), which could dampen opportunities for traditional corporate HR posts but increase opportunities in outsourcing firms.

Where to Learn More   Society for Human Resource Managers, www.shrm.org; Society for Human Resource Professionals, www.shrp.org.

Senior Executives

Senior executives guide each major functional area within a company, including marketing, finance, manufacturing, IT, and human resources. In some firms, the job titles are vice president (such as vice president of sales and marketing); others have adopted the "C" designation—chief marketing officer, chief information officer, and so on. Of course, the ultimate "C" positions are chief operating officer (who handles the day-to-day management of the company) and the chief executive officer (who handles long-term strategy).

Nature of the Work   OK, you're not going to get a senior executive position right out of college, but it's never too early to start dreaming—and planning. Senior executives hold some of the most powerful, prestigious, and highly paid positions in the world. These rewards and responsibilities don't come without heavy demands, of course. The hours are long, and the personal and professional stress can be quite high. However, executives who know how to lead large departments, divisions, or entire companies can make a dramatic impact on the lives of their employees, customers, and communities.

Qualifications   A proven record of success is the common thread you'll find on every senior executive's résumé. Although many top executives do have advanced degrees in business and other fields such as engineering or medicine, professional accomplishments tend to carry more weight than educational background at this level.

Before people are promoted into these positions, they have shown the ability to develop strategies, establish goals, and implement plans that meet those goals. They know how to communicate clearly and persuasively, both inside and outside the company, and they have the leadership skills needed to encourage good performance from the managers and professionals who report to them. Analysis and decision-making skills are critical.

Where the Jobs Are   Top executive jobs can be found in midsize and large companies in every industry. However, the growth rates are likely to vary widely, with expanding opportunities in areas such as medical equipment, high technology, and services, and declining opportunities in many areas of old-line manufacturing. In any industry, expect fierce competition for these top jobs—you're up against the best of the best.

Where to Learn More   American Management Association, www.amanet.org; National Management Association, www.nma1.org.

Connecting with Customers: The Art and Science of Marketing

C H A P T E R

12

LEARNING OBJECTIVES

After studying this chapter, you will be able to

1. Explain what marketing is

2. Describe the four utilities created by marketing

3. Explain how techniques such as permission-based marketing help companies nurture positive customer relationships

4. Explain why and how companies learn about their customers

5. Discuss how marketing research helps the marketing effort and highlight its limitations

6. Outline the three steps in the strategic marketing planning process

7. Define market segmentation and name seven factors used to identify segments

8. Identify the four elements of a company's marketing mix

www.prenhall.com/bovee

Everything from the shape of the cars to the
accessories available at dealerships to the style
of promotional activities is designed to establish Scion
as a unique brand in the automotive marketplace.

INSIDE BUSINESS TODAY

Toyota Scion: Connecting with a New Generation of Car Buyers

www.scion.com

If you're in your early twenties and in the market for your first new car, are you likely to rush out and buy the same car your parents drive? You know—that sensible, conventional car such as the Toyota they drive to the grocery store and to your little sister's soccer practice?

Toyota's U.S. sales manager, Brian Bolain, knows you probably won't, and he knows that because his company has already tried selling conventional cars to younger buyers using conventional advertising messages. Over the past few decades, Toyota has grown to a position of prominence in the United States by offering your parents refreshing alternatives to the cars that *their* parents drove; now Bolain and his colleagues want to continue that cycle of success with the next generation of drivers.

Bolain and his colleagues knew that the conventional Toyota approach wouldn't work with this new audience, but what approach would? The search for an answer started with research, research, and more research. And that approach to research had to be unconventional—for example, hiring 50 young Californians to record video diaries with their friends. The company even went so far as to learn how core groups of trendsetters discover new ideas and products before spreading them through the larger population. The research yielded a wide range of insights, including the fact that Japan has emerged as a new center of cool and the realization not only that young adults strongly resist being sold to but also that they put a high priority on individualism, self-expression, and authenticity.

The research results helped Toyota create a new line of cars called Scion, the most unconventional of which is the aggressively boxy xB model. The cars benefit from the Toyota heritage of top-notch quality at competitive prices, and Toyota created a wide range of accessories to let buyers personalize their cars—from illuminated cup holders to colored steering wheels. These accessories not only attract buyers from the "tuner car" generation but also help Toyota get sales that would normally go to *after-market* suppliers, and their high profit margins offset the lower profits made on the cars themselves.

Toyota's research discoveries have shaped virtually every aspect of its marketing efforts. The company downplays the "Toyota" name, even though it has a worldwide reputation for value and quality, and shuns most traditional mass-market advertising. Instead it favors small-scale, neighborhood-centered promotions that allow trendsetters to "discover" the Scion product line and share the word with other young adults (for example, putting posters near popular hangouts, bearing phrases such as "Ban Normality" and "No Clone Zone").

As part of the quest to reach younger buyers, Toyota even started a music label, Scion A/V, to help promote such groups as the DaKAH hip-hop orchestra from Los Angeles and to work with a variety of DJs in cities around the country whose Scion-sponsored concerts in turn present Scion as a cutting-edge brand for a new generation. Scion marketers also work with emerging fashion designers and artists to further align the brand with cultural forces that shape the buying influences of younger drivers. Scion owners can show off their cars at Scion VIP nights, gatherings designed, of course, to attract even more potential owners.

By virtue of these media and event choices, Scion marketing is virtually hidden from older buyers, although that hasn't stopped many of them from buying the eye-catching new cars, either. In fact, the number of buyers in their 50s and 60s has pushed the average age of Scion drivers into the mid-30s range.

By combining an appealing product, competitive pricing, and promotional efforts that tell the world that Scion is not your average automobile, the Scion launch exceeded Toyota's expectations, even during a time when the economy was still sputtering and most of the automotive world's attention was focused on SUVs and pickups. Scion did suffer some initial hiccups with minor but widespread quality issues, although Toyota said that was not unusual for a new line of cars. In spite of that glitch, Scion keeps adding to a loyal base of customers who are happy to buy a Toyota product even though buying a "Toyota" might be about the last thing they'd like to do with their hard-earned money.[1]

GET READY

The multiple threads of the Scion success story demonstrate how marketing has evolved into such a challenging and intriguing aspect of contemporary business. If you had Brian Bolain's assignment to introduce an entirely new line of cars to a generation of drivers who are skeptical about advertising and leery of buying products that make them feel old before their time, what kind of marketing strategy would you put in place? How would you shape the design of the products themselves to make sure they're different enough to attract the target audience but not so different as to become oddities that no one would buy? What steps would you take to make Scion part of the cultural landscape? How would you get the Scion message out to an audience that doesn't like to be advertised to or sold to? ▪

Chapter Overview

Toyota's strategy for introducing the Scion product line demonstrates both the careful analysis and the extensive effort required to launch new products in today's hotly competitive markets. Here in the first of four chapters covering the marketing function, you'll discover the role that marketing plays in contemporary society and the ways that successful businesses apply the marketing concept. After that introduction, you'll explore the steps that marketers take to understand their target customers and the process they use to create marketing strategies.

Marketing in a Changing World

Your experiences as a consumer may not have given you lots of insights into accounting, production, and other business functions, but you already know a lot about marketing. Companies have been targeting you as a customer since you were a young child, and if you're now a young adult about to enter your professional career, thousands of companies would like to get a piece of your future paycheck. You've been on the receiving end of plenty of marketing tactics—contests, advertisements, displays of merchandise, price markdowns, product giveaways, and maybe even mysterious offers and product advice from friends acting as the unpaid salesforce of major consumer goods marketers, to name just a few. However, marketing involves much more than displays, commercials, and contests. Successfully marketing a product line such as the Toyota Scion requires a wide range of skills, from research and analysis to strategic planning to persuasive communication.

The American Marketing Association (AMA) defines **marketing** as planning and executing the conception, pricing, promotion, and distribution of ideas, goods, and services to create exchanges that satisfy individual and organizational objectives.[2] With respect to products, marketing involves all the decisions related to a product's characteristics, price, production specifications, market-entry date, distribution, promotion, and sales. With respect to customers, marketing involves understanding customers' needs and their buying behavior, creating consumer awareness, providing **customer service**—which is everything a company does to satisfy its customers—and maintaining relationships with customers long after the sales transaction is complete (see Exhibit 12.1).

LEARNING OBJECTIVE 1

Explain what marketing is

marketing
Process of planning and executing the conception, pricing, promotion, and distribution of ideas, goods, and services to create and maintain customer relationships

customer service
Efforts a company makes to satisfy its customers to help them realize the greatest possible value from the products they are purchasing

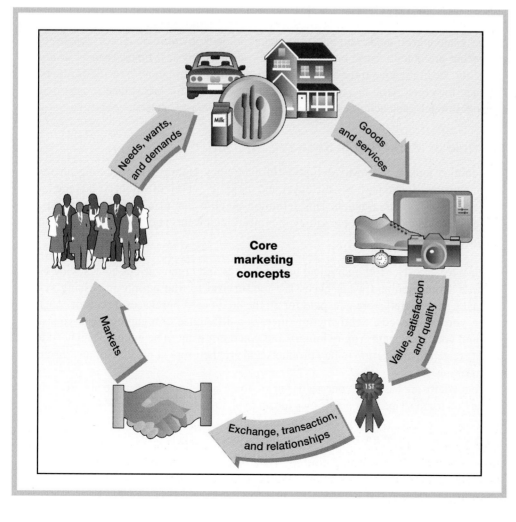

Exhibit 12.1
What Is Marketing?
Each of the core marketing concepts—needs, wants, demands, goods, services, value, satisfaction, quality, exchange, transaction, relationships, and markets—builds on the ones before it.

Avon has made breast cancer awareness and research funding a focus of its cause-related marketing.

Most people think of marketing in connection with selling tangible goods for a profit, but marketing applies to services, nonprofit organizations, people, places, and causes, too. Politicians constantly market themselves. So do places (such as Paris or Poland) that want to attract residents, tourists, and business investment. **Place marketing** describes efforts to market geographical areas ranging from neighborhoods to entire countries. **Cause-related marketing** promotes a cause or a social issue—such as physical fitness, cancer awareness, recycling, or highway safety—while also promoting a company and its products. For instance, for years, Avon has raised money and awareness for breast cancer screening and research through such activities as the Avon Walk for Breast Cancer.[3]

place marketing
Marketing efforts to attract people and organizations to a particular geographical area

cause-related marketing
Identification and marketing of a social issue, cause, or idea to selected target markets

The Role of Marketing in Society

Take another look at the AMA definition of marketing. Notice that marketing involves an exchange between two parties—the buyer and the seller—both of whom seek some level of satisfaction from the transaction. This definition suggests that marketing plays an important role in society by helping people satisfy their needs and wants and by helping organizations determine what to produce.

need
Difference between a person's actual state and his or her ideal state; provides the basic motivation to make a purchase

Needs and Wants Both individual human beings and organizations have a wide variety of needs, from food and water necessary for survival to transaction processing systems that make sure a retail store gets paid for all the credit card purchases it records. As a consumer, you experience a **need** anytime there is a difference or a gap between your actual state and your ideal state. You're hungry and you don't want to be hungry: You need to eat. Needs create the motivation to buy products and are therefore at the core of any discussion of marketing.

wants
Goods, services, experiences, or other entities that are desirable in light of a person's experiences, culture, and personality

Your **wants** are based on your needs but are more specific. Producers do not create needs, but they do try to shape your wants by exposing you to attractive choices. For instance, when you need some food, you may want a Snickers bar, an orange, or a seven-course dinner at the swankiest restaurant in town. If you have the means, or *buying power*, to then purchase the product that you want, you create *demand* for that product.[4]

exchange process
Act of obtaining a desired object or service from another party by offering something of value in return

Exchanges and Transactions When you participate in the **exchange process**, you trade something of value (usually money) for something else of value, whether you're

Utility	Example
Form utility	Kettle Valley's Fruit Snack bars provide the nutritional value of real fruit in a form that offers greater convenience and longer storage life.
Time utility	LensCrafters has captured a big chunk of the market for eyeglasses by providing on-the-spot, one-hour service.
Place utility	By offering convenient home delivery of the latest fashion apparel and accessories, the dELiA*s catalog and website have become favorites of teenaged girls.
Possession utility	RealNetworks, producer of software for listening to music from the Internet, allows customers to download and install its programs directly from the company's website.

Exhibit 12.2
Examples of the Four Utilities
The utility of a good or service has four aspects, each of which enhances the product's value to the consumer.

buying an airline ticket, a car, or a college education. When you make a purchase, you cast your vote for that item and encourage the producer of that item to make more of it. In this way, supply and demand tend toward balance, and society obtains the goods and services that are most satisfying.

When the exchange actually occurs, it takes the form of a **transaction**. Party A gives Party B $1.29 and gets a medium Coke in return. A trade of values takes place. Most transactions in today's society involve money, but money is not necessarily required. Bartering, which predates the use of cash, is making a comeback thanks to the Internet. The dot-com boom, which saw many cash-poor start-ups pay for goods and services with company stock instead of cash, seemed to open many eyes to the possibility of trading goods and services. A number of online exchanges now facilitate bartering using a trade credit system; members trade everything from office space to website design.[5]

The Four Utilities To encourage the exchange process, marketers enhance the appeal of their goods and services by adding **utility**, which is any attribute that increases the value that customers place on the product (see Exhibit 12.2). When organizations change raw materials into finished goods, they are creating **form utility** desired by consumers. For example, when Nokia combines plastic, computer chips, and other materials to make digital phones, the company is providing form utility. In other cases, marketers try to make their products available when and where customers want to buy them, creating **time utility** and **place utility**. Overnight couriers such as FedEx create time utility, whereas coffee carts in office buildings and ATM machines in shopping malls create place utility. The final form of utility is **possession utility**—the satisfaction that buyers get when they actually possess a product, both legally and physically. First Union Mortgage, for example, creates possession utility by offering loans that allow people to buy homes they could otherwise not afford.

The Marketing Concept

In earlier business eras, companies typically focused more on their own production or sales functions and less on long-term relationships with markets and customers. In contrast, many of today's companies try to embrace the **marketing concept**, the idea that companies should respond to customers' needs and wants while seeking long-term profitability and coordinating their own marketing efforts to achieve the company's long-term goals. These *customer-focused* companies build their marketing strategies around the goal of long-term relationships with satisfied customers.[6] The term **relationship marketing** is often applied to these efforts to distinguish them from efforts that emphasize production or sales transactions. One of the most significant goals of relationship marketing is

transaction
Exchange between parties

LEARNING OBJECTIVE 2

Describe the four utilities created by marketing

utility
Power of a good or service to satisfy a human need

form utility
Customer value created by converting raw materials and other inputs into finished goods and services

time utility
Customer value added by making a product available at a convenient time

place utility
Customer value added by making a product available in a convenient location

possession utility
Customer value created when someone takes ownership of a product

marketing concept
Approach to business management that stresses customer needs and wants, seeks long-term profitability, and integrates marketing with other functional units within the organization

relationship marketing
A focus on developing and maintaining long-term relationships with customers, suppliers, and distribution partners for mutual benefit

Exhibit 12.3
The Selling Concept Versus the Marketing Concept

Firms that practice the selling concept sell what they make rather than make what the market wants. In contrast, firms that practice the marketing concept determine the needs and wants of a market and deliver the desired product or service more effectively and efficiently than competitors do.

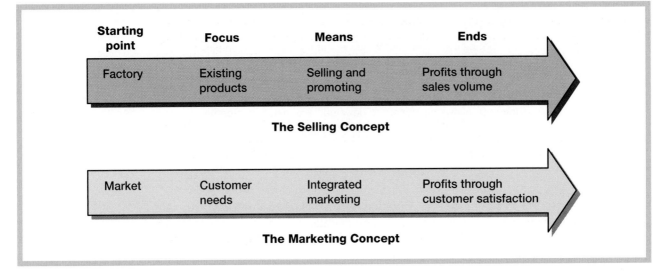

customer loyalty
Degree to which customers continue to buy from a particular retailer or buy the products of a particular manufacturer or service provider

customer loyalty, the degree to which customers continue to buy from a particular retailer or buy the products offered by a particular manufacturer. The payoff from becoming customer-focused can be considerable, but the process of transforming a product- or sales-driven company into one that embraces the marketing concept can take years and involve changes to major systems and processes throughout the company, as well as the basic culture of the company itself.[7]

Focusing on product features and quality, rather than working backwards from customers to create solutions that meet their needs and wants, is a risky strategy. If history were any guide, Sony should be the top dog in portable music players, not Apple—after all, Sony invented the entire product category and revolutionized the way people listen to music with its Walkman tape player and Discman CD player. However, critics claim that Sony's insistence on using its own digital file format, rather than the formats that the market has already accepted, has kept it a minor player in the new world of digital music players.[8]

Sony's approach is an example of pursuing the *product concept* instead of the marketing concept. Exhibit 12.3 compares the marketing concept with an another alternative, the *sales concept*, in which the emphasis is on building a business by generating as many sales transactions as possible, rather than on creating lasting relationships with customers.[9]

Why all the emphasis on customer service and customer satisfaction in the marketing concept, by the way? It's not just about being nice and helpful, although many firms are certainly motivated by those factors as well—satisfying customers is simply good business. The most successful companies often push to get a step beyond satisfaction with the goal of *delighting* their customers by exceeding expectations. Among the many positive results of satisfying and delighting your customers: (1) greater customer loyalty, which can sharply reduce marketing costs; (2) positive *word of mouth*, in which happy customers help promote your products to friends, family, and colleagues; (3) the opportunity to sell more different types of products to customers who are satisfied with the purchases they've made from you already; and (4) reduced sensitivity to price.[10] When Dave Meisburger of Mobile, Alabama, experienced the fast, reassuring service from Progressive Insurance after his wife had been in an automobile accident, he said that "they could double their rate, and I wouldn't care. Their customer service means more to me than anything." Even though its prices remain competitive, delighted customers have helped Progressive enjoy annual profit gains of as much as 75 percent in recent years.[11] Similarly, baseball legend Hank Aaron's highly regarded BMW dealership in Atlanta, Georgia, distinguishes itself through such special touches as offering customers free shuttle service to the airport and servicing their cars while they're away.[12]

In contrast, negative customer experiences can quickly damage a company's reputation and business prospects, particularly when competitors may be only a few mouse clicks away. One recent survey suggests that customers generally give a company one more chance after a bad experience, but after two mistakes, they're ready to take their business elsewhere. Moreover, the majority of customers share their bad experiences with friends, family, and colleagues, spreading the damage even further.[13]

After some rocky starts at the beginning of the dot-com era, online retailers learned that the need for relationships and service was every bit as strong online as it is offline—perhaps even more so. Consequently, successful online merchants such as Amazon.com, Landsend.com, and Dell.com offer a variety of support services, including self-help web pages, toll-free phone support, e-mail, online chat, and IM. Customers of Landsend.com, for example, simply click on the Lands' End Live button to immediately engage a customer service representative in an electronic chat. If customers would prefer to talk on the phone, they ask the representative to call them back. Called "personal shoppers," the online service reps can answer customer questions, solve problems, and even make suggestions about appropriate merchandise—all in real time. They can even split the computer screen and display apparel combinations (such as a skirt and a blouse) to help the customer make a decision.[14]

Marketing on the Leading Edge

As with every other functional area in business, marketing seems to get more complicated with each passing year. You'll read about some specific challenges in the next several chapters, but here are three issues that every successful, responsible marketing organization is wrestling with today: making marketing more accountable, using technology effectively without losing the human touch, and conducting marketing with greater concern for ethics and etiquette.

As part of the marketing concept, successful companies tend to invest heavily in customer service. This instant messaging system from InstantService is an example of the latest tools that companies can use to improve customer service.

Making Marketing More Accountable The marketing function has always been haunted by a lack of measurability and accountability; many decisions and activities are difficult if not impossible to measure, and even some that can be measured won't yield definitive answers for months after the fact. For instance, if you introduce a new product and it fails, is the reason the price, the advertising, the sales training, the product itself, the wrong market, or some other factor? And what about that expensive website or those millions you spent on advertising? How can you tell if those investments paid off in increased sales? Today's CEOs and CFOs are demanding that marketing find some way to justify these expenses and decisions.[15] Internet-based advertising has proven to be helpful in this quest, since it's much easier to track response patterns by following people's click trails, but measuring the effectiveness of many other marketing efforts remains a considerable challenge.

Employing Technology Effectively Without Losing the Human Touch For all the amazing technologies that marketers now have at their disposal, from virtual reality websites to mobile commerce that can put electronic coupons in customers' hands as they walk past a storefront, marketing always has been and always will be about the choices, beliefs, and emotions of human beings. When commerce first reached the Internet, many predicted that online technology would change the way people think, feel, and behave, and indeed change the very nature of business. As revolutionary as it has been, however, the Internet didn't and couldn't change the fact that people are still people—and marketers need to connect with them at a human level, no matter which technologies they might be using.[16]

LEARNING OBJECTIVE 3

Explain how techniques such as permission-based marketing help companies nurture positive customer relationships

permission-based marketing
Marketing approach in which firms first ask permission to deliver messages to an audience and then promise to restrict their communication efforts to those subject areas in which audience members have expressed interest

Business Buzz
viral marketing
Promotional strategy that relies on customers to spread the word, in much the same way that people spread actual viruses.

stealth marketing
The delivery of marketing messages to people who are not aware that they are being marketed to; these messages can be delivered by either acquaintances or strangers, depending on the technique

Conducting Marketing with Greater Concern for Ethics and Etiquette Let's face it: advertising, sales, public relations, and other activities within the marketing function don't always have a shining reputation with the general public—and often for good reason. Under pressure to reach and persuade buyers in a business environment that gets more fragmented and noisier all the time, marketers occasionally step over the line and engage in practices that are rude, manipulative, or even downright deceptive. The result is an increasing degree of skepticism of and hostility toward advertising and other marketing activities.[17] When Mazda published a blog supposedly written by some 22-year-old named Kid Halloween and showing a video of a break-dancing Mazda car, savvy readers quickly caught on and called the company's bluff. The blog was pulled down within three days.[18]

To avoid intensifying the vicious circle in which marketers keep doing the same old things, only louder and longer—leading customers to get more and more angry and defensive—some marketers are looking for a better way. One hopeful possibility is **permission-based marketing**, in which marketers invite potential or current customers to receive information in areas that genuinely interest them. Many websites now take this approach, letting visitors sign up for specific e-mail newsletters with the promise that they won't be bombarded with information they don't care about. Some go a step further with *reciprocation*, giving customers something of value in exchange for the opportunity to present promotional information.[19] Business-to-business technology marketers frequently do this through *white papers* and other materials that give readers valuable information they can use in running their businesses.

At the same time, the emergence of **stealth marketing**, in which customers don't know they're being marketed to, has raised an entirely new set of concerns about ethics and intrusion. Two common stealth marketing techniques are sending people into public places to use particular products in a conspicuous manner and then discuss them with strangers—as though they were just regular people on the street, when in fact they are employed by a marketing firm—and paying consumers (or plying them with insider information and other perks) to promote products to their friends without telling them it's a form of advertising. Critics complain that such techniques are deceptive because they don't give their targets the opportunity to raise their instinctive defenses against the

THINKING ABOUT ETHICS

MINING YOUR DEEPEST SECRETS

They know more about you than some of your closet friends and relatives might know, and you've probably never heard of them. Knowing where you live, where you work, how much you earn—yawn; that's all basic stuff. These organizations keep track of the deeper secrets: your medication, your online shopping habits, your religious and political affiliations, whether or not you gamble, and maybe even your sexual orientation.

Who are these organizations? They are companies such as ChoicePoint, Acxiom, Equifax, HNC Software, and LexisNexus that compile data files on consumers and resell the information to marketers, landlords, banks, government agencies, and others with the legal right to purchase it.

And how do they know all this about you? Every time you make a purchase using a credit card, a gift card, or a frequent-shopper card, the information about your transaction goes into databases. Unless you pay with cash, virtually every commercial transaction you make is recorded somewhere by somebody. Not buying anything today? No problem, just send in a warranty registration card, get married, buy a house, get arrested—every major and minor decision you make probably gets recorded. And whenever you venture online, from search engines to shopping sites, you leave electronic footprints all over the place. Spend a few minutes exploring a car-related website? Bingo—you've just been tagged as a potential car buyer. Reading up on some interesting stocks you might want to invest in? Don't be surprised if your web browser starts spitting out ads for mutual funds and stockbrokers.

Companies have been collecting information like this for years, but recent advances in web tracking and data mining make it easier than ever to cross-index multiple databases and to uncover relationships between your data points. In fact, most consumers would be stunned to discover (a) how much information various companies know about them, (b) how easy it is for companies to buy and sell this information, and (c) how little privacy protection they really have under current laws. In Europe, strict privacy regulations prevent companies from using data about individuals without asking permission and explaining how the data will be used. But in the United States and many other countries, marketers have few restrictions about using such information.

Things may change in the coming years, however, thanks to several recent high-profile instances involving theft or misappropriation of consumer data. In particular, the discovery that ChoicePoint had inadvertently sold data to a gang of identity thieves alerted the public and lawmakers alike to the weak oversight of the data collecting and mining industry. Expect a loud and long fight over database privacy, however. Companies claim that constitutionally protected freedom of speech gives them the right to market to consumers using publicly available information. Security experts say that the global fight against terrorism makes it imperative to give government agencies access to personal records. Meanwhile, if you don't want anybody to know what you're buying, you better pay cash.

Questions for Critical Thinking

1. Should a marketer selling long-distance telephone service be allowed to see your telephone records without your knowledge or permission?
2. Should web marketers be required to conspicuously post their privacy policies and ask consent before collecting and using visitors' personal data?

persuasive powers of marketing messages.[20] Stealth marketing may be successful in many cases, but it's likely to generate yet another backlash from parents, privacy watchdogs, and the general public.

CRITICAL THINKING CHECKPOINT

1. If customer service happens after the sale, how can it be considered part of the marketing effort?
2. In what ways does permission marketing reflect the spirit behind the marketing concept?
3. Why are some people upset about stealth marketing?

Is this a group of friends just talking, or is one of these boys a stealth marketing agent secretly promoting products to his classmates?

Understanding Today's Customers

L E A R N I N G
O B J E C T I V E 4

Explain why and how
companies learn about
their customers

To implement the marketing concept, companies must have good information about what customers want. This is a challenge because today's customers, both individual consumers and organizational buyers, are a diverse and demanding group, with little patience for marketers who do not understand them or will not adapt business practices to meet their needs. They expect goods and services to be delivered faster and more conveniently. And most have no qualms about switching to competitors if their demands are not met. Armed with facts, prices, data, product reviews, advice, how-to guides, and databases, today's customers are informed, which places them in an unprecedented position of control.[21] For instance, consumers faced with complex purchase decisions such as cars or homes can now find extensive information online about products, prices, competitors, customer service rankings, safety issues, and other factors. They no longer have to put their fate entirely in the hands of companies that once had the upper hand by hoarding all the information.

This phenomenon isn't limited to technical purchases, either. The fashion industry is experiencing an upheaval of its own as more and more customers no longer wait for a select few design houses to tell everyone what's "in" or "out" for the coming season. Hemlines, necklines, necktie widths, lapel widths, fabrics, colors, and other design elements used to ebb and flow with remarkable similarity across the industry. However, with visual images reaching around the globe through innumerable print, broadcast, cable, satellite, and online media, many shoppers follow the mix-and-match creativity of Susannah Brunings of Mission Viejo, California: "I'm interested in becoming my own trendsetter."[22]

consumer market
Individuals or households that buy goods and services for personal use

organizational market
Businesses, nonprofit organizations, and government agencies that purchase goods and services for use in their operations

customer buying behavior
Behavior exhibited by consumers as they consider, select, and purchase goods and services

The first step toward understanding customers is recognizing the different purchase and ownership habits of the **consumer market**, made up of individuals and families who buy for personal or household use, and the **organizational market**, composed of both companies and a variety of noncommercial institutions, from local school districts to the federal government.

The Consumer Decision Process

Think about several purchase decisions you've made recently or might make in the near future. What sort of process did you follow to arrive at the specific choice you made in each case? Classical economics suggests that your **customer buying behavior** would follow the rational process in Exhibit 12.4, first recognizing a need, gathering information, identifying alternative solutions, then making your choice from those alternatives. How often do you

Exhibit 12.4

The Rational Model of Buyer Decisions

In the classic, rational model of buyer behavior, customers work through several steps in logical order before making a purchase decision. However, new research shows that most consumer decisions are less rational and more subconscious than the classical model suggests.

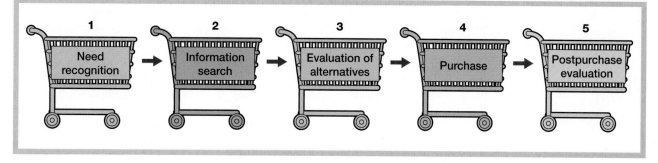

1	2	3	4	5
Need recognition	Information search	Evaluation of alternatives	Purchase	Postpurchase evaluation

make decisions like that? Or do you sometimes buy on impulse, like the $125 pair of basketball shoes that you saw in a shop window and purchased a few seconds later, or the black dress you bought because it was on sale, even though you already own nine black dresses? The classical, rational model serves as a helpful starting point, but researchers now realize that consumer behavior tends to be far less logical and far more complicated—and more interesting—than this model suggests.

Even in situations in which consumers gather lots of information and appear to be making a well-thought-out, rational decision, they often are acting more on gut feelings and emotional response. For instance, you might see one of those funky Scion xB models drive past on the street, and in that split second—before you even start "thinking" about it—you've already decided to buy one just like it. Sure, you'll gather brochures, do research on the Internet, test-drive other models, and so on, but chances are you're not really evaluating alternatives. Instead, your rational, conscious brain is just looking for evidence to support the decision that your emotional, semiconscious brain has already made.

Moreover, we consumers make all kinds of decisions that are hard to explain by any rational means: Does anybody really "need" 50 pairs of shoes or a car that can go 160 miles an hour? Sometimes we buy food that we know isn't healthy (sure tastes good) or furniture that isn't comfortable (sure looks good next to that expensive painting we don't like). We might spend two weeks gathering data on $200 MP3 players, then choose a college with $20,000 tuition because our best friend is going there. Sometimes we buy things for no apparent reason other than the fact that we have money in our pockets. As a result, at one time or another, all consumers suffer from **cognitive dissonance**, which occurs when our beliefs and behaviors don't match. A common form of this is *buyer's remorse*, when we make a purchase then regret doing so—sometimes immediately after the purchase.

This isn't to say that many purchases aren't rational or that consumers don't try to make rational decisions most of the time. But a significant portion of consumer decisions don't follow a strictly logical, conscious sequence. In fact, new research suggests that 95 percent of the decision-making process is subconscious and that sensory cues can play a much larger role than objective information.[23] You can start to understand why so many decisions seem mysterious from a rational point of view if you consider all the influences that affect purchases:

- *Culture.* The cultures (and subgroups within cultures) that people belong to shape their values, attitudes, and beliefs and influence the way they respond to the world around them. Understanding culture is therefore an increasingly important step in international business and in marketing to diverse populations within a country such as the United States. As you can see in the Case for Critical Thinking on pages 423–425, Levi Strauss has lost billions of dollars of business in the past decade because it failed to pay attention to the emergence of hip-hop fashion and other culture shifts.
- *Social class.* In addition to being members of a particular culture, people also perceive themselves as members of a certain social class—be it upper, middle, lower, or somewhere in between. In general, members of various classes pursue different

cognitive dissonance
Tension that exists when a person's beliefs don't match his or her behaviors; a common example is buyer's remorse, when someone regrets a purchase after making it

activities, buy different goods, shop in different places, and react to different media—or at least like to believe they do.

- **Reference groups.** Consumers are also influenced by *reference groups* that provide information about product choices and establish values that individual consumers perceive as important. Reference groups can be either *membership* or *aspirational*. As the name suggests, membership groups are those to which consumers actually belong; families, networks of friends, sports teams, clubs, and work groups are common examples. The term *tribal marketing* is sometimes used to describe efforts to present products to groups that are organized around a specific lifestyle element, such as skateboarding or cruising the highways on Harley-Davidson motorcycles. In contrast, consumers don't belong to aspirational reference groups but use them as role models for style, speech, opinions, and various other behaviors.[24] For instance, millions of consumers buy products that help them identify with popular musicians (hip-hop clothing styles are a great example) or professional athletes (such as wearing the logo of your favorite team).

- **Situational factors.** These factors include events or circumstances in people's lives that are more circumstantial but that can influence buying patterns. Such factors might include having a coupon, being in a hurry, celebrating a holiday, being in a bad mood, and so on. If you've ever practiced "retail therapy" to cheer yourself up, you know all about situational factors—and probably the buyer's remorse that comes with realizing you shouldn't have spent the money you just spent.

- **Self-image.** Many consumers tend to believe that "you are what you buy," so they make or avoid choices that support their desired self-images. Marketers capitalize on people's need to express their identity through their purchases by emphasizing the image value of goods and services (see "Learning from Business Blunders"). That's why professional athletes and musicians frequently appear as product endorsers—so that consumers will incorporate part of these celebrities' public image into their own self-images. Product owners can even grow angry with marketers if they engage in marketing tactics that run counter to the owners' images of themselves and those products. For instance, hundreds of Scion owners complained to the company after it ran a commercial on the reality show "The Bachelor," which the owners said "contaminated the brand."[25]

Of course, marketers don't sit idly by waiting for consumers to make their choices. Companies in every line of business try to influence customer behavior. These efforts can be particularly vigorous when an industry is in its infancy or undergoing significant upheaval, since permanent changes in consumer behavior can make or break products. For example,

LEARNING FROM BUSINESS BLUNDERS

OOPS On the surface, it looked like Hallmark Cards did about everything you're supposed to do. Its researchers, monitoring the demographic bulge of the baby boom generation, created the Time of Your Life product line to appeal specifically to people reaching the 50-year milestone in life. Their careful customer research showed that while boomers might be aging, they don't want to think of themselves as old. In response, the product line featured youthful, healthy images of people in the prime of life. The products were displayed in a special Time of Your Life section in Hallmark stores. Great idea? Hallmark has succeeded with other product lines aimed at specific groups of customers, such as Mahogany (African-American themes) and Tree of Life (Jewish themes). Time of Your Life sounded like another winner, but the product line was a flop.

WHAT YOU CAN LEARN While the products themselves may have been right on the mark in terms of customer wants and needs, the final piece of the puzzle—the retail presentation—put people off. Boomers who didn't want to think of themselves as old weren't about to shop in the "old people's" section of the card store. Marketers need to consider the entire consumer experience; a mistake at any stage can doom the entire effort.

digital photography created a huge opportunity for HP and other companies that sell photo-quality printers to consumers who want to print their own snapshots at home. At the same time, all this at-home photo printing is a competitive threat to Wal-Mart and other retailers that have sold photo-finishing services for years; as a result, many of these retailers now offer digital photo-printing services that compete directly with HP's printers. With billions of dollars at stake, each camp is highly motivated to convince consumers to adopt its way of photo printing.[26]

The Organizational Customer Decision Process

In a sense, the purchasing behavior of organizations is easier to understand because it's more clearly driven by economics and influenced less by subconscious, emotional factors. Here are some of the significant ways in which organizational purchasing differs from consumer purchasing:[27]

- *An emphasis on economic payback and other rational factors.* Most organizational purchases are carefully evaluated for financial impact, technical compatibility, reliability, and so forth. Businesses and other organizations don't always make the best choices, of course, but their choices are usually based on a more rational analysis of needs and alternatives. However, some business-to-business marketers make the mistake of assuming that customer emotions play little or no role in the purchase decision, forgetting that organizations don't make decisions, people do. Fear of change, fear of failure, excitement over new technologies, and the pride of being associated with world-class suppliers are just a few of the emotions that can influence organizational purchases.
- *A formal buying process.* From office supplies to new factories, most organizational purchases follow a formal buying process, particularly in government agencies and in mid- to large-size companies. In fact, the model in Exhibit 12.4 is a better representation of organizational purchasing than it is of consumer purchasing, although organizational purchasing often includes additional steps such as establishing budgets, analyzing potential suppliers, and requesting proposals.
- *The participation and influence of multiple people.* Except in the very smallest businesses, where the owner may make all the purchasing decisions, the purchase process usually involves a group of people. This team can include end users, technical experts, the manager with ultimate purchasing authority, and a professional purchasing agent whose job includes researching suppliers, negotiating prices, and evaluating supplier performance.
- *Closer relationships between buyers and sellers.* Close and long-lasting relationships between buyers and sellers are common in organizational purchasing. For example, a company might use the same advertising agency, accounting firm, and raw material suppliers for years or even decades. In some cases, employees from the seller even have offices inside the buyer's facility to promote close interaction.

Marketing Research and Customer Databases

LEARNING OBJECTIVE 5
Discuss how marketing research helps the marketing effort and highlight its limitations

Understanding customer purchase behavior is one of the many goals of **marketing research**—the process of gathering and analyzing information about customers, markets, and related marketing issues. As markets grow increasingly dynamic and open to competition from all corners of the globe, today's companies realize that information is the key to successful action. Without it, they're forced to use guesswork, analogies from other markets that may or may not apply, or experience from the past that may not correspond to the future.[28] At the same time, however, marketing research can't provide the answer to every strategic or tactical question. As a manager or entrepreneur, you'll find yourself in situations that require creative thinking and careful judgment to make the leap beyond what the data alone can tell you.

marketing research
The collection and analysis of information for making marketing decisions

Research techniques range from the basic to the exotic, from simple surveys to advanced statistical techniques to neurological scanning that tries to discover how and why customers' brains respond to visual and verbal cues about products. You can see a sample of techniques in Exhibit 12.5. As with other aspects of marketing, some research techniques raise ethical concerns over the invasion of consumer privacy. For instance, *video mining*, the visual counterpart of data mining, involves videotaping shoppers so that researchers can study their movements and behaviors throughout a store. Most consumers understand the need for security cameras in stores, but few are aware that these cameras are often used for marketing research, too.[29]

Another way to learn about customer preferences is to gather and analyze all kinds of customer-related data. **Database marketing** is the process of recording and analyzing customer interactions, preferences, and buying behavior for the purpose of contacting and transacting with customers. Capital One, for example, has become a leading credit card company by collecting extensive records on millions of consumers and using that information to plan its marketing strategies. Every credit card transaction, Internet sale, and frequent-buyer purchase leaves behind a trail of information that retailers can use to their advantage. Frequent-shopper card programs, good for a wealth of discounts at checkout, have convinced customers to share some of the most intimate details about their lives. For instance, customer grocery purchases reveal preferences for everything from hygiene

database marketing
Process of building, maintaining, and using customer databases for the purpose of contacting customers and transacting business

Exhibit 12.5
Marketing Research Techniques
Marketers can use a wide variety of techniques to learn more about customers, competitors, and threats and opportunities in the marketplace.

Technique	Examples
Observation	Any in-person, mechanical, or electronic technique that monitors and records behavior, from video mining to website usage tracking to devices that monitor TV program selection to monitoring what bloggers are writing online.
Surveys	Data collection efforts that measure responses from a representative subset of a larger group of people; can be conducted in person (when people with clipboards stop you in a mall, that's called a *mall intercept*), over the phone, by mail or e-mail, or online. Designing and conducting a meaningful survey requires thorough knowledge of statistical techniques such as *sampling* to ensure valid results that truly represent the larger group. For this reason, many of the simple surveys that you see online these days do not produce statistically valid results.
Interviews and focus groups	One-on-one or group discussions that try to probe deeper into issues than a survey typically does. *Focus groups* involve a small number of people guided by a facilitator while being observed or recorded by researchers. Unlike surveys, interviews and focus groups are not designed to collect statistics that represent a larger group; their real value is in uncovering issues that might require further study.
Process data collection	Any method of collecting data during the course of other business tasks, including warranty registration cards, sales transaction records, gift and loyalty program card usage, and customer service interactions.
Experiments	Controlled scenarios in which researchers adjust one or more variables to measure the affect these changes have on customer behavior. For instance, separate groups of consumers can be exposed to different ads to see which ad is most effective. *Test marketing*, the launch of a product under real-world conditions but on a limited scale (such as in a single city), is a form of experimental research.

TECHNOLOGIES THAT ARE REVOLUTIONIZING BUSINESS Data Mining

To find a few ounces of precious gold, you dig through a mountain of earth. To find a few ounces of precious information, you dig through mountains of data using data mining, a combination of technologies and techniques that extract important customer insights buried within thousands or millions of transaction records.

HOW IT'S CHANGING BUSINESS

As you read in Chapter 4, data mining is an essential part of business intelligence because it helps transform millions of pieces of individual data (including demographics, purchase histories, customer service record, and research results) accumulating in supersized databases known as *data warehouses* or department-specific subsections known as *data marts.* Data mining helps marketers identify who their most profitable customers are, which goods and services are in highest demand

in specific markets, how to structure promotional campaigns, where to target upcoming sales efforts, and which customers are likely to be high credit risks, among many other benefits (see also "Mining Your Deepest Secrets").

WHERE YOU CAN LEARN MORE

Intelligent Enterprise magazine, www.intelligententerprise.com, offers numerous articles and news updates on data mining, data warehousing, and other business intelligence topics. You can also learn about specific solutions from the companies that either offer stand-alone data mining products or incorporate the technology into databases and other products, including Angoss (www.angoss.com), Insightful (www.insightful.com), Megaputer Intelligence (www.megaputer.com), SAS (www.sas.com), SPSS (www.spss.com), IBM (www.ibm.com), Microsoft (www.microsoft.com), and Oracle (www.oracle.com).

products to junk food to magazines. The proliferation of gift cards in recent years has given marketers yet another source of electronic data.[30]

CRITICAL THINKING CHECKPOINT

1. Why do consumers sometimes make purchasing decisions that may not be in their best interests from a conscious, rational point of view?
2. If you were marketing a single model of laptop computer to both consumers and businesses, should you use a single advertisement in order to save costs? Why or why not?
3. Why is word of mouth so important to marketers today?

LEARNING OBJECTIVE 6

Outline the three steps in the strategic marketing planning process

strategic marketing planning
The process of examining an organization's current marketing situation, assessing opportunities and setting objectives, then developing a marketing strategy to reach those objectives

Planning Your Marketing Strategies

By now you can see why successful marketing rarely happens without carefully analyzing and understanding your customers. Once you have learned about your customers, you're ready to begin planning your marketing strategies. **Strategic marketing planning** is a process that involves three steps: (1) examining your current marketing situation, (2) assessing your opportunities and setting your objectives, and (3) developing your marketing strategy to reach those objectives (see Exhibit 12.6). Most companies record the results of their planning efforts in a document called the *marketing plan.*

A solid marketing strategy both flows from and supports the overall business strategy; it is also closely coordinated with other functional strategies. For instance, in order to reach out to younger drivers with the high-quality, low-cost Scion, Toyota not only needs an effective marketing strategy, but a manufacturing strategy that can create the necessary products, a financial strategy that supports the price levels required by the marketing strategy, a human resource strategy that makes sure the right workers are in place across all the functions, and so on. Here's a closer look at the three steps in the process.

Exhibit 12.6
The Strategic Marketing Planning Process
Strategic marketing planning comprises three steps: (1) examining your current marketing situation, (2) assessing your opportunities and setting objectives, and (3) developing your marketing strategy.

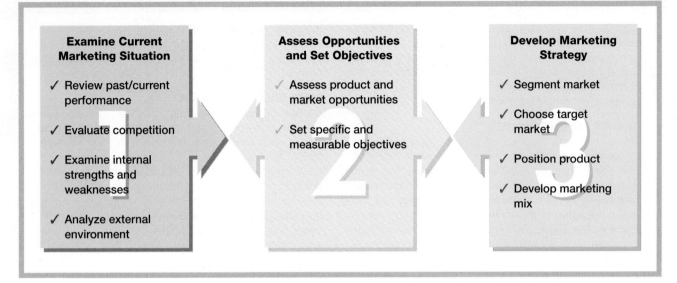

Examine Current Marketing Situation

✓ Review past/current performance

✓ Evaluate competition

✓ Examine internal strengths and weaknesses

✓ Analyze external environment

Assess Opportunities and Set Objectives

✓ Assess product and market opportunities

✓ Set specific and measurable objectives

Develop Marketing Strategy

✓ Segment market

✓ Choose target market

✓ Position product

✓ Develop marketing mix

Step 1: Examining Your Current Marketing Situation

Examining your current marketing situation includes reviewing your past performance (how well each product is doing in each market where you sell it), evaluating your competition, examining your internal strengths and weaknesses, and analyzing the external environment.

Reviewing Performance Unless you're starting a new business, your company has a history of marketing performance. Maybe sales have slowed in the past year; maybe you've had to cut prices so much that you're barely earning a profit; or maybe sales are going quite well and you have money to invest in new marketing activities. Reviewing where you are and how you got there is critical, because you will want to repeat your successes and learn from your past mistakes.

Evaluating Competition In addition to reviewing past performance, you must also evaluate your competition. If you own a Burger King franchise, for example, you need to watch what McDonald's and Wendy's are doing. You also have to keep an eye on Taco Bell, KFC, Pizza Hut, and other restaurants in addition to paying attention to any number of other ways your customers might satisfy their hunger—including fixing a sandwich at home. Furthermore, you need to watch the horizon for competitors that do not yet exist, such as the next big food craze. For instance, when low-carbohydrate diets caught on recently, established food companies such as Kraft and General Mills found themselves suddenly losing business to competitors they'd never heard of before, such as Atkins Nutritionals.[31]

Examining Internal Strengths and Weaknesses Successful marketers try to identify both sources of competitive advantage and areas that need improvement. They look at such factors as financial resources, production capabilities, distribution networks, business partnerships, managerial expertise, and promotional capabilities. This step is important because you can't develop a successful marketing strategy if you don't know your strengths as well as your limitations. On the basis of your internal analysis, you will be able to decide whether your business should (1) limit itself to those opportunities for which it possesses the required strengths or (2) challenge itself to reach higher goals by acquiring and developing new strengths. When Steven Nichols purchased the K-Swiss sneaker company, he didn't try to update the basic 40-year-old shoe designs to the leading edge of contemporary fashion. Instead, he went with its retro appeal and played up the conservative angle for people who don't want the flashy designs of Nike and other market leaders. Sales took off, and because the company doesn't try to constantly churn out new designs, K-Swiss's profits are much higher than those of Nike and Adidas.[32]

Understanding your strengths and weaknesses is especially important when evaluating the merits of global expansion. Selling products overseas requires not only managerial expertise and financial resources but also the ability to adjust your operation to different cultures, customs, legal requirements, and product specifications. Similarly, selling on the Internet often requires deep technological expertise and commitment as well as a thorough understanding of online buyer behavior.

Analyzing the External Environment Marketers must also analyze a number of external environment factors when planning their marketing strategies. These factors include:

- *Economic conditions.* Marketers are greatly affected by trends in interest rates, inflation, unemployment, personal income, and savings rates. In tough times, consumers put off buying expensive items such as major appliances, cars, and homes. They cut back on travel, entertainment, and luxury goods. Conversely, when the economy is good, consumers open their wallets and satisfy their pent-up demand for higher-priced goods and services.
- *Natural environment.* Changes in the natural environment can affect marketers, both positively and negatively. Interruptions in the supply of raw materials can upset even the most carefully conceived marketing plans. Floods, droughts, and cold weather can affect the price and availability of many products as well as the behavior of target customers.
- *Social and cultural trends.* Planners also study the social and cultural environment to determine shifts in consumer values. If social trends are running against a product, the producer might need more advertising to educate consumers about the product's benefits or may need to alter the product to make it more appealing. For example, diet fads and programs frequently affect the marketing efforts of food producers and retailers. When the extremely popular South Beach Diet books discouraged the consumption of orange juice (because of its fructose sugar content), the Florida Department of Citrus launched a counter-promotional campaign on behalf of the state's orange growers. Bob Crawford, the department's executive director, explained that "There are powerful, negative messages against us. We're not going to stand and take it."[33]
- *Laws and regulations.* Like every other function in business today, marketing is controlled by laws at the local, state, national, and international levels. From product design to pricing to advertising, virtually every task you'll encounter in marketing is affected in some way by laws and regulations.
- *Technology.* When technology changes, so must your marketing approaches. Encyclopaedia Britannica presents a classic case of how changing technology can turn an industry upside down—almost overnight. The 235-year-old publisher cruised into the 1990s with record sales of its flagship product, an encyclopedia set that cost over $1,400, weighed 118 pounds, and consumed four and a half feet of shelf space. But then along came CD-ROMs and the Internet, which enabled much cheaper—and sometimes free—solutions from competitors. Even though most of these alternatives couldn't deliver the comprehensive quality of Britannica, they quickly ate into the company's sales. After a stumble or two, including the common misstep of trying to support a site through advertising revenue, Britannica now has 200,000 paid subscribers online.[34] Marketers must not only keep on top of today's external environment, they must also think about tomorrow's changes. Car manufacturers, for example, are responding to increasing consumer and governmental pressure to reduce emissions by producing hybrid gas-and-electric vehicles.

Step 2: Assessing Your Opportunities and Setting Your Objectives

Once you've examined your current marketing situation, you're ready to assess your marketing opportunities and set your objectives. Successful companies are always on the lookout for new marketing opportunities, which can be classified into four options:[35]

- *Market penetration:* Selling more of your existing products in current markets
- *Product development:* Creating new products for your current markets
- *Market development:* Selling your existing products to new markets
- *Diversification:* Creating new products for new markets

These four options are listed in order of increasing risk; creating new products for unfamiliar markets is usually the riskiest choice of all because you encounter uncertainties in both dimensions (you may fail to create the product you need, and the market might not be interested in it). Once you've framed the opportunity you want to pursue, you are ready to set your marketing objectives. A common marketing objective is to achieve a certain level of **market share**, which is a firm's portion of the total sales within a market (market share can be defined by either number of units sold or by sales revenue).

Step 3: Developing Your Marketing Strategy

Using your current marketing situation and your objectives as your guide, you're ready to move to the third step. This is where you develop your **marketing strategy**, which consists of dividing your market into *segments,* choosing your *target markets* and the *position* you'd like to establish in those markets, and then developing a *marketing mix* to help you get there.

Dividing Markets into Segments A **market** contains all the customers or businesses that might be interested in a product and can pay for it. Most companies subdivide the market in an economical and feasible manner by identifying *market segments,* or homogeneous groups of customers within a market that are significantly different from each other. This process is called **market segmentation**; its objective is to group customers with similar characteristics, behavior, and needs. Each of these market segments can then be targeted by offering products that are priced, distributed, and promoted differently. For instance, Toyota knows that a 25-year-old whose primary interests are clubbing and mountain biking won't respond to the same marketing messages as a 50-year-old whose primary concerns are getting the kids through college and saving for retirement.

The overall goal of market segmentation is to understand why and how certain customers buy what they buy so that you use your limited resources to create and market products in the most efficient manner possible.[36] Here are seven of the most common factors marketers use to identify market segments:

- *Demographics.* When you segment a market using **demographics**, the statistical analysis of a population, you subdivide your customers according to characteristics such as age, gender, income, race, occupation, and ethnic group. Be aware, however, that according to recent studies, demographic variables are poor predictors of behavior. For instance, not all American men aged 35 to 44 making chage to $200,000 per year buy a Mercedes. In fact, some don't even buy a luxury car, and those who do may not purchase such cars for the same reasons.[37]
- *Geographics.* When differences in buying behavior are influenced by where people live, it makes sense to use **geographic segmentation**. Segmenting the market into different geographical units such as regions, cities, counties, or neighborhoods allows companies to customize and sell products that meet the needs of specific markets. Marketers need to stay on top of changing population patterns. For instance, responding to changes in small towns across the country, the U.S. Census Bureau recently created the "micropolis" designation for boom towns such as Silverthorne, Colorado, and Palm Coast, Florida, that are near major metropolitan centers but so self-contained that many residents no longer need to travel into the city for shopping and employment.[38]

market share
A firm's portion of the total sales in a market

marketing strategy
Overall plan for marketing a product; includes target market segments, a positioning strategy, and a marketing mix

LEARNING OBJECTIVE 7

Define market segmentation and name seven factors used to identify segments

market
A group of customers who need or want a particular product and have the money to buy it

market segmentation
Division of a diverse market into smaller, relatively homogeneous groups with similar needs, wants, and purchase behaviors

demographics
Study of statistical characteristics of a population

geographic segmentation
Categorization of customers according to their geographical location

THINKING ABOUT ETHICS

QUESTIONABLE MARKETING TACTICS ON CAMPUS

Alarmed by how quickly college students can bury themselves in debt and fed up with aggressive sales tactics, a growing number of universities are banning or restricting credit card marketing on campus.

College administrators complain that students are bombarded with credit card offers from the moment they step on campus as freshmen. Marketers have shown up on campuses unannounced and without permission to hawk cards in dorms and other areas. They stuff applications into bags at college bookstores. They entice students to apply for cards and take on debt with free T-shirts, music CDs, and promises of an easy way to pay for spring break vacations. Some yell at students to get their attention and follow them through hallways to make a sale. And they even get student organizations to work for them so that friends pressure friends.

College students are, of course, a prized target for the credit card industry because consumers tend to be loyal to their first credit card. And even though college students often have little or no income, they are not considered high-risk borrowers because parents generally bail them out if they get into trouble. As a result, an estimated 80 percent of full-time college students now have a credit card in their own name. But only about half of those students pay their bills in full each month, and the number who usually make just the minimum payment is rising. The average balance carried is now $3,000, and 10 percent of students carry balances of $8,000 or more.

Many young people can't even keep up with the minimum payment. In fact, it is estimated that in one year 150,000 people younger than 25 will declare personal bankruptcy. That means for 150,000 young people, their first significant financial event as an adult will be to declare themselves a failure—a failure that will complicate their lives for years. And for each one who goes into bankruptcy, there are dozens just behind them, struggling with credit card bills—like Katy Spivak, for instance. Within her first three years at college, Spivak ran up $9,000 in credit card debt—forcing her to work two part-time jobs just to pay off her credit card bills.

While some universities have banned credit card marketers from campus to protect students from their own potentially destructive credit practices, many students say it's paternalistic for schools to do so. After all, marketers don't give up. They just move across the street or to other locations frequented by students, such as spring break vacation hot spots. Moreover, credit cards have almost become a necessity in modern consumer life in recent years, since so many businesses require them as security or identification even when you don't use them for purchasing.

Questions for Critical Thinking

1. Should credit card companies be prohibited from soliciting on college campuses? Why or why not?
2. Why do credit card companies target students even though most have little or no income?

- **Psychographics.** Whereas demographic segmentation is the study of people from the outside, **psychographics** is the analysis of people from the inside, focusing on their psychological makeup, including attitudes, interests, opinions, and lifestyles. Psychographic analysis focuses on why people behave the way they do by examining such issues as brand preferences, media preferences, reading habits, values, and self-concept.

  psychographics
  Classification of customers on the basis of their psychological makeup

- **Geodemographics.** Dividing markets into distinct neighborhoods by combining geographical and demographic data is the goal of **geodemographics**. One of the geodemographic systems, developed by Claritas Corporation, divided the United States into 40 neighborhood types, with labels such as "Blue Blood Estates" and "Old Yankee Rows." This system, known as PRIZM, uses postal ZIP codes for the geographic segmentation part, making it easy to use specialized marketing programs to reach people in targeted neighborhoods. Responding to changes in the U.S. population, Claritas and other geodemographic researchers continue to devise new breakdowns that include such clusters as "Bright Lites, Li'l City" (child-free professional couples living in upscale

  geodemographics
  Method of combining geographical data with demographic data to develop profiles of neighborhood segments

communities near big cities) and "Young Digerati" (ethnically diverse and technically sophisticated young urbanites).[39]

- ***Behavior.*** Markets can also be segmented according to customers' knowledge of, attitude toward, use of, or response to products or product characteristics. This approach is known as **behavioral segmentation**. Many web-based companies ask first-time visitors to fill out a personal profile so they can gear product recommendations and even display customized webpages that appeal to certain behavioral segments.

- ***Loyalty.*** Segmenting your customer base by degree of loyalty can be an effective step toward planning the best way to interact with each type of customer. For instance, if you know that some customers buy from you some of the time but from your competitors at other times, you can study their needs more carefully to figure out how to capture a greater share of their business.[40]

- ***Usage.*** The manner in which customers use products or media such as the Internet can also tell you a lot about how to market to them effectively. For instance, someone who plays guitar in a professional band may respond differently to your promotional efforts than someone who plays at home for enjoyment, even though they play the exact same guitar. Similarly, many online marketers now try to categorize web users by their session length, time per page, content areas of interest, and so on to help define the types of marketing that are best suited for each user type.[41]

When you segment your market, you end up with several customer groups, each representing a potentially productive focal point for marketing efforts. A typical marketing niche might be young adult tennis players. Members of this niche would be interested in tennis goods such as rackets, shoes, and tennis wear and services such as club memberships and tennis-themed travel packages.

Choosing Your Target Markets Once you have segmented your market, the next step is to find appropriate target segments or **target markets** to focus your efforts on. Deciding exactly which segment to target—and when—is not an easy task. Sometimes the answer will be obvious, such as when you lack the necessary technological skills or financial power to enter a particular market segment. At other times, you'll have the resources to compete in several segments but not enough resources to compete in all of them. In general, marketers use a variety of criteria to narrow their focus to a few suitable market segments, including the magnitude of potential sales within each segment, the cost of reaching those customers, fit with existing core competencies, and any risks in the business environment. Identifying which customers you do want also implies identifying those you *don't* want. For instance, the retailer Best Buy identified a segment of customers that was costing the company through relentless bargain hunting, a high rate of product returns, and frequent calls for technical support. By reducing sales promotions and charging a small fee for restocking returned products, the company is effectively excluding this group of shoppers from its stores.[42]

Exhibit 12.7 diagrams three popular strategies for reaching target markets. Companies that practice *undifferentiated marketing* (or mass marketing) ignore differences among buyers and offer only one product or product line to satisfy the entire market. This strategy, which concludes that all buyers have similar needs that can be served with the same standardized product, was more popular in the past than it is today. Henry Ford, for instance, began by selling only one car type (the Model T Ford) and in one color (black) to the entire market.

By contrast, companies that manufacture or sell a variety of products to several target customer groups practice *differentiated marketing.* This is Toyota's approach, with the Scion brand aimed at young buyers, the Toyota brand for its core audience, and the Lexus brand for those wanting a luxury car. Differentiated marketing is a popular strategy, but it requires substantial resources because you have to tailor products, prices, promotional efforts, and distribution arrangements for each customer group.

---

behavioral segmentation
Categorization of customers according to their relationship with products or response to product characteristics

target markets
Specific customer groups or segments to whom a company wants to sell a particular product

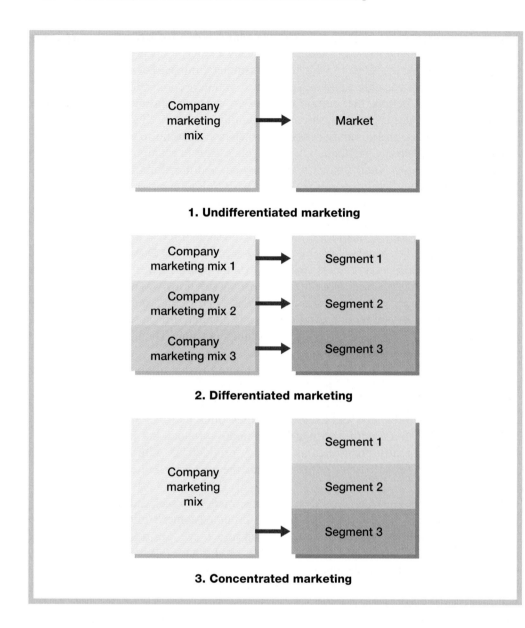

Exhibit 12.7
Market-Coverage
Strategies
*Three alternative
market-coverage strategies
are undifferentiated
marketing, differentiated
marketing, and
concentrated marketing.*

1. Undifferentiated marketing

2. Differentiated marketing

3. Concentrated marketing

When company resources are limited, *concentrated marketing* may be the best marketing strategy, which is why start-up companies usually use it to make sure they don't spread themselves too thin. With this approach, you acknowledge that various other market segments exist but you choose to target just one. Switzerland's Enzo Stretti started a rental car company that targets what might be the narrowest segment in the industry: drivers who temporarily lose their regular driving privileges but are allowed to drive slow-speed cars. Stretti rents them Smart cars that are limited to 28 miles per hour.[43] The biggest advantage of concentrated marketing is that it allows you to focus all your time and resources on a single type of customer. The strategy can be risky, however, because you've staked your fortunes on just one segment.

Moreover, it's important to understand whether you're going after a niche that will always be a niche or simply gaining a foothold in a small segment as part of a carefully sequenced plan to expand into other segments. For instance, Southwest Airlines started out as a niche player in a regional market but is now the nation's busiest airline in terms of number of passenger flights.[44]

Positioning Your Product Once you have decided which segments of the market to enter, your next step is to decide what position you want to occupy in those segments.

positioning
Using promotion, product, distribution, and price to differentiate a good or service from those of competitors in the mind of the prospective buyer

Positioning your product is the process of designing your company's offerings, messages, and operating policies so that both the company and its products occupy distinct and desirable competitive positions in your target customers' minds. For instance, for every product category that you care about as a consumer, you have some ranking of desirability in your mind—you believe that certain colleges are more prestigious than others, that certain brands of shoes are more fashionable than others, that one videogame system is better than the others, and so on. Successful marketers are careful to choose the position they'd like to occupy in buyers' minds. One of Toyota's goals in positioning the Scion brand was to make sure buyers *didn't* think it was a Toyota, and therefore the parent company name is rarely seen in Scion promotions (you'll have to look hard to see it on the Scion website, for instance).

A product can also be *repositioned* if the position it occupies is no longer favorable in some respect or new uses or qualities of the product make a different position more attractive to the marketer. For instance, you've probably seen Mountain Dew's hip commercials featuring skateboarders, snowboarders, and other extreme-sports figures who encourage you to "do the Dew." You might be surprised to learn that the soft drink was positioned quite differently a few decades ago, when the tagline was "It'll tickle your innards" and the spokesperson was a cartoon hillbilly who was usually pictured firing a shotgun at a government agent who had come to bust up his moonshine operation. The hillbilly disappeared after PepsiCo bought the brand in 1964.[45]

A vital and often overlooked aspect of positioning is that although marketers take all kinds of steps to position their products, it is the customers who ultimately decide on the positioning—they're the ones who interpret the many different messages they encounter in the marketplace and decide what they think and feel about each product. For example, you can advertise that you have a luxury product, but if consumers aren't convinced, it's not really positioned as a luxury product. As with everything else in marketing, the only result that matters is what the customer believes, not what the marketer believes.

In their attempts to secure favorable positions, marketers seek out positions that are both unique (no one else occupies that position in the customer's mind) and achievable (the firm can deliver the bundle of value needed to achieve that position).[46] They can position their products on specific product features or attributes (such as size, ease of use, style, performance, quality, durability, or design), on the services that accompany the product (such as convenient delivery, lifetime customer support, or installation methods), on the product's image (such as reliability or sophistication), on price (such as low cost or premium), on category leadership (such as the leading online bookseller), and so forth. For example, BMW and Porsche associate their products with performance, Mercedes Benz with luxury, and Volvo with safety. Organizing products and services into categories based on the perceived position helps consumers simplify the buying process. Instead of test-driving all cars, for instance, they may focus on those they perceive to be high-performance vehicles.

LEARNING OBJECTIVE 8

Identify the four elements of a company's marketing mix

marketing mix
The four key elements of marketing strategy: product, price, distribution, and promotion

product
Good or service used as the basis of commerce

Developing the Marketing Mix After you've segmented your market, selected your target market, and taken steps to position your product, your next task is to develop a marketing mix. A firm's **marketing mix** (often called the *four Ps*) consists of product, price, place (or distribution), and promotion (see Exhibit 12.8).

Products. The most basic marketing-mix element is *product,* which covers the product itself plus brand name, design, packaging, services, quality, and warranty. From a marketing standpoint, a **product** is anything offered for the purpose of satisfying a want or a need in a marketing exchange. If you were asked to name three popular products off the top of your head, you might think of Doritos tortilla chips, the Mini Cooper, and Gatorade drinks. You might not think of the Boston Celtics, Disney World, and *The Gilmore Girls*. That's because we tend to think of products as *tangible* objects, or things that we can actually touch and possess. Basketball teams, amusement parks, and television programs provide an *intangible*

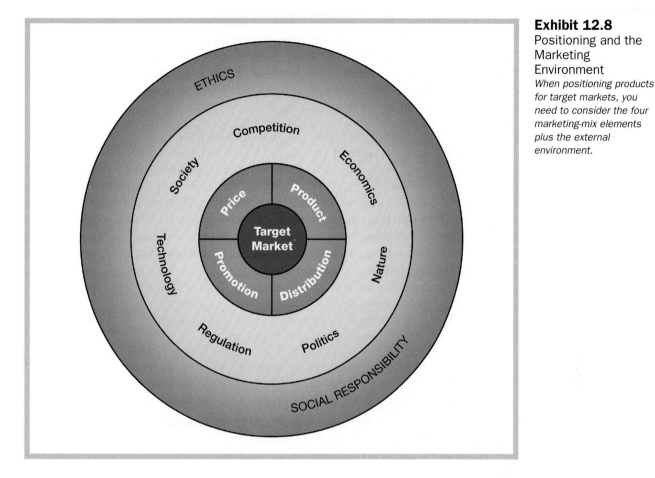

Exhibit 12.8
Positioning and the
Marketing
Environment
*When positioning products
for target markets, you
need to consider the four
marketing-mix elements
plus the external
environment.*

service for our use or enjoyment, not for our ownership; nevertheless, these and other services are products just the same. In fact, broadly defined, products can be persons, places, physical objects, ideas, services, and organizations. No matter what it is, every product possesses a number of *features* or *attributes* (what the product is or does) that create *benefits* (what it does for the customer). High-technology companies that create complex products face a recurring challenge in this respect; they need to keep one eye on the technology and the features and one eye on customer needs and benefits.[47]

Pricing. **Price**, the amount of money customers pay for the product (including any discounts), is the second major component of a firm's marketing mix. Developing a product's price is one of the most critical decisions a company must make, because price is the only element in a company's marketing mix that produces revenue—all other elements represent cost. Thus, setting a product's price not only determines the amount of income your company will generate from sales of that product but also can differentiate the product from competition. As you can imagine, determining the right price is not an easy task, and marketers constantly worry whether they've turned away profitable customers by charging too much or "left money on the table" by charging too little.

price
*The amount of money
charged for a product or
service*

Distribution. *Distribution* is the third marketing-mix element. It covers the organized network of firms that move goods and services from the producer to the consumer. This network is also known as *marketing channels, marketing intermediaries,* or **distribution channels**. As you can imagine, channel decisions are interdependent with virtually everything else in the marketing mix. For instance, low-priced software is often available for download from the Internet these days, and that may be the only channel through which customers can buy it. In contrast, high-end business and technical software products, which can cost hundreds of thousands or even millions of dollars, often have dedicated sales

distribution channels
*Systems for moving goods
and services from
producers to customers;
also known as marketing
channels*

teams that will visit most any customer interested in the products. In another example, to lower the risk for dealers with the new Scion brand, Toyota allows existing Toyota dealers to co-locate Scions retail facilities on the same sites where they sell the Toyota brand. However, to protect the exclusive image of its Lexus brand, the company requires any dealer that wants to carry Lexus to build and staff an entirely separate dealership that carries only Lexus.[48]

promotion
Wide variety of persuasive techniques used by companies to communicate with their target markets and the general public

Promotional Strategies. Promotion, the fourth marketing-mix element, includes all the activities the firm undertakes to communicate and promote its products to the target market. Among these activities are advertising, personal selling, public relations, and sales promotion. Promotion may take the form of direct, face-to-face communication or indirect communication through such media as television, radio, magazines, newspapers, direct mail, billboards, bus ads, the Internet, and other channels. Of the four components in a firm's marketing mix, promotion is perhaps the one most often associated with marketing. Although it is no guarantee of success, promotion does have a profound impact on a product's performance in the marketplace.

The next three chapters offer a closer look at each of the four major elements in the marketing mix. Chapter 13 introduces you to what's involved in developing product and pricing strategies, Chapter 14 discusses the steps involved in developing a firm's distribution strategies, and Chapter 15 discusses promotional strategies.

CRITICAL THINKING CHECKPOINT
1. Why is it important to examine your own business weaknesses while formulating a marketing strategy?
2. Who has the ultimate control over how your product is positioned in the minds of target customers? Why?
3. Is your college education a product? Why or why not?

CHECKLIST: Apply These Ideas When You're the Boss

✓ Remember that as in all successful relationships, successful marketing involves a willing exchange that meets the needs of both parties, leaving neither side feeling manipulated or exploited.

✓ Treat customers with respect, and they'll be the best salesforce you could ever hope for.

✓ The hard sell may generate sales in the short term, but it rarely creates customers for the long term.

✓ Include customer retention as a key element in your marketing and business strategy; it's nearly always cheaper to keep an existing customer than to attract a new one.

✓ Understand all the influences at work in the decisions and behaviors of your target customers, whether it's the influence of popular culture in a consumer market or the importance of technical standards in an organizational market.

✓ Build marketing research into business processes whenever you can, such as having customer service reps collect information about customers needs or having sales reps record why customers don't buy.

✓ Choose target markets carefully; you'll spend a considerable amount of time, money, and energy trying to connect with each market you choose.

✓ Remember that you don't have the final say-so about how your products are positioned in the minds of target customers, and they may end up with very different perceptions than the ones you're trying to create.

✓ Keep in mind that marketing sometimes has a bad reputation; don't contribute to the negative perceptions by engaging in manipulative or deceptive business practices.

Summary of Learning Objectives

1 **Explain what marketing is.** Marketing is the process of planning and executing the conception, pricing, promotion, and distribution of ideas, goods, and services to create exchanges that satisfy individual and organizational objectives. It involves all decisions related to a product's characteristics, price, production specifications, market-entry date, distribution, promotion, and sale. It involves understanding and satisfying customers' needs and buying behavior to encourage consumer purchases, in addition to maintaining long-term relationships with customers after the sale.

2 **Describe four utilities created by marketing.** Marketers enhance the appeal of their products and services by adding utility. Form utility is created when companies turn raw materials into finished goods desired by consumers. Time utility is created by making the product available when the consumer wants to buy it. Place utility is created when a product is made available at a location that is convenient for the consumer. Possession utility is created by facilitating the transfer of ownership from seller to buyer.

3 **Explain how techniques such as permission-based marketing help companies nurture positive customer relationships.** Permission-based marketing helps in the effort to build long-term relationships by demonstrating not only respect for customers but a willingness to meet *their* needs, as opposed to the marketer's need.

4 **Explain why and how companies learn about their customers.** Today's customers generally are sophisticated, price sensitive, demanding, more impatient, more informed, and difficult to satisfy. Companies learn about their customers so they can stay in touch with their current needs and wants, deliver quality products, and provide effective customer service. Such attention tends to keep customers satisfied and helps retain their long-term loyalty. Moreover, studies show that sales to repeat customers are more profitable. Most companies learn about their customers by studying consumer buying behavior, conducting marketing research, and capturing and analyzing customer data.

5 **Discuss how marketing research helps the marketing effort, and highlight its limitations.** Marketing research can help companies set goals, develop new products, segment markets, plan future marketing programs, evaluate the effectiveness of a marketing program, keep an eye on competition, and measure customer satisfaction. On the other hand, marketing research is a poor predictor of what will excite consumers in the future. It is sometimes ineffective because it is conducted in an artificial setting. And, it is not a substitute for good judgment.

6 **Outline the three steps in the strategic marketing planning process.** The three steps in the strategic marketing planning process are (1) examining your current marketing situation, which includes reviewing your past performance, evaluating your competition, examining your internal strengths and weaknesses, and analyzing the external environment; (2) assessing your opportunities and setting your objectives; and (3) developing your marketing strategy, which covers segmenting your market, choosing your target markets, positioning your product, and creating a marketing mix to satisfy the target market.

7 **Define market segmentation and name seven factors commonly used to identify segments.** Market segmentation is the process of subdividing a market into homogeneous groups to identify potential customers and to devise marketing approaches geared to their needs and interests. Seven factors commonly used to identify segments are demographics, geographics, psychographics, geodemographics, behavior, loyalty, and usage of both products and media.

8 **Identify the four elements of a company's marketing mix.** The four elements, sometimes known as the four Ps, are product, price, place (or distribution), and promotion. Products are persons, places, physical objects, ideas, services, organizations, or anything which is offered for the purpose of satisfying a want or need in a marketing exchange. Price is the amount of money customers pay for the product. Place (also known as distribution) is the organized network of firms that move the goods and services from the producer to consumer. Promotion involves the activities used to communicate and promote a product to the target market.

Toyota Scion: What's Next

Thanks to clever marketing and the resources of one of the world's premiere manufacturers, Toyota's launch of the Scion line surpassed the company's expectations. Scions are now being sold in a new way, too, with haggle-free pricing and commitments from dealers to shun the aggressive sales tactics some Toyota dealers are known for. By not requiring dealers to build entirely separate facilities, which it did for the Lexus launch in the 1990s, Toyota also dramatically lowered the cost of entry for dealers, which no doubt helps keep a lid on prices as well.

With its success in the long-neglected small car segment of the market, however, Toyota is sure to attract renewed competition from its Japanese compatriots Honda and Nissan, the Big Three U.S. makers, and the surging South Korean companies Kia and Hyundai. Another potential threat is being a victim of its own success. Both the Chrysler PT Cruiser and the new VW Beetle took off quickly when they were introduced in recent years, but sales for both tapered off as their unusual look became commonplace on U.S. streets. Scion also runs the risk of attracting so many older buyers that the brand loses its appeal to younger drivers.

Critical Thinking Questions

1. What other product categories would you apply the Scion marketing approach to?
2. Why would younger buyers possibly shun a brand that their parents remain loyal to?
3. As Scion sales grow, the newness wears off, and more owners come to grips with the fact that they're really driving Toyotas, do you think the allure of the Scion brand will diminish?

Learn More Online

Visit the Scion website by clicking on the hotlink at Chapter 12 of this text's website at **www.prenhall.com/bovee**. What is your first impression of Scion's online presence? How is the presentation of cars balanced with information about culture and community? What do you think of the ability to customize a Scion product online? Do you find any discussion of price? Overall, does the evidence of Scion's marketing mix make you intrigued to learn more about the cars?

Key Terms

behavioral segmentation (414)
cause-related marketing (398)
cognitive dissonance (405)
consumer market (404)
customer buying
   behavior (404)
customer loyalty (400)
customer service (397)
database marketing (408)
demographics (412)
distribution channels (417)
exchange process (398)
form utility (399)
geodemographics (413)
geographic segmentation (412)

market (412)
market segmentation (412)
market share (412)
marketing (397)
marketing concept (399)
marketing mix (416)
marketing research (407)
marketing strategy (412)
need (398)
organizational market (404)
permission-based
   marketing (402)
place marketing (398)
place utility (399)
positioning (416)

possession utility (399)
price (417)
product (416)
promotion (418)
psychographics (413)
relationship
   marketing (399)
stealth marketing (402)
strategic marketing
   planning (409)
target markets (414)
time utility (399)
transaction (399)
utility (399)
wants (398)

Test Your Knowledge

Questions for Review

1. What are some of the characteristics of today's customers?
2. How does the organizational market differ from the consumer market?
3. What is strategic marketing planning, and what is its purpose?
4. What external environmental factors affect strategic marketing decisions?
5. What are the four basic components of the marketing mix?

Questions for Analysis

6. If relationship marketing is such a good idea, why don't more businesses do it?

7. How can marketing research and database marketing help companies improve their marketing efforts?

8. Why does a marketer need to consider its current marketing situation, including competitive trends, when setting objectives for market share?

9. Why do companies segment markets?

10. **Ethical Considerations.** Thanks to the Internet you can contact a company for product information with a click of a mouse. But while many companies promote a variety of online customer service features, few respond in a timely manner to customers' questions and some don't respond at all. Companies claim that they simply can't keep up with the number of customer e-mail queries they receive. And they can't afford to increase their customer service staff either. Website promises such as "Click here to talk to customer service," or "Got a question, let us help" look good, but the reality is too many companies promote a service they can't support. Review a few of your favorite retail websites and analyze the different online customer service options these companies offer. Do they provide a projected response time? Do they send an auto reply message for e-mail queries? Do they offer a self-service help page for frequently asked questions. In your opinion, how could companies better handle online customer support when they are short of resources?

Questions for Application

11. How might a retailer use relationship and database marketing to improve customer loyalty?

12. Think of a product you recently purchased and review your decision process. Why did you need or want that product? How did the product's marketing influence your purchase decision? How did you investigate the product before making your purchase decision? Did you experience cognitive dissonance after your decision?

13. **Integrated:** Why is it important to analyze a firm's marketing plan before designing the production process for a service or a good? What kinds of information are generally included in a marketing plan that might affect the design of the production process as discussed in Chapter 9?

14. **Integrated:** How might these economic indicators, discussed in Chapter 1, affect a company's marketing decisions: consumer price index, inflation, unemployment?

Practice Your Knowledge

Handling Difficult Situations on the Job: Making Marketing Promotions Safer for Kids

Fast-food giveaways account for one-third of all toys distributed in the United States. So when two babies died in 1999 after suffocating on plastic Pokemon balls their parents got from Burger King, the fast-food industry took notice. Some restaurants implemented safety tests on the billions of free toys being distributed with kids' meals. But few took the strict steps now followed by Burger King and McDonald's. Burger King has hired independent testers, strengthened safety standards, and conducted tests before, during, and after manufacturing. McDonald's has developed a testing doll, "McBaby," with artificial lungs to check suffocation risks.

Ann W. Brown, the chairman of the Consumer Product Safety Commission (and your boss) wants other fast-food vendors to follow in their footsteps. "Just because a toy is inexpensive and is given away doesn't mean it shouldn't be as safe as the safest toys," Brown believes. Brown wants restaurants that profit from such promotions to be responsible for safety tests. After all, a popular giveaway can increase a restaurant's sales by about 4 percent; a really big hit, by 15 percent, so it's to their advantage to protect child safety. In addition to legal liabilities and reputation damage if children are injured or die from giveaway toys, restaurants can lose the millions they've spent to promote a toy that has to be recalled.[49]

Your task: Brown wants you to write to fast-food vendors in the United States, urging them to follow McDonald's and Burger King's lead in pretesting giveaway toys. She also wants you to think of other ways to encourage vendors to adopt stricter safety standards. Knowing that a variety of situational factors also influence a buyer's decision-making process, how might you put further pressure on fast-food vendors to test the toys?

Sharpening Your Communication Skills

In small groups as assigned by your instructor, take turns interviewing each person in the group about a product that each person absolutely loves or detests. Try to probe for the real reasons behind the emotions, touching on all the issues you read about in this chapter, from self-image to reference groups. Do you see any trends in the group's collective answers? Do people learn anything about themselves when answering the group's questions? Does anyone get defensive about his or her reasons for loving or hating a product? Be prepared to share with at least two marketing insights you learned through this exercise.

Building Your Team Skills

In the course of planning a marketing strategy, marketers need to analyze the external environment to consider how forces outside the firm may create new opportunities and challenges. One important environmental factor for merchandise buyers at Sears is weather conditions. For example, when merchandise buyers for lawn and garden products think about the assortment and number of products to purchase for the chain's stores, they don't place any orders without first poring over long-range weather forecasts for each market. In particular, temperature and precipitation predictions for the coming 12 months are critical to the company's marketing plan, because they offer clues to consumer demand for barbecues, lawn furniture, gardening tools, and other merchandise.

What other products would benefit from examining weather forecasts? With your team, brainstorm to identify at least three types of products (in addition to lawn and garden items) for which Sears should examine the weather as part of its analysis of the external environment. Share your recommendations with the entire class. How many teams identified the same products your team did?

Expand Your Knowledge

Discovering Career Opportunities

Jobs in marketing cover a wide range of activities, including a variety of jobs such as personal selling, advertising, marketing research, product management, and public relations. You can get more information about various marketing positions by consulting the Career Information Center guide to jobs and careers, the U.S. Employment Service's Dictionary of Occupational Titles, and online job-search websites such as Career Builder, www.careerbuilder.com.

1. Select a specific marketing job that interests you. Using one or more of the preceding resources, find out more about this chosen job. What specific duties and responsibilities do people in this position typically handle?
2. Search through help-wanted ads in newspapers, specialized magazines, or websites to find two openings in the field you are researching. What educational background and work experience are employers seeking in candidates for this position? What kind of work assignments are mentioned in these ads?
3. Now think about your talents, interests, and goals. How do your strengths fit with the requirements, duties, and responsibilities of this job? Do you think you would find this field enjoyable and rewarding? Why?

Developing Your Research Skills

From recent issues of business journals and newspapers (print or online editions), select an article that describes in some detail a particular company's attempt to build relationships with its customers (either in general or for a particular product or product line).

1. Describe the company's market. What geographic, demographic, behavioral, or psychographic segments of the market is the company targeting?
2. How does the company hold a dialogue with its customers? Does the company maintain a customer database? If so, what kinds of information does it gather?
3. According to the article, how successful has the company been in understanding its customers?

Exploring the Best of the Web

URLs for all Internet exercises are provided at the website for this book, www.prenhall.com/bovee. When you log on to this text's Companion Website, select Chapter 12. Then select "Featured Websites," click on the name of the featured website, and review the website to complete these exercises.

Explore these chapter-related websites, review their content, and answer the following questions for each website you visit:

1. What is the purpose of this website?
2. What kinds of information does this website contain? Please be specific.
3. How is the information provided at this website useful for businesspeople? Consumers?
4. How did you expand your knowledge of marketing and customers by reviewing the material at this website? What new things did you learn about these topics?

Sign Up for Electronic Commerce 101
Think you may be interested in moving your business onto the Net but you don't know where to start? Study the basics at Electronic Commerce 101 before you plan your marketing strategies. Find out how to succeed in electronic commerce. Read the beginners guide and the step-by-step process of becoming e-commerce enabled. Learn how to process payments, credit cards, and e-cash. Find out the top 10 ways websites lose customers. Still have a question? This site has free advice from over 7,000 experts. www.ecommerce.about.com/smallbusiness/ecommerce/library/bl101

Gather Some Demographical Data for Your Marketing Toolbox
How much does the typical family spend on food away from home? On entertainment? Are these consumer expenditures increasing each year? Find out by visiting the American Demographics Marketing Tools website and explore its toolbox of useful information. Read some of the current marketing articles. Follow the link to the Bureau of Labor Statistics (BLS) website. With all these sources, no wonder marketers today have more and better data about today's customers. www.marketingtools.com

See Why It's "As Easy As Dell"
Everybody talks about Dell's exceptional customer service and sales approach but few have been able to duplicate Dell's success. Dell's website demonstrates its commitment to customer service. The webpages include product benefits, product information, online help, and a variety of customer-care services. Log on and explore the website. See why the company has adopted the slogan "Easy as Dell." How does Dell use its website to build relationships with customers? How does the Dell website employ the marketing concept? What kinds of online customer service features does the Dell website offer? www.dell.com

Learning Interactively

Companion Website
Visit the Companion Website at www.prenhall.com/bovee. For Chapter 12, take advantage of the interactive "Learning Modules" to test your chapter knowledge. Get instant feedback on whether you need additional studying. Complete the exercises as specified by your instructor.

A Case for Critical Thinking

Can Levi Strauss Recover from Its Fashion Faux Pas?

Throughout most of the twentieth century, Levi Strauss had the jeans world sewn up. Its tough denim pants, created originally to meet the utilitarian demands of nineteenth century California gold miners, had evolved from work clothes to fashion must-haves. As the teenage generations from the 1950s through the 1980s reached adulthood, many continued to wear the classic five-pocket, straight-leg model 501 pants they'd grown up with. Levi's appeal was universal; along with Harley-Davidson, Coca-Cola, and a select few other brands, it came to symbolize the American lifestyle for consumers around the world.

The 1990s brought some seismic shifts in fashion, however. The emergence of hip-hop and other cultural forces, along with the rapid proliferation of discount retail powerhouses Wal-Mart and Target, changed the fashion landscape dramatically. Young consumers began to shun Levi's in favor of either low-cost pants from the discounters or trendier brands such as Diesel and Lucky. By 1998, only 7 percent of teenage boys considered Levi's to be a "cool" brand. Levi's hold on consumers grew even weaker as customers moved away from traditional department stores such as J.C. Penney and into discounters and upstart retailers that didn't carry Levi's products.

LISTENING WITHOUT HEARING
As customers began to look elsewhere, some of its retailers tried to tell Levi's managers that their market was slipping away. Here's how one retailer summed it up in late 1990s: "We told them what kids were asking for. They even attended some of our focus groups. But they didn't want to believe."

Sticking with its "one brand fits all" marketing strategy that had worked successfully for years, though, Levi's plowed ahead without addressing the fashion or budget demands of the next generation of potential customers. That decision would prove costly.

AN ICON FADES

As the youth segment turned to competitors for lower-cost clothes or fashion-statement jeans with baggier fits, wide pant legs, and bigger pockets, Levi's share of the market collapsed. Internally, the company was distracted by dissension between its wide-ranging social commitments and the need to generate profits, an enormous and costly project to re-engineer production and customer service, and a management style that emphasized consensus to such an extreme degree that some former executives claim it was next to impossible to get anything done. As the company grew further and further out of touch with key markets, sales would eventually plummet from a peak of $7 billion to $4 billion over the course of a 10-year slide.

"ONE BRAND FITS ALL" NO LONGER FITS

The message about meeting the unique needs of various market segments finally began to sink in. Levi's adopted a differentiated marketing approach that now varies from the low-cost Levi's Signature line, selling for around $20 through Wal-Mart and other discounters, on up through the classic straight-leg styles to premium pants that sell for more than $100 at Bloomingdales, Barneys New York, and other exclusive retailers.

The Levi's Signature line, first introduced through Target in 2003 and then through Wal-Mart in 2004, is proving to be a success so far. In keeping with the discount model, the company watches costs with a hawk eye in this product line, which includes choosing cheaper denim fabrics than those used in the mid-range and premium products. Selling into Wal-Mart also required Levi's to revamp its production and delivery systems, since the giant retailer demands accurate and timely shipments from all its suppliers—an area of performance at which Levi's had been notoriously weak in the past.

STRUGGLING BACK TO STABILITY

In 1999, Phil Marineau came on board as CEO with the mission of making the company less about manufacturing clothing and more about connecting with customers. While it worked to get back in touch with consumers, Levi's also had some serious internal housekeeping to tend to. Desperate to bring costs down in order to align with its severely reduced revenue levels, over the course of several years the company laid off thousands of employees worldwide and eventually shut down its remaining U.S. factories to outsource production overseas—a move it had long resisted as a matter of principle.

After losing $349 million in 2003, Marineau brought in a turnaround consultant who worked with the company for more than a year to continue paring costs and improving efficiency throughout the organization. The cuts continued in 2004, as a quarter of the remaining workforce was jettisoned. Marineau also attempted to sell the Docker's casual wear business but couldn't find a buyer at the right price, so it remains a part of the company.

In 2005, after nearly a decade of declining sales, Marineau said the situation had finally been stabilized. He now believes the company has the right products, the right retailers, and a design and production process that can respond to shifting market demands. While he continues to chew away at the $2 billion debt racked up during the tumultuous decade before, he's confident that Levi's is ready to grow again on a global scale.

LESSONS LEARNED

An entire business course could be built around the story of Levi Strauss, with important lessons in nearly every aspect from governance to finance to manufacturing. Within the marketing realm specifically, several issues demand attention:

- Even if you're a cultural icon, most consumers don't care about your glorious past; they're only interested in whether you can meet their wants and needs today.
- Manufacturers don't call the shots with nearly the influence they did in years gone by. To a large degree, Wal-Mart, Target, Amazon, and other retailers now dictate which products get offered to consumers.
- Consumer brands need to create an emotional connection with customers; as Levi's learned, making clothes that people want to wear involves a lot more than simply stitching together pieces of fabric.
- More than ever before, fashion is inextricably linked with music, movies, television, and the rest of popular culture—and fickle consumers are ready to change brands overnight if that's what it takes to stay on top of trends.

Critical Thinking Questions

1. Why did Levi's lose serious market share during the 1990s?
2. What steps did Levi's take to regain its market share?
3. What should Levi's do in the future to make sure it never again loses touch with its target markets?

4. Go to Chapter 12 of this text's website at www.prenhall.com/bovee. Click on the Levi's link to answer these questions: How is Levi's using its website to attract younger consumers? How do the graphics and content reflect the needs and interests of the targeted segment? What points of differentiation are emphasized?

Video Case

In Consumers' Shoes: Skechers USA

Learning Objectives

The purpose of this video is to help you:

1. Describe the role of the four Ps in a company's marketing mix
2. Explain how a company shapes its market research to fit its marketing goals
3. Discuss the effectiveness of target marketing and segmentation in analyzing consumers

Synopsis

Skechers USA enjoys a reputation for producing footwear that combines comfort with innovative design, and the company has built its product line into a globally recognized brand distributed in more than 110 countries and territories throughout the world. From its corporate headquarters in Manhattan Beach, California, Skechers has engineered steady growth in market share while competing against some powerful players in the high-ticket, branded athletic shoe industry.

Since its start in 1992, Skechers has solidified its image as a maker of hip footwear through a savvy marketing strategy that calls for catering to a closely targeted consumer base. Maintaining brand integrity and its reputation for innovation is a crucial goal in all of Skechers' product development and marketing activities.

Director of public relations Kelly O'Connor discusses her work and the marketing activities that are critical to maintaining Skechers' edge in the highly competitive footwear marketplace. She describes the company's goal of creating a megabrand with an image, personality, and "feel" that can be translated and marketed globally. Skechers has been successful in brand building by means of an "Ask, Don't Tell" approach to product development and marketing—that is, it aims to find out what the market wants and then appeal to customers' wants rather than trying to influence the market with the products that it makes available.

Discussion Questions

1. *For analysis:* Which of the four Ps of the marketing mix seems to govern Skechers' marketing strategy? Why?
2. *For analysis:* How do you suppose Skechers alters elements of its American marketing mix to attract consumers in international markets?
3. *For application:* Skechers collects a lot of *primary* data in its market research. What kinds of primary data does the company prefer to gather? Why do these kinds of data suit the company's marketing goals? How do the data suit its consumer base? Given Skechers' fairly limited consumer base, are there other types of research data that you would recommend to company marketers?
4. *For application:* Describe Skechers' target market and explain how company marketers segment it. How effective is this strategy in analyzing customers? How successful are Skechers' marketing efforts among 12- to 24-year-olds (and consumers wishing they were in that demographic segment)?
5. *For debate:* Building brand loyalty is a major effort that presents both opportunities and challenges to marketers and product developers. How might Skechers increase loyalty for its brand? Do you think Skechers should expand its current product lines to include other new products such as clothing or accessories? How could the company go about investigating the market potential for such products?

Online Exploration

Go online to find out about the product lines and target markets of such companies as Nike (www.nike.com), Reebok (www.reebok.com), Lady Foot Locker (www.ladyfootlocker.com), and FUBU (www.fubu.com). How does the approach to segmentation at these companies compare with that of Skechers?

Defining the Exchange: Product and Pricing Strategies

LEARNING OBJECTIVES

After studying this chapter, you will be able to

1. Describe the four stages in the life cycle of a product

2. Describe six stages of product development

3. Cite three levels of brand loyalty

4. Discuss the functions of packaging and labeling

5. Identify four ways of expanding a product line and discuss two risks that product-line extensions pose

6. List seven factors that influence pricing decisions and cite several common pricing strategies

7. Explain why cost-based pricing can be a flawed strategy

www.prenhall.com/bovee

INSIDE BUSINESS TODAY
Allergan Stumbles onto a Billion-Dollar Product

www.botoxcosmetic.com

Some companies spend million of dollars developing new products only to have them crash land in the marketplace, generating little or no revenue. Allergan took the opposite approach: It more or less stumbled onto a new market for an obscure medical treatment and within a few years had a billion-dollar hit on its hands.

That hit product was Botox Cosmetic, a temporary treatment for facial wrinkles that revolutionized cosmetic care. Botox was developed in the 1970s by a San Francisco doctor looking for ways to correct crossed eyes, or strabismus. He found that injections of small amounts of purified botulinum toxin (from the same bacterium that causes botulism) paralyzed the overactive muscles that cause strabismus, allowing other eye muscles to operate normally. The injections also improved uncontrollable eye blinking and uncontrollable neck spasms. Allergan, an Irvine, California, company, purchased the rights to the doctor's discovery in 1987 and started marketing Botox after receiving FDA approval for these uses in 1989.

Prior to Botox, Allergan was a small firm paddling the backwaters of the pharmaceuticals industry, selling little-known eye and skin drugs, some surgical devices, and a line of over-the-counter lens cleaners. Because it was too small to attract much attention from pharmaceutical giants 20 times its size, Allergan adopted a narrowcast marketing approach, focusing on two attractive submarkets: ophthalmology and dermatology. This narrow focus meant that Allergan didn't have to spend a fortune on marketing or hire a large sales force to call on hundreds of thousands of internists and family practitioners.

Then in the mid-1990s, doctors noticed something intriguing: Botox's paralyzing properties seemed to greatly reduce frown lines and wrinkles in patients using it for eye problems. As word of the Botox effect spread, more and more doctors began using it to relax the facial muscles that create eyebrow furrows, crow's feet, and horizontal forehead lines. Allergan conducted clinical trials and in 2002 received FDA regulatory approval to use a version of Botox for cosmetic procedures. (This version is formally known by its trademarked name, Botox Cosmetic.)

Nothing in Allergan's history could have prepared it for the transformation of one of its oddest products into a glamorous and profitable sensation. The injections, which can be given in just a few minutes, make a perfect lunch-hour treatment. Soon the early buzz and media splash boosted Botox sales in a few major urban areas. But Allergan recognized that selling the general public on Botox would require more than word-of-mouth promotion. The company would have to overcome several negative attributes: The treatment lasts for only four months or so, it's not covered by health insurance, and it does involve injecting a toxic substance into the face (although to be fair, most medicines are toxic in the wrong dosages). On the plus side, Botox is far less expensive and less invasive than cosmetic surgery, and it has proven to be a safe and fairly painless procedure.

To get the word out, Allergan decided to promote the entire Botox experience. It began training doctors on how to inject Botox. And the company showed doctors how to design and decorate their offices to appeal to patients who want to be pampered.

The timing was perfect. A goodly number of baby boomers don't seem inclined to grow old without a fight and are buying up Botox and other cosmetic treatments that help in that struggle. Several million people a year now get Botox treatments, spending about a billion dollars on them. Not bad for a product that started by accident.[1]

GET READY

Allergan's experience with Botox illustrates the challenges involved in defining a combination of product and price that will appeal to target markets—and the rewards that come to companies that make the right decisions. If you were faced with the challenge of bringing Botox to market, what decisions would you make? What would you call the product? What steps would you take to encourage people to continue using the product and thereby prevent it from becoming just a fad? How would you encourage trial use from people who might be leery of using such a radically different product? Would you set a high price to make a lot of money from a small number of sales, or set a lower price to reach a broad market? ▪

Chapter Overview

This chapter, the second of four on the marketing function, gives you a close look at two elements of the marketing mix: product and price. The exploration of price starts with a rundown of the major types of products, the life cycle that most products progress through from introduction to the point at which they're removed from the market, and the process companies use to create new products. Following that, you'll learn about the techniques used to identify products: branding, packaging, and labeling. The final product discussion involves the decisions companies make when managing multiple families of products. The chapter wraps up with a look at pricing strategies.

Characteristics of Products

As the central element in every company's exchanges with its customers, products naturally command considerable attention when managers plan new offerings and manage the marketing mixes for their existing offerings. To understand the nature of these decisions, it's important to recognize the various types of products and the stages that products go through during their "lifetime" in the marketplace.

Types of Products

Think about Botox, Doritos tortilla chips, Intel computer chips, and your favorite musical artist. You wouldn't market all these products in the same way, because buyer behavior, product characteristics, market expectations, competition, and other elements of the equation are entirely different.

Marketers frequently classify products on the basis of tangibility and use. Some products are predominantly tangible; others are mostly intangible. Most products, however, fall somewhere between those two extremes. The *product continuum* indicates the relative amounts of tangible and intangible components in a product (see Exhibit 13.1). Education is a product at the intangible extreme, whereas salt and shoes are at the tangible extreme. The complete Botox product includes both the tangible medication and the intangible services of the medical professionals who administer it. Similarly, digital music players such as the Apple iPod involve product elements that are both tangible (the music player itself) and intangible (the iTunes download service).

Deciding how much or how little to expand on the core product is one of the most important product strategy decisions that managers need to make. In many markets, competitors offer a wide range of possibilities, from "bare-bones" offerings to products with all the "bells and whistles," as marketers like to say. The discount online brokerage Ameritrade, for instance, offers the most basic stock buying and selling services, without the research and advice that stock brokers typically offer. Not all customers want these stripped-down offerings, of course, but Ameritrade has become quite profitable by appealing to customers who do want a less-expensive, no-frills product.[2] Exhibit 13.2 shows some of the ways marketers can *augment*, or enhance, a basic product with additional services and accessories.

Service Products

As you read in Chapter 9, the unique characteristics of service products require special consideration in every part of the business, and particularly in marketing. For instance, the intangibility of services makes them more difficult to demonstrate in advertisements (particularly in print ads). Services marketers often compensate for intangibility by using tangible symbols or by adding tangible components to their products. Prudential Financial (www.prudential.com), for example, uses the Rock of Gibraltar as a symbol of stability. Similarly, companies that deliver services often give clients tangible representations of the service, both to add to its value and to remind customers of the value they've received. Business consultants usually give their clients printed reports in addition to in-person presentations, for instance. Testimonials from satisfied customers are another important tactic marketers can use to compensate for the frequent inability to demonstrate services.

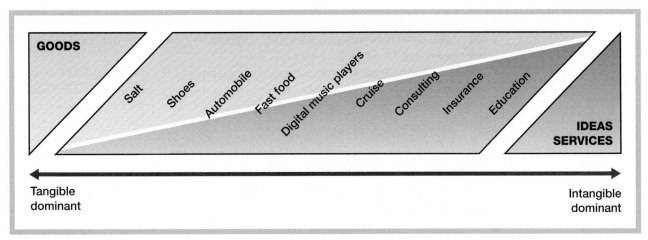

Exhibit 13.1
The Product Continuum
Products contain both tangible and intangible components; predominantly tangible products are categorized as goods, whereas predominantly intangible products are categorized as services.

Exhibit 13.2
Augmenting the
Basic Product
*Product decisions also
involve how much or how
little to augment the core
product with additional
goods and services.*

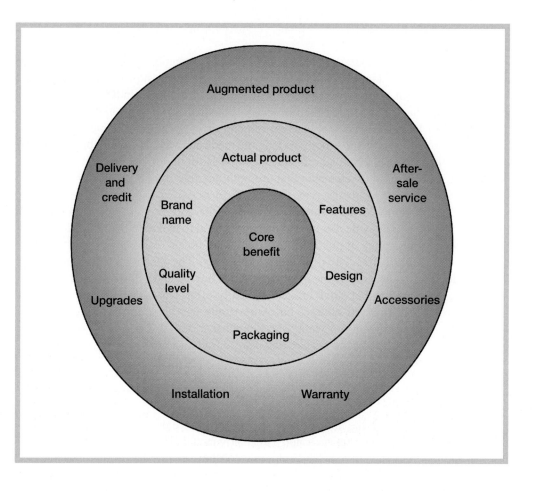

Consumer Products

Marketers also classify products by use as a way to channel marketing strategies toward specific market segments. Both organizations and consumers use many of the same products, but they use them for different reasons and in different ways. Individual consumers or households generally purchase smaller quantities of goods and services for personal use. Products that are primarily sold to consumers for personal consumption are known as *consumer products*. Consumer products can be classified into four subgroups, depending on how people shop for them:

- *Convenience products* are the goods and services that people buy frequently, without much conscious thought, such as toothpaste, dry cleaning, film developing, and photocopying.
- *Shopping products* are fairly important goods and services that people buy less frequently, such as music players, computers, refrigerators, and college educations. Such purchases require more thought and comparison shopping to check on price, features, quality, and reputation.
- *Specialty products* are particular brands that the buyer especially wants and will seek out, regardless of location or price, such as Prada clothing and accessories or Suzuki violin lessons. Even through a recent recession, the Danish firm Bang & Olufsen (www.bang-olufsen.com) fared well selling its world-renowned home entertainment gear, which includes $20,000 TV sets and $8,000 speakers.[3] Specialty products are not necessarily expensive, but they are products that customers go out of their way to buy and for which they rarely accept substitutes.
- *Unsought products* are products that many people do not normally think of buying, such as life insurance, cemetery plots, and new products. Part of the marketing challenge in these cases is simply making people aware of the product.

INNOVATING FOR BUSINESS SUCCESS

RINGING UP BUSINESS IN CREATIVE NEW WAYS

When engineers at Motorola debuted the first cell phone back in the 1980s, the two-pound, $4,000 brick-size unit was a technological marvel, but the designers probably couldn't imagine all the uses that their innovation would be put to one day. Ringtones alone have become a billion-dollar business as cell phone owners announce their musical tastes to the world with song snippets that can cost up to several dollars each. The music world is paying close attention, too; Ludicris, Snoop Dogg, and Aaliyah are among the stars who've signed exclusive contracts to create ring tones for Zingy (www.zingy.com), one of the leading ringtone suppliers.

Ringtones are only part of the industry growing up around mobile phone services—these days, talking seems like about the last thing some people do on their cell phones. From offering games to mobile blogs that let you share the sights and sounds of your latest vacation or business meeting, cell phones are morphing into multipurpose gadgets that defy categorization. Mforma (www.mforma.com), which is big in mobile games, is pushing the idea of media snacking, in which you consume short segments of films, news broadcasts, webcasts, and other content on your phone. Jamdat (www.jamdat.com) lets you play everything from baseball to Yahtzee. The National Basketball Association (www.nba.com) is betting heavily that consumers will feel a need to get scores and highlights on their phones. Other companies are racing to expand handheld travel guides so you'll never be lost, hungry, or out of places to shop.

The road to wireless riches does have a few rocky patches, though, as companies fight for control of the industry. Motorola (www.motorola.com) learned this lesson in 2005 when cellular companies initially refused to support its new Rokr music phone, which delivers Apple's iTunes service in a cellular handset, until they figured out how music downloads would fit into their business models. (Cingular eventually became the first carrier to offer Rokr.)

Whoever ends up in control, these mobile phone services are great examples of how a product developed for one purpose (giving business executives a way to stay in touch while they were on the move) can spawn countless other ideas in the hands of creative entrepreneurs. Next time you're playing around with your phone (you know, like, when you should be studying), maybe you'll dream up a new product idea of your own.

Questions for Critical Thinking

1. What other services can you think of that could be offered on cell phones?
2. Pick one of your ideas from the previous question and identify the infrastructure that would need to be in place in order to make that service a reality. Let's say your idea is a pet-tracking service, through which pet owners could keep track of the location of their pets. In addition to the cell phone itself, what other product elements would be required to launch such a service?

Industrial Products

In contrast to consumer products, *industrial products* are generally purchased by firms in large quantities and are used for further processing or in conducting a business. Two categories of industrial products are *expense items* and *capital items*. Expense items are relatively inexpensive goods and services that organizations generally use within a year of purchase. Examples are pencils and printer cartridges. Capital items are more expensive organizational products and have a longer useful life. Examples include computers, vehicles, and production machinery.

Aside from dividing products into expense and capital items, industrial buyers and sellers often classify products according to their intended use:

- **Raw materials** such as iron ore, crude petroleum, lumber, and chemicals are used in the production of final products.
- **Components** such as semiconductors and fasteners are similar to raw materials; they also become part of the manufacturers' final products. Many companies also buy completed

Business Buzz
prosumer
Refers to products that fall somewhere between consumer class and professional class. For example, a prosumer camcorder creates higher-quality movies than a mass-market consumer camcorder, but not quite as good as the complex, top-of-the-ine models that professional videographers use

subsystems that they then assemble into final products; Boeing buys complete engines for its aircraft, for instance.

- *Supplies* such as pencils, nails, and light bulbs that are used in a firm's daily operations are considered expense items.
- *Installations* such as factories, power plants, airports, production lines, and semiconductor fabrication machinery are major capital projects.
- *Equipment* includes less-expensive capital items such as desks, telephones, and fax machines that are shorter lived than installations.
- *Business services* range from simple and fairly risk-free services such as landscaping and cleaning to complex services such as management consulting and auditing.

The Product Life Cycle

LEARNING OBJECTIVE 1

Describe the four stages in the life cycle of a product

product life cycle
Four basic stages through which a product progresses: introduction, growth, maturity, and decline

Regardless of a product's classification, few products last forever. Most products go through a **product life cycle**, passing through four distinct stages in sales and profits: introduction, growth, maturity, and decline (see Exhibit 13.3). As the product passes from stage to stage, various marketing approaches become appropriate.

The product life cycle can describe a product class (gasoline-powered automobiles), a product form (sports-utility vehicles), or a brand (Ford Explorer). Product classes and forms tend to have the longest life cycles, whereas specific brands tend to have shorter life cycles. The amount of time that a product remains in any one stage depends on customer needs and preferences, economic conditions, the nature of the product, and the marketer's strategy. Still, the proliferation of new products, changing technology, globalization, and the ability to quickly imitate competitors is hurtling many product forms and brands through their life cycles much faster today than in the past.

Not only are existing products advancing through product life cycles at a rapid pace, but many companies are finding it increasingly hard to maintain a unique advantage long enough to make good profits on product innovations. Years ago, companies could milk an innovative product for years before less-expensive clones arrived. Now, new goods and services are often barely out the door before rivals are on their tails, bludgeoning prices. Procter & Gamble (**www.pg.com**), for example, had high profit hopes for its innovative $50 Swiffer WetJet mop, which sprays water on floors. But soon after the product's launch, Clorox Co. developed ReadyMop and priced it competitively. P&G was then forced to cut the price of its Swiffer WetJet mop price by half—only seven months after it was introduced into the marketplace.[4]

Exhibit 13.3
The Product Life Cycle
Most products and product categories move through a life cycle similar to the one represented by the curve in this diagram. However, the duration of each stage varies widely from product to product. Automobiles, crayons, and telephone service have been selling well in the maturity stage for decades, but faxing services barely made it into the introduction stage before being knocked out of the market by low-cost fax machines that every business and home office could afford.

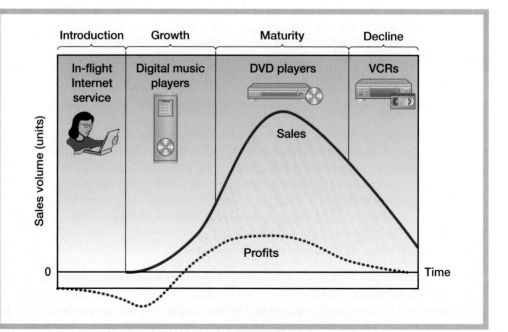

SAFETY AND SECURITY IN A COMPLEX WORLD

DESIGNING SAFER PRODUCTS

Drivers of ordinary cars and trucks can die in 30 or 40 mph crashes, but race car drivers routinely walk away from 150 or 200 mph crashes. Clearly, the technology exists to protect vehicle occupants better than the average automobile does, but few consumers are in a position to shell out millions of dollars for cars with carbon-fiber *safety cells* (a super-strong "pod" that encloses the driver and fuel tank). And few people would consent to wearing the harnesses, helmets, or head-and-neck restraint systems that protect racers.

Although most situations aren't this dramatic, product safety frequently involves *trade-offs* between costs and benefits. Moreover, this trade-off is just one of many judgment calls and decisions that designers must address during the product-development process:

- **Safety margins.** How far beyond normal conditions should your product be able to operate safely? For instance, airplanes are designed to withstand stresses and strains far beyond anything they're likely to encounter in everyday operation, but designing in such safety margins adds to the cost of the product.
- **Predictable use, abuse, and misuse.** How will customers use the product after it leaves your control? Used responsibly, *pocket bikes*, those miniatures motorcycles that teenagers like to zip around on these days, can be safe enough, but they become extremely dangerous when riders dart in and out of traffic (which is why many local governments are starting to ban or restrict them).
- **Maintenance and repair issues.** What are the customer's responsibilities in terms of keeping the product in safe working condition—and what might happen if the customer ignores these responsibilities? If you tell car owners to get the brakes serviced every 30,000 miles, but they don't—what will happen and whose fault will it be?

Thanks to a combination of activism, regulations, market pressures, engineering pride, and technological advances in design and testing, most of today's products have an admirable record of safety. For instance, with everything from antilock brakes to airbags, automobiles are safer today than they have ever been.

Autos are also a good example of how an entire industry sometimes has to change its attitude about product safety, from Lee Iacocca's infamous remark in the 1970s that "safety doesn't sell" to today's market, where companies constantly promote safety features. As one example, in 2005, General Motors (www.gm.com) announced that its StabiliTrak stability control system (which helps drivers maintain control on slippery roads or during emergency maneuvers) would be a standard feature on all GM cars by 2010. As Bob Austin of Rolls Royce recently put it, "Making safety a hallmark of all its brands is probably a good corporate strategy."

Questions for Critical Thinking

1. Think about Lee Iacocca's remark that "safety doesn't sell." Do manufacturers have a responsibility to create safe products even if customers don't care and don't want to pay for safety features? Why or why not?
2. What role do customers have in ensuring product safety?

Introduction The first stage in the product life cycle is the *introductory stage*, which extends from the research-and-development (R&D) phase through the product's first commercial availability. The introductory stage is a crucial phase that requires careful planning and often considerable investment. Marketing staffs often work long hours for weeks or months before a product launch, preparing promotional materials, training sales staff, completing packaging, finalizing the price, and wrapping up countless other tasks. In many markets, a vital activity in the prelaunch phase is generating "buzz" for the product by discussing it with journalists, demonstrating it to user groups, and other activities. Some markets offer the luxury of building demand over time if the introduction isn't a blockbuster, but in others, a weak introduction can doom a product. The opening weekend for a movie, for instance, often determines its success or failure—a tremendously stressful scenario for people who may have invested years and many millions of dollars making it.

Growth After the introductory stage comes the *growth stage*, marked by a rapid jump in sales—assuming the product is successful—and, usually, an increase in the number of competitors and distribution outlets. As competition increases, so does the struggle for market share. This situation creates pressure to introduce new product features and to maintain large promotional budgets and competitive prices. In fact, marketing in this stage is so expensive that it can drive out smaller, weaker firms. With enough growth, however, a firm can often produce and deliver its products more economically than in the introduction phase. Thus, the growth stage can reap handsome profits for those who survive.

Maturity During the *maturity stage*, usually the longest in the product life cycle, sales begin to level off or show a slight decline. Most products are in the maturity stage of the life cycle, where competition increases and market share is maximized—making further expansion difficult. Because the costs of introduction and growth have diminished in this stage, most companies try to keep mature products alive so they can use the resulting profits to fund the development of new products (which is often referred to as "milking a cash cow").

Adding new features that appeal to select segments of customers is a common way to squeeze more sales out of a mature product or product category. For instance, overall PC sales haven't grown much in the United States in recent years, but several companies have increased sales to serious game players. These consumers spend up to $10,000 or more on ultrafast computers with audio, video, and storage systems customized for game playing.[5]

Decline Although maturity can be extended for many years, most products eventually enter the *decline stage*, when sales and profits slip and then fade away. Declines occur for several reasons: changing demographics, shifts in popular taste, product competition, and advances in technology. When a product reaches this point in the life cycle, the company must decide whether to keep it and reduce the product's costs to compensate for declining sales or discontinue it and focus on developing newer products. Sometimes an entire product category begins to decline, which is currently happening to film-based cameras as digital cameras gain widespread acceptance. Eastman Kodak, which has been selling film cameras for more than a century, decided to phase out most of them in 2004, citing continued losses on the product line.[6]

LEARNING FROM BUSINESS BLUNDERS

OOPS For years, Kryptonite locks, produced by a company of the same name headquartered in Canton, Massachusetts, have had a reputation for near invincibility. The company's tubular U-shaped locks are particularly popular with bicycle owners. That reputation took a hit when an online bike forum posted videos showing how certain models of the locks could be opened with a simple Bic ballpoint pen.

WHAT YOU CAN LEARN Sometimes vulnerabilities pop up when and where you least expect them. Kryptonite's designers took great care to use special high-strength steel, for instance, since the presumed enemies were hacksaws and bolt cutters, not the flimsy plastic barrels of Bic pens. In any area of business, look beyond the obvious when you're trying to identify risks and threats. Not only did this mistake hurt Kryptonite's reputation, it also cost the company millions of dollars to replace defective products.

Product Makeovers

Marketers don't need to accept a product's decline as inevitable, however. Numerous products have been pulled back from the brink with reinvigorated designs and refreshed marketing efforts. For instance, when *Rolling Stone* (www.rollingstone.com) began to lose readers to both other music magazines (such as *Spin* and *Blender*) and "lad mags" (such as *FHM* and *Maxim*), publisher Jann Wenner launched a major redesign of the publication to make it more relevant and more appealing to contemporary audiences. The effort touched every aspect of the magazine: cover logo, photography, article length, music reviews, and more. "We're responding to an overall change in the media landscape, and an overall change in the way people use and consume media," explained Wenner. Within a few months, *Rolling Stone*'s circulation figures were on the rise once again.[7]

Jeffrey Himmel, chairman and CEO of New York's Himmel group, has made a business of seeking out and resuscitating deceased brands. As Himmel sees it, any brand that had lasted a long time must have had something going for it. "A company may have spent $10 million building up a brand, and then they let it slip," says Himmel. "But the value is still there, lodged in the backs of people's memory." Take Breck shampoo, for example. The 72-year-old brand peaked in the 1970s and then declined as the Breck Girl ads lost their power. The brand was taken off the shelf in 2000. But Himmel, who is licensing the marketing rights from Dial, has brought the brand back to life by focusing on the shampoo's light floral fragrance (which he thinks consumers will remember fondly) instead of introducing a new generation of Breck Girls.[8]

The New-Product Development Process

Mad scientists and basement inventors still create new products, but many of today's products appear on the market as a result of a rigorous, formal *product development process*—a series of stages through which a product idea passes (see Exhibit 13.4). Here are the six stages of the process:

- *Idea generation.* The first step is to come up with ideas that will satisfy unmet needs. Customers, competitors, and employees are often the best source of new-product ideas. Some ideas are sheer luck: The microwave oven was invented after a Raytheon engineer in the 1940s noticed that a chocolate bar in his pocket melted when he stood close to a radar component known as a magnetron.[9] Some consumer products companies employ thousands of teenagers to report back on what's hot and what's not all over the world.[10]

LEARNING OBJECTIVE 2

Describe six stages of product development

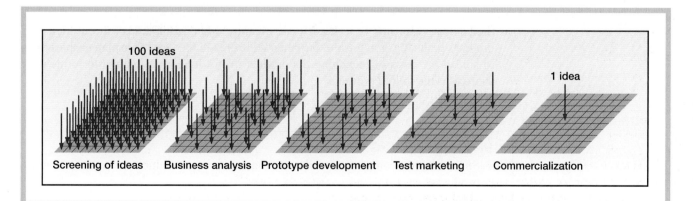

Exhibit 13.4

The Product Development Process

For every hundred ideas generated, only one or two salable products may emerge from the lengthy and expensive process of product development.

Of course, many "new" product ideas are simply improvements to or variations on existing products, but even those slight alterations can generate big revenues.

- *Idea screening.* From the mass of ideas suggested, the company culls a few that appear to be worthy of further development, applying broad criteria such as whether the product can use existing production facilities and how much technical and marketing risk is involved. In the case of industrial or technical products, this phase is often referred to as a "feasibility study," in which the product's features are defined and its workability is tested. In the case of consumer products, marketing consultants and advertising agencies are often called in to help evaluate new ideas. In some cases, potential customers are asked what they think of a new product idea—a process known as concept testing.

- *Business analysis.* A product idea that survives the screening stage is subjected to a business analysis. During this stage the company reviews the sales, costs, and profit projections to see if they meet the company's objectives. For instance, one question the company must answer is whether the company can make enough money on the product to justify the investment. To answer this question, the company forecasts the probable sales of the product, assuming various pricing strategies. In addition, it estimates the costs associated with various levels of production. Given these projections, the company calculates the potential profit that will be achieved if the product is introduced. If the product meets the company's objectives, it can then move to the product-development stage.

- *Prototype development.* At this stage the firm actually develops the product concept into a physical product. The firm creates and tests a few samples, or *prototypes*, of the product, including its packaging. During this stage, the various elements of the marketing mix are put together. In addition, the company evaluates the feasibility of large-scale production and specifies the resources required to bring the product to market.

- *Test marketing.* During **test marketing**, the firm introduces the product in selected areas of the country and monitors consumer reactions. Test marketing gives the marketer experience with marketing the product before going to the expense of a full introduction. Fisher-Price's Play Lab (www.fisher-price.com) is the centerpiece of the company's success. There, marketers observe as children and infants play with dozens of new toy concepts. "Kids are pretty humbling," notes one product designer. "You can have what you think is a great idea, and they shoot it down in minutes." Infants are even harsher critics. Show babies something that they don't like, and they'll cry, push it away, or throw it on the floor. Drool, however, is the highest praise.[11]

- *Commercialization.* The final stage of development is **commercialization**, the large-scale production and distribution of products that have survived the testing process. This phase (also referred to as a product launch) requires the coordination of many activities—manufacturing, packaging, distribution, pricing, and promotion. A classic mistake is letting marketing get out of phase with production by promoting the product before the company can supply it in adequate quantity. Many companies roll out their new products gradually, going from one geographic area to the next. This plan enables them to spread the costs of launching the product over a longer period and to refine their strategy as the rollout proceeds.

CRITICAL THINKING CHECKPOINT
1. Should laptop computers be classified as consumer products or organizational products? Explain your answer.
2. Why is the introductory phase so critical to a new product's success?
3. Why are most companies so careful to screen out product ideas that might not succeed?

TECHNOLOGIES THAT ARE REVOLUTIONIZING BUSINESS Digital Products

The category of digital products encompass an extremely broad range of product types, from e-books to music and movie files to product designs and instruction sets for automated machinery.

HOW THEY'RE CHANGING BUSINESS

Digital products are so pervasive that many people rarely even think about them anymore, but the ability to remotely deliver product value is quite a staggering concept when you think about it. In the near future, even *tangible* products might be delivered electronically: The technology that deposits layers of ink in ink-jet printers is being adapted to deposit layers of other materials in liquid form, and the step from two-dimensional printing to three-dimensional product fabrication is not all that far-fetched. Aside from the exotic possibilities, the economics, benefits, and concerns of digital product formats offer instructive insights into so many areas of contemporary business, from customer expectations to questions of ownership, privacy, and security, that it's worth the time to give them a second look.

WHERE YOU CAN LEARN MORE

The range of websites covering digital products is as diverse as the products themselves, so there's no one single place to look for information. For a business perspective, check out the Digital Media Association, www.dima.org. For news on a variety of business and technical issues, visit News.com's digital media section: www.news.com, then click on "The Net," then "Digital media." For privacy issues, start with Public Interest Research Group, www.uspirg.org, and Privacy International, www.privacyinternational.org.

Product Identities

Creating an identity for products is one of the most important decisions marketers make. That identity is encompassed in the **brand**, which can have meaning at three levels: (1) a unique name, symbol, or design that sets the product apart from those offered by competitors; (2) the legal protections afforded by a trademark and any relevant intellectual property; and (3) the overall company or organizational brand.[12] For instance, the Nike "swoosh" symbol is a unique identifier on every Nike product, a legally protected piece of property, and a symbol that represents the entire company.

Branding helps a product in many ways. It provides customers with a way of recognizing and specifying a particular product so that they can choose it again or recommend it to others. It provides consumers with information about the product. It facilitates the marketing of the product. And it creates value for the product. This notion of the value of a brand is also called **brand equity**.

Brand Equity

A brand name is often an organization's most valuable asset. Strong brands often command a premium price in the marketplace, as Nike shoes, North Face outdoor wear, Estée Lauder cosmetics, and Evian water do. Customers who buy the same brand again and again are evidence of the strength of **brand loyalty**, or commitment to a particular brand. Brand loyalty can be measured in degrees. The first level is **brand awareness**, which means that people are likely to buy a product because they are familiar with it. The next level is **brand preference**, which means people will purchase the product if it is available, although they may still be willing to experiment with alternatives if they cannot find the preferred brand. The third and ultimate level of brand loyalty is **brand insistence**, the stage at which buyers will accept no substitute.

brand
A name, term, sign, symbol, design, or combination of those used to identify and differentiate products and companies

brand equity
The value that a company has built up in a brand

LEARNING OBJECTIVE 3

Cite three levels of brand loyalty

brand loyalty
The degree to which customers continue to purchase a specific brand

brand awareness
Level of brand loyalty at which people are familiar with a product

brand preference
Level of brand loyalty at which people habitually buy a product if it is available

brand insistence
Level of brand loyalty at which people will accept no substitute for a particular product

Brands help consumers make confident choices from the thousands of products available in today's supermarkets.

Brand Name Selection

Botox Cosmetic, Jeep, Levi's 501, and iPod are **brand names**, the portion of a brand that can be spoken, including letters, words, or numbers. McDonald's golden arches and the Nike "swoosh" symbols are examples of a **brand mark**, the portion of a brand that cannot be expressed verbally. The choice of a brand name and any associated brand marks can be a critical success factor. A well-known brand name, for instance, can generate more sales than an unknown name. As a result, manufacturers zealously protect their names.

Brand names and brand symbols may be registered with the Patent and Trademark Office as **trademarks**, brands that have been given legal protection so that their owners have exclusive rights to their use. The Lanham Trademark Act, a federal law, prohibits the unauthorized use of a trademark on goods or services when the use would likely confuse consumers as to the origin of those goods and services. For trademark infringement, the evidence must show that an appreciable number of ordinary prudent purchasers are likely to be confused as to the source, sponsorship, affiliation, or connection of the goods or services.[13] Nonetheless, when a name becomes too widely used, it no longer qualifies for protection under trademark laws. Cellophane, kerosene, linoleum, escalator, zipper, shredded wheat, and raisin bran are just a few of the many brand names that have passed into public domain, much to their creators' dismay.

Brand Sponsorship

Brand names may be associated with a manufacturer, retailer, wholesaler, or a combination of business types. Brands offered and promoted by a national manufacturer, such as Procter & Gamble's Tide detergent and Pampers disposable diapers, are called **national brands**. **Private brands** are not linked to a manufacturer but instead carry a wholesaler's or a retailer's brand. DieHard batteries and Kenmore appliances are private brands sold by Sears. As an alternative to branded products, some retailers also offer **generic products**, which are packaged in plain containers that bear only the name of the product. Note that "generics" is also a term used in the pharmaceutical industry to describe products that are copies of an original drug (other companies are allowed to make these copies after the patent on the original drug expires).

Co-branding occurs when two or more companies team up to closely link their names in a single product. For example, the Internet company AOL and the satellite radio service XM recently teamed up on a co-branded online radio service that gives AOL fresh, new content to offer its subscribers and gives XM the opportunity to demonstrate its service to AOL's large customer base.[14]

Sometimes companies, such as Warner Brothers, **license** or sell the rights to specific well-known names and symbols—such as Looney Tunes cartoon characters—and then manufacturers use these licensed labels to help sell products. Licensing is an especially hot growth area for automotive marketers, where sales of licensed goods amount to over $6 billion annually. For instance, thousands of children now ride around in Jeep and Land Rover strollers, and thousands of adults ride around in Ford trucks sporting the Harley-Davidson logo.[15]

Packaging

Another way that marketers create an identity for their products is through packaging. Most products need some form of packaging to protect them from damage or tampering. Packaging can also make it convenient for customers to purchase or use a product. Examples of innovative packaging are Frito-Lay's Go Snacks—plastic canisters filled with 3-D Doritos, Cheetos, or Fritos Hoops—and 7-Eleven's Candy Gulp, a plastic cup filled with gummy animals. Both conveniently fit in a car's cup holder.[16] Other examples of innovative packaging with strong consumer appeal are Gatorade's ergonomically designed bottle, Quaker Oats cereal in bags, Hidden Valley Ranch Dressing's "Easy-Squeeze" inverted bottle, and Coca-Cola's 12-pak can refrigerator dispenser.

In some cases, packaging is an essential part of the product itself, such as microwave popcorn or toothpaste in pump dispensers. Besides function, however, packaging plays an important role in a product's marketing strategy. Packaging makes products easier to display, facilitates the sale of smaller products, serves as a means of product differentiation, and enhances the product's overall appeal and convenience. In addition, in an effort to reduce shoplifting, retailers have recently put a lot of pressure on manufacturers to adopt packages that are difficult to conceal or to open in the store. Those stiff plastic packages known as "clamshells" that consumers love to hate—and that account for hundreds of injuries every year as people attempt to slice them open—are one such response to shoplifting.[17]

Labeling

Labeling is an integral part of packaging. Whether the label is a separate element attached to the package or a printed part of the container, it serves to identify a brand. Labels also provide grading information about the product and information about ingredients, operating procedures, shelf life, and risks. The labeling of foods, drugs, cosmetics, and many health products is regulated under various federal laws, which often require disclosures about potential dangers, benefits, and other issues consumers need to consider when making a buying decision.

license
Agreement to produce and market another company's product in exchange for a royalty or fee

L E A R N I N G
O B J E C T I V E 4

Discuss the functions of packaging and labeling

Product packaging usually has a number of functions, from promoting and protecting the product to displaying legally required health and safety information to providing instructions for use.

Universal Product Codes (UPCs)
Bar codes on packaging that provide information read by optical scanners

Labels do more than communicate with consumers. They are also used by manufacturers and retailers as a tool for monitoring product performance and inventory. **Universal Product Codes (UPCs)**, those black stripes on packages, give companies a cost-effective method of tracking the movement of goods. Store checkout scanners read UPC codes and relay the identity, sales, and prices of all products to the retailer's computer system. Such data can help retailers and manufacturers measure the effectiveness of promotions such as coupons and in-store displays, as well as control inventory. Although they may eventually be replaced in many cases by RFID tags (see Chapter 9), UPC codes will go down in history as a simple concept that saved countless billions of dollars.[18]

Product-Line and Product-Mix Strategies

Why does General Motors offer a product in nearly every category from economy cars to giant SUVs, whereas Aston Martin offers only a handful of models, all of which are ultraexpensive sports cars? Why does L.L. Bean sell casual and outdoor clothing from head to toe but not tuxedos or evening gowns? Why is Nokia now an electronics company and not the paper and tire company it used to be? Why can't you buy a burger and fries at Starbucks or fettuccine Alfredo at McDonald's? The answers to these questions might seem obvious to consumers, but every company needs to address these product strategy questions at some point—and sometimes over and over again as managers try to increase sales and maintain competitiveness.

In addition to developing product identities, a company must decide how many and what kind of products it will offer. To stay competitive, most companies continually add and drop products to ensure that declining items will be replaced by growth products. Companies that offer more than one product also need to pay close attention to how those products are positioned in the marketplace relative to one another. The responsibility for managing individual products, product lines, and product mixes is usually assigned to one or more managers in the marketing department. In a smaller company, the *marketing manager* tackles this effort; in larger companies with more products to manage, individual products or groups of products are usually assigned to **brand managers**, known in some companies as *product managers* or *product line managers*.

brand managers
People who develop and implement strategies and marketing programs

Product Lines

product line
A series of related products offered by a firm

A **product line** is a group of products from a single manufacturer that are similar in terms of use or characteristics. The General Mills (**www.generalmills.com**) snack-food product line, for example, includes Bugles, Fruit Roll-Ups, Nature Valley Granola Bars, and Pop Secret Popcorn. Within each product line, a company confronts decisions about the number of goods and services to offer. Hewlett Packard must decide on how many different types of products to manufacture in its printer and personal computer product lines.

Product Mix

product mix
Complete list of all products that a company offers for sale

An organization with several product lines has a **product mix**—a collection of goods or services offered for sale. The General Mills product mix consists of cereals, baking products, desserts, snack foods, main meals, and so on (see Exhibit 13.5). Three important dimensions of a company's product mix are *width*, *length*, and *depth*, and each dimension presents its own set of challenges and opportunities. A product mix is *wide* if it has several different product lines. General Mills's product mix, for instance, is fairly wide, with a half dozen or more product lines. A company's product mix is *long* if it carries several items in its product lines, as General Mills does. For instance, General Mills carries a number of different cereal brands within the ready-to-eat cereal line. A product mix is *deep* if it has a number of versions of *each* product in a product line. The Cheerios brand, for example, currently has nine different varieties, including frosted, multi-grain, and honey nut. The same is true for many other products in the company's other product lines.[19]

Exhibit 13.5

The Product Mix at General Mills

Selected products from General Mills show a product mix that is fairly wide but that varies in length and depth within each product line.

	Ready-to-Eat Cereals	Snack Foods and Beverages	Baking Products and Desserts	Main Meals and Side Dishes	Dairy Products
Product lines	Cheerios Cinnamon Toast Crunch Cocoa Puffs Kix Oatmeal Crisp Raisin Nut Bran	Bugles Corn Snacks Chex Snack Mix Fruit by the Foot Fruit Roll-Ups Nature Valley Granola Bars Pop Secret Popcorn	Bisquick Gold Medal Flour Sunkist Lemon Bars HomeStyle Frosting Mix Cinnamon Streusel Quick Bread Mix Supermoist Cake Mix	Chicken Helper Green Giant Vegetables Hamburger Helper Potato Buds Suddenly Salad	Columbo Yogurt Yoplait Yogurt Yumsters Yogurt Trix Yogurt

When deciding on the dimensions of a product mix, a company must weigh the risks and rewards associated with various approaches. Some companies limit the number of product offerings and focus on selling a few selected items to be economical: Doing so keeps the production costs per unit down and limits selling expenses to a single sales force. However, counting too heavily on a narrow group of products leaves a company vulnerable to competitive threats and market shifts. Other companies diversify their product offerings as a protection against shifts in consumer tastes, economic conditions, and technology. For example, Fox is among the companies experimenting with TV shows for cell phones, and in response to the growing influence of online music outlets, a number of music labels have begun releasing online-only songs that aren't available on CD.[20]

The decisions are also influenced by such factors as a company's long-term strategy, competitive strengths and weaknesses, managerial depth, and financial resources. For instance, the personal computer company Gateway recently decided to pull back from an expansion into consumer electronics so it could refocus on PCs in an attempt to return to profitability. At the same time, competitor HP was busy expanding even further into home electronics as a way to broaden its presence in the consumer marketplace.[21]

Retailers often have considerable influence in manufacturers' product line decisions as well. In general, the more revenue a manufacturer represents, the better treatment it receives in the retail channel—particularly with regard to the all-important issue of shelf space. In the cereal segment, for instance, Kraft's Post brand is in third place behind General Mills and Kellogg's, so retailers tend to give Kraft less shelf space.[22] Consequently, manufacturers look for ways to build portfolios of major brands that can command attention at the retail level. After its acquisition of Gillette in 2005, for example, P&G boasted 21 brands with annual sales of at least a billion dollars each.[23] Conversely, these retail pressures can encourage manufacturers to drop products that aren't big sellers. Kraft, which has a major presence in food aisles but a weaker presence in candy aisles, recently put its Altoids and Life Savers brands up for sale because these two brands struggle to compete for space and attention with big candy brands from Wrigley, Mars, and Hershey.[24]

Product Expansion Strategies

As Exhibit 13.6 shows, you can expand your product line and mix in a number of ways. One approach is to introduce additional items in a given product category under the same brand name—such as new flavors, forms, colors, ingredients, or package sizes. Old Spice (www.oldspice.com), for example, put a new spin on its product line by entering the body-wash category with its Old Spice High Endurance.[25] And Heinz squeezed more sales out of ketchup by adding green ketchup to its product line after young consumers identified color change as a desirable selling feature.[26]

LEARNING OBJECTIVE 5

Identify four ways of expanding a product line and discuss two risks that product-line extensions pose

Exhibit 13.6
Expanding the Product Line
Knowing that no product or category has an unlimited life cycle, companies use one or more of these product-line expansion methods to keep sales strong.

Method of Expansion	How It Works	Example
Line filling	Developing items to fill gaps in the market that have been overlooked by competitors or have emerged as consumers' tastes and needs shift	Alka-Seltzer Plus cold medicine
Line extension	Creating a new variation of a basic product	Tartar Control Crest toothpaste
Brand extension	Putting the brand for an existing product category into a new category	Virgin Cola
Line stretching	Adding higher- or lower-priced items at either end of the product line to extend its appeal to new economic groups	Marriott Marquis hotel

family branding
Using a brand name on a variety of related products

brand extension
Applying a successful brand name to a new product category

Another approach to expanding a product line is to add new products with the same product name—a strategy known as **family branding**. Kraft, for example, has extended its Jell-O product line with new products such as gelatin in a cup, pudding in a cup, and cheesecake snacks in a cup. These products build on the convenience-with-quality image of the Jell-O family brand. Similarly, in a **brand extension**, a company applies a successful brand name to a new category in the hopes that the recognition and reputation of the brand will give it a head start in the new category. For instance, movie star Jackie Chan is applying his name to a variety of product lines, including healthy cookies and clothing.[27] Another option is translating a successful brand in a different product format, such as videogames that are based on movies. Caleador, which created the hit TV show *Who Wants to Be a Millionaire?* in the United Kingdom (where it originated before becoming a U.S. hit), recently re-created the show as a live theater event.[28]

Building on the name recognition of an existing brand cuts the costs and risks of introducing new products. However, there are limits to how far a brand name can be stretched to accommodate new products and still fit the buyer's perception of what the brand stands for. Snickers ice cream bars and Dr. Scholl's socks and shoes worked as brand extensions, but Bic perfume and Rubbermaid computer accessories did not. When Kraft tried to extend the Chips Ahoy! brand with Ooey Gooey Warm 'N Chewy Chips Ahoy! (a microwavable version), the new cookies failed on a wide scale, forcing the company to spend $5.5 million to pull them off retail shelves.[29]

Moreover, an overextended brand name can start to lose the meaning a company has spent years and millions building up. For instance, for years Nike (www.nike.com) has wanted to enter the discount retail channel, but it didn't want to risk devaluing its brand image, as Nike senior vice president Scott Olivet explained: "Nike's positioning is really as a premium performance brand, and what you always worry about with a brand is extending it too far." To avoid that risk, the company purchased Starter, a brand well-known to Wal-Mart shoppers, and began selling Nike-designed but Starter-branded shoes in 2005.[30] Similarly, after discounter Kmart acquired the mid-level retailer Sears, Nike pulled its Nike-branded shoes from Sears, fearing that they would start showing up in Kmart stores.[31]

Product Strategies for International Markets

As you read in Chapter 3, product adaptation is one of the key changes that companies need to consider when moving into other countries. First, they must decide on which products and services to introduce in which countries. When selecting a country, they must take into consideration the type of government, market-entry requirements, tariffs and other trade barriers, cultural and language differences, consumer preferences, foreign-exchange rates, and differing business

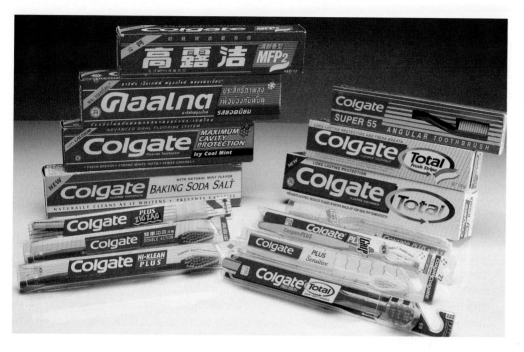

Notice how these localized versions of Colgate toothpaste packaging maintain key brand identifiers such as color and type style.

customs. Then they must decide whether to standardize the product, selling the same product everywhere, or to customize the product to accommodate the lifestyles and habits of local target markets. Keep in mind that the degree of customization can vary. A company may change only the product's name or packaging, or it can modify the product's components, size, and functions.

For example, French consumers have been eating McDonald's (www.mcdonalds.com) food from the moment the company first arrived in 1972, and France is now the company's third largest market in Europe. However, the burger giant has a unique look in that country. To accommodate a culture known for its cuisine and dining experience, many McDonald's outlets in France have upgraded their decor to a level that would make them almost unrecognizable in the United States. Gone are the Golden Arches, utilitarian chairs and tables, and other plastic fixtures. Instead the restaurants have hardwood floors, brick architecture, armchairs, and extras such as music videos that entice customers to linger over their meals. And while the basic burger offerings remain the same, menus at the upscale restaurants include a premiere line of sandwiches, espresso, and brioche (a soft bread common in France).[32]

CRITICAL THINKING CHECKPOINT
1. Why do companies such as Xerox and FedEx work so hard to make sure their brand names maintain legal protection?
2. Why would Ford introduce a pickup model with Harley-Davidson branding?
3. Does strong awareness for a given brand make brand extensions more or less risky? Explain your answer.

Pricing Strategies

LEARNING OBJECTIVE 6

List seven factors that influence pricing decisions and cite several common pricing strategies

The second key factor in the marketing mix is pricing. The pricing decisions for a product are determined by manufacturing and selling costs, competition, and the needs of wholesalers and retailers who distribute the product to the final customer. In addition, pricing is influenced by a firm's marketing objectives, government regulations, customer perceptions, and customer demand:

- *Marketing objectives.* The first step in setting a price is to match it to the objectives you set in your strategic marketing plan. Is your goal to increase market share, increase sales, improve profits, project a particular image, or combat competition? For instance, in order to compete with cut-rate credit cards, many banks and card issuers now offer low interest rates (a form of price) but make up for it with higher fees for late payments and other consumer mistakes.[33]

- **Government regulations.** Government plays a big role in pricing in many countries. To protect consumers and encourage fair competition, governments around the world have enacted various price-related laws over the years. These regulations are particularly important in three areas: (1) *price fixing*—an agreement among two or more companies supplying the same type of products as to the prices they will charge, (2) *price discrimination*—the practice of unfairly offering attractive discounts to some customers but not to others, and (3) *deceptive pricing*—pricing schemes that are considered misleading.

- **Customer perceptions.** Another consideration is the perception of quality that your price will elicit from your customers. When people shop, they usually have a rough price range in mind. An unexpectedly low price triggers fear that the item is of low quality. On the other hand, an unexpectedly high price makes buyers question whether the product is worth the money. Of course, in some consumer markets, high price is part of the appeal because it connotes exclusivity.

- **Customer demand.** Whereas a company's costs establish a floor for prices, demand for a product establishes a ceiling. Theoretically, if the price for an item is too high, demand falls and the producers reduce their prices to stimulate demand. Conversely, if the price for an item is too low, demand increases and the producers are motivated to raise prices. As prices climb and profits improve, producers boost their output until supply and demand are in balance and prices stabilize. Nonetheless, the relationship between price and demand isn't always this perfect. Some goods and services are relatively insensitive to changes in price; others are highly responsive. Marketers refer to this sensitivity as **price elasticity**—how responsive demand will be to a change in price. SanDisk (**www.sandisk.com**), which makes electronic memory cards for digital cameras and other devices, largely attributes a recent 40 percent increase in revenue to lower prices, which spurred demand from consumers.[34]

Marketers often take other financial and psychological factors into account, such as the "9 effect." You've probably noticed that many prices end in a 9, such as $9.99 or $5,999. Your conscious mind says, "Gimme a break; we all know that's really $10 or $6,000." However, research suggests that our minds equate that 9 with a bargain—even when it isn't. In one experiment, for example, a dress sold more when priced at $39 than when it was priced at $34.[35]

When companies set their prices, they take these factors—among others—into account before choosing a general pricing approach. Common pricing approaches include cost-based, price-based, optimal, skimming, and penetration pricing, and a variety of price adjustment methods.

price elasticity
A measure of the sensitivity of demand to changes in price

Prices—even on simple handwritten price tags—indicate more than mere monetary figures; they also send signals regarding a product's quality, exclusivity, and other.

Cost-Based Pricing

Many companies simplify the pricing task by using *cost-based pricing*, also known as *cost-plus pricing*. (As you'll see in a moment, however, cost-based pricing is not as simple as it seems.) Companies using this approach start with the cost of producing a good or a service and then add a markup to the cost of the product to produce a profit. How does a company determine the amount of profit it will earn by selling a certain product? **Break-even analysis** is a tool companies use to determine the number of units of a product they must sell at a given price to cover all manufacturing and selling costs, or to break even.

In break-even analysis, you consider two types of costs. **Variable costs** change with the level of production. These include raw materials, shipping costs, and supplies consumed during production. **Fixed costs**, by contrast, remain stable regardless of the number of products produced. These costs include rent payments, insurance premiums, and real estate taxes. The total cost of operating the business is the sum of a firm's variable and fixed costs. The **break-even point** is the minimum sales volume the company must achieve to avoid losing money. Sales volume beyond the break-even point will generate profits; sales volume below the break-even amount will result in losses.

You can determine the break-even point in number of units with this simple calculation:

$$\text{Break-even point} = \frac{\text{Fixed costs}}{\text{Selling price} - \text{Variable costs per unit}}$$

For example, if you wanted to price haircuts at $20 and you had fixed costs of $60,000 and variable costs per haircut of $5, you would need to sell 4,000 haircuts to break even:

$$\text{Break-even point} = \frac{\$60,000}{\$20 - \$5} = 4,000 \text{ units}$$

Of course, $20 isn't your only pricing option. Why not charge $30 instead? When you charge the higher price, you need to give only 2,400 haircuts to break even (see Exhibit 13.7). However, before you raise your haircut prices to $30, bear in mind that a lower price may attract more customers and enable you to make more money in the long run.

Break-even analysis doesn't dictate what price you should charge; rather, it provides some insight into the number of units you have to sell at a given price in order to start making a profit. This analysis is especially useful when you are trying to calculate the amount to mark up a price to earn a profit.

By this point you might've picked up on the two major weaknesses in cost-based pricing. First, in many industries, variable costs are often affected by volume, so your break-even equation could have two variables going in opposite directions at once, making it difficult to arrive at a stable answer.[36] As a simple example, the $30 haircut price might seem to lower your break-even point to 2,400, but at that lower level of sales, you might lose the volume purchasing discounts you'd been getting from your suppliers on shampoo, conditioner, and other materials. In other words, your break-even point is no longer what you thought it was because your variable costs changed. Second, cost-based pricing doesn't factor in either customers or competitors. What if customers think a $20 haircut is so inexpensive that it must be of poor quality? Or what if they're willing to pay $60 or $80? For these reasons, cost-based pricing is a risky approach, even if it is simple.

Price-Based Pricing

Companies that use *priced-based pricing* can maximize their profit by first establishing an optimal price for a product or service. The product's price is based on an analysis of a product's competitive advantages, the users' perception of the item, and the market being targeted. Once the desired price has been established, the firm focuses its energies on keeping costs at a level that will allow a healthy profit.

At Ikea (www.ikea.com), the price literally comes first. Ikea's corporate mantra is "Low price with meaning." The goal is to make products less expensive without making customers feel that

break-even analysis
Method of calculating the minimum volume of sales needed at a given price to cover all costs

variable costs
Business costs that increase with the number of units produced

fixed costs
Business costs that remain constant regardless of the number of units produced

break-even point
Sales volume at a given price that will cover all of a company's costs

LEARNING OBJECTIVE

Explain why cost-based pricing can be a flawed strategy

Exhibit 13.7

Break-Even Analysis

The break-even point is the point at which revenues just cover costs. After fixed costs and variable costs have been met, any additional income represents profit. The graphs show that at $20 per haircut, the break-even point is 4,000 haircuts; charging $30 yields a break-even point at only 2,400 haircuts.

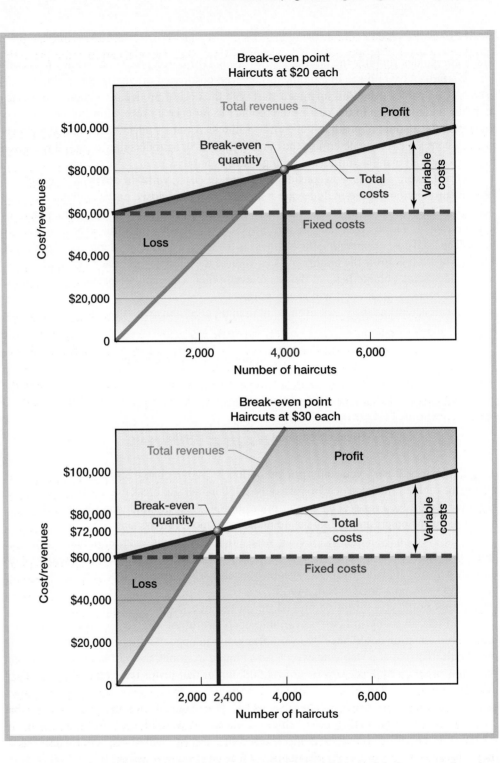

the products are cheap. Striking that balance demands a special kind of design, manufacturing, and distribution expertise. New products are born at Ikea by first establishing a price point. The company surveys competition to figure out how much the new product should cost and then targets a price 30 to 50 percent below that of rivals. After settling on a target price for a product, Ikea determines what materials will be used and what manufacturer will do the assembly work—even before the new item is actually designed. The company chooses among its 1,800 suppliers in 55 countries by posting a description of the product's target cost and basic specifications to suppliers. Once a manufacturer is selected, Ikea uses the same competitive process to find a designer and select a design for production. To reduce costs, Ikea designers focus on using materials as efficiently as possible; they analyze the function of every furniture surface to determine which materials, finishes, and construction techniques will work best for the least amount of money.

Ikea's price-driven manufacturing process is a key factor in its success. While the price of other companies' products tends to rise over time, Ikea has reduced its retail prices by about 20 percent during the past four decades.[37]

Optimal Pricing

Optimal pricing uses computer software to generate the ideal price for every item, at each individual store, at any given time. Research shows that many retailers routinely under-price or overprice the merchandise on their shelves. They generally set a price by marking up from cost, by benchmarking against the competition's prices, or simply by hunch.

A price-optimization program plugs reams of data from checkout scanners, seasonal sales figures, and so on into probability algorithms to come up with an individual demand curve for each product in each store. From that, retailers can identify which products are the most price sensitive. Then they can adjust prices up or down according to each store's priorities—profit, revenue, or market share—to achieve a theoretically maximum profit margin for their goals. This means that an item priced at $2.07 in one store's location might be going for $1.86 at a different location.

Longs Drug Stores in California have reported increased sales and margins after adopting a price-optimization program. But considerable obstacles stand in the way of broader adoption. First, the software can cost $1 million to $10 million depending on the number of stores and the complexity of the inventory. That limits price optimization to large retailers. Another problem is psychological: The software requires users to accept, on faith, pricing recommendations that are sometimes counterintuitive. "You have to trust it," says the chief operating officer of Longs Drug Stores.[38]

Skim Pricing

A product's price seldom remains constant and will vary depending on the product's stage in its life cycle. During the introductory phase, for example, the objective might be to recover product development costs as quickly as possible, before competitors can enter the market. To achieve this goal, the manufacturer might charge a high initial price—a practice known as **skim pricing**—with the intention of dropping the price later. *Early adopters*, those customers who tend to jump on new products quickly, are often willing to pay a premium to get their hands on the new products as soon as possible. In consumer markets, some people simply want to have the latest and greatest before anyone else; in organizational markets, new types of equipment can give companies a short-term competitive advantage.

skim pricing
Charging a high price for a new product during the introductory stage and lowering the price later

Penetration Pricing

Skim prices are set high with the understanding that many customers won't be willing to pay them. In contrast, companies use **penetration pricing** to build sales volume by charging a low initial price. This approach has the added advantage of discouraging competition, because the low price (which competitors would be pressured to match) limits the profit potential for everyone. Southwest Airlines uses this strategy when it enters new markets—partly because its lower cost structure enables it to charge lower prices.

penetration pricing
Introducing a new product at a low price in hopes of building sales volume quickly

Penetration pricing doesn't work if the company can't sustain the low price levels profitably or if customers weigh other factors more heavily than price. As mentioned earlier, prices that are far below the market's expectations can raise concerns about quality, reliability, and safety, for instance. Everyone would like to pay less for medical care, but few people would be willing to go to cut-rate clinics if they thought their health might be jeopardized.

Price Adjustment Strategies

Once a company has set a product's price, it may choose to adjust that price from time to time to account for changing market situations or changing customer preferences. Three common price adjustment strategies are price discounts, bundling, and dynamic pricing.

Customers who need to have the latest and greatest products are often willing to pay higher prices than those who wait until later in the product life cycle.

discount pricing
Offering a reduction in price

Price Discounts When you use **discount pricing**, you offer various types of temporary price reductions, depending on the type of customer being targeted and the type of item being offered. You may decide to offer a trade discount to wholesalers or retailers as a way of encouraging orders, or you may offer cash discounts to reward customers who pay cash or pay promptly. You may offer a quantity discount to buyers who buy large volumes, or you may offer a seasonal discount to buyers who buy merchandise or services out of season.

Another way to discount products is by *value pricing* them, charging a fairly affordable price for a high-quality offering. Many restaurants offer value menus for certain times of the day or certain customer segments, such as seniors. This strategy builds loyalty among price-conscious customers without damaging a product's quality image.

Although discounts are a popular way to boost sales of a product, the down side is that they can touch off *price wars* between competitors. Price wars can occur whenever (a) one supplier believes that underpricing the competition is the best way—or perhaps the only way—for it to increase sales volume and (b) customers believe that price is the only meaningful differentiator among the various suppliers. This situation occurs frequently in the air travel industry, which is why it has been wracked with price wars ever since the industry was deregulated years ago. Internet telephone service looks like it might be ready for a price war, even before the industry enters the mainstream.[39] Price wars present two significant dangers: that customers will begin to believe even more than they might've before that price is the only factor to care about in the market and that desperate competitors will cut prices so far that they'll damage their finances—perhaps beyond repair.

bundling
Combining several products and offering the bundle at a reduced price

Bundling Sometimes sellers combine several of their products and sell them at one reduced price. This practice, called **bundling**, can promote sales of products consumers might not otherwise buy—especially when the combined price is low enough to entice them to purchase the bundle. Examples of bundled products are season tickets, vacation packages, computer software with hardware, and wrapped packages of shampoo and conditioner. Bundling products and services can make it harder for consumers to make price comparisons.

dynamic pricing
Charging different prices depending on individual customers and situations

Dynamic Pricing **Dynamic pricing** is the opposite of fixed pricing. Using Internet technology, companies continually reprice their products and services to meet supply and demand. Dynamic pricing not only enables companies to move slow-selling merchandise instantly but also allows companies to experiment with different pricing levels. Because price changes are immediately posted to electronic catalogs or websites, customers always have the most current price information. Airlines and hotels have used this type of continually adjusted pricing for years, a technique often know as *yield management.*

Auctions are another form of dynamic pricing that used to be confined to a few market sectors such as fine art. That all changed when eBay came along and made selling and buying via auctions into a new national pastime. Consumers selling off old stuff from the basement aren't the only ones using eBay, either. Many companies now use eBay and other auction sites to sell everything from modular buildings to tractors to industrial equipment. *Procurement auctions* or *reverse auctions* are another twist on dynamic pricing, in which potential buyers post the goods or services they need and the prices they're willing to pay, then suppliers respond with offers at the prices they're willing to charge. In other words, in a regular auction, the price starts low and increases until only one buyer is left willing to buy at that price, while in a reverse auction, the price starts high and drops until there is only one seller left willing to sell at that price. A variation on the reverse auction is the name-your-price method, such as that used on the travel website Priceline.com. On Priceline, buyers can name a price for a desired travel service, then see if any sellers are willing to match it.[40]

CRITICAL THINKING CHECKPOINT

1. What message would a low price send to potential customers of a law firm?
2. Why do many experts consider cost-based pricing to be a flawed strategy?
3. Why might optimal pricing upset customers from time to time?

CHECKLIST: Apply These Ideas When You're the Boss

✓ Recognize that identical or similar products sold into both consumer and organizational markets may need different marketing strategies (for a good example to study, review the way Dell, www.dell.com, pitches its products to the home/home office, small business, large business, and education/government segments.

✓ Look for ways to augment your basic products with services and accessories to make them more appealing to target customers.

✓ Be ready to adjust your marketing strategy (and possibly other parts of your business strategy as well) as your products move through the product life cycle; moreover, don't wait until sales drop before you make such adjustments.

✓ Don't give up on a product just because sales are slipping; see if you can salvage the brand with some design changes or other adjustments to the marketing mix.

✓ On the other hand, if the market has moved on, don't spend heavily to prop up a brand that clearly isn't coming back.

✓ Consider every aspect of your products and your company, from graphic design to customer service, as components of your brand.

✓ Protect your brands with great care—from both external threats and internal mistakes.

✓ Before you attempt to set prices, make sure you understand the true value that you offer customers.

✓ Be wary of using cost-based pricing; you could end up leaving money on the table or making your products less competitive than they need to be.

✓ Be careful with discounts as well—use them too often, and customers quickly become trained to wait for them; you can lose the ability to ever sell at full price again.

Summary of Learning Objectives

1 Describe the four stages in the life cycle of a product. Products start in the introductory stage, during which marketers focus on stimulating demand for the new product. As the product progresses through the growth stage, marketers focus on increasing the product's market share. During the maturity stage, marketers try to extend the life of the product by highlighting improvements or by repackaging the product in different sizes. Eventually, all products move to a decline stage, where the marketer must decide whether to keep the product and reduce its costs to compensate for declining sales or to discontinue it.

2 **Describe six stages of product development.** The first two stages of product development involve generating and screening ideas to isolate those with the most potential. In the third stage, promising ideas are analyzed to determine their likely profitability. Those that appear worthwhile enter the fourth, or prototype development stage, in which a limited number of the products are created. In the fifth stage, the product is test marketed to determine buyer response. Products that survive the testing process are then commercialized, the final stage.

3 **Cite three levels of brand loyalty.** The first level of brand loyalty is brand awareness, in which the buyer is familiar with the product. The next level is brand preference, in which the buyer will select the product if it is available. The final level is brand insistence, in which the buyer will accept no substitute.

4 **Discuss the functions of packaging and labeling.** Packaging provides protection for the product, makes products easier to display, and attracts attention. In addition, packaging enhances the convenience of the product and communicates its attributes to the buyer. Labels help identify and distinguish the brand and product. They provide information about the product—including ingredients, risks, shelf life, and operating procedures. And they contain UPC codes, which are used for scanning sales information and monitoring inventory and pricing.

5 **Identify four ways of expanding a product line, and discuss two risks that product-line extensions pose.** A product line can be expanded by filling gaps in the market, extending the line to include new varieties of existing products, extending the brand to new product categories, and stretching the line to include lower- or higher-priced items. Two of the biggest risks with product-line extensions include a loss of brand identity (weakening of the brand's meaning), and cannibalization of sales of other products in the product line.

6 **List seven factors that influence pricing decisions, and cite several common pricing strategies.** Pricing decisions are influenced by manufacturing and selling costs, competition, the needs of wholesalers and retailers who distribute the product to the final customer, a firm's marketing objectives, government regulations, consumer perceptions, and consumer demand. Common pricing methods include cost-based, price-based, optimal pricing, price skimming, penetration pricing, and a number of price adjustment strategies such as discounting, bundling, and dynamic pricing. Cost-based pricing suffers from two major weaknesses. First, determining variable costs can be difficult since they often depend on production and sales volume. As the projected volume goes up or down, variable costs (necessary to compute the break-even point or profit margin) might be going down or up in response. Second, cost-based pricing doesn't take into account the influences of competitors or customers, both of which can dramatically affect the ability to sell at a given price point.

7 **Explain why cost-based pricing can be a flawed strategy.** Cost-based pricing suffers from two weaknesses. First, variable cost levels often change with volume (through discounts on higher-volume purchases of parts, for instance), so getting stable answers can be difficult. Second, cost-based pricing doesn't consider the expectations of customers or the tactics of competitors, so it can lead to under- or overpricing relative to market dynamics.

Botox Cosmetic: What's Next?

With a safe, simple, and fairly inexpensive way to diminish the visible effects of aging, Allergan is ideally positioned to profit as the Baby Boom generation advances in years. Of course, a huge market invites lots of competition from a variety of techniques and technologies. In addition to chemical peels, lasers, and a variety of other wrinkle-battling methods, a competitor called Inamid is bringing a Botox-like product to market. However, Allergan clearly has a head start with its product and the enormous brand equity built up in the Botox name.

Competitors aren't the only cloud on the horizon, though. The state of New Jersey recently began taxing Botox injections as a way to raise additional revenue, and other states are considering similar taxes.

Critical Thinking Questions

1. Would it be a good idea for Allergan to extend the Botox brand name to medical products outside of the cosmetics market, such as cold and flu medications?

2. Do you agree with New Jersey's decision to tax Botox injections? Why or why not?

3. A number of patients were recently injured when doctors around the country purchased and administered an unsafe product that its maker claimed was just like Botox. Even though

Allergan's product remains safe and it had nothing to do with the deceptive product, what steps, if any, should it take to protect the Botox brand name?

Learn More Online

Visit the Botox Cosmetic website by clicking on the hotlink at Chapter 13 of this text's website at www.prenhall.com/bovee. How is the product presented to potential customers? How does the website attempt to segment customers according to usage or loyalty patterns? What information is given about potential side effects and other safety issues? In what ways does Allergan promote the benefits of a product that is largely intangible?

Key Terms

brand (437)	bundling (448)	price elasticity (444)
brand awareness (437)	co-branding (438)	private brands (438)
brand equity (437)	commercialization (436)	product life cycle (432)
brand extension (442)	discount pricing (448)	product line (440)
brand insistence (437)	dynamic pricing (448)	product mix (440)
brand loyalty (437)	family branding (442)	skim pricing (447)
brand manager (440)	fixed costs (445)	test marketing (436)
brand mark (438)	generic products (438)	trademarks (438)
brand names (438)	license (439)	Universal Product Codes
brand preference (437)	national brands (438)	(UPCs) (440)
break-even analysis (445)	penetration pricing (447)	variable costs (445)
break-even point (445)		

Test Your Knowledge

Questions for Review

1. What are the four main subgroups of consumer products?
2. Why are most services perishable?
3. What are the functions of packaging?
4. How many books will a publisher have to sell to break even if fixed costs are $100,000, the selling price per book is $60, and the variable costs per book are $40?
5. How does cost-based pricing differ from price-based pricing?

Questions for Analysis

6. Why do businesses continually introduce new products, given the high costs of the introduction stage of the product life cycle?
7. How could a marketer confuse a consumer when developing a product's positioning strategies?
8. Why are brand names important?
9. Why is it important to review the objectives of a strategic marketing plan before setting a product's price?
10. **Ethical Considerations.** Why might an employee with high personal ethical standards act less ethically when developing packaging, labeling, or pricing strategies?

Questions for Application

11. In what ways might Mattel modify its pricing strategies during the life cycle of a toy product?
12. As the international marketing manager for Coca-Cola's Dasani bottled water, you are responsible for investigating the possibility of selling bottled water in other countries. What are some of the product-related issues you should consider during your study?
13. **Integrated.** Review the theory of supply and demand in Chapter 1 (see pages 34–39). How do skimming and penetration pricing strategies influence a product's supply and demand?

14. **Integrated.** Review the discussion of cultural differences in international business in Chapter 3 (see page 111). Which cultural differences do you think Disney had to consider when planning its product strategies for Disneyland Paris? Originally the company offered a standardized product but was later forced to customize many of the park's operations. What might have been some of the cultural challenges Disney experienced under a standardized product strategy?

Practice Your Knowledge

Handling Difficult Situations on the Job: Second Thoughts About Extended Warranties

A not-so-secret secret is getting more attention than you'd really like after an article in *BusinessWeek* gave the world an inside look at how much money you and other electronics retailers make from extended warranties (sometimes called service contracts). The article explained that typically half of the warranty price goes to the salesperson as a commission and that only 20 percent of the total amount customers pay for warranties eventually goes to product repair.

You also know why extended warranties are such a profitable business. Many electronics products follow a predictable pattern of failure: a high failure rate early in their lives, then a "midlife" period during which failures go way down, and concluding with an "old age" period when failure rates ramp back up again (engineers refer to the phenomenon as the *bathtub curve* because it looks like a bathtub from the side—high at both ends and low in the middle). Those early failures are usually covered by manufacturers' warranties, and the extended warranties you sell are designed to cover that middle part of the life span. In other words, many extended warranties cover the period of time during which consumers are *least* likely to need them and offer no coverage when consumers need them *most*. (Consumers can actually benefit from extended warranties in a few product categories, including laptop computers and plasma TVs. Of course, the more sense the warranty makes for the consumer, the less financial sense it makes for your company.)[41]

Your task: Worried that consumers will start buying fewer extended warranties, your boss has directed you to put together a sales training program that will help cashiers sell the extended warranties even more aggressively. The more you ponder this challenge, though, the more you're convinced that your company should change its strategy so it doesn't rely on profits from these warranties so much. In addition to offering questionable value to the consumer, they risk creating a consumer backlash that could lead to lower sales of all your products. Outline a discussion you plan to have with your boss, explaining why you think the sales training specifically and the warranties in general is a bad idea.

Sharpening Your Communication Skills

Now's your chance to play the role of a marketing specialist trying to convince a group of customers that your product concept is better than the competition's. You're going to wade into the industry battle over digital photo printing (see Chapter 12, page 407). Choose a side: either the photo printer manufacturers, who want consumers to buy printers to print their own digital photos (visit HP at www.hp.com for a good overview of photo-quality printers) or the service providers, who claim their way is better (visit one of the many retailers that offer a service-based approach, such as www.cvs.com or www.walmart.com). Prepare a short presentation on why the approach you've chosen is better for consumers. Feel free to segment the consumer market and choose a particular target segment if that bolsters your argument.

Building Your Team Skills

Select a high-profile product with which you and your teammates are familiar. Do some online research to learn more about that brand. Then answer these questions and prepare a short group presentation to your classmates summarizing your findings.

- Is the product a consumer product, industrial product, or both?
- At what stage in its life cycle is this product?
- Is the product a national brand or a private brand?
- How do the product's packaging and labeling help boost consumer appeal?
- How is this product promoted?
- Is the product mix to which this product belongs wide? Long? Deep?
- Is the product sold in international markets? If so, does the company use a standardized or a customized strategy?
- How is the product priced in relation to competing products?

Expand Your Knowledge

Discovering Career Opportunities

Being a marketing manager is a big responsibility, but it can be a lot of fun at the same time. Read what the U.S. Department of Labor has to say about the nature of the work, working conditions, qualifications, and job outlook for marketing managers by accessing the Bureau of Labor Statistics Occupational Outlook Handbook at www.bls.gov/oco.

1. What does a marketing manager do?
2. What are some key questions you might want to ask when interviewing for a job in marketing?
3. What training and qualifications should a marketing manager have?

Developing Your Research Skills

Scan recent business journals and newspapers (print or online editions) for an article related to one of the following:

- New-product development
- The product life cycle
- Pricing strategies
- Packaging

1. Does this article report on a development in a particular company, several companies, or an entire industry? Which companies or industries are specifically mentioned?
2. If you were a marketing manager in this industry, what concerns would you have as a result of reading the article? What questions do you think companies in this industry (or related ones) should be asking? What would you want to know?
3. In what ways do you think this industry, other industries, or the public might be affected by this trend or development in the next five years? Why?

Exploring the Best of the Web

URLs for all Internet exercises are provided at the website for this book, www.prenhall.com/bovee. When you log on to this text's Companion Website, select Chapter 13. Then select "Featured Websites," click on the name of the featured website, and review the website to complete these exercises.

Explore these chapter-related websites, review their content, and answer the following questions for each website you visit:

1. What is the purpose of this website?
2. What kinds of information does this website contain? Please be specific.
3. How is the information provided at this website useful for businesspeople? Consumers?
4. How did you expand your knowledge of marketing and customers by reviewing the material at this website? What new things did you learn about these topics?

Be a Sharp Shopper

Put your marketing knowledge to practice. Visit the Sharper Image website and think like a marketer. Evaluate the company's product mix. Is the product mix wide? Deep? What types of consumer products does this company sell? Who is its target market? Do the products have recognizable brand names? Which other stores carry this type of product? Be sure to read about the company's mission. And don't leave without checking out the new products. www.sharperimage.com

Protect Your Trademark

Got a winning idea for a new product? Don't forget to protect your trademark by registering it with the U.S. Patent and Trademark Office. Visit this government agency's website and learn the basic facts about registering a trademark, such as who is allowed to use the TM symbol and how a trademark differs from a service mark. Find out how the process works and how much it costs. In fact, why not search its database now to see whether anyone has already registered your trademark? www.uspto.gov

Uncover Hidden Costs

When you buy something online, the selling price is usually only part of your total cost. Factor in extra costs such as shipping and sales tax, and the total cost can vary dramatically from one website to another. Using comparison-shopping sites can help you ferret out hidden costs. Take a look at Best Book Buys, which compares the total cost of buying a book from a variety of Internet sources. Check out one of the best-selling books or search for your favorite book. Click to see a table comparing the item price, shipping cost, and total cost at different retail websites. Then simply click to buy. www.bestbookbuys.com

Learning Interactively

Companion Website

Visit the Companion Website at www.prenhall.com/bovee. For Chapter 13, take advantage of the interactive "Learning Modules" to test your chapter knowledge. Get instant feedback on whether you need additional studying. Complete the exercises as specified by your instructor.

A Case for Critical Thinking

Coke Unpacks a Winner

In 2002, Coca-Cola was a company in need of some good news. Although the company was still profitable and the Coca-Cola brand was one of the world's most valuable, as measured by future profit potential, bad news seemed to be bubbling over everywhere. A $300 million ad campaign failed to make much of an impression on consumers. An attempt to buy Quaker Oats, which would've brought Gatorade into the Coke beverage portfolio, got nixed at the last minute by Coke's board of directors; Quaker was then snatched up by Coke's arch rival, PepsiCo. A deal to partner Coke's Minute Maid orange juice brand with Procter & Gamble's Pringles potato chips—to better compete against PepsiCo's Frito-Lay and Tropicana brands—also fell apart.

Perhaps most troubling, sales were growing at only 2.4 percent a year, a far cry from the growth rates of 10 percent or more Coke enjoyed during its glory days. Among carbonated drinks, upstarts such as the repositioned Mountain Dew were growing at the expense of Coke's primary brands. PepsiCo (with its Aquafina brand) also moved into the surging bottled water market two years before Coke got there with Dasani. Coca-Cola's legendary marketing magic seemed to have fizzled out.

THINKING LIKE A CUSTOMER

Sometimes in marketing, good news can come from the smallest details. Researchers at Alcoa, which supplies aluminum cans to Coca-Cola, learned that the typical refrigerator is too full of food for the blocky 3 × 4 12-pack box—which was originally designed as a carrying case, not as a refrigerator storage case. Most beverage drinkers pull a few cans out of a box, throw them in the fridge, and shove the rest of the box in a pantry or other room-temperature storage. When the chilled cans are consumed, though, many people are slow to grab a few more from storage to restock the fridge. Consequently, the warm cans sit in storage longer, and people find something else in the fridge to drink.

Coke's product strategists picked up on this behavioral detail and reasoned that a package more compatible with today's refrigerators would let people keep the entire 12-pack chilled and ready to drink. The more chilled cans, the faster they get consumed and the faster those thirsty consumers would head back to the grocery store for more Coke.

A NEW FIT FOR THE FRIDGE

Conventional 12-packs stacked cans in a three-by-four configuration—too tall for many overloaded fridge shelves. Front to back, though, fridges tend to have more empty space. The solution was something shorter but deeper: two cans high by six cans deep. It was one of those simple ideas that everyone thinks is obvious once somebody else comes up with it.

While a product's package may seem far less important than the product itself, packaging can be a major influence if it affects consumer behavior. Coke's own research suggested that consumers could respond more to changes in packaging than to changes in branding.

The idea of the Fridge Pack is about as simple as ideas get, but execution is another matter entirely. The beverage business is both highly automated and complex, involving multiple local and regional bottlers who produce the beverage and deliver it to thousands of retail outlets. Just studying the system to figure out what needs to be modified can take months. For instance, everything from production lines to store shelves is set up for certain packaging sizes . Changes can ripple all the way through the system, from production facilities to in-store stacking procedures. Changing a single production line to accommodate the Fridge Pack costs a half million dollars, and Coca-Cola has some 80 production lines around the country. Executives needed to be reasonably sure such a large gamble would pay off.

PASSING THE TEST

Coke chose its hometown of Atlanta and the city of Chicago—a Pepsi stronghold—as sites to test the new package. It was a hit; sales of Coke in cans rose 10 percent at the two sites. The next step was rolling out regionally in the Southeastern United States. The success continued: Sales of 12-packs climbed 25 percent. Then Coke took the new 12-pack packaging nationwide. The packaging was also adapted for Dasani bottled water, Coke's fastest-growing brand, and that beverage is now "flying off the shelves," in the words of the regional bottler. Something as simple as a reconfigured box seems to have shaken up the fiercely competitive and generally stagnant soft drink market.

Coca-Cola still needs a few more success stories to get its marketing magic back, but the dramatic success of the Fridge Pack shows it can be done.

Critical Thinking Questions

1. Why was Alcoa interested in the behavior of Coca-Cola's customers?
2. Why were the market tests in Atlanta and Chicago so important?
3. Why would beverage consumers be more sensitive to packaging than branding?
4. Browse the websites of several beverage products and examine how they package their products. As a consumer, what other ways could beverage companies use packaging to make their products easier for you to purchase and consume?

Video Case

Sending Products into Space: MCCI

Learning Objectives

The purpose of this video is to help you:

1. Recognize how and why a company develops specialized products for organizational customers.
2. Describe some of the decisions a company faces in pricing specialized products under long-term contracts for organizational customers.
3. Understand how a company can use quality to differentiate its products.

Synopsis

MCCI designs and produces highly specialized products that are customized to the detailed specifications of its organizational customers. When a telecommunications company or government agency needs a radio frequency filter for a new satellite, it calls on MCCI to design one especially for that situation. Custom-made from tiny components and precious materials, this filter must be top quality to withstand powerful vibration and temperature extremes in space—and continue to perform exactly as promised for 20 years. Because some contracts cover products purchased over a decade or more, MCCI must carefully assess the risks of designing a product and pricing it for long-term profit. Yet speed is also a factor: MCCI once created a new product during a single weekend to win a contract from an important customer.

Discussion Questions

1. *For analysis:* Are MCCI's products capital or expense items? How do you know?
2. *For analysis:* Given its in-depth knowledge of the market, why does MCCI develop new products for individual customers rather than creating new products to meet general industry needs?
3. *For application:* The price of gold can fluctuate widely, depending on market conditions. How might this affect MCCI's pricing decisions for products that incorporate components made from gold?
4. *For application:* What factors must MCCI analyze as it prices a custom-designed product?
5. *For debate:* At the start of a long-term contract, should MCCI price a product to return little or no profit in the hope that it will be able to generate more profit from other products sold to this customer later in the contract period? Support your chosen position.

Online Exploration

One of MCCI's products went to Mars on the Sojourner Rover sent by NASA. What other kinds of goods and services does NASA buy? Visit its procurement website, acquisition.jpl.nasa.gov, and follow the link to see some of the requests for proposals on this site. Do any contain a document with questions and answers? Why would MCCI need to read such a document before preparing a proposal to develop a product for NASA? Now examine the listing of other links. How could MCCI use information from the sites on this listing in planning a product for NASA?

Costco prefers to offer name-brand products, but because many high-end suppliers such as Cartier and Cannondale flinch at the idea of their goods being sold in a warehouse setting, this isn't always possible. Some suppliers, hoping to protect their higher-end retail customers, have been known to spurn Costco's offers "officially," only to call back later to quietly cut a deal. In other cases, Costco goes on its own treasure hunts, using third-party distributors to track down hot products, even though these "gray market" channels can be unpredictable. And if that doesn't work, Costco can commission another manufacturer to create a look-alike product—leather handbags are one example—with its own Kirkland Signatures label.

To give its millions of members the best prices on everything, Costco negotiates directly—and fiercely—with suppliers. Aiming to be known as the toughest negotiators in the business, Costco's buyers won't let up until they get their target price on the merchandise. Often, the "right" price is determined by how much cheaper Costco can make a product itself. Using this approach, the company has managed to drive down price points in several categories, including photo film and over-the-counter drugs. Costco then passes on the savings to customers, who never pay more than 14 percent above its cost.

By coupling relentless drive with one of the most motivated and loyal workforces in the industry, Costco reigns supreme in the warehouse club business. With hundreds of stores across North America and a growing presence in the United Kingdom, Taiwan, South Korea, and Japan, Costco continues to make the good life affordable for millions of enthusiastic customers.[1]

GET READY

If you were in Costco CEO Jim Sinegal's shoes, would you steer Costco in the same directions he has chosen? Would you continue to offer a narrow selection of goods and services or expand into a full-line retailer? How would you decide where to locate new stores? Where would online retailing fit in your strategy? Plus, how would you maintain profitable growth when you're up against the mighty Wal-Mart?

Chapter Overview

This chapter explores retailing—one of the most visible aspects of marketing—along with wholesaling and physical distribution, two other vital parts of the marketing equation, but ones that many consumers never see in action. You'll start by learning about the role that all these marketing intermediaries play in the effort to move products from the companies that create them to the companies and consumers who buy them. You'll also see how the Internet continues to create both challenges and opportunities for every company in the distribution sector. The second part of the chapter explains the complex decisions that marketing managers need to make regarding distribution strategies, then the final section explores the process of physical distribution.

LEARNING OBJECTIVE 1

Explain the role of marketing intermediaries in contemporary business and list the seven primary functions that intermediaries can perform

distribution strategy
An overall plan for moving products to intermediaries and final customers

Understanding the Role of Marketing Intermediaries

Costco is just one example of how marketing intermediaries work. Getting products to customers (both consumers and organizational buyers) is the role of distribution, the third major element of the marketing mix. As Chapter 12 points out, a *distribution channel*, or *marketing channel*, is an organized network of firms that work together to get goods and services from producer to customer. Whether you're selling digital music files online or scrap iron stripped out of old ships, your **distribution strategy**, or overall plan for moving products to buyers, will play a major role in your success.

Think of all the products you buy: food, cosmetics, clothing, sports equipment, train tickets, haircuts, gasoline, stationery, appliances, music, books, and all the rest. How many of these products do you buy directly from the producer? For most people, the answer is not many. Most companies that create products do not sell these goods directly to the final users, even though the Internet is making that easier to do these days. Instead, producers in many industries work with **marketing intermediaries** (traditionally called *middlemen*) to bring their products to market.

Intermediaries can be grouped into two general types: wholesalers and retailers. **Wholesalers** sell to organizational customers, including other wholesalers, companies, government agencies, and educational institutions. In turn, the customers of wholesalers either resell the products or use them to make products of their own. Ingram Book Group, for example, the world's largest wholesaler of books and related products, supplies thousands of retail outlets from an inventory of more than 1 million items.[2]

Unlike wholesalers, **retailers** primarily sell products to consumers for personal use. Retailers can operate out of a physical facility (department store, gas station, kiosk), through vending equipment (soft drink machine, newspaper box, automated teller), or from a virtual store (via telephone, catalog, website). Note that even though Costco and other warehouse-type stores often use the "wholesale" label to describe themselves, they function as both wholesalers and retailers simultaneously. Small-business owners, for instance, are enthusiastic Costco shoppers since it's a low-cost place to buy supplies and equipment. In these cases, Costco is functioning as a wholesaler. However, when selling to consumers, Costco is technically operating as a retailer, not a wholesaler.

Wholesalers and retailers are instrumental in creating three of the four forms of utility mentioned in Chapter 12: They provide the items you need in a convenient location (place utility), they save you the time of having to contact each manufacturer to purchase a good (time utility), and they provide an efficient process for transferring products from the producer to the customer (possession utility). In addition to creating utility, wholesalers and retailers perform the following distribution functions (see Exhibit 14.1):

- *Matching buyers and sellers.* By making sellers' products available to multiple buyers, intermediaries such as Costco reduce the number of transactions between producers and

marketing intermediaries
Businesspeople and organizations that channel goods and services from producers to consumers

wholesalers
Firms that sell products to other firms for resale or for organizational use

retailers
Firms that sell goods and services to individuals for their own use rather than for resale

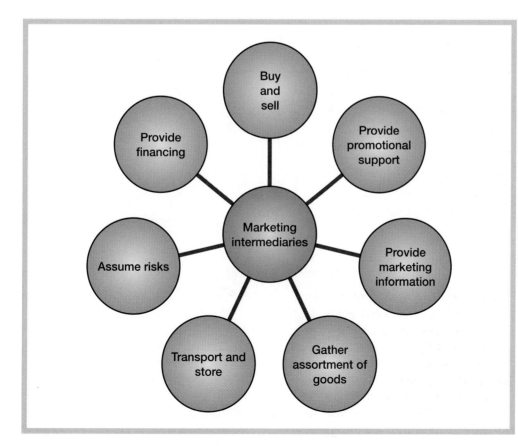

Exhibit 14.1
Seven Roles of Marketing Intermediaries
These important functions performed by marketing intermediaries make life easier for both producers and consumers.

customers. In the business-to-business market, giant online trading hubs such as Covisint (automotive parts, www.covisint.com) and ChemConnect (chemicals and plastics, www.chemconnect.com) bring together thousands of buyers and sellers.[3]

- *Providing market information.* Retail intermediaries, such as Amazon and Macy's, collect valuable data about customer purchases: who buys, how often, and how much. Many stores now use frequent shopper cards to help them spot buying patterns and share marketplace information with producers.
- *Providing promotional and sales support.* Many intermediaries, such as Pepsi distributors, create advertising, produce eye-catching displays, and use other promotional devices for some or all of the products they sell. Some also employ a salesforce, which can perform a number of selling functions.
- *Gathering an assortment of goods.* Nordstrom, Sportmart, Office Max, and other intermediaries receive bulk shipments from producers and break them into more convenient units by sorting, standardizing, and dividing bulk quantities into smaller packages.
- *Transporting and storing products.* Intermediaries such as Borders, Best Buy, and Pier 1 maintain an inventory of merchandise that they acquire from producers so they can quickly fill customers' orders. In many cases retailers purchase this merchandise from wholesalers who, in addition to *breaking bulk*, may also transport the goods from the producer to the retail outlets.
- *Assuming risks.* When intermediaries accept goods from manufacturers, they take on the risks associated with damage, theft, product perishability (in the sense of tangible goods that are vulnerable to rotting, for instance), and obsolescence. For example, if products stocked or displayed at Costco are stolen, Costco assumes responsibility for the loss.
- *Providing financing.* Large intermediaries sometimes provide loans to smaller producers.

As Exhibit 14.2 shows, without marketing intermediaries, the buying and selling process in many industries would be expensive and time-consuming.

Exhibit 14.2
How Intermediaries
Simplify Commerce
*Intermediaries actually
reduce the price customers
pay for many goods and
services, because they
reduce the number of
contacts between
producers and consumers
that would otherwise
be necessary. They also
create place, time,
and possession utility.*

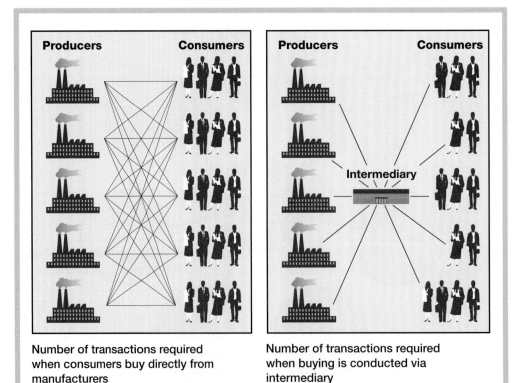

Number of transactions required when consumers buy directly from manufacturers

Number of transactions required when buying is conducted via intermediary

Wholesalers

Because wholesalers seldom deal directly with consumers, you may not be familiar with the various players in the wholesale distribution arena. Most U.S. wholesalers are independent companies that can be classified as *merchant wholesalers*, *agents*, or *brokers*. Beyond this simple distinction, the terminology surrounding wholesaling can be rather confusing. For instance, "agents" and "brokers" are also common in services retailing (including real estate agents and stockbrokers). Likewise, as mentioned earlier, many retail firms use "warehouse" or "wholesale" in their company or store names to convey low prices to consumers. Just remember the simple rule: When a marketing intermediary is selling to individual consumers, it's functioning as a retailer; when an intermediary sells to any type of organization, from a mom-and-pop store to the Pentagon, it's functioning as a wholesaler. (And just to add one more level of confusion to all this, some wholesaling firms now call themselves *supply chain* or *logistics* companies to reflect the broad range of services they offer.)

The majority of wholesalers are **merchant wholesalers**, independently owned businesses that buy from producers, take legal title to the goods, then resell them to retailers or to organizational buyers. For instance, Supervalu's (www.supervalu.com) grocery wholesaling operation is the intermediary between some 500 producers and more than 4,000 retailers.4 **Full-service merchant wholesalers** provide a wide variety of services, such as storage, selling, order processing, delivery, and promotional support. *Rack jobbers*, for example, are full-service merchant wholesalers that set up displays in retail outlets, stock inventory, and mark prices on merchandise displayed in a particular section of a store. **Limited-service merchant wholesalers**, on the other hand, provide fewer services. Natural resources such as lumber, grain, and coal are usually marketed through a class of limited-service wholesalers called *drop shippers*, which take ownership but not physical possession of the goods they handle.

Merchant wholesalers can also be distinguished by their customers. Supervalu and others that sell primarily to other intermediaries are usually known in the trade simply as *wholesalers*. In contrast, firms that sell goods to companies for use in their own products and operations are usually called *distributors*. For instance, Avnet (www.avnet.com) is a large distributor of electronic components. Avnet buys integrated circuits, wiring connectors, and thousands of other items from 300 different manufacturers, then resells these items to companies that build electrical and electronic products.5

Unlike merchant wholesalers, **agents and brokers** never actually own the products they handle, and they perform fewer services. Their primary role is to bring buyers and sellers together; they are generally paid a commission (a percentage of the money received) for arranging sales. Producers of industrial parts often sell to business customers through brokers. Manufacturers' representatives, another type of agent, sell various noncompeting products to customers in a specific region. By representing several manufacturers' products, these reps achieve enough volume to justify the cost of a direct sales call.

Retailers

In contrast to wholesalers, retailers are a highly visible element in the distribution chain. Retail stores provide many benefits to consumers. Some, such as Target, save people time and money by providing a huge assortment of merchandise and—increasingly, services—under one roof. Others, such as Trader Joe's, give shoppers access to goods and delicacies that they would have difficulty finding on their own. Still other retailers add convenience by diversifying their product lines, a practice known as **scrambled merchandising**. For example, you can rent videos, eat pizza, and buy T-shirts at Grand Union supermarkets, and you can buy cosmetics, stationery, and toys at Walgreens drugstores. Such mixed product assortments often cut across retail classifications and can blur store identities in the consumers' minds.

Many stores begin as discount operations and then upgrade their product offerings to become more like department stores in appearance, merchandise, and price. This process of

merchant wholesalers
Independent wholesalers that take legal title to goods they distribute

full-service merchant wholesalers
Merchant wholesalers that provide a wide variety of services to their customers, such as storage, delivery, and marketing support

limited-service merchant wholesalers
Merchant wholesalers that offer fewer services than full-service merchant wholesalers; they often specialize in particular markets, such as agriculture

agents and brokers
Independent wholesalers that do not take title to the goods they distribute but may or may not take possession of those goods

scrambled merchandising
Strategy of carrying merchandise that is ordinarily sold in a different type of outlet

Business Buzz
retail anthropology
Applying research methods from cultural anthropology to shopping behavior in the hope of increasing purchasing activity with store layouts, music, lighting, and other factors that promote buying

wheel of retailing
Evolutionary process by which stores that feature low prices gradually upgrade until they no longer appeal to price-sensitive shoppers and are replaced by new low-price competitors

store evolution, known as the **wheel of retailing**, follows a fairly predictable pattern: An innovative retailer with low operating costs attracts a following by offering low prices and limited service. As this store adds more services to broaden its appeal, its prices creep upward, opening the door for lower-priced competitors. Eventually, these competitors also upgrade their operations and are replaced by still other lower-priced stores that later follow the same upward pattern. For instance, Wal-Mart, which has reshaped retailing and much of the business world with low prices derived from its extraordinary abilities at cost control and efficiency, now finds itself facing new low-price competition from the likes of Dollar General and other so-called "dollar stores," which are multiplying across the retail landscape.[6]

Regardless of product offerings or target markets, all retailing efforts can be divided into *store* formats—based in physical store locations—and *nonstore* formats—which take place anywhere and everywhere outside of physical stores.

LEARNING OBJECTIVE 2

Identify the major types of both store and nonstore retailers

Store-Based Retailing Formats Stores may look similar on the outside to many consumers, but their marketing strategies and internal workings vary widely. Store retailers include everything from convenience stores to grocery stories to produce stands, but the most significant forms to study from a marketing perspective are *specialty stores*, *department stores*, *category killers*, and *discount stores*. These and other types that you're probably familiar with are listed in Exhibit 14.3.

Type of Retailer	Description	Examples
Online retailer	Web-based store offering anything from a single product line to comprehensive selections in multiple product areas; can be web-only (e.g., Amazon.com) or integrated with physical stores (e.g., REI.com)	REI.com Amazon.com
Category killer	Type of specialty store focusing on specific products on a giant scale and dominating retail sales in respective products categories	Office Depot Babies "R" Us Lowe's
Convenience store	Offers staple convenience goods, long service hours, quick checkouts	7-Eleven AM-PM
Department store	Offers a wide variety of merchandise under one roof in departmentalized sections and many customer services	Sears J.C. Penney Nordstrom
Discount store	Offers a wide variety of merchandise at low prices with relatively fewer services	Dollar General Target Wal-Mart
Factory/retail outlet	Large outlet store selling discontinued items, overruns, and factory seconds	Nordstrom Rack Nike outlet store
Hypermarket	Giant store offering both food and general merchandise at discount prices	Wal-Mart Supercenters Carrefour
Off-price store	Offers designer and brand-name merchandise at low prices and with relatively fewer services	T.J. Maxx Marshall's
Specialty store	Offers a complete selection in a narrow range of merchandise, often with extensive customer services	Payless Shoes REI
Supermarket	Large, self-service store offering a wide selection of food and nonfood merchandise	Kroger Safeway
Warehouse club	Large, warehouse-style store that sells food and general merchandise at discount prices; some require club membership	Sam's Club Costco

Exhibit 14.3
Types of Retail Stores
The term retailer *covers many types of outlets. This table shows some of the most common types.*

When you shop in a pet store, a shoe store, or a stationery store, for instance, you are in a **specialty store**—a store that carries only particular types of goods. The basic merchandising strategy of a specialty shop is to offer a limited number of product lines but an extensive selection of brands, styles, sizes, models, colors, materials, and prices within each line. The range and variety of specialty stores is practically endless, from florists and bridal shops to antique dealers and party-supply stores.

Department stores are the classic major retailers in the United States, with the likes of Bloomingdale's, Macy's, Nordstrom, Dillard's, Marshal Field, Kohl's, Sears, and J.C. Penney. These stores can have local, regional, or national presence and different price and quality offerings, but most tend to carry clothing, housewares, bedding, furniture in some cases, and similar items. Shopping malls often feature them as *anchors*, stores with wide appeal that mall developers hope will bring in business for all the shops in the mall.

Over the past few decades a new type of store has been reshaping retailing in a number of sectors. **Category killers** are superstores that dominate a particular product category by stocking every conceivable variety of merchandise in every important product line in that category. The Home Depot (tools and home improvement), Staples (office supplies), and Bed, Bath and Beyond (home products) are well-known category killers. These retailers are specialty stores in a sense, but their sheer size and market dominance—through which they occasionally drive specialty stores out of business—puts them in a category of their own.

Toys "R" Us, one of the stores that helped define the category killer label when it first appeared on the scene, is currently taking its own spin around the wheel of retailing as it finds itself under ferocious attack from Wal-Mart and other **discount stores**. Discounters come in various shapes and sizes, but they tend to be fairly large stores with a wide variety of aggressively priced merchandise. Some offer few services at all, whereas others offer a range of services from film processing to banking. Larger discount stores such as Wal-Mart and Kmart are often called *mass merchandisers*. The largest are known as *supercenters*, which combine discount stores with grocery stores. Wal-Mart now has more than 1,700 supercenters around the United States, with an average size of 190,000 square feet (in addition to 1,300 or so regular Wal-Marts), and is now one of the nation's largest food retailers.[7]

U.S. shoppers have migrated by the millions to both category killers and giant discounters—often known as "big box" stores—for the past several decades, but now some consumers are getting tired of trudging through stores the size of airplane hangars. To expand their customer base, some of the nation's leading discount stores and category killers—Wal-Mart, Home Depot, and Best Buy among them—are opening smaller versions of their big-box stores. At 41,000 square feet, Home Depot's new "urban format" design is less than one-third the size of the chain's typical orange warehouse.[8]

From specialty shops to classic department stores, many retail stores face a challenging future. For instance, some experts suggest that conventional music stores such as Tower Records will have to change dramatically if they hope to survive the onslaught of legitimate online music services such as RealNetwork's Rhapsody and Apple's iTunes, illegal file downloads and other piracy, online CD stores such as Amazon, and low-price competitors such as Wal-Mart.[9] And the shopping mall, that icon of American consumerism, is facing some changes as well. The department stores that typically anchor malls are losing market share to discounters and e-tailers, and as their number drops, some malls now look to Target and other discounters to serve as anchors.[10] In addition, there are simply too many malls in the United States, thanks to a decade or two of building that far outpaced the rate of population growth. The country now has about 1,800 malls, which industry watchers say is hundreds more than the consumer market can profitably support.[11]

E-Commerce and Other Nonstore Formats Nonstore retailing can trace its origin back to such classics as the mail-order catalogs sent out by Sears Roebuck and Montgomery Ward during the late 1800s, selling everything from household goods to ready-to-assemble houses. Today, Amazon, Apple iTunes, and thousands of other e-tailers carry on that tradition. Even venerable old Sears has a busy website (www.sears.com), and Montgomery Ward, which went bankrupt several years ago, has been reborn as an e-commerce operation (www.wards.com).

---

specialty store
Store that carries only a particular type of goods

department stores
Large stores that carry a variety of products in multiple categories, such as clothing, housewares, gifts, bedding, and furniture

category killers
Discount chains that sell only one category of products

discount stores
Retailers that sell a variety of goods below the market price by keeping their operating costs low

MINDING YOUR OWN BUSINESS

LOOKING FOR A GET-RICH-SLOW SCHEME?

So you wanna make a million on the Internet, eh? In the early days of e-commerce, *losing* a million (or two or three) was a lot easier than making a million. Many early e-tailers lost money for a variety of reasons, from suspect business models to supply-chain problems to a get-rich-quick mentality that overlooked the complexities of running a retail business.

Fortunately, you don't need to repeat any of those early mistakes. After several years of trial and error, today's successful online retailers have established workable models for turning a profit. Lesson number one: Making money online is no easier than making it anywhere else. Every time the Internet giveth (such as instant access to a huge market), it also taketh away (starting with price comparison websites that help customers find your competitors in an instant and virtually guarantee price wars in many categories). Lesson number two: Mimic the companies that have succeeded with these strategies:

- *Provide the information buyers need in order to make informed choices.* To take the mystery and uncertainty out of buying diamond jewelry, Blue Nile (www.bluenile.com) provides in-depth text and visuals to help people understand the complex system used to grade diamond quality. A number of clothing sites now use My Virtual Model (www.mvm.com) and similar technologies to let shoppers create 3-D versions of themselves in order to "try on" clothes.
- *Use the tools, from blogs to IM to chat rooms.* Clicks-and-bricks jewelry store owner Bill Pearlman (www.pearlmansjewelers.com) of Battle Creek, Michigan, says he can wait on 80 to 100 customers a day online—10 times as many as he can handle in his store location.
- *Offer unique or unusual goods and services.* Amazon.com, Wal-Mart.com, and other mass e-merchants are winning the competitive battle in mass-market products, but their business systems are geared around selling large quantities of mainstream products, which leaves plenty of room for e-tailers that offer unique or unusual products. Red Envelope (www.redenvelope.com) specializes in gift items that are difficult or impossible to find in stores. Wooden Toys and More (www.woodentoys-and-more.com) and Zebra Hall (www.zebrahall.com) are growing like crazy by offering toys that the big e-tailers would generally never carry. Timberland (www.timberland.com) lets customers design their own boots, complete with personalized monogramming.
- *Make it easy.* Customers who get confused or aggravated on your site will simply click away to a competitor. Amazon's "1-Click" ordering is a good example of making online shopping fast and simple, but you don't even need advanced technology—simple, customer-focused site design is the most important element.

As you can see, nothing on this list lends itself to a get-rich-quick mentality. However, by taking the time to do all these things well, you'll position yourself for long-term success.

Questions for Critical Thinking

1. Car buyers can get reams of information about new cars from sites such as Kelly Blue Book, www.kbb.com, and Edmunds.com, www.edmunds.com. As a local car dealer, what other information could you offer on your own site that would encourage shoppers to visit your dealership?
2. Why is it important for online retailers to create a pleasant online experience for shoppers?

Online sales are still less than 10 percent of U.S. retail sales and obviously can't replace all store-based retailing, but it's safe to say that e-tailing will continue to grow far into the future. "It's the new economic model," says John Seely Brown, an Amazon director.[12] That model is international in scope, too, as Amazon's multiple country-specific websites attest. However, any idea that U.S. e-commerce firms are going to dominate online retailing on a global scale is misguided. For instance, in the increasingly important realm of integrated online and offline operations, local companies with established store chains can have significant competitive advantages.[13]

Amazon's Jeff Bezos was a pioneer in recognizing the Internet's potential for making goods and services available to buyers. He reasoned that given a choice, many people would prefer the ease and convenience of online shopping to visiting a store every time they wanted to buy a book. Amazon has spent massive amounts of money for the past decade and has had more than its share of doubters, but Bezos and company are having the last laugh. Amazon not only helped redefine what retailing means, but it continues to expand far beyond books to dozens of product categories. Amazon isn't the only game on the web, of course; you can find thousands of e-tailers today selling every imaginable kind of product. Even luxury stores such as Barneys New York (www.barneys.com) and Bergdorf Goodman (www.bergdorfgoodman.com), which initially resisted the web, are now embracing it.[14]

Stores such as Amazon and Blue Nile, which sell exclusively online, are sometimes known as *clicks-only* or *pure-play* Internet retailers. Macy's, Nordstrom, and other stores that sell both online and offline are often called *clicks-and-bricks* or *clicks-and-mortar* (a wordplay on "bricks and mortar") operations. A clicks-and-bricks strategy integrates a company's website (clicks) with its existing physical stores (bricks) and other retail channels so that all logistics and marketing programs are shared. In a perfect mesh, all retail channels operate seamlessly so that consumers see the company as one operation. (This chapter's Case for Critical Thinking on page 481 offers a closer look at how REI has masterfully blended its offline and online operations.)

Meanwhile, the **mail-order firms** that inspired e-commerce are still going strong in many industries, as a look inside any mailbox in the country will verify. Attractive catalogs are a powerful marketing tool, but printing and mailing them is expensive, so many mail-order firms are working to integrate their catalog efforts with e-commerce.

Another common form of nonstore retailing is automatic vending, in which machines dispense everything from gasoline to candy bars to hot meals to train tickets. Vending machines are quite common in countries such as Japan, which boasts one vending machine for every 23 residents.[15] Interactive *kiosks*, freestanding electronic displays that combine elements of vending machines and e-commerce, also play a role in retailing. Located in showrooms or shopping areas, kiosks can inform customers about new products, availability, products, and store promotions; take and process orders; help people fill out applications; sell small items such as entertainment and transportation tickets; and even provide virtual product demonstrations. Scion customers, for example, can sample audio options, order accessories, and customize their cars using special Internet kiosks at Toyota dealerships.[16] Dell recently launched mall-based kiosks that allow customers to sample and select PCs, printers, and other peripheral devices. "We see [kiosks] as another marketing vehicle to extend the direct sales model," says a Dell senior vice president.[17]

Retailing Innovations The Internet is the biggest story to hit retailing in decades, but it's not the only area of innovation. Among the ongoing developments you can expect to encounter are multichannel retailing, hybrid store formats, retail theater, and pop-up stores:

- *Multichannel retailing.* The integration of offline and online operations is a good example of *multichannel retailing*, a term for any coordinated effort to reach customers through more than one retail channel. The upscale department store Saks Fifth Avenue (www.saksfifthavenue.com) reports that people who shop through multiple channels spend five times as much as those who shop through only one channel.[18] "This synchronization of multiple sales channels is absolutely the future of retail," says one industry consultant.[19]
- *Hybrid store formats.* The boundary-blurring tradition of scrambled merchandising is being taken to a new level in *hybrid retail formats*, which combine different types of retailers or different retail companies in the same facility. For instance, the MinuteClinics inside Target retail stores offer quick medical treatment for a limited number of common ailments such as strep throat and ear infections.[20] Staples, the leading category killer in office supplies, now has "Staples aisles" in more than 500 Stop & Shop and Giant-Landover grocery stores.[21]

LEARNING OBJECTIVE 3

Explain how a clicks-and-bricks distribution strategy differs from a clicks-only strategy

mail-order firms
Companies that sell products through catalogs and ship them directly to customers

Mall shoppers try out computers, printers, and other equipment at a Dell kiosk in Austin, Texas.

*   ***Retail theater.*** Increasingly, retail stores aren't just places to buy things; they're becoming places to research new technologies, learn about cooking, engage in arts and crafts, or simply be entertained for a few minutes while going through the drudgery of picking out the week's groceries—a tactic known as **retail theater**. At the Samsung Experience in New York City, for example, customers can explore the future of electronic gadgetry by playing around with some 300 Samsung products and prototypes.[22] Apple's newest outlets look more like art galleries than stores, and they've even become hot places to meet people and to spot celebrities.[23]

retail theater
The addition of entertainment or education aspects to the retail experience

*   ***Pop-up stores.*** The lifecycle of retail stores is usually measured in decades, but pop-up stores are designed to last as little as a week. As a combination of retail channel and marketing event, pop-ups appear in such places as empty storefronts, parking lots, and open spaces inside malls. For instance, a pop-up called Vacant appears for anywhere from a week to a month in an unadvertised location (you have to be on a newsletter mailing list or get the news by word of mouth), selling trendy clothing and footwear brands.[24]

No, this isn't some trendy new restaurant—it's a grocery store. Whole Foods Markets aims to make food shopping more enjoyable by making the retail environment more interesting and more pleasant.

> **CRITICAL THINKING CHECKPOINT**
> 1. How can Costco be both a wholesaler and a retailer at the same time?
> 2. Moving into the future, what effect is online retailing likely to have on the over-supply of retail store space in the United States?
> 3. Would it ever make sense for Amazon to open retail stores? Why or why not?

Setting Distribution Strategies

Should you sell directly to end users or rely on intermediaries? Which intermediaries should you choose? Should you try to sell your product in every available outlet or limit its distribution to a few exclusive outlets? Should you use more than one channel? These are some of the critical decisions that managers face when designing and selecting marketing channels for any product.

Building an effective channel system can take years and, as with all marketing relationships, requires commitment. Successful *trading partners*, a general term for any group of companies involved in a distribution network, work to establish relationships that are mutually beneficial and built on trust. For instance, General Motors has to trust that its dealerships (which are independent franchises, incidentally) will protect the reputation of the various GM brands with ethical sales practices and effective customer service. Conversely, dealers need to know that they can count on GM for quality cars in the right quantities and the training needed to sell and service those cars effectively.

The ideal **distribution mix**—number and type of intermediaries—varies widely from industry to industry and even from company to company within the same industry. For example, Black & Decker (www.blackanddecker.com) distributes its power tools through hundreds of hardware stores and home centers such as Lowe's and Home Depot along with a wide range of online retailers, including Amazon.com.[25] Black & Decker sells to both consumers and professionals, it wants to reach a broad audience, and its products don't require extensive support from retailers, so these mass market intermediaries make perfect sense. In contrast, Felder (www.felder.co.at), an Austrian company that manufactures top-of-the line woodworking machines for professional use, makes its products available through only two company-owned stores in the entire United States.[26]

distribution mix Combination of intermediaries and channels a producer uses to get a product to end customers

Black & Decker and Felder, like all producers, reach their respective distribution mix decisions by considering a wide variety of factors:

- *Customer needs and expectations.* How do customers want and expect to purchase your product? If you have a food product, for example, are customers willing to drive to specialty stores to buy it, or does it need to be available in their regular grocery stores if you're to have any hope of selling it? Do customers expect to test or try on products before they buy?
- *Product support requirements.* Consider a mass spectrometer, the laboratory instrument you see being used in TV shows such as *CSI* to identify unknown substances found at crime scenes. In real life, these complex machines require significant technical skills to sell and to support after the sale, which is why companies that make them, such as Agilent Technologies (www.agilent.com) generally sell them through their own salesforces.
- *Segmentation, targeting, and positioning.* Just as producers segment markets, choose target segments, and try to position their products within those segments, marketing intermediaries make strategic marketing decisions regarding their own businesses. For instance, Super Jock'n Jill, www.jocknjill.com, an athletic shoe retailer in Seattle, focuses on quality running shoes for people who are serious about physical fitness.[27] If you produce mass-market sneakers that are more about fashion than performance, this store won't help you reach your target audience.
- *Competitors' distribution channels.* In some industries, you'll wage an endless battle with your competitors within the distribution network. Food producers, for example,

LEARNING OBJECTIVE 4

Discuss the key factors that marketers should consider when choosing distribution channels

INNOVATING FOR BUSINESS SUCCESS

NAUTILUS BULKS UP THROUGH MULTIPLE CHANNELS

Adults in over half of all U.S. households own at least one piece of exercise equipment, and many of these home gyms contain equipment from Nautilus, which markets, develops, and manufactures health and fitness products under four well-known brands: Bowflex, Nautilus, Schwinn, and StairMaster.

Founded in 1986 as Bowflex of America, the company initially tried to sell its unusual-looking machine (which uses flexible resistance rods instead of weights) through traditional retail stores. However, the product proved to need more hands-on selling and support assistance than most stores could provide, so Bowflex switched to a direct-to-consumer mode featuring TV commercials and infomercials that invited potential buyers to contact the company directly. The new approach was a smashing success, and sales doubled every year—generating enough profits to help Bowflex expand even further through acquisitions, purchasing the industry classic Nautilus International in 1999, Schwinn Fitness in 2001, and StairMaster in 2002. By that point, sales had soared to nearly $600 million. Playing on the strength of the Nautilus brand name, Bowflex changed the company name to Nautilus, too.

Nautilus now uses a variety of distribution channels, with a mix tuned to the unique needs and opportunities of each brand. For example, Nautilus, Schwinn, and StairMaster commercial fitness equipment is sold to health clubs, universities, and other institutions through the company's own salesforce and via selected dealers. A diverse line of consumer fitness equipment under the same three brands is sold through a network of distributors and specialty dealers. And the product that was originally too unusual to sell through normal retail channels is now available in mainstream retailers nationwide, too; a version of the Bowflex is now sold through sporting goods stores.

However, the direct channel remains a key strategy for most of the Bowflex product line, with a finely tuned combination of television commercials, infomercials, response mailings, the Internet, toll-free call centers, and outbound telemarketing. The direct marketing process begins with thorough market research, centered on the company's extensive database of existing and potential customers. Next, it uses accumulated business intelligence and calculated estimates of consumer response rates to place carefully designed and targeted TV commercials and infomercials. A direct-selling team takes these leads and promotes the Bowflex brand one-on-one.

Overall, Nautilus's sales are currently split about 50/50 between direct to consumer and a variety of retailing channels, but executives hope to move retail sales up to 65 percent. As U.S. consumers pursue that never-ending quest to get in shape, they can find a Nautilus product at a retailer nearby to help.

Questions for Critical Thinking

1. How did Nautilus more fully utilize the distribution channels for the brands it acquired?
2. For the Bowflex line, what supporting activities make the direct channel so successful?

must compete with one another for the limited space available in grocery store shelves. In other cases, finding a new or unexpected channel might be the way to go.

- *The established patterns with your industry.* Over the years, all industries develop certain patterns of distribution. If you try to "buck the system," you might uncover a profitable new opportunity—or you might fail to reach your target customers entirely.

Specific industries have other considerations as well, such as the need to get perishable food items to retail locations quickly or government regulations that dictate how and where certain products (hazardous chemicals and pharmaceuticals, for example) can be sold. In addition, every manager involved in distribution channels needs to be aware of *channel length*, *market coverage*, *cost*, *control*, and *channel conflict*, all of which are addressed in the following sections. Exhibit 14.4 offers a summary of the major factors to consider regarding distribution channels.

Exhibit 14.4

Factors That Influence Distribution Channel Choices

Designing a distribution mix is rarely a simple task; here are some of the most important factors to consider.

Factor	Issues to Consider
Customer needs and expectations	Where are customers likely to look for your products? How much customer service do they expect from the channel? Can you make your offering more attractive by choosing an unconventional channel?
Product support requirements	How much training do salespeople need to present your products successfully? How much after-sale support is required? Who will answer questions when things go wrong?
Positioning and targeting	Which intermediaries—if any—can present your products to target customers while maintaining your positioning strategy?
Competitors' channels	Which channels do your competitors use? Do you need to use the same channels in order to reach your target customers or can you use different channels to distinguish yourself?
Established channel structure	Which intermediaries are already in place? Can you take advantage of them or do you need to find or create alternatives? Will retailers demand that you use specific wholesalers or distributors?
Channel length	Do you want to deal directly with customers? *Can* you? Do you need to engage other intermediaries to perform vital functions?
Market coverage	Are you going for intensive, selective, or exclusive distribution? Are the right intermediaries available in your target markets? Can they handle the volumes at which you hope to sell?
Cost	How much will intermediaries add to the price that final customers will eventually pay? Put another way, how much of a discount from the retail price will intermediaries expect from you?
Control	How much control do you need to maintain as products move through the channel—and how much can you expect to maintain with each potential intermediary? What happens if you lose control?
Channel conflict	What are the potential sources of channel conflict, both now and in the future? If such conflict can't be avoided, how will you minimize its effect?

Channel Length

As you no doubt sense by now, distribution channels come in all shapes and sizes. Some channels are short and simple; others are long and complex. Many businesses purchase goods they use in their operations directly from producers, so those distribution channels are short. Boeing, for example, purchases many of the parts and supplies it needs to build airplanes directly from over 15,000 companies, such as C&D Aerospace (stowage bins, lavatories, and baggage compartment liners) and Crissair (fuel-system components).[28] In contrast, the channels for consumer goods are usually longer and more complex (see Exhibit 14.5). The four primary channels for consumer goods are

- *Producer to consumer.* Producers that sell directly to consumers through catalogs, telemarketing, infomercials, and the Internet are using the shortest, simplest distribution channel. Dell is an excellent example of a company using a producer-to-consumer channel. By selling directly to consumers, Dell gains more control over pricing, promotion, service, and delivery. Although this approach eliminates payments to channel members, it also forces producers to handle distribution functions such as storing inventory and delivering products.

Exhibit 14.5
Common Distribution Channel Models
Producers of consumer and business goods and services must analyze the alternative channels of distribution available for their products so they can select the channels that best meet their marketing objectives and their customers' needs.

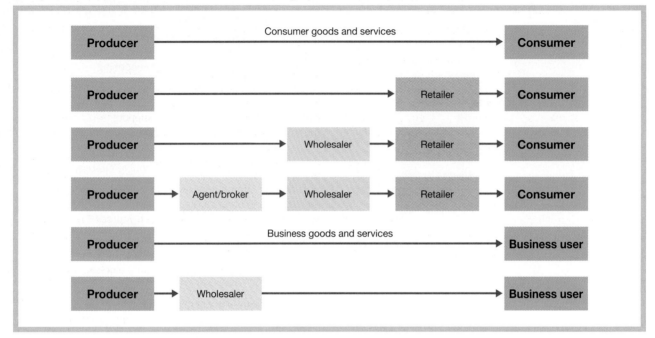

- *Producer to retailer to consumer.* Many producers create longer channels by selling their products to retailers, who then resell them to consumers. Weber grills, Benjamin Moore paint, and GE light bulbs are typical of the many products distributed in this way.
- *Producer to wholesaler to retailer to consumer.* Most manufacturers of supermarket and pharmaceutical items rely on longer channels when selling to such retailers as Albertsons, Safeway, and Walgreens. They sell their products to wholesalers such as Supervalu, which in turn sell to the retailers. This approach works particularly well for small producers that lack the resources to sell or deliver merchandise to individual retail sites. It is also beneficial to retailers that lack the space to store container-size shipments of each product they sell.
- *Producer to agent/broker to wholesaler to retailer to consumer.* Additional channel levels are common in certain industries, such as agriculture, where specialists are required to negotiate transactions or to perform interim functions such as sorting, grading, or subdividing the goods.

Market Coverage

The appropriate market coverage—the number of wholesalers or retailers that will carry a product—depends on a number of factors in the marketing strategy. Inexpensive convenience goods or organizational supplies such as computer paper and pens sell best if they are available in as many outlets as possible. Such **intensive distribution** requires wholesalers and retailers of many types. In contrast, shopping goods (goods that require some thought before being purchased) such as Sub-Zero refrigerators require different market coverage, because customers shop for such products by comparing features and prices. For these items, the best strategy is usually **selective distribution**, selling through a limited number of outlets that can give the product adequate sales and service support. If producers of expensive specialty or technical products do not sell directly to customers, they may choose **exclusive distribution**, offering products in only one outlet in each market area.

LEARNING OBJECTIVE 5

Differentiate between intensive, selective, and exclusive distribution strategies

intensive distribution
Market coverage strategy that tries to place a product in as many outlets as possible

selective distribution
Market coverage strategy that uses a limited number of outlets to distribute products

exclusive distribution
Market coverage strategy that gives intermediaries exclusive rights to sell a product in a specific geographical area

LEARNING FROM BUSINESS BLUNDERS

OOPS Krispy Kreme Doughnuts stormed out of its home base in Winston-Salem, North Carolina, and swept across the country, opening stores to accommodate hungry crowds who had heard about the wonders of the fresh-made pastries. In Rochester, New York, a hundred people waited in a predawn snowstorm to be the first in the city to buy the gooey sweet treats. Before long, though, it seemed the once-rare goodies were available everywhere, from hundreds of Krispy Kreme franchise outlets to Wal-Marts to truck stops. The fad cooled down, as fads always do, but the receding revenue tide exposed some questionable accounting practices, too. As of mid-2005, the company was battling trouble on multiple fronts: an SEC investigation into those accounting practices, a Justice Department inquiry that could lead to criminal charges, and lawsuits from shareholders claiming they'd been misled about earnings. Sales are down, and bankruptcy appears to be a distinct possibility.

WHAT YOU CAN LEARN As is too often the case for public companies, Krispy Kreme seems to have stepped too hard on the gas pedal in order to impress investors. By expanding into too many retail outlets too quickly—and particularly into retail stores, gas stations, and other places where it sold cold, boxed doughnuts instead of the hot, fresh-baked delicacies it was known for—it devalued the special appeal of the brand. Overexpansion was not the direct cause of the company's current financial crisis, but it no doubt put pressure on executives to keep showing strong financial results to the public. The investigations continue, but suspicions run high that doughnuts weren't the only things being cooked at Krispy Kreme.

Cost

Costs play a major role in determining channel selection. It takes money to perform all the functions that are handled by intermediaries. Small or new companies often cannot afford to hire a salesforce large enough to sell directly to end users or to call on a host of retail outlets. Neither can they afford to build large warehouses and distribution centers to store large shipments of goods. These firms need the help of intermediaries, who can spread the cost of such activities across a number of products. Of course, intermediaries don't perform all these services for free; to cover their costs and turn a profit, they expect to pay you less, sometimes far less, than their customers will pay them.

Control

A third issue to consider when selecting distribution channels is control over how, where, when, and for how much your product is sold. Longer distribution channels mean less control for producers, who become increasingly distant from sellers and buyers as the number of intermediaries multiplies. Shorter distribution channels, on the other hand, give producers more control over how the goods are sold in the market, but there is a trade-off. Concentrating too many distribution functions in the hands of too few intermediaries can increase the negotiating power of these firms.

Control becomes critical when a firm's reputation is at stake. For instance, a designer of high-priced purses, such as Kate Spade or Louis Vuitton, generally limits distribution to exclusive boutiques or high-end retail stores such as Neiman Marcus. If the purses were sold by mid-priced retailers such as J.C. Penney, the brand could lose some of its appeal. Similarly, producers of complex technical equipment don't want their products handled by unqualified intermediaries that can't provide adequate customer service.

Channel Conflict

Because the success of individual channel members depends on the overall channel success, ideally all channel members should work together smoothly. However, individual channel members must also run their own businesses profitably, which means that they often disagree on the roles each member should play. Such disagreements create **channel conflict**.[29]

channel conflict
Disagreement or tension between two or more members in a distribution channel, usually resulting from competition to reach the same group of customers

**LEARNING
OBJECTIVE 6**

Explain why channel
conflict can be such
a serious problem for
both producers and
intermediaries

Channel conflict may arise when producers provide inadequate support to their channel partners, when markets are oversaturated with intermediaries, or when producers try to expand sales by adding additional channels, either on their own or through new intermediaries. Such moves expand a manufacturer's reach into target markets but create new competition for its original distribution channel partners. In recent years, this sort of conflict has arisen in two areas in particular. The first occurs when manufacturers that have been selling through independent dealers start selling through mass discounters. For instance, Goodyear angered many of the independent dealers that carried its tires for years when it tried to increase sales by adding Wal-Mart, Sam's Club, and other discounters to its distribution mix. To compensate for the loss of revenue, many of the dealers added other tire brands, and some dropped Goodyear entirely. Under a new CEO, the company is working hard to repair the damage. "We lost sight of the fact that it's in our interest that our dealers succeed," admits a Goodyear executive.[30]

Retailers stuck in such situations often suffer a double whammy, in fact: Not only do they lose sales to discounters and online merchants but often wind up helplessly helping their new competitors make those sales. Independent dealers and specialty retailers frequently invest considerable time and money in showrooms and employee training in order to demonstrate new products to potential buyers, but many consumers take advantage of this situation by previewing products at these full-service retailers, then buying from discounters or e-tailers. In other words, the independents bear much of the cost of the sale, but the discounters get all of the revenue. To help minimize this problem, some manufacturers now create different product versions for different channels. For instance, Toro sells its lower-priced products through discount stores but reserves its high-end lawn equipment for independent dealers.[31]

The second competition conflict occurs when producers that have been selling through any combination of channels start selling directly to end customers via the Internet. Such was the case when Levi Strauss decided to sell its jeans on the company website. Worried that they might lose jeans sales, retail channel members protested. Some even fought back by giving Levi's jeans less prominent display space in their stores. Eventually Levi caved in to retailer pressure and stopped selling directly to consumers via its website.[32] Like Levi, a number of manufacturers that had hoped the Internet might let them reduce their dependence on traditional distribution channels have found that a cooperative effort that uses the web to everyone's benefit makes more sense.[33]

CRITICAL THINKING CHECKPOINT

1. Would you advise Dell to take advantage of its well-oiled producer-to-consumer distribution model by expanding beyond computers and related products to offer its customer base such products as car stereos or musical instruments (made by other companies in both cases)? Why or why not?
2. Does exclusive distribution limit the potential size of manufacturer's market? Why or why not?
3. Is the continuing growth of e-commerce likely to increase or decrease instances of channel conflict? Explain your answer.

**LEARNING
OBJECTIVE 7**

Highlight the major
components of a physical
distribution process and
the key factors to consider
when choosing a mode of
outbound transportation

physical distribution
*All the activities required
to move finished products
from the producer to the
consumer*

Managing Physical Distribution

Developing a distribution strategy involves more than selecting the most effective channels for selling your products. Companies must also decide on the best way to move goods through the channels so that they are available to the customers at the right place, at the right time, and in the right amount. **Physical distribution** encompasses all the activities required to move finished products from the producer to the consumer, including forecasting, order processing, inventory control, warehousing, materials handling, and outbound transportation (see Exhibit 14.6).

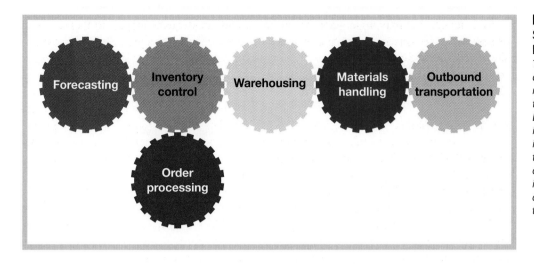

Exhibit 14.6
Steps in the Physical Distribution Process
The phases of a distribution system should mesh as smoothly as the cogs in a machine. Because the steps are interrelated, a change in one phase can affect the other phases. The objective of the process is to provide a target level of customer service at the lowest overall cost.

The physical movement of goods may not appear glamorous or exciting, but it is vital to most every company's success. Moreover, physical distribution isn't getting any easier. The surge of globalized manufacturing driven by outsourcing is putting heavy demands on the transportation infrastructure, and no place demonstrates this more dramatically than the port facilities at Los Angeles and Long Beach, California. More than 40 percent of the goods brought into the United States pass through these two ports, and when they have trouble, from the annual holiday rush to occasional labor disputes, the whole country has trouble. In 2004, MGA Entertainment lost $40 million when it couldn't get its hot-selling Bratz dolls into the country in time for holiday gift buying. Once things do get through port, the story doesn't always improve, either. For instance, rail travel between Los Angeles and Chicago, a major redistribution point in the middle of the country, is considerably slower now than it was 40 years ago. More than a few companies are starting to wonder if outsourcing manufacturing to Asia is worth all the costs and headaches.[34]

Moreover, so many physical distribution systems are burdened with duplication and inefficiency that in industry after industry executives have been placing one item near the top of the corporate agenda: **logistics**—the planning and movement of goods and information throughout the supply chain. Hard pressed to knock out competitors on quality or price, companies are trying to gain an edge by streamlining processes that traverse companies and continents—no easy task, although the payback can be enormous. The key to success in managing physical distribution is to coordinate the activities of everyone involved, from the sales staff who are trying to satisfy demanding customers to the production staff who are trying to manage factory workloads. The overriding objective should be to achieve a competitive level of *customer-service standards* (the quality of service that a firm provides for its customers) at the lowest total cost. In general, as the level of service improves, the cost of distribution increases. A producer must analyze whether it is worthwhile to deliver the product in, say, three days as opposed to five, if doing so increases the price of the item.

This type of trade-off can be difficult because the components of a physical distribution process are all interrelated. A change in one affects the others. For example, if you use slower forms of transportation, you reduce your shipping costs, but you probably increase your storage costs. Similarly, if you reduce the level of inventory to cut your storage costs, you run the risk of being unable to fill orders in a timely fashion. The trick is to optimize the total cost of achieving the desired level of service. This optimization requires a careful analysis of each component in the distribution process in relation to every other component. Let's take a closer look at each of these components.

logistics
The planning, movement, and flow of goods and related information throughout the supply chain

In-House Operations

The components of the distribution process can be divided into in-house operations and outbound transportation. The in-house steps include forecasting, order processing, inventory control, warehousing, and materials handling.

TECHNOLOGIES THAT ARE REVOLUTIONIZING BUSINESS | Supply-Chain Integration Standards

How do Amazon's computers know which book to reorder from its suppliers when you order one from Amazon's website? Who's going to make sure RFID readers know how to detect RFID tags (Chapter 4) accurately and make sure databases know what to do with the data? How does every one of the millions of barcodes now in use get the right combination of black and white stripes? All these decisions are guided by industry groups that define the standards and technologies that make sure supply chains work together, from producers to wholesalers to retailers.

HOW THEY'RE CHANGING BUSINESS

From a consumer's point of view, this standardization is probably the least exciting technology mentioned in this entire book, but global business simply wouldn't work without it—and consumers benefit from lower prices and better service. Moving forward, advances in supply-chain integration promise to remove billions of dollars of errors and inefficiencies from supply chains in many industries.

WHERE YOU CAN LEARN MORE

Much of the development of supply-chain standards takes place under the watchful eye of the Uniform Code Council, www.uc-council.org, and EPC Global, www.epcglobalus.org, two nonprofit organizations that oversee UPC barcodes, electronic product codes (EPC), RFID standards, the RosettaNet e-business standards, and the Global Data Synchronization Network (which helps manufacturers and retailers "stay on the same page" regarding product data).

Forecasting To control the flow of products through the distribution system, a firm must have an accurate estimate of demand. To some degree, historical data can be used to project future sales; however, the firm must also consider the impact of unusual events (such as special promotions) that might temporarily boost demand. For example, if Costco decided to offer a special discount price on television sets during September, management would need to project how many additional sets will be sold because of the sale and order enough sets so that they arrive in time for the promotion.

order processing
Functions involved in preparing and receiving an order

Order Processing **Order processing** involves preparing orders for shipment and receiving orders when shipments arrive. It includes a number of activities, such as checking the customer's credit, recording the sale, making the appropriate accounting entries, arranging for the item to be shipped, adjusting the inventory records, and billing the customer. Because order processing involves direct interaction with the customer, it affects a company's reputation for customer service. Most companies establish standards for filling orders within a specified time period.

Inventory Control As Chapter 9 discusses, in an ideal world a company would always have just the right amount of goods on hand to fill the orders it receives. In reality, however, inventory and sales are seldom in perfect balance. Most firms like to build a supply of finished goods so that they can fill orders in a timely fashion. But how much inventory is enough? If your inventory is too large, you incur extra expenses for storage space, handling, insurance, and taxes; you also run the risk of product obsolescence. On the other hand, if your inventory is too low, you may lose sales when the product is not in stock. The objective of inventory control is to resolve these issues. Inventory managers decide how much product to keep on hand and when to replenish the supply of goods in inventory. They also decide how to allocate products to customers if orders exceed supply.

warehouse
Facility for storing inventory

distribution centers
Warehouse facilities that specialize in collecting and shipping merchandise

Warehousing Products held in inventory are physically stored in a **warehouse**, which may be owned by the manufacturer, by an intermediary, or by a private company that leases space to others. Some warehouses are almost purely holding facilities, in which goods are stored for relatively long periods. Other warehouses, known as **distribution centers**, serve as command posts for moving products to customers. In a typical distribution center, goods produced at a variety of locations are collected, sorted, coded, and redistributed to fill customer orders. Leading-edge distribution centers use some of the most advanced technologies in business today, including satellite navigation and communication, voice-activated computers, wireless data services, machine vision, robots, and planning software that relies on artificial intelligence.

Materials Handling An important part of warehousing activities is **materials handling**, the movement of goods within and between physical distribution facilities. One main area of concern is storage method—whether to keep supplies and finished goods in individual packages, in large boxes, or in sealed shipping containers. The choice of storage method depends on how the product is shipped, in what quantities, and to which locations. For example, a company that typically sends small quantities of goods to widely scattered customers wouldn't want to use large containers. Materials handling also involves keeping track of inventory so that the company knows where in the distribution process its goods are located and when they need to be moved.

materials handling
Movement of goods within a firm's warehouse terminal, factory, or store

Outbound Transportation

For any business, the cost of transportation is normally the largest single item in the overall cost of physical distribution. When choosing a mode of transportation, managers must also evaluate other marketing issues: storage, financing, sales, inventory size, speed, product perishability, dependability, flexibility, and convenience—to name a few. The goal is to maximize the efficiency of the entire distribution process while minimizing overall cost. Each of the five major modes of transportation has distinct advantages and disadvantages:

- *Rail.* Railroads can carry heavier and more diverse cargo and a larger volume of goods than any other mode of transportation. However, trains are constrained to tracks, so they can rarely deliver goods directly to customers.
- *Truck.* Trucks are a preferred form of transportation for two reasons: (1) the convenience of door-to-door delivery, and (2) the ease and efficiency of travel on public highways, which do not require the use of expensive terminals or the execution of right-of-way agreements (customary for air and rail transportation). Trucks cannot, however, carry all types of cargo cost effectively; for example, commodities such as steel and coal are too large and heavy.
- *Water.* The cheapest method of transportation is via water, and is the preferred method for such low-cost bulk items as oil, coal, ore, cotton, and lumber. However, ships are slow, and

Moving goods quickly, accurately, and safely is a strategic priority for every company that depends on physical distribution.

service to any given location is infrequent. Furthermore, another form of transportation is usually needed to complete delivery to the final destination, as it is for rail.

- *Air.* Air transportation offers the advantage of speed—but at a price. Airports are not always convenient to the customers. Moreover, air transport imposes limitations on the size, shape, and weight of shipments and is the least dependable and most expensive form of transportation. Weather may cause flight cancellations (although air freight specialists such as FedEx are so good at weather forecasting that they rarely experience such delays), and even minor repairs may lead to serious delays. To give you an idea of how expensive air freight can be, delivering a shipping container full of goods from Los Angeles to Dallas costs $900 by rail, $4,000 by truck, and $40,000 by air.[35] But when speed is a priority, air is usually the only way to go.

- *Pipeline.* For products such as gasoline, natural gas, and coal or wood chips (suspended in liquid), pipelines are an effective mode of transportation. Although they are expensive to build, they are extremely economical to operate and maintain. The downside is transportation via pipeline is slow (three to four miles per hour), and routes are inflexible.

Shippers can combine the benefits of each mode by using *intermodal transportation* (a combination of multiple modes). For instance, a company may ship goods in over-the-road trailers that ride part of the way on flat bed railroad freight cars and part of the way on highways.

CRITICAL THINKING CHECKPOINT

1. If another high-tech company approached Dell with a partnership proposal to build and operate several distribution centers that would ship both companies' products to customers, what would you advise Dell to do? Why?
2. Given the huge volume of small packages that Amazon ships every year, should it consider starting its own transportation company instead of giving all that business to FedEx and other shipping companies? Why or why not?
3. Which mode of transportation would you use to transport clothes made in Asia to retail outlets in North America? Why?

CHECKLIST: Apply These Ideas When You're the Boss

✓ Distribution may not have the glamour of other areas of business, but don't make the mistake of overlooking its importance; top executives at successful companies such as Amazon devote considerable time and energy to distribution issues.

✓ No matter what your role is in the channel—manufacturer, wholesaler, distributor, or retailer—use the opportunity to learn from your trading partners; for instance, manufacturers can learn a lot about customer needs and behaviors by listening to retailers.

✓ If you're a manufacturer currently selling through marketing intermediaries and you're tempted by the possibility of selling directly to consumers online, think twice about the channel conflict this will create; the growth in sales through your new channel might not make up for the losses you'll experience in the existing channels.

✓ Look for opportunities in distribution innovation; can you deliver value to customers in ways that nobody else has thought of yet?

✓ Remember that e-commerce is only the visible surface of a business; without distribution systems in place to transfer tangible value to the customer (assuming you're not in a purely digital business), the business isn't going anywhere.

Summary of Learning Objectives

1 **Explain the role of marketing intermediaries in contemporary business, and list the seven primary functions that intermediaries can perform.** Intermediaries can be responsible for any and all aspects of distribution, one of the key elements in any firm's marketing mix. The two major categories are *wholesalers*, which buy from producers and sell to retailers, to other wholesalers, and to organizational customers such as businesses, government agencies, and institutions, and *retailers*, which buy from producers or wholesalers and sell the products to the final consumers. These marketing intermediaries bring products to market and help ensure that the goods and services are available in the right time, place, and amount. Depending on their position in the channel, intermediaries can perform up to seven key functions: matching buyers and sellers; providing market information; providing promotional and sales support; sorting, standardizing, and dividing merchandise; transporting and storing the product; assuming risks; and providing financing.

2 **Identify the major types of both store and nonstore retailers.** Retailers come in many shapes and sizes, but the four more significant store formats are specialty stores, department stores, category killers, and discount stores. The two most widely known nonstore retailers are online retailers (often called e-tailers) and mail-order firms.

3 **Explain how a clicks-and-bricks distribution strategy differs from a clicks-only strategy.** Clicks and bricks, or the integration of e-commerce with physical retail in a multichannel strategy, provides customers with more shopping options. Essentially, customers can get what they want, where they want it, and when they want it. A clicks-and-bricks approach also facilitates the product return process. Customers who buy on the web can return unwanted merchandise to physical stores. Traditional retailers benefit from a clicks-and-bricks strategy by using their existing name recognition and goodwill to attract e-commerce customers. Moreover, studies show that customers who shop at both a company's website and physical stores tend to spend more. In contrast, in a click-only approach, the company's presence is entirely virtual, with no physical locations to facilitate product demonstrations, returns, or customer service.

4 **Discuss the key factors that marketers should consider when choosing distribution channels.** Defining a distribution strategy requires consideration of such issues as customer needs and expectations; product support requirements; segmentation, targeting, and positioning objectives; competitors' distribution mixes; established distribution patterns within a given industry; channel length, market coverage needs (intense, selective, or exclusive), costs, control issues, and the potential for channel conflict.

5 **Differentiate between intensive, selective, and exclusive distribution strategies.** With an intensive distribution strategy, a company attempts to saturate the market with its products by offering them in every available outlet. Companies that use a more selective approach to distribution choose a limited number of retailers that can adequately support the product. Firms that use exclusive distribution grant a single wholesaler or retailer the exclusive right to sell the product within a given geographic area.

6 **Explain why channel conflict can be such a serious problem for both producers and intermediaries.** Channel conflict can raise costs and lower revenues and profits for everyone involved. Moreover, it can damage relationships that companies may have spent years or decades fostering and developing. Channel conflict can be particularly damaging to intermediaries that rely on sales of a particular producer's products because it creates sources of competition that didn't exist before.

7 **Highlight the major components of a physical distribution process and the key factors to consider when choosing a mode of outbound transportation.** The major components of a firm's distribution process are order processing, inventory control, warehousing, materials handling, and outbound transportation. When choosing the best method of outbound transportation, such as truck, rail, ship, airplane, and pipeline, you should consider cost, storage, sales, inventory size, speed, product perishability, dependability, flexibility, and convenience.

Costco: What's Next?

Costco is rolling through its third decade with strong financial health, a dominant market position, and millions of consumers and business customers that rely on Costco bargains. International expansion is one of the items on Costco's strategic menu for the next few years, although the company will maintain a sensible pace of only a few new international stores per year, including additional stores in Asia and expansion into Australia and across Europe. For instance, the company thinks Taiwan could support 20 Costco stores and Japan could support 50, but finding enough land for the giant footprint of a warehouse store—typically 15 acres—that is near population centers but not in areas with zoning regulations that prohibit big-box retailers is a particular challenge in some of these countries.

Critical Thinking Questions

1. If customers repeatedly ask Costco to carry certain items that the company thinks are outside its price/quality "comfort zone" (because they're too expensive or not of high enough quality), should it give in and carry the items? Why or why not?

2. Most of the items on Costco's website are available only through Costco; should it expand its online product selection to include more commonly available products, since an online store doesn't have the physical constraints of a brick-and-mortar location? Why or why not?

3. If Costco can't find enough land in, say, Japan, to build its usual store format, should it leverage the Costco brand name anyway and build something such as conventional department stores or grocery stores in these areas? Why or why not?

Learn More Online

Visit the Costco website by clicking on the hotlink at Chapter 14 of this text's website at **www.prenhall.com/bovee**. What evidence do you see of clicks-and-bricks integration? Are nonmembers allowed to make purchases online? How does the online experience compare to retailers such as eToys (**www.etoys.com**) or Apple iTunes (**www.itunes.com**), which sell exclusively online?

Key Terms

agents and brokers (461)
category killers (463)
channel conflict (471)
department stores (463)
discount stores (463)
distribution centers (474)
distribution mix (467)
distribution strategy (458)
exclusive distribution (470)
full-service merchant
   wholesalers (461)

intensive distribution (470)
limited-service merchant
   wholesalers (461)
logistics (473)
mail-order firms (465)
marketing intermediaries (459)
materials handling (475)
merchant wholesalers (461)
order processing (474)
physical distribution (472)

retail theater (466)
retailers (459)
scrambled merchandising (461)
selective distribution (470)
specialty store (463)
warehouse (474)
wheel of retailing (462)
wholesalers (459)

Test Your Knowledge

Questions for Review

1. What is a distribution channel?
2. What are the two main types of intermediaries and how do they differ?
3. What forms of utility do intermediaries create?
4. What are some of the main causes of channel conflict?
5. How does a specialty store differ from a category killer and a discount store?

Questions for Analysis

6. How does the presence of intermediaries in the distribution channel affect the price of products?
7. What are some of the challenges facing retailers and wholesalers today?
8. What trade-offs must you consider when adopting a physical distribution system?
9. If a manufacturer starts to sell its goods on its company website, why might this create channel conflict?
10. **Ethical Considerations.** Manufacturers that have been selling to wholesalers and other intermediaries occasionally decide to start selling directly to end customers, which of course puts them in competition with the channel partners that have been selling for them. Even if this is legal, do you think such moves are ethical? Why or why not?

Questions for Application

11. Imagine that you own a small specialty store selling handcrafted clothing and jewelry. What are some of the nonstore retail options you might explore to increase sales? What are the advantages and disadvantages of each option?
12. Compare the prices of three products offered at a retail outlet with the prices charged if you purchase those products by mail order (catalog or phone) or over the Internet. Be sure to include extra costs such as handling and delivery charges. Which purchasing format offers the lowest price for each of your products?
13. **Integrated.** Chapter 9 discussed the fact that supply chain management integrates all the activities involved in the production of goods and services from suppliers to customers. What are the benefits of involving wholesalers and retailers in the design, manufacturing, or sale of a company's product or service?
14. **Integrated.** Which of the four basic functions of management discussed in Chapter 7 would be involved in decisions that establish or change a company's channels of distribution? Explain your answer.

Practice Your Knowledge

Handling Difficult Situations on the Job: Retraining the Channel

Sales of your DJ equipment (turntables, amplifiers, speakers, mixers, and related accessories) have been falling for months, even as more and more music fans around the world try their hand at being DJs. Magazine reviews and professional DJs give your equipment high marks, your prices are competitive, and your advertising presence is as strong. Suspecting that the trouble is in the distribution channel, you and a half dozen fellow executives go on an undercover shopping mission at retail stores that carry your products—and you're quickly appalled by what you see. The salespeople in these stores clearly don't understand your products, so they either give potential customers bad information about your products or steer them to products from your competitors. No wonder sales are falling off a cliff.

Your task: The executive team is split over the best way to solve this dilemma, but based on your experience in this market, you know how difficult and expensive it is to recruit new retailers. Plus, other aspects of the trading relationship are in working order—order processing, physical distribution, invoicing, and all the other things you'd have to set up all over with new retailers. Outline a persuasive argument you could make to your follow executives to convince them that retraining your existing channel partners is the better idea. Explain how you could put together a "training swat team" that could visit major retailers and educate their sales reps on the best way to sell your products. At the very least, you should give training a try before abandoning these retailers.

Sharpening Your Communication Skills

You've convinced your fellow executives (see previous exercise) that retraining your existing channel partners is better than replacing them. Now you have to convince store managers to let you pull their staffs off the sales floor for a half day so you can train them. Each store will lose a half day's revenue, and each sales rep will lose commissions for that time as well. Draft a short e-mail for the store managers, explaining why the training would be well worth their time. Make up any details you need to complete the message.

Building Your Team Skills

Complicated, confusing, or downright dysfunctional shopping experiences are one of the biggest challenges for online retailing. Customers who can't find what they're looking for or who get lost filling out order forms, for instance, often just click away and leave their virtual shopping carts. Unfortunately, consumers don't always perceive the shopping experience the same way, so it's not always easy for website developers to craft the ideal e-retail experience.

Your team's task is to analyze the shopping experience on three competitive e-tail sites and from that analysis decide how a new competitor in the market could create a better customer experience. First, as a group, choose a product that the group finds interesting but that no one in the group has purchased online before, then identify three websites that are likely to offer the product; www.shopzilla.com, www.shopping.com, and www.pricegrabber.com can help with this step. Next, individually (so you can't guide each other), each person in the group should then shop the three sites for your chosen product (if you can't find the exact model, choose something similar). Answer the following questions about each site (if it'll help with your analysis, feel free to print out any of the webpages you encounter along the way):

1. Did you have any trouble finding the right website?
2. How difficult was it to find the product you wanted?
3. How much information was available? Complete product details or just a few highlights? A static photo or a 3-D virtual experience that let you explore the product from all angles?
4. How easy was it to compare this product to similar products?
5. Could you find the store's privacy and return policies? Were they acceptable to you?
6. How long did it take to get from the site's homepage to the point at which you could place an order for the specific product?
7. What forms of help are available in case you have questions or concerns?
8. Go ahead and place your item in the shopping cart to simulate placing an order (don't actually buy the product, of course!).

Summarize your impression of each of the three sites, then compare notes with your teammates. Based on the strengths and weaknesses of each site, identify four pieces of advice for a company that wants to compete against these sites.

Expand Your Knowledge

Discovering Career Opportunities

Retailing is a dynamic, fast-paced field with many career opportunities in both store and nonstore settings. In addition to hiring full-time employees when needed, retailers of all types often hire extra employees on a temporary basis for peak selling periods, such as the year-end holidays. You can find out about seasonal and year-round job openings by checking newspaper classified ads, looking for signs in store windows, and browsing the websites of online retailers.

1. Select a major retailer, such as a chain store in your area or a retailer on the Internet. Is this a specialty store, discount store, department store, or another type of retailer?
2. Visit the website of the retailer you selected. Does the site discuss the company's hiring procedures? If so, what are they? What qualifications are required for a position with the company?
3. Research your chosen retailer using library sources or online resources. Is this retailer expanding? Is it profitable? Has it recently acquired or been acquired by another firm? What are the implications of this acquisition for job opportunities?

Developing Your Research Skills

Find an article in a business journal or newspaper (online or print editions) discussing changes a company is making to its distribution strategy or channels. For example, is a manufacturer selling products directly to consumers? Is a physical retailer offering goods via a company website? Is a company eliminating an intermediary? Has a nonstore retailer decided to open a physical store? Is a category killer opening smaller stores? Has a major retail tenant closed its store in a mall?

1. What changes in the company's distribution structure or strategy have taken place? What additional changes, if any, are planned?
2. What were the reasons for the changes? What role, if any, did e-commerce play in the changes?
3. If you were a stockholder in this company, would you view these changes as positive or negative? What, if anything, might you do differently?

Exploring the Best of the Web

URLs for all Internet exercises are provided at the website for this book, www.prenhall.com/bovee. When you log on to the text's Companion Website, select Chapter 14. Then select "Featured Websites," click on the name of the featured website, and review the website to complete these exercises.

Explore these chapter-related websites, review their content, and answer the following questions for each website you visit:

1. What is the purpose of this website?
2. What kinds of information does this website contain? Please be specific.
3. How is the information provided at this website useful for businesspeople? Consumers?
4. How did you expand your knowledge of marketing and customers by reviewing the material at this website? What new things did you learn about these topics?

Explore the World of Wholesaling

Thinking about a career as a wholesale sales representative? The *Occupational Outlook Handbook* is a terrific source for learning about careers in business. Read the online material discussing the functions wholesale sales reps perform, the skills and experience manufacturers look for in candidates, and how to acquire any necessary training. Find out what a typical day on the job involves. How will you be compensated? Will travel be required? Will you be required to work long hours? What types of reports will you be expected to submit? Log on and learn now. A career in wholesale sales may be just the thing for you. www.bls.gov/oco

Explore the World of Retailing

Thinking about opening up a small store or building a career in retailing? Need some statistics? Find out what's hot in the retail industry by visiting the National Retail Federation website. Browse the FAQs and read the Washington Update. Learn which government proposals might affect your retail business and how to respond to them. Opening a retail store can be an exciting venture—especially if you're prepared. www.nrf.com

Get a Move On

How much freight are companies moving around the United States? To find the answer, visit the website of the U.S. Department of Transportation's Commodity Flow Survey Program. Read the results of the latest survey to find out how many billion tons of raw materials and finished goods—worth trillions of dollars—are being shipped within the country. Surprisingly, more than half the shipments (as measured by tonnage) are headed to a destination less than 50 miles from their point of origin; physical distribution is critical even when you are buying and selling locally. www.bts.gov/programs/commodity_flow_survey

Learning Interactively

Companion Website

Visit the Companion Website at www.prenhall.com/bovee. For Chapter 14, take advantage of the interactive "Learning Modules" to test your chapter knowledge. Get instant feedback on whether you need additional studying. Complete the exercises as specified by your instructor.

A Case for Critical Thinking

REI's Perfect Blend of Retail and E-Tail Channels

During the mid-1990s, many retailers were reluctant to establish an online presence for fear of competing against existing distribution channels. But Recreational Equipment, Inc. (REI) viewed the web as an exciting new channel that could reach markets far beyond the limits of its physical stores and paper catalogs. And the outdoor gear retailer quickly developed a winning multichannel approach that successfully blended its online store with its offline businesses.

ON SOLID GROUND

Established in 1938 by two Seattle mountain climbers as a consumer cooperative, REI developed a reputation for providing enthusiasts with high-quality sports equipment at reasonable prices. By the mid-1990s, REI had grown into the nation's largest supplier of specialty outdoor gear, serving customers nationwide through some 50 retail stores and a thriving catalog business.

Offering everything from canoes to hiking gear, each REI store was a true interactive experience. Spanning from 10,000 to 95,000 square feet, the stores gave shoppers an avalanche of opportunities to test, touch, and play with products most stores kept in boxes or behind glass. Footwear test trails, water filter testing stations, binocular demo stations, and rock climbing walls were just a few of the reasons that shoppers flocked to REI stores.

GEARING UP

Despite its success, REI was largely unknown outside the western United States. The catalog reached people across the country, but without a physical retail presence in most of the country, REI didn't have a powerful way to connect with the rest of the country. Moreover, the company needed to find a way to keep customers and employees informed of the rapidly changing array of products in the outdoor gear industry. The Internet seemed like a perfect channel for accomplishing both objectives, but in the mid-1990s it was still a wild frontier—largely populated by net surfers and techno-enthusiasts. Furthermore, experts warned retailers that opening an online store would likely steal business from a company's existing retail channels.

But the advantages of venturing into the world of e-tailing outweighed the risks for REI. Start-up costs for REI's website—$500,000 for all computers and programming—paled in comparison to building and equipping the typical $6 million REI store. And six decades of experience, powerful name recognition, and a loyal customer base placed REI in a strong position to move online. "We knew it was going to cannibalize our catalog and retail sales," CEO Dennis Madsen predicted at the time, "but our philosophy was we better cannibalize ourselves or somebody will do it to us." Fortunately, his prediction turned out to be wrong.

THE FIRST STEP

In true trailblazer style, REI pressed ahead with its web store in 1996. Launching www.rei.com in five languages to attract customers around the world, the company made every effort to integrate the online store with its established channels. Unlike pure-play retailers that must start from scratch, REI called on its existing retail and catalog distribution systems for processing e-tail orders. The co-op also extended its web strategy into its retail channels by placing Internet kiosks in stores. With in-store access to REI's website, retail shoppers can place online orders, interact with experts, or download customized items such as topographic hiking maps. Furthermore, store cash registers are web-linked, so clerks can look up product information or sell items that are out of stock at one store but available at another. And because REI's online and offline channels offer the same merchandise and use the same computer system, customers can return web purchases to REI's physical stores without any hassles.

With the success of its online store, the company launched a second site in 1998 to attract bargain hunters. The website, www.rei-outlet.com, carries limited quantities of manufacturers' overstocks, seconds, and product closeouts at rock-bottom prices. It features items that are not available at REI's physical stores, in its catalog, or on the main website, and it is linked to the company's main website. This strategy allows REI to tailor messages to each consumer segment.

FLYING HIGH

Named by *Fortune* magazine as one of the top corporate websites, REI.com offered some 78,000 products—more than any physical REI store—and soon spanned 45,000 pages of detailed product information. REI's top-rate service appeals to e-tail shoppers, including the night owls who place nearly one-third of online orders after regular retail hours. "Our value proposition for rei.com is to deliver any product, at any time, to any place, and to answer any question," says an REI executive.

And the strategy works. Online sales account for a significant portion of total sales—and are growing twice as fast as the sales of its busiest physical store. REI credits its multichannel approach to serving customers as one of the key reasons for the company's success. "We've recognized that we can't choose how our customers want to shop, but we can make it easier for them to access us and provide the same high-quality shopping experience however they interact with REI," says a company spokesperson. So what about REI's worry that the online stores would cannibalize their physical stores, that clicks would damage the bricks? According to Joan Broughton, REI's vice president in charge of multichannel programs, "Far from the concern of the web cannibalizing stores, we are using the Internet to measurably increase store sales while also lifting Internet sales." For instance, with nearly a quarter of the orders placed online, customers opt to have the merchandise delivered to their local REI store. And when they visit the stores to pick up their orders, more than a third of these customers buy additional merchandise in person. Broughton also says that the coordinated channel effort also helps build a sense of community between the company and its customers. "Some of the e-commerce world does not seem to consider the physical location of its customers. It's almost as if they think of their customers as floating out there in cyberspace." As REI continues to grow across the country, those customers have a home no matter where they are.

Critical Thinking Questions

1. Why did REI venture into e-commerce?
2. How has REI's success as a traditional retailer benefited its online business?
3. How does REI blend its online and offline channels?
4. Go to the REI website at www.rei.com. Review the website and then answer these questions: How does REI promote its physical stores? What are REI's return policies for online customers? What outdoor information does this site offer?

Video Case

Through the Grapevine: Clos du Bois Winery

Learning Objectives

The purpose of this video is to help you:

1. Understand how a company works with wholesalers and retailers to make its products available to consumers.
2. Discuss the factors that affect a company's distribution strategy.
3. Consider the goals and challenges of physical distribution.

Synopsis

Riding a tidal wave of U.S. consumer interest in California wines, Clos du Bois Winery sells its wines from coast to coast. The company now produces and ships more than one million cases of wine every year, although less than 20 percent is sold in California. The winery works through a network of statewide and regional distributors that sell to retailers and restaurants, which in turn sell the wine to consumers. For efficient order fulfillment and inventory management, Clos du Bois ships its wines from a central warehouse to more than 300 wholesalers' warehouses around the United States. The company also pays close attention to the details of physical distribution so wine quality is not compromised by temperature extremes. Now the company is tapping the infrastructure of parent company Allied Domecq to arrange for wider distribution in Europe.

Discussion Questions

1. *For analysis:* Why does Clos du Bois sell through wholesalers rather than selling directly to retailers and restaurants?
2. *For analysis:* How does the U.S. pattern of table wine consumption affect the winery's domestic distribution strategy?
3. *For application:* What might Clos du Bois do when its supply of a certain vintage is very limited?
4. *For application:* What effect does the cost of storing and shipping Clos du Bois wine have on the prices paid by retailers and, ultimately, consumers?
5. *For debate:* Given its long-term relationships with established wholesalers, should Clos du Bois lobby against direct sales of wine to U.S. consumers through Internet channels? Support your position.

Online Exploration

Visit the website of the Clos du Bois Winery at www.closdubois.com/home and (if you are of legal drinking age in your state) check out what the company says about its wines, winery, and wine club. Also follow the link to explore the trade site and find out where Clos du Bois wines are sold. Considering the winery's dependence on distributors, why would it invest so heavily in a consumer-oriented website? What channel conflict might be caused by this site? If you cannot legally enter the winery's website, use your favorite search engine (such as Google.com) to see whether other online retailers are selling this wine. If so, why would Clos du Bois make its wine available through these intermediaries?

Spreading the Message: Promotional Strategies

CHAPTER 15

LEARNING OBJECTIVES

After studying this chapter, you will be able to

1. Identify the five basic categories of promotion

2. Highlight factors you should consider when developing a promotional mix

3. List the seven steps in the personal-selling process

4. Identify five common types of advertising

5. Explain the difference between logical and emotional advertising appeals

6. Name three common types of online advertising

7. Distinguish between the two main types of sales promotion and give at least two examples of each

8. Explain the role of public relations in marketing

9. Discuss the importance of integrated marketing communications

www.prenhall.com/bovee

INSIDE BUSINESS TODAY

Profitable Search Results: Google Advances the Science of Online Advertising

www.google.com

The Internet has generated plenty of surprises in its relatively short history, but few can compete with the tale of how a group of computer experts obsessed with the arcane science of search algorithms suddenly became one of the most powerful forces in contemporary advertising. When Stanford graduate students Larry Page and Sergey Brin set out to create a better way to find information online, few people could've imagined that within a few years, advertisers ranging from individuals working at home in their sweats to the largest corporations in the would be signing up for its advertising services.

With its stated mission to "organize the world's information and make it universally accessible and useful," Google is well known to most web surfers, and certainly to anyone who conducts any kind of research online. Only a few years ago, it was just one of many search engines struggling to break out of the pack, but by putting some of the brightest minds in computer science to work on the challenge of analyzing and organizing billions of numbers, words, and images, Google soon became king of the search mountain.

While Google was honing its search capabilities, advertisers were trying to decide just what to make of the Internet in general and the World Wide Web in particular. Many tried simple banner ads on various websites and a few tried more creative multimedia efforts such as mini-movies and interactive "adver-games." In general, though, most of the major U.S. advertisers, including the 20 or 30 that regularly spend more than $1 billion a year on advertising, weren't quite sure yet how the Internet could—or even would—fit in their plans. At the same time, users were getting tired of annoying pop-up windows and fewer of them were clicking on banner ads. Some observers began to wonder just how wonderful this new medium would be from an advertiser's point of view.

Gradually, however, advertisers began to realize how powerful the new method of search engine advertising could be. Those small text ads that you see next to a search results listing on Google or near the content you see on other websites seem rather simple, but they actually address two fundamental problems in advertising: (1) putting the right message in front of the right people at the right time—and in a respectful way that won't cause them to resent the communication—and (2) measuring the effectiveness of the effort.

The keys to solving the first problem are content relevancy and unobtrusive presentation. For instance, if you search for "in-line skates," chances are you're interested in buying such a product, so the several ads that appear next to your search results are relevant to your search. Plus, they're off to the side, not obscuring your primary view, and they're static and silent, so you're not distracted by flashing colors and you don't need to worry about boisterous ad sounds suddenly blasting out of your computer's speakers. Similarly, if you're on a website for in-line skating enthusiasts, the appearance of a few skate ads next to the content you're reading are also relevant to the information you're seeking. And not only are the ads relevant to you; from the advertisers' perspective, the ads aren't wasted on people who aren't interested in in-line skates.

The second problem, measuring the effectiveness of the promotional effort, is solved by how you interact with the ads. In many other media, advertisers don't really know if their ad efforts are generating the sort of responses they hope for. With online ads, if you click on an ad, the advertiser immediately knows that the ad was at least effective enough to get your attention and create enough interest to prompt you to look for more information.

Can simple text ads really add up to a viable business, though? Just ask the accounting department at Google, which is probably going to need some computer experts of its own to tally up the billions of dollars the company generates through those seemingly simple ads.[1]

GET READY

Google's emergence as a major advertising force provides an educational look at an intriguing intersection of technology, marketing, finance, and customer behavior. For instance, it wasn't long ago that most companies thought online search was a low-level utility of no strategic importance. Until recently, in fact, Microsoft outsourced the search function on its MSN website rather than devote its own resources to search technology. Not anymore, though: Google's success and growing influence in the online world has opened plenty of eyes through the technology and advertising industries. If you were in charge of selling Google's services to advertisers around the world, how would you convince them to spend less of their finite budgets on traditional media and more on Google-driven ads? And what strategies would you take to persuade them to use Google instead of one of its search engine competitors? ▪

Chapter Overview

The rapid growth of search engine advertising is a great example of the creativity involved in the promotional element of the marketing mix. This chapter, the final discussion of the marketing function, explains how marketers set promotional goals and develop promotional mixes. The chapter then takes you through the major elements in the promotional mix: personal selling, advertising and direct marketing, sales promotion, and publication. The chapter wraps up with a look at integrated marketing communication.

What Is Promotion?

Of the four ingredients in the marketing mix (product, price, distribution, and promotion), promotion is perhaps the one element you associate most with the marketing function, since promotion is highly visible to consumers. Chapter 12 defined promotion as a form of persuasive communication that motivates people to buy whatever an organization is selling—goods, services, or ideas. Promotion may take the form of direct, face-to-face interaction or indirect communication through such media as television, radio, magazines, newspapers, direct mail, billboards, the Internet, and other vehicles. How does a firm decide on which forms of promotion to use? Most companies develop a **promotional strategy** that defines the direction and scope of the promotional activities they will take to meet their marketing objectives by setting promotional goals and developing a promotional mix.

Setting Your Promotional Goals

You can use promotion to achieve three basic goals: to inform, to persuade, and to remind. *Informing* is the first promotional priority, because people cannot buy something until they are aware of it and know what it can do for them. Potential customers need to know where the item can be purchased, how much it costs, and how to use it. *Persuading* is also an important priority, because most people need to be encouraged to purchase something new or to switch brands. Advertising that meets this goal is classified as **persuasive advertising**. *Reminding* the customer of the product's availability and benefits is also important, because such reminders stimulate additional purchases. The term for such promotional efforts is **reminder advertising**.

Beyond these general goals, your promotional goals should accomplish specific objectives, such as attracting new customers, increasing usage among existing customers, helping distributors pull in new business, stabilizing sales, boosting brand-name recognition, creating sales leads, differentiating products, and influencing decision makers.

Developing the Promotional Mix

A company's **promotional mix** consists of a specific blend of personal selling, sales promotion, advertising, direct-marketing tools, and public relations that work best for the firm's product variables, market, and desired objectives (see Exhibit 15.1).

- *Personal selling.* **Personal selling** is the interpersonal arm of the promotional mix. It involves person-to-person presentation—face-to-face, by phone, or by interactive media—for the purpose of making sales and building customer relationships. Personal selling allows for immediate interaction between the buyer and seller. It also enables the seller to adjust the message to the specific needs, interests, and reactions of the individual customer. **Telemarketing**, personal selling over the telephone, has long been popular with marketers, generating sales anywhere from 2 to 20 percent of the time. However, consumer

---

promotional strategy
Defines the direction and scope of the promotional activities that a company will use to meet its marketing objectives

persuasive advertising
Advertising designed to encourage product sampling and brand switching

reminder advertising
Advertising intended to remind existing customers of a product's availability and benefits

Identify the five basic categories of promotion

promotional mix
Particular blend of personal selling, advertising, direct marketing, sales promotion, and public relations that a company uses to reach potential customers

personal selling
In-person communication between a seller and one or more potential buyers

telemarketing
Selling or supporting the sales process over the telephone

Activity	Reach	Timing	Flexibility	Cost/Exposure
Personal selling	Direct personal interaction with limited reach	Regular, recurrent contact	Message tailored to customer and adjusted to reflect feedback	Relatively high
Advertising	Indirect interaction with large reach	Regular, recurrent contact	Standard, unvarying message	Low to moderate
Direct marketing	Direct personal interaction with large reach	Intermittent, based on short-term sales objectives	Customized, varying message	Relatively high
Sales promotion	Indirect interaction with large reach	Intermittent, based on short-term sales objectives	Standard, unvarying message	Varies
Public relations	Indirect interaction with large reach	Intermittent, as newsworthy events occur	Standard, unvarying message	No direct cost

Exhibit 15.1
The Five Elements of Promotion
The promotional mix typically includes a blend of elements. The most effective mix depends on the nature of the market and the characteristics of the good or service being marketed. Over time the mix for a particular product may change.

advertising
Paid, nonpersonal communication to a target market from an identified sponsor using mass communications channels

direct marketing
Direct communication other than personal sales contacts designed to effect a measurable response

direct mail
Advertising sent directly to potential customers, usually through the U.S. Postal Service

sales promotion
Promotional events and activities such as coupons, rebates, contests, and trade shows

public relations (PR)
Nonsales communication that businesses have with their various audiences

complaints about interruptions led to the creation of the National Do Not Call Registry in 2003, partially blocking telemarketing access to millions of U.S. homes. The registry does not affect nonprofit organizations or several specific industries, including, ironically enough, the telephone companies themselves. Also, telemarketers are still allowed to call their existing customers, homes not registered on the do not call list, and other businesses.[2]

- *Advertising.* **Advertising** consists of messages paid for by an identified sponsor and transmitted through a mass communication medium such as television, radio, or newspapers. The primary role of advertising is to create product awareness and stimulate demand by bringing a consistent message to a large targeted consumer group economically. As you'll see later in the chapter, advertising can take many forms—each with its own advantages and disadvantages.

- *Direct marketing.* **Direct marketing** involves the distribution of promotional materials to target customers with the goal of having them respond by placing an order, visiting a website, or performing some other desired action. Particularly when coupled with the personalization made possible by new data mining techniques, direct marketing helps marketers build mutually beneficial relationships with customers by focusing communication on each customer's specific interests.[3] The principal method of direct marketing is **direct mail**, which includes catalogs, brochures, DVDs, CD-ROMs, and other materials delivered through the U.S. Postal Service and private carriers.

- *Sales promotion.* **Sales promotion** includes a wide range of events and activities designed to either build the reputation of a company and its brands or to stimulate immediate interest in and encourage the purchase of a good or service. Sales promotions can be directed at either consumers or other businesses, including marketing intermediaries.[4]

- *Public relations.* **Public relations (PR)** encompasses all the nonsales communications that businesses have with their many audiences—communities, investors, industry analysts, government agencies and officials, and the news media. Companies rely on public relations to build a favorable corporate image and foster positive relations with these groups.

When developing a promotional mix, companies weigh the advantages and disadvantages of the five elements of promotion (which are highlighted throughout this chapter). They also consider a number of product and market variables.

LEARNING OBJECTIVE 2
Highlight factors you should consider when developing a promotional mix

Product Variables Various types of products lend themselves to differing forms of promotion. Simple, familiar items such as laundry detergent can be explained adequately through advertising, but personal selling is generally required to communicate the features of unfamiliar and sophisticated goods and services such as office-automation equipment or municipal waste-treatment facilities. Direct, personal contact is particularly important in promoting customized services such as interior design, financial advice, or legal counsel.

LEARNING FROM BUSINESS BLUNDERS

OOPS In one of the e-newsletters that it regularly sends out to suggest party ideas and thereby encourage use of its web-based event planning services, Evite suggested that the Yom Kippur holiday would be a good "reason to party." Not a move likely to foster a positive response from Jewish members of the company's audience, for whom Yom Kippur is a day of solemn atonement for one's sins. Evite responded with an apology the following day.

WHAT YOU CAN LEARN Whether Evite staffers failed to recognize the nature of the Yom Kippur holiday or simply made a mistake when compiling their newsletter, the result was an embarrassing promotional blunder. Promotional messages must take great care when referencing any aspect of an individual's cultural context, whether it's adhering to a particular religious faith, being a single parent, being young, being old—or any of the dozens of other variables that define the human experience.

As this chapter will later explain, the complexity of a product and its familiarity in the marketplace will dictate the best forms of promotion to use.

The product's price is another factor to consider in selecting an appropriate promotional mix. Inexpensive items such as shaving cream or breakfast cereal sold to a mass market are well suited to advertising and sales promotion, which have a relatively low per-unit cost. At the other extreme, products with a high unit price such as in-ground swimming pools lend themselves to personal selling because the high cost of a sales call is justified by the price of the product. Furthermore, the nature of the selling process often demands face-to-face interaction between the buyer and seller.

The product's position in its life cycle also influences promotional choices. Early on, when the seller is trying to inform the customer about the product and build the distribution network, promotional efforts are in high gear. Selective advertising, sales promotion, and public relations are good tools for building awareness and for encouraging early adopters to try the product, while personal selling is an effective tool for gaining the cooperation of intermediaries.

As the market expands during the growth phase, the seller broadens its advertising and sales-promotion activities to reach a wider audience and continues to use personal selling to expand the distribution network. When the product reaches maturity and competition is at its peak, the seller's primary goal is to differentiate the product from rival brands. Advertising generally dominates the promotional mix during this phase, but sales promotion is an important supplemental tool, particularly for low-priced consumer products. As the product begins to decline, the level of promotion generally tapers off.

Market Variables Selection of an appropriate promotional mix is also influenced by the size and concentration of the target market. In markets with many widely dispersed buyers, advertising is generally the most economical way of communicating the product's features. In markets with relatively few customers, particularly when they are clustered in a limited area, personal selling is a practical promotional alternative. Many marketers use a combination of methods, often relying on advertising and public relations to build awareness and interest, following up with personal selling to complete the sale.

When selecting a promotional mix, a firm must also decide whether it will focus its marketing effort on intermediaries or on final customers. If the focus is on intermediaries, the producer uses a **push strategy** to persuade wholesalers and retailers to carry the item. Producers may, for instance, offer wholesalers or retailers special discounts or incentives for purchasing larger quantities of the item. Thus, you would expect to see personal selling and trade promotions

push strategy
Promotional strategy that uses the salesforce and a number of trade promotions to motivate wholesalers and retailers to push products to end users

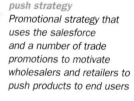

A product in a mature product category, such as blue jeans, requires a different promotional mix than a product in the introduction or growth phase.

INNOVATING FOR BUSINESS SUCCESS

TRACKING DOWN THE DISAPPEARING AUDIENCE

Looking around at today's media-saturated world, it's hard to imagine a time when "mass media" consisted of three nationwide television networks, radio, local newspapers, and a handful of popular magazines. If you wanted to launch a new product nationwide, you simply bought commercial time on ABC, CBS, or NBC, and you would've had a pretty good chance of reaching your target market. Advertisers didn't have to look very far to find consumers because consumers didn't have anywhere else to turn (and they didn't even have remote controls to mute commercials or change the channel).

Fast-forward to the twenty-first century, when advertisers wonder where everybody went. Consumers are still around, of course, but now they're scattered in smaller, isolated pockets all over the media landscape, from blogs to Internet radio to online e-zines to digital cable systems with hundreds of channels. With digital video recorders (DVRs) such as TiVo, they can zoom right past commercials they once had to sit through; 30 million households are expected to have DVRs by 2007. And many people, particularly younger consumers, are spending less time watching regular TV and more time playing video games or enjoying DVDs that NetFlix drops off in the mail. According to one study, in 1995, a national advertiser could reach 80 percent of U.S. women aged 18 to 49 by running a commercial just three times. To reach that same group in 2000 required 97 ads.

How can advertisers reach audiences that won't sit still and won't pay attention when they are sitting still? Nobody has the answer for every situation, but advertisers are trying plenty of possibilities. *Product placement,* in which advertisers put their products right into a TV show or movie, are more common than ever. Did you notice those Coke-logo beverage cups the judges drink from on *American Idol?* Coca-Cola paid $20 million to put them there. Another common move is taking the ads to

wherever the customers are, from posters in rest rooms to TV screens positioned near checkout lines, gas pumps, and other places people are forced to wait. Highway billboards have gone high tech, too, with flashy electronic displays that can be altered by remote control to catch the eye of drivers stuck in traffic. One company pays college students to wear company logos on their foreheads. Tremor, a promotions company started by consumer giant Procter & Gamble, has recruited several hundred thousand teenagers to help promote its products—without pay. These boys and girls are treated to sneak previews and inside information about various products, and they're only too happy to share the news with their friends.

Television commercials aren't going away, of course, but advertisers are working harder to make them more entertaining and more memorable, if sometimes more risqué or even disgusting in some eyes. If you don't like these new ads, don't think you can get away by switching off the TV to play a video game instead; a number of games now have ads built right into them (and if you play networked games over the Internet, somebody's probably measuring your response to these ads, too).

Of course, every new solution seems to create another round of problems. With ads everywhere, consumers are now complaining that there's nowhere to hide. Until somebody dreams up a better way to reach consumers, though, chances are that wherever you go, you'll find an ad waiting for you—and it might be delivered by your best friend.

Questions for Critical Thinking

1. Do fragmented media make it easier or harder for marketers to engage in segmented or concentrated marketing? Explain your answer.
2. Is it ethical to engage consumers to help promote your products without explicitly telling them you're doing so? Explain your answer.

pull strategy
Promotional strategy that stimulates consumer demand via advertising and a number of consumer promotions, thereby exerting pressure on wholesalers and retailers to carry a product

dominate the promotional mix aimed at intermediaries. These marketing intermediaries then use a number of promotional tools to push the products into the market channels.

If the marketing focus is on end users, the producer uses a **pull strategy** to appeal directly to the ultimate customer, using advertising, direct mail, contests, discount coupons, and so on. With this approach, consumers "pull" the product through the market channels by requesting it from retailers, who in turn request it from wholesalers, who request it from producers (see Exhibit 15.2). Most companies use a combination of push and pull tactics to increase the impact of their promotional efforts.

Exhibit 15.2
Push and Pull Strategies

In a push strategy, the manufacturer "pushes" products through the distribution channel, first promoting and distributing them to wholesalers, who then push them to retailers, who then push them to consumers. In a pull strategy, the manufacturer promotes its products directly to consumers who then "pull" the products through the distribution channel by requesting them from retailers, who then request them from wholesalers, who then request them from the manufacturer. Many companies use a combination of push and pull strategies.

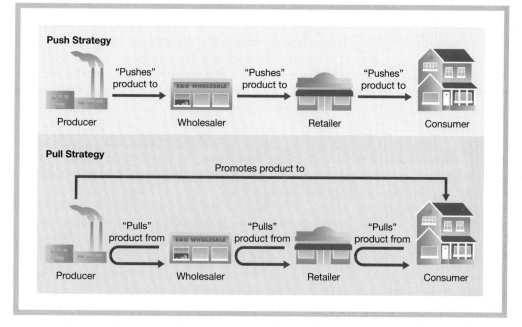

CRITICAL THINKING CHECKPOINT

1. Why would a company such as McDonald's, which is already well-known to virtually all consumers in the United States, continue to spend heavily on advertising?
2. Why does an entirely new sort of product need a different promotional strategy than a well-known product?
3. Would it be wise for a manufacturer that is new to a particular industry (and unknown within it) to invest most of its promotional resources in a pull strategy? Why or why not?

Personal Selling

Even with the rapid advance of e-commerce and other marketing technologies, personal selling remains a fundamentally important part of the promotional mix. As with other elements of the marketing mix, personal selling has evolved over the years to support the contemporary idea of the customer-oriented marketing concept. In this sense, personal selling has evolved from *peddling products* to *creating partnerships* with customers.[5]

Types of Sales Personnel

The people who do personal selling go by many names: salespeople, account executives, marketing representatives, sales representatives, and sales consultants, to cite only a few. Regardless of their title, salespeople can be categorized according to three broad areas of responsibility: order getting, order taking, and sales support services. Although some salespeople focus primarily on one area of responsibility, others may have broader responsibilities that span all three.

Order Getters **Order getters** are responsible for generating new sales and for increasing sales to existing customers. Order getters can range from telemarketers selling home security

order getters
Salespeople who are responsible for generating new sales and for increasing sales to existing customers

systems and stockbrokers selling securities to engineers selling computers and nuclear physicists selling consulting services. Order getting is sometimes referred to as *creative selling*, particularly if the salesperson must invest a significant amount of time in determining what the customer needs, devising a strategy to explain how the product can meet those needs, and persuading the customer to buy. This type of creative selling requires a high degree of empathy, and the salesperson focuses on building a long-term relationship with the customer.

Order Takers **Order takers** do little creative selling; they primarily process orders. Unfortunately, the term *order taker* has assumed negative overtones in recent years because salespeople often use it to refer to someone too lazy to work for new customers or actively close orders, or they use it to refer to someone whose territory is so attractive that the individual can just sit by the phone and wait for orders to roll in. Regardless of how salespeople use the term, order takers in the true sense play an important role in the sales function.

With the aim of generating additional sales, many companies are beginning to train their order takers to think more like order getters. You've probably noticed that nearly every time you order a meal at McDonald's and don't ask for French fries, the person at the counter will ask, "Would you like an order of fries to go with that?" Such suggestions can prompt customers to buy something they may not otherwise order.

Sales Support Personnel *Sales support personnel* generally don't sell products, but they facilitate the overall selling effort by providing a variety of services. Their responsibilities can include looking for new customers, educating potential and current customers, building goodwill, and providing service to customers after the sale. The three most common types of sales support personnel are missionary, technical, and trade salespeople.

Missionary salespeople are employed by manufacturers to disseminate information about new products to existing customers (usually wholesalers and retailers) and to motivate them to sell the product to their customers. Manufacturers of pharmaceuticals and medical supplies use missionary salespeople to call on doctors and pharmacists. They leave samples and information, answer questions, and persuade doctors to prescribe their products.

Technical salespeople contribute technical expertise and assistance to the selling function. They are usually engineers and scientists or have received specialized technical training. In addition to providing support services to existing customers, they may also participate in sales calls to prospective customers. Companies that manufacture computers, industrial equipment, and sophisticated medical equipment use technical salespeople to sell their products as well as to provide support services to existing customers.

Trade salespeople sell to and support marketing intermediaries. Producers such as Hormel, Nabisco, and Sara Lee use trade salespeople to give in-store demonstrations, offer samples to customers, set up displays, restock shelves, and work with retailers to obtain more shelf space. Increasingly, producers work to establish lasting, mutually beneficial relationships with their channel partners, and trade salespeople are responsible for building those relationships.

The Personal-Selling Process

Although it may look easy, personal selling is not a simple task, and successful sales professionals work hard to develop their skills. Some sales, of course, are made in a matter of minutes. However, other sales, particularly for large organizational purchases, can take months to complete. Many salespeople follow a carefully planned process from start to finish, as Exhibit 15.3 suggests. But personal selling involves much more than performing a series of steps. Successful salespeople help customers understand their problems and show them new and better solutions to those problems. In this sense, salespeople go beyond communicating value to actually creating value for their customers.[6]

Step 1: Prospecting **Prospecting** is the process of finding and qualifying potential customers. This step involves three activities: (1) *generating sales leads*—names of individuals and organizations that might be likely prospects for the company's product; (2) *identifying*

---

order takers
Salespeople who generally process incoming orders without engaging in creative selling

missionary salespeople
Salespeople who support existing customers, usually wholesalers and retailers

technical salespeople
Specialists who contribute technical expertise and other sales assistance

trade salespeople
Salespeople who sell to and support marketing intermediaries by giving in-store demonstrations, offering samples, and so on

L E A R N I N G
O B J E C T I V E   3

List the seven steps in the personal-selling process

prospecting
Process of finding and qualifying potential customers

Exhibit 15.3
The Personal Selling Process

The personal selling process can involve up to seven steps, starting with prospecting for sales leads and ending with following up after the sale has been closed.

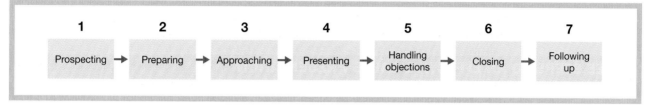

1		2		3		4		5		6		7
Prospecting	→	Preparing	→	Approaching	→	Presenting	→	Handling objections	→	Closing	→	Following up

prospects—potential customers who indicate a need or a desire for the seller's product; and (3) *qualifying prospects*—the process of figuring out which prospects have both the authority and the available money to buy. Those who pass the test are called **qualified prospects**.

Step 2: Preparing With a list of hot prospects in hand, the salesperson's next step is to prepare for the sales call (the call is not necessarily a phone call; the term also refers to in-person visits). Without this preparation, the chances of success are greatly reduced. Preparation starts with creating a prospect profile, which includes the names of key people, their role in the decision-making process, and other relevant information, such as the prospect's buying needs, motive for buying, current suppliers, income/revenue level, and so on.

Next, the salesperson decides how to approach the prospect. Possible options for a first contact include sending a letter or making a cold call in person or by telephone. For an existing customer, the salesperson can either drop by unannounced or call ahead for an appointment, which is generally preferred.

Before meeting with the prospect, the salesperson establishes specific objectives to achieve during the sales call. Depending on the situation, objectives can range anywhere from "getting the order today" to simply "persuading prospects to accept the company as a potential supplier." After establishing the objectives, the salesperson prepares the actual presentation, which can be as basic as a list of points to discuss or as elaborate as a product demonstration or multimedia presentation.

Step 3: Approaching the Prospect Whether the approach is by telephone, by letter, or in person, a positive first impression results from three elements. The first is an appropriate *appearance*—you wouldn't wear blue jeans to call on a banker, and you probably wouldn't wear a business suit to call on a farmer. Appearance also covers the things that represent you, including business cards, letters, and automobiles. Second, a salesperson's *attitude and behavior* can make or break a sale. A salesperson should come across as professional, courteous, and considerate. Third, a salesperson's *opening lines* should include a brief greeting and introduction, followed by a few carefully chosen words that get the prospect's attention and generate interest. The best way to get a prospect's attention is to focus on a benefit to the customer rather than on the product itself.

Step 4: Making the Presentation The most crucial step in the selling process is the presentation. It can take many forms, but its purpose never varies: to personally communicate a product message that will persuade a prospect to buy. Most sellers use one of two methods. The *canned approach* is a memorized presentation (easier for inexperienced sellers, but inefficient for complex products or for sellers who don't know the customer's needs). The *need-satisfaction approach* (now used by most professionals) identifies the customer's needs and creates a presentation to specifically address them.

Step 5: Handling Objections No matter how well a presentation is delivered, it doesn't always conclude with an immediate offer that might move the prospect to buy. Often the prospect will express various types of objections and concerns throughout the presentation. In fact, the absence of objections is often an indication that the prospect is not all that

qualified prospects
Potential buyers who have both the money needed to make the purchase and the authority to make the purchase decision

Types of Advertising

Business professionals generally refer to advertising by its type. Common types of advertising include product advertising, institutional advertising, national and local advertising, and word-of-mouth advertising. Here's a closer look at each.

product advertising
Advertising that tries to sell specific goods or services

Product Advertising Product advertising is the most common type, designed to sell specific goods or services, such as Kellogg's cereals, Sega video games, or Esteé Lauder cosmetics. **Product advertising** generally describes the product's features and may mention its price, but creative advertising teams can use a wide range of images and language to catch the eye of a target audience.

competitive advertising
Ads that specifically highlight how a product is better than its competitors

comparative advertising
Advertising technique in which two or more products are explicitly compared

You can argue that all product advertising is competitive, but the term **competitive advertising** is applied to ads that specifically highlight how a product is better than its competitors. When two or more products are directly contrasted in an ad, the technique being used is **comparative advertising**. In some countries, comparative ads are tightly regulated and sometimes banned; that is clearly not the case in the United States. Indeed, the Federal Trade Commission encourages advertisers to use direct product comparisons with the intent of better informing customers. Comparative advertising is frequently used by competitors vying with the market leader, but it is useful whenever a company believes it has some specific product strengths that are important to customers. Given the damage that unfair comparative advertising can cause, both federal regulations (principally the Lanham Act) and industry guidelines established by the American Association of Advertising Agencies address the issues of fairness and accuracy in comparative advertising.[8]

institutional advertising
Advertising that seeks to create goodwill and to build a desired image for a company rather than to sell specific products

Institutional Advertising **Institutional advertising** is designed to create goodwill and build a desired image for a company rather than to sell specific products. As discussed in Chapter 2, many companies are now spending large sums for institutional advertising that focuses on *green marketing*, creating an image of companies as corporate conservationists. Institutional advertisers tout their actions, contributions, and philosophies not only as supporting the environmental movement but as leading the way. When used as *corporate advertising*, institutional advertising often promotes an entire line of a company's products. Institutional ads can also be used to remind investors that the company is doing well.

In this example of competitive advertising, Napster makes a case for its music based on price. Do you find Napster's message to be compelling?

The Home Depot used the visual metaphor of diverse species of wood in this institutional ad to convey its commitment to an ethnically diverse supplier base.

Institutional ads that address public issues are called **advocacy advertising**. Advocacy advertising has recently expanded beyond issues in which the organization has a stake. Some companies now run advocacy ads that don't directly benefit their business, such as ads that project opinions and attitudes supporting those of their target audiences.

National Versus Local Advertising Advertising can also be classified according to the sponsor. **National advertising** is sponsored by companies that sell products on a nationwide basis. The term *national* refers to the level of the advertiser, not the geographic coverage of the ad. If a national manufacturer places an ad in only one city, the ad is still classified as a national ad. As Exhibit 15.4 shows, national advertisers spend well over $200 billion on advertising every year.[9]

advocacy advertising
Ads that present a company's opinions on public issues such as education and health

national advertising
Advertising sponsored by companies that sell products nationwide; refers to the geographic reach of the advertiser, not the geographic coverage of the ad

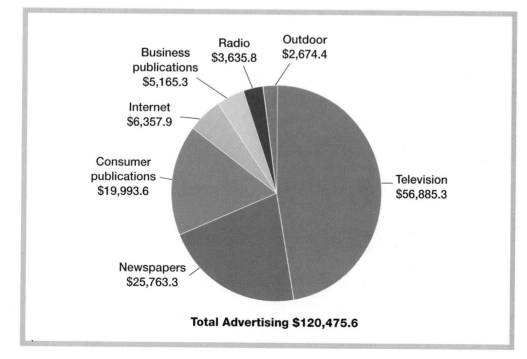

Total Advertising $120,475.6

Business publications $5,165.3
Radio $3,635.8
Outdoor $2,674.4
Internet $6,357.9
Consumer publications $19,993.6
Newspapers $25,763.3
Television $56,885.3

Exhibit 15.4
U.S. National Advertising Expenditures by Media Type ($millions)
In 2003, advertisers spent roughly $120 billion on national media; the Internet remains one of the smaller categories but it is growing the fastest. That same year, advertisers spent another $125 billion on local media, including Yellow Pages.

In contrast, **local advertising** is sponsored by a local merchant. Grocery store ads in the local newspaper are a good example. **Cooperative advertising** is a financial arrangement in which companies with products sold nationally share the costs of local advertising with local merchants and wholesalers. As a result, it is a cross between local and national advertising.

Word-of-Mouth Advertising Although it's not really advertising in the strict sense of the term, word-of-mouth advertising is important to every company. In fact, more consumers learn about new products from family members and friends than from any promotional activity.[10] Increasingly, marketers aren't leaving the word of mouth up to chance, either. For instance, the stealth marketing techniques you read about in Chapter 12 represent organized attempts at shaping word of mouth. Similarly, *buzz marketing* tactics try to generate "buzz" among consumers so they'll be motivated to learn more about a particular product.

Of course, word of mouth isn't just about people talking face to face or on the phone. Websites and blogs have become extremely influential disseminators of word of mouth communication as well—sometimes with positive results for marketers (when someone raves about a new product) and sometime with negative results (when a blogger trashes a product that he or she is unhappy about, for example). Many companies are now experimenting with blogs as a way to reach customers and influential people in their target markets.

Advertising Appeals

All well-designed ads make a carefully planned appeal to whatever is most likely to motivate the target audience. By segmenting along age, ethnic group, lifestyles, and other variables, advertisers try to identify which groups of people can be reached with logical or emotional appeals to get their points across.

Logical Appeal As the name implies, a logical appeal attempts to persuade the audience through reason and information. A logical appeal works best when the purchase involves rational decision making on the buyer's part, such as when a materials engineer for an auto company compares the attributes of various types of steel, which is why this approach is

The appeal is clear in this ad: Driving the right car can be a lot of fun.

They're gonna need it. S2000 HONDA

Slip into the S2000's race-inspired, driver-focused cockpit, and you'll wonder if this might just be the most exhilarating sports car ever built. Take its 237-hp engine up tp 8000 rpm, and you'll know for sure.

used extensively in business-to-business marketing and in *high-involvement* purchases by consumers. For the logical appeal to work in an advertising context specifically, however, the ad needs to catch the audience's attention and convince them to pay attention long enough to hear the reasoning behind the logical appeal.[11] For this reason, sometimes even highly logical and fact-filled ads may employ creative headlines, graphics, or other elements to pull the audience into the ad.

Emotional Appeal In your years as a consumer, you've been subjected to a dizzying array of emotional appeals. Even with the most unemotional sort of product, emotions can be a significant factor in the decision process because all people have hopes, fears, desires, and dreams, regardless of the products they buy. Emotional appeals range from the most syrupy and sentimental to the downright terrifying. On the lighter side, some companies try to convince you of how good it will feel to use their products. Flowers, greeting cards, and gifts are among the products usually sold with a positive emotional appeal. Other companies appeal to a broad range of fears: personal and family safety, financial security, social acceptance, and business success or failure. Insurance companies are notorious for using fear in advertising campaigns when they air commercials that show extensive losses from burglary, fire, hurricanes, or other catastrophic events. To be effective, appeals to fear must be managed carefully. Laying it on too thick can anger the audience or even cause them to block out the message entirely.

Celebrity Appeal Celebrity appeals are based on the notion of aspirational reference groups (see Chapter 12), those real or imaginary groups that consumers would like to consider themselves part of. The thinking behind the celebrity involvement in the ad is that people will be more inclined to use products endorsed by a celebrity because they will identify with and want to be like this person (no matter how far-fetched such aspirations might be at a purely logical level). Celebrities can also bring new excitement, humor, energy, and even perceived value to a product. In some cases the celebrity has a direct and obvious connection to the product, but in others the person's name, likeness, voice, or reputation are used more for the value of their association and recognition. For example, professional golfer Annika Sorenstam has endorsement contracts with a variety of companies (including Callaway Golf, Mercedes-Benz, Oakley, Cutter & Buck, Rolex, Kraft, and ADT),[12] but not all of them are in the golf industry. Celebrities have become so common in advertising—roughly 20 percent of all ads contain some element of celebrity involvement—that some advertisers have shifted back to "real people" as a way to connect with their audiences.[13]

Sex Appeal No discussion of advertising is complete with an examination of the sex appeal. Such appeals range from the subtle (such as when an attractive person poses next to an automobile) to the ridiculous (such as ads for male body sprays that suggest the wearer will immediately be trampled by a stampede of passionate women) to the arguably offensive (an accusation leveled at some ads from companies such as Calvin Klein[14]). Ironically, studies suggest that sex appeals are effective at capturing an audience's attention but often less effective than other appeals at creating long-term memory and recall of the brands being advertised—presumably because audience attention is focused on the sexual aspects of the advertising, rather than on the product being advertised. Sex appeals remain a subject of controversy for people concerned with both decency standards and the portrayal of women in advertising.[15]

Advertising Media

Choosing the right **media**, or channels of communication, can be as important as selecting the type of advertising. Your **media plan** is a document that shows your advertising budget, the schedule of when your ads will appear, and a discussion of the **media mix**, the combination of print, broadcast, online, and other media used for the advertising campaign. When selecting the media mix, the first step is to determine the characteristics of the target audience and the types of media that will reach the largest audience at the lowest cost per exposure. The choice is also based on what the medium can do, since the various media excel in different ways.

Although his days as a champion boxer are long past, George Foreman is still a popular celebrity for both product endorsements and advertising projects.

media
Communications channels, such as newspapers, radio, and television

media plan
Written plan that outlines how a company will spend its media budget, including how the money will be divided among the various media and when the advertisements will appear

media mix
Combination of print, broadcast, online, and other media used for an advertising campaign

For instance, since television is good at conveying the appeal of products in action, automakers such as GM and Ford spend a large percentage of their annual promotional budgets on TV commercials.[16] The second step in choosing the media mix is to pick specific vehicles in each of the chosen media categories, such as individual magazines, websites, or radio stations.

Exhibit 15.5 summarizes the strengths and weaknesses of seven major media. In addition to these seven, marketers can choose from an almost endless array of other delivery vehicles, from traditional means such as Yellow Pages and highway billboards to GPS-enabled shopping carts that display product messages as shoppers move through the grocery store.[17] As the Google story at the beginning of the chapter suggests, some of the most intriguing developments in advertising are taking place in electronic media. The following sections offer a glimpse at some of the challenges and opportunities in e-mail marketing and online media.

Developments in E-Mail Marketing As millions of consumers and business employees got connected to e-mail in recent years, e-mail looked to be a promising medium for advertising. The ability to reach people inexpensively and direct them to an e-commerce website was a

Medium	Advantages	Disadvantages
Newspapers	Extensive market coverage; low cost; short lead time for placing ads; good local market coverage; geographic selectivity	Poor graphic quality; short life span; cluttered pages; visual competition from other ads
Television	Great impact; broad reach; appealing to senses of sight, sound, and motion; creative opportunities for demonstration; high attention; entertainment carryover	High cost for production and air time; less audience selectivity; long preparation time; commercial clutter; short life for message; vulnerability to remote controls; losing ground to new media options
Direct mail	Can deliver large amounts of information to narrowly selected audiences; excellent control over quality of message; personalization	High cost per contact; delivery delays; difficulty of obtaining desired mailing lists; customer resistance; generally poor image (junk mail)
E-mail	Extremely low cost; fast preparation and delivery; ability to customize and to provide links back to websites	Deluge of spam, much of it illegal or offensive, has tainted this medium for general advertising use, possibly beyond repair; many legitimate marketers use only permission-based (opt-in) e-mail now
Radio	Low cost; high frequency; immediacy; highly portable; high geographic and demographic selectivity	No visual possibilities; short life for message; commercial clutter; lower attention than television; lower level of engagement makes it easier to switch stations
Magazines	Good production quality; long life; local and regional market selectivity; authority and credibility; multiple readers	Limited demonstration possibilities; long lead time between placing and publishing ads; high cost; less compelling than other major media
Internet	Rich media options and creative flexibility can make ads more compelling and more effective; changes and additions can be made quickly and easily in most cases; webpages can provide an almost unlimited amount of information; can be personalized more than any other medium	Difficulty in measuring audiences and ad effectiveness, although improvements are being made; customer resistance; increasing clutter (such as pop-up ads); extreme fragmentation (millions of websites)

Exhibit 15.5
Advantages and Disadvantages of Major Advertising Media
When selecting the media mix, companies attempt to match the characteristics of the media audiences with the characteristics of the customer segments being targeted. A typical advertising campaign involves the use of several media.

compelling combination. As anyone with an e-mail account knows, however, legitimate e-mail campaigns are now getting buried in a deluge of spam campaigns that vary from the suspicious to the down-and-out illegal. The CAN-SPAM Act of 2003 attempted to address the situation by prohibiting e-mail with misleading subject lines or fake return addresses, but the results are not encouraging. Not only does spam continue to grow, but attempts to stem the flow through automated filtering are increasingly blocking e-mail from legitimate sources.[18]

The e-mail issue has led some to steer away from e-mail as a mass medium. Mike Gilbert, of Three A.M. Advertising, a Seattle ad agency with such clients as Microsoft and T-Mobile, has abandoned mass e-mailing for his clients because it risks tainting a valuable brand by associating it with spammers.[19] To avoid such associations and to help potential customers get the information they really do want, many mainstream companies now emphasize permission marketing approaches, usually through *opt-in* choices that are displayed on their websites. Opt-in approaches also let recipients select the specific information they want, which benefits both recipients and marketers by making the communication more efficient. At Agilent Technologies' website, for instance, engineers and scientists who want e-mail updates on the company's products can select from dozens of specific topics that match their professional interests.[20]

When it is approached in a careful manner that respects both government regulations and customer preferences, e-mail marketing can be a powerful promotional method. Legitimate e-mail marketers take the time to develop lists of recipients who are truly interested in their messages and shun the use of both "harvested" address lists (in which e-mail addresses are automatically gathered from websites, blogs, chat groups, and so on) and "address guessing" (sending e-mail to every conceivable user name at a given domain name). Marketers that take the time to do it right can still reach receptive audiences through e-mail.[21]

Developments in Online Media Although online advertising represents just a small fraction of the total advertising dollars spent every year, it is by far the fastest growing advertising medium and continue to draw budget share away from magazines, newspapers, and direct mail.[22] It's the primary advertising medium for many small companies, and an increasingly important media choice for many midsize and large companies.

Online advertising offers a number of compelling benefits, including *timeliness* (ads can be updated at any time with minimal cost), *reach* (the web reaches hundreds of millions of people worldwide), *low cost* (web ads tend to be much cheaper than comparable print or broadcast ads), and *interactivity* (audiences can get involved with both the ads themselves and with sales personnel via instant messaging and chat options). In addition to using their own websites and blogs as promotional platforms, online marketers can purchase online advertising in a variety of ways:

- *Display ads.* *Display ad* is a general term for any ad that that includes both graphical elements in addition to text (the term also applies to print media). Online display ads are often called **banner ads**, although this also refers to one specific shape of ad (the wide, flat horizontal ad). Banner ads don't take full advantage of online technology, but they are inexpensive, easy to create, and easy to measure (every time someone clicks one). *Rich media* ads go beyond simple text and graphics to include animation, audio, video, and interactivity. Exhibit 15.6 offers a list of other common online advertising terms.
- *Search engine ads.* Google, Yahoo!, MSN, and other websites have clearly demonstrated the power of **search engine advertising**, ads that are related to either the results of an online search or the content being displayed on other webpages. Search engine ads began as small, text-only presentations, but Google and others now offer display ad services as well. Search-related ads account for more than a third of all online ad spending and continue to grow rapidly.[23]
- *Advertising on blogs.* Many advertisers are now trying to harness the popularity of blogging as a means to reach audiences. For instance, Audi signed on as the sole sponsor of the Jalopnik blog (www.jalopnik.com), a blog that caters to automobile enthusiasts.[24]

LEARNING OBJECTIVE 6

Name three common types of online advertising

banner ads
A rectangular display ad on a webpage that links to an advertiser's webpage

search engine advertising
Automatic presentation of ads that are related to either the results of an online search or the content being displayed on other webpages

Business Buzz
flog
A fake blog that is designed to deceive readers by hiding the identity of the blogger, such as when a marketing staffer writes raves reviews of his or her own company's products but tries to pass the effort off as the work of a satisfied customer

INNOVATING FOR BUSINESS SUCCESS

THE RISE, FALL—AND RISE—OF ONLINE ADVERTISING

As the World Wide Web began to evolve from an online meeting place for scientists into a global playground and shopping mall, the question of advertising was inevitable. Hundreds of dot-com businesses were founded and funded on the idea that the web would turn into a major advertising medium. Many gave away free content (and a few even gave away free PCs), in the hope of attracting enough "eyeballs" to attract big-budget advertisers. Millions of websites popped up, and millions of consumers and businesses logged on. Everything was ready to go.

Except somebody forgot to tell the advertisers. A number of major players, such as McDonald's, with its $1 billion-plus annual advertising budget, shunned web advertising. And advertisers who did plunge in often came away disappointed with low response rates. When the advertising revenue didn't materialize, most of the dot-coms struggled and many disappeared entirely.

With so many millions of people flocking to the web, why didn't it turn into the advertising dreamland that so many investors anticipated? After all, serious web surfers practically live online, their eyes glued to the screen. Sounds like a perfect advertising medium, but a combination of issues plagued early web advertising. One of the biggest was hyperfragmentation; with millions of new websites popping up all around, advertisers weren't sure where to place their bets. This only added to the general uncertainty surrounding the web. National advertisers had decades of experience with television and radio advertising, and many weren't about to jeopardize sales on an unproven medium.

Other issues included measurement questions (businesses weren't quite sure how to gauge the effectiveness of online ads), buyer behavior (you'd never believe it now, but the early web was a fairly noncommercial place, where many people shunned the whole idea of advertising and e-commerce), seller behavior (such as failing to respond when sales leads came in from their websites), and too many websites that didn't take advantage of the medium (the biggest culprit: stale, static "brochure-ware" sites that merely duplicated printed brochures). For many people, advertising started to look like one more empty promise of the dot-com boom.

Through it all, though, some of the online pioneers persevered, learning from those early experiments, fine-tuning business models and creative approaches, and improving the technology. By 2003, online ad spending started to grow again. As broadband Internet access reached more consumers and businesses, advertisers could increase the use of *rich media* ads that combine audio, video, and animation. The result is a new generation of ads that are more entertaining and more informative—and often more effective. These new ads entice web visitors to play games, download helpful information, customize product choices, or sit back and enjoy "minimovies" that are 5 or 10 times longer than typical TV commercials.

While these improvements were coming along, a whole new category of advertising appeared: paid keyword searches on Google, Yahoo! and other search engines—those "sponsored links" that you see alongside your search results. In addition to targeted search advertising, technology has also improved advertisers' ability to track online behavior and customize ads based on users' web habits. (You know those times you hop online to plan your spring break, then suddenly start seeing ads for air travel, condo rentals on the beach, and other related products? That's not a coincidence.) And "ad networks," collections of websites on which advertisers can buy ad space in a coordinated way (rather than site by site), makes ad purchasing easier than ever.

Moreover, the price for online ad space has dropped considerably from the dot-com fever days, giving advertisers one more reason to give the web another try. For instance, McDonald's is now spending an estimated 5 percent of its budget for ads on such youth-oriented sites as www.nick.com, www.disney.com, and www.foxkids.com. Five percent might not sound like a big commitment so far, but 5 percent of a billion dollars is a big number.

Online advertising will continue to evolve in the coming years as advertisers keep improving their tools and techniques—and continue to explore new options, such as advertising on blogs and Internet radio stations. It's been a bumpy ride, but this time the ride is going straight up.

Questions for Critical Thinking

1. Why wouldn't a major advertiser such as McDonald's just spread its massive ad budget all over the web, buying ad space on hundreds or thousands of sites?
2. Do you think the creative flexibility of web advertising makes it a more compelling advertising medium than television or radio? Why or why not?

Exhibit 15.6
Common Online Marketing Terms
Using the Internet as a marketing vehicle has given birth to a variety of online marketing terms.

Term	Explanation
Banner	Webpage ad; usually refers to short, wide ads displayed along the top or bottom of a page
Click stream	The "trail" a user follows through a website or across multiple sites
Click through	The act of clicking on an ad, which takes the user to a *landing page* (see below)
Cookie	A small data file stored on the user's computer that identifies the user's browser and can store various site parameters
Cost per click	The cost an advertiser pays for each click on an ad
CPM	Cost per thousand impressions; a pricing model for ads in which the advertiser pays according to the number of times its ads are displayed
Eyeballs	Slang for website visitors
Impression	A single instance of a webpage or webpage element being displayed
Interactive ad	General term for any ad that requires or encourages some type of action on the user's part, such as entering data, playing a game, or exploring a product image
Interstitials	Ad pages that temporarily display as a user is clicking from one content page to another
Landing page	A special webpage that a user arrives at after clicking on an online ad or typing in a URL from an offline ad; often created for specific advertising campaigns
Microsite	A multipage interactive ad embedded within a regular website
Opt-in	Website policy stating that users must specifically give their permission to receive promotional e-mails and other messages
Opt-out	Website policy in which users who register at a site are automatically sent promotional message unless they take some action to remove themselves from the mailing list
Podcasting	The broadcast distribution of audio files via the Internet and the RSS distribution method
Pop-under	A new window that is generated behind the browser window the user is currently viewing; often not visible until the main window is closed
Pop-up ad	A new window that displays on top of the browser window the user is currently viewing
Search engine optimization	Choosing keywords that are most likely to yield targeted hits when visitors enter requests into search engines
Skyscraper ad	A tall, narrow ad that is typically positioned beside webpage content
Splash screen	An interstitial page displayed temporarily when a visitor first links to a site; typically used to promote a particular brand
Stickiness	A website's ability to keep visitors coming back
Vlog	A blog with video content
Webcasting	Live or delayed delivery of the audio and video files of an event such as a presentation

Employee blogs are also showing promise as an effective way to put a "human face" on large corporations. The full potential of blogging has yet to be discovered, so expect to see many developments in this area in the years to come.

Advertising Ethics, Etiquette, and Regulations

Advertising is a powerful and pervasive force in modern life and, as such, it continues to generate concerns about ethics and etiquette. In response to these concerns, government bodies the world over have enacted a wide variety of regulations affecting both the content and delivery of advertising messages.

In spite of the negative image some consumers have of the advertising business, responsible companies and advertising agencies recognize the vital importance of ethical communication. Professional associations such as the American Association of Advertising Agencies (www.aaaa.org), the Direct Marketing Association (www.the-dma.org), and the American Marketing Association (www.marketingpower.com) devote considerable time and energy to ethical issues in marketing, including ongoing education for practitioners and self-regulation efforts aimed at avoiding or correcting ethical lapses. For instance, the National Advertising Review Council (www.narcpartners.org), whose members include advertisers, agencies, and the general public, works with the Better Business Bureau to investigate and resolve complaints of deceptive advertising in order to foster public trust.[25]

In addition to ethical concerns, advertisers should also consider the issue of simple etiquette, whether it's the decade-old problem of interrupting consumers at dinnertime with telemarketing calls or newer problems such as flooding electronic in-boxes with e-mail messages. This is a tough balancing act with no easy solution, however. Ads that don't get anyone's attention clearly have no value, but the techniques often used to get attention, from ultra-loud TV commercials to flashing electronic billboards that distract drivers on busy streets, are a frequent source of complaints about advertising's intrusive reach into people's lives. To protect the long-term value of their brands, advertisers need to seek a balance between effectiveness and sensitivity to their audiences. In fact, the same technology that is used to collect data about consumers can be used to craft marketing programs that are more sensitive. The British consumer data firm Bounty offers a great example. To avoid compounding the trauma of families that have recently lost an unborn or newborn child, Bounty maintains data on families that have suffered such loses so that direct marketers can avoid sending infant-related marketing materials to those households.[26]

Not all companies maintain high ethical standards in their advertising, and even those that do can't always agree on where to draw the line, so government regulators have enacted a variety of laws designed to prohibit deceptive and abusive promotion. In the United States, the Federal Trade Commission (www.ftc.gov) has regulations regarding such areas as misleading claims, supporting evidence, fairness in comparative ads, the use of expert endorsements, and the manner in which products are demonstrated in ads. Other agencies address concerns in specific industries, such as the Food and Drug Administration (www.fda.gov), whose concerns include packaging and labeling; the Federal Communications Commission (www.fcc.gov), which oversees radio and television; and the U.S. Postal Service (www.usps.gov), which has authority in areas of direct mail advertising.[27]

CRITICAL THINKING CHECKPOINT
1. Should your college advertise to attract new students? Why or why not?
2. Why have so many companies used celebrities in their ads?
3. Why has search engine advertising become such a popular way to reach audiences?

LEARNING OBJECTIVE 7

Distinguish between the two main types of sales promotion and give at least two examples of each

Sales Promotion

The fourth element of promotion, sales promotion, consists of short-term incentives to build the reputation of a brand or to encourage the purchase of a product or service. Sales promotion consists of two basic categories: consumer promotion and trade promotion.

Consumer Promotions

consumer promotion
Sales promotion aimed at final consumers

Consumer promotion is aimed directly at the final users of the product. Companies use a variety of consumer promotional tools and incentives to stimulate repeat purchases and to entice new users:

- **Coupons.** The biggest category of consumer promotion—and the most popular with consumers—is **coupons**, certificates that spur sales by giving buyers a discount when they purchase specified products. Couponing is a fairly inefficient technique, however, since only a small fraction of the coupons printed and delivered every year get redeemed. Most companies that use coupons are trying to figure out how to issue fewer of them with more precise targeting.[28] Many marketers are also concerned that coupons help foster a bargain-hunting mentality that eventually lowers the perceived value of a brand.

- **Rebates.** With rebates, buyers generally get reimbursement checks from the manufacturer by submitting proofs of purchase along with a rebate form. Rebates can be an effective way to boost sales, but like coupons, their value can diminish through overuse. For instance, automobile manufacturers have relied on rebates so heavily in recent years that many consumers won't buy a car until a rebate is offered, which effectively lowers the prices that the manufacturers can charge for their products and dampens sales activity when rebates aren't being offered.[29]

- **Point-of-purchase.** The **point-of-purchase (POP) display** is an in-store presentation designed to stimulate immediate sales. POP displays are a vital element in the marketing effort for many products sold at retail stores. Not only do they represent the manufacturer's last chance to communicate with the consumer, but they help capture *impulse purchases*—unplanned purchases that can make up as much as 50 percent of sales in mass merchandise stores and supermarkets.[30]

- **Samples.** Samples are an effective way to introduce a new product, encourage nonusers to try an existing product, encourage current buyers to use the product in a new way, or expand distribution into new areas. To help consumers in Japan try a variety of cosmetic products in the privacy of their own homes, the beauty magazine *ViVACO* includes 10 product samples in every issue.[31]

- **Special-event sponsorship.** Sponsoring special events has become one of the most popular sales promotion tactics. Thousands of companies spend billions of dollars to sponsor events ranging from golf to opera. Next time you watch the Olympic Games on television, take note of how many commercial sponsorships you see on display. Companies can apply for Olympic sponsorship at a variety of national and international levels. A dozen or so companies, including Coca-Cola, Panasonic, and Visa, currently have "worldwide sponsorship" status, meaning they can associate their brands with the Olympics (including the famous five-ring logo) across national boundaries. The Home Depot and Bank of America are among the companies that have "partner" status, allowing them to co-brand with the Olympics within the United States.[32]

- **Cross-promotion.** With **cross-promotion**, one brand is used to promote another, noncompeting brand. Movie studios frequently cross-promote with consumer products, from automobiles to fast food to toys. When *Revenge of the Sith*, the sixth and final movie in the Star Wars series hit the screen in 2005, Playskool offered kids a friendlier version of the arch-villain Darth Vader: a take-off on its classic Mr. Potato toy called Darth Tater.[33]

Other popular consumer sales promotion techniques include in-store demonstrations, loyalty and frequency programs such as frequent-flyer miles, and **premiums**, which are free or bargain-priced items offered to encourage the consumer to buy a product. Contests, sweepstakes, and games are also quite popular in some industries and can generate a great deal of public attention, particularly when valuable or unusual prizes are offered. **Specialty advertising** (on pens, calendars, T-shirts, mouse pads, and other items) helps keep a company's name in front of customers for a long period of time.

Trade Promotions

Although shoppers are more aware of consumer promotion, trade promotion actually accounts for the larger share of promotional spending. **Trade promotions** are aimed at inducing distributors or retailers to sell a company's products. The most popular trade promotion

---

coupons
Certificates that offer discounts on particular items and that are redeemed at the time of purchase

point-of-purchase (POP) display
Advertising or other display materials set up at retail locations to promote products to potential customers as they are making their purchase decisions

cross-promotion
Jointly advertising two or more noncompeting brands

premiums
Free or bargain-priced items offered to encourage consumers to buy a product

specialty advertising
Advertising that appears on various items such as coffee mugs, pens, and calendars

trade promotions
Sales-promotion efforts aimed at inducing distributors or retailers to push a producer's products

Once a mundane afterthought to costlier, more glamorous forms of advertising, product sampling is now seen by many marketers as a more cost-effective way to promote some products. Here an Odwalla representative serves up samples of the company's natural juice drinks.

trade allowance
Discount offered by producers to wholesalers and retailers

is a **trade allowance**, which involves a discount on the product's price or free merchandise that brings down the cost of the product. The wholesaler can either pocket the savings and increase company profits or pass the savings on to the consumer to generate additional sales. Trade allowances are commonly used when adopting a push marketing strategy. Their chief downside is that they can create the controversial practice of *forward buying*, in which the distributor stocks up on merchandise while the price is low. For example, say that the producer of Bumble Bee tuna offers retailers a 20 percent discount for a period of 6 weeks. A retailer might choose, however, to buy enough tuna to last 8 or 10 weeks. Purchasing this excessive amount at the lower price increases the retailer's profit, but at the expense of the producer's profit.

Besides trade allowances, other popular trade promotions are display premiums, dealer contests or sweepstakes, and travel bonus programs. All are designed to motivate distributors or retailers to push particular merchandise. Product samples are also common in many business marketing efforts. For instance, semiconductor manufacturers often provide samples of electronic components to engineers who are designing new products, knowing that if the prototype is successful, it could lead to full-scale production—and orders for thousands or millions of components. For a look at the sometimes-controversial role that product samples play in the marketing of pharmaceutical products, refer to the Case for Critical Thinking on page 513.

L E A R N I N G
O B J E C T I V E

Explain the role of public relations in marketing

press relations
Process of communicating with reporters and editors from newspapers, magazines, and radio and television networks and stations

Public Relations

Public relations (PR), the fifth element of promotion, plays a vital role in the success of most companies, and that role applies to more than just the marketing of goods and services. Smart businesspeople know that a good reputation is one of a business's most important assets, and PR helps build, maintain, and repair reputations as needed. The PR activity is as diverse as the company's range of stakeholders, including community relations, product publicity, government affairs ("lobbying"), investor relations, and **press relations**—the process of communicating with print, broadcast, and online media. In the personal computer industry, for example, manufacturers know that many people look to publications such as *PC Magazine* and websites such as CNET (www.cnet.com) when shopping for computers. Editors and reporters often review new products and then make recommendations to their readers, pointing out both strengths and weaknesses. Companies roll out the proverbial red carpet for these media figures, treating them to hospitality suites at conventions, factory tours, and interviews with company leaders. When introducing products, manufacturers often send samples to reporters and editors for review, or they visit the media offices themselves.

Two standard public relations tools are the news release and the news conference. A **news release**, or *press release*, is a short memo sent to the media covering topics that are of potential news interest; a video news release is a brief video clip sent to television stations. Companies use news releases to get favorable news coverage about themselves and their products. When a business has significant news to announce, it will often arrange a **news conference**. Both tools are used when the company's news is of widespread interest, when products need to be demonstrated, or when company officials want to be available to answer questions from the media.

Integrated Marketing Communications

With five major promotional methods available—personal selling, advertising, direct marketing, sales promotion, and public relations—how do you decide on the right mix for your product? There are no easy answers because you must take many factors into account. In fact, when you consider all the ways that audiences can receive marketing messages today, the potential for confusion is not all that surprising. Besides the traditional media—radio, television, billboards, print ads, and direct-mail promotions—marketers are using websites, e-mail, blogs, kiosks, sponsorships, and more to deliver messages to targeted audiences. Coordinating promotional and communication efforts is becoming vital if a company is to send a consistent message and boost that message's effectiveness.

When companies fail to integrate their various marketing communications, the result is confusing to audiences: Mass media advertisements may say one thing, a price promotion sends a different message, a product label creates yet another message, and company website says something altogether different. **Integrated marketing communications (IMC)** is a strategy of coordinating and integrating all of a company's communications and promotion efforts to provide customers with clarity, consistency, and maximum communications impact. The concept of IMC is quite simple: communicating with one voice and one message to the marketplace, as Exhibit 15.7 suggests, although the implementation can be quite involved for large organizations using multiple media.

news release
Brief statement or video program released to the press announcing new products, management changes, sales performance, and other potential news items; also called a press release

news conference
Gathering of media representatives at which companies announce new information; also called a press briefing

Discuss the importance of integrated marketing communications

integrated marketing communications (IMC)
Strategy of coordinating and integrating communications and promotions efforts with customers to ensure greater efficiency and effectiveness

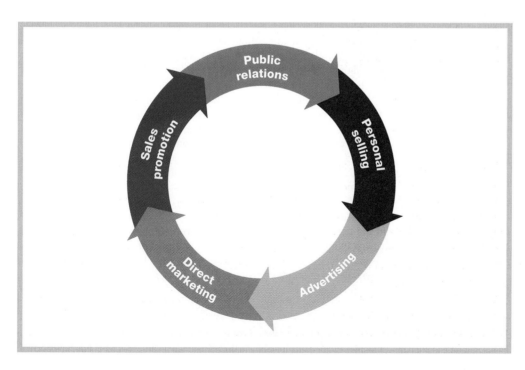

Exhibit 15.7
Integrated Marketing Communications
Coordinating the five elements of promotion delivers a consistent message to the marketplace.

CRITICAL THINKING CHECKPOINT
1. How can sales promotion reduce the uncertainty that buyers might feel about trying an unfamiliar product?
2. Why are press relations so critical to the launch of many new products?
3. Why does the integrated marketing communication philosophy place so much importance on delivering a consistent message through all communication channels?

CHECKLIST: Apply These Ideas When You're the Boss

✓ Don't try to make any single promotional vehicle do too many things at once because it will probably fail at all of them; even a multi-faceted effort such as a website should carefully divide its promotional tasks.

✓ Don't cut yourself off from customers if you rely heavily on a website for marketing; give people a way to reach you via telephone, e-mail, or instant messaging.

✓ Never base a promotional strategy on trickery; even if you're effective in the short term, it'll catch up with you sooner or later—audience trust is the most important asset a marketer can ever possess.

✓ Choose your promotional media and tools carefully; each has strengths but each also has weaknesses.

✓ Even if you aren't officially involved in personal selling, you can still benefit from the methods that sales professionals use—such as when pitching a business plan to venture capitalists when you're trying to secure financing for a start-up company.

✓ Commit to a policy of respecting your customers; this alone is enough to prevent most promotional blunders and improve the quality of your communications, too.

Summary of Learning Objectives

1 **Identify the five basic categories of promotion.** The five basic categories of promotion are (1) personal selling, which involves contacting customers by phone, interactive media, or in person to make a sale; (2) advertising, which consists of paid sponsored messages transmitted by mass communication media; (3) direct marketing, which is the distribution of promotional material to consumers via direct mail, e-mail, the Internet, telemarketing, or infomercials to generate an order or other consumer response; (4) sales promotion, which includes a number of consumer and promotional tools designed to stimulate consumer interest in a product and encourage a purchase; and (5) public relations (PR), which includes nonsales communications between businesses and their stakeholders to foster positive relationships.

2 **Highlight factors you should consider when developing a promotional mix.** When establishing a promotional mix you should consider a product's characteristics, price, and position in its life cycle. You should also consider the target market size and concentrations and whether you will focus your marketing efforts on intermediaries (using a push strategy) or on end users (adopting a pull strategy).

3 **List the seven steps in the personal-selling process.** The seven steps are (1) prospecting (finding prospects and qualifying them), (2) preparing (creating a prospect profile and deciding on the appropriate approach), (3) approaching the prospects (using appropriate behavior and language for your prospect), (4) making the sales presentation (using either a canned or personalized approach), (5) handling objections (using audience comments as an opportunity to strengthen the presentation), (6) closing (focusing on making a sale), and (7) following up after the sale has been made.

4 **Identify five common types of advertising.** Product advertising, which is the most common type, may be competitive or comparative. Institutional advertising creates goodwill

and focuses on building a company's image. National advertising is sponsored by companies that sell on a nationwide basis. Local advertising is sponsored by companies that sell locally. Cooperative advertising is an agreement to share the advertising costs with merchants and wholesalers. Word-of-mouth advertising focuses on providing customers with good experiences so that they will promote the product to other potential customers. Stealth advertising is the act of disguising an ad as normal programming material and may involve the everyday discussion of a product's benefits or the use of a branded product on TV programs or movie sets.

5 **Explain the difference between logical and emotional advertising appeals.** You can view the difference between logical and emotional appeals as the difference between appealing to the head and appealing to the heart. Logical appeals try to convince the audience with facts, reasons, and rational conclusions; they tend to focus on important product features and the product's price or value. Emotional appeals, as the name implies, persuade through emotion—which can range from heart-warming tenderness to stark fear. Use of celebrities and sex appeal are two ways marketers appeal to emotions. It's important to remember, however, that nearly all ads contain a mixture of both logic and emotion; most just lean heavily in one direction or the other.

6 **Name three common types of online advertising.** The nature of online advertising continues to evolve, but three major types of online advertising now in use are display ads (banner ads and rich media ads), search engine advertising, and advertising on blogs.

7 **Distinguish between the two main types of sales promotion, and give at least two examples of each.** The two main types of sales promotion are consumer promotion and trade promotion. Consumer promotions are intended to motivate the final consumer to try new products or to experiment with the company's brands. Examples include coupons, rebates, cross-promotion, specialty advertising, point-of-purchase displays, samples, and special event sponsorship. Trade promotions are designed to induce wholesalers and retailers to stimulate sales of a producer's products. Examples include trade allowances, trade shows, display premiums, dealer contests, and travel bonus programs.

8 **Explain the role of public relations in marketing.** Because consumers and investors support companies with good reputations, smart companies use public relations to build and protect their reputations. They communicate with consumers, investors, industry analysts, and government officials through the media. They pursue and maintain press relations with representatives of newspapers, television, and other broadcast media so that they can provide effective news releases (also known as press releases) and hold effective news conferences.

9 **Discuss the importance of integrated marketing communications.** When companies use a greater variety of marketing communications, the likelihood of sending conflicting marketing messages to consumers increases. Integrated marketing communications (IMC) is a process of coordinating all of a company's communications and promotions efforts so that they present only one consistent message to the marketplace. Properly implemented, IMC increases marketing and promotional effectiveness.

Google: What's Next?

As many in the online community were wondering whether banner ads and similar promotional endeavors would ever be a viable way to support a website, Google was gradually building a search-engine advertising capability that would soon generate enough cash to support one of the world's top high-tech companies.

Google has a huge head start in search-related advertising, but it does face challenges ahead. For starters, it's not the only game in town. Yahoo!, the second-most-popular search engine, also sells search-based advertising on its own search page and on customers' content pages via Overture, a company that Yahoo! recently purchased.

Google's rapid climb to the top of the search business and its growing role in both advertising and Internet usage in general has also caught the attention of Microsoft—a company feared far and wide for its aggressively competitive nature. Microsoft is now throwing its considerable financial and technical resources into a competitive scheme that it claims will eventually make Google's search technology look antiquated.

Larry Page and Sergey Brin aren't sitting still, of course. They've already expanded beyond search-linked text ads with their cost-per-click simplicity to begin offering regular online ads with color, animation, and other media richness. These new ads also use the traditional cost-per-thousand (CPM) pricing model, where advertisers pay according to the number of times an ad is displayed. The CPM method is less precise than paying for clicks, but Google and the rest of the ad industry know that simple text ads aren't enough for many advertisers. Most media mixes will probably combine precisely measured click-through ads with the less measurable but more emotionally effective full color and multimedia ads.

Like the rest of the online experience, every day seems to bring new developments in online marketing, and you can have a front-row seat as this new adventure in advertising continues.

Critical Thinking Questions

1. Simple text ads are easy to target, cost-effective, and highly measurable—so why do some advertisers feel the need to include other types of ads in their online advertising mixes?

2. Google became one of the best-known brands in the world almost entirely by word of mouth, joining that rare group of firms whose very names turn into verbs. Think about some of the lesser-known firms you are familiar with, such as the companies you frequent as a customer or perhaps your own employer. Assuming they're not already global brand names, could they also use Internet-assisted word of mouth to become known around the world? Why or why not?

3. If there were ever a contest for plain vanilla web design, Google would probably win by a wide margin. Review the look and feel of Google's home page; do you think it affects the company's marketing efforts in any way, either positively or negatively? If so, how?

Learn More Online

Visit the Google website by clicking on the hotlink at Chapter 15 of this text's website at **www.prenhall.com/bovee**. Click on the Advertising Programs link and explore the various programs presented there. How many different groups does Google target with these programs? How does it advertise its advertising services to these audiences? Does it provide examples of the various advertising vehicles?

Key Terms

advertising (488)	media (499)	promotional strategy (487)
advocacy advertising (497)	media mix (499)	prospecting (492)
banner ads (501)	media plan (499)	public relations (PR) (488)
closing (494)	missionary salespeople (492)	pull strategy (490)
comparative advertising (496)	national advertising (497)	push strategy (489)
competitive advertising (496)	news conference (507)	qualified prospects (493)
consumer promotion (504)	news release (507)	reminder advertising (487)
cooperative advertising (498)	order getters (491)	sales promotion (488)
coupons (505)	order takers (492)	search engine advertising (501)
cross-promotion (505)	personal selling (487)	specialty advertising (505)
direct mail (488)	persuasive advertising (487)	technical salespeople (492)
direct marketing (488)	point-of-purchase (POP)	telemarketing (487)
institutional advertising (496)	display (505)	trade allowance (506)
integrated marketing	premiums (505)	trade promotions (505)
communications	press relations (506)	trade salespeople (492)
(IMC) (507)	product advertising (496)	
local advertising (498)	promotional mix (487)	

Test Your Knowledge

Questions for Review

1. What are the three basic goals of promotion?
2. What is the difference between using a push strategy and using a pull strategy to promote products?

3. What is the biggest advantage of personal selling over other forms of promotion?

4. What techniques do skilled salespeople use when closing a sale?

5. What are some common types of consumer promotion?

Questions for Analysis

6. Why is it important to prepare for a sales call?

7. How do advertisers determine the type of appeal to use in designing an ad, and why must they use caution with celebrity appeals?

8. Why do some reputable companies shy away from e-mail marketing, particularly to noncustomers?

9. How does online advertising help marketers judge the effectiveness of their advertising efforts?

10. **Ethical Considerations.** Scan your local papers or favorite websites and highlight or clip ads that could possibly mislead the public. What do you find misleading about the ad? How would you improve the ad?

Questions for Application

11. If you were a real estate agent, how would you determine whether it's worth investing a significant amount of time in a particular prospect?

12. Find three print ads or online ads that you think are particularly effective and three more that you think are ineffective. What do you like about the effective ads? How might you improve the ineffective ads?

13. **Integrated.** Should companies involve their marketing channels in the design of their promotional programs? What are the advantages and disadvantages of doing so?

14. **Integrated.** Review the five forms of promotion discussed in this chapter. How can companies use each of these forms to build relationships with their customers?

Practice Your Knowledge

Handling Difficult Situations on the Job: Extolling a Better Way to Buy Insurance

The great thing about Insure.com is that no one is obligated to buy a thing, which makes your job in the company's marketing department easier. Free of charge, consumers can log on to your website, ask for dozens of insurance quotes, then go off and buy elsewhere. They can look at instant price-comparison quotes from more than 200 insurers, covering every kind of insurance from term life and medical, to private passenger auto insurance. All rates are guaranteed up-to-the-day accurate, against a $500 reward. And so far the online service has received positive press from *Nation's Business, Kiplinger's Personal Finance, Good Housekeeping, The Los Angeles Times, Money, U.S. News & World Report*, and *Forbes*.

Insure.com generates revenues primarily from the receipt of commissions and fees paid by insurers based on the volume of business produced. Customers can purchase insurance from the company of their choice via the Insure.com website or they can call a toll-free number to speak to one of the company's representatives. The reps are paid salaries versus commissions, and do not directly benefit by promoting one insurance company's product over another.[34]

Your task: It's your job to lure more insurance customers to Insure.com. How will you promote the site and the service it offers? Describe how you might use both logical and emotional appeals. Rate the potential effectiveness of each of the five promotional categories for Insure.com; explain your reasoning. Could you employ online ads effectively? What about blogs?

Sharpening Your Communication Skills

The good news: The current events blog you started as a hobby has become quite popular. The bad news: It now takes up so much of your time that you've had to quit a part-time job you were using to supplement your regular income. After some discussions with other bloggers, you decide to join Google's AdSense program to help pay for the costs of operating your blog. With this program, small ads triggered by keywords in the content you publish will appear on your site. However, you're worried that your audience will think you've "sold out" because you're now generating revenue from your blog. Write a short message that could be posted on your blog, explaining why you consider it necessary to run ads and assuring your readers of your continued objectivity, even if that means criticizing organizations whose ads might appear on your blog.

Building Your Team Skills

In small groups discuss three or four recent ads or consumer promotions (in any media) that you think were particularly effective. Using the knowledge you've gained from this chapter, try to come to agreement on which attributes contributed to the success of each ad or promotion. For instance: Was it persuasive? Informative? Competitive? Creative? Did it have logical or emotional appeal? Did it stimulate you to buy the product? Why? Compare your results with those of other teams. Did you mention the same ads? Did you list the same attributes?

Expand Your Knowledge

Discovering Career Opportunities

Jobs in promotion—personal selling, advertising, direct marketing, sales promotion, and public relations—are among the most exciting and challenging in all of marketing. Choose a particular job in one of these five areas, such as public relations or media planning. Using personal contacts, local directories of businesses or business professionals, or Internet resources such as company websites or search engines, arrange a brief phone, e-mail, or personal interview with a professional working in your chosen marketing field.

1. What are the daily activities of this professional? What tools and resources does this person use most often on the job? What does this professional like most and least about the job?
2. What talents and educational background does this professional bring to the job? How are the person's skills and knowledge applied to handle the job's daily activities?
3. What advice does the person you are interviewing have for newcomers entering this field? What can you do now to get yourself started on a career path toward this position?

Developing Your Research Skills

Choose an article from recent issues of business journals or newspapers (print or online editions) that describe the advertising or promotion efforts of a particular company or trade association.

1. Who is the company or trade association targeting?
2. What specific marketing objectives is the organization trying to accomplish?
3. What role does advertising play in the promotion strategy? What other promotion techniques does the article mention? Are any of them unusual or noteworthy? Why?

Exploring the Best of the Web

URLs for all Internet exercises are provided at the website for this book, www.prenhall.com/bovee. When you log on to this text's Companion Website, select Chapter 15. Then select "Featured Websites," click on the name of the featured website, and review the website to complete these exercises.

Explore these chapter-related websites, review their content, and answer the following questions for each website you visit:

1. What is the purpose of this website?
2. What kinds of information does this website contain? Please be specific.
3. How is the information provided at this website useful for businesspeople? Consumers?
4. How did you expand your knowledge of marketing and customers by reviewing the material at this website? What new things did you learn about these topics?

Learn the Consumer Marketing Laws
Visit the Federal Trade Commission (FTC) website and click on Consumer Protection to learn how this agency protects consumers against unfair and deceptive marketing practices. Do you know what the FTC's policies are on deceptive pricing, use of the word "free," or use of endorsements and testimonials? Find out what it means to substantiate product claims such as "tests prove" or "studies show." Learn what the rules are for unsolicited telephone calls and telephone slamming before you telemarket your product. www.ftc.gov

Find Out How Blogs are Transforming Business

With their potential to help—or hurt—virtually any company, blogs have rapidly caught the attention of the business community. As this medium develops and business professionals explore various ways of using blogs themselves and responding to the blogging efforts of others, you can follow their progress at *BusinessWeek's* Blogspotting site. www.businessweek.com/the_thread/blogspotting

Join the Revolution—In Interactive Advertising, That Is

Although the Internet has been employed for commercial uses for more than a decade, the field of interactive advertising is still being invented—sometimes on a daily basis. Visit the ClickZ Network to see what the innovators on the leading edge of promotion are learning by trial, error, and continuous experimentation. You'll find articles on search engine marketing, advertising technology, rich media, and other hot topics, along with frequently updated statistics that measure the universe of electronic advertising. www.clickz.com

Learning Interactively

Companion Website

Visit the Companion Website at www.prenhall.com/bovee. For Chapter 15, take advantage of the interactive "Learning Modules" to test your chapter knowledge. Get instant feedback on whether you need additional studying. Complete the exercises as specified by your instructor.

A Case for Critical Thinking

Polyclinic Closes the Door on Sales Reps

When you walk out of the doctor's office and head to the pharmacy to get that prescription filled, do you ever wonder if the doctor recommended the best medication possible? What if the person who visited the doctor right before you was not another patient but a sales rep pushing the very medication the doctor just prescribed for you?

Many organizations are concerned about the role of personal selling in medicine. They wonder how much personal selling—including the $7 billion worth of free samples the industry gives to doctors every year—influences both the choices doctors make and the overall cost of health care. The management team at Polyclinic, an 80-doctor clinic in Seattle, got so worried about personal selling that they took the drastic step of locking drug company sales reps out of the clinic.

INFORMATION VERSUS PERSUASION

A look inside the pharmaceutical sales process helps to shed some light on Polyclinic's bold decision. Doctors have two primary sources of information about drugs: professional medical journals and the marketing materials and sales presentations from drug companies. Information from a drug company, understandably, seeks to present that specific company's products in the most positive light possible. To the worry of many, though, studies show that doctors who rely heavily on drug company information tend to exhibit prescription patterns that are both more expensive than their peers and sometimes less effective.

THE COST OF SALES

For the past decade, Polyclinic and other health providers have watched as the cost of prescription drugs and supplies has increased an average of 13 percent per year, a rate significantly above the general rate of inflation. A number of factors contribute to rising costs, but two relate directly to personal selling. The first issue is the cost of all that marketing and selling, costs that must be covered by the prices patients pay. Drug companies spend $5 billion a year to send nearly 90,000 salespeople out on 60 million sales calls. And like many sales personnel, drug company reps employ a variety of promotional gifts as part of their effort to build customer relationships. These gifts can be as insignificant as pens and coffee cups or as expensive as trips to resorts for informational seminars.

The second issue involves the specific drug recommendations that doctors make. Because patients, not doctors, have to pay for the drugs, there is no systematic pressure on doctors to prescribe less-expensive drugs. Moreover, free samples make the problem even worse, according to Howard Springer, an associate administrator at Polyclinic. He suggests it's simply too easy for a doctor to hand a patient a few doses from the samples left by a sales rep, then prescribe a full course of treatment with that drug if the samples prove to be effective—even if it's not the least-expensive choice.

WEARING OUT THEIR WELCOME

As if an expensive selling process and expensive prescription choices weren't enough, drug reps were wearing out their welcome with their demands on doctors' time. On a slow day, more than a dozen sales reps visited Polyclinic's offices, and on busy days it could get a lot worse. This time crunch is a common complaint among doctors today, according to the American Medical Association.

Polyclinic decided it had had enough. Dr. Ralph Rossi, who chairs the clinic's pharmacy and therapeutics panel, said the onsite sales calls weren't benefiting patients, the clinic, or the community. Following the lead of some other clinics around the United States, the clinic first started charging reps $30 an hour just to enter the building, then announced a ban on sales calls entirely in January 2003.

THE RIGHT PRESCRIPTION?

Is Polyclinic's response the right answer to this complicated dilemma? Even the clinic's own doctors didn't all agree with it; many liked to give the free samples away to low-income patients. To counter that loss, the clinic will help low-income patients apply for free medication directly from drug companies. And to make sure doctors continue to get needed information, the clinic is planning quarterly seminars hosted by an outside consultant and an internal team of doctors.

Not surprisingly, pharmaceutical companies don't applaud the decision, saying that Polyclinic's doctors will lose access to vital information. With enormous pressure on one side to sell medications that cost millions to develop and enormous pressure on the other to contain health care costs, the battle over personal selling in the pharmaceutical industry has only just begun.

Critical Thinking Questions

1. Why did Polyclinic decide to ban drug company sales representatives?
2. How might drug companies continue to reach Polyclinic's doctors with persuasive messages about their products?
3. A new law in Vermont requires sales reps to report any gift to doctors worth more than $25 (not including samples); will this law reduce the inappropriate influence of promotional gifts?
4. Visit the Pharmaceutical Research and Manufacturers of America website at www.phrma.org and search for "marketing code." Does this code of ethics discourage the sort of problems that affected Polyclinic?

Video Case

Revving Up Promotion: BMW Motorcycles

Learning Objectives

The purpose of this video is to help you:

1. Describe the purpose of product promotion.
2. Understand how and why a company must coordinate all the elements in its promotional mix.
3. Discuss how the message and the media work together in an effective advertising campaign.

Synopsis

Although U.S. car buyers are extremely familiar with the BMW brand, the brand has much lower awareness among motorcycle buyers. Increasing customer awareness is a major challenge for BMW Motorcycles, which has been producing high-end motorcycles for more than 80 years. The company's main promotional goal is to attract serious buyers who are looking for an exceptional riding experience. To do so, its marketers carefully coordinate every promotional detail to convey a unified brand message positioning the BMW motorcycle as "the ultimate riding machine," as its advertising slogan states. Using print and television advertising, personal selling in dealerships, sales promotion, and a virtual showroom on the web, BMW is driving its brand message home to motorcycle enthusiasts across the United States.

Discussion Questions

1. *For analysis:* What are the advantages of using more personal advertising copy and encouraging customers to become missionaries for BMW motorcycles?
2. *For analysis:* Why would BMW use its website as a virtual showroom rather than also selling online directly to consumers?

3. *For application:* What are some ways that BMW might use public relations to build brand awareness?

4. *For application:* How might BMW use direct mail to bring potential buyers into its motorcycle dealerships?

5. *For debate:* Should BMW develop and promote a new brand to differentiate its motorcycles from competing motorcycle brands as well as from BMW cars? Support your chosen position.

Online Exploration

Visit the BMW Motorcycles site, www.bmwmotorcycles.com, and notice the links on the home page. Then look at the pages promoting new models and preowned motorcycles. Finally, follow the link to look at the contact page. Which elements of the promotional mix are in evidence on this site? How does this site support the company's "ultimate riding machine" brand message? How does the site make it easy for customers to obtain more information and ask questions about BMW motorcycles and dealer services?

E-Business in Action

CLICKS AND BRICKS: BRIDGING THE PHYSICAL AND VIRTUAL WORLDS

When established retailers started to ponder a move to the web a few years ago, many experts advised them to keep their fledgling e-businesses separate. The thinking was that the creation of separate e-businesses would allow the web entity to speed up decision making, be more flexible, be more entrepreneurial, act independently, and thus compete more effectively with pure-play e-businesses (those that exist only on the Internet, such as Amazon.com). While some retailers embraced this approach, others debated whether to sell online at all. They worried about spreading their human and financial resources too thin. They worried about competing with their existing distributors, their competitors, and themselves (because their e-sales could cannibalize their physical-store sales).

Mixing Clicks with Bricks

In hindsight, the experts were wrong. Although financially the separate e-businesses promised considerable shareholder potential, running separate online and offline operations did not work.

Consider Barnes & Noble. To compete with Amazon.com, the company established a completely separate division—barnesandnoble.com (www.bn.com)—and later spun the division off as a stand-alone company. But unlike pure-plays, barnesandnoble.com lacked a sense of urgency about the web and let Amazon capture the lion's share of initial e-business and publicity. Moreover, customers did not care that the two were separate entities. Web customers became confused and angry when they tried to return books purchased online to the physical Barnes & Noble bookstores, only to be turned away. Furthermore, the strategy forced the physical stores to compete with their online sibling and prevented them from sharing management teams, combining marketing programs, or achieving economies of scale.

It didn't take long for Barnes & Noble to realize its decision to separate its online and physical stores was flawed. So in 2000, Barnes & Noble integrated the two operations—making it possible for web customers to return purchases at a company's physical stores. In 2004, it took the final step and purchased barnesandnoble.com, folding it back into the main company. Other companies have since followed Barnes & Noble's lead by reeling in their separate e-businesses.

Creating the Perfect Blend

After much debate, experts now agree that integrating a retailer's physical store operation with its web operation is the most effective approach to e-commerce. Mixing clicks with bricks (also known as clicks-and-bricks or clicks-and-mortar) makes a store's physical and web operations transparent to the customer. A Sears customer, for instance, can gather product information from Sears.com before heading to the outlet at the local mall. Salespeople can then add value by doing things the website can't—such as answering specific product questions and demonstrating products. Similarly, Circuit City's and Office Depot's customers can purchase what they want online and then pick up the products at the stores to avoid delivery fees. "It's a tremendous convenience for the customer," says one e-tailing expert. "They've done their research, compared prices, and paid. They can walk up to the pickup counter with a receipt, and they don't have to stand in line with everyone else."

A clicks-and-bricks strategy is also a boon for retailers. Multichannel customers who shop both online and in stores tend to be more loyal and spend more. Eddie Bauer (which sells products through catalogs, retail stores, and its website) reports that shoppers who use all three methods to purchase from the company spend five times more than those who shop only by catalog. Moreover, clicks-and-bricks retailers can use their websites to advertise, test merchandise, suggest gifts, increase product awareness, cross-promote online and offline products, and drive traffic to their physical stores or vice versa. Some are even using their websites to provide specialty items not available in stores. "We don't have the same real estate issues," says one spokesperson for the Gap, which offers plus sizes for men and women exclusively online. "It's an easy, lower-cost way to get merchandise out there quickly."

However, there are limitations to mixing clicks with bricks. Not all retailers, especially those that don't have a catalog business, are able to offer their entire inventory online, because of the expense of photographing and describing every item. This confuses customers. And delivery fees continue to be a barrier to online purchases, which is why so many companies offer free delivery when you spend, say, $100. Still, if you don't mix clicks with bricks, "you literally won't exist as a retailer," declares one e-commerce expert. The web is where most consumers do their initial phases of shopping—whether it's as basic as price comparison or searching for store locations.

Questions for Critical Thinking

1. Why did retailers initially separate their physical and web stores?
2. Why did the strategy to separate online and offline stores fail?
3. What are the benefits of a clicks-and-bricks strategy?

Career Profiles

Here are brief glimpses at two career paths that relate to the chapters in Part V. You'll find other career profiles following Chapters 4, 6, 9, 11, and 18.

Marketing Professionals and Marketing Managers

Careers in marketing can cover any aspect of marketing that you read about in Chapters 12 through 15. (Sales careers are covered separately; see the next profile.)

Nature of the Work Marketing is one of the most diverse job categories in business, and the situation is further complicated by the fact that various companies use different terms to describe marketing positions. For instance, a "marketing representative" job is usually a sales position, not a marketing position in the usual sense of the term. Some marketing jobs are highly specialized (advertising copywriter and e-commerce architect, for instance), whereas others encompass several aspects of marketing (brand managers, for example, often deal with virtually every aspect of the marketing mix).

In addition to focusing on different parts of the marketing mix, marketing jobs also carry varying degrees of analytical, strategic, and creative components. Particularly for positions dealing with promotions, communications skills are obviously paramount for marketers. The ability to write and speak clearly and persuasively will serve you well throughout your career in marketing, even if you don't specialize in a job in which writing or speaking is the primary function. For example, marketing managers need to be able to communicate strategic plans to their own teams, as well as advertising agencies, public relations specialists, distribution channels, industry media, and other stakeholders.

Qualifications Because marketing jobs tend to be either generalist (brand managers, marketing managers) or specialist (videographer, art director), there is no single set of qualifications for marketing professionals and managers. Business degrees are commonly expected for generalist jobs; degrees in advertising, public relations, journalism, and art are more common for people applying to ad agencies and PR firms.

Where the Jobs Are Every company engages in marketing to some degree, although the staffing strategies can vary widely from industry to industry and company to company. Marketing also has a long history of outsourcing, so many marketing jobs exist in firms that provide marketing services to corporate clients. For example, if you're interested in advertising but want to focus more on the strategic, business aspects of marketing, a job on the "client side" might be more appealing because you'll be more involved with overall marketing and business strategy. In contrast, if the creative side (writing, designing, website design, and so on) is more appealing, a job on the "agency side" is probably the better choice because you'll have more opportunities to develop your craft working on multiple projects for multiple clients. Moving between the two sides is not uncommon.

Where to Learn More American Marketing Association, www.marketingpower.com; Public Relations Society of America, www.prsa.org; American Association of Advertising Agencies, www.aaaa.org.

Sales Professionals and Sales Managers

This category includes both sales professionals (including sales engineers) and sales managers, who oversee the work of multiple salespeople in a given geographic region, industry, or customer group.

Nature of the Work If you thrive on competition, enjoy solving problems, and get energized by working with a wide range of people, you should definitely consider a career in sales. As a consumer, your exposure to sales might be limited to the retail sector of professional selling, but the field is much more diverse. Salespeople sell everything from design services to pharmaceuticals to airliners.

Many salespeople enjoy a degree of day-to-day freedom and flexibility not usually found in office-bound jobs. On the other hand, the pressure is usually intense—few jobs have the immediate indicators of success or failure that sales has, and most salespeople have specific targets or *quotas* they are expected to meet. The rewards can be considerable, though. In some fields, top salespeople can earn as much as some senior executives.

Qualifications The qualifications for professional selling depend on the industry and the type of goods and services being sold. In many business-to-business selling situations, salespeople need a considerable amount of expertise in both their products and the customers' applications. In high technology, for instance, salespeople often have engineering degrees, and some have worked as engineers before moving into sales.

Personal characteristics are of utmost importance in the sales professional as well, including the ability to listen carefully to customers' needs and communicate information about solutions clearly and persuasively. Professional appearance and a trustworthy demeanor are both key. Moreover, being told "no" is a constant fact of life for salespeople, so they need the emotional ability to remain upbeat in the face of disappointment.

Where the Jobs Are Sales professionals work throughout the value chain: manufacturers selling to wholesalers, distributors selling to other manufacturers, wholesalers selling to retailers, retailers selling to consumers, and so on. Many companies have their own salesforces, but many also outsource the selling function to *manufacturers' agents* or *manufacturers' representatives*—typically small firms that sell a variety of product lines in the same industry.

Where to Learn More Manufacturers' Agents National Association, www.manaonline.org; Manufacturers' Representatives Educational Research Foundation, www.mrerf.org.

Getting to the Bottom Line: Basic Accounting Concepts

CHAPTER 16

LEARNING OBJECTIVES

After studying this chapter, you will be able to

1. Discuss how both managers and external stakeholders use financial information

2. Describe what accountants do

3. Summarize the impact of the Sarbanes-Oxley Act

4. State the basic accounting equation and explain the purpose of double-entry bookkeeping and the matching principle

5. Differentiate between cash basis and accrual basis accounting

6. Explain the purpose of the balance sheet and identify its three main sections

7. Explain the purpose of the income statement and statement of cash flows

8. Explain the purpose of ratio analysis and list the four main categories of financial ratios

www.prenhall.com/bovee

Massive accounting fraud at WorldCom, as MCI was known at the time, led to the largest bankruptcy in U.S. history.

INSIDE BUSINESS TODAY

When Giants Fall: The Collapse of WorldCom/MCI

www.mci.com

Telecommunications giant WorldCom was a company of big numbers: 20 million customers, a 98,000-mile fiber optic network connecting 100,000 buildings in 2,800 cities across 140 countries, business offices in 65 countries on every continent except Antarctica—and the biggest bankruptcy in U.S. history. The company had assets of more than $100 billion when it asked the courts in 2002 for debt relief and temporary protection from creditors because it was no longer able to pay its bills.

Founder Bernie Ebbers built WorldCom through numerous acquisitions of other telecom companies. Because WorldCom used its own stock to help pay for these acquisitions, it counted on continuous increases in the price of that stock; and to keep the stock price moving upward, it had to keep demonstrating profitable growth to keep investors interested. However, faced with ferocious competition and high costs, WorldCom eventually found it couldn't maintain that pace of growth.

When the real financial numbers wouldn't cooperate, a handful of high-ranking executives began to make up numbers that would. By understating expenses and overstating revenue, they created the illusion that WorldCom was doing much better than it really was. Everything went fine—until their scheme fell apart when a WorldCom employee blew the whistle. These executives had fooled the stock market, the company's board of directors, and most of WorldCom's workforce. The accounting frauds, which eventually totaled an estimated $11 billion, quickly caused the company's stock to tank as investors dumped their shares for any price they could get. Ebbers resigned under pressure in April 2002, trading in WorldCom stock was halted two months later, and WorldCom filed for bankruptcy a month after that.

While it would be tempting at this point in the story to relegate the company to the history books as a sorry case study in how not to run a business, the company didn't simply disappear when it declared bankruptcy. Even though it was broke, WorldCom still served millions of customers and still employed tens of thousands of people. What *does* happen when a giant falls flat on its face?

Michael Capellas, a seasoned high-tech executive, decided he'd like the challenge of rescuing WorldCom. He took over as CEO in November 2002, but it was hardly a glamorous new job—his new company was more than $30 billion in debt, investors and employees were angry and disillusioned, customers were worried about service disruptions, and prosecutors were banging on the door demanding justice.

The fiasco got the government's attention at the highest levels. In a report that outlined 78 proposed changes, former SEC chairman Richard Breeden pointedly summarized the cause of the problem: "One cannot say that the checks and balances against excessive [executive] power within the old WorldCom didn't work adequately. Rather, the sad fact is that there were no checks and balances."

Implementing Breeden's reforms became Capellas's top priority. He changed the organizational structure, tightened accounting policies, started work toward replacing the company's 27 separate accounting systems with a single system, and overhauled corporate governance—including replacing the entire board of directors. The effort to restore public confidence also included changing the name from WorldCom to MCI, the name of one of the firms Ebbers had acquired earlier.

As part of the bankruptcy settlement, WorldCom was allowed to keep all of its assets, rather than selling them to pay creditors. In a highly controversial agreement, the court also forgave most of the $30 billion debt by giving those creditors ownership portions, giving some creditors more than others, and giving shareholders nothing—although shareholders would receive a penalty payment assessed by the SEC. The rationale behind the agreement was that freeing the company from its huge debt would allow it to rebuild value for those creditor-owners and protect the jobs of its 55,000 employees.

MCI's recovery plan didn't sit well with everyone concerned, but it did keep the company running long enough for Capellas and the new board to stabilize the situation—and put the company up for sale in late 2004. Bernie Ebbers' role in the story reached its own conclusion in 2005, when he was convicted on a variety of criminal charges.[1]

GET READY

Does rescuing MCI sound like a business challenge you'd like to take on? If you were Michael Capellas, how would you get this giant back on its feet? What would you do to restore public confidence and protect the remaining jobs? Would you have made the decision to put the company up for sale, or would you have tried to stick it out as an independent company? Looking at the broader picture, what can you and other aspiring managers and entrepreneurs learn from the WorldCom/MCI debacle? ▪

Chapter Overview

As you'll see in this chapter (the first of three dealing with the financial aspects of running a business), WorldCom/MCI may be reaching the end of the line, but the story of this enormous scandal is far from over as it continues to affect every stock market investor and publicly traded company in the United States. At its core, WorldCom/MCI is a stark reminder of the degree to which investors, employees, regulators, and the economy in general depend on accurate financial information. The accounting principles that were violated are the very same ones you'll learn about in this chapter. After an introduction to what accountants do and the rules they are expected to follow, you'll learn about the fundamental concepts of the accounting equation and double-entry bookkeeping. After that you'll explore the primary "report cards" used in accounting: the balance sheet, the income statement, and the statement of cash flows. The chapter wraps up with a look at trend analysis and ratio analysis, the tools that managers, lenders, and investors use to predict a company's ongoing health.

Understanding Accounting

As Michael Capellas knows, it's difficult to manage a business today without accurate and up-to-date financial information. **Accounting** is the system a business uses to identify, measure, and communicate financial information to others, inside and outside the organization. Financial information is important to businesses such as MCI for two reasons: First, it helps managers and owners plan and control a company's operation and make informed business decisions. Second, it helps outsiders evaluate a business. Suppliers, banks, and other lenders want to know whether a business is creditworthy; investors and shareholders are concerned with a company's profit potential; government agencies are interested in a business's tax accounting.

Because outsiders and insiders use accounting information for different purposes, accounting has two distinct facets. **Financial accounting** is concerned with preparing financial statements and other information for outsiders such as *stockholders* and *creditors* (people or organizations that have lent a company money or have extended them credit); **management accounting** is concerned with preparing cost analyses, profitability reports, budgets, and other information for insiders such as management and other company decision makers. To be useful, all accounting information must be accurate, objective, consistent over time, and comparable to information supplied by other companies.

What Accountants Do

Some people confuse the work accountants do with **bookkeeping**, which is the clerical function of recording the economic activities of a business. Although some accountants do perform bookkeeping functions, their work generally goes well beyond the scope of this activity. Accountants design accounting systems, prepare financial statements, analyze and interpret financial information, prepare financial forecasts and budgets, and prepare tax returns. Some accountants specialize in certain areas of accounting, such as **cost accounting** (computing and analyzing production costs), **tax accounting** (preparing tax returns and interpreting tax law), or **financial analysis** (evaluating a company's performance and the financial implications of strategic decisions such as product pricing, employee benefits, and business acquisitions).

In addition to traditional accounting work, accountants may also help clients improve business processes, plan for the future, evaluate product performance, analyze profitability by customer and product groups, design and install new computer systems, assist companies with decision making, and provide a variety of other management consulting services. Performing these functions requires a strong business background and a variety of business skills beyond accounting, from leadership to information technology.

Most accountants (about 65 percent) are **private accountants** (sometimes called *corporate accountants*). Private accountants work for a business, a government agency (such as the Internal Revenue Service, a school, or a local police department), or a nonprofit corporation (such as a church, charity, or hospital).[2] Private accountants generally work together as a team under the supervision of the organization's **controller**, who reports to the vice president of finance or the chief financial officer (CFO). Exhibit 16.1 shows the typical finance department of a large company. In smaller organizations, the controller may be in charge of the company's entire finance operation and report directly to the president.

LEARNING OBJECTIVE 1

Discuss how both managers and external stakeholders use financial information

accounting
Measuring, interpreting, and communicating financial information to support internal and external decision making

financial accounting
Preparing financial information for users outside the organization

management accounting
Preparing data for use by managers within the organization

LEARNING OBJECTIVE 2

Describe what accountants do

bookkeeping
Recordkeeping; clerical aspect of accounting

cost accounting
Calculating the cost of creating and selling a company's goods and services

tax accounting
Area of accounting focusing on tax preparation and tax planning

financial analysis
Evaluating a company's performance and analyzing the costs and benefits of a strategic action

private accountants
In-house accountants employed by organizations and businesses other than a public accounting firm

controller
Highest-ranking accountant in a company, responsible for overseeing all accounting functions

Exhibit 16.1

Typical Finance
Department

*Here is a typical finance
department of a large
company. In smaller
companies, the controller
may be the highest-ranking
accountant and report
directly to the president.
The vice president in
charge of finance is often
called the chief financial
officer (CFO).*

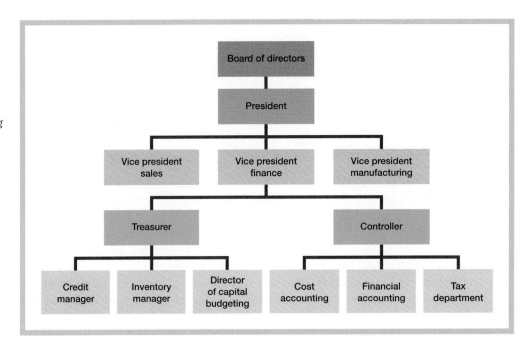

*certified public
accountants (CPAs)
Professionally licensed
accountants who meet
certain requirements
for education and
experience and who
pass a comprehensive
examination*

*certified management
accountants (CMAs)
Accountants who have
fulfilled the requirements
for certification as
specialists in
management accounting*

*public accountants
Professionals who provide
accounting services to
other businesses and
individuals for a fee*

*audit
Formal evaluation of the
fairness and reliability of a
client's financial statements*

Although certification is not required of private accountants, many are licensed **certified public accountants (CPAs)**, which means they have passed a rigorous state-certified licensing exam. To become eligible to sit for the exam, candidates must complete the equivalent of 120 to 150 semester hours of college-level course work and other requirements specified by the licensing state.[3] A growing number of private accountants are becoming **certified management accountants (CMAs)**; to do so they must pass a two-day exam (given by the Institute of Management Accountants) that is comparable in difficulty to the CPA exam.[4]

In contrast to private accountants, **public accountants** are independent of the businesses, organizations, and individuals they serve. Most public accountants are employed by public accounting firms that provide a variety of accounting and consulting services to their clients. The largest of these firms, commonly known as the "Big Four," are Deloitte & Touche (www.deloitte.com), Ernst & Young (www.ey.com), KPMG (www.kpmg.com), and PriceWaterhouseCoopers (www.pwcglobal.com). The Big Four were the Big Eight at one point, but mergers and the collapse of Arthur Andersen has reduced the number to four. Whether they belong to one of these giant firms or a smaller regional or local firm, public accountants generally are CPAs and must obtain CPA and state licensing certifications before they are eligible to conduct an **audit**—a formal evaluation of a company's accounting records and processes to ensure the integrity and reliability of a company's financial statements.

By the way, if you've shied away from accounting as a career choice because of popular stereotypes about it being a dull job fit only for "bean counters," it's time to take another look. Partly as a consequence of recent financial scandals, accounting specialists are now a hot commodity in the job market. Salaries and benefits are increasing as everybody from the Big Four accounting firms to the FBI to corporations both large and small actively recruit accountants to help navigate the increasingly complex landscape of contemporary business finance.[5]

The Rules of Accounting

In order to make informed decisions, investors, bankers, suppliers, and other parties need some means to verify the quality of the financial information that companies release to the public. They also need some way to compare information from one company to the next. To accommodate these needs, financial accountants are expected to follow a number of rules, some of which are voluntary and some of which are required by law. The two most significant sets of rules are known as *GAAP*, which has evolved over decades, and *Sarbanes-Oxley*, new legislation that was passed in the wake of Enron and other recent accounting scandals.

Accountants perform a variety of services for their clients beyond tax preparation and auditing. Many serve on strategic planning teams and help companies plan for the future. All are required to meet a variety of government regulations for financial decision making and reporting.

GAAP Companies whose stock is publicly traded in the United States are required to file audited financial statements with the Securities and Exchange Commission (SEC). During an audit, CPAs who work for an independent accounting firm, also known as **external auditors**, review a client's financial records to determine whether the statements that summarize these records have been prepared in accordance with **generally accepted accounting principles (GAAP)**, basic accounting standards and procedures that have been agreed on by regulators, auditors, and companies over decades. GAAP aims to give a fair and true picture of a company's financial position.

Once the auditors have completed an audit, they attach a report summarizing their findings to the client's published financial statements. Sometimes these reports disclose information that might materially affect the client's financial position, such as the bankruptcy of a major supplier, a large obsolete inventory, costly environmental problems, or questionable accounting practices. Most companies, however, receive a clean audit report, which means that to the best of the auditors' knowledge the company's financial statements are accurate.

To assist with the auditing process, many large organizations use **internal auditors**—employees who investigate and evaluate the organization's internal operations and data to determine whether they are accurate and whether they comply with GAAP, federal laws, and industry regulations. Although this self-checking process is vital to an organization's financial health, an internal audit is not a substitute for having an independent auditor look things over and render an unbiased opinion.

All U.S. public companies such as MCI must publish their financial statements in accordance with GAAP. This requirement makes it possible for external users to compare the financial results of one company with those of another and to gain a general idea of a firm's relative effectiveness and its standing within a particular industry. From time to time, companies experience special situations, such as incurring a significant onetime loss, which managers believe may distort the overall financial picture. In the recent past, it was common for companies in these situations to publish *pro forma* or *non-GAAP* numbers that removed the effect of these deviations from the financial results. Some companies claimed their investors wanted to see these numbers, but critics say that too often the technique was used to hide losses that would depress stock prices. The SEC now requires companies that publish pro forma results to also publish GAAP-equivalent results so that investors can compare the difference.[6]

In the United States, the Financial Accounting Standards Board (FASB) is responsible for overseeing GAAP. Among the FASB's responsibilities is the work of the Emerging Issues Task Force, which keeps an eye on developments in corporate accounting and issues

external auditors
Independent accounting firms that provide auditing services for public companies

generally accepted accounting principles (GAAP)
Professionally approved U.S. standards and practices used by accountants in the preparation of financial statements

internal auditors
Employees who analyze and evaluate a company's operations and data to determine their accuracy

new rules as required. For instance, one recent change affected how companies could classify debt as either short-term or long-term.[7] Although such changes may seem minor, they can affect such important factors as the interest rate a company gets charged on bank loans.

Other countries have similar governing boards with accounting rules that don't always match GAAP conventions, which means that foreign companies such as Nissan or Toyota may report accounting data using rules that are different from those used by U.S. companies such as Ford or General Motors. Foreign companies that list their securities on a U.S. stock exchange currently must convert financial statements prepared under foreign accounting rules to GAAP. This requirement ensures that all companies listed on U.S. stock exchanges are on even ground. But it can also create problems for foreign companies. For instance, when the German firm Daimler-Benz first listed its stock on the New York Stock Exchange, the company's $102 million profit changed to a $579 million loss for the same period because of a difference between German accounting rules and U.S. GAAP.[8]

The International Accounting Standards Board (IASB) has been working for years to develop a uniform set of global accounting rules known to help eliminate such differences but has not yet been able to iron out all the differences from country to country. The IASB's proposed guidelines would simplify accounting for multinational companies, give foreign companies easier access to U.S. stock markets, and help investors select stocks from companies around the world. For instance, European companies that comply with IASB standards are expected to be able to file reports with the U.S. SEC (thereby allowing them to offer stock on U.S. exchanges) without substantially modifying their financial reports.[9]

LEARNING OBJECTIVE 3

Summarize the impact of the Sarbanes-Oxley Act

Sarbanes-Oxley
Comprehensive legislation, passed in the wake of Enron and other scandals, designed to improve integrity and accountability of financial information

Business Buzz
Sox or Sarbox
Accounting slang for the Sarbanes-Oxley Act

Sarbanes-Oxley GAAP sets forth the principles and guidelines for companies and accountants to follow when preparing financial reports or recording accounting transactions, but high-profile scandals involving Enron, WorldCom, and other big corporations in recent years prove that it is still possible to get around the rules and deceive investors. To repair investor confidence, Congress passed the Public Company Accounting Reform and Investor Protection Act, usually referred to as **Sarbanes-Oxley**. The legislation aims to stop abuses and errors in several important areas. The act[10]

- Outlaws most loans by corporations to their own directors and executives
- Creates the Public Company Accounting Oversight Board (PCAOB) to oversee external auditors
- Requires corporate lawyers to report evidence of financial wrongdoing
- Prohibits external auditors from providing some nonaudit services
- Requires that audit committees on the board of directors have at least one financial expert and that the majority of board members be independent (not employed by the company in an executive position)
- Prohibits investment bankers from influencing stock analysts
- Requires CEOs and CFOs to sign statements attesting to the accuracy of their financial statements
- Requires companies to document and test their internal financial controls and processes

The last two items in particular have generated lots of interest and some controversy among businesses. In a few of the recent scandals, top executives claimed not to know what was going on in their own companies, although "the idea that a CEO doesn't know what's going on in his company is ridiculous," according to United Technologies CEO George David. In any event, signing their financial statements under oath should have the intended effect of ensuring close attention to the details. However, the requirement to document and test financial controls has generated perhaps the most widespread discussion—even though the requirement to have such controls in place has actually been part of federal law since the Foreign Corrupt Practices Act of the late 1970s. Estimates of the cost of complying with Sarbanes-Oxley vary widely, from a few hundred thousand dollars to many millions, depending on the size of the company and initial state of its financial systems. Large corporations, those with $4 billion or more in annual revenue, were expected to spend an average of $35 million each on compliance efforts in 2005 alone. Costs are forecast to drop as companies improve their systems and get

TECHNOLOGIES THAT ARE REVOLUTIONIZING BUSINESS Compliance Management Software

The Sarbanes-Oxley Act requires publicly traded companies to regularly verify their internal accounting controls. To assist in this recurring task, a number of software companies now offer *compliance management software.*

HOW IT'S REVOLUTIONIZING BUSINESS

Verifying accounting controls can be a considerable task for large or decentralized companies with multiple accounting systems. For instance, one recent study found that the average billion-dollar public company has 48 separate financial systems. Rather than creating their own software solutions to the problem or adapting existing accounting software, many companies now turn to ready-made compliance management software. The costs can be considerable (up to $100,000 or more just to purchase the software and possibly many times more than that to

have it customized and installed); the companies buying these solutions say it's cheaper and faster than building their own, plus they can take advantage of the compliance knowledge programmed into the software. Whether they build or buy, a number of firms are also using the new reporting requirements as an opportunity to streamline and improve their business operations.

WHERE YOU CAN LEARN MORE

Several professional publications are keeping an eye on the compliance software market, including *Computerworld* (**www.computerworld.com**), *CIO* (**www.cio.com**), *InformationWeek* (**www.informationweek.com**), *eWeek* (**www.eweek.com**), and *CFO* and *CFO IT* (**www.cfo.com**). Search their respective websites for "compliance software" to get the latest news.

accustomed to the regulations, but the U.S. Chamber of Commerce and other business interests are pressuring the government to revise the regulations to focus on major issues instead of trying to verify every single, detailed item.[11]

Is Sarbanes-Oxley the right idea—or even necessary? As you might expect with anything this complex and far-reaching, opinions vary widely. Most investors welcome the changes, while many executives find them unnecessary or overreaching. Some companies have already benefited from fixing problems that compliance efforts uncovered, including unnecessary spending and inconsistent reporting across divisions.[12] Moreover, in spite of all the thunder and lightning surrounding Sarbanes-Oxley, financial reporting and governance issues are a much smaller problem for investors than simple managerial mistakes. A recent survey by the consulting firm Booz Allen Hamilton indicated that in poorly performing corporations, strategic and tactical blunders, such as botched mergers or inaccurate forecasting, accounted for 87 percent of the decline in shareholder value, as compared to only 13 percent caused by compliance and governance issues.[13]

Regulations such as Sarbanes-Oxley represent an effort to improve **quality of earnings**, which is a general term for the degree of confidence that investors should have in the profits reported by public corporations. As you'll read in Chapter 18, earnings are the primary question that investors have regarding stocks they invest in, so it's a critical figure. However, in large companies that track millions of transactions across multiple divisions operating in dozens of countries, distilling all these data points down to a single figure is no easy task. Moreover, even while staying strictly within the law, companies often have considerable flexibility in how they report many of the numbers, particularly numbers that are estimates (such as predictions of future gains from investments or future losses from bad debts). Some company reports suffer from even more fundamental problems, such as complementary financial statements that are supposed to present different but simultaneous views of the company's financial health—but don't cover the same time periods, making it impossible to compare and consolidate numbers. The chief accounting analyst at investment banker Morgan Stanley goes so far as to say that "The financial reporting system is completely broken." Many investors are calling for new restrictions in such areas as the use of estimates.[14]

quality of earnings
General term for the degree of confidence that investors should have in the profits reported by public corporations

THINKING ABOUT ETHICS

PUTTING ACCOUNTABILITY BACK INTO PUBLIC ACCOUNTING

For a profession that is supposed to be all about trust and financial responsibility, public accounting seems to be lurching from one scandal to another: Billions of dollars in accounting fraud that slipped past auditors, multimillion-dollar fines for selling shady tax shelters, accountants arrested for destroying documents, accusations of over-billing, an endless parade of lawsuits from investors and clients—and the biggest black eye of them all, the collapse of the once-mighty accounting firm Arthur Andersen (see Case for Critical Thinking on page 546). How did all this happen, and how can the profession restore public confidence?

No situation this complex will surrender to a simple explanation, but observers point out several issues that have contributed to many of the recent problems:

- **Deliberate deception by corporate clients.** Auditors maintain that in many cases it's impossible to detect deliberately misleading bookkeeping, and it's unfair to hold them accountable when they don't. An auditor "cannot provide 100 percent guarantee against fraud," says Chuck Landes, director of auditing for the American Institute of Certified Public Accountants (AICPA).
- **Changes in accounting practices.** Some claim that auditors aren't looking in the right places. In the past, auditors used a labor-intensive process of sifting through thousands of transactions to determine if bookkeeping entries were correct. Now they focus on analyzing the computerized bookkeeping programs and internal controls. While this approach prevents low-level employees from swiping petty cash, it can't always catch executives who shift millions or billions around using creative accounting schemes.
- **Conflict of interest.** Others blame the conflict of interest that exists when an accounting firm earns millions performing consulting work for an audit client. "If you are auditing your own creations, it is very difficult to criticize them," says one accounting expert. Critics say these cozy relationships and lucrative consulting contracts discouraged some auditors from examining corporate books closely enough or challenging CEOs when potential irregularities did surface.

- **Overly aggressive business practices.** In 1991, the AICPA changed its code of conduct to allow tax accountants to charge performance-based fees, meaning that firms could charge a percentage of the money they saved clients by lowering their taxes. The IRS and industry insiders say this spawned a rash of overly aggressive tax shelters throughout the 1990s. When the IRS finally got its arms around the problem, it started banning these shelters, fining accountants who sold them, and recovering back taxes from clients who used them. Some of these clients are suing their accountants, claiming they were misled.

Between IRS crackdowns, new SEC requirements, and the numerous provisions of the Sarbanes-Oxley Act, the profession is certainly getting attention—some of it welcome, some of it not. For instance, auditors say Sarbanes-Oxley finally gives them the authority to stand up to executives who might be playing tricks with the numbers. The ban on selling certain kinds of consulting to auditing clients should help with the conflict of interest as well. At the same time, though, regulators and the AICPA are locking horns over the guidelines to implement Sarbanes-Oxley and other regulatory changes. The accountants say they have the expertise needed to write effective auditing rules; the regulators say the AICPA is more interested in protecting its members from lawsuits than in conducting proper audits.

Unfortunately, this story doesn't end with WorldCom and Enron. A new round of investigations and lawsuits involving clients in the insurance industry is bringing new problems to light. With billions of dollars and the financial health of millions of people on the line, this battle is likely to go on for years. And the past few years have given everyone a clear and important reminder: Auditing is a vital function upon which free enterprise and the health of the global economy depend.

Questions for Critical Thinking

1. Should accounting firms be allowed to perform management consulting functions for their audit clients? Why or why not?
2. Why is the auditing function of such vital importance to the global economy?

CRITICAL THINKING CHECKPOINT

1. What effect does unreliable or uncertain accounting have on the U.S. economy?
2. Do U.S. companies need to worry about accounting rules and regulations in other countries? Why or why not?
3. Will requiring CEOs to personally attest to the accuracy of financial statements eliminate errors and misrepresentations? Why or why not?

Fundamental Accounting Concepts

As pressure mounts for companies to produce cleaner financial statements and to disclose material information promptly, the need increases for all businesspeople—not just accountants—to understand basic accounting concepts. In the next sections we discuss the fundamental accounting concepts, explore the key elements of financial statements, and explain how managers and investors analyze a company's financial statements to make decisions.

In their work with financial data, accountants are guided by three basic concepts: the *fundamental accounting equation, double-entry bookkeeping,* and the *matching principle.* Here is a closer look at each of these concepts.

The Accounting Equation

For thousands of years, businesses and governments have kept records of their **assets**—valuable items they own or lease, such as equipment, cash, land, buildings, inventory, and investments. Claims against those assets are **liabilities**, or what the business owes to its creditors—such as banks and suppliers. For example, when a company borrows money to purchase a building, the lender or creditor has a claim against the company's assets. What remains after liabilities have been deducted from assets is **owners' equity**:

$$\text{Assets} - \text{Liabilities} = \text{Owners' equity}$$

Using the principles of algebra, this equation can be restated in a variety of formats. The most common is the simple **accounting equation**, which serves as the framework for the entire accounting process:

$$\text{Assets} = \text{Liabilities} + \text{Owners' equity}$$

This equation suggests that either creditors or owners provide all the assets in a corporation. Think of it this way: If you were starting a new business, you could contribute cash to the company to buy the assets you needed to run your business or you could borrow money from a bank (the creditor) or you could do both. The company's liabilities are placed before owners' equity in the accounting equation because creditors get paid first. After liabilities have been paid, anything left over belongs to the owners or, in the case of a corporation, to the shareholders. As a business engages in economic activity, the dollar amounts and composition of its assets, liabilities, and owners' equity change. However, the equation must always be in balance; in other words, one side of the equation must always equal the other side.

Double-Entry Bookkeeping and the Matching Principle

To keep the accounting equation in balance, most companies use a **double-entry bookkeeping** system that records every transaction affecting assets, liabilities, or owners' equity. For example, if MCI purchased a $6,000 computer system on credit, assets would increase by $6,000 (the cost of the system) and liabilities would also increase by $6,000 (the amount the company owes the vendor), keeping the accounting equation in balance. But if MCI paid cash outright for the

LEARNING OBJECTIVE 4

State the basic accounting equation and explain the purpose of double-entry bookkeeping and the matching principle

assets
Any things of value owned or leased by a business

liabilities
Claims against a firm's assets by creditors

owners' equity
Portion of a company's assets that belongs to the owners after obligations to all creditors have been met

accounting equation
Basic accounting equation that assets equal liabilities plus owners' equity

LEARNING OBJECTIVE 5

Differentiate between cash basis and accrual basis accounting

double-entry bookkeeping
Way of recording financial transactions that requires two entries for every transaction so that the accounting equation is always kept in balance

Accounting software designed for small businesses, such as QuickBooks from Intuit, simplifies bookkeeping and financial planning for small-business owners.

equipment (instead of arranging for credit), the company's total assets and total liabilities would not change, because the $6,000 increase in equipment would be offset by an equal $6,000 reduction in cash. In fact, the company would just be switching assets—cash for equipment.

matching principle
Fundamental principle requiring that expenses incurred in producing revenue be deducted from the revenues they generate during an accounting period

The **matching principle** requires that expenses incurred in producing revenues be deducted from the revenue they generated during the same accounting period. This matching of expenses and revenue is necessary for the company's financial statements to present an accurate picture of the profitability of a business. Accountants match revenue to expenses by adopting the **accrual basis** of accounting, which states that revenue is recognized when you make a sale or provide a service, not when you get paid. Similarly, your expenses are recorded when you receive the benefit of a service or when you use an asset to produce revenue—not when you pay for it. Accrual accounting focuses on the economic substance of the event instead of on the movement of cash. It's a way of recognizing that revenue can be earned either before or after cash is received and that expenses can be incurred when you receive a benefit (such as a shipment of supplies) whether before or after you pay for it.

accrual basis
Accounting method in which revenue is recorded when a sale is made and expense is recorded when it is incurred

cash basis
Accounting method in which revenue is recorded when payment is received and expense is recorded when cash is paid

If a business runs on a **cash basis**, the company records revenue only when money from the sale is actually received. Your checkbook is an easy-to-understand cash-based accounting system: You record checks at the time of purchase and deposits at the time of receipt. Revenue thus equals cash received, and expenses equal cash paid. The trouble with cash-based accounting, however, is that it can be misleading. You can misrepresent expenses and income by the way you time payments. It's easy to inflate income, for example, by delaying the payment of bills. For that reason, public companies are required to keep their books on an accrual basis. Unfortunately, as the earlier discussion of estimates suggests, the accrual method is also vulnerable to both intentional abuse and unintentional mistakes, particularly in complex, long-term sales contracts. When IMPAC Medical Systems, a software company based in Mountain View, California, couldn't figure out when to accrue revenue from some of its contracts, it asked three separate outside auditors for advice—and got three different answers. The company finally gave up and had to ask the SEC how to handle the accounting.[15]

depreciation
Accounting procedure for systematically spreading the cost of a tangible asset over its estimated useful life

Depreciation, or the allocation of the cost of a tangible long-term asset over a period of time, is another way that companies match expenses with revenue. During the normal course of business, a company enters into many transactions that benefit more than one accounting period—such as the purchase of buildings, inventory, and equipment. When you buy a piece of real estate or equipment, instead of deducting the entire cost of the item at the time of purchase, you depreciate it, or spread its cost over the asset's useful life (because the asset will likely generate income for years to come). If the company were to expense long-term assets at the time of purchase, the financial performance of the company would be distorted in the year of purchase as well as in all future years when these assets generate revenue.

CRITICAL THINKING CHECKPOINT

1. Would the current amount of the owners' equity be a reasonable price to pay for a company? Why or why not?
2. How does double-entry bookkeeping help to eliminate errors?
3. Why is accrual-based accounting considered more fraud-proof than cash-based accounting?

Using Financial Statements

A typical corporate accounting system handles thousands or even millions of individual transactions—debits and credits to be exact. During the accounting process, sales, purchases, and other transactions are recorded and classified into individual accounts. Once these individual transactions are recorded and then summarized, accountants must review the resulting transaction summaries and adjust or correct all errors or discrepancies before they can **close the books**, or transfer net revenue and expense items to *retained earnings.* Exhibit 16.2 presents the process for putting all of a company's financial data

close the books
The act of transferring net revenue and expense account balances to retained earnings for the period

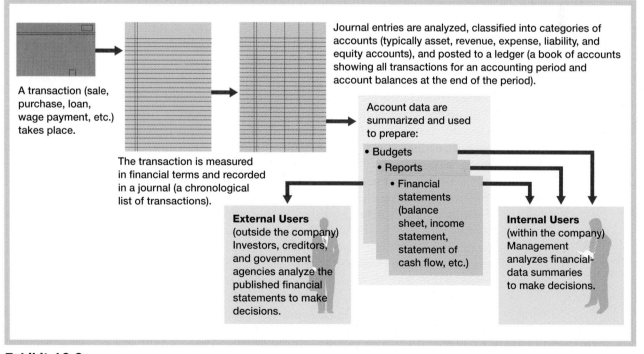

A transaction (sale, purchase, loan, wage payment, etc.) takes place.

The transaction is measured in financial terms and recorded in a journal (a chronological list of transactions).

Journal entries are analyzed, classified into categories of accounts (typically asset, revenue, expense, liability, and equity accounts), and posted to a ledger (a book of accounts showing all transactions for an accounting period and account balances at the end of the period).

Account data are summarized and used to prepare:
- Budgets
- Reports
- Financial statements (balance sheet, income statement, statement of cash flow, etc.)

External Users (outside the company) Investors, creditors, and government agencies analyze the published financial statements to make decisions.

Internal Users (within the company) Management analyzes financial-data summaries to make decisions.

Exhibit 16.2
The Accounting Process
The accounting process involves numerous steps between recording the sales and other transactions to the internal and external reporting of summarized financial results. (The paper forms illustrated here are classic accounting forms; today, nearly all companies record this information on computers.)

into standardized formats that can be used for decision making, analysis, and planning. To make sense of these individual transactions, accountants summarize them by preparing financial statements.

Understanding Financial Statements

Financial statements consist of three separate yet interrelated reports: the *balance sheet,* the *income statement,* and the *statement of cash flows.* Together these statements provide information about an organization's financial strength and ability to meet current obligations, the effectiveness of its sales and collection efforts, and its effectiveness in managing its assets. Organizations and individuals use financial statements to spot opportunities and problems, to make business decisions, and to evaluate a company's past performance, present condition, and future prospects. Whether the company is a one-person consulting firm or a multinational with a hundred thousand employees, financial statements are a vital tool.

The following sections examine the financial statements of Computer Central, a company engaged in direct sales and distribution of brand-name personal computers (such as HP, Toshiba, and Apple) and related computer products (such as software, printer cartridges, and scanners). The company conducts its primary business from a combined telemarketing, corporate office, warehouse, and showroom facility in Denver, Colorado. There, Computer Central's 600-plus account executives service over 634,000 customers annually. In 2005, the company shipped over 2.3 million orders, amounting to more than $1.7 billion in sales—a 35 percent increase in sales from the prior year. The company's daily sales volume has grown considerably over the last decade—from $232,000 to $6.8 million. Because of this tremendous growth and the increasing demand for new computer products, the company recently purchased a 276,000-square-foot building. Keep these points in mind as you explore Computer Central's financial statements in the next sections.

LEARNING OBJECTIVE 6

Explain the purpose of the balance sheet and identify its three main sections

balance sheet
Statement of a firm's financial position on a particular date; also known as a statement of financial position

Balance Sheet The **balance sheet**, also known as the *statement of financial position,* is a snapshot of a company's financial position on a particular date, such as December 31, 2005. In effect, it freezes all business actions and provides a baseline from which a company can measure change. This statement is called a balance sheet because it includes all elements in the accounting equation and shows the balance between assets on one side of the equation and liabilities and owners' equity on the other side. In other words, as in the accounting equation, a change on one side of the balance sheet means changes elsewhere. Exhibit 16.3 is the balance sheet for Computer Central as of December 31, 2005.

In reality, however, no business can stand still while its financial condition is being examined. A business may make hundreds of transactions of various kinds every working day. Even during a holiday, office fixtures grow older and decrease in value and interest on savings accounts accumulates. Yet the accountant must set up a balance sheet so that managers and other interested parties can evaluate the business's financial position as if it were static, rather than ever changing.

calendar year
Twelve-month accounting period that begins on January 1 and ends on December 31

Every company prepares a balance sheet at least once a year, most often at the end of the **calendar year**, covering from January 1 to December 31. However, many business and government bodies use a **fiscal year**, which may be any 12 consecutive months. For example, a company may use a fiscal year of June 1 to May 31 because its peak selling season ends in May. Its fiscal year would then correspond to its full annual cycle of manufacturing and selling. Some companies prepare a balance sheet more often than once a year, perhaps at the end of each month or quarter. Thus, every balance sheet is dated to show the exact date when the financial snapshot was taken.

fiscal year
Any 12 consecutive months used as an accounting period

By reading a company's balance sheet you should be able to determine the size of the company, the major assets owned, any asset changes that occurred in recent periods, how the company's assets are financed, and any major changes that have occurred in the company's debt and equity in recent periods. Most companies classify assets, liabilities, and owners' equity into categories such as those shown in the Computer Central balance sheet.

Exhibit 16.3
Balance Sheet for Computer Central

The categories used on Computer Central's year-end balance sheet are typical.

Computer Central
Balance Sheet
As of December 31, 2005
(in thousands)

ASSETS

Current Assets		
Cash	$ 4,230	
Marketable Securities	36,458	
Accounts Receivable	158,204	
Inventory	64,392	
Miscellaneous Prepaid and Deferred Items	6,504	
Total Current Assets		$269,788
Fixed Assets		
Property and Equipment	53,188	
Less: Accumulated Depreciation	−16,132	
Total Fixed Assets		37,056
Other Assets		4,977
Total Assets		**$311,821**

Current Assets
Cash and other items that will or can be converted to cash within one year.

Fixed Assets
Long-term investments in buildings, equipment, furniture, and any other tangible property expected to be used in running the business for a period longer than one year.

LIABILITIES AND SHAREHOLDERS' EQUITY

Current Liabilities		
Accounts Payable	$ 41,358	
Accrued Expenses	29,700	
Total Current Liabilities		71,058
Long-Term Liabilities		
Loans Payable	15,000	
Total Long-Term Liabilities		15,000
Total Liabilities		86,058
Shareholders' Equity		
Common Stock		
(21,571 shares @ $.01 par value)	216	
Less: Treasury Stock (50,000 shares)	−2,089	
Paid-in Capital	81,352	
Retained Earnings	146,284	
Total Shareholders' Equity		225,763
Total Liabilities and Shareholders' Equity		**$311,821**

Current Liabilities
Amounts owed by the company that are to be repaid within one year.

Long-Term Liabilities
Debts that are due a year or more after the date of the balance sheet.

Shareholders' Equity
Money contributed to the company for ownership interests, as well as the accumulation of profits that have not been paid out as dividends (retained earnings).

Assets. As discussed earlier in this chapter, an asset is something owned by a company that will be used to generate income. Assets can be both *tangible*, such as equipment and buildings, and *intangible*, such as cash, patents, skilled workers and managers, and strong brand names. Intangible, nonfinancial assets are a particularly thorny issue, by the way. While they consume enormous amounts of investment (such as in training, advertising, and research), are responsible for much of the revenue that a company can generate, and make up an increasingly important part of the value of many contemporary companies, their true value rarely shows up in a balance sheet.[16] For instance, the real value of a company such as Google is not in its tangible assets, but in its search engine algorithms, software designs, and the brainpower of its workforce.

Most often, the asset section of the balance sheet is divided into *current assets* and *fixed assets*. **Current assets** include cash and other items that will or can become cash within the following year. **Fixed assets** (sometimes referred to as *property*, *plant*, and *equipment*) are long-term investments in buildings, equipment, furniture and fixtures, transportation equipment, land, and other tangible property used in running the business. Fixed assets have a useful life of more than one year. Computer Central's principal fixed asset is the company's warehouse facility.

Assets are listed in descending order by *liquidity,* or the ease with which they can be converted into cash. Thus, current assets are listed before fixed assets. The balance sheet gives a subtotal for each type of asset and then a grand total for all assets. Computer Central's current assets consist primarily of cash, investments in short-term marketable securities such as money-market funds, accounts receivable (or amounts due from customers), and inventory (such as computers, software, and other items the company sells to customers).

Liabilities. Liabilities come after assets because they represent claims against the company's assets, as shown in the basic accounting equation: Assets = Liabilities + Owners' equity. Liabilities may be current or long-term, and they are listed in the order in which they will come due. The balance sheet gives subtotals for **current liabilities** (obligations that will have to be met within one year of the date of the balance sheet) and **long-term liabilities** (obligations that are due one year or more after the date of the balance sheet), and then it gives a grand total for all liabilities.

Current liabilities include accounts payable, short-term financing, and accrued expenses. *Accounts payable* includes the money the company owes its suppliers (such as Compaq and Toshiba) as well as money it owes vendors for miscellaneous services (such as electricity and telephone charges). *Short-term financing* consists of trade credit—the amount owed to suppliers for products purchased but not yet paid for—and commercial paper—short-term promissory notes of major corporations sold in denominations of $100,000 or more, with maturities of up to 270 days (the maximum allowed by the SEC without registration). *Accrued expenses* are expenses that have been incurred but for which bills have not yet been received. For example, because Computer Central's account executives earn commissions on computer sales to customers, the company has a liability to its account executives once the sale is made—regardless of when a check is issued to the employee. Thus, the company must record this liability because it represents a claim against company assets. If such expenses and their associated liabilities were not recorded, the company's financial statements would be misleading and would violate the matching principle (because the commission expenses that were earned at the time of sale would not be matched to the revenue generated from the sale).

Long-term liabilities include loans, leases, and bonds. As Chapter 17 points out, bank loans may be secured or unsecured. The borrowing company makes principal and interest payments to the bank over the term of the loan, and its obligation is limited to these payments (see the "Debt Versus Equity Financing" discussion in Chapter 17 on pages 558–559). Leases are an alternative to loans. Rather than borrowing money to buy a piece of equipment, a firm may enter into a long-term **lease**, under which the owner of an item allows another party to use it in exchange for regular payments. Bonds are certificates that obligate the company to repay a certain sum, plus interest, to the bondholder on a specific date. Bonds are traded on organized securities exchanges and are discussed in detail in Chapter 18.

Computer Central's long-term liabilities are relatively small for a company its size. In 2005, the company purchased a new $30 million warehouse facility with $15 million in cash it had saved over many years and a five-year, $15 million bank loan. The company invests its excess cash in short-term marketable securities so it can earn interest on these funds until they are needed for future projects.

Owners' Equity. The owners' investment in a business is listed on the balance sheet under owners' equity (or shareholders' equity for a corporation such as Computer Central). Sole

---

current assets
Cash and items that can be turned into cash within one year

fixed assets
Assets retained for long-term use, such as land, buildings, machinery, and equipment; also referred to as property, plant, and equipment

current liabilities
Obligations that must be met within a year

long-term liabilities
Obligations that fall due more than a year from the date of the balance sheet

Businesses rely on bank loans as a chief source of long-term financing. Here bankers review a company's financial statements to determine if the firm is creditworthy.

lease
Legal agreement that obligates the user of an asset to make payments to the owner of the asset in exchange for using it

proprietorships list owner's equity under the owner's name with the amount (assets minus liabilities). Small partnerships list each partner's share of the business separately, and large partnerships list the total of all partners' shares. Shareholders' equity for a corporation is presented in terms of the amount of common stock that is outstanding, meaning the amount that is in the hands of the shareholders. The combined amount of the assigned or par value of the common stock plus the amount paid over the par value (paid-in capital) represents the shareholders' total investment. Roughly $81 million was paid into the corporation by Computer Central shareholders at the time the company's shares were issued. In 2005, the company repurchased 50,000 shares of the company's own stock in the open market for $948,000. The company will use this *treasury stock* for its employee stock option plan and other general corporate purposes.

Shareholders' equity also includes a corporation's **retained earnings**—the portion of shareholders' equity that is not distributed to its owners in the form of dividends. Computer Central's retained earnings amount to $146 million. The company did not pay dividends. Instead, it is building its cash reserves for future asset purchases and to finance future growth.

Income Statement If the balance sheet is a snapshot, the income statement is a movie. The **income statement** shows an organization's profit performance over a specific period of time, typically one year. It summarizes all **revenues** (or sales), the amounts that have been or are to be received from customers for goods or services delivered to them, and all **expenses**, the costs that have arisen in generating revenues. Expenses and income taxes are then subtracted from revenues to show the actual profit or loss of a company, a figure known as **net income**—profit, or the *bottom line.* By briefly reviewing a company's income statements you should have a general sense of the company's size, its trend in sales, its major expenses, and the resulting net income or loss. Owners, creditors, and investors can evaluate the company's past performance and future prospects by comparing net income for one year with net income for previous years. Exhibit 16.4 is the 2005 income statement for Computer Central, showing net income of almost $66 million. This is a 32 percent increase over the company's net income of $50 million for the previous year. Of course, as the WorldCom debacle illustrated, outsiders will get a distorted picture of profits if a company doesn't provide accurate and honest reports of revenues and expenses.

Expenses, the costs of doing business, include both the direct costs associated with creating or purchasing products for sale and the indirect costs associated with operating the business. Whether a company manufactures or purchases its inventory, the cost of storing the product for sale (such as heating the warehouse, paying the rent, and buying insurance on the storage facility) is added to the difference between the cost of the beginning inventory and the cost of the ending inventory in order to compute the actual cost of items that were sold during a period—or the **cost of goods sold**. The computation can be summarized as follows:

Cost of goods sold = Beginning inventory + Net purchases – Ending inventory

As shown in Exhibit 16.4, cost of goods sold is deducted from sales to obtain a company's **gross profit**—a key figure used in financial statement analysis. In addition to the costs directly associated with producing goods, companies deduct **operating expenses**, which include both *selling expenses* and *general expenses,* to compute a firm's *net operating income.* Net operating income is often a better indicator of financial health because it gives you an idea of how much cash the company is able to generate. For instance, a company with a sizable gross profit level can actually be losing money if its operating expenses are out of control—and if it doesn't have enough cash on hand to cover the shortfall, it could soon find itself bankrupt.[17] **Selling expenses** are operating expenses incurred through marketing and distributing the product (such as wages or salaries of salespeople, advertising, supplies, insurance for the sales operation, depreciation for the store and sales equipment, and other sales department expenses such as telephone charges).

LEARNING OBJECTIVE 7

Explain the purpose of the income statement and statement of cash flows

retained earnings
The portion of shareholders' equity earned by the company but not distributed to its owners in the form of dividends

income statement
Financial record of a company's revenues, expenses, and profits over a given period of time

revenues
Amount earned from sales of goods or services and inflow from miscellaneous sources such as interest, rent, and royalties

expenses
Costs created in the process of generating revenues

net income
Profit earned or loss incurred by a firm, determined by subtracting expenses from revenues; casually referred to as the bottom line

cost of goods sold
Cost of producing or acquiring a company's products for sale during a given period

gross profit
Amount remaining when the cost of goods sold is deducted from net sales; also known as gross margin

operating expenses
All costs of operation that are not included under cost of goods sold

selling expenses
All the operating expenses associated with marketing goods or services

Trend Analysis The process of comparing financial data from year to year in order to see how they have changed is known as *trend analysis*. You can use trend analysis to uncover shifts in the nature of the business over time. Most large companies provide data for trend analysis in their annual reports. Their balance sheets and income statements typically show three to five years or more of data (making comparative statement analysis possible). Changes in other key items—such as revenues, income, earnings per share, and dividends per share—are usually presented in tables and graphs.

Of course, when you are comparing one period with another, it's important to take into account the effects of extraordinary or unusual items such as the sale of major assets, the purchase of a new line of products from another company, weather, or economic conditions that may have affected the company in one period but not the next. These extraordinary items are usually disclosed in the text portion of a company's annual report or in the notes to the financial statements.

LEARNING OBJECTIVE 8

Explain the purpose of ratio analysis and list the four main categories of financial ratios

ratio analysis
Use of quantitative measures to evaluate a firm's financial performance

profitability ratios
Ratios that measure the overall financial performance of a firm

return on sales
Ratio between net income after taxes and net sales

return on investment (ROI)
Ratio between net income after taxes and total owners' equity; also known as return on equity

earnings per share
Measure of profitability calculated by dividing net income after taxes by the average number of shares of common stock outstanding

Ratio Analysis Managers and others compute financial ratios to facilitate the comparison of one company's financial results with those of competing firms and with industry averages. **Ratio analysis** compares two elements from the same year's financial figures. They are called *ratios* because they are computed by dividing one element of a financial statement by another. The advantage of using ratios is that it puts companies on the same footing; that is, it makes it possible to compare different-size companies and changing dollar amounts. For example, by using ratios, you can easily compare a large supermarket's ability to generate profit out of sales with a similar statistic for a small grocery store.

The benefit of converting numbers into ratios can be explained by the following example: Suppose you wanted to know how well your favorite baseball player was performing this year. To find out, you would check the player's statistics—batting average, runs batted in (RBIs), hits, and home runs. In other words, you would look at data that have been arranged into meaningful statistics that allow you to compare present performance with past performance and with the performance of other players in the league. Financial ratios do the same thing. They convert the raw numbers from the current and prior years' financial statements into ratios that highlight important relationships or measures of performance.[19]

Just as baseball statistics focus on various aspects of performance (such as hitting or pitching), financial ratios help companies understand their current operations and answer key questions: Is inventory too large? Are credit customers paying too slowly? Can the company pay its bills? Ratios also set standards and benchmarks for gauging future business by comparing a company's scores with industry averages that show the performance of competition. Every industry tends to have its own "normal" ratios, which act as yardsticks for individual companies. Dun and Bradstreet, a credit rating firm, and Robert Morris Associates publish both average financial figures and ratios for a variety of industries and company sizes.

Before reviewing specific ratios, consider two rules of thumb: First, avoid drawing too strong a conclusion from any one ratio. For instance, even with a low batting average, a baseball player's RBIs may prove valuable in the team's lineup. Second, once ratios have presented a general indication, refer back to the specific data involved to see whether the numbers confirm what the ratios suggest. In other words, do a little investigating, because statistics can be misleading.

Types of Financial Ratios Financial ratios can be organized into the following groups, as Exhibit 16.6 shows: profitability, liquidity, activity, and leverage (or debt).

Profitability Ratios. You can analyze how well a company is conducting its ongoing operations by computing **profitability ratios**, which show the state of the company's financial performance or how well it's generating profits. Three of the most common profitability ratios are **return on sales**, or profit margin (the net income a business makes per unit of sales); **return on investment (ROI)**, or return on equity (the income earned on the owner's investment); and **earnings per share** (the profit earned for each share of stock outstanding). Exhibit 16.6 shows how to compute these profitability ratios by using the financial information from Computer Central.

Exhibit 16.6
How Well Does This Company Stack Up?

Nearly all companies use ratios to evaluate how well the company is performing in relation to prior performance, the economy as a whole, and the company's competitors.

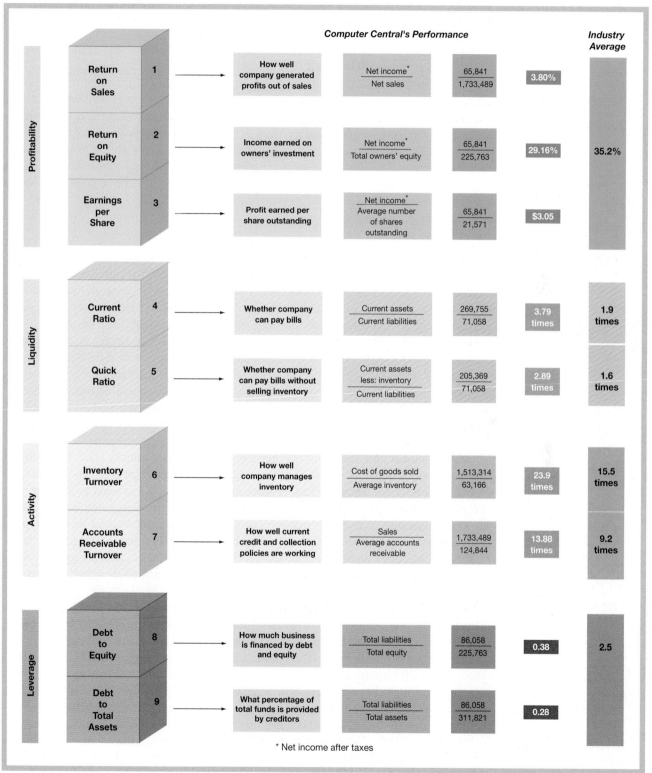

			Computer Central's Performance		Industry Average
Profitability	Return on Sales	1	How well company generated profits out of sales	Net income* / Net sales	65,841 / 1,733,489 = 3.80%	
	Return on Equity	2	Income earned on owners' investment	Net income* / Total owners' equity	65,841 / 225,763 = 29.16%	35.2%
	Earnings per Share	3	Profit earned per share outstanding	Net income* / Average number of shares outstanding	65,841 / 21,571 = $3.05	
Liquidity	Current Ratio	4	Whether company can pay bills	Current assets / Current liabilities	269,755 / 71,058 = 3.79 times	1.9 times
	Quick Ratio	5	Whether company can pay bills without selling inventory	Current assets less: inventory / Current liabilities	205,369 / 71,058 = 2.89 times	1.6 times
Activity	Inventory Turnover	6	How well company manages inventory	Cost of goods sold / Average inventory	1,513,314 / 63,166 = 23.9 times	15.5 times
	Accounts Receivable Turnover	7	How well current credit and collection policies are working	Sales / Average accounts receivable	1,733,489 / 124,844 = 13.88 times	9.2 times
Leverage	Debt to Equity	8	How much business is financed by debt and equity	Total liabilities / Total equity	86,058 / 225,763 = 0.38	2.5
	Debt to Total Assets	9	What percentage of total funds is provided by creditors	Total liabilities / Total assets	86,058 / 311,821 = 0.28	

* Net income after taxes

Liquidity Ratios. **Liquidity ratios** measure the ability of the firm to pay its short-term obligations. As you might expect, lenders and creditors are keenly interested in liquidity measures. Liquidity can be judged on the basis of *working capital,* the *current ratio,* and the *quick ratio.* A company's **working capital** (current assets minus current liabilities) is an indicator of liquidity because it represents current assets remaining after the payment of all current liabilities. The dollar amount of working capital can be misleading, however. For example, it may include the value of slow-moving inventory items that cannot be used to help pay a company's short-term debts.

A different picture of the company's liquidity is provided by the **current ratio**—current assets divided by current liabilities. This figure compares the current debt owed with the current assets available to pay that debt. The **quick ratio**, also called the *acid-test ratio,* is computed by subtracting inventory from current assets and then dividing the result by current liabilities. This ratio is often a better indicator of a firm's ability to pay creditors than the current ratio because the quick ratio leaves out inventories—which at times can be difficult to sell. Analysts generally consider a quick ratio of 1.0 to be reasonable, whereas a current ratio of 2.0 is considered a safe risk for short-term credit. Exhibit 16.6 shows that both the current and quick ratios of Computer Central are well above these benchmarks and industry averages.

Activity Ratios. A number of **activity ratios** may be used to analyze how well a company is managing its assets. The most common is the **inventory turnover ratio**, which measures how fast a company's inventory is turned into sales; in general, the quicker the better, because holding excess inventory can be expensive. When inventory sits on the shelf, money is tied up without earning interest; furthermore, the company incurs expenses for its storage, handling, insurance, and taxes. For instance, in 2004 Staples turned inventory over 7.5 times while competitor Office Depot turned its stock over only 6.2 times.[20] The ability to generate more revenue during the same time frame gives Staples an important competitive advantage. In addition, there is always a risk that the inventory will become obsolete before it can be converted into finished goods and sold. The firm's goal is to maintain enough inventory to meet customer demand in a timely fashion at the lowest cost.

Keep in mind that it's difficult to judge a company by its inventory level. For example, lower inventories might mean one of many things: You're running an efficient operation, the right inventory is not being stocked, or sales are booming and you need to increase your orders. Likewise, higher inventories could signal a decline in sales, careless ordering, or stocking up because of favorable pricing. The "ideal" turnover ratio varies with the type of operation. In 2005, Computer Central turned its inventory 23.9 times (see Exhibit 16.6). This rate is unusually high when compared with industry averages, and it suggests that the company stocks only enough inventory to fill current orders and cover a product's reorder time, as discussed in Chapter 8.

Another popular activity ratio is the **accounts receivable turnover ratio**, which measures how well a company's credit and collection policies are working by indicating how frequently accounts receivable are converted to cash. The volume of receivables outstanding depends on the financial manager's decisions regarding several issues, such as who qualifies for credit and who does not, how long customers are given to pay their bills, and how aggressive the firm is in collecting its debts. Be careful here as well. If the ratio is going up, you need to determine whether the company is doing a better job of collecting or sales are rising. If the ratio is going down, it may be because sales are decreasing or because collection efforts are lagging. In 2005, Computer Central turned its accounts receivable 13.88 times—considerably higher than the industry average (see Exhibit 16.6).

Leverage, or Debt, Ratios. You can measure a company's ability to pay its long-term debts by calculating its **debt ratios**, or leverage ratios. Lenders look at these ratios to determine whether the potential borrower has put enough money into the business to serve as a protective cushion for the loan. The **debt-to-equity ratio** (total liabilities

MINDING YOUR OWN BUSINESS

HOW TO READ AN ANNUAL REPORT

Whether you're thinking of investing, becoming a supplier, or applying for a job, knowing how to read a company's annual report will be an important skill throughout your career. Thus, it's worth your while to consider the advice of *Newsweek* columnist Jane Bryant Quinn, who provided these pointers.

READ THE LETTERS

First, turn to the report of the certified public accountant. This third-party auditor will tell you right off the bat if the report conforms with generally accepted accounting principles. Now turn to the letter from the chairman, which should tell you how the company fared this year—and why. Keep an eye out for sentences that start with "Except for . . ." and "Despite the . . ." They're clues to problems. The chairman's letter should also give you insights into the company's future. For example, look for what's new in each line of business. Is management getting the company in good shape to weather the tough and competitive years ahead?

DIG INTO THE NUMBERS

Check out the trend in the company's working capital (the difference between current assets and current liabilities). If working capital is shrinking, it could mean trouble. One possibility: The company may not be able to keep dividends growing rapidly.

Another important number to analyze is earnings per share. Management can boost earnings by selling off a plant or by cutting the budget for research or advertising. See the footnotes; they often tell the whole story. If earnings are down only because of a change in

accounting, maybe that's good! The company owes less tax and has more money in its pocket. If earnings are up, maybe that's bad. They may be up because of a special windfall that won't happen again next year. One good indicator is the trend in net sales. If sales increases are starting to slow, the company may be in trouble.

GET OUT YOUR CALCULATOR AND COMPARE

High and rising debt, relative to equity, may be no problem for a growing business. But it shows weakness in a company that's leveling out. So get out your calculator and divide long-term liabilities by shareholders' equity. That's the debt-to-equity ratio. A high ratio means the company borrows a lot of money to fund its growth. That's okay—if sales grow too, and if there's enough cash on hand to meet the payments. But if sales fall, watch out. The whole enterprise may slowly sink.

Remember, one ratio, one annual report, one chairman's letter won't tell you much. You have to compare. Is the company's debt-to-equity ratio better or worse than it used to be? Better or worse than the industry norms? In company watching, comparisons are all. They tell you if management is staying on top of things.

Questions for Critical Thinking

1. Why might a job seeker want to read a company's annual report before applying for a job with that company?
2. What types of valuable nonfinancial information might an annual report disclose to a potential supplier?

divided by total equity) indicates the extent to which a business is financed by debt as opposed to invested capital (equity). From the lender's standpoint, the lower this ratio, the safer the company, because the company has less existing debt and may be able to repay additional money it wants to borrow. However, a company that is conservative in its long-term borrowing is not necessarily well managed; often a low level of debt is associated with a low growth rate. Computer Central's low debt-to-equity ratio of 38 percent (as shown in Exhibit 16.6) reflects the company's practice of financing its growth by using excess cash flow from operations and by selling shares of common stock to the public.

The **debt-to-total-assets ratio** (total liabilities divided by total assets) also serves as a simple measure of a company's ability to carry long-term debt. As a rule of thumb, the amount of debt should not exceed 50 percent of the value of total assets. For Computer

debt-to-total-assets ratio
Measure of a firm's ability to carry long-term debt, calculated by dividing total liabilities by total assets

LEARNING FROM BUSINESS BLUNDERS

OOPS With a nationwide advertising campaign and free financing, Mitsubishi Motors went all out to entice young drivers to buy an Eclipse. The strategy worked—worked so well in fact that it cost the company nearly a billion dollars. Those young drivers took Mitsubishi up on the offer, then thousands of them defaulted on their loans when they couldn't make the payments. The bad debts cost the company $469 million. After fixing the credit problem, Mitsubishi then watched sales drop in half and had to spend $432 million more to buy back unsold inventory from its dealers.

WHAT YOU CAN LEARN Two lessons: Credit can be as dangerous for buyers as it is for sellers, and there is such a thing as a bad customer. Companies that go overboard in efforts to attract customers can find themselves in Mitsubishi's shoes, losing money on customers who couldn't afford their products in the first place.

Central, this ratio is a very low 28 percent and again reflects the company's policy of using retained earnings to finance its growth (see Exhibit 16.6). However, this ratio, too, is not a magic formula. Like grades on a report card, ratios are clues to performance. Managers, creditors, lenders, and investors can use them to get a fairly accurate idea of how a company is doing. But remember, one ratio by itself doesn't tell the whole story.

CRITICAL THINKING CHECKPOINT

1. Why is it so important to be aware of extraordinary items when analyzing a company's finances?
2. Why is the quick ratio frequently a better indicator than the current ratio of a firm's ability to pay its bills?
3. Why do you need to consider different factors when evaluating a company's ability to repay short-term versus long-term debt?

CHECKLIST: Apply These Ideas When You're the Boss

✓ The various accounting problems of recent years are a good reminder of the critical role that accurate financial information plays in every business; make sure your business systems are giving you the information you need.

✓ While accuracy and dependability are paramount considerations in accounting, be aware that you'll encounter some situations that aren't clearly defined and will require you to apply your sense of both managerial judgment and business ethics.

✓ Be careful when you try to compare accounting results from different countries (such as the profit margins of two companies); different accountant rules can generate results that are difficult to compare.

✓ Whether you're buying a company, selling a company, or just trying to figure out what a company might be worth, don't overlook the value of intangible assets.

✓ Aggressive accounting may be tempting when you need to produce attractive numbers, but remember how many companies have gotten themselves in trouble in recent years by pushing the numbers too far.

Summary of Learning Objectives

1 **Discuss how both managers and external stakeholders use financial information.** Managers use financial information to control a company's operation and to make informed business decisions. Outsiders use financial information to evaluate whether a business is creditworthy or a good investment. Specifically, banks want to know if a business is able to pay back a loan, investors want to know if the company is earning a profit, and governments want to be assured the company is paying the proper amount of taxes.

2 **Describe what accountants do.** Accountants design and install accounting systems, prepare financial statements, analyze and interpret financial information, prepare financial forecasts and budgets, prepare tax returns, interpret tax law, compute and analyze production costs, evaluate a company's performance, and analyze the financial implications of business decisions. In addition to these functions, accountants help managers improve business procedures, plan for the future, evaluate product performance, analyze the firm's profitability, and design and install computer systems. Auditors are licensed certified public accountants (CPAs) who review accounting records and processes to assess whether they conform to GAAP and whether the company's financial statements fairly present the company's financial position and operating results.

3 **Summarize the impact of the Sarbanes-Oxley Act.** In response to several high-profile cases of accounting fraud, including Enron and WorldCom, Sarbanes-Oxley introduced a number of rules covering the way publicly traded companies manage and report their finances, including restricting loans to directors and executives, creating a new board to oversee public auditors, requiring corporate lawyers to report financial wrongdoing, requiring CEOs and CFOs to sign financial statements under oath, and requiring companies to document their financial systems.

4 **State the basic accounting equation, and explain the purpose of double-entry bookkeeping and the matching principle.** The basic accounting equation is Assets = Liabilities + Owners' equity. Double-entry bookkeeping is a system of recording financial transactions to keep the accounting equation in balance. The matching principle makes sure that expenses incurred in producing revenues are deducted from the revenue they generated during the same accounting period.

5 **Differentiate between cash basis and accrual basis accounting.** Cash basis accounting recognizes revenue at the time payment is received, whereas accrual basis accounting recognizes revenue at the time of sale, even if payment is not made.

6 **Explain the purpose of the balance sheet, and identify its three main sections.** The balance sheet provides a snapshot of the business at a particular point in time. It shows the size of the company, the major assets owned, how the assets are financed, and the amount of owners' investment in the business. Its three main sections are assets, liabilities, and owners' equity.

7 **Explain the purpose of the income statement and the statement of cash flows.** The income statement reflects the results of operations over a period of time. It gives a general sense of a company's size and performance. The statement of cash flows shows how a company's cash was received and spent in three areas: operations, investments, and financing. It gives a general sense of the amount of cash created or consumed by daily operations, fixed assets, investments, and debt over a period of time.

8 **Explain the purpose of ratio analysis, and list the four main categories of financial ratios.** Financial ratios provide information for analyzing the health and future prospects of a business. Ratios facilitate financial comparisons among different-size companies and between a company and industry averages. Most of the important ratios fall into one of four categories: profitability ratios, which show how well the company generates profits; liquidity ratios, which measure the company's ability to pay its short-term obligations; activity ratios, which analyze how well a company is managing its assets; and debt ratios, which measure a company's ability to pay its long-term debt.

MCI: What's Next?

Even though MCI emerged from bankruptcy in 2004 with realistic accounting measures and a stronger balance sheet, controversy and uncertainty continued to be constant companions. For instance, the U.S. government prohibited the company from taking on new federal contracts, saying MCI still lacked sufficient ethical controls. (Noting that MCI still had progress to make in that respect, CEO Michael Capellas didn't appeal the decision.) Investigations also continue into charges leveled by competitors that MCI has been improperly labeling or routing long-distance phone calls to avoid paying fees owed to these other companies.

After MCI put itself up for sale, its considerable assets and customer base attracted both Verizon, the nation's largest phone company, and Qwest, a regional phone company. Both companies figured they could expand their markets and reduce overall costs by incorporating MCI's huge phone and data network into their existing operations (although the rapidly aging technology in that network is of some concern). In mid-2005, Verizon won the bidding war and now faces the enormous task of combining two large, complex companies—one of which is in shaky financial condition.

Even if the remnants of WorldCom live on under a new brand name, the devastation that WorldCom's fraud wreaked on its employees and investors—and the billions of dollars of added costs that WorldCom-inspired regulations heaped on thousands of other companies—won't be forgotten for years.[21]

Critical Thinking Questions

1. Should the old WorldCom's outside auditors have been able to detect the $11 billion accounting fraud? Why or why not?
2. Why would the old WorldCom's 27 separate accounting systems likely have contributed to its financial problems?
3. Why would companies such as Qwest and Verizon be interested in buying MCI when it was in such deep financial trouble?

Learn More Online

Visit the MCI website by going to Chapter 16 of this text's website at www.prenhall.com/bovee. Click on the company's hotlink, and review the company's current status (chances are good it won't be called MCI anymore by the time you read this). Is Verizon still in good financial shape after the acquisition? Look for its latest quarterly or annual report, then calculate the company's accounts receivable turnover, quick ratio, current ratio, and return on sales for the current and preceding year or quarter. What does each of these ratios show? How are the ratios trending from one period to the next? What might the trends indicate?

Key Terms

accounting (521)
accounting equation (527)
accounts receivable turnover
   ratio (538)
accrual basis (528)
activity ratios (538)
assets (527)
audit (522)
balance sheet (530)
bookkeeping (521)
calendar year (530)
cash basis (528)
certified management
   accountants (CMAs) (522)
certified public accountants
   (CPAs) (522)

close the books (529)
controller (521)
cost accounting (521)
cost of goods sold (533)
current assets (532)
current liabilities (532)
current ratio (538)
debt ratios (538)
debt-to-equity ratio (538)
debt-to-total-assets
   ratio (539)
depreciation (528)
double-entry
   bookkeeping (527)
earnings per share (536)
EBITDA (534)

expenses (533)
external auditors (523)
financial accounting(521)
financial analysis (521)
fiscal year (530)
fixed assets (532)
general expenses (534)
generally accepted
   accounting principles
   (GAAP) (523)
gross profit (533)
income statement (533)
internal auditors (523)
inventory turnover
   ratio (538)
lease (532)

liabilities (527)
liquidity ratios (538)
long-term liabilities (532)
management
    accounting (521)
matching principle (528)
net income (533)
operating expenses (533)
owners' equity (527)
private accountants (521)

profitability ratios (536)
public accountants (522)
quality of earnings (525)
quick ratio (538)
ratio analysis (536)
retained earnings (533)
return on investment
    (ROI) (536)
return on sales (536)

revenues (533)
Sarbanes-Oxley (524)
selling expenses (533)
statement of cash
    flows (534)
tax accounting (521)
working capital (538)

Test Your Knowledge

Questions for Review

1. What is GAAP?
2. What is an audit and why is it performed?
3. What is the matching principle?
4. What are the three main profitability ratios, and how is each calculated?
5. What is the primary goal of financial management?

Questions for Analysis

6. Why is accounting important to business?
7. Why do some companies resort to accounting tricks, and what steps are being taken to clamp down on such wrongdoings?
8. Why are the costs of fixed assets depreciated?
9. Why do companies prepare budgets?
10. **Ethical Considerations.** In the process of closing the company books, you encounter a problematic transaction. One of the company's customers was charged twice for the same project materials, resulting in a $1,000 overcharge. You immediately notify the controller, whose response is, "Let it go, it happens often." What should you do now?

Questions for Application

11. The senior partner of an accounting firm is looking for ways to increase the firm's business. What other services besides traditional accounting can the firm offer to its clients? What new challenges might this additional work create?
12. Visit the websites of Ford Motor Company and General Motors Corporation and retrieve their annual reports. Using these financials, compute the working capital, current ratio, and quick ratio for each company. Does one company appear to be more liquid than the other? Why?
13. **Integrated.** Review the discussion of corporate governance in Chapter 5. How will Sarbanes-Oxley affect corporate boards and their relationship with CEOs?
14. **Integrated.** Your appliance manufacturing company recently implemented a just-in-time inventory system (see Chapter 9) for all parts used in the manufacturing process. How might you expect this move to affect the company's inventory turnover rate, current ratio, and quick ratio?

Practice Your Knowledge

Handling Difficult Situations on the Job: Raising Funds for a Nonprofit

For nearly 50 years, New Jersey's nonprofit Morris County Senior Center has relied on financial support from government, businesses, and individuals. Unfortunately, recent state and federal cutbacks have dug into the organization's budget despite the center's growing needs. For many of the county's roughly 1,000 seniors who live alone, it's the only place where they can meet their peers, use a special library, avoid extreme weather, or get a well-balanced meal. Most individuals get to the facility on one of the three shuttle-type buses belonging to the center. The buses are also used for day trips to museums, plays, and similar functions, or to help the temporarily disabled get to doctors' offices or pharmacists.

Unfortunately, the buses are old and constant repairs are costing the center an average of $300 per month per bus. When buses aren't working, seniors can't get to the center, trips are canceled, and drivers are sometimes paid for coming to work even though they aren't able to drive. Conservatively, it would cost about $28,000 to replace each van with a new one: $84,000 total, including trade-in value on the old buses. Your board of directors believes that buying new vans is a better choice than continuously repairing the old ones or risking the purchase of used ones.

Your task: As director of the center, you'll be drafting a fundraising letter to send to county businesses, seeking donations to pay for the new buses. You'll stress the good work the center does and the fact that this is a special fundraising effort. But what specific financial information should you include in your letter?

Sharpening Your Communication Skills

Obtain a copy of the annual report of a business and examine what the report shows about finances and current operations. In addition to other chapter material, use the information in "How to Read an Annual Report" on page 539 as a guideline for understanding the annual report's content.

- Consider the statements made by the CEO regarding the past year: Did the company do well, or are changes in operations necessary to its future well-being? What are the projections for future growth in sales and profits?
- Examine the financial summaries for information about the fiscal condition of the company: Did the company show a profit?
- If possible, obtain a copy of the company's annual report from the previous year, and compare it with the current report to determine whether past projections were accurate.
- Prepare a brief written summary of your conclusions.

Building Your Team Skills

Divide into small groups and compute the following financial ratios for Alpine Manufacturing using the company's balance sheet and income statement. Compare your answers to those of your classmates:

- Profitability ratios: return on sales; return on equity; earnings per share
- Liquidity ratios: current ratio; quick ratio
- Activity ratios: inventory turnover; accounts receivable turnover
- Leverage ratios: debt to equity; debt to total assets

ALPINE MANUFACTURING
INCOME STATEMENT
YEAR ENDED DECEMBER 31, 2006

Sales	$1,800
Less: Cost of Goods Sold	1,000
Gross Profit	$ 800
Less: Total Operating Expenses	450
Net Operating Income Before Income Taxes	350
Less: Income Taxes	50
NET INCOME AFTER INCOME TAXES	$ 300

ALPINE MANUFACTURING
BALANCE SHEET
DECEMBER 31, 2006

ASSETS

Cash	$ 100
Accounts Receivable (beginning balance $350)	300
Inventory (beginning balance $250)	300
Current Assets	700
Fixed Assets	2,300
Total Assets	**$3,000**

LIABILITIES AND SHAREHOLDERS' EQUITY

Current Liabilities (beginning balance $300)	$ 400
Long-Term Debts	1,600
Shareholders' Equity (100 common shares outstanding valued at $12 each)	1,000
Total Liabilities and Shareholders' Equity	**$3,000**

Expand Your Knowledge

Discovering Career Opportunities

People interested in entering the field of accounting can choose among a wide variety of careers with diverse responsibilities and challenges. Select one of the occupations mentioned in this chapter or in the Prologue, under the section "Careers in Finance and Accounting." Using the Prologue, library sources, or Internet websites from one of the major accounting firms or the AICPA, dig deeper to learn more about your chosen occupation.

1. What are the day-to-day duties of this occupation? How would these duties contribute to the financial success of a company?
2. What skills and educational qualifications would you need to enter this occupation? How do these qualifications fit with your current plans, skills, and interests?
3. What kinds of employers hire people for this position? According to your research, does the number of employers seem to be increasing or decreasing? How do you think this trend will affect your employment possibilities if you choose this career?

Developing Your Research Skills

Select an article from a business journal or newspaper (print or online editions) that discusses the quarterly or year-end performance of a company that industry analysts consider notable for either positive or negative reasons.

1. Did the company report a profit or a loss for this accounting period? What other performance indicators were reported? Is the company's performance improving or declining?
2. Did the company's performance match industry analysts' expectations, or was it a surprise? How did analysts or other experts respond to the firm's actual quarterly or year-end results?
3. What reasons were given for the company's improvement or decline in performance?

Exploring the Best of the Web

URLs for all Internet exercises are provided at the website for this book, www.prenhall.com/bovee. When you log on to this text's Companion Website, select Chapter 16. Then select "Featured Websites," click on the name of the featured website, and review the website to complete these exercises.

Explore these chapter-related websites, review their content, and answer the following questions for each website you visit:

1. What is the purpose of this website?
2. What kinds of information does this website contain? Please be specific.
3. How is the information provided at this website useful for businesspeople? Consumers?
4. How did you expand your knowledge of marketing and customers by reviewing the material at this website? What new things did you learn about these topics?

Link Your Way to the World of Accounting

Looking for one accounting supersite packed with information and links to financial resources? Check out the WebCPA, an online launching point for accountants. This is the place to find answers to all kinds of questions about accounting, financial analysis, taxes, and more. Participate in one of the many focused discussion groups. Visit the niche sites for information on financial planning, practice management, technology consulting, or CPA requirements. Read the latest issues of *Accounting Today, Accounting Technology,* and the *Practical Accountant.* Don't leave without checking out the Career Center where you'll find information on the latest accounting hot jobs and opportunities. www.webcpa.com

Sharpen Your Pencil

Take a virtual field trip to the Report Gallery, where you can click to view the annual reports of Allstate, Boeing, and many other U.S. and international firms. Select an annual report for any company and examine the financial statements, chairman's letter, and auditor's report. Was it a good or bad year for the company? Who are the company's auditors? Did they issue a clean audit report? www.reportgallery.com

Think Like an Accountant

Find out how the world of accounting is changing by exploring the valuable links at CPAnet. Learn about the many facets of accounting such as taxes, finance, auditing, and more. Follow the link to your state CPA society, and discover what it takes to become a CPA or how to prepare for the CPA exam. Learn how to read a financial report, and discover what financial statements say about your business. Check out the financial calculators. Increase your knowledge of accounting terms and accounting basics before participating in one of the site's discussion forums. CPAnet claims to be a complete resource for the accounting profession. www.cpanet.com

Learning Interactively

Companion Website

Visit the Companion Website at www.prenhall.com/bovee. For Chapter 16, take advantage of the interactive "Learning Modules" to test your chapter knowledge. Get instant feedback on whether you need additional studying. Complete the exercises as specified by your instructor.

A Case for Critical Thinking

Consulting Pushes Arthur Andersen out of Balance

The descent of accounting firm Arthur Andersen from role model to convicted felon didn't happen overnight. It stemmed from external forces and internal decisions that gradually eroded the company's core values. Founded in 1913 by Arthur Andersen, the firm built its reputation by putting integrity ahead of profits. Its new hires recited the founder's motto, "Think straight, talk straight." And they learned Andersen's four cornerstones: provide good service, produce quality audits, manage staff well, and generate profits.

ASSETS AND LIABILITIES

As the firm grew from a close-knit partnership to a globe-spanning giant, its auditing services practically sold themselves. Andersen also offered business consulting, but this service was considered secondary to the accounting practice.

In the early 1970s businesses started clamoring for computers, and Andersen was ready: Its small consulting practice had been helping clients set up computer systems since 1954. As more clients began using computers to automate bookkeeping, Andersen's consulting practice exploded. It was soon bringing in as much money as the firm's accounting business; meanwhile, however, the rise of computers was driving down the demand for auditing.

As the consulting business grew larger and more profitable, the accountants struggled to retain control of the company. This conflict put a tremendous strain on the partnership, and in 1989 the consultants made their break. The firm separated into two units: Arthur Andersen and Andersen Consulting. Both reported to a new parent company called Andersen Worldwide SC, but under a complex formula, the less profitable unit would receive a share of the other's profits.

SIBLING RIVALRY

The annual race for profits turned into a brutal internal battle. When efforts to expand the accounting business faltered, the accountants began offering consulting to audit clients—sometimes competing head-to-head with Andersen Consulting. The accountants couldn't keep pace with their sibling, though, which by 1994 was contributing twice as much revenue to the parent. Worse yet, the separation agreement required Andersen Consulting to subsidize the Arthur Andersen partners by $200 million annually. This understandably upset Andersen Consulting, which in 1997 voted unanimously to sever all ties with the accounting side. The siblings battled for three years over the terms of separation until an arbitrator finally settled the dispute. Andersen Consulting won its freedom but lost the prize it wanted most: the Andersen name. Reborn reluctantly as Accenture, the consultants would soon be glad they had a new name.

UNSETTLING SETTLEMENTS

During the separation fight, pressure mounted at Arthur Andersen to make up for the $200 million it was about to lose every year. Auditors were pushed to sell more audit work or to recommend that clients outsource their internal bookkeeping operations to Andersen. Critics of this practice believed such services would damage the firm's integrity because Andersen would in effect be checking its own work.

Ultimately, partners who faced accounting dilemmas with clients had much more at stake when deciding whether to reject questionable practices uncovered by audits. Some fell short of the founder's high standards. In 1997, audit and consulting client Waste Management reported an unprecedented earnings restatement, wiping out $1.7 billion in profits. Securities regulators alleged that Andersen had bent rules so badly that it had committed fraud; Andersen paid $75 million to settle the shareholder suits that followed. In 2001, Andersen paid investors $110 million for its botched 1997 audit of home-appliance maker Sunbeam, and in 2002, the firm paid $10.3 million to settle a shareholders' lawsuit related to audit client Boston Market. But it was Andersen's role in the Enron scandal that sealed the firm's fate.

PAYING THE PIPER

During the 1990s Arthur Andersen formed unusually close ties with energy-trading company Enron, serving as its external auditors, internal auditors, and consultants. Not only did Andersen's staff maintain permanent offices at Enron's headquarters, but Andersen's Houston office became a recruiting pool for Enron. In fact, the hiring became so relentless, Andersen had to cap the number of people Enron could hire away.

In 2001, the scandal surrounding Enron exploded. The U.S. Justice Department rejected Andersen's settlement overtures, citing its repeated offenses, and took the company to court. After a six-week trial, a jury convicted Andersen of federal obstruction of justice for interfering with the Enron investigation. The court imposed the maximum punishment—a $500,000 fine and five years of court monitoring—for obstructing the government's investigation into Enron's collapse. But the fine was just the tip of the iceberg for Andersen.

During the scandal and the ensuing trial, audit clients and employees bolted from the firm to protect their own integrity and seek new relationships before Andersen went under. After its conviction, the firm surrendered its licenses to practice accounting in every U.S. state, essentially ending its

89-year history. That conviction was eventually overturned by the U.S. Supreme Court, but it seems unlikely that the firm will ever again practice public accounting. With that sad ending, the story of Arthur Andersen has made an indelible mark on the public image of accounting and prompted a tidal wave of reform within the industry.

Critical Thinking Questions

1. How did the growth of consulting services seal Arthur Andersen's fate?
2. How did Arthur Andersen's troubles affect the accounting industry?
3. Why was Andersen Consulting ultimately relieved to have a new name?
4. Visit the AICPA website at www.aicpa.org and review the AICPA Code of Professional Conduct. Which sections of the Code did Arthur Andersen accountants violate in their dealings with clients?

Video Case

Accounting for Billions of Burgers: McDonald's

Learning Objectives

The purpose of this video is to help you:

1. Understand the challenges a company may face in managing financial information from operations in multiple countries.
2. Consider how management and investors use the financial information reported by a public company.
3. Recognize how different laws and monetary systems can affect the accounting activities of a global corporation.

Synopsis

Collecting, analyzing, and reporting financial data from 30,000 restaurants in more than 100 countries is no easy task, as the accounting experts at McDonald's know all too well. Every month, the individual restaurants send their sales figures to be consolidated with data from other restaurants at the local or country level. From there, the figures are sent to country-group offices and then to one of three major regional offices before going to their final destination at the McDonald's headquarters in Oak Brook, Illinois. In the past, financial information arrived in Illinois in bits and pieces, sent by courier, mail, or fax. Today, local and regional offices log on to a special secure website and enter their month-end figures, enabling the corporate controller to quickly produce financial statements and projections for internal and external use.

Discussion Questions

1. *For analysis:* Why does McDonald's use "constant currency" comparisons when reporting its financial results?
2. *For analysis:* What types of assets might McDonald's list for depreciation in its financial statements?
3. *For application:* What effect do the corporate income tax rates in the countries where McDonald's operates have on the income statements prepared in local offices?
4. *For application:* What problems might arise if individual McDonald's restaurants were required to enter sales data directly on the company's centralized accounting website, instead of following the current procedure of sending it through country and regional channels?
5. *For debate:* To help investors and analysts better assess the company's worldwide financial health, should McDonald's be required to disclose detailed financial results for every country and region? Support your chosen position.

Online Exploration

Visit the McDonald's corporate website at www.mcdonalds.com/corp, locate the most recent financial report (quarterly or annual), and examine both overall and regional results. What aspects of its results does McDonald's highlight in this report? What does McDonald's say about its use of constant currency reporting? Which regions are doing particularly well? Which are lagging? How does management explain any differences in performance? What does McDonald's say about its use of constant currency reporting?

Keeping the Engine Running: Financial Management and Banking

LEARNING OBJECTIVES

After studying this chapter, you will be able to

1. Identify the responsibilities of a financial manager

2. Discuss how financial managers improve a company's cash flow

3. Differentiate between a master budget and a capital budget

4. Cite three factors financial managers must consider when selecting an appropriate funding vehicle

5. Identify five common types of debt financing

6. Identify three common financial services that banks provide customers and list electronic banking vehicles that facilitate these services

7. Explain how banks are involved in efforts to combat crime and terrorism

8. Describe four ways the Federal Reserve System influences the U.S. money supply

www.prenhall.com/bovee

Microsoft chairman Bill Gates and CEO Steve Ballmer recently faced an extraordinary dilemma: what to do with $60 billion in cash.

INSIDE BUSINESS TODAY

A Nice Problem to Have: Microsoft Wonders What to Do with Too Much Cash

www.microsoft.com

On the list of nice problems to have, this one has to rank very near the top: After more than two decades of growing sales and careful management of its finances, by 2004, Microsoft found itself sitting on $60 billion—and couldn't figure out what to do with it. (This amount included both cash and *cash equivalents*, assets the company could quickly convert to cash if needed.)

Publicly owned companies such as Microsoft have three basic choices for using cash that the business generates above and beyond its day-to-day operational needs: (1) save it for a rainy day; (2) invest it in the company's future through new research, acquisition of other companies, or other efforts aimed at expanding revenue; or (3) distribute it to stockholders in the form of *dividends*, which are regular payments at a designated amount per share.

Microsoft is known for its fiscally conservative management, which includes the habit of keeping enough cash on hand to deal with emergencies and unexpected expenses. However, it's hard to imagine any emergency dire enough to soak up $60 billion, so the rainy day option wasn't realistic—particularly when the company continues to generate a billion dollars more new cash every month.

The second option, reinvesting in the company's growth, makes sense in principle, but spending $60 billion is not as easy as you might think. Even if executives wanted to dramatically expand the workforce, it would be virtually impossible to hire fast enough to consume that kind of money. Acquisitions are another possibility, and Microsoft has purchased a number of companies over the years. However, it has always done so for strategic reasons—to acquire emerging technologies or to fill in gaps in its product mix. In other words, it's not a conglomerate that's interested in building a diverse portfolio of businesses in a variety of unrelated industries. Any addition must complement its strategic focus, which severely limits the number of companies that would qualify as sensible acquisitions.

Microsoft went with option number three. In a move one analyst termed "breathtaking," the company initiated a plan to distribute the bulk of the money to its shareholders, who had been clamoring for some of that ever-expanding pile of cash. These investors have had good reason to clamor, too. Stocks fall into two general categories: *growth stocks*, which investors buy in the hope that the price of their shares will increase, and *income stocks*, which aren't expected to increase in value as much but that do pay regular cash dividends. By the early years of the twenty-first century, Microsoft's stock had wandered into a gray area between the two—it was no longer growing at the torrid pace of previous years, but it hadn't yet begun to pay serious dividends, either. The company had finally initiated a $0.08/share annual dividend in 2003 and raised that to $0.16/share in 2004 (meaning that if you owned a thousand shares, you received $160), but that was far below the best income stocks and also not enough to make a meaningful dent in the growing billions sitting in the bank.

A dramatic step was needed, and it came in the form of a special, one-time three dollar per share dividend. If you held a thousand shares, in other words, you received a $3,000 payment. With more than 10 billion shares to cover, the payout totaled $32.6 billion—a sum so large that it helped lift the national personal income total by 3.7 percent the month it was distributed. (Bill Gates donated his own $3 billion windfall to the Bill & Melinda Gates Foundation, which is one of the world's premiere charitable organizations.) Microsoft also doubled the annual dividend payment again and pegged another large pile of cash to buy back many of its own shares, which should also help shareholders by nudging the stock price up. In all, the company figures it will transfer $75 billion of value to shareholders over the course of several years.[1]

GET READY

Microsoft's situation is extraordinary, to say the least, but it is not the only company with lots of cash and nowhere to spend it these days. In 2004, the largest corporations in the country were sitting on a total of a half-*trillion* dollars of cash and cash equivalents.[2] If you were the CFO of one of these corporations, what would you recommend? Acquire a competitor? Give employees a bonus? Invest in real estate? Save it all? Your own financial management challenges may never be quite this dramatic, but who knows? Apply all the lessons in this book well enough and long enough, and you might end up with the problem of getting rid of $60 billion, too. ▪

Chapter Overview

John Connor, who was Microsoft's CFO at the time of the dividend distribution, had the pleasant task of managing extra cash. Of course, most CFOs and other managers struggle with the opposite problem much of the time, that of having too many demands on a limited supply of money. In this chapter, you'll learn more about the decisions they make, starting with the process of developing a financial plan, creating and maintaining budgets, and finding ways to finance both ongoing operations and growth opportunities. The second part of the chapter offers an overview of the U.S. financial system, from the basics of bank accounts to the latest developments in the banking environment. The chapter wraps up with a look at the Federal Reserve, the government institution responsible for managing the nation's money supply.

The Role of Financial Management

Financial management starts with the simple fact that all companies need to pay their bills and still have some money left over to improve the business and provide a cushion in case of emergencies. Furthermore, a key goal of any business is to increase the value to its owners by making it grow; most companies also try to keep growing and developing as a way to provide fresh opportunities for employees. Maximizing owner wealth sounds simple enough: just sell a good product for more than it costs to make. Before you can earn any revenue, however, you need money to get started. Once the business is off the ground, your need for money continues—whether it's to buy parts and supplies or to build a new warehouse.

Planning for a firm's current and future money needs is the foundation of **financial management**, or finance. In most smaller companies, the owner is responsible for the firm's financial decisions, whereas in larger operations financial management is the responsibility of the finance department, which reports to a vice president of finance or a chief financial officer (CFO). This department also includes the accounting function. In fact, most financial managers are accountants.

Financial management involves making decisions about alternative sources and uses of funds, with the goal of maximizing a company's value (see Exhibit 17.1). To achieve this goal, financial managers develop and implement a firm's financial plan; monitor a firm's cash flow and decide how to create or use excess funds; budget for current and future expenditures and for capital investments; raise capital to finance the enterprise for future growth; and interact with banks and capital markets. Here's a closer look at these important tasks.

L E A R **1** N I N G
O B J E **C** T I V E

Identify the responsibilities of a financial manager

financial management
Effective acquisition and use of money

Developing and Implementing a Financial Plan

Successful financial management starts with a **financial plan**, a document that shows the funds a firm will need for a period of time as well as the sources and uses of those funds. An underlying concept of any financial plan is that all money should be used productively. When you prepare a financial plan for a company, you have two objectives: achieving a positive cash flow and efficiently investing excess cash flow to make your company grow. Financial planning requires answers to such questions as: Is the company introducing a new product in the near future or expanding its market? Is the industry growing? Is the global

financial plan
A forecast of financial requirements and the financing sources to be used

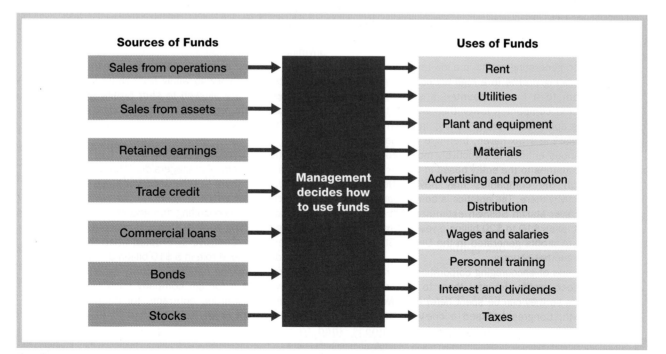

Exhibit 17.1
Sources and Uses of a Company's Funds
Financial management involves finding suitable sources of funds and deciding on the most appropriate uses for those funds.

Budgeting

In addition to developing a financial plan and monitoring cash flow, financial managers are responsible for developing a **budget**, a financial blueprint for a given period (often one year). Master (or operating) budgets help financial managers estimate the flow of money into and out of the business by structuring financial plans within a framework of a firm's total estimated revenues, expenses, and cash flows. Accountants provide much of the data required for budgets and are important members of the budget development team because they have a complete understanding of the company's operating costs.

The master budget sets a standard for expenditures, provides guidelines for controlling costs, and offers an integrated and detailed plan for the future. For example, by reviewing the budget of any airline, you can determine whether the company plans on increasing its fleet of aircraft, adding more routes, hiring more employees, increasing employees' pay, or continuing or abandoning any discounts for travelers. No wonder companies like to keep their budgets confidential.

Once a budget has been developed, the finance manager compares actual results with projections to discover variances and recommends corrective action—a process known as **financial control**. Companies also periodically adjust their budgets to meet their changing financial needs and goals. After Jamie Dimon, a banking executive widely known for his cost-control prowess, joined J. P. Morgan, he looked at everything from company-issued cell phones to executive aircraft to charitable contributions as a way to reduce the company's noncritical expenses.[4]

Capital Budgeting In contrast to operating budgets, capital budgets forecast and plan for a firm's **capital investments**, such as major expenditures in buildings or equipment. Capital investments generally cover a period of several years and help the company grow. Before investments can be made, however, a firm must decide on which of the many possible capital investments to make, how to finance those that are undertaken, and even whether to make any capital investments at all. This process is called **capital budgeting**.

The process generally begins by having all divisions within a company submit their capital requests—essentially, "wish lists" of investments that would make the company more profitable and thus more valuable to its owners over time. Next, the financial manager decides which investments need evaluating and which don't. For example, the routine replacement of old equipment probably wouldn't need evaluating; however, the construction of a new manufacturing facility would. Finally, a financial evaluation is performed to

determine whether the amount of money required for a particular investment will be greater than, equal to, or less than the amount of revenue it will generate. On the basis of this analysis, the financial manager can determine which projects to recommend to senior management for purchase approval.

Forecasting Capital Requirements As with any poorly made decision, an erroneous forecast of capital requirements can have serious consequences. If the firm invests too much in assets, it can end up with excess capacity that doesn't generate enough revenue to pay for itself. In contrast, if it invests too little, such as by not replacing or upgrading existing assets, the assets can become obsolete and leave the firm in a weaker competitive situation. For example, old manufacturing equipment may be incapable of handling new technologies needed for a new generation of products. For these important reasons, firms try to match capital investments with the company's goals. In other words, if the firm is growing, projects that would produce the greatest growth rates would receive the highest priority. However, if the company is trying to reduce costs, priority would go to projects that enhance the company's efficiency and productivity. Because asset expansion frequently involves large sums of money and affects the company's productivity for an extended period of time, finance managers must carefully evaluate the best way to finance or pay for these investments, another major responsibility of financial managers.

Financing Operations and Growth

As you can imagine, financing the ongoing needs of an enterprise is a complex undertaking. Just consider the many options you have for buying a car, for example. Depending on your circumstances, you might buy it with cash from your savings, cash you generate from a home equity loan, cash advances from credit cards, an informal loan from a family member, or a traditional car loan. Each of these options has different qualification requirements, different costs, and different effects on your monthly cash flow. For businesses, the process begins by assessing the firm's financing needs and determining whether funds are needed for the short or the long term. Next, the firm must assess the cost of obtaining those funds. Finally, it must weigh the advantages and disadvantages of financing through debt or equity, taking into consideration the firm's special needs and circumstances. The financing process is further complicated by the fact that many sources of long-term and short-term financing exist—each with their own special attributes, risks, and costs.

Length of Term Financing can be either short term or long term. **Short-term financing** is any financing that will be repaid within one year, whereas **long-term financing** is any financing that will be repaid in a period longer than one year. The primary purpose of short-term financing is to ensure that a company maintains its liquidity, or its ability to meet financial obligations (such as inventory payments) as they become due. By contrast, long-term financing is used to acquire long-term assets such as buildings and equipment or to fund expansion via any number of growth options. Long-term financing can come from both internal and external sources, as Exhibit 17.2 highlights.

Cost of Capital In general, a company wants to obtain money at the lowest cost and least amount of risk. However, lenders and investors want to receive the highest possible return on their investment, also at the lowest risk. A company's **cost of capital**, the average rate of interest it must pay on its debt and equity financing, depends on three main factors: the risk associated with the company, the prevailing level of interest rates, and management's selection of funding vehicles.

Risk. Lenders that provide money to businesses expect their returns to be in proportion to the two types of risk they face: the quality and length of time of the venture. Obviously, the more financially solid a company is, the less risk investors face. However, time also plays a vital role. Because a dollar will be worth less tomorrow than it is today, lenders need to be

Companies plan for construction projects years in advance and reflect the costs of such long-term projects in their capital budgets.

LEARNING OBJECTIVE 4

Cite three factors financial managers must consider when selecting an appropriate funding vehicle

short-term financing
Financing used to cover current expenses (generally repaid within a year)

long-term financing
Financing used to cover long-term expenses such as assets (generally repaid over a period of more than one year)

cost of capital
Average rate of interest a firm pays on its combination of debt and equity

Exhibit 17.2
Sources of Long-Term
Financing
*To finance long-term
projects, financial
managers rely on both
internal and external
sources of capital.*

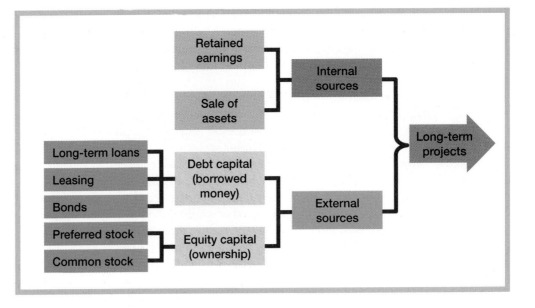

compensated for waiting to be repaid. As a result, long-term financing generally costs a company more than short-term financing.

Interest Rates. Regardless of how financially solid a company is, the cost of money will vary over time because interest rates fluctuate. The **prime interest rate** (often called simply the *prime*) is the lowest interest rate offered on short-term bank loans to preferred borrowers. The prime changes irregularly and, at times, quite frequently. Sometimes it changes because of supply and demand; at other times it changes because the prime rate is closely tied to the **discount rate**, the interest rate that the Federal Reserve charges on loans to commercial banks and other depository institutions (see "The Functions of the Federal Reserve System" on page 567).

Companies must take such interest rate fluctuations into account when making financing decisions. For instance, a company planning to finance a short-term project when the prime rate is 3 percent would want to reevaluate the project if the prime rose to 6 percent a few months later. Even though companies try to time their borrowing to take advantage of drops in interest rates, this option is not always possible. A firm's need for money doesn't always coincide with a period of favorable rates. At times, a company may be forced to borrow when rates are high and then renegotiate the loan when rates drop. Sometimes projects must be put on hold until interest rates become more affordable.

Opportunity Cost. Using a company's own cash to finance its growth has one chief attraction: No interest payments are required. Nevertheless, such internal financing is not free; using this money has an *opportunity cost*. That is, a company might be better off investing its excess cash in external opportunities, such as stocks of other companies, and borrowing money to finance its own growth. Doing so makes sense as long as the company can earn a greater *rate of return* (the percentage increase in the value of an investment) on those investments than the rate of interest paid on borrowed money. This concept is called **leverage** because the loan acts like a lever: It magnifies the power of the borrower to generate profits (see Exhibit 17.3). However, leverage works both ways: Borrowing may magnify your losses as well as your gains. Because most companies require some degree of external financing from time to time, the issue is not so much whether to use outside money; rather, it's a question of how much should be raised, by what means, and when. The answers to such questions determine the firm's **capital structure**, the mix of debt and equity.

Debt Versus Equity Financing *Debt financing* refers to financing by borrowing money: A creditor agrees to lend money to a debtor in exchange for repayment, with

prime interest rate
*Lowest rate of interest
charged by banks for
short-term loans to their
most creditworthy
customers*

discount rate
*Interest rate charged by
the Federal Reserve on
loans to commercial
banks and other financial
institutions*

leverage
*Technique of increasing
the rate of return on an
investment by financing
it with borrowed funds*

capital structure
Financing mix of a firm

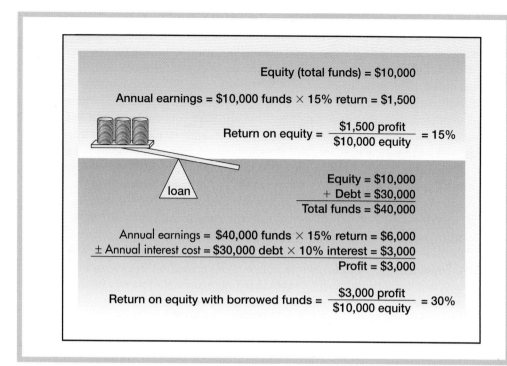

Exhibit 17.3
How Leverage Works
If you invest $10,000 of your own money in a business venture and it yields 15 percent (or $1,500), your return on equity is 15 percent. However, if you borrow an additional $30,000 at 10 percent interest and invest a total of $40,000 with the same 15 percent yield, the ultimate return on your $10,000 equity is 30 percent (or $3,000). The key to using leverage successfully is to try to make sure that your profit on the total funds is greater than the interest you must pay on the portion of it that is borrowed.

accumulated interest, at some future date. In contrast, *equity financing* is achieved by selling shares of a company's stock. When choosing between debt and equity financing, companies consider a variety of issues, including the prevailing interest rates, maturity, the claim on income, the claim on assets, and the desire for ownership control. Exhibit 17.4 summarizes these issues.

Characteristic	Debt	Equity
Maturity	**Specific:** Specifies a date by which it must be repaid.	**Nonspecific:** Specifies no maturity date.
Claim on income	**Fixed cost:** Company must pay interest on debt held by bondholders and lenders before paying any dividends to shareholders. Interest payments must be met regardless of operating results.	**Discretionary cost:** Shareholders may receive dividends after creditors have received interest payments; however, company is not required to pay dividends.
Claim on assets	**Priority:** Lenders have prior claims on assets.	**Residual:** Shareholders have claims only after the firm satisfies claims of lenders.
Influence over management	**Little:** Lenders are creditors, not owners. They can impose limits on management only if interest payments are not received.	**Varies:** As owners of the company, shareholders can vote on some aspects of corporate operations. Shareholder influence varies, depending on whether stock is widely distributed or closely held.

Exhibit 17.4
Debt Versus Equity
When choosing between debt and equity financing, companies evaluate the characteristics of both types of funding.

LEARNING OBJECTIVE 5

Identify five common types of debt financing

trade credit
Credit obtained by the purchaser directly from the supplier

secured loans
Loans backed up with something of value that the lender can claim in case of default, such as a piece of property

collateral
Tangible asset a lender can claim if a borrower defaults on a loan

unsecured loans
Loan requiring no collateral but a good credit rating

compensating balance
Portion of an unsecured loan that is kept on deposit at the lending institution to protect the lender and increase the lender's return

line of credit
Arrangement in which the financial institution makes money available for use at any time after the loan has been approved

commercial paper
An IOU, backed by the corporation's reputation, issued to raise short-term capital

Common Types of Debt Financing Financial managers have a number of options when it comes to debt financing, including *trade credit, leases, loans, commercial paper*, and *bonds*. (As a consumer in search of debt financing, you can opt for leases, loans, and the consumer equivalent of trade credit in some cases, but you don't have the option of commercial paper or bonds).

Trade credit, often called *open-account purchasing*, is the business equivalent of "running a tab." Suppliers that extend trade credit provide goods and services to their customers without demanding immediate payment; this approach can also save both the buyer and seller money by consolidating a number of smaller transactions into a single invoice and payment activity.

Loans come in a variety of shapes and sizes, either long term or short term and secured or unsecured. **Secured loans** are those backed by something of value, known as **collateral**, which may be seized by the lender in the event that the borrower fails to repay the loan. The most common type of secured loan is a *mortgage*, in which a piece of property such as a building is used as collateral. Other types of loan collateral are accounts receivable, inventories, securities, and other assets. **Unsecured loans** are ones that require no collateral. Instead, the lender relies on the general credit record and the earning power of the borrower. To increase the returns on such loans and to obtain some protection in case of default, most lenders insist that the borrower maintain some minimum amount of money on deposit at the bank—a **compensating balance**—while the loan is outstanding.

A common example of an unsecured loan is a **line of credit**, which is an agreed-on maximum amount of money a bank is willing to lend a business during a specific period of time, usually one year. Once a line of credit has been established, the business may obtain unsecured loans for any amount up to that limit. Regular lines of credit can be canceled at any time, so companies that want to be sure of obtaining credit when needed should arrange a *revolving line of credit*, which guarantees that the bank will honor the line of credit up to the stated amount.

Rather than borrowing from a commercial lender to buy a piece of property or equipment, a firm may enter into a lease, under which the owner of an item allows another party to use it in exchange for regular payments. Leasing may be a good alternative for a company that has difficulty obtaining loans because of a poor credit rating. Creditors are more willing to provide a lease than a loan because, should the company fail, the lessor need not worry about a default on loan payments; it can simply repossess equipment it legally owns. Some firms use leases to finance significant portions of their assets, particularly in industries such as airlines, where assets are mostly large, expensive pieces of equipment.

When businesses need a sizable amount of money for short period of time, they can issue **commercial paper**—short-term promissory notes of major corporations usually sold in denominations of $100,000 or more, with maturities of up to 270 days (the maximum allowed by the SEC without a formal registration process). Commercial paper is normally issued by established corporations (with strong credit ratings) that use the funds for such short-term needs as buying supplies, rather than financing major expansion projects. Because the amounts are generally so large, these notes are usually purchased by various investments funds and not by individual investors.

When a company needs to borrow a large sum of money, it may not be able to get the entire amount from a single source. Under such circumstances, it may borrow from many individual investors by issuing *bonds*—certificates that obligate the company to repay a certain sum, plus interest, to the bondholder on a specific date. (Both bonds and stocks are traded on organized securities exchanges and are discussed in detail in Chapter 18.)

CRITICAL THINKING CHECKPOINT
1. What are the some of the risks of failing to create and manage budgets? Identify as many risks as you can think of.
2. Does it ever make sense for a profitable company with positive cash flow to seek external financing (through either debt or equity)? Why or why not?
3. What factors might lead a company to gain additional funds through debt financing rather than through equity financing?

The U.S. Financial System

Whether a company finances with debt, equity, or cash reserves, financial managers must interact with financial institutions to satisfy their financial needs. The variety of financial institutions that operate within the U.S. banking environment can be classified into two broad categories: *deposit institutions* and *nondeposit institutions*. Deposit institutions accept deposits from customers or members and offer checking and savings accounts, loans, and other banking services. Among the many deposit institutions are

- *Commercial banks.* These are the institutions people are usually talking about when they talk about "banks."
- *Thrifts.* These include savings and loan associations (which use most of their deposits to make home mortgage loans) and mutual savings banks (which are owned by their depositors).
- *Credit unions.* These include institutions that take deposits only from members, such as one company's employees or one union's members or another designated group.

Nondeposit institutions offer specific financial services but do not accept deposits. Among the many nondeposit institutions are

- *Insurance companies.* These institutions provide insurance coverage for life, property, and other potential losses; they invest the payments they receive in real estate, in construction projects, and in other ways.
- *Pension funds.* These institutions are set up by companies to provide retirement benefits for employees; money contributed by the company and its employees is put into securities and other investments.
- *Finance companies.* These institutions lend money to consumers and businesses for home improvements, expansion, purchases, and other purposes.
- *Brokerage firms.* These institutions buy and sell stocks, bonds, and other investments for investors; many also offer checking accounts, high-paying savings accounts, and loans to buy securities. (Brokerage firms are discussed more fully in Chapter 18.)

In the past, services such as checking accounts, savings accounts, and loans were not offered at all financial institutions; instead, each institution focused on offering a particular set of financial services for specific customer groups. However, the competitive situation changed dramatically after the passage of the Depository Institutions Deregulation and Monetary Control Act of 1980. This law deregulated banking and made it possible for all financial institutions to offer a wider range of services—blurring the line between banks and other financial institutions and encouraging more competition between various types of institutions.

Financial Services

No matter where in the world you live, work, or travel, today's businesses and individuals require a wide range of financial services. Banks of all sizes—from the largest multinational bank to the tiniest community bank—provide customers with a variety of financial services that include checking and savings accounts, loans, and credit and debit cards. Moreover, thanks to technological advances and the Internet, customers can now access their money and account information at any hour and from almost anywhere. Of course, the human touch is still a big part of banking. But in today's time-pressured world, more people want to handle banking transactions from different locations and at different times, not during traditional bankers' hours.

Checking and Savings Accounts
Money you put into your checking account is a *demand deposit*, available immediately (on demand) through the use of **checks**, written orders that direct your bank to pay the stated amount of money to you or to someone else. Banks traditionally paid no interest on money in checking accounts. Since the laws changed in 1980, however, financial institutions have been allowed to offer interest-bearing NOW (Negotiable Order of Withdrawal) checking accounts.

LEARNING OBJECTIVE 6

Identify three common financial services that banks provide customers and list electronic banking vehicles that facilitate these services

checks
Written orders that tell the customer's bank to pay a specific amount to a particular individual or business

Many banks now offer a bewildering range of checking accounts, with various balance requirements, check writing privileges, online banking features, and so on. Along with the profusion of account types is an even greater profusion of fees associated with them—fees for talking to tellers, using telephone banking, dropping below minimum balances, triggering overdraft protection, and so on. In fact, many banks now earn more from fees than they do from lending money; collectively, U.S. banks earned $32 billion in account-related fees in 2004.[5] (As you can read in Appendix C, "Personal Finances: Getting Set for Life" on A-25–A-46, minimizing your exposure to these fees through careful money management is one of the most important skills you need to develop as a consumer.)

On the plus side, you earn interest on the money you put away in savings accounts. Originally, these accounts were known as *passbook savings accounts* because customers received a small passbook in which the bank recorded all deposits, withdrawals, and interest. Today, banks send out statements instead of passbooks, so these accounts have become known as *statement savings accounts.* In general, money in savings accounts can be withdrawn at any time. Money in a *money-market deposit account* earns more interest, but you are allowed only a limited number of monthly withdrawals. Money held in a *certificate of deposit (CD)* earns an even higher interest rate, but you cannot withdraw the funds for a stated period, such as six months or more. If you want to make an early withdrawal from a CD, you will lose some or all of the interest you've earned.

Loans Businesses of all sizes rely on banks to provide loans for expansion, purchases of new equipment, construction or renovation of plants and facilities, or other large-scale projects. As you read in Chapter 5, however, banks tend to loan money to established businesses with predictable cash flows, so bank loans aren't an option for every company.

Credit and Debit Cards Most of the money that consumers and businesses spend every year is still delivered via cash or checks, but banks and other financial services firms are waging an all-out effort to encourage the use of "plastic"—as in credit cards and debit cards.[6] As a consumer, you've seen this in both the number of credit card offers you receive in your mailbox and the number of businesses that accept plastic now. The motivation is simple: The companies that issue these cards want a piece of the action, so they're doing everything they can to encourage the use of cards rather than cash or checks. Card issuers collect money in a variety of ways, including a small percentage of the transaction value (which they collect from the retailer), as well as annual "membership fees," interest on unpaid balances, and fees for paying late or going over your credit limit (which they collect from cardholders).

Although the various types of cards look similar, the way they work and the impact they have on your finances varies. **Credit cards** give the cardholder the flexibility of making purchases now and paying for them later; if the balance isn't paid in full each month, interest begins to accrue. Credit cards are now so easy to get and so easy to use that they've helped create debt crises for many consumers, particularly college students and recent graduates. (Appendix C offers more insights into the risks of credit card debt.) *Charge cards* such as the regular American Express cards offer the same buy-now, pay-later flexibility but don't let you carry a balance from month to month. **Debit cards** are used in much the same way as credit and charge cards, but they actually operate like instantaneous checks, immediately subtracting, or debiting, the purchase amount from the cardholder's bank account and transferring it to the retailer's account.

You may have encountered some of the other types of cards that financial services firms and various retailers now offer as well. *Prepaid* cards are common in telephone services, for instance, letting you load up a card with a certain value of money, then using it to make long-distance calls until the money is used up. Similarly, prepaid credit cards work like regular credit cards until the prepaid amount is exhausted. A number of financial companies are also experimenting with **smart cards**, credit cards, or debit cards with tiny computer chips that can perform such functions as maintaining up-to-date information about account balances and providing additional levels of security (deactivating a card if an incorrect PIN is entered, for example).

credit cards
Plastic cards that allow the customer to buy now and pay back the loaned amount at a future date

debit cards
Plastic cards that allow the bank to take money from the user's demand-deposit account and transfer it to a retailer's account

smart cards
Plastic cards that include an embedded chip to store money drawn from the user's demand-deposit account and information that can be used for purchases

TECHNOLOGIES THAT ARE REVOLUTIONIZING BUSINESS Credit Scoring Software

Credit scoring software is a type of business intelligence software that measures the credit worthiness of applications for credit cards, mortgages, and other forms of credit. It has the dual objective of filtering out applications that don't meet a lender's criteria while speeding up the process for applications that do meet the criteria. Most of these packages use variations on a scoring system originally developed by Fair Isaac Corporation.

HOW IT'S CHANGING BUSINESS

Using sophisticated mathematical models based on historical records, credit scoring software helps lenders decide which applicants to accept and how much credit to extend to each one. In addition, software with *predictive modeling* or *predictive analytics* helps predict which applicants will make the best customers (lowest risk and highest profit potential) for a given lender. For instance, customers who receive credit cards but never use them or who pay off their balance every month are less profitable than customers who tend to carry a balance and therefore pay interest charges every month. The software can also help detect fraudulent credit card applications, which cost card issuers $1 billion a year—a cost that gets passed on to consumers and businesses in the form of higher interest rates, higher fees, and tighter credit availability. Variations on credit scoring software are also used in the insurance industry to predict the likelihood that an applicant will file a claim in the future.

WHERE YOU CAN LEARN MORE

The details of the FICO model are confidential, but you can read more about the products offered by Fair Isaac at **www.fairisaac.com**. If you'd like to see what your own credit score is, you can buy a report at **www.myfico.com**.

Online Payment Systems The growth of e-commerce prompted a number of companies to explore online payment systems that would give buyers an alternative to sending their credit or debit card numbers over the Internet or mailing paper checks. This effort took on added urgency with the rise of eBay, which created a widespread need for a mechanism that would allow consumers to buy and sell from one another. A variety of approaches were tried, but in recent years, PayPal (**www.paypal.com**, which is now owned by eBay) has emerged as the clear leader in online payment methods. PayPal buyers and sellers can transfer funds without the need to set up *merchant accounts*, which are required when sellers want to accept credit cards. PayPal now boasts millions of users and processes millions of transactions a month, roughly 70 percent of which involve online auctions.[7]

PayPal is the market leader in online payments, but it has had its share of glitches along the way. Its attempts to prevent fraud have occasionally locked merchants out of their accounts, leading to a class-action lawsuit that was settled for $9 million. In October 2004, some sellers were locked out of their accounts for as long as a week because of a faulty software upgrade. Moreover, PayPal is a money transfer service, not a bank, so it is not governed by the same strict consumer protection measures that all banks must adhere to.[8]

Electronic Banking Credit, debit, and smart cards are part of the larger financial world of electronic banking, which can be defined as any banking activity conducted from sites other than a physical bank location. For instance, customers rely on **automated teller machines (ATMs)** to withdraw money from their demand-deposit accounts at any hour. By linking with regional, national, and international ATM networks, banks let customers withdraw cash far from home, make deposits, and handle other transactions such as check cashing, purchasing prepaid wireless phone cards or gift cards, and transferring funds between bank and brokerage accounts.[9]

Electronic funds transfer systems (EFTS) are another form of electronic banking. These computerized systems allow users to conduct financial transactions efficiently from remote locations. For instance, more than half of all U.S. workers take advantage of EFTS when their employers use direct deposit to transfer wages directly into employees' bank accounts. Workers with direct deposit won't find a check inside their pay envelopes

automated teller machines (ATMs)
Electronic terminals that permit people with plastic cards to perform simple banking transactions 24 hours a day without the aid of a human teller

electronic funds transfer systems (EFTS)
Computerized systems for performing financial transactions

THINKING ABOUT ETHICS

SURPRISE! YOU'VE BEEN SWIPED

Phishing (coaxing people to reveal their credit card numbers via deceptive e-mail and fake websites) gets a lot of attention these days, but thanks to some clever technology and bold thieves, your credit card number can also be stolen right under your nose. Using a technique called *skimming*, a thief steals card data by swiping the credit card through a small, handheld magnetic card reader. The reader copies the cardholder's name, account number, and even the card validation code—stored on the magnetic stripe—giving the counterfeiter all the data needed to create a perfect clone of the credit card. Readers can be purchased for as little as $100 over the Internet and are intended for legitimate use by banks, restaurants, retailers, and hotels. Unfortunately, some end up in the wrong hands.

Thieves and, increasingly, organized crime groups pay waiters and store clerks to steal information from credit cards using the concealed devices. By skimming 14 to 20 accounts, crooks can generate $50,000 to $60,000 worth of fraud that will probably go undiscovered until the victims get their bills—30 to 60 days after the crime. Moreover, skimmed data from, say, a customer in New York City or Washington can be e-mailed to Taiwan, Japan, or Europe and used for mail-order, telephone-order, or e-commerce overseas transactions within 24 to 48 hours of the theft. Professionals can even encode the stolen codes into a strip and use equipment to produce an electronically indistinguishable counterfeit card.

While credit card issuers decline to say how much they are losing to skimmers—in part because they don't want to scare consumers out of using their plastic—industry analysts estimate skimmers reap over $125 million annually.

To curb the fraud, major credit card issuers are cooperating with the U.S. Secret Service to pool information about fraudulent transactions. For example, issuers can generate computer analyses that flag locations where numerous cards may have been skimmed. Or if someone in Hong Kong tries to buy something with a credit card that was used two hours earlier in Chicago, the computer will reject the transaction.

In the latest twist on skimming, thieves have begun attaching tiny memory devices to the card readers in gas pumps and privately owned ATMs (the type you often see in convenience stores). They sneak the recorder into the machine, temporarily wire it to the existing card reader, wait until it fills up with credit card data, then break into the machine again and retrieve the recorder.

What can you do to prevent your credit cards from getting skimmed? Not much, say experts, besides reading your bills closely, checking your accounts on the web or by phone during the month to make sure there are no surprises, and reporting improper charges promptly. Although you're not liable for fraudulent charges made to your accounts by skimmers or other scam artists, you do have to face the hassle of getting the unauthorized transactions removed from your bills. Of course, you can always pay with old-fashioned cash. But if you carry lots of that around, you may have to worry about the old-fashioned robber.

Questions for Critical Thinking
1. To curb the abuse, why don't all retailers require customers to present additional personal validation data at the time of sale?
2. Why don't thieves skim debit cards too?

on payday. Instead, they get a stub showing the amounts earned, withheld, deducted, and directly deposited into their bank account. Some companies are even eliminating the pay stub and instead giving employees a password so they can access their personal payroll records online. Such methods are more convenient for both employers and employees, and they usually save employers money, too.[10]

In addition to automated teller machines and electronic funds transfer systems, most major banks and many thrifts and community banks now offer Internet or online banking to accommodate the growing number of individuals and businesses that want to transfer money between accounts, check account balances, pay bills, apply for loans, and handle other transactions at any hour.

Individuals can also transfer funds electronically to family and friends without using banks. Western Union (**www.westernunion.com**) lets you send money online, although the

LEARNING FROM BUSINESS BLUNDERS

OOPS Mark Guthrie, who delivers newspapers for the *Hartford Courant*, must've thought he'd received the biggest wage increase in history when he discovered that his employer had direct-deposited his latest paycheck—in the amount of $301,102.50. He's probably quite good at his job, but not that good, unfortunately. Tribune Co., which owns both the *Courant* and the Chicago Cubs baseball team, had accidentally deposited Cub's pitcher Mark Guthrie's paycheck into delivery guy Mark Guthrie's account.

WHAT YOU CAN LEARN This blunder made headlines because it involved a professional athlete, but mistakes like this happen with disturbing regularity, and they're often unpleasant, too. Instead of getting unexpected riches, consumers can get tagged with other people's unpaid bills, credit problems, and even legal entanglements. In a world in which bits and bytes stored on unseen disk drives can affect people's lives in dramatic ways, every company needs to take all necessary precautions to ensure data accuracy (such as cross-checking employee names with Social Security numbers, in this case).

receiver needs to visit a Western Union office to pick up the funds. Another online transfer service, Ikobo (www.ikobo.com), mails the recipient a debit card instead.[11]

Bank Safety and Regulation

After thousands of banks failed in the United States during the Great Depression (1929–1934), bank safety understandably became a vital concern for government leaders, regulators, the financial community—anybody who ever worried if the money he or she put in the bank would be there when it was time to withdraw it. In response to these concerns, the government established the Federal Deposit Insurance Corporation (FDIC) to protect money in customer accounts. Banks pay a fee to join the FDIC network, and in turn the FDIC guarantees to cover any losses from bank failure up to a maximum of $100,000 per account.[12] (Banks that are members of FDIC display a sign indicating this; if you're not sure about a specific bank, you can verify its membership at www.fdic.gov.) Similar organizations exist for other types of banking institutions: the Savings Association Insurance Fund for thrifts, the Bank Insurance Fund for commercial banks, and the National Credit Union Association for credit unions.

In addition, a number of government agencies supervise and regulate banks. State-chartered banks come under the watchful eyes of each state's banking commission, nationally chartered banks are under the federal Office of the Comptroller of the Currency, and thrifts are under the federal Office of Thrift Supervision. The overall health of the country's banking system is, ultimately, the responsibility of the Federal Reserve System.

The Future of Banking

The U.S. banking industry has experienced radical changes over the past few decades—and the changes and challenges aren't over yet. Here are some of the key issues that bankers and their business and consumer clients face in the coming years:

- *Competitive structure of the industry.* For a half century following the Great Depression, banks, insurance companies, and investment firms operated under strict regulations that defined the scope of services each could offer, and various state laws limited the degree to which banks could operate across state lines. The situation started to change in 1994, when the Riegle–Neal Interstate Banking and Branching Efficiency Act overrode those state restrictions on interstate banking and allowed true nationwide banking operations. Banking companies began to consolidate on a massive scale, and continue to do so today.

LEARNING OBJECTIVE 7

Explain how banks are involved in efforts to combat crime and terrorism

Then in 1999, the Financial Services Modernization Act repealed the Glass–Steagall Act, which had prevented the various types of financial services companies from invading each other's industries—and the financial services industry has been in a constant state of change ever since. Banks offer insurance, insurance companies offer investments, investment houses offer banking services, you name it. A number of companies soon tried to become *financial supermarkets*, offering a variety of services from insurance to stock market investing. For instance, E*Trade, www.etrade.com, started as an online stock brokerage but now offers investing, bank accounts, credit cards, home mortgages, car loans, and more. Meanwhile, many credit unions have grown beyond their original scope (pooling members' deposits for the purposes of granting loans) to become full-service financial companies virtually indistinguishable from banks. To top it off, Internet-only banks are trying to lure business away from the clicks-and-bricks operations set up by traditional banks (see E-Business in Action on page 610 for more on Internet-only banks).[13]

- *Banking ethics.* Some banks also face a rash of ethical and legal issues, from the roles that several large banks played in the Enron and WorldCom scandals to complaints about high fees to the problem of *predatory lending*, in which consumers are talked into highly unfavorable loan terms that lead to serious financial damage. The banking industry is addressing some of these issues, such as predatory lending, by educating banks and encouraging lenders to avoid problematic practices. Both state and federal regulators have put the industry on notice about high fees and excessive interest rates as well.[14]

- ***The role of banks in the struggles against crime and terrorism.*** Because money factors into many criminal activities, from *money laundering* (concealing the source of money obtained through illegal means) to identity theft to support of terrorist groups, banks often inadvertently enable these crimes. In most cases, the bank is an unwitting participant. However, banks are required to report suspicious activities by their customers, such as large cash transfers to or from obscure organizations—particularly those based in countries with weak banking regulations. Banks are also required to report all cash transactions that involve $10,000 or more. In a few recent instances, banks that failed to follow these reporting requirements got themselves into trouble. J. P. Morgan, Bank of New York, Bank of America, and AmSouth are among the institutions recently investigated for their roles in suspicious money transfers; several

While the rest of the financial industry swirls with change, independent community banks continue to be strong forces of support in towns and neighborhoods, helping both consumers and small business owners with advice and financing opportunities often not available through larger banks. Community banks often cater to markets that some large banks have traditionally neglected or ignored, such as minorities, small businesses, rural communities, and inner cities.

have been hit with multimillion-dollar fines. Banks are beefing up internal training and procedures to avoid such mishaps, but some complain that government regulations aren't precise enough to help identify exactly which types of transactions and which customers they should be scrutinizing.[15]

CRITICAL THINKING CHECKPOINT

1. Why would a company choose the direct deposit method for paying its employees?
2. How might the fact that PayPal is not a bank affect consumers' willing to use it for online transactions?
3. Do banks have an ethical responsibility to find out if their customers are using bank services to support criminal activity? Why or why not?

The Functions of the Federal Reserve System

Like the FDIC, the Federal Reserve System was created (in 1913) in response to fear, uncertainty, and doubt regarding banking in the United States. However, the Federal Reserve, or the "Fed," as it is commonly called, has a much broader set of responsibilities and much more direct influence on the financial well-being of both consumers and businesses. The Fed's role in the nation's economy is pervasive:[16]

- Conducting monetary policy (see Chapter 1) by influencing both money and credit markets
- Supervising and regulating financial institutions in order to maintain the stability of the nation's banking system and to protect the rights of creditors
- Maintaining the overall stability of the economy
- Serving as a clearinghouse for checks

Decisions made by the Fed will affect your personal and professional lives time and again, because the Fed influences the money supply and interest rates, which determine everything from your house payment to whether or not your company can get a loan to expand its manufacturing capacity.

The Fed's two main components are a network of 12 district banks that controls the nation's banking system and a seven-member board of governors that determine Fed policy. To preserve the board's political independence, the members are appointed by the president to 14-year terms, staggered at 2-year intervals. Although all national banks are required to be members of the Federal Reserve System, membership for state-chartered banks is optional. Still, the Fed exercises regulatory power over all deposit institutions, members and nonmembers alike.

Influencing the U.S. Money Supply

Money is anything generally accepted as a means of paying for goods and services. To be an effective medium for exchange, money must have these important characteristics: It must be divisible, portable (easy to carry), durable, and difficult to counterfeit, and it should have a stable value. In addition, money must perform three basic functions: First, it must serve as a medium of exchange—a tool for simplifying transactions between buyers and sellers. Second, it must serve as a measure of value so that you don't have to negotiate the relative worth of dissimilar items every time you buy something. Finally, money must serve as a temporary store of value—a way of accumulating your wealth until you need it.

The Fed's main job is to establish and implement monetary policy, the guidelines for handling the nation's economy and the money supply. The U.S. money supply has three major components:

- **Currency**: Money in the form of coins, bills, traveler's checks, cashier's checks, and money orders

money
Anything generally accepted as a means of paying for goods and services

currency
Bills and coins that make up the cash money of a society

demand deposits
Money in checking accounts that can be used by customers at any time

time deposits
Bank accounts that pay interest and require advance notice before money can be withdrawn

M1
That portion of the money supply consisting of currency and demand deposits

M2
That portion of the money supply consisting of currency, demand deposits, and small time deposits

M3
That portion of the money supply consisting of M1 and M2 plus large time deposits and other restrictive deposits

- **Demand deposits**: Money available immediately on demand, such as checking accounts
- **Time deposits**: Accounts that pay interest and restrict the owner's right to withdraw funds on short notice, such as savings accounts, certificates of deposit, and money-market deposit accounts

The Fed influences the money supply to make certain that enough money and credit are available to fuel a healthy economy. However, it must act carefully, because altering the money supply affects interest rates, inflation, and the economy. When the money supply is increased, more money is available for loans, so banks can charge lower interest rates to borrowers. On the other hand, an increased money supply can lead to more consumer spending and can result in the demand for goods exceeding supply. When demand exceeds supply, sellers may raise their prices, leading to inflation. In turn, inflation can slow economic growth—a situation the Fed wants to avoid. And, because so many companies now buy and sell across national borders, Fed changes may affect the interlinked economies of many countries, not just the United States. That's why the Fed moves cautiously and keeps a close eye on the size of the money supply. In turn, businesses and investors keep a close eye on the Fed to see where interest rates might be heading.

How the Money Supply Is Measured To get a rough idea of the size of the money supply, the Fed looks at various combinations of currency, demand deposits, and time deposits (see Exhibit 17.5). The narrowest measure, known as **M1**, consists of currency, demand deposits, and NOW accounts that are common forms of payment. **M2**, a broader measure of the money supply, includes M1 plus savings deposits, money-market funds, and time deposits under $100,000. **M3**, the broadest measure of the money

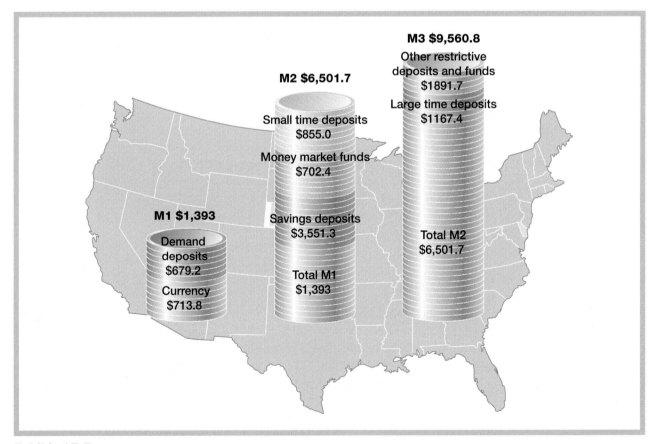

Exhibit 17.5
The Total Money Supply
The U.S. money supply is measured at three levels: M1, M2, and M3. Here's a snapshot of the three fund balances at one point during 2005 (in billions of dollars).

supply, includes M2 plus time deposits of $100,000 and higher and other restricted deposits.

Tools for Influencing the Money Supply The Fed can use four basic tools to influence the money supply:

LEARNING OBJECTIVE

Describe four ways the Federal Reserve System influences the U.S. money supply

reserve requirement
Percentage of a bank's deposit that must be set aside

- *Changing the reserve requirement.* All financial institutions must set aside reserves, sums of money equal to a certain percentage of their deposits. The Fed can change the **reserve requirement**, the percentage of deposits that banks must set aside, to influence the money supply. However, the Fed rarely uses this technique because a small change can have a drastic effect. Increasing the reserve requirement slows down the economy: Banks have less money to lend, so businesses can't borrow to expand and consumers can't borrow to buy goods and services. Conversely, reducing this requirement boosts the economy, because banks have more money to lend to businesses and consumers (see Exhibit 17.6).

- *Changing the discount rate.* The Fed can also change the discount rate, the interest rate it charges on loans to commercial banks and other depository institutions. When the Fed raises the discount rate, member banks generally raise the prime interest rate. This situation discourages loans, and in so doing tightens the money supply, which can slow down economic growth. By contrast, lowering the discount rate results in lower lending rates, which can encourage more borrowing and stimulate economic growth. Is lower always better when it comes to interest rates, then? Not necessarily. Sustained periods of

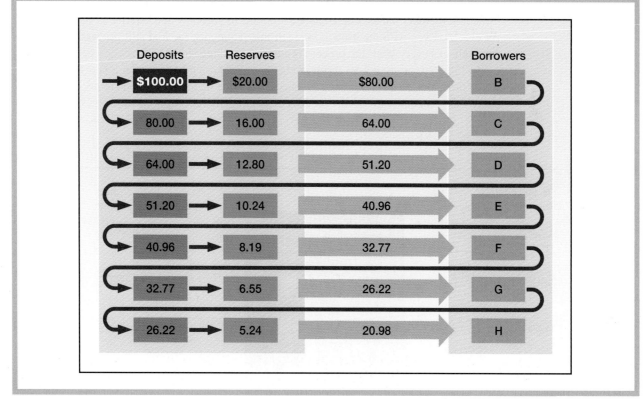

Exhibit 17.6
How Banks Generate Income Through Interest
Banks generate interest income by earning more on interest from loans than they pay out in the form of interest on deposits. When customer A deposits $100, the bank must keep some in reserve but can lend, say, $80, to customer B (and earn interest on that loan). If customer B deposits the borrowed $80 in the same bank, the bank can lend 80 percent of that amount to borrower C. The initial $100 deposit, therefore, creates a much larger pool of funds from which customer loans may be made. (Note that many banks now earn more from service and penalty fees than they do from interest accumulation, however.)

low interest rates and the resulting increase in the money supply can drive prices artificially high as new money continues to pour in—which is exactly what some observers fear has already happened with the U.S. housing market.[17] They worry that the boom in recent years has turned into a "bubble," a term used to describe a market situation where prices have grown far beyond the real value of the product in question. When a market bubble bursts, values collapse, often below real value, which can spell trouble for millions of consumers and the economy in general.

open-market operations
Activity of the Federal Reserve in buying and selling government bonds on the open market

selective credit controls
Federal Reserve's power to set credit terms on various types of loans

- **Conducting open-market operations.** The tool the Fed uses most often to influence the money supply is the power to buy and sell U.S. government bonds. Because anyone can buy these bonds on the open market, this tool is known as **open-market operations**. If the Fed is concerned about inflation, it can reduce the money supply by selling U.S. government bonds, which takes cash out of circulation. And when the Fed wants to boost the economy, it can buy back government bonds, putting cash into circulation and increasing the money supply.

- **Establishing selective credit controls.** The Fed can also use **selective credit controls** to set the terms of credit for various kinds of loans. This tool includes the power to set margin requirements, the percentage of the purchase price that an investor must pay in cash when purchasing a stock or a bond on credit. By altering the margin requirements, the Fed is able to influence how much cash is tied up in stock market transactions.

Exhibit 17.7 summarizes the effects of using these four tools.

Supplying Currency and Clearing Checks

In addition to monetary policy, the Fed also has numerous tactical responsibilities, including providing member banks with adequate amounts of currency and serving as a clearinghouse for checks. Even with the growth in electronic payments, the Fed still processes billions of paper checks every year; the process is summarized in Exhibit 17.8.

In the past, anyone who wrote a check could probably count on a short delay, often called *float*, before the amount of the check would be deducted from his or her account. The delay was principally due to the process of sending all those billions of pieces of paper from

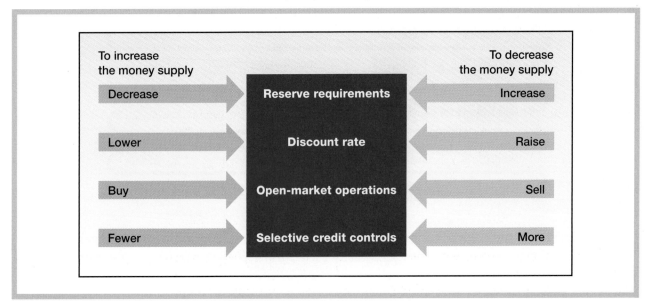

Exhibit 17.7
Influencing the Money Supply
The Federal Reserve uses four tools to influence the money supply as it attempts to stimulate economic growth while keeping inflation and interest rates at acceptable levels.

Exhibit 17.8

How the Fed Clears Checks

The Federal Reserve acts as a clearinghouse for checks in the United States. This example shows how the Fed clears a check that has been drawn on a bank in one city but deposited by a store in a bank in another city.

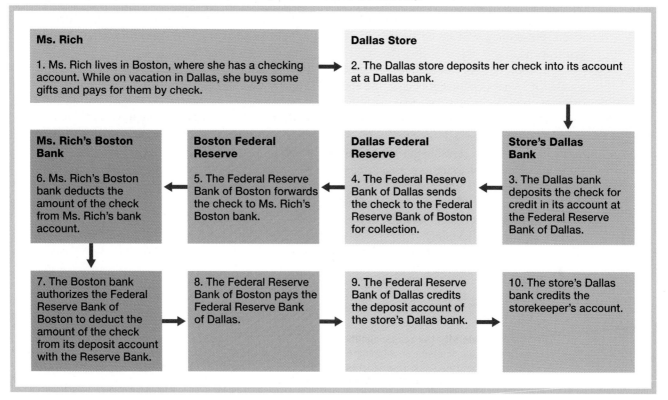

Ms. Rich

1. Ms. Rich lives in Boston, where she has a checking account. While on vacation in Dallas, she buys some gifts and pays for them by check.

Dallas Store

2. The Dallas store deposits her check into its account at a Dallas bank.

Ms. Rich's Boston Bank

6. Ms. Rich's Boston bank deducts the amount of the check from Ms. Rich's bank account.

Boston Federal Reserve

5. The Federal Reserve Bank of Boston forwards the check to Ms. Rich's Boston bank.

Dallas Federal Reserve

4. The Federal Reserve Bank of Dallas sends the check to the Federal Reserve Bank of Boston for collection.

Store's Dallas Bank

3. The Dallas bank deposits the check for credit in its account at the Federal Reserve Bank of Dallas.

7. The Boston bank authorizes the Federal Reserve Bank of Boston to deduct the amount of the check from its deposit account with the Reserve Bank.

8. The Federal Reserve Bank of Boston pays the Federal Reserve Bank of Dallas.

9. The Federal Reserve Bank of Dallas credits the deposit account of the store's Dallas bank.

10. The store's Dallas bank credits the storekeeper's account.

one institution to the next around the country. Check writers occasionally enjoyed the flexibility of writing checks they didn't yet have money in their accounts to cover, figuring they had a few days to deposit the necessary funds. However, from the perspective of banks and the people on the receiving end of all those checks, the manual, paper-based system was not only slow but expensive to operate.

That system is now in the midst of a major overall in which all that shuttling around of paper checks is being replaced with electronic delivery. As specified in the Check Clearing for the 21st Century Act, commonly called *Check 21*, banks or companies that receive paper checks can convert them to electronic images, which can then zip around at the speed of e-mail. The system will eventually be able to clear checks in 24 hours or so, compared to the two or three days it has traditionally taken to clear out-of-town checks. Substitute checks can then be printed when any party in the system requires a paper copy.[18] If you receive copies of your printed checks from your bank, you may have already seen one of these substitutes.

CRITICAL THINKING CHECKPOINT

1. Would a CFO put a company's emergency funds in a demand deposit account or a time deposit account? Why?

2. If the Federal Reserve was worried about the economy overheating (possibly triggering an inflationary trend), would it raise or lower the discount rate? Why?

3. Will Check 21 change the way consumers and businesses pay their bills? Why or why not?

CHECKLIST: Apply These Ideas When You're the Boss

✓ Always have a financial plan that itemizes how much money you'll need to achieve your goals, where the money will come from, and how you'll spend it.

✓ Always know where the money is going, whether it's your department budget, the entire corporate budget, or just your household budget; it's easy for even small expenses to add up to a giant hole in your cash flow.

✓ Don't let accounts receivable get out of hand; although it's never pleasant to press customers to pay their bills, it's a vital task.

✓ Be very cautious about taking on debt; the wrong kind or the wrong amount can severely limit your strategic and tactical flexibility.

✓ Lenders will demand to see a repayment plan, but don't view that as just paperwork for their benefit—make sure you're confident about your ability to repay, too.

✓ Just as in your personal finances, your company's credit rating affects your cost of capital, so protect your credit rating through sensible borrowing and careful repayment.

✓ If you own a small company and are considering equity financing, try to keep your ownership share at 51 percent or higher so that you can retain managerial control of the company.

Summary of Learning Objectives

1 Identify the responsibilities of a financial manager. The responsibilities of a financial manager include developing and implementing a firm's financial plan; monitoring a firm's cash flow and deciding how to create or use excess funds; budgeting for current and future expenditures and capital investments; raising capital to finance the enterprise for future growth; and interacting with banks and capital markets.

2 Discuss how financial managers improve a company's cash flow. Monitoring working capital accounts is one way financial managers improve a company's cash flow. Such monitoring includes establishing effective accounts receivable credit and collection policies; paying bills strategically to obtain discounts and to conserve cash; establishing inventory procedures to maintain enough inventory to fill orders on time at the lowest purchase cost; and investing excess cash so it earns as much interest as possible.

3 Differentiate between a master budget and a capital budget. Master or operating budgets handle all revenues, expenses, and cash flows of the firm. Moreover, they provide guidelines for a firm's total expenditures. By contrast, capital budgets forecast and plan for a firm's capital investments such as buildings and equipment while matching a firm's capital investments with the company's overall long-term goals.

4 Cite three factors financial managers must consider when selecting an appropriate funding vehicle. Finance managers must determine whether the financing is for the short term or the long term. They must minimize the cost of capital by weighing the risk, interest costs, and opportunity costs of different financing alternatives. Finally, they must evaluate the merits of debt versus equity financing in light of their own needs.

5 Identify five common types of debt financing. Five common types of debt financing are trade credit (paying for products after they are purchased), commercial paper (short-term promissory notes of major corporations), loans (money borrowed from the bank which is secured or unsecured, long term or short term), leases (paying for the use of someone else's property over a fixed term), and bonds (issuing corporate certificates to individual investors that obligate the company to repay a certain sum plus interest on a specific date).

6 Identify three common financial services that banks provide customers, and list electronic banking vehicles that facilitate these services. Banks provide customers with checking and savings accounts so they can pay bills and earn interest on money they save. They provide loans so customers can purchase homes, cars, and finance educational expenses, among other things. They issue credit cards so customers can purchase now and repay the loaned amount later, as well as debit and smart cards, which facilitate retail transactions without the physical use of money. Banks facilitate these services by providing a number of electronic banking options. These include ATMs, electronic funds transfers, and online banking.

7 **Explain how banks are involved in efforts to combat crime and terrorism.** Banks sometimes get involved unknowingly in crime and terrorism simply because criminals and terrorists use banking services to transfer funds or to launder money. However, banks are required to report suspicious financial activities to government investigators, particularly those that involve obscure organizations based in countries with weak banking regulations.

8 **Identify four ways the Federal Reserve System influences the U.S. money supply.** The Fed influences the U.S. money supply by changing reserve requirements (the percentage of deposits that banks must set aside), by changing the discount rate (the interest rate it charges on loans to commercial banks and other depository institutions), by carrying out open-market operations (selling and buying government bonds), and by setting selective credit controls (setting the amount of cash investors must pay when purchasing a stock or bond on credit).

Microsoft: What's Next?

Microsoft's dilemma of having too much cash is an interesting side effect of a larger strategic issue: Is Microsoft still a hot growth company, or has it already matured into one of the country's "old line" corporations, joining the likes of General Motors, General Electric, and other behemoths? Stock analysts are split on the question, with some saying the fact that the company has so much cash is an indication that it's a mature business, with fewer interesting new ways to grow and evolve (the thinking here is that a dynamic, growing company would by definition have more places to invest). The other side says that the mountain of cash was simply a measure of the company's success as the king of the software industry. Either way, both Microsoft stockholders and industry observers should have an intriguing drama to watch over the next few years, as the company continues to generate billions of dollars of cash annually.[19]

Critical Thinking Questions

1. Why wouldn't Microsoft just lower its prices in order to stop generating so much cash?
2. Would giving every employee a big raise be a smart thing to do with the extra cash? Why or why not?
3. Microsoft will always have some cash on hand, of course, which leaves the question of how to manage this reserve. Should the company put that money in riskier investments that might pay off more in the long run but could lose value, or leave it in safer investments that won't return as much? Why?

Learn More Online

Visit the Microsoft website by going to Chapter 17 of this text's website at www.prenhall.com/bovee. Click on the company's hotlink, and visit the Investor Relations section. What does the company say about its stock dividend? What trends do you see in revenue and net income over the past several years (look for Financial Highlights in the latest annual reports)? How might those trends affect Microsoft's cash management issues in the near future?

Key Terms

accounts payable (555)	capital structure (558)	currency (567)
accounts receivable (555)	checks (561)	debit cards (562)
automated teller machines (ATMs) (563)	collateral (560)	demand deposits (568)
	commercial paper (560)	discount rate (558)
budget (556)	compensating balance (560)	electronic funds transfer system (EFTS) (563)
capital budgeting (556)	cost of capital (557)	
capital investments (556)	credit cards (562)	financial control (556)

financial management (553)   M3 (568)   selective credit controls (570)
financial plan (553)   marketable securities (555)   short-term financing (557)
leverage (558)   money (567)   smart cards (562)
line of credit (560)   open-market operations (570)   time deposits (568)
long-term financing (557)   prime interest rate (558)   trade credit (560)
M1 (568)   reserve requirement (569)   unsecured loan (560)
M2 (568)   secured loans (560)

Test Your Knowledge

Questions for Review

1. What is the primary goal of financial management?
2. What types of projects are typically considered in the capital budgeting process?
3. What is the difference between a secured and an unsecured loan?
4. How do credit cards, debit cards, and smart cards work?
5. What is the main function of the Federal Reserve System?

Questions for Analysis

6. Why do companies prepare budgets?
7. Why does internal financing have an opportunity cost?
8. How can smaller community banks compete with large commercial banks?
9. Besides shipping information and credit card information, what types of customer information might smart cards store in their chip that would be useful to e-businesses?
10. **Ethical Considerations.** What issues regarding privacy of personal information must E*Trade and other financial supermarkets address to protect consumers?

Questions for Application

11. The financial manager for a small manufacturing firm wants to improve the company's cash flow position. What steps can he or she take?
12. Why might a company's board of directors decide to lease a piece of property even though it would be more economical to purchase the property and finance it with a long-term loan?
13. **Integrated.** Which of the four forms of utility discussed in Chapter 12 do ATMs and online banking create?
14. **Integrated.** How does the money supply affect the economy and inflation? (Hint: Think about the theory of supply and demand discussed in Chapter 1.)

Practice Your Knowledge

Handling Difficult Situations on the Job: Dealing with Electronic Banking Errors

The ATM Error Resolution Department at Union Bank of California (where you work as an operations officer) often adjusts customer accounts for multiple electronic debit errors. Such errors are usually the result of an honest mistake: A merchant will run a customer's debit card two or three times through the card machine, thinking the first few times didn't "take," when in fact the machine was working. For genuine errors, your routine is to authorize a correcting credit.

This time, you're questioning a claim from customer Margaret Caldwell. According to her letter and bank statement, her account was debited three times on the same day, using her debit card and crediting the same market, Wilson's Gourmet. The amounts differed: $23.02, $110.95, and $47.50. That doesn't strike you as a multiple-card-swipe situation. She hasn't enclosed any store receipt, and she claims that Wilson's Gourmet was trying to steal from her.

The store manager, Ronson Tibbits, tells you on the phone that his equipment is working fine, so it's unlikely that any card could be run repeatedly. He also mentions that food shoppers often return on the same day to make additional purchases, particularly for highly consumable products, or to pick up merchandise they forgot. Some buy a deli lunch at noon, then return later to shop for dinner.[20]

Your task: Margaret Caldwell and her husband are wealthy customers who keep large sums on deposit; they also use your investment and lending services. You're convinced that Mrs. Caldwell is merely mistaken or confused. But bank roles are clear: Deny the request politely. How will you convey your decision to the Caldwells without losing their valued business?

Sharpening Your Communication Skills

You've just been hired as the CFO of a start-up company that is just a few months away from launching its first products. Unfortunately, the company is running short of cash and doesn't have enough to pay for initial manufacturing costs. Your boss, Connie Washington, is getting frantic. She has worked for several years to get to this point, and she doesn't want the company to collapse before it even starts selling products. She comes to you asking for ideas to generate some funds—immediately, if not sooner. Several investors have expressed interest in helping with financing, but Connie doesn't want to surrender any control by using equity financing. She wants to start applying for loans, even stacks of credit cards if that's what it takes.

However, you don't think piling on debt is such a wise idea at this point. The company doesn't have any revenue yet, and there's no guarantee that the new products will be successful. You'd rather share the risk with some equity investors, even if that means that Connie will have to give up some of her managerial authority. Draft a short memo to Connie explaining why you think equity financing is a better option at this stage (make up any details you need).

Building Your Team Skills

You and your team are going to build an operating expense budget worksheet for a neighborhood Domino's pizza franchise. Begin by brainstorming a list of expenses that are typical of a franchise delivery restaurant. One way to do so is to think about the company's process—from making the pizza to delivering it. List the types of expenses and then group your list into categories such as delivery, marketing, manufacturing, financing, and so on. Leave the budget dollar amounts blank. Finally, develop a list of capital investments your company will make over the next three to five years. Compare your budget worksheets to those of the other teams in your class. Which operating and capital expenses did other teams have that your team did not? Which expenses did your team have that other teams omitted? Did all the teams categorize the expenses in a similar manner?

Expand Your Knowledge

Discovering Career Opportunities

Is a career in community banking for you? Bankers in smaller banks deal with a wide variety of customers, products, transactions, and inquiries every working day. To get a better idea of what community bankers do, explore the Independent Community Bankers of America website at www.icba.org and visit a local independent bank branch.

1. Talk with a customer service representative or an officer about the kinds of customers this bank serves. Does it handle a high volume of business banking transactions, or is it more geared to consumer banking needs? How does the mix of consumer and business customers affect the branch's staffing and working hours?
2. What banking services are offered by this bank? Does the bank have specialized experts on staff to service these customers? What kind of skills, experience, education, and licenses must these experts have?
3. What kinds of entry-level jobs in this bank are appropriate for your background? What are the advancement opportunities within the bank and within the bank organization? Now that you have a better idea of what branch banking is, how does this career fit with your interests and goals?

Developing Your Research Skills

Choose a recent article from a business journal or newspaper (print or online editions) that discusses the financing arrangements or strategies of a particular company.

1. What form of financing did the company choose? Did the article indicate why the company selected this form of financing?
2. Who provided the financing for the company? Was this arrangement considered unusual, or was it routine?
3. What does the company intend to do with the arranged financing—purchase equipment or other assets, finance a construction project, finance growth and expansion, or do something else?

Exploring the Best of the Web

URLs for all Internet exercises are provided at the website for this book, www.prenhall.com/bovee. When you log on to this text's Companion Website, select Chapter 17. Then select "Featured Websites," click on the name of the featured website, and review the website to complete these exercises.

Explore these chapter-related websites, review their content, and answer the following questions for each website you visit:

1. What is the purpose of this website?
2. What kinds of information does this website contain? Please be specific.
3. How is the information provided at this website useful for businesspeople? Consumers?
4. How did you expand your knowledge of marketing and customers by reviewing the material at this website? What new things did you learn about these topics?

It's In Your Best Interest to Shop Around

Don't automatically settle for whatever interest rate a bank or other financial corporation offers you—the web makes it easy shop around. Whether you want to maximize the interest on money you're saving in a certificate of deposit or minimize the interest on a car loan, mortgage, or credit card, find the best rates around at Bankrate.com. Also, take advantage of the site's extensive educational resources and the free online financial calculators. www.bankrate.com

Take a Field Trip to the Fed

Visit the Fed. Find out what the Board of Governors of the Federal Reserve System does. Read summaries of their regulations. Learn what "Truth in Lending" means or how to file a consumer complaint against a bank. Brush up on your credit card knowledge. Learn more about Check 21 and how it affects your personal finances. www.federalreserve.gov

Protect Yourself from Identity Theft

Identity theft is on the rise, but you can take steps to avoid becoming one of the unfortunate statistics. Visit the Federal Trade Commission's ID Theft website and learn about the problem, the steps you can take to protect yourself (including avoiding phishing scams), and what to do if you do become a victim of identity theft. www.consumer.gov/idtheft

Learning Interactively

Companion Website

Visit the Companion Website at www.prenhall.com/bovee. For Chapter 17, take advantage of the interactive "Learning Modules" to test your chapter knowledge. Get instant feedback on whether you need additional studying. Complete the exercises as specified by your instructor.

A Case for Critical Thinking

Cablevision Survives a Financial Crisis—Then Creates a Few More

It's a dilemma most college students can certainly relate to: running a few dollars short when expenses pile up faster than income. If you can't earn more, the only choices are to spend less or to borrow enough to bridge the gap. James L. Dolan and the management team at Cablevision Systems ran into this problem in 2002. But in their case the gap was $600 million wide.

FINANCING HIGH-SPEED GROWTH

In recent years, the name of the game in the media business has been size—bigger is better and biggest is best of all. From local cable companies to international giants such as Time Warner and Viacom, media firms acquired smaller companies and grew on the theory that market share was the key to success. One by one, though, many of these behemoths began to struggle under the challenge of financing their complex, far-flung operations.

New York–based Cablevision Systems started as a tiny local cable service with 1,500 subscribers and grew into a multibillion-dollar conglomerate with 3 million cable customers, a chain of electronics stores (The Wiz), a local telephone company, Rainbow Media Holdings (whose cable channels include American Movie Classics and the Independent Film Channel), a chain of movie theaters (Clearview Cinemas), stakes in a fledging wireless phone service, entertainment properties (Madison Square Garden and Radio City Music Hall), and—if all that weren't enough—the New York Knicks and several other professional sports teams.

REPAIRING A WEAK SIGNAL

Like most public companies, Cablevision relies heavily on sales of its own stock as a potential source of cash and as collateral for loans (if it needs to borrow). Unfortunately, like too many media and technology-related stocks, in the summer of 2002 Cablevision's market value took a nasty tumble, from a typical range of $60 to $70 a share to as low as $5 a share. It was also losing cable subscribers, thanks in large part to its refusal to carry New York Yankees games. (Cablevision certainly wanted to carry the games, but not at the price the Yankees channel was demanding.) Moreover, advertising business was down as a result of a general recession stretching back to 2001. The company was losing money, and the trend was not encouraging.

At the same time, Cablevision needed to keep investing in new cable and Internet technologies in order to retain existing customers and attract new subscribers. By midsummer, the cash-flow crunch reached a critical point, with cable revenues in danger and the company's ability to generate funds by selling stocks or securing attractive loans on the decline. Financial projections showed the company would need a cash infusion of $600 million in 2003. Borrowing enough to close the gap would be tough, given the company's sinking stock-collateral value and the fact that it was already $7 billion in debt after acquiring all those business units over the years.

BANKING ON NEW BUSINESS

The company had to act, both to shore up its finances and to give investors some reason to buy Cablevision stock and thereby help push the price back up. Dolan knew how much money he needed to find; the question was how to get it. Cutting capital investments in the cable operation would delay attractive new features and run the risk of losing more subscribers to the competition. Reducing staff could affect customer service at a time when Cablevision was already in hot water with many New Yorkers for not carrying the Yankees games.

With no single place to make enough cuts to solve the problem, Dolan developed a multipart plan for increasing revenues and cutting costs. To both protect and grow the core cable business, which offered multiple opportunities for selling new digital services such as high-speed Internet access and video on demand, Cablevision announced plans to accelerate completion of its advanced broadband network. Meanwhile, the company maintained existing staff in the customer service call centers and field service operations to handle increased customer inquiries. Then Dolan sold the wireless phone licenses, sold the Bravo cable channel, closed down The Wiz chain, refocused the Lightpath business, and laid off 3,000 employees.

WILL CABLEVISION SURVIVE?

The drastic moves began to produce positive results in 2003, and stakeholders might've been tempted to think Cablevision was moving toward solid financial footing. However, over the past few years, questionable strategic decisions and a seemingly endless series of internal and external disputes have pushed the company's finances to the brink. For instance, company founder and chairman of the board Charles Dolan—who just happens to be CEO James Dolan's father—insisted on pumping millions into a money-losing satellite broadcasting venture for two years before shutting it down in 2005. Meanwhile, James Dolan spent tens of millions of dollars trying to block construction of a new football stadium that he feared would pose too much competition for Madison Square Garden. With ongoing governance battles between the Dolans and between Cablevision and fierce criticism from shareholders upset by the collapse of the company's stock, the breakup of Cablevision could come soon and could be the final chapter for this pioneer in the cable TV industry.

Critical Thinking Questions

1. Why did Dolan decide not to reduce customer service staff in the cable operation?
2. How did the company's sinking stock price affect its financial management?
3. Why couldn't Cablevision simply borrow $600 million to close the cash flow gap?
4. Visit the investor information section of Cablevision's website, www.cablevision.com, and check out the financial news. How has the company performed financially in recent quarters?

Video Case

Singing a More Profitable Tune at Song Airlines

Learning Objectives

The purpose of this video is to help you:

1. See how Delta Airlines, a company burdened with a heavy cost structure, has been able to compete in the low-cost market segment by creating a new sub-brand with more-efficient operations.
2. Understand the critical importance of process efficiency in a services business such as airline, with its high fixed costs and capacity-management issues.
3. Recognize the opportunity in converting product aspects that are traditionally viewed as unavoidable costs (serving food and offering movies, in the case of airlines) into profitable business activities.

Synopsis

Delta Airlines, like all major U.S. carriers in recent years, has struggled to maintain profitability in the face of relentless price competition and high costs for landing fees, equipment, fuel, and labor. Discounters, led by Southwest Airlines, have steadily taken market share away from the majors by offering lower fares—fares made possible by efficient, lower-cost operations. Unencumbered with the massive debt loads and *legacy costs* (including more-expensive labor contracts and inefficient mixed fleets, which are more expensive to operate than the single-model fleets typically used by discounters) of the majors, these newer, nimbler discounters have been able to engage in nearly endless price wars. As a result, the majors face a vastly changed marketplace, in which the discounters largely define the rules. In classic "if you can't beat 'em, join 'em" style, Delta decided to launch its own discount airline, only with a twist. Unlike the no-frills approach of Southwest, Delta's new Song Airlines operation offers low fares with such amenities as leather seats, healthy food, and personal entertainment systems. Flying large planes to popular destinations helps boost sales volume, which Song says makes up for the cost of providing these additional benefits. Moreover, by charging for gourmet meals and premium entertainment services, Song makes money on services that are traditionally viewed as costly necessities in the airline industry.

Discussion Questions

1. *For analysis:* How has Song been able to increase the return on its fixed investments (planes, gate-leasing fees, and so on)?
2. *For analysis:* Given that first-class fares are often many times higher than coach fares, why would Song choose not to offer first-class seats in its planes?
3. *For application:* Would the Delta-Song approach, of starting a new company or new brand that offers lower prices or an otherwise more appealing product than the parent, work across all other industries? For example, would it help Microsoft to offer a stripped-down, discount version of Microsoft Word? Should Porsche offer an economy car? Why or why not?
4. *For application:* Would an emphasis on process efficiency, which has helped Song operate more profitably, also help a fast-food restaurant boost its profits? What about a fine-dining restaurant? Explain your answers.
5. *For debate:* What is likely to happen to air travel in the United States if more and more carriers focus on the highest-volume routes, such as those between New York and Florida?

Online Exploration

Visit the Song Airlines website at www.flysong.com and explore the way Song presents itself to the traveling public. What steps does it take to emphasize low fares without making the service seem cheap or unappealing? How does Song address the perennial complaint about confusing and often unfair differences in air fares for the same flight (hint: find the page entitled "How We Price")?

Investing in the Future: Securities and Investment Strategies

CHAPTER 18

LEARNING OBJECTIVES

After studying this chapter, you will be able to

1. Differentiate among a stock's par value, its market value, and its book value

2. Highlight the distinguishing features of common stock, preferred stock, bonds, and mutual funds

3. List five types of bonds issued by governments

4. Differentiate among an auction exchange, a dealer exchange, and an electronic communication network (ECN)

5. Explain how government regulation of securities trading tries to protect investors

6. Name five criteria to be considered when making investment decisions

7. Explain how to find information about potential securities investments

www.prenhall.com/bovee

INSIDE BUSINESS TODAY

Schwab Reinvents an Industry—Then Has to Reinvent Itself

www.schwab.com

Since its founding in 1974, Charles Schwab has been at the leading edge of a series of industry-transforming changes—sometimes to its benefit, but sometimes not. When the Securities and Exchange Commission (SEC) ended fixed-stock commissions in the 1970s, the company forged new ground by opening the discount brokerage house that bears the founder's name. When mutual funds became popular in the 1980s, the trendsetter revolutionized the mutual-fund industry by creating a mutual-fund supermarket where investors could buy and sell hundreds of mutual funds in one account without incurring heavy fees. And, when e-commerce took off in the mid-1990s, Schwab took a giant leap of faith by leveraging the power of the Internet and the company's nationwide network of customer centers to provide a convenient and economical way for investors to trade stocks online.

Through it all, Schwab developed a reputation as a bold innovator that responds to market changes and isn't afraid to take on anybody in the business. That attitude was put to the test time and again after the dot-com collapse in 2000 and 2001, the persistent recession that followed soon after, corporate financial scandals that scared investors away, and the market-depressing effects of terrorist attacks and global political uncertainty. Schwab responded in true character, redefining the company to meet changing conditions and taking on old-school Wall Street at every step. The internal changes were painful: The company laid off nearly a quarter of its staff in 2001, and the cuts continued into 2002.

But the company didn't simply retreat. With the online discount business in trouble, Schwab expanded from its discounter roots in order to recapture wealthier customers who had been migrating to Merrill Lynch and other full-service firms. Schwab purchased U.S. Trust Co., an old-line money-management firm that focused on the needs of the wealthiest (and most profitable) investment customers. With the addition of other services, such as financial planning and portfolio evaluations, Schwab was steadily moving closer to becoming a full-service financial services provider. It also expanded beyond individual investors to institutional investing, acquiring firms that provided research and advice to pension funds and other big organizational investors. "The changes we're making are profound," said then-CEO David Pottruck at the time. "We are retesting what the company stands for."

Unfortunately, the results of that test were not altogether encouraging. Profits never really recovered, and the institutional effort in particular never got off the ground. Both it and Pottruck were jettisoned in 2004, when founder and company namesake Charles Schwab came out of semiretirement to retake the reins and refocus the firm on meeting the needs of individual investors.

Meanwhile, as if the battle between full-service and discount brokers wasn't enough, additional competitive forces emerged from two other directions. The first involved brokers that operate exclusively or almost entirely online, such as E-Trade and Ameritrade. With lower operating costs, these new players quickly put downward pressure on brokerage fees. The second involved Fidelity Investments, the nation's largest mutual fund company. For years, Fidelity had been viewed as a "sleeping giant" in the brokerage business, emphasizing its own mutual funds business more than the business of helping customers buy and sell. Along about 2003, however, the giant woke up. After having quietly expanded its online systems and customer service capabilities, Fidelity unleashed an aggressive marketing campaign and quickly began adding new clients. Schwab lost 10 percent of its clients and E-Trade lost 20 percent of its clients during the onslaught. Moreover, half of Fidelity's brokerage clients' assets are in the company's own mutual funds, which helps make Fidelity "ragingly more profitable than Schwab," in the creative words of one industry analyst. Fidelity is now going after one of Schwab's key strengths—its close ties to hundreds of independent investment advisers, each of whom can bring hundreds of clients to a brokerage house.

In response to these challenges, Schwab's sights are now clearly focused on building long-term relationships with individual investors. It now offers a range of services, from simple stock trading to financial planning, and has even added home mortgages and other banking services. By 2005, the approach was showing signs of success, with the company reporting its highest profits in five years.[1]

GET READY

As a central player in the ever-evolving securities business over the past several decades, Charles Schwab has instigated some major changes and has been forced to respond to others. As those changes rolled through the industry, Schwab has benefited from some and suffered from others. From a big-picture perspective, it's a classic example of how a firm interacts with a dynamic business environment. Within the financial services industry specifically, Schwab is also a good case study of the changing nature of the stock markets and the way that both individuals and organizations invest for the future. If you were asked to take over Charles Schwab so that "Chuck" could return to his retirement, how would you respond to the changes in the industry? Would you try to slug it out on the low end, matching the cheapest discounters on price? Or would you go head to head with Merrill Lynch and other full-service firms? And where would the business of buying and selling stocks—your original mission—fit in your overall product portfolio? ■

Chapter Overview

Whether you're working as corporate financial manager who needs to invest your company's funds, as the CEO of a publicly traded company who needs to understand the expectations of company shareholders, or simply as an individual investor building your own nest egg, you'll need to understand securities markets and investment strategies. This chapter introduces you to the most common types of securities investments—stocks, bonds, and mutual funds—as well as a few others of interest to more advanced investors and corporate finance managers. Next, it describes the markets where these investments are bought and sold, along with the all-important issues of government regulations aimed at protecting investors. The final section of the chapter provides an overview of investing strategies, including setting your investment objectives, creating a balanced portfolio, buying and selling securities, and analyzing financial news.

Types of Securities Investments

With the line between banks and brokerage houses such as Schwab blurring, consumers now have more choices as to where they can purchase **securities**—stocks, bonds, and other investments—to meet their investment goals. Securities are traded in organized markets. Corporations sell stocks or bonds to finance their operations or expansion, while governments and municipalities issue bonds to raise money for building or public expenses—from national defense to road improvements. Here's a closer look at these three principal types of securities investments.

securities
Investments such as stocks, bonds, options, futures, and commodities

Stocks

As discussed in Chapter 5, a share of stock represents ownership in a corporation and is evidenced by a stock certificate. The number of stock shares a company sells depends on the amount of equity capital the company requires and on the price of each share it sells. A corporation's board of directors sets a maximum number of shares into which the business can be divided. In theory, all these shares—called *authorized stock*—may be sold at once. In practice, however, the company sells only a part of its authorized stock. The part sold and held by shareholders is called *issued stock*; the unsold portion is called *unissued stock*.

From time to time a company may announce a **stock split**, in which it increases the number of shares that each stock certificate represents while proportionately lowering the value of each share. Companies generally use a stock split to make the share price more affordable. For instance, if a company with 1 million shares outstanding and a stock price of $50 per share announces a two-for-one split, it is doubling the number of shares. After the split, the company will have 2 million shares outstanding, and each original share will become two shares worth $25 each.

When stock is first issued, the company assigns a **par value**, or dollar value, to the stock primarily for bookkeeping purposes. Par value is also used to calculate dividends (for certain kinds of stock). Keep in mind that par value is not the same as the stock's *market value,* the price at which a share currently sells, or its *book value,* the amount of net assets of a corporation represented by one share of common stock.

stock split
Increase in the number of shares of ownership that each stock certificate represents, at a proportionate drop in each share's value

LEARNING OBJECTIVE 1
Differentiate among a stock's par value, its market value, and its book value

par value
As shown on the stock certificate, a value assigned to a stock for use in bookkeeping and in calculating dividends

Common Stock Most investors buy common stock, which represents an ownership interest in a publicly traded corporation. As Chapter 4 points out, shareholders of this class of stock vote to elect the company's board of directors, vote on other important corporate issues, and receive dividend payments from the company's profits. But they have no say in the day-to-day business activities. Still, common shareholders have the advantage of limited liability if the corporation gets into trouble, and as part owners, they share in the fortunes of the business and are eligible to receive dividends as long as they hold the stock. In addition, common shareholders stand to make a profit if the stock price goes up and they sell their shares for more than the purchase price. The reverse is also true: Shareholders of common stock can lose money if the market price drops and they sell the stock for less than they paid for it.

Preferred Stock Investors who own preferred stock, the second major class of stock, enjoy higher dividends and a better claim (after creditors) on assets if the corporation fails. The amount of the dividend on preferred stock is printed on the stock certificate and set when the stock is first issued. If interest rates fluctuate, the market price of preferred stock

LEARNING OBJECTIVE 2
Highlight the distinguishing features of common stock, preferred stock, bonds, and mutual funds

Stock certificates represent a share of ownership of a company.

will go up or down to adjust for the difference between the market interest rate and the stock's dividend. Preferred stock often comes with special privileges. *Convertible preferred stock* can be exchanged, if the shareholder chooses, for a certain number of shares of common stock issued by the company. *Cumulative preferred stock* has an additional advantage: If the issuing company stops paying dividends for any reason, the dividends on these shares will be held (accumulate) until preferred shareholders have been paid in full—before common stockholders are paid.

Bonds

Unlike stock, which gives the investor an ownership stake in the corporation, bonds are debt financing. A **bond** is a method of raising money in which the issuing organization borrows from an investor and issues a written pledge to make regular interest payments and then repay the borrowed amount later. When you invest in this type of security, you are lending money to the company, municipality, or government agency that issued the bond. Bonds are usually issued in multiples of $1,000, such as $5,000, $10,000, and $50,000. Also like stocks, bonds are evidenced by a certificate, which shows the issuer's name, the amount borrowed (the **principal**), the date this principal amount will be repaid, and the annual interest rate investors receive.

The interest is stated in terms of an annual percentage rate but is usually paid at six-month intervals. For example, the holder of a $1,000 bond that pays 8 percent interest due January 15 and July 15 could expect to receive $40 on each of those dates. A look at the financial section of any newspaper will show that some corporations sell new bonds at an interest rate two or three percentage points higher than that offered by other companies. Yet the terms of the bonds seem similar. Why? Because bonds are not guaranteed investments. The variations in interest rates reflect the degree of risk associated with the bond, which is closely tied to the financial stability of the issuing company. Agencies such as Standard & Poor's (S&P) and Moody's rate bonds on the basis of the issuers' financial strength. Exhibit 18.1 shows that the safest corporate bonds are rated AAA (S&P) and Aaa (Moody's). Low-rated bonds, known as *junk bonds,* pay higher interest rates to compensate investors for the higher risk.

Corporate Bonds Companies issue a variety of corporate bonds. **Secured bonds** are backed by company-owned property (such as airplanes or plant equipment) that will pass to

bond
Method of funding in which the issuer borrows from an investor and provides a written promise to make regular interest payments and repay the borrowed amount in the future

principal
Amount of money a corporation borrows from an investor through the sale of a bond

secured bonds
Bonds backed by specific assets that will be given to bondholders if the borrowed amount is not repaid

Bell South Telecommunications bond certificate: (1) Name of corporation issuing bond; (2) type of bond (debenture); (3) face value of the bond; (4) annual interest rate (8.25%); (5) maturity date (due 2032).

the bondholders if the issuer does not repay the amount borrowed. *Mortgage bonds,* one type of secured bond, are backed by real property owned by the issuing corporation. **Debentures** are unsecured bonds, backed only by the corporation's promise to pay. Because debentures are riskier than other types of bonds, investors who buy these bonds receive higher interest rates. **Convertible bonds** can be exchanged at the investor's option for a certain number of shares of the corporation's common stock. Because of this feature, convertible bonds generally pay lower interest rates.

debentures
Corporate bonds backed only by the reputation of the issuer

convertible bonds
Corporate bonds that can be exchanged at the owner's discretion into common stock of the issuing company

Exhibit 18.1
Corporate Bond Ratings
Standard & Poor's (S&P) and Moody's Investors Service are two companies that rate the safety of corporate bonds. When its bonds receive a low rating, a company must pay a higher interest rate to compensate investors for the higher risk.

S&P	Interpretation	Moody's	Interpretation
AAA	Highest rating	Aaa	Prime quality
AA	Very strong capacity to pay	Aa	High grade
A	Strong capacity to pay; somewhat susceptible to changing business conditions	A	Upper-medium grade
BBB	More susceptible than A-rated bonds	Baa	Medium grade
BB	Somewhat speculative	Ba	Somewhat speculative
B	Speculative	B	Speculative
CCC	Vulnerable to nonpayment in default	Caa	Poor standing; may be in default
CC	Highly vulnerable to nonpayment	Ca	Highly speculative; often in default
C	Bankruptcy petition filed or similar action taken	C	Lowest rated; extremely poor chance of ever attaining real investment standing
D	In default		

U.S. Government Securities and Municipal Bonds Just as corporations raise money by issuing bonds, so too do federal, state, city, and local governments and agencies. As an investor, you can buy a variety of U.S. government securities, including three types of bonds issued by the U.S. Treasury, U.S. savings bonds, and bonds issued by various U.S. municipalities.

Treasury bills (also referred to as *T-bills*) are short-term U.S. government bonds that are repaid in less than one year. Treasury bills are sold at a discount and redeemed at face value. The difference between the purchase price and the redemption price is, in effect, the interest earned for the time periods. **Treasury notes** are intermediate-term U.S. government bonds that are repaid from 1 to 10 years after they were initially issued. **Treasury bonds** are long-term U.S. government bonds that are repaid more than 10 years after they were initially issued. Both treasury notes and treasury bonds pay a fixed amount of interest twice a year. But in general, U.S. government securities pay lower interest than corporate bonds because they are considered safer: There is very little risk that the government will fail to repay bondholders as promised. Another benefit is that investors pay no state or local income tax on interest earned on these bonds. Also, these bonds can easily be bought or sold through the Treasury or in organized securities markets.

A traditional choice for many individual investors, **U.S. savings bonds** are issued by the U.S. government in amounts ranging from $50 to $10,000. Investors who buy Series EE savings bonds pay just 50 percent of the stated value and receive the full face amount in as little as 17 years (the difference being earned interest). Once the bond's face value equals its redemption value, the bond continues to earn interest but only until 30 years after the bonds were issued (the bond's final maturity date). Other savings bonds are Series HH, which can be bought only by exchanging Series EE bonds, and Series I, which pay interest indexed to the inflation rate.

Municipal bonds (often called *munis*) are issued by states, cities, and special government agencies to raise money for public services such as building schools, highways, and airports. Investors can buy two types of municipal bonds: general obligation bonds and revenue bonds. A **general obligation bond** is a municipal bond backed by the taxing power of the issuing government. When interest payments come due, the issuer makes payments out of its tax receipts. In contrast, a **revenue bond** is a municipal bond backed by the money to be generated by the project being financed. As an example, revenue bonds issued by a city airport are paid from revenues raised by the airport's operation. To encourage investment, the federal government doesn't tax the interest that investors receive from municipal bonds. Also exempt from state income tax is the interest earned on municipal bonds that are issued by the governments within the taxpayer's home state. However, **capital gains**—the return investors get from selling a security for more than its purchase price—are taxed at both the federal and state levels.

Retirement of Debt Of course, organizations that issue bonds must eventually repay the borrowed amount to the bondholders. Normally, this repayment is done when the bonds mature—say, 10, 15, or 20 years after the bond is issued. The cost of retiring the debt can be staggering, because bonds are generally issued in quantity—perhaps thousands of individual bonds in a single issue. To ease the cash flow burden of redeeming its bonds all at once, a company sometimes issues *serial bonds,* which mature at various times, as opposed to *term bonds,* which mature all at the same time.

Another way of relieving the financial strain of retiring many bonds all at once is to set up a **sinking fund**. When a corporation issues a bond payable by a sinking fund, it must set aside a certain sum of money each year to pay the debt. This money may be used to retire a few bonds each year, or it may be set aside to accumulate until the issue matures.

With most bond issues, a corporation retains the right to pay off the bonds before maturity. Bonds containing this provision are known as *callable bonds,* or *redeemable bonds.* If a company issues bonds when interest rates are high and then rates fall later on, it may want to pay off its high-interest bonds and sell a new issue at a lower rate. However, this feature carries a price tag: Investors must be offered a higher interest rate to encourage them to buy callable bonds. The portion of the percentage rate that is above market rates is actually a "call premium."

Mutual Funds

Individual stocks and bonds can be great investments, but researching every company of interest and deciding which ones to include in your portfolio can literally be a full-time job. Fortunately, there's a fairly easy way to invest in securities without researching and monitoring individual companies. **Mutual funds** are financial organizations that pool money from many investors to buy a diversified mix of stocks, bonds, or other securities; the term *mutual fund* also applies to the individual funds themselves. You can buy shares in mutual funds through your broker or directly from the mutual-fund company. Charles Schwab helped make this type of investment even more popular when the company launched its OneSource no-fee mutual-fund supermarket in 1992. Mutual funds are particularly well suited for investors who wish to spread a limited amount of money over a variety of investments and do not have the time or experience to search out and manage investment opportunities. Investing in mutual funds does save you the trouble of researching individual securities, but you still need to select from the thousands of mutual funds available today, so while mutual funds may make investing simpler, they certainly don't make it *easy*.

Naturally, the companies that do all this research and investing on your behalf expect to be compensated for their time and expertise, which has led to a confusing array of fees associated with mutual funds. These fees are a common source of complaints about mutual funds and can take a considerable bite out of your gains (or add to your losses if a fund declines in value), so you need to understand them before you invest. Fees come in two basic flavors: *annual operating expenses* and *shareholder fees*. The annual expenses are usually assessed as a percentage of your balance in the fund and cover both the fund manager's compensation and the company's marketing costs. All funds charge these fees, but the percentage varies widely from fund to fund. Shareholder fees, commonly called *loads*, are triggered whenever you buy or sell shares in the fund. Loads are essentially sales commissions. However, not all funds have this load feature; those that don't are called *no-load funds*. To find out the true cost of owning any fund, the only alternative is to add up the various fees yourself. Fortunately, the SEC provides a handy online calculator to help you do this: visit www.sec.gov, click on Investor Information, then click on Mutual Fund Cost Calculator.

Mutual funds are also distinguished by whether or not they continue to solicit new investors. An *open-end fund* issues additional shares as new investors ask to buy them. The number of shares outstanding changes daily as investors buy new shares or redeem old ones. *Closed-end funds,* on the other hand, raise all their money at once by distributing a fixed number of shares that trade much like stocks on major security exchanges. As soon as a certain number of shares are sold, the fund closes its books.

Various mutual funds have different investment priorities. Among the most popular mutual funds are **money-market funds**, which invest in short-term securities and other liquid investments. *Growth funds* invest in stocks of rapidly growing companies. *Income funds* invest in securities that pay high dividends and interest. *Balanced funds* invest in a carefully chosen mix of stocks and bonds. *Sector funds* (also known as *specialty* or *industry funds*) invest in companies within a particular industry. *Global funds* invest in foreign and U.S. securities, whereas *international funds* invest strictly in foreign securities. And *index funds* buy stocks in companies included in specific market averages, such as the Standard & Poor's 500. An alternative to the index fund is the exchange-traded fund (ETF), which also tracks a market index but trades on a stock exchange just as a company's stock trades.

mutual funds
Financial organizations pooling money to invest in diversified blends of stocks, bonds, or other securities; the term also applies to the funds themselves

money-market funds
Mutual funds that invest in short-term securities and other liquid investments

Other Investments

A quick look at just about any financial periodical or website will show you that stocks, bonds, and mutual funds are not the only investment opportunities that individuals and organizations have. Three other major categories of investments are options, financial futures, and commodities. However, it must be emphasized that these opportunities are for advanced investors only. And even experts recommend that you never invest your core nest egg in such areas—only money that you can afford to lose without getting wiped out financially.[2]

MINDING YOUR OWN BUSINESS

IS AN INDEX FUND RIGHT FOR YOUR FUTURE?

Life doesn't present many opportunities in which the less work you do, the more successful you can be, but index funds offer just that promise. Index funds are mutual funds that replicate a broad swath of the stock market, such as the NASDAQ Composite or the 500 stocks in the S&P 500.

The appeal of index funds is based on evidence showing that many actively managed funds (meaning that a fund manager is actively choosing which stocks to include or exclude), often don't perform as well as the stock market as a whole, so why not skip all that picking and choosing and just ride the market as a whole. Proponents of index investing admit that the *best* active mutual funds will always outperform index funds, but identifying these high performers ahead of time is so difficult that the average investor is better off just sticking with an index. They argue that stocks have historically risen around 10 percent on average over the course of many decades, so an index fund that tracks the broader market should give the long-term investor a healthy 10 percent return. That's not a spectacular return, but it's enough to build a safe retirement if you start early and invest regularly.

The argument against index funds is also compelling: The best actively managed funds do beat the market, sometimes by a wide margin. Moreover, even though stocks have risen an average of 10 percent a year or so, there have been extended periods when the overall stock market went nowhere or declined for extended periods of time. In other words, riding an index is certainly no guarantee of success—particularly if you're investing for a short-term goal, such as saving for a house.

Aside from the long-term performance question, index funds have an advantage when it comes to cost. In any mutual fund, you pay a portion of your balance every year to cover the company's cost of managing the fund. In an actively managed fund, you'll pay an average of 1.5 percent or so per year, whereas the cost of many index funds is 0.5 percent or less. Does a single percentage point matter? Assume you invest $500 a month starting at age 25 and continue until you're 55, and the fund gains an average of 10 percent a year. That extra percentage point in costs will lower your retirement nest egg by roughly $150,000. So, yes, small percentages do matter.

The arguments for and against indexing often devolve into statistical boxing matches in which either side can find numbers to support its case. However, the argument in favor of index investing is compelling enough that it warrants your attention. If you plan to invest for the long term but don't have the time or inclination for research, index funds make a lot of sense. Even if you do have the time and resources to actively pick stocks yourself or pick mutual funds that actively pick stocks, an index find still might be a sensible part of your overall portfolio.

Questions for Critical Thinking

1. Why do you suppose so many people continue to invest in actively managed mutual funds even though most don't do as well as the market overall (and hence don't do as well as index funds)?
2. Why are index funds recommended particularly for long-term, buy-and-hold investors?

Options and Financial Futures An option is the purchased right—but not the obligation—to buy or sell a specified number of shares of a stock at a predetermined price during a specified period. Options can be used for speculation, or they can be used to **hedge** your positions—that is, partially protect against the risk of a sudden loss. By trading options, the investor doesn't have to own shares of stock in a company—only an option to buy or sell those shares. Investors who trade stock options are betting that the price of the stock will either rise or fall. The cost of buying an option on shares of stock is only the premium paid to the seller, or the price of the option.

All options fall into two broad categories: *puts* and *calls.* Exhibit 18.2 explains the rights acquired with each type of option. **Financial futures** are similar to options, but they are legally binding contracts to buy or sell a financial instrument (stocks, Treasury bonds, foreign currencies) for a set price at a future date.

hedge
To make an investment that protects the investor from suffering loss on another investment

financial futures
Legally binding agreements to buy or sell financial instruments at a future date

Exhibit 18.2

Options

All stock options fall into two broad categories: puts and calls.

Right	Buyer's Belief	Seller's Belief
	CALL OPTION	
The right to buy the stock at a fixed price until the expiration date.	Buyer believes price of underlying stock will increase. Buyer can buy stock at a set price and sell it at a higher price for a capital gain.	Seller believes price of underlying stock will decline and that the option will not be exercised. Seller earns a premium.
	PUT OPTION	
The right to sell the stock at a fixed price until the expiration date.	Buyer believes price of underlying stock will decline and wants to lock in a fixed profit. Buyer usually already owns shares of underlying stock.	Seller believes price of underlying stock will rise and that the option will not be exercised. Seller earns a premium.

Commodities Another option for investors who are comfortable with risky investments is speculating in **commodities**—raw materials and agricultural products, such as petroleum, gold, coffee beans, pork bellies, beef, and coconut oil. Commodities markets originally sprang up as a convenience for buyers and sellers interested in trading the actual commodities. A manufacturer of breakfast cereals, for example, must buy wheat, rye, oats, and sugar from hundreds of farmers. The easiest way to arrange these transactions is to meet in a forum where many buyers and sellers come to trade. Because the commodities are too bulky to bring to the marketplace, the traders buy and sell contracts for delivery of a given amount of these raw materials at a given time.

Trading contracts for immediate delivery of a commodity is called *spot trading,* or *cash trading.* Most commodity trading is for future delivery, usually months in advance, sometimes a year or more; this is called trading commodities futures. The original purpose of futures trading was to allow producers and consumers of commodities to hedge their position, or protect themselves against violent price swings. For example, say you're a cattle rancher in Montana and each month you purchase 20,000 bushels of feed corn. A big rise in corn prices resulting from a flood in the Midwest could ruin you. To

commodities
Raw materials used in producing other goods

At the Chicago Mercantile Exchange (CME) orders stream in from customers trading futures and options from all over the world. Each CME trader acts as buyer and seller, communicating with hand signals and by shouting bids to buy and offers to sell.

hedge against such risk, you purchase futures contracts guaranteeing you 20,000 bushels of corn at a given price when you need them at a later date. Now you know what you'll have to pay. But for every hedger, there must be a speculator—a person willing to take on the risk the hedger wants to shed. The person on the other end of your corn trade probably has no business interest in corn or cattle; he simply wants to gamble that he can buy an offsetting corn contract at a lower price and thus make a profit on the deal.[3] But such speculation is risky—even seasoned veterans have been known to lose literally millions of dollars within a few days.

CRITICAL THINKING CHECKPOINT
1. Why are mutual funds considered a good choice for investors who don't have much time to do their own investment research?
2. Why do so-called junk bonds usually pay higher dividends than higher-quality bonds?
3. Would options and futures be a wise investment for someone getting close to retirement who wants to create a final boost to his or her nest egg before retiring? Why or why not?

Securities Markets

primary market
Market where firms sell new securities issued publicly for the first time

investment banks
Financial institutions that raise capital for corporations and government bodies

secondary market
Market where subsequent owners trade previously issued shares of stocks and bonds

LEARNING OBJECTIVE 4

Differentiate among an auction exchange, a dealer exchange, and an electronic communication network (ECN)

stock exchanges
Location where traders buy and sell stocks and bonds

Securities are bought and sold in two kinds of marketplaces: primary markets and secondary markets. Newly issued shares or initial public offerings (IPOs) are sold in the **primary market** with the assistance of **investment banks**, financial institutions that specialize in raising capital for both corporations and government bodies. Once these shares have been issued, subsequent investors can buy and sell them from each other in the **secondary market**. This section offers a look at the dynamic changes in the secondary market and the efforts to protect investors through regulation of securities markets.

Evolution of Securities Markets

Investors sometimes refer to the "stock market" as if it were a single entity or organization, but in reality, there are a number of different stock markets involved in the buying and selling of securities. Organizations that facilitate the buying and selling are known as **stock exchanges**. Some of these are actual physical facilities, whereas others are little more than computer networks. The most famous of the physical variety is the New York Stock Exchange (NYSE), also known as the "Big Board," which is located on Wall Street in New York City (leading to the frequent use of "Wall Street" as a metaphor for either the NYSE itself or the larger community of financial companies in the immediate area). Other major cities around the world, including Tokyo, London, Frankfurt, Paris, Toronto, and Montreal, also have stock exchanges with national or international importance. *Regional stock exchanges* also play a role in buying and selling many lesser-known stocks.

The NYSE is an example of an *auction exchange*, in which all buy and sell orders (and all information concerning companies traded on that exchange) are funneled onto an auction floor. There, buyers and sellers are matched by a *stock specialist*, a broker who occupies a post on the trading floor and conducts all the trades in specific stocks via a central clearinghouse. These specialists not only help match buyers and sellers but also help minimize the *volatility* of a stock price by controlling buying and selling in a way that prevents prices climbing or falling out of control. The stocks of roughly 3,000 companies are currently sold on the NYSE, including such well-known firms as Campbell Soup, Coca-Cola, Ford Motor, Nike, and Walt Disney.[4] Stocks that sell on the NYSE and other exchanges are said to be *listed* on that exchange.

Thousands of other stocks are sold outside of organized stock exchanges in what is known as the **over-the-counter (OTC) market** (the name dates from the time such stocks were literally sold over the counter in banks and other places).[5] Most of these stocks are sold through the well-known *NASDAQ* (*National Association of Securities Dealers Automated Quotations*). In contrast to auction exchanges such as the NYSE, NASDAQ is a *dealer exchange* that has no physical marketplace for making transactions. Instead, all buy and sell orders are executed through a computer network by *market makers*, registered stock and bond representatives who sell securities out of their own inventories. NASDAQ, which is owned by the National Association of Securities Dealers (NASD), is a significant competitor to the NYSE and home to such high-profile stocks as Amazon.com, Apple Computer, Electronic Arts, Intel, and Microsoft.[6]

In addition to auction and dealer exchanges, a third major type of marketplace is involved in the buying and selling of securities. **Electronic communication networks (ECNs)** use the Internet to link buyers and sellers; they have no exchange floors, specialists, or market makers (see Exhibit 18.2). In fact, they are nothing more than computer networks with software programs that match buy and sell orders directly, bypassing the once-dominant market makers and specialists.

ECNs are taking on an increasingly important role in the securities industry—so much so, in fact, that both the NYSE and NASDAQ are joining the party. In 2005, the NYSE announced a merger with Archipelago, which owned one of the fastest growing ECNs, and NASDAQ announced the acquisition of Instinet, at the time the largest ECN.[7] You can read more about NYSE's moves in the Case for Critical Thinking on page 607. These developments are just two examples of how the securities industry continues to evolve in the face of increasing competition and advancing technology.

Regulation of Securities Markets

Whether you buy and sell securities online or use a traditional full-service broker, your trades are governed by a variety of state and federal laws; Exhibit 18.3 lists some of the most significant of these. Combined with industry self-regulation, these laws are designed to ensure that you and all investors receive accurate information and that no one artificially manipulates the market price of a given security. Trading in stocks and bonds is monitored by the SEC, which works closely with the stock exchanges and the NASD to

over-the-counter (OTC) market
Network of dealers who trade securities on computerized linkups rather than a trading floor

electronic communication networks (ECNs)
Internet-based networks that match up buy and sell orders without using an intermediary

LEARNING OBJECTIVE 5

Explain how government regulation of securities trading tries to protect investors

More than 3,000 companies trade their stock on the NASDAQ exchange, including such well-known firms as Merrill-Lynch, 1-800 Flowers, Microsoft, and Apple Computer.

Exhibit 18.3

Major Federal Legislation Governing the Securities Industry

Although you have no guarantee that you'll make money on your investments, you are protected by laws against unfair securities trading practices.

Legislation	Provision
Securities Act (1933)	Requires full disclosure of relevant financial information from companies that want to sell new stock or bond issues to the general public; also known as the Truth in Securities Act
Securities Exchange Act (1934)	Creates the Securities and Exchange Commission (SEC) to regulate the national stock exchanges and to establish trading rules
Maloney Act (1938)	Creates the National Association of Securities Dealers to regulate over-the-counter securities trading
Investment Company Act (1940)	Extends the SEC's authority to cover the regulation of mutual funds
Amendment to the Securities Exchange Act (1964)	Extends the SEC's authority to cover the over-the-counter market
Securities Investor Protection Act (1970)	Creates the Securities Investor Protection Corporation (SIPC) to insure individual investors against losses in the event of dealer fraud or insolvency
Commodity Futures Trading Commission Act (1974)	Creates the Commodity Futures Trading Commission (CFTC) to establish and enforce regulations governing futures trading
Insider Trading and Securities Fraud Act (1988)	Toughens penalties, authorizes bounties for information, requires brokerages to establish written policies to prevent employee violations, and makes it easier for investors to bring legal action against violators
Securities Market Reform Act (1990)	Increases SEC market control by granting additional authority to suspend trading in any security for 10 days, to restore order in the event of a major disturbance, to establish a national system for settlement and clearance of securities transactions, to adapt rules for actions affecting market volatility, and to require more detailed record keeping and reporting of brokers and dealers
Private Securities Litigation Reform Act (1995)	Protects companies from frivolous lawsuits by investors: limits how many class-action suits can be filed by the same person in a three-year period, and encourages judges to penalize plaintiffs who bring meritless cases
Sarbanes-Oxley Act of 2002	Among its far-reaching efforts aimed at reforming corporate accounting and the securities industry, the act prohibits investment bankers from influencing stock analysts and requires CEOs and CFOs to sign statements attesting to the accuracy of their financial statements

police securities transactions and maintain the system's integrity. As recent scandals have shown, however, even all these watchdog efforts can't always catch people who are determined to manipulate the market in some way.

SEC Filing and Disclosure Requirements One of the most significant protections afforded by the SEC is the requirement that all companies wishing to sell securities to the public (including foreign companies that want to sell securities in the United States) must file a number of detailed financial reports with the SEC, which then makes all these reports available to the public at no charge. Exhibit 18.4 lists the major types of reports, but this is just a small sample of the various reports that the SEC requires. You can access the reports on any company or mutual fund through the SEC's Electronic Data Gathering, Analysis, and Retrieval (EDGAR) database: visit the SEC website at www.sec.gov, then click on Filings & Forms (EDGAR).

These filing requirements are part of the SEC's mission to ensure *full and fair disclosure*, which means that all investors get all the relevant information they need—and they can all get it at the same time. For instance, Regulation FD (Full Disclosure) was

10K ➡ The official version of a company's annual report, with a comprehensive overview of the business.

10Q ➡ An abridged version of the 10K, filed quarterly for the first three quarters of a company's fiscal year.

8K ➡ An interim report disclosing significant company events that occur before the company files its next 10Q or 10K.

12B-25 ➡ Request for a deadline extension to file a required report, like a 10K or 10Q. When the late report is ultimately filed, NT is appended to the report's name.

S1 ➡ Basic registration form for new securities, most often initial or secondary public offerings.

Proxy Statement ➡ Information and ballot materials for shareholder votes, including election of directors and approval of mergers and acquisitions when required.

Forms 3, 4, and 5 ➡ Directors, officers, and owners of more than 10 percent of a company's stock report their initial purchases on Form 3 and subsequent purchases or sales on Form 4; they file an annual statement of their holdings on Form 5.

Exhibit 18.4
An Edgar Scorecard
To successfully navigate the Securities and Exchange Commission's Edgar database of corporate filings, it helps to know the most common filings required of publicly traded companies and their content.

adopted to prohibit companies from "selectively disclosing" important information (such as earnings estimates) to big institutional shareholders and Wall Street analysts before giving the information to individual investors.[8] SEC regulations also make it illegal to engage in **insider trading**, buying or selling a stock based on information that is not available to the general public, such as an upcoming merger or government approval of a new wonder drug.

insider trading
Illegal use of nonpublic information to make an investment profit

Securities Fraud In spite of the constant effort by the SEC, the NASD, and others to police the financial markets, as long as dishonest people can find a way to reach trusting targets, fraud will always be a problem. As mentioned earlier, the tremendous freedom that the Internet gives individual investors has also created seemingly endless opportunities for crooks to devise new ways to scam people.

For instance, in a variation on the increasingly common technique of phishing, crooks can lure people to fake websites that appear to be legitimate stock brokerage sites. Some even claim to be affiliated with the NASD or other industry watchdog groups. Once the unsuspecting visitors have reached the site, they'll be sold on the prospects of some "hot stock" that's just about to skyrocket. One scam artist even tried to convince people to swap their shares of Yahoo! for shares of several unknown companies—and deposit cash in an overseas bank account while the trade was taking place.[9] As an investor, your best defenses against fraud are to carefully research securities before you buy and to steer clear of any investment that seems too good to be true (see Exhibit 18.5).

Business Buzz
pump and dump
An illegal stock manipulation maneuver in which a small group of people buy a stock, "pump" the price up by talking it up enthusiastically in chat rooms and other web forums, wait until enough receptive listeners jump on the bandwagon to push the price up, then "dump" it by selling out before the price inevitably falls again

CRITICAL THINKING CHECKPOINT

1. As an individual investor, do you need to worry about which exchanges your stocks are traded on? Why or why not?
2. If a required financial report has been filed with the SEC, can you safely assume that the information it contains is complete and accurate? Why or why not?
3. Why is insider trading illegal?

Exhibit 18.5
Ten Questions to Ask Before You Invest
You can avoid getting taken in an online stock scam by asking yourself these 10 questions before you invest.

1. Is the investment registered with the SEC and your state's securities agency?
2. Have you read the company's audited financial statements?
3. Is the person recommending this investment a registered broker?
4. What does the person promoting the investment have to gain?
5. If the tip came from an online bulletin board or e-mail, is the author identifiable or using an alias? Is there any reason to trust that person?
6. Are you being pressured to act before you can evaluate the investment?
7. Does the investment promise you'll get rich quick, using words like "guaranteed," "high return," or "risk free"?
8. Does the investment match your objectives? Could you afford to lose all of the money you invest?
9. How easy would it be to sell the investment later? Remember, stocks with fewer shares are easy for promoters to manipulate and hard for investors to sell if the price starts falling.
10. Does the investment originate overseas? If yes, beware: It is tougher to track money sent abroad and harder for burned investors to have recourse to justice.

Investment Strategies and Techniques

Done wisely, investing in stocks and bonds can help you meet your financial goals, whether you're investing as an individual or on behalf of your company. But you must first make decisions about how much you want to invest and where to invest it. To choose wisely, you need to know what choices you have and what risks they entail. Before you start to trade, take time to think about your objectives, both long term and short term. Next, look at how various securities match your objectives and your attitude toward risk, because investing in stocks and bonds can involve potential losses.

Establishing Investment Objectives

All investment opportunities are not created equal, not by a long shot. You can keep your money in a bank savings account, where it'll stay safe for decades but earn so little interest that you won't even keep up with inflation. At the other extreme, you can invest in risky high-growth stocks that might increase in value a hundred times over—or might collapse right after you buy them. In between are thousands of investment opportunities with a wide range of potential risks and rewards.

LEARNING OBJECTIVE 6

Name five criteria to be considered when making investment decisions

Given this wide spectrum of investments, it's absolutely critical to establish objectives before you invest any money. Are you saving up to buy a business, to put your children through college, to care for your parents, to prepare for your own retirement, or several of these reasons at once? By identifying your goals you can then start to select investments based on five factors: *income* (regular cash payments that an investment provides, such as quarterly dividends from a stock), *growth* (gains in the market value of the investment), *safety* (the risk that the value of the investment might decline, even below the amount that you paid for it), *liquidity* (the ease and speed with which you can sell the investment when you need to), and *tax consequences* (investments have markedly different tax ramifications, and some are designed specifically to minimize taxes). As with all well-crafted goals, you need to establish a timeframe for your investment objectives, too. Real estate is a good long-term investment but generally not a good short-term investment because of its poor liquidity (real estate can take a long time to sell).

For example, investors who are entering retirement and need to generate regular income, or those who have large recurring expenses such as college tuition payments, usually emphasize income over growth. In other words, investments that provide high **yield** (the annual rate of income from an investment such as stock dividends), are more attractive than stocks that might grow in value over time but pay little or nothing in dividends now. Common investment choices for income investors include certificates of deposit, government securities, corporate bonds, and preferred stocks.

yield
Income received from securities, calculated by dividing dividend or interest income by market price

In contrast, investors who still need to build their personal wealth are more interested in growth than income and often look to **growth stocks** issued by younger companies that have the potential to expand sales rapidly. These companies often pay no dividends because they reinvest earnings in the company to expand operations. However, high-growth stocks attract a breed of investors who tend to buy stocks with rapidly accelerating earnings and sell them on the slightest hint of bad news. For this reason, these stocks are usually the most volatile in the market.

growth stocks
Equities issued by small companies with unproven products or services

Both income and growth investors care about safety, of course. Generally, the higher the potential for income or growth, the greater the risk of the investment. Government bonds are safer than corporate bonds, which are safer than common stocks, which are safer than futures contracts, which are safer than commodities. **Speculators** operate at the extreme end of the safety spectrum; they are willing to take the highest risks in the hopes of achieving the highest returns. *Long-term* or *buy-and-hold investors*, in contrast, stick with their investments for years, riding out the inevitable ups and downs.

speculators
Investors who purchase securities in anticipation of making large profits quickly

Two additional investment objectives you should consider when selecting investments are liquidity and tax consequences. Liquidity is the measure of how quickly you can convert an investment into cash. For example, common stock is more liquid than real estate; most financial assets can be changed into cash within a day. Some, like certificates of deposit, can be cashed in before maturity, but only after paying a penalty. All investors must consider the tax consequences of their decisions as well. For instance, long-term capital gains are usually taxed at a lower rate than short-term gains. Similarly, income from most state and local municipal bonds is exempt from federal income tax as an incentive for people to invest in major public projects such as sports stadiums, schools, and other facilities.

LEARNING FROM BUSINESS BLUNDERS

OOPS You know that e-commerce has truly spanned the globe when you can get scammed out of money from halfway around the world. Anyone with an e-mail account has probably seen the Nigerian investment scam. Someone claiming to be connected to somebody connected to the Nigerian government or the national oil company claims to have a way to shuttle millions of dollars out of the country if only you'll provide some up-front money to shake the whole thing loose. Sounds crazy, but the scheme has already defrauded hopeful e-mail recipients out of more than $100 million in the United States alone. One retired man from Florida shelled out more than $300,000 before he realized he'd been had.

WHAT YOU CAN LEARN If it sounds too good to be true, it is. This rule applies in the stock market, in the grocery market—pretty much anywhere on planet Earth. If you're ever tempted by this or any other investment pitch, stop and ask yourself a couple of questions: (1) Why are they offering this to *me,* out of the 5 or 6 billion people in the world? (2) What would have to happen for me to make any money from this deal? If you can't make the connection between your investment and the promised payoff, that's a good sign there won't be one.

Creating an Investment Portfolio

investment portfolios
Assortment of investment instruments

Unfortunately, no single investment provides an ideal combination of income, growth potential, safety, liquidity, and tax consequences. For this reason, investors build **investment portfolios**, or collections of various types of investments. Money managers and financial advisers are often asked to determine which investments should be in an investor's portfolio and to buy and sell securities and maintain the client's portfolio. Sometimes they must structure a portfolio to provide a desired **rate of return**, the percentage of gain or interest yield on investments.

rate of return
Percentage increase in the value of an investment

asset allocation
Method of shifting investments within a portfolio to adapt them to the current investment environment

Managing a portfolio to gain the highest rates of return while reducing risk as much as possible is known as **asset allocation**. A portion of the portfolio might be devoted to cash instruments such as money-market mutual funds, a portion to income instruments such as government and corporate bonds, and a portion to equities (mainly common stock). Investors then determine how much each portion should be, on the basis of both his or her objectives and prevailing economic and market conditions—not an easy task. For instance, someone who believes that the stock market is heading for a sharp decline might shift a major portion of assets out of stock (before share prices drop) and into cash.

diversification
Assembling investment portfolios in such a way that a loss in one investment won't cripple the value of the entire portfolio

Asset allocation is related to another major portfolio concern, which is **diversification**—reducing the risk of overall loss by investing in several areas in the hope that a loss in one area will be balanced by gains or at least stability in others. One way to diversify is by investing in securities from unrelated industries and a variety of countries. Another way is by allocating your assets among different investment types.

Buying and Selling Securities

Once you've set your goals and decided which types of investments to purchase, you're ready to enter the market. How you make these purchases depends on what you're buying. For instance, you can purchase mutual funds directly from the mutual fund company, or you can buy them through a broker such as Charles Schwab. However, to purchase specific stocks or bonds, you must buy them through a broker.

broker
An expert who has passed specific tests and is registered to trade securities for investors

Securities Brokers A **broker** is an expert who has passed a series of formal examinations and is legally registered to buy and sell securities on behalf of individual and institutional investors. As an investor, you pay *transaction costs* for every buy or sell order, to cover the broker's commission, which varies with the type of broker and the size of your trade. A *full-service broker* provides financial management services such as investment counseling and planning, whereas a *discount broker* provides fewer or limited services and generally charges lower commissions than a full-service broker. As you probably gathered from the Charles Schwab story at the beginning of the chapter, however, the brokerage market seems to be in a state of ongoing upheaval, so the once-clear line between full-service and discount is anything but clear these days.

Most brokers give you several ways to execute trades: online, over the phone, or in person at their offices. The choice is a matter of cost, convenience, and personal preference. You should also consider whether access to customer service personnel is important to you, or if you're comfortable doing everything yourself online or on the phone—brokerages vary widely in the quality and availability of support personnel.

market order
Authorization for a broker to buy or sell securities at the best price that can be negotiated at the moment

limit order
Market order that stipulates the highest or lowest price at which the customer is willing to trade securities

stop order
An order to sell a stock when its price falls to a particular point to limit an investor's losses

Orders to Buy and Sell Securities Regardless of which broker you use and how you access its services, you can place a variety of different types of buy and sell orders. A **market order** tells the broker to buy or sell at the best price that can be negotiated at the moment. A **limit order** specifies the highest price you are willing to pay when buying or the lowest price at which you are willing to sell. A **stop order**, or *stop-loss order*, tells the broker to sell if the price of your security drops to or below the price you set, protecting

TECHNOLOGIES THAT ARE REVOLUTIONIZING BUSINESS | Online Investing

HOW IT'S CHANGING BUSINESS

Online investing has turned much of the securities industry on its head, giving individual investors information and control they never had before and introducing price competition that continues to help investors and hurt brokerage firms. At the same time, online investing has exposed individual investors to greater risk than they might've experienced when going through traditional brokers. When you invest online, no one is there to ask, "Are you *sure* about that?" before you buy or sell a security. Moreover, in the vast proliferation of chat rooms, blogs, and websites that discuss investing, plenty of misinformation (both confused and downright dishonest) is floating around. In other cases, investors simply misuse the tools, such as trying to use online brokerage sites to conduct *day trading*, a risky technique that requires ultrafast processing available only through specialized terminals connected directly to exchanges. Online investing gives individual investors more power, but to keep from hurting themselves, they need to use that power wisely.

WHERE YOU CAN LEARN MORE

All of the websites listed in "Put Your Money Where Your Mouse Is" on page 598 offer useful information for online investors. In addition, check out the sites listed at Winning Investing, **www.winninginvesting.com**.

---

you from losing more money if prices are dropping. You can also place a time limit on your orders. An **open order** instructs the broker to leave the order open until you cancel it. A **day order** is valid only on the day you place it. All of these orders can have a significant effect on your finances, so make sure you understand the specific details of how your broker implements each type.

If you have special confidence in your broker's ability, you may place a **discretionary order**, which gives the broker the right to buy or sell your securities at the broker's discretion. In some cases, discretionary orders can save you from taking a loss, because the broker may have a better sense of when to sell a stock. If the broker's judgment proves wrong, however, you cannot hold the broker legally responsible for the consequences; so investigate your broker's background and think carefully before you give anyone the right to trade your securities.

Investors sometimes borrow cash to buy stocks, a practice known as **margin trading**. Instead of paying for the stock in full, you borrow some of the money from your stockbroker, paying interest on the borrowed money and leaving the stock with the broker as collateral. The Federal Reserve establishes limits on how much you can borrow on margin, and many brokers have their own limits.[10] Be aware, however, that margin trading increases risk. If the price of a stock you bought on margin goes down far enough to exceed those margin limits, you'll get a *margin call* notice from the broker, meaning you need to put more cash in your account or sell your stock if you don't have the cash—even if that means selling at a steep loss.

If you believe that a stock's price is about to drop, you may choose a trading procedure known as **short selling**. With this procedure, you sell stock you borrow from a broker in the hope of buying it back later at a lower price. After you return the borrowed stock to the broker, you keep the price difference. For example, you might decide to borrow 25 shares that are selling for $30 per share and sell short because you think the share price is going to plummet. When the stock's price declines to $15, you buy 25 shares on the open market and make $15 profit on every share (minus transaction costs). Selling short is also risky. If the stock climbs instead, you may be forced to buy shares at higher prices, even though you would be losing money.

Analyzing Financial News

Whether you are purchasing, holding, or selling securities, as an investor you will want to keep current on the overall economy, the stock market, and the performance of specific

open order
Limit order that does not expire at the end of a trading day

day order
Any order to buy or sell a security that automatically expires if not executed on the day the order is placed

discretionary order
Market order that allows the broker to decide when to trade a security

margin trading
Borrowing money from brokers to buy stock, paying interest on the borrowed money, and leaving the stock with the broker as collateral

short selling
Selling stock borrowed from a broker with the intention of buying it back later at a lower price, repaying the broker, and keeping the profit

LEARNING OBJECTIVE 7

Explain how to find information about potential securities investments

INNOVATING FOR BUSINESS SUCCESS

PUT YOUR MONEY WHERE YOUR MOUSE IS

The Internet has been hailed as the great equalizer between individual investors and Wall Street. Today's investors have access to a staggering amount of valuable information and investment tools—many of which are used by Wall Street professionals. But having access to information is one thing; using it wisely is another. So before you put money into any investment, learn as much as possible about the market, the security, its issuer, and its potential. Here are some of the many websites that can help you succeed.

For "how-to" advice, try the Motley Fool (www.fool.com), Investopedia (www.investopedia.com), or *CNN/Money*'s website (http://money.cnn.com). For the latest online news and commentary about stocks, check out The Street (www.thestreet.com), CBS Market Watch (www.marketwatch.com), or Yahoo! Finance (http://finance.yahoo.com). Be sure to research individual companies using your favorite search engine; stop by each company's website to read its press releases and financial statements. Dig into specialty areas such as Morningstar's mutual fund reports (www.morningstar.com) or bond prices and market performance (www.investinginbonds.com).

Before you invest real money, construct a hypothetical portfolio on Investopedia, Yahoo!, or another financial website and watch how your investments fare. Track your favorite market index on MSN MoneyCentral (http://moneycentral.msn.com), and compare it to your personal investment portfolio. Are your proposed investments meeting, missing, or beating the market index?

Now you're in a better position to buy securities, but your research shouldn't end here. Even after you start trading, you need to stay on top of the latest news and industry developments that can affect the securities in which you have invested. And if a potential investment seems too good to be true, point your web browser to the North American Securities Administrators Association (www.nasaa.org) and get some tips on investment fraud. Remember, when it comes to investments, your web surfing can really pay off.

Questions for Critical Thinking

1. Why is it important to learn about a company's financial results and background before buying its stock or bonds?
2. What are the risks involved in searching for investment information on the Internet?

companies and industries. Good sources of financial information include daily newspaper reports on securities markets, newspapers aimed specifically at investors (such as *Investor's Business Daily* and *Barron's*), and general-interest business publications that follow the corporate world and give hints about investing (such as the *Wall Street Journal, Forbes, Fortune,* and *Business Week*). Standard & Poor's, Moody's Investor Service, and Value Line also publish newsletters and special reports on securities. Online sources include your brokerage firm's website, the websites of all the financial periodicals just listed, plus a growing number of excellent financial websites listed in "Put Your Money Where Your Mouse Is."

The list of specific types of information you might want to follow could fill a book and, in fact, has filled several thousand investing books. Before you invest any of your hard-earned money, check out several investing books in the library and visit websites that offer free tutorials for beginners, such as www.investopedia.com or www.fool.com. Don't be put off if it all seems confusing at first—it's confusing to everyone in the beginning. But you'll gradually pick up on the terminology and start to identify which topics you need to care about and which of the many arcane topics you can leave to the specialists. For instance, you'll soon get familiar with the general conditions of the stock market and learn the terms that define its ups and downs. If stock prices have been rising over a long period, the industry and the media will often describe

Exhibit 18.6

The Stock Market's Ups and Downs

The peaks and valleys on this chart represent swings in the Dow Jones Industrial Average, the most widely used indicator of U.S. stock prices.

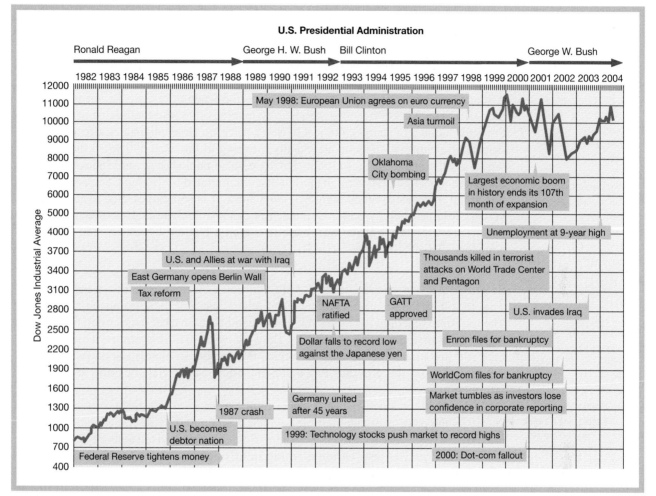

this situation as a **bull market**. The reverse is a **bear market**, one characterized by a long-term trend of falling prices. You can see these broad market movements in Exhibit 18.6. You'll hear about stocks being *overvalued* and *corrections* that occur when enough people realize a stock is overpriced and sell, pushing the price down.

All beginners can learn from **institutional investors**—such as pension funds, insurance companies, investment companies, banks, and colleges and universities—that buy and sell securities in large quantities, often in blocks of at least 10,000 shares per transaction. Because these institutions have such large pools of money to work with, their investment decisions have a major impact on the marketability of a company's shares as well as the overall behavior of the securities market. If the stock market is down on heavy volume (that is, if prices are moving downward and a lot of trading is going on), institutional investors may be trying to sell before prices go down further—a bearish sign. At the same time, don't think that you should necessarily mimic institutional investors; they usually don't pay attention to smaller stocks that could fit nicely in a growth-oriented portfolio, for instance.

Watching Market Indexes and Averages One way to determine whether the market is bullish or bearish is to watch **market indexes** and averages, which use the performance

bull market
Rising stock market

bear market
Falling stock market

institutional investors
Companies and other organizations that invest money entrusted to them by others

market indexes
Measures of market activity calculated from the prices of a selection of securities

of a representative sampling of stocks, bonds, or commodities as a gauge of broader market activity. The most famous U.S. stock index is the Dow Jones Industrial Average (DJIA), which tracks the prices of 30 *blue-chip* or well-established stocks, each representing a particular sector of the U.S. economy. The DJIA currently contains such bedrock companies as Microsoft, Intel, Home Depot, and SBC Communications, but the editors of the *Wall Street Journal*, who oversee the index, periodically replace companies to keep the index relevant.[11]

Many other indexes have developed over the years in attempts to better reflect either the overall stock market or specific sectors within it. The Standard & Poor's 500 Stock Average (S&P 500), for instance, tracks the performance of 500 stocks, many more than the DJIA. The S&P 500 is also weighed by market value (the total value of share price times the number of shares), not just by stock price, so large companies affect it far more than small companies. People are usually referring to the S&P 500 when they say such things as "the market is up today."[12] NASDAQ also publishes several indexes related to the stocks in its trading system, including the often-quoted NASDAQ Composite; because this group includes so many high-tech companies, it is sometimes used as a measure of how well the technology sector is doing. You can also look at indexes to learn about the performance of foreign markets, such as Japan's Nikkei 225 Index and the United Kingdom's FT-SE 100 Index.

Interpreting the Financial News In addition to watching market trends, you will want to follow the securities you own and others that look like promising investments. The traditional method for doing this is by reading the market pages published in most major daily newspapers. Exhibit 18.7 shows how to read this report, which includes high and low prices for the past 52 weeks, the number of shares traded (volume), and the change from the previous day's closing price. Many websites now offer similar information.

price-earnings ratio
Ratio calculated by dividing a stock's market price by its prior year's earnings per share

Included in the stock exchange report is the **price-earnings ratio**, or *p/e ratio* (also known as the price-earnings multiple), which is computed by dividing a stock's market price by its *prior* year's earnings per share. Some investors also calculate a forward p/e ratio using *expected* year earnings in the ratio's denominator. Bear in mind that if a stock's p/e ratio is well below the industry norm, either the company is in trouble or it's an undiscovered gem with a relatively low stock price. For more detailed data on a stock, consult the company's annual reports, documents filed with the SEC, or your favorite financial website.

To follow specific bonds, you can check the bond quotation tables in major newspapers (see Exhibit 18.8). When reading these tables, remember that the price is quoted as a percentage of the bond's value. For example, a $1,000 bond shown closing at 65 actually sold at $650.

Newspapers and business publications also include tables of price quotations for investments such as mutual funds, commodities, options, and government securities (see Exhibit 18.9). These same publications also carry news about current challenges the securities industry is facing, securities regulations, reported frauds, and proposals to improve investor protection.

CRITICAL THINKING CHECKPOINT
1. Why is liquidity a concern for investors?
2. If you want to buy a particular stock but are worried that demand from investors could push the price to an unreasonably high level before your order is executed, which type of order would you specify? Why?
3. Does a low p/e ratio mean that a stock is a good buy? Explain your answer.

Exhibit 18.7
How to Read a Newspaper Stock Quotation
Even before you invest, you will want to follow the latest quotations for your stock. This table shows you how to read the newspaper stock quotation tables.

(1) 52-WEEK HIGH	(1) 52-WEEK LOW	(2) STOCK	(3) SYM	(4) DIV	(5) YLD %	(6) PE	(7) VOL 100s	(8) HI	(8) LOW	(9) LAST	(10) NET CHG
43.84	34.45	JPMorgan Chase	JPM	1.37	3.6	20	9282	38.18	37.03	38.10	+0.61
47.94	22.25	Maytag	MYG	.72	2.3	33	9027	31.48	29.40	31.36	+1.16
39.50	23.53	Neiman Marc	NMGA	...	...	18	4217	27.03	23.75	27.03	+2.15
21.96	10.06	Office Depot	ODP	...	...	15	33898	12.80	11.05	12.77	+0.98

1. **52-week high/low:** Indicates the highest and lowest trading price of the stock in the past 52 weeks plus the most recent week but not the most recent trading day (adjusted for splits). Stocks are quoted in dollars and cents. In most newspapers, boldfaced entries indicate stocks whose price changed by at least 4% but only if the change was at least 75 cents a share.

2. **Stock:** The company's name may be abbreviated. A capital letter usually means a new word. In this example, Neiman Marc is Neiman Marcus.

3. **Symbol:** Symbol under which this stock is traded on stock exchanges.

4. **Dividend:** Dividends are usually annual payments based on the last quarterly or semiannual declaration, although not all stocks pay dividends. Special or extra dividends or payments are identified in footnotes.

5. **Yield:** The percentage yield shows dividends as a percentage of the share price.

6. **PE:** Price-to-earnings ratio, calculated by dividing the stock's closing price by the earnings per share for the latest four quarters.

7. **Volume:** Daily total of shares traded, in hundreds. A listing of 888 indicates 88,800 shares were traded during that day.

8. **High/Low:** The stock's highest and lowest price for that day.

9. **Last:** Closing price of the stock that day.

10. **Net change:** Change in share price from the close of the previous trading day.

Common Stock Footnotes: d—new 52-week low; n—new; pf—preferred; s—stock split or stock dividend of 25 percent or more in previous 52 weeks; u—new 52-week high; v—trading halted on primary market; vi—in bankruptcy; x—ex dividend (the buyer won't receive a recently declared dividend, but the seller will)

Exhibit 18.8
How to Read a Newspaper Bond Quotation
When newspapers carry bond quotations, they show prices as a percentage of the bond's value, which is typically $1,000.

(1) COMPANY	(2) CUR YLD	(3) VOL	(4) CLOSE	(5) NET CHG
NYTel 6 1/8 10	6.6	11	93.40	−.25
PacBell 6 1/4 05	6.4	10	98.40	+.25
Safwy 9 7/8 07	8.4	20	117.50	+3.60
StoneC 11 1/4 06	11.1	24	103.50	−1.10
TimeWar 9 1/8 13	8.3	30	109.75	−.50

1. **Company:** Name of company issuing the bond, such as New York Telephone, and bond description, such as 6 1/8 percent bond maturing in 2010.

2. **Current yield:** Annual interest of $1,000 bond divided by the closing price shown. The yield for New York Telephone is $61.25 + $933.75 = 0.06559, or approximately 6.6 percent.

3. **Volume:** Number of bonds traded (in thousands) that day.

4. **Close:** Price of the bond at the close of the last day's business.

5. **Net change:** Change in bond price from the close of the previous trading day.

Exhibit 18.9
How to Read a Newspaper Mutual Fund Quotation
A mutual fund listing shows the new asset value of one share (the price at which one share is trading) and the change in trading price from one day to the next.

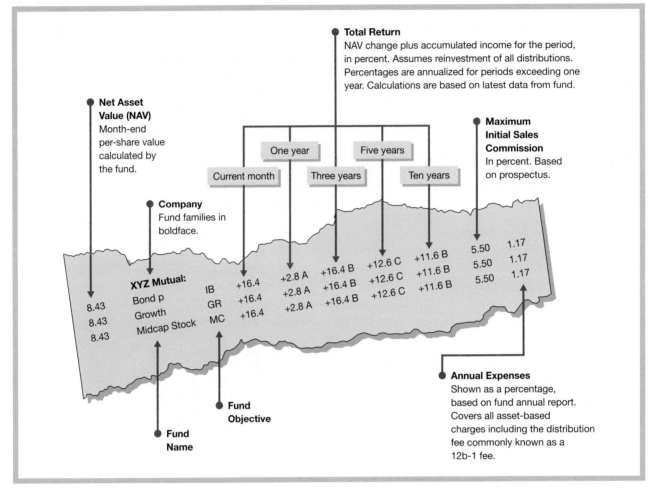

CHECKLIST: Apply These Ideas When You're the Boss—Or Investing for Yourself

✓ Never invest on emotion.

✓ If you can't explain in realistic, financial terms why a particular investment should increase in value, you're not ready to buy it.

✓ Keep in mind that investing in mutual funds isn't necessarily any easier than investing in individual stocks; you still need to do considerable research to select which of the several thousand mutual funds available today is right for you.

✓ Day trading, short selling, buying on margin, trading futures and commodities, and other techniques have made some people wealthy, but they've also wiped out people who didn't know what they were doing or took on more risk than they could handle, so think twice (or three or four times) before taking the plunge in any of these areas.

✓ Never invest without an objective; for instance, do you want a stock to grow in value 20 or 30 years from now, or do you need dividend income this year?

✓ Understand the tax implications of every investment before you buy.

✓ Identify the costs of buying, holding, and selling an investment; in a mutual fund with weak performance, for instance, these costs can erase any gain the fund might make.

✓ If something sounds too good to be true, it's more than likely a scam—run fast, run far.

✓ Don't let the complexities of some investments scare you away; using the many resources now available for little or no cost, millions of people without financial backgrounds now invest successfully.

Summary of Learning Objectives

1 **Differentiate among a stock's par value, its market value, and its book value.** Par value is the dollar value assigned to a stock for bookkeeping and for dividend calculations. Market value is the price at which a share of stock is currently selling. Book value is the portion of a corporation's net assets represented by a single share of common stock.

2 **Highlight the distinguishing features of common stock, preferred stock, bonds, and mutual funds.** Common stock gives shareholders an ownership interest in the company, the right to elect directors and vote on important issues, and the chance to earn dividends and share in the fortunes of the company—while limiting the shareholder's liability to the price paid for the shares. Preferred stock gives shareholders a higher dividend than common stock and a preferred claim over creditors if the corporation fails. Special types of preferred stock have certain privileges. Bonds are long-term loans investors make to the issuing entity in return for a stated interest amount. The loan or principal is paid back to the bondholder over the life of the bond. Bonds may be secured, unsecured, or convertible. They may be issued by corporations or federal, state, city, and local agencies. Mutual funds are pools of money drawn from many investors to buy a variety of stocks, bonds, and other marketable securities. The primary benefit of this investment is diversification.

3 **List five types of bonds issued by governments.** The U.S. government issues treasury bills (short-term bonds), treasury notes (intermediate-term bonds), and treasury bonds (long-term bonds). In addition, the U.S. government issues U.S. savings bonds. These bonds are issued at a discount and grow to their full redemption value at maturity (generally 17 years or more). Cities, states, and special government agencies issue municipal bonds to fund public services such as building schools, highways, and airports. Municipal bonds backed by the taxing power of the issuing government are general obligation bonds. Municipal bonds backed by money to be generated from the financial project are revenue bonds.

4 **Differentiate among an auction exchange, a dealer exchange, and an electronic communication network (ECN).** Auction exchanges such as the New York Stock Exchange funnel all buy and sell orders into one centralized location. Dealer exchanges such as NASDAQ are decentralized marketplaces in which dealers, known as market makers, are connected electronically to handle buy and sell orders without a single, centralized trading floor. Electronic computerized networks (ECNs) match buy and sell orders directly (cutting out the market makers and specialists); ECNs operate globally, and they operate economically.

5 **Explain how government regulation of securities trading tries to protect investors.** The government tries to prevent fraud in the securities markets by requiring companies to file registration papers, fulfill certain requirements, and file periodic information reports so that investors receive accurate information. Government regulations also control the listing of companies on stock exchanges and prohibit such fraudulent acts as improper release of information, insider trading, stock scams, and other acts designed to deceive investors.

6 **Name five criteria to be considered when making investment decisions.** Investors should consider the income, growth, safety, liquidity, and tax consequences of all potential investments.

7 **Explain how to find information about potential securities investments.** Daily newspaper reports on securities markets, general-interest business publications, investor newsletters, and special reports are good sources of investment information. So are online resources such as brokerage firm websites, company websites, and a number of financial websites, chat rooms, and blogs. Market indexes are another source of financial information and are good indicators of market performance and market trends. Reports filed with the SEC such as prospectuses and annual reports are other good information sources.

Charles Schwab: What's Next?

Somewhere in the middle of a triangle defined by the well-oiled machine of Fidelity, the traditional full-service brokers, and the low-cost online brokers, Schwab is working to solidify a new position. Prices for online brokerage services are now so low—Schwab recently lowered its commission prices three times in a single year—that some in the industry believe brokerage-only services will struggle to survive (although Ameritrade, with its rigorous attention to cost control, was earning strong profits as of 2005). To lower its dependence on brokerage services, Schwab continues to develop a differentiated marketing strategy that offers a range of services and pricing plans for investors with different needs. In a sign of how much things have changed since its founding three decades ago, Schwab is now counting on profits from its bank to help supplement the razor-thin margins from the brokerage business.[13]

Critical Thinking Questions

1. Why has Charles Schwab continued to reinvent itself?
2. If simple stock transactions aren't all that profitable, why would Schwab bother catering to this market need?
3. How does the wheel of retailing (see page 462 in Chapter 14) apply to Schwab's experiences over the past decade or so?

Learn More Online

Visit the corporate website of Charles Schwab by going to Chapter 18 of this text's website at www.prenhall.com/bovee, and clicking on the Charles Schwab hotlink. Review the website. What evidence of differentiated marketing can you find? What services does Schwab offer individual investors? How do the new banking services fit in with Schwab's other offerings? What tools and resources do you find that could help you with your own financial planning?

Key Terms

asset allocation (596)
bear market (599)
bond (584)
broker (596)
bull market (599)
capital gains (586)
commodities (589)
convertible bonds (585)
day order (597)
debentures (585)
discretionary order (597)
diversification (596)
electronic communication
  networks (ECNs) (591)
financial futures (588)
general obligation bond (586)
growth stocks (595)
hedge (588)

insider trading (593)
institutional investors (599)
investment banks (590)
investment portfolios (596)
limit order (596)
margin trading (597)
market indexes (599)
market order (596)
money-market funds (587)
municipal bonds (586)
mutual funds (587)
open order (597)
over-the-counter (OTC)
  market (591)
par value (583)
price-earnings ratio
  (p/e ratio) (600)
primary market (590)

principal (584)
rate of return (596)
revenue bond (586)
secondary market (590)
securities (583)
secured bonds (584)
short selling (597)
sinking fund (586)
speculators (595)
stock exchanges (590)
stock split (583)
stop order (596)
Treasury bills (586)
Treasury bonds (586)
Treasury notes (586)
U.S. savings bonds (586)
yield (595)

Test Your Knowledge

Questions for Review

1. What are the differences among a Treasury bill, a Treasury note, and a U.S. savings bond?
2. What is the difference between a general obligation bond and a revenue bond?
3. What happens during a 2-for-1 stock split?
4. What is a p/e ratio, and what does it signify to an investor?
5. What is the function of the Securities and Exchange Commission?

Questions for Analysis

6. What are some of the advantages of mutual funds?
7. What are some of the ways an investor can diversify investments to reduce risk of loss?

8. Why are debentures considered riskier than other types of bonds?

9. When might an investor sell a stock short? What risks are involved in selling short?

10. **Ethical Considerations.** You work in the research-and-development department of a large corporation and have been involved in a discovery that could lead to a new, profitable product. News of the discovery has not been made public. Is it legal for you to buy stock in the company? Now assume the same scenario, but you talk to your friend about your discovery while dining at a restaurant. The person at the next table overhears the conversation. Is it legal for the eavesdropper to buy the company's stock before the public announcement of the news?

Questions for Application

11. If an investor wants a steady, predictable flow of cash, what types of investments should she seek and why?

12. If you were thinking about buying shares of AT&T, under what circumstances would you place a market order, a limit order, an open order, and a discretionary order?

13. **Integrated.** Look back at Chapter 7 and review the discussion of mission statements. Suppose you were thinking about purchasing 100 shares of common stock in General Electric. Why might you want to first review the company's mission statement? What would you be looking for in the company's mission statement that could help you decide whether or not to invest?

14. **Integrated.** Chapter 5 mentioned that one disadvantage of going public was the burdensome SEC filing requirements. Why do you think the SEC requires companies to file the documents listed in Exhibit 18.4, page 590?

Practice Your Knowledge

Handling Difficult Situations on the Job—Calming an Angry Online Trader

You are a customer service representative for a popular online broker. One of the company's investors, Ian Stevens, placed an online market order for a hot new biomedical stock, thinking it would cost between $15 and $25 a share. His order was filled for 2,300 shares, but at a price of $90 a share and a bill of $207,000—nearly $150,000 more than he expected. Irate, Stevens called E*Trade—and you're the lucky rep to get his call.

Your company prominently posts statements on its website warning customers about possible delays and other potential problems with online trades. For example, it warns customers that high trading volume can delay the execution of an order, which may mean that a stock's price is significantly different from when the order was placed. It also informs customers of the difference between a market order and a limit order. Doesn't matter. Stevens is making all kinds of threats and he wants to speak to the president of the company NOW! You have been told to turn over situations such as these to your department manager, but only after you input all the facts in an electronic customer file.[14]

Your task: To complete the file, you need to ask Stevens a series of questions, but first you have to calm him down—without making any promises, of course. What kinds of information should you try to obtain from Stevens?

Sharpening Your Communication Skills

Interviewing a broker is one of the most important steps you can take before hiring that broker to execute your trades or manage your funds and investment portfolio. Practice your communication skills by developing two sets of questions:

1. Questions you might ask a stockbroker to help you decide whether you would use his or her services.

2. Questions you might pose to that broker to help you evaluate the merits of purchasing a specific security.

Building Your Team Skills

You and your team are going to pool your money and invest $5,000. Before you plunge into any investments, how can you prepare yourselves to be good investors? First, consider your group's goals. What will you and your teammates do with any profits generated by your investments? Once you have agreed on a goal for your team's profits, think about how much money you will need to achieve this goal and how soon you want to achieve it.

Next, think about how much risk you personally are willing to take to achieve the goal. Bear in mind that safer investments generally offer lower returns than riskier investments—and certain investments, such as stocks, can lose money. Now hold a group discussion to find a level of risk that feels comfortable for everyone on your team.

Once your team has decided how much risk to take, consider which investments are best suited to your group's goals and chosen risk level. Will you choose stocks, bonds, a combination of both, or other securities? What are the advantages and disadvantages of each type of investment for your team's situation? Then come to a decision about specific investment opportunities—particular stocks, for example—that your group would like to investigate further.

Compare your group's goal, risk level, and investment possibilities with those of the other teams in your class and discuss the differences and similarities you see.

Expand Your Knowledge

Discovering Career Opportunities

Think you might be interested in a job in the securities and commodities industry? This industry has one of the most highly educated and skilled workforces of any industry. And the requirements for entry are high—most brokerage clerks have a college degree. Log on to the Bureau of Labor Statistics, Career Guide to Industries, at www.bls.gov/oco.cg, and click on Financial and Insurance, then click on Securities and Commodities. Read the article, then answer these questions:

1. What are the licensing and continuing education requirements for securities brokers?
2. What is the typical starting position for many people in the securities industry?
3. What factors are expected to contribute to the projected long-term growth of this industry?

Developing Your Research Skills

Stock market analysts advise investors (both individuals and institutions) on which stocks to buy, sell, or hold. Changes in their opinions are called *upgrades* or *downgrades*, depending on the direction of their outlook. Changing a "hold" recommendation to a "buy" recommendation is an upgrade, for example. Find a stock that has been recently upgraded or downgraded (you can use Research Center at Yahoo! Finance, http://biz.yahoo.com/r, New Ratings, www.newratings.com, or a similar source) then perform some research on that company so you can answer the following questions:

1. On what exchange do the company's shares trade and under what ticker symbol?
2. Why did the analyst(s) change their opinion of the stock? Was it in response to something the company said or did? Is the company performing better or worse than its competitors? Do you think the rating change is fair to the company?
3. How did the rating change affect the company's stock price?
4. How has the company's stock been performing relative to the DJIA and S&P 500 indexes?

Exploring the Best of the Web

URLs for all Internet exercises are provided at the website for this book, www.prenhall.com/bovee. When you log on to this text's Companion Website, select Chapter 18. Then select "Featured Websites," click on the name of the featured website, and review the website to complete these exercises.

Explore these chapter-related websites, review their content, and answer the following questions for each website you visit:

1. What is the purpose of this website?
2. What kinds of information does this website contain? Please be specific.

3. How is the information provided at this website useful for businesspeople? Consumers?
4. How did you expand your knowledge of marketing and customers by reviewing the material at this website? What new things did you learn about these topics?

Stock Up at the NYSE
Tour the New York Stock Exchange at www.nyse.com. Visit the trading floor and learn about the hectic pace of trading. Find out why having a seat doesn't necessarily mean you'll have a chance to sit down. Listen in on a stock transaction and discover how a stock is bought and sold. Learn how investors are protected and how unusual stock transactions are spotted. Get the latest market information as well as a historical perspective of the exchange. www.nyse.com

Open an Encyclopedia of Investing Information
Don't know where to start when it comes to investing? Sounds like you could use a look inside the Investopedia, a cornucopia of online investing information. Look up unfamiliar terms in the investing dictionary. Click on the Beginners section for great advice on learning from successful investors. Read the Stock Basics and Bond Basics tutorials to make sure you know what you're buying. www.investopedia.com

Invest Wisely—Like a Fool
Here's a fun securities website you can fool around at for a while. Visit the Motley Fool and don't be afraid to ask a foolish investment question or two. (The idea of an investing Fool is somebody who's not afraid to ask tough questions of the rich and powerful.) Roll up your sleeves and do a little work on your own. Discover the strategies, ideas, and information needed to make investment decisions at Fool's School. Learn the steps to investing foolishly. Read the investing basics and learn how to value stocks, analyze stocks, or pick a stockbroker. Expand your knowledge of stocks, bonds, and mutual funds. Finally, discover the keys to successful investing. www.fool.com

Learning Interactively

Companion Website
Visit the Companion Website at www.prenhall.com/bovee. For Chapter 18, take advantage of the interactive "Learning Modules" to test your chapter knowledge. Get instant feedback on whether you need additional studying. Complete the exercises as specified by your instructor.

Case for Critical Thinking

NYSE: An 18th-Century Institution Embraces the 21st

Ever since a group of brokers gathered on Wall Street to trade stocks in 1792, the New York Stock Exchange (NYSE) has provided a central marketplace for buying and selling securities. Its floor-based auction system met the needs of large and small investors for years. But at the close of the twentieth century new technologies threatened its established trading system, and the world's largest and most prestigious securities exchange seemed under assault from all angles.

At the height of Internet mania, its chief competitor, NASDAQ, touted itself as the "stock market for the next 100 years." Its volume was bigger than the NYSE's, and its top companies—technology giants Microsoft, Intel, Dell, Sun, Oracle, and Cisco—seemed more important. Moreover, the NASDAQ seemed to be more efficient. Trades were either completed by market markers sitting at banks of computer screens, or increasingly, by computerized systems. The NYSE, by contrast, looked like something Normal Rockwell would have painted. Jackets and ties were still required on the trading floor. Uniformed porters in cloakrooms took members' coats and shined their shoes. And while many parts of the exchange were computerized, stocks still traded more or less the same way they had since the specialist system was invented in 1871—at a trading post in a sea of paper on the floor. "The exchange simply looked like it wasn't going to be able to compete," said a former SEC commissioner.

As more and more customers bypassed the Big Board in favor of trading through electronic markets, NYSE's chairman and CEO at the time acknowledged that the NYSE could no longer cling to its old ways. "These are no longer the days of old, when we were the only game in town. . . . Reinvention is absolutely essential." Still, the exchange had no desire to switch to an all-electronic market that would turn its venerable trading floor into a museum.

THE BIG BOARD TAKES A STAND

To meet demands for change without abolishing the existing auction system, the NYSE began investing heavily in a strategy that combined both human and electronic services. Its Direct Plus service, for example, automatically executes orders for up to 1,099 shares on the NYSE without human intervention, enabling floor traders to devote their attention to larger orders.

That human element took on new symbolic importance in the uncertain days of 2000 and 2001. After the dot-com miracle crumbled, the Enron and WorldCom scandals rocked Wall Street, and terrorists attacked New York City, many of the exchange's critics began to view it as the place where companies of quality list their stocks. In particular, the NYSE's reopening on September 17, 2001, six days after the terrorist attacks, was emblematic of the august institution's solidity and resolve.

A SURPRISE MOVE INTO THE WORLD OF ECNS

As much respect as the NYSE might've gained during those dark days, ECN competitors weren't about to sit still. In 2004, the NYSE applied to the SEC to institute an expanded hybrid model that would combine the speed of electronic exchange with the judgment and control of specialists on the trading floor. More than 50 companies moved their stock from NASDAQ to NYSE in 2003 and 2004, and NYSE says the main reason was to reduce volatility. During the opening and closing of the trading day (when prices can fluctuate more than usual) and whenever the price of a stock starts to swing too wildly, the hybrid system passes control from automated electronic trading to the floor traders.

Then in 2005, the NYSE surprised the financial world by announcing a merger with Archipelago, which owns one of the fastest growing ECNs—and handles 25 percent of archrival NASDAQ's trades. The new organization, to be named NYSE Group, is planned to be a publicly traded, for-profit corporation with a significant presence in electronic trading. In essence, the NYSE simply joined forces with one of its major competitive threats. As before, even as it pushes even deeper into the ECN realm, the exchange has no plans to eliminate its trading floor.

However, not all of NYSE's members are pleased at the way the Archipelago merger was negotiated, nor are they all thrilled with the idea of keeping the trading floor in operation. In mid-2005, these members were considering launching a counter-bid to purchase NYSE outright. No matter which way the struggle for NYSE turns out, the organization that started with a few local business leaders meeting under a buttonwood tree on Wall Street more than two centuries ago is likely to end up as a major player in electronic trading.

Critical Thinking Questions

1. Why did the NYSE merge with Archipelago when it already had elements of electronic trading?
2. Why does the NYSE want to maintain the existing auction system with floor specialists, even as it expands into electronic trading?
3. How important do you think the NYSE is in the U.S. economy?
4. Go to New York Stock Exchange's website at www.nyse.com. Review the site to answer these questions: Was the NYSE's merger with Archipelago completed? What mix of auction and electronic trading does the NYSE now offer? Has the new entity remained an independent, for-profit entity?

Video Case

Learn More to Earn More with Motley Fool

Learning Objectives

The purpose of this video is to help you:

1. Identify the wide variety of investments available to individuals.
2. Describe the process by which securities are bought and sold.
3. Recognize the risks involved in commodities and other investments.

Synopsis

Despite news reports about lottery winners and others who have become millionaires overnight, individuals have a better chance of getting rich if they learn to select investments that are appropriate for their long-term financial goals. Experts advise looking for investments that will beat inflation and keep up with or—ideally—beat general market returns. Individuals can invest in preferred or common stock, newly issued stock from initial public offerings (IPOs), managed or index mutual funds, bonds, or commodities. These investments are far from risk-free, however; commodities and IPOs can be particularly risky. Therefore, individuals should become educated about securities and investment strategies by surfing Web sites such as the Motley Fool (www.fool.com).

Discussion Questions

1. *For analysis:* Why is the Securities and Exchange Commission concerned about stock rumors that circulate on the Internet?
2. *For analysis:* Why do Motley Fool's experts advise individuals to invest in index funds rather than in actively managed mutual funds?
3. *For application:* What should you consider when deciding whether to buy and sell stock through a broker, through a web-based brokerage, or directly through the company issuing the stock?
4. *For application:* If you were about to retire, why might you invest in preferred stock rather than common stock?
5. *For debate:* Should stock rumors that circulate on the Internet be covered by the individual's constitutional right to freedom of speech rather than being regulated by the SEC? Support your chosen position.

Online Exploration

Mutual funds that seek out environmentally and socially conscious firms in which to invest are becoming more popular because they offer investors a way to earn returns that don't offend their principles. Investigate the following websites: www.socialfunds.com, www.ethicalfunds.com, and www.domini.com. What types of firms does each fund avoid? What type does each prefer to invest in? Would you choose one of these funds if you wanted to invest in a mutual fund? Explain your answer.

E-Business in Action

INTERNET BANKS HIT A BRICK WALL

When online-only banks began popping up in the late 1990s, many believed they would revolutionize retail banking. Lower transaction costs, no physical building costs, and smaller staffs than physical banks meant that online banks could afford to offer customers higher interest rates on deposits, little or no transaction fees, and lower interest rates on loans. Furthermore, customers could bank at home 24 hours a day, seven days a week. They could move money from a savings account to a checking account—or even into the stock market—whenever they pleased. But the promise that banking customers would flock to online banks and abandon traditional banks never quite materialized. Online *banking* has taken off like a wildfire in the past few years, but most of the business has been won by traditional banks such as Bank of America and Wells Fargo, not by online-only start-ups.

Tough Sell

Why didn't online banks take off as some expected? As with a number of new Internet-only businesses, online banks faced these roadblocks:

- *Lack of name recognition.* To attract new customers, online banks launched their e-businesses with expensive marketing campaigns, eliminating much of the Internet cost advantage.
- *No in-person service.* Customers appreciated the cost advantages online banks offered, but without branches, many online banks lacked a concrete place for customers to resolve problems. Customers wanted the assurance that someone was there (in person) if they needed help.
- *Limited services.* Customers still needed to venture into the physical world to get services online banks did not offer: ATMs, safe deposit boxes, or business loans. Moreover, without access to a network of ATMs, customers faced hefty fees when using other banks' machines and were required to deposit money into their accounts by mail.

To overcome these challenges, some online banks got physical by opening service centers, setting up kiosks, and establishing ATM networks. Others offered rebates on ATM surcharges their customers paid to other banks. Still others, such as Juniper Financial, formed alliances with stores such as Mail Boxes Etc. (now known as The UPS Store) so customers could deposit checks nationwide. But these actions were not enough to fend off the awakening giants.

Bricks-and-Mortar Banks Wake Up

Rather than give traditional (bricks-and-mortar) banks a run for their money, online banks gave them ideas. Some traditional banks established partnerships with key online players or swallowed them up altogether. Others, such as Bank One, established their own virtual banks— keeping them separate entities. But in spite of their efforts, few traditional banks generated profits from their online banking ventures. Online-only banking did not reach the mass appeal needed to justify the huge investment and operating costs involved. So most traditional banks eventually folded their online ventures into the parent organization. For instance, in 2001 WingspanBank.com, Bank One's highly publicized online venture, was folded into the parent organization. And customers of Security First Network Bank became a part of RBC Centura, a North Carolina-based physical bank.

From Competitive Edge to Commodity

The playing field has changed considerably since virtual banking first emerged. Online banking has moved from becoming a competitive edge to a commodity. Today, roughly 40 million U.S. households do at least some of their banking online, and online banking continues to grow rapidly. More than half of all banks offer some form of online banking services, such as money transfer, bill payment, loan applications, and account management. Some, such as Citibank, allow customers to set up a personal account and aggregate all the services they use into one webpage interface at the My Citi site.

Online-only banks didn't disappear entirely, of course, and several still compete with better rates on savings deposits than their bricks-and-mortar competitors frequently offer. However, in a slightly surprising twist, even as online banking becomes ever more popular, so do physical bank branches. The top six U.S. banks built more than 500 new branches in 2004 alone. Clicks-and-bricks seems to be the preferred approach for millions of U.S. consumers, which could be the ultimate reason that Internet banks never quite revolutionized the banking business the way many people predicted.[15]

Questions for Critical Thinking

1. What challenges did online-only banking face in the competitive banking environment, and what steps did they take to overcome these challenges?
2. Why did most pure Internet banks close up or fold into their parent organizations?
3. What banking services, if any, do you perform online? What do you like and dislike about banking online?

Career Profiles

Here are brief glimpses at two career paths that relate to the chapters in Part 6. You'll find other career profiles following Chapters 4, 6, 9, 11, and 15.

Accountants

Accountants fulfill a variety of roles in business, including serving as management accountants and internal auditors within companies, as public accountants and external auditors who perform services for individual and corporate clients, and as forensic accountants who investigate financial crimes. Financial managers, who often direct the work of accountants, are covered in the next column.

Nature of the Work The spate of financial scandals in recent years has raised the profile of the accounting profession, making more people aware of the critical importance of accurate, ethical accounting—and not only to individual businesses but to the national and global economy as well. If working at the intersection of mathematics and business sounds appealing, then a career in accounting or finance could be just the place for you. Accounting tasks vary by job and industry, but in general, management accountants are responsible for collecting, analyzing, and reporting on financial matters—such as analyzing budgets, assessing the manufacturing costs of new products, and preparing state and federal tax returns. Internal auditors not only verify the work of the company's accounting effort but also look for opportunities for efficiency and cost-effectiveness. Public accountants offer accounting, tax preparation, and investment advice to individuals, companies, and other organizations. And external auditors verify the financial reports of public companies as required by law.

Qualifications Most jobs in accounting require a bachelor's degree in accounting as a minimum, and many employers now except a master's. Professional certifications also play an important role in the careers of accountants, including certified public accountant (CPA), certified management accountant (CMA), certified internal auditor (CIA), and certified information systems auditor (CISA).

Accounting professionals need to have an affinity for numbers, an analytical mind, and attention to detail. Their work can have wide-ranging effects on investors, employees, and executives, so accuracy and timeliness are critical. Communication skills are important in virtually every accounting function. Computer skills are also increasingly important, particularly for accountants closely involved with the design or operation of accounting systems.

Where the Jobs Are Every company has accounting needs, so accounting opportunities can be found in every industry. Most accountants work within the accounting departments of small, medium, and large companies, but a sizable portion work for accounting firms or as independent entrepreneurs.

Where to Learn More American Institute of Certified Public Accountants, www.aicpa.org; National Association of State Boards of Accountancy (CPA licensing information), www.nasba.org; Institute of Management Accountants, www.imanet.org; Accreditation Council for Accountancy and Taxation, www.acatcredentials.org; Institute of Internal Auditors, www.theiia.org; Information Systems Audit and Control Association, www.isaca.org.

Financial Managers

Financial managers perform a variety of leadership and strategic functions.

Nature of the Work The responsibilities of the financial manager vary somewhat by the specific job. *Controllers* oversee the preparation of income statements, balance sheets, and other financial reports; they frequently manage accounting departments as well. *Treasurers* and *finance officers* have a more strategic role, establishing long-term financial goals and budgets, investing the firm's funds, and raising capital as needed. They also get closely involved with any merger and acquisition activity, including estimating the value of other companies and analyzing the ramifications of business combinations. Other financial management positions include *credit managers*, who supervise credit accounts established for customers, and *cash managers*, who monitor and control cash flow. Financial managers can rise to the upper echelons of a corporation, and many CEOs reach their position by excelling in finance.

Qualifications As one of the most important positions in a corporation, financial management naturally carries some rigorous qualifications. A bachelor's degree is a bare minimum; many organizations require a master's in business, finance, risk management, or a related field. Financial managers also need to stay on top of government regulations, banking developments, and new investment vehicles, so most pursue continuing education through industry associations and other organizations.

The work of a financial manager touches every part of the company, so a broad understanding of the various functional areas in business is a key attribute for this position. The ability to communicate with people who aren't financial experts is also vital. Moreover, awareness of information technology developments is important for chief financial officers and other top financial managers, so that they can direct their companies' investments in new or improved accounting systems as needed.

Where the Jobs Are Roughly a quarter of all financial managers work in insurance and financial services. The rest can be found across the entire business landscape, in virtually every industry. Unlike accounting tasks, for which there is a long tradition of outsourcing, the work of financial managers is generally kept "in house," particularly in midsize and large companies.

Where to Learn More Financial Management Association International, www.fma.org; Association for Financial Professionals, www.afponline.org; Chartered Financial Analyst Institute, www.cfainstitute.org; Institute of Management Accountants, www.imanet.org.

The U.S. Legal System

Throughout this textbook, you encountered a number of regulatory agencies, such as the FDA, FTC, EPA, and SEC, whose function is to protect society from the potential abuses of business. Federal, state, and local governments work in numerous ways to protect both individuals and other businesses from corporate wrongdoing. Laws also spell out accepted ways of performing many essential business functions—along with the penalties for failing to comply. In other words, like the average person, companies must obey the law or face the consequences.

As you read this material, keep in mind that many U.S. companies also conduct business in other countries, so executives in these firms must also be familiar with **international law**, the principles, customs, and rules that govern the relationships between sovereign states and international organizations and persons.[1] Successful global business requires an understanding of the domestic laws of trading partners as well as of established international trading standards and legal guidelines.

*international law
Principles, customs, and rules that govern the international relationships between states, organizations, and persons*

Sources of Law

A *law* is a rule developed by a society to govern the conduct of, and relationships among, its members. The U.S. Constitution, including the Bill of Rights, is the foundation for U.S. laws. Because the Constitution is a general document, laws offering specific answers to specific problems are constantly embellishing its basic principles. However, law is not static; it develops in response to changing conditions and social standards. Individual laws originate in various ways: through legislative action (*statutory law*), through administrative rulings (*administrative law*), and through customs and judicial precedents (*common law*). To one degree or another, all three forms of

Global companies, such as Coca-Cola, must have a firm grasp of international law.

contracts, agency, property transactions, patents, trademarks, copyrights, negotiable instruments, and bankruptcy.

Torts

tort
Noncriminal act (other than breach of contract) that results in injury to a person or to property

damages
Financial compensation to an injured party for loss and suffering

A **tort** is a noncriminal act (other than breach of contract) that results in injury to a person or to property.[6] A tort can be either intentional or the result of negligence. The victim of a tort is legally entitled to some form of financial compensation, or **damages**, for his or her loss and suffering. This compensation is also known as a *compensatory damage award.* In some cases, the victim may also receive a *punitive damage award* to punish the wrongdoer if the misdeed was deemed particularly bad. Extremely large punitive damages occasionally grab headlines and generate criticism and calls for reform of the tort process. However, a Cornell University study found that punitive damages are awarded in only about 6 percent of cases nationwide and that the majority of such awards are in line with compensatory damage awards.[7]

intentional tort
Willful act that results in injury

Intentional Torts An **intentional tort** is a willful act that results in injury. For example, accidentally hitting a softball through someone's window is a tort, but purposely cutting down someone's tree because it obscures your view is an intentional tort. Note that *intent* in this case does not mean the intent to cause harm; it is the intent to commit a specific act. Some intentional torts involve communication of false statements that harm another's reputation. If the communication is in writing or on television, it is called *libel;* if it is spoken, it is *slander.*[8] For example, Jose Santos, the winning jockey in the 2003 Kentucky Derby, recently sued the *Miami Herald* for printing an article that accused him of using an electrical prod during the race. Although race officials subsequently cleared Santos of any improper behavior, the outcome of his case will depend on whether he can prove that the paper knowingly published false information.[9]

negligence
Tort in which a reasonable amount of care to protect others from risk of injury is not used

product liability
The capacity of a product to cause harm or damage for which the producer or seller is held accountable

Negligence and Product Liability In contrast to intentional torts, torts of **negligence** involve a failure to use a reasonable amount of care necessary to protect others from unreasonable risk of injury.[10] Cases of alleged negligence often involve **product liability**, which is a product's capacity to cause damages or injury for which the producer or seller is held responsible. Product liability is one of the most hotly contested aspects of business law today, with consumer advocates pointing to the number of product-related injuries and deaths every year—some 28 million injuries and 22,000 deaths—and business advocates pointing to the high cost of product-liability lawsuits—as much as $150 billion every year.[11]

strict product liability
Liability for injury caused by a defective product when all reasonable care is used in its manufacture, distribution, or sale; no fault is assigned

A company may also be held liable for injury caused by a defective product even if the company used all reasonable care in the manufacture, distribution, or sale of its product. Such **strict product liability** makes it possible to assign liability without assigning fault. It must only be established that (1) the company is in the business of selling the product, (2) the product reached the customer or user without substantial change in its condition, (3) the product was defective, (4) the defective condition rendered the product unreasonably dangerous, and (5) the defective product caused the injury.[12]

With so much at stake, including the magnitude of legal fees in many cases, it's no surprise that product-liability lawsuits generate so much controversy. Although few people would argue that individual victims of harmful goods and services shouldn't be entitled to some sort of compensation, many people now ask whether the system needs reforms. For instance, a recent survey suggested a majority of U.S. consumers favor such reforms as limiting the fees that lawyers can earn in product-liability lawsuits, placing limits on the amount of money awarded for pain and suffering, and enacting sanctions against attorneys who file frivolous lawsuits.[13] In addition, business leaders point out that the billions of dollars consumed by legal fees and damage awards raise prices for all consumers and, in some cases, limit the product choices available in the marketplace. As is often the case in complex situations such as this, both sides have valid points to make.

Contracts

Broadly defined, a **contract** is an exchange of promises between two or more parties that is enforceable by law. Many business transactions—including buying and selling products, hiring employees, purchasing group insurance, and licensing technology—involve contracts. Contracts may be either express or implied. An **express contract** is derived from the words (either oral or written) of the parties; an **implied contract** stems from the actions or conduct of the parties.[14]

Elements of a Contract
The law of contracts deals largely with identifying the exchanges that can be classified as contracts. The following factors must usually be present for a contract to be valid and enforceable:

- *An offer must be made.* One party must propose that an agreement be entered into. The offer may be oral or written, but it must be firm, definite, and specific enough to make it clear that someone intends to be legally bound by the offer. Finally, the offer must be communicated to the intended party or parties.
- *An offer must be accepted.* For an offer to be accepted, there must be clear intent (spoken, written, or by action) to enter into the contract. An implied contract arises when a person requests or accepts something and the other party has indicated that payment is expected. If, for example, your car breaks down on the road and you call a mobile mechanic and ask him or her to repair it, you are obligated to pay the reasonable value for the services, even if you didn't agree to specific charges beforehand. However, when a specific offer is made, the acceptance must satisfy the terms of the offer. For example, if someone offers you a car for $18,000, and you say you would take it for $15,000, you have not accepted the offer. Your response is a *counteroffer,* which may or may not be accepted by the salesperson.
- *Both parties must give consideration.* A contract is legally binding only when the parties have bargained with each other and have exchanged something of value, which is called the **consideration**. The relative value of each party's consideration does not generally matter to the courts. In other words, if you make a deal with someone and later decide you didn't get enough in the deal, that result is not the court's concern. You entered into the deal with the original consideration in mind, and that fact is legally sufficient.[15]
- *Both parties must give genuine assent.* To have a legally enforceable contract, both parties must agree to it voluntarily. The contract must be free of fraud, duress, undue influence, and mutual mistake.[16] If only one party makes a mistake, it ordinarily does not affect the contract. On the other hand, if both parties make a mistake, the agreement would be void. For example, if both the buyer and the seller of a business believed the business was profitable, when in reality it was operating at a loss, their agreement would be void.
- *Both parties must be competent.* The law gives certain classes of people only a limited capacity to enter into contracts. Minors, people who are senile or insane, and in some cases those who are intoxicated cannot usually be bound by a contract for anything but the bare necessities: food, clothing, shelter, and medical care.
- *The contract must not involve an illegal act.* Courts will not enforce a promise that involves an illegal act. For example, a drug dealer cannot get help from the courts to enforce a contract to deliver illegal drugs at a prearranged price.

contract
Legally enforceable exchange of promises between two or more parties

express contract
Contract derived from words, either oral or written

implied contract
Contract derived from actions or conduct

consideration
Negotiated exchange necessary to make a contract legally binding

Exhibit A.2
Elements of
a Contract
This simple document contains all the essential elements of a valid contract.

The band titled XYZ agrees to provide entertainment at the Club de Hohenzollern on April 30, 2006, between 8:30 p.m. and midnight.

The band will be paid $500.00 for its performance.

Signed on the date of

February 19, 2006

Violetta Harvey

Violetta Harvey,
Manager,
Club de Hohenzollern
and

Ralph Perkins

Ralph Perkins,
Manager, XYZ

- *The contract must be in proper form.* Most contracts can be made orally, by an act, or by a casually written document; however, certain contracts are required by law to be in writing. For example, the transfer of goods worth $500 or more must be accompanied by a written document. The written form is also required for all real estate contracts.

A contract need not be long; all these elements of a contract may be contained in a simple document (see Exhibit A.2). In fact, a personal check is one type of simple contract.

Contract Performance Contracts normally expire when the agreed-to conditions have been met, called *performance* in legal terms. However, not all contracts run their expected course. Both parties involved can agree to back out of the contract, for instance. In other cases, one party fails to live up to the terms of the contract, a situation called **breach of contract**. The other party has several options at that point:

breach of contract
Failure to live up to the terms of a contract, with no legal excuse

- *Discharge.* When one party violates the terms of the agreement, generally the other party is under no obligation to continue with his or her end of the contract. In other words, the second party is discharged from the contract.
- *Damages.* A party has the right to sue in court for damages that were foreseeable at the time the contract was entered into and that result from the other party's failure to fulfill the contract. The amount of damages awarded usually reflects the amount of profit lost and often includes court costs as well, although figuring out fair amounts is not always easy. When talk-show host Rosie O'Donnell and publisher

Gruner + Jahr USA sued each other for more than $100 million each over the collapse of the magazine *Rosie,* a judge determined that neither side deserved anything.[17]

- *Specific performance.* A party can be compelled to live up to the terms of the contract if money damages would not be adequate.

To control the increasing costs of litigation, more and more companies are now experimenting with alternatives to the courtroom. These include independent mediators, who sit down with the two parties and try to hammer out a satisfactory solution to contract problems, and mandatory arbitration, in which an impartial arbitrator or arbitration panel hears evidence from both sides and makes a legally binding decision. However, mandatory arbitration has come under fire by consumer groups because it can wipe out a customer's right to sue. For example, Gateway includes a clause in the purchase agreement documents it ships with every computer stating that any dispute or controversy arising from an agreement to purchase a Gateway product "shall be settled exclusively and finally by arbitration." Moreover, the courts have ruled that failure to read such documents constitutes acceptance of Gateway's terms. Although some consumers prefer to use alternative dispute resolution, those who do not wish to waive their right to sue are advised to read the fine print of all contracts and purchase agreements. The same advice applies to employment and service contracts.[18]

Warranties The Uniform Commercial Code specifies that everyday sales transactions are a special kind of contract (although this provision applies only to tangible goods, not to services), even though they may not meet all the exact requirements of regular contracts. Related to the sales contract is the notion of a **warranty**, which is a statement specifying what the producer of a product will do to compensate the buyer if the product is defective or if it malfunctions. Warranties come in several flavors. One important distinction is between *express warranties,* which are specific, written statements, and *implied warranties*, which are unwritten but involve certain protections under the law. Also, warranties are either *full* or *limited.* The former obligates the seller to repair or replace the product, without charge, in the event of any defect or malfunction, whereas the latter imposes restrictions on the defects or malfunctions that will be covered. Warranty laws also address a number of other details, including giving consumers instructions on how to exercise their rights under the warranty.[19]

Agency

Many creative and athletic professionals engage the services of agents to promote their services, negotiate contracts, and conduct other business affairs. These relationships illustrate a common legal association known as **agency**, which exists when one party, known as the *principal*, authorizes another party, known as the *agent*, to act on his or her behalf in contractual matters.[20]

All contractual obligations come into play in agency relationships. The principal usually creates this relationship by explicit authorization. In some cases—when a transfer of property is involved, for example—the authorization must be written in the form of a document called **power of attorney**, which states that one person may legally act for another (to the extent authorized).

Usually, an agency relationship is terminated when the objective of the relationship has been met or at the end of a period specified in the contract between agent and principal. It may also be ended by a change of circumstances, by the agent's breach of duty or loyalty, or by the death of either party.

After the massive "Big Dig" highway project in Boston ran billions of dollars over budget, the state of Massachusetts sued the company in charge of the project, claiming it had withheld financial information that might have changed the state's decision to approve the project.

warranty
Statement specifying what the producer of a product will do to compensate the buyer if the product is defective or if it malfunctions

agency
Business relationship that exists when one party (the principal) authorizes another party (the agent) to enter into contracts on the principal's behalf

power of attorney
Written authorization for one party to legally act for another

Property Transactions

property
Rights held regarding any tangible or intangible object

real property
Land and everything permanently attached to it

personal property
All property that is not real property

Anyone interested in business must know the basics of property law. Most people think of property as some object they own (a book, a car, a house). However, **property** is actually the relationship between the person having the rights to any tangible or intangible object and all other persons. The law recognizes two primary types of property: real and personal. **Real property** is land and everything permanently attached to it, such as trees, fences, or mineral deposits. **Personal property** is all property that is not real property; it may be tangible (cars, jewelry, or anything having a physical existence) or intangible (bank accounts, stocks, insurance policies, customer lists). A piece of marble in the earth is real property until it is cut and sold as a block, when it becomes personal property. Property rights are subject to various limitations and restrictions. For example, the government monitors the use of real property for the welfare of the public, to the point of explicitly prohibiting some property uses and abuses.[21]

deed
Legal document by which an owner transfers the title, or ownership rights, to real property to a new owner

Two types of documents are important in obtaining real property for factory, office, or store space: a deed and a lease. A **deed** is a legal document by which an owner transfers the *title*, or right of ownership, to real property to a new owner. A lease is used for a temporary transfer of interest in real property. The party that owns the property is commonly called the *landlord*; the party that occupies or gains the right to occupy the property is the *tenant.* The tenant pays the landlord, usually in periodic installments, for the use of the property. Generally, a lease may be granted for any length of time that the two parties agree on.

Patents, Trademarks, and Copyrights

intellectual property
Intangible personal property, such as ideas, songs, trade secrets, and computer programs, that are protected by patents, trademarks, and copyrights

If you invent a product, write a book, develop some new software, or simply come up with a unique name for your business, you probably want to prevent other people from using or prospering from your **intellectual property** without fairly compensating you. Several forms of legal protection are available for your creations. They include patents, trademarks, and copyrights. Which one you should use depends on what you have created. Having a patent, copyright, or trademark still doesn't guarantee that your idea or product will not be copied. However, they do provide you with legal recourse if your creations are infringed upon.

One of the most recognized trademarks in the world is the Nike Swoosh.

Patents A patent protects the invention or discovery of a new and useful process, an article of manufacture, a machine, a chemical substance, or an improvement on any of these. Issued by the U.S. Patent Office, a patent grants the owner the right to exclude others from making, using, or selling the invention for 20 years from the date the patent application is filed.[22] After that time, the patented item becomes available for common use. On the one hand, patent law guarantees the originator the right to use the discovery exclusively for a relatively long period of time, thus encouraging people to devise new machines, gadgets, and processes. On the other hand, it also ensures that rights to the new item will be released eventually, allowing other enterprises to discover even more innovative ways to use it.

Trademarks A trademark is any word, name, symbol, or device used to distinguish the product of one manufacturer from those made by others. A service mark is the same thing for services. McDonald's golden arches are one of the most visible of modern trademarks. Brand names can also be registered as trademarks.

If properly registered and renewed every 20 years, a trademark generally belongs to its owner forever. Among the exceptions are popular brand names that have become generic terms, meaning that they describe a whole class of products. A brand-name trademark can become a generic term if the trademark has been allowed to expire, if it has been incorrectly used by its owner (as in the case of Borden's ReaLemon lemon juice, which the

Federal Trade Commission ruled was being used by Borden to maintain a monopoly in bottled lemon juice), or if the public comes to equate the name with the class of products, as was the case with zipper, linoleum, aspirin, and many other common terms that started out as brand names.

Trade dress, defined as the general appearance or image of a product, has been easier to legally protect since 1992 when the U.S. Supreme Court extended trademark protection to products with "inherently distinctive" appearances. For instance, Apple Computer filed suit against Future Power for allegedly infringing on the iMac trade dress with its look-alike E-Power PC. Apple Computer asked the court to prohibit the sale of E-Power in addition to an award of actual and punitive damages. A U.S. District Court granted a preliminary injunction against Future Power from making, distributing, and selling a 15-inch all-in-one computer with a colored plastic cover while the case was being heard. The two parties settled the lawsuit in 2001 when Future Power agreed to refrain from producing the look-alike until 2004.[23]

Copyrights Copyrights protect the creators of literary, dramatic, musical, artistic, scientific, and other intellectual works. Any printed, filmed, or recorded material can be copyrighted. The copyright gives its owner the exclusive right to reproduce (copy), sell, or adapt the work he or she has created. Copyright law covers reproduction by photocopying, videotape, and magnetic storage.

The Library of Congress Copyright Office will issue a copyright to the creator or to whomever the creator has granted the right to reproduce the work. (A book, for example, may be copyrighted by the author or the publisher.) Copyrights issued through 1998 are good for 75 years from the date of publication. Copyrights issued after 1998 are valid for the lifetime of the creator plus 70 years.[24]

Copyright protection on the Internet has become an especially important topic as more businesses and individuals include original material on their websites. Technically, copyright protection exists from the moment material is created. Therefore, anything you post on a website is protected by copyright law. However, loose Internet standards and a history of sharing information via the Net has made it difficult for some users to accept this situation. But the No Electronic Theft Act (enacted in 1998) makes it clear that the sanctity of the copyright extends to online publishing. This law makes it a crime to possess or distribute multiple copies of online copyrighted material for profit or not. Specifically, it closes the loophole that had allowed the distribution of copyrighted material as long as the offender didn't seek profit. Penalties include fines up to $250,000 and five years in prison.[25] To avoid potential copyright infringements, experts suggest that authors include copyright and trademark notices on webpages that contain protected material, include a link on each page to a detailed copyright notice that explains what users can and cannot do, and place disclaimers on all pages that contain links to other sites.[26]

After copyright-infringement lawsuits from music companies shut down Napster's free music service, the company filed for Chapter 11 bankruptcy protection. Napster reemerged several years later, marketing paid music downloads.

Negotiable Instruments

Whenever you write a personal check, you are creating a **negotiable instrument**, a transferable document that represents a promise to pay a specified amount. (*Negotiable* in this sense means that it can be sold or used as payment of a debt; an *instrument* is simply a written document that expresses a legal agreement.) In addition to checks, negotiable instruments include certificates of deposit, promissory notes, and commercial paper. To be negotiable, an instrument must meet several criteria:[27]

- It must be in writing and signed by the person who created it.
- It must have an unconditional promise to pay a specified sum of money.
- It must be payable either on demand or at a specified date in the future.
- It must be payable either to some specified person or organization or to the person holding it (the bearer).

negotiable instrument
Transferable document that represents a promise to pay a specified amount

Exhibit A.3
Steps in Chapter 11 Bankruptcy Proceedings
Chapter 11 bankruptcy may buy a debtor time to reorganize finances and continue operating. However, using this device to evade financial obligations is extremely risky from a legal standpoint, and declaring bankruptcy may severely damage the reputation and credit rating of a firm or an individual.

Step 1: All current legal proceedings against the firm are halted. A decision is made to either liquidate or reorganize the firm, based on the value of the firm's assets. If liquidation is chosen, the firm's assets are transferred to a trustee, who sells them to pay the firm's debts. If reorganization is chosen, go to step 2.

Step 2: The courts may appoint a trustee to operate the firm, or current management may continue to operate it. A reorganization plan is developed either by current management, by the trustee, or by a committee of creditors. When plan is developed, go to step 3.

Step 3: Creditors and shareholders vote on the reorganization plan. Plan is ratified if (1) at least one-half of creditors vote in favor and if their claims against the company represent at least two-thirds of total claims; (2) at least two-thirds of shareholders approve the plan; and (3) the plan is confirmed by the court. When plan is ratified, go to step 4.

Step 4: The plan guarantees creditors new securities, and sometimes cash, in exchange for dismissal of their claims. With the firm discharged from its debts, it is free to start anew without the weight of past failures.

You can see how a personal check meets those criteria; when you write one, you are agreeing to pay the amount of the check to the person or organization to whom you're writing it.

Bankruptcy

bankruptcy
Legal procedure by which a person or a business that is unable to meet financial obligations is relieved of debt

Even though the U.S. legal system establishes the rules of fair play and offers protection from the unscrupulous, it can't prevent most consumers or businesses from taking on too much debt. The legal system does, however, provide help for parties that find themselves in deep financial trouble. **Bankruptcy** is the legal means of relief for debtors who are unable to meet their financial obligations.[28] (Consumer bankruptcy, including the 2005 law that makes it more difficult for consumers to file for bankruptcy and to avoid paying debts if they do file, is covered in Appendix C.)

Voluntary bankruptcy is initiated by the debtor; *involuntary bankruptcy* is initiated by creditors. The law provides for several types of bankruptcy, which are commonly referred to by chapter number of the Bankruptcy Reform Act. In a Chapter 7 bankruptcy, the debtor's assets will be sold and the proceeds divided equitably among the creditors. Under Chapter 11 (which is usually aimed at businesses but does not exclude individuals other than stockbrokers), a business is allowed to get back on its feet and continue functioning while it arranges to pay its debts.[29] For the steps involved in a Chapter 11 bankruptcy, see Exhibit A.3. If a company emerges from Chapter 11 as a leaner, healthier organization, creditors generally benefit. That's because once a company is back on its financial feet it can resume payments to creditors. For instance, after Polaroid reorganized its finances during nine months of Chapter 11 bankruptcy

Exhibit A.4
Largest U.S.
Bankruptcies
Since 1990
*Companies in banking,
energy, and technology
dominate the list of the
largest U.S. corporate
bankruptcies in recent
years.*

Company	Year of Bankruptcy	Assets Prior to Bankruptcy ($ billions)
WorldCom, Inc.	2002	$103.9
Enron Corp.	2001	63.4
Conseco, Inc.	2002	61.4
Global Crossing Ltd.	2002	30.2
Pacific Gas and Electric Co.	2001	29.8
UAL Corp.	2002	25.2
Adelphia Communications	2002	21.5
Mirant Corporation	2003	19.4
First Executive Corp.	1991	15.2
Gibraltar Financial Corp.	1990	15.0
Kmart Corp.	2002	14.6
FINOVA Group, Inc.	2001	14.1
HomeFed Corp.	1992	13.9
Southeast Banking Corporation	1991	13.4
NTL, Inc.	2002	13.0
Reliance Group Holdings, Inc.	2001	12.6
Imperial Corp. of America	1990	12.3
Federal-Mogul Corp.	2001	10.2
First City Bancorp of Texas	1992	9.9
First Capital Holdings	1991	9.7

protection, the courts approved the sale of substantially all of Polaroid's business to One Equity Partners. Both the secured and unsecured creditors supported the sale in anticipation of receiving payments on their outstanding debt balances.[30]

As Exhibit A.4 shows, a number of Chapter 11 bankruptcies of epic proportions have been filed in the past few years. Banking failures dominated the early 1990s, whereas technology and energy failures dominated in the early years of the new millennium.

Test Your Knowledge

Questions for Review

1. What are the three types of U.S. laws, and how do they differ? What additional laws must global companies consider?
2. What is the difference between negligence and intentional torts?
3. What are the seven elements of a valid contract?
4. How can companies protect their intellectual property?
5. What criteria must an instrument meet to be negotiable?

Questions for Analysis

6. What is precedent, and how does it affect common law?
7. What does the concept of strict product liability mean to businesses?
8. Why is agency important to business?
9. What is the advantage of declaring Chapter 11 bankruptcy? What is the disadvantage?
10. **Ethical Considerations.** Should products that can be used in the commission of a crime be declared illegal? For example, DVD burners can be used to make illegal copies of movies pirated from the Internet. Why wouldn't the government simply ban such devices?

Reducing Exposure to Risk

All businesses face the risk of loss. Fire, lawsuits, accidents, natural disasters, theft, illness, disability, and death are common occurrences that can devastate any business—large or small—if it is not prepared. Of course, managers cannot guard against every conceivable threat of loss. Still, they know that in any given situation, the greater the number of outcomes that may occur, the greater their company is at risk.

Understanding Risk

Risk is a daily fact of life for both businesses and individuals. Most businesses accept the possibility of losing money in order to make money. In fact, risk prompts people to go into business in the first place. Although the formal definition of **risk** is the variation, based on chance, in possible outcomes of an event, it's not unusual to sometimes hear the term used to mean exposure to loss. This second definition is helpful, because it explains why people purchase **insurance**, a contractual arrangement whereby one party agrees to compensate another party for losses.

Speculative risk refers to those exposures that offer the prospect of making a profit or loss—such as investments in stock. Because in most cases speculative risks are not insurable, the idea is to identify the risks, take steps to minimize them, and provide for the funding of potential losses. **Pure risk**, on the other hand, is the threat of loss without the possibility of gain. Disasters such as an earthquake or a fire at a manufacturing plant are examples of pure risk. Nothing good can come from an exposure to pure risk.

An **insurable risk** is one that meets certain requirements in order for the insurer to provide protection, whereas an **uninsurable risk** is one that an insurance company will not cover (see Exhibit B.1). For example, most insurance companies are unwilling to cover potential losses that can occur from general economic conditions such as a recession. Such uncertainties are beyond the realm of insurance. In general, a risk is insurable if it meets these requirements:

- ***The loss must be accidental and beyond the insured's control.*** For example, a fire insurance policy excludes losses caused by the insured's own arson, but losses caused by an employee's arson would be covered.
- ***The loss must be financially measurable.*** Although the loss of an apartment building is financially measurable, the loss suffered by having an undesirable tenant is not.
- ***A large number of similar cases must be subject to the same peril.*** In order for the likelihood of a loss to be predictable, insurance companies must have data on the frequency and severity of losses caused by a given peril. If this information covers a long period of time and is based on a large number of cases or observations, the **law of large numbers** will usually allow insurance companies to predict accurately how many losses will occur in the future. For example, insurers keep track of the number of automobile accidents by age group in the United States so they can estimate the likelihood of a customer's becoming involved in a collision. Young drivers often complain about relatively higher insurance rates, but these rates are based on accident rates in this age group.
- ***The possible loss must be financially serious to the insured.*** An insurance company could not afford the paperwork involved in handling numerous small **claims** (demands by the insured that the insurance company pay for a loss) of a few dollars each, nor would a business be likely to insure such a small loss. For this reason, many policies have a

risk
Uncertainty of an event or exposure to loss

insurance
Written contract that transfers to an insurer the financial responsibility for losses up to specified limits

speculative risk
Risk that involves the chance of both loss and profits

pure risk
Risk that involves the chance of loss only

insurable risk
Risk for which an acceptable probability of loss may be calculated and that an insurance company might, therefore, be willing to cover

uninsurable risk
Risk that few, if any, insurance companies will assume because of the difficulty of calculating the probability of loss

law of large numbers
Principle that the larger the group on which probabilities are calculated, the more accurate the predictive value

claims
Demands for payments from an insurance company because of some loss by the insured

Exhibit B.1
Insurable and Uninsurable Risk

Insurance companies consider some pure risks insurable. They usually view speculative risks as uninsurable. (Some pure risks, such as flood and strike, are considered uninsurable in some cases.)

Insurable	Uninsurable
Property risks: Uncertainty surrounding the occurrence of loss from perils that cause	Market risks: Factors that may result in loss of property or income, such as
1. Direct loss of property	1. Price changes, seasonal or cyclical
2. Indirect loss of property	2. Consumer indifference
Personal risks: Uncertainty surrounding the occurrence of loss due of	3. Style changes
	4. Competition offered by a better product
1. Premature death	Political risks: Uncertainty surrounding the occurrence of
2. Physical disability	1. Overthrow of the government
3. Old age	2. Restrictions imposed on free trade
Legal liability risks: Uncertainty surrounding the occurrence of loss arising out of	3. Unreasonable or punitive taxation
	4. Restrictions of free exchange of currencies
1. Use of automobiles	Production risks: Uncertainties surrounding the occurrence of
2. Occupancy of buildings	1. Failure of machinery to function economically
3. Employment	2. Failure to solve technical problems
4. Manufacture of products	3. Exhaustion of raw-material resources
5. Professional misconduct	4. Strikes, absenteeism, labor unrest
	Personal risks: Uncertainty surrounding the occurrence of
	1. Unemployment
	2. Poverty from factors such as divorce, lack of education or opportunity, loss of health from military service

deductible
Amount of loss that must be paid by the insured before the insurer will pay for the rest

risk management
Process used by business firms and individuals to deal with their exposures to loss

loss exposures
Areas of risk in which a potential for loss exists

clause specifying that the insurance company will pay only that part of a loss greater than an amount stated in the policy. This amount, the **deductible**, represents small losses (such as the first $250 of covered repairs) that the insured has agreed to absorb.

In other words, businesses can't insure themselves against every potential loss, and even when they can buy coverage, insurance represents a recurring financial burden. Consequently, most companies do everything they can to reduce the financial exposure created by risk through **risk management**, which includes assessing risk, controlling risk, and financing risk by shifting it to an insurance company or by self-insuring to cover possible losses.

Assessing Risk

One of the first steps in managing risk is to identify where it exists. Those areas of risk in which a potential for loss exists, called **loss exposures**, fall under four headings: (1) loss of property (due to destruction or theft of tangible or intangible assets), (2) loss of income (either through decreased revenues or through increased expenses resulting from an accidental event), (3) legal liability to others, including employees, and (4) loss of the services of key personnel (through accidental injury or death).

Consider just one of the many loss exposures that a manufacturer of stuffed toys must face: First, the manufacturer must identify the ways a consumer (most likely a child) can be

Theft and destruction of company information are two loss exposures that more and more companies are taking seriously. "High-tech crime is the wave of the future," says the head of FBI's computer crime department.

injured by a stuffed toy. The child might choke on button eyes, get sick from eating the stuffing, or have an allergic reaction to any material in the toy. Second, the company must identify any possible flaws in the production or marketing of the toy that might lead to one of these injuries. For example, a child may have an allergic reaction to the toy if its materials are not carefully tested for allergenic substances, if impurities enter the toy during manufacture, or if the toy is not properly packaged (allowing foreign substances to reach it). Third, the manufacturer must analyze these possibilities in order to predict product-liability losses accurately.

Once you have identified your potential for risk, you have three reasonable choices: you can accept risk, eliminate or control it, or shift the responsibility for it.

Controlling Risk

Whereas some companies choose to fully accept the financial consequences of a loss themselves—especially when the potential loss costs are small or can be financed by the company itself—others choose to control risk by using a number of *risk-control techniques* to minimize the organization's losses:

- *Risk avoidance.* A risk manager might try to eliminate the chance of a particular type of loss. With rare exceptions, such risk avoidance is not practical. The stuffed-toy manufacturer could avoid being sued for a child's allergic reaction by not making stuffed toys, but, of course, the company would also be out of business.
- *Loss prevention.* A risk manager may try to reduce (but not totally eliminate) the *chance* of a given loss by removing hazards or taking preventive measures. Security guards at banks, warnings on medicines and dangerous chemicals, and safety locks are examples of loss prevention measures.
- *Loss reduction.* A risk manager may try to reduce the *severity* of the losses that do occur. Examples include installing overhead sprinklers to reduce damage during a fire and paying the medical expenses of an injured consumer to reduce the likelihood of litigation and punitive damages.
- *Risk-control transfer.* A risk manager may try to eliminate risk by transferring to some other person or group either (1) the actual property or activity responsible for the risk or (2) the responsibility for the risk. For example, a firm can sell a building to eliminate the risks of ownership.

Of course, not all risk is controllable. Thus, many companies will shift risk to an outside insurance company or self-insure against risk.

Avoiding accidents and injuries through such measures as protective clothing is an important step in managing corporate risk.

Shifting Risk to an Insurance Company

When companies purchase insurance, they transfer a group's (but not an individual's) predicted losses to an insurance pool. The pool combines the cost of the potential losses to be financed and then redistributes them back to the individuals exposed (in advance) by charging them a fee known as an **insurance premium**.

Actuaries determine how much income insurance companies need to generate from premiums by compiling statistics of losses, predicting the amount needed to pay claims over a given period, and calculating the amount needed to cover these expenses plus any anticipated operating costs. Insurance companies don't count on making a profit on any particular policy, nor do they count on paying for a single policyholder's losses out of the premium paid by that particular policyholder. Rather, the insurance company pays for a loss by drawing the money out of the pool of funds it has received from all its policyholders in the form of premiums (see Exhibit B.2). In this way, the insurance company redistributes the cost of predicted losses from a single individual or company to a large number of policies.

If you were starting a business, what types of insurance would you need? To some extent, the answer to that question would depend on the nature of your business and your potential for loss. In general, however, you would probably want to protect yourself against the loss of property, loss of income, liability, and loss of services of key personnel (see Exhibit B.3).

insurance premium
Fee that the insured pays the insurer for coverage against loss

actuaries
People employed by an insurance company to compute expected losses and to calculate the cost of premiums

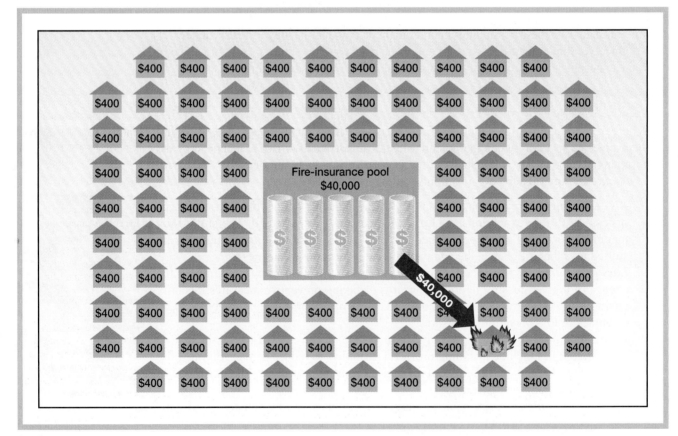

Exhibit B.2
How Insurance Works
An insurance company covers the cost of a policyholder's loss out of the premiums paid by a large pool of policyholders. Thus, if 100 policyholders pay $400 each to insure against fire damage, the insurance company can afford to compensate one policyholder who actually suffers fire damage with $40,000 (not including the costs associated with managing the insurance fund).

Risk	Protection
Loss of property	
Due to destruction or theft	Fire insurance
	Disaster insurance
	Marine insurance
	Automobile insurance
Due to dishonesty or nonperformance	Fidelity bonding
	Surety bonding
	Credit life insurance
	Crime insurance
Loss of income	Business interruption insurance
	Extra-expense insurance
	Contingent business-interruption insurance
Liability	Comprehensive general liability insurance
	Automobile liability insurance
	Workers' compensation insurance
	Umbrella liability insurance
	Professional liability insurance
Loss of services of key personnel	Key-person insurance

Exhibit B.3
Business Risks and Protection
Here are some of the more common types of business insurance purchased.

Property Insurance Property loss can have a variety of causes, including accidental damage, natural disaster, and theft. Property can also be lost through employee dishonesty and nonperformance. When a cannery in California ships jars of pizza sauce by a truck to New York, for example, the goods face unavoidable risks in transit. One wrong turn could cover a whole hillside with broken glass and gallons of sauce, which would represent a sizable loss to the manufacturer. The factory itself is vulnerable to fire, flood, and (especially in California) earthquakes.

Property insurance covers the insured for physical damage to or destruction of property and also for its loss by theft. When purchasing property insurance, the buyer has three coverage options: replacement cost, actual cash value, or functional replacement cost. **Replacement-cost coverage** means that the insurer promises to pay an amount equal to the full cost of repairing or replacing the property even if the property was old or run-down before the loss occurred. Because the insured is often better off after the loss, the premium for this type of coverage is generally quite expensive.

Actual cash value coverage assumes that the property that was lost or damaged was worth less than new property because of normal aging or use. Thus, the insurance company will pay the amount that allows the insured to return the property to its same state before the incident. Sometimes, however, it does not pay to restore a property to its same state because the replacement cost of a building is greater than its market value (as is often the case with older, inner-city structures). **Functional-replacement-cost coverage** allows for the substitution of modern construction materials such as wallboard instead of plaster to restore a property to a similar, functioning state.

Consequential Loss Insurance When a disaster strikes, such as a fire or a flood or terrorism, property loss is only one part of the story. Disasters not only disrupt the business operation; they often result in a temporary shutdown, costing the company far more than the

property insurance
Insurance that provides coverage for physical damage to or destruction of property and for its loss by theft

replacement-cost coverage
Property insurance in which the insurer pays for the full cost of repairing or replacing the property rather than the actual cash value

actual cash value coverage
Property insurance in which the insurer pays for the replacement cost of property at the time of loss, less an allowance for depreciation

functional-replacement-cost coverage
Property insurance that allows for the substitution of construction materials to restore a property to a similar, functioning state

equipment repairs or replacement of damaged stock. That's because expenses continue—salaries, interest payments, rent—even though the company is not earning revenues. Disruption also results in extra expenses: leasing of temporary space, paying overtime to meet work schedules with a reduced capacity, buying additional advertising to assure the public that the business is still a going concern. In fact, a prolonged interruption of business could even cause bankruptcy.

For this reason, many companies carry *consequential loss insurance*. Available coverage includes **business-interruption insurance**, which protects the insured against lost profits and pays continuing expenses when a fire or other disaster causes a company to shut down temporarily; **extra-expense insurance**, which pays the additional costs of maintaining the operation in temporary quarters; and **contingent business-interruption insurance**, which protects against a company's loss of profit due to the misfortune of another business, such as a fire or other disaster that interrupts the operation of an important supplier or the closing of an anchor store in the mall where the business is located.

Liability Insurance Liability insurance provides protection against a number of perils. **Liability losses** are financial losses suffered by firms or individuals held responsible for property damage or for injuries suffered by others. In general, liability losses arise from three sources: (1) the costs of legal damages awarded by a court to the injured party if the company is found negligent; (2) the costs of a legal defense, which can be quite expensive; and (3) the costs of loss prevention or identifying potential liability problems so they may be handled in an appropriate way. To accommodate these sources of liability, the insurance industry has created these types of liability policies:

- *Commercial general liability.* This basic coverage automatically provides protection against all forms of liability not specifically excluded under the terms of the policy. Examples would be liability for operations on business premises, product liability, completed operations, and operations of independent contractors.
- *Product liability.* Manufacturers of a product have a legal duty to design and produce a product that will not injure people in normal use. In addition, products must be packaged carefully and accompanied by adequate instructions and warnings, so consumers may use them properly and avoid injury. If these duties are not fulfilled and result in an injured user, a potential for a product-liability lawsuit exists. **Product-liability coverage** protects insured companies from being threatened financially when someone claims that one of their products caused damage, injury, or death.
- *Automobile liability.* Many companies also carry insurance that specifically covers liability connected with any vehicles owned or operated by the company. Some states have **no-fault insurance laws**, which means that all parties involved in an automobile accident receive compensation for their injuries from their own insurer, regardless of who causes the accident. According to current no-fault plans, after some threshold of damage has been reached, the injured party may revert to the liability system to seek compensation for loss.
- *Professional liability.* Also known as *malpractice insurance* or *errors and omissions insurance*, **professional liability insurance** covers people who are found liable for professional negligence. Because this type of coverage protects professionals from financial ruin if sued by dissatisfied clients, it tends to be very expensive.
- *Employment practices liability.* Recent increases in employee lawsuits and hefty judgments against employers have generated increased interest in employment practices liability insurance. Such insurance reimburses employers for defense costs, settlements, and judgments arising from employment claims related to discrimination, sexual harassment, wrongful termination, breach of employment contract,

business-interruption insurance
Insurance that covers losses resulting from temporary business closings

extra-expense insurance
Insurance that covers the added expense of operating the business in temporary facilities after an event such as a fire or a flood

contingent business-interruption insurance
Insurance that protects a business from losses due to losses sustained by other businesses such as suppliers or transportation companies

liability losses
Financial losses suffered by a business firm or individual held responsible for property damage or injuries suffered by others

product-liability coverage
Insurance that protects companies from claims for injuries or damages that result from use of a product the company manufactures or distributes

no-fault insurance laws
Laws limiting lawsuits connected with auto accidents

professional liability insurance
Insurance that covers losses arising from damages or injuries caused by the insured in the course of performing professional services for clients

negligent evaluation, failure to employ or promote, wrongful discipline, deprivation of career opportunity, wrongful infliction of emotional stress, and mismanagement of employee benefits.

- *Umbrella liability.* Because many liability policies have limits, or maximum amounts that may be paid out, businesses sometimes purchase **umbrella policies** to provide coverage after underlying liability policies have been exhausted. Sometimes an umbrella policy is called *excess liability insurance.*

umbrella policies
Insurance that provides businesses with coverage beyond what is provided by a basic liability policy

Key-Person Insurance Sometimes one executive or employee has expertise or experience that is crucial to the company's operation. If a business loses this key person by illness, disability, death, or unplanned retirement, the effect may be felt in lost income. **Key-person insurance** can be purchased to protect a company against the financial impact of losing such a key employee under the circumstances described. Part of identifying the key-employee exposure is developing an estimate of where, at what cost, and how quickly a replacement may be hired and trained.

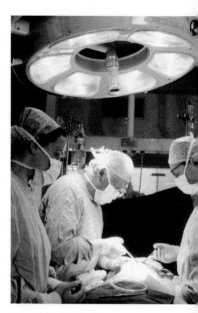

Self-Insuring Against Risk

Self-insurance is becoming an increasingly popular method of insuring against risk. Because self-insurance plans are not subject to state regulation, mandates, and premium taxes (typically 2 percent), companies that use **self-insurance** often save quite a bit of money. Deciding to self-insure with a liability reserve fund means putting aside a certain sum each year to cover predicted liability losses. Unless payments to the self-insurance fund are calculated scientifically and paid regularly, a true self-insurance system does not exist.

Keep in mind that self-insurance differs greatly from "going bare," or having no reserve funds. Self-insurance implies an attempt by business to combine a sufficient number of its own similar exposures to predict the losses accurately. It also implies that adequate financial arrangements have been made in advance to provide funds to pay for losses should they occur. For instance, companies that self-insure often set aside a revenue or self-insurance contingency fund to cover any unexpected or large losses. That way, if disaster strikes, companies won't have to borrow funds to cover their losses, or be forced out of business. In addition, they generally protect themselves from unexpected losses or disasters by purchasing excess insurance from commercial insurers, called *stop-loss insurance.* This additional insurance is designed to cover losses that would exceed a company's own financial capabilities.

Experts advise companies to consider self-insurance plans only if they are prepared to handle the worst-case scenario (usually the point at which stop-loss insurance kicks in) and to use self-insurance only as a long-term strategy. That's because in some years the cost to self-insure will be lower than the cost of commercial insurance, whereas in other years it will be higher. In the long run, however, statistics show that the good and bad years should average out in the company's favor.[1]

Professional liability insurance is a must for health care providers, in order to avoid the financially devastating effects of malpractice lawsuits. The high cost of this type of insurance is a major reason that health care costs have risen so rapidly in recent years.

key-person insurance
Insurance that provides a business with funds to compensate for the loss of a key employee by unplanned retirement, resignation, death, or disability

self-insurance
Accumulating funds each year to pay for predicted losses, rather than buying insurance from another company

Monitoring the Risk-Management Program

Risk management is an ongoing activity. Managers must periodically reevaluate the company's loss exposures by asking these questions: What does the company have? What can go wrong? What's the minimum we need to stay in business? What's the best way to protect the company's assets? By answering these questions, managers can then revise a company's risk-management program to address changing needs and circumstances. As new threats appear, new types of insurance often appear as well, so risk management specialists also need to evaluate new categories of insurance, such as insurance that covers acts of terrorism or identity theft. Of course, smart managers recognize that risk management is really everybody's job. Practically every employee can take steps to reduce his or her company's exposure to risk by preventing it or controlling it.

Insuring the Health and Well-Being of Employees

Besides protecting company property and assets, many businesses look out for the well-being of employees by providing them with health, disability, workers' compensation, and life insurance coverage. Disease and disability may cost employees huge sums of money unless they are insured. In addition, death carries the threat of financial hardship for an employee's family.

Health Insurance

As you read in Chapter 11, health care costs are one of the most pressing issues facing managers today, and health insurance represents one of the biggest concerns in health care—both for people who are covered by health insurance and for the 45 million Americans who aren't covered. Exhibit B.4 identifies the most common forms of health insurance.

Health insurance and health care services are available from a variety of sources, including government programs, private nonprofit organizations, and for-profit commercial providers. The largest health insurer in the United States is the Blue Cross and Blue Shield Association, www.bcbs.com, an association of independent, local insurance providers (most of which are nonprofit organizations, but some are converting to for-profit status).[2] Another major source of health coverage are **health maintenance organizations (HMOs)**, which are comprehensive, prepaid, group-practice medical plans in which consumers pay a set fee (called a *capitation payment*) and in return receive most of their health care at little or no additional costs. Because the capitation payment does not change with usage, HMOs shift the risk from the employer to the health care provider. Consequently, HMOs place a high priority on wellness and disease prevention.[3] Certain HMOs (called "open HMOs") allow members the option of using hospitals and

health maintenance organizations (HMOs)
Prepaid medical plans in which consumers pay a set fee in order to receive a full range of medical care from a group of medical practitioners

Exhibit B.4
Common Types of Health Insurance
Here are five of the most common types of health insurance policies sold by insurers.

Basic medical	Designed to pay for most inpatient and some outpatient hospital costs
Major medical	Protects the insured against catastrophic financial losses by covering medical expenses that exceed the coverage limits of the basic policies
Disability income	Designed to protect against the loss of short-term or long-term income while the insured is disabled as a result of an illness or accident
Medicare supplemental	Designed specifically to supplement benefits provided under the Medicare program
Long-term care	Designed to cover stays in long-term care facilities

doctors outside the network. These variations are actually a form of **managed care** programs where employers (usually through an insurance carrier) set up their own network of doctors and hospitals that agree to discount the fees they charge in return for the flow of patients.

As an alternative to HMOs, some employers opt for **preferred-provider organizations (PPOs)**, health care providers that contract with employers, insurance companies, or other third-party payers to deliver health care services to an employee group at a reduced fee. In most companies, employees are not required to use preferred providers, but they are offered incentives to do so—such as reduced deductibles (the amount the patient must pay before insurance kicks in) or lower *copayments* (small per-visit or per-service fees). Preferred-provider organizations not only save employers money but also allow them to control the quality and appropriateness of services provided. However, employees are restricted in their choice of hospitals and doctors, and preventive services are generally not covered.

As employers and other parties continue to wrestle with high costs of health care, you can expect to see continuing developments in health care financing. Two of the newest innovations are *health savings accounts (HSAs)*, which allow employees to save a portion of their earnings in a special account that can be used for medical expenses, and *health reimbursement arrangements (HRAs)*, in which an employer sets aside funds to reimburse employees for covered medical expenses.[4]

managed care
Health care set up by employers (usually through an insurance carrier) who provide networks of doctors and hospitals that agree to discount the fees they charge in return for the flow of patients

preferred-provider organizations (PPOs)
Health care providers offering reduced-rate contracts to groups that agree to obtain medical care through the providers' organization

Disability Income Insurance

Disability income insurance, which replaces income not earned because of illness or accident, is often included as part of the health insurance package provided by employers. Such policies are designated as either short-term or long-term, depending on the period for which coverage is provided. Short-term policies are more common and provide a specific number of weeks of coverage (often 30), after a brief waiting or elimination period—a period that must elapse before an employee is eligible to receive insurance payments. The purpose of the elimination period is to exclude payments for minor illness. Long-term disability income, on the other hand, provides a number of years of protection after a substantial elimination period has elapsed (generally six months of continuous disability).

The amount of disability payment depends on whether the disability is partial or total, temporary or permanent, short-term or long-term. In general, the amount received is decreased by the amount of disability payments received from Social Security. To encourage employees to return to work as soon as possible, some policies will continue partial payments if an employee is able to perform some type of work, even if he or she is unable to maintain the same pace of career advancement or hours of labor per week as before the disability.

disability income insurance
Short-term or long-term insurance that protects an individual against loss of income while that individual is disabled as the result of an illness or accident

Workers' Compensation Insurance

As Chapter 2 points out, each year thousands of workers die or are injured on the job. To protect employees from medical costs and related expenses that they might incur as a result of these mishaps, all 50 states require employers to cover their employees with **workers' compensation insurance**. This form of insurance covers loss of income by occupationally injured or diseased workers, full payment of medical expenses, and rehabilitation expenses for these workers. Plus, it provides death benefits to the survivors of any employee killed on the job. In most cases, it covers both full- and part-time employees.

workers' compensation insurance
Insurance that partially replaces lost income and that pays for employees' medical costs and rehabilitation expenses for work-related injuries

Premiums for workers' compensation insurance are based largely on the employer's ongoing health and safety performance. Thus, employers with relatively good safety records will pay lower workers' compensation insurance rates than employers with poor safety records. This approach rewards loss prevention and loss reduction efforts. Insurers also classify employers by industry, giving recognition to the fact that some industries involve more danger to workers than others do. For instance, an employer in a mining industry would pay higher rates than an employer in the food services industry.

Like other types of insurance, costs for "workers' comp" insurance has skyrocketed in recent years. Because coverage is legally mandated, employers can't drop it when premiums increase, so some have been forced to reduce their workforces when insurance rates rise. Reasons cited for the steep increases include higher medical costs associated with injury claims, fraudulent claims, and reduced competition among insurers in states where providing coverage has become so expensive that some insurers have stopped doing business.[5]

Life Insurance

One of the most unfortunate circumstances that could strike a family would be the loss of its main source of income. Life insurance policies provide some protection against the financial problems associated with premature death by paying predetermined amounts to **beneficiaries** when the covered individual dies.

beneficiaries
People named in a life insurance policy who receive the proceeds of an insurance contract when the insured dies

There are many types of life insurance, and each is used for a variety of purposes. For example, *credit life insurance* is required by many lending institutions to guarantee that a mortgage or other large loan will be paid off in the case of the borrower's death. Some life insurance policies provide a type of savings fund for retirement or other purposes by building a *cash value* from excess premiums. In some policies, owners can borrow against the cash value by paying interest to the insurer (sometimes at a lower rate than banks charge), and they can withdraw the accumulated cash value in one lump sum or in annual payments if they want to end the policy.

term insurance
Life insurance that provides death benefits for a specified period

Term insurance, as the name implies, covers a person for a specific period of time—the *term* of the policy. In other words, if the insured person dies after the term expires, no payment is made to beneficiaries. Group life insurance is term insurance that is commonly purchased by employers for their employees. It may generally be renewed without the proof of insurability (also known as guaranteed renewable), but not past the age of 65. **Whole life insurance** provides a combination of insurance and savings. The policy stays in force until the insured dies, provided that the premiums are paid. In addition to paying death benefits, whole life insurance accumulates cash value over time. Policyholders can borrow some or all of this money during the life of the policy, or they can use it to help defray the costs of increasing premiums as they age.[6]

whole life insurance
Insurance that provides both death benefits and savings for the insured's lifetime, provided premiums are paid

variable life insurance
Whole life insurance policy that allows the policyholder to decide how to invest the cash value

Variable life insurance was developed in response to the soaring inflation of the late 1970s and early 1980s. The difference between variable life insurance and whole life insurance is that variable is most often associated with an investment portfolio because the underlying investments are securities, and the policy owner has some investment choice. If the insured's investment decisions are good, the policy's cash value and death benefit (the amount paid at death) will increase. On the other hand, if the investments do poorly, the cash value may drop to $0 and the death benefit may decrease—although not below the original amount purchased (the face value) as long as the policy remains in force and accumulates cash value.

universal life insurance
Combination of term life insurance policy and a savings plan with flexible interest rates and flexible premiums

Universal life insurance is another combination life insurance and investment product, in which customers purchase a term insurance policy and invest additional funds (typically in government bonds). The combination of insurance and investments gives customers some flexibility—depending on the performance of the investments—in the size and frequency of premiums and the size of the death benefits.[7]

Social Insurance Programs

When most people think of insurance, they think of the kind of insurance purchased from a private insurance company. Actually, the largest single source of insurance in the United States is the government, which accounts for nearly half of the total insurance premiums collected for all types of coverage combined. Most social insurance programs are designed to protect people from loss of income, either because they have reached retirement age or because they have lost their jobs or become disabled. Unlike private insurance, which is voluntarily chosen by the insured, government-sponsored programs are compulsory.

Social Security

Social Security was created by the federal government following the Great Depression of the 1930s. Officially known as Old-Age, Survivors, Disability, and Health Insurance, this program covers just about every wage earner in the United States.

The basic purpose of the Social Security program is to provide a minimum level of income for retirees, their survivors, and their dependents, as well as for the permanently disabled. The program also provides hospital and supplemental medical insurance—known as Medicare—for people age 65 and over. Social Security benefits vary, depending on a worker's average indexed monthly earnings and number of dependents. The program is funded by a payroll tax paid half by workers and half by their employers. In most cases, these taxes are automatically deducted from each paycheck. Self-employed people pay the full amount of the tax as part of their federal income tax liability. It's important to note that Social Security is not a needs-based program; every eligible person is entitled to the benefits of the system, regardless of his or her financial status.

As Chapter 2 pointed out, the long-term future of Social Security is a subject of intense analysis and debate at the national level. As the population ages and the ratio of active to retired employees changes, the system's current funding model may not be adequate to sustain payments at their current levels. A solution is likely to involve increased funding from other sources, reduced benefits for at least some segments of the population (possibly making benefits tied to need), or some combination of the two.

Unemployment Insurance

Under the terms of the Social Security Act of 1935, employers in all 50 states finance special **unemployment insurance** to benefit employees who become unemployed. The cost is borne by employers. Currently, the unemployment insurance program is a joint federal-state program, with about 90 percent of the funding coming from the states.

unemployment insurance
Government-sponsored program for assisting employees who are laid off for reasons not related to performance

The unemployment insurance program is designed to meet the peril of short-term unemployment caused by the business cycle and other factors over which workers have little control. Thus, an employee who becomes unemployed for reasons not related to performance is entitled to collect benefits—typically for 26 weeks, which may be extended during periods of very high unemployment.

Test Your Knowledge

Questions for Review

1. What is the difference between pure risk and speculative risk?
2. What are the five characteristics of insurable risks?
3. What are the four types of loss exposure?
4. How can you control risk?
5. What is the difference between workers' compensation insurance and disability income insurance?

Questions for Analysis

6. How do insurance companies calculate their premiums?

7. What is self-insurance, and why is it becoming an increasingly popular risk-shifting technique?

8. Why is it a good idea to purchase consequential loss insurance?

9. If you were starting a new accounting practice with 15 employees, what types of insurance might you need?

10. **Ethical Consideration.** A survey by the Society of Chartered Property Casualty Underwriters rated ethical behavior as the number-one attribute insurance industry employers look for in job candidates when making hiring decisions.[8] Why is ethics of such critical concern in the insurance industry? (Hint: Think about the nature and length-of-term of the product.)

Will You Control Your Money, or Will Your Money Control You?

In your years as a consumer and a wage earner, even if it has only been from part-time jobs so far, you've already established a relationship with money. How would you characterize that relationship? Positive or negative? Are you in control of your money, or does money—and a frequent lack of it—control you? Unfortunately, too many people in the United States find themselves in the second situation, with heavy debt loads, a constant cycle of struggle from one paycheck to the next, and worries about the future. In a recent survey, 64 percent of U.S. adults said they were living paycheck to paycheck, and 71 percent said that getting out of debt is their primary financial goal.[1] When people get stuck in this mode, money often controls their lives because it's a constant source of worry.

The good news is that with some basic information in hand, you can almost always improve your financial well-being and take control of your money. The timing might seem ironic, but the best time to establish a positive relationship with money is right now, when you're still a student. If you build good habits now, when money is often scarce, you'll be taking a major step toward getting set for life. Conversely, if you fall into bad habits now, you could find yourself struggling and worrying for years to come. You'd be amazed at how many graduates think that their financial lives will improve dramatically when they start earning a "real" paycheck, only to discover that their bills and their debts increase even faster than their earnings.

This appendix will help you understand the basic principles of personal finances and give you a solid foundation for managing your money. Before exploring some helpful strategies for each stage of your life, the following sections emphasize three lessons that every consumer and wage earner needs to know and offer a brief look at the financial planning process.

By establishing positive financial habits now, you can avoid the money worries that plague millions of U.S. consumers.

Three Simple—but Vital—Financial Lessons

If you've ever read a copy of the *Wall Street Journal, Barron's,* or another financial publication, you might have gotten the sense that money management is complex and jargon infested. However, unless you become a financial professional, you don't need to worry about the intricacies of "high finance." A few simple lessons will serve you well, starting with three ideas that will have enormous impact on your financial future: (1) the value of your money is constantly changing, so you need to understand how time affects your financial health; (2) small sacrifices early in life can have huge payback later in life; and (3) every financial decision you make involves trades-offs. Taking these three ideas to heart will improve every aspect of your money management efforts, no matter how basic or sophisticated your finances.

The Value of Your Money Is Constantly Changing

If you remember only one thing from this discussion of personal finance, make sure this thought stays with you: A dollar today does not equal a dollar tomorrow. If you've successfully invested a dollar, it will be worth a little more tomorrow. However, if you charged a dollar's worth of purchases on a credit card, you're going to owe a little more than a dollar tomorrow. And even if you hold it tightly in your hand, that dollar will be worth a little less tomorrow, thanks to **inflation**—the tendency of prices to increase over

inflation
The tendency of prices to increase over time

time. When prices go up, your **buying power** goes down, so that dollar will buy less and less with each passing day.

These effects are so gradual that they are usually impossible to notice from one day to the next, but they can have a staggering impact on your finances over time. Put time to work for you, and you'll join that happy segment of the population whose finances are stable and under control. Let time work against you, and you could get trapped in an endless cycle of stress and debt.

A simple example will demonstrate the power of time. Let's say you inherit $10,000 today and have two choices: hide it under your mattress or invest it in the stock market. Now fast-forward 10 years. If you hid the $10,000 under your mattress, it'll now be worth only $7,000 or so (assuming today's inflation rates stay about the same). It will still *look* like $10,000, but because of inflation, it'll *spend* like $7,000. On the other hand, if you invested it in the stock market, you could have $18,000 or more, assuming stock market returns track historical patterns. That's a difference of $11,000 between the two choices, more than your inheritance to begin with.

Now let's say you didn't get that inheritance but you did get the urge to treat your best friends to a relaxing vacation. You don't have the cash, but lucky you—a shiny new credit card with a $10,000 limit just arrived in the mail, so away you go. The bill arrives a few days after you return home, and you start paying a modest amount, say $150 a month. At 13 percent interest, which is not unusual for a credit card, it'll take you just about 10 years to pay off the $10,000 you borrowed—and you'll end up paying $18,000, nearly twice what you thought that vacation was costing you. Doesn't seem so relaxing now, does it?

Depending on the financial decisions you make, then, time can be your best friend or your worst enemy. The **time value of money** refers to increases in money as a result of accumulating interest.[2] Time is even more powerful when your investment or debt is subject to **compounding**, which occurs when new interest is applied to interest that has already accumulated. Financial planners often talk about the "magic of compounding," and it really can feel like magic—good magic if it's compounded interest on savings, bad magic if it's compounded interest on debt. For example, Exhibit C.1 shows how $10,000 grows in a savings account that pays 3 percent annually, compounded monthly.

Granted, you're not going to get wealthy with 3 percent interest, but if you leave your money in this account for 10 years, you'd accumulate more than $1,600 in compounded

Exhibit C.1
Compounding and the Time Value of Money
The "magic of compounding" accelerates savings (or debt) by calculating new interest on both the existing balance and previously accumulated interest.

Month	Balance	Interest
(1) Opening balance — 0	$10,000.00	$0.00
1	10,025.00	25.00
(3) Balance at beginning of 2nd month: $10,000.00 + 25.00 — 2	10,050.06	25.06
3	10,075.19	25.13
(5) Balance at beginning of 3rd month: $10,025.00 + 25.06 — 4	10,100.38	25.19
5	10,125.63	25.25
6	10,150.94	25.31
7	10,176.32	25.38
8	10,201.76	25.44
9	10,227.26	25.50
10	10,252.83	25.57
11	10,278.46	25.63
12	10,304.16	25.70

(2) Interest after 1st month: $10,000.00 × 0.25%

(4) Interest after 2nd month: $10,025.00 × 0.25%

interest. (Unfortunately, inflation would probably erode all your gains in this case, which is why you don't want to keep much of your savings in a savings account, as you'll see later.)

Small Sacrifices Early in Life Can Produce Big Payoffs

If you're currently living the life of a typical college student, you probably can't wait to move on and move up in life. You'll land that first "real" job, then get a nicer apartment, buy a new car, replace those ratty clothes you've been wearing for four years, and stop eating ramen seven nights a week. This might be the last thing you want to hear, but if you can convince yourself to continue your frugal ways for a few more years, you'll benefit tremendously in the long run.

Let's say that by age 65 you'd like to have a retirement fund of $1 million in *today's dollars,* which means it's adjusted for inflation. Compare the scenarios in Exhibit C.2 (which assume 10 percent annual return on your investments, which is in line with historical stock market investments, and 4 percent annual inflation). If you start investing at age 25, you'll need to invest $904 a month. If you wait until age 35 to start, you'll need to invest $1,643 a month to reach $1 million. Wait until age 45, and you'll need to invest $3,188 a month. In other words, the longer you wait, the more painful it gets. But that's not all. The longer you wait, the more you need to invest in total dollars, too—$330,000 more if you start at age 45 instead of age 25.

Of course, saving $904 a month during the early years of your career is no easy task, and it may be impossible, depending on your starting salary. In addition to the endless temptations to spend, you may also face the costs of starting a family, for instance. However, you'd be amazed at how much you can save every month by forgoing that new car, renting a cheaper apartment, buying modestly priced clothes, and watching your entertainment expenses closely. A few simple choices can often free up hundreds of dollars every month. And if you join the growing number of college graduates who plan to move back in with their parents during the initial years of their careers, you can really pile up the savings.[3] Even if you can save only a few hundred dollars every month early in your career, the earlier you start, the better off you'll be. Just keep increasing your monthly investment every time your salary increases and do everything you can to take advantage of the time value of money.

Every Decision Involves Trade-Offs

By now, you've probably noticed that the time value of money and frugal living involve lots of choices. In fact, virtually every financial decision you make, from buying a cup of coffee to buying a house, involves a **trade-off**, in which you have to give up one thing to gain something else. If your family and friends give you $2,000 for graduation, should you run right out and buy alloy wheels and a custom exhaust system for your car? Or should you invest that $2,000 in the stock market and invest another $200 every month, so that in five or six years you could have enough to buy a new car—in cash, with no monthly payments? Then, while your friends are shelling out $300 or $400 in payments for their

trade-off
A decision-making condition in which you have to give up one or more benefits to gain other benefits

Starting Age	Monthly Investment	Total Investment
25	$ 904	$434,880
35	$1,643	$591,480
45	$3,188	$765,120

Exhibit C.2
Building a Million
To amass $1 million by age 65 (assuming 10 percent return on your investments and 4 percent inflation), you can save $330,000 by starting 20 years earlier.

new cars, you can be investing that amount every month and build up enough money to start your own business or perhaps retire a few years early.

Even the smallest habits and choices have consequences. Addicted to potato chips? Let's say you spend $3.19 for a big bag two or three times a week. Kick that habit now and invest the money instead. Over the course of 40 years, you could earn enough to treat yourself to a new car when you retire. Sounds crazy, but over the course of many years, even tiny amounts of money can add up to large sums.

Not all your choices will be so simple, of course. Most of the examples presented so far have involved trading current pleasures and luxuries for future financial gain—a dilemma you'll be facing most of your life, by the way. Other choices involve risks versus rewards. Should you buy life insurance to provide for your family or invest the money and hope it'll grow fast enough to provide your loved ones with enough to get by on in the event of your death? Should you invest your money in a safe but slow-growing investment or an investment that offers the potential for high growth—but the risk that you could lose everything? As you gain experience with financial choices, you'll recognize your own level of *risk tolerance.* For instance, if you're lying awake at night worrying about a high-risk stock you just purchased, you may have a lower level of risk tolerance and you'll probably want to stick with safer, saner investments.

Figuring out the best choice is difficult in many cases, but simply recognizing that every decision involves a trade-off will improve your decision making. Too often, people get into trouble by looking at *only* the risk (which can stop them from making choices that might in fact be better for them in the long run) or *only* the potential rewards (which can lure them into making choices that are too risky). Consider all the consequences of every choice you make, and you'll start making better financial decisions.

You'll pick up many other financial tips as you start investing, buying houses, selecting insurance, and making other financial choices, but these three concepts will always apply. With those thoughts in mind, it's time to take a look at the financial planning process.

Creating Your Personal Financial Plan

Creating and following a sensible financial plan is the only sure way to stay in control of your finances. A good plan can help you get the most from whatever amount of money you have, identify the funds you'll need to get through life's major expenses, increase your financial independence and confidence, minimize the time and energy you need to manage your finances, and answer a question that vexes millions of people every year: Where did all my money go?

Many people discover they'd rather turn the planning task over to a professional financial planner. And even if you do most of your planning yourself, you may encounter special situations or major transactions in which you'd like the advice of an expert. The right advice at the right time can mean all the difference. Unfortunately, finding the right adviser is not a simple task: Some 250,000 people in the United States offer their services as financial advisers.[4] Before you sign on with anyone, make sure you understand what advice you need and who can provide it. Ask for references, professional credentials, investing strategies, and most important of all, how the adviser is paid.[5]

fee-only planners
Financial advisers who charge a fee for their services, rather than earning a commission on financial services they sell you

commission-based planners
Financial advisers who are paid commissions on the financial products they sell you, such as insurance policies and mutual funds

Fee-only planners charge you for their services, either an hourly rate or a percentage of the assets they're managing for you. In theory, the major advantage of fee-only planners is complete objectivity, as they don't make money on the specific decisions they recommend for you. In contrast, **commission-based planners** are paid commissions on the financial products they sell you, such as insurance policies and mutual funds. While you can certainly receive good advice from a commission-based planner, make sure he or she has a wide range of offerings for you. Otherwise, you're likely to by hampered by limited choices.[6] Of course, since these types of planners are selling you something, make sure their recommendations are really the best choices for your financial needs. If you can't get a good recommendation from family members or colleagues, consider a matchmaker such as www.wiseradvisor.com, an impartial service that helps investors find advisers.

Even if you decide to rely on a full-service financial adviser to guide your decisions, stay informed and actively involved. Lawsuits against financial advisers have risen dramatically in recent years, as clients seek compensation for losses in the stock market, for tax shelters (investments designed primarily to reduce tax obligations) that the Internal Revenue Service (IRS) later ruled were "abusive," or for other financial missteps. Some observers attribute this trend to clients who are simply angry and frustrated that many stocks crumbled after the dot-com boom. In other cases, however, clients have sued advisers who led them into overly complex or even illegal investment and tax schemes.[7] Keep in mind that even if you get advice, you are ultimately responsible for—and in control of—the choices involving your money. Don't count on anyone else to secure your financial future for you.

Planning can be as simple or as complex as you're inclined to make it, as long as you follow the basic steps shown in Exhibit C.3.[8] The following sections discuss each step in more detail.

Figure Out Where You Are Now

Successful financial planning starts with a careful examination of where you stand right now, financially speaking. Before you can move ahead, you need to add up what you own and what you owe, where your money is going, and how you're using credit. You might not like what you see, but if your finances are heading downhill, the sooner you learn that, the sooner you can fix it.

Start by listing your **assets**—the things you own—and your **liabilities**—the amounts of money you owe. Assets include both *financial assets,* such as bank accounts, mutual funds, retirement accounts, and money that people owe you, and *physical assets,* such as cars, houses, and artwork. Liabilities include credit card debts, car loans, home mortgages, and student loans. After you've itemized everything you own and everything you owe, calculate your **net worth** by subtracting your liabilities from your assets. The **balance sheet** in Exhibit C.4 shows Devon Anderson's net worth. Her net worth is currently negative, but that's certainly not uncommon for college students. The important thing for Devon at this point is that she knows how much she's worth, so she has a baseline to build on.

Your balance sheet gives you a snapshot of where you stand at a particular point in time. The second major planning tool is your **income and expense statement**, or simply *income statement.* This statement answers that all-important question of where your money is going month by month. Start by adding up all your sources of income from jobs, parents, investments, and so on. If you have irregular income, such as a onetime cash infusion from your parents at the beginning of each semester, divide it by the number of months it needs

assets
The physical things, such as real estate and artwork, and financial elements, such as cash and stocks, that you own

liabilities
Amounts of money you owe

net worth
The difference between your assets and your liabilities

balance sheet
A summary of your assets and liabilities; the difference between the two subtotals is your net worth

income and expense statement
A listing of your monthly inflows (income) and outflows (expenses); also called an income statement

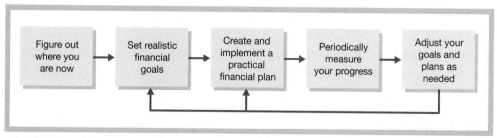

Exhibit C.3
The Financial Planning Process
The financial planning process starts with an honest assessment of where you are now, followed by setting goals, defining and implementing plans, measuring your progress, then adjusting if needed.

Exhibit C.4
Devon Anderson's
Net Worth
Devon Anderson's net worth is currently negative, driven in large part by her school loans. However, she now knows exactly where she stands and can start working to improve her balance.

Assets

Cash accounts	Checking account	$ 450.67
	Savings account	927.89
Investments	50 shares Microsoft	1,302.50
Retirement accounts	(none)	
Automobiles	2001 Escort	5,500.00
Personal property	Jewelry	1,800.00
	Furniture	2,000.00
	Computer	450.00
Total assets		**$12,431.06**

Liabilities

Current bills (due within 30 days)	Rent	$ 650.00
	Visa	120.00
	MasterCard	195.00
	Car payment	327.25
Credit card debt	Visa	1,185.34
	MasterCard	2,431.60
Housing debt	(none)	
Automobile loans	2001 Escort	3,880.10
Other debt	Student loans	22,560.00
Total liabilities		**$31,349.29**
Net worth (total assets − total liabilities)		**($18,918.23)**

to cover to give you an average monthly value. Next, list all your expenses. If you're in the habit of using debit cards, credit cards, or a checkbook for most of your expenses, this task is fairly easy, since your statements will show where the money is going. However, if you tend to use cash for a lot of purchases, you'll need to get in the habit of recording those purchases. (Using cash has the major advantage of limiting your spending to money that you actually have, but it doesn't leave a "paper trail," so you have to keep track of the spending yourself.) Exhibit C.5 shows Devon's income and expense statement.

Assembling your balance sheet and your income and expense statement can be a chore the first time around, but updating it as you make progress is much easier. By the way, software such as Intuit Quicken or Microsoft Money can simplify these tasks, but it's not absolutely necessary. You can do all your record keeping in a spreadsheet (the software is probably already on your computer), or simply keep records in a notebook. How you record your data is less important than making sure you do it.

Set Realistic Financial Goals

Now that you've gotten through the chore of assessing your current financial situation, the next step is setting goals. Take some time with this step. Your goals will drive all your financial decisions from here on out, so make sure they're the right ones for you. For instance, saving up for an early retirement requires a different financial strategy than saving up to take a year off in the middle of your career. Think carefully about what you really value in life. Discuss your dreams and plans with family and friends. Is making a million dollars by the time you're 40 your most important goal, and are you willing to work around the clock to get there? Or would you rather accumulate wealth more slowly and live at a more relaxed pace? Do you want to start a family when you're 25? 35?

Income	
Wages (take home, average per month)	$1,230.00
Help from the parents	450.00
Total income	**$ 1,680.00**
Expenses (average monthly)	
Rent	$ 650.00
Gas bill	34.00
Electric bill	76.00
Cell phone	98.00
Food	315.00
Misc. household supplies	45.00
School materials & supplies	22.00
Car payment	327.25
Gasoline	38.00
Sailing club	78.25
Clothes	188.00
Entertainment & fast food	325.00
Visa payment	120.00
MasterCard payment	195.00
Total expenses	**$2,511.50**
Monthly difference	**($ 831.50)**

Exhibit C.5
Devon Anderson's
Income and Expense
Statement
Devon was surprised to learn that she has been spending over $800 more every month than she takes in. Since she can't work any more hours without compromising her studies and she is reluctant to ask her parents for more, the only solution is to cut expenses. After some careful thought, she realizes that by cutting her cell phone usage in half (or finding a better deal), dropping the sailing club, economizing on groceries, and cutting way back on entertainment, fast food, and new clothes, she can almost break even every month.

Perhaps being able to take care of an aging relative is important. In spite of what you might hear in TV commercials, you can't have it all, but you can make trade-offs that are compatible with your personal goals and values.

No matter what they might be, effective financial goals have two aspects in common: They are *specific* and they are *realistic*. "I want to be rich" and "I just don't want to have to worry about money" are not good goal statements because both are too general to give you any guidance. For one person, "not worrying about money" could require $100,000 a year, but another person might get by on only $50,000 a year. You can certainly start with a general desire, such as wealth or freedom from worry, but you need to translate that into real numbers so you can craft a meaningful plan.

In addition to making them specific, make sure your goals are realistic. Lots of young people start out life saying they'd like to make a million by age 30 or retire by age 40. These are wonderful desires, but for most people, they simply aren't realistic. The problem with having unrealistic goals is that you'll be repeatedly frustrated by your inability to meet them, and you're more likely to give up on your financial plan as a result.[9] While amassing a million dollars in the first 10 years of your career is highly unlikely, amassing a million dollars in 40, 30, or sometimes even 20 years is quite attainable for many professional wage earners. A few minutes with a financial calculator will help you assess the various possibilities and determine what is reasonable for you. (If you don't have a calculator with financial functions or software such as Quicken or Money, visit www.choosetosave.org/tools, which offers a wide variety of online calculators. In fact, just playing around with the many calculators on this site will teach you a fair amount about financial planning.)

You can find a wide range of free financial-planning tools online, such as these calculators offered by the "Choose to Save" program at www. choosetosave.org.

Many people find it helpful to divide financial goals into short, medium, and long term. Your personal time frame for each might vary, but in general, short-term goals will get you through your current financial situation, medium-term goals will get you into the next stage in your life, and long-term goals will get you completely set for life. For some people, this planning might split up into 1 year or less, 2 to 5 years, and 6 years and beyond. For others, short term might be the next 5 years, medium could be 6 to 10, and long term beyond 10 years.[10] The important thing is to consider the phases in your life and establish goals for each phase. Also, think carefully about the type of goals you wish to achieve. For instance, acquiring a ranch might be a significant goal for you, whereas someone who loves to travel may have little interest in real estate. Similarly, if you find that you have a low tolerance for risk or a number of loved ones depend on you, comprehensive insurance coverage might be a significant goal. So go ahead and earn that million if you want to, but make sure you know *why* you're earning it.

Create and Implement a Practical Plan to Meet Your Goals

You've thought about your goals and defined some that are specific and realistic. You're inspired and ready to start. What's next? For all the thousands of books, television shows, magazines, software products, and websites devoted to money, financial success really boils down to one beautifully—and brutally—simple formula: Earn more, spend less, and make better choices with what you have left over. On the plus side, this is an easy concept to understand. On the minus side, it's completely unforgiving. If you're spending more than you're earning or making bad choices with your savings and investments, you're never going to reach your goals until you can turn things around. The sections on life stages later in this appendix explore some of the details of these three components, but here's a brief overview to put it all in context.

- *Earn more.* Particularly in the early stages of your career, income from your job will probably provide most or all of your income, so be sure to maximize your earning potential. As you get more established and have the opportunity to invest, you can start earning income from real estate, stocks and other investments, and perhaps businesses that you either own yourself or own a share of. As you move into retirement, your sources of income will shift to returns from your own investments, along with both

In fact, if you're like most college students, you'll go through at least four major stages in your financial life: getting through college, establishing a financial foundation, building your net worth and preparing for life's major expenses, and planning for retirement. (If you're back in college after having been in the workforce for a while, your situation might vary.) The following sections give you an overview of the decisions to consider at each major stage in your life.

Life Stage 1: Getting Through College

The most important financial advice for college students can be summed up in a single phrase: Make sure you graduate. With tuition and expenses rising so rapidly these days, completing your education can be a mammoth struggle, to be sure, but if you leave school early, you will dramatically reduce your earning power throughout your entire career. In today's job market, the average difference between having a bachelor's degree and not having one is at least $15,000 a year. Advanced degrees add even more to your earning power.[14] Multiply those numbers by 40 or 45 years in the workforce, and a college diploma can be worth a half million dollars or more. No matter how desperate things might be, do everything possible to stay in school. Ask for advice—and help—if you need it. Many people find doing so uncomfortable or embarrassing, but you're almost guaranteed to regret it later if you don't ask when you really do need help. Talk to a counselor in your school's financial aid office. Ask friends and family for advice. If you have a job, see whether your employer is willing to assist with school expenses. Make sure you're getting all the financial aid you're eligible for, too. A number of websites can help you explore all the options, including www.fastweb.com, www.fafsa.gov, and www.loans4students.org.

Is it a good idea to borrow money to get through college? Absolutely, as long as the money goes toward the essential elements of your education and not toward the weekend's entertainment possibilities. This point leads to the second most important piece of advice for college students: Don't dig yourself into a giant hole with credit card debt. The average U.S. college student today has over $3,000 in credit card debt, and one in 10 has nearly $8,000.[15] If you're already in a hole, don't panic, but do stop digging.

Your first step to recovery is to recognize that you're at a make-or-break point in both your college career and your life as a whole. No amount of extracurricular fun is worth the damage that a credit card mess can inflict on your life. Excessive credit card debt from college can follow you for decades, limiting your ability to pay off student loans and purchase a car or a house, warns Sophia Jackson, a North Carolina financial adviser who counsels many students from schools in the area. She describes debt problems with college-age consumers as "absolutely epidemic."[16] Too many students drop out of college because of credit card debt, and many more spend years after graduation paying off debt they probably shouldn't have accumulated in the first place. Don't assume you can ring up a big balance during college and easily pay it off when you start working, either. Many graduates entering the workforce are disappointed to find themselves bringing home less and paying out more than they expected. You'll be facing student loan repayments and a host of new expenses, from housing to transportation to a business-quality wardrobe; you can't afford to devote a big chunk of your new salary to paying off your beer and pizza bills from the previous four years.

Your second step is to compile your income and expense statement as described earlier so you know where all that borrowed money is going. Do a thorough and honest evaluation of your expenses: How much of your spending is going toward junk food, clubbing, concert tickets, video games, and other nonessentials? At first, it won't seem possible that these small-ticket items can add up to big trouble, but it happens to thousands of

*Do you really need it?
Every purchase you
make now means you
have less money to
save and invest for the
future.*

college students every year. Most colleges and college towns offer a wide spectrum of free
and low-cost entertainment options. With a little effort and creativity, anyone can find
ways to reduce nonessential expenses, often by hundreds of dollars a month. As noted earlier, a few sacrifices now can make all the difference.

Life Stage 2: Building Your Financial Foundation

Whew, you made it. You scraped by to graduation, found a decent job, and now are ready
to get really serious about financial planning. First, give yourself a pat on the back; it's a
major accomplishment in life. Second, dust off that financial plan you put together in
college. It's time to update it to reflect your new status in life. Third, don't lose those frugal habits you learned in college. Keep your *fixed expenses,* those bills you have to pay
every month no matter what, as low as possible. Some of these expenses are mandatory,
such as transportation and housing, but others may not be. Such things as gym and club
memberships, additional phone lines, and subscriptions have a tendency to creep into
your budget and gradually raise your expenses. Before you know it, you could be
shelling out hundreds of dollars a month on these recurring but often nonessential
expenses.

Among the important decisions you may need to make at this stage involve paying for
transportation and housing, taking steps to maximize your earning power, and managing
your cash and credit wisely.

Paying for Transportation

Transportation is likely to be one of your biggest ongoing expenses, if transportation for
you means owning or leasing a vehicle. The *true cost* of owning a vehicle is significantly higher than the price tag. You'll probably have to finance it, you'll definitely need
to insure it, and you'll face recurring costs for fuel and maintenance. And unfortunately,
unlike houses, which often *appreciate* in value, cars always *depreciate* in value (with

extremely rare exceptions, such as classic cars). In fact, that lovely new ride can lose as much as 20 percent of its value the instant you drive away from the dealership. If you pay $25,000 for a car, for example, your net worth could drop $5,000 before you've driven your first mile. And if you took out a five-, six-, or seven-year loan, you'll probably owe more than the car is worth for the first several years, a situation known as having an "upside-down" loan. In fact, 40 percent of new-car buyers now owe more on their trade-ins than those cars are worth.[17]

There is good news, however. Most cars tend not to depreciate much during their second, third, and fourth years, then plummet again after five years. You can take advantage of this effect by looking for a used car that is one year old, driving it for three years, then selling it.[18] Automotive websites such as www.edmunds.com offer a wealth of information about depreciation and other costs, including the true cost of owning any given model. Also check with your insurance company before buying any car, as some models cost considerably more to insure.

Negotiating the purchase of a car ranks high on most consumers' list of dreaded experiences. You can level the playing field, at least somewhat, by remembering two important issues. First, most buyers worry only about the monthly payment, which can be a costly mistake. Salespeople usually negotiate with four or even five variables at once, including the monthly payment, purchase price, down payment, value of your trade-in, and terms of your loan. If you don't pay attention to these other variables, you can get a low monthly payment and still get a bad deal. Experts suggest arranging your financing ahead of time, then negotiating only the purchase price when you're at the dealership.[19] If you're not comfortable negotiating, consider using a car-buying service such as CarsDirect.com (www.carsdirect.com).

Leasing, rather than buying, is a popular option with many consumers. In general, the biggest advantage of leasing is lower monthly payments than with a purchase (or a nicer car for the same monthly payment, depending on how you look at it). However, leases are even more complicated than purchases, so it's even more important to know what you're getting into. Also, leases usually aren't the best choice for consumers who want to minimize their long-term costs. To learn more about leasing, visit www.leaseguide.com.

Paying for Housing

Housing also presents you with a lease-versus-buy decision, although purchasing a house has two huge advantages that purchasing a car doesn't have: Most houses appreciate in value, and the interest on the **mortgage** reduces taxable income. And compared to renting, buying your own place also lets you build **equity**, the portion of the house's value that you own. These three factors mean that real estate is nearly always a recommended investment for anyone who can afford it. However, there are times when renting makes better financial sense. The **closing costs** for real estate—all the fees and commissions associated with buying or selling a house—can be considerable. Closing costs can represent from 3 to 6 percent of the price of a home. Depending on how fast your house's value rises, you may need to stay there two or three years just to recoup your closing costs before selling.

If you think that a job change, an upcoming marriage, or any other event in your life might require you to move in the near future, plug your numbers into a "rent versus own" calculator to see which option makes more sense. You can find several of these calculators online; two handy examples are at HomeLoanCenter.com (www.homeloancenter.com/loancalculator/maincalculator.aspx, then select "Rent vs. Own") and Choose to Save (www.choosetosave.org/tools/fincalcs.htm#bud, then select "Am I Better Off Renting?" from the list of home mortgage calculators).

mortgage
A loan used to purchase real estate

equity
The portion of a house's current value that you own

closing costs
Fees associated with buying and selling a house

When you are ready to buy, take your time. Choosing a house to buy is the most complicated financial decision many people will ever make, involving everything from property values in the neighborhood to the condition of the house to the details of the financial transaction. Fortunately, you can learn more about home ownership from a number of sources. Check local lenders and real estate agencies for free seminars. Online sources include the U.S. Department of Housing and Urban Development (www.hud.gov) and MSN House and Home (http://houseandhome.msn.com). Buying your own house can and should be a wonderful experience, but don't let emotional factors lead you to a decision that doesn't make financial sense. Keep in mind that a house is both a home and an investment.

Maximizing Your Earning Power

Why do some people peak at earning $40,000 or $50,000 a year while others go on to earn 2 or 3 or 10 times that much? Because your salary is likely to be the primary "engine" of your financial success, this question warrants careful consideration. The profession you choose is one of the biggest factors, of course, but even within a given profession, you'll often find a wide range of income levels. A number of factors influence these variations, including education, individual talents, ambition, location, contacts, and good old-fashioned luck. You can change some of these factors throughout your career, but some you can't. However, compensation experts stress that virtually everyone can improve his or her earning power by following these tips:[20]

- *Know what you're worth.* The more informed you are about your competitive value in the marketplace, the better chance you have of negotiating a salary that reflects your worth. Several websites offer salary-level information that will help you decide your personal value, including www.bls.gov, www.salary.com, www.vault.com, and www.salaryexpert.com. (Some of these sites charge a modest fee for customized reports, but the information could be worth many times what you pay for it.)
- *Be ready to articulate your value.* In addition to knowing what other people in your profession make, you need to be able to explain to your current employer or a potential

Buying a house could be the one of the most important financial decisions you ever make.

new employer why you're worth the money you think you deserve. Collect concrete examples of how you've helped companies earn more or spend less in the past—and be ready to explain how you can do so in the future. Moreover, seek out opportunities that let you increase and demonstrate your worth.

- ***Don't overlook the value of employee benefits, performance incentives, and perks.*** For instance, even if you can't negotiate the salary you'd really like, maybe you can negotiate extra time off or a flexible schedule that would allow you to run a home-based business on the side. Or perhaps you can negotiate a bonus arrangement that rewards you for higher-than-average performance.
- ***Understand the salary structure in your company.*** If you hope to rise through the ranks and make $200,000 as a vice president, for instance, but the CEO is making only $150,000, your goal is obviously unrealistic. Some companies pay top performers well above market average, whereas others stick closely to industry norms.
- ***Study top performers.*** Some employees have the misperception that top executives must have "clawed their way" to the top or stepped on everyone else on their way up. In most cases, the opposite is true. Employees and managers who continue to rise through the organization do so because they make people around them successful. Being successful on your own is one thing; helping an entire department or an entire company be successful is the kind of behavior that catches the attention of the people who write the really big paychecks.

Managing Cash

When those paychecks start rolling in, you'll need to set up a system of **cash management**, your personal system for handling cash and other **liquid assets**, which are those that can be quickly and easily converted to cash. You have many alternatives nowadays for storing cash, from a basic savings account to a variety of investment funds, but most offer interest rates that are below the average level of inflation. In other words, if you were to keep all your money in such places, your buying power would slowly but surely erode over time. Consequently, the basic challenge of cash management is keeping enough cash or other liquid assets available to cover your near-term needs without keeping so much cash that you lose out on investment growth opportunities or fall prey to inflation. Once again, your budget planning will come to the rescue by showing you how much money you need month to month. Financial experts also recommend keeping anywhere from three to six months' worth of basic living expenses in an *emergency fund* that you can access if you find yourself between jobs or have other unexpected needs.

Chapter 17 introduced the wide variety of financial institutions that offer ways to store and protect your cash. Just as there are a number of alternatives to the traditional bank these days, you can also choose from several different options for holding cash (see Exhibit C.6 for a summary of their advantages and disadvantages):[21]

- ***Checking accounts.*** Whether it's a traditional checking account from your neighborhood bank, an online account at an Internet bank, or a brokerage account with check-writing privileges, your checking account will serve as your primary cash management tool. A checking account can be either a demand deposit, which doesn't pay interest, or an interest-bearing or negotiable order of withdrawal (NOW) account.
- ***Savings accounts.*** Savings accounts are convenient places to store small amounts of money. Many savings accounts can be linked to a checking account for quick access to your cash. Although they're convenient and safe, savings accounts nearly always offer interest rates below average inflation rates, so the buying power of your account steadily diminishes.

cash management
All of the planning and activities associated with managing your cash and other liquid assets

liquid assets
Assets that can be quickly and easily converted to cash

Exhibit C.6
Places to Stash Your Cash
You can find quite a few places to park your cash, but they're not all created equal.

Type of Account	Advantages	Disadvantages
Checking account (demand deposit)	Convenient, usually no minimum balance needed to open, often provides online banking and access via ATMs, insured against losses due to bank failure	Does not earn any interest
Checking account (NOW account)	Convenience of a regular checking account, plus you earn interest on your balance; insured	Some institutions require a minimum balance to open an account; modest interest rates
Savings account	Slightly higher interest rate than on typical checking account, often linked to a checking account for simple transfers; insured	Low interest rates; not as liquid as checking accounts (except for linked accounts, in which you can easily transfer funds to checking)
Money market deposit account	Higher interest rates than checking or savings accounts; insured	High minimum balances; limited check writing; fees can limit real returns
Money market mutual fund	Higher interest rates than many other cash management options	Not insured (but limited exposure to risk); minimum balance requirements; limited check writing
Asset management account	Convenience of having cash readily available for investment purposes; higher interest rates than regular checking or savings accounts; consolidated statements show most of your cash management and investing activity	Expensive (high monthly fees); large minimum balances; restrictions on check writing privileges (such as high minimum amounts) can limit usefulness as regular checking account; not insured against losses
Certificate of deposit	Higher interest rates that are fixed and therefore predictable; insured	Minimum balance requirements; limited liquidity (your money is tied up for weeks, months, or years)

- *Money market accounts.* Money market accounts, sometimes called money market deposit accounts, are an alternative to savings accounts; the primary difference is that they have variable interest rates that are usually higher than savings account rates.
- *Money market mutual funds.* Money market mutual funds, sometimes called money funds, are similar to stock mutual funds, although they invest in *debt instruments* such as bonds, rather than stocks.
- *Asset management accounts.* Brokerage firms and mutual fund companies frequently offer **asset management accounts** as a way to manage cash that isn't currently invested in stocks or stock mutual funds.
- *Certificate of deposits.* With a certificate of deposit (CD), you are essentially lending a specific amount of money to a bank or other institution for a specific length of time and a specific interest rate. The length of time can range from a week to several years; the longer the time span and the larger the amount, the higher the interest rate.

No matter which types of accounts you choose, make sure you understand all the associated fees—which might not be clearly labeled as fees, either. Some accounts charge a fee every month, some charge fees when your balance drops below a certain amount or you write too many checks, and so on. For accounts with checking capability, **overdraft fees**

asset management accounts
Cash management accounts offered by brokerage firms and mutual fund companies, frequently as a way to manage cash that isn't currently invested elsewhere

overdraft fees
Penalties charged against your checking account when you write checks that total more than your available balance

can chew up hundreds of dollars if you bounce checks frequently. Also, be sure to verify your account statement every month and **reconcile** your checking account to make sure you and the bank agree on the balance.

Managing Credit

Even if you never want to use a credit card or borrow money, it's increasingly difficult to get by without credit in today's consumer environment. For instance, car rental companies usually require a credit card before you can rent a car, and landlords want to verify your **credit history**, a record of your mortgages, consumer loans (such as financing provided by a home appliance store), credit card accounts, and bill-paying performance. Banks and other companies voluntarily provide this information to **credit bureaus**, businesses that compile **credit reports**. As you read in Chapter 11, an increasing number of employers are looking into the credit history of job applicants as well. Moreover, you may find yourself in need of a loan you didn't anticipate, and getting a loan without a credit history is not easy. Consequently, building and maintaining a solid credit history needs to be a part of your lifetime financial plan.

To build a good credit history, apply for a modest amount of sensible credit (a credit card, auto loan, or a line of credit at a bank, for instance), use that credit periodically, and make sure that at least some credit is being established in your name. If an account is in someone else's name, such as a parent, spouse, or domestic partner, you won't "get credit" for a good payment history, even if you provide some or all of the money.[22] This situation can be a troublesome one for married women in households where most of the accounts are in the husband's name. Applying for credit after a divorce or death of the husband can be difficult for women who haven't built up credit in their own names. Most important of all is to pay all your bills on time. If you find that you can't pay a particular bill on time, call the company and explain your situation. You may get some leniency by showing that you're making a good faith effort to pay your bill.

Experts also recommend that you verify the accuracy of your credit report once a year. Mistakes do creep into credit reports from time to time, and you also need to make sure you haven't been a victim of identity theft, in which someone illegally applies for credit using your name. Actually, you don't have just one credit report. The three major credit reporting agencies in the United States each keep a file on you and provide their own credit reports to lenders, landlords, and others with a valid need to see them. For more information, visit Experian (www.experian.com), TransUnion (www.transunion.com), or Equifax (www.equifax.com).

Managing your credit wisely will help you avoid one of the most traumatic events that can befall a consumer: **personal bankruptcy**. You have several options for declaring bankruptcy, but none of them is desirable and all should be avoided by every means possible. Declaring bankruptcy, even if for an unavoidable reason such as medical costs or loss of a spouse, is sometimes called "the 10-year mistake" because it stays on your credit record for 10 years.[23] Bankruptcy is not a simple cure-all, as it is sometimes presented. If you are considering bankruptcy, talk to a counselor first. Start with the National Foundation for Credit Counseling (www.nfcc.org). Wherever you turn for advice, make sure you understand it thoroughly and understand why the organization would be motivated to give you that particular advice. You've probably seen ads (and a torrent of spam e-mail) offering ways to get out from under your debt. Many of these schemes involve declaring bankruptcy, which may not be the right choice for you.[24]

After years of growing concern about the number of U.S. consumers filing for personal bankruptcy, Congress modified the bankruptcy filing process in 2005—and made it considerably more difficult for many people to file for bankruptcy. Consumers wishing to file for

reconcile
The process of comparing the balance you believe is in your account with the balance the bank believes is in your account

credit history
A record of your mortgages, consumer loans, credit card accounts (including credit limits and current balances), and bill-paying performance

credit bureaus
Businesses that compile credit information on businesses and individual consumers

credit reports
Reports generated by credit bureaus, showing an individual's credit usage and payment history

personal bankruptcy
A condition in which a consumer is unable to repay his or her debts; depending on the type of bankruptcy, a court will either forgive many of the person's debts or establish a compatible repayment plan

bankruptcy protection must first submit to *credit counseling,* which is designed to explore alternatives to bankruptcy. The outcome of credit counseling is likely to depend largely on household income: those with high incomes will be encouraged to get their spending under control, those with moderate incomes will be encouraged to apply for a *debt-management plan* (an agreement to stop using credit cards and pay off existing balances, possibly in exchange for reduced interest rates), and those with lower incomes and therefore less hope of paying off their debts over time will be directed toward bankruptcy filing. For anyone who still seeks bankruptcy, the popular *Chapter 7* bankruptcy, in which all debts are wiped out, is now more difficult to obtain. Consumers with income above a certain threshold (which varies by state) are now required to file for *Chapter 13* bankruptcy instead, in which debts are consolidated but still must be repaid over a number of years.[25]

Stage 3: Increasing Your Net Worth and Preparing for Life's Major Expenses

With your basic needs taken care of and a solid foundation under your feet, the next stage of your financial life is increasing your net worth and preparing for both expected and unexpected expenses. Some of the major decisions at this stage include investments, taxes, insurance, your children's education, and emergency planning.

Investing: Building Your Nest Egg

The various cash management options described earlier can be an effective way to store and protect money you already have, but they aren't terribly good at generating more money. That's the goal of *investing,* in which you buy something of value with the idea that it will increase in value before you sell it to someone else. You read about the most common financial investment vehicles in Chapter 18: stocks, mutual funds, and bonds. Real estate is the other major category of investment for most people, not only their own homes but also rental properties and commercial real estate. The final category of investments includes precious metals (primarily gold), gems, and collectibles such as sports or movie memorabilia.

The details of successful investing in these various areas differ widely, but six general rules apply to all of them:

- ***Don't invest cash that you may need in the short term.*** You may not be able to *liquidate* the investment (selling it to retrieve your cash) in time, or the value may be temporarily down, in which case you'll permanently lose money.
- ***Don't invest in anything you don't understand or haven't thoroughly evaluated.*** If you can't point to specific reasons that the investment should increase in value, you're simply guessing or gambling.
- ***Don't invest on emotion.*** You might love eating at a certain restaurant chain, shopping at a particular online retailer, or collecting baseball cards, but that doesn't mean any of these is automatically a good investment.
- ***Understand the risks.*** Aside from Treasury bills and U.S. savings bonds, virtually no investment can guarantee that you'll make money or even protect the money you originally invested. You could lose most or all of your money, thanks to the risk/reward trade-off discussed earlier. To give yourself the opportunity to realize higher gains, you nearly always need to accept higher levels of risk.
- ***Beware of anybody who promises guaranteed results or instant wealth.*** Chances are that person will profit more by snaring you into the investment than you'll earn from the investment yourself.
- ***Given the risks involved, don't put all your eggs in one basket.*** Diversify your investments to make sure you don't leave yourself vulnerable to downturns in a single stock or piece of real estate, for instance.

If you plan to invest in a specific area, you would be wise to take a course in that area or commit to learning on your own. Most of the websites mentioned throughout this appendix offer information, and some offer formal courses you can take online. Investment clubs are an increasingly popular way to learn and pool your resources with other individual investors, too. In the beginning, don't worry about the details of particular stocks or the intricacies of real estate investment trusts and other more advanced concepts. Focus on the fundamentals: Why do stock prices increase or decrease? What effect do interest rates have on bonds? How can a particular house increase in value dramatically while another in the same neighborhood stays flat?

You can also practice investing without risking any money. This is a smart move early in your career, when you're still getting on your feet and may not have much money to invest yet. After you've learned the basics of stock investing, for instance, set up a "mock portfolio" on one of the many online sites that provide free portfolio tracking. Month by month, monitor the performance of your choices. Whenever you see a big increase or decrease, dig deeper to understand why. By practicing first, you can learn from your mistakes before those mistakes cost you any money.

Taxes: Minimizing the Bite

Taxes will be a constant factor in your personal financial planning. You pay *sales tax* on many of the products you buy (in all but five states at present); you pay federal *excise taxes* on certain purchases such as gasoline and phone service; you pay *property tax* on real estate; and you pay *income tax* on both earned income (wages, salaries, tips, bonuses, commissions, and business profits) and investment income. The total taxes paid by individuals vary widely, but you can safely assume that taxes will consume 30 to 40 cents of every dollar you make.

Your personal tax strategy should focus on minimizing the taxes you are required to pay, without running afoul of the law or harming your financial progress (for instance, you usually don't want to skip an investment opportunity just because you'll have to pay tax on your gains). Put another way, you are expected to pay your fair share of taxes, but no one expects you to pay more than your share.

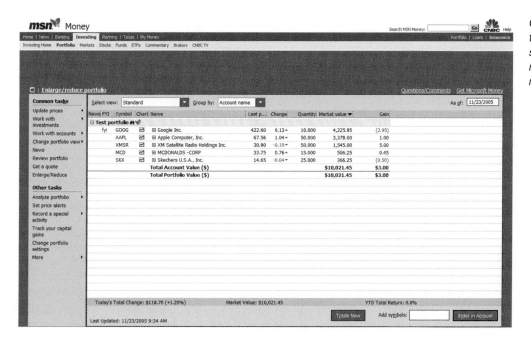

Create a mock portfolio to test your stock-market skills before you invest real money in the market.

deductions
Opportunities to reduce taxable income by subtracting the cost of a specific item, such as business expenses or interest paid on home mortgages

exemptions
Reductions to taxable income based on the number of dependents in the household

tax-exempt investments
Investments (usually municipal bonds) whose income is not subject to federal income tax

tax-deferred investments
Investments such as 401(k) plans and IRAs that let you deduct the amount of your investments from your gross income (thereby lowering your taxable income); you don't have to pay tax on any of the income from these investments until you start to withdraw money during retirement

tax credits
Direct reductions in your tax obligation

will
A legal document that specifies what happens to your assets, who will execute your estate (carry out the terms of your will), and who will be the legal guardian of your children, if you have any, in the event of your death

You can reduce taxes in three basic ways: (1) by reducing your consumption of goods and services that are subject to either sales tax or excise taxes, (2) by reducing your *taxable income,* or (3) by reducing your tax through the use of *tax credits.* Reducing consumption is a straightforward concept, although there are obviously limits to how far you can reduce consumption and therefore this portion of your tax obligation.

Reducing your taxable income is more complicated but can have a great impact on your finances (by the way, reducing your taxable income means reducing the part of your income that is subject to local, state, or federal income tax, not reducing your overall income level). Authorities such as the IRS allow a variety of **deductions**, such as interest paid on home mortgages and the costs associated with using part of your home for office space. Qualifying deductions can be subtracted from your *gross income* to lower your taxable income. A portion of your income is also *exempt* from federal income tax, based on the number of dependents in your household. The more **exemptions** you can legally claim, the lower your taxable income. You can also lower your taxable income by investing a portion of your income in *tax-exempt* or *tax-deferred* investments. With **tax-exempt investments** (which are primarily bonds issued by local governments), you don't have to pay federal income tax on any income you earn from the investment. With **tax-deferred investments**, such as 401(k) plans and individual retirement accounts (IRAs), you can deduct the amount of money you invest every year from your gross income, and you don't have to pay tax on income from the investment until you withdraw money during retirement.

Unlike deductions, which only reduce your taxable income and therefore reduce your tax burden by your tax rate, **tax credits** reduce your tax obligation directly. In other words, a $100 *deduction* reduces your tax bill by $28 (if you're in the 28 percent tax bracket, for instance), whereas a $100 *credit* reduces your tax bill by $100.

Personal tax software such as TurboTax (www.turbotax.com) or TaxCut (www.taxcut.com) can guide you through the process of finding deductions and credits. For more complex scenarios, though, it's always a good idea to get the advice of a professional tax adviser.

Insurance: Protecting Yourself, Your Family, and Your Assets

Unfortunately, things go wrong in life, from accidents to health problems to the death of an income provider. Insurance is designed to protect you, your family, and your assets if and when these unpleasant events occur. In a sense, insurance is the ultimate risk/reward trade-off decision. If you had an ironclad guarantee that you would never get sick or injured, you would have no need for health insurance. However, there's a reasonable chance that you will need medical attention at some point, and major injuries and illness can generate many thousands of dollars of unplanned expenses. Consequently, most people consider it a reasonable trade-off to pay for health insurance to protect themselves from catastrophic financial blows. Exhibit C.7 provides a brief overview of your most significant insurance options.

Another vital step to protecting your family, and one that is often overlooked by younger people, is preparing a **will**, a legal document that specifies what happens to your assets (as well as who will be legal guardian of your children, if you have any) in the event of your death.

Stage 4: Plan for a Secure, Independent Retirement

Retirement? You're only 25 years old (or 35 or 45). Yes, but as you saw earlier in the discussion of compound interest, it's never too early to start planning for retirement. It's tempting to picture retirement as a carefree time when you can finally ditch your job and

Category	Highlights
Medical insurance	Usually purchased as part of group coverage, such as through an employer or a union; individual or single family is available but often more expensive; most plans offer a variety of cost and coverage options—for instance, to lower your monthly costs you can select a higher deductible, which is the amount you have to pay before insurance coverage kicks in; selecting the right plan requires a careful analysis of your needs and financial circumstances
Disability insurance	Temporarily replaces a portion of your salary if you are unable to work; various policies have different definitions of "disability" and restrictions on coverage and payments
Auto insurance	Most states now have *compulsory liability insurance laws*, meaning that you have to prove that you are covered for any damage you might cause as a driver; coverage for your vehicle can be both *collision* (damages resulting from collisions) and *comprehensive* (other damages or theft); you can also buy coverage to protect yourself from illegally uninsured motorists
Homeowners' insurance	Most policies include both *property loss coverage* (to replace or repair the home and its contents) and *liability coverage* (to protect you in case someone sues you); often required by the lender when you have a mortgage
Life insurance	Primary purpose is to provide for others in the event that your death would create a financial hardship for them; common forms are *term life* (limited duration, less expensive, no investment value), *whole-life* (permanent coverage, builds cash value over time, more expensive than term life), and *universal life* (similar to whole-life but more flexible)

Exhibit C.7
Understanding Your Insurance Options
You can buy insurance for every eventuality from earthquake damage to vacation interruptions, but the most common and most important types include medical, disability, auto, home owners', and life insurance.

focus on hobbies, travel, volunteer work, and the hundred other activities you haven't had time for all your life. Sadly, the reality for millions of retired people today is much different. Between skyrocketing medical costs, the dot-com devastation in the stock market, and lower than expected company pensions in some cases, retirement for many people is a never-ending financial struggle with little hope for improvement.

Perhaps the most important step you can take toward a more positive retirement is to shed all of the misconceptions that people often have about retirement planning:[26]

- *My living expenses will drop so I'll need less money.* Some of your expenses may well drop, but rising health care costs will probably swamp any reductions you have in housing, clothing, transportation, and other personal costs.
- *I'll live for roughly 15 years after I retire.* The big advantage of that expensive health care is that people are living longer and longer. You could live for 20 or 30 years after you retire.
- *Social Security will cover my basic living expenses.* Social Security probably won't cover even your basic requirements, and the entire system is in serious financial trouble. While it's unlikely that political leaders would ever let Social Security collapse, the safest bet is to not count on it at all.
- *My employer will keep funding my pension and health insurance.* Thousands of retirees in recent years have been devastated by former employers who either curtailed or eliminated pension and health coverage.
- *I can't save much right now, so there's no point in saving anything at all.* If you find yourself thinking this, remind yourself of the magic of compounding. Over

time, small amounts grow into large amounts of money. Do whatever it takes to get started now.

- ***I have plenty of time to worry about retirement later.*** Unfortunately, you don't. The longer you wait, the harder it will become to ensure a comfortable retirement. If you're not prepared, your only option will be to continue working well into your 70s or 80s.

In other words, the situation is serious. However, that doesn't mean it's hopeless—not by any means. You control your destiny, and you don't need to abandon all pleasures and comforts now to make it happen. However, you do need to put a plan together and start saving now. Make retirement planning a positive part of your personal financial planning, part of your dream of living the life you want to live.

Getting Started with Business PlanPro Software

Business PlanPro (BPP) software is a template for crafting a winning business plan. The software is designed to stimulate your thinking about the many tasks and decisions that go into planning and running a business. The software does not do your thinking for you. Instead, it leads you through a thought process by asking you to respond to questions about your business and to provide data for the preformatted tables and charts. Accompanying instructions, examples, and sample business plans provide you with a full range of assistance you can use to draft your own comprehensive business plan. By working these exercises, you will gain a practical skill for your business career.

When installing BPP, be sure to install Adobe Acrobat Reader, so you can view the sample business plans included with the disk and download them from the web. You can get an overview of the BPP software by clicking on the Help menu from the main screen, then selecting About Business PlanPro. Under the Help menu, you can click on Contents and then Getting Help for operational instructions or to look up business terms in the software's Glossary. For quick answers to questions about using the software, look under the How Do I menu at the top right of the screen. An overview of the software's features is also on the web at www.paloalto.com/prenticehall.

Navigating the Software

One of the best ways to become familiar with the BPP software is by navigating one of the BPP sample business plans. Launch the BPP software, then click on Create a New Business Plan to reach the main screen. Now choose File from the menu and click Open Sample. This brings you to the Sample Plan Browser. An alternate way to get to this screen is by clicking on the Research It menu along the left of the screen, then selecting Sample Plan Browser.

The names of the sample plans are listed on the left, and the first page of plans bundled with the software can be seen on the right. To view a sample plan, double-click on the plan name. To page through a plan, simply click on the arrows on the bottom of the frame in which the plan pages appear. If you have an Internet connection, the software will download the latest version of the sample plan. You can also check the web at www.bplans.com/sp to search through dozens of sample plans created using BPP software.

To see how a sample plan in the BPP software is organized or to move between sections in your order, click the Show/Hide Navigation icon to the right of the printer icon on the menu above the sample plan page. When you click on a section name, the plan displays that page.

As you will see when exploring the sample plans, the Executive Summary section provides a brief overview of the business plan. The Company Summary discusses company specifics such as the mission and ownership. The Products and Services section describes exactly what the company is selling. The Market Analysis examines the company's market, including competitors and customers. The Strategy and Implementation section indicates the company's broad course of action in the market, its sales goals, and how it will implement the plan. The Management Summary introduces the organizational structure and management personnel. Finally, the Financial Plan section presents profit-and-loss projections and other financial plans.

You may find it helpful to print out a full copy of the sample plan you have selected and review it as you navigate its contents on your screen. This way you can see how the software uses the information to construct a formal business plan. To print out the sample plan, click on the Printer icon and select Plan. You may also choose to print selected sections or the instructions or examples for a business plan. Once you've finished viewing or printing sample plans, click to close the frame and return to the main screen.

You have multiple options for accessing the same information, as shown under the View menu. The Plan Manager option guides you through the process of researching a plan, building it, distributing and delivering it, and making it happen. The Plan Outline option allows you to develop the plan section by section in outline form. To access the text mode option, where you write your business plan's text, select Text Mode from the View menu. You can move between sections by selecting from topics in the Topic drop-down menu above the text screen or using the forward and backward arrows at the right of the Topic menu. To view related tables and charts, click the Table mode or the Chart mode under the View menu.

Creating a Winning Business Plan

The exercises included in this appendix allow you to use the knowledge you've gained from reading a specific part in this textbook. Each exercise has two tasks: Think Like a Pro tasks require you to navigate the software, find and review information in the sample business plans, and evaluate and critique some of the thinking that went behind these plans. By reviewing these sample plans with a critical eye you will begin to sharpen your own business planning skills. Create Your Own Business Plan tasks are an opportunity for you to apply your business planning skills to create your own winning business plan. So begin thinking now about the type of business you'd like to own or manage some day. Then develop and refine your business strategies as you work through the exercises on the pages that follow.

Part 1: Conducting Business in the Global Economy

Think Like a Pro

Objective: By completing these exercises you will become acquainted with the sections of a business plan that address forms of competition, company and product/service descriptions, and the economic outlook for the related industry. You will use the sample business plan for Adventure Excursions Unlimited (listed as Travel Agency-Adventure Sports in the Sample Plan Browser) in this exercise. Use the table of contents to move from section to section as you explore the plan and answer these questions.

1. What products and services does Adventure Excursions provide? Will the company compete on the basis of price, speed, quality, service, or innovation to gain a competitive advantage?
2. What is the economic outlook for the travel industry? What competition does Adventure Excursions face?
3. How does Adventure Excursions plan to use the Internet?

Create Your Own Business Plan

Now start a new plan for your own business. Answering the following questions will help you think about different aspects of your business plan. Enter your answers in the appropriate sections of the new business plan.

What information should you include about your product or service when creating a business plan? Describe in detail the product or service your company will provide. Indicate whether you will compete on price, speed, quality, service, or innovation. What are some of the things you should discuss about your competition in a business plan? In what industry will you compete? What is the economic outlook for that industry? What kinds of competition do you expect to face?

Part 2: Starting and Organizing a Small Business

Think Like a Pro

Objective: By completing these exercises you will become acquainted with the sections of a business plan that address forms of ownership, financing the enterprise, and the franchising alternative. You will use the sample business plan for Pegasus Sports (listed as Inline Skating Products in the Sample Plan Browser) in this exercise.

1. What form of ownership does Pegasus currently use? What are the advantages of selecting that form of ownership? What change in ownership form is Pegasus planning to make?
2. How is Pegasus financing its start-up operations? Has the company gone public (or does the plan indicate it wants to go public)?
3. Would you recommend that Pegasus use franchising to grow its business? Explain your answer.

Create Your Own Business Plan

Think about your own business. What form of ownership will you choose? Why? How much start-up money will you need? How will you finance your start-up costs? Where will you obtain the money you will need to grow your business? Enter your answers in the appropriate sections of your business plan.

Part 3: Managing a Business

Think Like a Pro

Objective: By completing these exercises you will become acquainted with the sections of a business plan that address a company's mission, goals and objectives, and management team. You will use the sample business plan for JavaNet (listed as Internet Cafe in the Sample Plan Browser) in this exercise.

1. Evaluate JavaNet's mission statement. Does it summarize why the organization exists, what it seeks to accomplish, and the principles that the company will adhere to as it tries to reach its goals? How might you improve this mission statement?
2. Evaluate JavaNet's objectives. Are they clearly stated? Are they measurable? Do they seem realistic? Which objectives might need some refining?
3. Assess the risks facing JavaNet. How do you expect these threats to affect the company's ability to compete?
4. Read about the company's management structure and personnel plan. What challenges might JavaNet face as a result of its chosen structure and personnel plan?

Create Your Own Business Plan

Return to the plan you are creating for your own business. List your company's goals and objectives, and be sure they are clearly stated and measurable. How will you reach these goals and objectives? What might prevent you from achieving them? What information should you include about your management team? Should you mention the team's weaknesses in addition to its strengths? Why?

Part 4: Managing Human Resources and Employee Relations

Think Like a Pro

Objective: By completing these exercises you will become acquainted with the sections of a business plan that address staffing the enterprise and managing employees. You will use the sample business plan for Sagebrush Sam's (listed as Restaurant-Steak Buffet in the Sample Plan Browser) in this exercise.

1. What do the mission statement and keys to success sections say about Sagebrush Sam's approach to employee relations? Why are good relations with employees so important to the success of this type of business?
2. What workforce challenges is Sagebrush Sam's likely to encounter as it grows?
3. What are the company's estimates for manager and employee compensation, and how do these estimates change over the years covered by the plan?
4. According to the business plan, Sagebrush Sam's will need a director of store operations when it has more than five units. How might the company recruit a manager with the appropriate experience and background for this position?

Create Your Own Business Plan

The success of your business depends on hiring, training, and motivating the right employees. Answer these questions as you continue developing your own business plan. How many employees will your business require? Of these, how many will be managers? How will you motivate your staff? Will you pay them a salary or a commission? Will you offer alternative work arrangements? If so, which ones? Will you use part-time and temporary employees? Will you provide your employees with benefits? Which ones?

Part 5: Developing Marketing Strategies to Satisfy Customers

Think Like a Pro

Objective: By completing these exercises you will become acquainted with the sections of a business plan that address a firm's product, pricing, promotion, and distribution strategies. You will use the sample business plan for Boulder Stop (listed as Sports Equipment-Cafe in the Sample Plan Browser) in this exercise.

1. Define the target market for Boulder Stop. How will the company differentiate its products and services from those of its competitors?
2. Describe the company's pricing, promotion, sales, and distribution strategies. Which distribution channels will the company use to deliver its products?
3. Rank the company's three market segmentation categories according to their importance.
4. According to the Keys to Success section, what must Boulder Stop do to be successful?

Create Your Own Business Plan

Consider your own target market and customers as you continue working on the business plan you are creating. How will you segment your target market? Which customers are likely to buy your product or service? Describe your product, pricing, promotion, and distribution strategies. Now make some preliminary sales forecasts. Under which section headings will you present this information?

Part 6: Managing Financial Information and Resources

Think Like a Pro

Objective: By completing these exercises you will become acquainted with the sections of a business plan that address a company's financial and operational projections. You will use the sample business plan for Fantastic Florals (listed as Import-Artificial Flowers in the Sample Plan Browser) in this exercise.

1. Identify the source(s) Fantastic Florals will use to fund its start-up costs. Why is it important to indicate how much start-up money will be used to fund assets versus expenses?
2. Review the financial assumptions, sales tables and graphs, and other financial information included in the Fantastic Florals plan. Assuming the financial projections are on target, would an investment of $75,000 for a 20 percent ownership stake in the company be prudent? Explain your answer. Which financial statement(s) did you use to make your decision?
3. Examine the company's projected gross margin for the years covered by the plan. How does Fantastic Florals' gross margin compare with the industry profile? How might a potential investor view this comparison?

Create Your Own Business Plan

Return to the plan you are developing for your own business. How will you categorize your revenue and expense items? Will you break down your sales by product type, by service, or by location? What general operating and product-related expenses will you incur? Set up your basic revenue and expense categories, and build the framework for your profit and loss statement. How do the categories in your plan compare with those used by Fantastic Florals?

Prologue

1. Jeffrey R. Young, "'E-Portfolios' Could Give Students a New Sense of Their Accomplishments," *The Chronicle of Higher Education*, 8 March 2002, A31.

2. Nancy M. Somerick, "Managing a Communication Internship Program," *Bulletin of the Association for Business Communication* 56, no. 3 (1993): 10–20.

3. Bureau of Labor Statistics, *2004-2005 Occupational Outlook Handbook* [accessed 13 June 2005] www.bls.gov/oco.

4. Caroline A. Drakeley, "Viral Networking: Tactics in Today's Job Market," *Intercom*, September–October 2003, 4–7.

5. Cheryl L. Noll, "Collaborating with the Career Planning and Placement Center in the Job-Search Project," *Business Communication Quarterly* 58, no. 3 (1995): 53–55.

6. Rockport Institute, "How to Write a Masterpiece of a Résumé" [accessed 16 October 1998] www.rockportinstitute.com/résumés.html.

7. Janice Tovey, "Using Visual Theory in the Creation of Résumés: A Bibliography," *The Bulletin of the Association for Business Communication* 54, no. 3 (September 1991): 97–99.

8. "Resume Fraud Gets Slicker and Easier," CNN.com [accessed 11 March 2004] www.cnn.com.

9. "Resume Fraud Gets Slicker and Easier," Employment Screening Resources website [accessed 18 March 2004] www.erscheck.com.

10. Pam Stanley-Weigand, "Organizing the Writing of Your Resume," *Bulletin of the Association for Business Communication* 54, no. 3 (September 1991): 11–12.

11. Susan Vaughn, "Answer the Hard Questions Before Asked," *Los Angeles Times*, 29 July 2001, W1–W2.

12. Richard H. Beatty and Nicholas C. Burkholder, *The Executive Career Guide for MBAs* (New York: Wiley, 1996), 133.

13. Adapted from Burdette E. Bostwick, *How to Find the Job You've Always Wanted* (New York: Wiley, 1982), 69–70.

14. Norma Mushkat Gaffin, "Recruiters' Top 10 Resume Pet Peeves," Monster.com [accessed 19 February 2004] www.monster.com; Beatty and Burkholder, *The Executive Career Guide for MBAs*, 151.

15. Rockport Institute, "How to Write a Masterpiece of a Résumé."

16. Beverly Culwell-Block and Jean Anna Sellers, "Résumé Content and Format—Do the Authorities Agree?" *Bulletin of the Association for Business Communication* 57, no. 4 (1994): 27–30.

17. Ellen Joe Pollock, "Sir: Your Application for a Job Is Rejected; Sincerely, Hal 9000," *Wall Street Journal*, 30 July 1998, A1, A12.

18. "Scannable Resume Design," ResumeEdge.com [accessed 19 February 2004] www.resumeedge.com.

19. Kim Isaacs, "Tips for Creating a Scannable Resume," Monster.com [accessed 19 February 2004] www.monster.com.

20. William J. Banis, "The Art of Writing Job-Search Letters," *CPC Annual*, 36th ed., 2 (1992): 42–50.

21. Robert Gifford, Cheuk Fan Ng, and Margaret Wilkinson, "Nonverbal Cues in the Employment Interview: Links Between Applicant Qualities and Interviewer Judgments," *Journal of Applied Psychology* 70, no. 4 (1985): 729.

22. Amanda Bennett, "GE Redesigns Rungs of Career Ladder," *Wall Street Journal*, 15 March 1993, B1, B3.

23. Robin White Goode, "International and Foreign Language Skills Have an Edge," *Black Enterprise*, May 1995, 53.

24. Nancy M. Somerick, "Managing a Communication Internship Program," *Bulletin of the Association for Business Communication* 56, no. 3 (1993): 10–20.

25. Noll, "Collaborating with the Career Planning and Placement Center in the Job-Search Project."

26. Joan Lloyd, "Changing Workplace Requires You to Alter Your Career Outlook," *Milwaukee Journal Sentinel*, 4 July 1999, 1; Camille DeBell, "Ninety Years in the World of Work in America," *Career Development Quarterly* 50, no. 1 (September 2001): 77–88

Chapter 1

1. "iTunes Music Store Downloads Top 200 Million," 16 December 2004 [accessed 6 January 2005] www.apple.com/itunes; Apple iTunes website [accessed 6 January 2005] www.apple.com/itunes; Pui-Wing Tam, "Apple, Paced by Sales of iPods, Sees Profit and Revenue Surge," *Wall Street Journal*, 14 October 2004, B4; David Pringle and Charles Goldsmith, "Cellphone Companies Chime in With Music Downloading," *Wall Street Journal*, 1 November 2004, B1, B4; Nick Wingfield, "Online Music's Latest Tune," *Wall Street Journal*, 27 August 2004, B1–B2; Jeff Leeds, "Online Song Sales, Though Rising Fast, Are at Most a Hopeful Blip," *Los Angeles Times*, 1 February 2004, C1; Pui-Wing Tam and Nick Wingfield, "Apple's iTunes to Fall Short on Song Sales, *Wall Street Journal*, 16 March 2004, B3; Bob Tedeschi, "Music at Your Fingertips, but a Battle Among Those Selling It to You," *New York Times*, 1 December 2003, C21; Gloria Goodale, "'Don't Call Me a Pirate. I'm an Online Fan'; One Girl's Downloading Habits Reveal the Gulf Between the Music Industry and Teens," *Christian Science Monitor*, 18 July 2003, 13; John Schwartz and John Markoff, "Power Players: Big Names Are Jumping into the Crowded Online Music Field," *New York Times*, 12 January 2004 [accessed 30 March 2004] www.nytimes.com; Peter Lewis, "Gadgets: Drop a Quarter in the Internet," *Fortune*, 14 March 2004 [accessed 30 March 2004] www.fortune.com.

2. Ken Stammen, "Where Big Planes Are Born," *Cincinnati Post*, 12 September 2000, 7C.

3. IBM 2002 Annual Report [accessed 29 March 2004] www.ibm.com.

4. David Cay Johnson, "In the New Economics: Fast-Food Factories?" *Wall Street Journal*, 20 February 2004, C2.

5. *Gross-Domestic-Product-by-Industry Accounts*, U.S. Bureau of Economic Analysis website [accessed 6 January 2005] www.bea.doc.gov; "U.S. Service Sector Grows But Factory Orders Decline," *Los Angeles Times*, 4 November 2004, C5.

6. U.S. Bureau of Labor Statistics website [accessed 29 March 2004] www.bls.gov.

7. Mike Sunnucks, "Service Industries Keeping Valley Ahead in Job Gains," *Business Journal (Phoenix)*, 25 June 2004 [accessed 10 January 2005] www.bizjournals.com.

8. "The 2004 Fortune 500," *Fortune* [accessed 13 January 2005] www.fortune.com.

9. Cromwell Schubarth, "Autoheroes Handle Hassle of Haggling," *Boston Herald*, 24 July 2003 [accessed 30 June 2004] www.highbeam.com.

10. Robert L. Heilbroner and Lester C. Thurow, *Economics Explained* (New York: Simon & Schuster, 1994), 29–30.

11. Ronald M. Ayers and Robert A. Collinge, *Economics: Explore and Apply* (Upper Saddle River, N.J.: Pearson Prentice Hall, 2005), 97–103.

12. Heilbroner and Thurow, *Economics Explained*, 250.

13. Heilbroner and Thurow, *Economics Explained*, 250.

14. Michael Mandel, "The Politics of Risk," *BusinessWeek*, 4 October 2004 [accessed 12 January 2005] www. businessweek.com; Carol Matlack, "Can A Lame Duck Keep French Reform Alive?" *BusinessWeek*, 12 April 2004 [accessed 12 January 2005] www.businessweek.com; Greg Steinmetz, "Her Majesty May Sell Part of London's Tube, Angering Some in U.K.," *Wall Street Journal*, 14 October 1999, A1, A12; Erik Eckholm, "Chinese Restate Goals to Reorganize State Companies," *New York Times*, 23 September 1999, A10; Dexter Roberts, "China's New Revolution," *BusinessWeek*, 27 September 1999, 72–78.

15. Ethan Smith, "Concert Industry Blames Creeping Prices for Slow Summer," *Wall Street Journal*, 11 October 2004, B1.

16. Eric A. Taub, "Signs of a Glut and Lower Prices in Thin TVs," *New York Times*, 29 November 2004, C1, C7.

17. Martin Peers, "Show of Strength: How Media Giants Are Reassembling the Old Oligopoly," *Wall Street Journal*, 15 September 2003, A1, A11.

18. Erin Joyce, "Court Upholds EU's Penalties Against Microsoft," *Internetnews.com*, 22 December 2004 [accessed 12 January 2005] www.internetnews.com; Brier Dudley and Kim Peterson, "Microsoft Legal Maneuvers Could Offset EU Sanctions," *Seattle Times*, 25 March 2004 [accessed 27 March 2004] www.seattletimes.com.

19. Kenneth N. Gilpin, "Antitrust Challenge Stops United Merger with U.S. Airways," *New York Times*, 26 July 2001, B1, B2; Patrick M. Reilly, "Barnes & Noble Closes Book on Attempt to Buy Ingram Amid FTC Objections," *Wall Street Journal*, 3 June 1999, B16.

20. Elizabeth Hurt, "AOL/Time Warner Merger Approved," *Business 2.0*, 11 January 2001 [accessed 29 March 2004] www.business2.com.

21. Jim Rossi, "The Electric Deregulation Fiasco: Looking to Regulatory Federalism to Promote a Balance Between Markets and the Provision of Public Goods," *Michigan Law Review*, May 2002, 1768–1790; Ferdinand E. Banks, "A Simple Economic Analysis of Deregulation Failure," *OPEC Review*, June 2002, 169–181.

22. Ken Brown and Scott Thurm, "Drag on High-Tech Recovery: Companies Do More With Less," *Wall Street Journal*, 9 November 2004, A1, A8.

23. "No Longer the 'Jobless Recovery,'" *BusinessWeek*, 7 May 2004 [accessed 12 January 2005] www.businessweek.com.

24. Anna Bernasek, "The $44 Trillion Abyss," *Fortune*, 24 November 2003, 113–116; Mike Allen, "Bush Pledges Effort to Balance Budget by 2004," *Washington Post*, 17 April 2002, A6; Richard W. Stevenson, "2 Parties Predict a Sharp Increase in Spending by U.S.," *New York Times*, 12 May 2002, sec. 1, 1; Martin Kasindorf and Ken Fireman, "The Clinton Budget/2002 Solution," *Newsday*, 7 February 1997, A4; Gilbert C. Alston, "Balancing the Federal Budget," *Los Angeles Times*, 14 February 1997, B8.

25. Kathleen Madigan, "Keep Your Nest Egg Safe—Watch Housing Data," *BusinessWeek*, 17 April 2000, 208–210.

26. Kevin Maney, "The Economy According to eBay," *USA Today*, 29 December 2003, B1.

27. Sue Kirchhoff, "Delicate Balance Helps USA Battle Deflation, Inflation," *USA Today*, 5 March 2003, B1–B2.

28. U.S. Bureau of Labor Statistics website [accessed 29 March 2004] www.bls.gov; Jyoti Thottam, "Why Aren't Your Prices Falling?" *Time*, 26 May 2003, 53.

29. Jon E. Hilsenrath, "Producer-Price Drop Signals Change in Inflation Dynamics," *Wall Street Journal*, 13 September 2004, A2.

30. Karen Mazurkewich, "In Bhutan, Happiness Is King," *Wall Street Journal*, 13 October 2004, A14.

31. Elizabeth Becker, "Record Deficit for a Crucial Trade Figure," *New York Times*, 15 September 2004, C1, C9.

32. U.S. Census Bureau website [accessed 12 January 2005] www.census.gov.

33. William A. Sahlman, "The New Economy Is Stronger Than You Think," *Harvard Business Review*, November–December 1999, 99–106.

34. Sahlman, "The New Economy is Stronger Than You Think," 99–106.

35. Moynihan, *The Coming American Renaissance*, 42–43; "Through Seven Decades, Tracking Business Around the World," *BusinessWeek*, 4 October 1999, 118A–118P.

36. Steve Hamm, "Big Blue's Bold Step into China," *BusinessWeek*, 20 December 2004 [accessed 12 January 2005] www.businessweek.com; Bruce Einhorn, "Rethinking the China Threat," *BusinessWeek*, 4 January 2005 [accessed 12 January 2005] www.businessweek.com.

37. Rich Miller, "High Expansion. Low Inflation. What Gives?" *BusinessWeek*, 18 October 2004, 44+.

38. Einhorn, "Rethinking the China Threat."

39. Clay Chandler, "Inside the New China," *Fortune*, 2 October 2004, 84–98.

40. Stephen Baker, "Where Danger Lurks," *BusinessWeek*, 25 August 2003, 114–118.

41. See Note 1.

42. Adapted from Bruce Horovitz, "Booksellers Wild About Harry Pre-Sales," USA Today, 21 December 2004 [accessed 7 January 2005] www.usatoday.com; Bernard Weinraub, "New Harry Potter Book Becoming a Publishing Phenomenon," *New York Times*, 3 July 2000 [accessed 12 July 2000] www.nytimes.com; Laura Miller, "Pottermania at Midnight," Salon.com, 8 July 2000 [accessed 12 July 2000] www.salon.com; David D. Kirkpatrick, "Harry Potter Magic Halts Bedtime for Youngsters," *New York Times,* 9 July 2000 [accessed 12 July 2000] www.nytimes.com; David D. Kirkpatrick, "Vanishing Off the Shelves," *New York Times,* 10 July 2000 [accessed 10 July 2000] www.nytimes.com.

Chapter 2

1. "Patagonia Company History," Patagonia website [accessed 14 January 2005] www.patagonia.com; Lisa Gardiner, "From Synchilla to School Support," *Issues in Ethics*, Winter 1997 [accessed 14 January 2005] www.scu.edu/ethics/publications; "Warm, Fuzzy, and Highly Profitable," *Fortune*, 15 November 2004, 194; Robert Smith (interviewer), "Profile: Patagonia Clothing Company and Founder Yvon Chouinard," National Public Radio, 12 November 2002 [accessed 14 January 2005] www.ebsco.com; Linda Hutchinseon, "Patagonia's Pasadena, Calif., Store Makes Good Use of Recycled Materials," *San Gabriel Valley Tribune*, 19 April 2004 [accessed 14 January 2005] www.ebsco.com; Jim McLain, "Ventura, Calif.-Based Clothing Firm Again Ranks Among Nation's Best Workplaces," *Ventura County Star*, 5 July 2004 [accessed 14 January 2005] www.ebsco.com; Monte Burke, "The World According to Yvon," *Forbes*, 26 November 2001, 236; Dianna Edwards, "A Mountain of Trust," *Step-By-Step Graphics*, September–October 2001, 30–39; Jennifer Laabs, "Mixing Business With Passion," *Workforce*, March 2000, 80–87; Roger Rosenblatt, "The Root of All Good: Reaching the Top by Doing the Right Thing," *Time*, 18 October 1999, 88–91; Michael Lear-Olimpi, "Management Mountaineer," *Warehousing Management*, January–February 1999, 23–30; Larry Armstrong, "Patagonia Sticks to Its Knitting," *BusinessWeek*, 7 December 1998, 68; Nancy Rivera Brooks, "Companies Give Green Power the Green Light," *Los Angeles Times*, 27 September 1998, D8; Charlene Marmer Solomon, "A Day in the Life of Terri Wolfe: Maintaining Corporate Culture," *Workforce*, June 1998, 94–95; Jacqueline Ottman, "Proven Environmental Commitment Helps Create Committed Customers," *Marketing News*, 2 February 1998, 5–6; Dawn Hobbs, "Patagonia Ranked 24th by Magazine," *Los Angeles Times*, 23 December 1997, B1; Jim Collins, "The Foundation for Doing Good," *Inc.*, December 1997, 41–42; "It's Not Easy Being Green," *BusinessWeek*, 24 November 1997, 180; Paul C. Judge and Melissa Downing, "A Lean, Green Fulfillment Machine," *Catalog Age*, June 1997, 63; "Patagonia, A Green Endeavor," *Apparel Industry Magazine*, February 1997, 46–48; Polly LaBarre, "Patagonia Comes of Age," *IndustryWeek*, 3 April 1995, 42; John Steinbreder, "Yvon Chouinard, Founder and Owner of Patagonia Outdoor," *Sports Illustrated*, 2 November 1991, 200.

2. Aaron Bernstein, Brian Grow, Darnell Little, Stanley Holmes, and Diane Brady, "Bracing for a Backlash," *BusinessWeek*, 4 February 2002, 32–36.

3. John R. Emshwiller and Kara Scannell, "Enron Trial Results in Five Guilty Verdicts," *Wall Street Journal*, 4 November 2004, C1; "Timeline of Enron's Collapse," *Washington Post*, 27 January 2004 [accessed 2 April 2004] www.washingtonpost.com; Ellen Florian, "Scandal Cheat Sheet," *Fortune*, 7 July 2003, 48–49.

4. Hope Yen, "High Court Overturns Arthur Andersen's Conviction," *Seattle Times*, 31 May 2005 [accessed 31 May 2005] www.seattletimes.com; Carrie Johnson and Peter Behr, "Andersen Guilty of Obstruction: Accounting Firm Will End Audit Work," *Washington Post*, 16 June 2002, A1+.

5. Joseph B. Treaster, "Marsh Settles for $850 Million," *New York Times*, 1 February 2005, A1, C5; Carrie Coolidge and Neil Weinberg, "Pulling the Plug on Marsh," *Forbes*, 15 November 2004, 126-132; Ian McDonald, "Marsh & McLennan, Squeezed by Charges, Will Lay Off 3,000," *Wall Street Journal*, 10 November 2004, C3; Monica Langley and Ian McDonald, "Marsh Averts Criminal Case With New CEO," *Wall Street Journal*, 26 November 2004, A1, A10.

6. Erin Mcclam, "Former WorldCom Chief Ebbers Convicted of All Counts," *Seattle Times*, 15 March 2005 [accessed 15 March 2005] www.seattletimes.com; Christopher Stern, "WorldCom Plans New Job Cuts," *Washington Post*, 16 January 2004, E1.

7. Andrew Morse and Mitchell Pacelle, "Japan Orders Citibank to Halt Private Banking," *Wall Street Journal*, 20 September 2004, A3, A16; Carol J. Loomis, "Citi Still Has a Few Tabs to Settle Up," *Fortune*, 31 May 2004, 38; Mitchell Pacelle, "An Alarming Year for Citi's CEO," *Wall Street Journal*, 28 September 2004, C1, C4; Andrew Morse, "Citigroup Extends Apology to Japan," *Wall Street Journal*, 26 October 2004, A3, A16.

8. "Staying Current: Sarbanes-Oxley Compliance Cost," *The Controller's Report,* November 2003, 2–3; Jorge E. Guerra, "The Sarbanes-Oxley Act and Evolution of Corporate Governance," *CPA Journal*, March 2004, 14+; Justin Schack, "The Anti-IPO," *Institutional Investor*, June 2003, 24.

9. Peter Asmus, "100 Best Corporate Citizens: 2003," *Business Ethics*, Spring 2003, 6–10.

10. Elaine Appleton Grant, "Let the Good Works Roll," *Inc.*, February 2003, 51–54.

11. Karen Bells, "Engineering an Ethical Firm," *Cincinnati Business Courier*, 26 March 2004 [accessed 17 January 2005] www.bizjournals.com.

12. Melanie Wells, "Kid Nabbing," *Forbes*, 2 February 2004, 84–88; Michelle Conlin, "The Stepford Kids," *BusinessWeek*, 27 September 2004, 26–27.

13. Anick Jesdanun, "How Bloggers Handle Ethics and Disclosure Varies Greatly," *Seattle Times*, 24 January 2005 [accessed 24 January 2005] www.seattletimes.com.

14. Paul Elias, "'Gene Flow' Worries Farmers," *San Diego Union-Tribune*, 23 September 2004, C-3; Scott Kilman, "New Scotts Grass Is Dealt a Setback," *Wall Street Journal*, 9 September 2004, A-17.

15. Elizabeth MacDonald, "Crony Capitalism," *Forbes*, 21 June 2004, 140–146; John R. Emshwiller, "Many Companies Report Transactions with Top Officers," *Wall Street Journal*, 29 December 2003, A1, A10.

16. Heather Tesoriero, "Drug Maker Helps the Police Fight Abuse," *Wall Street Journal*, 9 September 2004, B1, B4; Debra Rosenberg, "Kentucky's Pain," *Newsweek*, 20 September 2004, 44–45.

17. John S. McClenahen, "Your Employees Know Better," *IndustryWeek*, 1 March 1999, 12–14.

18. Betsy Stevens, "Communicating Ethical Values: A Study of Employee Perceptions," *Journal of Business Ethics*, June 1999, 113–120.

19. Steven Greenhouse, "Time Records Often Altered, Job Experts Say," *New York Times*, 4 April 2004 [accessed 4 April 2004] www.nytimes.com.

20. Milton Bordwin, "The Three R's of Ethics," *Management Review*, June 1998, 59–61.

21. Joanne Sammer, "United Technologies Offers a Model for Reporting Ethical Issues," *Workforce Management*, August 2004, 64–66.

22. Richard Lacayo and Amanda Ripley, "Persons of the Year," *Time*, 20 December 2002/6 January 2003, 60.

23. Mahzarin R. Banaji, Max H. Bazerman, and Dolly Chugh, "How (Un)Ethical Are You?" *Harvard Business Review*, December 2003, 56–64.

24. See letters in *New York Times*, 25 August 1918, and *New York Herald*, 1 October 1918.

25. "Business of Social Responsibility," *Businessline*, 3 August 1999, 1.

26. "Does It Pay to Be Ethical?" *Business Ethics*, March–April 1997, 14–16; Don L. Boroughs, "The Bottom Line on Ethics," *U.S. News & World Report*, 20 March 1995, 61–66.

27. Ann Graham, "Lynn Sharp Paine: The Thought Leader Interview," *Strategy + Business*, Summer 2003, 97–105.

28. Joseph Weber, "3M's Big Cleanup," *BusinessWeek*, 5 June 2000, 96–98.

29. Stephanie Strom, "Gates Aims Billions To Attack Illnesses of World's Neediest," *New York Times*, 13 July 2003, 1, 15.

30. Jim Carlton, "Once Targeted by Protesters, Home Depot Plays Green Role," *Wall Street Journal*, 6 August 2004, A1+.

31. Jessi Hempel and Lauren Gard, "The Corporate Givers," *BusinessWeek*, 29 November 2004, 100–104.

32. Hempel and Gard, "The Corporate Givers."

33. Jill Meredith Ginsberg and Paul N. Bloom, "Choosing the Right Green Marketing Strategy," *MIT Sloan Management Review*, Fall 2004, 79+.

34. U.S. Department of Energy website [accessed 3 April 2004] www.energy.gov.

35. John A. Fialka, "Report Questions EPA's Progress on Reducing Smog," *Wall Street Journal*, 1 October 2004, A4.

36. Bruce Barcott, "Changing All the Rules," *New York Times Magazine*, 4 April 2004 [accessed 4 April 2004] www.nytimes.com.

37. "Hummer Mania," CBSNews.com [accessed 3 April 2004] www.cbsnews.com; Danny Hakim, "To Avoid Fuel Limits, Subaru Is Turning a Sedan into a Truck," *New York Times*, 13 January 2004 [accessed 13 January 2004] www.nytimes.com.

38. Traci Watson, "Smoggy Skies Persist Despite Decade of Work," *USA Today*, 16 October 2003, 6A.

39. "Human Impacts on Climate," American Geophysical Union website [accessed 15 March 2005] www.agu.org.

40. Jonathan Ledgard, "Bjorn Lomborg Is the World's Most Optimistic Statistician," *Strategy + Business*, Issue 38, 72–81; John Carey, "Global Warming," *BusinessWeek*, 16 August 2004, 60–69.

41. "Tap Water at Risk: Bush Administration Actions Endanger America's Drinking Water Supplies," Natural Resources Defense Council website [accessed 4 April 2004] www.ndrc.org.

42. "What's on Tap? Grading Drinking Water in U.S. Cities," Natural Resources Defense Council website [accessed 4 April 2004] www.ndrc.org.

43. Elizabeth Weise and Traci Watson, "Mercury in Many Lakes, Rivers," *USA Today*, 25 August 2004, 1A; Traci Watson, "States Looks Harder for Mercury," *USA Today*, 25 August 2004, 3A.

44. Paul Rauber, "Saving the Environment," *The Nation*, 8 March 2004 [accessed 3 April 2004] www.highbeam.com.

45. Michelle Conlin, "From Plunderer to Protector," *BusinessWeek*, 19 July 2004.

46. Marc Gunther, "Tree Huggers, Soy Lovers, and Profits," *Fortune*, 23 June 2003, 98–103.

47. "The IW Survey: Encouraging Findings," *IndustryWeek*, 19 January 1998, 62.

48. Chris Prystay, "Recycling 'E-Waste'," *Wall Street Journal*, 23 September 2004, B1, B6; "Waste Electrical and Electronic Equipment," Europa (European Union website) [accessed 19 January 2005] www.europa.eu.int; John S. McClenahen, "HP Doubles Recycling Efforts," *IndustryWeek*, July 2004, 58; John Markoff, "Technology's Toxic Trash Is Sent to Poor Nations," *New York Times*, 25 February 2002, C1, C4.

49. Barry Meier, "Earlier Merck Study Indicated Risks of Vioxx," *New York Times*, 18 November 2004, C1, C9; Barbara Martinez, Anna Wilde Mathews, Joann S. Lublin, and Ron Winslow, "Merck Pulls Vioxx from Market After Link to Heart Problems," *Wall Street Journal*, 1 October

2004, A1, A12; Raymond V. Gilmartin, "An Open Letter from Merck" (advertisement), *Wall Street Journal*, 19 November 2004, A11; Amy Barrett, "Merck: How Much Misery After Vioxx?" *BusinessWeek*, 22 November 2004, 48–50; Anna Wilde Mathews and Barbara Martinez, "E-Mails Suggest Merck Knew Vioxx's Dangers at Early Stage," *Wall Street Journal*, 1 November 2004, A1, A10; Matt Harper and Robert Langreth, "Merck's Mess," *Forbes*, 1 November 2004, 50–51.

50. Patricia R. Olsen, "Women's Concerns Push Hotels to Improve Security," *New York Times*, 25 November 2003, C4.

51. Rachel Konrad, "Hackers Steal Personal Data from Tens of Thousands," *Seattle Times*, 16 February 2005 [accessed 16 February 2005] www.seattletimes.com; "Thieves Steal Consumer Info Database," CNNMoney, 15 February 2005 [accessed 15 February 2005] www.cnn.com; Jennifer Saranow, "Guarding Identities: Banks Fall Short," *Wall Street Journal*, 17 November 2004, D2.

52. Diana B. Henriques, "Insurer to Refund Money to Soldiers Who Bought High-Cost Life Policies," *New York Times*, 23 September 2004, C1, C4; Diana B. Henriques, "Going Off to War, and Vulnerable to the Pitches of Salesmen," *New York Times*, 20 July 2004, C1, C6.

53. Action on Smoking and Health website [accessed 15 March 2005] www.ash.org; Chris Burritt, "Fallout from the Tobacco Settlement," *Atlanta Journal and Constitution*, 22 June 1997, A14; Jolie Solomon, "Smoke Signals," *Newsweek*, 28 April 1997, 50–51; Marilyn Elias, "Mortality Rate Rose Through '80s," *USA Today*, 17 April 1997, B3; Mike France, Monica Larner, and Dave Lindorff, "The World War on Tobacco," *BusinessWeek*, 11 November 1996; Richard Lacayo, "Put Out the Butt, Junior," *Time*, 2 September 1996, 51; Elizabeth Gleick, "Smoking Guns," *Time*, 1 April 1996, 50.

54. John A. Byrne, Leslie Brown, and Joyce Barnathan, "Directors in the Hot Seat," *BusinessWeek*, 8 December 1997, 100, 102, 104.

55. Lorraine Woellert, "Anger on the Right, Opportunity for Bush," *BusinessWeek*, 7 July 2003 [accessed 24 January 2005] www.businessweek.com; Roger O. Crockett, "The Great Race Divide," *BusinessWeek*, 14 July 2003 [accessed 24 January 2005] www.businessweek.com; Earl Graves, "Celebrating the Best and the Brightest," *Black Enterprise*, February 2005, 16;

56. "Disability Discrimination," Equal Employment Opportunity Commission website [accessed 24 January 2005] www.eeoc.gov.

57. "Injuries, Illnesses, and Fatalities," Bureau of Labor Statistics [accessed 26 February 2002] www.bls.gov/iif.

58. Asmus, "100 Best Corporate Citizens: 2003," 6–10.

59. Abigail Goldman, "Sweat, Fear, and Resignation Amid All the Toys," *Los Angeles Times*, 26 November 2004, A1, A30–A32.

60. Cheryl Dahle, "Gap's New Look: The See-Through," *Fast Company*, September 2004, 70–71.

61. Goldman, "Sweat, Fear, and Resignation Amid All the Toys."

62. "Independent Monitoring & Assessment," Nike website [accessed 19 January 2005] www.nike.com.

63. See Note 1.

64. Dean Starkman, "Cities Use Eminent Domain to Clear Lots for Big-Box Stores," *Wall Street Journal*, 8 December 2004, B1, B4.

65. Adapted from Associated Press, "Children's Painkiller Recalled," CNN.com/Health, 16 August 2001 [accessed on 22 August 2001] www.cnn.com/2001/HEALTH/parenting/ 08/16/ kids.drug.recalled.ap/index.html; Perrigo Company website, www.perrigo.com [accessed on 29 August 2001].

66. Geanne Rosenberg, "Truth and Consequences," *Working Woman*, June/August 1998, 79–80.

Chapter 3

1. Adapted from John Crenshaw, "Trek Completes Move from Ireland to Germany," *Bicycle Retailer*, May 2004, 52; John Crenshaw, "Trek Bicycles Goes Dealer Direct in France," *Bicycle Retailer*, October 2002, 86; Bonnie Miller Rubin, "Quite a Ride for Trek," *Chicago Tribune,* 23 July 2002, sec. 3, 1, 4; Trek website [accessed 26 January 2005] www.trekbikes.com; Michele Wucker, "Keep on Trekking," *Working Woman,* December/January 1998, 32–36; Christopher Elliott, "Zero Defects Through Design," *Chief Executive*, 1998, 36–38; Randy Weston, "Trek Design System Cranks Out Changes," *Computerworld*, 15 December 1997, 37; "A Trek Through Time—The History of Trek Bicycles," Vintage Trek website [accessed 26 January 2005] www.vintage-trek.com.

2. Peter Wonacott, "China's Buick Infatuation," *Wall Street Journal*, 22 July 2004, B1–B2; Ginny Parker, "Learning Japanese, Once About Résumés, Is Now About Cool," *Wall Street Journal*, 5 August 1004, A1–A2; Christopher Palmeri and Nanette Byrnes, "Is Japanese Style Taking Over the World?" *BusinessWeek*, 26 July 2004, 56–58; Timothy Aeppel, "Red Wing Digs In Its Heels," *Wall Street Journal*, 28 September 2004, B1, B6; Alex Taylor III, "Shanghai Auto Wants to Be the World's Next Great Car Company," *Fortune*, 4 October 2004, 103–110.

3. Michael Freedman, "Something to Talk About," *Forbes*, 29 November 2004, 131–137.

4. Geri Smith, "Can Televisa Conquer the U.S.?" *BusinessWeek*, 4 October 2004, 70–73; Deborah Orr, "Delivering America," *Forbes*, 4 October 2004, 78–80.

5. Bob Parks, "Technology Map of the World," *Business 2.0*, August 2004, 111–118.

6. Alexei Barrionuevo, "Joining Film Fight, Hungary Tries to Go Hollywood," *Wall Street Journal*, 26 August 2004, A1, A6.

7. Eric Bellman, "Indian Scooters Zip to the Global Market," *Wall Street Journal*, 10 August 2004, A8.

8. Holley H. Ulbrich and Mellie L. Warner, *Managerial Economics* (New York: Barron's Educational Series, 1990), 190.

9. Patrick Lane, "World Trade Survey: Why Trade Is Good for You," *The Economist*, 3 October 1998, S4–S6.

10. John Heilemann, "In Through the Outsourcing Door," *Business 2.0*, November 2004, 54–57; Shailaja Neelakantan, "Teaching Tech," *Wall Street Journal*, 27 September 2004, R7; Om Malik, "McProgrammers," *Business 2.0*, August 2004, 96–102; John Carey, "Flying High?" *BusinessWeek*, 11 October 2004, 116–122; Spencer E. Ante, "Keeping Out the Wrong People," *BusinessWeek*, 4 October 2004, 90–94; Richard Florida, "America's Looming Creativity Crisis," *Harvard Business Review*, October 2004, 122–136.

11. Aaron Bernstein, "Shaking Up Trade Theory," *BusinessWeek*, 6 December 2004, 116–120.

12. "U.S. International Transactions," U.S. Bureau of Economic Analysis website [accessed 5 April 2004] www.bea.doc.gov.

13. Pete Engardio and Dexter Roberts, "The China Price," *BusinessWeek*, 6 December 2004, 102–112.

14. "Twelve Myths About Hunger," Institute for Food and Development Policy website [accessed 27 January 2005] www.foodfirst.com.

15. Steve Stecklow and Erin White, "At Some Retailers, 'Fair Trade' Carries a Very High Cost," *Wall Street Journal*, 8 June 2004, A1, A10.

16. Robert J. Samuelson, "Trading with the Enemy," *Newsweek*, 1 April 1996, 41; Amy Borrus, Pete Engardio, and Dexter Roberts, "The New Trade Superpower," *BusinessWeek*, 16 October 1995, 56–57; David A. Andelman, "Marco Polo Revisited," *American Management Journal*, August 1995, 10–12; John Greenwald, "Get Asia Now, Pay Later," *Time*, 10 October 1994, 61; Simons, "High-Tech Jobs for Sale," 59.

17. Ginger Thompson, "Fraying of a Latin Textile Industry," *New York Times*, 25 March 2005, C1, C4; Jonathan Steiman, "Expiration of Textile Quota Act Takes Toll on U.S. Manufacturers," *Inc.com*, 13 January 2005 [accessed 28 January 2005] www.inc.com; Mei Fong, "Garment Traders Seek New Roles As Quotas End," *Wall Street Journal*, 26 November 2004, B1, B3; James Cox, "Tariffs Shield Some U.S. Products," *USA Today*, 6 May 1999, 1B.

18. Andrew Pollack, "U.S. Permits 3 Cancer Drugs from Cuba," *New York Times*, 15 July 2004, 1, 4.

19. Eric Schmitt, "U.S. Backs off Sanctions, Seeing Poor Effect Abroad," *New York Times*, 31 July 1998, A1, A6; Robert T. Gray, "Book Review," *Nation's Business*, January 1999, 47.

20. "Saudi Arabia Hopes to Join WTO by 2002," *Reuters Business Report*, 3 August 1997.

21. Elizabeth Becker, "U.S. Will Cut Farm Subsidies in Trade Deal," *New York Times*, 31 July 2004, B1, B3;

22. Elizabeth Becker and Paul Meller, "On Subsidies, the Sky Wasn't the Limit," *New York Times*, 12 January 2005, C1, C5; Paul Daniel Michaels and J. Lynn Lunsford, "Globalization Blunts Air Trade Rivalry," *Wall Street Journal*, 19 July 2004, A3; Carol Matlack and Stanley Holmes, "Boeing Vs. Airbus: It's Getting Ugly," *BusinessWeek*, 20 September 2004, 50–51; Neil King, Jr., Scott Miller, Daniel Michaels, and J. Lynn Lunsford,

"U.S., Europe Sue Each Other at WTO over Aircraft Subsidies," *Wall Street Journal*, 7 October 2004, A2, A6.

23. John D. Daniels, Lee H. Radebaugh, and Daniel P. Sullivan, *International Business*, 10th ed. (Upper Saddle River, N.J.: Prentice-Hall, 2004), 182.

24. "10 Common Misunderstandings About the WTO," World Trade Organization website [accessed 28 January 2005] www.wto.org.

25. "APEC Ministers Commit to Sustainable Development," *Xinhau News Agency*, 11 June 1997; Fred C. Bergsten, "An Asian Push for World-Wide Free Trade: The Case for APEC," *The Economist*, 6 January 1996, 62; "U.S. Must Press to Reduce Trade Barriers in Asia, Pacific, Congress Told," *Gannett News Service*, 1995.

26. Michael M. Phillips, "One by One," *Wall Street Journal*, 26 April 1999, R4, R7.

27. International Finance Corporation website [accessed 28 January 2005] www.ifc.org; World Bank Group website [accessed 28 January 2005] www.worldbank.org.

28. Masaaki Kotabe and Maria Cecilia Coutinho de Arruda, "South America's Free Trade Gambit," *Marketing Management*, Spring 1998, 3936.

29. "Grand Illusions," *The Economist*, 4 March 1995, 87; Bob Davis, "Global Paradox: Growth of Trade Binds Nations, But It Also Can Spur Separatism," *Wall Street Journal*, 20 June 1994, A1, A6; Barbara Rudolph, "Megamarket," *Time*, 10 August 1992, 43–44; Peter Truell, "Free Trade May Suffer from Regional Blocs," *Wall Street Journal*, 1 July 1991, A1.

30. Patrice M. Jones, "Leaving Trade Pact's Woes Behind," *Chicago Tribune*, 10 May 2000, sec. 3, 42.

31. Rafael A. Lecuona, "Economic Integration: NAFTA and MERCOSUR, A Comparative Analysis." *International Journal of World Peace,* December 1999, 27–49.

32. "North American Free Trade Agreement (NAFTA)," Public Citizen website [accessed 28 January 2005] www.publiccitizen.org; Debra Beachy, "A Decade of NAFTA," *Hispanic Business*, July/August 2004, 24–25; Geri Smith and Cristina Lindblad, "Mexico: Was NAFTA Worth It?" *BusinessWeek*, 22 December 2003, 66–72; Charles J. Walen, "NAFTA's Scorecard: So Far, So Good," *BusinessWeek*, 9 July 2001, 54–56.

33. Patricia Guadalupe, "CAFTA Prospects Brighter in Next Congress," *Hispanic Business*, December 2004, 14; Evelyn Iritani, "In U.S., Latino Discord Over Trade Accord," *Los Angeles Times*, 23 August 2004, C1, C5; Smith and Lindblad, "Mexico: Was NAFTA Worth It?" 68; Geri Smith, "Betting on Free Trade," *BusinessWeek*, 23 April 2001, 60–62.

34. Europa (European Union website) [accessed 5 April 2004] www.europa.eu.int.

35. Thomas Kamm, "EU Certifies Participants for Euro," *Wall Street Journal*, 26 March 1998, A14; Mitchener, "Increasingly Rules of Global Economy Are Set in Brussels," A1, A10.

36. Mark Landler, "In Eastern Europe, Skepticism Over the Euro," *New York Times*, 6 December 2006, C3; Thane

Peterson, "The Euro," *BusinessWeek*, 27 April 1998, 90–94; Joan Warner, "The Great Money Bazaar," *BusinessWeek*, 27 April 1998, 96–98; Gail Edmondson, "Industrial Evolution," *BusinessWeek*, 27 April 1998, 100–101.

37. David Welch and Ian Rowley, "How Honda Is Stalling in the U.S.," *BusinessWeek*, 24 May 2004, 62–63.

38. Mark Landler and Simon Romero, "Diverging Fortunes, Tied to the Dollar," *New York Times*, 11 December 2004, B1, B2.

39. Elizabeth Becker, "I.M.F. Asks China to Free Its Currency from Dollar," *New York Times*, 30 September 2004, C1, C9.

40. John Alden, "What in the World Drives UPS?" *International Business*, March/April 1998, 6–7; UPS website [accessed 4 March 2002] www.ups.com.

41. Diana Farrell, "Beyond Offshoring: Assess Your Company's Global Potential," *Harvard Business Review*, December 2004, 82–90.

42. "Getting It Right in Japan," *International Business*, May–June 1997, 19.

43. Daniels, et al., *International Business*, 93–94.

44. Michael Freedman, "Judgment Day," *Forbes*, 7 June 2004, 97–98.

45. Daniels, et al., *International Business*, 335.

46. "FAQs for Journalists; Facts and Figures on Corruption," Transparency International website [accessed 30 January 2005] www.transparency.org.

47. Christopher Rhoads, "Lucent Faces Bribery Allegations in Giant Saudi Telecom Project," *Wall Street Journal*, 16 November 2004, A1, A18.

48. "Frequently Asked Questions About Corruption," Transparency International website [accessed 30 January 2005] www.transparency.org.

49. Daniels, et al., *International Business*, 334.

50. James Wilfong and Toni Seger, *Taking Your Business Global* (Franklin Lakes, N.J.: Career Press, 1997), 289.

51. Jules Abend, "Jockey Colors Its World," *Bobbin*, February 1999, 50–54.

52. Ricky W. Griffin and Michael W. Pustay, *International Business* (Reading, Mass.: Addison-Wesley, 1999), 415.

53. "Padgett Surveys Franchise/Small Business Sectors," *Franchising World*, March–April 1995, 46; John Stansworth, "Penetrating the Myths Surrounding Franchise Failure Rates—Some Old Lessons for New Business," *International Small Business Journal*, January–March 1995, 59–63; Laura Koss-Feder, "Building Better Franchise Relations," *Hotel & Motel Management*, 6 March 1995, 18; Carol Steinberg, "Franchise Fever," *World Trade*, July 1992, 86, 88, 90–91; John O'Dell, "Franchising America," *Los Angeles Times*, 25 June 1989, sec. IV, 1.

54. Geoffrey A. Fowler, "Viacom, Boosting China Toehold, Enter Beijing Television Venture," *Wall Street Journal*, 24 September 2004, B4.

55. Ginny Parker and Robert Guy Matthews, "Carrefour Retreat Points Up Pitfalls of Flying Solo into Japanese Market," *Wall Street Journal*, 13 October 2004, A14.

56. Daniels, et al., *International Business*, 253.

57. Ernest Beck and Emily Nelson, "As Wal-Mart Invades Europe, Rivals Rush to Match Its Formula," *Wall Street Journal*, 6 October 1999, A1, A6.

58. Fred Vogelstein, "How Intel Got Inside," *Fortune*, 4 October 2004, 127–136.

59. Tracie Rozhon, "Luxury Market Blooms Near Red Square," *New York Times*, 17 September 2004, C1, C10; Clay Chandler, "China Deluxe," *Fortune*, 26 July 2004, 150–156.

60. Ginny Parker, "Going Global Can Hit Snags, Vodafone Finds," *Wall Street Journal*, 16 June 2004, B1, B2.

61. Geoffrey A. Fowler and Ramin Setoodeh, "Outsiders Get Smarter About China's Tastes," *Wall Street Journal*, 5 August 2004, B1.

62. Erin White and Jeffrey A. Trachtenberg, "'One Size Doesn't Fit All': At WPP, Sir Martin Sorrell Sees Limits to Globalization," *Wall Street Journal*, 1 October 2003, B1, B2.

63. Om Malik, "The New Land of Opportunity," *Business 2.0*, July 2004, 72–79.

64. Joel Millman and Ann Zimmerman, "'Repats' Help Payless Shoes Branch Out in Latin America," *Wall Street Journal*, 24 December 2003, B1, B2.

65. Paul Magnusson and Mike McNamee, "Welcome to Security Nation," *BusinessWeek*, 14 June 2004, 32–35; Robert Block, Jonathan Karp, and Joann S. Lublin, "Accenture Team Wins Pact to Create Virtual Border," *Wall Street Journal*, 2 June 2004, A1, A11; Elliot Blair Smith, "Money Fled to Security Sector After 9/11; Anyone Feel Safer?" *USA Today*, 10 September 204, B1–B3.

66. Paul Magnusson, "Your Jitters Are Their Lifeblood," *BusinessWeek*, 14 April 2003, 41; Del Jones, "Executives Pessimistic About Disaster Readiness, Survey Finds," *USA Today*, 5 August 2003, 12B; Gary Fields, "FedEx Takes Direct Approach to Terrorism," *Wall Street Journal*, 9 October 2003, A4.

67. Paul Magnusson, "What Companies Need to Do," *BusinessWeek*, 16 August 2004, 26–29.

68. Toni Locy, "Anti-Terror Law Puts New Demands on Business," *USA Today*, 26 February 2004, 5A.

69. Stephen E. Flynn, "Terrorism and the Bottom Line," *Forbes*, 4 October 2004, 48.

70. Nicholas Stein, "America's 21st-Century Borders," *Fortune*, 6 September 2004, 114–120.

71. Robert Lenzner and Nathan Vardi, "Terror Inc.," *Forbes*, 18 October 2004, 52–54.

72. See Note 1.

73. Adapted from Courtland L. Bovée and John V. Thill, "Should Companies Stress English Only on the Job?" *Business Communication Today*, 6th ed. (Upper Saddle River, N.J.: Prentice Hall, 2000), 74.

74. Marc Gunther, "MTV's Passage to India," *Fortune*, 9 August 2004, 117–125.

75. "USAJobs: International Trade Specialist," USA Jobs website [accessed 17 June 1999] www.usajobs.opm.gov/wfjic/jobs/BL2896.htm.

76. Adapted from Adam Aston and Michael Arndt, "A New Goliath in Big Steel," *BusinessWeek*, 8 November 2004 [accessed 24 January 2005] www.businessweek.com; "Electrolux, Whirlpool See Lower Profits, *BusinessWeek*, 10 October 2004 [accessed 24 January 2005] www.businessweek.com; "Building a Global Loyal Following," *Appliance*, April 2003, W1–W4; "About Whirlpool Corp.," Whirlpool website [accessed 5 April 2004] www.whirlpool.com; Regina Fazio Maruca, "The Right Way to Go Global," *Harvard Business Review*, March–April 1994, 135–145; Deborah Duarte and Nancy Snyder, "From Experience: Facilitating Global Organizational Learning in Product Development at Whirlpool Corporation," *Journal of Product Innovation Management* 14, no. 1 (January 1997): 48–55; Joe Jancsurak, "Whirlpool: U.S. Leader Pursues Global Blueprint," *Appliance Manufacturer* 45, no. 2 (February 1997): G21; Carl Quintanilla, "Despite Setbacks, Whirlpool Pursues Overseas Markets," *Wall Street Journal*, 9 December 1997, B4; Ian Katz, "Whirlpool: In the Wringer," *BusinessWeek*, 14 December 1998, 83+; Gale Cutler, "Asia Challenges Whirlpool Technology," *Research Technology Management*, September–October 1998, 4–6; "Whirlpool Europe and Tupperware Europe Announce Strategic Alliance," *Investor Relations*, 28 April 1999.

Chapter 4

1. "New UPS Technology Helps Businesses Navigate Complexities of Global Trade," "UPS Fact Sheet," and "Technology Facts: UPS," UPS website [accessed 12 February 2005] www.ups.com; Michael Liedtke, "UPS Moves Beyond Delivering Packages," *USA Today*, 7 November 2002, 19A; Erick Schonfeld, "The Total Package," www.ecompany.com, June 2001, 91–97; Samuel Greengard, "UPS Delivers on Wireless Connectivity," *IQ Magazine*, May–June 2001, 63; Kelly Barron, "UPS Company of the Year," *Forbes*, 10 January 2000, 79–83; Jack Ewing and Dean Faust, "DHL's American Adventure," *BusinessWeek*, 29 November 2004, 126–127; Deborah Orr, "Delivering America," *Forbes*, 4 October 2004, 78–80.

2. Daniel Lyons, "Too Much Information," *Forbes*, 13 December 2004, 110–115.

3. Irma Becerra-Fernandez, Avelino Gonzalez, and Rajiv Sabherwal, *Knowledge Management* (Upper Saddle River, N.J.: Pearson Education, 2004), 200.

4. Quentin Hardy, "Data of Reckoning," *Forbes*, 10 May 2004, 151–154

5. Hardy, "Data of Reckoning."

6. Daniel Lyons, "Speed Demon," *Forbes*, 13 December 2004, 114–115.

7. Kenneth C. Laudon and Jane P. Laudon, *Management Information Systems*, 8th ed. (Upper Saddle River, N.J.: Pearson Education, 2004), 236.

8. Abrahm Lustgarten, "Getting Ahead of the Weather," *Fortune*, 87–94.

9. Elizabeth Esfahani, "7-Eleven Gets Sophisticated," *Business 2.0*, January/February 2005, 93–100.

10. InnoCentive website [accessed 7 February 2005] www.innocentive.com.

11. Timothy J. Mullaney and Robert D. Hof, "E-Tailing Finally Hits Its Stride," *BusinessWeek*, 20 December 2004, 36–37.

12. Kevin Laws, "Whither mCommerce?" *VentureBlog*, 30 March 2004 [accessed 6 February 2005] www.ventureblog.com.

13. Brian Steinberg, "Online Ad Dollars Set to Match, Then Go Ahead of Magazines," *Wall Street Journal*, 27 July 2004, B7.

14. Stephen Baker, "Where the Real Internet Money Is Made," *BusinessWeek*, 27 December 2004, 98–100.

15. Andy Reinhardt, "The Paperless Manual," *BusinessWeek e.Biz*, 18 September 2000, EB92.

16. Bob Tedeschi, "E-Commerce Report," *New York Times*, 31 January 2005, C4.

17. Sebastian Rupley, "WebEx Exposed," *PC Magazine*, 7 September 2004 [accessed 5 February 2005] www.pcmag.com.

18. Kris Maher, "The Jungle," *Wall Street Journal*, 5 October 2004, B10.

19. Erika D. Smith, "Online Chat Companies Offer Way out of Phone Frustration," *San Diego Union-Tribune*, 5 July 2004, E5.

20. Douglas P. Shuit, "A Few Years Behind Schedule, Employee Portals Gain Ground," *Workforce Management*, September 2004, 57.

21. Heather Green, "The Underground Internet," *BusinessWeek*, 15 September 2003, 80–82.

22. Michael Fitzgerald, "The Next Best Thing to Being There," *Inc.*, July 2004, 44–45.

23. David Kirkpatrick, "It's Hard to Manage If You Don't Blog," *Fortune*, 4 October 2004, 46; Lee Gomes, "How the Next Big Thing in Technology Morphed into a Really Big Thing," *Wall Street Journal*, 4 October 2004, B1; Jeff Meisner, "Cutting Through the Blah, Blah, Blah," 19–25 November 2004, 27–28; Lauren Gard, "The Business of Blogging," *BusinessWeek*, 13 December 2004, 117–119; Heather Green, "Online Video: The Sequel," *BusinessWeek*, 10 January 2005, 40; Michelle Conlin and Andrew Park, "Blogging with the Boss's Blessing," *BusinessWeek*, 28 June 2004, 100–102.

24. Kara Swisher, "'Wiki' May Alter How Employees Work Together," *Wall Street Journal*, 29 July 2004, B1; Robert D. Hof, "Hate Your Software? Write Your Own," *BusinessWeek*, 18 October 2004, 120–121.

25. Daniel Roth, "Catch Us If You Can," *Fortune*, 9 February 2004, 65–74; Stephanie N. Mehta, "The Future Is on the Line," *Fortune*, 26 July 2004, 121–130; Mary Kathleen Flynn, "Courting Calls," *U.S. News & World Report*, 2 February 2004, 40–42; James Fallows, "In Internet Calling, Skype Is Living Up to the Hype," *New York Times*, 5 September 2004, C5; Andy Reinhardt, "Net Phone Calls, Free and Clear," 1 November 2004, 60–61.

26. Open Directory [accessed 13 December 2003] www.dmoz.com.

27. LookSmart.com [accessed 13 December 2003] www.looksmart.com.

28. AllTheWeb.com advanced search page [accessed 13 December 2003] www.alltheweb.com; Google advanced search page [accessed 13 December 2003] www.google.com; Yahoo! advanced search page [accessed 13 December 2003] www.yahoo.com.

29. Saul Hansell, "Search Sites Play a Game of Constant Catch-Up," *New York Times*, 31 January 2005, C1, C4; Robert D. Hof, "Amazon Joins the Search Party," *BusinessWeek*, 27 September 2004, 52.

30. Heather Green, "Your Online Paperboy," *BusinessWeek*, 20 December 2004, 104; Kim Peterson, "Software Programs Called RSS Readers Creating a Blog Jam," *Seattle Times*, 20 September 2004 [accessed 20 September 2004] www.seattletimes.com; Gavin Shearer, "Syndication Services Become More Popular," *Puget Sound Business Journal*, 17–23 September 2004, 29; Heather Green, "All the News You Choose—On One Page," *BusinessWeek*, 25 October 2004; NewsGator website [accessed 6 February 2005] www.newsgator.com; NewzCrawler website [accessed 6 February 2005] www.newzcrawler.com.

31. Darrell K. Rigby and Dianne Ledingham, "CRM Done Right," *Harvard Business Review*, November 2004, 118–129.

32. Laudon and Laudon, *Management Information Systems*, 325.

33. "Technology Facts: UPS."

34. William M. Bulkeley, "The Office PC Slims Down," *Wall Street Journal*, 17 January 2005, R3.

35. Roger Parloff, "Gunning for Linux," *Fortune*, 17 May 2004, 88–102.

36. Peter Lewis, "Broadband Wonderland," *Fortune*, 20 September 2004, 191–198; Catherine Tang, "Behind in Broadband," *BusinessWeek*, 6 September 2004, 88–89.

37. Leslie Cauley, "Small Towns Tired of Slow Rollout Create Own High-Speed Networks," *USA Today*, 22 September 2004, B1, B2.

38. Internet2 website [accessed 8 February 2005] www.internet2.edu.

39. Steven Levy, "Something in the Air," *Newsweek*, 7 June 2004, 46–54.

40. Scott Woolley and Quentin Hardy, "Into Thin Air," *Forbes*, 26 April 2004 [accessed 9 February 2005] www.forbes.com.

41. Jesse Drucker and Almar Latour, "Internet and Phone Companies Plot Wireless-Broadband Push," *Wall Street Journal*, 20 January 2005, A1, A10; Wade Roush, "Why WiMax?" *Technology Review*, November 2004, 20–21.

42. Don Clark, "A New Tech Battle for the Home," *New York Times*, 3 January 2005, B1, B4; Stephen Baker and Heather Green, "Big Bang," *BusinessWeek*, 21 June 2004, 68–76; Catherine Yang, "Easy Broadband—and Smarter Power," *BusinessWeek*, 22 November 2004, 132–134; Catherine Yang, "Cable vs. Fiber," *BusinessWeek*, 1 November 2004,

36–39; Almar Latour, "Free for All," *Wall Street Journal*, 13 September 2004, R1, R4; Christopher Rhoads, "Cellphones Become 'Swiss Army Knives' as Technology Blurs," *Wall Street Journal*, 4 January 2005, B1, B3.

43. Jon Swartz, "Crooks Slither into Net's Shady Nooks and Crannies," *USA Today*, 21 October 2004, B1–B2.

44. Benjamin Fulford, "Ware Protection," *Forbes*, 4 October 2004, 82–86.

45. Bruce Schneier, "The Witty Worm: A New Chapter in Malware," *Computerworld*, 2 June 2004 [accessed 10 February 2005] www.computerworld.com; Scott Berinato, "Why Wasn't the Witty Worm Widely Worrisome?" *CIO*, 14 January 2005 [accessed 10 February 2005] www.cio.com.

46. Ken Belson, "Hackers Are Discovering a New Frontier: Internet Telephone Service," *New York Times*, 2 August 2004, C4; Yuki Noguchi, "Hold the Phone: Hackers Starting to Infect Our Cells," *Seattle Times*, 26 November 2004 [accessed 26 November 2004] www.seattletimes.com; Steven Ranger, "Mobile Virus Epidemic Heading This Way," *Test Bed Blog*, 10 February 2005, [accessed 10 February 2005] www.vnunet.com; Stephanie N. Mehta, "Wireless Scrambles to Batten Down the Hatches," *Fortune*, 18 October 2004, 275–280.

47. Jon Swartz, "Identity Thieves Can Lurk at Wi-Fi Spots," *USA Today*, 7 February 2005, B1; Ken Monroe, "Bugwatch: Access Point Impersonation," *Test Bed Blog*, 8 December 2004 [accessed 10 February 2005] www.vnunet.com.

48. Richard Behar, "Never Heard of Acxiom? Chances Are It's Heard of You," *Fortune*, 23 February 2004, 140–148.

49. Dennis Blank, "When the Hacker Is on the Inside," *BusinessWeek*, 13 December 2000 [accessed 11 February 2005] www.businessweek.com.

50. Yuki Noguchi, "Online Search Engines Tap into Privacy," *Seattle Times*, 20 February 2004 [accessed 10 February 2004] www.seattletimes.com.

51. Anick Jesdunan, "You're Being Followed—By Web Ads," *Seattle Times*, 14 June 2004 [accessed 14 June 2004] www.seattletimes.com; Bill Gossman, "Changing the Privacy Paradigm," Revenue Science website [accessed 11 February 2005] www.revenuescience.com.

52. Jon Swartz, "More Firms Keep an Eye on Outgoing E-Mail," *USA Today*, 14 July 2004, B1.

53. Steven Levy, "A Future with Nowhere to Hide," *Newsweek*, 7 June 2004, 76.

54. John Teresko, "Too Much Data, Not Enough Info?" *IndustryWeek*, September 2004, 16.

55. "Bill Gates Gets 4 Million E-Mails a Day," *Seattle Times*, 18 November 2004 [accessed 18 November 200] www.seattletimes.com; Riva Richmond, "Pre-Emptive Strike," *Wall Street Journal*, 18 November 2004, R13; Anita Hamilton, "You've Got Spim!" *Time*, 2 February 2004 [accessed 30 January 2004] www.time.com.

56. Chris Gaither, "Searching for Ways to Fight Junk E-Mail," *Los Angeles Times*, 15 July 2004, C1, C4; Jon Swartz and Byron Acohido, "E-Mail Carriers Sign On to Anti-Spam

Efforts," *USA Today*, 23 June 2004, B1; Jon Swartz, "Spam Can Hurt in More Ways Than One," *USA Today*, 8 July 2004, B1; Katie Hafner, "Delete: Bathwater. Undelete: Baby," *New York Times*, 5 August 2004, E1, E7; "Spam Invasion Targets Mobile Phones," *CNN.com*, 5 February 2004 [accessed 4 February 2004] www.cnn.com; "Study: Spam Costing Companies $22 Billion a Year," *CNN.com*, 3 February 2004 [accessed 3 February 2005] www.cnn.com; John Swartz, "Is the Future of E-Mail Under Cyberattack?" *USA Today*, 15 June 2004, 4B.

57. Sushil K. Sharma and Jatinder N. D. Gupta, "Improving Workers' Productivity and Reducing Internet Abuse," *Journal of Computer Information Systems*, Winter 2003–2004, 74–78.

58. Laudon and Laudon, *Management Information Systems*, 208.

59. Andrew McAfee, "Do You Have Too Much IT?" *MIT Sloan Management Review*, Spring 2004, 18–21.

60. Stuart Crainer and Des Dearlove, "Making Yourself Understood," *Across the Board*, May/June 2004, 23–27.

61. Gregory A Maciag, "Finding the Right Medium for the Message," *National Underwriter*, 20 October 1997, 19–21.

62. Weld Royal, "Is Your CEO a Computer Geek?" *IndustryWeek*, 5 March 2001, 26+.

63. Stephanie Armour, "Some Firms Trade E-mail for Face Time," *USA Today*, 7 December 2004, B1.

64. See note 1.

65. Adapted from Stephanie Armour, "Technology's Burps Give Workers Heartburn," *USA Today*, 16 August 1999, B1–B2; "COMPAQ: Employees Get 'IT' Out of Their Systems," *M2 Presswire*, 27 May 1999; Jack Gordon, Kim Kiser, Michele Picard, and David Stamps," Take That, You @!%#!* Machine!" *Training*, May 1999, 20.

Chapter 5

1. Adapted from *Business Wire*, "FedEx Completes Acquisition of Kinko's; Strategic Move Allows FedEx to Capitalize on Key Business Trends," 12 February 2004 [accessed 7 April 2004] www.highbeam.com; Woody Baird, "FedEx Buying Kinko's for $2.4 Billion," *AP Online*, 31 December 2003 [accessed 7 April 2004] www.highbeam.com; "Kinko Deal Yields Payoff for Buyout Firm," *AP Online*, 30 December 2003 [accessed 7 April 2004] www.highbeam.com; Kinko's website [accessed 7 April 2004] www.kinkos.com; Shawn Tully, "A Better Taskmaster than the Market," *Fortune*, 26 October 1998, 277–286; Laurie J. Flynn, "For the Officeless, a Place to Call Home," *New York Times*, 6 July 1998, 1, 4; Michele Marchetti, "Getting the Kinks Out," *Sales and Marketing Management*, March 1997, 56–64; "Man of Few Words," *Sales and Marketing Management*, March 1997, 63; "Kinko's Improves Image of Businesses with Top-Notch Proposals and Presentations Capabilities; Presentations a Growing Percentage of Customer Work at Kinko's," *Business Wire*, 28 September 1997; "Kinko's Strengthens Office Product Assortment," *Discount Store News*, 17 November 1997, 6, 70; Ann Marsh, "Kinko's

Grows Up—Almost," *Forbes*, 1 December 1997, 270–272; "Kinko's Strikes Deal for Mideast Growth," *Graphic Arts Monthly*, January 1998, 22; Lori Ioannou and Paul Orfalea, "Interview: The Brains Behind Kinko's," *Your Company*, 1 May 1999, 621.

2. Mitchell Pacelle and Ianthe Jeanne Dugan, "Partners Forever? Within Andersen, Personal Liability May Bring Ruin," *Wall Street Journal*, 2 April 2002, C1, C16.

3. Norman M. Scarborough and Thomas W. Zimmerer, *Effective Small Business Management* (Upper Saddle River, N.J.: Prentice Hall, 2000), 84.

4. James W. Cortada, "Do You Take This Partner," *Total Quality Review*, November–December 1995, 11.

5. Laurence Zuckerman, "UPS Hears Market's Song, and Plans to Sell Some Stock," *New York Times*, 22 July 1999, A1, C23.

6. Emily Thornton, "A Little Privacy, Please," *BusinessWeek*, 24 May 2004, 74–75; John H. Christy and Shlomo Reifman, "The Importance of Being Private," *Forbes*, 29 November 2004, 201–202.

7. Dimitra Kessenides, "Happy Together," *Inc.*, November 2004, 54–56.

8. "The 2004 Fortune 500," *Fortune.com* [accessed 22 February 2005] www.fortune.com.

9. Wal-Mart website [accessed 18 February 2005] www.walmart.com; U.S. Census Bureau website [accessed 18 February 2005] www.census.gov.

10. Scarborough and Zimmerer, *Effective Small Business Management*, 90.

11. Robert G. Goldstein, Russell Shapiro, and Edward A. Hauder, "So Many Choices of Business Entities—Which One Is Best for Your Needs?" *Insight (CPA Society)*, February/March 1999, 10–16.

12. John M. Cunningham, "What's Behind New Hampshire's LLC 'Revolution'?" *New Hampshire Business Review*, 19 September–2 October 2003, 27A.

13. Jeffrey E. Garten, "Put Your Money Where Your Mouth Is," *BusinessWeek*, 27 January 2003 [accessed 19 February 2005] www.businessweek.com; *Business Wire*, "CalPERS to Vote Proxy Against Safeway Directors," 7 April 2004, [accessed 8 April 2004] www.highbeam.com.

14. David A. Nadler, "Building Better Boards," *Harvard Business Review*, May 2004, 102–111.

15. Brent Schlender, "Inside Andy Grove's Latest Crusade," *Fortune*, 23 August 2004, 68–78.

16. Floyd Norris, "Ebbers and Passive Directors Blamed for WorldCom Woes: Board That Made Decisions in Haste with No Questioning," *Wall Street Journal*, 10 June 2003, C1, C2.

17. Cora Daniels, "Finally in the Director's Chair," *Fortune*, 4 October 2004, 42–44; Nadler, "Building Better Boards"; Judy B. Rosener, "Women on Corporate Boards Make Good Business Sense," *Directorship*, May 2003 [accessed 18 February 2005] www.womensmedia.com.

18. Joann S. Lublin, "Back to School," *Wall Street Journal*, 21 June 2004, R3.

19. Joann S. Lublin, Theo Francis, and Jonathan Weil, "Directors Are Getting the Jitters," *Wall Street Journal*, 13 January 2005, B1, G6; Jack Milligan, "Targeting the Board," *Bank Director*, 4th Quarter 2003 [accessed 18 February 2005] www.bankdirector.com.

20. "Mergers & Acquisitions Explained," Thomson Investors Network [accessed 8 April 2004] www.thomsoninvest.net.

21. "Mergers & Acquisitions Explained."

22. *The PSI Opportunity* (online newsletter), PSI website [accessed 8 April 2004] www.psiusa.com.

23. Amy Merrick and Dennis K. Berman, "Kmart to Buy Sears for $11.5 Billion," *Wall Street Journal*, 18 November 2004, A1, A8.

24. Nancy K. Kubasek, Bartley A. Brennan, and M. Neil Browne, *The Legal Environment of Business*, 3d ed. (Upper Saddle River, N.J.: Pearson Education, 2003), 691.

25. Irene Macauley, "Corporate Governance: Crown Charters to Dotcoms," Museum of American Financial History website [accessed 8 April 2004] www.financialhistory.org.

26. Mark Maremont, "More Can Be More," *Wall Street Journal*, 25 October 2004, R4.

27. *PR Newswire*, "Bank of America Completes FleetBoston Merger; Starting Today, Customers Have Access to Full ATM Network" [accessed 8 April 2004] www.highbeam.com.

28. Nick Wingfield and Robert A. Guth, "Videogame Makers Are Playing 'Takeover 2005'," *Wall Street Journal*, 29 December 2004, C1, C3.

29. Ben Elgin, "Can Anyone Save HP?" *BusinessWeek*, 21 February 2005 [accessed 19 February 2005] www.businessweek.com; Carol J. Loomis, "Why Carly's Big Bet Is Failing," *Fortune*, 7 February 2005, 50–62; Brian Caulfield, "Saving $3 Billion the HP Way," *Business 2.0*, May 2003, 52–54.

30. Stephen Labaton, "800-Pound Gorillas," *New York Times*, 11 June 2000, sec. 4, 1; Martin Peers, Nick Wingfield, and Laura Landro, "AOL, Time Warner Set Plan to Link in Mammoth Merger," *Wall Street Journal*, 11 January 2000, A1, A6; Thomas E. Weber, Martin Peers, and Nick Wingfield, "Two Titans in a Strategic Bind Bet on a Futuristic Megadeal," *Wall Street Journal*, 11 January 2000, B1, B12; "AOL and Time Warner Will Merge to Create World's First Internet-Age Media and Communications Company," America Online website [accessed 11 January 2000] media.web.aol.com/media/press.cfm.

31. March Gunther, "A Big Win for the Little Guys," *Fortune*, 16 January 2003 [accessed 19 February 2005] www.fortune.com.

32. Erin White and Jason Singer, "Old-Line Retailer Learns New Tricks to Evade Takeover," *Wall Street Journal*, 19 July 2004, A1, A6.

33. Michael Hickins, "Searching for Allies," *Management Review*, January 2000, 54–58.

34. "Cisco and IBM Pave Way for Customers to Easily Adopt Voice and Video IP Services," IBM press release, 18 May 2004, IBM website [accessed 19 February 2005] www.ibm.com.

35. Christina Binkley and Alessandra Galloni, "A Bitter Suite Mix," *Wall Street Journal*, 8 October 2004, B1, B3.

36. Dominic M. Palmer and Patrick Mullaney, "Strategy: Building Better Alliances," *Outlook Journal*, July 2001 [accessed 10 August 2005] www.accenture.com.

37. Binkley and Galloni, "A Bitter Suite Mix."

38. Adapted from advertisement, *Atlantic Monthly*, January 2000, 119; Endless Pools website [accessed 31 August 2000] www.endlesspools.com.

Chapter 6

1. "Forbes.com Best of the Web Directory," Forbes.com [accessed 20 February 2005] www.forbes.com; GeniusBabies.com website [accessed 20 February 2005] www.geniusbabies.com; Abigail Leichman, "Oh, Baby—Novel Gifts for the Newborn," *The Record* (Bergen County, N.J.), 7 September 2002, F01; Isabel M Isidro, "GeniusBabies.com: Turning Passion Into a Successful Business," PowerHomeBiz.com [accessed 10 November 2002] www.powerhomebiz.com; Isabel M Isidro, "What Works on the Web? 12 Lessons from Successful Home-based Online Entrepreneurs," PowerHomeBiz.com [accessed 10 November 2002] www.powerhomebiz.com; Karen Dash, "Dotcom Moms: Many Parents Have Discovered the Perfect Place to Balance Work and Family—the Web," *Raleigh News & Observer*, 14 May 2000 [accessed online 10 November 2002] www.babyuniversity.com/about_us/ raleigh_n_o.shtml; Barbara Whitaker, "For the Small Retailer, Life on the Internet Is One Big Bazaar," *New York Times*, 29 March 2000 [accessed online 10 November 2002] www.nytimes.com.

2. Irwin Speizer, "Going to Ground," *Workforce Management*, December 2004, 39–44.

3. Alan Hughes, "Funny Money," *Black Enterprise*, December 2004, 130–144; Bo Burlingham, "Don't Call Her an Entrepreneur," *Inc.*, September 2004, 97–102.

4. Bernard Stamler, "Redefinition of Small Leads to a Huge Brawl," *New York Times*, 21 September 2004, G8.

5. U.S. Small Business Administration website [accessed 11 April 2004] www.sba.gov; Jim Hopkins, "Entrepreneur 101: Supervising Employees," *USA Today*, 12 September 2001, 9B; Claudia H. Deutsch, "When a Big Company Hatches a Lot of Little Ideas," *New York Times*, 23 September 1998, D4.

6. Small Business Administration Office of Advocacy website [accessed 17 March 2002] www.sba.gov/advo.

7. Malik Singleton, "Same Markets, New Marketplaces," *Black Enterprise*, September 2004, 34; Edmund L. Andrews, "Where Do the Jobs Come From?" *New York Times*, 21 September 2004, E1, E11; Small Business Administration website [accessed 11 April 2004] www.sba.gov.

8. Scott Kirsner, "4 Leaders You Need to Know," *Fast Company*, February 2005, 68–69.

9. Om Malik, "The New Road to Riches," *Business 2.0*, October 2004, 84–94.

10. Norman M. Scarborough and Thomas W. Zimmerer, *Effective Small Business Management*, 7th ed. (Upper Saddle River, N.J.: Prentice Hall, 2003), 22.

11. Matthew Maier, "A Store for Cereal (Seriously)," *Business 2.0*, October 2004, 42; Cereality website [accessed 21 February 2005] www.cereality.com.

12. Heidi Dietrich, "Online Radio Venture Bets on African Tunes," *Puget Sound Business Journal*, 27 August–2 September 2004, 14–15; Chondo website [accessed 21 February 2005] www.chondo.net.

13. Malik, "The New Road to Riches."

14. Intrapreneur.com website [accessed 20 February 2005] www.intrapreneur.com.

15. Joe Mullich, "Warming Up for Leadership," *Workforce Management*, November 2004, 63–66.

16. Ross Wehner, "'Intrapreneurs' to Spread Their Gospel at Thornton, Colo., Summit," *Denver Post*, 21 September 2004 [accessed 20 February 2005] www.ebsco.com.

17. Jim Hopkins, "Female-Owned Companies Flourish," *USA Today*, 6 May 2003, B1.

18. Mary Ellen Egan, "Big Shot in Bangalore," *Forbes*, 18 October 2004, 88–89.

19. Small Business Association website [accessed 17 March 2002] www.sba.gov.

20. Small Business Administration Office of Advocacy website [accessed 11 April 2004] www.sba.gov/advo.

21. Jim Hopkins, "Hispanic-Owned Companies See Strong Growth Spurt," *USA Today*, 2 July 2003, B1.

22. David J. Dent, "Coming to America," *Inc.*, November 2004, 100–107.

23. Scarborough and Zimmerer, *Effective Small Business Management*, 16.

24. Tiana Velez, "New Generation of High-Tech Entrepreneurs Gathers Steam," *Arizona Daily Star*, 31 January 2005 [accessed 21 February 2005] www.ebsco.com.

25. Jim Hopkins, "Bad Times Spawn Great Start-Ups," *USA Today*, 18 December 2001, 1B; Alan Cohen, "Your Next Business," *FSB*, February 2002, 33–40.

26. Louise Nicholson and Alistair R. Anderson, "New and Nuances of the Entrepreneurial Myth and Metaphor: Linguistic Games in Entrepreneurial Sense-Making and Sense-Giving," *Entrepreneurship Theory and Practice*, March 2005, 153–172.

27. "Are You Ready?" SBA website [accessed 21 February 2005] www.sba.gov; "Entrepreneurial Test," SBA Online Women's Business Center, SBA website [accessed 21 February 2005] www.sba.gov; Scarborough and Zimmerer, *Effective Small Business Management*, 4.

28. Zakiyyah El-Amin, "The New Look on the Greens," *Black Enterprise*, June 2004, 64; Urban Golf Gear website [accessed 21 February 2005] www.urbangolfgear.com.

29. Joshua Hyatt, "The Real Secrets of Entrepreneurs," *Fortune*, 15 November 2004, 185–202.

30. Jessica Mintz, "First Things First," *Wall Street Journal*, 29 November 2004, R10–R11.

31. Maggie Overfelt, "Ready to Operate," *FSB*, November 2004, 70–76.

32. Norm Brodsky, "Caveat Emptor," *Inc.*, August 1998, 31–32; "Why Buy a Business?" CCH Toolkit website [accessed 20 May 1999] http://aol.toolkit.cch.com/text/PO1_0820.asp.

33. Wendy Harris, "10 Hottest Deals in Franchising," *Black Enterprise*, September 2004, 77–88.

34. Harris, "10 Hottest Deals in Franchising."

35. Papa John's website [accessed 20 March 2002] www.papajohns.com.

36. Eve Tahmincioglu, "When Franchisees Lose Part of Their Independence," *New York Times*, 3 February 2005, C6.

37. Great Harvest Bread website [accessed 21 February 2005] www.greatharvest.com; Michael Hopkins, "Zen and the Art of the Self-Managed Company," *Inc.*, November 2000, 54–63.

38. "Study: Restaurant Failure Rate Lower Than Thought," *Baltimore Business Journal*, 10 September 2003 [accessed 21 February 2005] www.bizjournals.com; "McBusiness," *Inc. State of Small Business 2001*, 58.

39. Joseph W. Duncan, "The True Failure Rate of Start-Ups," *D&B Reports*, January–February 1994; Maggie Jones, "Smart Cookies," *Working Woman*, April 1995, 50–52; Janice Maloney, "Failure May Not Be So Bad After All," *New York Times*, 23 September 1998, 12.

40. Zina Moukheiber, "Slim Pickings," *Forbes*, 26 July 2004, 134–135.

41. Hyatt, "The Real Secrets of Entrepreneurs."

42. Kiri Blakely, "A Dog's Life," *Forbes*, 7 June 2004, 132.

43. Daniel McGinn, "Why Size Matters," *Inc. 500*, Fall 2004, 33–36.

44. SCORE website [accessed 11 April 2004] www.score.org.

45. National Business Incubation Association website [accessed 21 February 2005] www.nbia.com; Louisiana Technology Park website [accessed 21 February 2005] www.lactechpark.com.

46. Gwendolyn Bounds, "The Great Money Hunt," *Wall Street Journal*, 29 November 2004, R1, R4.

47. Paulette Thomas, "It's All Relative," *Wall Street Journal*, 29 November 2004, R4, R8.

48. Reed Albergotti, "Long Shot," *Wall Street Journal*, 29 November 2004, R4; Scarborough and Zimmerer, *Effective Small Business Management*, 439.

49. Bob Zider, "How Venture Capital Works," *Harvard Business Review*, November/December 1998, 131–139.

50. Amy Chozick, "A Helping Hand," *Wall Street Journal*, 29 November 2004, R9, R11.

51. Association for Enterprise Opportunity website [accessed 22 February 2005] www.microenterpriseworks.org.

52. Robert A. Guth, "Mobile-Game Companies Are Shown the Money," *Wall Street Journal*, 17 August 2004, C3–C4.

53. Arlene Weintraub, "Biotech's Tough New Taskmasters," *BusinessWeek*, 14 June 2004, 42; Turney Stevens, "What Do VC Firms Look for When They Invest?" *Puget Sound Business Journal*, 1–7 October 2004, 48.

54. William Payne, "What to Expect from Angel Networks," *American Venture*, September/October 2004, 38–39; Kaufman Foundation, "Business Angel Investing Groups Growing in North America," October 2002 [accessed 21 February 2005] www.angelcapitalassociation.org.

55. Peter Loftus, "Charge It!" *Wall Street Journal*, 29 November 2004, R6; Bobbie Gossage, "Charging Ahead," *Inc.*, January 2004, 42.

56. Kent Hoover, "Small SBA Loans Cost More; Large Loans Harder," *Puget Sound Business Journal*, 8–14 October 2004, 18.

57. Small Business Administration website [accessed 22 February 2005] www.sba.gov.

58. Small Business Administration website [accessed 22 February 2005] www.sba.gov.

59. Adapted from "Top 10 Franchises for 2005," *Entrepreneur* [accessed 20 February 2005] www.entrepreneur.com; Subway website [accessed 20 February 2005] www.subway.com; Robert Maynard, "Choosing a Franchise," *Nation's Business*, October 1996, 54–55.

Chapter 7

1. Adapted from Lawrence M. Fisher, "How Dell Got Soul," *Strategy + Business*, Fall 2004, 46–59; Cathy Booth Thomas, "Dell Wants Your Home," *Time*, 6 October 2003, 48–49; Adam Lashinsky, "Where Dell Is Going Next," *Fortune*, 18 October 2004, 115–120; Justin Martin, "Dancing with Elephants, *FSB*, October 2004, 84–92; Andrew Park, "Thinking Out of the Box," *BusinessWeek*, 22 November 2004, 22; Kathryn Jones, "The Dell Way," *Business 2.0*, February 2003, 61–66; Linda Tischler, "Can Kevin Rollins Find the Soul of Dell?," *Fast Company*, November 2002, 110–114; Pui-Wing Tam, Gary McWilliams, Scott Thurm, "Out of the Box: As Alliances Fade, Computer Firms Toss Out Playbook," *Wall Street Journal*, 15 October 2002, A1; John G. Spooner, "Dell Dives into Printer Market," *News.com*, 24 September 2002, http://news.com.com; Andrew Park, Faith Keenan, and Cliff Edwards, "Whose Lunch Will Dell Eat Next?," *BusinessWeek*, 12 August 2002, 66–67; Dell Inc. website [accessed 5 March 2005] www.dell.com.

2. Anne Fisher, "Starting a New Job? Don't Blow It," *Fortune*, 24 February 2005 [accessed 26 February 2005] www.fortune.com.

3. Daft, *Management*, 533.

4. Melanie Warner, "How a Meek Comic Book Company Became a Hollywood Superpower," *New York Times*, 19 July 2004, C7.

5. Cornelus A. de Kluyver and John A. Pearce II, *Strategy: A View from the Top* (Upper Saddle River, N.J.: Prentice-Hall, 2003), 6–7.

6. Michael C. Mankins, "Stop Wasting Valuable Time," *Harvard Business Review*, September 2004, 58–65.

7. Daft, *Management*, 533.

8. Hydrogen Power Inc., website [accessed 8 March 2005] www.hydrogenpowerinc.com.

9. Translink website [accessed 8 March 2005] www.translink.co.uk.

10. Geoff Keighley, "New Life for Old Games," *Business 2.0*, September 2004, 64.

11. W. Chan Kim and Renée Mauborgne, "Blue Ocean Strategy," *Harvard Business Review*, October 2004, 76–84.

12. Tonya Vinas and Jill Jusko, "5 Threats That Could Destroy Your Company," *IndustryWeek*, September 2004, 52–61.

13. Daniel Lyons, "Kill Bill," *Forbes*, 7 June 2004, 86–96.

14. Robert D. Hof, "Building an Idea Factory," *BusinessWeek*, 11 October 2004, 194–200.

15. Barbara Kiviat, "The End of Management?" *Time Bonus Section: Inside Business*, August 2004.

16. Kiviat, "The End of Management?"

17. Julie Schlosser, "How Target Does It," *Fortune*, 18 October 2004, 100–112.

18. de Kluyver and Pearce, *Strategy: A View From the Top*, 55–56.

19. Harry R. Weber, "Tighter Regulation Sought for Data-Collection Industry," *Seattle Times*, 25 February 2005 [accessed 25 February 2005] www.seattletimes.com; "Thieves Steal Consumer Info Database," CNNMoney.com [accessed 15 February 2005] www.cnn.com.

20. "Throw Out the Old Handbook in Favor of Today's Crisis Drills," *PR News*, 27 January 2003, 1.

21. Daft, *Management*, 13.

22. Daft, *Management*, 514–515.

23. Alex Taylor III, "Toyota's Secret Weapon," *Fortune*, 23 August 2004, 60–66.

24. James G. Clawson, *Level Three Leadership: Getting Below the Surface*, 2nd ed. (Upper Saddle River, N.J.: Prentice Hall, 2003), 112–119.

25. "Sometimes, EQ Is More Important Than IQ," CNN.com, 14 January 2005 [accessed 14 January 2005] www.cnn.com; Daniel Goleman, "What Makes a Leader?" *Harvard Business Review*, November–December 1998, 92–102; Shari Caudron, "The Hard Case for Soft Skills," *Workforce*, July 1999, 60–66.

26. Andrew Park, "Thinking Out of the Box," *BusinessWeek*, 22 November 2004, 22.

27. Clawson, *Level Three Leadership: Getting Below the Surface*, 116.

28. Clawson, *Level Three Leadership: Getting Below the Surface*, 118.

29. G. Pascal Zachary, "The Survivor," *Business 2.0*, December 2004, 133–140.

30. Patricia Sellers, "eBay's Secret," *Fortune,* 18 October 2004, 161–178; Nick Wingfield, "Auctioneer to the World," *Wall Street Journal*, 5 August 2004, B1, B6.

31. Matthew Boyle, "The Wegmans Way," *Fortune*, 24 January 2005, 62–68.

32. Daniel Goleman, "Leadership That Gets Results," *Harvard Business Review*, March–April 2000, 78–90.

33. Daft, *Management*, 526.

34. Stephen P. Robbins and David A. De Cenzo, *Fundamentals of Management*, 4th ed. (Upper Saddle River, N.J.: Prentice Hall, 2004), 325.

35. Eve Tahmincioglu, "Group Mentoring: A Cost-Effective Option," *Workforce Management*, December 2004 [accessed 10 March 2005] www.workforce.com; Eve Tahmincioglu, "When Women Rise," *Workforce Management*, September 2004, 26–32.

36. David Welch and Kathleen Kerwin, "Rick Wagoner's Game Plan," *BusinessWeek*, 10 February 2003, 52–60.

37. Daft, *Management*, 382; Robbins and De Cenzo, *Fundamentals of Management*, 209.

38. Michael Been and Nitin Nohria, "Cracking the Code of Change," *Harvard Business Review*, May–June 2000, 133–141.

39. Robbins and De Cenzo, *Fundamentals of Management*, 211; Daft, *Management*, 384, 396.

40. Robbins and De Cenzo, *Fundamentals of Management*, 4th ed., 210–211.

41. Patrick J. Sauer, "Open-Door Management," *Inc.*, June 2003, 44.

42. Melanie Trottman, "Inside Southwest Airlines, Storied Culture Feels Strains," *Wall Street Journal*, 11 July 2003, A1, A6.

43. Kevin J. Gregson, "Converting Strategy to Results," *American Venture*, September/October 2004, 16–18.

44. Parija Bhatnagar, "Toys 'R' Us Sold for $6.6B," CNNMoney.com, 17 March 2005 [accessed 17 March 2005] http://cnnmoney.com; Clayton M. Christensen and Scott D. Anthony, "Toys 'R' History," *Wall Street Journal*, 31 August 2004, B4.

45. Mitchell Pacelle, Martin Fackler, and Andrew Morse, "For Citigroup, Scandal in Japan Shows Dangers of Global Sprawl," *Wall Street Journal*, 22 December 2004, A1, A10.

46. Robert E. Kaplan and Robert B. Kaiser, "Developing Versatile Leadership," *MIT Sloan Management Review*, Summer 2003, 19–26.

47. Louis Lavelle, "How to Groom the Next Boss," *BusinessWeek*, 10 May 2004, 93–94.

48. Courtland L. Bovée and John V. Thill, *Business Communication Today*, 8th ed. (Upper Saddle River, N.J.: Pearson Prentice Hall, 2005), 4.

49. Daft, *Management*, 128; Kathryn M. Bartol and David C. Martin, *Management* (New York: McGraw-Hill, 1991), 268–272.

50. Jeff Cole, "Wing Commander," *Wall Street Journal*, 10 January 2001, A1, A12.

51. "Airbus Says Its A380 Jet Is over Budget," *New York Times*, 13 December 2004, C2; "Boeing Puts a Price on Speedier Flights: $25," *Chicago Sun-Times*, 4 August 2002, 42.

52. Stanley Holmes and Wendy Zellner, "Boeing: A Flight to Safety," *BusinessWeek*, 29 July 2002, 70.

53. Holmes and Zellner, "Boeing: A Flight to Safety," 70; J. Lynn Lunsford, "Boeing Explores Plan B," *Wall Street Journal*, 11 June 2002, D5.

54. Boeing website [accessed 14 March 2005] www.boeing.com.

55. See Note 1.

56. Adapted from Walt Bogdanich, "Criminals Focus on A.T.M.'s, Weak Link in Banking System," *New York Times*, 3 August 2003, 1, 22; Richard Burnett, "Florida Warns of Credit Card Fraud at Gasoline Pumps," *Orlando Sentinel*, 26 January 2004 [accessed 10 May 2004] www.highbeam.com; Tom Lowry, "Thieves Swipe Credit With Card Readers," *USA Today*, 28 June 1999, 1B; Elaine Shannon, "A New Credit-Card Scam," *Time*, 5 June 2000, 54–55; Linda Punch, "Card Fraud: Down But Not Out," *Credit Card Management*, June 1999, 30–42; Bill Orr, "Will E-Commerce Reverse Card Fraud Trend?" *American Bankers Association*, April 2000, 59–62.

Chapter 8

1. "2005: Best Companies to Work For," *Fortune*, 24 January 2005 [accessed 11 March 2005] www.fortune.com; Bob Nelson, "Can't Contain Excitement at The Container Store," BizJournals.com [accessed 11 March 2005] www.bizjournals.com; Mike Duff, "Top-Shelf Employees Keep Container Store on Track," *DSN Retailing Today*, 8 March 2004, 7, 49; Bob Nelson, "The Buzz at The Container Store," *Corporate Meetings & Incentives*, June 2003, 32; Jennifer Saba, "Balancing Act," *Potentials*, 1 October 2003 [accessed 15 April 2004] www.highbeam.com; Peter S. Cohan, "Corporate Heroes," *Financial Executive*, 1 March 2003 [accessed 15 April 2004] www.highbeam.com; Margaret Steen, "Container Store's Focus on Training a Strong Appeal to Employees," *Mercury News* (San Jose, CA), 6 November 2003 [accessed 15 April 2004] www.highbeam.com; Holly Hayes, "Container Store Brings Clutter Control to San Jose, Calif.," 17 October 2003, *Mercury News* (San Jose, CA), 1F; "Performance Through People Award," press release, 10 September 2003; David Lipke, "Container Store's CEO: People Are Most Valued Asset," 13 January 2003, *HFN* [accessed 9 March 2003] www.highbeam.com; Lorrie Grant, "Container Store's Workers Huddle Up to Help You Out," 30 April 2002, *USA Today*, B1; The Container Store website [accessed 11 March 2005] www.containerstore.com.

2. Jonathan Fahey, "First, Heal Thyself," *Forbes*, 4 October 2004, 72–76.

3. Maryann Hammers, "The Company Picnic Is Alive and Well," *Workforce Management*, July 2004, 70–73.

4. Peter F. Drucker, "Management's New Paradigms," *Forbes*, 5 October 1998, 152–176.

5. Stephen P. Robbins and David A DeCenzo, *Management*, 4th ed. (Upper Saddle River, N.J.: Pearson Prentice Hall, 2004), 142–143.

6. Charles R. Greer and W. Richard Plunkett, *Supervision: Diversity and Teams in the Workplace*, 10th ed. (Upper Saddle River, N.J.: Prentice-Hall, 2003), 77.

7. Caroline Ellis, "The Flattening Corporation," *MIT Sloan Management Review*, Summer 2003, 5.

8. Jeffrey Pfeffer, "How Companies Get Smart," *Business 2.0*, January/February 2005, 74.

9. Gareth R. Jones, *Organizational Theory, Design, and Change* 4th ed. (Upper Saddle River, N.J.: Pearson Prentice Hall, 2004), 109.

10. Kevin Kelleher, "The Drug Pipeline Flows Again," *Business 2.0*, April 2004 [accessed 15 April 2004] www.business2.com.

11. Jones, *Organizational Theory, Design, and Change*, 109–111.

12. Lee Hawkins, Jr., "Reversing 80 Years of History, GM Is Reining in Global Fiefs," *Wall Street Journal*, 6 October 2004, A1, A14; Jonathan Fahey, "Come Home to Momma," *Forbes*, 21 June 2004, 56.

13. Richard L. Daft, *Management*, 6th ed. (Mason, Ohio: South-Western, 2003), 320.

14. Systems Integration/Modeling & Simulation website [accessed 12 March 2005] www.sim-s.com.

15. Jones, *Organizational Theory, Design, and Change*, 163.

16. Jones, *Organizational Theory, Design, and Change*, 167.

17. Don Clark, "Intel Restructures into 5 Units, Putting Focus on Succession Issue," *Wall Street Journal*, 18 January 2005, A3.

18. "Company Leadership," ChevronTexaco website [accessed 12 March 2005] www.chevrontexaco.com.

19. Daft, *Management*, 324–327.

20. Thomas A. Stewart and Louise O'Brien, "Execution Without Excuses," *Harvard Business Review*, March 2005 [accessed 12 March 2005] www.ebsco.com.

21. Jerald Greenberg and Robert A. Baron, *Behavior in Organizations*, 8th ed (Upper Saddle River, N.J.: Prentice-Hall, 2003), 558–560; Daft, *Management*, 329.

22. Pete Engardio and Bruce Einhorn, "Outsourcing Innovation," *BusinessWeek*, 21 March 2005, 84–94.

23. Inergy website [accessed 12 March 2005] www.inergy.com.

24. Stephen P. Robbins, *Essentials of Organizational Behavior*, 6th ed. (Upper Saddle River, N.J.: Prentice Hall, 2000), 105.

25. Greer and Plunkett, *Supervision*, 293.

26. Erin White, "To Make Your Pitch at U.K. Ad Agencies, You'll Need a Partner," *Wall Street Journal*, 3 September 2004, A1, A5.

27. David Kiley, "Can VW Find Its Beetle Juice?" *BusinessWeek*, 31 January 2005, 76+.

28. Daft, *Management*, 594; Robbins and De Cenzo, *Fundamentals of Management*, 336.

29. Steven Wilhelm, "Cutting Edge: 7E7 Program Chief Outlines Plans," *Puget Sound Business Journal*, 15 August 2003 [accessed 12 March 2005] www.bizjournals.com.

30. Daft, *Management*, 618; Robbins and De Cenzo, *Fundamentals of Management*, 262.

31. "Nanotech Task Force to Promote Silicon Valley," *San Francisco Business Times*, 16 December 2004 [accessed 12 March 2005] www.bizjournals.com.

32. Chuck Salter, "Ford's Escape Route," *Fast Company*, October 2004, 106–110.

33. Barbara De Lollis, "Virtual Meeting Companies Get Boost as Travel Wanes," *USA Today*, 18 March 2003, B10.

34. Jenny Goodbody, "Critical Success Factors for Global Virtual Teams," *Strategic Communication Management*, February/March 2005, 18–21; Ann Majchrzak, Arvind Malhotra, Jeffrey Stamps, and Jessica Lipnack, "Can Absence Make a Team Grow Stronger?" *Harvard Business Review*, May 2004, 131–137.

35. Robbins and De Cenzo, *Fundamentals of Management*, 257–258; Daft, *Management*, 634–636.

36. Robert Kreitner, *Management*, 9th ed. (Boston: Houghton Mifflin, 2004), 475–481; Daft, *Management*, 635–636.

37. Jon R. Katzenbach and Douglas K. Smith, "The Discipline of Teams," *Harvard Business Review*, July/August 2005, 162–171; Laird Mealiea and Ramon Baltazar, "A Strategic Guide for Building Effective Teams," *Public Personnel Management*, Summer 2005, 141–160; Larry Cole and Michael Cole, "Why is the Teamwork Buzz Word Not Working?" *Communication World*, February/March 1999, 29; Patricia Buhler, "Managing in the 90s: Creating Flexibility in Today's Workplace," *Supervision*, January 1997, 24+; Allison W. Amason, Allen C. Hochwarter, Wayne A. Thompson, and Kenneth R. Harrison, "Conflict: An Important Dimension in Successful Management Teams," *Organizational Dynamics*, Autumn 1995, 20+.

38. Jared Sandberg, "Some Ideas Are So Bad That Only a Team Effort Can Account for Them," *Wall Street Journal*, 29 September 2004, B1.

39. Robbins and De Cenzo, *Fundamentals of Management*, 258–259; Daft, *Management*, 625–627.

40. Jones, *Organizational Theory, Design, and Change*, 112–113; Greenberg and Baron, *Behavior in Organizations*, 280–281; Daft, *Management*, 629–631.

41. Greenberg and Baron, *Behavior in Organizations*, 418–419.

42. Daft, *Management*, 631–632.

43. Salter, "Ford's Escape Route."

44. Kreitner, *Management*, 547–548.

45. Courtland L. Bovée and John V. Thill, *Business Communication Today*, 8th ed. (Upper Saddle River, N.J.: Pearson Prentice Hall, 2005), 42–43.

46. See Note 1.

47. Adapted from Dan Goodin, "Graduating Students Weigh New Job Incentive: Money to Stay Away," *Wall Street Journal*, 4 May 2001, B1; Mark Larson, "Intel Offering Buy-outs to Workers, College Recruits," *Sacramento Business Journal*, 4 May 2001, 1; Barbara Clements, "The Workplace: This Year's College Grads Will Face a More Challenging Job Hunt," *News Tribune*, Tacoma, Wash., 7 May 2001, D1.

Chapter 9

1. "Carvin AW175" (product reviews), Harmony Central website [accessed 18 March 2005] www.harmonycentral.com; "Carvin CT6M California Carved Top," *Guitar Player*, December 2004 [accessed 18 March 2005] www.guitarplayer.com; Carvin website [accessed 17 March 2005] www.carvin.com; Rich Krechel, "Some Custom-Made Guitars Can Cost $4,000 to $8,000," *St. Louis Post Dispatch*, 27 September 2001, 16.

2. Roberta A. Russell and Bernard W. Taylor III, *Operations Management: Focusing on Quality and Competitiveness*, 4th ed. (Upper Saddle River, N.J.: Prentice Hall, 2003), 19–23.

3. Stephen P. Robbins and David A. DeCenzo, *Fundamentals of Management*, 4th ed. (Upper Saddle River, N.J.: Pearson Prentice-Hall, 2004), 405.

4. Lee Hawkins, Jr., "U.S. Auto Makers Get Better Grades for Productivity," *Wall Street Journal*, 11 June 2004, A3.

5. Robert Kreitner, *Management*, 9th ed. (Boston: Houghton-Mifflin, 2004), 576–578; Robert Johnston and Graham Clark, *Service Operations Management*, 2d ed. (Harlow, England: Pearson Education Limited, 2005), 249–251.

6. Milt Freudenheim, "Digital Rx: Take Two Aspirins and E-Mail Me in the Morning," *New York Times*, 2 March 2005 [accessed 7 March 2005] www.nytimes.com.

7. Meridian Golf website [accessed 17 March 2005] www.meridiangolf.com; T. J. Becker, "Have It Your Way," *The Edward Lowe Report*, February 2002, 1–3, 12.

8. Julie Schlosser, "Cashing In on the New World of Me," *Fortune*, 13 December 2004, 244–250.

9. Philip Reed, "The Smart Invasion: A New Smart Line of Cars Is Coming to the U.S.," Edmunds.com, 9 March 2004 [accessed 21 March 2005] www.edmunds.com; Philip Siekman, "The Smart Car Is Looking More So," *Fortune*, 15 April 2002, 310(I)–310(P).

10. "Solectron to Manufacture the Personal Internet Communicator Introduced by AMD," Solectron website [accessed 21 March 2005] www.solectron.com.

11. Rod Kurtz, "Case Study," *Inc.*, July 2004, 48–49.

12. Jon Swartz, "Inmates Vs. Outsourcing," *USA Today*, 7 July 2004, B1–B2.

13. Boeing website [accessed 21 March 2005] www.boeing.com.

14. Robert J. Trent, "What Everyone Needs to Know About SCM," *Supply Chain Management Review*, 1 March 2004 [accessed 16 April 2004] www.manufacturing.net.

15. Jane C. Linder, "Transformational Outsourcing," *MIT Sloan Management Review*, Winter 2004, 52–58.

16. Jeffrey K. Liker and Thomas Y. Choi, "Building Deeper Supplier Relationships," *Harvard Business Review*, December 2004, 104–113.

17. Lee J. Krajewski and Larry P. Ritzman, *Operations Management: Processes and Value Chains*, 7th ed (Upper Saddle River, N.J.: Pearson Prentice Hall, 2005), 244–245.

18. G. Pascal Zachary, "More Green from Green Beans," *Business 2.0*, August 2004, 64–66.

19. Mark M. Davis, Nicholas J. Aquilano, and Richard B. Chase, *Fundamentals of Operations Management* (Boston: Irwin McGraw-Hill, 1999), 241–242.

20. Karen M. Kroll, "Life on the Island," *IndustryWeek*, July 2004, 51–52.

21. Mark Landler, "Slovakia No Longer a Laggard in Automaking," *New York Times*, 13 April 2004 [accessed 15 April 2004] www.nytimes.com.

22. Krajewski and Ritzman, *Operations Management: Processes and Value Chains*, 299–300.

23. Russell and Taylor, *Operations Management: Focusing on Quality and Competitiveness*, 161.

24. Russell and Taylor, *Operations Management: Focusing on Quality and Competitiveness*, 161–165, 176.

25. Davis, Aquilano, and Chase, *Fundamentals of Operations Management*, 254; Ravi Anupindi, Sunil Chopra, Sudakar D. Deshmukh, Jan A. Van Mieghem, and Eitan Zemel, *Managing Business Process Flows*, 2d ed. (Upper Saddle River, N.J.: Pearson Prentice Hall, 2006), 290–291.

26. Kreitner, *Management*, 202–203.

27. Tom Lecklider, "Vision Sensors Decide for Themselves," *Evaluation Engineering*, February 2005 [accessed 21 March 2005] www.evaluationengineering.com.

28. Daren Fonda, "Sole Survivor," *Time*, 8 November 2004, 48–49.

29. John Teresko, "Making a Pitch for PLM," *IndustryWeek*, August 2004, 57–62.

30. Russell and Taylor, *Operations Management*, 101–102.

31. Davis, Aquilano, and Chase, *Fundamentals of Operations Management*, 64.

32. UGS, "Palm, Inc. Cut Engineering Expenditures in Half by Developing the Palm i705 Handheld Exclusively in NX" (case study), UGS website [accessed 21 March 2005] www.ugs.com.

33. Teresko, "Making a Pitch for PLM."

34. Russell and Taylor, *Operations Management*, 147–148.

35. "Online Extra: Porsche's CEO Talks Shop," *BusinessWeek*, 22 December 2003 [accessed 18 March 2005] www.businessweek.com.

36. James A. Senn, *Information Technology: Principles, Practices, Opportunities*, 3d ed. (Upper Saddle River, N.J.: Prentice Hall, 2004), 328.

37. Helen Gurevich, "Surviving the Enterprise Integration War," *Health Management Technology*, February 2004, 66+; Mark Jones, "Ingram Micro: The Trouble with XML and Web Services," *InfoWorld*, 9 November 2001 [accessed 17 April] www.infoworld.com; "Companies Continue to Find Benefit In EDI Investments," *Electronic Commerce News*, 1 March 2004, 1; Ian Mount, "Why EDI Won't Die," *Business 2.0*, August 2003 [accessed 16 March 2005] www.business2.com.

38. Jae K. Shim and Joel G. Siegel, *Operations Management* (Hauppauge, N.Y.: Barron's Educational Series, 1999), 326.

39. Anupindi, et al, *Managing Business Process Flows*, 289; Russell and Taylor, *Operations Management*, 532.

40. Jonathan Fahey, "Just in Time Meets Just Right," *Forbes*, July 2004, 66–68.

41. Russell and Taylor, *Operations Management*, 549.

42. Trent, "What Everyone Needs to Know About SCM."

43. David Hughes, "Life-Cycle Software," *Aviation Week & Space Technology*, 18 August 2003 [accessed 17 April 2004] www.ebsco.com.

44. Tim Laseter and Keith Oliver, "When Will Supply Chain Management Grow Up?" *Strategy + Business*, Fall 2003, 32–36; Trent, "What Everyone Needs to Know About SCM."

45. Laura Rock Kopczak and M. Eric Johnson, "The Supply-Chain Management Effect," *MIT Sloan Management Review*, Spring 2003, 27–34.

46. George Taninecz, "Forging the Chain," *IndustryWeek*, 15 May 2000, 40–46.

47. Laseter and Oliver, "When Will Supply Chain Management Grow Up?"

48. Alan Young, "Healing Corrupted by Practices of Big Pharma," *Toronto Star*, 11 April 2004 [accessed 17 April 2004] www.highbeam.com; Kathleen Longcore, "Group Aims to Fix Medical Mistakes, Shorten Recovery with Technology," *Grand Rapids Press* (Grand Rapids, MI), 3 April 2004 [accessed 17 April 2004] www.highbeam.com.

49. Jonathan Fahey, "Over-Engineering 101," *Forbes*, 13 December 2004, 62.

50. Moon Ihlwan, "Hyundai: Kissing Clunkers Goodbye," *BusinessWeek*, 17 May 2004, 45.

51. Davis, Aquilano, and Chase, *Fundamentals of Operations Management*, 177–179; Russell and Taylor, *Operations Management*, 131.

52. Russell and Taylor, *Operations Management*, 131.

53. Dale H. Besterfield, Carol Besterfield-Michna, Glen H. Besterfield, and Mary Besterfield-Sacre, *Total Quality Management*, 3d ed., (Upper Saddle River, N.J.: Prentice Hall, 2003), 2–3.

54. Besterfield, et al, *Total Quality Management*, 10–13.

55. John McQuaig, "Whatever Happened to TQM?" *Wenatchee Business Journal*, October 2004, C8.

56. Tom McCarty, "Six Sigma at Motorola," *European CEO*, September–October 2004 [accessed 21 March 2005] www.motorola.com.

57. McCarty, "Six Sigma at Motorola"; General Electric, "What Is Six Sigma?" GE website [accessed 21 March 2005] www.ge.com.

58. International Organization for Standardization website [accessed 21 March 2005] www.iso.org.

59. See Note 1.

60. Gina Imperato, "How Microsoft Reviews Suppliers," *Fast Company*, September 1998, 148.

Chapter 10

1. Adapted from Atlas Container website [accessed 24 March 2005] www.atlascontainer.com; John Case, "The Power of Listening," *Inc.*, March 2003, 76–84; Esther Durkalski, "Workplace Perks Spark Happy Employees," *Paperboard Packaging*, May 2001, p28+; Steven Averett, "Provocative Politics," *Industrial Engineer*, May 2003, p28+; Esther Durkalski, "Mapping Its Future," *Paperboard Packaging*, October 2001 [accessed 30April 2004] www.highbeam.com; Richard McGill Murphy, "The Persuaders," *Fortune Small Business*, May 2004, 74+.

2. Leigh Buchanan, "The Things They Do for Love," *Harvard Business Review*, December 2004, 19–20.

3. Stephen P. Robbins and David A. DeCenzo, *Fundamentals of Management*, 4th ed. (Upper Saddle River, N.J.: Prentice Hall, 2004), 284.

4. Edwin A. Locke and Gary P. Latham, "What Should We Do About Motivation Theory? Six Recommendations for Twenty-First Century," *Academy of Management Review*, July 2004, 388+.

5. Robbins and DeCenzo, *Fundamentals of Management*, 27–29.

6. Andrew J. DuBrin, *Applying Psychology: Individual & Organizational Effectiveness*, 6th ed. (Upper Saddle River, N.J.: Pearson Prentice-Hall, 2004), 122–124.

7. Richard L. Daft, *Management,* 6th ed. (Mason, Ohio: Thomson South-Western, 2003), 552–553.

8. Kerry Hannon, "Praise Cranks Up Productivity," *USA Today*, 20 August 2004, B6.

9. Matthew Gilbert, "The Insider: Awards & Recognition," *Workforce Management*, November 2004, 82–83.

10. Daft, *Management,* 547; Robbins and DeCenzo, *Fundamentals of Management*, 283–284; DuBrin, *Applying Psychology: Individual & Organizational Effectiveness*, 15–16.

11. John Grossmann, "Location, Location, Location," *Inc.*, August 2004, 83–86.

12. Richard L. Daft, "Theory Z: Opening the Corporate Door for Participative Management," *Academy of Management Executive*, November 2004, 117–121.

13. Todd Raphael, "Think Twice: HR's New Guru? An NBA Bigmouth," *Workforce Management*, 6 July 2004 [accessed 25 March 2005] www.workforce.com.

14. Daft, *Management*, 554–555.

15. Eryn Brown, "How to Get Paid What You're Worth," *Business 2.0*, May 2004, 102–110.

16. Robbins and DeCenzo, *Fundamentals of Management*, 289.

17. Bob Parks, "Where the Customer Service Rep Is King," *Business 2.0*, June 2003, 70–72.

18. Thomas Nelson, "High Impact for Low-Wage Workers," *Workforce Management*, August 2004, 47–49.

19. James A. Dinsmoor, "The Etymology of Basic Concepts in the Experimental Analysis of Behavior," *Journal of the Experimental Analysis of Behavior*, November 2004, 311–316.

20. Stephanie Armour, "Companies Hire Even As They Lay Off," *USA Today*, 15 May 2001, A1.

21. Carlos Tejeda and Gary McWilliams, "New Recipe for Cost Savings: Replace Expensive Workers," *Wall Street Journal*, 11 June 2003, A1, A6.

22. Lauren Keller Johnson, "The New Loyalty: Make It Work for Your Company," *Harvard Management Update*, March 2005, 3–5.

23. Johnson, "The New Loyalty: Make It Work for Your Company."

24. Randall Stross, "When Long Hours at a Video Game Stop Being Fun," *New York Times*, 21 November 2004, sec. 3, 3; Mark Schwanhauser, "Electronic Arts Hit with Lawsuit on OT," *Mercury News*, 19 February 2005 [accessed 30 March 2005] www.siliconvalley.com.

25. DuBrin, *Applying Psychology: Individual & Organizational Effectiveness*, 159.

26. Dan Seligman, "New Crisis—Junk Statistics," *Forbes*, 18 October 2004, 118–120.

27. Jeffrey Pfeffer, "All Work, No Play? It Doesn't Pay." *Business 2.0*, August 2004, 50.

28. Jane Sturges, "Working to Live or Living to Work? Work/Life Balance Early in the Career," *Human Resource Management Journal*, 2004, Vol. 14, Issue 4, 5+.

29. Keith H. Hammonds, "Balance Is Bunk!" *Fast Company*, October 2004, 68–76.

30. Fiona Haley, "Mutual Benefit," *Fast Company*, October 2004, 98–99.

31. Rona Gindin, "Dealing with a Multicultural Workforce," *Nation's Restaurant News*, September–October 1998, 31, 83; Howard Gleckman, "A Rich Stew in the Melting Pot," *BusinessWeek*, 31 August 1998, 76+; Toby B. Gooley, "A World of Difference," *Logistics Management and Distribution Report*, June 2000, 51–55; William H. Miller, "Beneath the Surface," *IndustryWeek*, 20 September 1999, 13–16.

32. Linda Beamer and Iris Varner, *Intercultural Communication in the Workplace*, 2d ed. (New York: McGraw-Hill Irwin, 2001), xiii.

33. "A Trend to Watch: Rehiring Retirees," *Workforce Management*, November 2004, 27; Kelly Greene, "Many Older Workers to Delay Retirement Until After Age 70," *Wall Street Journal*, 23 September 2003, D2.

34. Kim Clark, "A Fondness for Gray Hair," *U.S. News & World Report*, 8 March 2004, 56–58; Donna Fenn, "Respect Your Elders," *Inc.*, September 2003, 29–30; "Work Force Facts," *Chicago Tribune*, 10 September 2000, sec. 6, 1.

35. Catrine Johansson, "Older Workers, Retirees Build New Careers at Home Depot," *San Diego Union-Tribune*, 21 June 2004, C5.

36. Clark, "A Fondness for Gray Hair," 56; Stephanie Armour, "Maturing Boomers Smack 'Silver Ceiling,'" *USA Today*, 16 August 2001, 1A, 2A.

37. Norm Alster, "When Gray Heads Roll, Is Age Bias at Work?" *New York Times*, 30 January 2005, Sunday Business, 3.

38. Hope Yen, "Court Rules Deliberate Bias Not Needed to Win Age Discrimination Suits," *Seattle Times*, 30 March 2005 [accessed 30 March 2005] www.seattletimes.com.

39. Julie Connelly, "Youthful Attitudes, Sobering Realities," *New York Times*, 28 October 2003, E1, E6; Stephanie Armour, "Young Workers Say Their Age Holds Them Back," *USA Today*, 8 October 2003, A1–A2.

40. Michael Kinsman, "Respect Helps Mix of Generations Work Well Together," *San Diego Union-Tribune*, 19 September 2004, H2.

41. Betsy Morris, "How Corporate America Is Betraying Women," *Fortune*, 10 January 2005, 64–74.

42. Patrick McGeehan, "What Merrill's Women Want," *New York Times*, 22 August 2004, sec. 3, 1, 4; "Morgan Stanley Settles Claims of Gender Bias for $54 Million," *Los Angeles Times*, 13 July 2004, C5.

43. Stephanie Armour, "'Rife with Discrimination'," *USA Today*, 24 June 2004, 3B; Lisa Takeuchi Cullen, "Wal-Mart's Gender Gap," *Time*, 5 July 2004, 44.

44. Louis Uchitelle, "Gaining Ground on the Wage Front," *New York Times*, 31 December 2004, C1–C2; Morris, "How Corporate America Is Betraying Women"; Aaron Bernstein, "Women's Pay: Why the Gap Remains a Chasm," *BusinessWeek*, 14 June 2004, 25–59; Judy B. Rosener, "Women on Corporate Boards Make Good Business Sense," *Directorship*, May 2003, 7+; United Press International, "Women Increase Employment, Not Salaries," 8 March 2004 [accessed 29 April 2004] www.highbeam.com; Gary Strauss and Del Jones, "Too Bright Spotlight Burns Female CEOs," *USA Today*, 18 December 2000, 3B.

45. Ann Harrington and Petra Bartosiewicz, "50 Most Powerful Women," *Fortune*, 18 October 2004, 181–190.

46. "Gender Diversity Linked to Bottom-Line Performance," *MSI*, 1 April 2004 [accessed 29 April 2004] www.highbeam.com.

47. M. June Allard, "Theoretical Underpinnings of Diversity," in Carol Harvey and M. June Allard, *Understanding and Managing Diversity*, 2d ed. (Upper Saddle River, N.J.: Prentice-Hall, 2002), 7.

48. Robert Kreitner, *Management*, 9th ed. (Boston: Houghton Mifflin, 2004), 375–377; "One-Fifth of Women Are Harassed Sexually," *HR Focus*, April 2002, 2.

49. Kreitner, *Management*, 84.

50. Roger O. Crockett, "For Blacks, Progress Without Parity," *BusinessWeek*, 14 July 2003 [accessed 1 April 2005] www.businessweek.com.

51. Cora Daniels, "Finally in the Director's Chair," *Fortune*, 4 October 2004.

52. Todd Henneman, "A New Approach to Faith at Work," *Workforce Management*, October 2004, 76–77.

53. David A. Thomas, "Diversity as Strategy," *Harvard Business Review*, September 2004, 98–108; Joe Mullich, "Hiring Without Limits," *Workforce Management*, June 2004, 53–58; Mike France and William G. Symonds, "Diversity Is About to Get More Elusive, Not Less," 7 July 2003, *BusinessWeek* [accessed 24 January 2005] www. businessweek.com; Anne Papmehl, "Diversity in Workforce Paying Off, IBM Finds," *Toronto Star*, 7

October 2002 [accessed 4 November 2003], www.elibrary.com.

54. "Anne Fisher, "How You Can Do Better on Diversity," *Fortune*, 15 November 2004, 60.

55. Carol Hymowitz, "Managers Err If They Limit Their Hiring to People Like Them," *Wall Street Journal*, 12 October 2004, B1.

56. Stephanie Armour, "Fewer Working Flex-Time Hours, Report Says," *USA Today*, 25 July 2005, B1; Stephanie Armour, "Working 9-to-5 No Longer," *USA Today*, 6 December 2004, B1–B2.

57. Samuel Greengard, "Sun's Shining Example," *Workforce Management*, March 2005, 48–49.

58. Kemba J. Dunham, "Telecommuters' Lament," *Wall Street Journal*, 31 October 2000, B1, B8.

59. Doreen Carvajal, "It's All About the Coffeepot," *International Herald Tribune*, 4 February 2004 [accessed 24 April 2004] www.highbeam.com.

60. ITAC press release, "Home-Based Telework by U.S. Employees Grows Nearly 40% Since 2001," International Telework Association and Council website, 4 September 2003 [accessed 24 April 2004] www.telecommute.org.

61. Susan Campbell ,"More Hartford, Conn.-Area Workers Telecommute to Beat Winter Blues," *Hartford Courant*, 5 February 2004 [accessed 24 April 2004] www.highbeam.com.

62. Carvajal, "It's All About the Coffeepot."

63. Clare Brennan, "What Is Job-Sharing?" iVillage [accessed 31 March 2005] www.ivillage.co.uk.

64. Cynthia R. Cunningham and Shelley S. Murray, "Two Executives, One Career," *Harvard Business Review*, February 2005, 125–131.

65. Diane Brady, "Hopping Aboard the Daddy Track," *BusinessWeek*, 8 November 2004, 100–101.

66. Sylvia Ann Hewlett and Carolyn Buck Luce, "Off-Ramps and On-Ramps," *Harvard Business Review*, March 2005, 43–54.

67. Stephanie Armour, "Moms Find It Easier to Pop Back Into Workforce," *USA Today*, 23 September 2004, B1–B2.

68. Demographia.com [accessed 22 August 2005] www.demographia.com.

69. UAW Local 1853 website [accessed 31 March 2005] www.uawlocal1853.org.

70. Murphy, "The Persuaders."

71. Paul D. Staudohar, "Labor Relations in Basketball: The Lockout of 1998–99," *Monthly Labor Review*, April 1999, 3–9; E. Edward Herman, *Collective Bargaining and Labor Relations*, 4th ed. (Upper Saddle River, N.J.: Prentice Hall, 1998), 61; "NLRB Permits Replacements During Legal Lockout," *Personnel Journal*, January 1987, 14–15.

72. CBC Sports website [accessed 31 March 2005] www.cbc.ca.

73. Nancy Cleeland, "Union Membership Steady in 2001 at 13.5% of Nation's Workforce," *Los Angeles Times*, 18 January 2002, C3; Steven Greenhouse, "Unions Hit Lowest Point in 6 Decades," *New York Times*, 21 January 2001, 1, 20.

74. Steven Greenhouse, "Unions to Push to Make Organizing Easier," *New York Times*, 31 August 2003, 16.

75. Ron Fournier, "Teamsters, SEIU to Bolt AFL-CIO as Part of Four-Union Rift," *Seattle Times*, 24 July 2005 [accessed 24 July 2005] www.seattletimes.com; Aaron Bernstein, "Can This Man Save Labor?" *BusinessWeek*, 13 September 2004, 80–88.

76. Cora Daniels, "Up Against the Wal-Mart," 17 May 2004, *Fortune*, 112–120; Steven Greenhouse, "Wal-Mart, Driving Workers and Supermarkets Crazy," *New York Times*, 19 October 2003, 3; Janet Adamy, "Supermarkets Get Concessions; Wal-Mart Wage Gap Remains," *Wall Street Journal*, 1 March 2004, B2; Martin Kasindork, "Strikes Strain Southern California, *USA Today*, 20 October 2003, 3A.

77. Michael Arndt, "Salvation from the Shop Floor," *BusinessWeek*, 3 February 2003, 100–101; Stanley Holmes, "Boeing: Putting Out Labor Fires," *BusinessWeek*, 29 December 2003, 43; Jill Jusko, "Nature Versus Nurture," *IndustryWeek*, July 2003, 40–42; David Kiley, "Foreign Companies Cast Long Shadow on UAW Negotiations," *USA Today*, 6 August 2003, B1.

78. See Note 1.

79. Adapted from Hewlett and Luce, "Off-Ramps and On-Ramps."

Chapter 11

1. Jamba Juice website [accessed 2 April 2005] www.jambajuice.com; Michelle V. Rafter, "Restaurant Workers in the Drive-Thru Lane," *Workforce Management*, April 2005 [accessed 2 April 2005] www.workforce.com; Alan J. Liffle, "Jamba Juice Sets Big Growth Goals as Segment's Leader," *Nation's Restaurant News*, 20 December 2004, 8+; Dina Berta, "Confab Forecast: Labor Shortage, Turnover to Worsen Soon," *Nation's Restaurant News*, 15 November 2004, 8, 16; Megan Rowe, "Jamba Juice," *Restaurant Business*, 1 July 2001, 42; Janet Moore, "Juicy Prospects," *Star Tribune*, 17 August 2001, 1D; "Here's How Jamba Juice Unsnagged a New Incentive Plan," *IOMA's Report on Managing Customer Service*, April 2001, 6–7; Brenda Paik Sunoo, "Blending a Successful Workforce," *Workforce*, March 2000, 44–48; Karyn Strauss, "Perron: Jamba's Juiced for Growth, Plans IPO," *Nation's Restaurant News*, 24 January 2000, 1, 76; Karyn Strauss, "Report: Smoothie Indies Face Rocky Road as Chains Slurp Up Market Share," *Nation's Restaurant News*, 14 June 1999, 8, 138; "Best Healthy Choice Menu Selection: Jamba Juice: Jambola Bread Is on the Rise," *Nation's Restaurant News*, 24 March 1999, 168; Michael Adams, "Kirk Perron: Jamba Juice," *Restaurant Business*, 15 March 1999, 38; Victor Wishna, "Leaving for Good," *Restaurant Business*, 1 May 2000, 64–74.

2. Gary Dessler, *A Framework for Human Resource Management*, 3d ed. (Upper Saddle River, N.J.: Pearson Prentice-Hall, 2004), 2.

3. "Data Bank Annual 2004: Flexibility Moves to Center Stage," *Workforce Management*, December 2004, 86–92; Kris Maher, "Human-Resources Directors Are Assuming Strategic Roles," *Wall Street Journal*, 17 June 2003, B8.

4. Dessler, *A Framework for Human Resource Management*, 74–75.

5. Shari Randall, "Succession Planning Is More Than a Game of Chance," *Workforce Management* [accessed 1 May 2004] www.workforce.com.

6. "Have You Upgraded Your Retention Plan Yet?" *HRFocus*, July 2004, 6–10.

7. David Koeppel, "The New Cost of Keeping Workers Happy," *New York Times*, 7 March 2004, 11.

8. Dessler, *A Framework for Human Resource Management*, 82–83.

9. Daniel Nasaw, "Companies Are Hedging Their Best by Hiring Contingent Employees," *Wall Street Journal*, 14 September 2004, B10.

10. "Employee or Independent Contractor? How to Tell," *HR Focus*, January 2004, 7, 10.

11. Robert J. Bohner, Jr. and Elizabeth R. Salasko, "Beware the Legal Risks of Hiring Temps," *Workforce Management*, October 2002, 50–57.

12. Henry R. Cheeseman, *Contemporary Business and E-Commerce Law*, 4th ed. (Upper Saddle River, N.J.: Prentice Hall, 2003), 625; Bohner, Jr. and Salasko, "Beware the Legal Risks of Hiring Temps."

13. United States Immigration Support website [accessed 1 May 2004] www.immigrationconsultant.org; Barry Newman, "Safe Crossing: One Solution to Illegal Workers Takes Form: H-2B," *Wall Street Journal*, 14 April 2004, A1, A12.

14. Spencer E. Ante and Paul Magnusson, "Too Many Visas for Techies?" *BusinessWeek*, 25 August 2003, 39.

15. Dean Calbreath, "Foreign-Worker Visa Cap Met in 1 Day," *San Diego Union-Tribune*, 5 October 2004, C1.

16. "Data Bank Annual 2004: Flexibility Moves to Center Stage."

17. Joellen Perry, "Help Wanted," *U.S. News & World Report*, 8 March 2004, 48–54.

18. Dessler, *A Framework for Human Resource Management*, 66.

19. Dessler, *A Framework for Human Resource Management*, 72.

20. Samuel Greengard, "Quality of Hire: How Companies Are Crunching the Numbers," *Workforce Management*, July 2004 [accessed 8 July 200] www.workforce.com.

21. Jeff Meisner, "Cutting Through the Blah, Blah, Blah," *Puget Sound Business Journal*, 19–25 November 2004, 27–28.

22. Patrick J. Kiger, "Eliyon Steps Up the Search," *Workforce Management*, January 2005, 41–43.

23. "How to Make Your Recruitment & Applicant Tracking System Pay Off," *HR Focus*, December 2003, 3–4.

24. Kerry J. Sulkowicz, "The Corporate Shrink," *Fast Company*, January 2005, 38.

25. Samuel Greengard, "Gimme Attitude," *Workforce Management*, July 2003, 56–60.

26. Ann Zimmerman, "Wal-Mart to Toughen Job Screening," *Wall Street Journal*, 12 August 2004, A3, A6; Kris Maher, "The Jungle: Focus on Recruitment, Pay and Getting Ahead," *Wall Street Journal*, 20 January 2004, B8.

27. Laura Cutland, "Hiring Hoops," *Puget Sound Business Journal*, 16–22 July 2004, 27–28.

28. Samuel Greengard, "Cracking the Hiring Code," *Workforce Management*, January 2004, 15.

29. Eilene Zimmerman, "Getting to Know You Is as Easy as A, B, C, or D," *New York Times*, 30 November 2003, 8.

30. Barbara Rose, "Employers Test a Gatekeeper," *San Diego Union-Tribune*, 13 December 2004, C6.

31. Andy Meisler, "Negative Results," *Workforce Management*, October 2003, 35–40.

32. "Employers' Use of Drug Screening on the Decline," *Industrial Health and Safety News*, March 2005, 12; Meisler, "Negative Results," 35–40.

33. Tammy Galvin, "2003 Industry Report," *Training*, October 2003, 21+.

34. Michelle V. Rafter, "Liberal Arts Grads Get the Business," *Workforce Management*, September 2004, 20.

35. Carol A. Hacker, "New Employee Orientation: Make It Pay Dividends for Years to Come," *Information Systems Management*, Winter 2004, 89–92.

36. Galvin, "2003 Industry Report."

37. Galvin, "2003 Industry Report."

38. Dessler, *A Framework for Human Resource Management*, 198.

39. PerformanceNow.com website [accessed 2 May 2004] www.performancenow.com; Dessler, *A Framework for Human Resource Management*, 199.

40. Andrew Park and Peter Burrows, "What You Don't Know About Dell," *BusinessWeek*, 3 November 2003, 76+.

41. Dessler, *A Framework for Human Resource Management*, 198–199.

42. Andrew E. Jackson, "Recognizing the "I" in Team," *Industrial Engineer*, March 2005, 38–42.

43. Jeff St. John, "Kennewick, Wash., 'Snoop' Software Maker Also Protects Privacy," *Tri-City Herald* (Kennewick, Wash.), 17 April 2004 [accessed 2 May 2004] www.highbeam.com; Dessler, *A Framework for Human Resource Management*, 204–205.

44. Dessler, *A Framework for Human Resource Management*, 223–225.

45. Arlene Weintraub, "Revenge of the Overworked Nerds," *BusinessWeek*, 8 December 2003, 41.

46. Pui-Wing Tam and Nick Wingfield, "As Tech Matures, Workers File a Spate of Salary Complaints," *Wall Street Journal*, 24 February 2005, A1, A11; Kris Maher, "Changes U.S. Rules for Overtime Pay Roil the Workplace," *Wall Street Journal*, 7 July 2004, B1, B6.

47. Matthew Grim, "Wal-Mart Uber Alles," *American Demographics*, October 2003, 38–39; Jeffrey E. Garten,

"Wal-Mart Gives Globalism a Bad Name," *BusinessWeek*, 8 March 2004, 24; Jerry Useem, "Should We Admire Wal-Mart?" *Fortune*, 8 March 2004, 118–120.

48. Michelle V. Rafter, "Welcome to the Club," *Workforce Management*, April 2005, 41–46; Elayne Robertson Demby, "Two Stores Refuse to Join the Race to the Bottom for Benefits and Wages," *Workforce Management*, February 2004, 57–59; Stanley Holmes and Wendy Zellner, "The Costco Way," *BusinessWeek*, 12 April 2004, 76–77.

49. Gary Strauss and Barbara Hansen, "CEO Pay Packages 'Business as Usual'," *USA Today*, 31 March 2005, B1–*Business 2.0.*

50. Silvia Ascarelli, "Mannesmann Trial Ends, but Pay Furor Burns On," *Wall Street Journal*, 23 July 2004, A8.

51. Jennifer Reingold, "CEOs Who Should Lose Their Jobs," *Fast Company*, October 2003, 68–80; Louis Lavelle, "Executive Pay," *BusinessWeek*, 21 April 2003, 86–90; Jerry Useem, "Have They No Shame?" *Fortune*, 28 April 2003, 57–64.

52. Jeff D. Opdyke, "Getting a Bonus Instead of a Raise," *Wall Street Journal*, 29 December 2004, D1–D2.

53. Steven Wilhelm, "The Protector," *Puget Sound Business Journal*, 24–30 December 2004, 8–9.

54. Janet Wiscombe, "Can Pay for Performance Really Work?," *Workforce Management*, August 2001, 28–34.

55. Dessler, *A Framework for Human Resource Management*, 231–232.

56. Karen Kroll, "Paying for Performance," *Inc.*, November 2004, 46.

57. John S. McClenahen and Traci Purdum, "Making Variable Pay Pay," *IndustryWeek*, September 2004, 72.

58. Sarah Skidmore, "Jack Puts Health Plan on Employees' Menu," *San Diego Union-Tribune*, 16 December 2004, C1, C5.

59. Joseph Weber, "Health Insurance: Small Biz Is in a Bind," *BusinessWeek*, 27 September 2004, 47–48; Joseph Pereira, "Parting Shot: To Save on Health-Care Costs, Firms Fire Disabled Workers," *Wall Street Journal*, 14 July 2003, A1, A7; Timothy Aeppel, "Ill Will: Skyrocketing Health Costs Start to Pit Worker vs. Worker," *Wall Street Journal*, 17 July 2003, A1, A6; Vanessa Furhmans, "To Stem Abuses, Employers Audit Workers' Health Claims," *Wall Street Journal*, 31 March 2004, B1, B7; Milt Freudenheim, "Employees Paying Ever-Bigger Share for Health Care," *New York Times*, A1, C2; Julie Appleby, "Employers Get Nosy About Workers' Health," *USA Today*, 6 March 2003, B1–B2; Ellen E. Schultz and Theo Francis, "Employers' Caps Raise Retirees' Health-Care Costs," *Wall Street Journal*, 25 November 2003, B1, B11; Vanessa Fuhrmans, "Company Health Plans Try to Drop Spouses," *Wall Street Journal*, 9 September 2003, D1, D2.

60. Jeremy W. Peters, "Company's Smoking Ban Means Off-Hours, Too," *New York Times*, 8 February 2005, C5.

61. Steve Lohr, "The Disparate Consensus on Health Care for All," *New York Times*, 6 December 2004, C16; Sara Schaefer and Laurie McGinley, "Census Sees a Surge in Americans Without Insurance," *Wall Street Journal*,

30 September 2003, B1, B6; "Half of Health Care Spending Is Wasted, Study Finds," *Detroit News*, 10 February 2005 [accessed 5 April 2005] www.detnews.com.

62. Cheeseman, *Contemporary Business and E-Commerce Law*, 625.

63. James H. Dulebohn, Brian Murray, and Minghe Sun, "Selection Among Employer-Sponsored Pension Plans: The Role of Individual Differences," *Personal Psychology*, Summer 2000, 405–432.

64. Carroll Lachnit, "The Drowning Pool," *Workforce Management*, October 2004, 12.

65. Keith Naughton, "Business's Killer I.O.U.," *Newsweek*, 6 October 2003, 42–44; Christine Dugas, "Companies Consider Pension Freezes," *USA Today*, 7 January 2004, B1.

66. Jeffrey Pfeffer, "The Confidence Game," *Business 2.0*, November 2004, 94.

67. Mary Williams Walsh, "Taking the Wheel Before a Pension Runs into Trouble," *New York Times*, 30 January 2005, Sunday Money, 5; Amy Borrus, "Will the Bough Break?" *BusinessWeek*, 14 April 2003, 62–63; Barbara De Lollis and Marilyn Adams, "Fed Up with Pension Defaults," *USA Today*, 9 September 2004, B1; Janice Revell, "New Math: Don't Pay As You Go Under," *Fortune*, 4 October 2004, 38.

68. Dessler, *A Framework for Human Resource Management*, 282.

69. George Van Dyke, "Examining Your 401k," *Business Credit*, January 2000, 59.

70. Paul J. Lim, "Losing Altitude," *U.S. News & World Report*, 21 April 2003, 58–60; Paul J. Lim and Matthew Benjamin, "The 401(k) Stumbles," *U.S. News & World Report*, 24 December 2001, 30–32.

71. Tom Lauricella, "A Lesson for Social Security: Many Mismanage Their 401(k)s," *Wall Street Journal*, 1 December 2004, A1, A4; Carroll Lachnit, "The 401(k) Gamble," *Workforce Management*, June 2004, 10.

72. Robert A Guth and Joann S. Lublin, "Tarnished Gold: Microsoft Ushers Out Era of Options," *Wall Street Journal*, 9 July 2003, A1, A9; John Markoff and David Leonhardt, "Microsoft Will Award Stock, Not Options, to Employees," *New York Times*, 9 July 2003, A1, C4.

73. Cheeseman, *Contemporary Business and E-Commerce Law*, 626.

74. Sara Schaefer Muñoz, "A Good Idea, but . . . ," *Wall Street Journal*, 24 January 2005, R6.

75. Patrick J. Kiger, "A Case for Child Care," *Workforce Management*, April 2004, 34–40.

76. Patrick J. Kiger, "Child-Care Models," *Workforce Management*, April 2004, 38.

77. "Employer-Sponsored Daycare Can Be Profitable, New Study Shows," Bowdoin College website [accessed 6 April 2005] www.bowdoin.edu; Erin L. Kelly, "The Strange History of Employer-Sponsored Child Care: Interested Actors, Uncertainty, and the Transformation of Law in Organizational Fields," *American Journal of Sociology*, November 2003, 606–649.

78. Stephanie Armour, "Employers Stepping Up in Elder Care," *USA Today*, 3 August 2000, 3B.

79. Agilent Technologies website [accessed 6 April 2005] www.agilent.com.

80. Andy Meisler, "A Matter of Degrees," *Workforce Management*, May 2004, 32–38; Stephanie Armour, "More Firms Help Workers Find Home Sweet Home," *USA Today*, 30 August 2004, C1–C2.

81. Atkinson, "Wellness, Employee Assistance Programs"; Kevin Dobbs, Jack Gordon, and David Stamps, "EAPs Cheap But Popular Perk," *Training*, February 2000, 26.

82. Laila Karamally, "The Insider: Employee Assistance," *Workforce Management*, September 2004, 60–63.

83. Alison Stein Wellner, "The Pickup Artists," *Workforce Management*, July 2004 [accessed 6 April 2005] www.workforce.com.

84. Adam Cohen and Cathy Booth Thomas, "Inside a Layoff," *Time*, 16 April 2001, 38–40.

85. Challenger, Gray & Christmas website [accessed 6 April 2005] www.challengergray.com.

86. John Jude Moran, *Employment Law: New Challenges in the Business Environment*, 2d ed. (Upper Saddle River, N.J.: Prentice Hall, 2002), 127; Dan Seligman, "The Right to Fire," *Forbes*, 10 November 2003, 126–128.

87. Del Jones, "Let People Know Where They Stand, Welch Says," *USA Today*, 18 April 2005, B5; Del Jones, "Study: Thinning Herd from Bottom Helps," *USA Today*, 14 March 2005, B1.

88. Cheeseman, *Contemporary Business and E-Commerce Law*, 649.

89. See Note 1.

Chapter 12

1. Michael Paoletta, "Toyota's Scion Starts Label," *Billboard*, 26 March 2005, 8+; "2005 Scion tC," Edmunds.com [accessed 12 April 2005] www.edmunds.com; "10 Hottest Cars and Trucks in 2004," *Advertising Age*, 20 December, 28; David Welch, "Not Your Father's . . . Whatever," *BusinessWeek*, 15 March 2004, 82–84; Daren Fonda, "Scion Grows Up," *Time (Canada)*, 16 August 2004, 61; Katherine Zachery, "The Makings of a Hit," *Ward's Auto World*, June 2004, 42; Christopher Palmeri, "Toyota's Youth Models Are Having Growing Pains," *BusinessWeek*, 31 May 2004, 32; Steven Kichen, "Scion's Smart Moves," *Forbes*, 12 October 2004 [accessed 12 April 2005] www.forbes.com; Norihiko Shirouzu, "Scion Plays Hip-Hop Impresario to Impress Young Drivers," *Wall Street Journal*, 5 October 2004, B1+; Phil Patton, "As Authentic as 'The Matrix' or Menudo," *New York Times*, 25 July 2004, sec. 12, 1+; Dan Lienert, "What's New? With Toyota's Scion, Youth Must Be Served," *New York Times*, 19 October 2003 [accessed 12 November 2003] www.nytimes.com; Fara Warner, "Learning How to Speak to Gen Y," *Fast Company*, July 2003, 36; Darren Fonda, "Baby, You Can Drive My Car," *Time*, 30 June 2003, 46; Christopher Palmeri, Ben Elgin, Kathleen Kerwin, "Toyota's Scion: Dude, Here's Your Car," *BusinessWeek*, 9 June 2003, 44; Jonathan Fahey, "For the Discriminating Body Piercer," *Forbes*, 12 May 2003, 136;

George Raine, "Courting Generation Y," *San Francisco Chronicle*, 11 May 2003, I3.

2. "AMA Board Approves New Marketing Definition," *Marketing News*, 1 March 1985, 1.

3. Avon website [accessed 13 April 2005] www.avon.com.

4. Philip Kotler and Gary Armstrong, *Principles of Marketing*, 10th ed. (Upper Saddle River, N.J.: Pearson Prentice Hall, 2004), 6.

5. Stan Choe, "Businesses Still Barter, in Simple or Complex Exchanges," *Charlotte Observer*, 30 March 2004 [accessed 5 May 2004] www.highbeam.com.

6. June Lee Risser, "Customers Come First," *Marketing Management*, November/December 2003, 22–26.

7. Ranjay Gulati and James B. Oldroyd, "The Quest for Customer Focus," *Harvard Business Review*, April 2005, 92–101.

8. Peter Kafka, "Sony Sings Off-Key," *Forbes*, 13 December 2004 [accessed 12 April 2005] www.forbes.com.

9. Kotler and Armstrong, *Principles of Marketing*, 12–13.

10. Kotler and Armstrong, *Principles of Marketing*, 19–21.

11. Fiona Haley, "Profitable Player Winner: Progressive," *Fast Company*, October 2004, 84–85.

12. Tanisha A. Sykes, "Power Hitter," *Black Enterprise*, June 2004, 161–169.

13. "Two Strikes and You're Out," *Marketing Management*, September/October 2004, 5.

14. Lands End website [accessed 12 April 2005] www.landsend.com.

15. Gordon A. Wyner, "The Journey to Marketing Effectiveness," *Marketing Management*, March/April 2004, 8–9; Lawrence A. Crosby and Sheree L. Johnson, "The Three Ms of Customer Loyalty," *Marketing Management*, July/August 2004, 12–13.

16. Alan Middleton, "The Evolution of Marketing," *Marketing*, 28 February 2005, 9.

17. "Marketing Under Fire," *Marketing Management*, July/August 2004, 5.

18. "Blog Power," *Marketing*, 17 January 2005, 4.

19. J. Walker Smith, "Permission Is Not Enough," *Marketing Management*, May/June 2004, 52.

20. "Undercover Marketing Uncovered," *CBSnews.com*, 25 July 2004 [accessed 11 April 2005] www.cbsnews.com; Stephanie Dunnewind, "Teen Recruits Create Word-of-Mouth 'Buzz' to Hook Peers on Products," *Seattle Times*, 20 November 2004 [accessed 11 April 2005] www.seattletimes.com.

21. Peter Fingar, Harsha Kumar, and Tarun Sharma, *Enterprise E-Commerce* (Tampa, Fla.: Meghan-Kiffer Press, 2000), 24, 109.

22. Teri Agins, "As Consumers Mix and Match, Fashion Industry Starts to Fray," *Wall Street Journal*, 8 September 2004, A1, A6.

23. Dan Hill, "Why They Buy," *Across the Board*, November–December 2003, 27–32; Eric Roston, "The Why of Buy," *Time*, April 2004.

24. Michael R. Solomon, *Consumer Behavior*, 6th ed. (Upper Saddle River, N.J.: Pearson Prentice Hall, 2004), 366–372.

25. "Motoring Online," *Economist*, 2 April 2005, 11+.

26. Pui-Wing Tam, "As Cameras Go Digital, a Race to Shape Habits of Consumers," *Wall Street Journal*, 19 November 2004, A1+.

27. James C. Anderson and James A. Narus, *Business Market Management: Understanding, Creating, and Delivering Value*, 2d ed. (Upper Saddle River, N.J.: Pearson Prentice Hall, 2004), 114–116; Kotler and Armstrong, *Principles of Marketing*, 215, 224–226.

28. Eric Almquist, Martin Kon, and Wolfgang Bock, "The Science of Demand," *Marketing Management*, March/April 2004, 20–26; David C. Swaddling and Charles Miller, "From Understanding to Action," *Marketing Management*, July/August 2004, 31–35.

29. Joseph Pereira, "Spying on the Sales Floor," *Wall Street Journal*, 21 December 2004, B1, B4.

30. Eric Dash, "The Gift That Keeps Giving," *Inc.*, September 2004, 32.

31. Brain Grow and Gerry Khermouch, "The Low-Carb Fight Ahead," *BusinessWeek*, 22 December 2003, 48.

32. Christopher Palmeri, "Teach an Old Sneaker New Tricks—and the Kids Will Come Running," *BusinessWeek*, 7 June 2004, 92–94.

33. Mike Schneider, "Florida Orange Growers Fight Back Against Low-Carb Diets," *Atlanta Journal-Constitution*, 22 January 2004 [accessed 29 April 2005] www.ajc.com.

34. May Wong, "Encyclopedias Gather Dust in Internet Age," *AP Online* [accessed 5 May 2004] www.high-beam.com; Encyclopaedia Britannica website [accessed 5 May 2004] www.britannica.com; Leslie Kaufman, "Playing Catch-Up at the On-Line Mall," *New York Times*, 21 February 1999, sec. 3, 1, 6; Gary Samuels, "CD-ROMs First Big Victim," *Forbes*, 28 February 1994, 42–44; Richard A. Melcher, "Dusting Off the Britannica," *BusinessWeek*, 20 October 1997, 143–146.

35. Kotler and Armstrong, *Principles of Marketing*, 47–48.

36. Gordon A. Wyner, "Pulling the Right Levers," *Marketing Management*, July/August 2004, 8–9.

37. Jennifer Barron and Jill Hollingshead, "Making Segmentation Work," *Marketing Management*, January/February 2002, 24–28.

38. Michael J. McCarthy, "Granbury, Texas, Isn't a Rural Town: It's a 'Micropolis'," *Wall Street Journal*, 3 June 2004, A1, A6.

39. Haya El Nassar and Paul Overberg, "Old Labels Just Don't Stick in 21st Century," *USA Today*, 17 December 2003; Michael J. Weiss, *The Clustering of America* (New York: Harper & Row, 1988), 41.

40. Lawrence A. Crosby and Sheree L. Johnson, "Redefine Your Customer Base," *Marketing Management*," April 2004, 12–13.

41. Susie Harwood, "Targeting," *New Media Age*, 3 March 2005, 6–7; Horacio D. Rozanski, Gerry Bollman, and Martin Lipman, "Seize the Occasion," *Strategy + Business*, Third Quarter 2001, 42–51.

42. Duff McDonald, "Best Buy's Brilliant Bouncer," *Business 2.0*, January/February 2005, 60.

43. Hélène Fouquet, "Making Money Fast on Very Slow Cars," *New York Times*, sec. 3, 6.

44. Michael E. Raynor and Howard S. Weinberg, "Beyond Segmentation," *Marketing Management*, December 2004, 22–28.

45. Mountain Dew website [accessed 12 April 2005] www.mountaindew.com.

46. Kotler and Armstrong, *Principles of Marketing*, 55–56.

47. Steve Hamm, "Why High Tech Has to Stay Humble," *BusinessWeek*, 19 January 2004, 76–77.

48. Kichen, "Scion's Smart Moves."

49. Adapted from Julian E. Barnes, "Fast-Food Giveaway Toys Face Rising Recalls," *New York Times*, 16 August 2001, A1; Shirley Leung, "Burger King Recalls 2.6 Million Kids Meal Toys," *Wall Street Journal*, 1 August 2001, B2.

Chapter 13

1. Jennifer Clark, "Botulinum Toxin Type A Safety Review Remains Positive," *Dermatology Times*, February 2005, 105, 110; Melissa Foss, "Botox and Beyond," *InStyle*, March 2005, 427+; John Jesitus, "Bogus Botox Sounds Wake-Up Call," *Cosmetic Surgery Times*, March 2005, 1, 10; Harriet Tramer, "Docs Detecting How to Boost Botox Profitability," *Crain's Cleveland Business*, 7 March 2005, 17; Julie Schmit, "Medicis Tightens Face of Vanity Race with $2.8 Billion Bid for Inamed," *USA Today*, 22 March 2005 [accessed 14 April 2005] www.usatoday.com; "Smooth Moves: Medical Treatments for Facial Wrinkles," Mayo Clinic website [accessed 14 April 2005] www.mayoclinic.com; David Lipschultz, "When Facial Wrinkles Are Ironed Away for Good," *New York Times*, 11 February 2003, D6; Brian O'Reilly, "Facelift in a Bottle," *Fortune*, 24 June 2002, 101–104; Ronald D. White, "Allergan Bets on Botox Lift," *Los Angeles Times*, 23 May 2002, C1; Michael McCarthy, "Botox Maker Plans $50 Million Ad Campaign," *USA Today*, 29 April 2002, B1; Reed Abelson, "FDA Approves Allergan Drug for Fighting Wrinkles," *New York Times*, 16 April 2002, C4; Carol Lewis, "Botox Cosmetic: A Look at Looking Good," *FDA Consumer*, July–August 2002 [accessed 14 April 2005] www.fda.gov.

2. Keven Kelleher, "The No-Service Broker," *Business 2.0*, July 2004, 50–51.

3. Poul Funder Larsen, "Better Is . . . Better," *Wall Street Journal*, 22 September 2003, R6, R11.

4. Pete Engardio and Faith Keenan, "The Copycat Economy," *BusinessWeek*, 26 August 2002, 94–96.

5. Brendan Coffey, "Tangerine Flake Streamline Baby," *Forbes*, 18 October 2004, 78–80.

6. James Bandler, "Ending Era, Kodak Will Stop Selling Most Film Cameras," *Wall Street Journal*, 14 January 2004, B1, B4.

7. Allison Fass, "Reality Bites," *Forbes*, 25 November 2002, 242; Lisa Granatstein, "Not Fade Away," *Brandweek*, 21 October 2002, SR6; Jenna Schnuer, "Launch of the Year," *Advertising Age*, October 21, 2002, S8; Michael Grossman, "Rolling Revisions," *Folio*, October 2002, 66; Anthony Violanti, "Rolling Stone Losing the Youth Battle," *Buffalo News*, 21 June 2002, C.1.

8. Rogier Van Bakel, "The Art of Brand Revival," *Business 2.0*, September 2002, 45–48.

9. David Armstrong, Monte Burke, Emily Lambert, Nathan Vardi, and Rob Wherry, "85 Innovations," *Forbes*, 23 December 2002, 122–202.

10. Lev Grossman, "The Quest for Cool," *Time*, 8 September 2003, 48–54.

11. Douglas McGray, "Babes in R&D Toyland," *Fast Company*, December 2002, 46.

12. David Haigh and Jonathan Knowles, "How to Define Your Brand and Determine Its Value," *Marketing Management*, May/June 2004, 22–28.

13. Janell M. Kurtz and Cynthia Mehoves, "Whose Name Is It Anyway," *Marketing Management*, January/February 2002, 31–33.

14. Julia Angwin and Sarah McBride, "AOL and XM to Jointly Create Online Radio Service," *Wall Street Journal*, 11 April 2005, A10.

15. Rick Barrett, "Harley-Davidson, Ford Extend Pact; Automaker to Use Harley's Colors, Logos," *Milwaukee Journal Sentinel*, 5 February 2004 [accessed 17 April 2005] www.ebsco.com; Laura Clark Geist, "Licensing Links Brands, People with Goods," *Automotive News*, 16 September 2002, 2M.

16. Roy Evans, "The Year in Ideas: Cup-Holder Cuisine," *New York Times Magazine*, 15 December 2002, 6, 80.

17. Jennifer Saranow, "The Puncture Wound I Got for Christmas," *Wall Street Journal*, 30 December 2004, D1+.

18. Bernard Silver, "Bar Codes Grow in Use at Age 30; Keeping Track of Almost Everything," *Seattle Times*, 3 July 2004 [accessed 17 April 2005] www.ebsco.com.

19. General Mills website [accessed 17 April 2005] www.generalmills.com.

20. Jeff Leeds, "Music Industry Is Trying Out New Releases as Digital Only," *New York Times*, 22 November 2004, C1+; "Fox to Create Drama Series for Cell Phones," *San Diego Union-Tribune*, 11 November 2004, C3.

21. Mike Freeman, "Gateway to Cut Back Selling Electronics to Focus on Core PCs," *San Diego Union-Tribune*, 14 September 2004, C1, C4.

22. Sarah Ellison, "Retailers' Appetite for Top Sellers Has Food Firms Slimming Down," *Wall Street Journal*, 28 October 2004, A1+.

23. Stan Sutter, "Billion Dollar Brands," *Marketing*, 14 February 2005, 2.

24. Ellison, "Retailers' Appetite for Top Sellers Has Food Firms Slimming Down."

25. Jack Neff, "P & G Shores Up Old Spice with Body-Wash Extension," *Advertising Age*, 30 December 2002, 8.

26. Gary Strauss, "Squeezing New from Old," *USA Today*, 4 January 2001, B1–B2.

27. "Jackie Chan Eyes Business Empire Ranging from Clothes to Cookies," *Business CustomWire*, 6 April 2005 [accessed 15 April] www.ebsco.com.

28. Ben Carter, "Celador Extends Millionaire Format to Theatre Tour," *Marketing (UK)*, 31 March 2005, 3.

29. Sarah Ellison, "Kraft's Stale Strategy," *Wall Street Journal*, 18 December 2003, B1, B6.

30. Rukmini Callimachi, "Nike sans Swoosh Enters Wal-Mart," *Seattle Times*, 15 April 2005 [accessed 15 April 2005] www.seattletimes.com.

31. "Nike Says No to Blue-Light Specials," *CNNMoney*, 4 May 2005 [accessed 4 May 2005] http://cnnmoney.com.

32. Carol Matlack, "What's This? The French Love McDonald's?" *BusinessWeek*, 13 January 2003, 50; Shirley Leung, "Armchairs, TVs and Espresso—Is It McDonald's?" *Wall Street Journal*, 30 August 2002, A1, A6.

33. Mitchell Pacelle, "Growing Profit Source for Banks: Fees from Riskiest Card Holders," *Wall Street Journal*, 6 July 2004, A1+.

34. "Q2 2004 SanDisk Corp. Earnings Conference Call," *Fair Disclosure Wire*, 14 July 2004 [accessed 3 August 2004] www.highbeam.com.

35. Eric Anderson and Duncan Simester, "Mind Your Pricing Cues," *Harvard Business Review*, September, 96–103.

36. Thomas T. Nagle and Reed K. Holden, *The Strategy and Tactics of Pricing*, 3d ed. (Upper Saddle River, N.J.: Prentice-Hall, 2002), 2–4.

37. Lisa Margonelli, "How Ikea Designs Its Sexy Price Tags," *Business 2.0*, October 2002, 106–112.

38. Amy Cortese, "The Power of Optimal Pricing," *Business 2.0*, September 2002, 68–70.

39. Shawn Young, "A Price War Hits Internet Calling," *Wall Street Journal*, 26 August 2004, D1, D3.

40. Priceline website [accessed 18 April 2005] www.priceline.com.

41. Adapted from "Bathtub Curve," *Engineering Statistics Handbook*, National Institute of Standards and Technology website [accessed 16 April 2005] www.nist.gov; Robert Berner, "The Warranty Windfall," *BusinessWeek*, 20 December 2004, 84–86; Larry Armstrong, "When Service Contracts Make Sense," *BusinessWeek*, 20 December 2004, 86

Chapter 14

1. Costco website [accessed 19 April 2005] www.costco.com; Michelle V. Rafter, "Welcome to the Club," *Workforce Management*, April 2005, 41–46; David Meier, "It's the Employees, Stupid," MotleyFool.com, 17 September 2004 [accessed 7 October 2004] www.fool.com; Jeff Malester, "Costco Sales Rise 10%, Hit $12.4 Billion in Fis. Q2," *Twice*, Ilana Polyak, "Warehouse Sale," *Kiplinger's Personal Finance*, May 2005, 67; 7 March 2005, 53;

Suzanne Wooley, "Costco? More Like Costgrow," *Money*, August 2002, 44–46; "Costco: A Cut Above," *Retail Merchandiser*, July 2002, 44; Pete Hisey, "Costco.com Means Business," *Retail Merchandiser*, October 2001, 36; Shelly Branch, "Inside the Cult of Costco," *Fortune*, 6 September 1999, 184–188.

2. Ingram Book Group website [accessed 7 May 2004] www.ingrambook.com.

3. Robert M. Grant and Anjali Bakhru, "The Limits of Internationalisation in E-Commerce," *European Business Journal*, 3rd Quarter 2004, 95–104.

4. Supervalu website [accessed 21 April 2005] www.supervalu.com.

5. Avnet website [accessed 21 April 2005] www.avnet.com.

6. Robert Berner and Brain Grow, "Out-Discounting the Discounter," *BusinessWeek*, 10 May 2004, 78–79.

7. Wal-Mart home page [accessed 21 April 2005], www.walmart.com; Mike Troy, "Wal-Mart Supercenters: The Combo with the Midas Touch," *DSN Retailing Today*, 8 May 2000, 113–114.

8. Daniel McGinn, "Honey, I Shrunk the Store," *Newsweek*, 3 June 2002, 36–37.

9. Louise Lee and Kerry Capell, "Taps for Music Retailers?" *BusinessWeek*, 23 June 2003, 40; Paul Keegan, "Is the Music Store Over?" *Business 2.0*, March 2004, 115–119.

10. Glen A. Bere, "Big Boxes Pop Up in Regional Malls, Altering Landscape for Chain Stores," *National Jeweler*, 16 May 2005, 1+; Bruce Horovitz and Lorrie Grant, "Changes in Store for Department Stores?" *USA Today*, 21 January 2005, B1-B2.

11. Dean Starkman, "As Malls Multiply, Developers Fight Fiercely for Turf," *Wall Street Journal*, 19 April 2002, A1, A6; Robert Berner and Gerry Khermouch, "Retail Reckoning," *BusinessWeek*, 10 December 2001, 72–77.

12. Timothy J. Mullaney and Robert D. Hof, "E-Tailing Finally Hits Its Stride," *BusinessWeek*, 20 December 2004, 36–37.

13. Grant and Bakhru, "The Limits of Internationalisation in E-Commerce."

14. Cheryl Lu-Lien Tan and Sally Beatty, "Surfing for Jimmy Choo: Luxury Hits the Web," *Wall Street Journal*, 21 October 2004, D1, D4.

15. Japan Guide website [accessed 22 April 2005] www.japan-guide.com.

16. "Toyota Takes Aim at Young Buyers," *Grand Rapids Press*, 3 June 2002, A7.

17. Gary McWilliams and Ann Zimmerman, "Dell Plans to Peddle PCs Inside Sears, Other Large Chains," *Wall Street Journal*, 30 January 2003, B1, B3.

18. Cate T. Corcoran, "What Works: Retailers Share Strategies for Online Success," *Women's Wear Daily*, 9 March 2005, 6.

19. Maryanne Murray Buechner, "Recharging Sears," *Time*, 27 May 2002, 46.

20. Michelle Andrews, "Next to the Express Checkout, Express Medical Care," *New York Times*, 28 July 2004, Sunday Money, 5.

21. Lorrie Grant, "Staples Makes Plans to Stock Grocery Aisles with Supplies," *USA Today*, 10 March 2005 [accessed 19 April 2005] www.ebsco.com.

22. Jennifer Ordoñez, "Shop Till You're Cool," *Newsweek*, 22 November 2004, 58.

23. Andy Serwer, "The iPod People Have Invaded Apple's Stores," *Fortune*, 13 December 2004, 79.

24. "Why Pop-Up Shops Are Hot," *Business 2.0*, December 2004, 34.

25. Black & Decker website [accessed 21 April 2005] www.blackanddecker.com.

26. Felder website [accessed 21 April 2005] www.felder.co.at.

27. Super Jock'n Jill website [accessed 21 April 2005] www.superjocknjill.com.

28. Felix Sanchez, "Boeing Honors Its Top Suppliers," *Press-Telegram* (Long Beach, Calif.), 15 February 2002 [accessed 7 May 2004] www.highbeam.com.

29. Philip Kotler and Gary Armstrong, *Principles of Marketing*, 9th ed. (Upper Saddle River, N.J.: Prentice Hall, 2001), 435.

30. Kevin Kelleher, "Giving Dealers a Raw Deal," *Business 2.0*, December 2004, 82–84.

31. Kelleher, "Giving Dealers a Raw Deal."

32. Michael S. Katz and Jeffrey Rothfeder, "Crossing the Digital Divide," *Strategy + Business*, First Quarter 2000, 26–41; Anne Stuart, "Clicks & Bricks," *CIO*, 15 March 2000, 76–84."

33. Andrew J. Rohm and Fareena Sultan, "The Evolution of E-Business," *Marketing Management*, January/February 2004, 32–37.

34. Barney Gimbel, "Yule Log Jam," *Fortune*, 13 December 2004, 163–170.

35. Gimbel, "Yule Log Jam."

Chapter 15

1. Dave Morgan, "Impressions Count," *ClickZ*, 5 May 2005 [accessed 6 May 2005] www.clickz.com; Kevin Newcomb, "Google Doubles Revenue, Extends Focus on Big Advertisers," *ClickZ*, 21 April 2005 [accessed 6 May 2005] www.clickz.com; Kevin Newcomb, "Google's CPM Ads Meet Lukewarm Reception," *ClickZ*, 27 April 2005 [accessed 6 May 2005] www.clickz.com; Pamela Parker, "Google Targets Ads by Site, Sells by CPM," *ClickZ*, 25 April 2005 [accessed 6 May 2005] www.clickz.com; Krysten Crawford, "Google: Biting the Hand That Feeds It?" *CNN/Money*, 3 May 2005 [accessed 6 May 2005] www.cnnmoney.com; Google website [accessed 6 May 2005] www.google.com; Jefferson Graham, "Google's AdSense a Bonanza for Some Web Sites," *USA Today*, 11 March 2005 [accessed 6 May 2005] www.usatoday.com; Verne Kopytoff, "Google Earnings Juiced by Ads," *San Francisco Chronicle*, 22 April 2005, C1; Fred Vogelstein, "Search and Destroy," *Fortune*, 2 May 2005, 72–82; Fred Vogelstein, "Google Shifts Gears," *Fortune*, 26 April 2005 [accessed 6 May 2005] www.fortune.com.

2. Ellen Neuborne, "Telemarketing After 'Do Not Call,'" *Inc.*, November 2003, 32–34.

3. Philip Kotler and Gary Armstrong, *Principles of Marketing*, 10th ed. (Upper Saddle River, N.J.: Pearson Prentice Hall, 2004), 544.

4. Kenneth E. Clow and Donald Baack, *Integrated Advertising, Promotion, and Marketing Communications*, 2d ed. (Upper Saddle River, N.J.: Pearson Prentice Hall, 2004). 338.

5. Gerald L. Manning and Barry L. Reece, *Selling Today*, 9th ed. (Upper Saddle River, N.J.: Pearson Prentice Hall, 2004), 7–8.

6. Manning and Reece, *Selling Today*, 53.

7. William Wells, John Burnett, and Sandra Moriarty, *Advertising: Principles & Practice*, 6th ed. (Upper Saddle River, N.J.: Prentice Hall, 2003), 31.

8. Wells, Burnett, and Moriarty, *Advertising: Principles & Practice*, 47–48.

9. Craig R. Endicott, "100 Leading National Advertisers," *Advertising Age*, 28 June 2004, S1+.

10. "Money Where Your Mouth Is," *Marketing Management*, March/April 2004, 7.

11. Clow and Baack, *Integrated Advertising, Promotion, and Marketing Communications*, 215–216.

12. LPGA website [accessed 5 May 2005] www.lpga.com.

13. Clow and Baack, *Integrated Advertising, Promotion, and Marketing Communications*, 244–247.

14. Clow and Baack, *Integrated Advertising, Promotion, and Marketing Communications*, 207.

15. Clow and Baack, *Integrated Advertising, Promotion, and Marketing Communications*, 208–212.

16. Endicott, "100 Leading National Advertisers."

17. Libby Quaid, "Smart Grocery Carts Help Shoppers Live Life in the Fast Aisle," *Seattle Times*, 4 May 2005 [accessed 4 May 2005] www.seattletimes.com.

18. Paul Soltoff, "Does CAN-SPAM Hurt Compliant Marketers?" *ClickZ*, 7 March 2005 [accessed 5 May 2005] www.clickz.com.

19. Heidi Dietrich, "Direct Marketer Steers Away from E-Mail Ads," *Puget Sound Business Journal*, 23–29 April 2004, 28.

20. Agilent Technologies website [accessed 6 May 2004] www.agilent.com.

21. Jeanne Jennings, "Let's Do the Numbers," *ClickZ*, 3 January 2005 [accessed 5 May 2005] www.clickz.com; Anne Mitchell, "Getting and Staying CAN-SPAM Compliant," *ClickZ*, 30 August 2004 [accessed 5 May 2005] www.clickz.com.

22. Pamela Parker, "Online Ad Budgets to Swell to $26 Billion by 2010," *ClickZ*, 3 May 2005 [accessed 5 May 2005] www.clickz.com.

23. Zachary Rogers, "Online Ad Revenues Up 33 Percent in 2004," *ClickZ*, 28 April 2005 [accessed 5 May 2005] www.clickz.com.

24. Zachary Rogers, "Measuring Blog Marketing," *ClickZ*, 12 January 2005 [accessed 5 May 2005] www.clickz.com.

25. National Advertising Review Council website [accessed 6 May 2005] www.narcpartners.org.

26. James Quilter, "Bounty Launches Baby Suppression File for Bereaved Families," *PrecisionMarketing*, 1 April 2005, 1.

27. Wells, Burnett, and Moriarty, *Advertising: Principles & Practice*, 45–53.

28. Kotler and Armstrong, *Principles of Marketing*, 511–512.

29. Clow and Baack, *Integrated Advertising, Promotion, and Marketing Communications*, 349.

30. Clow and Baack, *Integrated Advertising, Promotion, and Marketing Communications*, 322.

31. "Shoppers Become Product Advisers," *Yomiuri Shimbun*, 7 February 2005 [accessed 7 May 2005] www.ebsco.com.

32. U.S. Olympic Committee website [accessed 7 May 2005] www.usoc.org.

33. Ben Mathis-Lilley and Marc Silver, "Jabba the Spud Is Next," *U.S. News & World Report*, 18 April 2005, D16.

34. Adapted from Insure.com website [accessed 6 May 2005] www.insure.com.

Chapter 16

1. Adapted from Dana Cimilluca, "MCI Board Wants Verizon to Up Bid," *Seattle Times*, 12 April 2005, C1; James S. Granelli, "Shareholders May Decide MCI's Fate," *Los Angeles Times*, 7 April 2005, C1; Erin McClam, "Former WorldCom Chief Ebbers Convicted of All Counts," *Seattle Times*, 15 March 2005 [accessed 15 March 2005] www.seattletimes.com; Leslie Cauley, "MCI Reports Loss, Shows How Tough Carriers Have It," *USA Today*, 5 November 2004, B3; Christopher Stern, "WorldCom Plans New Job Cuts," *Washington Post*, 16 January 2004, E1; Peter J. Howe, "MCI Chief Unveils Global Vision for Telecom Giant," *Boston Globe*, 24 September 2004 [accessed 15 October 2004] www.highbeam.com; Andrew Backover, "MCI Monitor Calls for Power Shift, *USA Today*, 23 August 2003 [accessed 15 October 2004] www.usatoday.com; Liesbeth Evers, "Capellas Faces Cuts to £24m WorldCom Pay Package," *Accountancy Age*, 12 November 2002 [accessed 15 October 2004] www.accountancyage.com; Craig Schneider, "MCI: Ringing in Reform," *CFO*, 21 October 2003 [accessed 15 October 2004] www.cfo.com; "Ebbers to Face WorldCom Fraud Charges," *Accountancy Age*, 3 March 2004 [accessed 13 October 2004] www.accountancyage.com; "Ex-WorldCom Execs Face Criminal Charges," *Accountancy Age*, 28 August 2003 [accessed 13 October 2004] www.accountancyage.com; Kevin Maney, Andrew Backover, and Elliot Blair Smith, "Straightening Out the Story on Telecom's Routing Game," *USA Today*, 26 August 2003 [accessed 15 October 2004] www.usatoday.com; Larry Schlesinger, "WorldCom Report: Recovery Is on Track," *Accountancy Age*, 6 October 2003 [accessed 13 October 2004] www.accountancyage.com; James Hester, "U.S. Draws Up Corporate Governance Blueprint," *Accountancy Age*, 26 August 2003 [accessed 13 October 2004] www.accountancyage.com; Robert Jaques, "Customers Set to Abandon WorldCom/MCI," *Accountancy Age*, 6 October 2003 [accessed 13 October

2004] www.accountancyage.com; Liz Loxton, "Judge Approves MCI Recovery Plans," *Accountancy Age*, 11 April 2003 [accessed 13 October 2004] www.accountancyage.com; "MCI Just Can't Escape Its Past," *Accountancy Age*, 8 July 2003 [accessed 13 October 2004] www.accountancyage.com; Paul Grant, "MCI Excluded from U.S. Government Work," *Accountancy Age*, 8 January 2003 [accessed 13 October 2004] www.accountancyage.com; "Emergence News," MCI website [accessed 13 October 2004] www.mci.com; Om Malik, "One Scandal That Won't Die," *Business 2.0*, 29 July 2003 [accessed 13 October 2004] www.business2.com; Susie Gharib, interview with Michael Capellas on *Nightly Business Report*, 20 April 2004 [access 15 October 2004] www.highbeam.com.

2. Robert Stuart, "Accountants in Management—A Globally Changing Role," *CMA Magazine*, 1 February 1997, 5.

3. Melody Petersen, "Shortage of Accounting Students Raises Concern on Audit Quality," *New York Times*, 19 February 1999, C1, C3.

4. Jack L. Smith, Robert M. Keith, and William L. Stephens, *Accounting Principles*, 4th ed. (New York: McGraw-Hill, 1993), 16–17.

5. Nanette Byrnes, "Green Eyeshades Never Looked So Sexy," *BusinessWeek*, 10 January 2005, 44; "Rules Make Accountants Newly Hot Commodity," *Oregonian*, 13 April 2005 [accessed 24 April 2005] www.ebsco.com.

6. Matt Krantz, "Some Major Companies Still Use Pro Forma Accounting," *USA Today*, 11 August 2003, B1; "Pro Forma Financial Information: Tips for Investors," SEC website [accessed 9 May 2004] www.sec.gov; David Henry and Robert Berner, "Ouch! Real Numbers," *BusinessWeek*, 24 March 2003, 72–73.

7. Diya Gullapalli, "Which Companies Were Tripped Up?" *Wall Street Journal*, 10 September 2004, C3.

8. Steve Zwick, "The Price of Transparency," *Time*, 19 February 2001, B8–B11.

9. Floyd Norris, "Europe Welcomes Accounting Plan; U.S. Remains a Bit Wary," *New York Times*, 23 April 2005 [accessed 25 April 2005] www.nytimes.com; Kerry Capell and David Henry, "When Bankers Keep Saying *Non*," *BusinessWeek*, 1 March 2004, 54.

10. "Summary of SEC Actions and SEC Related Provisions Pursuant to the Sarbanes-Oxley Act of 2002," SEC website [accessed 9 May 2004] www.sec.gov; "Sarbanes-Oxley Act's Progress," *USA Today*, 26 December 2002 [accessed 9 May 2004] www.highbeam.com.

11. David Henry and Amy Borrus, "Death, Taxes & Sarbanes-Oxley," *BusinessWeek*, 17 January 2005, 28–30; David Henry and Amy Borrus, "Honesty Is a Pricey Policy," *BusinessWeek*, 27 October 2003, 100–101.

12. Henry and Borrus, "Death, Taxes & Sarbanes-Oxley"; Ben Worthen, "A Funny Thing Happened on the Way to Compliance (It Got Easier for CIOs)," *CIO*, 1 December 2003 [accessed 9 May 2004] www.cio.com; "SEC Approves Listing Exchange Rules," *Internal Auditor*, 1 December 2003 [accessed 9 May 2004]

www.highbeam.com; Henry and Borrus, "Honesty Is a Pricey Policy."

13. Paul Kocourek, Jim Newfrock, and Reggie Van Lee, "SOX Rocks, But Won't Block Shocks," *Strategy + Business*, 38, 8–10.

14. David Henry, "Fuzzy Numbers," *BusinessWeek*, 4 October 2004, 79–88.

15. Henry, "Fuzzy Numbers."

16. Baruch Lev, "Sharpening the Intangibles Edge," *Harvard Business Review*, June 2004, 109–116.

17. "How to Spot Trouble in Your Financials," *Inc.*, October 2004, 96.

18. "Bobbie Gossage," Cranking Up the Earnings," *Inc.*, October 2004, 54; Rick Wayman, "EBITDA: The Good, the Bad, and the Ugly," Investopedia.com [accessed 25 April 2005] www.investopedia.com.

19. Frank Evans, "A Road Map to Your Financial Report," *Management Review*, October 1993, 39–47.

20. Robert Barker, "A Surprise in Office Depot's In-Box," *BusinessWeek*, 25 October 2004, 122.

21. See Note 1.

Chapter 17

1. Adapted from *Microsoft 2004 Annual Report* [accessed 26 April 2005] www.microsoft.com; Elliot Blair Smith, Matt Krantz, and Jon Swartz, "Microsoft's Flush, with Nothing to Splurge On," *USA Today*, 22 July 2004, B1–B2; Brier Dudley, Microsoft Shareholders to Vote on Lucrative Dividend," *Seattle Times*, 7 November 2004 [accessed 26 April 2005] www.ebsco.com; Microsoft teleconference, 20 July 2004 [accessed 26 April 2005] www.microsoft.com; Marcia Vickers, "A Dividend from Microsoft's Dividend?" *BusinessWeek Online*, 22 July 2004 [accessed 26 April 2005] www.businessweek.com; Jay Greene, "Checking Out Microsoft's New CEO," *BusinessWeek Online*, 26 April 2005 [accessed 26 April 2005] www.businessweek.com; Patrice Hill, "Microsoft Lifts Economy," *Washington Times*, 1 February 2005, C6.

2. Smith, Krantz, and Swartz, "Microsoft's Flush, with Nothing to Splurge On."

3. Gabriel Kahn, "Financing Goes Just-in-Time," *Wall Street Journal*, 4 June 2004, A10.

4. Robin Sidel, "J.P. Morgan: If It Moves, Try to Cut It," *Wall Street Journal*, 13 January 2005, C1, C4.

5. Dean Foust, "'Protection' Racket?" *BusinessWeek*, 2 May 2005, 68–69.

6. Robin Sidel, "Cash? What's Cash?" *Wall Street Journal*, 31 January 2005, R3.

7. Anne Kandra, "The Problem with PayPal," *PC World*, February 2005 [accessed 2 May 2005] www.pcworld.com.

8. Kandra, "The Problem with PayPal."

9. Michelle Higgins, "ATMs to Go Far Beyond Cash," *Wall Street Journal*, 6 June 2002, D1.

10. Jerri Stroud, "Paperless Paydays Put Money in the Bank for Large Employers," *St. Louis Post-Dispatch*, 15 December 2002, G1.

11. Ikobo website [accessed 2 May 2005] www.ikobo.com; Western Union website [accessed 2 May 2005] www.westernunion.com.

12. FDIC website [accessed 28 April 2005] www.fdic.gov.

13. "Bank Geographic Structure," State of Connecticut Department of Banking [accessed 30 April 2005] www.state.ct.us; E-Trade website [accessed 28 April 2005] www.etrade.com; American Bankers Association website [accessed 28 April 2005] www.aba.com.

14. American Bankers Association website [accessed 28 April 2005] www.aba.com; Foust, "'Protection' Racket?"

15. Glenn R. Simpson, "As Investigations Proliferate, Big Banks Feel Under the Gun," *Wall Street Journal*, 30 December 2004, A1, A4.

16. Federal Reserve website [accessed 28 April 2005] www.federalreserve.gov.

17. Gretchen Morgenson, "Housing Bust: It Won't Be Pretty," *New York Times*, 25 July 2004 [accessed 12 January 2005] www.nytimes.com; *Interest Rate and Currency Trader* (newsletter), 5 January 2005.

18. Laura Bruce, "Check 21: New Law Ends Checking Traditions," Bankrate.com, 28 October 2004 [accessed 29 April 2005] www.bankrate.com.

19. See Note 1.

20. Adapted from Union Bank of California teleservices, personal communication, 16 August 2001.

Chapter 18

1. Adapted from Aaron Pressman, "The Busiest Broker on Earth," *BusinessWeek*, 18 April 2005, 84+; Jim Cole, "Despite Letdown, Schwab Likes Its Bank's Situation," *American Banker*, 18 April 2005, 8; Gaston F. Ceron, "Online Brokers Are Taking Hit from Price War," *Wall Street Journal*, 11 April 2005, C1; Ruth Simon, "Discount Brokers Cut Prices," *Wall Street Journal*, 16 March 2005, D1; "Schwab's Earnings Fall; Big Increase in Profit at Ameritrade," *New York Times*, 19 January 2005, C2; Gregory Bresiger, "Why Did Schwab Sell Capital Markets?" *Traders Magazine*, 1 November 2004, 1; Patrick McGeehan, "Charles Schwab to Give Up Title at Brokerage Firm," *New York Times*, 1 February 2003, C1; "Company News; Charles Schwab Reports a $79 Million Loss in Quarter," *New York Times*, 22 January 2003, C1; Patrick McGeehan, Seeing Long Trading Slump, Schwab Sets More Cutbacks," *New York Times*, 13 August 2002, C2; Louise Lee and Emily Thorton, "Schwab vs. Wall Street," *BusinessWeek*, 3 June 2002, 62–71; Louise Lee, "Will Investors Pay for Schwab's Advice?" *BusinessWeek*, 21 January 2002, 36; Fred Vogelstein, "Can Schwab Get Its Mojo Back?" *Fortune*, 17 September 2001, 93–98; Susanne Craig, "Schwab Unveils a New Service, Chides Brokers," *Wall Street Journal*, 17 May 2002, C1, C13; Charles Gasparino and Ken Brown, "Discounted, Schwab's Own Stock Suffers from Move into Online Trading," *Wall Street Journal*, 19 June 2001, A1, A6; Rebecca Buckman, "Schwab, Once a Predator, Is Now Prey," *Wall Street Journal*, 8 December 1999, C1; Louise Lee, "When You're No.1, You Try Harder," *BusinessWeek E.Biz*, 18 September 2000, EB88.

2. "Options," Investopedia.com [accessed 4 May 2005] www.investopedia.com.

3. David Rynecki, "CBOT Gazes Into the Pit," *Fortune*, 15 May 2000, 279–294.

4. Jack R. Kapoor, Les R. Dlabay, and Robert J. Hughes, *Personal Finance*, 7th ed. (Boston: McGraw-Hill Irwin, 2004), 474–477; "Your Specialist and the Auction Market," NYSE website [accessed 4 May 2005] www.nyse.com.

5. Kapoor, Dlabay, and Hughes, *Personal Finance*, 474.

6. NASDAQ website [accessed 4 May 2005] www.nasdaq.com

7. Heidi Moore and Vipal Monga, "NYSE-ArcaEx Confounds Street," *The Deal.com* [accessed 3 May 2005] www.thedeal.com.

8. SEC website [accessed 4 May 2005] www.sec.gov.

9. National Association of Securities Dealers website [accessed 4 May 2005] www.nasd.com.

10. "Margin Trading: The Dreaded Margin Call," Investopedia.com [accessed 4 May 2005] www.investopedia.com.

11. "Calculating The Dow Jones Industrial Average," Investopedia.com [accessed 4 May 2005] www.investopedia.com.

12. "Standard and Poor's 500 Index—S&P 500," Investopedia.com [accessed 4 May 2005] www.investopedia.com.

13. See Note 1.

14. Adapted from Stephen Labaton, "On-Line Trades Rise and So Do the Complaints," *New York Times*, 28 January 1999, A1, C21.

15. John Kimelman, "How Internet Banks Have Inched Ahead on Rates," *New York Times*, 28 December 2003, 6; Rick Brooks and Charles Forelle, "Despite Online-Banking Boom, Branches Remain King," *Wall Street Journal*, 29 October 2003, B1–B2; Christine Dugas, "Banks Race to Add Branches," *USA Today*, 20–22 January 2003, 1A; Pallavi Gogoi, "The Hot News in Banking: Bricks and Mortar," *BusinessWeek*, 21 April 2003, 83–84; Mark Sievewright, "Traditional vs. Virtual Service," *Credit Union Magazine*, February 2002, 26; Eileen Colkin, "Citibank," *Information Week*, 27 August 2001, 30; Andrew Ross Sorkin, "Put Your Money Where Your Modem Is," *New York Times*, 30 May 2002, G1; Erica Garcia, "What's Left of the Online Banks," *Money*, October 2001, 167; Jathon Sapsford, "Consumers Take Notice of Online Banks," *Wall Street Journal*, 28 November 2000, C1, C19; Lauren Bielski, "Online Banking Yet to Deliver," American Bankers Association, *ABA Banking Journal*, September 2000, 6, 12+; Heather Timmons, "Online Banks Can't Go It Alone," *BusinessWeek*, 31 July 2000, 86–87; Mark Skousen, "Online Banking's Goodies," *Forbes*, 12 June 2000, P366+; Tony Stanco, "Internet Banking—Some Big Players, But Little Returns So Far," *Boardwatch*, March

2000, 86–90; Carrick Mollenkamp, "Old-Line Banks Advance in Bricks-vs.-Clicks Battle," *Wall Street Journal*, 21 January 2000, C1.

Appendix A

1. Bill Shaw and Art Wolfe, *The Structure of the Legal Environment: Law, Ethics, and Business*, 2d ed. (Boston: PWS-Kent, 1991), 635.

2. Shaw and Wolfe, *The Structure of the Legal Environment*, 146.

3. "Pfizer Fined for False Advertising; Company to Pay $430 Million U.S.," *Toronto Star*, 14 May 2004 [accessed 16 May 2004] www.highbeam.com.

4. George A. Steiner and John F. Steiner, *Business, Government, and Society* (New York: McGraw-Hill, 1991), 149.

5. Paula Burkes Erickson, "Oklahoma Bill Proposes Business Courts," *Daily Oklahoman*, 23 February 2004 [accessed 16 May 2004] www.highbeam.com.

6. Thomas W. Dunfee, Frank F. Gibson, John D. Blackburn, Douglas Whitman, F. William McCarty, and Bartley A. Brennan, *Modern Business Law* (New York: Random House, 1989), 164.

7. Jacqueline Bueno, "Home Depot to Fight Sex-Bias Charges," *Wall Street Journal*, 19 September 1997, B5; Edward Felsenthal, "Punitive Awards Are Called Modest, Rare," *Wall Street Journal*, 17 June 1996, B2.

8. Bartley A. Brennan and Nancy K. Kubasek, *The Legal Environment of Business* (New York: McGraw-Hill, 1990), 183.

9. "'03 Derby Controversy' Santos Seeks $48M in Damages for Libel," *Newsday*, 10 May 2004 [accessed 16 May 2004] www.highbeam.com.

10. Brennan and Kubasek, *The Legal Environment of Business*, 184.

11. Nancy K. Kubasek, Bartley A. Brennan, and M. Neil Browne, *The Legal Environment of Business*, 3d ed. (Upper Saddle River, N.J.: Prentice Hall, 2003), 325; "Reasonable Product-Liability Reform," *Nation's Business*, 1 September 1997, 88.

12. Dunfee et al., *Modern Business Law*, 569.

13. Michael Ha, "Public Banks Many Tort Reforms," *National Underwriter*, 19 April 2004, 10.

14. Dunfee et al., *Modern Business Law*, 236.

15. Dunfee et al., *Modern Business Law*, 284–297; Brennan and Kubasek, *The Legal Environment of Business*, 125–127; Douglas Whitman and John William Gergacz, *The Legal Environment of Business*, 2d ed. (New York: Random House, 1988), 196–197; *The Lawyer's Almanac* (Englewood Cliffs, N.J.: Prentice Hall Law & Business, 1991), 888.

16. Brennan and Kubasek, *The Legal Environment of Business*, 128.

17. Samuel Maull, "Judge Rules No Damages to Rosie, Publisher," *AP Online*, 20 February 2004 [accessed 16 May 2004] www.highbeam.com.

18. Roy Furchgott, "Opposition Builds to Mandatory Arbitration at Work," *New York Times*, 20 July 1997, F11; Barry Meier, "In Fine Print, Customers Lose Ability to Sue," *New York Times*, 10 March 1997, A1, C7.

19. Richard M. Steuer, *A Guide to Marketing Law: What Every Seller Should Know* (New York: Harcourt Brace Jovanovich, 1986), 151–152.

20. Dunfee et al., *Modern Business Law*, 745, 749.

21. Brennan and Kubasek, *The Legal Environment of Business*, 160; Whitman and Gergacz, *The Legal Environment of Business*, 260.

22. Henry R. Cheeseman, *Business Law*, 4th ed. (Upper Saddle River, N.J.: Prentice Hall, 2001), 324.

23. James Connell, "Tech Brief: Apple Look-Alike Suit Settled," *International Herald Tribune*, 7 June 2001, 17; David P. Hamilton, "Apple Sues Future Power and Daewood, Alleging They Copied Design of iMac," *Wall Street Journal*, 2 July 1999, B4; "Injunction Is Issued Against Makers of iMac Look Alikes," *Wall Street Journal*, 9 November 1999, B25.

24. Cheeseman, *Business Law*, 330.

25. Mike Snider, "Law Targets Copyright Theft Online," *USA Today*, 18 December 1998, A1.

26. Tariq K. Muhammad, "Real Law in a Virtual World," *Black Enterprise*, December 1996, 44.

27. Jerry M. Rosenberg, *Dictionary of Business and Management* (New York: Wiley, 1983), 340.

28. Ronald A. Anderson, Ivan Fox, and David P. Twomey, *Business Law* (Cincinnati: South-Western Publishing, 1987), 635.

29. Brennan and Kubasek, *The Legal Environment of Business*, 516–517.

30. "Polaroid Finalizes Sale, Emerges From Chapter 11," *TWICE*, 8 July 2002, 37; Polaroid website [accessed 29 July 2002] www.polaroid.com.

Appendix B

1. Laura M. Litvan, "Switching to Self-Insurance," *Nation's Business*, March 1996, 16–21; Joseph B. Treaster, "Protecting Against the Little Risks," *New York Times*, 31 December 1996, C1, C15.

2. Blue Cross and Blue Shield Association website [accessed 13 June 2005] www.bcbs.com.

3. Mark S. Dorfman, *Introduction to Risk Management and Insurance*, 8th ed. (Upper Saddle River, N.J.: Pearson Prentice Hall, 2005), 73.

4. Haneefa T. Saleem, "Health Spending Accounts," U.S. Bureau of Labor Statistics website [accessed 13 June 2005] www.bls.gov.

5. Joseph B. Treaster, "Cost of Insurance for Work Injuries Soars Across U.S.," *New York Times*, 23 June 2003, A1, A18.

6. Dorfman, *Introduction to Risk Management and Insurance*, 261.

7. Dorfman, *Introduction to Risk Management and Insurance*, 265.

8. Amanda Levin, "Ethics Rates Highest When Hiring Insurance Staff," *National Underwriter,* 12 April 1999, 4, 65.

Appendix C

1. Lawrence J. Gitman and Michael D. Joehnk, *Personal Financial Planning*, 10th ed. (Mason, Ohio: Thomson South-Western, 2005), 27.

2. Jack R. Kapoor, Les R. Dlabay, and Robert J. Hughes, *Personal Finance*, 7th ed. (New York: McGraw-Hill/Irwin, 2004), 18.

3. Anne Kim, "Moving In, Moving On," *Seattle Times*, 8 May 2004 [accessed 13 May 2004] www.seattletimes.com.

4. Kapoor et al., *Personal Finance*, 33.

5. "How to Choose a Financial Advisor," WiserAdvisor.com [accessed 21 May 2004] www.wiseradvisor.com.

6. Arthur J. Keown, *Personal Finance: Turning Money into Wealth*, 3d ed. (Upper Saddle River, N.J.: Prentice Hall, 2003), 52–53.

7. Albert B. Crenshaw and Brooke A. Masters, " Big Four Face Legal Trouble, Lost Business; IRS, Clients Challenge Tax-Shelter Advice," *Washington Post*, 12 February 2003 [accessed 21 May 2004] www.highbeam.com; Jerry L. Reiter, "The Blame Game," *Registered Rep*, 2 January 2003 [accessed 21 May 2004] www.highbeam.com.

8. Kapoor et al., *Personal Finance*, 11; Gitman and Joehnk, *Personal Financial Planning*, 5.

9. Gitman and Joehnk, *Personal Financial Planning*, 15.

10. Deborah Fowles, "Financial Advice for Your 20s," About.com [accessed 22 May 2004] www.about.com; Gitman and Joehnk, *Personal Financial Planning*, 15.

11. Ana M. Aizcorbe, Arthur B. Kennickell, and Keven B. Moore, "Recent Changes in U.S. Family Finances: Evidence from the 1998 and 2001 Survey of Consumer Finances," *Federal Reserve Bulletin*, January 2003, 4.

12. Deborah Fowles, "The Psychology of Spending Money," About.com [accessed 22 May 2004] www.about.com.

13. Gitman and Joehnk, *Personal Financial Planning*, 15.

14. "More College Grads, Fewer Home-Grown," *Seattle Times*, 17 May 2004 [accessed 17 May 2004] www.seattletimes.com.

15. Kimberly E. Mock, *Athens Banner-Herald*, "Good Credit Skills Are Essential for Georgia's College Students," 23 February 2004 [accessed 4 May 2004] www.highbeam.com.

16. Lucy Lazarony, "Credit Cards Teaching Students a Costly Lesson," Bankrate.com, 5 June 1998 [accessed 22 May 2004] www.bankrate.com.

17. David Kiley, "Car Buyers Pay More, Owe More Longer," *USA Today*, 17 February 2004, B1; Lucy Lazarony, "It's a Good Time to Be a New-Car Shopper," Bankrate.com, 5 March 2003 [accessed 22 May 2004] www.bankrate.com.

18. Philip Reed, "Drive a (Nearly) New Car for (Almost) Nothing," Edmunds.com [accessed 22 May 2004] www.edmunds.com.

19. Chandler Phillips, "Confessions of a Car Salesman," Edmunds.com [accessed 22 May 2004] www.edmunds.com.

20. Eryn Brown, "Hot to Get Paid What You're Worth," *Business 2.0*, May 2004, 102–110, 134.

21. Keown, *Personal Finance: Turning Money into Wealth*, 143–148; Gitman and Joehnk, *Personal Financial Planning*, 140–147.

22. "How To Establish Credit," CreditInfoWeb.com [accessed 23 May 2004] www.creditinfoweb.com.

23. Kapoor et al., *Personal Finance*, 222.

24. "Ads Promising Debt Relief May Be Offering Bankruptcy," FTC Consumer Alert [accessed 23 May 2004] www.ftc.gov.

25. Christopher Conkey, "Bankruptcy Overall Means Tougher Choices," *Wall Street Journal*, 22 May 2005 [accessed 10 June 2005] www.wsj.com.

26. Kapoor et al., *Personal Finance*, 582.

Prologue

Photo Credit

8 PhotoEdit

Exhibits

7 (Exhibit 1) Adapted from Daniel E. Hecker, "Occupational Employment Projections to 2012," *Monthly Labor Review,* February 2004, 80–105.
19 (Exhibit 7) Adapted from Marilyn Sherman, "Questions R Us: What to Ask at a Job Interview," *Career World,* January 2004, 20; H. Lee Rust, *Job Search: The Complete Manual for Jobseekers* (New York: American Management Association, 1979), 56.

Chapter 1

Photo Credits

25 AP Wide World Photos; **28** Corbis/Bettmann, Richard T. Nowitz; **41** AP Wide World Photos; **44** Masterfile Corporation, Roy Ooms; **49** Corbis/Bettman, UPI

Exhibits

31 (Exhibit 1.1) Adapted from Christopher Caggiano, "Will the Real Bootstrappers Please Stand Up?" Inc., August 1995, 34; Mike Hofman, "Capitalism—A Bootstrappers' Hall of Fame," Inc., August 1997, 54–57; Hoover's [accessed 27 March 2004] www.hoovers.com; Gateway website [accessed 6 January 2005] www.gateway.com; Limited Brands website [accessed 6 January 2005] www.limited.com.
32 (Exhibit 1.2) Adapted from Monica Kearns, "Whatever Happened to the New Economy?" *State Legislatures,* February 2002, 24–27.

Boxes and Case for Critical Thinking

28 (Business Buzz) Adapted from Wordspy.com [accessed 15 April 2004] www.wordspy.com.
29 (Technologies That Are Revolutionizing Business) Adapted from Jefferson Graham, "Instant Messaging Programs Are No Longer Just for Messages," *USA Today,* 20 October 2003, 5D; Todd R. Weiss, "Microsoft Targets Corporate Instant Messaging Customers," *Computerworld,* 18 November 2002, 12; "Banks Adopt Instant Messaging to Create a Global Business Network," *Computer Weekly,* 25 April 2002, 40; Michael D. Osterman, "Instant Messaging in the Enterprise," *Business Communications Review,* January 2003, 59–62; John Pallato, "Instant Messaging Unites Work Groups and Inspires Collaboration," *Internet World,* December 2002, 14+; Mark Gibbs, "Racing to Instant Messaging," *NetworkWorld,* 17 February 2003, 74.
42 (Learning from Business Blunders) Adapted from Adam Horowitz, Mark Athitakis, Mark Lasswell, and Owen Thomas, "The 101 Dumbest Moments in Business," Business 2.0 [accessed 27 March 2004] www.business2.com.
51 (The Electronic Economy: Redefining Reality) Adapted from Stephen Baker, "Where Danger Lurks," *BusinessWeek,* 25 August 2003, 114–118; W. Brian Arthur, "Why Tech Is Still the Future," *Fortune,* 24 November 2003, 119–125;

Kevin Anderson, "Delivery at Internet Speed," *BBC News Online,* 22 December 1999 [accessed 30 March 2004] news.bbc.co.uk.
58 (Turmoil in the Airline Industry) Adapted from Susan Carey and Scott McCartney, "Long Flight: How Airlines Resisted Change for 25 Years, and Finally Lost," *Wall Street Journal,* 5 October 2004, A1, A15; Dan Reed, "United Pension Debate Goes On," *USA Today,* 2 January 2005 [accessed 7 January 2005] www.usatoday.com; Janice Revell, "New Math: Don't Pay As You Go Under," *Fortune,* 4 October 2004, 38; Daniel Michaels and Melanie Trottman, "Surging Fuel Costs Hit Struggling Airlines Hard," *Wall Street Journal,* 19 August 2004, A1, A6; Scott McCartney, "On Rising Fares and Airplane Food," *Wall Street Journal,* 12 October 2004, D4; Mark Tatge and Neil Weinberg, "What Goes Up . . . " *Forbes,* 18 October 2004, 116–118; John Helyar, "Why Is This Man Smiling?" *Fortune,* 18 October 2004, 130–138; Kelly K. Spors, "New Horizons," *Wall Street Journal,* 25 October 2004, R11; Chris Woodward, "United Launches Premium Service," *USA Today,* 29 October 2004, B1; Jennifer Davies, "Major Airlines' Survival up in Air," *San Diego Union-Tribune,* 7 November 2004, H1, H3; Wendy Zellner and Michael Arndt, "Holding Steady," *BusinessWeek,* 3 February 2003, 66–68; Shawn Tully, "Friendly Skies Aren't Out of the Picture," *Fortune,* 30 December 2002, 42–43; Edward Wong, "Winter's Frustrations Linger On Stubbornly for U.S. Airline Industry," *New York Times,* 15 June 2002, C1; George F. Will, "Always A Bumpy Ride," *Washington Post,* 9 May 2002, A31; Susan Carey, "Costly Race in the Sky," *Wall Street Journal,* 9 September 2002, B1, B3; Laurence Zuckerman, "A New Sense of Urgency in Debating the Future of Airlines," *New York Times,* 17 December 2001, C10; Adam Bryant, "The Cruel New Math," *Newsweek,* 26 November 2001, 22; "Business: Too Many Here, Too Few There," *Economist,* 13 January 2001, 58–59; Wendy Zellner, "It's Showtime for the Airlines," *BusinessWeek,* 2 September 2002, 36–37; Peter Coy, "The Airlines: Caught Between A Hub and A Hard Place," *BusinessWeek,* 5 August 2002, 83; Michael E. Levine, "Another Airline Nose-dives. Who's Next?" *Wall Street Journal,* 13 August 2002, A20; Scott McCartney, "Clipped Wings: American Airlines to Retrench In Bid to Beat Discount Carriers," *Wall Street Journal,* 13 August 2002, A1, A8; Melanie Trottman and Scott McCartney, "Executive Flight: The Age of 'Wal-Mart' Airlines Crunches the Biggest Carriers," *Wall Street Journal,* 18 June 2002, A1, A8. Shawn Tully, "From Bad to Worse," *Fortune,* 15 October 2001, 119–126; Alex Berenson, "Cry for Help: This Industry Doesn't Fly," *New York Times,* 18 November 2001, A5; Perry Flint, "Hard Times," *Air Transport World,* November 2001, 22–28; Cynthia Wilson, "U.S. Airline Industry Faced Big Losses Even Before Terrorists Hijacked Jets," *St. Louis Post-Dispatch,* 23 September 2001, A13.

Chapter 2

Photo Credits

61 Patagonia, Inc., Scott Willson/Patagonia; **64** Landov LLC, Yuriko Nakao/Reuters; **75** Landov LLC, Jeff Christensen/

Reuters/Landov; **79** Photo researchers, Inc., Calvin Larsen; **80** Basel Action Network (BAN); **84** Getty Images, Inc.—Liaison

Exhibits

68 (Exhibit 2.1) Adapted from "eHealth Code of Ethics," Internet Healthcare Coalition website [accessed 20 January 2005] www.ihealthcoalition.org.

70 (Exhibit 2.2) "American Workers Do the Right Thing," *HRFocus*, March 1999, 4.

71 (Exhibit 2.3) Adapted from Manuel G. Velasquez, *Business Ethics: Concepts and Cases* (Upper Saddle River, N.J.: Prentice Hall, 1998), 87; Joseph L. Badaracco, Jr., "Business Ethics: Four Spheres of Executive Responsibility," *California Management Review*, Spring 1992, 64–79; Kenneth Blanchard and Norman Vincent Peale, *The Power of Ethical Management* (Reprint, 1989; New York: Fawcett Crest, 1991), 7–17; John R. Boatright, *Ethics and the Conduct of Business* (Upper Saddle River, N.J.: Prentice Hall, 1996), 35–39, 59–64, 79–86.

73 (Exhibit 2.4) Weld Royal, "Real Expectations," *IndustryWeek*, 4 September 2000, 32.

86 (Exhibit 2.8) 2002 Census of Fatal Occupational Injuries, U.S. Bureau of Labor Statistics [accessed 1 April 2004] www.bls.gov.

Boxes and Case for Critical Thinking

63 (Business Buzz) Adapted from Wordspy.com [accessed 15 April 2004] www.wordspy.com.

66 (Learning from Business Blunders) Adapted from Adam Horowitz, Mark Athitakis, Mark Lasswell, and Owen Thomas, "The 101 Dumbest Moments in Business," *Business 2.0* [accessed 27 March 2004] www.business2.com; Bob Garfield, "KFC Serves Big, Fat Bucket of Nonsense in 'Healthy' Spots," *Advertising Age*, 3 November 2003, 61; "KFC Blunders in Healthy Ads," *Advertising Age*, 3 November 2003, 22.

69 (Lead Your Team With Ethical Behavior) Adapted from Melissa Ingwersen, *Columbus Business First*, 23 January 2004 [accessed 17 January 2005] www.bizjournals.com; Harold Tinkler, "Execs Must Embed Ethics into Company Culture," *Puget Sound Business Journal*, 16 April 2004 [accessed 17 January 2005] www.bizjournals.com; Marc Gunther, "Money and Morals at GE," *Fortune*, 15 November 2004, 176–182; Craig Dreilinger, "Get Real (and Ethics Will Follow)," *Workforce*, August 1998, 101–102; Louisa Wah, "Workplace Conscience Needs a Boost," *American Management Association International*, July–August 1998; "Ethics Are Questionable in the Workplace," *HRFocus*, June 1998, 7.

77 (Ben & Jerry's: A Double Scoop of Irony?) Adapted from Ben & Jerry's website [accessed 1 April 2004] www.benjerry.com; George F. Will, "Being Green and Ben & Jerry's," *Newsweek*, 6 May 2002, 72; Edward O. Welles, "Ben's Big Flop," *Inc.*, September 1998, 40+; Constance L. Hays, "Getting Serious at Ben & Jerry's," *New York Times*, 22 May 1998, C1, C3; Constance L. Hays, "Ben & Jerry's To Unilever, With Attitude," *New York Times*, 13 April 2000, C1, C20; Fred Bayles, "Reviews In on Ben & Jerry's Sweet Deal," *USA Today*, 20 April 2000, 3A.

83 (Technologies That Are Revolutionizing Business) Adapted from "Benetton Explains RFID Privacy Flap," *RFID Journal* [accessed 1 April 2004] www.rfidjournal.com; David LaGress, "They Know Where You Are," *U.S. News & World Report*, 8 September 2003, 32–38; Christopher Elliott, "Some Rental Cars Are Keeping Tabs on Drivers," *New York Times*, 13 January 2004, C6; Kristi Heim, "Microchips in People, Packaging and Pets Raise Privacy Questions," *Seattle Times*, 18 October 2004 [accessed 18 October 2004] www.seattletimes.com; Andrew Heining and Christa Case, "Are Book Tags a Threat?" *Christian Science Monitor*, 5 October 2004 [accessed 7 October 2004] www.csmonitor.com; Corie Lok, "Wrist Radio Tags," *Technology Review*, November 2004, 25; Brian Albright, "RFID Dominates Frontline's Supply Chain Week," *Frontline Solutions*, November 2003, 10–13.

93 (Enron: A Case Study in Unethical Behavior) Adapted from John R. Emshwiller and Kara Scannell, "Enron Trial Results in Five Guilty Verdicts," *Wall Street Journal*, 4 November 2004, C1; "Timeline of Enron's Collapse," *Washington Post*, 27 January 2004 [accessed 2 April 2004] www.washingtonpost.com; Ellen Florian, "Scandal Cheat Sheet," *Fortune*, 7 July 2003, 48–49; Gabrielle Solomon, "Enron Book Excerpt: Greed, Love, Hate, Sex—and Massive Amounts of Ego," *Fortune.com*, 10 October 2003 [accessed 23 January 2005] www.fortune.com; Bethany Mclean, "Is Enron Overpriced?" *Fortune*, 5 March 2001 [accessed 23 January 2005] www.fortune.com; Bethany Mclean, "Why Enron Went Bust," *Fortune*, 24 December 2001, 59–68; Michael Tackett, "Enron's Fall Piques Congress' Interest in 401(k) Rules," *Chicago Tribune*, 25 January 2002, 1-1, 1-12; Fred Tam, "Proper Controls Needed After Enron Debacle," *Business Times*, 14 February 2002, 18; Leslie Wayne, "Before Debacle, Enron Insiders Cashed in $1.1 Billion in Shares," *New York Times*, 13 January 2002, A1; Jacob M. Schlesinger, "O'Neill Weighs Stricter Corporate Penalties," *Wall Street Journal*, 25 February 2002, A1; Bethany McLean, "Monster Mess," *Fortune*, 4 February 2002, 93–96; Grag Hitt and Tom Hamburger, "Skilling Denies He Misled Enron Officials," *Wall Street Journal*, 27 February 2002, A3, A8. Daniel Kadlec, "Who's Accountable?" *Time*, 21 January 2002, 28–34; Jonathan Weil, "Enron's Auditors Debated Partnership Losses," *Wall Street Journal*, 3 April 2002, C1, C12; Kurt Eichenwald, "Andersen Guilty in Effort to Block Inquiry on Enron," *New York Times*, 16 June 2002 [accessed 19 June 2002] www.nytimes.com; E.A. Torriero and Robert Manor, "Jury Finds Andersen Guilty," *Chicago Tribune*, 16 June 2002, sec. 1-1, 1-12; David Futrelle, "Who Called Enron First?," *Business 2.0*, 24 May 2002 [accessed 23 January 2005] www.business2.com.

Chapter 3

Photo Credits
97 Getty Images, Inc.—Hulton Archive Photos, Reuters/Jacky Naegelen; **104** Corbis—NY; **108** Getty Images, Inc.—Liaison, Michel Poro; **118** AP Wide World Photos; **119** Getty Images, Inc.—Agence France Presse, Mehdi Fedouach/AFP

Exhibits
100 (Exhibit 3.1) World Economic Forum, "Global Competitiveness Report 2004–2005," World Economic Forum website [accessed 28 January 2005] www.weforum.org.

101 (Exhibit 3.2) U.S. Bureau of Economic Analysis website [accessed 5 April 2004]

102 (Exhibit 3.3) "U.S. International Transactions," U.S. Bureau of Economic Analysis website [accessed 30 January 2005] www.bea.doc.gov.

110 (Exhibit 3.5) "Strong Dollar, Weak Dollar: Foreign Exchange Rates and the U.S. Economy." Federal Reserve Bank of Chicago website [accessed 29 January 2005] www.chicagofed.org.

113 (Exhibit 3.6) John V. Thill and Courtland L. Bovée, *Excellence in Business Communication* (Upper Saddle River, N.J.: Prentice Hall, 2002), 33.

Boxes and Case for Critical Thinking

103 (Business Buzz) Adapted from Wordspy.com [accessed 15 April 2004] www.wordspy.com.

105 (Technologies That Are Revolutionizing Business) Adapted from Rick Whiting, "Innovation: Videoconferencing's Virtual Room," *InformationWeek*, 1 April 2002, 14; Mark Alpert, "Long-Distance Robots," *Scientific American*, December 2001, 94; Teliris website [accessed 8 August 2003] www.teliris.com.

112 (How to Avoid Business Mistakes Abroad) Adapted from David Ricks, "How to Avoid Business Blunders Abroad," *Business*, April–June 1984, 3–11.

116 (China's Counterfeit Economy) Adapted from Frederik Balfour, "Fakes!" *BusinessWeek*, 7 February 2005, 54–64; Robyn Meredith, "Microsoft's Long March," *Forbes*, 17 February 2003, 78–86; Chris Buckley, "Helped by Technology, Piracy of DVD's Runs Rampant in China," *New York Times*, 18 August 2003, C9; Todd Zaun and Karen Leggert, "Road Warriors," *Wall Street Journal*, 25 July 2001, A1, A4; Steve Friess, "Product Piracy Poses Biggest Threat to China's Economic Status," *USA Today*, 28 June 2001, 6B; Richard Behar, "Beijing's Phony War On Fakes," *Fortune*, 30 October 2000, 188+; Susan V. Lawrence, "For Better or Worse," *Far Eastern Economic Review*, 5 October 2000, 60; Lorien Holland, "A Brave New World," *Far Eastern Economic Review*, 5 October 2000, 46–48; Trish Saywell, "Fakes Cost Real Cash," *Far Eastern Economic Review*," 5 October 2000, 57–58; Dexter Roberts, Frederik Balfour, Paul Magnusson, Pete Engardio, and Jennifer Lee, "China's Piracy Plague," *BusinessWeek*, 5 June 2000, 44–48.

120 (Learning From Business Blunders) Adapted from Glenn R. Simpson, "Expanding in an Age of Terror, Western Union Faces Scrutiny," *Wall Street Journal*, 20 October 2004, A1, A14.

121 (Cyberterror: Could the Next Attack Happen Online?) Adapted from Scott Berinato, "The Truth About Cyberterrorism," *CIO*, 15 May 2002, [accessed 31 January 2005] www.cio.org; Robert Lenzner and Nathan Vardi, "The Next Threat," *Forbes*, 20 September 2004; Andrew Donoghue, "Cyberterror: Clear and Present Danger or Phantom Menace?" ZDNet UK website [accessed 31 January 2005] www.zdnet.co.uk; John Blau, "The Battle Against Cyberterror," *Industry Standard*, 29 November 2004 [accessed 31 January 2005] www.thestandard.com.

127 (Doing Everybody's Wash—Whirlpool's Global Lesson) Adapted from Adam Aston and Michael Arndt, "A New Goliath In Big Steel," *BusinessWeek*, 8 November 2004 [accessed 24 January 2005] www.businessweek.com; "Electrolux, Whirlpool See Lower Profits, *BusinessWeek*, 10 October 2004 [accessed 24 January 2005] www.businessweek.com; "Building a Global Loyal Following," *Appliance*, April 2003, W1–W4; "About Whirlpool Corp.," Whirlpool website [accessed 5 April 2004] www.whirlpool.com; Regina Fazio Maruca, "The Right Way to Go Global," *Harvard Business Review*, March–April 1994, 135–145; Deborah Duarte and Nancy Snyder, "From Experience: Facilitating Global Organizational Learning in Product Development at Whirlpool Corporation," *Journal of Product Innovation Management* 14, no. 1 (January 1997): 48–55; Joe Jancsurak, "Whirlpool: U.S. Leader Pursues Global Blueprint," *Appliance Manufacturer* 45, no. 2 (February 1997): G21; Carl Quintanilla, "Despite Setbacks, Whirlpool Pursues Overseas Markets," *Wall Street Journal*, 9 December 1997, B4; Ian Katz, "Whirlpool: In the Wringer," *BusinessWeek*, 14 December 1998, 83+; Gale Cutler, "Asia Challenges Whirlpool Technology," *Research Technology Management*, September–October 1998, 4–6; "Whirlpool Europe and Tupperware Europe Announce Strategic Alliance," *Investor Relations*, 28 April 1999.

Chapter 4

Photo Credits

97 Getty Images, Inc.—Hulton Archive Photos, Reuters; Jacky Naegelen; **104** Corbis—NY; **108** Getty Images, Inc.—Liaison, Michel Poro; **131** PhotoEdit, Mary Kate Denny; **135** Bernd Auers; **146** Corbis/ Bettmann, Walter Hodges; **152** Webroot Software, Inc.

Boxes and Case for Critical Thinking

138 (LivePerson Puts a Pulse on the Web) Adapted from Erika D. Smith, "Online Chat Companies Offer Way out of Phone Frustration," *San Diego Union-Tribune*, 5 July 2004, E5; LivePerson website [accessed 27 March 2004] www.liveperson.com; Mary Wagner, "The Long Road to Online Checkout," *Internet World*, April 2001 [accessed 7 May 2001] www.internetretailer.com; Karen J. Bannan, "Burning Up the Wires," *PSINet eBusiness*, Winter 2001, 48–51; Bruce Horovitz, "Site Untangles E-Customer Service Mess," *USA Today*, 23 November 1999 [accessed 7 May 2001] www.usatoday.com; "LivePerson Reels in $19 Million," *Red Herring*, 10 August 1999 [accessed 7 May 2001] www.redherring.com; Connie Guglielmo, "LivePerson Puts a Pulse into Web Interaction," *ZDNet*, 21 June 1999 [accessed 7 May 2001] www.zdnet.com; Vanessa Geneva Melter, "Closing the Sale with Interactive Chat," *ShopGuide News*, 7 June 1999 [accessed 7 May 2001] www.shopguide.com; Jennifer Gilbert, "LivePerson Focuses on the Human Touch," *Advertising Age*, 1 June 1999 [accessed 7 May 2001] www.adage.com; Craig Bicknell, "Somebody Freakin' Talk to Me!" *Wired*, 1 June 1999 [accessed 7 May 2001] www.wired.com.

145 (Technologies That Are Revolutionizing Business) Adapted from "Cryptography," Tech-Encyclopedia [accessed 15 February 2005] www.techweb.com; Kenneth C. Laudon and Jane P. Laudon, *Management Information Systems*, 8th ed. (Upper Saddle River, N.J.: Pearson Education, 2004), 463-464; *System Developer Guide, Using LAN in Test Systems: Applications*, Agilent Technologies, February 2005, 6.

153 (Learning from Business Blunders) Adapted from Bob Tedeschi, "After Catalog Blunder, Eziba.com Suspends Business," New York Times, 24 January 2005, C4; Mark Del Franco, "Eziba Suspends Operations, Goes Up for Sale," *Catalog Age*, 18 January 2005 [accessed 14 February 2005] www.catalogagemag.com; "Cataloger, Online Marketer Eziba to Liquidate Holdings: Reports," 25 January 2005 [accessed 14 February 2005] www.directmag.com.

154 (Say, Is That Stolen Data You're Listening to on Your iPod?) Adapted from Ruggero Contu, "Tackling the Threat from Portable Storage Devices," *ZDNet UK*, 5 July 2004 [accessed 15 February 2005] www.zdnet.co.uk; Stephanie

Armour, "Camera Phones Don't Click at Work," *USA Today*, 12 January 2004 [accessed 15 February 2005] www.usatoday.com; "U.K. Military Issues iPod Ban to Foil Data Thieves," News.com, 14 July 2004 [accessed 15 February 2005] www.news.com; David Ralkow, "No Easy Fix for Internal Security," *eWeek*, 16 August 2004 [accessed 15 February 2005] www.thechannelinsider.com; Chris Mellor, "The USB Key Drive Data Security Nightmare," *TechWorld*, [accessed 15 February 2005] www.techworld.com.

154 (Business Buzz) (*Wardriving*) Adapted from "Glossary: Decoding the Jargon," CNN.com [accessed 25 October 2004] www.cnn.com; (Zombie PC) Adapted from Jon Swartz and Byron Acohido, "E-Mail Carriers Sign On to Anti-Spam Efforts," *USA Today*, 23 June 2004, B1.

160 (Nokia Dials Up Wireless Innovations) Adapted from "Nokia Moves Forward with Management Succession Plan," 1 August 2005 [accessed 9 August 2005] www.nokia.com; Kevin Maney, "CEO Ollila Says Nokia's 'Sisu' Will See It Past Tough Times," *USA Today*, 21 July 2004, B1–B2; Nelson D. Schwartz, "Has Nokia Lost It?" *Fortune*, 24 January 2005, 98–106; Andy Reinhardt, "Can Nokia Get the Wow Back," *BusinessWeek*, 31 May 2004, 48–50; "About Nokia," Nokia website [accessed 14 February 2005] www.nokia.com; David Pringle and Matt Pottinger, "Nokia's China Connection May Grow Turbulent," *Wall Street Journal*, 29 August, 2002, B4; David Pringle, "Nokia Widens Gap With Its Rivals," *Wall Street Journal*, 20 August 2002, B6; Alan Cowell, "Nokia Lowers Sales Target But Is Optimistic on Profits, *New York Times*, 11 September 2002, 1; Andy Reinhardt, "Nokia's Next Act," *BusinessWeek*, 1 July, 2002, 56–58; Stephen Baker with Inka Resch and Roger O. Crockett, "Nokia's Costly Stumble," *BusinessWeek*, 14 August 2000, 42; "Business: Star Turn," *The Economist*, 5 August 2000, 60; Maryanne Murry Buechner, "Making the Call," *Time*, 29 May 2000, 64–65; Justin Fox, "Nokia's Secret Code," *Fortune*, 1 May 2000; 160–174; Adrian Wooldridge, "Survey: Telecommunications: To the Finland Base Station," *The Economist*, 9 October 1999, S23–S27; Stephen Baker and Robert McNatt, "Now Nokia is Net Crazy," *BusinessWeek*, 5 April 1999, 6; "Jorma Ollila: Finn Fatale," *BusinessWeek*, 11 January 1999, 78; Stephen Baker with Roger O. Crockett and Neil Gross, "Nokia," *BusinessWeek*, 10 August 1998, 54.

163 E-Business in Action
Adapted from Charles Hutzler, "China Finds New Ways to Restrict Access to the Internet," *Wall Street Journal*, 1 September 2004, B1–B2; "China Is World's No.2 Spam Receiver," ChinaTechNews.com, 17 March 2004 [accessed 5 April 2004] www.chinatechnews.com; Bruce Einhorn, "The Net's Second Superpower," *BusinessWeek*, 15 March 2004, 54–56; David J. Lynch, "Surf's Up in China, Where Millions Are Going Online," *USA Today*, 8 October 2003, B1–B2; "China Pulls Plug On Internet Blogs," ChinaTechNews.com, 17 March 2004 [accessed 5 April 2004] www.chinatechnews.com; "China Suspends Registration of New Net Cafés," 3 March 2004 [accessed 5 April 2004] www.chinatechnews.com.

Career Profiles
165 (Business Economist) Adapted from U.S. Department of Labor, Bureau of Labor Statistics website, *Occupational Outlook Handbook* [accessed 16 May 2005] www.bls.gov.

165 (Information Technology Manager) Adapted from U.S. Department of Labor, Bureau of Labor Statistics website, *Occupational Outlook Handbook* [accessed 16 May 2005] www.bls.gov; "Job Profile for Computer and Information Systems Managers," Careers.org [accessed 16 May 2005] www.careers.org; Association of Information Technology Professionals website [accessed 16 May 2005] www.aitp.org.

Chapter 5

Photo Credits
167 FedEx Corporation, FedEx Global Corporate Identity; **172** Jodi L. Jacobson; **174** AP Wide World Photos; **178** Corbis/Sygma, Gary I. Rothstein; **181** Corbis/Bettmann, Joe Pugliese

Exhibits
171 (Exhibit 5.2) Business Enterprise," *2004–2005 Statistical Abstract of the United States*, 483.
175 (Exhibit 5.3) "The 2004 Fortune 500," *Fortune.com* [accessed 18 February 2005] www.fortune.com.
184 (Exhibit 5.5) Mergerstat, "M&A Activity: U.S. and U.S. Cross-Border Transactions" [accessed 11 April 2004] www.mergerstat.com.

Boxes and Case for Critical Thinking
171 (Technologies That Are Revolutionizing Business) Adapted from Tony Kontzer, "Learning to Share," *InformationWeek*, 5 May 2003, 28; Jon Udell, "Uniting Under Groove," *InfoWorld*, 17 February 2003 [accessed 9 September 2003] www.elibrary.com; Alison Overholt, "Virtually There?" *Fast Company*, 14 February 2002, 108.
173 (Business Buzz) Adapted from Wordspy.com [accessed 15 April 2004] www.wordspy.com.
182 (Hey, Wanna Lose a Few Billion? We've Got a Sure Deal For You) Adapted from Emily Thornton, "Why Consumers Hate Mergers," *BusinessWeek*, 6 December 2004, 58–63; Steven Hamm, "The Soft Underbelly of Software Deals," *BusinessWeek*, 27 December 2004, 48; Larry Selden and Geoffrey Colvin, "M&A Needn't Be a Loser's Game," *Harvard Business Review*, June 2003, 70–79; Amy Kover, "Big Banks Debunked," *Fortune*, 21 February 2000, 187–194; Erick Schonfeld, "Have the Urge to Merge? You'd Better Think Twice," *Fortune*, 31 March 1997, 114–116; Phillip L. Zweig et al., "The Case Against Mergers," *BusinessWeek*, 30 October 1995, 122–130; Kevin Kelly et al., "Mergers Today, Trouble Tomorrow?" *BusinessWeek*, 12 September 1994; "How to Merge," *The Economist*, 9 January 1999, 21–23; "Study Says Mergers Often Don't Aid Investors," *New York Times*, 1 December 1999, C9.
183 (DaimlerChrysler: Merger of Equals or Global Fender Bender?) Adapted from Alex Taylor III, "The Nine Lives of Jürgen Schrempp," *Fortune*, 10 January 2005, 86–92; Christiaan Hetzner and Chang-Ran Kim, "Daimler Boss Set To Ride Out Storm," *Birmingham Post*, 6 April 2004 [accessed 7 April 2004] www.highbeam.com; Roberto A. Weber and Colin F. Camerer, "Cultural Conflict and Merger Failure: An Experimental Approach," *Management Science*, April 2003, 400–415; Bill Vlasic and Bradley A. Stertz, "How the DaimlerChrysler Marriage of Equals Got Taken for a Ride," *BusinessWeek*, 5 June 2000, 86–92; Jeffrey Ball and Scott Miller, "Full Speed Ahead: Stuttgart's Control Grows With Shakeup at DaimlerChrysler," *Wall Street Journal*,

24 September 1999, A1, A8; Robert L. Simison and Scott Miller, "Making Digital Decisions," *Wall Street Journal*, 24 September 1999, B1, B4; Keith Bradsher, "A Struggle Over Culture and Turf at Auto Giant," *New York Times*, 25 September 1999, B1, B14; Message from DaimlerChrysler Chairman to Company Employees, *Wall Street Journal*, 24 September 1999, A15; Joann Muller, Kathleen Kerwin, and Jack Ewing, "Man With a Plan," *BusinessWeek*, 4 October 1999, 34–35; Frank Gibney, Jr., "Worldwide Fender Bender," *Time*, 24 May 1999, 58–62; Daniel McGinn and Stefan Theil, "Hands on the Wheel," *Newsweek*, 12 April 1999, 49–52; Alex Taylor III, "The Germans Take Charge," *Fortune*, 11 January 1999, 92–96; Barrett Seaman and Ron Stodghill II, "The Daimler-Chrysler Deal: Here Comes the Road Test," *Time*, 18 May 1999, 66–69; Bill Vlasic, Kathleen Kerwin, David Woodruff, Thane Peterson, and Leah Nathans Spiro, "The First Global Car Colossus," *BusinessWeek*, 18 May 1998, 40–43; Joann Muller, "Lessons From a Casualty of the Culture Wars," *BusinessWeek*, 29 November 1999, 198; Rovert McNatt, "Chrysler: Not Quite So Equal," *BusinessWeek*, 13 November 2000, 14.

185 (Learning from Business Blunders) Adapted from Ed Garsten and Christine Tierney, "GM Will Pay $2 Billion to Dump Fiat," Detroit News, 14 February 2005 [accessed 17 February 2005] www.detnews.com; Aidan Lewis, "GM, Fiat Agree to End Partnership," *Washington Post*, 14 February 2005 [accessed 17 February 2005] www.washingtonpost.com; "GM, Fiat Reach Settlement Agreement," General Motors press release, 13 February 2005, GM website [accessed 17 February 2005] www.gm.com.

191 (AOL Time Warner: From Deal of the Century to Disaster of a Lifetime?) Adapted from Tom Lowry, "Time Warner's Settling Day, Sort Of," *BusinessWeek*, 16 December 2004 [accessed 17 February 2005] www.businessweek.com; Time Warner website [accessed 17 February 2005] www.timewarner.com; Andy Holloway, "Wasting Time," *Canadian Business*, 1 March 2004, 95+; John Motavalli, "More AOL Woes for Time Warner," *Television Week*, 5 January 2004, 1+; Martin Peers and Julia Angwin, "AOL Reports Record Annual Loss and Says Ted Turner Will Resign," *Wall Street Journal*, 30 January 2003, A1, A2; Martin Peers and Julia Angwin, "Steve Case Quits As AOL Chairman Under Pressure," *Wall Street Journal*, 13 January 2003, A1, A8; Catherine Yang, "AOL: Anatomy of a Long Shot," *BusinessWeek*, 16 December 2002, 58–60; Andy Kessler, "Here's the Sinking Case of AOL Time Warner," *Wall Street Journal Online*, October 8, 2002; Frank Ahrens, "At AOL and Disney, Uneasy Chairs," *Washington Post*, September 18, 2002, E01; Martin Peers, "Will Steve Case Leave AOL?," *Wall Street Journal*, September 12, 2002, B1, B7; Jeremy Kahn and Bill Powell, "Can These Guys Fix AOL?," *Fortune*, September 2, 2002, 95–100; Tom Lowry, "The Sinkhole of 'Synergy'," *BusinessWeek*, August 26, 2002, 22; Catherine Yang, "Can Miller Put the Oomph Back in AOL?," *BusinessWeek*, August 26, 2002, 42; Frank Ahrens, Merissa Marr, "Old-School Media Reassert Control," *Toronto Star*, July 30, 2002; "Big Media Mergers Raise Big Doubts; Is Synergy Achievable—or Even Desirable?," *Washington Post*, May 14, 2002, A01.

Chapter 6

Photo Credits

195 New York Times Agency, Nancy Pierce; **197** Aria Pictures, Mamoru Tsukada/Aria Pictures; **199** Namas Bhojani; **208** Subway Restaurants, DAI; **210** Corbis/Bettmann; **212** Native Ground Music, Tim Barnwell

Exhibits

198 (Exhibit 6.1) Adapted from Carrie Dolan, "Entrepreneurs Often Fail as Managers," *Wall Street Journal*, 15 May 1989, B1. Reprinted by permission of The Wall Street Journal, © 1989 Dow Jones & Company, Inc. All Rights Reserved Worldwide.

201 (Exhibit 6.2) From Anne R. Carey and Grant Jerding, *USA Snapshot, USA Today*, 26 March 1998, B1.

203 (Exhibit 6.3) From Norman M. Scarborough and Thomas W. Zimmerer, *Effective Small Business Management*, 7th ed. (Upper Saddle River, N.J.: Prentice-Hall, 2003), 4; Dun and Bradstreet, *19th Annual Small Business Survey*, 2000.

204 (Exhibit 6.4) Based on "Checklist for Going into Business," SBA website [accessed 20 February 2005] www.sba.gov; Janet Attard, "Business Start-Up Checklist, Business Know How website [accessed 20 February 2005] www.businessknowhow.com.

207 (Exhibit 6.5) Adapted from Norman M. Scarborough and Thomas W. Zimmerer, *Effective Small Business Management*, 7th ed. (Upper Saddle River, N.J.: Prentice Hall, 2003), 9–14.

210 (Exhibit 6.7) Adapted from Norman M. Scarborough and Thomas W. Zimmerer, *Effective Small Business Management*, 7th ed. (Upper Saddle River, N.J.: Prentice Hall, 2003), 27–29.

Boxes and Case for Critical Thinking

198 (Business Buzz) Adapted from Wordspy.com [accessed 15 April 2004] www.wordspy.com.

202 (Technologies That Are Revolutionizing Business) Adapted from David Pescovitz, "Technology of the Year: Social Network Applications," *Business 2.0*, November 2003, 113–114; Spoke website [accessed 11 April 2004] www.spoke.com; LinkedIn website [accessed 11 April 2004] www.linkedin.com; Ryze website [accessed 11 April 2004] www.ryze.com.

205 (Learning from Business Blunders) Adapted from Eve Tahmincioglu, *New York Times*, 9 October 2003, C9.

206 (Blueprint for a Comprehensive Business Plan) Adapted from Michael Gerber, "The Business Plan That Always Works," *Her Business*, May/June 2004, 23–25; J. Tol Broome, Jr., "How to Write a Business Plan," *Nation's Business*, February 1993, 29–30; Albert Richards, "The Ernst & Young Business Plan Guide," *R & D Management*, April 1995, 253; David Lanchner, "How Chitchat Became a Valuable Business Plan," *Global Finance*, February 1995, 54–56; Marguerita Ashby-Berger, "My Business Plan—And What Really Happened," *Small Business Forum*, Winter 1994–1995, 24–35; Stanley R. Rich and David E. Gumpert, *Business Plans That Win $$$* (New York: Harper Row, 1985).

220 (Why is Papa John's Rolling in Dough?) Adapted from Papa John's website [accessed 22 February 2005] www.papajohns.com; "Papa John's Hires President from Blockbuster," *Business First*, 1 February 2005 [accessed 22 February 2005] www.bizjournals.com; Kate MacArthur, "Pizza Rut," *Advertising Age*, 21 January 2002, 4, 39; Susan Gosselin, "Pizza Wars," *The Lane Report*, 1 September 2001, 46; Kirsten Haukebo, "Papa John's Dad Finds His Calling," *USA Today*, 22 February 2000, 3B; Ron Ruggles, "John Schnatter: Mom Never Thought There'd Be Days Like This, But Papa John's CEO Is Rolling In Dough," *Nation's Restaurant News*, January 2000, 158–160; Amy Zuber, "Papa John's European Expansion to

Mushroom via Perfect Pizza Buy," *Nation's Restaurant News,* 13 December 1999, 8; Alynda Wheat, "Striking It Rich the Low-Tech Way," *Fortune,* 27 September 1999, 86; Amy Zuber, "Papa John's Acquires Minnesota Pizza Co.," *Nation's Restaurant News,* 12 April 1999, 4, 91; Anne Field, "Piping-Hot Performance," *Success,* March 1999, 76–80; John Greenwald, "Slice, Dice, and Devour," *Time,* 26 October 1998, 64–66.

222 E-Business in Action
Adapted from Jennifer Reingold, Carleen Hawn, Keith H. Hammonds, Ryan Underwood, and Linda Tischler, "What We Learned in the New Economy," *Fast Company,* March 2003, 9+; AP Worldstream, "Ebay Tops Wall Street Expectations, Improves Outlook for 2004," 21 January 2004 [accessed 10 April 2004] www.highbeam.com; David Moschella, "Revenge of the Dot-coms," *Computerworld,* 26 January 2004 [accessed 10 April 2004] www.highbeam.com; Paulette Thomas, "The Morning After," *Wall Street Journal,* 27 March 2002, R12; Michael Totty and Ann Grimes, "If at First You Don't Succeed," *Wall Street Journal,* 11 February 2002, R6–R7; J. William Gurley, "Startups, Beware: Obey the Law of Supply and Demand," *Fortune,* 29 May 2000, 278; William M. Bulkeley and Jim Carlton, "E-Tail Gets Derailed: How Web Upstarts Misjudged the Game," *Wall Street Journal,* 5 April 2000, A1, A6; Leslie Kaufman, "After Taking a Beating, Dot-Coms Now Seek Financial Saviors," *New York Times,* 18 April 2000, C1, C18; Kevin Maney, "Net Start-Ups Pull Out of the Garage," *USA Today,* 1 October 1999, 1B, 2B; Matt Krantz, "E-Retailers Run Low on Fuel," *USA Today,* 26 April 2000, 1B, 2B; "Survival of the Fastest," *Inc. Tech,* 16 November 1999, 44–58; Darnell Little, "Peapod Is in a Pickle," *BusinessWeek,* 3 April 2000, 41; Heather Green, Nanette Byrnes, Norm Alster, and Arlene Weintraub, "The Dot.Coms Are Falling To Earth," *BusinessWeek,* 17 April 2000, 48–49; John A. Byrne, "The Fall of A Dot-Com," *BusinessWeek,* 1 May 2000, 150–160; Stephanie N. Mehta, "As Investors Play VC, It's Dot-Com Doomsday," *Fortune,* 1 May 2000, 40–41; David P. Hamilton and Mylene Mangalindan, "Angels of Death," *Wall Street Journal,* 25 May 2000, A1, A8; Luisa Kroll, "When the Music Stops," *Forbes,* 15 May 2000, 182; Chris Farrell, "Death of the Dot-Coms?" *BusinessWeek,* 22 May 2000, 104E6; John Steele Gordon, "The Golden Spike," *Forbes ASAP,* 21 February 2000, 118–122; Eric W. Pfeiffer, "Where Are We in the Revolution?" *Forbes ASAP,* 21 February 2000, 68–70; James Lardner and Paul Sloan, "The Anatomy of Sickly IPOs," *U.S. News and World Report,* 29 May 2000, 42; Hillary Stout, "Crunch Time," *Wall Street Journal,* 7 June 2000, B1; Jerry Useem, "Dot-Coms—What Have We Learned?" *Fortune,* 30 October 2000, 82–104; Heather Green and Norm Alster, "Guess What—Venture Capitalists Aren't Geniuses," *BusinessWeek,* 10 July 2000, 98; Thomas E. Weber, "What Were We Thinking?" *Wall Street Journal,* 18 July 2000, B1, B4; Greg Ip, Susan Pulliam, Scott Thurm, and Ruth Simon, "The Color Green," *Wall Street Journal,* 14 July 2000, A1, A8; "Business Brief—Value America: Bankruptcy–Code Filing is Made by the Company," *Wall Street Journal,* 14 August 2000, B2.

Career Profiles
224 (Marketing Researcher and Research Manager) Adapted from U.S. Department of Labor, Bureau of Labor Statistics website, *Occupational Outlook Handbook* [accessed 20 May 2005] www.bls.gov.

224 (Administrative Services Manager) Adapted from U.S. Department of Labor, Bureau of Labor Statistics website, *Occupational Outlook Handbook* [accessed 20 May 2005] www.bls.gov; "Job Profile for Administrative Services Managers," Careers.org [accessed 20 May 2005] www.careers.org; International Facility Management Association website [accessed 20 May 2005] www.ifma.org.

Chapter 7

Photo Credits
227 Dell, Inc.; **230** Landov LLC, Peter Endig/DPA; **235** PhotoEdit, Felicia Martinez; **240** Getty Images, Inc.—Hulton Archive Photos, David McNew; **246** Evan Kafka

Exhibits
231 (Exhibit 7.3) Adapted from Kodak website [accessed 11 March 2005] www.kodak.com.
233 (Exhibit 7.4) Adapted from Fred Vogelstein, "Mighty Amazon," *Fortune,* 26 May 2003, 60–74; Stuart Crainer, "The 75 Greatest Management Decisions Ever Made," *Management Review,* November 1998, 17–23.
241 (Exhibit 7.6) Adapted from and reprinted by permission of *Harvard Business Review,* an exhibit from "How to Choose a Leadership Pattern" by Robert Tannenbaum and Warren H. Schmidt, May–June 1973. Copyright © 1973 by the President and Fellows of Harvard College, all rights reserved.

Boxes and Case for Critical Thinking
238 (Do You Have What It Takes to Be a Leader?) Adapted from Peter F. Drucker, "What Makes an Effective Executive," *Harvard Business Review,* June 2004, 58–63; Nicholas Varchaver, "Glamour! Fortune! Org Charts!" *Fortune,* 15 November 2004, 136–148; Carl Robinson, "What They Don't Teach You at Harvard or Kindergarten," *Puget Sound Business Journal,* 16–22 July 2004, 29; Alison Stein Wellner, "Who Can You Trust?" *Inc.,* October 2004, 39–40; Michael C. Mankins, "Stop Wasting Valuable Time," *Harvard Business Review,* September 2004, 58–65; Larry Bossidy and Ram Charan, "Confronting Reality," *Fortune,* 18 October 2004, 225–231.
243 (Creating the Ideal Culture in Your Company) Adapted from Andrew Bird, "Do You Know What Your Corporate Culture Is?" *CPA Insight,* February, March 1999, 25–26; Gail H. Vergara, "Finding a Compatible Corporate Culture," *Healthcare Executive,* January/February 1999, 46–47; Hal Lancaster, "To Avoid a Job Failure, Learn the Culture of a Company First," *Wall Street Journal,* 14 July 1998, B1.
245 (Learning from Business Blunders) Adapted from Richard Pérez-Peña and Matthew L. Wald, "Basic Failures by Ohio Utility Set Off Blackout, Report Finds," *New York Times,* 20 November 2003, A1; "US Blackout: Interim Report," *Power Economics,* January 2004, 9; Edward Iwata, "Report: Major Blackout Could Have Been Prevented," *USA Today,* 6 April 2004, A1.
245 (Business Buzz) Adapted from Wordspy.com [accessed 15 April 2004] www.wordspy.com.
248 (Technologies That Are Revolutionizing Business) Adapted from TechEncyclopedia.com [accessed 13 April 2004] www.techweb.com/encyclopedia; Business Objects websites [accessed 13 April 2004] www.businessobjects.com; Cognos website [accessed 13 April 2004] www.cognos.com.

254 (Wegmans Satisfies Customers by Putting Employees First) Adapted from Wegmans website [accessed 8 March 2005] www.wegmans.com; William Conroy, "Rochester, N.Y.-Based Grocer Tops Magazine's Best Employer Rankings," *Asbury Park (NJ) Press*, 11 January 2005 [accessed 8 March 2005] www.ebsco.com; Matthew Boyle, "The Wegmans Way," *Fortune*, 24 January 2005, 62–68; "UCCNet Designated as U.S. Data Pool of Choice by Leading Retailers," UCCNet website [accessed 8 March 2005] www.uccnet.org; Joy Davis, "Caring for Employees Is Wegmans' Best Selling Point," *Democrat and Chronicle (Rochester, NY)*, 6 February 2005 [accessed 8 March 2005] www.democratandchronicle.com; Michael A. Prospero, "Employee Innovator: Wegmans," *Fast Company*, October 2004, 88; Matt Glynn, "Employees of Rochester, N.Y.-Based Grocer Celebrate Firm's Top Ranking," *Buffalo (NY) News*, 11 January 2005 [accessed 8 March 2005] www.ebsco.com.

Chapter 8

Photo Credits
259 Joe McDonald; **269** Getty Images, Inc.—Stone Allstock, Terry Vine; **273** Stock Boston, John Coletti; **274** Getty Images, Inc.—Image Bank, Lockyet, Romilly; **279** PhotoEdit, Spencer Grant

Exhibit
267 (Exhibit 8.4) Adapted from Steven Burke, "Acer Restructures into Six Divisions," *Computer Reseller News*, 13 July 1998, 10.

Boxes and Case for Critical Thinking
262 (Technologies That Are Revolutionizing Business) Adapted from Wavelink case study, "Tesco Picks Wavelink to Manage Over 5000 Wireless Access Points Across More Than 600 Stores," Wavelink website [accessed 14 April 2004] www.wavelink.com; Cisco case study, "University of Wyoming—Rocky Mountain Campus Builds Rock-Solid Wireless Network," Cisco website [accessed 14 April 2004] www.cisco.com; "Wireless Access Point (WLAN) Basics," Caltech Information Technology Services website [accessed 14 April 2004] www.its.caltech.edu.
266 (Learning from Business Blunders) Adapted from Clayton M. Christensen and Michael E. Raynor, "Why Hard-Nosed Executives Should Care About Management Theory," *Harvard Business Review*, September 2003, 67–74; Martha McKay, "Lucent Turns Its First Profit in 14 Quarters," *The Record* (Bergen County, NJ), 23 October 2003 [accessed 14 April 2004] www.highbeam.com.
266 (Business Buzz) Adapted from Wordspy.com [accessed 15 April 2004] www.wordspy.com.
270 (E-SoftSys Stays Connected Around the Globe) Adapted from E-SoftSys website [accessed 30 May 2004] www. e-softsys.com; Bob Davis, "With Software Jobs Migrating to India, Think Long Term," 6 October 2003, *The Wall Street Journal* [accessed 6 October 2003] http://online.wsj.com; Carolyn A. April, "App-Dev Megatrends: New Tools and Techniques Take the Drudgery Out of Development Work," 15 September 2003, *VAR Business*, 28; Larry Dignan, "How to Manage a Globally Staffed Project," 1 September 2003, *Baseline*, 17.
272 (Don't Leave Home: American Express's Virtual Environment) "American Express Takes Control of Their Office Space," Archibus website [accessed 11 March 2005] www.archibus.com; American Express Company website [accessed 11 April 2005] www. americanexpress.com; Sally Richards, "Make the Most of Your First Job," *InformationWeek*, 21 June 1999, 183–186; Tim Greene, "American Express: Don't Leave Home to Go to Work," *Network World*, 8 March 1999, 25; Mahlon Apgar IV, "The Alternative Workplace: Changing Where and How People Work," *Harvard Business Review*, May/June 1998, 121–130; "How Senior Executives at American Express View the Alternative Workplace," *Harvard Business Review*, May/June 1998, 132–133; Michelle Marchetti, "Master Motivators," *Sales and Marketing Management*, April 1998, 38–44; Carrie Shook, "Leader, Not Boss," *Forbes*, 1 December 1997, 52–54.
285 (Harley-Davidson Drives from Dysfunctional to Cross-Functional) Adapted from Pallavi Gogoi, "I Am Woman, Hear Me Shop," *BusinessWeek*, 14 February 2005 [accessed 12 March 2005] www.businessweek.com; Joseph Weber, "Thirty Years in Hog Heaven," *BusinessWeek*, 21 March 2005 [accessed 12 March 2005] www.businessweek.com; Harley-Davidson website [accessed 12 March 2005] www.harley-davidson.com; John Teresko, "Fueled by Innovation," *IndustryWeek*, December 2002, 52–57; John Helyar, "Will Harley Davidson Hit the Wall?" *Fortune*, 12 August 2002, 120–124; Jonathan Fahey, "Love into Money," *Forbes*, 7 January 2002, 60–65; Rich Teerlink, "Harley's Leadership U-Turn," *Harvard Business Review*, July–August 2000, 43+; Kevin R. Fitzgerald, "Purchasing at Harley Links Supply with Design," *Purchasing*, 13 February 1997, 56–57; Machan Dyan, "Is the Hog Going Soft?," *Forbes*, 10 March 1997, 114–115; Ronald B. Lieber, "Selling the Sizzle," *Fortune*, 23 June 1997, 80; Clyde Fessler, "Rotating Leadership at Harley-Davidson: From Hierarchy to Interdependence," *Strategy & Leadership*, July–August 1997, 42–43; Tim Minahan, "Harley-Davidson Revs Up Development Process," *Purchasing*, 7 May 1998, 44S18–44S23; Michael A. Verespej, "Invest in People," *IndustryWeek*, 1 February 1999, 6–7; Leslie P. Norton, "Potholes Ahead?," *Barron's*, 1 February 1999, 16–17; Mark A. Brunelli, "How Harley-Davidson Uses Cross-Functional Teams," *Purchasing*, 4 November 1999, 148.

Chapter 9

Photo Credits
289 Carvin Customized Guitars; **294** Alamy Images, Jeff Morgan/Alamy; **299** Corbis/Bettmann; **304** Think3, Inc; **305** Alamy Images, Leslie Garland Picture Library/Alamy; **306** Corbis/Bettmann

Exhibit
293 (Exhibit 9.2) Adapted from Mark M. Davis, Nicholas J. Aquilano, and Richard B. Chase, *Fundamentals of Operations Management* (Boston: Irwin McGraw-Hill, 1999), 7.

Boxes and Case for Critical Thinking
296 (Offshoring: Profits, Yes, But at What Cost?) Adapted from Jeffrey E. Garten, "Offshoring: You Ain't Seen Nothin' Yet," *BusinessWeek*, 21 June 2004, 28; Jim Hopkins, "To Start Up Here, Companies Hire Over There," *USA Today*, 11 February 2005, B1–B2; Marc Lacey, "Accents of Africa: A New Outsourcing Frontier," *New York Times*, 2 February 2005, C1, C6; Susan Carey and Alex Frangos, "Airlines, Facing Cost Pressure, Outsource Crucial Safety Tasks," *Wall Street Journal*, 21 January 2005, A1, A5; Barbara Hagenbaugh, "U.S. Layoffs

Not a Result of Offshoring, Data Show," *USA Today*, 11 June 2004, B1; Jay Solomon, "India's Latest: Debt Collection," *Wall Street Journal*, 6 December 2004, A14; Stephanie Amour and Michelle Kessler, "USA's New Money-Saving Export: White-Collar Jobs," *USA Today*, 5 August 2003, B1–B2; Steve Lohr, "Offshore Jobs in Technology: Opportunity or Threat?" *New York Times*, 22 December 2003, C1, C6; Kris Maher, "Next on the Outsourcing List," *Wall Street Journal*, 28 March 2004, B1, B8; Jennifer Reingold, "Into Thin Air," *Fast Company*, April 2004, 76–82; Paul Craig Roberts, "The Harsh Truth About Outsourcing," 22 March 2004, *BusinessWeek*, 48; Craig Karmin, "'Offshoring' Can Generate Jobs in the U.S.," *Wall Street Journal*, 16 March 2004, B1, B7; Bernard J. La Londe, "From Outsourcing to '''Offshoring'—Part 1," *Supply Chain Management Review*, 1 March 2004 [accessed 16 April 2004] www.manufacturing.net; Paul Kaihla, "Straws in the Wind," *Business 2.0*, 27 April 2004 [accessed 22 July 2004] www.business2.com.

303 (Technologies That Are Revolutionizing Business) Adapted from Barnaby J. Feder, "Technology: Bashful vs. Brash in the New Field of Nanotech," *New York Times*, 15 March 2004 [accessed 16 April 2004] www.nytimes.com; "Nanotechnology Basics," Nanotechnology Now website [accessed 16 April 2004] www.nanotech-now.com; Center for Responsible Nanotechnology website [accessed 16 April 2004] www.crnano.org; Gary Stix, "Little Big Science," *Scientific American*, 16 September 2001 [accessed 16 April 2004] www.sciam.com; Tim Harper, "Small Wonders," *Business 2.0*, July 2002 [accessed 16 April 2004] www.business2.com; Erick Schonfeld, "A Peek at IBM's Nanotech Research," *Business 2.0*, 5 December 2003 [accessed 16 April 2004] www.business2.com; David Pescovitz, "The Best New Technologies of 2003," *Business 2.0*, November 2003, 109–116.

304 (Business Buzz) Adapted from Wordspy.com [accessed 15 April 2004] www.wordspy.com.

308 (Your Inventory Wants to Talk to You) Adapted from Mark Roberti, "Wal-Mart Begins RFID Process Change, *RFID Journal*, 1 February 2005 [accessed 20 March 2005] www.rfidj-ournal.com; "The Wal-Mart Factor," *RFID Journal*, 17 March 2003, [accessed 20 March 2005] www.rfidjournal.com; George Spohrer, "Seven Steps to an RFID Deployment," *RFID Journal*, 14 March 2005 [accessed 20 March 2005] www.rfidjournal.com; "Benetton Explains RFID Privacy Flap," *RFID Journal* [accessed 1 April 2004] www.rfidjournal.com; Kristi Heim, "Microchips in People, Packaging and Pets Raise Privacy Questions," *Seattle Times*, 18 October 2004 [accessed 18 October 2004] www.seattletimes.com; Brian Albright, "RFID Dominates Frontline's Supply Chain Week," *Frontline Solutions*, November 2003, 10–13.

310 (Learning From Business Blunders) Adapted from Adam Horowitz, Mark Athitakis, Mark Lasswell, and Owen Thomas, "The 101 Dumbest Moments in Business," *Business 2.0* [accessed 27 March 2004] www.business2.com; David Lazarus, "Pakistani Threatened UCSF to Get Paid, She Says," *San Francisco Chronicle,* 12 November 2003 [accessed 17 April 2004] www.sfgate.com.

318 (Porsche—Back in the Fast Lane) Adapted from Porsche AG website [accessed 18 March 2005] www.porsche.com; Diana T. Kurylko, "Porsche Plans Cayman for Younger Buyers," *Automotive News*, 7 March 2005 [accessed 18 March 2005] www.ebsco.com; Jens Meiners, "Porsche Coupe Contract Will Buoy Valmet," *Automotive News,* 7 February 2005 [accessed 18 March 2005] www.ebsco.com; "Online Extra: Porsche's CEO Talks Shop," *BusinessWeek*, 22 December 2003 [accessed 18 March 2005] www.businessweek.com; Gail Edmondson, "This SUV Can Tow an Entire Carmaker," *BusinessWeek*, 22 December 2003 [accessed 18 March 2005] www.businessweek.com; "Online Extra: Q&A with Porsche's Wendelin Wiedeking," *BusinessWeek*, 28 June 2004 [accessed 18 March 2005] www.businessweek.com; Alex Taylor III, "Porsche's Risky Recipe," *Fortune*, 17 February 2003, 91–94; Scott Miller, "Porsche Gambling That Cayenne Will Be Hot SUV," *Chicago Sun Times*, 26 August 2002, 4; "The Selling of an Anachronistic Dream; Porsche Is Now the World's Most Profitable Car Maker," *Irish Times*, 21 August 2002, 53; "The Stars of Europe: Turnaround Artists: Wendelin Wiedeking," *BusinessWeek*, 19 June 2000, 186; Tom Mudd, "Back in High Gear," *IndustryWeek*, 21 February 2000, 38–46; Matthew Karnitschnig, "That Van You're Driving May Be Part Porsche," *BusinessWeek*, 27 December 1999, 72; Peter Morgan, "Back to Winning Ways," *Professional Engineering*, 28 April 1999, 30–31; Karen Abramic Dilger, "Gear Up and Go," Manufacturing Systems, A24–A28; "Porsche Gears Up for Faster Parts Distribution," *Material Handling Engineering*, July 1998, 34–40; Richard Feast, "The Road Ahead for Porsche," *Independent*, 6 September 1996, 17.

321 E-Commerce in Action
Adapted from Erik Heinrich, "What Can Work: One Buyer, Many Sellers," *Toronto Sun,* 23 October 2003 [accessed 17 April] www.highbeam.com; Peter Loftus, "E-Commerce: Business to Business—Exchanges Making It Work," *Wall Street Journal*, 11 February 2002, R16; Ralph Kisiel, "Automakers Saving by Using Covisint," *Crain's Detroit Business*, 21 January 2002, 12; Eric Young, "Web Marketplaces That Really Work," *Fortune Tech Review*, Winter 2002, 10; J. William Gurley, "Big Company.com: Should You Start a B2B Exchange?" *Fortune*, 3 April 2000, 260+; Peter D. Henig, "Revenge of the Bricks," *Red Herring*, August 2000, 121–134; Daniel Lyons, "B2Bluster," *Forbes*, 1 May 2000, 122–126; Steven Kaplan and Mohanbir Sawhney, "E-hubs: The New B2B Marketplaces," *Harvard Business Review*, May–June 2000, 97–100; Robert D. Hof, "Who Will Profit from the Internet Agora?" *BusinessWeek E.Biz*, 5 June 2000, EB56–EB62; Joseph B. White, "Getting Into Gear," *Wall Street Journal*, 17 April 2000, R65; Douglas A. Blackmon, "Where the Money Is," *Wall Street Journal*, 17 April 2000, R30–R32; Edward Iwata, "Despite the Hype, B2B Marketplaces Struggle," *USA Today*, 10 May 2000, 1B–2B; Jack Trout, "Stupid Net Tricks," *Business 2.0*, May 2000, 76–77; John W. Verity, "Invoice? What's an Invoice?" *BusinessWeek*, 10 June 1996, 110–112; Christina Binkley, "Hyatt Plans Internet Firm with Marriott," *Wall Street Journal*, 2 May 2000, A3, A6; Clint Willis, "B2B to Be?" *Forbes ASAP*, 21 August 2000, 125–130; Jason Anders, "Yesterday's Darling," *Wall Street Journal*, 23 October 2000, R8.

Career Profiles
322 (Buying, Purchasing Agent, and Purchasing Manager) Adapted from U.S. Department of Labor, Bureau of Labor Statistics website, *Occupational Outlook Handbook* [accessed 20 May 2005] www.bls.gov; Institute for Supply Management website [accessed 23 May 2005] www.ism.ws.

322 (Manufacturing and Operations Managers) Adapted from U.S. Department of Labor, Bureau of Labor Statistics website, *Occupational Outlook Handbook* [accessed 25 May 2005] www.bls.gov.

Chapter 10

Photo Credits
325 Atlas Container Corporation; **327** Corbis—NY; **336** Getty Images, Inc.—Taxi, Michael Krasowitz; **340** Landov LLC, MTV Networks/via Bloomberg News/Landov; **341** PhotoEdit, Tom McCarthy; **342** Omni-Photo Communications, Inc., Jeff Greenberg; **348** Corbis—NY

Exhibits
329 (Exhibit 10.2) *Management, Fourth Edition*, by Richard L. Daft copyright © 1997 by Harcourt Inc., reproduced by permission of the publisher.
330 (Exhibit 10.3) Douglas McGregor, *The Human Side of Enterprise* (New York: McGraw-Hill, 1960).
333 (Exhibit 10.4) Adapted from Stephen P. Robbins and David A. DeCenzo, *Fundamentals of Management*, 4th ed. (Upper Saddle River, N.J.: PrenticeHall, 2004), 289.

Boxes and Case for Critical Thinking
331 (Which Theory Will Solve the Problem of Employee Theft?) Adapted from "Embezzlement/Employee Theft," *Business Credit*, February 2005, 41–42; "Shrink Is Shrinking—But So Are the Loss-Prevention Budgets," *IOMA's Security Director's Report*, December 2004, 7–11; James E. Merklin, "Thieves at Work," *Industrial Distribution*, September 2004, 53–54; "Common-Sense Measures Preventing Employee Theft," SBA website [accessed 27 March 2005] www.sba.gov.
332 (Learning from Business Blunders) Adapted from Adam Horowitz, Mark Athitakis, Mark Lasswell, and Owen Thomas, "The 101 Dumbest Moments in Business," *Business 2.0* [accessed 24 April 2004] www.business2.com; "The Best & Worst Managers of 2003," *BusinessWeek*, 12 January 2004, 55–85; Gretchen Morgenson, " It's Awards Time on Wall Street: From Epic to Comic Wall Street Watch," *International Herald Tribune*, 30 December 2003 [accessed 24 April 2004] www. highbeam.com; Rick Moriarty, "Low-Flying Airline; American Struggles to Recover from 9/11, Bankruptcy, Executive Pay Scandal," *The Post-Standard* (Syracuse, NY), 15 December 2003 [accessed 24 April 2004] www.highbeam.com.
337 (Are We Having Fun Yet?) Adapted from Jyoti Thottam, "Thank God It's Monday!" *Time,* 17 January 2005, A58+; Tim Larimer, "Having Any Fun?" *Time,* November 2003; Harvey Meyer, "Fun for Everyone," *Journal of Business Strategy,* March–April 1999, 13–17; Erika Rasmusson, "A Funny Thing Happened on the Way to Work," *Sales and Marketing Management*, March 1999, 97–98; Peter Baker, "Work: Have Fun. And That's An Order," *The Observer*, 3 January 1999, 11+; Melanie Payne, "Chuckle While You Work," *San Diego Union-Tribune*, 19 October 1998, E1–E2; Maggie Jackson, "Corporate America Lightens Up: Laughing Workers are Happy Workers," *The Salt Lake Tribune*, 4 May 1997, E1; Diane E. Lewis, "Employers Find Humor Can Improve Morale, Profits," *Boston Globe*, 1 April 1997, C5; R. J. King, "Here's A Laugh: Speaker Shows How Office Humor Helps," *Detroit News*, 15 February 1996, B3; Katy Robinson, "Use Laughter to Brighten Your Office," *Idaho Statesman*, 18 October 1995, 1.

339 (Too Many Workers? Not for Long) Adapted from David Streitfeld, "Jobs, but Few Workers," *Los Angeles Times*, 31 October 2004, C1, C4; Eduardo Porter, "Coming Soon: The Vanishing Work Force," *New York Times*, 29 August 2004, sec. 3, 1, 4; John S. McClenahen, "The Next Crisis: Two Few Workers," *Industry Week*, May 2003, 41–45; Ken Dychtwald, Tamara Erickson, and Bob Morison, "It's Time to Retire Retirement," *Harvard Business Review*, March 2004, 48–57; Paul Kaihla, "The Coming Job Boom," *Business 2.0*, September 2003, 97–105; Stephanie Armour, "More Moms Make Kids Their Career of Choice," *USA Today*, 12 March 2002, 1B; Aaron Bernstein, "Too Many Workers? Not for Long," *BusinessWeek*, 20 May 2002, 126–130; Steven A. Nyce and Sylvester J. Schieber, "The Decade of the Employee: The Workforce in the Coming Decade," *Benefits Quarterly*, First Quarter 2002, 60–79; Paul Gores, "Economist Calls Recession Mild, Predicts Labor Shortage Will Return," *Knight Ridder Tribune Business News*, 10 February 2002; Nancy Pounds, "Nation Expert Sees Skilled Worker Need Despite Recent Layoffs," *Alaska Journal of Commerce*, 28 October 2001, 19.
343 (Technologies That Are Revolutionizing Business) Adapted from Rich Karlgaard, "Outsource Yourself," *Forbes*, 19 April 2004 [accessed 24 April 2004] www.highbeam.com; David Kirkpatrick, "Big-League R&D Gets Its Own eBay," *Fortune*, 3 May 2004 [accessed 24 April 2004] www. highbeam.com; Joseph N. Pelton, "The Rise of Telecities: Decentralizing the Global Society," *The Futurist,* 1 January 2004 [accessed 24 April 2004] www.highbeam.com.
349 (Business Buzz) Adapted from Wordspy.com [accessed 25 April 2004] www.wordspy.com.
355 (Brewing Up People Policies at Starbucks) Adapted from Starbucks website [accessed 25 March 2005] www. starbucks.com; John Hollon, "A Simple Philosophy," *Workforce Management,* December 2004, 12; Maryann Hammers, "Pleasing Employees, Pouring Profits," *Workforce Management,* October 2003, 58–59; Peter Briefer and Sean O'Shea, "Private Blog Wasn't; Man Fired for Blasting Boss," *National Post and Global News*, 3 September 2004; Kate Bonamici and Andy Serwer, "Hot Starbucks to Go," *Fortune*, 26 January 2004, 58+; Peter Kafka, "Bean Counter," Forbes.com, 28 February 2005 [accessed 25 March 2005] www.forbes.com; Phyllis Feinberg, "From Starbucks to the Oakland A's, 18 DC Plans Exhibit 'Best Practices'," *Pensions & Investments*, 23 February 2004, 3+; Stanley Homes, Drake Bennett, Kate Carlisle, and Chester Dawson, "Planet Starbucks," *BusinessWeek,* 9 September 2002, 99–110; Ranjay Gulati, Sarah Huffman, and Gary Neilson, "The Barista Principle," *Strategy + Business,* Quarter 3 2002, 58–69; "Mr. Coffee," Context, August–September 2001, 20–25; Jennifer Ordonez, "Starbucks' Schultz to Leave Top Post, Lead Global Effort," *Wall Street Journal*, 7 April 2000, B3; Karyn Strauss, "Howard Schulz: Starbucks' CEO Serves a Blend of Community, Employee Commitment," *Nation's Restaurant News,* January 2000, 162–163; Carla Joinson, "The Cost of Doing Business?" *HR Magazine*, December 1999, 86–92; "Interview with Howard Schulz: Sharing Success," *Executive Excellence*, November 1999, 16–17; Kelly Barron, "The Cappuccino Conundrum," *Forbes*, 22 February 1999, 54–55; Naomi Weiss, "How Starbucks Impassions Workers to Drive Growth," *Workforce*, August 1998, 60–64; Scott S. Smith, "Grounds for Success," *Entrepreneur*, May 1998,

120–126; "Face Value: Perky People," *The Economist,* 30 May 1998, 66; Howard Schulz and Dori Jones Yang, "Starbucks: Making Values Pay," *Fortune,* 29 September 1997, 261–272.

Chapter 11

Photo Credits
359 PhotoEdit, Amy C. Etra; **363** AP Wide World Photos, Melanie Einzig; **370** Photo Researchers, Inc., EIK Image; **371** Corbis—NY, Lester Lefkowitz; **377** The Image Works, Jeff Greenberg; **380** Getty Images, Inc.—Agence France Presse; **382** SAS Institute Inc.

Exhibits
369 (Exhibit 11.5) Adapted from Henry R. Cheeseman, *Contemporary Business and E-Commerce Law,* 4th ed. (Upper Saddle River, N.J.: Prentice Hall, 2003), 628–631.
379 (Exhibit 11.7) Adapted from Sarah Rubenstein, "Keeping Coverage," *Wall Street Journal,* 24 January 2005, R5; "Multiple Employer Initiatives: Working for Better Health Care," *HRFocus,* July 2004, 11–15; Traci Purdum, "Health Care for All," *IndustryWeek,* August 2004, 12; Milt Freudenheim, "60 Companies Plan to Sponsor Health Coverage for Uninsured," *New York Times,* 27 January 2005, C1, C17; Michelle Rafter, "The Insider: Health Care Benefits," *Workforce Management,* December 2004, 72; Maryann Hammers, "Sliding-Scale Plans Seeing a Renaissance," *Workforce Management,* January 2005, 22; Vanessa Furhmans, "One Cure for High Health Costs: In-House Clinics at Companies," *Wall Street Journal* 11 February 2005, A1, A8; Charlotte Huff, "The Insider: Health Benefits," *Workforce Management,* November 2004, 69–70; Eve Tahmincioglu, "Tackling the High Cost of Health Benefits Takes Some Creativity," *New York Times,* 26 August 2004, C6; Carrie Coolidge, "Saving for Your Health," *Forbes,* 13 December 2004, 240–244; Sara Horowitz, "Ensure They're Insured," *Harvard Business Review,* December 2004, 24; Kris Maher, "Popular . . . but Cheap," *Wall Street Journal,* 24 January 2005, R4.

Boxes and Case for Critical Thinking
364 (Technologies That Are Revolutionizing Business) Adapted from IBM Accessibility Center [accessed 30 April 2004] www-3.ibm.com/able; AssistiveTech.net [accessed 30 April 2004] www.assistivetech.net; Business Leadership Network website [accessed 30 April 2004] www.usblin.com; National Institute on Disability and Rehabilitation Research website [accessed 30 April 2004] www.ed.gov/about/offices/list/osers/nidrr; Rehabilitation Engineering and Assistive Technology Society of North America website [accessed 30 April 2004] www.resna.org.
368 (When Employees Turn on Each Other) Adapted from Anne Fisher, "How to Prevent Workplace Violence," *Fortune,* 21 February 2005, 42; "How to Predict and Prevent Workplace Violence," *HRFocus,* April 2005, 10–11; "Threat Assessments Prove Effective and Curbing Violence," *IOMA Security Director's Report,* April 2005, 8–9; Tonya Vinas and Jill Jusko, "5 Threats That Could Sink Your Company," *IndustryWeek,* September 2004, 52+; Laila Karamally, "The Insider: Employee Assistance," *Workforce Management,* September 2004, 60–63; Stephanie Armour, "The Mind of a Killer," *USA Today,* 15 July 2004, A1–A2; Stephanie Armour, "Stopping a Killer," *USA Today,* 16–18 July 2004, A1, 62; Stephanie Armour, "Life After Workplace Violence," *USA Today,* 15 July 2004, 3B.

370 (Learning from Business Blunders) Adapted from Steven Greenhouse, "Workers Assail Night Lock-Ins by Wal-Mart," *New York Times,* 18 January 2004, 1, 23; Steven Greenhouse, "Wal-Mart Raids by U.S. Aimed at Illegal Aliens, "*New York Times,* 24 October 2003, A1, A19; Jeffrey E. Garten, "Wal-Mart Gives Globalism a Bad Name," *BusinessWeek,* 8 March 2004, 24; "Wal-Mart Suit Gets Class-Action Status in Massachusetts," *Wall Street Journal,* 19 January 2004, A2.
372 (Click and Learn: E-Training Today's Employees) Adapted from "Home Depot Says E-Learning Is Paying for Itself," *Workforce Management,* 25 February 2004 [accessed 28 February 2004] www.workforce.com; Robert Celaschi, "The Insider: Training," *Workforce Management,* August 2004, 67–69; Joe Mullich, "A Second Act for E-Learning," *Workforce Management,* February 2004, 51–55; Gail Johnson, "Brewing the Perfect Blend," *Training,* December 2003, 30+; Michael A. Verespej, "Click and Learn," *Industry Week,* 15 January 2001, 31–36; Elisabeth Goodridge, "Slowing Economy Sparks Boom in E-Learning," 12 November 2001, 100–104; Cynthia Pantazis, "Maximizing E-Learning to Train the 21st Century Workforce," *Public Personnel Management,* Spring 2002, 21–26; Mary Lord, "They're Online and on the Job," *U.S. News & World Report,* 15 October 2001, 72–78.
375 (Somebody's Watching (and Listening and Reading and Monitoring and Recording)) Adapted from Pui-Wing Tam, Erin White, Nick Wingfield, and Kris Maher, "Snooping E-Mail by Software Is Now a Workplace Norm," *Wall Street Journal,* 9 March 2005, B1, B3; TrueActive website [accessed 4 April 2005] www.winwhatwhere.com; Jon Swartz, "Boeing Scandal Highlights E-Mail Checks," *USA Today,* 11 March 2005 [accessed 3 April 2005] www.usatoday.com; John Schwartz, "Snoop Software Gains Power and Raises Privacy Concerns," *New York Times,* 10 October 2003 [accessed 4 April 2005] www.nytimes.com.
383 (Business Buzz) Adapted from Wordspy.com [accessed 30 April 2004] www.wordspy.com.
389 (General Motors: Will Taking Care of Employees Sink This Industrial Titan?) Adapted from David Welch, "Will the UAW Cut GM Some Slack?" *BusinessWeek,* 11 April 2005, 72–73; Alex Taylor III, "At GM, There's Health to Pay," *Fortune,* 7 February 2005, 22–23; Danny Hakim, "Carmakers in for Long Haul in Paying Retiree Health Care," *New York Times,* 15 September 2004, C1–C2; UAW website [accessed 5 April 2005] www.uaw.org; Nanette Byrnes, "The Benefits Trap," *BusinessWeek,* 19 July 2004, 64+; Ceci Connolly, "U.S. Firms Losing Health Care Battle, GM Chairman Says," *Washington Post,* 11 February 2005, E1; Joseph Szczesny, "GM Executive: Rising Health Care Costs Are Troublesome," *News Herald,* 19 September 2004 [accessed 5 April 2005] www.thenewsherald.com; Ed Garsten, "GM: Repair Health Care," *Detroit News,* 10 February 2005 [accessed 5 April 2005] www.detnews.com; "Half of Health Care Spending Is Wasted, Study Finds," *Detroit News,* 10 February 2005 [accessed 5 April 2005] www.detnews.com; Barbara Wieland, "GM Health Care Concerns Top Wagoner's Worry List," *Lansing State Journal,* 10 January 2005 [accessed 5 April 2005]

www.lsj.com; David Welch and Nanette Byrnes, "GM Is Losing Traction," *BusinessWeek*, 7 February 2005, 74–76.

392 E-Business in Action

Adapted from Douglas Wolk, "As the Big Three Job Boards Battle It Out, DirectEmployers Quietly Wheels and Deals," *Workforce Management*, July 2004 [accessed 8 July 2004] www.workforce.com; Donald P. Shuit, "Board Games," *Workforce Management,* November 2003, 37–44; "The Pros and Cons of Online Recruiting," *HR Focus*, April 2004, S2; Efraim Turban, Jae Lee, David King, and H. Michael Chung, *Electronic Commerce*: *A Managerial Perspective* (Upper Saddle River, N.J.: Prentice Hall, 2000), 164–168; Marlene Piturro, "The Power of E-Cruiting," *Management Review*, January 2000, 33–38; "Online Recruiting: What Works, What Doesn't," *HR Focus*, March 2000, 11–15; "More Pros and Cons to Internet Recruiting," *HR Focus*, May 2000, 8; Christopher Caggiano, "The Truth About Internet Recruiting," *Inc.*, December 1999, 156; Peter Buxbaum, "Where's Dilbert?" *Chief Executive* [accessed 2 March 2000] www.chiefexecutive.net/mag/150tech/part1c.htm; James R. Borck, "Recruiting Systems Control Résumé Chaos," *InfoWorld*, 24 July 2000, 47–48; Bill Leonard, "Online and Overwhelmed," *HR Magazine*, August 2000, 36–42; Milton Zall, "Internet Recruiting," *Strategic Finance*, June 2000, 66–72; "Why Your Web Site Is More Important Than Ever to New Hires," *HR Focus*, June 2000, 9; Rachel Emma Silverman, "Recruiters' Hunt for Résumés Is Nocturnal Game," *Wall Street Journal*, 20 September 2000, B1–B4.

Career Profiles

393 (Human Resources Managers) Adapted from U.S. Department of Labor, Bureau of Labor Statistics website, *Occupational Outlook Handbook* [accessed 20 May 2005] www.bls.gov

393 (Senior Executives) Adapted from U.S. Department of Labor, Bureau of Labor Statistics website, *Occupational Outlook Handbook* [accessed 25 May 2005] www.bls.gov.

Chapter 12

Photo Credits

395 Toyota Motor Sales, USA, Inc., Toyota Motor Sales; **398** AP Wide World Photos; **401** Getty Images, Inc.—Stockbyte, AARP; **404** PhotoEdit, Mary Kate Denny.

Exhibits

397 (Exhibit 12.1) Gary Armstrong and Philip Kotler, *Marketing: An Introduction*, 5th ed. (Upper Saddle River, N.J.: Prentice Hall, 2000), 5 (Figure 1.1—Core marketing concepts).

400 (Exhibit 12.3) Gary Armstrong and Philip Kotler, *Marketing: An Introduction,* 5th ed. (Upper Saddle River, New Jersey: Prentice Hall, 2000), 19.

408 (Exhibit 12.5) Adapted from Dick Bucci, "Recording Systems Add More Depth When Capturing Answers," *Marketing News*, 1 March 2005, 50; Laurence Bernstein, "Enough Research Bashing!" *Marketing*, 24 January 2005, 10; Naresh K. Malhotra, *Basic Marketing Research,* (Upper Saddle River, N.J.: Prentice-Hall, 2002), 110–112, 208–212, 228–29.

415 (Exhibit 12.7) Exhibit 12.3, Gary Armstrong and Philip Kotler, *Marketing: An Introduction*, 5th ed. (Upper Saddle River, N.J.: Prentice Hall, 2000), 201.

Boxes and Case for Critical Thinking

402 (Business Buzz) Adapted from Wordspy.com [accessed 11 May 2005] www.wordspy.com.

403 (Mining Your Deepest Secrets) Adapted from Paul Magnusson, "They're Watching You," *BusinessWeek*, 24 January 2005, 22–23; Anick Jesdanun, "You're Being Followed—by Web Ads," *Seattle Times*, 14 June 2004 [accessed 14 June 2004] www.seattletimes.com; Harry R. Weber, "Tighter Regulation Sought for Data-Collection Industry," *Seattle Times*, 25 February 2005 [accessed 25 February 2005] www.seattletimes.com; Tom Zeller, "Breach Points Up Flaws in Security Laws," *New York Times*, 24 February 2005, C1, C6; Richard Behar, "Never Heard of Acxiom? Chances Are Its' Heard of You," *Fortune*, 23 February 2004, 140–148; Linda Stern, "Is Orwell Your Banker?" *Newsweek*, 8 April 2002, 59; Mike France and Heather Green, "Privacy in an Age of Terror," *BusinessWeek*, 5 November 2001, 83–87; Amy Harmon, "F.T.C. to Propose Laws to Protect Children Online," *New York Times*, 4 June 1998, C1, C6; Andrew L. Shapiro, "Privacy for Sale," *The Nation*, 23 June 1997, 11–16; Bruce Horovitz, "Marketers Tap Data We Once Called Our Own," *USA Today*, 19 December 1995, 1A–2A; Stephen Baker, "Europe's Privacy Cops," *BusinessWeek*, 2 November 1998, 49, 51.

406 (Learning from Business Blunders) Adapted from Pamela Paul, "It's Mind Vending," *Time,* 15 September 2003; Hallmark website [accessed 4 May 2004] www.hallmark.com; "Every Day, 10,000 Baby Boomers Turn 50; Nobody Said Getting Old Would Be Easy," *Seattle Post-Intelligencer,* 27 March 1997 [accessed 4 May 2004] www.highbeam.com.

409 (Technologies That Are Revolutionizing Business) Adapted from TechEncyclopedia, TechWeb.com [accessed 4 May 2004] www.techweb.com; Ganesh Variar, "Only the Best Survive: The Combination of Integration and BI Were the Standouts of the 2003 IT Landscape," *Intelligent Enterprise*, January 2004 [accessed 4 May 2004] www.highbeam.com; Angoss website [accessed 4 May 2004] www.angoss.com.

413 (Questionable Marketing Tactics on Campus) Adapted from Kimberly E. Mock, "Good Credit Skills Are Essential for Georgia's College Students," *Athens Banner-Herald,* 23 February 2004 [accessed 4 May 2004] www.highbeam.com; Charles Haddad, "Congratulations, Grads—You're Bankrupt," *BusinessWeek*, 21 May 2001, 48; Christine Dugas, "Colleges Target Card Solicitors," *USA Today*, 12 March 1999, B1; Lisa Toloken, "Turning the Tables on Campus," *Credit Card Management*, May 1999, 76–79; "Credit Cards Given to College Students a Marketing Issue," *Marketing News*, 27 September 1999, 38.

423 (Can Levi Strauss Recover from Its Fashion Faux Pas?) Adapted from "Levi's Loss Narrows," *Los Angeles Times*, 18 February 2005, C2+; James Covert, "Levi Strauss Stitches In Its Loss as It Quits Unprofitable," *Wall Street Journal*, 18 February, B4+; Leslie Earnest, "Levi Strauss Folds Plan to Sell Dockers Brand," *Los Angeles Times*, 19 October 2004, C2+; Leslie Earnest, "Levi Strauss Posts Profit Despite Slump in Sales," *Los Angeles Times*, 13 October 2004, C2; "Fitting In: in Bow to Retailers' New Clout, Levi Strauss Makes Alternations," *Wall Street Journal*, 17 June 2004, A1+; "Levi Strauss Walks with a Swagger into New Markets," *Finance CustomWire*, 17 March 2005; Evan Clark, "Changing Retail Market: Vendors Eye Discounters to Bolster Bottom Line," *Women's Wear Daily*, 1+; Scott Malone, "Levi's Returns to

Black," *Women's Wear Daily*, 18 February 2005, 5; Fara Warner, "Levi's Fashions a New Strategy," *Fast Company*, November 2002, 48–49; Susan Chandler, "Low-Rise a Boon to Levi," *Seattle Times*, 21 September 2002, C1; Louise Lee, "Why Levi's Still Looks Faded," *BusinessWeek*, 22 July 2002, 54; Brad Stone, "Jean Therapy For Levi's," *Newsweek*, 15 April 2002, 42–43; Louise Lee, "Can Levi's Be Cool Again?," *BusinessWeek*, 13 March 2000, 144, 148; Nina Munk, "How Levi's Trashed a Great American Brand," *Fortune*, 12 April 1999, 83–90; Betsy Spethmann, "Can We Talk?," *American Demographics*, March 1999, 42–44; Wayne D'Orio, "Clothes Make the Teen," *American Demographics*, March 1999, 34–37; Murray Forester, "Levi's Weaves a Tangled Web," *Chain Store Age*, January 1999, 10; Suzette Hill, "Levi Strauss & Co.: Icon in Revolution," *Apparel Industry Magazine*, January 1999, 66–69; "Keep Reinventing the Brand or Risk Facing Extinction," *Marketing*, 25 February 1999, 5.

Chapter 13

Photo Credits
427 AP Wide World Photos; 438 David R. Frazier Photolibrary, Inc.; 439 AP Wide World Photos; 443 Colgate-Palmolive Company; 444 Robert Harding World Imagery, Norma Joseph; 448 Getty Images, Inc.—Liaison, Koichi Kamoshida

Exhibits
430 (Exhibit 13.2) Adapted from Philip Kotler and Gary Armstrong, *Principles of Marketing,* 10th ed. (Upper Saddle River, N.J.: Pearson Prentice Hall, 2004), 279.

432 (Exhibit 13.3) Adapted from Philip Kotler and Gary Armstrong, *Principles of Marketing,* 10th ed. (Upper Saddle River, N.J.: Pearson Prentice Hall, 2004), 330.

Boxes and Case for Critical Thinking
431 (Ringing Up Business in Creative New Ways) Adapted from Jyoti Thottam, "How Kids Set the (Ring) Tone," *Time*, 4 April 2005, 40+; Zingy website [accessed 16 April 2005] www.zingy.com; Jamdat website [accessed 16 April 2005] www.jamdat.com; "Battling for Mobile iTunes," *Om Malik on Broadband* (blog), 14 March 2005 [accessed 16 April 2005] www.gigaom.com.

431 (Business Buzz) Adapted from Cnet.com [accessed 15 April 2005] www.cnet.com.

433 (Designing Safer Products) Adapted from Chris Ayres and Nicola Woolcock, "America in Rush to Ban Mini-Bikes as Teenage Racers Dice with Death," *Times (UK)*, 19 March 2005 [accessed 15 April 2005] www.ebsco.com; Dan Deitz, "A Wider Margin of Safety," *Mechanical Engineering*; March 1995, 68+; Lanny Berke, "Designing Safer Products," *Machine Design*, 17 March 2005, 61; Formula 1 website [accessed 15 April 2005] www.formula1.com.

434 (Learning from Business Blunders) Adapted from BikeForums.net [accessed 16 April 2005] www.bikeforums.net; Hannah Hickey, "Many Monterey County, Calif., Cyclists Unaware of Lock Scare," *Monterey County Herald*, 4 October 2004 [accessed 16 April 2005] www.ebsco.com; J.J Jensen, "Massachusetts-Based Bike-Lock Maker to Offer Customers Free Upgrades," *Seattle Times*, 23 September 2004, [accessed 16 April 2005] www.ebsco.com.

454 (Coke Unpacks a Winner) Adapted from "Fridge Vendor: A Cool Idea That's Paying Off," Alcoa website [accessed 14 April] www.alcoa.com; Dean Foust and Gerry Khermouch, "Shaking up the Coke Bottle," *BusinessWeek*, 3 December 2001, 74–75; Patricia Sellers, "Who's in Charge Here?" *Fortune*, 24 December 2001, 77–86; Gerry Khermouch, "The Best Global Brands," *BusinessWeek*, 5 August 2002, 92+; Daniel Fisher, "Gone Flat," *Forbes*, 15 October 2001, 77–79; Betsy McKay, "Thinking Inside the Box—'Big Idea' Behind Fridge Pack is That Consumers Will Drink More When Soft Drinks Are Kept Cold," *Wall Street Journal*, 2 August 2002, B1+; Scott Leith, "CCE Puts 'Fridge Pack' on Store Shelves Today," *Atlanta Journal – Constitution*, 1 May 2002, D1+.

Chapter 14

Photo Credits
457 Landov LLC, Susan Goldman/Bloomberg News; 466 AP Wide World Photos; 466 Mark Matson Photography; 475 Getty Images, Inc.—Taxi, Chris Salvo

Exhibit
460 (Exhibit 14.2) Adapted from Philip Kotler, *Marketing Management,* 10th ed. (Upper Saddle River, N.J.: Prentice Hall, 2000), 491.

Boxes and Case for Critical Thinking
461 (Business Buzz) Adapted from Wordspy.com [accessed 18 April 2005] www.wordspy.com

464 (Looking for a Get-Rich-Slow Scheme?) Adapted from Mylene Mangalindan, "Web Retailers Try New Game," *Wall Street Journal*, 2 December 2004, B1, B7; Cate T. Corcoran, "What Works: Retailers Share Strategies for Online Success," *Women's Wear Daily*, 9 March 2005, 6; Sarah Lacy, "A Double Bind for E-Tailers," *BusinessWeek*, 25 October 2004 [accessed 19 April 2005] www.ebsco.com; Glenn Law, "Finding Sales in Chat Rooms, Blogs," *National Jeweler*, 1 March 2005, 1+; Blue Nile website [accessed 19 April 2005] www.bluenile.com; Timberland website [accessed 19 April 2005] www.timberland.com; My Virtual Model website [accessed 19 April 2005] www.tvm.com; Timothy J. Mullaney and Robert D. Hof, "E-Tailing Finally Hits Its Stride," *BusinessWeek*, 20 December 2004, 36–37.

468 (Nautilus Bulks Up Through Multiple Channels) Adapted from Nautilus website [accessed 19 April 2005], www.nautilus.com; Helen Jung, "Nautilus Shows New Fiscal Fitness," *Oregonian*, 3 February 2005 [accessed 19 April 2005] www.ebsco.com; Nicole Urso, "Getting Pumped Up About Direct Response," *Response*, January 2005, 30–36; Matthew Creamer, "Nautilus Bulks Up to Move Beyond Direct Response," *Advertising Age*, 1 November 2004, 4+; Rukmini Callimachi, "Bowflex Recoils After Patent Expires," *Spokesman-Review* (Spokane, WA), 25 August 2004 [accessed 19 April 2005] www.ebsco.com; Elizabeth MacDonald, "Fiscal Fitness," *Forbes*, 11 November 2002, 80.

471 (Learning from Business Blunders) Adapted from Rick Brooks and Mark Maremont, "Sticky Situation: Ovens Are Cooling at Krispy Kreme as Woes Multiply," *Wall Street Journal*, 3 September 2004, A1, A5; Richard Connor, "Hot Doughnuts When?" *Fort Worth Business Press*, 24–30 January 2005, 46; Jonathan Nelson, "Troubled Krispy Kreme Pulls Out of Doughnut Shop Deal," *Columbian* (Vancouver, WA), 28 February 2005 [accessed 19 April 2005] www.ebsco.com; Frank Maley, "New CEO Won't Do an Enron on Krispy," *Business North Carolina*, March 2005, 18–19.

474 (Technologies That Are Revolutionizing Business) Adapted from Uniform Code Council website [accessed 18 April 2005] www.uc-council.org; EPC Global website [accessed 18 April 2005] www.epcglobalus.org; RosettaNet website [accessed 18 April 2005] www.rosettanet.org.

481 (REI's Perfect Blend of Retail and E-Tail Channels) Adapted from REI website [accessed 7 May 2004] www.rei.com; "REI Store Pickup Lifts Store and Internet Sales," *BusinessWire,* 22 September 2003 [accessed 7 May 2004] www.highbeam.com; "Ken Yamada, "Web Trails," *Forbes Best of the Web,* 3 December 2001, 15; Mike Troy, "REI.com Scales On-Line Heights," *DSN Retailing Today,* 8 May 2000, 6; Kellee Harris, "Online Travel Revs Up Revenues," *Sporting Goods Business,* 1 February 2000, 16; Lawrence M. Fisher, "REI Climbs Online: A Clicks-and-Mortar Chronicle," *Strategy + Business,* First Quarter 2000 [accessed 13 October 2000] www.strategy-business.com; "REI Scales New Heights with Second-Generation Web Sites and IBM," IBM E-Business Case Studies [accessed 10 March 2000] www.ibm.com; Kristin Carpenter, "REI.com," *Sporting Goods Business,* 6 July 1999, 57; David Orenstein, "Retailers Find Uses for Web Inside Stores," *Computerworld,* 11 January 1999, 41; Sharon Machlis, "Outdoor Goods Seller Creates Online Outlet," *Computerworld,* 14 December 1998, 51–53; Kerry A. Dolan, "Backpackers Meet Bottom Line," *Forbes,* 16 November 1998, 161; Kristin Carpenter, "REI Venturing Out with Off-Price Web Site," *Sporting Goods Business,* 10 August 1998, 22.

Chapter 15

Photo Credits

485 Google Inc.; **489** The Image Works, Margot Granitsas; **499** Karin Leitza; **506** PhotoEdit, Bill Aron

Exhibits

497 (Exhibit 15.4) "Domestic Advertising Spending by Category," *Advertising Age,* 28 June 2004, S21.

503 (Exhibit 15.6) Adapted from *Web Hosting Glossary,* Marketingterms.com [accessed 4 May] www.marketingterms.com; Internet Ad Sales [accessed 4 May] www.internetadsales.com; *Glossary of Interactive Advertising Terms,* Interactive Advertising Bureau [accessed 4 May] www.iab.net.

Boxes and Case for Critical Thinking

488 (Learning from Business Blunders) Adapted from Evite website [accessed 6 May 2004] www.evite.com; "Desktop," *Rocky Mountain News* (Denver), 1 September 2003 [accessed 6 May 2004] www.highbeam.com; Adam Horowitz, Mark Athitakis, Mark Lasswell, and Owen Thomas, "The 101 Dumbest Moments in Business," *Business 2.0* [accessed 6 May 2004] www.business2.com.

490 (Tracking Down the Disappearing Audience) Adapted from Mike Drexler, "Media Midlife Crisis: The Changes are Monumental," *Adweek,* 9 February 2004 [accessed 6 May 2004] www.highbeam.com; Kevin J. Delaney and Robert A. Guth, "Beep. Foosh. Buy Me. Pow." *Wall Street Journal,* 8 April 2004, B1, B7; Stuart Elliot, "Advertising," *New York Times,* 14 April 2004, C8; Melanie Wells, "Kid Nabbing," *Forbes,* 2 February 2004, 84–88; Kimberly Palmer, "Highway Ads Take High-Tech Turn," *Wall Street Journal,* 13 September 2003, B5; Brian Hindo, "Ad Space," *BusinessWeek,* 12 January 2004, 14; Ellen Neuborne, "Dude, Where My Ad?" *Inc.,* April 2004, 56–57; Erin White, "Look Up for New Products in Aisle 5," *Wall Street Journal,* 23 March 2004, B11; Ronald Grover, "Can Mad Ave.

Make Zap-Proof Ads?" *BusinessWeek,* 2 February 2004, 36; Mathew Boyle, "Brand Killers," *Fortune,* 88–100.

495 (Technologies That Are Revolutionizing Business) Adapted from "Nick Gillespie Discusses the Personalized Cover of *Reason* Magazine and the Possibilities of Database Technology" (interview), Talk of the Nation, National Public Radio, 4 May 2003 [accessed 6 May 2004] www.highbeam.com; Kevin J. Delaney, "Will Users Care if Gmail Invades Privacy?" *Wall Street Journal,* 6 April 2004, B1, B3; Allison Fass, "Spot On," *Forbes,* 23 June 2003, 140; "Hey You! How About Lunch?" *Wall Street Journal,* 1 April 2004, B1, B5.

501 (Business Buzz) Adapted from Susan Getgood, "Flogging a Dead Horse & *BusinessWeek,*" *Marketing Roadmaps* (blog), 26 April 2005 [accessed 7 May 2005] www.getgood.com.

502 (The Rise, Fall—and Rise—of Online Advertising) Adapted from David Utter, "Zooming Sales for Online Ads," *WebProNews.com,* 31 August 2005 [accessed 31 August 2005] www.webpronews.com; Sean Michael Kerner, "Online Ad Spending Swells," *ClickZ,* 1 April 2005 [accessed 30 August 2005] www.clickz.com; Heather Green and Pallavi Gogoi, "Online Ads Take Off—Again," *BusinessWeek,* 5 May 2003 [accessed 30 August 2005] www.businessweek.com; Pamela Parker, "Yahoo! Results Reveal Trends Behind Recovery," *ClickZ,* 8 April 2004 [accessed 30 August 2005] www.clickz.com; Jack Komperda, Buying Time Online: Internet Advertising Is Back, But This Time Name Companies Are Paving the Way," *U.S. News & World Report,* 6 October 2003 [accessed 30 August 2005] www.usenews.com; Stefanie Olsen, "Online Ad Outlook Brightens," 21 April 2003, *News.com* [accessed 30 August 2005] www.news.com.

513 (Polyclinic Closes the Door on Sales Reps) Adapted from Carol M. Ostrom, "Polyclinic Shuts Out Drug Reps, Samples," *Seattle Times,* 16 January 2003 [www.seattletimes .com]; Pharmaceutical Research and Manufacturers of America website [accessed 5 May 2005] www.phrma.org; Helen Jung, "Clinic Charges Drug Reps for Access," *AP Online,* 14 June 2002 [accessed 16 January 2003] www.elibrary.com; Jeffrey Kahn, "The Double-Edged Sword of Drug Marketing," *CNN Health,* Ethics Matters, 9 August 1999 [accessed 16 January 2003] www.cnn.com; Abigail Zuger, "Fever Pitch: Getting Doctors To Prescribe Is Big Business," *New York Times,* 11 January 1999 [accessed 16 January 2003] www. nyt.com; Michael A. Steinman, "Gifts to Physicians in the Consumer Marketing Era," *MSJAMA—Review,* 1 November 2000, 2243 [accessed 16 January 2003] www.ama-assn.org; Tony Pugh, "Drug Reps Get the Cold Shoulder," *Toronto Star,* 6 September 2002 [accessed 16 January] www.elibrary.com; "Sales Pitch: Drug Firms Use Perks to Push Pills; Companies Ply Doctors to Write Prescriptions," *USA Today,* 16 May 2001, 1B.

516 E-Business in Action
Adapted from Jim Milliot, "B&N-B&N.com Closing Delayed," *Publishers Weekly,* 4 March 2004 [accessed 7 May 2004] www.publishersweekly.com; Allison Kaplan, "Retailers Taking New Approach to Internet," *Knight Ridder Tribune News Service,* 11 June 2002, 1; Gerry Khermouch and Nanette Byrnes, "Come Back to Papa," *BusinessWeek,* 19 February 2001, 42; Rebecca Quick, "Returns to Sender," *Wall Street Journal,* 17 July 2000, R8; Greg Farrell, "Clicks-and Mortar World Values Brands," *USA Today,* 5 October 1999, B1, B2; Ranjay Gulati and Jason Garino, "Get the Right Mix of Bricks and Clicks," *Harvard*

Business Review, May–June 2000, 107–114; Anne Stuart, "Clicks & Bricks," *CIO*, 15 March 2000, 76–84; Jason Anders, "Sibling Rivalry," *Wall Street Journal*, 17 July 2000, R16; William M. Bulkeley, "Clicks and Mortar," *Wall Street Journal*, 17 July 2000, R4; Allanna Sullivan, "From a Call to a Click," *Wall Street Journal*, 17 July 2000, R30; Suein L. Hwang, "Clicks and Bricks," *Wall Street Journal*, 17 April 2000, R8, R10; Jeffrey Rothfeder, "Toys 'R' Us Battles Back," *Strategy and Business*, Quarter 2, 2000; Dennis K. Berman and Heather Green, "Cliff Hanger Christmas," *BusinessWeek E.Biz*, 23 October 2000, EB30–EB38; Jerry Useem, "Dot-Coms What Have We Learned?" *Fortune*, 30 October 2000, 82–104.

Career Profiles

517 (Marketing Professionals and Marketing Managers) Adapted from U.S. Department of Labor, Bureau of Labor Statistics website, *Occupational Outlook Handbook* [accessed 25 May 2005] www.bls.gov

517 (Sales Professionals and Sales Managers) Adapted from U.S. Department of Labor, Bureau of Labor Statistics website, *Occupational Outlook Handbook* [accessed 25 May 2005] www.bls.gov.

Chapter 16

Photo Credits

519 AP Wide World Photos, Evan Vucci; **523** SuperStock, Inc.; **532** Getty Images Inc.—Stone Allstock, Terry Vine

Exhibit

522 (Exhibit 16.1) Adapted from Gary Siegel and Bud Kulesza, "The Practice of Management Accounting," *Management Accounting*, April 1996, 20; "Up the Ladder of Success," *Journal of Accountancy,"* November 2000, 24.

Boxes and Case for Critical Thinking

525 (Technologies That Are Revolutionizing Business) Adapted from Dennis Callaghan, "Sarbanes-Oxley: Road to Compliance," *eWeek,* 16 February 2004 [accessed 8 May 2004] www.eweek.com; Ellen Florian, "Can Tech Untangle Sarbanes-Oxley?" *Fortune,* 29 September 2003, 125–128; Thomas Hoffman, "Big Companies Turn to Packaged Sarb-Ox Apps," *Computerworld,* 1 March 2004 [accessed 8 May 2004] www.computerworld.com.

526 (Putting Accountability Back into Public Accounting) Adapted from Mark Maremont, "Deloitte Faces $2 Billion Claim Over Audits of Reinsurance Firm," *Wall Street Journal*, 11 November 2004, A1, A10; Daren Fonda, "Revenge of the Bean Counters," *Time,* 29 March 2004, 38–39; Greg Farrell and Andrew Backover, "Stage Is Set for Auditors, Management to Clash," *USA Today*, 20 February 2003 [accessed 9 May 2004] www.highbeam.com; Thomas A. Fogarty, "Accounting Oversight Agency Targets Abusive Tax Shelters," *USA Today*, 21 November 2003, 3B; Janice Revell, "The Fires That Won't Go Out," *Fortune,* 13 October 2003, 139–142; Jeremy Kahn, "Do Accountants Have a Future?" *Fortune,* 3 March 2003, 115–116; David Henry and Mike McNamee, "Bloodied and Bowed," *BusinessWeek,* 20 January 2003, 56–57; "Auditors' Methods Make It Hard to Catch Fraud By Executives," *Wall Street Journal*, 8 July 2002, C1, C16; Thaddeus Herrick and Alexei Barrionuevo, "Were Auditor and Client Too Close-Knit?" *Wall Street Journal*, 21 January 2002, C1, C5; Jeremy Kahn, "One Plus One Makes What?" *Fortune,*

7 January 2002, 88–90; Nanette Byrnes, "Auditing Here, Consulting Over There," *BusinessWeek*, 8 April 2002, 34–36; Nanette Byrnes, "Accounting in Crisis," *BusinessWeek*, 28 January 2002, 42–48.

539 (How to Read an Annual Report) Adapted from Manual Schiffres, "All the Good News That Fits," *U.S. News and World Report*, 14 April 1998, 50–51; Janice Revell, "Annual Reports Decided," *Fortune*, 25 June 2001, 176; "The P&L: Your Score Card of Profitability," *The Edward Lowe Report*, August 2001, 1–3.

540 (Learning from Business Blunders) Adapted from Adam Horowitz, Mark Athitakis, Mark Lasswell, and Owen Thomas, "The 101 Dumbest Moments in Business," *Business 2.0* [accessed 3 August 2004] www.business2.com.

546 (Consulting Practice Pushes Arthur Andersen Out of Balance) Adapted from Mary Flood, "Arthur Andersen Appeal to Go Before Justices in April," 23 February 2005 [accessed 24 April 2005] www.ebsco.com; Ameet Sachdev, "Judge Gives Andersen $500,000 Fine, Probation," *Chicago Tribune,* 17 October 2002, sec.1, 1; Flynn McRoberts, "Repeat Offender Gets Stiff Justice," *Chicago Tribune*, 4 September 2002, 1, 12, 13; Flynn McRoberts, "Ties to Enron Blinded Andersen," *Chicago Tribune*, 3 September 2002, 1; "Andersen Surrenders Accounting Licenses," *Wall Street Journal*, 3 September 2002, A6; Flynn McRoberts, "Civil War Splits Andersen," *Chicago Tribune*, 2 September 2002, 1; Flynn McRoberts, "The Fall of Andersen," *Chicago Tribune*, 1 September 2002, 1; Deepa Babington, "Curtain to Fall on Once-Proud Andersen," *Reuters Business*, 29 August 2002; Ken Brown and Ianthe Jeanne Dugan, "Andersen's Fall From Grace Is a Tale of Greed and Miscues," *Wall Street Journal,* 7 June 2002, A1, A6; Andrew Countryman and Delroy Alexander, "Bailing Out," *Chicago Tribune,* 2 June 2002, sec. 5, 1, 4; Ken Brown and Jonathan Weil, "How Andersen's Embrace of Consulting Altered the Culture of the Auditing Firm," *Wall Street Journal,* 12 March 2002, C1, C16; Thaddeus Herrick and Alexei Barrionuevo, "Were Auditor and Client Too Close-Knit?" *Wall Street Journal,* 21 January 2002, C1, C5; Deepa Babington, "Accenture Now a Clear Winner Without Andersen Name," *Reuters Business*, 17 January 2002.

Chapter 17

Photo Credits

551 Rich Frishman Photography and Videograph Inc.; **555** Omni-Photo Communications, Inc., Fotopic; **556** Michael Mitchell Photographic Works, Inc., Shotgun; **557** ImageState/International Stock Photography Ltd., Bob Firth Photography; **566** Corbis—NY, Ariel Skelley

Exhibit

568 (Exhibit 17.5) From "Money Stock Measures," Federal Reserve website, 21 April 2005 [accessed 28 April 2005] www.federalreserve.gov.

Boxes and Case for Critical Thinking

554 (There's a Reason They Call Them Havens) Adapted from David Cay Johnson, "Study Finds U.S. Companies Shifting Profits Overseas," *New York Times*, 13 September 2004, C2; Lynnley Browning, "Foreign Tax Havens Costly to U.S., Study Says," *New York Times*, 27 September 2004, C2; "Corporate Welfare Run Amok," *New York Times*, 30 January 2005, sec. 4, 16; Steven D. Jones, "Outside Audit: U.S. Firms Are Posting

Record Foreign Results," *Wall Street Journal*, 30 September 2004, C3+; Edmund L. Andrews, "Hitting the Tax-Break Jackpot," *New York Times*, 1 February 2005, C1-C2.

563 (Technologies That Are Revolutionizing Business) Adapted from "Fair Isaac Launches Strategy Science Institute; First Educational Forum Spurs Client Empowerment in Applying Advanced Analytics to Improve Critical Business Decisions," *BusinessWire* [accessed 10 May 2004] www.highbeam.com; Fair Isaac website [accessed 10 May 2004] www.fairisaac.com; "Idea Bank," *Orlando Sentinel,* 5 August 2002 [accessed 10 May 2004] www.highbeam.com.

564 (Surprise! You've Been Swiped) Adapted from Walt Bogdanich, "Criminals Focus on A.T.M.'s, Weak Link in Banking System," *New York Times*, 3 August 2003, 1, 22; Richard Burnett, "Florida Warns of Credit Card Fraud at Gasoline Pumps," *Orlando Sentinel,* 26 January 2004 [accessed 10 May 2004] www.highbeam.com; Tom Lowry, "Thieves Swipe Credit with Card Readers," *USA Today*, 28 June 1999, 1B; Elaine Shannon, "A New Credit-Card Scam," *Time*, 5 June 2000, 54–55; Linda Punch, "Card Fraud: Down But Not Out," *Credit Card Management*, June 1999, 30–42; Bill Orr, "Will E-Commerce Reverse Card Fraud Trend?" *American Bankers Association*, April 2000, 59–62.

565 (Learning from Business Blunders) Adapted from Adam Horowitz, Mark Athitakis, Mark Lasswell, and Owen Thomas, "The 101 Dumbest Moments in Business," *Business 2.0*, January/February 2005 [accessed 28 April 2005] www.business2.com.

576 (Cablevision Survives a Financial Crisis—Then Creates a Few More) Adapted from "Boards and Megalomaniacs," *Crain's New York Business*, 4 April 2005, 10; Leslie Cauley, "CEO Stands Up to Critics—and His Dad," *USA Today*, 29 March 2005, B3; Barney Gimbel, "Dolan's Daddy Dearest Act," *Fortune* (Europe), 21 March 2005, 14; Anne Michaud and Aaron Elstein, "Jets, Others Eye Bids for MSG and Teams," *Crain's New York Business*, 7 March 2005, 2+; NewsEdge, "Cablevision Clicks: Sales Strong, Earnings Up, Debt Down in 4Q," 12 February 2003 [accessed 13 February 2003] www.hoovers.com; Erin Joyce, "Digital Data Drives Cablevision's Outlook," Internetnews.com, 11 February 2003 [accessed 13 February 2003] www.internetnews.com; "Cablevision Puts 'For Sale' Sign on Wireless Unit," Internetnews.com, 9 August 2002 [accessed 13 February 2003] www.internetnews.com; Richard Sandomir, "Suit Dismissed Against Cablevision," *New York Times*, 15 June 2002, D7; Seth Schiesel, "Cablevision Will Retrench by Shedding Jobs and Stores," *New York Times*, 9 August 2002 [accessed 13 February 2003] www.nyt.com; Seth Schiesel, "Cablevision, Its Stock Price Battered, Will Retire Tracking Shares," *New York Times*, 6 August 2002, C3; Cablevision press release, "Cablevision Issues Statement Regarding Accounting," 10 June 2002; Ronald Grover, "Adelphia's Fall Will Bruise a Crowd," *BusinessWeek*, 8 July 2002 [accessed 14 February 2003] www.businessweek.com; Cablevision press release, "Cablevision Systems Corporation Announces Fully-Funded Growth Plan," 8 August 2002.

Chapter 18

Photo Credits

581 Corbis/SABA Press Photos, Inc., James Leynse; **584** BellSouth Advertising & Publishing; **585** Ron Sherman, Photographer; **589** Getty Images Inc.—Stone Allstock, Mark Joseph; **591** Corbis—NY

Boxes and Case for Critical Thinking

588 (Is an Index Fund Right for Your Financial Future?) Adapted from "Index Funds," SEC website [accessed 2 May 2005] www.sec.gov; "The S&P 500 Index Fund" and "Index Fund Anatomy Lesson," *Motley Fool* [accessed 2 May 2005] www.fool.com; Bill Mann, "Index Funds: Still Your Best Bet," *Motley Fool* [accessed 2 May 2005] www.fool.com; Nathan Slaughter, "The Case Against Index Funds," *Motley Fool* [accessed 2 May 2005] www.fool.com; Meir Stratman, "Odds Say You Can't Beat Index Funds," *MSN Money* [accessed 2 May 2005] http://moneycentral.msn.com.

593 (Business Buzz) Adapted from Investopedia.com [accessed 10 May 2004] www.investopedia.com.

595 (Learning from Business Blunders) Adapted from Peter Carbonara, "The Scam That Will Not Die," *Business Credit,* 1 July 2003 [accessed 10 May 2004] www.highbeam.com; "Profile: Recent Confidence Scams from Nigeria Have Their Roots in Depression-Era Scam that Targeted the Midwest," All Things Considered, National Public Radio, 29 July 2002 [accessed 10 May 2004] www.highbeam.com; Jim Stratton, "Notorious E-Mail Scam Snares Savings of Volusia, Fla., Retiree," *Orlando Sentinel,* 23 December 2003 [accessed 10 May 2004] www.highbeam.com.

607 (NYSE: An 18th-Century Institution Embraces the 21st) Adapted from Philip Boroff, "Langone Wants to Shut NYSE's Trading Floor," *Seattle Times*, 27 April 2005, E3; Heidi Moore and Vipal Monga, "NYSE-ArcaEx Confounds Street," *The Deal.com* [accessed 3 May 2005] www.thedeal.com; Holman W. Jenkins, Jr., "BusinessWorld: Antique for Sale," *Wall Street Journal*, 27 April 2005, A15; NYSE website [accessed 3 May 2005] www.nyse.com; Theresa W. Carey, "Big Merger Turns NYSE from Prey to Predator," eWeek, 22 April 2005 [accessed 3 May 2005] www.cioinsight.com; Charles Gasparino, "A Rival Bid for the Big Board?" *Newsweek*, 2 May 2005, 54. Aaron Lucchetti, "Moving the Market: NYSE, Archipelago Face Hurdles on Road to Combined Company," *Wall Street Journal*, 2 May 2005, C3; Fred Vogelstein, "The Man Who Saved the New York Stock Exchange," *Fortune*, 15 April 2002, 168–174; Neil Weinberg, "The Big Board Comes Back from the Brink," *Forbes*, 13 November 2000, 274–280; Pimm Fox, "Floored by Technology," *Computerworld*, 23 October 2000, 41; "Stock Exchanges: The Battle for Efficient Markets," *The Economist*, 17 June 2000, 69–71; Marcia Trombly, "Under Pressure, the NYSE Moves Online," *Computerworld*, 27 March 2000, 48; Marcia Vickers, "Getting off the NYSE Floor," *BusinessWeek*, 7 February 2000, 80–81; Randall Smith, "Will NYSE Get Bowled Over by Rivals?," *Wall Street Journal*, 19 January 2000, C1; Greg Ip and Randall Smith, "Tense Exchange: Big Board's Members Face Off on the Issue of Automated Trading," *Wall Street Journal*, 15 November 1999, A, 1:6; William P. Barrett, "End of an Era," *Forbes*, 11 October 1999, 121–126.

Career Profiles

611 (Accountants and Accounting Managers) Adapted from U.S. Department of Labor, Bureau of Labor Statistics website, *Occupational Outlook Handbook* [accessed 25 May 2005] www.bls.gov.

611 (Career Profiles: Financial Managers) Adapted from U.S. Department of Labor, Bureau of Labor Statistics website, *Occupational Outlook Handbook* [accessed 25 May 2005] www.bls.gov.

Appendix A

Photo Credits
A-1 Panos Pictures; **A-7** Corbis—NY, Ed Quinn; **A-8** Getty Images, Inc.—Allsport Photography, Harry How/Getty Images; **A-9** Corbis—NY

Exhibits
A-3 (Exhibit A.1) Adapted from Bartley A. Brennan and Nancy Kubasek, *The Legal Environment of Business* (New York: Macmillan, 1988), 24; Douglas Whitman and John Gergacz, *The Legal Environment of Business*, 2d ed. (New York: Random House, 1988), 22, 25.
A-10 (Exhibit A.3) Adapted from Richard A. Brealely and Stewart C. Myers, *Principles of Corporate Finance*, 4th ed. (New York: McGraw-Hill, 1991), 761–765.
A-11 (Exhibit A.4): Adapted from BankruptcyData.Com [accessed 11 June 2005] www.bankruptcy data.com.

Appendix B

Photo Credits
A-15 Stan Godlewski Photography; **A-15** Getty Images Inc.— Stone Allstock; **A-19** Photo Researchers, Inc., Tim Beddow

Exhibits
A-20 (Exhibit B.4) Adapted from Mark S. Dorfman, *Introduction to Risk Management and Insurance*, 8th ed., (Upper Saddle River, N.J.: Pearson Prentice-Hall, 2005), 296–301.

Appendix C

Photo Credits
A-25 Corbis—NY, Rob Lewine; **A-36** Creative Eye/MIRA.com, George H. Long; **A-38** Corbis—NY

Exhibits
A-40 (Exhibit C.6) Adapted from Lawrence J. Gitman and Michael D. Joehnk, *Personal Financial Planning,* 10th ed. (Mason, Ohio: Thomson South-Western, 2005), 139–143; Jack R. Kapoor, Les R. Dlabay, and Robert J. Hughes, *Personal Finance,* 7th ed. (New York: McGraw-Hill/Irwin, 2004), 141; Arthur J. Keown, *Personal Finance: Turning Money into Wealth,* 3d ed. (Upper Saddle River, N.J.: Prentice Hall, 2003), 150.

GLOSSARY

absolute advantage   A nation's ability to produce a particular product with fewer resources per unit of output than any other nation.

accountability   Obligation to report results to supervisors or team members and to justify outcomes that fall below expectations.

accounting   Measuring, interpreting, and communicating financial information to support internal and external decision making.

accounting equation   Basic accounting equation that assets equal liabilities plus owners' equity.

accounts payable   Amounts that a firm currently owes to other parties.

accounts receivable   Amounts that are currently owed to a firm

accounts receivable turnover ratio   Measure of time a company takes to turn its accounts receivable into cash, calculated by dividing sales by the average value of accounts receivable for a period.

accrual basis   Accounting method in which revenue is recorded when a sale is made and expense is recorded when it is incurred.

acquisition   Form of business combination in which one company buys another company's voting stock.

activity ratios   Ratios that measure the effectiveness of the firm's use of its resources.

actual cash value coverage   Property insurance in which the insurer pays for the replacement cost of property at the time of loss, less an allowance for depreciation.

actuaries   People employed by an insurance company to compute expected losses and to calculate the cost of premiums.

administrative law   Rules, regulations, and interpretations of statutory law set forth by administrative agencies and commissions.

administrative skills   Technical skills in information gathering, data analysis, planning, organizing, and other aspects of managerial work.

advertising   Paid, nonpersonal communication to a target market from an identified sponsor using mass communications channels.

advocacy advertising   Ads that present a company's opinions on public issues such as education and health.

affirmative action   Activities undertaken by businesses to recruit and promote women and minorities, based on an analysis of the workforce and the available labor pool.

agency   Business relationship that exists when one party (the principal) authorizes another party (the agent) to enter into contracts on the principal's behalf.

agents and brokers   Independent wholesalers that do not take title to the goods they distribute but may or may not take possession of those goods.

analytic system   Production process that breaks incoming materials into various component products and divisional patterns simultaneously.

arbitration   Process for resolving a labor-contract dispute in which an impartial third party studies the issues and makes a binding decision.

artificial intelligence   The ability of computers to solve problems through reasoning and learning and to simulate human sensory perceptions.

asset allocation   Method of shifting investments within a portfolio to adapt them to the current investment environment.

asset management accounts   Cash management accounts offered by brokerage firms and mutual fund companies, frequently as a way to manage cash that isn't currently invested elsewhere.

assets   Any things of value owned or leased by a business; the physical things, such as real estate and artwork, and financial elements, such as cash and stocks, that you own.

attrition   Loss of employees for reasons other than termination.

auction exchange   Centralized marketplace where securities are traded by specialists on behalf of investors.

audit   Formal evaluation of the fairness and reliability of a client's financial statements.

authority   Power granted by the organization to make decisions, take actions, and allocate resources.

authorized stock   Maximum number of ownership shares into which a corporation's board of directors decides the business can be divided.

authorization cards   Sign-up cards designating a union as the signer's preferred bargaining agent.

autocratic leaders   Leaders who do not involve others in decision making.

automated teller machines (ATMs)   Electronic terminals that permit people with plastic cards to perform simple banking transactions 24 hours a day without the aid of a human teller.

balance of payments   Sum of all payments one nation receives from other nations minus the sum of all payments it makes to other nations, over some specified period of time.

balance of trade   Total value of the products a nation exports minus the total value of the products it imports, over some period of time.

balance sheet   A summary of your assets and liabilities; the difference between the two subtotals is your net worth.

balance sheet   Statement of a firm's financial position on a particular date; also known as a *statement of financial position.*

bankruptcy   Legal procedure by which a person or a business that is unable to meet financial obligations is relieved of debt.

banner ads   A rectangular display ad on a webpage that links to an advertiser's webpage.

barriers to entry   Factors that make it difficult to launch a business in a particular industry.

bear market   Falling stock market.

behavior modification   Systematic use of rewards and punishments to change human behavior.

behavioral segmentation   Categorization of customers according to their relationship with products or response to product characteristics.

beneficiaries   People named in a life insurance policy who receive the proceeds of an insurance contract when the insured dies.

blogs   Web-based logs or journals.

board of directors   Group of people, elected by the share-holders, who have the ultimate authority in guiding the affairs of a corporation.

bond   Method of funding in which the issuer borrows from an investor and provides a written promise to make regular interest payments and repay the borrowed amount in the future.

bonus   Cash payment, in addition to regular wage or salary, that serves as a reward for achievement.

bookkeeping   Recordkeeping; clerical aspect of accounting.

boycott   Union activity in which members and sympathizers refuse to buy or handle the product of a target company.

brain drain   Term used to describe the loss of experienced employees from an organization.

brand   A name, term, sign, symbol, design, or combination of those used to identify and differentiate products and companies.

brand awareness   Level of brand loyalty at which people are familiar with a product.

brand equity   The value that a company has built up in a brand

brand extension   Applying a successful brand name to a new product category.

brand insistence   Level of brand loyalty at which people will accept no substitute for a particular product.

brand loyalty   The degree to which customers continue to purchase a specific brand.

brand managers   People who develop and implements strate-gies and marketing program.

brand mark   Portion of a brand that cannot be expressed verbally.

brand names   Portion of a brand that can be expressed orally, including letters, words, or numbers.

brand preference   Level of brand loyalty at which people habitually buy a product if it is available.

breach of contract   Failure to live up to the terms of a contract, with no legal excuse.

break-even analysis   Method of calculating the minimum volume of sales needed at a given price to cover all costs.

break-even point   Sales volume at a given price that will cover all of a company's costs.

broadband   A term applied to higher speed network connections.

broker   An expert who has passed specific tests and is regis-tered to trade securities for investors.

budget   Planning and control tool that reflects expected rev-enues, operating expenses, and cash receipts and outlays.

bull market   Rising stock market.

bundling   Combining several products and offering the bun-dle at a reduced price.

business   A profit-seeking enterprise that provides goods and services that a society wants or needs.

business agent   Full-time union staffer who negotiates with man-agement and enforces the union's agreements with companies.

business cycle   Fluctuations in the rate of growth that an economy experiences over a period of several years.

business law   Those elements of law that directly influence or control business activities.

business model   The fundamental design of the company, explaining how the enterprise plans to generate revenue.

business plan   A written document that provides an orderly statement of a company's goals and a plan for achieving those goals.

business-interruption insurance   Insurance that covers losses resulting from temporary business closings.

business-to-business e-commerce   E-commerce between companies; often referred to as B2B.

business-to-consumer e-commerce   E-commerce between a company and consumers; often referred to as B2C.

buying power   The real value of money, adjusted for inflation; inflation raises prices, which in turn reduces buying power.

cafeteria plans   Benefit plans that let employees choose from a flexible menu of health care, retirement, and other benefits.

calendar year   Twelve-month accounting period that begins on January 1 and ends on December 31.

capacity planning   The long-term strategic decisions that determine the level of resources available to an organization to meet customer demand.

capital   A collective term for both the funds used to finance a company's operations and its physical, human-made assets such as factories and computers.

capital budgeting   Process for evaluating proposed investments in select projects that provide the best long-term financial return.

capital gains   Return that investors receive when they sell a security for a higher price than the purchase price.

capital investments   Money paid to acquire something of per-manent value in a business.

capital structure   Financing mix of a firm.

capital-intensive businesses   Businesses that require large investments in capital assets.

capitalism   Economic system based on economic freedom, private ownership, and competition.

cash basis   Accounting method in which revenue is recorded when payment is received and expense is recorded when cash is paid.

cash management   All of the planning and activities associ-ated with managing your cash and other liquid assets.

category killers   Discount chains that sell only one category of products.

cause-related marketing   Identification and marketing of a social issue, cause, or idea to selected target markets.

cause-related marketing   Marketing campaigns that donate a portion of their proceeds to a charitable organization or other public cause.

cellular layout   Method of arranging a facility so that parts with similar shapes or processing requirements are processed together in work centers.

centralization   Concentration of decision-making authority at the top of the organization.

certification   Process by which a union is officially recog-nized by the National Labor Relations Board as the bargaining agent for a group of employees.

certified management accountants (CMAs)   Accountants who have fulfilled the requirements for certification as special-ists in management accounting.

certified public accountants (CPAs)   Professionally licensed accountants who meet certain requirements for education and experience and who pass a comprehensive examination.

chain of command   Pathway for the flow of authority from one management level to the next.

channel conflict   Disagreement or tension between two or more members in a distribution channel, usually resulting from competition to reach the same group of customers.

checks   Written orders that tell the customer's bank to pay a specific amount to a particular individual or business.

chief executive officer (CEO)   Person appointed by a corporation's board of directors to carry out the board's policies and supervise the activities of the corporation.

chief information officer (CIO)   A high-level executive responsible for understanding the company's information needs and creating systems and procedures to deliver that information to the right people at the right time.

chronological résumé   Most traditional type of résumé, listing employment history sequentially in reverse order so that the most recent experience is listed first.

claims   Demands for payments from an insurance company because of some loss by the insured.

close the books   The act of transferring net revenue and expense account balances to retained earnings for the period.

closing   Point at which a sale is completed.

closing costs   Fees associated with buying and selling a house

coaching   Helping employees reach their highest potential by meeting with them, discussing problems that hinder their ability to work effectively, and offering suggestions and encouragement.

co-branding   Partnership between two or more companies to closely link their brand names together for a single product.

code of ethics   Written statement setting forth the principles that guide an organization's decisions.

cognitive dissonance   Tension that exists when a person's beliefs don't match his or her behaviors; a common example is *buyer's remorse*, when someone regrets a purchase after making it.

cohesiveness   A measure of how committed the team members are to their team's goals.

collateral   Tangible asset a lender can claim if a borrower defaults on a loan.

collective bargaining   Process used by unions and management to negotiate work contracts.

combination résumé   A hybrid of a chronological and functional résumé that contains elements of both.

commercial paper   An IOU, backed by the corporation's reputation, issued to raise short-term capital.

commercialization   Large-scale production and distribution of a product.

commission-based planners   Financial advisers who are paid commissions on the financial products they sell you, such as insurance policies and mutual funds.

commissions   Employee compensation based on a percentage of sales made.

committee   Team that may become a permanent part of the organization and is designed to deal with regularly recurring tasks

commodities   Raw materials used in producing other goods.

common law   Law based on the precedents established by judges' decisions.

common stock   Shares whose owners have voting rights and have the last claim on distributed profits and assets.

communism   Economic system in which the government owns and operates all productive resources and determines all significant economic choices.

comparative advantage theory   Theory that states that a country should produce and sell to other countries those items it produces most efficiently.

comparative advertising   Advertising technique in which two or more products are explicitly compared.

compensating balance   Portion of an unsecured loan that is kept on deposit at the lending institution to protect the lender and increase the lender's return.

compensation   Money, benefits, and services paid to employees for their work.

competition   Rivalry among businesses for the same customer.

competitive advantage   A company's ability to perform in one or more ways that competitors cannot match.

competitive advertising   Ads that specifically highlight how a product is better than its competitors.

compounding   The acceleration of balances caused by applying new interest to interest that has already accumulated.

computer-aided design (CAD)   Use of computer graphics and mathematical modeling in the development of products.

computer-aided engineering (CAE)   Use of computers to test products without building an actual model.

computer-aided manufacturing (CAM)   Use of computers to control production equipment.

computer-integrated manufacturing (CIM)   Computer-based systems, including CAD and CAM, that coordinate and control all the elements of design and production.

conceptual skills   Ability to understand the relationship of parts to the whole.

conflict of interest   Situation in which a business decision may be influenced by the potential for personal gain.

consent order   Settlement in which an individual or organization promises to discontinue some illegal activity without admitting guilt.

consideration   Negotiated exchange necessary to make a contract legally binding.

consolidation   Combination of two or more companies in which the old companies cease to exist and a new enterprise is created.

consumer market   Individuals or households that buy goods and services for personal use.

consumer price index (CPI)   Monthly statistic that measures changes in the prices of about 400 goods and services that consumers buy.

consumer promotion   Sales promotion aimed at final consumers.

consumerism   Movement that pressures businesses to consider consumer needs and interests.

consumer-to-consumer e-commerce   E-commerce between consumers; often referred to as C2C.

contingent business-interruption insurance   Insurance that protects a business from losses due to losses sustained by other businesses such as suppliers or transportation companies.

contingent employee   As a general team, applies to any nonpermanent employee, including temporary workers and independent contractors; also applied specifically to workers hired on a probationary basis.

contract   Legally enforceable exchange of promises between two or more parties.

controller   Highest-ranking accountant in a company, responsible for overseeing all accounting functions.

controlling   Process of measuring progress against goals and objectives and correcting deviations if results are not as expected.

convertible bonds   Corporate bonds that can be exchanged at the owner's discretion into common stock of the issuing company.

cooperative advertising   Joint efforts between local and national advertisers, in which producers of nationally sold products share the costs of local advertising with local merchants and wholesalers.

corporate culture   A set of shared values and norms that support the management system and that guide management and employee behavior.

corporate governance   In a broad sense, describes the policies, procedures, relationships, and systems in place to oversee the successful and legal operation of the enterprise; in a narrow sense, describes the responsibilities and performance of the board of directors.

corporate social responsibility   The concern of businesses for the welfare of society as a whole.

corporation   Legally chartered enterprise having most of the legal rights of a person, including the right to conduct business, to own and sell property, to borrow money, and to sue or be sued.

cost accounting   Area of accounting focusing on the calculation of manufacturing and storage costs of products for use or sale in a business.

cost of capital   Average rate of interest a firm pays on its combination of debt and equity.

cost of goods sold   Cost of producing or acquiring a company's products for sale during a given period.

coupons   Certificates that offer discounts on particular items and are redeemed at the time of purchase.

credit bureaus   Businesses that compile credit information on businesses and individual consumers.

credit cards   Plastic cards that allow the customer to buy now and pay back the loaned amount at a future date.

credit history   A record of your mortgages, consumer loans, credit card accounts (including credit limits and current balances), and bill-paying performance.

credit reports   Reports generated by credit bureaus, showing an individual's credit usage and payment history.

crisis management   Plan for minimizing the harm that might result from some unusually threatening situations.

critical path   In a PERT network diagram, the sequence of operations that requires the longest time to complete.

cross-functional teams   Teams that draw together employees from different functional areas.

cross-promotion   Jointly advertising two or more noncompeting brands.

currency   Bills and coins that make up the cash money of a society.

current assets   Cash and items that can be turned into cash within one year.

current liabilities   Obligations that must be met within a year.

current ratio   Measure of a firm's short-term liquidity, calculated by dividing current assets by current liabilities.

customer buying behavior   Behavior exhibited by consumers as they consider, select, and purchase goods and services.

customer divisions   Divisional structure that focuses on customers or clients.

customer loyalty   Degree to which customers continue to buy from a particular retailer or buy the products of a particular manufacturer or service provider.

customer service   Efforts a company makes to satisfy its customers to help them realize the greatest possible value from the products they are purchasing.

customized production   Production of individual goods and services for individual customers.

damages   Financial compensation to an injured party for loss and suffering.

data   Facts, numbers, statistics, and other individual bits and pieces that by themselves don't necessarily constitute useful information.

data mining   A method of extracting previously unknown relationships among individual data points in a database.

database marketing   Process of building, maintaining, and using customer databases for the purpose of contacting customers and transacting business.

databases   Computerized files that collect, sort, and cross-reference data.

day order   Any order to buy or sell a security that automatically expires if not executed on the day the order is placed.

dealer exchanges   Decentralized marketplaces where securities are bought and sold by dealers out of their own inventories.

debentures   Corporate bonds backed only by the reputation of the issuer.

debit cards   Plastic cards that allow the bank to take money from the user's demand-deposit account and transfer it to a retailer's account.

debt ratios   Ratios that measure a firm's reliance on debt financing of its operations (sometimes called *leverage ratios*).

debt-to-equity ratio   Measure of the extent to which a business is financed by debt as opposed to invested capital, calculated by dividing the company's total liabilities by owners' equity.

debt-to-total-assets ratio   Measure of a firm's ability to carry long-term debt, calculated by dividing total liabilities by total assets.

decentralization   Delegation of decision-making authority to employees in lower-level positions.

decertification   Process employees use to take away a union's official right to represent them.

decision-making skills   The ability to make decisions by following the process of identifying a decision situation, analyzing the problem, weighing the alternatives, choosing an alternative and implementing it, and evaluating the results.

deductible   Amount of loss that must be paid by the insured before the insurer will pay for the rest.

deductions   Opportunities to reduce taxable income by subtracting the cost of a specific item, such as business expenses or interest paid on home mortgages.

deed   Legal document by which an owner transfers the title, or ownership rights, to real property to a new owner.

deflation   Economic condition in which prices fall steadily throughout the economy.

delegation   Assignment of work and the authority and responsibility required to complete it.

demand   Buyers' willingness and ability to purchase products.

demand curve   Graph of the quantities of product that buyers will purchase at various prices.

demand deposits   Money in checking accounts that can be used by customers at any time.

democratic leaders   Leaders who delegate authority and involve employees in decision making.

demographics   Study of statistical characteristics of a population.

department stores   Large stores that carry a variety of products in multiple categories, such as clothing, housewares, gifts, bedding, and furniture.

departmentalization   Grouping people within an organization according to function, division, matrix, or network.

depreciation   Accounting procedure for systematically spreading the cost of a tangible asset over its estimated useful life.

devaluation A move by one government to drop the value of its currency relative to the value of other currencies.

direct mail Advertising sent directly to potential customers, usually through the U.S. Postal Service.

direct marketing Direct communication other than personal sales contacts designed to effect a measurable response.

disability income insurance Short-term or long-term insurance that protects an individual against loss of income while that individual is disabled as the result of an illness or accident.

discount pricing Offering a reduction in price.

discount rate Interest rate charged by the Federal Reserve on loans to commercial banks and other financial institutions.

discount stores Retailers that sell a variety of goods below the market price by keeping their operating costs low.

discretionary order Market order that allows the broker to decide when to trade a security.

discrimination In a social and economic sense, denial of opportunities to individuals on the basis of some characteristic that has no bearing on their ability to perform in a job.

distribution centers Warehouse facilities that specialize in collecting and shipping merchandise.

distribution channels Systems for moving goods and services from producers to customers; also known as marketing channels.

distribution mix Combination of intermediaries and channels a producer uses to get a product to end customers.

distribution strategy A overall plan for moving products to intermediaries and final customers.

diversification Assembling investment portfolios in such a way that a loss in one investment won't cripple the value of the entire portfolio.

diversity initiatives Efforts to attract and support diverse workforces, expand supplier bases, and reach out to diverse markets.

dividends Distributions of corporate assets to shareholders in the form of cash or other assets.

divisional structure Grouping departments according to similarities in product, process, customer, or geography.

double-entry bookkeeping Way of recording financial transactions that requires two entries for every transaction so that the accounting equation is always kept in balance.

dumping Charging less than the actual cost or less than the home-country price for goods sold in other countries.

drop shippers Limited-service merchant wholesalers that assume ownership of goods but don't take physical possession; commonly used to market agricultural and mineral products.

dynamic pricing Charging different prices depending on individual customers and situations.

earnings per share Measure of profitability calculated by dividing net income after taxes by the average number of shares of common stock outstanding.

EBITDA Earnings before interest, taxes, depreciation, and amortization; a simpler and more direct measure of income.

e-business Taking advantage of information technology, particularly the Internet, across all major business functions.

ecology Study of the relationships among living things in the water, air, and soil; their environments; and the nutrients that support them.

e-commerce Short for electronic commerce, which refers to marketing and selling products over the Internet.

economic indicators Statistics that measure significant variables in the economy.

economic system Means by which a society distributes its resources to satisfy its people's needs.

economics The study of how society uses scarce resources to produce and distribute goods and services.

economies of scale savings gained from the increased efficiency of manufacturing, marketing, purchasing, or otherwise operating with large quantities.

economies of scale Savings from buying parts and materials, manufacturing, or marketing in large quantities.

electronic commerce (e-commerce) The general term for the buying and selling of goods and services on the Internet.

electronic communication networks (ECNs) Internet-based networks that match up buy and sell orders without using an intermediary.

electronic data interchange (EDI) Use of information systems that transmit documents such as invoices and purchase orders between computers, thereby lowering ordering costs and paperwork.

electronic funds transfer system (EFTS) Computerized systems for performing financial transactions.

electronic performance monitoring (EPM) Real-time, computer-based evaluation of employee performance.

embargo Total ban on trade with a particular nation (a sanction) or of a particular product.

employee assistance programs (EAPs) Company-sponsored counseling or referral plans for employees with personal problems.

employee benefits Compensation other than wages, salaries, and incentive programs.

employee empowerment Granting decision-making and problem-solving authorities to employees so they can act without getting approval from management.

employee retention Efforts to keep current employees.

employee stock-ownership plan (ESOP) Program enabling employees to become partial owners of a company.

employment interview Formal meeting during which an employer and an applicant ask questions and exchange information to see whether the applicant and the organization are a good match.

engagement An employee's rational and emotional commitment to his or her work.

enterprise resource planning (ERP) A comprehensive database system that expands beyond the production function to include other groups such as sales and accounting.

entrepreneurs Businesspeople who create and run new businesses and accept the risks involved in the private enterprise system.

equilibrium price Point at which quantity supplied equals quantity demanded.

equity The portion of a house's current value that you own.

equity theory A theory that suggests employees base their level of satisfaction on the ratio of their inputs to the job and the outputs or rewards they receive from it.

ethical dilemma Situation in which both sides of an issue can be supported with valid arguments.

ethical lapse Situation in which an individual makes a decision that is morally wrong, illegal, or unethical.

ethics The rules or standards governing the conduct of a person or group.

ethnocentrism Judging all other groups according to your own group's standards, behaviors, and customs.

euro A unified currency used by most nations in the European Union.

exchange process Act of obtaining a desired object or service from another party by offering something of value in return.

exchange rate Rate at which the money of one country is traded for the money of another.

exclusive distribution Market coverage strategy that gives intermediaries exclusive rights to sell a product in a specific geographical area.

exemptions Reductions to taxable income based on the number of dependents in the household.

expectancy theory Suggests that the effort employees put into their work depends on expectations about their own ability to perform, expectations about the rewards that the organization will give in response to that performance, and the attractiveness of those rewards relative to their individual goals.

expenses Costs created in the process of generating revenues.

exporting Selling and shipping goods or services to another country.

express contract Contract derived from words, either oral or written.

external auditors Independent accounting firms that provide auditing servicing for public companies.

extra-expense insurance Insurance that covers the added expense of operating the business in temporary facilities after an event such as a fire or a flood.

extranets Websites that are similar to intranets but also allow access by trusted outside business partners.

fair trade A voluntary approach to trading with artisans and farmers in developing countries, guaranteeing them above-market prices as a way to protect them from exploitation by larger, more-powerful trading partners.

family branding Using a brand name on a variety of related products.

fee-only planners Financial advisers who charge a fee for their services, rather than earning a commission on financial services they sell you.

financial accounting Preparing financial information for users outside the organization.

financial analysis Evaluating a company's performance and analyzing the costs and benefits of a strategic action.

financial control The process of analyzing and adjusting the basic financial plan to correct for forecasted events that do not materialize.

financial futures Legally binding agreements to buy or sell financial instruments at a future date.

financial management Effective acquisition and use of money.

financial plan A forecast of financial requirements and the financing sources to be used.

first-line managers Those at the lowest level of the management hierarchy; they supervise the operating employees and implement the plans set at the higher management levels.

fiscal policy Use of government revenue collection and spending to influence the business cycle.

fiscal year Any 12 consecutive months used as an accounting period.

fixed assets Assets retained for long-term use, such as land, buildings, machinery, and equipment; also referred to as *property, plant, and equipment.*

fixed costs Business costs that remain constant regardless of the number of units produced.

fixed-position layout Method of arranging a facility so that the product is stationary and equipment and personnel come to it.

flat organizations Organizations with a wide span of management and few hierarchical levels.

flextime Scheduling system in which employees are allowed certain options regarding time of arrival and departure.

foreign direct investment (FDI) Investment of money by foreign companies in domestic business enterprises.

form utility Customer value created by converting raw materials and other inputs into finished goods and services.

formal organization A framework officially established by managers for accomplishing tasks that lead to achieving the organization's goals.

franchise Business arrangement in which a company or entrepreneur obtains rights to sell the goods or services of the supplier (franchisor).

franchisee Business owner who contracts for the right to sell goods or services of the supplier (franchisor) in exchange for some payment.

franchisor Supplier that grants a franchise to an individual or group (franchisee) in exchange for payments.

free riders Team members who do not contribute sufficiently to the group's activities because members are not being held individually accountable for their work.

free trade International trade unencumbered by restrictive measures.

free-market system Economic system in which decisions about what to produce and in what quantities are decided by the market's buyers and sellers.

full-service merchant wholesalers Merchant wholesalers that provide a wide variety of services to their customers, such as storage, delivery, and marketing support.

functional résumé Résumé organized around a list of skills and accomplishments, subordinating employers and academic experience in order to stress individual areas of competence; frowned on by many recruiters.

functional structure Grouping workers according to their similar skills, resource use, and expertise.

functional teams Teams whose members come from a single functional department and that are based on the organization's vertical structure.

functional-replacement-cost coverage Property insurance that allows for the substitution of construction materials to restore a property to a similar, functioning state.

gain sharing Plan for rewarding employees not on the basis of overall profits but in relation to achievement of goals such as cost savings from higher productivity.

Gantt chart Bar chart used to control schedules by showing how long each part of a production process should take and when it should take place.

general expenses Operating expenses, such as office and administrative expenses, not directly associated with creating or marketing a good or a service.

general obligation bond Municipal bond that is backed by the government's authority to collect taxes.

general partnership Partnership in which all partners have the right to participate as co-owners and are individually liable for the business's debts.

generally accepted accounting principles (GAAP) Professionally approved U.S. standards and practices used by accountants in the preparation of financial statements.

generic products Products characterized by a plain label, with no advertising and no brand name.

geodemographics Method of combining geographical data with demographic data to develop profiles of neighborhood segments.

geographic divisions Divisional structure based on location of operations.

geographic segmentation Categorization of customers according to their geographical location.

glass ceiling Invisible barrier attributable to subtle discrimination that keeps women out of the top positions in business.

global warming A gradual rise in average temperatures around the planet; caused by increases in carbon dioxide emissions.

globalization Tendency of the world's economies to act as a single interdependent economy.

goal Broad, long-range target or aim.

goal-setting theory Motivational theory suggesting that setting goals can be an effective way to motivate employees.

goods-producing businesses Businesses that produce tangible products.

green marketing Marketing strategies that highlight a company's efforts to minimize damage to the natural environment.

gross domestic product (GDP) Value of all the final goods and services produced by businesses located within a nation's borders; excludes receipts from overseas operations of domestic companies.

gross national product (GNP) Value of all the final goods and services produced by domestic businesses that includes receipts from overseas operations and excludes receipts from foreign-owned businesses within a nation's borders.

gross profit Amount remaining when the cost of goods sold is deducted from net sales; also known as *gross margin.*

growth stocks Equities issued by small companies with unproven products or services.

hardware The tangible equipment used in information systems.

health maintenance organizations (HMOs) Prepaid medical plans in which consumers pay a set fee in order to receive a full range of medical care from a group of medical practitioners.

hedge To make an investment that protects the investor from suffering loss on another investment.

hostile takeovers Situations in which an outside party buys enough stock in a corporation to take control against the wishes of the board of directors and corporate officers.

human resources All the people who work for an organization.

human resources management (HRM) Specialized function of planning how to obtain employees, oversee their training, evaluate them, and compensate them.

hybrid structure Structure designs that combine elements of functional, divisional, matrix, and network organizations.

hygiene factors Aspects of the work environment that are associated with dissatisfaction.

identity theft Crimes in which thieves steal personal information and use it to take out loans and commit other types of fraud.

implied contract Contract derived from actions or conduct.

importing Purchasing goods or services from another country and bringing them into one's own country.

incentives Cash payments to employees who produce at a desired level or whose unit (often the company as a whole) produces at a desired level.

income and expense statement A listing of your monthly inflows (income) and outflows (expenses); also called an *income statement.*

income statement Financial record of a company's revenues, expenses, and profits over a given period of time.

incubators Facilities that house small businesses during their early growth phase.

inflation Economic condition in which prices rise steadily throughout the economy.

inflation The tendency of prices to increase over time.

informal organization Network of informal employee interactions that are not defined by the formal structure.

information Useful knowledge, often extracted from data.

information systems (IS) A collective label for all technologies and processes used to manage business information; many organizations now refer to this as information technology (IT).

information technology (IT) A generally accepted substituted term for information systems.

initial public offering (IPO) Corporation's first offering of stock to the public.

injunction Court order prohibiting certain actions by striking workers.

insider trading The use of unpublicized information that an individual gains from the course of his or her job to benefit from fluctuations in the stock market.

insight A deep level of understanding about a particular subject or situation.

instant messaging (IM) Real-time text conversations between computers; IM is similar in concept to text messaging on cell phones, but it's a more powerful and more flexible technology.

institutional advertising Advertising that seeks to create goodwill and to build a desired image for a company rather than to sell specific products.

institutional investors Companies and other organizations that invest money entrusted to them by others.

insurable risk Risk for which an acceptable probability of loss may be calculated and that an insurance company might, therefore, be willing to cover.

insurance Written contract that transfers to an insurer the financial responsibility for losses up to specified limits.

insurance premium Fee that the insured pays the insurer for coverage against loss.

integrated marketing communications (IMC) Strategy of coordinating and integrating communications and promotions efforts with customers to ensure greater efficiency and effectiveness.

intellectual property A wide range of creative outputs with commercial value, such as design ideas, manufacturing processes, brands, and chemical formulas.

intellectual property Intangible personal property, such as ideas, songs, trade secrets, and computer programs, that are protected by patents, trademarks, and copyrights.

intensive distribution Market coverage strategy that tries to place a product in as many outlets as possible.

intentional tort Willful act that results in injury.

internal auditors Employees who analyze and evaluate a company's operations and data to determine their accuracy.

international law Principles, customs, and rules that govern the international relationships between states, organizations, and persons.

internet A network of networks that spans the entire globe.

internet service providers (ISPs) Companies that provide access to the Internet through dial-up, DSL, cable, or wireless networking.

internet telephone service Telephone service that converts voice to digital data for transmission across the Internet; also known as Internet telephony or VoIP.

interpersonal skills Skills required to understand other people and to interact effectively with them.

intranets Websites that are accessible by employees only.

inventory Goods kept in stock for the production process or for sales to final customers.

inventory control System for determining the right quantity of various items to have on hand and keeping track of their location, use, and condition.

inventory turnover ratio Measure of the time a company takes to turn its inventory into sales, calculated by dividing cost of goods sold by the average value of inventory for a period.

investment banks Financial institutions that raise capital for corporations and government bodies.

investment portfolios Assortment of investment instruments.

issued stock Portion of authorized stock sold to and held by shareholders.

job analysis Process by which jobs are studied to determine the tasks and dynamics involved in performing them.

job description Statement of the tasks involved in a given job and the conditions under which the holder of the job will work.

job enrichment Reducing work specialization and making work more meaningful by adding to the responsibilities of each job.

job redesign Designing a better fit between employees' skills and their work to increase job satisfaction.

job sharing Splitting a single full-time job between two employees.

job specification Statement describing the kind of person who would be best for a given job—including the skills, education, and previous experience that the job requires.

joint venture Cooperative partnership in which organizations share investment costs, risks, management, and profits in the development, production, or selling of products.

justice The resolution of ethical questions and other dilemmas in a manner that is consistent with generally accepted standards of right and wrong.

just-in-time (JIT) Continuous system that pulls materials through the production process, making sure that all materials arrive just when they are needed with minimal inventory and waste.

key-person insurance Insurance that provides a business with funds to compensate for the loss of a key employee by unplanned retirement, resignation, death, or disability.

knowledge Expertise gained through experience or research.

knowledge-based pay Pay tied to an employee's acquisition of knowledge or skills; also called competency-based pay or skill-based pay.

labor federation Umbrella organization of national unions and unaffiliated local unions that undertakes large-scale activities on behalf of their members and that resolves conflicts between unions.

labor unions Organizations of employees formed to protect and advance their members' interests.

labor-intensive businesses Businesses in which labor costs are more significant than capital costs.

laissez-faire leaders Leaders who leave the actual decision making up to employees.

law of large numbers Principle that the larger the group on which probabilities are calculated, the more accurate the predictive value.

layoffs Termination of employees for economic or business reasons.

leading Process of guiding and motivating people to work toward organizational goals.

lease Legal agreement that obligates the user of an asset to make payments to the owner of the asset in exchange for using it.

leverage Technique of increasing the rate of return on an investment by financing it with borrowed funds.

leveraged buyouts (LBO) Situation in which individuals or groups of investors purchase companies primarily with debt secured by the company's assets.

liabilities Amounts of money you owe; claims against a firm's assets by creditors.

liability losses Financial losses suffered by a business firm or individual held responsible for property damage or injuries suffered by others.

license Agreement to produce and market another company's product in exchange for a royalty or fee.

licensing Agreement to produce and market another company's product in exchange for a royalty or fee.

limit order Market order that stipulates the highest or lowest price at which the customer is willing to trade securities.

limited liability companies (LLCs) Organizations that combine the benefits of S corporations and limited partnerships without the drawbacks of either.

limited partnership Partnership composed of one or more general partners and one or more partners whose liability is usually limited to the amount of their capital investment.

limited-service merchant wholesalers Merchant wholesalers that offer fewer services than full-service merchant wholesalers; they often specialize in particular markets, such as agriculture.

line of credit Arrangement in which the financial institution makes money available for use at any time after the loan has been approved.

line organization Organization with a clear line of authority flowing from the top down.

line-and-staff organization Organization system that combines a clear chain of command with functional groups that provide advice and specialized services.

liquid assets Assets that can be quickly and easily converted to cash.

liquidity The level of ease with which an asset can be converted to cash.

liquidity ratios Ratios that measure a firm's ability to meet its short-term obligations when they are due.

local advertising Advertising sponsored by a local merchant.

local area network (LAN) A network that connects computers within a limited local range, such as within a single department or single building.

locals Relatively small union groups, usually part of a national union or a labor federation, that represent members who work in a single facility or in a certain geographic area.

lockouts Management tactics in which union members are prevented from entering a business during a strike.

logistics The planning, movement, and flow of goods and related information throughout the supply chain.

long-term financing Financing used to cover long-term expenses such as assets (generally repaid over a period of more than one year).

long-term liabilities Obligations that fall due more than a year from the date of the balance sheet.

loss exposures Areas of risk in which a potential for loss exists.

M1 That portion of the money supply consisting of currency and demand deposits.

M2 That portion of the money supply consisting of currency, demand deposits, and small time deposits.

M3 That portion of the money supply consisting of M1 and M2 plus large time deposits and other restrictive deposits.

macroeconomics The study of "big picture" issues in an economy, including competitive behavior among firms, the effect of government policies, and overall resource allocation issues.

mail-order firms Companies that sell products through catalogs and ship them directly to customers.

malware Short for malicious software; an umbrella term for illicit software with destructive, invasive, or criminal intent.

managed care Health care set up by employers (usually through an insurance carrier) who provide networks of doctors and hospitals that agree to discount the fees they charge in return for the flow of patients.

management Process of coordinating resources to meet organizational goals.

management accounting Preparing data for use by managers within the organization.

management by objectives (MBO) A motivational approach in which managers and employees work together to structure personal goals and objectives for every individual, department, and project to mesh with the organization's goals.

management information system (MIS) A system that provides managers with information and support for making routine decisions; sometimes used to describe information systems in general.

management pyramid Organizational structure comprising top, middle, and lower management.

mandatory retirement Required dismissal of an employee who reaches a certain age.

manufacturing resource planning (MRP II) Computer-based system that integrates data from all departments to manage inventory and production planning and control.

margin trading Borrowing money from brokers to buy stock, paying interest on the borrowed money, and leaving the stock with the broker as collateral.

market A group of customers who need or want a particular product and have the money to buy it.

market indexes Measures of market activity calculated from the prices of a selection of securities.

market makers registered representatives who trade securities from their own inventories on dealer exchanges, making a ready market for buyers and sellers.

market order Authorization for a broker to buy or sell securities at the best price that can be negotiated at the moment.

market segmentation Division of a diverse market into smaller, relatively homogeneous groups with similar needs, wants, and purchase behaviors.

market share A firm's portion of the total sales in a market.

marketable securities Short-term investments that can be easily and quickly converted to cash.

marketing Process of planning and executing the conception, pricing, promotion, and distribution of ideas, goods, and services to create and maintain relationships.

marketing concept Approach to business management that stresses customer needs and wants, seeks long-term profitability, and integrates marketing with other functional units within the organization.

marketing intermediaries Businesspeople and organizations that channel goods and services from producers to consumers.

marketing mix The four key elements of marketing strategy: product, price, distribution, and promotion.

marketing research The collection and analysis of information for making marketing decisions.

marketing strategy Overall plan for marketing a product; includes target market segments, a positioning strategy, and a marketing mix.

mass customization Producing partially customized goods and services by combining mass production techniques with individual customization.

mass production Production of uniform products in large quantities.

matching principle Fundamental principle requiring that expenses incurred in producing revenue be deducted from the revenues they generate during an accounting period.

material requirements planning (MRP) Method of getting the correct materials where they are needed, on time, and without carrying unnecessary inventory.

materials handling Movement of goods within a firm's warehouse terminal, factory, or store.

matrix structure Structure in which employees are assigned to both a functional group and a project team (thus using functional and divisional patterns simultaneously).

media Communications channels, such as newspapers, radio, and television.

media mix Combination of print, broadcast, online, and other media used for an advertising campaign.

media plan Written plan that outlines how a company will spend its media budget, including how the money will be divided among the various media and when the advertisements will appear.

mediation Process for resolving a labor-contract dispute in which a neutral third party meets with both sides and attempts to steer them toward a solution.

mentoring Formal program of career guidance in which an experienced manager or employee with a wide network of industry colleagues explains office politics, serves as a role model for appropriate business behavior, and helps other employees negotiate the corporate structure.

merchant wholesalers Independent wholesalers that take legal title to goods they distribute.

merger Combination of two companies in which one company purchases the other and assumes control of its property and liabilities.

metacrawlers Online tools that format search requests for the specific requirements of multiple search engines.

microeconomics The study of how consumers, businesses, and industries collectively determine the quantity of goods and services demanded and supplied at different prices.

middle managers Those in the middle of the management hierarchy; they develop plans to implement the goals of top managers and coordinate the work of first-line managers.

mission statement A statement of the organization's purpose, basic goals, and philosophies.

missionary salespeople Salespeople who support existing customers, usually wholesalers and retailers.

mobile commerce (m-commerce) E-commerce that uses wireless Internet access and wireless handheld devices.

monetary policy Government policy and actions taken by the Federal Reserve Board to regulate the nation's money supply.

money Anything generally accepted as a means of paying for goods and services.

money-market funds Mutual funds that invest in short-term securities and other liquid investments.

monopolistic competition Situation in which many sellers differentiate their products from those of competitors in at least some small way.

monopoly Market in which there are no direct competitors so that one company dominates.

morale Attitude an individual has toward his or her job and employer.

mortgage A loan used to purchase real estate.

motivation The combination of forces that moves individuals to take certain actions and behaviors and avoid other actions or behaviors.

motivators In Herzberg's two-factor model, factors that may increase motivation.

multinational corporations (MNCs) Companies with operations in more than one country.

municipal bonds Bonds issued by city, state, and government agencies to fund public services.

mutual funds Financial organizations pooling money to invest in diversified blends of stocks, bonds, or other securities; the term also applies to the funds themselves.

NASDAQ (national association of securities dealers automated quotations) National over-the-counter securities trading network.

national advertising Advertising sponsored by companies that sell products nationwide; refers to the geographic reach of the advertiser, not the geographic coverage of the ad.

national brands Brands owned by the manufacturers and distributed nationally.

national union Nationwide organization made up of local unions that represent employees in locations around the country.

natural resources Land, forests, minerals, water, and other tangible assets usable in their natural state.

need Difference between a person's actual state and his or her ideal state; provides the basic motivation to make a purchase.

negligence Tort in which a reasonable amount of care to protect others from risk of injury is not used.

negotiable instrument Transferable document that represents a promise to pay a specified amount.

net income Profit earned or loss incurred by a firm, determined by subtracting expenses from revenues; casually referred to as the *bottom line.*

net worth The difference between your assets and your liabilities.

network A collection of specialized hardware and software that links computers together to share data and information.

network structure Structure in which individual companies are connected electronically to perform selected tasks for a small headquarters organization.

news conference Gathering of media representatives at which companies announce new information; also called a *press briefing.*

news release Brief statement or video program released to the press announcing new products, management changes, sales performance, and other potential news items; also called a *press release.*

no-fault insurance laws Laws limiting lawsuits connected with auto accidents.

nonprofit organizations Organizations whose primary objective is something other than returning a profit to their owners.

norms Informal standards of conduct that guide team behavior.

objective Specific, short-range target or aim.

oligopoly Market dominated by a few producers.

open order Limit order that does not expire at the end of a trading day.

open-market operations Activity of the Federal Reserve in buying and selling government bonds on the open market.

operating expenses All costs of operation that are not included under cost of goods sold.

operational plans Plans that lay out the actions and the resource allocation needed to achieve operational objectives and to support tactical plans; they are usually defined for less than one year and developed by middle managers.

order getters Salespeople who are responsible for generating new sales and for increasing sales to existing customers.

order processing Functions involved in preparing and receiving an order.

order takers Salespeople who generally process incoming orders without engaging in creative selling.

organization chart Diagram showing how employees and tasks are grouped and where the lines of communication and authority flow.

organization structure Framework enabling managers to divide responsibilities, ensure employee accountability, and distribute decision-making authority.

organizational market Businesses, nonprofit organizations, and government agencies that purchase goods and services for use in their operations.

organizing Process of arranging resources to carry out the organization's plans.

orientation programs Formal programs for acclimating new employees to an organization.

outsourcing Subcontracting work to outside companies.

overdraft fees Penalties charged against your checking account when you write checks that total more than your available balance.

over-the-counter (OTC) market Network of dealers who trade securities on computerized linkups rather than a trading floor.

owners' equity Portion of a company's assets that belongs to the owners after obligations to all creditors have been met.

par value As shown on the stock certificate, a value assigned to a stock for use in bookkeeping and in calculating dividends.

parent company Company that owns most, if not all, of another company's stock and that takes an active part in managing that other company.

participative management Sharing information with employees and involving them in decision making.

partnership Unincorporated business owned and operated by two or more persons under a voluntary legal association.

pay for performance Incentive program that rewards employees for meeting specific, individual goals.

penetration pricing Introducing a new product at a low price in hopes of building sales volume quickly.

pension plans Generally refers to traditional, defined benefit retirement plans.

performance appraisals Evaluation of an employee's work according to specific criteria.

permission-based marketing Marketing approach in which firms first ask permission to deliver messages to an audience and then promise to restrict their communication efforts to those subject areas in which audience members have expressed interest.

personal bankruptcy A condition in which a consumer is unable to repay his or her debts; depending on the type of bankruptcy, a court will either forgive many of the person's debts or establish a compatible repayment plan.

personal digital assistants (PDAs)   Handheld computers; some *smartphones* now have PDA capabilities as well.

personal property   All property that is not real property.

personal selling   In-person communication between a seller and one or more potential buyers.

persuasive advertising   Advertising designed to encourage product sampling and brand switching.

philanthropy   Altruistic actions such as donating money, time, goods, or services to charitable, humanitarian, or educational institutions.

physical distribution   All the activities required to move finished products from the producer to the consumer.

picketing   Strike activity in which union members march before company entrances to communicate their grievances and to discourage people from doing business with the company.

place marketing   Marketing efforts to attract people and organizations to a particular geographical area.

place utility   Customer value added by making a product available in a convenient location.

planned system   Economic system in which the government controls most of the factors of production and regulates their allocation.

planning   Establishing objectives and goals for an organization and determining the best ways to accomplish them.

point-of-purchase (POP) display   Advertising or other display materials set up at retail locations to promote products to potential customers as they are making their purchase decisions.

pollution   Damage to or destruction of the natural environment caused by the discharge of harmful substances.

positioning   Using promotion, product, distribution, and price to differentiate a good or service from those of competitors in the mind of the prospective buyer.

possession utility   Customer value created when someone takes ownership of a product.

power of attorney   Written authorization for one party to legally act for another.

preferred stock   Shares that give their owners first claim on a company's dividends and assets after paying all debts.

preferred-provider organizations (PPOs)   Health care providers offering reduced-rate contracts to groups that agree to obtain medical care through the providers' organization.

preliminary screening interview   Meeting between an employer's representative and a candidate for the purpose of eliminating unqualified applicants from the hiring process.

premiums   Free or bargain-priced items offered to encourage consumers to buy a product.

press relations   Process of communicating with reporters and editors from newspapers, magazines, and radio and television networks and stations.

price   The amount of money charged for a product or service.

price elasticity   A measure of the sensitivity of demand to changes in price.

price-earnings ratio   Ratio calculated by dividing a stock's market price by its prior year's earnings per share.

primary market   Market where firms sell new securities issued publicly for the first time.

prime interest rate   Lowest rate of interest charged by banks for short-term loans to their most creditworthy customers.

principal   Amount of money a corporation borrows from an investor through the sale of a bond.

private accountants   In-house accountants employed by organizations and businesses other than a public accounting firm.

private brands   Brands that carry the label of a retailer or a wholesaler rather than a manufacturer.

private corporation   Company owned by private individuals or companies.

privatizing   The conversion of public ownership to private ownership.

problem-solving team   Informal team to find ways of improving quality, efficiency, and the work environment.

process divisions   Divisional structure based on the major steps of a production process.

process layout   Method of arranging a facility so that production tasks are carried out in separate departments containing specialized equipment and personnel.

producer price index (PPI)   A statistical measure of price trends at the producer and wholesaler levels.

product   Good or service used as the basis of commerce

product advertising   Advertising that tries to sell specific goods or services.

product divisions   Divisional structure based on products.

product layout   Method of arranging a facility so that production proceeds along a line of workstations.

product liability   The capacity of a product to cause harm or damage for which the producer or seller is held accountable.

product-liability coverage   Insurance that protects companies from claims for injuries or damages that result from use of a product the company manufactures or distributes.

product life cycle   Four basic stages through which a product progresses: introduction, growth, maturity, and decline.

product lifecycle management (PLM)   A computerized approach to linking all the information flows throughout the value chain, from initial product concepts through maintenance and on to obsolescence.

product line   A series of related products offered by a firm.

product mix   Complete list of all products that a company offers for sale.

production   Transformation of resources into goods or services that customers need or want.

production and operations management (POM)   Coordination of an organization's resources for the manufacture of goods or the delivery of services.

production forecasts   Estimates of how much of a company's goods and services must be produced in order to meet future demand.

productivity   A measure of the efficiency with which a company transforms inputs into outputs.

professional liability insurance   Insurance that covers losses arising from damages or injuries caused by the insured in the course of performing professional services for clients.

profit   Money left over after expenses and taxes have been deducted from revenue generated by selling goods and services.

profit sharing   The distribution of a portion of the company's profits to employees.

profitability ratios   Ratios that measure the overall financial performance of a firm.

program evaluation and review technique (PERT)   A planning tool that managers of complex projects use to determine the optimal order of activities, the expected time for project completion, and the best use of resources.

promotion   Wide variety of persuasive techniques used by companies to communicate with their target markets and the general public.

promotional mix   Particular blend of personal selling, advertising, direct marketing, sales promotion, and public relations that a company uses to reach potential customers.

promotional strategy   Defines the direction and scope of the promotional activities that a company will use to meet its marketing objectives.

property   Rights held regarding any tangible or intangible object.

property insurance   Insurance that provides coverage for physical damage to or destruction of property and for its loss by theft.

prospecting   Process of finding and qualifying potential customers.

protectionism   Government policies aimed at shielding a country's industries from foreign competition.

proxy   Document authorizing another person to vote on behalf of a shareholder in a corporation.

psychographics   Classification of customers on the basis of their psychological makeup.

public accountants   Professionals who provide accounting services to other businesses and individuals for a fee.

public corporation   Corporation that actively sells stock on the open market.

public relations (PR)   Nonsales communication that businesses have with their various audiences.

pull strategy   Promotional strategy that stimulates consumer demand via advertising and a number of consumer promotions, thereby exerting pressure on wholesalers and retailers to carry a product.

purchasing   Acquiring the raw materials, parts, components, supplies, and finished products needed to produce goods and services.

pure competition   Situation in which so many buyers and sellers exist that no single buyer or seller can individually influence market prices.

pure risk   Risk that involves the chance of loss only.

push strategy   Promotional strategy that uses the salesforce and a number of trade promotions to motivate wholesalers and retailers to push products to end users.

qualified prospects   Potential buyers who have both the money needed to make the purchase and the authority to make the purchase decision.

quality   A measure of how closely a product conforms to predetermined standards and customer expectations.

quality assurance   System of policies, practices, and procedures implemented throughout the company to create and produce quality goods and services.

quality control   Routine checking and testing of a finished product for quality against an established standard.

quality of earnings   General term for the degree of confidence that investors should have in the profits reported by public corporations.

quality of work life (QWL)   Overall environment that results from job and work conditions.

quick ratio   Measure of a firm's short-term liquidity, calculated by adding cash, marketable securities, and receivables, then dividing that sum by current liabilities.

quotas   Limits placed on the quantity of imports a nation will allow for a specific product.

rack jobbers   Merchant wholesalers that are responsible for setting up and maintaining displays in a particular section of a retail store.

radio frequency identification (RFID)   A wireless tracking technology based on small tags that combine a memory chip with a tiny antenna.

rate of return   Percentage increase in the value of an investment.

ratio analysis   Use of quantitative measures to evaluate a firm's financial performance.

real property   Land and everything permanently attached to it

recession   Period during which national income, employment, and production all fall.

reconcile   The process of comparing the balance you believe is in your account with the balance the bank believes is in your account.

recovery   Period during which income, employment, production, and spending rise.

recruiting   Process of attracting appropriate applicants for an organization's jobs.

reinforcement theory   A motivational approach based on the idea that managers can motivate employees by influencing their behaviors with positive and negative reinforcement.

relationship marketing   A focus on developing and maintaining long-term relationships with customers, suppliers, and distribution partners for mutual benefit.

reminder advertising   Advertising intended to remind existing customers of a product's availability and benefits.

replacement chart   A planning tool that identifies the most vital employees in the organization and any available information related to their potential replacement.

replacement-cost coverage   Property insurance in which the insurer pays for the full cost of repairing or replacing the property rather than the actual cash value.

reserve requirement   Percentage of a bank's deposit that must be set aside.

responsibility   Obligation to perform the duties and achieve the goals and objectives associated with a particular position.

résumé   Form of advertising that lists a person's education, employment background, and job qualifications in order to obtain an interview.

retail theater   The addition of entertainment or education aspects to the retail experience.

retailers   Firms that sell goods and services to individuals for their own use rather than for resae.

retained earnings   The portion of shareholders' equity earned by the company but not distributed to its owners in the form of dividends.

retirement plans   Company-sponsored programs for providing retirees with income.

return on investment (ROI)   Ratio between net income after taxes and total owners' equity; also known as *return on equity.*

return on sales   Ratio between net income after taxes and net sales; also known as *profit margin.*

revenue bond   Municipal bond backed by revenue generated from the projects it is financing.

revenues   Amount earned from sales of goods or services and inflow from miscellaneous sources such as interest, rent, and royalties.

risk   Uncertainty of an event or exposure to loss.

risk management   Process used by business firms and individuals to deal with their exposures to loss.

S corporation   Corporation with no more than 75 shareholders that may be taxed as a partnership; also known as a subchapter S corporation.

salary   Fixed cash compensation for work, usually by yearly amount; independent of the number of hours worked.

sales promotion   Promotional events and activities such as coupons, rebates, contests, and trade shows.

Sarbanes-Oxley   Comprehensive legislation, passed in the wake of Enron and other scandals, designed to improve integrity and accountability of financial information.

scientific management   Management approach designed to improve employees' efficiency by scientifically studying their work.

scrambled merchandising   Strategy of carrying merchandise that is ordinarily sold in a different type of outlet.

search engine advertising   Automatic presentation of ads that are related to either the results of an online search or the content being displayed on other webpages.

search engines   Web-based research tools that identify individual webpages containing specific words or phrases.

secondary market   Market where subsequent owners trade previously issued shares of stocks and bonds.

secured bonds   Bonds backed by specific assets that will be given to bondholders if the borrowed amount is not repaid.

secured loans   Loans backed up with something of value that the lender can claim in case of default, such as a piece of property.

securities   Investments such as stocks, bonds, options, futures, and commodities.

selective credit controls   Federal Reserve's power to set credit terms on various types of loans.

selective distribution   Market coverage strategy that uses a limited number of outlets to distribute products.

self-insurance   Accumulating funds each year to pay for predicted losses, rather than buying insurance from another company.

self-managed teams   Teams in which members are responsible for an entire process or operation.

selling expenses   All the operating expenses associated with marketing goods or services.

service businesses   Businesses that provide intangible products or perform useful labor on behalf of their customers

sexism   Discrimination on the basis of gender.

sexual harassment   Unwelcome sexual advance, request for sexual favors, or other verbal or physical conduct of a sexual nature within the workplace.

shareholders   Owners of a corporation.

shop steward   Union member and employee who is elected to represent other union members and who attempts to resolve employee grievances with management.

short selling   Selling stock borrowed from a broker with the intention of buying it back later at a lower price, repaying the broker, and keeping the profit.

short-term financing   Financing used to cover current expenses (generally repaid within a year).

sinking fund   Account into which a company makes annual payments for use in redeeming its bonds in the future.

Six Sigma   A quality management program that strives to eliminate deviations between the actual and desired performance of a business system.

skills inventory   A list of the skills a company needs from its workforce, along with the specific skills that individual employees currently possess.

skim pricing   Charging a high price for a new product during the introductory stage and lowering the price later.

small business   Company that is independently owned and operated, is not dominant in its field, and meets certain criteria for the number of employees and annual sales revenue.

smart cards   Plastic cards that include an embedded chip to store money drawn from the user's demand-deposit account and information that can be used for purchases.

social audit   Assessment of a company's performance in the area of social responsibility.

socialism   Economic system characterized by public ownership and operation of key industries combined with private ownership and operation of less-vital industries.

software   The programmed instructions that direct the activity of the hardware; the intangible part of information systems.

sole proprietorship   Business owned by a single individual

spam   Unsolicited bulk e-mail.

span of management   Number of people under one manager's control; also known as span of control.

special-purpose teams   Temporary teams that exist outside the formal organization hierarchy and are created to achieve a specific goal.

specialty advertising   Advertising that appears on various items such as coffee mugs, pens, and calendars.

specialty store   Store that carries only a particular type of goods.

speculative risk   Risk that involves the chance of both loss and profits.

speculators   Investors who purchase securities in anticipation of making large profits quickly.

spyware   Malware that sneaks onto computers with the intent of capturing passwords, credit card numbers, and other valuable information.

stakeholders   Individuals or groups to whom business has a responsibility.

standards   Criteria against which performance is measured.

stare decisis   Concept of using previous judicial decisions as the basis for deciding similar court cases.

start-up companies   New business ventures.

statement of cash flows   Statement of a firm's cash receipts and cash payments that presents information on its sources and uses of cash.

statistical process control (SPC)   Use of random sampling and control charts to monitor the production process.

statistical quality control (SQC)   Monitoring all aspects of the production process to see whether the process is operating as it should.

statutory law   Statute, or law, created by a legislature.

stealth marketing   The delivery of marketing messages to people who are not aware that they are being marketed to; these messages can be delivered by either acquaintances or strangers, depending on the technique.

stereotyping   Assigning a wide range of generalized attributes, which are often superficial or even false, to an individual based on his or membership in a particular culture or social group.

stock certificate   Document that proves stock ownership.

stock exchanges   Location where traders buy and sell stocks and bonds.

stock options   Contract allowing the holder to purchase or sell a certain number of shares of a particular stock at a given price by a certain date.

stock split   Increase in the number of shares of ownership that each stock certificate represents, at a proportionate drop in each share's value.

stock specialist   Intermediary who trades in particular security on the floor of an auction exchange; "buyer of last resort."

stop order   An order to sell a stock when its price falls to a particular point to limit an investor's losses.

strategic alliance   Long-term relationship in which two or more companies share ideas, resources, and technologies in order to establish competitive advantages.

strategic marketing planning   The process of examining an organization's current marketing situation, assessing opportunities and setting objectives, then developing a marketing strategy to reach those objectives.

strategic plans   Plans that establish the actions and the resource allocation required to accomplish strategic goals; they're usually defined for periods of two to five years and developed by top managers.

strict product liability   Liability for injury caused by a defective product when all reasonable care is used in its manufacture, distribution, or sale; no fault is assigned.

strike   Temporary work stoppage by employees who want management to accept their union's demands.

strikebreakers   Nonunion workers hired to replace striking workers.

subsidiary corporations   Corporations whose stock is owned entirely or almost entirely by another corporation.

succession planning   Workforce planning efforts that identify possible replacements for specific employees, usually senior executives.

supply   Specific quantity of a product that the seller is able and willing to provide.

supply chain   The collection of suppliers and systems that provide all of the materials and supplies required to create finished products and deliver them to final customers; can refer to both the supply chain of an individual company and the supply chain of an entire industry.

supply curve   Graph of the quantities that sellers will offer for sale, regardless of demand, at various prices.

supply-chain management (SCM)   An approach to coordinating and optimizing the flow of goods, services, information, and capabilities throughout the entire supply chain, including outside business partners.

synthetic system   Production process that combines two or more materials or components to create finished products; the reverse of an analytic system.

tactical plans   Plans that define the actions and the resource allocation necessary to achieve tactical objectives and to support strategic plans; they're usually defined for a period of one to three years and developed by middle managers.

tall organizations   Organizations with a narrow span of management and many hierarchical levels.

target markets   Specific customer groups or segments to whom a company wants to sell a particular product.

tariffs   Taxes levied on imports.

task force   Team of people from several departments who are temporarily brought together to address a specific issue.

tax accounting   Area of accounting focusing on tax preparation and tax planning.

tax credits   Direct reductions in your tax obligation.

tax-deferred investments   Investments such as 401(k) plans and IRAs that let you deduct the amount of your investments from your gross income (thereby lowering your taxable income); you don't have to pay tax on any of the income from these investments until you start to withdraw money during retirement.

tax-exempt investments   Investments (usually municipal bonds) whose income is not subject to federal income tax.

team   A unit of two or more people who share a mission and collective responsibility as they work together to achieve a goal.

technical salespeople   Specialists who contribute technical expertise and other sales assistance.

technical skills   Ability and knowledge to perform the mechanics of a particular job.

telecommuting   Working at home while staying connected to the office via electronic networking.

telemarketing   Selling or supporting the sales process over the telephone.

term insurance   Life insurance that provides death benefits for a specified period.

termination   process of getting rid of an employee through layoff or firing.

test marketing   Product-development stage in which a product is sold on a limited basis—a trial introduction.

Theory X   Managerial assumption that employees are irresponsible, are unambitious, and dislike work and that managers must use force, control, or threats to motivate them.

Theory Y   Managerial assumption that employees like work, are naturally committed to certain goals, are capable of creativity, and seek out responsibility under the right conditions.

Theory Z   Leadership approach that emphasizes involving employees at all levels and treating them like family.

time deposits   Bank accounts that pay interest and require advance notice before money can be withdrawn.

time utility   Customer value added by making a product available at a convenient time.

time value of money   The increasing value of money as a result of accumulating interest.

top managers   Those at the highest level of the organization's management hierarchy; they are responsible for setting strategic goals, and they have the most power and responsibility.

tort   Noncriminal act (other than breach of contract) that results in injury to a person or to property.

total quality management (TQM)   A management philosophy and strategic management process that focuses on delivering the optimal level of quality to customers by building quality into every organizational activity.

trade allowance   Discount offered by producers to wholesalers and retailers.

trade credit   Credit obtained by the purchaser directly from the supplier.

trade deficit   Unfavorable trade balance created when a country imports more than it exports.

trade promotions   Sales-promotion efforts aimed at inducing distributors or retailers to push a producer's products.

trade salespeople   Salespeople who sell to and support marketing intermediaries by giving in-store demonstrations, offering samples, and so on.

trade surplus   Favorable trade balance created when a country exports more than it imports.

trademarks   Brands that have been given legal protection so that their owners have exclusive rights to their use.

trade-off   A decision-making condition in which you have to give up one or more benefits to gain other benefits.

trading blocs Organizations of nations that remove barriers to trade among their members and that establish uniform barriers to trade with nonmember nations.

transaction Exchange between parties.

treasury bills Short-term debt securities issued by the federal government; also referred to as *T-bills.*

treasury bonds Debt securities issued by the federal government that are repaid more than 10 years after issuance.

treasury notes Debt securities issued by the federal government that are repaid within 1 to 10 years after issuance.

U.S. savings bonds Debt instruments sold by the federal government in a variety of amounts.

umbrella policies Insurance that provides businesses with coverage beyond what is provided by a basic liability policy.

unemployment insurance Government-sponsored program for assisting employees who are laid off for reasons not related to performance.

Uniform Commercial Code (UCC) Set of standardized laws, adopted by most states, that govern business transactions.

uninsurable risk Risk that few, if any, insurance companies will assume because of the difficulty of calculating the probability of loss.

unissued stock Portion of authorized stock not yet sold to shareholders.

universal life insurance Combination of term life insurance policy and a savings plan with flexible interest rates and flexible premiums.

universal Product Codes (UPCs) A bar code on a product's package that provides information read by optical scanners.

unlimited liability Legal condition under which any damages or debts attributable to the business can also be attached to the owner because the two have no separate legal existence.

unsecured loan Loan requiring no collateral but a good credit rating.

utilitarianism A decision-making approach that seeks to create the greatest good for the greatest number of people affected by the decisions.

utility Power of a good or service to satisfy a human need.

value chain All of the functions required to transform inputs into outputs (goods and services), along with the business functions that support the transformation process.

variable costs Business costs that increase with the number of units produced.

variable life insurance Whole life insurance policy that allows the policyholder to decide how to invest the cash value.

venture capitalists (VCs) Investment specialists who provide money to finance new businesses or turnarounds in exchange for a portion of the ownership, with the objective of making a considerable profit on the investment.

virtual teams Teams that use communication technology to bring geographically distant employees together to achieve goals.

viruses Invasive computer programs that reproduce by infecting legitimate programs.

vision A viable view of the future that is rooted in but improves on the present.

wages Cash payment based on the number of hours the employee has worked or the number of units the employee has produced.

wants Goods, services, experiences, or other entities that are desirable in light of a person's experiences, culture, and personality.

warehouse Facility for storing inventory.

warranty Statement specifying what the producer of a product will do to compensate the buyer if the product is defective or if it malfunctions.

web directories Categorized lists of suggested websites on specific topics.

wheel of retailing Evolutionary process by which stores that feature low prices gradually upgrade until they no longer appeal to price-sensitive shoppers and are replaced by new low-price competitors.

whistle-blowing The disclosure of information by a company insider that exposes illegal or unethical behavior on the part of the organization.

whole life insurance Insurance that provides both death benefits and savings for the insured's lifetime, provided premiums are paid.

wholesalers Firms that sell products to other firms for resale or for organizational use.

Wi-Fi A wireless alternative for LANs; short for *wireless fidelity.*

will A legal document that specifies what happens to your assets, who will execute your estate (carry out the terms of your will), and who will be the legal guardian of your children, if you have any, in the event of your death.

work specialization Specialization in or responsibility for some portion of an organization's overall work tasks; also called division of labor.

work-life balance Efforts to help people balance the competing demands of their professional and personal lives.

worker buyout Distribution of financial incentives to employees who voluntarily depart; usually undertaken in order to reduce the payroll.

workers' compensation insurance Insurance that partially replaces lost income and that pays for employees' medical costs and rehabilitation expenses for work-related injuries.

working capital Current assets minus current liabilities.

yield Income received from securities, calculated by dividing dividend or interest income by market price.